Green type indicates global example

ECONOMICS IN ACTION

BUSINESS CASES

See the inside back cover for Sections 15–26

ECONOMICS

IN MODULES

THIRD EDITION

ECONOMICS IN MODULES

Paul Krugman • Robin Wells

Princeton University

WORTH PUBLISHERS

A Macmillan Higher Education Company

Vice President, Editing, Design, and Media Production: Catherine Woods

Vice President, Editorial—Sciences & Social Sciences: Charles Linsmeier

Publisher, Social and Behavioral Sciences: Kevin Feyen

Associate Publisher, Economics & Geography: Steven A. Rigolosi

Executive Development Editor: Sharon Balbos

Associate Development Editor: Mary Walsh

Editorial Assistant: Fay Kelly

Marketing Manager: Thomas Digiano

Marketing Assistant: Tess Sanders

Executive Media Editor: Rachel Comerford

Media Editor: Lukia Kliossis

Director of Development for Print and Digital: Tracey Kuehn

Product Owner—LaunchPad: Marie McHale

Managing Editor: Lisa Kinne

Project Editor: Liz Geller

Art Director: Babs Reingold

Cover Designers: Lyndall Culbertson and Babs Reingold

Interior Layout: Paul Lacy

Interior Design: Charles Yuen

Photo Editor: Cecilia Varas

Photo Researcher: Elyse Rieder

Production Manager: Barbara Anne Seixas

Supplements Production Manager: Stacey Alexander

Supplements Project Editor: Edgar Bonilla

Composition and Illustration: TSI Graphics

Printing and Binding: RR Donnelley

See page xlv for credits information. Page xlv is an extension of this copyright page.

ISBN-13: 978-1-4641-3903-1

ISBN-10: 1-4641-3903-2

Library of Congress Control Number: 2014935920

©2014, 2012, 2006 by Worth Publishers

All rights reserved.

Printed in the United States of America

Second printing

Worth Publishers

41 Madison Avenue

New York, NY 10010

www.worthpublishers.com

ABOUT THE AUTHORS

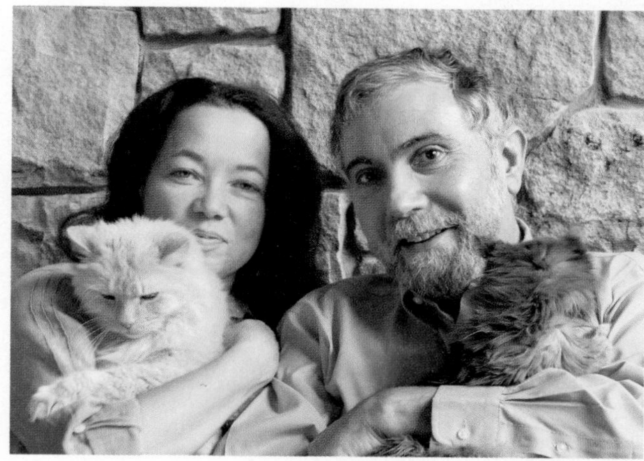

Paul Krugman, recipient of the 2008 Nobel Memorial Prize in Economic Sciences, is Professor of Economics at Princeton University, where he regularly teaches the principles course. In the summer of 2015 he will join the faculty of the Graduate Center, City University of New York, and become a distinguished scholar at the Graduate Center's Luxembourg Income Study Center. Krugman received his BA from Yale and his PhD from MIT. Prior to his current position, he taught at Yale, Stanford, and MIT. He also spent a year on the staff of the Council of Economic Advisers in 1982–1983. His research is mainly in the area of international trade, where he is one of the founders of the "new trade theory," which focuses on increasing returns and imperfect competition. He also works in international finance, with a concentration in currency crises. In 1991, Krugman received the American Economic Association's John Bates Clark medal. In addition to his teaching and academic research, Krugman writes extensively for nontechnical audiences. He is a regular op-ed columnist for the *New York Times*. His latest trade books, both best sellers, include *End This Depression Now!*, a look at the recent global financial crisis and recovery, and *The Return of Depression Economics and the Crisis of 2008*, a history of recent economic troubles and their implications for economic policy. His earlier books, *The Conscience of a Liberal, Peddling Prosperity,* and *The Age of Diminished Expectations,* have become modern classics.

Robin Wells was a Lecturer and Researcher in Economics at Princeton University. She received her BA from the University of Chicago and her PhD from the University of California at Berkeley; she then did postdoctoral work at MIT. She has taught at the University of Michigan, the University of Southampton (United Kingdom), Stanford, and MIT. The subject of her teaching and research is the theory of organizations and incentives.

To beginning students everywhere,
which we all were at one time.

BRIEF CONTENTS

CONTENTS

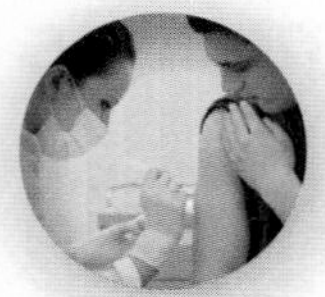

Section 3

Elasticity and the Law of Demand 71

Section 4

Market Efficiency 101

Section 5

Government Policy and Taxes 127

Section 20
Aggregate Demand and Aggregate Supply

Section 21
Fiscal Policy

Section 22

Section 23

PREFACE

"It is not how much empty space there is, but rather how it is used. It is not how much information there is, but rather how effectively it is arranged."

—*Edward R. Tufte*

An Innovative Modular Format

For a long while, we have been hearing from instructors who wanted to use the Krugman/Wells text in their principles course, but needed a less comprehensive version: a book that was shorter overall, with a focus on the essential principles of economics, and with less in the way of theory and analytics. We've responded to these requests, and you are holding the result in your hands.

***Economics in Modules* is a streamlined textbook that incorporates an innovative format geared toward how students learn today.** Instead of tackling 24 chapters of about 25 to 40 pages each, students encounter 6- to 10-page *modules* designed to be read in a single sitting. What exactly is a module? We think users and reviewers have come up with the best definition. They consistently describe modules as "short, digestible chunks" of text that students actually read. We should also add that shorter does not mean taking shortcuts. Although each module is a short, easy-to-manage reading assignment, each is also informative and thorough, with adequate rigor.

This text includes carefully crafted pedagogy that works within the modular format to enhance the student learning experience. The modular format offers a unique opportunity for structured learning and assessment. Each module concentrates on a specific topic using a learning-objectives approach and then concludes with three types of self-assessment questions: "Check Your Understanding" and multiple-choice questions that allow students to test their comprehension of module content, followed by critical-thinking questions that encourage reflection and analysis. Answers to these questions appear at the end of the book, so students can actually see how well they've mastered concepts.

There is additional opportunity for assessment at the end of each section (a section is a grouping of modules): thoughtful problems that test related concepts across all of the modules in a section, encouraging students to make connections among ideas as well as apply and practice what they've learned.

We've refined the modular structure in this edition to offer even greater flexibility. We've added several new sections to help unpack some of the more module-heavy sections. The result: more focused sections with fewer modules in each. Important topics are contained within their own sections, making it easier for instructors to navigate through the book and assign the topics they want to teach without breaking chapters apart (often done with non-modular texts), which can undermine narrative flow and diminish comprehension.

The Science Behind Modules

We see it for ourselves, we have heard it from reviewers, and the research confirms it: students are reading less, for shorter periods of time, and they continue to struggle with comprehension. So, when we began thinking about the idea of developing a more streamlined principles text, we also thought a lot about the best way to format it.

The modular format, which is popular in other disciplines, appealed to us. It was in keeping with the findings of cognitive psychologists who have demonstrated that comprehension is best attained when material is "chunked" into smaller reading assignments, reinforced with frequent questioning (the "testing effect"), and incentivized by a sense of accomplishment earned from completing discrete reading tasks. These findings are at the heart of the modular format of this text and its pedagogy.

Comments from users confirm the benefits of this new way of presenting economic concepts. Each user reported an almost identical story: students were actually completing their reading assignments, something that was rare when traditional textbook chapters were assigned. Overall, they found students coming to lectures better prepared. And, each of these users couldn't imagine returning to a textbook with a more traditional format.

This result makes intuitive sense. Why wouldn't students prefer to read short modules instead of long chapters? Of course it would enrich the learning experience if students could check their comprehension more frequently, at the end of short modules.

For a closer look at the text's format and feature set, see the walkthrough on pages xxxii–xxxv.

About the Revision

This edition of *Economics in Modules* represents a major revision. We had three goals in mind as we worked: adding important new content, improving the organization of sections, and updating examples and data to keep the book current and relevant. We even added a new feature.

Decisions about many of the changes were made with the help of feedback from a devoted group of adopters and reviewers—all fans of the modular format who offered us excellent suggestions for how we could make the text an even better match for their principles courses. Here is an overview of the major revisions.

New Coverage of Decision Making and Behavioral Economics

We devote an entire new section to this important topic. Section 7, "Economics and Decision Making" includes two new modules: Module 18 on the types of decisions made by individuals and firms, as well as the process of making decisions that leads to the best possible economic outcomes; and Module 19 on behavioral economics, which looks at types of irrational decision making. We've moved our module on utility maximization into this section to round out the coverage.

New Coverage of the Keynesian Cross

This was an omission that prompted the most vocal response from instructors and we've remedied it in this edition with **new Module 62, "The Income-Expenditure Model."** The module offers a detailed look at the aggregate-expenditure model and presents the famous 45-degree diagram. We worked hard to keep this module focused and free of unnecessary complexity.

New Modules and Organizational Improvements

In addition to the new coverage of economic decision making and the Keynesian cross, we've included several other new modules on topics that we hope will allow you to enrich your own teaching.

New Modules New **Module 15, "Taxes,"** has allowed us to devote a separate module to this topic and expand our coverage to include more detail on tax rates and revenues.

Section 6, "International Trade," includes two new fully integrated and up-to-date modules: Module 16, "Gains from Trade," and Module 17, "Supply, Demand, and International Trade," for those who wish to delve deeper into trade topics than is possible with the coverage of comparative advantage and trade presented in Module 4.

Module 39, "The Economics of the Welfare State," addresses a timely topic that is very much in the news and of particular importance to us. This module includes coverage of health care policy as well as a fully updated discussion of poverty, inequality, and welfare state programs.

And **Module 78, "Crises and Consequences,"** offers a unique look at the financial crisis of 2008, examining the aspects of the banking system that allowed the crisis to happen, the reasons why banking crises are so bad for so many, and the role that government and regulation play in crises.

Organizational Improvements We made the following changes in this edition. But for those who prefer to teach using a different order, the sections and modules remain completely flexible.

Many new sections: We've already touched on the benefits of more sections. Those of you familiar with the second edition will notice that we've virtually doubled the number of them, a structural change that alters the look of our table of contents, we think, for the better. Topics that had been submerged previously, such as elasticity, ADAS, and fiscal policy, are now prominent.

New early growth coverage: Following the section on unemployment and inflation is an early, all-new section devoted to economic growth (Section 17). This early coverage allows us to emphasize the idea that economic growth, along with low unemployment and stable inflation, are important policy goals. In addition, early coverage of long-run economic growth in real GDP helps students understand why the business cycle involves fluctuations around an upward trend. And we are now able to highlight the role that the markets and institutions covered next, in Section 18, play in economic growth.

New Feature: Business Case Studies

Now, more than ever, students need a strong understanding of economic principles and their applications to business decisions. To meet this need, virtually every section now concludes with a real-world business case that illustrates how the economic principles just covered play out in the world of entrepreneurs and bottom lines.

Each case concludes with "Questions for Thought" that help students engage more deeply with economic concepts by seeing them applied in actual business situations. A list of the new Business Cases appears on the inside front and back covers.

Extensive Updates

This edition includes over 30 new "Economics in Actions" (formerly called "In Real Life"). Many of those not replaced outright have been updated to include recent developments and research. Every module includes at least one "Economics in Action" feature. In addition, many of our section-opening stories have been updated or replaced outright. We have also undertaken a thorough updating of examples, data, and applications.

It is important to us to emphasize currency and to use stories from real life and the news. This makes every revision a work-intensive endeavor, but we believe that currency drives student interest.

A Closer Look at the Table of Contents and Feature Set

The annotated table of contents that follows shows how the modular format works and explains the focus of each section. Although the sections are grouped into building blocks in which conceptual material learned at one stage is built upon and then integrated into the next stage, the coverage is also flexible enough to allow instructors to organize content to best meet their needs.

Following the table of contents is a visual tour of our feature set that clarifies how well the content of this text is supplemented by real-world examples and ample opportunity for practice and review (pages xxxii–xxxv).

Annotated Table of Contents . . . A Closer Look at Content and Format

The text contains 26 sections with two to five modules in each.

An introduction to basic economic principles that will help students develop an understanding of economic modeling and the nature of markets.

Individual modules are devoted to each component of the supply and demand model so students can master the model incrementally.

Introduces the various elasticity measures, including income and substitution effects and price, cross-price, and income elasticity of demand.

Introduces students to market efficiency, the ways markets fail, the role of prices as signals, and property rights.

This new stand-alone section focuses on market interventions, price and quantity controls, and inefficiency. It also includes a **new module** devoted to taxes.

NEW TO THIS EDITION This new section on trade offers integrated early coverage for those who wish to expand on the coverage of comparative advantage and trade in Module 4.

NEW TO THIS EDITION This new section includes two **new modules:** one on rational choice and another on behavioral economics.

Develops the production function and various cost measures of the firm, including coverage of the differences between average cost and marginal cost.

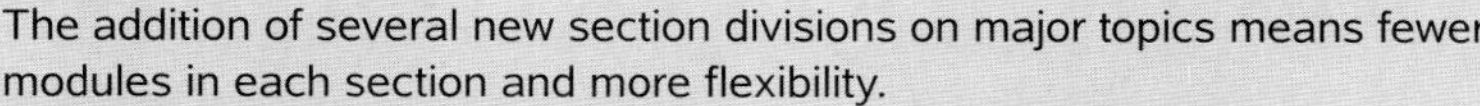
The addition of several new section divisions on major topics means fewer modules in each section and more flexibility.

Section 9
Market Structure and Perfect Competition

Explains the output decision of the perfectly competitive firm, its entry/exit decision, the industry supply curve, and long-run outcomes.

Section 10
Monopoly

A thorough treatment of monopoly, including coverage of price discrimination and the welfare effects of monopoly.

Section 11
Imperfect Competition

These manageable modules offer coverage on game theory, monopolistic competition, and product differentiation.

Section 12
Market Failure and the Role of Government

The section focuses on externalities and solutions to them. Also examined: positive externalities and public goods. The section concludes with a **new module** on applications within the welfare state.

Section 13
Factor Markets and the Distribution of Income

Covers the efficiency wage model of the labor market, market power, and a discussion of income distribution.

Section 14
Additional Topics in Microeconomics

These additional topics appear for those instructors who typically cover them. The modules are easily integrated into earlier discussions.

Annotated Table of Contents . . . A Closer Look at Content and Format, Continued

Introduces macroeconomics and explains how macroeconomic aggregates are measured.

A **new** stand-alone section examining unemployment, how it's measured, and the problems posed by inflation.

NEW TO THIS EDITION Early treatment of long-run growth. The section looks at sources of economic growth and explains why some countries have been more successful than others.

An introduction to the financial system with the background students will need to tackle upcoming topics such as monetary policy and international capital flows.

NEW TO THIS EDITION coverage of Keynesian cross analysis in **new Module 62.** It is preceded by a look at the logic of the multiplier and determinants of consumer and investment spending.

A thorough treatment of AD–AS focusing on the aggregate price level using the traditional approach to AD–AS, with coverage on the ability of economies to recover in the long run.

A **new** stand-alone section devoted to how fiscal policy can be used to manage the ups and downs of the business cycle, with an in-depth look at discretionary fiscal policy and automatic stabilizers.

This section examines the roles of money, money creation, and the structure and role of the Federal Reserve System—including historical background on the evolution of money and monetary institutions.

A **new** stand-alone section examining the use of monetary policy in the face of recession or inflation, with a close look at the Fed's role in driving interest rates and aggregate demand.

This section addresses the causes and consequences of inflation, deflation, and the dangers of disinflation. NEW TO THIS EDITION **Module 78** on financial crises, offering a detailed and up-to-date look at the recent crisis and its aftermath.

Analyzes the special issues raised by an open economy: a weak dollar, foreign accumulation of dollar reserves, and debates about the euro.

A unique overview of the history of macroeconomic thought set in the context of changing policy concerns and current macroeconomic debates.

These appendices offer a helpful review of graphing skills and easy access to macroeconomic data for reference.

Solutions allow students to independently test their mastery of concepts.

Tools for Learning . . . Getting the Most from This Book

Each section consists of interrelated modules with a consistent set of features and pedagogy. Each module is self-contained giving students discrete reading assignments to complete. Instructors have the freedom to assign only those modules that are important to their course.

Module 5: Demand
Module 6: Supply and Equilibrium
Module 7: Changes in Equilibrium

SECTION 2

The **SECTION-OPENING OUTLINE** offers a quick opening preview of the modules in each section.

Supply and Demand

BLUE JEAN BLUES

If you bought a pair of blue jeans in 2011, you may have been shocked at the price. Or maybe not: fashions change, and maybe you thought you were paying the price for being fashionable. But you weren't—you were paying for cotton. Jeans are made of denim, which is a particular weave of cotton, and by December 2010, the price ... had hit a 140-year high, the highest ... cords began in 1870.

... ton prices so high?

... and for clothing of all kinds was surg... s the world struggled with the effects ... nervous consumers cut back on cloth... y 2010, with the worst apparently over, ... force. On the supply side, Pakistan, ... rgest cotton producer, was hit by dev... put one-fifth of the country underwa... troyed its cotton crop.

... umers had limited tolerance for large increases in the price of cotton clothing, apparel makers began scrambling to find ways to reduce costs. They adopted changes like smaller buttons, cheaper linings, and—yes—polyester, doubting that consumers would be willing to pay more for cotton goods. In fact, some experts on the cotton market warned that the sky-high prices of cotton in 2010–2011 might lead to a permanent shift in tastes, with consumers becoming more willing to wear synthetics even when cotton prices came down.

At the same time, it was not all bad news for everyone connected with the cotton trade. In the United States, cotton producers had not been hit by bad weather and were relishing the higher prices. American farmers responded to sky-high cotton prices by sharply increasing the acreage devoted to the crop. None of this was enough, however, to produce immediate price relief.

Wait a minute: how, exactly, does flooding in Pakistan translate into higher jeans prices and more polyester in your T-shirts? It's a matter of supply and demand—but what does that mean? Many people use "supply and demand" as a sort of catchphrase to mean "the laws of the marketplace at work." To economists, however, the concept of supply and demand has a precise meaning: it is a *model of how a market behaves*.

In this section, we lay out the pieces that make up the *supply and demand model*, put them together, and show how this model can be used to understand how many—but not all—markets behave.

SECTION-OPENING STORY Each section begins with a compelling story that often extends through the modules. The opening stories are designed to illustrate important concepts, to build intuition with realistic examples, and then to encourage students to read on and learn more.

35

MODULE 5 Demand

Thinkstock

WHAT YOU WILL LEARN

1. What a competitive market is and how it is described by the supply and demand model
2. What the demand curve is
3. The difference between movements along the demand curve and changes in demand
4. The factors that shift the demand curve

Each module begins with WHAT YOU WILL LEARN, a numbered list of learning objectives in an easy-to-review format that alerts students to critical concepts in the pages ahead.

Supply and Demand: A Model of a Competitive Market

Cotton sellers and cotton buyers constitute a *market*—a group of producers and consumers who exchange a good or service for payment. In this section, we'll focus on a particular type of market known as a *competitive market*. Roughly, a **competitive market** is a market in which there are many buyers and sellers of the same good or service. More precisely, the key feature of a competitive market is that no individual's actions have a noticeable effect on the price at which the good or service is sold. It's important to understand, however, that this is not an accurate description of every market.

For example, it's not an accurate description of the market for cola beverages. That's because in the market for cola beverages, Coca-Cola and Pepsi account for such a large proportion of total sales that they are able to influence the price at which cola beverages are bought and sold. But it *is* an accurate description of the market for cotton. The global marketplace for cotton is so huge that even a jeans maker as large as Levi Strauss & Co. accounts for only a tiny fraction of transactions, making it unable to influence the price at which cotton is bought and sold.

It's a little hard to explain why competitive markets are different from other markets until we've seen how a competitive market works. For now, let's just say that it's ...ets. When taking an exam, it's ...r questions. In this book, we're ...etitive markets.

...l described by the **supply and** ...titive, the supply and demand

A competitive market is a market in which there are many bu... ers of the same good or ... of whom can influence th... which the good or servic...

The supply and deman... a model of how a compet... works.

KEY TERMS Every key term is defined in the text and then again in the margin, making it easier for students to study and review important vocabulary.

There are f...
- The *dema*...
- The *suppl*...
- The set of ... cause the ...
- The *mark*... *quantity*
- The way t... shifts

To explain ... in turn. In this...

The De...

How many pc... around the w... answer this qu... around the w... make a pair o... question, beca... cotton—consu...

When the p... higher price c... switching com... linen. In gener... want to buy, d... people want t... purchase.

So the answ... to buy?" depe... price will be, ... would want to ... *schedule*. This... elements of the...

The Dema...

A **demand sch**... want to buy at ... demand sched... world demand ...

According t... will want to pu... is $1.25 a pou... $0.75 a pound, ... price, the fewe... the price rises, ... willing to buy ...

The graph i... (For a refreshe... vertical axis sh... quantity of cot... tries in the tab... curve is a grap... the relationshi...

ECONOMICS IN ACTION — WORLD VIEW

GLOBAL STAMPS identify features that are global in focus.

BEATING THE TRAFFIC

All big cities have traffic problems, and many local authorities try to discourage driving in the crowded city center. If we think of an auto trip to the city center as a good that people consume, we can use the economics of demand to analyze anti-traffic policies.

One common strategy is to reduce the demand for auto trips by lowering the prices of substitutes. Many metropolitan areas subsidize bus and rail service, hoping to lure commuters out of their cars. An alternative is to raise the price of complements: several major U.S. cities impose high taxes on commercial parking garages and impose short time limits on parking meters, both to raise revenue and to discourage people from driving into the city.

A few major cities—including Singapore, London, Oslo, Stockholm, and Milan—have been willing to adopt a direct and politically controversial approach: reducing congestion by raising the price of driving. Under "congestion pricing" (or "congestion charging" in the United Kingdom), a charge is imposed on cars entering the city center during business hours. Drivers buy passes, which are then debited electronically as they drive by monitoring stations. Compliance is monitored with automatic cameras that photograph license plates.

charging
zone
C
Mon - Fri
7 am - 6.30 pm

Citie... raisi...

The current daily cost of driving in London ranges from £8 to £10 (about $13 to $16). And drivers who don't pay and are caught pay a fine of £120 (about $195) for each transgression.

Not surprisingly, studies have shown that after the implementation of congestion pricing, traffic does indeed decrease. In the 1990s, London had some of the worst traffic in Europe. The introduction of its congestion charge in 2003 immediately reduced traffic in the London city center by about 15%, with overall traffic falling by 21% between 2002 and 2006. And there was increased use of substitutes, such as public

ECONOMICS IN ACTION This feature, which appears in every module, provides a compelling real-life application of major concepts covered in the module. Students experience an immediate payoff when they can apply concepts they've just read about to real phenomena.

Each module concludes with a unique set of **REVIEW QUESTIONS.**

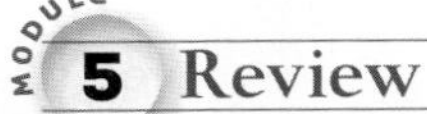

Review

Solutions appear at the back of the book.

Check Your Understanding

1. Explain whether each of the following events represents (i) a *change in demand* (a *shift of* the demand curve) or (ii) a *change in the quantity demanded* (a *movement* ... e).

... that customers are willing to pay ... on rainy days.

..., a long-distance telephone ... ered reduced rates on weekends, ... d calling increased sharply.

c. People buy more long-stem roses the week of Valentine's Day, even though the prices are higher than at other times during the year.

d. A sharp rise in the price of gasoline leads many commuters to join carpools in order to reduce their gasoline purchases.

CHECK YOUR UNDERSTANDING review questions allow students to immediately test their understanding of a module. By checking their answers with those found in the back of the book, students will know when they need to reread the module before moving on.

SECTION 2 SUPPLY AND DEMAND

Multiple-Choice Questions

1. Which of the following would increase demand for a normal good? A decrease in
   a. price.
   b. income.
   ... price of a substitute.
   ... sumer taste for a good.
   ... price of a complement.

... ease in the price of butter would most likely ... se the demand for
   ... garine.
   ... els.
   c. jelly.
   d. milk.
   e. syrup.

3. If an increase in income leads to a decrease in demand, the good is
   a. a complement.
   b. a substitute.
   c. inferior.
   d. abnormal.
   e. normal.

4. Which of the following will occur if consumers expect the price of a good to fall in the coming months?
   a. The quantity demanded will rise today.
   b. The quantity demanded will remain the same today.
   c. Demand will increase today.
   d. Demand will decrease today.
   e. No change will occur today.

5. Which of the following will increase the demand for disposable diapers?
   a. a new "baby boom"
   b. concern over the environmental effect of landfills
   c. a decrease in the price of cloth diapers
   d. a move toward earlier potty training of children
   e. a decrease in the price of disposable diapers

MULTIPLE-CHOICE QUESTIONS offer students additional opportunity to practice what they've learned.

Critical-Thinking Question

... correctly labeled graph showing the demand for ... On your graph, illustrate what happens to the de- ... or apples if a new report from the Surgeon General ... at an apple a day really *does* keep the doctor away.

CRITICAL-THINKING QUESTIONS offer students an opportunity to think more deeply about content in the module.

PITFALLS

DEMAND VERSUS QUANTITY DEMANDED

Consider how the term *demand* is used in the following sentence. Why is the sentence incorrect?

If the price of the good goes up then people will buy less and this will lead to a fall in demand which shifts the demand curve to the left.

THIS STATEMENT MISTAKES A CHANGE IN QUANTITY DEMANDED FOR A CHANGE IN DEMAND. WHEN DOING ECONOMIC ANALYSIS, IT IS IMPORTANT TO MAKE THE DISTINCTION BETWEEN CHANGES IN *DEMAND*, WHICH MEAN SHIFTS OF THE DEMAND CURVE, AND CHANGES IN *QUANTITY DEMANDED*. When economists say "an increase in demand," they mean a rightward shift of the demand curve, and when they say "a decrease in demand," they mean a leftward shift of the demand curve—that is, when they're being careful. In or- ... st people, including professional econ- ... ord *demand* casually. For example, an ... ay "the demand for air travel has dou- ... fifteen years, partly because of falling ... r she really means that the *quantity de-* ... led. The key point to remember is that ... causes a *movement along the demand* ... ift of the demand curve.

... Figure 5.3 for an illustration of a movement ... ve versus a shift of the demand curve. For an ... rence, see pages 38–40.

NEW The **PITFALLS** feature, appearing at the end of select modules, helps students come to a better understanding of commonly misunderstood concepts, using a question-and-answer format.

Solutions to all module-review questions can be found at the back of the book.

BUSINESS CASE

The Chicago Board of Trade

Around the world, commodities are bought and sold on "exchanges," markets organized in a specific location, where buyers and sellers meet to trade. But it wasn't always like this.

The first modern commodity exchange was the Chicago Board of Trade, founded in 1848. At the time, the United States was already a major wheat producer. And St. Louis, not Chicago, was the leading city of the American West and the dominant location for wheat trading. But the St. Louis wheat market suffered from a major flaw: there was no central marketplace, no specific location where everyone met to buy and sell wheat. Instead, sellers would sell their grain from various warehouses or from stacked sacks of grain on the river levee. Buyers would wander around town, looking for the best price.

In Chicago, however, sellers had a better idea. The Chicago Board of Trade, an association of the city's leading grain dealers, created a much more efficient method for trading wheat. There, traders gathered in one place—the "pit"—where they called out offers to sell and accepted offers to buy. The Board guaranteed that these contracts would be fulfilled, removing the need for the wheat to be physically in place when a trade was agreed upon.

This system meant that buyers could very quickly find sellers and vice-versa, reducing the cost of doing business. It also ensured that everyone could see the latest price, leading the price to rise or fall quickly in response to market conditions. For example, news of bad weather in a wheat-growing area hundreds of miles away would send the price in the Chicago pit soaring in a matter of minutes.

The Chicago Board of Trade went on to become the world's most important trading center for wheat and many other agricultural commodities, a distinction it retains to this day. And the Board's rise helped the rise of Chicago, too. The city, as Carl Sandburg put it in his famous poem, "Chicago," became:

Jim West

NEW BUSINESS CASES appear at the end of virtually every section, applying key economic principles to real-life business situations in both American and international companies. Each case concludes with critical-thinking questions.

Questions for Thought

1. In Module 6 we mention how prices can vary in a tourist trap. Which market, St. Louis or Chicago, was more likely to behave like a tourist trap? Explain.
2. What was the advantage to buyers from buying their wheat in the Chicago pit instead ... e advantage to sellers?
3. ... ned from this case, explain why the online auction site eBay ... as it been so successful as a marketplace for second-hand ... composed of various flea markets and dealers?

SECTION 2 REVIEW

Summary

Demand

1. The **supply and demand model** illustrates how a **competitive market,** one with many buyers and sellers of the same product, works.
2. The **demand schedule** shows the **quantity demanded** at each price and is represented graphically by a **demand curve.** The **law of demand** says that demand curves slope downward, meaning that as price decreases, the quantity demanded increases.
3. A **movement along the demand curve** occurs when the price changes and causes a change in the quantity demanded. When economists talk of **changes in demand,** they mean shifts of the demand curve—a change in the quantity demanded at any given price. An increase in demand causes a rightward shift of the demand curve. A decrease in demand causes a leftward shift.
4. There are five main factors that shift the demand curve:
   - A change in the prices of related goods, such as **substitutes** or **complements**
   - A change in income: when income rises, the demand for **normal goods** increases and the demand for **inferior goods** decreases
   - A change in tastes
   - A change in expectations
   - A change in the number of consumers

Supply and Equilibrium

5. The **supply schedule** shows the **quantity supplied** at each price and is represented graphically by a **supply curve.** Supply curves usually slope upward.
6. A **movement along the supply curve** occurs when the price changes and causes a change in the quantity supplied. When economists talk of **changes in supply,** they mean shifts of the supply curve—a change in the quantity supplied at any given price. An increase in supply causes a rightward shift of the supply curve. A decrease in supply causes a left...
7. There are five main factors tha...
   - A change in **input** prices
   - A change in the prices of rel...
   - A change in technology
   - A change in expectations
   - A change in the number of p...
8. The supply and demand mode... ple that the price in a market n... **price,** or **market-clearing pr...** the quantity demanded is equ... plied. This quantity is the **equil...** the price is above its market-clearing level, there is a **surplus** that pushes the price down. When the price is below its market-clearing level, there is a **shortage** that ...

Cha...

9. ...

10. ...

END-OF-SECTION REVIEW AND PROBLEMS
In addition to the opportunities for review at the end of every module, each section ends with a brief but complete summary of concepts, a list of key terms, and a comprehensive problem set that includes concepts from across all of the modules in the section.

Key Terms

Competitive market, p. 36
Supply and demand model,
Movement along the demand curve, p. 39
Supp...
Supp...

Problems

1. A survey indicated that chocolate ice cream is America's favorite ice-cream flavor. For each of the following, indicate the possible effects on the demand and/or supply, equilibrium price, and equilibrium quantity of chocolate ice cream.
   a. A severe drought in the Midwest causes dairy farmers to reduce the number of milk-producing cows in their herds by a third. These dairy farmers supply cream that is used to manufacture chocolate ice cream.
   b. A new report by the American Medical Association reveals that chocolate does, in fact, have significant health benefits.
   c. The discovery of cheaper synthetic vanilla flavoring lowers the price of vanilla ice cream.
   d. New technology for mixing and freezing ice cream lowers manufacturers' costs of producing chocolate ice cream.

a. the market for newspapers in your town
   Case 1: The salaries of journalists go up.
   Case 2: There is a big news event in your town, which is reported in the newspapers, and residents want to learn more about it.

b. the market for St. Louis Rams cotton T-shirts
   Case 1: The Rams win the championship.
   Case 2: The price of cotton increases.

c. the market for bagels
   Case 1: People realize how fattening bagels are.
   Case 2: People have less time to make themselves a cooked breakfast.

5. Find the flaws in reasoning in the following statements, paying particular attention to the distinction between changes in and movements along the supply and demand curves. Draw a diagram to illustrate what actually hap-

Supplements and Media

Worth Publishers is pleased to offer an enhanced and completely revised supplements and media package to accompany this textbook. The package has been crafted to help instructors teach their principles course and to give students the tools to develop their skills in economics.

For Instructors

Instructor's Resource Manual with Solutions Manual

The Instructor's Resource Manual, revised by Nora Underwood, University of Central Florida, is a resource meant to provide materials and tips to enhance the classroom experience.

The Instructor's Resource Manual provides the following:

- Module objectives
- Module outlines
- Teaching tips and ideas that include:
  - Hints on how to create student interest
  - Tips on presenting the material in class
- Discussion of the examples used in the text, including points to emphasize with your students
- Activities that can be conducted in or out of the classroom
- Hints for dealing with common misunderstandings that are typical among students
- Web resources (includes tips for using LaunchPad)
- Solutions manual with detailed solutions to all of the end-of-section problems from the textbook

The files for the Instructor's Resource Manual will be available for download by adopting instructors.

Test Bank

The Test Bank, coordinated by Doris Bennett, Jacksonville State University, provides a wide range of questions appropriate for assessing your students' comprehension, interpretation, analysis, and synthesis skills. The Test Bank offers multiple-choice, true/false, and short-answer questions designed for comprehensive coverage of the text concepts. Questions have been checked for continuity with the text content, overall usability, and accuracy.

The Test Bank features include the following:

- To aid instructors in building tests, each question has been categorized according to its general *degree of difficulty*. The three levels are*: easy, moderate,* and *difficult.*
  - *Easy* questions require students to recognize concepts and definitions. These are questions that can be answered by direct reference to the textbook.
  - *Moderate* questions require some analysis on the student's part.
  - *Difficult* questions usually require more detailed analysis by the student.
- Each question has also been categorized according to a *skill descriptor.* These include: *Fact-Based, Definitional, Concept-Based, Critical Thinking,* and *Analytical Thinking.*
  - *Fact-Based* questions require students to identify facts presented in the text.
  - *Definitional* questions require students to define an economic term or concept.
  - *Concept-Based* questions require a straightforward knowledge of basic concepts.
  - *Critical Thinking* questions require the student to apply a concept to a particular situation.
  - *Analytical Thinking* questions require another level of analysis to answer the question. Students must be able to apply a concept and use this knowledge for further analysis of a situation or scenario.
- To further aid instructors in building tests, each question is conveniently cross-referenced to the appropriate topic heading in the textbook. Questions are presented in the order in which concepts are presented in the text.
- The Test Bank includes questions with tables that students must analyze to solve for numerical answers. It also contains questions based on the graphs that appear in the book. These questions ask students to use the graphical models developed in the textbook and to interpret the information presented in the graph. Selected questions are paired with scenarios to reinforce comprehension.

The Diploma Computerized Test Bank and software is available in CD-ROM format for both Windows and Macintosh users. With this program, instructors can easily create and print tests and write and edit questions. Tests can be printed in a wide range of formats. The software's unique synthesis of flexible word-processing and database features creates a program that is extremely intuitive and capable.

Lecture PowerPoint Presentation

Created by Tori Knight, Carson-Newman University, these PowerPoint presentation slides are designed to assist with lecture preparation and presentations. The slides are organized by topic and contain graphs, data tables, and bulleted lists of key concepts suitable for lecture presentation. Key figures from the text are replicated and animated to demonstrate how they build. These slides can be customized to suit your individual needs by adding your own data, questions, and lecture notes.

Dynamic PowerPoint Presentation

This dynamic set of slides, designed by Solina Lindahl, CalPoly San Luis Obispo, is available as an alternative to the traditional lecture outline slides. The slides are brief, interactive, and visually interesting to keep students' attention in class. The slides utilize additional graphics and animations to demonstrate key concepts. The slides include additional (and interesting) real-world examples. The slides include hyperlinks to other relevant outside sources to illustrate real world examples and key concepts (including links to videos!). The slides also include opportunities to incorporate active learning in your classroom.

For Students

Study Guide

Prepared by Elizabeth Sawyer Kelly, University of Wisconsin–Madison, the Study Guide reinforces the topics and key concepts covered in the text. For each module, the Study Guide is organized as follows:

Before You Read the Module

- Summary: an opening paragraph that provides a brief overview of the module.
- Objectives: a numbered list outlining and describing the material that the student will learn in the module. These objectives can be easily used as a study tool for students.
- Key Terms: a list of boldface key terms with their definitions—including room for note-taking.

After You Read the Module

- Tips: numbered list of learning tips with graphical analysis.
- Worked Problems: A set of worked-out problems that take the student step-by-step through a particular problem/exercise.
- Problems and Exercises: a set of comprehensive problems.

Before You Take the Test

- Module Review Questions: a set of multiple-choice questions that focus on the key concepts students should grasp after reading the module. These questions are designed for student exam preparation.

Answer Key

- Answers to Problems and Exercises: detailed solutions to the Problems and Exercises in the Study Guide.
- Answers to Module Review Questions: solutions to the multiple-choice questions in the Study Guide—along with thorough explanations.

Online Offerings

www.saplinglearning.com

Sapling Learning provides the most effective interactive homework and instruction that improves student-learning outcomes for the problem-solving disciplines.

Sapling Learning offers an enjoyable teaching and effective learning experience that is distinctive in three important ways:

- **Ease of Use:** Sapling Learning's easy-to-use interface keeps students engaged in problem-solving, not struggling with the software.
- **Targeted Instructional Content:** Sapling Learning increases student engagement and comprehension by delivering immediate feedback and targeted instructional content.
- **Unsurpassed Service and Support:** Sapling Learning makes teaching more enjoyable by providing a dedicated Masters- or PhD-level colleague to service instructors' unique needs throughout the course, including content customization.

CoursePacks

Plug our content into your course management system. Registered instructors can download cartridges with no hassle, no strings attached. For more information, go to http://worthpublishers.com/catalog/Other/Coursepack.

Further Resources Offered

CourseSmart eTextbooks

http://www.coursesmart.com/ourproducts

CourseSmart textbooks offer the complete book in PDF format. Students can save money, up to 60% off the price of print textbooks. With the CourseSmart textbook, students have the ability to take notes, highlight, print pages, and more. A great alternative to renting print textbooks!

Worth Noting

Worth Noting keeps you connected to your textbook authors in real time. Whether they were just on CNBC or published in the *New York Times*, this is the place to find out about it. Visit Worth Noting at http://blogs.worthpublishers.com/econblog/.

i>clicker

Developed by a team of University of Illinois physicists, i>clicker is the most flexible and reliable classroom response system available. It is the only solution created *for* educators, *by* educators—with continuous product improvements made through direct classroom testing and faculty feedback. You'll love i>clicker, no matter your level of technical expertise, because the focus is on *your* teaching, *not the technology*. To learn more about packaging i>clicker with this textbook, please contact your local sales rep or visit www.iclicker.com.

Dismal Scientist

A high-powered business database and analysis service comes to the classroom! Dismal Scientist offers real-time monitoring of the global economy, produced locally by economists and professionals at Economy.com's London, Sydney, and West Chester offices. Dismal Scientist is *free* when packaged with the Krugman/Wells textbook. Please contact your local sales rep for more information or go to www.economy.com.

ECONPORTAL IS NOW LAUNCHPAD

Because Technology Should Never Get in the Way

LaunchPad

http://www.worthpublishers.com/launchpad

LaunchPad is an online homework, e-Book, and teaching and learning system that can be used as a stand-alone course management system or integrated into many campus course management systems such as Blackboard, Canvas, Desire2Learn, and others. And now, drawing on what we've learned from thousands of instructors and hundreds of thousands of students over the past several years, we are proud to introduce a new generation of Macmillan's Portals—***LaunchPad***.

LaunchPad features include:

- **LaunchPad Units** that provide the ability to build a course in minutes. LaunchPad offers selected resources compiled into ready-to-use teaching units, complete with problem sets, activities, e-Book sections, and state-of-the-art online homework and testing. Instructors can quickly set up their course using precreated LaunchPad units. They can also enhance LaunchPad units or create their own original assignments, adding selections from our extensive resource library of questions and activities, and their own materials as well.
- **LearningCurve:** A popular student resource, LearningCurve is an adaptive quizzing engine that automatically adjusts questions to the student's mastery level. With LearningCurve activities, each student follows a unique path to understanding the material. The more questions a student answers correctly, the more difficult the questions become. Each question is written specifically for the text and is linked to the relevant e-Book section. LearningCurve also provides a personal study plan for students as well as complete metrics for instructors. Proven to raise student performance, LearningCurve serves as an ideal formative assessment and learning tool. For detailed information, visit http://learningcurveworks.com.

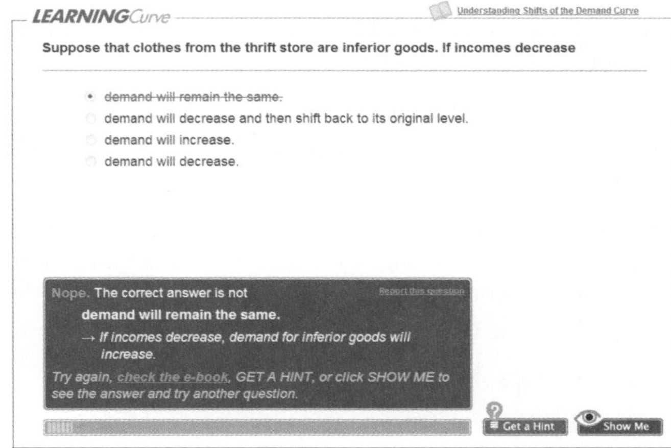

- **Clear, consistent interface:** LaunchPad integrates and unifies a consistent series of resources—LaunchPad units, the e-Book, media, assessment tools, instructor materials, and other content—to a degree unmatched by other online learning systems.
- **Robust, interactive e-Book:** The e-Book offers powerful study tools for students and easily customizable features for instructors. Our simple note-taking tool allows instructors to post notes, hyperlinks, content and more with a few simple clicks. Students can also take their own notes and can view all notes within each module to allow for easy study and review. Students can also highlight, access a glossary, and enlarge images within the text.

- **Powerful online quizzing and homework:** In addition to the LaunchPad units, instructors can create their own assignments using their own questions or drawing on quiz items within LaunchPad, including:
  - **The complete test bank** for the textbook for use in creating exams, quizzes, or homework problems. Instructors can use built-in filters and settings to ensure the right questions are chosen and displayed to their preferences.
  - **The end-of-section problem sets** are carefully edited and available in a self-graded format—perfect for in-class quizzes and homework assignments.
  - **Electronically gradable graphing problems** using a robust graphing engine. Students will be asked to draw their response to a question, and the software will automatically grade that response. Graphing questions are tagged to appropriate textbook sections and range in difficulty level and skill.

Get your feet wet with our graphing tools: Let's imagine a market for Tabloid Newspapers.

Part 1: Select the Line tool and draw a downward-sloping line. Label it "Demand 1". Next, using the same tool, draw an upward-sloping line that intersects "Demand 1" and label it "Supply 1".

Part 2: Use the Double Drop Line tool to identify the price and quantity where the two lines intersect. Label it "Equilibrium 1".

Part 3: With the Line tool, draw a new downward-sloping line that is to the LEFT of "Demand 1". Label it "Demand 2". Use the Double Drop Line tool to show the new equilibrium price and quantity in the global market for this Alien Bigfoot journalism. Label this point "Equilibrium 2."
Feel momentarily happy that demand for sensational stories has fallen, then remember that it's only because of the rise in demand for substitute goods like reality TV.

Continue to play with the graph if you like. We know you are an economist, after all.

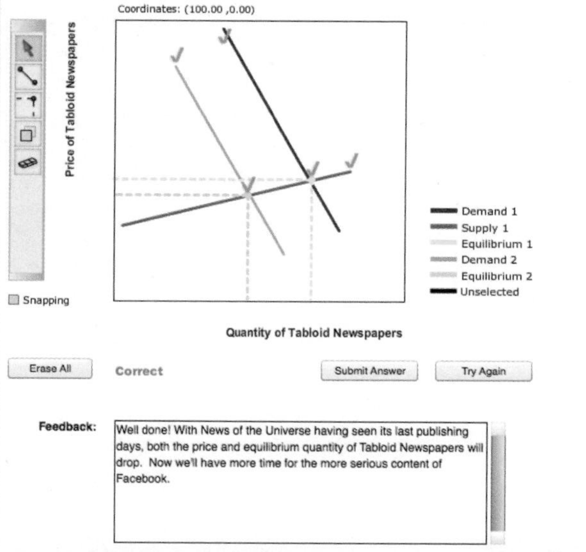

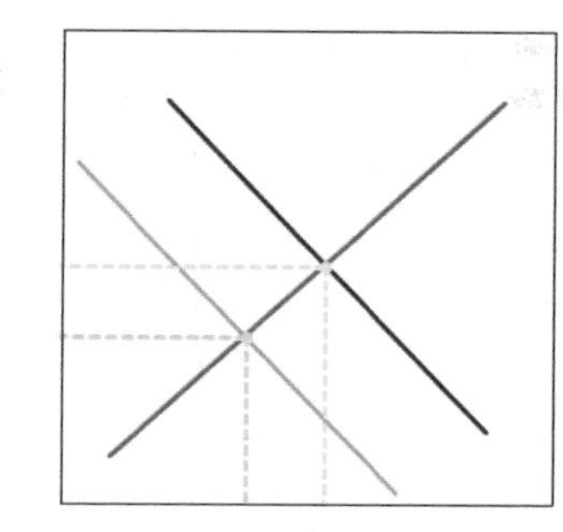

Next Question

ACKNOWLEDGMENTS

Our deep appreciation and heartfelt thanks go out to Margaret Ray, University of Mary Washington, and David Anderson, Centre College, for their hard work on the previous edition. Their efforts and innovations, inspired by many years of working with students in the classroom, provided us with a foundation for the modular approach that we have extended and built upon in this third edition. Thank you, Margaret and Dave, for doing such an exceptional job.

We must also thank Brian Peterson, Central College, for his contributions to the microeconomics portion of this book, and Nora Underwood, University of Central Florida, for her extensive contributions to the macroeconomic sections in this edition. Both Brian and Nora were involved during all stages of the revision. They supplied input as we were planning this edition, helping us make important decisions about sequencing and adding new content. This revision involved a lot of updating and Nora's contributions here were invaluable, as was her role in putting the final touches on the book in the page-proof stage. The efforts of Brian and Nora have helped us craft a third edition that is current and has even broader appeal.

We would also like to thank the following instructors who helped us with the revision of the third edition. Your enthusiasm for this project has been infectious.

Giuliana Campanelli Andreopoulos, *William Paterson University*
Becca Arnold, *San Diego Mesa College*
Margaret apRoberts-Warren, *University of California–Santa Cruz*
Robert Baden, *University of California–Santa Cruz*
Bryce Casavant, *University of Connecticut*
Dixie Dalton, *College of the Low Country*
Julie Gonzalez, *University of California–Santa Cruz*
Janet Koscianski, *Shippensburg University*
Sang Lee, *Southeastern Louisiana University*
Bill McLean, *Oklahoma State University*
Christopher McMahan, *University of Colorado–Boulder*
Joan Nix, *Queens College*
Dimitrios Pachis, *Eastern Connecticut State University*
Matthew S. Rutledge, *Boston College*
Robert Schlack, *Carthage College*
Fahlino Sjuib, *Framingham State University*
Bryan Snyder, *Bentley University*
Cheryl Wachenheim, *North Dakota State University*

We are indebted to the following reviewers, focus group participants, and other consultants for their suggestions and advice on earlier editions of this book.

Miki Brunyer Anderson, *Pikes Peak Community College*
Myra L. Moore, *University of Georgia*
Elizabeth Sawyer-Kelly, *University of Wisconsin, Madison*
Carlos Aguilar, *El Paso Community College*
Terence Alexander, *Iowa State University*
Morris Altman, *University of Saskatchewan*
Farhad Ameen, *State University of New York, Westchester Community College*
Christopher P. Ball, *Quinnipiac University*
Sue Bartlett, *University of South Florida*
Scott Beaulier, *Mercer University*
David Bernotas, *University of Georgia*
Marc Bilodeau, *Indiana University and Purdue University, Indianapolis*
Kelly Blanchard, *Purdue University*
Emily Blank, *Howard University*
Anne Bresnock, *California State Polytechnic University*
Douglas M. Brown, *Georgetown University*
Joseph Calhoun, *Florida State University*
Douglas Campbell, *University of Memphis*
Kevin Carlson, *University of Massachusetts, Boston*
Andrew J. Cassey, *Washington State University*
Shirley Cassing, *University of Pittsburgh*
Sewin Chan, *New York University*
Mitchell M. Charkiewicz, *Central Connecticut State University*
Joni S. Charles, *Texas State University, San Marcos*
Adhip Chaudhuri, *Georgetown University*
Eric P. Chiang, *Florida Atlantic University*
Hayley H. Chouinard, *Washington State University*
Kenny Christianson, *Binghamton University*
Lisa Citron, *Cascadia Community College*
Steven L. Cobb, *University of North Texas*
Barbara Z. Connolly, *Westchester Community College*
Stephen Conroy, *University of San Diego*
Thomas E. Cooper, *Georgetown University*
Cesar Corredor, *Texas A&M University and University of Texas, Tyler*
Jim F. Couch, *University of Northern Alabama*
Daniel Daly, *Regis University*
H. Evren Damar, *Pacific Lutheran University*
Satarupa Das, *Montgomery College, Takoma Park*
Antony Davies, *Duquesne University*
Greg Delemeester, *Marietta College*
Patrick Dolenc, *Keene State College*
Christine Doyle-Burke, *Framingham State College*
Ding Du, *South Dakota State University*
Jerry Dunn, *Southwestern Oklahoma State University*
Robert R. Dunn, *Washington and Jefferson College*
Ann Eike, *University of Kentucky*
Tisha L. N. Emerson, *Baylor University*
Hadi Salehi Esfahani, *University of Illinois*
William Feipel, *Illinois Central College*

Rudy Fichtenbaum, *Wright State University*
David W. Findlay, *Colby College*
Mary Flannery, *University of California, Santa Cruz*
Robert Francis, *Shoreline Community College*
Shelby Frost, *Georgia State University*
Frank Gallant, *George Fox University*
Robert Gazzale, *Williams College*
Seth Gitter, *Towson University*
Robert Godby, *University of Wyoming*
Michael Goode, *Central Piedmont Community College*
Douglas E. Goodman, *University of Puget Sound*
Marvin Gordon, *University of Illinois at Chicago*
Kathryn Graddy, *Brandeis University*
Mike Green, *College of Southern Maryland*
Yoseph Gutema, *Howard Community College*
Alan Day Haight, *State University of New York, Cortland*
Mehdi Haririan, *Bloomsburg University*
Clyde A. Haulman, *College of William and Mary*
Richard R. Hawkins, *University of West Florida*
Michael Heslop, *Northern Virginia Community College, Annandale*
Mickey A. Hepner, *University of Central Oklahoma*
Michael Hilmer, *San Diego State University*
Tia Hilmer, *San Diego State University*
Jane Himarios, *University of Texas, Arlington*
Jim Holcomb, *University of Texas, El Paso*
Don Holley, *Boise State University*
Alexander Holmes, *University of Oklahoma*
Julie Holzner, *Los Angeles City College*
Robert N. Horn, *James Madison University*
Steven Husted, *University of Pittsburgh*
John O. Ifediora, *University of Wisconsin, Platteville*
Hiro Ito, *Portland State University*
Mike Javanmard, *Rio Hondo Community College*
Robert T. Jerome, *James Madison University*
Shirley Johnson-Lans, *Vassar College*
David Kalist, *Shippensburg University*
Lillian Kamal, *Northwestern University*
Roger T. Kaufman, *Smith College*
Herb Kessel, *St. Michael's College*
Rehim Kiliç, *Georgia Institute of Technology*
Grace Kim, *University of Michigan, Dearborn*
Michael Kimmitt, *University of Hawaii, Manoa*
Robert Kling, *Colorado State University*
Sherrie Kossoudji, *University of Michigan*
Andrew Kozak, *St. Mary's College of Maryland*
Charles Kroncke, *College of Mount Saint Joseph*
Reuben Kyle, *Middle Tennessee State University (retired)*
Katherine Lande-Schmeiser, *University of Minnesota, Twin Cities*
David Lehr, *Longwood College*
Mary Jane Lenon, *Providence College*
Mary H. Lesser, *Iona College*
Solina Lindahl, *California Polytechnic State University, San Luis Obispo*
Haiyong Liu, *East Carolina University*
Jane S. Lopus, *California State University, East Bay*
María José Luengo-Prado, *Northeastern University*
Rotua Lumbantobing, *North Carolina State University*
Ed Lyell, *Adams State College*
Mireille Makambira, *Montgomery College, Rockville*
John Marangos, *Colorado State University*
Ralph D. May, *Southwestern Oklahoma State University*
Wayne McCaffery, *University of Wisconsin, Madison*
Dennis McCornac, *Anne Arundel Community College*
Bill McLean, *Oklahoma State University*
Larry McRae, *Appalachian State University*
Mary Ruth J. McRae, *Appalachian State University*
Ellen E. Meade, *American University*
Meghan Millea, *Mississippi State University*
Norman C. Miller, *Miami University (of Ohio)*
Khan A. Mohabbat, *Northern Illinois University*
Myra L. Moore, *University of Georgia*
Jay Morris, *Champlain College in Burlington*
Akira Motomura, *Stonehill College*
Kevin J. Murphy, *Oakland University*
Robert Murphy, *Boston College*
Ranganath Murthy, *Bucknell University*
Anthony Myatt, *University of New Brunswick, Canada*
Randy A. Nelson, *Colby College*
Charles Newton, *Houston Community College*
Daniel X. Nguyen, *Purdue University*
Dmitri Nizovtsev, *Washburn University*
Thomas A. Odegaard, *Baylor University*
Constantin Oglobin, *Georgia Southern University*
Charles C. Okeke, *College of Southern Nevada*
Terry Olson, *Truman State University*
Una Okonkwo Osili, *Indiana University and Purdue University, Indianapolis*
Chris Osuanah, *J. Sargeant Reynolds Community College, Downtown*
Maxwell Oteng, *University of California, Davis*
P. Marcelo Oviedo, *Iowa State University*
Jeff Owen, *Gustavus Adolphus College*
James Palmieri, *Simpson College*
Walter G. Park, *American University*
Elliott Parker, *University of Nevada, Reno*
Michael Perelman, *California State University, Chico*
Nathan Perry, *Utah State University*
Dean Peterson, *Seattle University*
Ken Peterson, *Furman University*
Paul Pieper, *University of Illinois at Chicago*
Dennis L. Placone, *Clemson University*
Michael Polcen, *Northern Virginia Community College*
Raymond A. Polchow, *Zane State College*
Linnea Polgreen, *University of Iowa*
Michael A. Quinn, *Bentley University*
Eileen Rabach, *Santa Monica College*
Matthew Rafferty, *Quinnipiac University*
Jaishankar Raman, *Valparaiso University*
Margaret Ray, *Mary Washington College*
Helen Roberts, *University of Illinois, Chicago*
Jeffrey Rubin, *Rutgers University, New Brunswick*
Rose M. Rubin, *University of Memphis*
Lynda Rush, *California State Polytechnic University, Pomona*
Michael Ryan, *Western Michigan University*

Sara Saderion, *Houston Community College*
Djavad Salehi-Isfahani, *Virginia Tech*
Elizabeth Sawyer-Kelly, *University of Wisconsin, Madison*
Jesse A. Schwartz, *Kennesaw State University*
Chad Settle, *University of Tulsa*
Steve Shapiro, *University of North Florida*
Robert L. Shoffner III, *Central Piedmont Community College*
Joseph Sicilian, *University of Kansas*
Judy Smrha, *Baker University*
John Solow, *University of Iowa*
John Somers, *Portland Community College*
Stephen Stageberg, *University of Mary Washington*
Monty Stanford, *DeVry University*
Rebecca Stein, *University of Pennsylvania*
William K. Tabb, *Queens College, City University of New York (retired)*
Sarinda Taengnoi, *University of Wisconsin, Oshkosh*
Henry Terrell, *University of Maryland*
Rebecca Achée Thornton, *University of Houston*
Michael Toma, *Armstrong Atlantic State University*
Brian Trinque, *University of Texas, Austin*
Boone A. Turchi, *University of North Carolina, Chapel Hill*
Nora Underwood, *University of Central Florida*
J. S. Uppal, *State University of New York, Albany*
John Vahaly, *University of Louisville*
Jose J. Vazquez-Cognet, *University of Illinois at Urbana-Champaign*
Daniel Vazzana, *Georgetown College*
Roger H. von Haefen, *North Carolina State University*
Andreas Waldkirch, *Colby College*
Christopher Waller, *University of Notre Dame*
Gregory Wassall, *Northeastern University*
Robert Whaples, *Wake Forest University*
Thomas White, *Assumption College*
Jennifer P. Wissink, *Cornell University*
Mark Witte, *Northwestern University*
Kristen M. Wolfe, *St. Johns River Community College*
Larry Wolfenbarger, *Macon State College*
Louise B. Wolitz, *University of Texas, Austin*
Gavin Wright, *Stanford University*
Bill Yang, *Georgia Southern University*
Jason Zimmerman, *South Dakota State University*

In the past, we always trusted Andreas Bentz and his indefatigable eye for detail while we focused on big-picture issues in the sections. We count ourselves extremely fortunate that Michael Reksulak, Georgia Southern University, stepped in when Andreas was unavailable to devote as much time to this project as in the past. Andreas was a helpful advisor during early stages of the revision. Michael turned out to be more than capable of providing expert-level guidance in the page-proof stage, when tending to accuracy and details is paramount. Michael's efforts as accuracy checker and coordinator were supported by the invaluable contributions of accuracy checkers Dixie Dalton, Southside Virginia Community College, Matthew S. Rutledge, Boston College, Sang Lee, Southeastern Louisiana University, Becca Arnold, San Diego Mesa College, Janet Koscianski, Shippensburg University, Stephanie Riche, North Carolina State University, and Cheryl Wachenheim, North Dakota State University. Many thanks to Solina Lindahl, California Polytechnic State University, who provided expert guidance on the media program associated with the textbook, and to Scott Houser, California State University, for his involvement.

We must also thank the many people at Worth Publishers for their contributions. Elizabeth Widdicombe and Catherine Woods for their role in planning this revision. Charles Linsmeier, who ably oversaw the revision and contributed throughout, and now Steve Rigolosi, who will have an important role to play post publication. A special thanks to Craig Bleyer, our original publisher and now national sales manager, who put so much effort into making all of our textbooks a success. And to Scott Guile, associate director of digital marketing, who recognized a need for a more streamlined version of our text and whose enthusiasm for the modular format helped to bring an innovative approach to fruition.

Once again, we have an incredible production and design team. Thank you all: Tracey Kuehn, Lisa Kinne, Barbara Seixas, and Liz Geller for producing this book; Babs Reingold, Lyndall Culbertson, Chuck Yuen, Diana Blume, and Paul Lacy for their beautiful interior design, layout, and cover; Deborah Heimann for her thoughtful copyedit; Cecilia Varas and Elyse Rieder, who work so hard and with lightning speed to get photos permissioned and just right; Stacey Alexander and Edgar Bonilla for coordinating the supplemental materials; Mary Walsh, associate editor, who made invaluable editorial contributions to this revision; and Fay Kelly, editorial assistant, who did a fine job preparing the manuscript for production.

Many thanks to Lukia Kliossis and Marie McHale for devising and coordinating the impressive collection of media and supplements. With each edition you've shown how far we've come in supporting instructors who choose to adopt our textbook. Thanks to the incredible team of writers and coordinators who worked with Lukia and Marie on the supplements and media package.

Thanks to Tom Digiano, marketing manager, and to Tom Acox for his many contributions. We must also extend our heartfelt thanks to the many members of the sales force, some who have been with us from the beginning, on your tireless efforts in promoting our book.

And most of all, special thanks to Sharon Balbos, executive development editor on each of our editions. Much of the success of this book is owed to Sharon's dedication and professionalism; in this edition, perhaps more so than most. Sharon, we're not sure we deserved an editor as good as you, but we're sure that everyone involved as well as our adopters and their students have been made better off by your presence.

Paul Krugman

Robin Wells

Photo Credits

Front cover *Welder:* Thinkstock. *City of Shanghai:* iStockphoto/Thinkstock. *Diesel prices:* © Laura Gangi Pond/iStockphoto/Thinkstock. *Group of friends carrying shopping bags on city street:* Monkey Business Images/Shutterstock. *Loading dock*: Glow Images/Superstock. *Cotton field:* © Fábio Salles/Dreamstime.com. *Girl writing on graph:* iStockphoto/Thinkstock. Fish: iStockphoto. **p. xiii** *Young woman and young man in TV store:* iStockphoto. *Cotton boll:* iStockphoto/Thinkstock. **p. xiv** *Vaccination:* iStockphoto/Thinkstock. *Used books:* Thinkstock. *Yellow cab:* iStockphoto. **p. xv** *Container ship:* © Juice Images/Alamy. *Portrait of young woman:* Ashley Hildreth. **p. xvi** *Wheat field:* Vaclav Volrab/Shutterstock. *Strawberry pickers:* Thinkstock. **p. xvii** *Model with enormous diamond ring:* Icogenic/Getty Images. *Office corridor:* Pressmaster/Shutterstock. **p. xviii** *No fishing sign:* iStockphoto/Thinkstock. *Students on graduation day:* Exactostock/Superstock. **p. xix** *Female café owner:* © Tetra Images/Alamy. *City of Shanghai:* iStockphoto/Thinkstock. **p. xx** *Bank of England:* Thinkstock. *Crowd in Hong Kong:* Red Chopsticks/Getty Images. **p. xxi** *Money pouring our of bank vault:* Jund Lund/Getty Images. *Warehouse worker:* Moodboard/Alamy. **p. xxii** *Need job sign:* Thinkstock. *Tax return check:* Shutterstock. **p. xxiii** *Detail of dollar bill:* ©Anna Delaw/Alamy. *Ben Bernanke:* Britt Leckman/Official Federal Reserve Photo. **p. xxiv** *Zimbabwe money:* Trevor Kelly/Shutterstock. *Map/coins:* © Sadik Demiroz/Thinkstock. **p. xxv** *Archival Depression photo (Looking for Work):* Everett Collection/Shutterstock. **p. xlviii** *Portrait:* Rubberball/Superstock. *Young woman and young man in TV store:* iStockphoto. *Young woman writing on glass graph:* iStockphoto/Thinkstock. *Boeing plane:* UPI/Alan Marts/Boeing/Landov. *Chinese package:* Kees Metselaar/Alamy. **p. 1** *Wright Brothers:* Landov Photos. **p. 34** *Portrait:* iStockphoto. *Jeans-clad legs:* Thinkstock. *Cotton field:* Casadphoto/Dreamstime.com. *Crowd carrying things through floodwater:* AP Photo/Khalid Tanveer. **p. 35** *Cotton boll:* iStockphoto/Thinkstock. **p. 70** *Red-capped bottles:* iStockphoto/Thinkstock. *Open house:* © Monkey Business Images/Dreamstime.com. *Hot dogs:* Msheldrake/Dreamstime.com. **p. 71** *Vaccination:* iStockphoto/Thinkstock. **p. 100** *Portrait:* Malyugin/Shutterstock. *Two people in textbook store:* Peter Huoppi. *Outdoor produce market:* iStockphoto/Thinkstock. **p. 101** *Used books:* Thinkstock. **p. 126** *Portrait:* © Simon Stanmore/Blend Images/Corbis. *Fire escapes:* Thinkstock/Photodisc. *Man hailing cab:* Alamy Images. *Uncle Sam* image courtesy of Library of Congress. **p. 127** *Yellow cab:* iStockphoto. **p. 164** *Portrait:* © Sherrie Nickol/Citizen Stock/Corbis. *Ford Mustang:* Scott Olsen/Getty Images. *Repairman:* Susana Gonzalez/Bloomberg via Getty Images. *Container ship dock:* Glow Images/Superstock. **p. 165** *Container ship:* © Juice Images/Alamy. **p. 190** *Portrait:* Tim Roberts/Getty Images. *Highway direction signs:* Vividpixel/Dreamstime. *3-D brain map:* Thinkstock. *Man eating hamburgers:* craftvision/Getty Images. **p. 191** *Portrait of a young woman:* Ashley Hildreth. **p. 228** *Portrait:* Thinkstock. *Harvesters:* Terrance Klassen/AgePhotostock. *Strawberry pickers:* Ilene MacDonald/Alamy. *Cookie packagers:* iStockphoto. **p. 229** *Wheat field:* Vaclav Volrab/Shutterstock. **p. 258** *Portrait:* Luis Alvarez/Getty Images. *Coca Cola: Tomatillos and tomatoes:* iStockphoto. **p. 259** *Strawberries:* Thinkstock. **p. 300** *Portrait:* © Ocean/Corbis. *Loose diamonds:* iStockphoto. *Seated woman with bills:* Sacks/Getty Images. *Airport lounge:* Exactostock/Superstock. **p. 301** *Model with enormous diamond ring:* Icogenic/Getty Images. **p. 328** *Portrait:* gulfimages/Alamy. *Office conference:* Martin Barraud/Getty Images. *Chess game:* Photosindia/Getty Images. *Mobil sign:* AP Photo/Steven Senne. *Exxon sign:* Tim Sloan/AFP/Getty Images/Newscom. *Mall:* iStockphoto. *Mall advertisements:* Andrew Moore/Gallery Stock. **p. 329** *Office corridor:* Pressmaster/Shutterstock. **p. 370** *Portrait:* © Image Source. *Smokestacks:* iStockphoto/Thinkstock. *Oil spill cleanup workers:* © AccentAlaska.com/Alamy. *Steamroller:* Telekhovskyi/Shutterstock. **p. 371** *No fishing sign:* iStockphoto/Thinkstock. **p. 422** *Portrait:* © Martin Palombini/Corbis. Fallow field: iStockphoto/Thinkstock. *Large imaging machine:* iStockphoto/Thinkstock. *Two young men:* iStockphoto/Thinkstock. *People of different professions in hardhats:* Kurhan/Shutterstock. *Office workers at desks with computers and telephones:* AAGIA/Getty Images. **p. 423** *Students on graduation day:* Exactostock/Superstock. **p. 452** *Portrait:* © Paul Burns/Corbis. *Robot worker:* Beth Hail/Bloomberg via Getty Images. *Human worker:* iStockphoto. *Lemons:* iStockphoto. **p. 453** *Female café owner:* Tetra Images/Alamy. **p. 466** *Portrait:* Rubberball/Superstock. *Photo of Hooverville:* American Stock/Getty Images. *Calculator:* Thinkstock. *Crowd in an urban setting:* SFC/Shutterstock. *Shelves of boxes:* Andersen Ross/Getty Images. *Shopping cart:* Corbis/Superstock. **p. 467** *City of Shanghai:* iStockphoto/Thinkstock. **p. 502** *Portrait:* Stockbyte/Getty Images. *Cutting staff and employee job reduction concept:* Lightspring/Shutterstock. *Job seekers at a career fair:* Frances Roberts/Alamy. *Supermarket check:* Oleg Doroshin/Shutterstock. *Gas station sign:* AP Photo/Paul Sakuma. **p. 503** *Bank of England:* Thinkstock. **p. 542** *Portrait:* Chris Schmidt/Getty Images. *The Iron Foundry, Burmeister & Wain, 1885 by Peder Severin Kroyer:* Prisma/UIG via Getty Images. *Smelting of the metal in a foundry:* Kaband/Shutterstock. *Circuit board manufacturing:* Kim Steele/Getty Images. *Busy streets in Shibuya Tokyo 2006:* FocusJapan/Alamy. **p. 543** *Crowd in Hong Kong:* Red Chopsticks/Getty Images. **p. 576** *Portrait:* Sherrie Nickol/age fotostock. *Conceptual money symbols with large group of people:* Shutterstock. *Wall Street bull statue:* © Michael Belardo/Alamy. *Time is money:* Shutterstock. *U.S. Savings Bonds:* NoDerog/Getty Images. *Stock market:* Tupungato/Thinkstock. **p. 577** *Facebook:* Knut Knipser/Media Bakery. **p. 612** *Portrait:* © Klaus Mellenthin/Westend61/Corbis. *People window shopping:* Thinkstock. *People carrying shopping bags:* Monkey Business Images/Shutterstock. *People window shopping:* Thinkstock. *Logs on truck:* Johner Images/Alamy. *Worker checking inventory:* Moodboard/Alamy. **p. 612** *Foreclosure bus tour:* AP Photo/Chris O'Meara. **p. 644** *Portrait:* Luis Alvarez/Getty Images. *Man shopping for laptop:* PhotoAlto/Alamy. *Welder cutting track rail:* Tristan Savatier/Getty Images. *Store closing sale:* Dorset Media Service/Alamy. **p. 645** *Need job sign:* Thinkstock. **p. 684** *Portrait:* Yuri Arcurs Media/Superstock. *U.S. dollars:* Shutterstock. *Tax return check:* Shutterstock. *National Debt clock:* Marmaduke St. John/Alamy. *Payment by credit card:* Dmitriy Shironosov/Alamy. **p. 685** *Highway sign:* AP Photo/The Plain Dealer, Scott Shaw. **p. 716** *Portrait:* Tom Fullum/Getty Images. *Paper money:* Shutterstock. *Money pouring out of bank vault:* Jund Lund/Getty Images. *Federal Reserve building:* Visions of America/JoeSohm/Getty Images. **p. 717** *Detail of dollar bill:* © Anna Delaw/Alamy. **p. 748** *Portrait:* © HBSS/Corbis. *Meeting room:* AP Photo/Britt K. Leckman, Federal Reserve. *Janet Yellen:* Drew Angerer/Bloomberg via Getty Images. *Hands with money:* Shutterstock. *Money graph:* Jezper/Shutterstock. **p. 749** *Ben Bernanke:* Britt Leckman/Official Federal Reserve Photo. **p. 784** *Portrait:* Luis Alvarez/Getty Images. *Printing U.S. dollar banknotes:* Thinkstock. *Tokyo street scene:* Tom Bonaventure/ Photographer's Choice RF /Getty Images. *Businessman with umbrella:* Igor Stevanovic/Shutterstock. **p. 785** *Zimbabwe money:* Trevor Kelly/Shutterstock. **p. 842** *Portrait:* Tim Kitchen/Getty Images. *Map and coins:* © Sadik Demiroz/Thinkstock. *Currency exchange board:* © Image Source Plus/Alamy. *Travelex Currency Exchange:* Greg Balfour Evans/Alamy. *Stacks of British currency:* Millennium Images/SuperStock. **p. 825** *Exterior of Swiss bank:* © Prisma Bildagentur AG/Alamy. **p. 860** *Portrait:* Justin Horrocks/Getty Images. *Children carrying picket signs:* © Minnesota Historical Society/CORBIS. *Man holding sign:* Thomas W. Elliott. *President Obama with senior advisors:* White House Photo/Alamy. **p. 861** *Roosevelt signing Social Security bill:* Universal History Archive/Getty Images.

ECONOMICS
IN MODULES

Basic Economic Concepts

THINKING LIKE AN ECONOMIST

All economic analysis is based on a set of common principles that apply to many different issues. Some of these principles involve *individual choice*—for economics is, first of all, about the choices that individuals make. Do you save your money and take the bus or do you buy a car? Do you keep your old smart phone or upgrade to a new one?

But in a market economy we make decisions in an environment shaped by the decisions of others—through *economic interaction*. Even the simplest decisions—like what to have for breakfast—are shaped by the decisions of thousands of other people, from the banana grower in Costa Rica who decided to grow the fruit we eat to the farmer in Iowa who provided the corn in our cornflakes.

To arrive at their theories about markets, economists use models, simplified representations of economic reality that allow for an understanding of a variety of economic issues. How helpful are models in the study of economics? To answer this question, let's consider the experience of the Wright brothers.

In 1901, Wilbur and Orville Wright built a device that would change the world. It was not the airplane—their successful flight at Kitty Hawk (pictured above) would come two years later. What made the Wright brothers true visionaries was their wind tunnel, an apparatus that let them experiment with many different designs for wings and control surfaces. These experiments gave them the knowledge that would make heavier-than-air flight possible.

A miniature airplane sitting motionless in a wind tunnel isn't the same thing as an actual aircraft in flight. But it is a very useful *model* of a flying plane. Needless to say, testing an airplane design in a wind tunnel is cheaper and safer than building a full-scale version and hoping it will fly. More generally, models play a crucial role in almost all scientific research—economics very much included. In fact, you could say that economic theory consists mainly of a collection of models.

In this section, we'll introduce you to the study of economics, including the role of individual choice. We'll look at how economists think and, in particular, how they use models in their work. We will then consider two economic models that are crucially important in their own right and also illustrate why such models are so useful.

The Study of Economics

iStockphoto

WHAT YOU WILL LEARN

1. How scarcity and choice are central to the study of economics
2. The importance of opportunity cost in individual choice and decision making
3. The difference between positive economics and normative economics
4. When economists agree and why they sometimes disagree
5. What makes macroeconomics different from microeconomics

Individual Choice: The Core of Economics

Economics is the study of scarcity and choice. Every economic issue involves, at its most basic level, **individual choice**—decisions by individuals about what to do and what *not* to do. In fact, you might say that it isn't economics if it isn't about choice.

Step into a big store such as Walmart or Target. There are thousands of different products available, and it is extremely unlikely that you—or anyone else—could afford to buy everything you might want to have. And anyway, there's only so much space in your home. Given the limitations on your budget and your living space, you must choose which products to buy and which to leave on the shelf.

The fact that those products are on the shelf in the first place involves choice—the store manager chose to put them there, and the manufacturers of the products chose to produce them. The **economy** is a system that coordinates choices about production with choices about consumption, and distributes goods and services to the people who want them. The United States has a **market economy,** in which production and consumption are the result of decentralized decisions by many firms and individuals. There is no central authority telling people what to produce or where to ship it. Each individual producer makes what he or she thinks will be most profitable, and each consumer buys what he or she chooses.

All economic activities involve individual choice. Let's take a closer look at what this means for the study of economics.

Economics is the study of scarcity and choice.

Individual choice is decisions by individuals about what to do, which necessarily involve decisions about what not to do.

An **economy** is a system for coordinating a society's productive and consumptive activities.

In a **market economy,** the decisions of individual producers and consumers largely determine what, how, and for whom to produce, with little government involvement in the decisions.

Resources Are Scarce

You can't always get what you want. Almost everyone would like to have a beautiful house in a great location (and help with the housecleaning), two or three luxury cars, and frequent vacations in fancy hotels. But even in a rich country like the United States, not many families can afford all of that. So they must make choices—whether to go to Disney World this year or buy a better car, whether to make do with a small backyard or accept a longer commute in order to live where land is cheaper.

Limited income isn't the only thing that keeps people from having everything they want. Time is also in limited supply: there are only 24 hours in a day. And because the time we have is limited, choosing to spend time on one activity also means choosing not to spend time on a different activity—spending time studying for an exam means forgoing a night at the movies. Indeed, many people feel so limited by the number of hours in the day that they are willing to trade money for time. For example, convenience stores usually charge higher prices than larger supermarkets. But they fulfill a valuable role by catering to customers who would rather pay more than spend the time traveling farther to a supermarket where they might also have to wait in longer lines.

Why do individuals have to make choices? The ultimate reason is that *resources are scarce*. A **resource** is anything that can be used to produce something else. The economy's resources, sometimes called *factors of production*, can be classified into four categories: **land** (including timber, water, minerals, and all other resources that come from nature), **labor** (the effort of workers), **physical capital** (machinery, buildings, tools, and all other manufactured goods used to make other goods and services), and **human capital** (the educational achievements and skills of the labor force, which enhance its productivity).

A resource is **scarce** when there is not enough of it available to satisfy the various ways a society wants to use it. For example, there are limited supplies of oil and coal, which currently provide most of the energy used to produce and deliver everything we buy. And in a growing world economy with a rapidly increasing human population, even clean air and water have become scarce resources.

Just as individuals must make choices, the scarcity of resources means that society as a whole must make choices. One way for a society to make choices is simply to allow them to emerge as the result of many individual choices. For example, there are only so many hours in a week, and Americans must decide how to spend their time. How many hours will they spend going to supermarkets to get lower prices rather than saving time by shopping at convenience stores? The answer is the sum of individual decisions: each of the millions of individuals in the economy makes his or her own choice about where to shop, and society's choice is simply the sum of those individual decisions.

For various reasons, there are some decisions that a society decides are best not left to individual choice. For example, two of the authors live in an area that until recently was mainly farmland but is now being rapidly built up. Most local residents feel that the community would be a more pleasant place to live if some of the land were left undeveloped. But no individual has an incentive to keep his or her land as open space, rather than sell it to a developer. So a trend has emerged in many communities across the United States of local governments purchasing undeveloped land and preserving it as open space. Decisions about how to use scarce resources are often best left to individuals but sometimes should be made at a higher, community-wide, level.

A **resource** is anything that can be used to produce something else.

Land refers to all resources that come from nature, such as minerals, timber, and petroleum.

Labor is the effort of workers.

Physical capital refers to manufactured goods used to make other goods and services.

Human capital refers to the educational achievements and skills of the labor force, which enhance its productivity.

A **scarce** resource is not available in sufficient quantities to satisfy all the various ways a society wants to use it.

The real cost of an item is its **opportunity cost:** what you must give up in order to get it.

Opportunity Cost: The Real Cost of Something Is What You Must Give Up to Get It

It is the last term before you graduate, and your class schedule allows you to take only one elective. There are two, however, that you would really like to take: Intro to Computer Graphics and History of Jazz.

Suppose you decide to take the History of Jazz course. What's the cost of that decision? It is the fact that you can't take the computer graphics class, your next best alternative choice. Economists call that kind of cost—what you must give up in order to get an item you want—the **opportunity cost** of that item. So the opportunity cost of taking the History of Jazz class is the benefit you would have derived from the Intro to Computer Graphics class.

.shock/Dreamstime

AP Photo/Paul Sakuma, FILE

Mark Zuckerberg understood the concept of opportunity cost.

The concept of opportunity cost is crucial to understanding individual choice because, in the end, all costs are opportunity costs. That's because every choice you make means forgoing some other alternative. Sometimes critics claim that economists are concerned only with costs and benefits that can be measured in dollars and cents. But that is not true. Much economic analysis involves cases like our elective course example, where it costs no extra tuition to take one elective course—that is, there is no direct monetary cost. Nonetheless, the elective you choose has an opportunity cost—the other desirable elective course that you must forgo because your limited time permits taking only one. More specifically, the opportunity cost of a choice is what you forgo by not choosing your next best alternative.

You might think that opportunity cost is an add-on—that is, something *additional* to the monetary cost of an item. Suppose that an elective class costs additional tuition of $750; now there is a monetary cost to taking History of Jazz. Is the opportunity cost of taking that course something separate from that monetary cost?

Well, consider two cases. First, suppose that taking Intro to Computer Graphics also costs $750. In this case, you would have to spend that $750 no matter which class you take. So what you give up to take the History of Jazz class is still the computer graphics class, period—you would have to spend that $750 either way. But suppose there isn't any fee for the computer graphics class. In that case, what you give up to take the jazz class is the benefit from the computer graphics class *plus* the benefit you could have gained from spending the $750 on other things.

Either way, the real cost of taking your preferred class is what you must give up to get it. As you expand the set of decisions that underlie each choice—whether to take an elective or not, whether to finish this term or not, whether to drop out or not—you'll realize that all costs are ultimately opportunity costs.

Sometimes the money you have to pay for something is a good indication of its opportunity cost. But many times it is not. One very important example of how poorly monetary cost can indicate opportunity cost is the cost of attending college. Tuition and housing are major monetary expenses for most students; but even if these things were free, attending college would still be an expensive proposition because most college students, if they were not in college, would have a job. That is, by going to college, students *forgo* the income they could have earned if they had worked instead. This means that the opportunity cost of attending college is what you pay for tuition and housing plus the forgone income you would have earned in a job.

It's easy to see that the opportunity cost of going to college is especially high for people who could be earning a lot during what would otherwise have been their college years. That is why star athletes like LeBron James and entrepreneurs like Mark Zuckerberg, founder of Facebook, often skip or drop out of college.

ECONOMICS IN ACTION

GOT A PENNY?

At many cash registers there is a little basket full of pennies. People are encouraged to use the basket to round their purchases up or down. If an item costs $5.02, you give the cashier $5.00 and take two pennies from the basket to give to the cashier. If an item costs $4.99, you pay $5.00 and the cashier throws a penny into the basket. It makes everyone's life a bit easier. Of course, it would be easier still if we just abolished the penny, a step that some economists have urged.

But why do we have pennies in the first place? If it's too small a sum to worry about, why calculate prices that precisely?

The answer is that a penny wasn't always such a negligible sum: the purchasing power of a penny has been greatly reduced by *inflation,* a general rise in the prices of all goods and services over time. Forty years ago, a penny had more purchasing power than a nickel does today.

Why does this matter? Well, remember the saying "A penny saved is a penny earned"? Of course, there are other ways to earn money, so you must decide whether saving a penny is a productive use of your time. Could you earn more by devoting that time to other uses?

Almost seventy years ago, the average wage was about $1.20 an hour. A penny was equivalent to 30 seconds' worth of work, so it was worth saving a penny if doing so took less than 30 seconds. But wages have risen along with overall prices, so that the average worker is now paid more than $23 per hour. A penny is therefore equivalent to just a little under 2 seconds of work, so it's not worth the opportunity cost of the time it takes to worry about a penny more or less.

In short, the rising opportunity cost of time in terms of money has turned a penny from a useful coin into a nuisance.

Microeconomics is the study of how people make decisions and how those decisions interact.

Macroeconomics is concerned with the overall ups and downs in the economy.

Economic aggregates are economic measures that summarize data across many different markets.

Microeconomics versus Macroeconomics

We have presented economics as the study of choices and described how, at its most basic level, economics is about individual choice. The branch of economics concerned with how individuals make decisions and how these decisions interact is called **microeconomics.** Microeconomics focuses on choices made by individuals, households, or firms—the smaller parts that make up the economy as a whole.

Macroeconomics focuses on the bigger picture—the overall ups and downs of the economy. When you study macroeconomics, you learn how economists explain these fluctuations and how governments can use economic policy to minimize the damage they cause. Macroeconomics focuses on **economic aggregates**—economic measures such as the unemployment rate, the inflation rate, and gross domestic product—that summarize data across many different markets.

Table 1-1 lists some typical questions that involve economics. A microeconomic version of the question appears on the left, paired with a similar macroeconomic question on the right. By comparing the questions, you can begin to get a sense of the difference between microeconomics and macroeconomics.

As these questions illustrate, microeconomics focuses on how individuals and firms make decisions, and the consequences of those decisions. For example, a school will use microeconomics to determine how much it would cost to offer a new course, which includes the instructor's salary, the cost of class materials, and so on. By weighing the costs and benefits, the school can then decide whether or not to offer the course. Macroeconomics, in contrast, examines the *overall* behavior of the economy—how the actions of all of the individuals and firms in the economy interact to produce a particular economy-wide level of economic performance. For example, macroeconomics is concerned with the general level of prices in the economy and how high or low they are relative to prices last year, rather than with the price of a particular good or service.

TABLE 1-1

Microeconomic versus Macroeconomic Questions

Microeconomic Questions	Macroeconomic Questions
Should I go to business school or take a job right now?	How many people are employed in the economy as a whole this year?
What determines the salary offered by Citibank to Cherie Camajo, a new MBA?	What determines the overall salary levels paid to workers in a given year?
What determines the cost to a university or college of offering a new course?	What determines the overall level of prices in the economy as a whole?
What government policies should be adopted to make it easier for low-income students to attend college?	What government policies should be adopted to promote employment and growth in the economy as a whole?
What determines whether Citibank opens a new office in Shanghai?	What determines the overall trade in goods, services, and financial assets between the United States and the rest of the world?

Positive economics is the branch of economic analysis that describes the way the economy actually works.

Normative economics makes prescriptions about the way the economy should work.

Positive versus Normative Economics

Economic analysis, as we will see throughout this book, draws on a set of basic economic principles. But how are these principles applied? That depends on the purpose of the analysis. Economic analysis that is used to answer questions about the way the world works, questions that have definite right and wrong answers, is known as **positive economics.** In contrast, economic analysis that involves saying how the world *should* work is known as **normative economics.**

Imagine that you are an economic adviser to the governor of your state and the governor is considering a change to the toll charged along the state turnpike. Below are three questions the governor might ask you.

1. How much revenue will the tolls yield next year?
2. How much would that revenue increase if the toll were raised from $1.00 to $1.50?
3. Should the toll be raised, bearing in mind that a toll increase would likely reduce traffic and air pollution near the road but impose some financial hardship on frequent commuters?

There is a big difference between the first two questions and the third one. The first two are questions about facts. Your forecast of next year's toll revenue without any increase will be proved right or wrong when the numbers actually come in. Your estimate of the impact of a change in the toll is a little harder to check—the increase in revenue depends on other factors besides the toll, and it may be hard to disentangle the causes of any change in revenue. Still, in principle there is only one right answer.

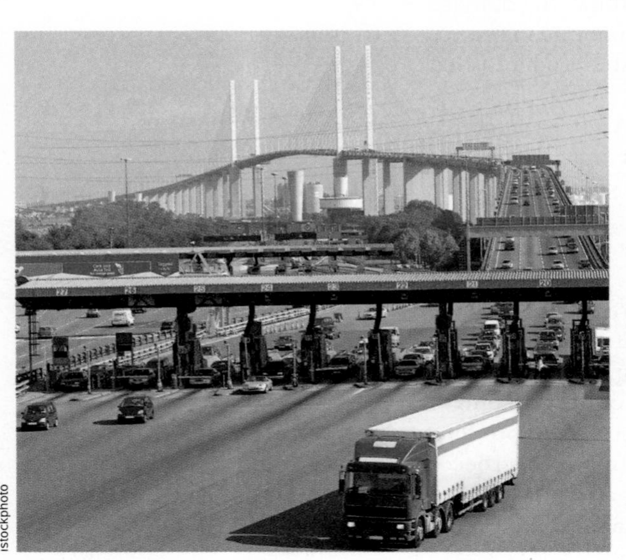

istockphoto

Should the toll be raised?

But the question of whether or not tolls should be raised may not have a "right" answer—two people who agree on the effects of a higher toll could still disagree about whether raising the toll is a good idea. For example, someone who lives near the turnpike but doesn't commute on it will care a lot about noise and air pollution but not so much about commuting costs. A regular commuter who doesn't live near the turnpike will have the opposite priorities.

This example highlights a key distinction between the two roles of economic analysis and presents another way to think about the distinction between positive and normative analysis: positive economics is about description, and normative economics is about prescription. Positive economics occupies most of the time and effort of the economics profession.

Looking back at the three questions the governor might ask, it is worth noting a subtle but important difference between questions 1 and 2. Question 1 asks for a simple prediction about next year's revenue—a forecast. Question 2 is a "what if" question, asking how revenue would change if the toll were to change. Economists are often called upon to answer both types of questions. Economic *models,* which provide simplified representations of reality such as graphs or equations, are especially useful for answering "what if" questions.

The answers to such questions often serve as a guide to policy, but they are still predictions, not prescriptions. That is, they tell you what will happen if a policy is changed, but they don't tell you whether or not that result is good. Suppose that your economic model tells you that the governor's proposed increase in highway tolls will raise property values in communities near the road but will tax or inconvenience people who currently use the turnpike to get to work. Does that information make this proposed toll increase a good idea or a bad one? It depends on whom you ask. As we've just seen, someone who is very concerned with the communities near the road will support the increase, but someone who is very concerned with the welfare of drivers will feel differently. That's a value judgment—it's not a question of positive economic analysis.

Still, economists often do engage in normative economics and give policy advice. How can they do this when there may be no "right" answer? One answer is that economists are also citizens, and we all have our opinions. But economic analysis can often be used to show that some policies are clearly better than others, regardless of individual opinions.

Suppose that policies A and B achieve the same goal, but policy A makes everyone better off than policy B—or at least makes some people better off without making other people worse off. Then A is clearly more efficient than B. That's not a value judgment: we're talking about how best to achieve a goal, not about the goal itself.

For example, two different policies have been used to help low-income families obtain housing: rent control, which limits the rents landlords are allowed to charge, and rent subsidies, which provide families with additional money with which to pay rent. Almost all economists agree that subsidies are the more efficient policy. (In a later module we'll see why this is so.) And so the great majority of economists, whatever their personal politics, favor subsidies over rent control.

When policies can be clearly ranked in this way, then economists generally agree. But it is no secret that economists sometimes disagree.

When and Why Economists Disagree

Economists have a reputation for arguing with each other. Where does this reputation come from?

One important answer is that media coverage tends to exaggerate the real differences in views among economists. If nearly all economists agree on an issue—for example, the proposition that rent controls lead to housing shortages—reporters and editors are likely to conclude that there is no story worth covering, and so the professional consensus tends to go unreported. But when there is some issue on which prominent economists take opposing sides—for example, whether cutting taxes right now would help the economy—that does make a good news story. So you hear much more about the areas of disagreement among economists than you do about the many areas of agreement.

It is also worth remembering that economics is, unavoidably, often tied up in politics. On a number of issues, powerful interest groups know what opinions they want to hear. Therefore, they have an incentive to find and promote economists who profess those opinions, which gives these economists a prominence and visibility out of proportion to their support among their colleagues.

Although the appearance of disagreement among economists exceeds the reality, it remains true that economists often *do* disagree about important things. For example, some highly respected economists argue vehemently that the U.S. government should replace the income tax with a *value-added tax* (a national sales tax, which is the main source of government revenue in many European countries). Other equally respected economists disagree. What are the sources of this difference of opinion?

One important source of differences is in values: as in any diverse group of individuals, reasonable people can differ. In comparison to an income tax, a value-added tax typically falls more heavily on people with low incomes. So an economist who values a society with more social and income equality will likely oppose a value-added tax. An economist with different values will be less likely to oppose it.

A second important source of differences arises from the way economists conduct economic analysis. Economists base their conclusions on models formed by making simplifying assumptions about reality. Two economists can legitimately disagree about which simplifications are appropriate—and therefore arrive at different conclusions.

THE GLASS IS HALF FULL.
HALF EMPTY.
ECONOMISTS
TOLES
UNIVERSAL PRESS SYND.
8©2001 THE BUFFALO NEWS
THE CONSUMER IS HALF ALIVE.

Toles © 2001 The Buffalo News. Reprinted with permission of Universal Press Syndicate. All rights reserved.

ECONOMICS IN ACTION

WHEN ECONOMISTS AGREE

"If all the economists in the world were laid end to end, they still couldn't reach a conclusion." So goes one popular economist joke. But do economists really disagree that much?

Not according to a classic survey of members of the American Economic Association, reported in the May 1992 issue of the *American Economic Review*. The authors asked respondents to agree or disagree with a number of statements about the economy; what they found was a high level of agreement among professional economists on many of the statements. At the top of the list, with more than 90% of the economists agreeing, were the statements "Tariffs and import quotas usually reduce general economic welfare" and "A ceiling on rents reduces the quantity and quality of housing available." What's striking about these two statements is that many noneconomists disagree: tariffs and import quotas to keep out foreign-produced goods are favored by many voters, and proposals to do away with rent control in cities like New York and San Francisco have met fierce political opposition.

So is the stereotype of quarreling economists a myth? Not entirely. Economists do disagree quite a lot on some issues, especially in macroeconomics, but there is a large area of common ground.

Suppose that the U.S. government was considering a value-added tax. Economist A may rely on a simplification of reality that focuses on the administrative costs of tax systems—that is, the costs of monitoring compliance, processing tax forms, collecting the tax, and so on. This economist might then point to the well-known high costs of administering a value-added tax and argue against the change. But economist B may think that the right way to approach the question is to ignore the administrative costs and focus on how the proposed law would change individual savings behavior. This economist might point to studies suggesting that value-added taxes promote higher consumer saving, a desirable result. Because the economists have made different simplifying assumptions, they find themselves on different sides of the issue.

Most such disputes are eventually resolved by the accumulation of evidence that shows which of the various simplifying assumptions made by economists does a better job of fitting the facts. However, in economics, as in any science, it can take a long time before research settles important disputes—decades, in some cases. And since the economy is always changing in ways that make old approaches invalid or raise new policy questions, there are always new issues on which economists disagree. The policy maker must then decide which economist to believe.

MODULE 1 Review

Solutions appear at the back of the book.

Check Your Understanding

1. What are the four categories of resources? Give an example of a resource from each category.
2. What type of resource is each of the following?
   a. time spent flipping hamburgers at a restaurant
   b. a bulldozer
   c. a river
3. You make $45,000 per year at your current job with Whiz Kids Consultants. You are considering a job offer from Brainiacs, Inc., which would pay you $50,000 per year. Which of the following are elements of the opportunity cost of accepting the new job at Brainiacs, Inc.? Answer yes or no, and explain your answer.
   a. the increased time spent commuting to your new job
   b. the $45,000 salary from your old job
   c. the more spacious office at your new job

4. Identify each of the following statements as positive or normative, and explain your answer.
   a. Society should take measures to prevent people from engaging in dangerous personal behavior.
   b. People who engage in dangerous personal behavior impose higher costs on society through higher medical costs.

Multiple-Choice Questions

1. Which of the following is an example of a resource?
   I. petroleum
   II. a factory
   III. a cheeseburger dinner
   a. I only
   b. II only
   c. III only
   d. I and II only
   e. I, II, and III

2. Which of the following situations represent(s) resource scarcity?
   I. Rapidly growing economies experience increasing levels of water pollution.
   II. There is a finite amount of petroleum in the physical environment.
   III. Cassette tapes are no longer being produced.
   a. I only
   b. II only
   c. III only
   d. I and II only
   e. I, II, and III

3. Suppose that you prefer reading a book you already own to watching TV and that you prefer watching TV to listening to music. If these are your only three choices, what is the opportunity cost of reading?
   a. watching TV and listening to music
   b. watching TV
   c. listening to music
   d. sleeping
   e. the price of the book

4. Which of the following statements is/are normative?
   I. The price of gasoline is rising.
   II. The price of gasoline is too high.
   III. Gas prices are expected to fall in the near future.
   a. I only
   b. II only
   c. III only
   d. I and III only
   e. I, II, and III

5. Which of the following questions is studied in microeconomics?
   a. Should I go to college or get a job after I graduate?
   b. What government policies should be adopted to promote employment in the economy?
   c. How many people are employed in the economy this year?
   d. Has the overall level of prices in the economy increased or decreased this year?
   e. What determines the overall salary levels paid to workers in a given year?

Critical-Thinking Question

In what type of economic analysis do questions have a "right" or "wrong" answer? In what type of economic analysis do questions not necessarily have a "right" answer? On what type of economic analysis do economists tend to disagree most frequently? Why might economists disagree? Explain.

MODULE 2

Models and the Circular Flow

istockphoto/Thinkstock

WHAT YOU WILL LEARN

1. Why models are an important tool in the study of economics
2. How to interpret the circular-flow diagram of the economy
3. How individual decisions affect the larger economy

In the section opener, you saw how the Wright brothers' experimenting with a miniature airplane in a wind tunnel—a simplified representation of the real thing—served as a very useful model of a flying plane. In this module, we will look at why models are so useful to economists. We'll also examine one important simplified representation of economic reality—the circular-flow diagram.

Models Take Flight in Economics

A **model** is any simplified version of reality that is used to better understand real-world situations. But how do we create a simplified representation of an economic situation?

One possibility—an economist's equivalent of a wind tunnel—is to find or create a real but simplified economy. For example, economists interested in the economic role of money have studied the system of exchange that developed in World War II prison camps, in which cigarettes became a universally accepted form of payment, even among prisoners who didn't smoke.

Another possibility is to simulate the workings of the economy on a computer. For example, when changes in tax law are proposed, government officials use *tax models*—large mathematical computer programs—to assess how the proposed changes would affect different groups of people.

Models are important because their simplicity allows economists to focus on the effects of only one change at a time. That is, they allow us to hold everything else constant and to study how one change affects the overall economic outcome. So when building economic models, an important assumption is the **other things equal assumption,** which means that all other relevant factors remain unchanged. Sometimes the Latin phrase *ceteris paribus,* which means "other things equal," is used.

A **model** is a simplified representation used to better understand a real-world situation.

The **other things equal assumption** means that all other relevant factors remain unchanged. This is also known as the *ceteris paribus* assumption.

But it isn't always possible to find or create a small-scale version of the whole economy, and a computer program is only as good as the data it uses. (Programmers have a saying: garbage in, garbage out.) For many purposes, the most effective form of economic modeling is the construction of "thought experiments": simplified, hypothetical versions of real-world situations.

As you will see throughout this book, economists' models are often in the form of a graph. In Module 3 we will look at graphs of the *production possibility frontier,* a model that helps economists think about the choices made in every economy. In Module 4 we turn to *comparative advantage,* a model that clarifies the principle of gains from trade—trade both between individuals and between countries. Models can also be represented in diagrams. In this module we will use the circular-flow diagram to better understand the workings of the economy.

ECONOMICS IN ACTION

THE MODEL THAT ATE THE ECONOMY

A model is just a model, right? So how much damage can it do? Economists probably would have answered that question differently before the financial meltdown of 2008–2009 than after it. It turns out that a *bad* economic model played a significant role in the origins of the crisis.

"The model that ate the economy" originated in finance theory, the branch of economics that seeks to understand what assets like stocks and bonds are worth. Financial theorists often devise complex mathematical models to help investment companies decide what assets to buy and sell and at what price.

Finance theory has become increasingly important as Wall Street (a district in New York City where nearly all major investment companies have their headquarters) has shifted from trading simple assets like stocks and bonds to more complex assets—notably, mortgage-backed securities (or MBSs for short). An MBS is an asset that entitles its owner to a stream of earnings based on the payments made by thousands of people on their home loans. Investors wanted to know how risky these complex assets were. That is, how likely was it that an investor would lose money on an MBS?

Although we won't go into the details, estimating the likelihood of losing money on an MBS is a complicated problem. It involves calculating the probability that a significant number of the thousands of homeowners backing your security will stop paying their mortgages. Until that probability could be calculated, investors didn't want to buy MBSs.

In 2000, a Wall Street financial theorist announced that he had solved the problem by devising a simple model for estimating the risk of buying an MBS. Financial traders loved the model, as it opened up a huge and extraordinarily profitable market for them. Using this simple model, Wall Street was able to create and sell billions of MBSs, generating billions in profits for itself.

Or investors *thought* they had calculated the risk of losing money on an MBS. Some financial experts warned from the sidelines that the estimates of risk calculated by this simple model were just plain wrong. They said that in the search for simplicity, the model underestimated the likelihood that many homeowners would stop paying their mortgages at the same time, leaving MBS investors in danger of incurring huge losses.

Billions of dollars worth of MBSs were sold to investors both in the United States and abroad. In 2008–2009, the problems critics warned about exploded in catastrophic fashion. Over the previous decade, American home prices had risen too high, and mortgages had been extended to many who were unable to pay. As home prices fell, millions of homeowners didn't pay their mortgages. With losses mounting for MBS investors, it became all too clear that the model had indeed underestimated the risks. When investors and financial institutions around the world realized the extent of their losses, the worldwide economy ground to an abrupt halt.

Nikada/iStockphoto

The **circular-flow diagram** represents the transactions in an economy by flows around a circle.

A **household** is a person or a group of people who share income.

A **firm** is an organization that produces goods and services for sale.

Product markets are where goods and services are bought and sold.

Factor markets are where resources, especially capital and labor, are bought and sold.

The Circular-Flow Diagram

The U.S. economy is a vastly complex entity, with more than 155 million workers employed by more than 27 million companies, producing millions of different goods and services. Yet you can learn some very important things about the economy by considering the simple graphic shown in Figure 2-1. This **circular-flow diagram** is a simplified representation of the way money, goods and services, and factors of production flow through the economy. The yellow arrows show how goods, services, labor, and raw materials flow in one direction, and the bluish–green arrows show how the money that pays for these things flows in the opposite direction. The underlying principle is that the flow of money into each market or sector is equal to the flow of money coming out of that market or sector.

This simple model illustrates an economy that contains only two types of participants: households and firms. A **household** consists of either an individual or a group of people (typically a family) who share their income. A **firm** is an organization or business that produces goods or services for sale—and that employs members of households.

As shown in Figure 2-1, there are two kinds of markets in this simple economy. On the left side are markets for goods and services, also known as **product markets,** in which households buy the goods and services they want from firms. This produces a flow of goods and services to households and a return flow of money to firms.

On the right side are **factor markets** in which firms buy the resources they need to produce goods and services. Recall from the preceding module that the factors of production are land, labor, physical capital, and human capital.

The best known factor market is the *labor market,* in which workers are paid for their time and effort. Besides labor, we can think of households as owning the other factors of production as well, and selling them to firms. For example, when a corporation pays dividends to its stockholders, who are members of households, it is in effect paying them for the use of the machines and buildings that belong to those investors.

FIGURE 2-1 **The Circular-Flow Diagram**

This diagram represents the flows of money and of goods and services in the economy. In the markets for goods and services, households purchase goods and services from firms, generating a flow of money to the firms and a flow of goods and services to the households. The money flows back to households as firms purchase factors of production from the households in factor markets.

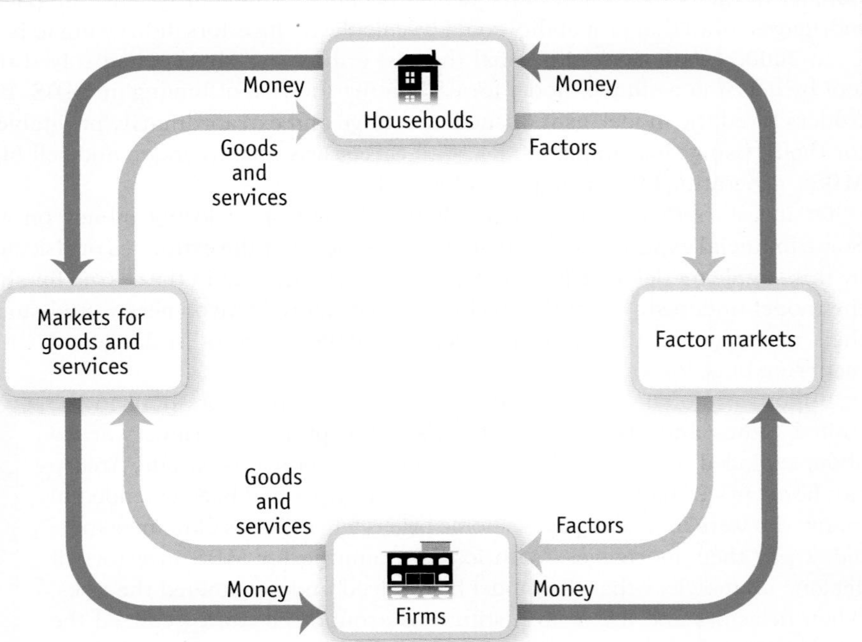

In the interest of simplicity, the circular-flow diagram in Figure 2-1 does not include a number of real-world complications. A few examples:

- In the real world, the distinction between firms and households isn't always that clear-cut. Consider a small, family-run business—a farm, a shop, a small hotel. Is this a firm or a household? A more complete picture would include a separate box for family businesses.
- A more complete picture would include the flows of goods, services, and money within the business sector.
- A more complete picture would include the sale of goods by firms to other firms; for example, steel companies sell mainly to other companies such as auto manufacturers, not to households.
- The diagram doesn't show the government, which takes money out of the circular flow in the form of taxes and injects it back into the flow as spending.

Figure 2-1, in other words, is by no means a complete picture of the economy's participants and the flows that take place among them. But despite its simplicity, the circular-flow diagram is a useful guide to how the economy works and how the participants are interconnected. Next we'll take a closer look at the relationship between individual decision making and broader economic outcomes.

One Person's Spending Is Another Person's Income

The circular-flow diagram shows that what goes around comes around. The circularity of spending magnifies the importance of individual and firm behavior at every level. And it helps to explain why reduced spending by one segment of the economy can lead to problems for almost everyone in the economy.

Consider Wichita, Kansas, known as the "Air Capital of the World" because so many airplanes are made there. In 2010, even as the economy recovered from the recession of 2007–2009, several corporations that had been buying a lot of airplanes decided to cut back on their purchases. These cuts bruised the Wichita economy, and spending dropped off at the city's retail stores. A similar problem occurred at the national level in 2001 and 2008, when cuts in business investment spending fueled a sharp downfall in retail sales.

But why should cuts in spending on airplanes by businesses mean empty stores in the shopping malls? After all, malls are places where families, not businesses, go to shop. The answer is that lower business spending led to lower incomes throughout the economy, because people who had been making those airplanes lost their jobs or were forced to take pay cuts. Between 2008 and 2010, Wichita's aviation industry lost about 13,000 jobs. As incomes evaporated in the aviation industry, so did spending by consumers who worked in the aviation industry. And then incomes and spending in industries supported by aviation workers—retail sales, day care, home construction, and so on—fell, and the domino effect of falling consumption and falling incomes continued.

This story illustrates a general principle: *One person's spending is another person's income.* In a market economy, people make a living selling things—including their labor—to other people. If some group in the economy decides, for whatever reason, to spend more, the income of other groups will rise. If some group decides to spend less, the income of other groups will fall.

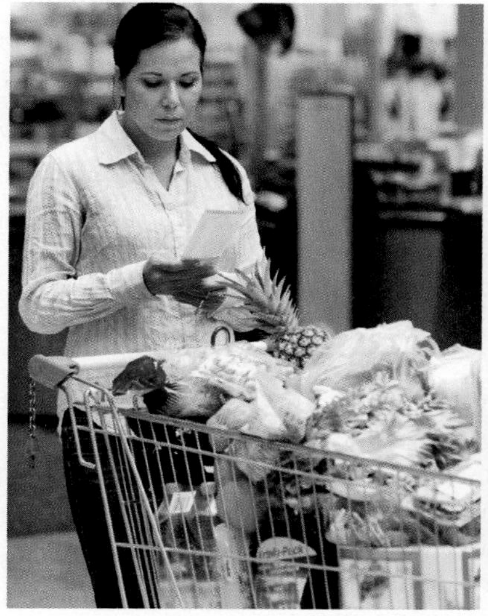

If one group in the economy spends more, the income of other groups will rise.

If one group spends less, the income of other groups will fall.

Because one person's spending is another person's income, a chain reaction of changes in spending behavior occurs. Spending cuts lead to reduced family incomes; families respond by reducing consumer spending, which leads to reductions in hiring by firms, and another round of income cuts; and so on.

Through these repercussions, individual and firm decisions send ripple effects throughout the economy. Keep in mind that behavior on the micro level can have macro consequences.

MODULE 2 Review

Solutions appear at the back of the book.

Check Your Understanding

1. Use the circular-flow diagram to explain how an increase in the amount of money spent by households results in an increase in the number of jobs in the economy.
2. Oil companies are investing heavily in projects that will extract oil from the "oil sands" of Canada. Near these projects, in Edmonton, Alberta, restaurants and other consumer businesses are booming. Explain why on the basis of a principle you learned about in this module.

Multiple-Choice Questions

1. The other things equal assumption allows economists to
   a. avoid making assumptions about reality.
   b. focus on the effects of only one change at a time.
   c. oversimplify.
   d. allow nothing to change in their model.
   e. reflect all aspects of the real world in their model.
2. Which of the following is true? The simple circular-flow diagram
   I. includes only the product markets.
   II. includes only the factor markets.
   III. is a simplified representation of the macroeconomy.
   a. I only
   b. II only
   c. III only
   d. I and III only
   e. none of the above
3. A firm is necessarily
   a. an employer of lawyers or accountants.
   b. a service provider.
   c. an organization.
   d. a corporation or business.
   e. a manufacturer of goods.
4. In the United States, we can think of the factors of production as being owned by
   a. firms.
   b. the government.
   c. factor markets.
   d. households.
   e. economists.
5. Economists are drawn to models by their
   a. good looks.
   b. realism.
   c. high level of detail.
   d. snap-on parts.
   e. simplicity.

Critical-Thinking Question

The inhabitants of the fictional economy of Atlantis use money in the form of cowry shells. Draw a circular-flow diagram showing households and firms. Firms produce potatoes and fish, and households buy potatoes and fish. Households also provide the land and labor to firms. Identify where, within the flows of cowry shells, goods and services, or resources, each of the following impacts would occur. Describe how this impact spreads around the circle.

a. A devastating hurricane floods many of the potato fields.
b. A productive fishing season yields an especially large number of fish.
c. The inhabitants of Atlantis discover the music of singer Beyoncé and spend several days a month at dancing festivals.

The Production Possibility Frontier Model

UPI/Alan Marts/Boeing/Landov

WHAT YOU WILL LEARN

1. The importance of trade-offs in economic analysis
2. What the production possibility frontier model tells us about efficiency, opportunity cost, and economic growth
3. The two sources of economic growth—increases in the availability of resources and improvements in technology

On December 15, 2009, Boeing's newest jet, the 787 Dreamliner, took its first three-hour test flight. It was a historic moment: the Dreamliner was the result of an aerodynamic revolution—a superefficient airplane designed to cut airline operating costs and the first to use superlight composite materials. The jet underwent over 15,000 hours of wind tunnel tests that resulted in subtle design changes to improve its performance. Boeing engineers owe an enormous debt to the Wright brothers' wind tunnel, which they used to model actual aircraft in flight. It made modern airplanes, including the Dreamliner, possible.

A good economic model can be a tremendous aid to understanding. In this module, we look at the *production possibility frontier,* a model that helps economists think about the *trade-offs* every economy faces. The production possibility frontier helps us understand three important aspects of the real economy: efficiency, opportunity cost, and economic growth.

Trade-offs: The Production Possibility Frontier

One of the important principles of economics we introduced in Module 1 was that resources are scarce. As a result, any economy—whether it contains one person or millions of people—faces trade-offs. You make a **trade-off** when you give up something in order to have something else. No matter how lightweight the Boeing Dreamliner is, and no matter how efficient Boeing's assembly line, producing Dreamliners means using resources that therefore can't be used to produce something else.

To think about the trade-offs necessary in any economy, economists often use the **production possibility frontier** model. The idea behind this model is to improve our

You make a **trade-off** when you give up something in order to have something else.

The **production possibility frontier (PPF)** illustrates the trade-offs facing an economy that produces only two goods. It shows the maximum quantity of one good that can be produced for each possible quantity of the other good produced.

understanding of trade-offs by considering a simplified economy that produces only two goods. This simplification enables us to show the trade-offs graphically.

Suppose, for a moment, that the United States was a one-company economy, with Boeing its sole employer and aircraft its only product. But there would still be a choice of what kinds of aircraft to produce—say, Dreamliners versus small commuter jets.

Figure 3-1 shows a hypothetical production possibility curve representing the trade-off this one-company economy would face. The curve—the dark-blue line in the diagram—shows the maximum quantity of small jets that Boeing can produce per year *given* the quantity of Dreamliners it produces per year, and vice versa. That is, it answers questions of the form, "What is the maximum quantity of small jets that Boeing can produce in a year if it also produces Dreamliners that year?"

There is a crucial distinction between points *inside* or *on* the production possibility curve (the shaded area) and *outside* the curve. If a production point lies inside or on the curve—like point *C*, at which Boeing produces 20 small jets and 9 Dreamliners in a year—it is feasible. After all, the curve tells us that if Boeing produces 20 small jets, it could also produce a maximum of 15 Dreamliners that year, so it could certainly make 9 Dreamliners. However, a production point that lies outside the curve—such as the hypothetical production point *D*, where Boeing produces 40 small jets and 30 Dreamliners—isn't feasible.

In Figure 3-1 the production possibility curve intersects the horizontal axis at 40 small jets. This means that if Boeing dedicated all its production capacity to making only small jets, it could produce 40 small jets per year. The production possibility curve intersects the vertical axis at 30 Dreamliners. This means that if Boeing dedicated all its production capacity to making Dreamliners, it could produce a maximum of 30 Dreamliners per year.

The figure also shows less extreme trade-offs. For example, if Boeing's managers decide to make 20 small jets this year, they can produce at most 15 Dreamliners; this production choice is illustrated by point *A*. And if Boeing's managers decide to produce 28 small jets, they can make at most 9 Dreamliners, as shown by point *B*.

Thinking in terms of a production possibility frontier simplifies the complexities of reality. The real-world U.S. economy produces millions of different goods. Even Boeing produces more than two different types of planes. Yet it's important to realize that even in its simplicity, this stripped-down model gives us important insights about the real world.

By simplifying reality, the production possibility frontier helps us understand some aspects of the real economy better than we could without the model: efficiency, opportunity cost, and economic growth.

FIGURE 3-1 **The Production Possibility Frontier**

The production possibility frontier illustrates the trade-offs Boeing faces in producing Dreamliners and small jets. It shows the maximum quantity of one good that can be produced given the quantity of the other good produced. Here, the maximum quantity of Dreamliners manufactured per year depends on the quantity of small jets manufactured that year, and vice versa. Boeing's feasible production is shown by the area *inside* or *on* the curve. Production at point *C* is feasible but not efficient. Points *A* and *B* are feasible and efficient in production, but point *D* is not feasible.

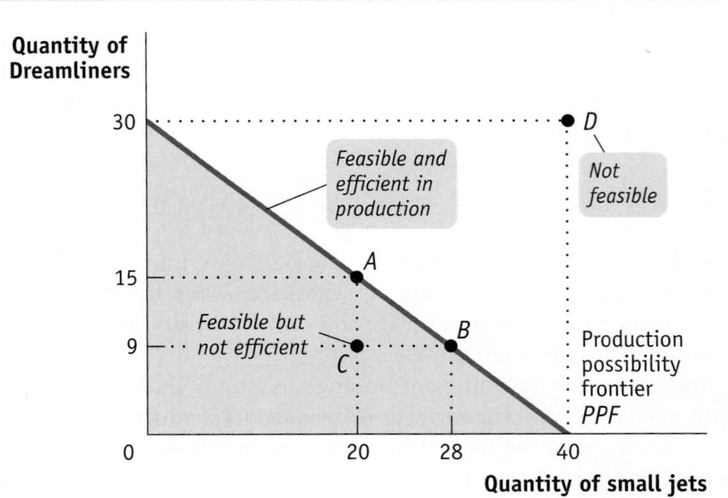

Efficiency

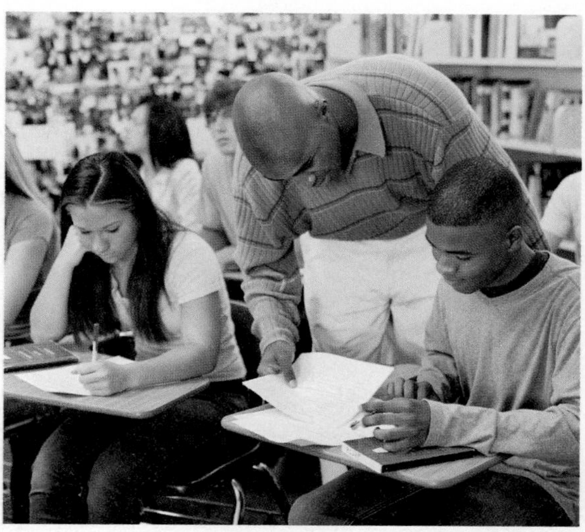
Alamy RF

Crowded classrooms reflect inefficiency if switching to a larger space would make some students better off without making anyone worse off.

The production possibility frontier is useful for illustrating the general economic concept of efficiency. An economy is **efficient** if there are no missed opportunities—meaning that there is no way to make some people better off without making other people worse off. For example, suppose a course you are taking meets in a lecture hall or classroom that is too small for the number of students—some may be forced to sit on the floor or stand—despite the fact that a larger space nearby is empty during the same period. Economists would say that this is an *inefficient* use of resources because there is a way to make some people better off without making anyone worse off—after all, the larger space is empty. The school is not using its resources efficiently.

When an economy is using all of its resources efficiently, the only way one person can be made better off is by rearranging the use of resources in such a way that the change makes someone else worse off. So in our classroom example, if all larger classrooms or lecture halls were already fully occupied, we could say that the school was run in an efficient way; your classmates could be made better off only by making people in the larger classroom worse off—by moving them to the room that is too small.

Returning to our Boeing example, as long as Boeing operates on its production possibility curve, its production is efficient. At point *A*, 15 Dreamliners are the maximum quantity feasible given that Boeing has also committed to producing 20 small jets; at point *B*, 9 Dreamliners are the maximum number that can be made given the choice to produce 28 small jets; and so on.

But suppose for some reason that Boeing was operating at point *C*, making 20 small jets and 9 Dreamliners. In this case, it would not be operating efficiently and would therefore be *inefficient:* it could be producing more of both planes.

Another example of inefficiency in production occurs when people in an economy are involuntarily unemployed: they want to work but are unable to find jobs. When that happens, the economy is not efficient in production because it could produce more output if those people were employed. The production possibility frontier shows the amount that can *possibly* be produced if all resources are fully employed. In other words, changes in unemployment move the economy closer to, or further away from, the PPF. But the curve itself is determined by what would be possible if there were full employment in the economy. Greater unemployment is represented by points farther below the PPF—the economy is not reaching its possibilities if it is not using all of its resources. Lower unemployment is represented by points closer to the PPF—as unemployment decreases, the economy moves closer to reaching its possibilities.

Although the production possibility frontier helps clarify what it means for an economy to be efficient in production, it's important to understand that efficiency in production is only *part* of what's required for the economy as a whole to be efficient. Efficiency also requires that the economy allocate its resources so that consumers are as well off as possible. If an economy does this, we say that it is *efficient in allocation*.

To see why efficiency in allocation is as important as efficiency in production, notice that points *A* and *B* in Figure 3-1 both represent situations in which the economy is efficient in production, because in each case it can't produce more of one good without producing less of the other. But these two situations may not be equally desirable. It may be more desirable to have more small jets and fewer Dreamliners than at point *A;* such as 28 small jets and 9 Dreamliners, corresponding to point *B*. In this case, point *A* is inefficient from the point of view of the economy as a whole: it is possible to move from point *A* to point *B*, and have some be made better off without making anyone else worse off.

This example shows that efficiency for the economy as a whole requires *both* efficiency in production and efficiency in allocation. To be efficient, an economy must produce as much of each good as it can, given the production of other goods, and it must also produce the mix of goods that people want to consume.

An economy is **efficient** if there is no way to make anyone better off without making anyone else worse off.

Opportunity Cost

The production possibility frontier is also useful as a reminder that the true cost of any good isn't the money it costs to buy, but what must be given up in order to get that good—the *opportunity cost.* If, for example, Boeing decides to change its production from point *A* to point *B,* it will produce 8 more small jets but 6 fewer Dreamliners. So the opportunity cost of 8 small jets is 6 Dreamliners—the 6 Dreamliners that can't be produced if Boeing produces 8 more small jets. This means that each small jet has an opportunity cost of $6/8 = 3/4$ of a Dreamliner.

iStockphoto

If Boeing decides to produce more small jets, the opportunity cost is the Dreamliners it must forego producing.

Is the opportunity cost of an extra small jet in terms of Dreamliners always the same, no matter how many small jets and Dreamliners are currently produced? In the example illustrated by Figure 3-1, the answer is yes. If Boeing increases its production of small jets from 28 to 40, the number of Dreamliners it produces falls from 9 to zero. So Boeing's opportunity cost per additional small jet is $9/12 = 3/4$ of a Dreamliner, the same as it was when Boeing went from 20 small jets produced to 28. The fact that the opportunity cost is always the

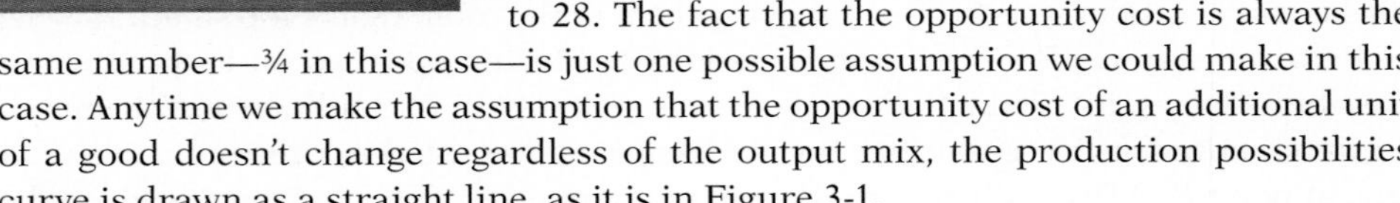

same number—$3/4$ in this case—is just one possible assumption we could make in this case. Anytime we make the assumption that the opportunity cost of an additional unit of a good doesn't change regardless of the output mix, the production possibilities curve is drawn as a straight line, as it is in Figure 3-1.

Moreover, as you might have already guessed, the slope of a straight-line production possibility curve is equal to the opportunity cost—specifically, the opportunity cost for the good measured on the horizontal axis in terms of the good measured on the vertical axis. In Figure 3-1, the production possibility curve has a *constant slope* of $-3/4$, implying that Boeing faces a *constant opportunity cost* for 1 small jet equal to $3/4$ of a Dreamliner. (A review of how to calculate the slope of a straight line is found in Appendix A at the back of the book.) This is the simplest case, but the production possibility frontier model can also be used to examine situations in which opportunity costs change as the mix of output changes.

Figure 3-2 illustrates a different assumption, a case in which Boeing faces *increasing opportunity cost.* Here, the more small jets it produces, the more costly it is to

FIGURE 3-2 **Increasing Opportunity Cost**

The bowed-out shape of the production possibility frontier reflects increasing opportunity cost. In this example, to produce the first 20 small jets, Boeing must give up producing 5 Dreamliners. But to produce an additional 20 small jets, Boeing must give up manufacturing 25 more Dreamliners.

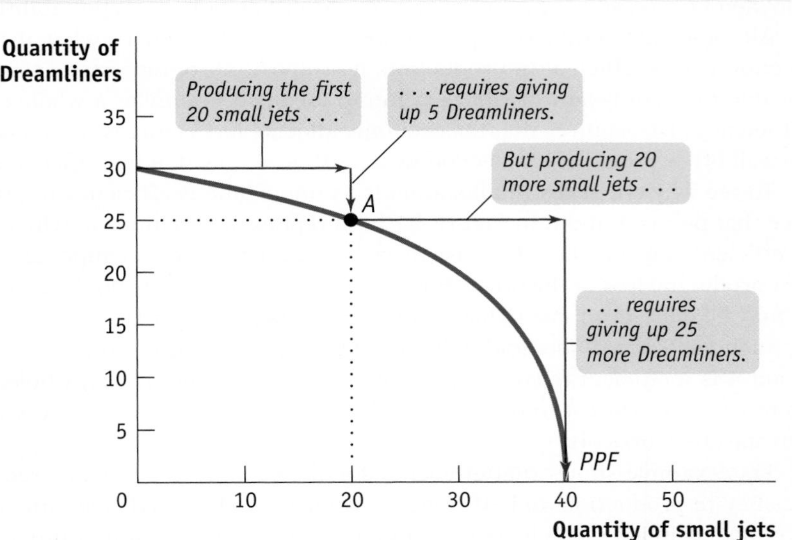

produce yet another small jet in terms of reduced production of a Dreamliner. For example, to go from producing zero small jets to producing 20, Boeing has to give up producing 5 Dreamliners. That is, the opportunity cost of those 20 small jets is 5 Dreamliners. But to increase its production of small jets to 40—that is, to produce an additional 20 small jets—it must produce 25 fewer Dreamliners, a much higher opportunity cost. And the same holds true in reverse: the more Dreamliners Boeing produces, the more costly it is to produce yet another Dreamliner in terms of reduced production of small jets. As you can see in Figure 3-2, when opportunity costs are increasing rather than constant, the production possibility curve is bowed outward rather than a straight line.

Although it's often useful to work with the simple assumption that the production possibility curve is a straight line, economists believe that in reality, opportunity costs are typically increasing. When only a small amount of a good is produced, the opportunity cost of producing that good is relatively low because the economy needs to use only those resources that are especially well suited for its production. For example, if an economy grows only a small amount of corn, that corn can be grown in places where the soil and climate are perfect for growing corn but less suitable for growing anything else, such as wheat.

So growing that corn involves giving up only a small amount of potential wheat output. Once the economy grows a lot of corn, however, land that is well suited for wheat but isn't so great for corn must be used to produce corn anyway. As a result, the additional corn production involves sacrificing considerably more wheat production. In other words, as more of a good is produced, its opportunity cost typically rises because well-suited inputs are used up and less adaptable inputs must be used instead.

Economic Growth

Finally, the production possibility frontier helps us understand what it means to talk about *economic growth,* which economists describe as creating *a sustained rise in aggregate output.* Economic growth is one of the fundamental features of the economy. But are we really justified in saying that the economy has grown over time? After all, although the U.S. economy produces more of many things than it did a century ago, it produces less of other things—for example, horse-drawn carriages. In other words, production of many goods is actually down. So how can we say for sure that the economy as a whole has grown?

The answer, illustrated in Figure 3-3, is that economic growth means an *expansion of the economy's production possibilities:* the economy *can* produce more of everything. In it, we assume again that our economy is only made up of Boeing, and therefore, our economy only produces two goods, Dreamliners and small jets. For example, if Boeing's production is initially at point *A* (20 small jets and 25 Dreamliners) economic growth means that Boeing could move to point *E* (25 small jets and 30 Dreamliners). Point *E* lies outside the original curve, so in the production possibility frontier model, growth is shown as an outward shift of the curve.

What can lead the production possibility curve to shift outward? There are basically

FIGURE 3-3 Economic Growth

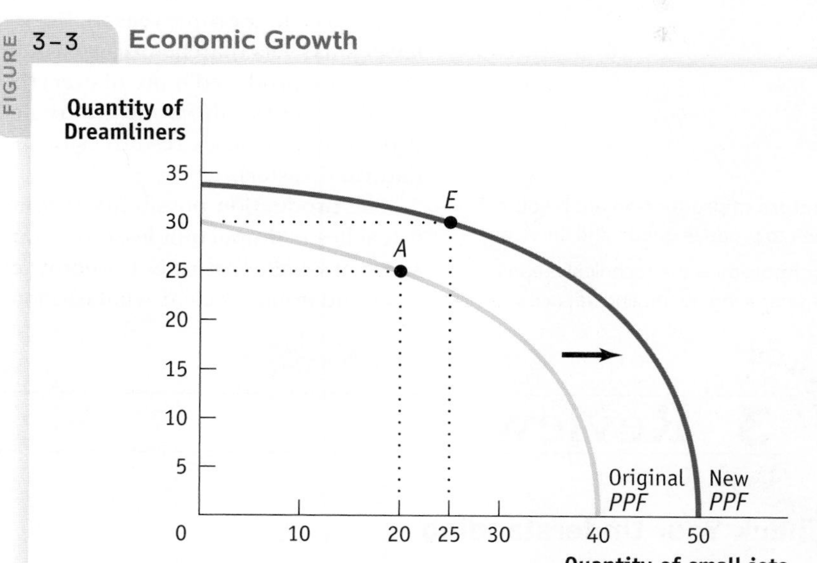

Economic growth results in an *outward shift* of the production possibility curve because production possibilities are expanded. The economy can now produce more of everything. For example, if production is initially at point *A* (25 Dreamliners and 20 small jets), economic growth means that the economy could move to point *E* (30 Dreamliners and 25 small jets).

iStockphoto

Comstock/Thinkstock

iStockphoto/Thinkstock

iStockphoto/Thinkstock

The four factors of production: land, labor, physical capital, and human capital.

two sources of economic growth. One is an increase in the economy's **factors of production,** the resources used to produce goods and services. Broadly speaking, the main factors of production are the resources land, labor, physical capital, and human capital. As you learned in Module 1, land is a resource supplied by nature; labor is the economy's pool of workers; physical capital refers to created resources such as machines and buildings; and human capital refers to the educational achievements and skills of the labor force, which enhance its productivity.

To see how adding to an economy's factors of production leads to economic growth, suppose that Boeing builds another construction hangar that allows it to increase the number of planes—small jets or Dreamliners or both—it can produce in a year. The new construction hangar is a factor of production, a resource Boeing can use to increase its yearly output. We can't say how many more planes of each type Boeing will produce; that's a management decision that will depend on, among other things, customer demand. But we can say that Boeing's production possibility curve has shifted outward because it can now produce more small jets without reducing the number of Dreamliners it makes, or it can make more Dreamliners without reducing the number of small jets produced.

The other source of economic growth is progress in **technology,** the technical means for the production of goods and services. Composite materials had been used in some parts of aircraft before the Boeing Dreamliner was developed. But Boeing engineers realized that there were large additional advantages to building a whole plane out of composites. The plane would be lighter, stronger, and have better aerodynamics than a plane built in the traditional way. It would therefore have longer range, be able to carry more people, and use less fuel, in addition to being able to maintain higher cabin pressure. So in a real sense Boeing's innovation—a whole plane built out of composites—was a way to do more with any given amount of resources, pushing out the production possibility curve.

But even if, for some reason, Boeing chooses to produce either fewer Dreamliners or fewer small jets than before, we would still say that this economy has grown, because it *could* have produced more of everything. At the same time, if an economy's production possibility curve shifts inward, the economy has become smaller. This could happen if the economy loses resources or technology (for example, if it experiences war or a natural disaster).

The production possibility frontier is a very simplified model of an economy. Yet it teaches us important lessons about real-world economies. It gives us our first clear sense of what constitutes economic efficiency, it illustrates the concept of opportunity cost, and it makes clear what economic growth is all about.

Factors of production are resources used to produce goods and services.

Technology is the technical means for producing goods and services.

MODULE 3 Review

Solutions appear at the back of the book.

Check Your Understanding

1. True or false? Explain your answer.
   a. An increase in the amount of resources available to Boeing for use in producing Dreamliners and small jets does not change its production possibility curve.
   b. A technological change that allows Boeing to build more small jets for any amount of Dreamliners built results in a change in its production possibility curve.
   c. The production possibility frontier is useful because it illustrates how much of one good an economy must give up to get more of another good regardless of whether resources are being used efficiently.

Multiple-Choice Questions

Refer to the accompanying graph to answer the following questions.

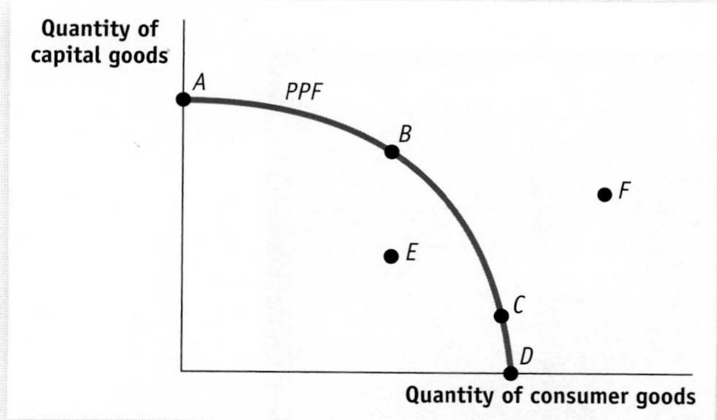

1. Which point(s) on the graph represent efficiency in production?
   a. *B* and *C*
   b. *A* and *D*
   c. *A*, *B*, *C*, and *D*
   d. *A*, *B*, *C*, *D*, and *E*
   e. *A*, *B*, *C*, *D*, *E*, and *F*

2. For this economy, an increase in the quantity of capital goods produced without a corresponding decrease in the quantity of consumer goods produced
   a. cannot happen because there is always an opportunity cost.
   b. is represented by a movement from point *E* to point *A*.
   c. is represented by a movement from point *C* to point *B*.
   d. is represented by a movement from point *E* to point *B*.
   e. is only possible with an increase in resources or technology.

3. An increase in unemployment could be represented by a movement from point
   a. *D* to point *C*.
   b. *B* to point *A*.
   c. *C* to point *F*.
   d. *B* to point *E*.
   e. *E* to point *B*.

4. Which of the following might allow this economy to move from point *B* to point *F*?
   a. more workers
   b. discovery of new resources
   c. building new factories
   d. technological advances
   e. all of the above

5. This production possibility curve shows the trade-off between consumer goods and capital goods. Since capital goods are a resource, an increase in the production of capital goods today will increase the economy's production possibilities in the future. Therefore, all other things being equal, producing at which point today will result in the largest outward shift of the PPF in the future?
   a. *A*
   b. *B*
   c. *C*
   d. *D*
   e. *E*

Critical-Thinking Questions

Assume that an economy can choose between producing food and producing shelter at a constant opportunity cost. Graph a correctly labeled production possibility curve for the economy. On your graph:

1. Use the letter *E* to label one of the points that is efficient in production.
2. Use the letter *U* to label one of the points at which there might be unemployment.
3. Use the letter *I* to label one of the points that is not feasible.

Comparative Advantage and Trade

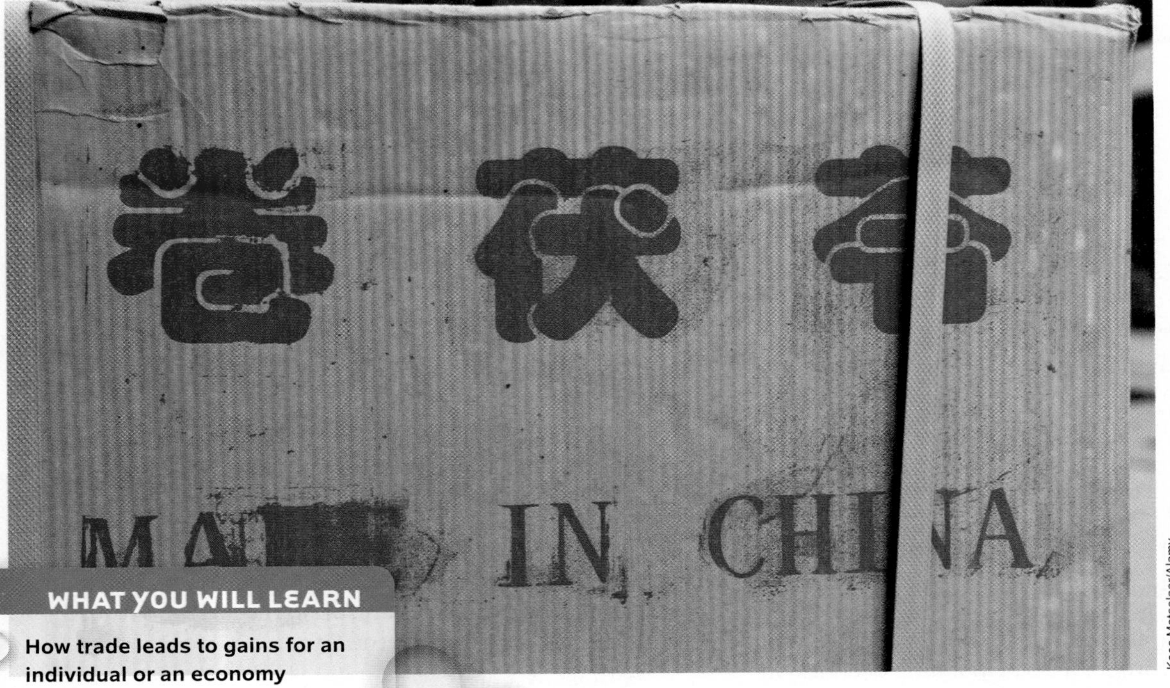

Kees Metselaar/Alamy

WHAT YOU WILL LEARN

1. How trade leads to gains for an individual or an economy
2. The difference between absolute advantage and comparative advantage
3. How comparative advantage leads to gains from trade in the global marketplace

Gains from Trade

A family could try to take care of all its own needs—growing its own food, sewing its own clothing, providing itself with entertainment, and writing its own economics textbooks. But trying to live that way would be very hard. The key to a much better standard of living for everyone is **trade,** in which people divide tasks among themselves and each person provides a good or service that other people want in return for different goods and services that he or she wants.

The reason we have an economy is that there are **gains from trade:** by dividing tasks and trading, two people (or 7 billion people) can each get more of what they want than they could get by being self-sufficient. Gains from trade arise, in particular, from this division of tasks, which economists call **specialization:** each person engages in a different task that he or she is good at performing.

In a market economy, individuals engage in **trade:** they provide goods and services to others and receive goods and services in return.

There are **gains from trade:** people can get more of what they want through trade than they could if they tried to be self-sufficient. This increase in output is due to **specialization:** each person engages in the task that he or she is good at performing.

The advantages of specialization, and the resulting gains from trade, were the starting point for Adam Smith's 1776 book *The Wealth of Nations,* which many regard as the beginning of economics as a discipline. Smith's book begins with a description of an eighteenth-century pin factory where, rather than each of the 10 workers making a pin from start to finish, each worker specialized in one of the many steps in pin-making:

> One man draws out the wire, another straights it, a third cuts it, a fourth points it, a fifth grinds it at the top for receiving the head; to make the head requires two or three distinct operations; to put it on, is a particular business, to whiten the pins is another; it is even a trade by itself to put them into the paper; and the important business of making a pin is, in this manner, divided into about eighteen distinct operations. . . . Those ten persons, therefore, could make among them upwards of forty-eight thousand pins in a day. But if they had all wrought separately and independently, and without any of them having been

educated to this particular business, they certainly could not each of them have made twenty, perhaps not one pin a day. . . .

The same principle applies when we look at how people divide tasks among themselves and trade in an economy. The economy, as a whole, can produce more when each person *specializes* in a task and *trades* with others.

The benefits of specialization are the reason a person typically focuses on the production of only one type of good or service. It takes many years of study and experience to become a doctor; it also takes many years of study and experience to become a commercial airline pilot. Many doctors might have the potential to become excellent pilots, and vice versa, but it is very unlikely that anyone who decided to pursue both careers would be as good a pilot or as good a doctor as someone who specialized in only one of those professions. So it is to everyone's advantage when individuals specialize in their career choices.

"I hunt and she gathers—otherwise, we couldn't make ends meet."

© The New Yorker Collection 1991 Ed Frascino from cartoonbank.com. All Rights Reserved.

Markets are what allow a doctor and a pilot to specialize in their respective fields. Because markets for commercial flights and for doctors' services exist, a doctor is assured that she can find a flight and a pilot is assured that he can find a doctor. As long as individuals know that they can find the goods and services that they want in the market, they are willing to forgo self-sufficiency and are willing to specialize.

Comparative Advantage and Gains from Trade

One of the most important insights in all of economics is that there are gains from trade—that it makes sense to produce the things you're especially good at producing and to buy from other people the things you aren't as good at producing. This would be true even if you could produce everything for yourself: even if a brilliant brain surgeon *could* repair her own dripping faucet, it's probably a better idea for her to call in a professional plumber.

How can we model the gains from trade? Let's stay with our aircraft example and once again imagine that the United States is a one-company economy where everyone works for Boeing, producing either large jets or small jets. Let's now assume, however, that the United States has the ability to trade with Brazil—another one-company economy where everyone works for the Brazilian aircraft company Embraer, which is, in the real world, a successful producer of small commuter jets.

Both countries could produce either kind of jet. But as we'll see in a moment, they can gain by producing different things and trading with each other. Let's return to the simpler case of straight-line production possibility curves. America's production possibilities are represented by the production possibility curve in panel (a) of Figure 4-1, which is similar to the production possibility curve in Figure 3-1 (page 16). According to this diagram, the United States can produce 40 small jets or 30 large jets, or some combination of the two. Recall that this means that the slope of the U.S. production possibility frontier is $-3/4$: its opportunity cost of 1 small jet is $3/4$ of a large jet.

Panel (b) of Figure 4-1 shows Brazil's production possibilities. Like the United States, Brazil's production possibility curve is a straight line. Brazil's production possibility curve has a constant slope of $-1/3$. Brazil can't produce as much of anything as the United States can: at most it can produce 30 small jets or 10 large jets. But it is relatively better at manufacturing small jets than the United States. While the United States sacrifices $3/4$ of a large jet per small jet produced, for Brazil the opportunity cost of a small jet is only $1/3$ of a large jet. Table 4-1 summarizes the two countries' opportunity costs of small jets and large jets.

Now, the United States and Brazil could each choose to make their own large and small jets, not trading any airplanes at all. Let's suppose that the two countries start out this way and make the consumption choices shown in

TABLE 4-1

U.S. and Brazilian Opportunity Costs of Small Jets and Large Jets

	U.S. Opportunity Cost		Brazilian Opportunity Cost
One small jet	¾ large jet	>	⅓ large jet
One large jet	4/3 small jets	<	3 small jets

FIGURE 4-1 Production Possibilities for Two Countries

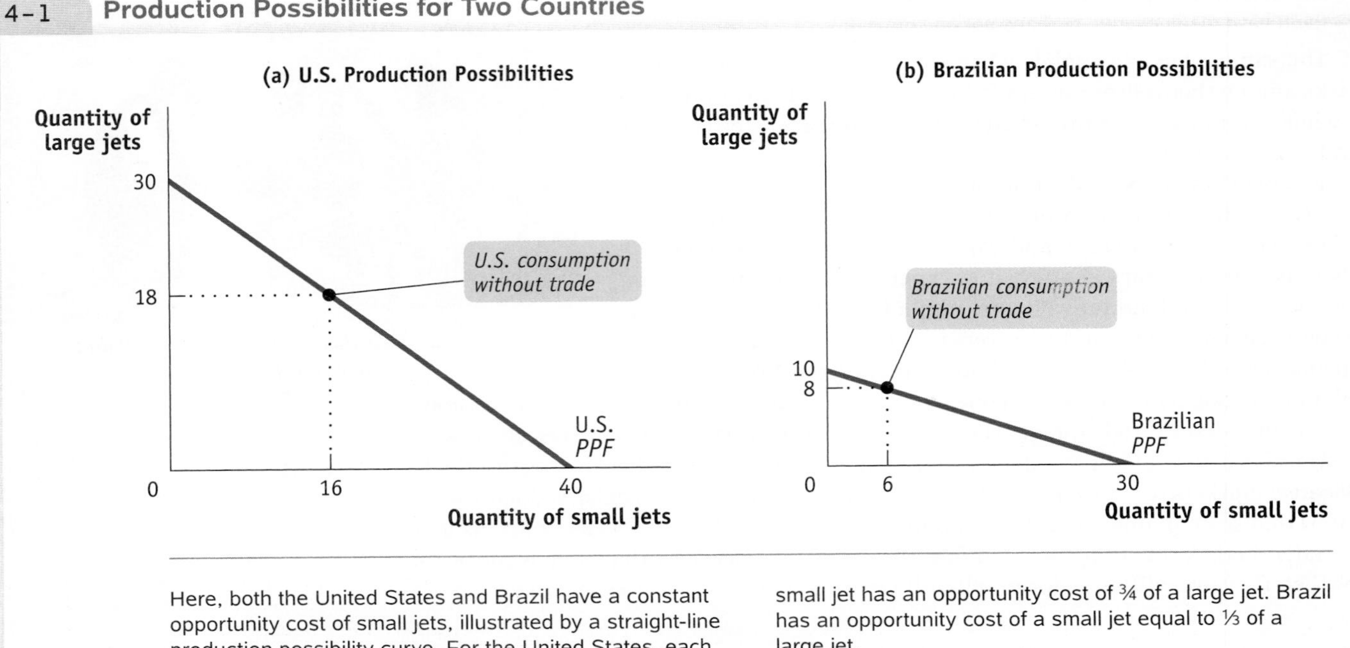

Here, both the United States and Brazil have a constant opportunity cost of small jets, illustrated by a straight-line production possibility curve. For the United States, each small jet has an opportunity cost of ¾ of a large jet. Brazil has an opportunity cost of a small jet equal to ⅓ of a large jet.

Figure 4-1: in the absence of trade, the United States produces and consumes 16 small jets and 18 large jets per year, while Brazil produces and consumes 6 small jets and 8 large jets per year.

But is this the best the two countries can do? No, it isn't. Given that the two producers—and therefore the two countries—have different opportunity costs, the United States and Brazil can strike a deal that makes both of them better off.

Table 4-2 shows how such a deal works: the United States specializes in the production of large jets, manufacturing 30 per year, and sells 10 to Brazil. Meanwhile, Brazil specializes in the production of small jets, producing 30 per year, and sells 20 to the United States. The result is shown in Figure 4-2. The United States now consumes more of both small jets and large jets than before: instead of 16 small jets and 18 large jets, it now consumes 20 small jets and 20 large jets. Brazil also consumes more, going from 6 small jets and 8 large jets to 10 small jets and 10 large jets. As Table 4-2 also shows, both the United States and Brazil reap gains from trade, consuming more of both types of plane than they would have without trade.

Both countries are better off when they each specialize in what they are good at and trade. It's a good idea for the United States to specialize in the production of large jets because its opportunity cost of a large jet is smaller than Brazil's: $4/3 < 3$. Correspondingly, Brazil should specialize in the production of small jets because its opportunity cost of a small jet is smaller than the United States': $1/3 < 3/4$.

TABLE 4-2

How the United States and Brazil Gain from Trade

		Without Trade		With Trade		Gains from Trade
		Production	Consumption	Production	Consumption	
United States	Large jets	18	18	30	20	+2
	Small jets	16	16	0	20	+4
Brazil	Large jets	8	8	0	10	+2
	Small jets	6	6	30	10	+4

FIGURE 4-2 Comparative Advantage and Gains from Trade

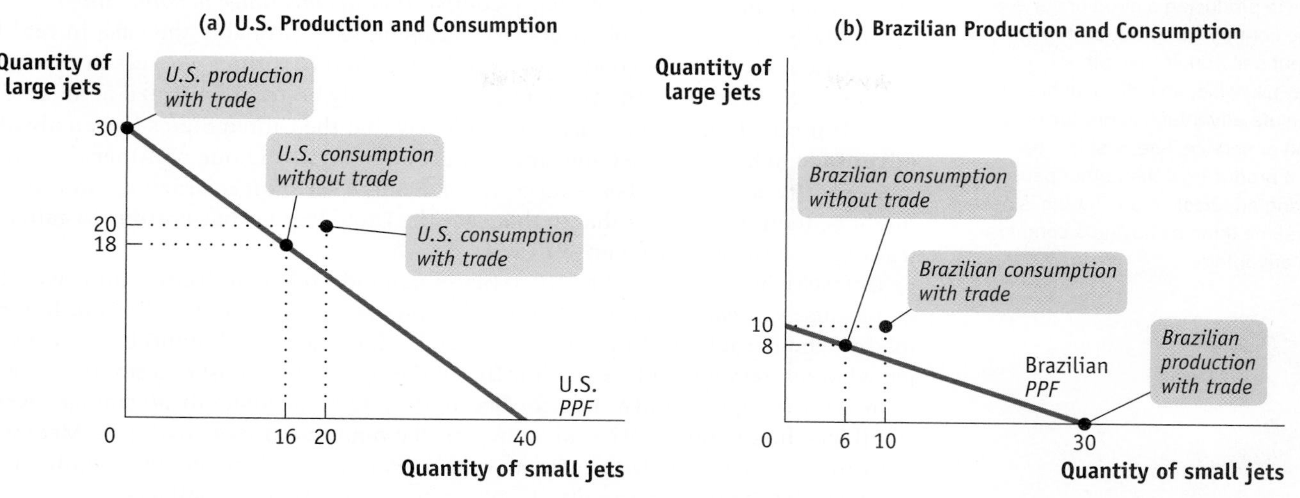

By specializing and trading, the United States and Brazil can produce and consume more of both large jets and small jets. The United States specializes in manufacturing large jets, its comparative advantage, and Brazil—which has an *absolute* disadvantage in both goods but a *comparative* advantage in small jets—specializes in manufacturing small jets. With trade, both countries can consume more of both goods than either could without trade.

What we would say in this case is that the United States has a comparative advantage in the production of large jets and Brazil has a comparative advantage in the production of small jets. A country has a **comparative advantage** in producing something if the opportunity cost of that production is lower for that country than for other countries. The same concept applies to firms and people: a firm or an individual has a comparative advantage in producing something if its, his, or her opportunity cost of production is lower than for others.

One point of clarification before we proceed further. You may have wondered why the United States traded 10 large jets to Brazil in return for 20 small jets. Why not some other deal, like trading 10 large jets for 12 small jets? The answer to that question has two parts. First, there may indeed be other trades that the United States and Brazil might agree to. Second, there are some deals that we can safely rule out—one like 10 large jets for 10 small jets.

To understand why, reexamine Table 4-1 and consider the United States first. Without trading with Brazil, the U.S. opportunity cost of a small jet is $3/4$ of a large jet. So it's clear that the United States will not accept any trade that requires it to give up more than $3/4$ of a large jet for a small jet. Trading 10 large jets in return for 12 small jets would require the United States to pay an opportunity cost of $10/12 = 5/6$ of a large jet for a small jet. Because $5/6 > 3/4$, this is a deal that the United States would reject. Similarly, Brazil won't accept a trade that gives it less than $1/3$ of a large jet for a small jet.

The point to remember is that the United States and Brazil will be willing to trade only if the "price" of the good each country obtains in the trade is less than its own opportunity cost of producing the good domestically. Moreover, this is a general statement that is true whenever two parties—countries, firms, or individuals—trade voluntarily.

While our story clearly simplifies reality, it teaches us some very important lessons that apply to the real economy, too.

First, the model provides a clear illustration of the gains from trade: through specialization and trade, both countries produce more and consume more than if they were self-sufficient.

Second, the model demonstrates a very important point that is often overlooked in real-world arguments: each country has a comparative advantage in producing

A country has a **comparative advantage** in producing a good or service if its opportunity cost of producing the good or service is lower than other countries'.

A country has an **absolute advantage** in producing a good or service if the country can produce more output per worker than other countries. Likewise, an individual has an absolute advantage in producing a good or service if he or she is better at producing it than other people. Having an absolute advantage is not the same thing as having a comparative advantage.

something. This applies to firms and people as well: *everyone has a comparative advantage in something, and everyone has a comparative disadvantage in something.*

Crucially, in our example it doesn't matter if, as is probably the case in real life, U.S. workers are just as good as or even better than Brazilian workers at producing small jets. Suppose that the United States is actually better than Brazil at all kinds of aircraft production. In that case, we would say that the United States has an **absolute advantage** in both large-jet and small-jet production: in an hour, an American worker can produce more of either a large jet or a small jet than a Brazilian worker. You might be tempted to think that in that case the United States has nothing to gain from trading with the less productive Brazil.

But we've just seen that the United States can indeed benefit from trading with Brazil because *comparative, not absolute, advantage is the basis for mutual gain.* It doesn't matter whether it takes Brazil more resources than the United States to make a small jet; what matters for trade is that for Brazil the opportunity cost of a small jet is lower than the U.S. opportunity cost. So Brazil, despite its absolute disadvantage, even in small jets, has a comparative advantage in the manufacture of small jets. Meanwhile the United States, which can use its resources most productively by manufacturing large jets, has a comparative *dis*advantage in manufacturing small jets.

If comparative advantage were relevant only to airplane manufacturers, it might not be that interesting. However, the idea of comparative advantage applies to many activities in the economy. Perhaps its most important application is in trade—not between individuals, but between countries. So let's look briefly at how the model of comparative advantage helps in understanding both the causes and the effects of international trade.

ECONOMICS ▶ IN ACTION

RICH NATION, POOR NATION

Try taking off your clothes—at a suitable time and in a suitable place, of course—and take a look at the labels inside that say where the clothes were made. It's a very good bet that much, if not most, of your clothing was manufactured overseas, in a country that is much poorer than the United States is—say, in El Salvador, Sri Lanka, or Bangladesh.

Why are these countries so much poorer than the United States? The immediate reason is that their economies are much less *productive*—firms in these countries are just not able to produce as much from a given quantity of resources as comparable firms in the United States or other wealthy countries. Why countries differ so much in productivity is a deep question—indeed, one of the main questions that preoccupy economists. But in any case, the difference in productivity is a fact.

But if the economies of these countries are so much less productive than ours, how is it that they make so much of our clothing? Why don't we do it for ourselves?

Although less productive than American workers, Bangladeshi workers have a comparative advantage in clothing production.

Robert Nickelsberg/Getty Images

The answer is "comparative advantage." Just about every industry in Bangladesh is much less productive than the corresponding industry in the United States. But the productivity difference between rich and poor countries varies across goods; there is a very great difference in the production of sophisticated goods such as aircraft but not as great a difference in the production of simpler goods such as clothing. So Bangladesh's position with regard to clothing production is like Brazil's position with respect to producing smaller jets. While Brazil is not as good as the United States at making either small or large jets, producing smaller jets is what Brazil does comparatively well.

Although Bangladesh is at an absolute disadvantage compared with the United States in almost everything, it has a comparative advantage in clothing production. This means that both the United States and Bangladesh are able to consume more because they specialize in producing different things, with Bangladesh supplying our clothing and the United States supplying Bangladesh with more sophisticated goods.

Comparative Advantage and International Trade, in Reality

Look at the label on a manufactured good sold in the United States, and there's a good chance you will find that it was produced in some other country. On the other side, many U.S. industries sell a large fraction of their output overseas.

Should all this international exchange of goods and services be celebrated, or is it cause for concern? Politicians and the public often question the desirability of international trade, arguing that the nation should produce goods for itself rather than buy them from foreigners. Industries around the world demand protection from foreign competition: Japanese farmers want to keep out American rice, American steelworkers want to keep out European steel. And these demands are often supported by public opinion.

Economists, however, have a very positive view of international trade. Why? Because they view it in terms of comparative advantage. As we learned from our example of U.S. large jets and Brazilian small jets, international trade benefits both countries. Each country can consume more than if it didn't trade and remained self-sufficient. Moreover, these mutual gains don't depend on each country being better than other countries at producing one kind of good. Even if one country has, say, higher output per worker in both industries—that is, even if one country has an absolute advantage in both industries—there are still gains from trade.

Thomas Lenne/Alamy

MODULE 4 Review

Solutions appear at the back of the book.

Check Your Understanding

1. In Italy, an automobile can be produced by 8 workers in one day and a washing machine by 3 workers in one day. In the United States, an automobile can be produced by 6 workers in one day, and a washing machine by 2 workers in one day.
   a. Which country has an absolute advantage in the production of automobiles? In washing machines?
   b. Which country has a comparative advantage in the production of washing machines? In automobiles?
   c. What type of specialization results in the greatest gains from trade between the two countries?
2. Using the numbers from Table 4-1, explain why the United States and Brazil are willing to engage in a trade of 10 large jets for 15 small jets.

Multiple-Choice Questions

Refer to the graph below to answer the following questions.

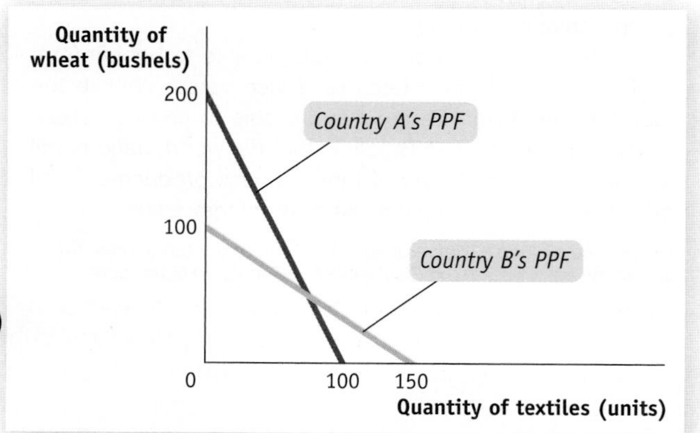

1. Use the graph to determine which country has an absolute advantage in producing each good.

	Absolute advantage in wheat production	*Absolute advantage in textile production*
a.	Country A	Country B
b.	Country A	Country A
c.	Country B	Country A
d.	Country B	Country B
e.	Country A	Neither Country

2. For Country A, the opportunity cost of a bushel of wheat is
   a. ½ units of textiles
   b. ⅔ units of textiles
   c. 1⅓ units of textiles
   d. 1½ units of textiles
   e. 2 units of textiles

3. Use the graph to determine which country has a comparative advantage in producing each good.

	Comparative advantage in wheat production	*Comparative advantage in textile production*
a.	Country A	Country B
b.	Country A	Country A
c.	Country B	Country A
d.	Country B	Country B
e.	Country A	Neither Country

4. If the two countries specialize and trade, which of the choices below describes the countries' imports?

	Import Wheat	*Import Textiles*
a.	Country A	Country A
b.	Country A	Country B
c.	Country B	Country B
d.	Country B	Country A
e.	Neither Country	Country B

5. What is the highest price Country B is willing to pay to buy wheat from Country A?
   a. ½ unit of textiles
   b. ⅔ unit of textiles
   c. 1 unit of textiles
   d. 1½ units of textiles
   e. 2 units of textiles

Critical-Thinking Questions

Refer to the table below to answer the following questions. These two countries are producing textiles and wheat using equal amounts of resources.

	Weekly output per worker	
	Country A	Country B
Bushels of Wheat	15	10
Units of Textiles	60	60

1. What is the opportunity cost of producing a bushel of wheat for each country?
2. Which country has the absolute advantage in wheat production?
3. Which country has the comparative advantage in textile production? Explain.

PITFALLS

? Back in the 1980s, when the U.S. economy seemed to be lagging behind that of Japan, one often heard commentators warn that if we didn't improve our productivity, we would soon have no comparative advantage in anything. What is wrong with this statement?

> IT IS INACCURATE; THOSE COMMENTATORS MISUNDERSTOOD COMPARATIVE ADVANTAGE. It happens all the time. Students, pundits, and politicians confuse *comparative* advantage with *absolute* advantage. What the commentators meant was that we would have no *absolute* advantage in anything—that there might come a time when the Japanese were able to produce more goods in an absolute sense than we were. (It didn't turn out that way, but that's another story.) And they had the idea that in that case we would no longer be able to benefit from trade with Japan.

A country has an absolute advantage in producing a good or service if the country can produce more output per worker than other countries. Likewise, an individual has an absolute advantage in producing a good or service if he or she is better at producing it than other people. Having an absolute advantage is not the same thing as having a comparative advantage.

Just as Brazil, in our example, is able to benefit from trade with the United States (and vice versa) despite the fact that the United States may be able to produce absolutely more goods than Brazil, in the real world, nations will still gain from trade even if they are less productive in all industries than the countries with whom they trade.

Review the section "Comparative Advantage and International Trade, in Reality" on page 27, and Figure 4-2 on page 25, to learn more.

BUSINESS CASE • Efficiency, Opportunity Cost, and the Logic of Lean Production

WORLD VIEW

Corbis/Photolibrary

In the summer and fall of 2010, workers were rearranging the furniture in Boeing's final assembly plant in Everett, Washington, in preparation for the production of the Boeing 767. It was a difficult and time-consuming process, however, because the items of "furniture"—Boeing's assembly equipment—weighed on the order of 200 tons each. It was a necessary part of setting up a production system based on "lean manufacturing," also called "just-in-time" production. Lean manufacturing, pioneered by Toyota Motors of Japan, is based on the practice of having parts arrive on the factory floor just as they are needed for production. This reduces the amount of parts Boeing holds in inventory as well as the amount of the factory floor needed for production—in this case, reducing the square footage required for manufacture of the 767 by 40%.

Boeing had adopted lean manufacturing in 1999 in the manufacture of the 737, the most popular commercial airplane. By 2005, after constant refinement, Boeing had achieved a 50% reduction in the time it takes to produce a plane and a nearly 60% reduction in parts inventory. An important feature is a continuously moving assembly line, moving products from one assembly team to the next at a steady pace and eliminating the need for workers to wander across the factory floor from task to task or in search of tools and parts.

Toyota's lean production techniques have been the most widely adopted of all manufacturing techniques and have revolutionized manufacturing worldwide. In simple terms, lean production is focused on organization and communication. Workers and parts are organized so as to ensure a smooth and consistent workflow that minimizes wasted effort and materials. Lean production is also designed to be highly responsive to changes in the desired mix of output—for example, quickly producing more sedans and fewer minivans according to changes in customers' demands.

Toyota's lean production methods were so successful that they transformed the global auto industry and severely threatened once-dominant American automakers. Until the 1980s, the "Big Three"—Chrysler, Ford, and General Motors—dominated the American auto industry, with virtually no foreign-made cars sold in the United States. In the 1980s, however, Toyotas became increasingly popular in the United States due to their high quality and relatively low price—so popular that the Big Three eventually prevailed upon the U.S. government to protect them by restricting the sale of Japanese autos in the United States. Over time, Toyota responded by building assembly plants in the United States, bringing along its lean production techniques, which then spread throughout American manufacturing.

Questions for Thought

1. What is the opportunity cost associated with having a worker wander across the factory floor from task to task or in search of tools and parts?
2. How does lean manufacturing improve the economy's efficiency in allocation?
3. How will the shift in location of Toyota's production from Japan to the United States alter the pattern of comparative advantage in automaking between the two countries?

SECTION 1 REVIEW

Summary

The Study of Economics

1. Everyone has to make choices about what to do and what *not* to do. **Individual choice** is the basis of **economics**—if it doesn't involve choice, it isn't economics. The **economy** is a system that coordinates choices about production and consumption. In a **market economy,** these choices are made by many firms and individuals.
2. The reason choices must be made is that **resources**—anything that can be used to produce something else—are **scarce.** The four categories of resources are **land, labor, physical capital,** and **human capital.** Individuals are limited in their choices by money and time; economies are limited by their supplies of resources.
3. Because you must choose among limited alternatives, the true cost of anything is what you must give up to get it—all costs are **opportunity costs.**
4. Economists use economic models for both **positive economics,** which describes how the economy works, and for **normative economics,** which prescribes how the economy *should* work. Positive economics often involves making forecasts. Economics can determine correct answers for positive questions, but typically not for normative questions, which involve value judgments. Exceptions occur when policies designed to achieve a certain prescription can be clearly ranked in terms of efficiency.
5. There are two main reasons economists disagree. One, they may disagree about which simplifications to make in a model. Two, economists may disagree—like everyone else—about values.
6. **Microeconomics** is the branch of economics that studies how people make decisions and how those decisions interact. **Macroeconomics** is concerned with the overall ups and downs of the economy, and focuses on **economic aggregates** such as the unemployment rate and gross domestic product, that summarize data across many different markets.

Models and the Circular Flow

7. Almost all economics is based on **models,** "thought experiments" or simplified versions of reality, many of which use analytical tools such as mathematics and graphs. An important assumption in economic models is the **other things equal (*ceteris paribus*) assumption,** which allows analysis of the effect of change in one factor by holding all other relevant factors unchanged.
8. In the simplest economies, people trade goods and services for one another rather than trade them for money, as in a modern economy. The **circular-flow diagram** represents transactions within the economy as flows of goods, services, and money between **households** and **firms.** These transactions occur in **markets for goods and services** and **factor markets,** markets for **factors of production**—land, labor, physical capital, and human capital. It is useful in understanding how spending, production, employment, income, and growth are related in the economy.

The Production Possibility Frontier

9. One important economic model is the **production possibility frontier,** which illustrates the **trade-offs** facing an economy that produces only two goods. The PPF illustrates three elements: opportunity cost (showing how much less of one good must be produced if more of the other good is produced), **efficiency** (an economy is efficient in production if it produces on the production possibility curve and efficient in allocation if it produces the mix of goods and services that people want to consume), and economic growth (an outward shift of the production possibility curve).
10. There are two basic sources of growth in the production possibility frontier model: an increase in resources and improved **technology.**

Comparative Advantage and Trade

11. There are **gains from trade:** by engaging in the **trade** of goods and services with one another, the members of an economy can all be made better off. Underlying gains from trade are the advantages of **specialization,** of having individuals engage in the tasks they are comparatively good at.
12. **Comparative advantage** explains the source of gains from trade between individuals and countries. Everyone has a comparative advantage in something—some good or service in which that person has a lower opportunity cost than everyone else. But it is often confused with **absolute advantage,** an ability to produce more of a particular good or service than anyone else. This confusion leads some to erroneously conclude that there are no gains from trade between people or countries.

Key Terms

Problems

1. Imagine a firm that manufactures textiles (pants and shirts). List the four categories of resources, and for each category, give an example of a specific resource that the firm might use to manufacture textiles.

2. Describe some of the opportunity costs of the following choices.

a. Attend college instead of taking a job.

b. Watch a movie instead of studying for an exam.

c. Ride the bus instead of driving your car.

3. Use the concept of opportunity cost to explain the following situations.

a. More people choose to get graduate degrees when the job market is poor.

b. More people choose to do their own home repairs when the economy is slow and hourly wages are down.

c. There are more parks in suburban areas than in urban areas.

d. Convenience stores, which have higher prices than supermarkets, cater to busy people.

4. A representative of the U.S. clothing industry recently made this statement: "Workers in Asia often work in sweatshop conditions earning only pennies an hour. American workers are more productive and, as a result, earn higher wages. In order to preserve the dignity of the American workplace, the government should enact legislation banning imports of low-wage Asian clothing."

a. Which parts of this quotation are positive statements? Which parts are normative statements?

b. Is the policy that is being advocated consistent with the statement about the wages and productivities of American and Asian workers?

c. Would such a policy make some Americans better off without making any other Americans worse off? That is, would this policy be efficient from the viewpoint of all Americans?

d. Would low-wage Asian workers benefit from or be hurt by such a policy?

5. Are the following statements true or false? Explain your answers.

a. "When people must pay higher taxes on their wage earnings, it reduces their incentive to work" is a positive statement.

b. "We should lower taxes to encourage more work" is a positive statement.

c. Economics cannot always be used to determine what society ought to do.

d. "The system of public education in this country generates greater benefits to society than the cost of running the system" is a normative statement.

e. All disagreements among economists are generated by the media.

6. Evaluate this statement: "It is easier to build an economic model that accurately reflects events that have already occurred than to build an economic model to forecast future events." Do you think that this is true or not? Why? What does this imply about the difficulties of building good economic models?

7. An economist might say that colleges and universities "produce" education, using faculty members and students as inputs. According to this line of reasoning, education is then "consumed" by households.

a. Construct a circular-flow diagram to represent the sector of the economy devoted to college education: colleges and universities represent firms, and households both consume education and provide faculty and students to universities. What are the relevant markets in this diagram? What is being bought and sold in each direction?

b. Now suppose that the government decided to subsidize 50% of all college students' tuition. How would this affect the circular-flow diagram that you created in part a?

8. Suppose Atlantis is a small, isolated island in the South Atlantic. The inhabitants grow potatoes and catch fish. The accompanying table shows the maximum annual output combinations of potatoes and fish that can be produced. Obviously, given their limited resources and available technology, as they use more of their resources for potato production, there are fewer resources available for catching fish.

Maximum annual output options	Quantity of potatoes (pounds)	Quantity of fish (pounds)
A	1,000	0
B	800	300
C	600	500
D	400	600
E	200	650
F	0	675

a. Draw a production possibility curve with potatoes on the horizontal axis and fish on the vertical axis, and illustrate these options, showing points *A–F.*

b. Can Atlantis produce 500 pounds of fish and 800 pounds of potatoes? Explain. Where would this point lie relative to the production possibility curve?

c. What is the opportunity cost of increasing the annual output of potatoes from 600 to 800 pounds?

d. What is the opportunity cost of increasing the annual output of potatoes from 200 to 400 pounds?

e. Explain why the answers to parts c and d are not the same. What does this imply about the slope of the production possibility curve?

9. Two important industries on the island of Bermuda are fishing and tourism. According to data from the World Resources Institute and the Bermuda Department of Statistics, in the year 2009 the 306 registered fishermen in Bermuda caught 387 metric tons of marine fish. And the 2,719 people employed by hotels produced 554,400 hotel stays (measured by the number of visitor arrivals). Suppose that this production point is efficient in production. Assume also that the opportunity cost of one additional metric ton of fish is 2,000 hotel stays and that this opportunity cost is constant (the opportunity cost does not change).

a. If all 306 registered fishermen were to be employed by hotels (in addition to the 2,719 people already working in hotels), how many hotel stays could Bermuda produce?

b. If all 2,719 hotel employees were to become fishermen (in addition to the 306 fishermen already working in the fishing industry), how many metric tons of fish could Bermuda produce?

c. Draw a production possibility curve for Bermuda, with fish on the horizontal axis and hotel stays on the vertical axis, and label Bermuda's actual production point for the year 2009.

10. In the ancient country of Roma, only two goods, spaghetti and meatballs, are produced. There are two tribes in Roma, the Tivoli and the Frivoli. By themselves, the Tivoli each month can produce either 30 pounds of spaghetti and no meatballs, or 50 pounds of meatballs and no spaghetti, or any combination in between. The Frivoli, by themselves, each month can produce 40 pounds of spaghetti and no meatballs, or 30 pounds of meatballs and no spaghetti, or any combination in between.

a. Assume that all production possibility curves are straight lines. Draw one diagram showing the monthly production possibility curve for the Tivoli and another showing the monthly production possibility curve for the Frivoli.

b. Which tribe has the comparative advantage in spaghetti production? In meatball production?

In A.D. 100, the Frivoli discovered a new technique for making meatballs that doubled the quantity of meatballs they could produce each month.

c. Draw the new monthly production possibility curve for the Frivoli.

d. After the innovation, which tribe had an absolute advantage in producing meatballs? In producing spaghetti? Which had the comparative advantage in meatball production? In spaghetti production?

11. In recent years, the United States used 124 million acres of land for wheat or corn farming. Of those 124 million acres, farmers used 50 million acres to grow 2.158 billion bushels of wheat, and 74 million acres of land to grow 11.807 billion bushels of corn. Suppose that U.S. wheat and corn farming is efficient in production. At that production point, the opportunity cost of producing one additional bushel of wheat is 1.7 fewer bushels of corn. However, farmers have increasing opportunity costs, so additional bushels of wheat have an opportunity cost greater than 1.7 bushels of corn. For each of the production points described below, decide whether that production point is (i) feasible and efficient in production, (ii) feasible but not efficient in production, (iii) not feasible, or (iv) uncertain as to whether or not it is feasible.

a. From their original production point, farmers use 40 million acres of land to produce 1.8 billion bushels of wheat, and they use 60 million acres of land to produce 9 billion bushels of corn. The remaining 24 million acres are left unused.

b. From their original production point, farmers transfer 40 million acres of land from corn to wheat production. They now produce 3.158 billion bushels of wheat and 10.107 billion bushels of corn.

c. From their original production point, farmers reduce their production of wheat to 2 billion bushels and increase their production of corn to 12.044 billion bushels. Along the production possibility curve, the opportunity cost of going from 11.807 billion bushels of corn to 12.044 billion bushels of corn is 0.666 bushel of wheat per bushel of corn.

12. The Hatfield family lives on the east side of the Hatatoochie River, and the McCoy family lives on the west side. Each family's diet consists of fried chicken and corn-on-the-cob, and each is self-sufficient, raising their own chickens and growing their own corn. Explain the conditions under which each of the following statements would be true.

 a. The two families are made better off when the Hatfields specialize in raising chickens, the McCoys specialize in growing corn, and the two families trade.

 b. The two families are made better off when the McCoys specialize in raising chickens, the Hatfields specialize in growing corn, and the two families trade.

13. According to the U.S. Census Bureau, back in July 2006 the United States exported aircraft worth $1 billion to China and imported aircraft worth only $19,000 from China. During the same month, however, the United States imported $83 million worth of men's trousers, slacks, and jeans from China but exported only $8,000 worth of trousers, slacks, and jeans to China. Using what you have learned about how trade is determined by comparative advantage, answer the following questions.

 a. Which country has the comparative advantage in aircraft production? In production of trousers, slacks, and jeans?

 b. Can you determine which country has the absolute advantage in aircraft production? In production of trousers, slacks, and jeans?

14. Peter Pundit, an economics reporter, states that the European Union (EU) is increasing its productivity very rapidly in all industries. He claims that this productivity advance is so rapid that output from the EU in these industries will soon exceed that of the United States and, as a result, the United States will no longer benefit from trade with the EU.

 a. Do you think Peter Pundit is correct or not? If not, what do you think is the source of his mistake?

 b. If the EU and the United States continue to trade, what do you think will characterize the goods that the EU exports to the United States and the goods that the United States exports to the EU?

SECTION 2

Supply and Demand

BLUE JEAN BLUES

If you bought a pair of blue jeans in 2011, you may have been shocked at the price. Or maybe not: fashions change, and maybe you thought you were paying the price for being fashionable. But you weren't—you were paying for cotton. Jeans are made of denim, which is a particular weave of cotton, and by December 2010, the price of a pound of cotton had hit a 140-year high, the highest cotton price since records began in 1870.

And why were cotton prices so high?

On one side, demand for clothing of all kinds was surging. In 2008–2009, as the world struggled with the effects of a financial crisis, nervous consumers cut back on clothing purchases. But by 2010, with the worst apparently over, buyers were back in force. On the supply side, Pakistan, the world's fourth-largest cotton producer, was hit by devastating floods that put one-fifth of the country underwater and virtually destroyed its cotton crop.

Fearing that consumers had limited tolerance for large increases in the price of cotton clothing, apparel makers began scrambling to find ways to reduce costs. They adopted changes like smaller buttons, cheaper linings, and—yes—polyester, doubting that consumers would be willing to pay more for cotton goods. In fact, some experts on the cotton market warned that the sky-high prices of cotton in 2010–2011 might lead to a permanent shift in tastes, with consumers becoming more willing to wear synthetics even when cotton prices came down.

At the same time, it was not all bad news for everyone connected with the cotton trade. In the United States, cotton producers had not been hit by bad weather and were relishing the higher prices. American farmers responded to sky-high cotton prices by sharply increasing the acreage devoted to the crop. None of this was enough, however, to produce immediate price relief.

Wait a minute: how, exactly, does flooding in Pakistan translate into higher jeans prices and more polyester in your T-shirts? It's a matter of supply and demand—but what does that mean? Many people use "supply and demand" as a sort of catchphrase to mean "the laws of the marketplace at work." To economists, however, the concept of supply and demand has a precise meaning: it is a *model of how a market behaves*.

In this section, we lay out the pieces that make up the *supply and demand model*, put them together, and show how this model can be used to understand how many—but not all—markets behave.

MODULE

5 Demand

Thinkstock

WHAT YOU WILL LEARN

1. What a competitive market is and how it is described by the supply and demand model
2. What the demand curve is
3. The difference between movements along the demand curve and changes in demand
4. The factors that shift the demand curve

Supply and Demand: A Model of a Competitive Market

Cotton sellers and cotton buyers constitute a *market*—a group of producers and consumers who exchange a good or service for payment. In this section, we'll focus on a particular type of market known as a *competitive market*. Roughly, a **competitive market** is a market in which there are many buyers and sellers of the same good or service. More precisely, the key feature of a competitive market is that no individual's actions have a noticeable effect on the price at which the good or service is sold. It's important to understand, however, that this is not an accurate description of every market.

For example, it's not an accurate description of the market for cola beverages. That's because in the market for cola beverages, Coca-Cola and Pepsi account for such a large proportion of total sales that they are able to influence the price at which cola beverages are bought and sold. But it *is* an accurate description of the market for cotton. The global marketplace for cotton is so huge that even a jeans maker as large as Levi Strauss & Co. accounts for only a tiny fraction of transactions, making it unable to influence the price at which cotton is bought and sold.

It's a little hard to explain why competitive markets are different from other markets until we've seen how a competitive market works. For now, let's just say that it's easier to model competitive markets than other markets. When taking an exam, it's always a good strategy to begin by answering the easier questions. In this book, we're going to do the same thing. So we will start with competitive markets.

When a market is competitive, its behavior is well described by the **supply and demand model.** Because many markets *are* competitive, the supply and demand model is a very useful one indeed.

A **competitive market** is a market in which there are many buyers and sellers of the same good or service, none of whom can influence the price at which the good or service is sold.

The **supply and demand model** is a model of how a competitive market works.

There are five key elements in this model:

- The *demand curve*
- The *supply curve*
- The set of factors that cause the demand curve to shift and the set of factors that cause the supply curve to shift
- The *market equilibrium,* which includes the *equilibrium price* and *equilibrium quantity*
- The way the market equilibrium changes when the supply curve or demand curve shifts

To explain the supply and demand model, we will examine each of these elements in turn. In this module we begin with demand.

The Demand Curve

How many pounds of cotton, packaged in the form of blue jeans, do consumers around the world want to buy in a given year? You might at first think that we can answer this question by looking at the total number of pairs of blue jeans purchased around the world each day, multiply that number by the amount of cotton it takes to make a pair of jeans, and then multiply by 365. But that's not enough to answer the question, because how many pairs of jeans—in other words, how many pounds of cotton—consumers want to buy depends on the price of a pound of cotton.

When the price of cotton rises, as it did in 2010, some people will respond to the higher price of cotton clothing by buying fewer cotton garments or, perhaps, by switching completely to garments made from other materials, such as synthetics or linen. In general, the quantity of cotton clothing, or of any good or service that people want to buy, depends on the price. The higher the price, the less of the good or service people want to purchase; alternatively, the lower the price, the more they want to purchase.

So the answer to the question "How many pounds of cotton do consumers want to buy?" depends on the price of a pound of cotton. If you don't yet know what the price will be, you can start by making a table of how many pounds of cotton people would want to buy at a number of different prices. Such a table is known as a *demand schedule*. This, in turn, can be used to draw a *demand curve,* which is one of the key elements of the supply and demand model.

The Demand Schedule and the Demand Curve

A **demand schedule** is a table showing how much of a good or service consumers will want to buy at different prices. On the right side of Figure 5-1, we show a hypothetical demand schedule for cotton. It's hypothetical in that it doesn't use actual data on the world demand for cotton and it assumes that all cotton is of equal quality.

According to the table, if a pound of cotton costs $1, consumers around the world will want to purchase 10 billion pounds of cotton over the course of a year. If the price is $1.25 a pound, they will want to buy only 8.9 billion pounds; if the price is only $0.75 a pound, they will want to buy 11.5 billion pounds; and so on. So, the higher the price, the fewer pounds of cotton consumers will want to purchase. In other words, as the price rises, the **quantity demanded** of cotton—the actual amount consumers are willing to buy at some specific price—falls.

The graph in Figure 5-1 is a visual representation of the information in the table. (For a refresher on graphs in economics, see Appendix A at the back of the book.) The vertical axis shows the price of a pound of cotton and the horizontal axis shows the quantity of cotton in pounds. Each point on the graph corresponds to one of the entries in the table. The curve that connects these points is a **demand curve.** A demand curve is a graphical representation of the demand schedule, another way of showing the relationship between the quantity demanded and the price.

A **demand schedule** shows how much of a good or service consumers will want to buy at different prices.

The **quantity demanded** is the actual amount of a good or service consumers are willing to buy at some specific price.

A **demand curve** is a graphical representation of the demand schedule. It shows the relationship between quantity demanded and price.

FIGURE 5-1 **The Demand Schedule and the Demand Curve**

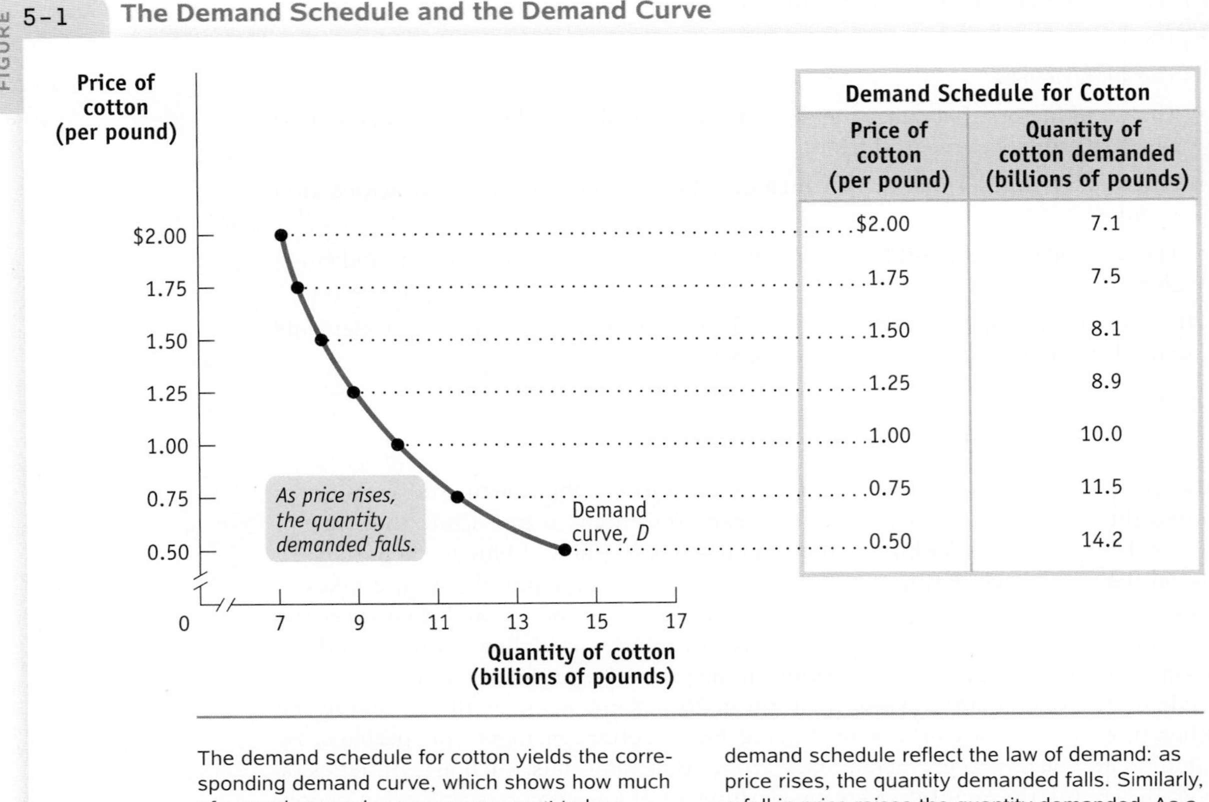

Demand Schedule for Cotton	
Price of cotton (per pound)	Quantity of cotton demanded (billions of pounds)
$2.00	7.1
1.75	7.5
1.50	8.1
1.25	8.9
1.00	10.0
0.75	11.5
0.50	14.2

The demand schedule for cotton yields the corresponding demand curve, which shows how much of a good or service consumers want to buy at any given price. The demand curve and the demand schedule reflect the law of demand: as price rises, the quantity demanded falls. Similarly, a fall in price raises the quantity demanded. As a result, the demand curve is downward sloping.

The **law of demand** says that a higher price for a good or service, all other things being equal, leads people to demand a smaller quantity of that good or service.

Note that the demand curve shown in Figure 5-1 slopes downward. This reflects the general proposition that a higher price reduces the quantity demanded. For example, jeans-makers know that they will sell fewer pairs when the price of a pair of jeans is higher, reflecting a $2 price for a pound of cotton, compared to the number they will sell when the price of a pair is lower, reflecting a price of only $1 for a pound of cotton. In the real world, demand curves almost always *do* slope downward. (The exceptions are so rare that for practical purposes we can ignore them.) Generally, the proposition that a higher price for a good, all other things equal, leads people to demand a smaller quantity of that good is so reliable that economists are willing to call it a "law"—the **law of demand.**

Higher prices for jeans will reduce the quantity demanded.

Image Source/Alamy

Shifts of the Demand Curve

Even though cotton prices in 2010 were higher than they had been in 2007, total world consumption of cotton was higher in 2010. How can we reconcile this fact with the law of demand, which says that a higher price reduces the quantity demanded, all other things being equal?

The answer lies in the crucial phrase all other things being equal. In this case, all other things weren't equal: the world had changed between 2007 and 2010, in ways that increased the quantity of cotton demanded at any given price. For one thing, the world's population, and therefore the number of potential cotton clothing wearers, increased. In addition, the growing popularity of cotton clothing, as well as higher incomes in countries like China that allowed people to buy more clothing than before, led to an increase in the quantity of cotton demanded at any given price. Figure 5-2 illustrates this

FIGURE 5-2 **An Increase in Demand**

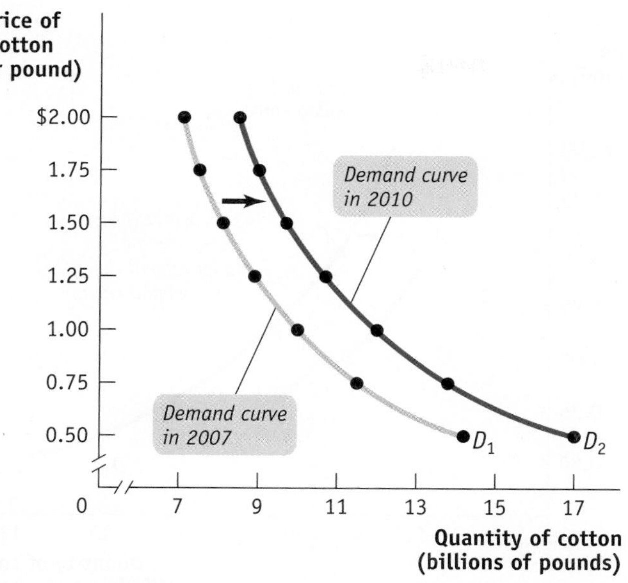

Demand Schedules for Cotton		
Price of cotton (per pound)	Quantity of cotton demanded (billions of pounds)	
	in 2007	in 2010
$2.00	7.1	8.5
1.75	7.5	9.0
1.50	8.1	9.7
1.25	8.9	10.7
1.00	10.0	12.0
0.75	11.5	13.8
0.50	14.2	17.0

An increase in the population is one factor that generates an increase in demand—a rise in the quantity demanded at any given price. This is represented by the two demand schedules—one showing demand in 2007, before the rise in population, the other showing demand in 2010, after the rise in population—and their corresponding demand curves. The increase in demand shifts the demand curve to the right.

phenomenon using the demand schedule and demand curve for cotton. (As before, the numbers in Figure 5-2 are hypothetical.)

The table in Figure 5-2 shows two demand schedules. The first is the demand schedule for 2007, the same as shown in Figure 5-1. The second is the demand schedule for 2010. It differs from the 2007 demand schedule due to factors such as a larger population and the increased popularity of cotton clothing, factors that led to an increase in the quantity of cotton demanded at any given price. So at each price the 2010 schedule shows a larger quantity demanded than the 2007 schedule. For example, the quantity of cotton consumers wanted to buy at a price of $1 per pound increased from 10 billion to 12 billion pounds per year, the quantity demanded at $1.25 per pound went from 8.9 billion to 10.7 billion, and so on.

What is clear from this example is that the changes that occurred between 2007 and 2010 generated a *new* demand schedule, one in which the quantity demanded was greater at any given price than in the original demand schedule. The two curves in Figure 5-2 show the same information graphically. As you can see, the demand schedule for 2010 corresponds to a new demand curve, D_2, that is to the right of the demand schedule for 2007, D_1. This **change in demand** shows the increase in the quantity demanded at any given price, represented by the shift in position of the original demand curve D_1 to its new location at D_2.

It's crucial to make the distinction between such changes in demand and **movements along the demand curve,** changes in the quantity demanded of a good that result from a change in that good's price. Figure 5-3 illustrates the difference.

The movement from point *A* to point *B* is a movement along the demand curve: the quantity demanded rises due to a fall in price as you move down D_1. Here, a fall in the price of cotton from $1.50 to $1 per pound generates a rise in the quantity demanded from 8.1 billion to 10 billion pounds per year. But the quantity demanded can also rise when the price is unchanged if there is an *increase in demand*—a rightward shift

A **change in demand** is a shift of the demand curve, which changes the quantity demanded at any given price.

A **movement along the demand curve** is a change in the quantity demanded of a good that is the result of a change in that good's price.

FIGURE 5-3 **Movement Along the Demand Curve versus Shift of the Demand Curve**

The rise in quantity demanded when going from point *A* to point *B* reflects a movement along the demand curve: it is the result of a fall in the price of the good. The rise in quantity demanded when going from point *A* to point *C* reflects a shift of the demand curve: it is the result of a rise in the quantity demanded at any given price.

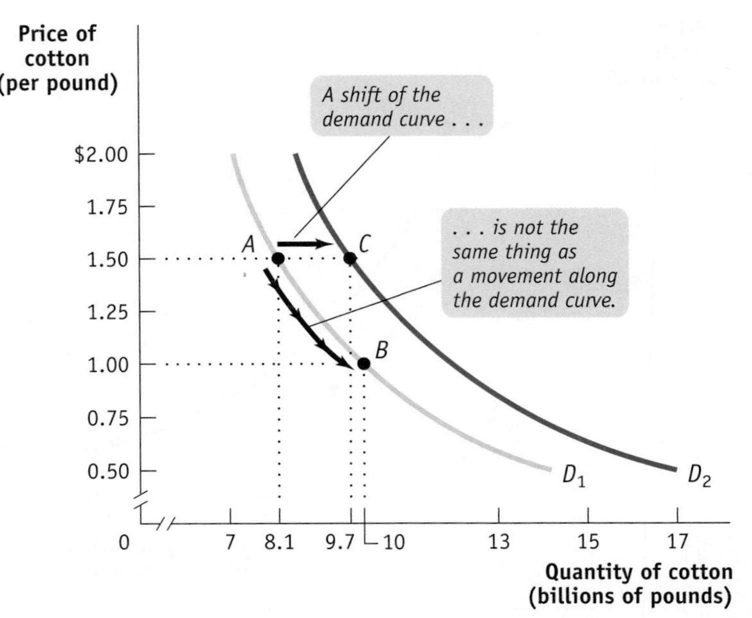

of the demand curve. This is illustrated in Figure 5-3 by the shift of the demand curve from D_1 to D_2. Holding the price constant at $1.50 a pound, the quantity demanded rises from 8.1 billion pounds at point *A* on D_1 to 9.7 billion pounds at point *C* on D_2.

When economists talk about a "change in demand," saying for example "the demand for *X* increased" or "the demand for *Y* decreased," they mean that the demand curve for *X* or *Y* shifted—*not* that the quantity demanded rose or fell because of a change in the price.

Understanding Shifts of the Demand Curve

Figure 5-4 illustrates the two basic ways in which demand curves can shift. When economists talk about an "increase in demand," they mean a *rightward* shift of the demand curve: at any given price, consumers demand a larger quantity of the good or service than before. This is shown by the rightward shift of the original demand curve D_1 to D_2. And when economists talk about a "decrease in demand," they mean a *leftward* shift of the demand curve: at any given price, consumers demand a smaller quantity of the good or service than before. This is shown by the leftward shift of the original demand curve D_1 to D_3.

What caused the demand curve for cotton to shift? We have already mentioned two reasons: changes in population and a change in the popularity of cotton clothing. If you think about it, you can come up with other things that would be likely to shift the demand curve for cotton. For example, suppose that the price of polyester rises. This will induce some people who previously bought polyester clothing to buy cotton clothing instead, increasing the demand for cotton.

Economists believe that there are five principal factors that shift the demand curve for a good or service:

- Changes in the prices of related goods or services
- Changes in income
- Changes in tastes
- Changes in expectations
- Changes in the number of consumers

FIGURE 5-4 **Shifts of the Demand Curve**

Any event that increases demand shifts the demand curve to the right, reflecting a rise in the quantity demanded at any given price. Any event that decreases demand shifts the demand curve to the left, reflecting a fall in the quantity demanded at any given price.

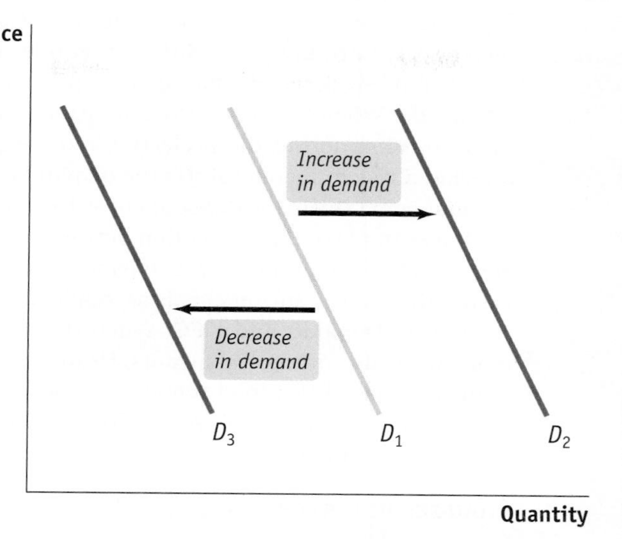

Although this is not an exhaustive list, it contains the five most important factors that can shift demand curves. So when we say that the quantity of a good or service demanded falls as its price rises, all other things being equal, we are in fact stating that the factors that shift demand are remaining unchanged. Let's now explore, in more detail, how those factors shift the demand curve.

Two goods are **substitutes** if a rise in the price of one of the goods leads to an increase in the demand for the other good.

Two goods are **complements** if a rise in the price of one good leads to a decrease in the demand for the other good.

CHANGES IN THE PRICES OF RELATED GOODS OR SERVICES While there's nothing quite like a comfortable pair of all-cotton blue jeans, for some purposes khakis—generally made from polyester blends—aren't a bad alternative. Khakis are what economists call a *substitute* for jeans. A pair of goods are **substitutes** if a rise in the price of one good (jeans) makes consumers more willing to buy the other good (khakis). Substitutes are usually goods that in some way serve a similar function: concerts and theater plays, muffins and doughnuts, train rides and air flights. A rise in the price of the alternative good induces some consumers to purchase the original good *instead* of it, shifting demand for the original good to the right.

But sometimes a rise in the price of one good makes consumers *less* willing to buy another good. Such pairs of goods are known as **complements.** Complements are usually goods that in some sense are consumed together: computers and software, cappuccinos and croissants, cars and gasoline. Because consumers like to consume a good and its complement together, a change in the price of one of the goods will affect the demand for its complement. In particular, when the price of one good rises, the demand for its complement decreases, shifting the demand curve for the complement to the left. So, for example, when the price of gasoline rises, the demand for gas-guzzling cars falls.

CHANGES IN INCOME When individuals have more income, they are normally more likely to purchase a good at any given price. For example, if a family's income rises, it is more likely to take that long-anticipated summer trip to Disney World—and therefore also more likely to buy plane tickets. So a rise in consumer incomes will cause the demand curves for most goods to shift to the right.

Thinkstock

When a rise in income increases the demand for a good—the normal case—it is a **normal good.**

When a rise in income decreases the demand for a good, it is an **inferior good.**

Why do we say "most goods," not "all goods"? Most goods are **normal goods**—the demand for them increases when consumer income rises. However, the demand for some products falls when income rises. Goods for which demand decreases when income rises are known as **inferior goods.** Usually an inferior good is one that is considered less desirable than more expensive alternatives—such as a bus ride versus a taxi ride. When they can afford to, people stop buying an inferior good and switch their consumption to the preferred, more expensive alternative. So when a good is inferior, a rise in income shifts the demand curve to the left. And, not surprisingly, a fall in income shifts the demand curve for inferior goods to the right.

One example of the distinction between normal and inferior goods that has drawn considerable attention in the business press is the difference between so-called casual-dining restaurants such as Applebee's or Olive Garden and fast-food chains such as McDonald's and KFC. When their incomes rise, Americans tend to eat out more at casual-dining restaurants. However, some of this increased dining out comes at the expense of fast-food venues—to some extent, people visit McDonald's less once they can afford to move upscale. So casual dining is a normal good, while fast-food appears to be an inferior good.

CHANGES IN TASTES Why do people want what they want? Fortunately, we don't need to answer that question—we just need to acknowledge that people have certain preferences, or tastes, that determine what they choose to consume and that these tastes can change. Economists usually lump together changes in demand due to fads, beliefs, cultural shifts, and so on under the heading of changes in *tastes* or *preferences*.

istockphoto/thinkstock

As tastes change, styles come and go.

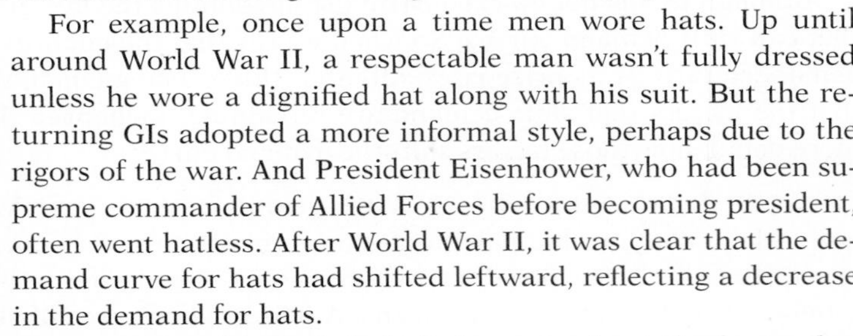

For example, once upon a time men wore hats. Up until around World War II, a respectable man wasn't fully dressed unless he wore a dignified hat along with his suit. But the returning GIs adopted a more informal style, perhaps due to the rigors of the war. And President Eisenhower, who had been supreme commander of Allied Forces before becoming president, often went hatless. After World War II, it was clear that the demand curve for hats had shifted leftward, reflecting a decrease in the demand for hats.

Economists have relatively little to say about the forces that influence consumers' tastes. (Marketers and advertisers, however, have plenty to say about them!) However, a *change* in tastes has a predictable impact on demand. When tastes change in favor of a good, more people want to buy it at any given price, so the demand curve shifts to the right. When tastes change against a good, fewer people want to buy it at any given price, so the demand curve shifts to the left.

CHANGES IN EXPECTATIONS When consumers have some choice about when to make a purchase, current demand for a good is often affected by expectations about its future price. For example, savvy shoppers often wait for seasonal sales—say, buying next year's holiday gifts during the post-holiday markdowns. In this case, expectations of a future drop in price lead to a decrease in demand today. Alternatively, expectations of a future rise in price are likely to cause an increase in demand today. For example, as cotton prices began to rise in 2010, many textile mills began purchasing more cotton and stockpiling it in anticipation of further price increases.

Expected changes in future income can also lead to changes in demand: if you expect your income to rise in the future, you will typically borrow today and increase your demand for certain goods; if you expect your income to fall in the future, you are more likely to save today and reduce your demand for some goods.

CHANGES IN THE NUMBER OF CONSUMERS As we've already noted, one of the reasons for rising cotton demand between 2007 and 2010 was a growing world population.

Because of population growth, overall demand for cotton would have risen even if the demand of each individual wearer of cotton clothing had remained unchanged.

Let's introduce a new concept: the **individual demand curve,** which shows the relationship between quantity demanded and price for an individual consumer. For example, suppose that Darla is a consumer of cotton blue jeans; also suppose that all pairs of jeans are the same, so they sell for the same price. Panel (a) of Figure 5-5 shows how many pairs of jeans she will buy per year at any given price. Then D_{Darla} is Darla's individual demand curve.

An **individual demand curve** illustrates the relationship between quantity demanded and price for an individual consumer.

The *market demand curve* shows how the combined quantity demanded by all consumers depends on the market price of that good. (Most of the time, when economists refer to the demand curve, they mean the market demand curve.) The market demand curve is the *horizontal sum* of the individual demand curves of all consumers in that market.

FIGURE 5-5 **Individual Demand Curves and the Market Demand Curve**

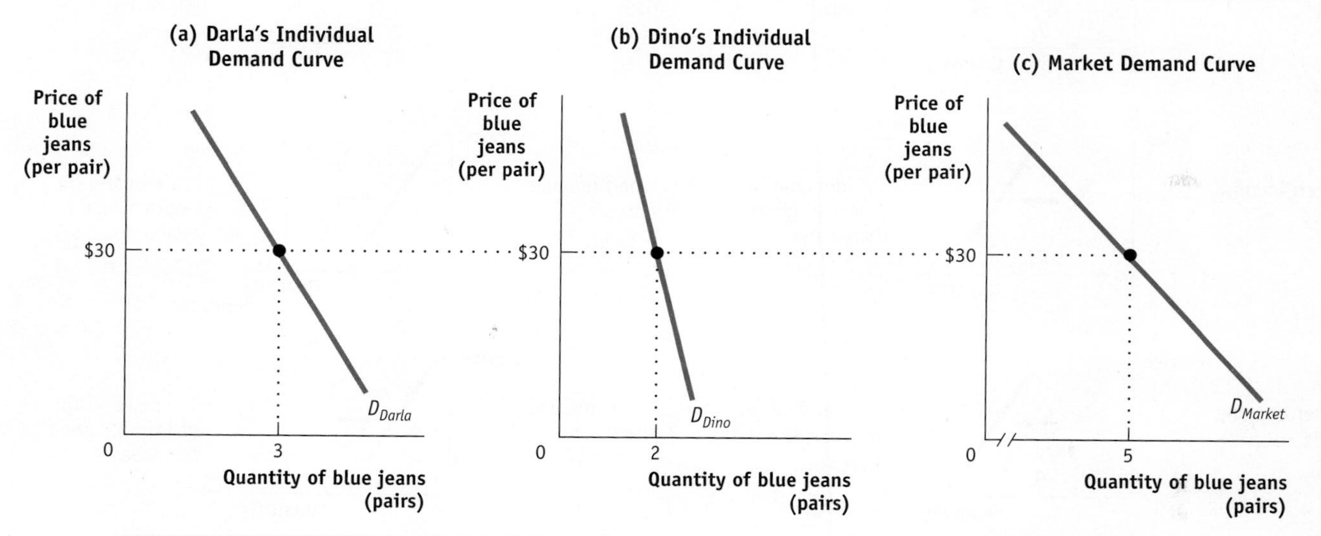

Darla and Dino are the only two consumers of blue jeans in the market. Panel (a) shows Darla's individual demand curve: the number of pairs of blue jeans she will buy per year at any given price. Panel (b) shows Dino's individual demand curve. Given that Darla and Dino are the only two consumers, the *market demand curve*, which shows the quantity of blue jeans demanded by all consumers at any given price, is shown in panel (c). The market demand curve is the *horizontal sum* of the individual demand curves of all consumers. In this case, at any given price, the quantity demanded by the market is the sum of the quantities demanded by Darla and Dino.

To see what we mean by the term *horizontal sum*, assume for a moment that there are only two consumers of blue jeans, Darla and Dino. Dino's individual demand curve, D_{Dino}, is shown in panel (b). Panel (c) shows the market demand curve. At any given price, the quantity demanded by the market is the sum of the quantities demanded by Darla and Dino. For example, at a price of $30 per pair, Darla demands 3 pairs of jeans per year and Dino demands 2 pairs per year. So the quantity demanded by the market is 5 pairs per year.

Clearly, the quantity demanded by the market at any given price is larger with Dino present than it would be if Darla were the only consumer. The quantity demanded at any given price would be even larger if we added a third consumer, then a fourth, and so on. So an increase in the number of consumers leads to an increase in demand.

For a review of the factors that shift demand, see Table 5-1.

TABLE 5-1

Factors That Shift Demand

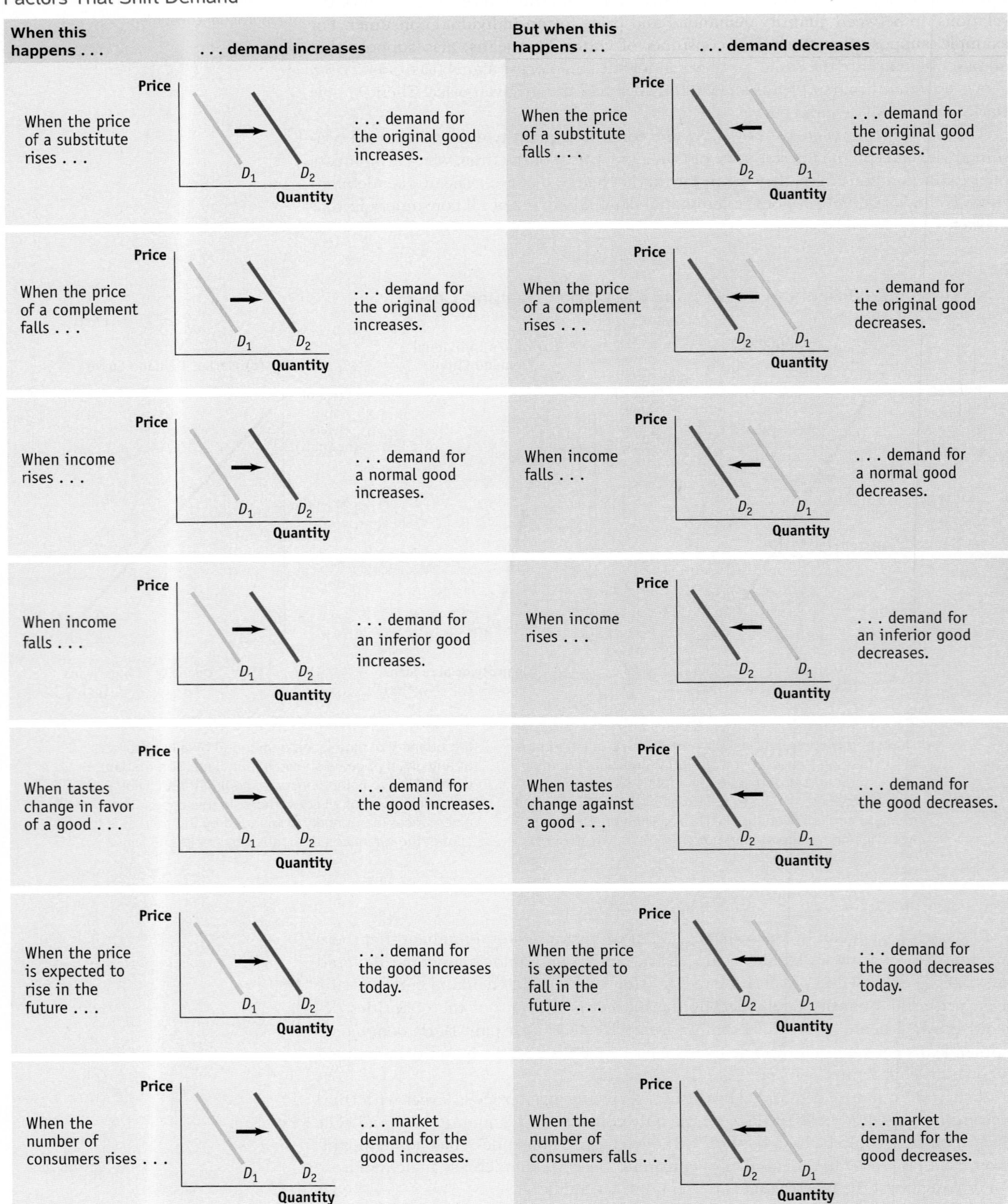

When this happens . . .	. . . demand increases	But when this happens . . .	. . . demand decreases
When the price of a substitute rises . . .	. . . demand for the original good increases.	When the price of a substitute falls . . .	. . . demand for the original good decreases.
When the price of a complement falls . . .	. . . demand for the original good increases.	When the price of a complement rises . . .	. . . demand for the original good decreases.
When income rises . . .	. . . demand for a normal good increases.	When income falls . . .	. . . demand for a normal good decreases.
When income falls . . .	. . . demand for an inferior good increases.	When income rises . . .	. . . demand for an inferior good decreases.
When tastes change in favor of a good . . .	. . . demand for the good increases.	When tastes change against a good . . .	. . . demand for the good decreases.
When the price is expected to rise in the future . . .	. . . demand for the good increases today.	When the price is expected to fall in the future . . .	. . . demand for the good decreases today.
When the number of consumers rises . . .	. . . market demand for the good increases.	When the number of consumers falls . . .	. . . market demand for the good decreases.

ECONOMICS IN ACTION

WORLD VIEW

BEATING THE TRAFFIC

All big cities have traffic problems, and many local authorities try to discourage driving in the crowded city center. If we think of an auto trip to the city center as a good that people consume, we can use the economics of demand to analyze anti-traffic policies.

One common strategy is to reduce the demand for auto trips by lowering the prices of substitutes. Many metropolitan areas subsidize bus and rail service, hoping to lure commuters out of their cars. An alternative is to raise the price of complements: several major U.S. cities impose high taxes on commercial parking garages and impose short time limits on parking meters, both to raise revenue and to discourage people from driving into the city.

A few major cities—including Singapore, London, Oslo, Stockholm, and Milan—have been willing to adopt a direct and politically controversial approach: reducing congestion by raising the price of driving. Under "congestion pricing" (or "congestion charging" in the United Kingdom), a charge is imposed on cars entering the city center during business hours. Drivers buy passes, which are then debited electronically as they drive by monitoring stations. Compliance is monitored with automatic cameras that photograph license plates.

Cities can reduce traffic congestion by raising the price of driving.

The current daily cost of driving in London ranges from £8 to £10 (about $13 to $16). And drivers who don't pay and are caught pay a fine of £120 (about $195) for each transgression.

Not surprisingly, studies have shown that after the implementation of congestion pricing, traffic does indeed decrease. In the 1990s, London had some of the worst traffic in Europe. The introduction of its congestion charge in 2003 immediately reduced traffic in the London city center by about 15%, with overall traffic falling by 21% between 2002 and 2006. And there was increased use of substitutes, such as public transportation, bicycles, motorbikes, and ride-sharing.

In the United States, the U.S. Department of Transportation has implemented pilot programs to study congestion pricing. The programs were so successful that congestion pricing has become policy in some states. Other states, taking suggestions from traffic experts, are trying variable congestion prices, raising prices during peak commuting hours. So even though congestion pricing has been controversial, it appears to be gaining acceptance.

MODULE 5 Review

Solutions appear at the back of the book.

Check Your Understanding

1. Explain whether each of the following events represents (i) a *change in demand* (a *shift of* the demand curve) or (ii) a *change in the quantity demanded* (a *movement along* the demand curve).
   a. A store owner finds that customers are willing to pay more for umbrellas on rainy days.
   b. When XYZ Telecom, a long-distance telephone service provider, offered reduced rates on weekends, its volume of weekend calling increased sharply.
   c. People buy more long-stem roses the week of Valentine's Day, even though the prices are higher than at other times during the year.
   d. A sharp rise in the price of gasoline leads many commuters to join carpools in order to reduce their gasoline purchases.

Multiple-Choice Questions

1. Which of the following would increase demand for a normal good? A decrease in
   a. price.
   b. income.
   c. the price of a substitute.
   d. consumer taste for a good.
   e. the price of a complement.

2. A decrease in the price of butter would most likely decrease the demand for
   a. margarine.
   b. bagels.
   c. jelly.
   d. milk.
   e. syrup.

3. If an increase in income leads to a decrease in demand, the good is
   a. a complement.
   b. a substitute.
   c. inferior.
   d. abnormal.
   e. normal.

4. Which of the following will occur if consumers expect the price of a good to fall in the coming months?
   a. The quantity demanded will rise today.
   b. The quantity demanded will remain the same today.
   c. Demand will increase today.
   d. Demand will decrease today.
   e. No change will occur today.

5. Which of the following will increase the demand for disposable diapers?
   a. a new "baby boom"
   b. concern over the environmental effect of landfills
   c. a decrease in the price of cloth diapers
   d. a move toward earlier potty training of children
   e. a decrease in the price of disposable diapers

Critical-Thinking Question

Draw a correctly labeled graph showing the demand for apples. On your graph, illustrate what happens to the demand for apples if a new report from the Surgeon General finds that an apple a day really *does* keep the doctor away.

PITFALLS

DEMAND VERSUS QUANTITY DEMANDED

? Consider how the term *demand* is used in the following sentence. Why is the sentence incorrect?

If the price of the good goes up then people will buy less and this will lead to a fall in demand which shifts the demand curve to the left.

\> THIS STATEMENT MISTAKES A CHANGE IN QUANTITY DEMANDED FOR A CHANGE IN DEMAND. WHEN DOING ECONOMIC ANALYSIS, IT IS IMPORTANT TO MAKE THE DISTINCTION BETWEEN CHANGES IN *DEMAND*, WHICH MEAN SHIFTS OF THE DEMAND CURVE, AND CHANGES IN *QUANTITY DEMANDED*. When economists say "an increase in demand," they mean a rightward shift of the demand curve, and when they say "a decrease in demand," they mean a leftward shift of the demand curve—that is, when they're being careful. In ordinary speech, most people, including professional economists, use the word *demand* casually. For example, an economist might say "the demand for air travel has doubled over the past fifteen years, partly because of falling airfares" when he or she really means that the *quantity demanded* has doubled. The key point to remember is that a change in price causes a *movement along the demand curve*, and not a shift of the demand curve.

To learn more, see Figure 5.3 for an illustration of a movement along the demand curve versus a shift of the demand curve. For an explanation of the difference, see pages 38–40.

Supply and Equilibrium

Casadphoto/Dreamstime.com

WHAT YOU WILL LEARN

1. What the supply curve is
2. The difference between movements along the supply curve and changes in supply
3. The factors that shift the supply curve
4. How supply and demand curves determine a market's equilibrium price and equilibrium quantity
5. In the case of a shortage or surplus, how price moves the market back to equilibrium

The Supply Curve

Some parts of the world are especially well suited to growing cotton, and the United States is one of those. But even in the United States, some land is better suited to growing cotton than other land. Whether American farmers restrict their cotton-growing to only the most ideal locations or expand it to less suitable land depends on the price they expect to get for their cotton. Moreover, there are many other areas in the world where cotton could be grown—such as Pakistan, Brazil, Turkey, and China. Whether farmers there actually grow cotton depends, again, on the price.

So just as the quantity of cotton that consumers want to buy depends on the price they have to pay, the quantity that producers are willing to produce and sell—the **quantity supplied**—depends on the price they are offered.

The Supply Schedule and the Supply Curve

The table in Figure 6-1 shows how the quantity of cotton made available varies with the price—that is, it shows a hypothetical **supply schedule** for cotton.

A supply schedule works the same way as the demand schedule shown in Figure 5-1 (page 38): in this case, the table shows the number of pounds of cotton farmers are willing to sell at different prices. At a price of $0.50 per pound, farmers are willing to sell only 8 billion pounds of cotton per year. At $0.75 per pound, they're willing to sell 9.1 billion pounds. At $1, they're willing to sell 10 billion pounds, and so on.

In the same way that a demand schedule can be represented graphically by a demand curve, a supply schedule can be represented by a **supply curve,** as shown in Figure 6-1. Each point on the curve represents an entry from the table.

Suppose that the price of cotton rises from $1 to $1.25; we can see that the quantity of cotton farmers are willing to sell rises from 10 billion to 10.7 billion pounds. This

The **quantity supplied** is the actual amount of a good or service people are willing to sell at some specific price.

A **supply schedule** shows how much of a good or service would be supplied at different prices.

A **supply curve** shows the relationship between quantity supplied and price.

FIGURE 6-1 The Supply Schedule and the Supply Curve

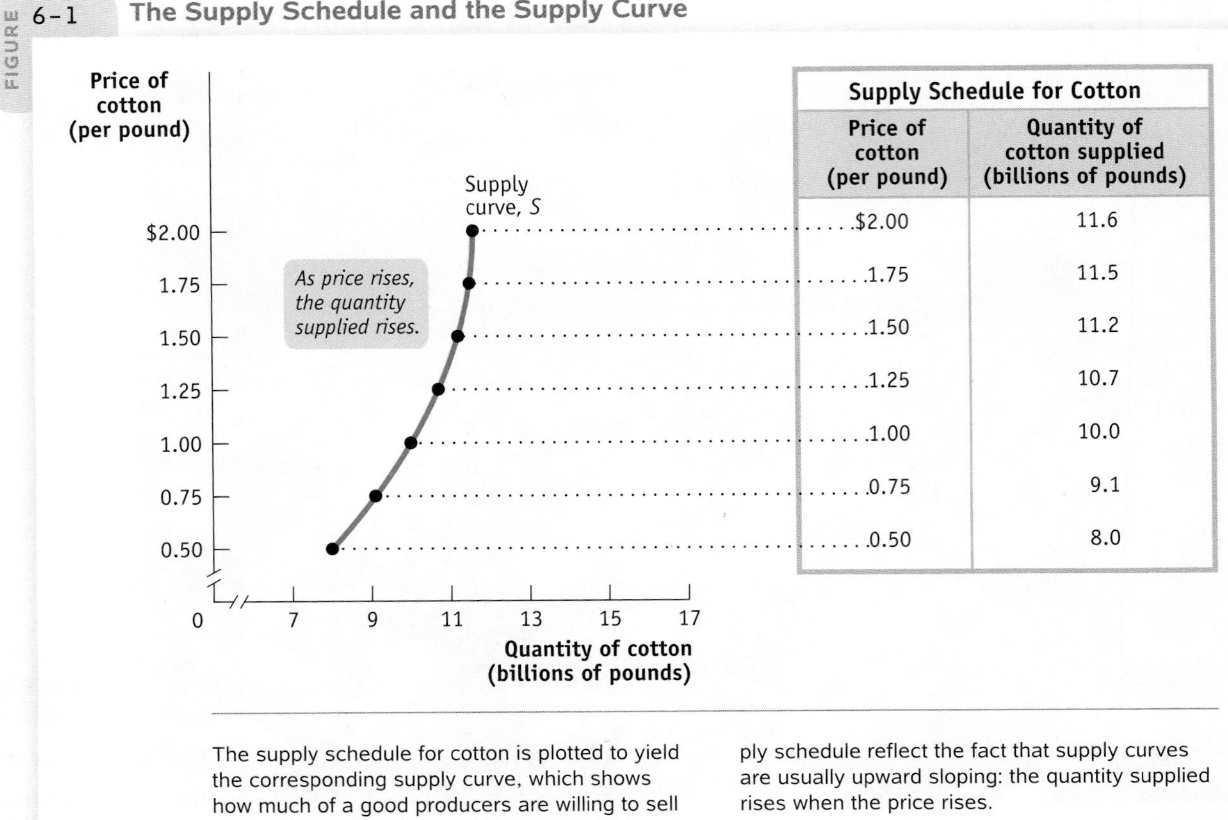

Supply Schedule for Cotton	
Price of cotton (per pound)	Quantity of cotton supplied (billions of pounds)
$2.00	11.6
1.75	11.5
1.50	11.2
1.25	10.7
1.00	10.0
0.75	9.1
0.50	8.0

The supply schedule for cotton is plotted to yield the corresponding supply curve, which shows how much of a good producers are willing to sell at any given price. The supply curve and the supply schedule reflect the fact that supply curves are usually upward sloping: the quantity supplied rises when the price rises.

is the normal situation for a supply curve, reflecting the general proposition that a higher price leads to a higher quantity supplied. Some economists refer to this relationship as the **law of supply.**

Shifts of the Supply Curve

Until recently, cotton remained relatively cheap for several decades. One reason is that the amount of land cultivated for cotton expanded by more than 35% from 1945 to 2007. However, the major factor accounting for cotton's relative cheapness was advances in the production technology, with output per acre more than quadrupling from 1945 to 2007. Figure 6-2 illustrates these events in terms of the supply schedule and the supply curve for cotton.

The table in Figure 6-2 shows two supply schedules. The schedule before improved cotton-growing technology was adopted is the same one as in Figure 6-1. The second schedule shows the supply of cotton *after* the improved technology was adopted. Just as a change in demand schedules leads to a shift of the demand curve, a change in supply schedules leads to a shift of the supply curve—a **change in supply.** This is shown in Figure 6-2 by the shift of the supply curve before the adoption of new cotton-growing technology, S_1, to its new position after the adoption of new cotton-growing technology, S_2. Notice that S_2 lies to the right of S_1, a reflection of the fact that quantity supplied rises at any given price.

As in the analysis of demand, it's crucial to draw a distinction between such shifts of the supply curve and **movements along the supply curve**—changes in the quantity supplied arising from a change in price. We can see this difference in Figure 6-3. The movement from point *A* to point *B* is a movement along the supply curve: the quantity supplied rises along S_1 due to a rise in price. Here, a rise in price from $1 to

The **law of supply** is the general proposition that, all else constant, a higher price leads to higher quantity supplied, and a lower price leads to lower quantity supplied.

A **change in supply** is a shift of the supply curve, which changes the quantity supplied at any given price.

A **movement along the supply curve** is a change in the quantity supplied of a good arising from a change in the good's price.

FIGURE 6-2 **An Increase in Supply**

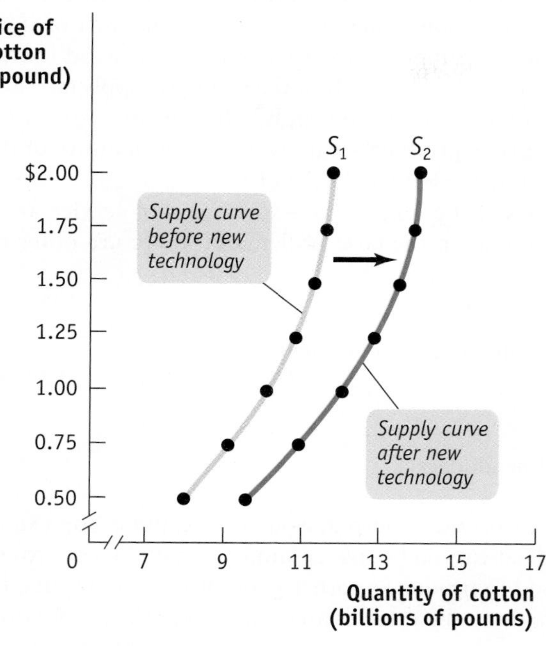

Supply Schedules for Cotton

Price of cotton (per pound)	Quantity of cotton supplied (billions of pounds)	
	Before new technology	After new technology
$2.00	11.6	13.9
1.75	11.5	13.8
1.50	11.2	13.4
1.25	10.7	12.8
1.00	10.0	12.0
0.75	9.1	10.9
0.50	8.0	9.6

The adoption of improved cotton-growing technology generated an increase in supply—a rise in the quantity supplied at any given price. This event is represented by the two supply schedules—one showing supply before the new technology was adopted, the other showing supply after the new technology was adopted—and their corresponding supply curves. The increase in supply shifts the supply curve to the right.

$1.50 leads to a rise in the quantity supplied from 10 billion to 11.2 billion pounds of cotton. But the quantity supplied can also rise when the price is unchanged if there is an increase in supply—a rightward shift of the supply curve. This is shown by the rightward shift of the supply curve from S_1 to S_2. Holding the price constant at $1, the quantity supplied rises from 10 billion pounds at point *A* on S_1 to 12 billion pounds at point *C* on S_2.

FIGURE 6-3 **Movement Along the Supply Curve versus Shift of the Supply Curve**

The increase in quantity supplied when going from point *A* to point *B* reflects a movement along the supply curve: it is the result of a rise in the price of the good. The increase in quantity supplied when going from point *A* to point *C* reflects a shift of the supply curve: it is the result of an increase in the quantity supplied at any given price.

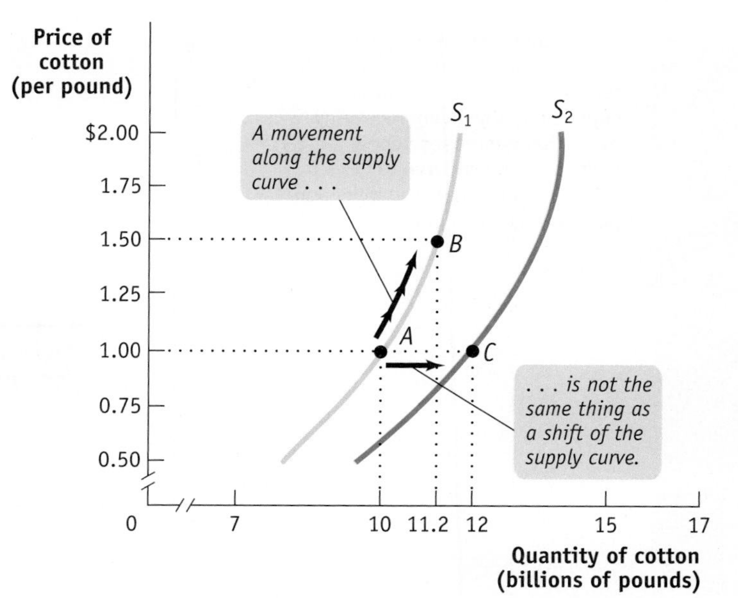

An **input** is a good or service that is used to produce another good or service.

Understanding Shifts of the Supply Curve

Figure 6-4 illustrates the two basic ways in which supply curves can shift. When economists talk about an "increase in supply," they mean a *rightward* shift of the supply curve: at any given price, producers supply a larger quantity of the good than before. This is shown in Figure 6-4 by the rightward shift of the original supply curve S_1 to S_2. And when economists talk about a "decrease in supply," they mean a *leftward* shift of the supply curve: at any given price, producers supply a smaller quantity of the good than before. This is represented by the leftward shift of S_1 to S_3.

Economists believe that shifts of the supply curve for a good or service are mainly the result of five factors (though, as in the case of demand, there are other possible causes):

- Changes in input prices
- Changes in the prices of related goods or services
- Changes in technology
- Changes in expectations
- Changes in the number of producers

CHANGES IN INPUT PRICES To produce output, you need inputs. For example, to make vanilla ice cream, you need vanilla beans, cream, sugar, and so on. An **input** is any good or service that is used to produce another good or service. Inputs, like outputs, have prices. And an increase in the price of an input makes the production of the final good more costly for those who produce and sell it. So producers are less willing to supply the final good at any given price, and the supply curve shifts to the left. For example, fuel is a major cost for airlines. When oil prices surged in 2007–2008, airlines began cutting back on their flight schedules and some went out of business. Similarly, a fall in the price of an input makes the production of the final good less costly for sellers. They are more willing to supply the good at any given price, and the supply curve shifts to the right.

CHANGES IN THE PRICES OF RELATED GOODS OR SERVICES A single producer often produces a mix of goods rather than a single product. For example, an oil refinery produces gasoline from crude oil, but it also produces heating oil and other products

FIGURE 6-4 **Shifts of the Supply Curve**

Any event that increases supply shifts the supply curve to the right, reflecting a rise in the quantity supplied at any given price. Any event that decreases supply shifts the supply curve to the left, reflecting a fall in the quantity supplied at any given price.

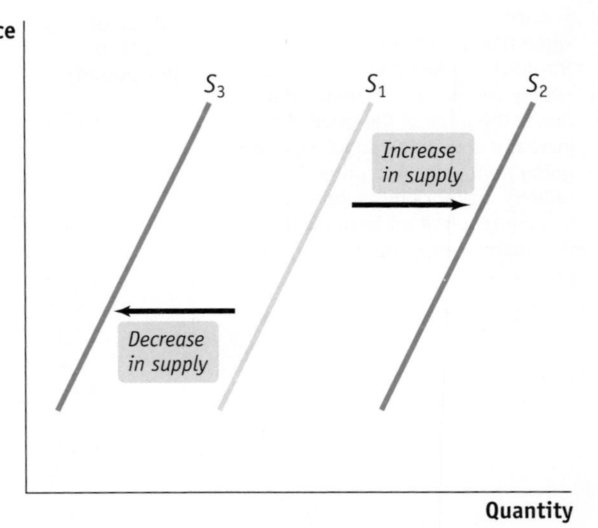

from the same raw material. When a producer sells several products, the quantity of any one good it is willing to supply at any given price depends on the prices of its other co-produced goods.

This effect can run in either direction. An oil refiner will supply less gasoline at any given price when the market price of heating oil rises, shifting the supply curve for gasoline to the left. But it will supply more gasoline at any given price when the market price of heating oil falls, shifting the supply curve for gasoline to the right. This means that gasoline and other co-produced oil products are *substitutes in production* for refiners.

istockphoto

In contrast, due to the nature of the production process, other goods can be *complements in production*. For example, producers of crude oil—oil-well drillers—often find that oil wells also produce natural gas as a by-product of oil extraction. The higher the price at which a driller can sell its natural gas, the more oil wells it will drill and the more oil it will supply at any given price for oil. As a result, natural gas is a complement in production for crude oil.

CHANGES IN TECHNOLOGY When economists talk about "technology," they don't necessarily mean high tech—they mean all the methods people can use to turn inputs into useful goods and services. In that sense, the whole complex sequence of activities that turn cotton from Pakistan into the pair of jeans hanging in your closet is technology.

Improvements in technology enable producers to sell more of their product at the same price. When a better technology becomes available, reducing the cost of production, supply increases, and the supply curve shifts to the right. Improved technology enabled farmers to more than quadruple cotton output per acre planted over the past several decades. Improved technology is also the main reason that, until recently, cotton remained relatively cheap even as worldwide demand grew.

CHANGES IN EXPECTATIONS Just as changes in expectations can shift the demand curve, they can also shift the supply curve. When suppliers have some choice about when they put their good up for sale, changes in the expected future price of the good can lead a supplier to supply less or more of the good today.

For example, consider the fact that gasoline and other oil products are often stored for significant periods of time at oil refineries before being sold to consumers. In fact, storage is usually part of producers' business strategy. Knowing that the demand for gasoline peaks in the summer, oil refiners usually store some of their gasoline produced during the spring for summer sale. Similarly, knowing that the demand for heating oil peaks in the winter, they usually store some of their heating oil produced during the fall for winter sale. In each case, there's a decision to be made between selling the product now versus storing it for later sale. Which choice a producer makes depends on a comparison of the current price versus the expected future price. This example illustrates how changes in expectations can alter supply: an increase in the anticipated future price of a good or service reduces supply today, a leftward shift of the supply curve. But a fall in the anticipated future price increases supply today, a rightward shift of the supply curve.

CHANGES IN THE NUMBER OF PRODUCERS Just as changes in the number of consumers affect the demand curve, changes in the number of producers affect the supply curve. Let's examine the **individual supply curve,** which shows the relationship between quantity supplied and price for an individual producer. For example, suppose

An **individual supply curve** illustrates the relationship between quantity supplied and price for an individual producer.

that Mr. Silva is a Brazilian cotton farmer and that panel (a) of Figure 6-5 shows how many pounds of cotton he will supply per year at any given price. Then S_{Silva} is his individual supply curve.

The *market supply curve* shows how the combined total quantity supplied by all individual producers in the market depends on the market price of that good. Just as the market demand curve is the horizontal sum of the individual demand curves of all consumers, the market supply curve is the horizontal sum of the individual supply curves of all producers. Assume for a moment that there are only two producers of cotton, Mr. Silva and Mr. Liu, a Chinese cotton farmer. Mr. Liu's individual supply curve is shown in panel (b). Panel (c) shows the market supply curve. At any given price, the quantity supplied to the market is the sum of the quantities supplied by Mr. Silva and Mr. Liu. For example, at a price of $2 per pound, Mr. Silva supplies 3,000 pounds of cotton per year and Mr. Liu supplies 2,000 pounds per year, making the quantity supplied to the market 5,000 pounds.

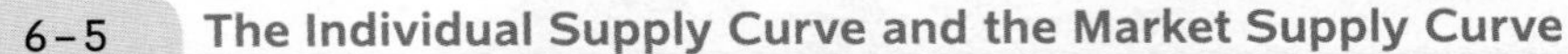

FIGURE 6-5 The Individual Supply Curve and the Market Supply Curve

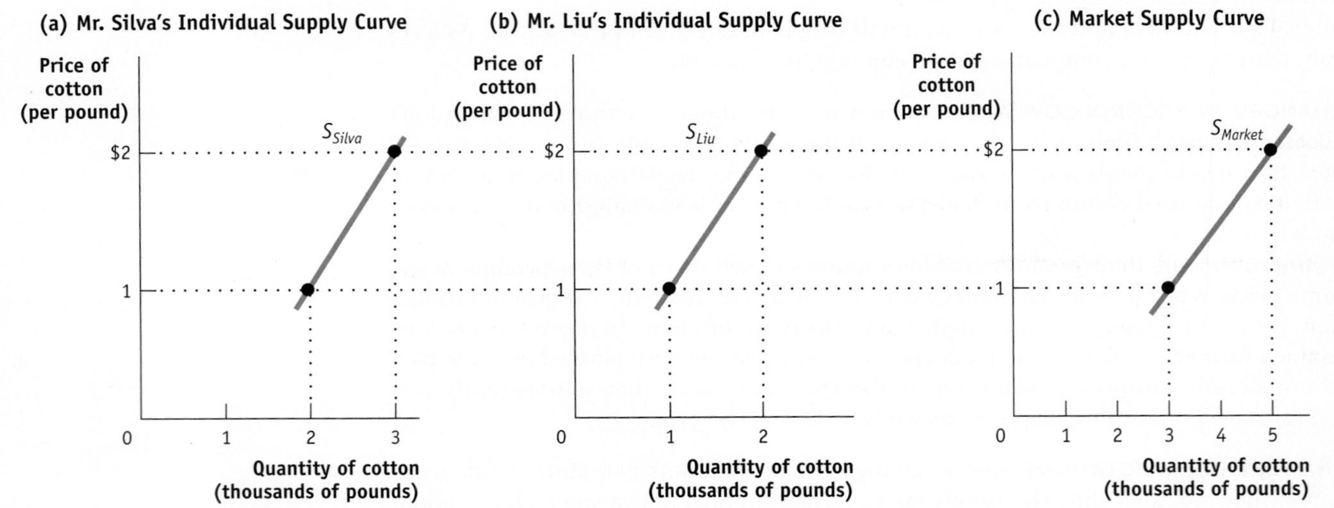

Panel (a) shows the individual supply curve for Mr. Silva, S_{Silva}, the quantity of cotton he will sell at any given price. Panel (b) shows the individual supply curve for Mr. Liu, S_{Liu}. The market supply curve, which shows the quantity of cotton supplied by all producers at any given price, is shown in panel (c). The market supply curve is the horizontal sum of the individual supply curves of all producers.

Clearly, the quantity supplied to the market at any given price is larger with Mr. Liu present than it would be if Mr. Silva were the only supplier. The quantity supplied at a given price would be even larger if we added a third producer, then a fourth, and so on. So an increase in the number of producers leads to an increase in supply and a rightward shift of the supply curve.

For a review of the factors that shift supply, see Table 6-1.

TABLE 6-1

Factors That Shift Supply

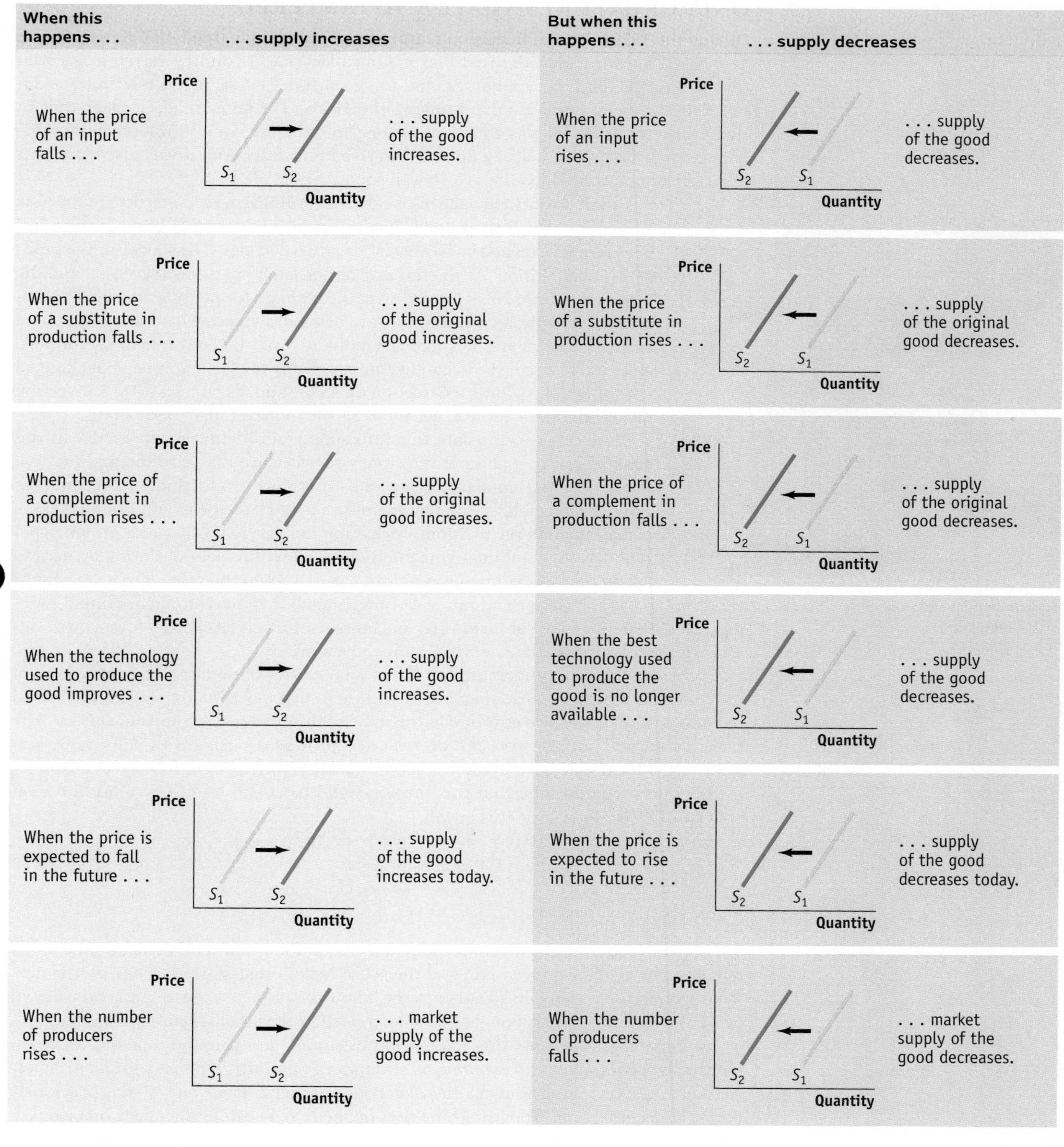

When this happens . . .	. . . supply increases	But when this happens . . .	. . . supply decreases
When the price of an input falls . . .	. . . supply of the good increases.	When the price of an input rises . . .	. . . supply of the good decreases.
When the price of a substitute in production falls . . .	. . . supply of the original good increases.	When the price of a substitute in production rises . . .	. . . supply of the original good decreases.
When the price of a complement in production rises . . .	. . . supply of the original good increases.	When the price of a complement in production falls . . .	. . . supply of the original good decreases.
When the technology used to produce the good improves . . .	. . . supply of the good increases.	When the best technology used to produce the good is no longer available . . .	. . . supply of the good decreases.
When the price is expected to fall in the future . . .	. . . supply of the good increases today.	When the price is expected to rise in the future . . .	. . . supply of the good decreases today.
When the number of producers rises . . .	. . . market supply of the good increases.	When the number of producers falls . . .	. . . market supply of the good decreases.

ECONOMICS IN ACTION

ONLY CREATURES SMALL AND PAMPERED

During the 1970s, British television featured a popular show titled *All Creatures Great and Small*. It chronicled the real life of James Herriot, a country veterinarian who tended to cows, pigs, sheep, horses, and the occasional house pet, often under arduous conditions, in rural England during the 1930s. The show made it clear that in those days the local vet was a critical member of farming communities, saving valuable farm animals and helping farmers survive financially. And it was also clear that Mr. Herriot considered his life's work well spent.

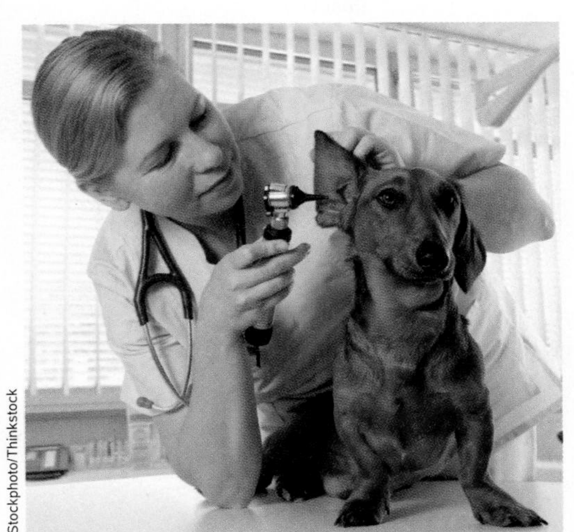
iStockphoto/Thinkstock

Higher spending on pets means fewer veterinarians are available to tend to farm animals.

But that was then and this is now. According to a recent article in the *New York Times*, the United States has experienced a severe decline in the number of farm veterinarians over the past two decades. The source of the problem is competition. As the number of household pets has increased and the incomes of pet owners have grown, the demand for pet veterinarians has increased sharply. As a result, vets are being drawn away from the business of caring for farm animals into the more lucrative business of caring for pets. As one vet stated, she began her career caring for farm animals but changed her mind after "doing a C-section on a cow and it's 50 bucks. Do a C-section on a Chihuahua and you get $300. It's the money. I hate to say that."

How can we translate this into supply and demand curves? Farm veterinary services and pet veterinary services are like gasoline and fuel oil: they're related goods that are substitutes in production. A veterinarian typically specializes in one type of practice or the other, and that decision often depends on the going price for the service. America's growing pet population, combined with the increased willingness of doting owners to spend on their companions' care, has driven up the price of pet veterinary services. As a result, fewer and fewer veterinarians have gone into farm animal practice. So the supply curve of farm veterinarians has shifted leftward—fewer farm veterinarians are offering their services at any given price.

In the end, farmers understand that it is all a matter of dollars and cents; they get fewer veterinarians because they are unwilling to pay more. As one farmer, who had recently lost an expensive cow due to the unavailability of a veterinarian, stated, "The fact that there's nothing you can do, you accept it as a business expense now. You didn't used to. If you have livestock, sooner or later you're going to have deadstock." (Although we should note that this farmer could have chosen to pay more for a vet who would have then saved his cow.)

Supply, Demand, and Equilibrium

We have now covered the first three key elements in the supply and demand model: the demand curve, the supply curve, and the set of factors that shift each curve. The next step is to put these elements together to show how they can be used to predict the actual price at which the good is bought and sold, as well as the actual quantity transacted.

In competitive markets this interaction of supply and demand tends to move toward what economists call *equilibrium*. Imagine a busy afternoon at your local supermarket; there are long lines at the checkout counters. Then one of the previously closed registers opens. The first thing that happens is a rush to the newly opened register. But soon enough things settle down and shoppers have rearranged themselves so that the line at the newly opened register is about as long as all the others. This situation—all the checkout lines are now the same length, and none of the shoppers can be better off by doing something different—is what economists call **equilibrium.**

An economic situation is in **equilibrium** when no individual would be better off doing something different.

The concept of equilibrium helps us understand the price at which a good or service is bought and sold as well as the quantity transacted of the good or service. A competitive market is in equilibrium when the price has moved to a level at which the quantity of a good demanded equals the quantity of that good supplied. At that price, no individual seller could make herself better off by offering to sell either more or less of the good and no individual buyer could make himself better off by offering to buy more or less of the good. Think of shoppers at the supermarket who cannot make themselves better off (cannot save time) by changing lines. Similarly, at the market equilibrium, the price has moved to a level that exactly matches the quantity demanded by consumers to the quantity supplied by sellers.

A competitive market is in equilibrium when price has moved to a level at which the quantity demanded of a good equals the quantity supplied of that good. The price at which this takes place is the **equilibrium price,** also referred to as the **market-clearing price.** The quantity of the good bought and sold at that price is the **equilibrium quantity.**

The price that matches the quantity supplied and the quantity demanded is the **equilibrium price;** the quantity bought and sold at that price is the **equilibrium quantity.** The equilibrium price is also known as the **market-clearing price:** it is the price that "clears the market" by ensuring that every buyer willing to pay that price finds a seller willing to sell at that price, and vice versa. So how do we find the equilibrium price and quantity?

Finding the Equilibrium Price and Quantity

The easiest way to determine the equilibrium price and quantity in a market is by putting the supply curve and the demand curve on the same diagram. Since the supply curve shows the quantity supplied at any given price and the demand curve shows the quantity demanded at any given price, the price at which the two curves cross is the equilibrium price: the price at which quantity supplied equals quantity demanded.

Figure 6-6 combines the demand curve from Figure 5-1 (page 38) and the supply curve from Figure 6-1. They *intersect* at point *E,* which is the equilibrium of this market; \$1 is the equilibrium price and 10 billion pounds is the equilibrium quantity.

Let's confirm that point *E* fits our definition of equilibrium. At a price of \$1 per pound, cotton farmers are willing to sell 10 billion pounds a year and cotton consumers want to buy 10 billion pounds a year. So at the price of \$1 a pound, the quantity of cotton supplied equals the quantity demanded. Notice that at any other price the market would not clear: every willing buyer would not be able to find a willing seller, or vice versa. More specifically, if the price were more than \$1, the quantity supplied would exceed the quantity demanded; if the price were less than \$1, the quantity demanded would exceed the quantity supplied.

FIGURE 6-6 **Market Equilibrium**

Market equilibrium occurs at point *E*, where the supply curve and the demand curve intersect. In equilibrium, the quantity demanded is equal to the quantity supplied. In this market, the equilibrium price is \$1 per pound and the equilibrium quantity is 10 billion pounds per year.

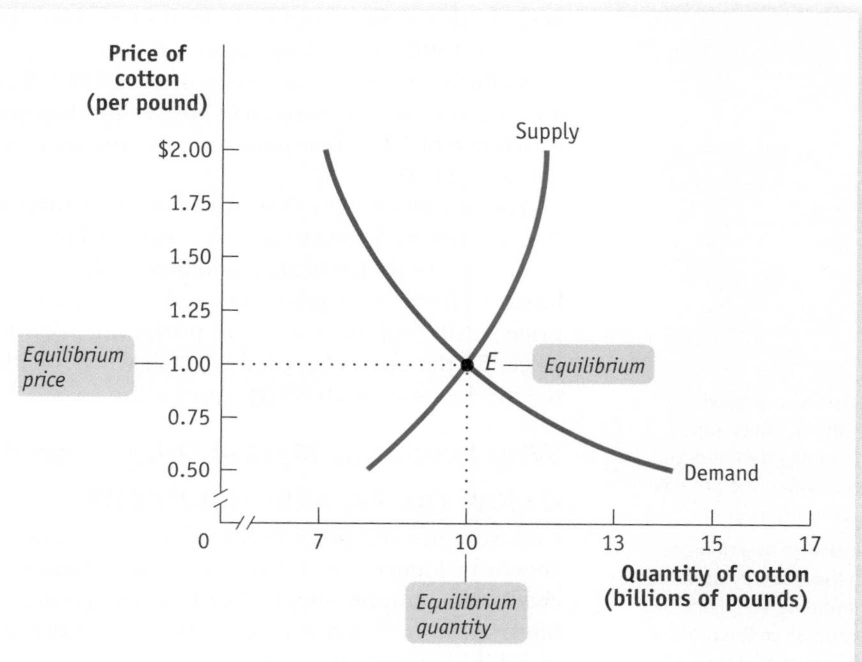

YEAH, I KNOW IT'S PRICEY, BUT I ONLY GOTTA SELL ONE GLASS AND I'M SET FOR LIFE.
Lemonade $1,000,000 a glass
©DAN PIRARO.1996 DIST. BY UNIVERSAL PRESS SYND.
WWW.CREWSOURCE.COM/BIZARRO

© Dan Piraro, 1996 Dist. by Universal Press Syndicate

The model of supply and demand, then, predicts that given the demand and supply curves shown in Figure 6-6, 10 billion pounds of cotton would change hands at a price of $1 per pound. But how can we be sure that the market will arrive at the equilibrium price? We begin by answering three simple questions:

1. Why do all sales and purchases in a market take place at the same price?
2. Why does the market price fall if it is above the equilibrium price?
3. Why does the market price rise if it is below the equilibrium price?

Why Do All Sales and Purchases in a Market Take Place at the Same Price?

There are some markets where the same good can sell for many different prices, depending on who is selling or who is buying. For example, have you ever bought a souvenir in a "tourist trap" and then seen the same item on sale somewhere else (perhaps even in the shop next door) for a lower price? Because tourists don't know which shops offer the best deals and don't have time for comparison shopping, sellers in tourist areas can charge different prices for the same good.

But in any market where the buyers and sellers have both been around for some time, sales and purchases tend to converge at a generally uniform price, so we can safely talk about *the* market price. It's easy to see why. Suppose a seller offered a potential buyer a price noticeably above what the buyer knew other people to be paying. The buyer would clearly be better off shopping elsewhere—unless the seller were prepared to offer a better deal. Conversely, a seller would not be willing to sell for significantly less than the amount he knew most buyers were paying; he would be better off waiting to get a more reasonable customer. So in any well-established, ongoing market, all sellers receive and all buyers pay approximately the same price. This is what we call the *market price.*

Why Does the Market Price Fall if It Is Above the Equilibrium Price?

Suppose the supply and demand curves are as shown in Figure 6-6 but the market price is above the equilibrium level of $1—say, $1.50. This situation is illustrated in Figure 6-7. Why can't the price stay there?

As the figure shows, at a price of $1.50 there would be more pounds of cotton available than consumers wanted to buy: 11.2 billion pounds versus 8.1 billion pounds. The difference of 3.1 billion pounds is the **surplus**—also known as the *excess supply*—of cotton at $1.50.

This surplus means that some cotton farmers are frustrated: at the current price, they cannot find consumers who want to buy their cotton. The surplus offers an incentive for those frustrated would-be sellers to offer a lower price in order to poach business from other producers and entice more consumers to buy. The result of this price cutting will be to push the prevailing price down until it reaches the equilibrium price. So the price of a good will fall whenever there is a surplus—that is, whenever the market price is above its equilibrium level.

There is a **surplus** of a good or service when the quantity supplied exceeds the quantity demanded. Surpluses occur when the price is above its equilibrium level.

There is a **shortage** of a good or service when the quantity demanded exceeds the quantity supplied. Shortages occur when the price is below its equilibrium level.

Why Does the Market Price Rise if It Is Below the Equilibrium Price?

Now suppose the price is below its equilibrium level—say, at $0.75 per pound, as shown in Figure 6-8. In this case, the quantity demanded, 11.5 billion pounds, exceeds the quantity supplied, 9.1 billion pounds, implying that there are would-be buyers who cannot find cotton: there is a **shortage,** also known as an *excess demand,* of 2.4 billion pounds.

FIGURE 6-7 Price Above Its Equilibrium Level Creates a Surplus

The market price of $1.50 is above the equilibrium price of $1. This creates a surplus: at a price of $1.50, producers would like to sell 11.2 billion pounds but consumers want to buy only 8.1 billion pounds, so there is a surplus of 3.1 billion pounds. This surplus will push the price down until it reaches the equilibrium price of $1.

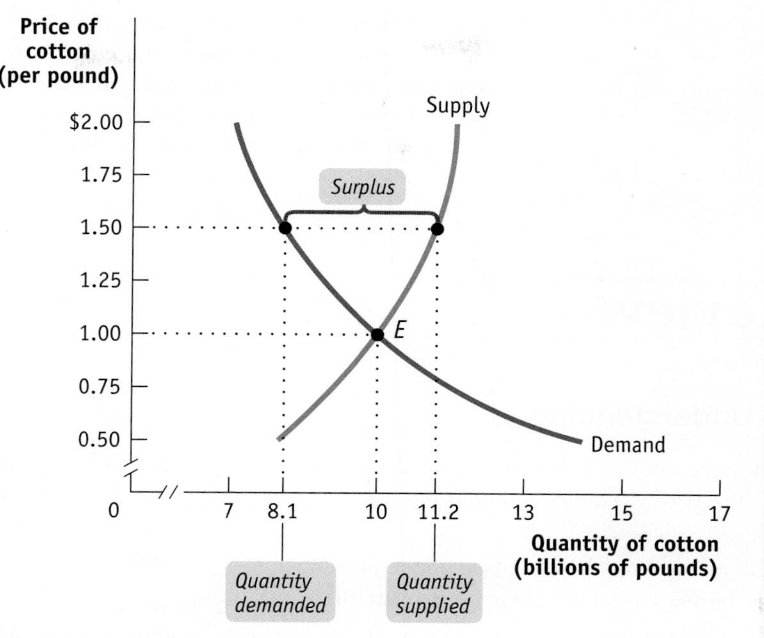

When there is a shortage, there are frustrated would-be buyers—people who want to purchase cotton but cannot find willing sellers at the current price. In this situation, either buyers will offer more than the prevailing price or sellers will realize that they can charge higher prices. Either way, the result is to drive up the prevailing price. This bidding up of prices happens whenever there are shortages—and there will be shortages whenever the price is below its equilibrium level. So the market price will always rise if it is below the equilibrium level.

FIGURE 6-8 Price Below Its Equilibrium Level Creates a Shortage

The market price of $0.75 is below the equilibrium price of $1. This creates a shortage: consumers want to buy 11.5 billion pounds, but only 9.1 billion pounds are for sale, so there is a shortage of 2.4 billion pounds. This shortage will push the price up until it reaches the equilibrium price of $1.

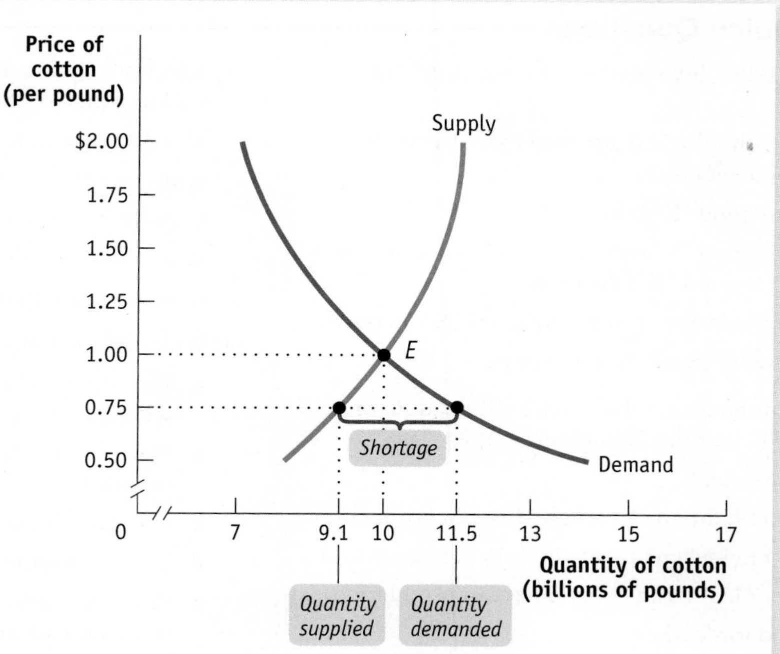

Using Equilibrium to Describe Markets

We have now seen that a market tends to have a single price, the equilibrium price. If the market price is above the equilibrium level, the ensuing surplus leads buyers and sellers to take actions that lower the price. And if the market price is below the equilibrium level, the ensuing shortage leads buyers and sellers to take actions that raise the price. So the market price always *moves toward* the equilibrium price, the price at which there is neither surplus nor shortage.

MODULE 6 Review

Solutions appear at the back of the book.

Check Your Understanding

1. Explain whether each of the following events represents (i) a *change in* supply or (ii) a *movement along* the supply curve.
   - a. During a real estate boom that causes house prices to rise, more homeowners put their houses up for sale.
   - b. Many strawberry farmers open temporary roadside stands during harvest season, even though prices are usually low at that time.
   - c. Immediately after the school year begins, fewer young people are available to work. Fast-food chains must raise wages, which represent the price of labor, to attract workers.
   - d. Many construction workers temporarily move to areas that have suffered hurricane damage, lured by higher wages.
   - e. Since new technologies have made it possible to build larger cruise ships (which are cheaper to run per passenger), Caribbean cruise lines have offered more cabins, at lower prices, than before.
2. In the following three situations, the market is initially in equilibrium. After each event described below, does a surplus or shortage exist at the original equilibrium price? What will happen to the equilibrium price as a result?
   - a. In 2013 there was a bumper crop of wine grapes.
   - b. After a hurricane, Florida hoteliers often find that many people cancel their upcoming vacations, leaving them with empty hotel rooms.
   - c. After a heavy snowfall, many people want to buy second-hand snowblowers at the local tool shop.

Multiple-Choice Questions

1. Which of the following will decrease the supply of good "X"?
   - a. There is a technological advance that affects the production of *all* goods.
   - b. The price of good "X" falls.
   - c. The price of good "Y" (which consumers regard as a substitute for good "X") decreases.
   - d. The wages of workers producing good "X" increase.
   - e. The demand for good "X" decreases.
2. An increase in the demand for steak will lead to an increase in which of the following?
   - a. the supply of steak
   - b. the supply of hamburger (a substitute in production)
   - c. the supply of chicken (a substitute in consumption)
   - d. the supply of leather (a complement in production)
   - e. the demand for leather
3. A technological advance in textbook production will lead to which of the following?
   - a. a decrease in textbook supply
   - b. an increase in textbook demand
   - c. an increase in textbook supply
   - d. a movement along the supply curve for textbooks
   - e. an increase in textbook prices
4. Which of the following is true at equilibrium?
   - a. The supply schedule is identical to the demand schedule at every price.
   - b. The quantity demanded is the same as the quantity supplied.
   - c. The quantity is zero.
   - d. Every consumer who enjoys the good can consume it.
   - e. Producers could not make any more of the product regardless of the price.

5. The market price of a good will tend to rise if
   a. demand decreases.
   b. supply increases.
   c. it is above the equilibrium price.
   d. it is below the equilibrium price.
   e. demand shifts to the left.

Critical-Thinking Question

Draw a correctly labeled graph showing the market for oranges in equilibrium. Show on your graph how a hurricane that destroys large numbers of orange groves in Florida will affect supply and demand, if at all.

PITFALLS

SUPPLY VERSUS QUANTITY SUPPLIED

? Where does the writer of this statement go wrong?

Economists generally agree that when demand decreases, the price falls. But a fall in price leads to a decrease in supply that, in turn, causes the price to rise again.

> THE WRITER CONFUSES A SHIFT OF THE SUPPLY CURVE (A DECREASE IN SUPPLY) AND A MOVEMENT ALONG THE SUPPLY CURVE (A CHANGE IN THE QUANTITY SUPPLIED). While economists agree that a decrease in demand leads to a fall in price, the fall in price leads only to a *movement along the supply curve*, not a shift of the supply curve. So that part of the statement is false. Always be careful to distinguish between a shift of the supply curve and a movement along the supply curve. A corrected statement would read:

Economists generally agree that when there is a decrease in demand, the price falls. And when the price falls, this leads to a decrease in the quantity supplied. It's as simple as that!

To learn more, see Figure 6-3, which illustrates a movement along the supply curve versus a shift of the supply curve. An explanation of the difference is on pages 48–49.

Changes in Equilibrium

AP Photo/Khalid Tanveer

WHAT YOU WILL LEARN

1. How equilibrium price and quantity are affected when there is a change in either supply or demand
2. How equilibrium price and quantity are affected when there is a simultaneous change in both supply and demand

Changes in Supply and Demand

The 2010 floods in Pakistan came as a surprise, but the subsequent increase in the price of cotton was no surprise at all. Suddenly there was a fall in supply: the quantity of cotton available at any given price fell. Predictably, a fall in supply raises the equilibrium price.

The flooding in Pakistan is an example of an event that shifted the supply curve for a good without having much effect on the demand curve. There are many such events. There are also events that shift the demand curve without shifting the supply curve. For example, a medical report that chocolate is good for you increases the demand for chocolate but does not affect the supply. Events often shift either the supply curve or the demand curve, but not both; it is therefore useful to ask what happens in each case.

We have seen that when a curve shifts, the equilibrium price and quantity change. We will now concentrate on exactly how the shift of a curve alters the equilibrium price and quantity.

What Happens When the Demand Curve Shifts

Cotton and polyester are substitutes: if the price of polyester rises, the demand for cotton will increase, and if the price of polyester falls, the demand for cotton will decrease. But how does the price of polyester affect the *market equilibrium* for cotton?

Figure 7-1 shows the effect of a rise in the price of polyester on the market for cotton. The rise in the price of polyester increases the demand for cotton. Point E_1 shows the equilibrium corresponding to the original demand curve, with P_1 the equilibrium price and Q_1 the equilibrium quantity bought and sold.

An increase in demand is indicated by a *rightward* shift of the demand curve from D_1 to D_2. At the original market price P_1, this market is no longer in equilibrium: a shortage occurs because the quantity demanded exceeds the quantity supplied. So the

FIGURE 7-1 **Equilibrium and Shifts of the Demand Curve**

The original equilibrium in the market for cotton is at E_1, at the intersection of the supply curve and the original demand curve, D_1. A rise in the price of polyester, a substitute, shifts the demand curve for cotton products rightward to D_2. A shortage exists at the original price, P_1, causing both the price and quantity supplied to rise, a movement along the supply curve. A new equilibrium is reached at E_2, with a higher equilibrium price, P_2, and a higher equilibrium quantity, Q_2. When demand for a good or service increases, the equilibrium price and the equilibrium quantity of the good or service both rise.

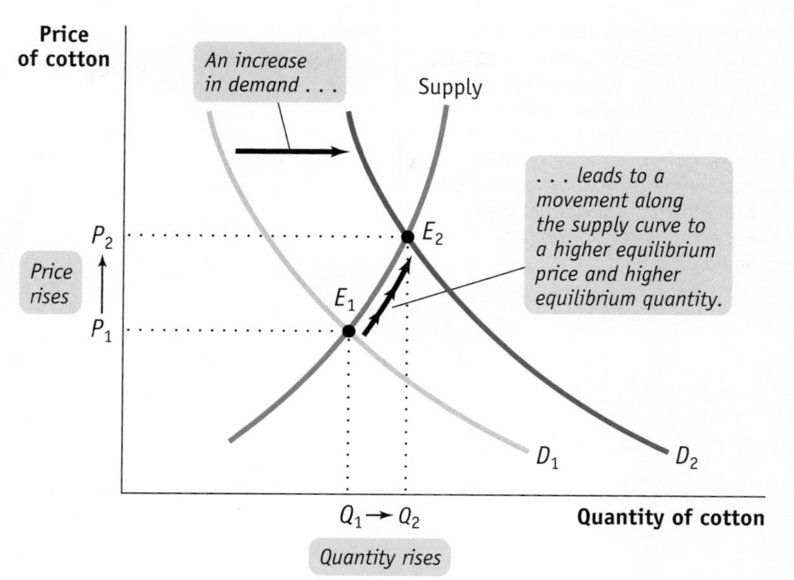

price of cotton rises and generates an increase in the quantity supplied, an upward *movement along the supply curve.* A new equilibrium is established at point E_2, with a higher equilibrium price, P_2, and higher equilibrium quantity, Q_2. This sequence of events reflects a general principle: *When demand for a good or service increases, the equilibrium price and the equilibrium quantity of the good or service both rise.*

What would happen in the reverse case, a fall in the price of polyester? A fall in the price of polyester reduces the demand for cotton, shifting the demand curve to the *left.* At the original price, a surplus occurs as quantity supplied exceeds quantity demanded. The price falls and leads to a decrease in the quantity supplied, resulting in a lower equilibrium price and a lower equilibrium quantity. This illustrates another general principle: *When demand for a good or service decreases, the equilibrium price and the equilibrium quantity of the good or service both fall.*

To summarize how a market responds to a change in demand: *An increase in demand leads to a rise in both the equilibrium price and the equilibrium quantity. A decrease in demand leads to a fall in both the equilibrium price and the equilibrium quantity.*

iStockphoto/Thinkstock

A fall in the price of polyester reduces the demand for cotton, shifting the demand curve to the left.

What Happens When the Supply Curve Shifts

In the real world, it is a bit easier to predict changes in supply than changes in demand. Physical factors that affect supply, like the availability of inputs, are easier to get a handle on than the fickle tastes that affect demand. Still, with supply as with demand, what we can best predict are the *effects* of shifts of the supply curve.

As we mentioned in this chapter's opening story, devastating floods in Pakistan sharply reduced the supply of cotton in 2010. Figure 7-2 shows how this shift affected the market equilibrium. The original equilibrium is at E_1, the point of intersection of the original supply curve, S_1, and the demand curve, with an equilibrium price P_1 and equilibrium quantity Q_1. As a result of the bad weather, supply falls and S_1 shifts *leftward* to S_2. At the original price P_1, a shortage of cotton now exists and the market is no longer in equilibrium. The shortage causes a rise in price and a fall in quantity demanded, an upward movement along the demand curve. The new equilibrium is at E_2, with an equilibrium price P_2 and an equilibrium quantity Q_2. In the new equilibrium,

FIGURE 7-2 Equilibrium and Shifts of the Supply Curve

The original equilibrium in the market for cotton is at E_1. Bad weather in cotton-growing areas causes a fall in the supply of cotton and shifts the supply curve leftward from S_1 to S_2. A new equilibrium is established at E_2, with a higher equilibrium price, P_2, and a lower equilibrium quantity, Q_2.

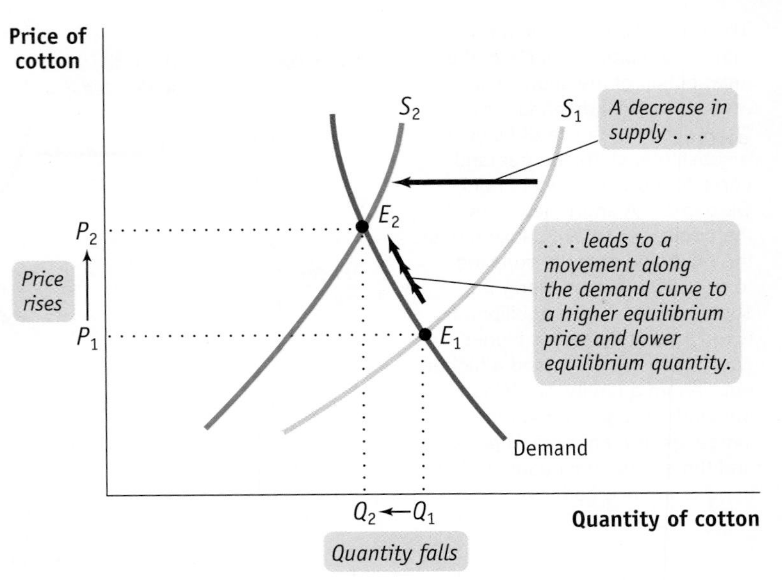

E_2, the price is higher and the equilibrium quantity lower than before. This can be stated as a general principle: *When supply of a good or service decreases, the equilibrium price of the good or service rises and the equilibrium quantity of the good or service falls.*

What happens to the market when supply increases? An increase in supply leads to a *rightward* shift of the supply curve. At the original price, a surplus now exists; as a result, the equilibrium price falls and the quantity demanded rises. This describes what happened to the market for cotton as new technology increased cotton yields. We can formulate a general principle: *When supply of a good or service increases, the equilibrium price of the good or service falls and the equilibrium quantity of the good or service rises.*

To summarize how a market responds to a change in supply: *An increase in supply leads to a fall in the equilibrium price and a rise in the equilibrium quantity. A decrease in supply leads to a rise in the equilibrium price and a fall in the equilibrium quantity.*

Simultaneous Shifts of Supply and Demand Curves

Finally, it sometimes happens that events shift *both* the demand and supply curves at the same time. This is not unusual; in real life, supply curves and demand curves for many goods and services shift quite often because the economic environment continually changes. Figure 7-3 illustrates two examples of simultaneous shifts. In both panels there is an increase in demand—that is, a rightward shift of the demand curve, from D_1 to D_2—say, for example, representing an increase in the demand for cotton due to changing tastes. Notice that the rightward shift in panel (a) is larger than the one in panel (b): we can suppose that panel (a) represents a year in which many more people than usual choose to buy jeans and cotton T-shirts and panel (b) represents a normal year. Both panels also show a decrease in supply—that is, a leftward shift of the supply curve from S_1 to S_2. Also notice that the leftward shift in panel (b) is relatively larger than the one in panel (a): we can suppose that panel (b) represents the effect of particularly bad weather in Pakistan and panel (a) represents the effect of a much less severe weather event.

iStockphoto/Thinkstock

In both cases, the equilibrium price rises from P_1 to P_2, as the equilibrium moves from E_1 to E_2. But what happens to the equilibrium quantity, the quantity of cotton bought and sold? In panel (a) the increase in demand is large relative to the decrease in supply, and the equilibrium quantity rises as a result. In panel (b), the decrease in

FIGURE 7-3 **Simultaneous Shifts of the Demand and Supply Curves**

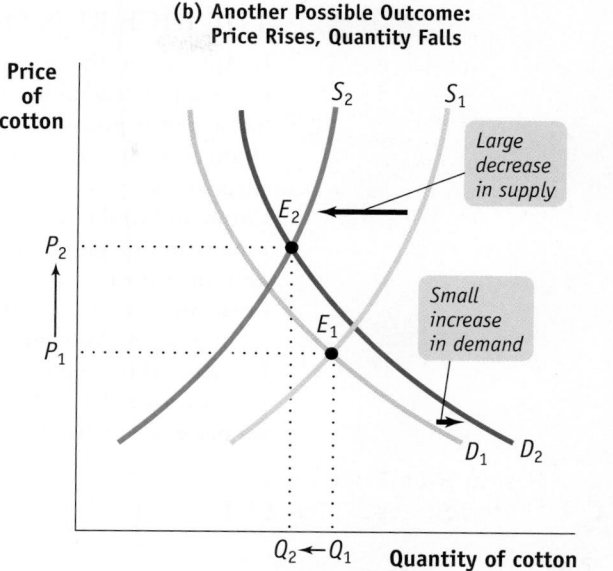

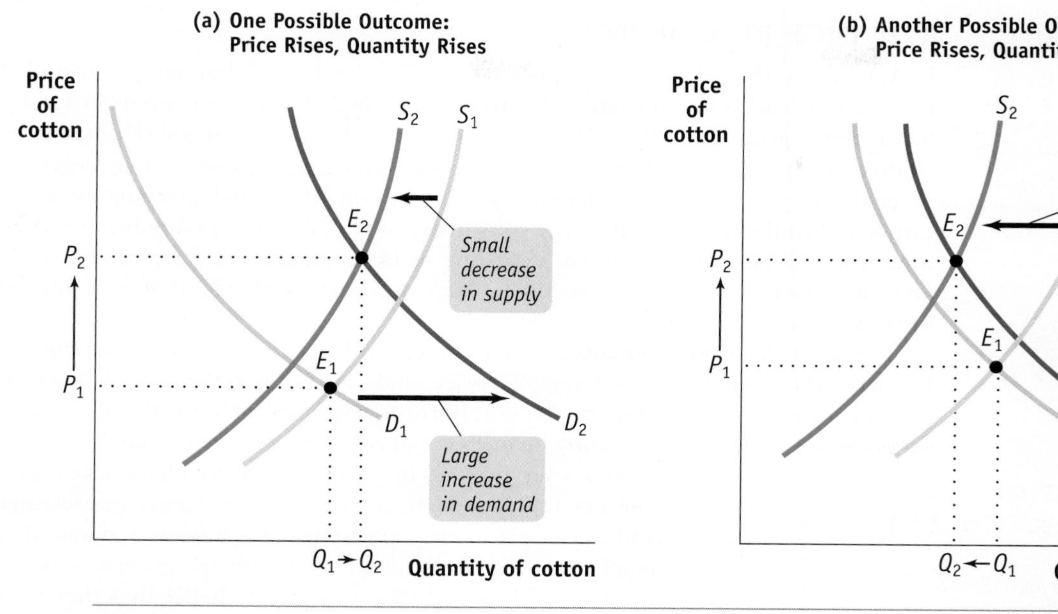

In panel (a) there is a simultaneous rightward shift of the demand curve and leftward shift of the supply curve. Here the increase in demand is relatively larger than the decrease in supply, so the equilibrium price and equilibrium quantity both rise. In panel (b) there is also a simultaneous rightward shift of the demand curve and leftward shift of the supply curve. Here the decrease in supply is relatively larger than the increase in demand, so the equilibrium price rises and the equilibrium quantity falls.

supply is large relative to the increase in demand, and the equilibrium quantity falls as a result. That is, when demand increases and supply decreases, the actual quantity bought and sold can go either way, depending on *how much* the demand and supply curves have shifted.

In general, when supply and demand shift in opposite directions, we can't predict what the ultimate effect will be on the quantity bought and sold. What we can say is that a curve that shifts a disproportionately greater distance than the other curve will have a disproportionately greater effect on the quantity bought and sold. That said, we can make the following prediction about the outcome when the supply and demand curves shift in opposite directions:

- When demand increases and supply decreases, the equilibrium price rises but the change in the equilibrium quantity is ambiguous.
- When demand decreases and supply increases, the equilibrium price falls but the change in the equilibrium quantity is ambiguous.

But suppose that the demand and supply curves shift in the same direction. Before 2010, this was the case in the global market for cotton, where both supply and demand had increased over the past decade. Can we safely make any predictions about the changes in price and quantity? In this situation, the change in quantity bought and sold can be predicted, but the change in price is ambiguous. The two possible outcomes when the supply and demand curves shift in the same direction (which you should check for yourself) are as follows:

- When both demand and supply increase, the equilibrium quantity rises but the change in equilibrium price is ambiguous.
- When both demand and supply decrease, the equilibrium quantity falls but the change in equilibrium price is ambiguous.

ECONOMICS ▶ IN ACTION

THE RICE RUN OF 2008

In April 2008, the price of rice exported from Thailand—a global benchmark for the price of rice traded in international markets—reached $950 per ton, up from $360 per ton at the beginning of 2008. Within hours, prices for rice at major rice-trading exchanges around the world were breaking record levels. The factors that lay behind the surge in rice prices were both demand-related and supply-related: growing incomes in China and India, traditionally large consumers of rice; drought in Australia; and pest infestation in Vietnam. But it was hoarding by farmers, panic buying by consumers, and an export ban by India, one of the largest exporters of rice, that explained the breathtaking speed of the rise in price.

In much of Asia, governments are major buyers of rice. They buy rice from their rice farmers, who are paid a government-set price, and then sell it to the poor at subsidized prices (prices lower than the market equilibrium price). In the past, the government-set price was better than anything farmers could get in the private market.

FIGURE 7-4 Rising Rice Prices in the United States, 2003–2011

Source: U.S. Bureau of Labor Statistics.

Now, even farmers in rural areas of Asia have access to the Internet and can see the price quotes on global rice exchanges. And as rice prices rose in response to changes in demand and supply, farmers grew dissatisfied with the government price and instead hoarded their rice in the belief that they would eventually get higher prices. This was a self-fulfilling belief, as the hoarding shifted the supply curve leftward and raised the price of rice even further.

At the same time, India, one of the largest growers of rice, banned Indian exports of rice in order to protect its domestic consumers, causing yet another leftward shift of the supply curve and pushing the price of rice even higher.

As shown in Figure 7-4, the effects even spilled over to the United States, which had not suffered any fall in its rice production. American rice consumers grew alarmed when large retailers limited some bulk rice purchases in response to the turmoil in the global rice market.

Fearful of paying even higher prices in the future, panic buying set in. As one woman who was in the process of buying 30 pounds of rice said, "We don't even eat that much rice. But I read about it in the newspaper and decided to buy some." In San Francisco, some Asian markets reported runs on rice. And, predictably, this led to even higher prices as panic buying shifted the demand curve rightward, further feeding the buying frenzy. As one market owner said, "People are afraid. We tell them, 'There's no shortage yet' but it was crazy in here."

MODULE 7 Review

Solutions appear at the back of the book.

Check Your Understanding

1. For each of the following examples, explain how the indicated change affects supply or demand for the good in question and how the shift you describe affects equilibrium price and quantity.
   a. As the price of gasoline fell in the United States during the 1990s, more people bought large cars.
   b. As technological innovation has lowered the cost of recycling used paper, fresh paper made from recycled stock is used more frequently.
   c. When a local cable company offers cheaper pay-per-view films, local movie theaters have more unfilled seats.

2. Periodically, a computer chip maker like Intel introduces a new chip that is faster than the previous one. In response, demand for computers using the earlier chip decreases as customers put off purchases in anticipation of machines containing the new chip. Simultaneously, computer makers increase their production of computers containing the earlier chip in order to clear out their stocks of those chips.

   Draw two diagrams of the market for computers containing the earlier chip: (a) one in which the equilibrium quantity falls in response to these events and (b) one in which the equilibrium quantity rises. What happens to the equilibrium price in each diagram?

Multiple-Choice Questions

1. Which of the following describes what will happen in the market for tomatoes if a salmonella outbreak is attributed to tainted tomatoes?
   a. Supply will increase and price will increase.
   b. Supply will increase and price will decrease.
   c. Demand will decrease and price will increase.
   d. Demand will decrease and price will decrease.
   e. Supply and demand will both increase.

2. Which of the following will lead to an increase in the equilibrium price of product "X"? A(n)
   a. increase in consumer incomes if product "X" is an inferior good
   b. increase in the price of machinery used to produce product "X"
   c. technological advance in the production of good "X"
   d. decrease in the price of good "Y" (a substitute for good "X")
   e. expectation by consumers that the price of good "X" is going to fall

3. The equilibrium price will rise, but equilibrium quantity may increase, decrease, or stay the same if
   a. demand increases and supply decreases.
   b. demand increases and supply increases.
   c. demand decreases and supply increases.
   d. demand decreases and supply decreases.
   e. demand increases and supply does not change.

4. An increase in the number of buyers and a technological advance will cause
   a. demand to increase and supply to increase.
   b. demand to increase and supply to decrease.
   c. demand to decrease and supply to increase.
   d. demand to decrease and supply to decrease.
   e. no change in demand and an increase in supply.

5. Which of the following is certainly true if demand and supply increase at the same time?
   a. The equilibrium price will increase.
   b. The equilibrium price will decrease.
   c. The equilibrium quantity will increase.
   d. The equilibrium quantity will decrease.
   e. The equilibrium quantity may increase, decrease, or stay the same.

Critical-Thinking Question

Draw a correctly labeled graph showing the market for cotton in equilibrium. On your graph, show the effect of an increase in the supply of cotton on equilibrium price and equilibrium quantity in the market for cotton.

BUSINESS CASE: The Chicago Board of Trade

Around the world, commodities are bought and sold on "exchanges," markets organized in a specific location, where buyers and sellers meet to trade. But it wasn't always like this.

The first modern commodity exchange was the Chicago Board of Trade, founded in 1848. At the time, the United States was already a major wheat producer. And St. Louis, not Chicago, was the leading city of the American West and the dominant location for wheat trading. But the St. Louis wheat market suffered from a major flaw: there was no central marketplace, no specific location where everyone met to buy and sell wheat. Instead, sellers would sell their grain from various warehouses or from stacked sacks of grain on the river levee. Buyers would wander around town, looking for the best price.

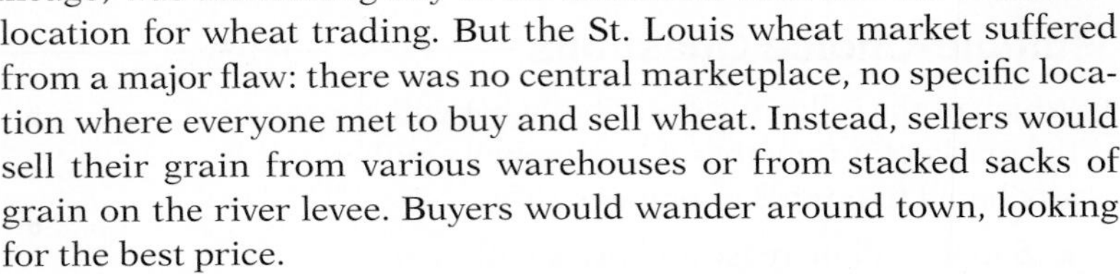

Jim West

In Chicago, however, sellers had a better idea. The Chicago Board of Trade, an association of the city's leading grain dealers, created a much more efficient method for trading wheat. There, traders gathered in one place—the "pit"—where they called out offers to sell and accepted offers to buy. The Board guaranteed that these contracts would be fulfilled, removing the need for the wheat to be physically in place when a trade was agreed upon.

This system meant that buyers could very quickly find sellers and vice-versa, reducing the cost of doing business. It also ensured that everyone could see the latest price, leading the price to rise or fall quickly in response to market conditions. For example, news of bad weather in a wheat-growing area hundreds of miles away would send the price in the Chicago pit soaring in a matter of minutes.

The Chicago Board of Trade went on to become the world's most important trading center for wheat and many other agricultural commodities, a distinction it retains to this day. And the Board's rise helped the rise of Chicago, too. The city, as Carl Sandburg put it in his famous poem, "Chicago," became:

Hog Butcher for the World,
Tool Maker, Stacker of Wheat,
Player with Railroads and the Nation's Freight Handler;
Stormy, husky, brawling,
City of the Big Shoulders

By 1890, Chicago had more than a million people, second only to New York and far out-pacing St. Louis. Making a better market, it turned out, was very good business indeed.

Questions for Thought

1. In Module 6 we mention how prices can vary in a tourist trap. Which market, St. Louis or Chicago, was more likely to behave like a tourist trap? Explain.
2. What was the advantage to buyers from buying their wheat in the Chicago pit instead of in St. Louis? What was the advantage to sellers?
3. Based on what you have learned from this case, explain why the online auction site eBay is like the Chicago pit. Why has it been so successful as a marketplace for second-hand items compared to a market composed of various flea markets and dealers?

SECTION 2 REVIEW

Summary

Demand

1. The **supply and demand model** illustrates how a **competitive market,** one with many buyers and sellers of the same product, works.
2. The **demand schedule** shows the **quantity demanded** at each price and is represented graphically by a **demand curve.** The **law of demand** says that demand curves slope downward, meaning that as price decreases, the quantity demanded increases.
3. A **movement along the demand curve** occurs when the price changes and causes a change in the quantity demanded. When economists talk of **changes in demand,** they mean shifts of the demand curve—a change in the quantity demanded at any given price. An increase in demand causes a rightward shift of the demand curve. A decrease in demand causes a leftward shift.
4. There are five main factors that shift the demand curve:
   - A change in the prices of related goods, such as **substitutes** or **complements**
   - A change in income: when income rises, the demand for **normal goods** increases and the demand for **inferior goods** decreases
   - A change in tastes
   - A change in expectations
   - A change in the number of consumers

Supply and Equilibrium

5. The **supply schedule** shows the **quantity supplied** at each price and is represented graphically by a **supply curve.** Supply curves usually slope upward.
6. A **movement along the supply curve** occurs when the price changes and causes a change in the quantity supplied. When economists talk of **changes in supply,** they mean shifts of the supply curve—a change in the quantity supplied at any given price. An increase in supply causes a rightward shift of the supply curve. A decrease in supply causes a leftward shift.
7. There are five main factors that shift the supply curve:
   - A change in **input** prices
   - A change in the prices of related goods and services
   - A change in technology
   - A change in expectations
   - A change in the number of producers
8. The supply and demand model is based on the principle that the price in a market moves to its **equilibrium price,** or **market-clearing price,** the price at which the quantity demanded is equal to the quantity supplied. This quantity is the **equilibrium quantity.** When the price is above its market-clearing level, there is a **surplus** that pushes the price down. When the price is below its market-clearing level, there is a **shortage** that pushes the price up.

Changes in Equilibrium

9. An increase in demand increases both the equilibrium price and the equilibrium quantity; a decrease in demand has the opposite effect. An increase in supply reduces the equilibrium price and increases the equilibrium quantity; a decrease in supply has the opposite effect.
10. Shifts of the demand curve and the supply curve can happen simultaneously. When they shift in opposite directions, the change in price is predictable but the change in quantity is not. When they shift in the same direction, the change in quantity is predictable but the change in price is not. In general, the curve that shifts the greater distance has a greater effect on the changes in price and quantity.

Key Terms

Competitive market, p. 36
Supply and demand model, p. 36
Demand schedule, p. 37
Quantity demanded, p. 37
Demand curve, p. 37
Law of demand, p. 38
Change in demand, p. 39
Movement along the demand curve, p. 39
Substitutes, p. 41
Complements, p. 41
Normal good, p. 42
Inferior good, p. 42
Individual demand curve, p. 43
Quantity supplied, p. 47
Supply schedule, p. 47
Supply curve, p. 47
Law of supply, p. 48
Change in supply, p. 48
Movement along the supply curve, p. 48
Input, p. 50
Individual supply curve, p. 51
Equilibrium, p. 54
Equilibrium price, p. 55
Market-clearing price, p. 55
Equilibrium quantity, p. 55
Surplus, p. 56
Shortage, p. 56

Problems

1. A survey indicated that chocolate ice cream is America's favorite ice-cream flavor. For each of the following, indicate the possible effects on the demand and/or supply, equilibrium price, and equilibrium quantity of chocolate ice cream.

   a. A severe drought in the Midwest causes dairy farmers to reduce the number of milk-producing cows in their herds by a third. These dairy farmers supply cream that is used to manufacture chocolate ice cream.

   b. A new report by the American Medical Association reveals that chocolate does, in fact, have significant health benefits.

   c. The discovery of cheaper synthetic vanilla flavoring lowers the price of vanilla ice cream.

   d. New technology for mixing and freezing ice cream lowers manufacturers' costs of producing chocolate ice cream.

2. In a supply and demand diagram, draw the change in demand for hamburgers in your hometown due to the following events. In each case show the effect on equilibrium price and quantity.

   a. The price of tacos increases.

   b. All hamburger sellers raise the price of their french fries.

   c. Income falls in town. Assume that hamburgers are a normal good for most people.

   d. Income falls in town. Assume that hamburgers are an inferior good for most people.

   e. Hot dog stands cut the price of hot dogs.

3. The market for many goods changes in predictable ways according to the time of year, in response to events such as holidays, vacation times, seasonal changes in production, and so on. Using supply and demand, explain the change in price in each of the following cases. Note that supply and demand may shift simultaneously.

   a. Lobster prices usually fall during the summer peak harvest season, despite the fact that people like to eat lobster during the summer months more than during any other time of year.

   b. The price of a Christmas tree is lower after Christmas than before and fewer trees are sold.

   c. The price of a round-trip ticket to Paris on Air France falls by more than $200 after the end of school vacation in September. This happens despite the fact that generally worsening weather increases the cost of operating flights to Paris, and Air France therefore reduces the number of flights to Paris at any given price.

4. Show in a diagram the effect on the demand curve, the supply curve, the equilibrium price, and the equilibrium quantity of each of the following events on the designated market.

   a. the market for newspapers in your town

      Case 1: The salaries of journalists go up.

      Case 2: There is a big news event in your town, which is reported in the newspapers, and residents want to learn more about it.

   b. the market for St. Louis Rams cotton T-shirts

      Case 1: The Rams win the championship.

      Case 2: The price of cotton increases.

   c. the market for bagels

      Case 1: People realize how fattening bagels are.

      Case 2: People have less time to make themselves a cooked breakfast.

5. Find the flaws in reasoning in the following statements, paying particular attention to the distinction between changes in and movements along the supply and demand curves. Draw a diagram to illustrate what actually happens in each situation.

   a. "A technological innovation that lowers the cost of producing a good might seem at first to result in a reduction in the price of the good to consumers. But a fall in price will increase demand for the good, and higher demand will send the price up again. It is not certain, therefore, that an innovation will really reduce price in the end."

   b. "A study shows that eating a clove of garlic a day can help prevent heart disease, causing many consumers to demand more garlic. This increase in demand results in a rise in the price of garlic. Consumers, seeing that the price of garlic has gone up, reduce their demand for garlic. This causes the demand for garlic to decrease and the price of garlic to fall. Therefore, the ultimate effect of the study on the price of garlic is uncertain."

6. In *Rolling Stone* magazine, several fans and rock stars, including Pearl Jam, were bemoaning the high price of concert tickets. One superstar argued, "It just isn't worth $75 to see me play. No one should have to pay that much to go to a concert." Assume this star sold out arenas around the country at an average ticket price of $75.

   a. How would you evaluate the argument that ticket prices are too high?

   b. Suppose that due to this star's protests, ticket prices were lowered to $50. In what sense is this price too low? Draw a diagram using supply and demand curves to support your argument.

   c. Suppose Pearl Jam really wanted to bring down ticket prices. Since the band controls the supply of its services, what do you recommend they do? Explain using a supply and demand diagram.

d. Suppose the band's next CD was a total dud. Do you think they would still have to worry about ticket prices being too high? Why or why not? Draw a supply and demand diagram to support your argument.

e. Suppose the group announced their next tour was going to be their last. What effect would this likely have on the demand for and price of tickets? Illustrate with a supply and demand diagram.

7. After several years of decline, the market for handmade acoustic guitars is making a comeback. These guitars, which are normal goods, are usually made in small workshops employing relatively few highly skilled luthiers. Assess the impact on the equilibrium price and quantity of handmade acoustic guitars as a result of each of the following events. In your answers, indicate which curve(s) shift(s) and in which direction.

   a. Environmentalists succeed in having the use of Brazilian rosewood banned in the United States, forcing luthiers to seek out alternative, more costly woods.

   b. A foreign producer reengineers the guitar-making process and floods the market with identical guitars.

   c. Music featuring handmade acoustic guitars makes a comeback as audiences tire of heavy metal and grunge music.

   d. The country goes into a deep recession and the income of the average American falls sharply.

8. Will Shakespeare is a struggling playwright in sixteenth-century London. As the price he receives for writing a play increases, he is willing to write more plays. For the following situations, use a diagram to illustrate how each event affects the equilibrium price and quantity in the market for Shakespeare's plays.

   a. The playwright Christopher Marlowe, Shakespeare's chief rival, is killed in a bar brawl.

   b. The bubonic plague, a deadly infectious disease, breaks out in London.

   c. To celebrate the defeat of the Spanish Armada, Queen Elizabeth declares several weeks of festivities, which involves commissioning new plays.

9. The small town of Middling experiences a sudden doubling of the birth rate. After three years, the birth rate returns to normal. Use a diagram to illustrate the effect of these events on the following:

   a. the market for an hour of babysitting services in Middling today

   b. the market for an hour of babysitting services 14 years into the future, after the birth rate has returned to normal, by which time children born today are old enough to work as babysitters

   c. the market for an hour of babysitting services 30 years into the future, when children born today are likely to be having children of their own

10. Use a diagram to illustrate how each of the following events affects the equilibrium price and quantity of pizza.

   a. The price of mozzarella cheese rises.

   b. The health hazards of hamburgers are widely publicized.

   c. The price of tomato sauce falls.

   d. The incomes of consumers rise and pizza is an inferior good.

   e. Consumers expect the price of pizza to fall next week.

11. Although he was a prolific artist, Pablo Picasso painted only 1,000 canvases during his "Blue Period." Picasso is now dead, and all of his Blue Period works are currently on display in museums and private galleries throughout Europe and the United States.

   a. Draw a supply curve for Picasso Blue Period works. Why is this supply curve different from ones you have seen?

   b. Given the supply curve from part a, the price of a Picasso Blue Period work will be entirely dependent on what factor(s)? Draw a diagram showing how the equilibrium price of such a work is determined.

   c. Suppose that rich art collectors decide that it is essential to acquire Picasso Blue Period art for their collections. Show the impact of this on the market for these paintings.

FOR
RENT

Module 8: Income Effects, Substitution Effects, and Elasticity

Module 9: Interpreting Price Elasticity of Demand

Module 10: Other Elasticities

SECTION 3

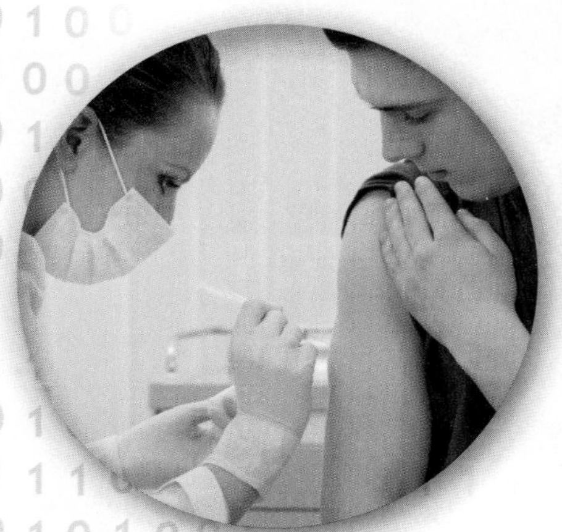

Elasticity and the Law of Demand

MORE PRECIOUS THAN A FLU SHOT

If you've ever had a real case of the flu, you know just how unpleasant an experience it is. And it can be worse than unpleasant: every year the flu kills around 36,000 Americans and sends another 200,000 to the hospital.

So, it was no surprise that panic was the only word to describe the situation at hospitals, clinics, and nursing homes across America in October 2004. Early that month, Chiron Corporation, one of only two suppliers of flu vaccine for the entire U.S. market, announced that contamination problems would force the closure of its manufacturing plant.

With that closure, the U.S. supply of vaccine for the 2004–2005 flu season was suddenly cut in half, from 100 million to 50 million doses. Because making flu vaccine is a costly and time-consuming process, no more doses could be made to replace Chiron's lost output. And since every country jealously guards its supply of flu vaccine for its own citizens, none could be obtained from other countries.

Victims of the flu are most commonly children, senior citizens, or those with compromised immune systems. In a normal flu season, this part of the population, along with health care workers, are immunized first. But the flu vaccine shortfall of 2004 upended those plans. As news of it spread, there was a rush to get the shots. People lined up in the middle of the night at the few locations that had somehow obtained the vaccine and were offering it at a reasonable price: the crowds included seniors with oxygen tanks, parents with sleeping children, and others in wheelchairs.

Meanwhile, some pharmaceutical distributors—the companies that obtain vaccine from manufacturers and then distribute it to hospitals and pharmacies—detected a profit-making opportunity in the frenzy. One company, Med-Stat, which normally charged $8.50 for a dose, began charging $90, more than 10 times the normal price. A survey of pharmacists found that price-gouging was fairly widespread.

Although most people refused or were unable to pay such a high price for the vaccine, many others undoubtedly did. Med-Stat judged, correctly, that consumers of the vaccine were relatively *unresponsive* to price; that is, the large increase in the price of the vaccine left the quantity demanded by consumers relatively unchanged.

Clearly, the demand for flu vaccine is unusual in this respect. For many, getting vaccinated meant the difference between life and death. Let's consider a very different and less urgent scenario. Suppose, for example, that the supply of a particular type of breakfast cereal was halved due to manufacturing problems. It would be extremely unlikely, if not impossible, to find a consumer willing to pay 10 times the original price for a box of this particular cereal. In other words, consumers of breakfast cereal are much more responsive to price than consumers of flu vaccine. But how do we define *responsiveness?* Economists measure consumers' responsiveness to price with a particular number, called the *price elasticity of demand.*

In this section we take a closer look at the supply and demand model developed early in this book and present several economic concepts used to evaluate market results. We will see how the price elasticity of demand is calculated and why it is the best measure of how the quantity demanded responds to changes in price. We will then discover that the price elasticity of demand is only one of a family of related concepts, including the *income elasticity of demand* and the *price elasticity of supply.*

Module 8 Income Effects, Substitution Effects, and Elasticity

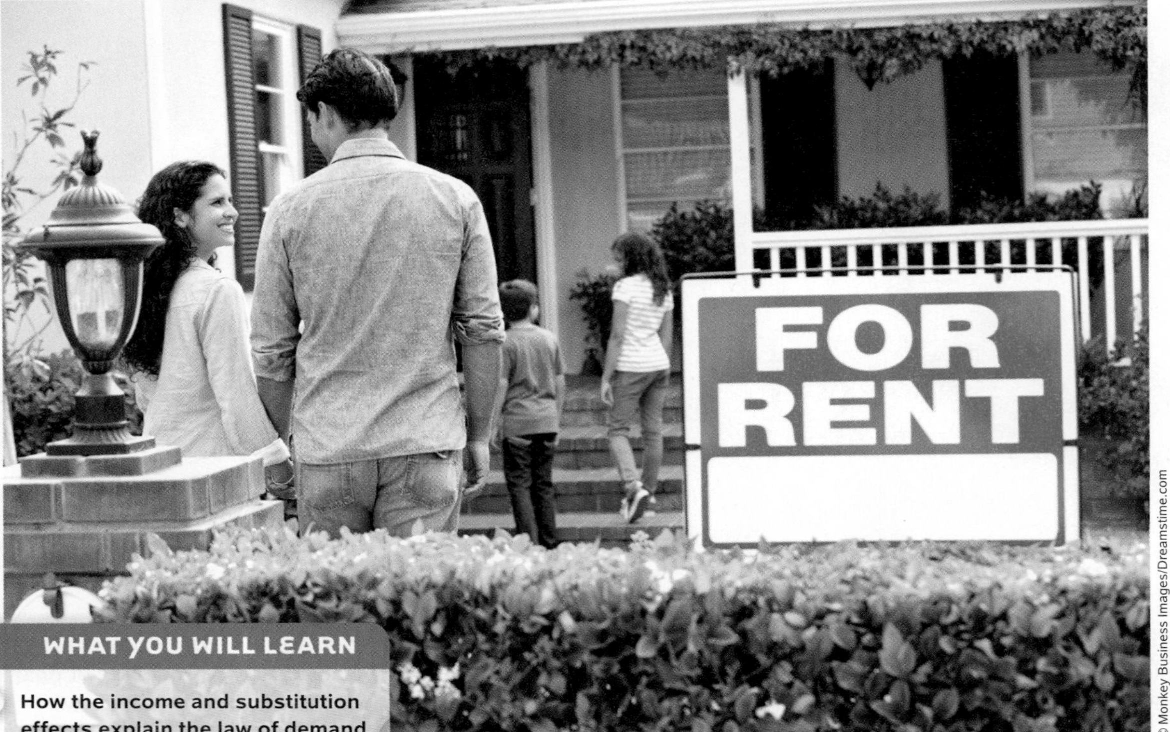

© Monkey Business Images/Dreamstime.com

WHAT YOU WILL LEARN

1. How the income and substitution effects explain the law of demand
2. The definition of elasticity, a measure of responsiveness to changes in prices or incomes
3. The importance of the price elasticity of demand, which measures the responsiveness of the quantity demanded to changes in price
4. How to calculate the price elasticity of demand

Explaining the Law of Demand

We introduced the demand curve and the law of demand in the previous section on supply and demand. To this point, we have accepted that the demand curve has a negative slope. And we have drawn demand curves that are somewhere in the middle between flat and steep (with a negative slope). In this module, we present more detail about why demand curves slope downward and what the slope of the demand curve tells us. We begin with the *income* and *substitution effects,* which explain why the demand curve has a negative slope.

The Substitution Effect

When the price of a good increases, an individual will normally consume less of that good and more of other goods. Correspondingly, when the price of a good decreases, an individual will normally consume more of that good and less of other goods. This explains why the individual demand curve, which relates an individual's consumption of a good to the price of that good, normally slopes downward—that is, it obeys the law of demand.

An alternative way to think about why demand curves slope downward is to focus on opportunity costs. For simplicity, let's suppose there are only two goods between which to choose. When the price of one good decreases, an individual doesn't have to give up as many units of the other good in order to buy one more unit of the first good. That makes it attractive to buy more of the good whose price has gone down. Conversely, when the price of one good increases, one must give up more units of the other good to buy one more unit of the first good, so consuming that good becomes less attractive and the consumer buys fewer.

The change in the quantity demanded as the good that has become relatively cheaper is substituted for the good that has become relatively more expensive is known as the **substitution effect.** When a good absorbs only a small share of the typical consumer's income, as with pillow cases and swim goggles, the substitution effect is essentially the sole explanation of why the market demand curve slopes downward. There are, however, some goods, like food and housing, that account for a substantial share of many consumers' incomes. In such cases another effect, called the *income effect,* also comes into play.

The **substitution effect** of a change in the price of a good is the change in the quantity of that good demanded as the consumer substitutes the good that has become relatively cheaper for some other good that has become relatively more expensive.

The **income effect** of a change in the price of a good is the change in the quantity of that good demanded that results from a change in the consumer's purchasing power when the price of the good changes.

The Income Effect

Consider the case of a family that spends half of its income on rental housing. Now suppose that the price of housing increases everywhere. This will have a substitution effect on the family's demand: other things equal, the family will have an incentive to consume less housing—say, by moving to a smaller apartment—and more of other goods. But the family will also, in a real sense, be made poorer by that higher housing price—its income will buy less housing than before.

When income is adjusted to reflect its true purchasing power, it is called *real income,* in contrast to *money income* or *nominal income,* which has not been adjusted. And this reduction in a consumer's real income will have an additional effect, beyond the substitution effect, on the family's consumption choices, including its consumption of housing. The **income effect** is the change in the quantity of a good demanded that results from a change in the overall purchasing power of the consumer's income due to a change in the price of that good.

It's possible to give more precise definitions of the substitution effect and the income effect of a price change, but for most purposes, there are only two things you need to know about the distinction between these two effects.

1. For the majority of goods and services, the income effect is not important and has no significant effect on individual consumption. Thus, most market demand curves slope downward solely because of the substitution effect—end of story.
2. When it matters at all, the income effect usually reinforces the substitution effect. That is, when the price of a good that absorbs a substantial share of income rises, consumers of that good become a bit poorer because their purchasing power falls. And the vast majority of goods are *normal* goods, goods for which demand decreases when income falls. So this effective reduction in income leads to a reduction in the quantity demanded and reinforces the substitution effect.

However, in the case of an *inferior* good, a good for which demand increases when income falls, the income and substitution effects work in opposite directions. Although the substitution effect decreases the quantity of any good demanded as its price increases, the income effect of a price increase for an inferior good is an *increase* in the quantity demanded. This makes sense because the price increase lowers the real income of the consumer, and as real income falls, the demand for an inferior good increases.

If a good were so inferior that the income effect exceeded the substitution effect, a price increase would lead to an increase in the quantity demanded. There is controversy over whether such goods, known as "Giffen goods," exist at all. (See the following Economics in Action for more on "Giffen goods"). If they do, they are very rare. You can generally assume that the income effect for an inferior good is smaller than the substitution effect, and so a price increase will still lead to a decrease in the quantity demanded.

ECONOMICS ▶ IN ACTION

GIFFEN GOODS

Two hundred years ago, when Ireland was under British rule and desperately poor, it was claimed that the Irish would eat *more* potatoes when the price of potatoes went up. That is, some observers claimed that Ireland's demand curve for potatoes sloped upward, not downward.

Can this happen? In theory, yes. If Irish demand for potatoes actually sloped upward, it would have been a real-life case of a "Giffen good," named after a nineteenth-century statistician who thought (probably wrongly) that he saw an upward-sloping demand curve in some data he was studying.

Here's the story. Suppose that there is some good that absorbs a large share of consumers' budgets and that this good is also *inferior*—people demand less of it when their income rises. The classic supposed example was, as you might guess, potatoes in Ireland, back when potatoes were an inferior good—they were what poor people ate—and when the Irish were very poor.

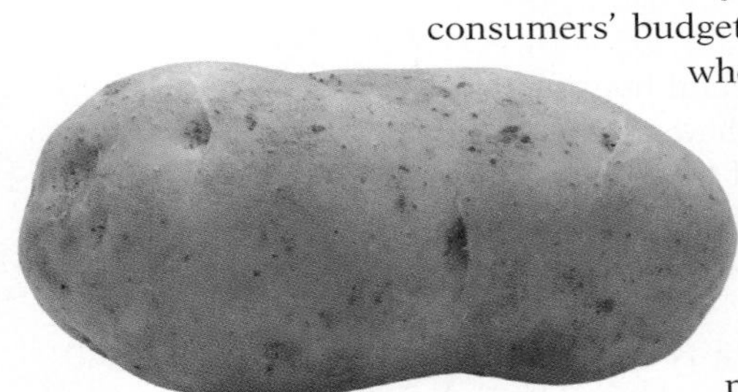
iStockphoto/Thinkstock

Now suppose that the price of potatoes increases. This would, *other things being equal,* cause people to substitute other goods for potatoes. But other things are not equal: given the higher price of potatoes, people are poorer. And this *increases* the demand for potatoes, because potatoes are an inferior good.

If this income effect outweighs the substitution effect, a rise in the price of potatoes would increase the quantity demanded; the law of demand would not hold.

In a way the point of this story—which has never been validated in any real situation, nineteenth-century Ireland included—is how unlikely such an event is. The law of demand really is a law, with few exceptions.

Defining and Measuring Elasticity

Most graphs in economics depict relationships between two variables: the value of one determining variable (the *independent variable*) directly influences the value of the other (the *dependent variable*). If two variables are negatively related and the independent variable increases, the dependent variable will respond by decreasing. (For a review of graphing variables, see Appendix A on graphs in economics, at the back of the book.) But often the important question is not whether the variables are negatively or positively related, but how responsive the dependent variable is to changes in the independent variable (that is, ***by how much*** will the dependent variable change?). If price increases, we know that quantity demanded will decrease (that is the *law of demand*). The question in this context is *by how much* will quantity demanded decrease if price goes up?

Economists use the concept of *elasticity* to measure the responsiveness of one variable to changes in another. For example, *price elasticity of demand* measures the responsiveness of quantity demanded to changes in price—something a firm considering changing its price would certainly want to know! Elasticity can be used to measure responsiveness using any two related variables. We will start by looking at the price elasticity of demand and then move on to other examples of elasticities commonly used by economists.

Think back to the opening story of the 2004 flu shot panic. In order for Flunomics, a hypothetical flu vaccine distributor, to know whether it could raise its revenue by significantly raising the price of its flu vaccine during the 2004 flu vaccine panic, it would have to know whether the price increase would decrease the quantity demanded by a lot or a little. That is, it would have to know the price elasticity of demand for flu vaccinations.

Calculating the Price Elasticity of Demand

Figure 8-1 shows a hypothetical demand curve for flu vaccinations. At a price of $20 per vaccination, consumers would demand 10 million vaccinations per year (point *A*); at a price of $21, the quantity demanded would fall to 9.9 million vaccinations per year (point *B*).

Figure 8-1, then, tells us the change in the quantity demanded for a particular change in the price. But how can we turn this into a measure of price responsiveness? The answer is to calculate the price elasticity of demand. The **price elasticity of demand** compares the *percent change in quantity demanded* to the *percent change in price* as we move along the demand curve. As we'll see later, the reason economists use percent changes is to get a measure that doesn't depend on the units in which a good is measured (say, a child-size dose versus an adult-size dose of vaccine). But before we get to that, let's look at how elasticity is calculated.

FIGURE 8-1 The Demand for Vaccinations

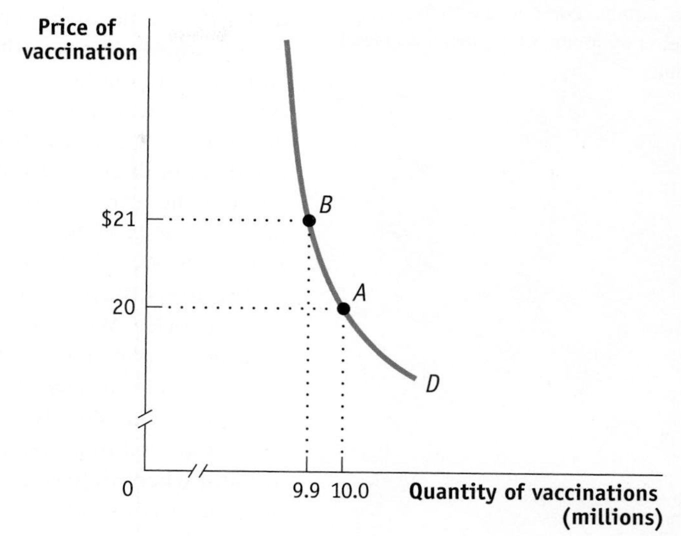

At a price of $20 per vaccination, the quantity of vaccinations demanded is 10 million per year (point *A*). When price rises to $21 per vaccination, the quantity demanded falls to 9.9 million vaccinations per year (point *B*).

To calculate the price elasticity of demand, we first calculate the *percent change in the quantity demanded* and the corresponding *percent change in the price* as we move along the demand curve. These are defined as follows:

$$\textbf{(8-1)} \quad \text{\% change in quantity demanded} = \frac{\text{Change in quantity demanded}}{\text{Initial quantity demanded}} \times 100$$

and

$$\textbf{(8-2)} \quad \text{\% change in price} = \frac{\text{Change in price}}{\text{Initial price}} \times 100$$

In Figure 8-1, we see that when the price rises from $20 to $21, the quantity demanded falls from 10 million to 9.9 million vaccinations, yielding a change in the quantity demanded of 0.1 million vaccinations. So the percent change in the quantity demanded is

$$\text{\% change in quantity demanded} = \frac{-0.1 \text{ million vaccinations}}{10 \text{ million vaccinations}} \times 100 = -1\%$$

The initial price is $20 and the change in the price is $1, so the percent change in the price is

$$\text{\% change in price} = \frac{\$1}{\$20} \times 100 = 5\%$$

To calculate the price elasticity of demand, we find the ratio of the percent change in the quantity demanded to the percent change in the price:

$$\textbf{(8-3)} \quad \text{Price elasticity of demand} = \frac{\text{\% change in quantity demanded}}{\text{\% change in price}}$$

In Figure 8-1, the price elasticity of demand is therefore

$$\text{Price elasticity of demand} = \frac{1\%}{5\%} = 0.2$$

Notice that the minus sign has been dropped from this equation. Why have we done this?

The **price elasticity of demand** is the ratio of the percent change in the quantity demanded to the percent change in the price as we move along the demand curve.

The **midpoint method** is a technique for calculating the percent change. In this approach, we calculate changes in a variable compared with the average, or midpoint, of the initial and final values.

The *law of demand* says that demand curves slope downward, so price and quantity demanded always move in opposite directions. In other words, a positive percent change in price (a rise in price) leads to a negative percent change in the quantity demanded; a negative percent change in price (a fall in price) leads to a positive percent change in the quantity demanded. This means that the price elasticity of demand is, in strictly mathematical terms, a negative number. However, it is inconvenient to repeatedly write a minus sign. So when economists talk about the price elasticity of demand, they usually drop the minus sign and report the *absolute value* of the price elasticity of demand. In other words, the absolute value of a negative number appears without the minus sign. In this case, for example, economists would usually say "the price elasticity of demand is 0.2," taking it for granted that you understand they mean *minus* 0.2. We follow this convention here.

The larger the price elasticity of demand, the more responsive the quantity demanded is to the price. When the price elasticity of demand is large—when consumers change their quantity demanded by a large percentage compared to the percent change in the price—economists say that demand is highly elastic.

As we'll see shortly, a price elasticity of 0.2 indicates a small response of quantity demanded to price. That is, the quantity demanded will fall by a relatively small amount when price rises. This is what economists call *inelastic* demand. And inelastic demand was exactly what Flunomics needed for its strategy to increase revenue by raising the price of its flu vaccines.

An Alternative Way to Calculate Elasticities: The Midpoint Method

We've seen that price elasticity of demand compares the *percent change in quantity demanded* with the *percent change in price*. When we look at some other elasticities, which we will do shortly, we'll see why it is important to focus on percent changes. But at this point we need to discuss a technical issue that arises when you calculate percent changes in variables and how economists deal with it.

The best way to understand the issue is with a real example. Suppose you were trying to estimate the price elasticity of demand for gasoline by comparing gasoline prices and consumption in different countries. Because of high taxes, gasoline usually costs about three times as much per gallon in Europe as it does in the United States. So what is the percent difference between American and European gas prices?

Well, it depends on which way you measure it. Because the price of gasoline in Europe is approximately three times higher than in the United States, it is 200 percent higher. Because the price of gasoline in the United States is one-third as high as in Europe, it is 66.7 percent lower.

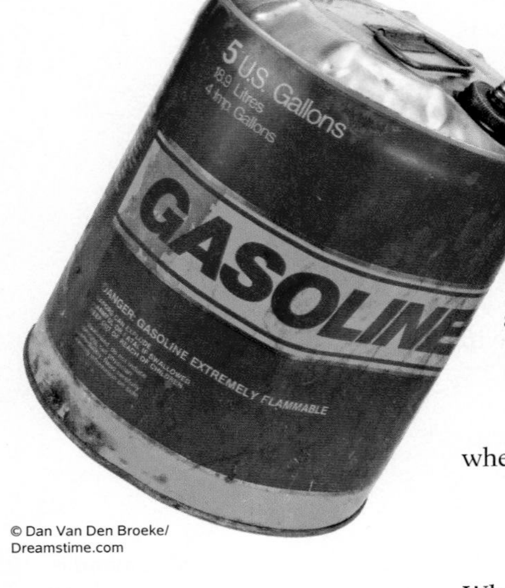

© Dan Van Den Broeke/ Dreamstime.com

This is a nuisance: we'd like to have a percent measure of the difference in prices that doesn't depend on which way you measure it. A good way to avoid computing different elasticities for rising and falling prices is to use the *midpoint method* (sometimes called the *arc method*).

The **midpoint method** replaces the usual definition of the percent change in a variable, X, with a slightly different definition:

$$\textbf{(8-4)} \quad \% \text{ change in } X = \frac{\text{Change in } X}{\text{Average value of } X} \times 100$$

where the average value of X is defined as

$$\text{Average value of } X = \frac{\text{Starting value of } X + \text{Final value of } X}{2}$$

When calculating the price elasticity of demand using the midpoint method, both the percent change in the price and the percent change in the quantity demanded are found using average values in this way. To see how this method works, suppose you have the following data for some good:

	Price	Quantity demanded
Situation A	$0.90	1,100
Situation B	$1.10	900

To calculate the percent change in quantity going from situation A to situation B, we compare the change in the quantity demanded—a fall of 200 units—with the *average* of the quantity demanded in the two situations. So we calculate

$$\% \text{ change in quantity demanded} = \frac{-200}{(1{,}100 + 900)/2} \times 100 = \frac{-200}{1{,}000} \times 100 = -20\%$$

In the same way, we calculate the percent change in price as

$$\% \text{ change in price} = \frac{\$0.20}{(\$0.90 + \$1.10)/2} \times 100 = \frac{\$0.20}{\$1.00} \times 100 = 20\%$$

So in this case we would calculate the price elasticity of demand to be

$$\text{Price elasticity of demand} = \frac{\% \text{ change in quantity demanded}}{\% \text{ change in price}} = \frac{20\%}{20\%} = 1$$

again dropping the minus sign.

The important point is that we would get the same result, a price elasticity of demand of 1, whether we went up the demand curve from situation A to situation B or down from situation B to situation A.

ECONOMICS IN ACTION

ESTIMATING ELASTICITIES

You might think it's easy to estimate price elasticities of demand from real-world data: just compare percent changes in prices with percent changes in quantities demanded. Unfortunately, it's rarely that simple because changes in price aren't the only thing affecting changes in the quantity demanded: other factors—such as changes in income, changes in population, and changes in the prices of other goods—shift the demand curve, thereby changing the quantity demanded at any given price.

To estimate price elasticities of demand, economists must use careful statistical analysis to separate the influence of these different factors, holding other things equal.

The most comprehensive effort to estimate price elasticities of demand was a mammoth study by the economists Hendrik S. Houthakker and Lester D. Taylor. Some of their results are summarized in Table 8-1. These estimates show a wide range of price elasticities. There are some goods, like eggs, for which demand hardly responds at all to changes in the price; there are other goods, most notably foreign travel, for which the quantity demanded is very sensitive to the price.

Notice that Table 8-1 is divided into two parts: inelastic and elastic demand. We'll explain in the next module the significance of that division.

TABLE 8-1

Some Estimated Price Elasticities of Demand

Good	Price elasticity of demand
Inelastic demand	
Eggs	0.1
Beef	0.4
Stationery	0.5
Gasoline	0.5
Elastic demand	
Housing	1.2
Restaurant meals	2.3
Airline travel	2.4
Foreign travel	4.1

Source: Hendrick S. Houthakker and Lester D. Taylor, *Consumer Demand in the United States, 1929–1970* (Cambridge: Harvard University Press, 1970)

To arrive at a more general formula for price elasticity of demand, suppose that we have data for two points on a demand curve. At point 1 the quantity demanded and price are (Q_1, P_1); at point 2 they are (Q_2, P_2). Then the formula for calculating the price elasticity of demand is:

$$\textbf{(8-5)} \quad \text{Price elasticity of demand} = \frac{\dfrac{Q_2 - Q_1}{(Q_1 + Q_2)/2}}{\dfrac{P_2 - P_1}{(P_1 + P_2)/2}}$$

As before, when reporting a price elasticity of demand calculated by the midpoint method, we drop the minus sign and report the absolute value.

Module 8 Review

Solutions appear at the back of the book.

Check Your Understanding

1. In each of the following cases, state whether the income effect, the substitution effect, or both are significant. In which cases do they move in the same direction? In opposite directions? Why?
   a. Orange juice represents a small share of Clare's spending. She buys more lemonade and less orange juice when the price of orange juice goes up. She does not change her spending on other goods.
   b. Apartment rents have risen dramatically this year. Since rent absorbs a major part of her income, Delia moves to a smaller apartment. Assume that rental housing is a normal good.
   c. The cost of a semester-long meal ticket at the student cafeteria rises, representing a significant increase in living costs. As a result, many students have less money to spend on weekend meals at restaurants and eat in the cafeteria instead. Assume that cafeteria meals are an inferior good.
2. The price of strawberries falls from \$1.50 to \$1.00 per carton, and the quantity demanded goes from 100,000 to 200,000 cartons. Use the midpoint method to find the price elasticity of demand.
3. At the present level of consumption, 4,000 movie tickets, and at the current price, \$5 per ticket, the price elasticity of demand for movie tickets is 1. Using the midpoint method, calculate the percentage by which the owners of movie theaters must reduce the price in order to sell 5,000 tickets.
4. The price elasticity of demand for ice-cream sandwiches is 1.2 at the current price of \$0.50 per sandwich and the current consumption level of 100,000 sandwiches. Calculate the change in the quantity demanded when price rises by \$0.05. Use Equations 8-1 and 8-2 to calculate percent changes and Equation 8-3 to relate price elasticity of demand to the percent changes.

Multiple-Choice Questions

1. Which of the following statements is true?
   I. When a good absorbs only a small share of consumer spending, the income effect explains the demand curve's negative slope.
   II. A change in consumption brought about by a change in purchasing power describes the income effect.
   III. In the case of an inferior good, the income and substitution effects work in opposite directions.

   a. I only
   b. II only
   c. III only
   d. II and III only
   e. I, II, and III

2. The income effect is most likely to come into play for which of the following goods?
   a. water
   b. clothing
   c. housing
   d. transportation
   e. entertainment

3. If a decrease in price from $2 to $1 causes an increase in quantity demanded from 100 to 120, using the midpoint method, price elasticity of demand equals
   a. 0.17.
   b. 0.27.
   c. 0.40.
   d. 2.5.
   e. 3.72.

4. Which of the following is likely to have the highest price elasticity of demand?
   a. eggs
   b. beef
   c. housing
   d. gasoline
   e. foreign travel

5. If a 2% change in the price of a good leads to a 10% change in the quantity demanded of a good, what is the value of price elasticity of demand?
   a. 0.02
   b. 0.2
   c. 5
   d. 10
   e. 20

Critical-Thinking Questions

Assume the price of an inferior good increases.

1. In what direction will the substitution effect change the quantity demanded? Explain.
2. In what direction will the income effect change the quantity demanded? Explain.
3. Given that the demand curve for the good slopes downward, what is true of the relative sizes of the income and substitution effects for the inferior good? Explain.

Interpreting Price Elasticity of Demand

iStockphoto/Thinkstock

WHAT YOU WILL LEARN

1. The difference between elastic and inelastic demand
2. The relationship between elasticity and total revenue
3. Changes in the price elasticity of demand along a demand curve
4. The factors that determine price elasticity of demand

A Closer Look at the Price Elasticity of Demand

Med-Stat and other pharmaceutical distributors believed they could sharply drive up flu vaccine prices in the face of a shortage because the price elasticity of vaccine demand was low. But what does that mean? How low does a price elasticity have to be for us to classify it as low? How high does it have to be for us to consider it high? And what determines whether the price elasticity of demand is high or low, anyway? To answer these questions, we need to look more deeply at the price elasticity of demand.

How Elastic Is Elastic?

As a first step toward classifying price elasticities of demand, let's look at the extreme cases.

First, consider the demand for a good when people pay no attention to the price of, say, shoelaces. Suppose that consumers would buy 1 billion pairs of shoelaces per year regardless of the price. If that were true, the demand curve for shoelaces would look like the curve shown in panel (a) of Figure 9-1: it would be a vertical line at 1 billion pairs of shoelaces. Since the percent change in the quantity demanded is zero for *any* change in the price, the price elasticity of demand in this case is zero. The case of a zero price elasticity of demand is known as **perfectly inelastic** demand.

Demand is **perfectly inelastic** when the quantity demanded does not respond at all to changes in the price. When demand is perfectly inelastic, the demand curve is a vertical line.

The opposite extreme occurs when even a tiny rise in the price will cause the quantity demanded to drop to zero or even a tiny fall in the price will cause the quantity demanded to get extremely large.

Panel (b) of Figure 9-1 shows the case of pink tennis balls; we suppose that tennis players really don't care what color their balls are and that other colors, such as neon

FIGURE 9-1 Two Extreme Cases of Price Elasticity of Demand

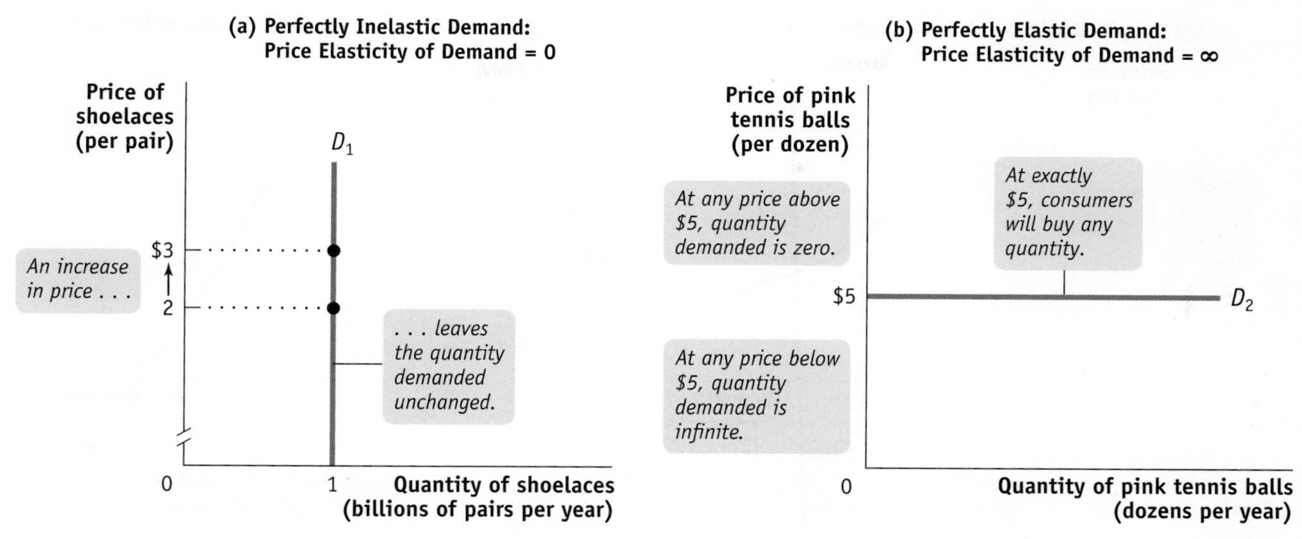

Panel (a) shows a perfectly inelastic demand curve, which is a vertical line. The quantity of shoelaces demanded is always 1 billion pairs, regardless of price. As a result, the price elasticity of demand is zero—the quantity demanded is unaffected by the price. Panel (b) shows a perfectly elastic demand curve, which is a horizontal line. At a price of $5, consumers will buy any quantity of pink tennis balls, but will buy none at a price above $5. If the price falls below $5, they will buy an extremely large number of pink tennis balls and none of any other color.

green and vivid yellow, are available at $5 per dozen balls. In this case, consumers will buy no pink balls if they cost more than $5 per dozen but will buy only pink balls if they cost less than $5. The demand curve will therefore be a horizontal line at a price of $5 per dozen balls. As you move back and forth along this line, there is a change in the quantity demanded but no change in the price. When you divide a number by zero, you get infinity, denoted by the symbol ∞. So a horizontal demand curve implies an infinite price elasticity of demand. When the price elasticity of demand is infinite, economists say that demand is **perfectly elastic.**

Demand is **perfectly elastic** when any price increase will cause the quantity demanded to drop to zero. When demand is perfectly elastic, the demand curve is a horizontal line.

Demand is **elastic** if the price elasticity of demand is greater than 1, **inelastic** if the price elasticity of demand is less than 1, and **unit-elastic** if the price elasticity of demand is exactly 1.

The price elasticity of demand for the vast majority of goods is somewhere between these two extreme cases. Economists use one main criterion for classifying these intermediate cases: they ask whether the price elasticity of demand is greater or less than 1. When the price elasticity of demand is greater than 1, economists say that demand is **elastic.** When the price elasticity of demand is less than 1, they say that demand is **inelastic.** The borderline case is **unit-elastic** demand, where the price elasticity of demand is—surprise—exactly 1.

To see why a price elasticity of demand equal to 1 is a useful dividing line, let's consider a hypothetical example: a toll bridge operated by the state highway department. Other things being equal, the number of drivers who use the bridge depends on the toll, the price the highway department charges for crossing the bridge: the higher the toll, the fewer the drivers who use the bridge.

Figure 9-2 shows three hypothetical demand curves—one in which demand is unit-elastic, one in which it is inelastic, and one in which it is elastic. In each case, point *A* shows the quantity demanded if the toll is $0.90 and point

©Rorem/Dreamstime.com

Knowing the price elasticity of demand allows the highway department to determine the drop in bridge use that would result from higher tolls.

FIGURE 9-2 Unit-Elastic Demand, Inelastic Demand, and Elastic Demand

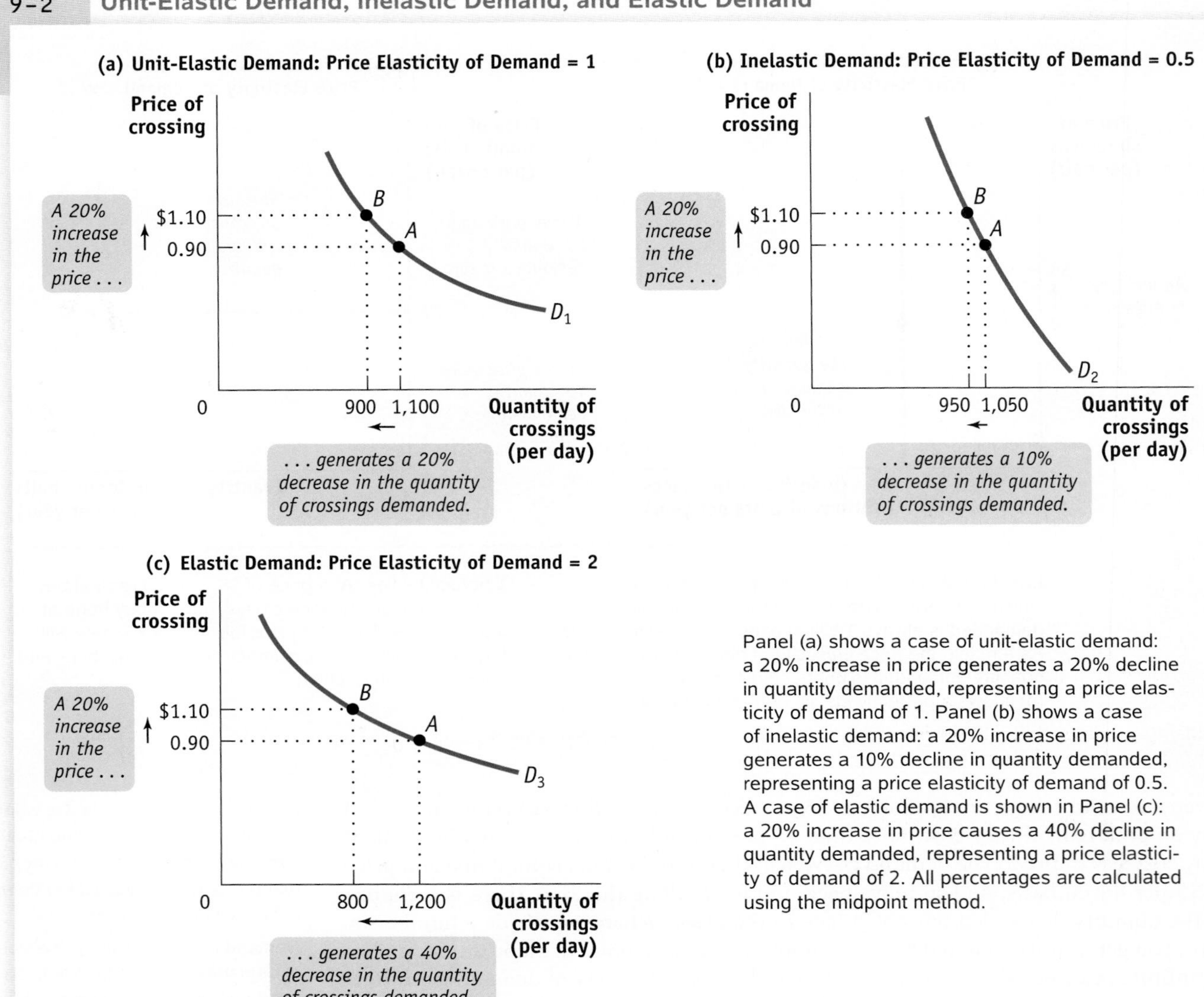

Panel (a) shows a case of unit-elastic demand: a 20% increase in price generates a 20% decline in quantity demanded, representing a price elasticity of demand of 1. Panel (b) shows a case of inelastic demand: a 20% increase in price generates a 10% decline in quantity demanded, representing a price elasticity of demand of 0.5. A case of elastic demand is shown in Panel (c): a 20% increase in price causes a 40% decline in quantity demanded, representing a price elasticity of demand of 2. All percentages are calculated using the midpoint method.

B shows the quantity demanded if the toll is $1.10. An increase in the toll from $0.90 to $1.10 is an increase of 20% if we use the midpoint method to calculate percent changes.

Panel (a) shows what happens when the toll is raised from $0.90 to $1.10 and the demand curve is unit-elastic. Here the 20% price rise leads to a fall in the quantity of cars using the bridge each day from 1,100 to 900, which is a 20% decline (again using the midpoint method). So the price elasticity of demand is 20%/20% = 1.

Panel (b) shows a case of inelastic demand when the toll is raised from $0.90 to $1.10. The same 20% price rise reduces the quantity demanded from 1,050 to 950. That's only a 10% decline, so in this case the price elasticity of demand is 10%/20% = 0.5.

Panel (c) shows a case of elastic demand when the toll is raised from $0.90 to $1.10. The 20% price increase causes the quantity demanded to fall from 1,200 to 800, a 40% decline, so the price elasticity of demand is 40%/20% = 2.

Why does it matter whether demand is unit-elastic, inelastic, or elastic? Because this classification predicts how changes in the price of a good will affect the *total revenue* earned by producers from the sale of that good. In many real-life situations, such as the one faced by Med-Stat, it is crucial to know how price changes affect total revenue. **Total revenue** is defined as the total value of sales of a good or service: the price multiplied by the quantity sold.

Total revenue is the total value of sales of a good or service. It is equal to the price multiplied by the quantity sold.

(9-1) Total revenue = Price × Quantity sold

Total revenue has a useful graphical representation that can help us understand why knowing the price elasticity of demand is crucial when we ask whether a price rise will increase or reduce total revenue. Panel (a) of Figure 9-3 shows the same demand curve as panel (a) of Figure 9-2. We see that 1,100 drivers will use the bridge if the toll is \$0.90. So the total revenue at a price of \$0.90 is \$0.90 × 1,100 = \$990. This value is equal to the area of the green rectangle, which is drawn with the bottom left corner at the point (0, 0) and the top right corner at (1,100, 0.90). In general, the total revenue at any given price is equal to the area of a rectangle whose height is the price and whose width is the quantity demanded at that price.

To get an idea of why total revenue is important, consider the following scenario. Suppose that the toll on the bridge is currently \$0.90 but that the highway department must raise extra money for road repairs. One way to do this is to raise the toll on the bridge. But this plan might backfire, since a higher toll will reduce the number of drivers who use the bridge. And if traffic on the bridge dropped a lot, a higher toll would actually reduce total revenue instead of increasing it. So it's important for the highway department to know how drivers will respond to a toll increase.

We can see graphically how the toll increase affects total bridge revenue by examining panel (b) of Figure 9-3. At a toll of \$0.90, total revenue is given by the sum of the areas *A* and *B*. After the toll is raised to \$1.10, total revenue is given by the sum of areas *B* and *C*. So when the toll is raised, revenue represented by area *A* is lost but revenue represented by area *C* is gained.

These two areas have important interpretations. Area *C* represents the revenue gain that comes from the additional \$0.20 paid by drivers who continue to use the bridge. That is, the 900 drivers who continue to use the bridge contribute an additional \$0.20 × 900 = \$180 per day to total revenue, represented by area *C*. But 200 drivers who would have used the bridge at a price of \$0.90 no longer do so, generating

FIGURE 9-3 Total Revenue

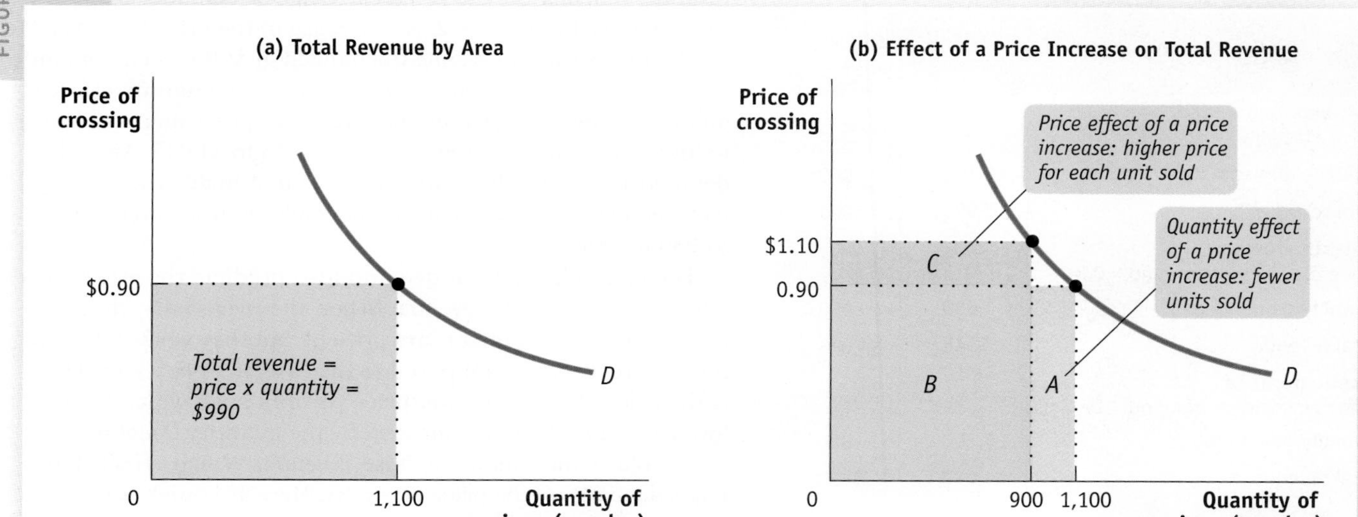

The green rectangle in panel (a) represents total revenue generated from 1,100 drivers who each pay a toll of \$0.90. Panel (b) shows how total revenue is affected when the price increases from \$0.90 to \$1.10. Due to the quantity effect, total revenue falls by area *A*. Due to the price effect, total revenue increases by area *C*. In general, the overall effect can go either way, depending on the price elasticity of demand.

a loss to total revenue of $\$0.90 \times 200 = \$180$ per day, represented by area *A*. (In this particular example, because demand is unit-elastic between the two points—the same as in panel (a) of Figure 9-2—the rise in the toll has no effect on total revenue; areas *A* and *C* are the same size.)

Except in the rare case of a good with perfectly elastic or perfectly inelastic demand, when a seller raises the price of a good, two countervailing effects are present:

- *A price effect.* After a price increase, each unit sold sells at a higher price, which tends to raise revenue.
- *A quantity effect.* After a price increase, fewer units are sold, which tends to lower revenue.

But then, you may ask, what is the net ultimate effect on total revenue: does it go up or down? The answer is that, in general, the effect on total revenue can go either way—a price rise may either increase total revenue or lower it. If the price effect, which tends to raise total revenue, is the stronger of the two effects, then total revenue goes up. If the quantity effect, which tends to reduce total revenue, is the stronger, then total revenue goes down. And if the strengths of the two effects are exactly equal—as in our toll bridge example, where a \$180 gain offsets a \$180 loss—total revenue is unchanged by the price increase.

The price elasticity of demand tells us what happens to total revenue when price changes: its size determines which effect—the price effect or the quantity effect—is stronger. Specifically:

- If demand for a good is *unit-elastic* (the price elasticity of demand is 1), an increase in price does not change total revenue. In this case, the quantity effect is weaker than the price effect.
- If demand for a good is *inelastic* (the price elasticity of demand is less than 1), a higher price increases total revenue. In this case, the quantity effect is weaker than the price effect.
- If demand for a good is *elastic* (the price elasticity of demand is greater than 1), an increase in price reduces total revenue. In this case, the quantity effect is stronger than the price effect.

TABLE 9-1

Price Elasticity of Demand and Total Revenue

	Price of crossing = \$0.90	Price of crossing = \$1.10
Unit-elastic demand (price elasticity of demand = 1)		
Quantity demanded	1,100	900
Total revenue	\$990	\$990
Inelastic demand (price elasticity of demand = 0.5)		
Quantity demanded	1,050	950
Total revenue	\$945	\$1,045
Elastic demand (price elasticity of demand = 2)		
Quantity demanded	1,200	800
Total revenue	\$1,080	\$880

Table 9-1 shows how the effect of a price increase on total revenue depends on the price elasticity of demand, using the same data as in Figure 9-2. An increase in the price from \$0.90 to \$1.10 leaves total revenue unchanged at \$990 when demand is unit-elastic. When demand is inelastic, the quantity effect is dominated by the price effect; the same price increase leads to an increase in total revenue from \$945 to \$1,045. And when demand is elastic, the quantity effect dominates the price effect; the price increase leads to a decline in total revenue from \$1,080 to \$880.

The price elasticity of demand also predicts the effect of a *fall* in price on total revenue. When the price falls, the same two countervailing effects are present, but they work in the opposite directions as compared to the case of a price rise. There is the price effect of a lower price per unit sold, which tends to lower revenue. This is countered by the quantity effect of more units sold, which tends to raise revenue. Which effect dominates depends on the price elasticity. Here is a quick summary:

- When demand is *unit-elastic,* the two effects exactly balance each other out; so a fall in price has no effect on total revenue.
- When demand is *inelastic,* the quantity effect is dominated by the price effect; so a fall in price reduces total revenue.
- When demand is *elastic,* the quantity effect dominates the price effect; so a fall in price increases total revenue.

Price Elasticity Along the Demand Curve

Suppose an economist says that "the price elasticity of demand for coffee is 0.25." What he or she means is that *at the current price* the elasticity is 0.25. In the previous discussion of the toll bridge, what we were really describing was the elasticity *at a specific price*. Why this qualification? Because for the vast majority of demand curves, the price elasticity of demand at one point along the curve is different from the price elasticity of demand at other points along the same curve.

To see this, consider the table in Figure 9-4, which shows a hypothetical demand schedule. It also shows in the last column the total revenue generated at each price and quantity combination in the demand schedule. The upper panel of the graph in Figure 9-4 shows the corresponding demand curve. The lower panel illustrates the same data on total revenue: the height of a bar at each quantity demanded—which corresponds to a particular price—measures the total revenue generated at that price.

In Figure 9-4, you can see that when the price is low, raising the price increases total revenue: starting at a price of $1, raising the price to $2 increases total revenue from $9 to $16. This means that when the price is low, demand is inelastic. Moreover, you can see that demand is inelastic on the entire section of the demand curve from a price of $0 to a price of $5.

FIGURE 9-4 The Price Elasticity of Demand Changes Along the Demand Curve

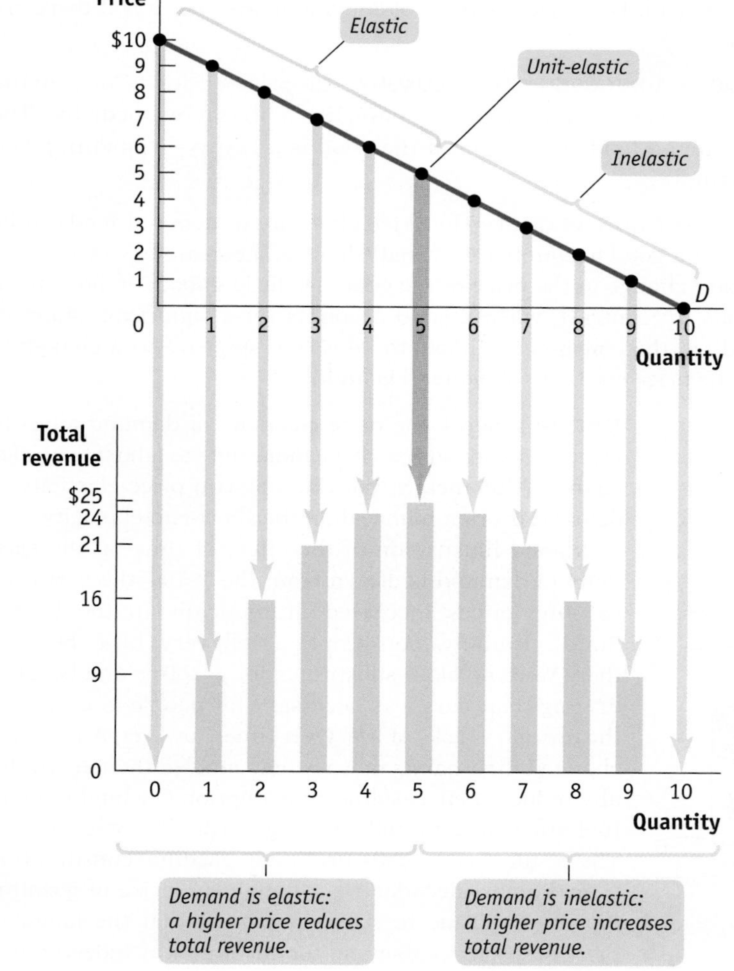

Demand Schedule and Total Revenue for a Linear Demand Curve

Price	Quantity demanded	Total revenue
$0	10	$0
1	9	9
2	8	16
3	7	21
4	6	24
5	5	25
6	4	24
7	3	21
8	2	16
9	1	9
10	0	0

The upper panel shows a demand curve corresponding to the demand schedule in the table. The lower panel shows how total revenue changes along that demand curve: at each price and quantity combination, the height of the bar represents the total revenue generated. You can see that at a low price, raising the price increases total revenue. So demand is inelastic at low prices. At a high price, however, a rise in price reduces total revenue. So demand is elastic at high prices.

When the price is high, however, raising it further reduces total revenue: starting at a price of $8, for example, raising the price to $9 reduces total revenue, from $16 to $9. This means that when the price is high, demand is elastic. Furthermore, you can see that demand is elastic over the section of the demand curve from a price of $5 to $10.

For the vast majority of goods, the price elasticity of demand changes along the demand curve. So whenever you measure a good's elasticity, you are really measuring it at a particular point or section of the good's demand curve.

What Factors Determine the Price Elasticity of Demand?

The flu vaccine shortfall of 2004–2005 allowed vaccine distributors to significantly raise their prices for two important reasons: there were no substitutes, and for many people the vaccine was a medical necessity.

People responded in various ways. Some paid the high prices, and some traveled to Canada and other countries to get vaccinated. Some simply did without (and over time often changed their habits to avoid catching the flu, such as eating out less often and avoiding mass transit). This experience illustrates the four main factors that determine elasticity: whether close substitutes are available, whether the good is a necessity or a luxury, the share of income a consumer spends on the good, and how much time has elapsed since the price change. We'll briefly examine each of these factors.

WHETHER CLOSE SUBSTITUTES ARE AVAILABLE The price elasticity of demand tends to be high if there are other goods that consumers regard as similar and would be willing to consume instead. The price elasticity of demand tends to be low if there are no close substitutes.

WHETHER THE GOOD IS A NECESSITY OR A LUXURY The price elasticity of demand tends to be low if a good is something you must have, like a life-saving medicine. The price elasticity of demand tends to be high if the good is a luxury—something you can easily live without.

SHARE OF INCOME SPENT ON THE GOOD The price elasticity of demand tends to be low when spending on a good accounts for a small share of a consumer's income. In that case, a significant change in the price of the good has little impact on how much the consumer spends. In contrast, when a good accounts for a significant share of a consumer's spending, the consumer is likely to be very responsive to a change in price. In this case, the price elasticity of demand is high.

TIME In general, the price elasticity of demand tends to increase as consumers have more time to adjust to a price change. This means that the long-run price elasticity of demand is often higher than the short-run elasticity.

A good illustration of the effect of time on the elasticity of demand is drawn from the 1970s, the first time gasoline prices increased dramatically in the United States. Initially, consumption fell very little because there were no close substitutes for gasoline and because driving their cars was necessary for people to carry out the ordinary tasks of life. Over time, however, Americans changed their habits in ways that enabled them to gradually reduce their gasoline consumption (by buying more fuel-efficient cars and forming carpools, for example). The result was a steady decline in gasoline consumption over the next decade, even though the price of gasoline did not continue to rise, confirming that the long-run price elasticity of demand for gasoline was indeed much larger than the short-run elasticity.

© David Sipress/The New Yorker Collection/www.cartoonbank.com

"Three hundred dollars' of regular."

ECONOMICS ▶ IN ACTION

RESPONDING TO YOUR TUITION BILL

College costs more than ever—and not just because of overall inflation. Tuition has been rising faster than the overall cost of living for years. But does rising tuition keep people from going to college? Two studies found that the answer depends on the type of college. Both studies assessed how responsive the decision to go to college is to a change in tuition.

A 1988 study found that a 3% increase in tuition led to an approximately 2% fall in the number of students enrolled at four-year institutions, giving a price elasticity of demand of 0.67 (2%/3%). In the case of two-year institutions, the study found a significantly higher response: a 3% increase in tuition led to a 2.7% fall in enrollments, giving a price elasticity of demand of 0.9. In other words, the enrollment decision for students at two-year colleges was significantly more responsive to price than for students at four-year colleges. The result: students at two-year colleges are more likely to forgo getting a degree because of tuition costs than students at four-year colleges.

Photodisc

How responsive are college enrollment rates to changes in tuition?

A 1999 study confirmed this pattern. In comparison to four-year colleges, it found that two-year college enrollment rates were significantly more responsive to changes in state financial aid (a decline in aid leading to a decline in enrollments), a predictable effect given these students' greater sensitivity to the cost of tuition. Another piece of evidence suggests that students at two-year colleges are more likely to be paying their own way and making a trade-off between attending college and working: the study found that enrollments at two-year colleges are much more responsive to changes in the unemployment rate (an increase in the unemployment rate leading to an increase in enrollments) than enrollments at four-year colleges. So is the cost of tuition a barrier to getting a college degree in the United States? Yes, but more so at two-year colleges than at four-year colleges.

Interestingly, the 1999 study found that for both two-year and four-year colleges, price sensitivity of demand had fallen somewhat since the 1988 study. One possible explanation is that because the value of a college education has risen considerably over time, fewer people forgo college, even if tuition goes up.

MODULE 9 Review

Solutions appear at the back of the book.

Check Your Understanding

1. For each case, choose the condition that characterizes demand: elastic demand, inelastic demand, or unit-elastic demand.
   a. Total revenue decreases when price increases.
   b. When price falls, the additional revenue generated by the increase in the quantity sold is exactly offset by the revenue lost from the fall in the price received per unit.
   c. Total revenue falls when output increases.
   d. Producers in an industry find they can increase their total revenues by working together to reduce industry output.
2. For the following goods, is demand elastic, inelastic, or unit-elastic? Explain. What is the shape of the demand curve?
   a. demand by a snake-bite victim for an antidote
   b. demand by students for blue pencils

Multiple-Choice Questions

1. A perfectly elastic demand curve is
   - a. upward sloping.
   - b. vertical.
   - c. not a straight line.
   - d. horizontal.
   - e. downward sloping.

2. Which of the following would cause the demand for a good to be relatively inelastic?
   - a. The good has a large number of close substitutes.
   - b. Expenditures on the good represent a large share of consumer income.
   - c. There is ample time to adjust to price changes.
   - d. The good is a necessity.
   - e. The price of the good is in the upper left section of a linear demand curve.

3. Which of the following is true if the price elasticity of demand for a good is zero?
   - a. The slope of the demand curve is zero.
   - b. The slope of the demand curve is one.
   - c. The demand curve is vertical.
   - d. The demand curve is horizontal.
   - e. The price of the good is high.

4. Which of the following is correct for a price increase? When demand is ___________, total revenue will ___________.

	Demand	*Total Revenue*
a.	inelastic	decrease
b.	elastic	decrease
c.	unit-elastic	increase
d.	unit-elastic	decrease
e.	elastic	increase

5. Total revenue is maximized when demand is
   - a. elastic.
   - b. inelastic.
   - c. unit-elastic.
   - d. zero.
   - e. infinite.

Critical-Thinking Questions

Draw a correctly labeled graph illustrating a demand curve that is a straight line and is neither perfectly elastic nor perfectly inelastic.

1. On your graph, indicate the half of the demand curve along which demand is elastic.
2. In the elastic range, how will an increase in price affect total revenue? Explain.

Other Elasticities

(left) Msheldrake/Dreamstime.com • (right) © Lauri Pattersoni/iStockphoto

WHAT YOU WILL LEARN

1. **How the cross-price elasticity of demand measures the responsiveness of demand for one good to changes in the price of another good**
2. **The meaning and importance of the income elasticity of demand, a measure of the responsiveness of demand to changes in income**
3. **The significance of the price elasticity of supply, which measures the responsiveness of the quantity supplied to changes in price**
4. **The factors that influence the size of these various elasticities**

Using Other Elasticities

We stated earlier that economists use the concept of *elasticity* to measure the responsiveness of one variable to changes in another. However, up to this point we have focused on the price elasticity of demand. Now that we have used elasticity to measure the responsiveness of quantity demanded to changes in price, we can go on to look at how elasticity is used to understand the relationship between other important variables in economics.

The quantity of a good demanded depends not only on the price of that good but also on other variables. In particular, demand curves shift because of changes in the prices of related goods and changes in consumers' incomes. It is often important to have a measure of these other effects, and the best measures are—you guessed it—elasticities. Specifically, we can best measure how the demand for a good is affected by prices of other goods using a measure called the *cross-price elasticity of demand,* and we can best measure how demand is affected by changes in income using the *income elasticity of demand.*

Finally, we can also use elasticity to measure supply responses. The *price elasticity of supply* measures the responsiveness of the quantity supplied to changes in price.

The Cross-Price Elasticity of Demand

The demand for a good is often affected by the prices of other, related goods—goods that are substitutes or complements. A change in the price of a related good shifts the demand curve of the original good, reflecting a change in the quantity demanded at any given price. The strength of such a "cross" effect on demand can be measured by the **cross-price elasticity of demand,** defined as the ratio of the percent change in the quantity demanded of one good to the percent change in the price of another.

The **cross-price elasticity of demand** between two goods measures the effect of the change in one good's price on the quantity demanded of the other good. It is equal to the percent change in the quantity demanded of one good divided by the percent change in the other good's price.

$$\textbf{(10-1)}\ \text{Cross-price elasticity of demand between goods A and B} = \frac{\%\ \text{change in quantity of A demanded}}{\%\ \text{change in price of B}}$$

When two goods are substitutes, like hot dogs and hamburgers, the cross-price elasticity of demand is positive: a rise in the price of hot dogs increases the demand for hamburgers—that is, it causes a rightward shift of the demand curve for hamburgers. If the goods are close substitutes, the cross-price elasticity will be positive and large; if they are not close substitutes, the cross-price elasticity will be positive and small. So when the cross-price elasticity of demand is positive, its size is a measure of how closely substitutable the two goods are, with a higher number meaning the goods are closer substitutes.

When two goods are complements, like hot dogs and hot dog buns, the cross-price elasticity is negative: a rise in the price of hot dogs decreases the demand for hot dog buns—that is, it causes a leftward shift of the demand curve for hot dog buns. As with substitutes, the size of the cross-price elasticity of demand between two complements tells us how strongly complementary they are: if the cross-price elasticity is only slightly below zero, they are weak complements; if it is very negative, they are strong complements.

Note that in the case of the cross-price elasticity of demand, the sign (plus or minus) is very important: it tells us whether the two goods are complements or substitutes. So we cannot drop the minus sign as we did for the price elasticity of demand.

Our discussion of the cross-price elasticity of demand is a useful place to return to a point we made earlier: elasticity is a *unit-free* measure—that is, it doesn't depend on the units in which goods are measured.

To see the potential problem, suppose someone told you that "if the price of hot dog buns rises by $0.30, Americans will buy 10 million fewer hot dogs this year." If you've ever bought hot dog buns, you'll immediately wonder: is that a $0.30 increase in the price *per bun*, or is it a $0.30 increase in the price *per package* of buns? It makes a big difference what units we are talking about! However, if someone says that the cross-price elasticity of demand between buns and hot dogs is −0.3, it doesn't matter whether buns are sold individually or by the package. So elasticity is defined as a ratio of percent changes, which avoids confusion over units.

The Income Elasticity of Demand

The **income elasticity of demand** measures how changes in income affect the demand for a good. It indicates whether a good is normal or inferior and specifies how responsive demand for the good is to changes in income. Having learned the price and cross-price elasticity formulas, the income elasticity formula will look familiar:

$$\textbf{(10-2)}\ \text{Income elasticity of demand} = \frac{\%\ \text{change in quantity demanded}}{\%\ \text{change in income}}$$

Just as the cross-price elasticity of demand between two goods can be either positive or negative, depending on whether the goods are substitutes or complements, the income elasticity of demand for a good can also be either positive or negative. Recall that goods can be either *normal goods,* for which demand increases when income rises, or *inferior goods,* for which demand decreases when income rises. These definitions relate directly to the sign of the income elasticity of demand:

- When the income elasticity of demand is positive, the good is a normal good—that is, the quantity demanded at any given price increases as income increases.
- When the income elasticity of demand is negative, the good is an inferior good—that is, the quantity demanded at any given price decreases as income increases.

Economists often use estimates of the income elasticity of demand to predict which industries will grow most rapidly as the incomes of consumers grow over time. In doing this, they often find it useful to make a further distinction among normal goods, identifying which are *income-elastic* and which are *income-inelastic.*

The **income elasticity of demand** is the percent change in the quantity of a good demanded when a consumer's income changes divided by the percent change in the consumer's income.

The demand for a good is **income-elastic** if the income elasticity of demand for that good is greater than 1. When income rises, the demand for income-elastic goods rises *faster* than income. Luxury goods such as second homes and international travel tend to be income-elastic. The demand for a good is **income-inelastic** if the income elasticity of demand for that good is positive but less than 1. When income rises, the demand for income-inelastic goods rises, but more slowly than income. Necessities such as food and clothing tend to be income-inelastic.

The demand for a good is **income-elastic** if the income elasticity of demand for that good is greater than 1.

The demand for a good is **income-inelastic** if the income elasticity of demand for that good is positive but less than 1.

ECONOMICS IN ACTION — WORLD VIEW

WILL CHINA SAVE THE U.S. FARMING SECTOR?

In the days of the Founding Fathers, the great majority of Americans lived on farms. As recently as the 1940s, one American in six—or approximately 17%—still did. But in 2007, the official number was less than 1%. Why do so few people now live and work on farms in the United States? There are two main reasons, both involving elasticities.

First, the income elasticity of demand for food is much less than 1—it is income-inelastic. As consumers grow richer, other things being equal, spending on food rises less than income. As a result, as the U.S. economy has grown, the share of income it spends on food—and therefore the share of total U.S. income earned by farmers—has fallen.

Second, the demand for food is price-inelastic. This is important because technological advances in American agriculture have steadily raised yields over time and led to a long-term trend of lower U.S. food prices for most of the past century and a half. The combination of price inelasticity and falling prices led to falling total revenue for farmers. That's right: progress in farming has been good for American consumers but bad for American farmers.

Cultura Limited/SuperStock

Why do so few Americans live and work on farms?

The combination of these effects explains the long-term relative decline of farming in the United States. The low income elasticity of demand for food ensures that the income of farmers grows more slowly than the economy as a whole. And the combination of rapid technological progress in farming with price-inelastic demand for foodstuffs reinforces this effect, further reducing the growth of farm income.

That is, up until now. Starting in the mid-2000s, increased demand for foodstuffs from rapidly growing developing countries like China has pushed up the prices of agricultural products around the world. And American farmers have benefited, with U.S. farm net income rising 47% in 2011 alone. Eventually, as the growth in developing countries tapers off and agricultural innovation continues to progress, it's likely that the agricultural sector will resume its downward trend. But for now and for the foreseeable future, American farmers are enjoying the sector's revival.

The Price Elasticity of Supply

In the wake of the flu vaccine shortfall of 2004, attempts by vaccine distributors to drive up the price of vaccines would have been much less effective if a higher price had induced a large increase in the output of flu vaccines by flu vaccine manufacturers other than Chiron. In fact, if the rise in price had precipitated a significant increase in flu vaccine production, the price would have been pushed back down. But that didn't happen because, as we mentioned earlier, it would have been far too costly and technically difficult to produce more vaccine for the 2004–2005 flu season. (In reality, the production of flu vaccine is begun a year before it is to be distributed.)

The **price elasticity of supply** is a measure of the responsiveness of the quantity of a good supplied to the price of that good. It is the ratio of the percent change in the quantity supplied to the percent change in the price as we move along the supply curve.

There is **perfectly inelastic supply** when the price elasticity of supply is zero, so that changes in the price of the good have no effect on the quantity supplied. A perfectly inelastic supply curve is a vertical line.

There is **perfectly elastic supply** if the quantity supplied is zero below some price and infinite above that price. A perfectly elastic supply curve is a horizontal line.

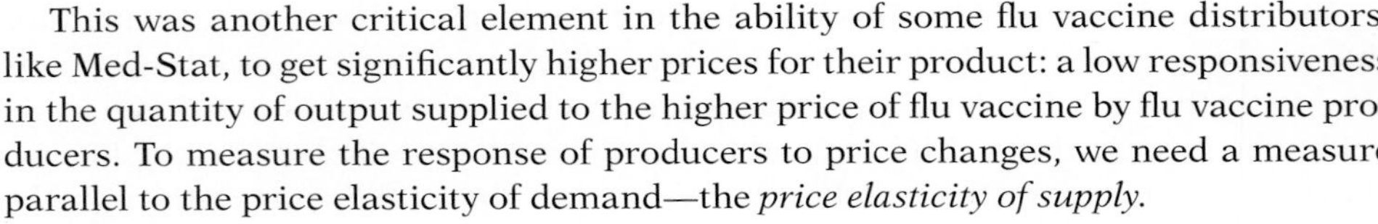

This was another critical element in the ability of some flu vaccine distributors, like Med-Stat, to get significantly higher prices for their product: a low responsiveness in the quantity of output supplied to the higher price of flu vaccine by flu vaccine producers. To measure the response of producers to price changes, we need a measure parallel to the price elasticity of demand—the *price elasticity of supply.*

Measuring the Price Elasticity of Supply

The **price elasticity of supply** is defined the same way as the price elasticity of demand (although there is no minus sign to be eliminated here):

$$\textbf{(10-3)}\quad \text{Price elasticity of supply} = \frac{\%\text{ change in quantity supplied}}{\%\text{ change in price}}$$

The only difference is that now we consider movements along the supply curve rather than movements along the demand curve.

Suppose that the price of tomatoes rises by 10%. If the quantity of tomatoes supplied also increases by 10% in response, the price elasticity of supply of tomatoes is 1 (10%/10%) and supply is unit-elastic. If the quantity supplied increases by 5%, the price elasticity of supply is 0.5 and supply is inelastic; if the quantity supplied increases by 20%, the price elasticity of supply is 2 and supply is elastic.

As with the demand side, the extreme values of the price elasticity of supply have a simple graphical representation. Panel (a) of Figure 10-1 shows the supply of cell phone frequencies, the portion of the radio spectrum that is suitable for sending and receiving cell phone signals. Governments own the right to sell the use of this part of the radio spectrum to cell phone operators inside their borders. But governments can't increase or decrease the number of cell phone frequencies they have to offer—for technical reasons, the quantity of frequencies suitable for cell phone operation is fixed.

So the supply curve for cell phone frequencies is a vertical line, which we have assumed is set at the quantity of 100 frequencies. As you move up and down that curve, the change in the quantity supplied by the government is zero, whatever the change in price. So panel (a) illustrates a case of **perfectly inelastic supply,** meaning that the price elasticity of supply is zero.

Panel (b) shows the supply curve for pizza. We suppose that it costs $12 to produce a pizza, including all opportunity costs. At any price below $12, it would be unprofitable to produce pizza and all the pizza parlors would go out of business. At a price of $12 or more, there are many producers who could operate pizza parlors. The ingredients—flour, tomatoes, cheese—are plentiful. And if necessary, more tomatoes could be grown, more milk could be produced to make mozzarella cheese, and so on. So by allowing profits, any price above $12 would elicit the supply of an extremely large quantity of pizzas. The implied supply curve is therefore a horizontal line at $12.

Since even a tiny increase in the price would lead to an enormous increase in the quantity supplied, the price elasticity of supply would be virtually infinite. A horizontal supply curve such as this represents a case of **perfectly elastic supply.**

As our cell phone frequencies and pizza examples suggest, real-world instances of both perfectly inelastic and perfectly elastic supply are easier to find than their counterparts in demand.

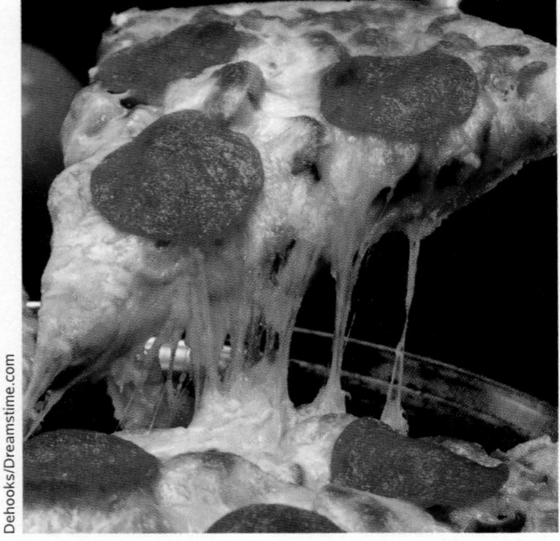

Dehooks/Dreamstime.com

The price elasticity of supply for pizza is very high because the inputs needed to make more of it are readily available.

What Factors Determine the Price Elasticity of Supply?

Our examples tell us the main determinant of the price elasticity of supply: the availability of inputs. In addition, as with the price elasticity of demand, time may also play a role in the price elasticity of supply. Here we briefly summarize the two factors.

THE AVAILABILITY OF INPUTS The price elasticity of supply tends to be large when inputs are readily available and can be shifted into and out of production at a relatively

FIGURE 10-1 Two Extreme Cases of Price Elasticity of Supply

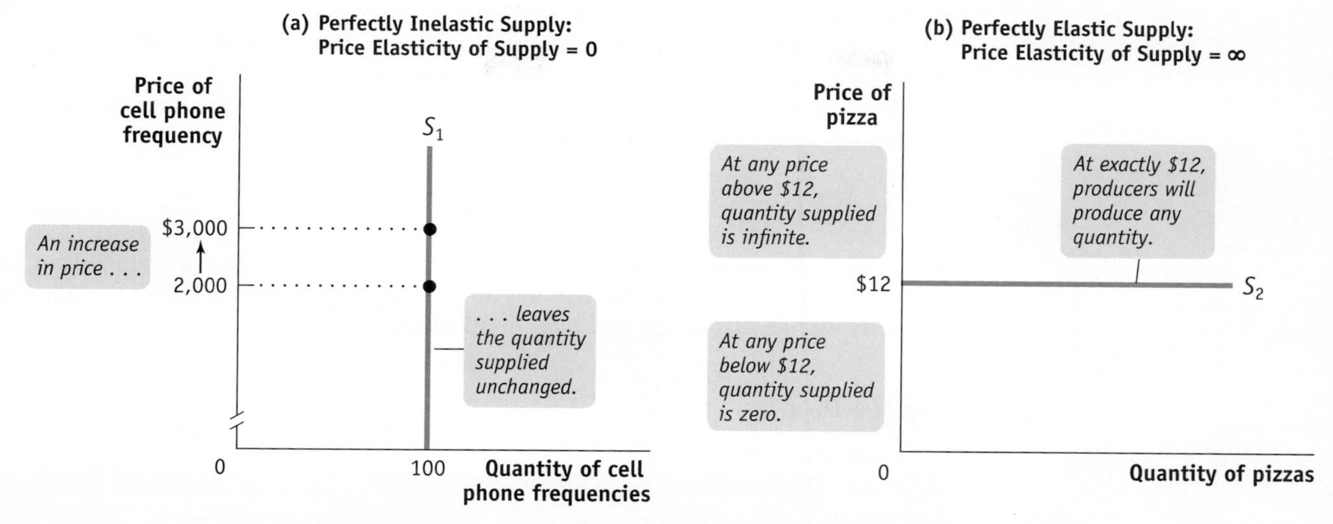
(a) Perfectly Inelastic Supply:
Price Elasticity of Supply = 0
Price of cell phone frequency
S_1
An increase in price . . .
$3,000
2,000
. . . leaves the quantity supplied unchanged.
0
100
Quantity of cell phone frequencies
(b) Perfectly Elastic Supply:
Price Elasticity of Supply = ∞
Price of pizza
At any price above $12, quantity supplied is infinite.
At exactly $12, producers will produce any quantity.
$12
S_2
At any price below $12, quantity supplied is zero.
0
Quantity of pizzas

Panel (a) shows a perfectly inelastic supply curve, which is a vertical line. The price elasticity of supply is zero: the quantity supplied is always the same, regardless of price. Panel (b) shows a perfectly elastic supply curve, which is a horizontal line. At a price of $12, producers will supply any quantity, but they will supply none at a price below $12. If the price rises above $12, they will supply an extremely large quantity.

low cost. It tends to be small when inputs are available only in a more-or-less fixed quantity or can be shifted into and out of production only at a relatively high cost.

TIME The price elasticity of supply tends to grow larger as producers have more time to respond to a price change. This means that the long-run price elasticity of supply is often higher than the short-run elasticity. In the case of the flu vaccine shortfall, time was the crucial element because flu vaccine must be grown in cultures over many months.

The price elasticity of the supply of pizza is very high because the inputs needed to make more pizza are readily available. The price elasticity of cell phone frequencies is zero because an essential input—the radio spectrum—cannot be increased at all.

Many industries are like pizza and have large price elasticities of supply: they can be readily expanded because they don't require any special or unique resources. On the other hand, the price elasticity of supply is usually substantially less than perfectly elastic for goods that involve limited natural resources: minerals like gold or copper, agricultural products like coffee that flourish only on certain types of land, and renewable resources like ocean fish that can be exploited only up to a point without destroying the resource.

iStockphoto

The price elasticity of supply is usually less than perfectly elastic for goods, such as ocean fish, that are limited natural resources.

But given enough time, producers are often able to significantly change the amount they produce in response to a price change, even when production involves a limited natural resource. For example, consider again the effects of a surge in flu vaccine prices, but this time focus on the supply response. If the price were to rise to $90 per vaccination and stay there for a number of years, there would almost certainly be a substantial increase in flu vaccine production. Producers such as Chiron would eventually respond by increasing the size of their manufacturing plants, hiring more lab technicians, and so on. But significantly enlarging the capacity of a biotech manufacturing lab takes several years, not weeks or months or even a single year.

For this reason, economists often make a distinction between the short-run elasticity of supply, usually referring to a few weeks or months, and the long-run elasticity of supply, usually referring to several years. In most industries, the long-run elasticity of supply is larger than the short-run elasticity.

An Elasticity Menagerie

We've just run through quite a few different types of elasticity. Keeping them all straight can be a challenge. So in Table 10-1 we provide a summary of all the types of elasticity we have discussed and their implications.

TABLE 10-1

An Elasticity Menagerie

Price elasticity of demand = $\frac{\text{\% change in quantity demanded}}{\text{\% change in price}}$ (dropping the minus sign)	
0	**Perfectly inelastic:** price has no effect on quantity demanded (vertical demand curve).
Between 0 and 1	**Inelastic:** a rise in price increases total revenue.
Exactly 1	**Unit-elastic:** changes in price have no effect on total revenue.
Greater than 1, less than ∞	**Elastic:** a rise in price reduces total revenue.
∞	**Perfectly elastic:** any rise in price causes quantity demanded to fall to 0. Any fall in price leads to an infinite quantity demanded (horizontal demand curve).
Cross-price elasticity of demand = $\frac{\text{\% change in quantity } \textit{of one good} \text{ demanded}}{\text{\% change in price } \textit{of another good}}$	
Negative	**Complements:** quantity demanded of one good falls when the price of another rises.
Positive	**Substitutes:** quantity demanded of one good rises when the price of another rises.
Income elasticity of demand = $\frac{\text{\% change in quantity demanded}}{\text{\% change in income}}$	
Negative	**Inferior good:** quantity demanded falls when income rises.
Positive, less than 1	**Normal good, income-inelastic:** quantity demanded rises when income rises, but not as rapidly as income.
Greater than 1	**Normal good, income-elastic:** quantity demanded rises when income rises, and more rapidly than income.
Price elasticity of supply = $\frac{\text{\% change in quantity supplied}}{\text{\% change in price}}$	
0	**Perfectly inelastic:** price has no effect on quantity supplied (vertical supply curve).
Greater than 0, less than ∞	ordinary upward-sloping supply curve.
∞	**Perfectly elastic:** any fall in price causes quantity supplied to fall to 0. Any rise in price elicits an infinite quantity supplied (horizontal supply curve).

MODULE 10 Review

Solutions appear at the back of the book.

Check Your Understanding

1. After Chelsea's income increased from $12,000 to $18,000 a year, her purchases of DVDs increased from 10 to 40 DVDs a year. Calculate Chelsea's income elasticity of demand for DVDs using the midpoint method.

2. As the price of margarine rises by 20%, a manufacturer of baked goods increases its quantity of butter demanded by 5%. Calculate the cross-price elasticity of demand between butter and margarine. Are butter and margarine substitutes or complements for this manufacturer?

3. Using the midpoint method, calculate the price elasticity of supply for web-design services when the price per hour rises from $100 to $150 and the number of hours supplied increases from 300,000 hours to 500,000. Is supply elastic, inelastic, or unit-elastic?

Multiple-Choice Questions

1. If the cross-price elasticity between two goods is negative, this means that the two goods are
   a. substitutes.
   b. complements.
   c. normal.
   d. inferior.
   e. luxuries.

2. If Kylie buys 200 units of good X when her income is $20,000 and 300 units of good X when her income increases to $25,000, her income elasticity of demand, using the midpoint method, is
   a. 0.06.
   b. 0.5.
   c. 1.65.
   d. 1.8.
   e. 2.00.

3. The income elasticity of demand for a normal good is
   a. zero.
   b. 1.
   c. infinite.
   d. positive.
   e. negative.

4. A perfectly elastic supply curve is
   a. positively sloped.
   b. negatively sloped.
   c. vertical.
   d. horizontal.
   e. U-shaped.

5. Which of the following leads to a more inelastic price elasticity of supply?
   I. the use of inputs that are easily obtained
   II. a high degree of substitutability between inputs
   III. a shorter time period in which to supply the good
   a. I only
   b. II only
   c. III only
   d. I and II only
   e. I, II, and III

Critical-Thinking Questions

Assume the price of corn rises by 20% and this causes suppliers to increase the quantity of corn supplied by 40%.

1. Calculate the price elasticity of supply.
2. In this case, is supply elastic or inelastic?
3. Draw a correctly labeled graph of a supply curve illustrating the most extreme case of the category of elasticity you found in part b (either perfectly elastic or perfectly inelastic supply).
4. What would likely be true of the availability of inputs for a firm with the supply curve you drew in part c? Explain.

BUSINESS CASE: The Airline Industry: Fly Less, Charge More

The recession that began in 2008 hit the airline industry very hard as both businesses and households cut back their travel plans. According to the International Air Transport Association, the industry lost $11 billion in 2008. However, by 2009, despite the fact that the economy was still extremely weak and airline traffic was still well below normal, the industry's profitability began to rebound. And by 2010, even in the midst of continued economic weakness, the airline industry's prospects had definitely recovered, with the industry achieving an $8.9 billion profit that year, with continued profitability in 2011 and 2012. As Gary Kelly, CEO of Southwest Airlines said, "The industry is in the best position—certainly in a decade—to post profitability."

Chris Sweda/Chicago Tribune/MCT via Getty Images

How did the airline industry achieve such a dramatic turnaround? Simple: fly less and charge more. In 2011, fares were 14% higher than they had been the previous year, and flights were more crowded than they had been in decades, with fewer than one in five seats empty on domestic flights.

In addition to cutting back on the number of flights—particularly money-losing ones—airlines implemented more extreme variations in ticket prices based on when a flight departed and when the ticket was purchased. For example, the cheapest day to fly is Wednesday, with Friday and Saturday the most expensive days to travel. The first flight of the morning (the one that requires you to get up at 4 A.M.) is cheaper than flights departing the rest of the day. And the cheapest time to buy a ticket is Tuesday at 3 P.M. Eastern Standard Time, with tickets purchased over the weekend carrying the highest prices.

And it doesn't stop there. As every beleaguered traveler knows, airlines have tacked on a wide variety of new fees and increased old ones—fees for food, for a blanket, for checked bags, for carry-on bags, for the right to board a flight first, for the right to choose your seat in advance, and so on. Airlines have also gotten more inventive in imposing fees that are hard for travelers to track in advance—such as claiming that fares have not risen during the holidays while imposing a "holiday surcharge." In 2011, airlines collected more than $22.6 billion from fees for checking baggage and changing tickets, up 66% from 2010.

But the question in the minds of industry analysts is whether airlines can manage to maintain their currently high levels of profitability. In the past, as travel demand picked up, airlines increased capacity—added seats—too quickly, leading to falling airfares. "The wild card is always capacity discipline," says William Swelbar, an airline industry researcher. "All it takes is one carrier to begin to add capacity aggressively, and then we follow and we undo all the good work that's been done."

Questions for Thought

1. How would you describe the price elasticity of demand for airline flights following the 2008 recession given the information in this case? Explain.
2. Using the concept of elasticity, explain why airlines would create such great variations in the price of a ticket depending on when it is purchased and the day and time the flight departs. Assume that some people are willing to spend time shopping for deals as well as fly at inconvenient times, but others are not.
3. Using the concept of elasticity, explain why airlines have imposed fees on things such as checked bags. Why might they try to hide or disguise fees?
4. Use an elasticity concept to explain under what conditions the airline industry will be able to maintain its high profitability in the future. Explain.

SECTION 3 REVIEW

Summary

Income Effects, Substitution Effects, and Elasticity

1. Changes in the price of a good affect the quantity consumed as a result of the **substitution effect,** and in some cases the **income effect.** Most goods absorb only a small share of a consumer's spending; for these goods, only the substitution effect—buying less of the good that has become relatively more expensive and more of the good that has become relatively cheaper—is significant. The income effect becomes substantial when there is a change in the price of a good that absorbs a large share of a consumer's spending, thereby significantly changing the purchasing power of the consumer's income.
2. Many economic questions depend on the size of consumer or producer responses to changes in prices or other variables. *Elasticity* is a general measure of responsiveness that can be used to answer such questions.
3. The **price elasticity of demand**—the percent change in the quantity demanded divided by the percent change in the price (dropping the minus sign)—is a measure of the responsiveness of the quantity demanded to changes in the price. In practical calculations, it is usually best to use the **midpoint method,** which calculates percent changes in prices and quantities based on the average of the initial and final values.

Interpreting Price Elasticity of Demand

4. Demand can fall anywhere in the range from **perfectly inelastic,** meaning the quantity demanded is unaffected by the price, to **perfectly elastic,** meaning there is a unique price at which consumers will buy as much or as little as they are offered. When demand is perfectly inelastic, the demand curve is a vertical line; when it is perfectly elastic, the demand curve is a horizontal line.
5. The price elasticity of demand is classified according to whether it is more or less than 1. If it is greater than 1, demand is **elastic;** if it is less than 1, demand is **inelastic;** if it is exactly 1, demand is **unit-elastic.** This classification determines how **total revenue,** the total value of sales, changes when the price changes. If demand is elastic, quantity demanded is relatively more responsive to changes in price, total revenue falls when the price increases and rises when the price decreases. If demand is inelastic, quantity demanded is relatively less responsive to changes in price, total revenue rises when the price increases and falls when the price decreases.
6. The price elasticity of demand depends on whether there are close substitutes for the good in question, whether the good is a necessity or a luxury, the share of income spent on the good, and the length of time that has elapsed since the price change.

Other Elasticities

7. The **cross-price elasticity of demand** measures the effect of a change in one good's price on the quantity of another good demanded. The cross-price elasticity of demand can be positive, in which case the goods are substitutes, or negative, in which case they are complements.
8. The **income elasticity of demand** is the percent change in the quantity of a good demanded when a consumer's income changes divided by the percent change in income. The income elasticity of demand indicates how intensely the demand for a good responds to changes in income. It can be negative; in that case the good is an inferior good. Goods with positive income elasticities of demand are normal goods. If the income elasticity is greater than 1, a good is **income-elastic;** if it is positive and less than 1, the good is **income-inelastic.**
9. The **price elasticity of supply** is the percent change in the quantity of a good supplied divided by the percent change in the price. If the quantity supplied does not change at all, we have an instance of **perfectly inelastic supply;** the supply curve is a vertical line. If the quantity supplied is zero below some price but infinite above that price, we have an instance of **perfectly elastic supply;** the supply curve is a horizontal line.
10. The price elasticity of supply depends on the availability of resources to expand production and on time. It is higher when inputs are available at relatively low cost and when more time has elapsed since the price change.

Key Terms

Problems

1. In each of the following situations, describe the substitution effect and, if it is significant, the income effect. In which direction does each of these effects move? Why?

   a. Ed spends a large portion of his income on his children's education. Because tuition fees rise, one of his children has to withdraw from college.

   b. Homer spends much of his monthly income on home mortgage payments. The interest on his adjustable rate mortgage falls, lowering his mortgage payments, and Homer decides to move to a larger house.

   c. Pam thinks that Spam is an inferior good. Yet as the price of Spam rises, she decides to buy less of it.

2. Nile.com, the online bookseller, wants to increase its total revenue. One strategy is to offer a 10% discount on every book it sells. Nile.com knows that its customers can be divided into two distinct groups according to their likely responses to the discount. The accompanying table shows how the two groups respond to the discount.

	Group A (sales per week)	Group B (sales per week)
Volume of sales before the 10% discount	1.55 million	1.50 million
Volume of sales after the 10% discount	1.65 million	1.70 million

   a. Using the midpoint method, calculate the price elasticities of demand for group A and group B.

   b. Explain how the discount will affect total revenue from each group.

   c. Suppose Nile.com knows which group each customer belongs to when he or she logs on and can choose whether or not to offer the 10% discount. If Nile.com wants to increase its total revenue, should discounts be offered to group A or to group B, to neither group, or to both groups?

3. Do you think the price elasticity of demand for Ford sport-utility vehicles (SUVs) will increase, decrease, or remain the same when each of the following events occurs? Explain your answer.

   a. Other car manufacturers, such as General Motors, decide to make and sell SUVs.

   b. SUVs produced in foreign countries are banned from the American market.

   c. Due to ad campaigns, Americans believe that SUVs are much safer than ordinary passenger cars.

   d. The time period over which you measure the elasticity lengthens. During that longer time, new models such as four-wheel-drive cargo vans appear.

4. In the United States, 2007 was a bad year for growing wheat. And as wheat supply decreased, the price of wheat rose dramatically, leading to a lower quantity demanded (a movement along the demand curve). The accompanying table describes what happened to prices and the quantity of wheat demanded.

	2006	2007
Quantity demanded (bushels)	2.2 billion	2.0 billion
Average price (per bushel)	$3.42	$4.26

   a. Using the midpoint method, calculate the price elasticity of demand for winter wheat.

   b. What is the total revenue for U.S. wheat farmers in 2006 and 2007?

   c. Did the bad harvest increase or decrease the total revenue of U.S. wheat farmers? How could you have predicted this from your answer to part a?

5. What can you conclude about the price elasticity of demand in each of the following statements?

   a. "The pizza delivery business in this town is very competitive. I'd lose half my customers if I raised the price by as little as 10%."

   b. "I owned both of the two Jerry Garcia autographed lithographs in existence. I sold one on eBay for a high price. But when I sold the second one, the price dropped by 80%."

   c. "My economics professor has chosen to use the Krugman/Wells textbook for this class. I have no choice but to buy this book."

   d. "I always spend a total of exactly $10 per week on coffee."

6. The accompanying table gives part of the supply schedule for personal computers in the United States.

Price per computer	Quantity of computers supplied
$1,100	12,000
900	8,000

   a. Using the midpoint method, calculate the price elasticity of supply when the price increases from $900 to $1,100.

   b. Suppose firms produce 1,000 more computers at any given price due to improved technology. As price increases from $900 to $1,100, is the price elasticity of supply now greater than, less than, or the same as it was in part a?

   c. Suppose a longer time period under consideration means that the quantity supplied at any given price is 20% higher than the figures given in the table. As price increases from $900 to $1,100, is the price elasticity of supply now greater than, less than, or the same as it was in part a?

7. The accompanying table lists the cross-price elasticities of demand for several goods, where the percent quantity change is measured for the first good of the pair, and the percent price change is measured for the second good.

Good	Cross-price elasticities of demand
Air-conditioning units and kilowatts of electricity	−0.34
Coke and Pepsi	+0.63
High-fuel-consuming sport-utility vehicles (SUVs) and gasoline	−0.28
McDonald's burgers and Burger King burgers	+0.82
Butter and margarine	+1.54

a. Explain the sign of each of the cross-price elasticities. What does it imply about the relationship between the two goods in question?

b. Compare the absolute values of the cross-price elasticities and explain their magnitudes. For example, why is the cross-price elasticity of McDonald's burgers and Burger King burgers less than the cross-price elasticity of butter and margarine?

c. Use the information in the table to calculate how a 5% increase in the price of Pepsi affects the quantity of Coke demanded.

d. Use the information in the table to calculate how a 10% decrease in the price of gasoline affects the quantity of SUVs demanded.

8. The accompanying table shows the price and yearly quantity sold of souvenir T-shirts in the town of Crystal Lake according to the average income of the tourists visiting.

Price of T-shirt	Quantity of T-shirts demanded when average tourist income is $20,000	Quantity of T-shirts demanded when average tourist income is $30,000
$4	3,000	5,000
5	2,400	4,200
6	1,600	3,000
7	800	1,800

a. Using the midpoint method, calculate the price elasticity of demand when the price of a T-shirt rises from $5 to $6 and the average tourist income is $20,000. Also calculate it when the average tourist income is $30,000.

b. Using the midpoint method, calculate the income elasticity of demand when the price of a T-shirt is $4 and the average tourist income increases from $20,000 to $30,000. Also calculate it when the price is $7.

9. In each of the following cases, do you think the price elasticity of supply is (i) perfectly elastic; (ii) perfectly inelastic; (iii) elastic, but not perfectly elastic; or (iv) inelastic, but not perfectly inelastic? Explain using a diagram.

a. An increase in demand this summer for luxury cruises leads to a huge jump in the sales price of a cabin on the Queen Mary 2.

b. The price of a kilowatt of electricity is the same during periods of high electricity demand as during periods of low electricity demand.

c. Fewer people want to fly during February than during any other month. The airlines cancel about 10% of their flights as ticket prices fall about 20% during this month.

d. Owners of vacation homes in Maine rent them out during the summer. Due to a soft economy, a 30% decline in the price of a vacation rental leads more than half of homeowners to occupy their vacation homes themselves during the summer.

10. There is a debate about whether sterile hypodermic needles should be passed out free of charge in cities with high drug use. Proponents argue that doing so will reduce the incidence of diseases, such as HIV/AIDS, that are often spread by needle sharing among drug users. Opponents believe that doing so will encourage more drug use by reducing the risks of this behavior. As an economist asked to assess the policy, you must know the following: (i) how responsive the spread of diseases like HIV/AIDS is to the price of sterile needles and (ii) how responsive drug use is to the price of sterile needles. Assuming that you know these two things, use the concepts of price elasticity of demand for sterile needles and the cross-price elasticity between drugs and sterile needles to answer the following questions.

a. In what circumstances do you believe this is a beneficial policy?

b. In what circumstances do you believe this is a bad policy?

11. Worldwide, the average coffee grower has increased the amount of acreage under cultivation over the past few years. The result has been that the average coffee plantation produces significantly more coffee than it did 10 to 20 years ago. Unfortunately for the growers, however, this has also been a period in which their total revenues have plunged. In terms of an elasticity, what must be true for these events to have occurred? Illustrate these events with a diagram, indicating the quantity effect and the price effect that gave rise to these events.

Module 11: Consumer and Producer Surplus
Module 12: Efficiency and Markets

SECTION 4

Market Efficiency

MAKING GAINS BY THE BOOK

There is a lively market in second-hand college textbooks. At the end of each term, some students who took a course decide that the money they can make by selling their used books is worth more to them than keeping the books. And some students who are taking the course next term prefer to buy a somewhat battered but less expensive used textbook rather than pay full price for a new one.

Textbook publishers and authors are not happy about these transactions because they cut into sales of new books. But both the students who sell used books and those who buy them clearly benefit from the existence of the market. That is why many college bookstores facilitate their trade, buying used textbooks and selling them alongside the new books.

But can we put a number on what used textbook buyers and sellers gain from these transactions? Can we answer the question "*How much* do the buyers and sellers of textbooks gain from the existence of the used-book market?"

Yes, we can. In this section we will see how to measure benefits, such as those to buyers of used textbooks, from being able to purchase a good—known as *consumer surplus*. And we will see that there is a corresponding measure, *producer surplus,* of the benefits sellers receive from being able to sell a good.

The concepts of consumer surplus and producer surplus are useful for analyzing a wide variety of economic issues. They let us calculate how much benefit producers and consumers receive from the existence of a market. They also allow us to calculate how the welfare of consumers and producers is affected by changes in market prices. Such calculations play a crucial role in evaluating many economic policies.

What information do we need to calculate consumer and producer surplus? Surprisingly, all we need are the demand and supply curves for a good. That is, the supply and demand model isn't just a model of how a competitive market works—it's also a model of how much consumers and producers gain from participating in that market. Our first step will be to learn how consumer and producer surplus can be derived from the demand and supply curves. We will then see how these concepts can be applied to actual economic issues.

MODULE

11 Consumer and Producer Surplus

Peter Huoppi

WHAT YOU WILL LEARN

1. The meaning of consumer surplus and its relationship to the demand curve
2. The meaning of producer surplus and its relationship to the supply curve

Consumer Surplus and the Demand Curve

First-year college students are often surprised by the prices of the textbooks required for their classes. The College Board estimates that in 2011–2012 students at four-year schools spent, on average, about $1,200 for books and supplies. But at the end of the semester, students might again be surprised to find out that they can sell back at least some of the textbooks they used for the semester for a percentage of the purchase price (offsetting some of the cost of textbooks).

The ability to purchase used textbooks at the start of the semester and to sell back used textbooks at the end of the semester is beneficial to students on a budget. In fact, the market for used textbooks is a big business in terms of dollars and cents—approximately $3 billion in 2009. This market provides a convenient starting point for us to develop the concepts of consumer and producer surplus. We'll use these concepts to understand exactly how buyers and sellers benefit from a competitive market and how big those benefits are. In addition, these concepts assist in the analysis of what happens when competitive markets don't work well or there is interference in the market.

So let's begin by looking at the market for used textbooks, starting with the buyers. The key point, as we'll see in a minute, is that the demand curve is derived from their tastes or preferences—and that those same preferences also determine how much they gain from the opportunity to buy used books.

Willingness to Pay and the Demand Curve

A used book is not as good as a new book—it will be battered and coffee-stained, may include someone else's highlighting, and may not be completely up to date. How much this bothers you depends on your preferences. Some potential buyers would prefer to buy the used book even if it is only slightly cheaper than a new one, while others would buy the used book only if it is considerably cheaper.

A consumer's **willingness to pay** for a good is the maximum price at which he or she would buy that good.

Let's define a potential buyer's **willingness to pay** as the maximum price at which he or she would buy a good, in this case a used textbook. An individual won't buy the good if it costs more than this amount but is eager to do so if it costs less. If the price is just equal to an individual's willingness to pay, he or she is indifferent between buying and not buying. For the sake of simplicity, we'll assume that the individual buys the good in this case.

The table in Figure 11-1 shows five potential buyers of a used book that costs $100 new, listed in order of their willingness to pay. At one extreme is Aleisha, who will buy a second-hand book even if the price is as high as $59. Brad is less willing to have a used book and will buy one only if the price is $45 or less. Claudia is willing to pay only $35 and Darren only $25. Edwina, who really doesn't like the idea of a used book, will buy one only if it costs no more than $10.

How many of these five students will actually buy a used book? It depends on the price. If the price of a used book is $55, only Aleisha buys one; if the price is $40, Aleisha and Brad both buy used books, and so on. So the information in the table can be used to construct the *demand schedule* for used textbooks.

We can use this demand schedule to derive the market demand curve shown in Figure 11-1. Because we are considering only a small number of consumers, this curve doesn't look like the smooth demand curves we have seen previously, for markets that contained hundreds or thousands of consumers. This demand curve is step-shaped, with alternating horizontal and vertical segments. Each horizontal segment—each step—corresponds to one potential buyer's willingness to pay. However, we'll see

FIGURE 11-1 **The Demand Curve for Used Textbooks**

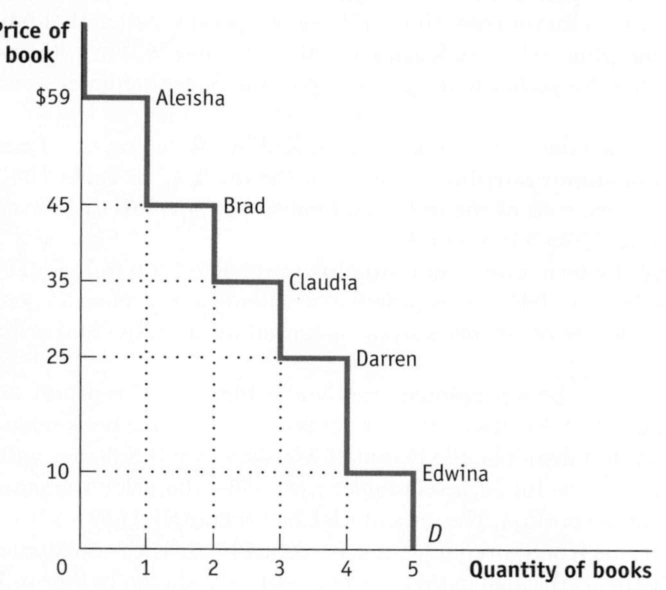

Potential buyers	Willingness to pay
Aleisha	$59
Brad	45
Claudia	35
Darren	25
Edwina	10

With only five potential consumers in this market, the demand curve is step-shaped. Each step represents one consumer, and its height indicates that consumer's willingness to pay—the maximum price at which each will buy a used textbook—as indicated in the table. Aleisha has the highest willingness to pay at $59, Brad has the next highest at $45, and so on down to Edwina with the lowest willingness to pay at $10. At a price of $59, the quantity demanded is one (Aleisha); at a price of $45, the quantity demanded is two (Aleisha and Brad); and so on until you reach a price of $10, at which all five students are willing to purchase a book.

shortly that for the analysis of consumer surplus it doesn't matter whether the demand curve is step-shaped, as in this figure, or whether there are many consumers, making the curve smooth.

Willingness to Pay and Consumer Surplus

Suppose that the campus bookstore makes used textbooks available at a price of $30. In that case Aleisha, Brad, and Claudia will buy used books. Do they gain from their purchases, and if so, how much?

The answer, shown in Table 11-1, is that each student who purchases a used book does achieve a net gain but that the amount of the gain differs among students.

TABLE 11-1

Consumer Surplus When the Price of a Used Textbook = $30

Potential buyer	Willingness to pay	Price paid	Individual consumer surplus = Willingness to pay – Price paid
Aleisha	$59	$30	$29
Brad	45	30	15
Claudia	35	30	5
Darren	25	—	—
Edwina	10	—	—
All buyers			**Total consumer surplus = $49**

Aleisha would have been willing to pay $59, so her net gain is $59 – $30 = $29. Brad would have been willing to pay $45, so his net gain is $45 – $30 = $15. Claudia would have been willing to pay $35, so her net gain is $35 – $30 = $5. Darren and Edwina, however, won't be willing to buy a used book at a price of $30, so they neither gain nor lose.

The net gain that a buyer achieves from the purchase of a good is called that buyer's **individual consumer surplus.** What we learn from this example is that whenever a buyer pays a price less than his or her willingness to pay, the buyer achieves some individual consumer surplus.

The sum of the individual consumer surpluses achieved by all the buyers of a good is known as the **total consumer surplus** achieved in the market. In Table 11-1, the total consumer surplus is the sum of the individual consumer surpluses achieved by Aleisha, Brad, and Claudia: $29 + $15 + $5 = $49.

Economists often use the term **consumer surplus** to refer to both individual and total consumer surplus. We will follow this practice; it will always be clear in context whether we are referring to the consumer surplus achieved by an individual or by all buyers.

Total consumer surplus can be represented graphically. Figure 11-2 reproduces the demand curve from Figure 11-1. Each step in that demand curve is one book wide and represents one consumer. For example, the height of Aleisha's step is $59, her willingness to pay. This step forms the top of a rectangle, with $30—the price she actually pays for a book—forming the bottom. The area of Aleisha's rectangle, ($59 – $30) × 1 = $29, is her consumer surplus from purchasing one book at $30. So the individual consumer surplus Aleisha gains is the *area of the dark blue rectangle* shown in Figure 11-2.

In addition to Aleisha, Brad and Claudia will also each buy a book when the price is $30. Like Aleisha, they benefit from their purchases, though not as much, because they each have a lower willingness to pay. Figure 11-2 also shows the consumer surplus gained by Brad and Claudia; again, this can be measured by the areas of the appropriate rectangles. Darren and Edwina, because they do not buy books at a price of $30, receive no consumer surplus.

The total consumer surplus achieved in this market is just the sum of the individual consumer surpluses received by Aleisha, Brad, and Claudia. So total consumer surplus is equal to the combined area of the three rectangles—the entire shaded area

Individual consumer surplus is the net gain to an individual buyer from the purchase of a good. It is equal to the difference between the buyer's willingness to pay and the price paid.

Total consumer surplus is the sum of the individual consumer surpluses of all the buyers of a good in a market.

The term **consumer surplus** is often used to refer to both individual and to total consumer surplus.

FIGURE 11-2 **Consumer Surplus in the Used-Textbook Market**

At a price of $30, Aleisha, Brad, and Claudia each buy a book but Darren and Edwina do not. Aleisha, Brad, and Claudia get individual consumer surpluses equal to the difference between their willingness to pay and the price, illustrated by the areas of the shaded rectangles. Both Darren and Edwina have a willingness to pay that is less than $30, so they are unwilling to buy a book at this market price; they receive zero consumer surplus. The total consumer surplus is given by the entire shaded area—the sum of the individual consumer surpluses of Aleisha, Brad, and Claudia—equal to $29 + $15 + $5 = $49.

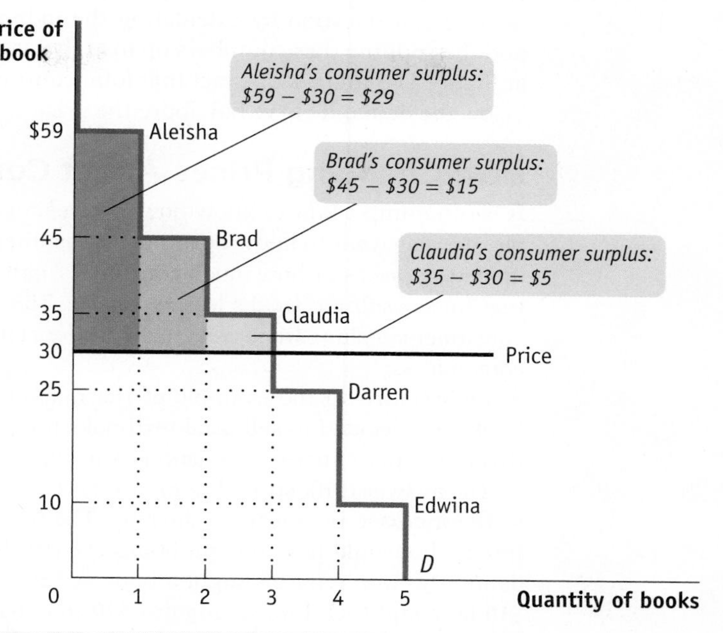

in Figure 11-2. Another way to say this is that total consumer surplus is equal to the area below the demand curve but above the price.

This is worth repeating as a general principle: *The total consumer surplus generated by purchases of a good at a given price is equal to the area below the demand curve but above that price*. The same principle applies regardless of the number of consumers.

When we consider large markets, this graphical representation becomes particularly helpful. Consider, for example, the sales of iPads to millions of potential buyers. Each potential buyer has a maximum price that he or she is willing to pay. With so many potential buyers, the demand curve will be smooth, like the one shown in Figure 11-3.

FIGURE 11-3 **Consumer Surplus**

The demand curve for iPads is smooth because there are many potential buyers. At a price of $500, 1 million iPads are demanded. The consumer surplus at this price is equal to the shaded area: the area below the demand curve but above the price. This is the total net gain to consumers generated from buying and consuming iPads when the price is $500.

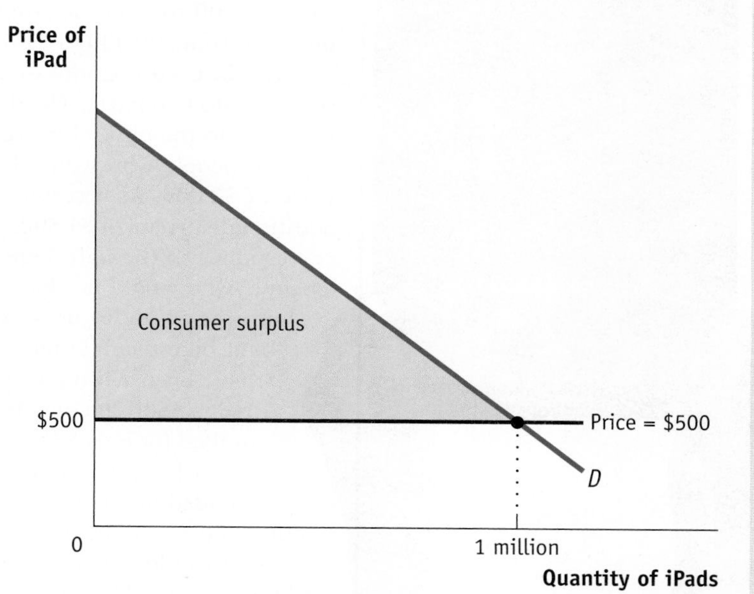

Suppose that at a price of $500 per iPad a total of 1 million iPads are purchased. How much do consumers gain from being able to buy those 1 million iPads? We could answer that question by calculating the individual consumer surplus of each buyer and then adding these numbers up to arrive at a total. But it is much easier just to look at Figure 11-3 and use the fact that total consumer surplus is equal to the shaded area below the demand curve but above the price.

How Changing Prices Affect Consumer Surplus

It is often important to know how price *changes* affect consumer surplus. For example, we may want to know how much consumers are hurt if a flood in Pakistan drives up cotton prices or how much consumers' gain from the introduction of fish farming that makes salmon steaks less expensive. The same approach we have used to derive consumer surplus can be used to answer questions about how changes in prices affect consumers.

Let's return to the example of the market for used textbooks. Suppose that the bookstore decided to sell used textbooks for $20 instead of $30. By how much would this fall in price increase consumer surplus?

The answer is illustrated in Figure 11-4. As shown in the figure, there are two parts to the increase in consumer surplus. The first part, shaded dark blue, is the gain of those who would have bought books even at the higher price of $30. Each of the students who would have bought a book at $30—Aleisha, Brad, and Claudia—now pays $10 less, and therefore each gains $10 in consumer surplus from the fall in price to $20. So the dark blue area represents the $10 × 3 = $30 increase in consumer surplus to those three buyers.

The second part, shaded light blue, is the gain to those who would not have bought a book at $30 but are willing to pay more than $20. In this case that gain goes to Darren, who would not have bought a book at $30 but does buy one at $20. He gains $5—the difference between his willingness to pay of $25 and the new price of $20. So the light blue area represents a further $5 gain in consumer surplus.

The total increase in consumer surplus is the sum of the shaded areas, $35. Likewise, a rise in price from $20 to $30 would decrease consumer surplus by an amount equal to the sum of the shaded areas.

Figure 11-4 illustrates that when the price of a good falls, the area under the demand curve but above the price—the total consumer surplus—increases. Figure 11-5 shows the same result for the case of a smooth demand curve, the demand for iPads. Here we assume that the price of iPads falls from $2,000 to $500, leading to an increase in the quantity demanded from 200,000 to 1 million units.

As in the used-textbook example, we divide the gain in consumer surplus into two parts. The dark blue rectangle in Figure 11-5 corresponds to the dark blue area in Figure 11-4: it is the gain to the 200,000 people who would have bought iPads even at the higher price of $2,000. As a result of the price reduction, each receives additional surplus of $1,500. The light blue triangle in Figure 11-5 corresponds to the light blue area in Figure 11-4: it is the gain to people who would not have bought the good at the higher price but are willing to do so at a price of $500. For example, the light blue triangle includes the gain to someone who would have been willing to pay $1,000 for an iPad and therefore gains $500 in consumer surplus when it is possible to buy an iPad for only $500.

As before, the total gain in consumer surplus is the sum of the shaded areas, the increase in the area under the demand curve but above the price.

What would happen if the price of a good were to rise instead of fall? We would do the same analysis in reverse. Suppose, for

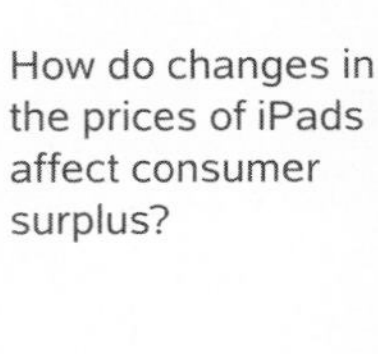
How do changes in the prices of iPads affect consumer surplus?

iStockphoto/Thinkstock

FIGURE 11-4 **Consumer Surplus and a Fall in the Price of Used Textbooks**

There are two parts to the increase in consumer surplus generated by a fall in price from $30 to $20. The first is given by the dark blue rectangle: each person who would have bought at the original price of $30—Aleisha, Brad, and Claudia—receives an increase in consumer surplus equal to the total reduction in price, $10. So the area of the dark blue rectangle corresponds to an amount equal to 3 × $10 = $30. The second part is given by the light blue area: the increase in consumer surplus for those who would *not* have bought at the original price of $30 but who buy at the new price of $20—namely, Darren. Darren's willingness to pay is $25, so he now receives consumer surplus of $5. The total increase in consumer surplus is 3 × $10 + $5 = $35, represented by the sum of the shaded areas. Likewise, a rise in price from $20 to $30 would decrease consumer surplus by an amount equal to the sum of the shaded areas.

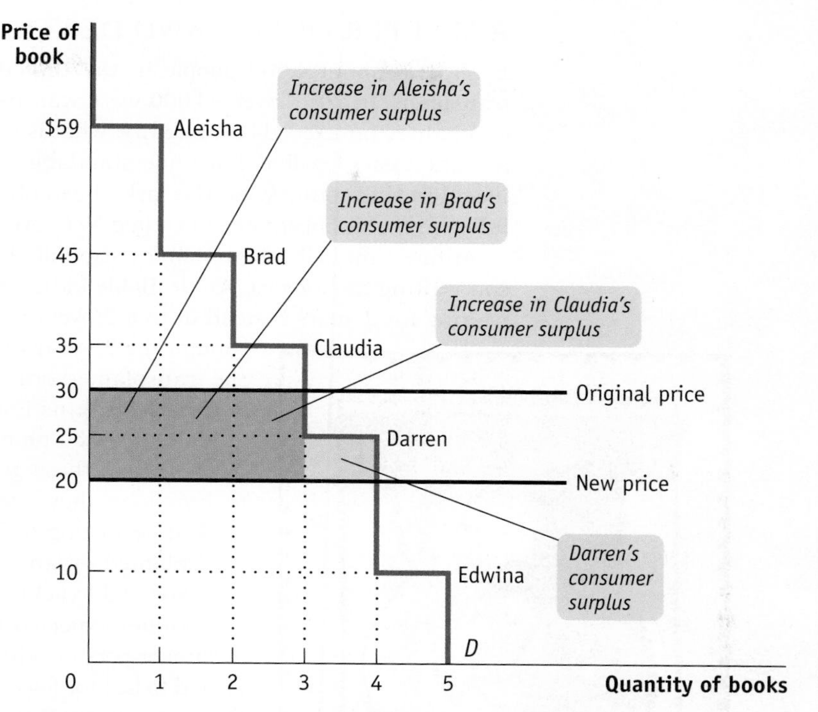

example, that for some reason the price of iPads rises from $500 to $2,000. This would lead to a fall in consumer surplus equal to the sum of the shaded areas in Figure 11-5. This loss consists of two parts. The dark blue rectangle represents the loss to consumers who would still buy an iPad, even at a price of $2,000. The light blue triangle represents the loss to consumers who decide not to buy an iPad at the higher price.

FIGURE 11-5 **A Fall in the Price Increases Consumer Surplus**

A fall in the price of an iPad from $2,000 to $500 leads to an increase in the quantity demanded and an increase in consumer surplus. The change in total consumer surplus is given by the sum of the shaded areas: the total area below the demand curve and between the old and new prices. Here, the dark blue area represents the increase in consumer surplus for the 200,000 consumers who would have bought an iPad at the original price of $2,000; they each receive an increase in consumer surplus of $1,500. The light blue area represents the increase in consumer surplus for those willing to buy at a price equal to or greater than $500 but less than $2,000. Similarly, a rise in the price of an iPad from $500 to $2,000 generates a decrease in consumer surplus equal to the sum of the two shaded areas.

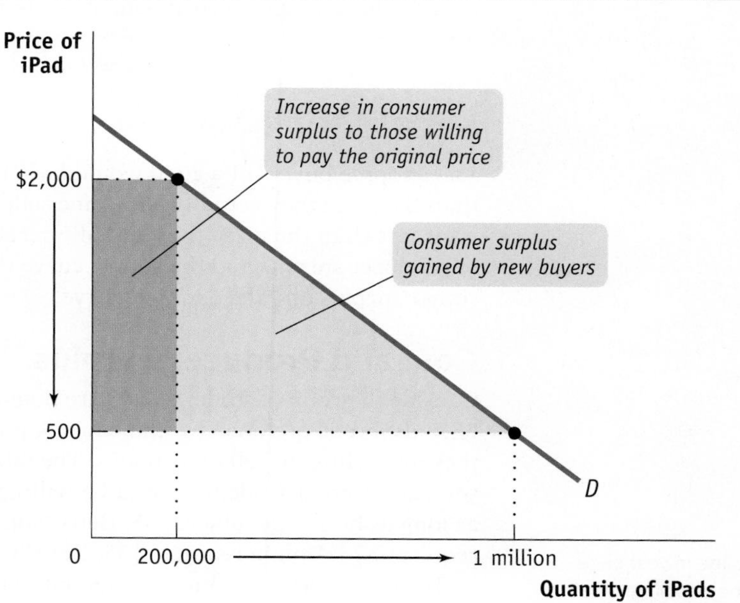

ECONOMICS ▶ IN ACTION

A MATTER OF LIFE AND DEATH

Each year about 4,000 people in the United States die while waiting for a kidney transplant. In 2013, over 90,000 were wait listed. Since the number of those in need of a kidney far exceeds availability, what is the best way to allocate available organs? A market isn't feasible. For understandable reasons, the sale of human body parts is illegal in this country. So the task of establishing a protocol for these situations has fallen to the nonprofit group United Network for Organ Sharing (UNOS).

At one time, UNOS guidelines stipulated that a donated kidney went to the person waiting the longest. An available kidney would go to a 75-year-old who had been waiting for 2 years instead of to a 25-year-old who had been waiting 6 months, even though the 25-year-old will likely live longer and benefit from the transplanted organ for a longer period of time.

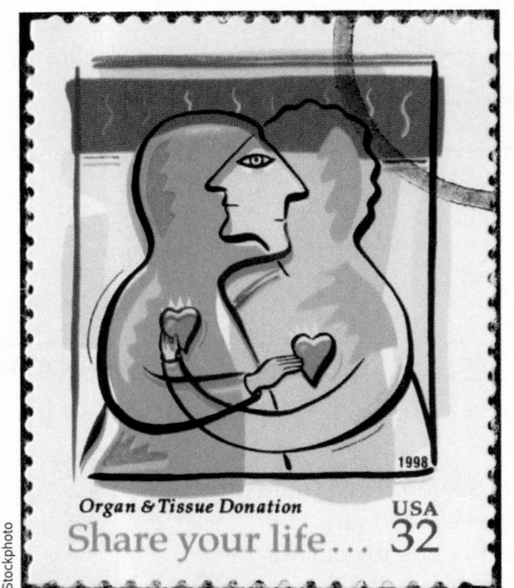

iStockphoto

To address this issue, in 2013 UNOS adopted a new set of guidelines based on a concept it called "net survival benefit." According to these guidelines, kidneys are ranked according to how long they are likely to last; similarly, recipients are ranked according to how long they are likely to live with the transplanted organ. Each kidney is then matched to the person expected to achieve the greatest survival time from it.

A kidney expected to last many decades will be allocated to a younger person, while older recipients will receive kidneys expected to last for fewer years. This way, UNOS tries to avoid situations in which (1) recipients outlive their transplants, creating the need for another transplant and reducing the pool of kidneys available and (2) a kidney "outlives" its recipient, thereby wasting years of kidney function that could have benefited someone else.

What does this have to do with consumer surplus? As you may have guessed, the UNOS concept of "net survival benefit" is a lot like individual consumer surplus—the individual consumer surplus generated from getting a new kidney. In essence, UNOS devised a system that allocates donated kidneys according to who gets the greatest individual consumer surplus from it. In this way, the new UNOS guidelines attempt to maximize the total consumer surplus available from the existing pool of kidneys. In terms of results, then, a "net survival benefit" system operates a lot like a competitive market.

Producer Surplus and the Supply Curve

Just as some buyers of a good would have been willing to pay more for their purchase than the price they actually pay, some sellers of a good would have been willing to sell it for less than the price they actually receive. We can therefore carry out an analysis of producer surplus and the supply curve that is almost exactly parallel to that of consumer surplus and the demand curve.

Cost and Producer Surplus

Consider a group of students who are potential sellers of used textbooks. Because they have different preferences, the various potential sellers differ in the price at which they are willing to sell their books. The table in Figure 11-6 shows the prices at which several different students would be willing to sell. Andrew is willing to sell the book as long as he can get at least $5; Betty won't sell unless she can get at least $15; Carlos requires $25; Donna requires $35; Engelbert $45.

A seller's **cost** is the lowest price at which he or she is willing to sell a good.

The lowest price at which a potential seller is willing to sell is called the seller's **cost.** So Andrew's cost is $5, Betty's is $15, and so on.

Using the term *cost,* which people normally associate with the monetary cost of producing a good, may sound a little strange when applied to sellers of used textbooks. The students don't have to manufacture the books, so it doesn't cost the student who sells a book anything to make that book available for sale, does it?

Yes, it does. A student who sells a book won't have it later, as part of his or her personal collection. So there is an *opportunity cost* to selling a textbook, even if the owner has completed the course for which it was required. And remember that one of the basic principles of economics is that the true measure of the cost of doing something is always its opportunity cost. That is, the real cost of something is what you must give up to get it.

So it is good economics to talk of the minimum price at which someone will sell a good as the "cost" of selling that good, even if he or she doesn't spend any money to make the good available for sale. Of course, in most real-world markets the sellers are also those who produce the good and therefore *do* spend money to make the good available for sale. In this case the cost of making the good available for sale *includes* monetary costs, but it may also include other opportunity costs.

Getting back to the example, suppose that Andrew sells his book for $30. Clearly he has gained from the transaction: he would have been willing to sell for only $5, so he has gained $25. This net gain, the difference between the price he actually gets and his cost—the minimum price at which he would have been willing to sell—is known as his **individual producer surplus.**

Individual producer surplus is the net gain to an individual seller from selling a good. It is equal to the difference between the price received and the seller's cost.

Just as we derived the demand curve from the willingness to pay of different consumers, we can derive the supply curve from the cost of different producers. The step-shaped curve in Figure 11-6 shows the supply curve implied by the costs shown in the accompanying table. At a price less than $5, none of the students are willing to sell; at a price between $5 and $15, only Andrew is willing to sell, and so on.

FIGURE 11-6 The Supply Curve for Used Textbooks

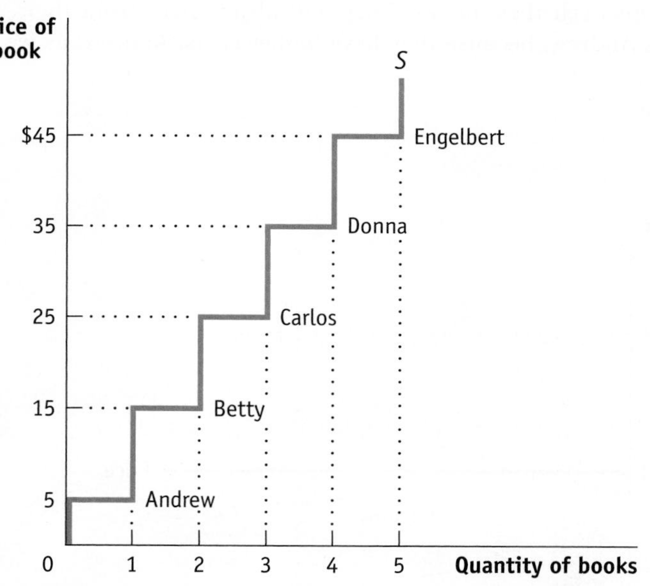

Potential sellers	Cost
Andrew	$5
Betty	15
Carlos	25
Donna	35
Engelbert	45

The supply curve illustrates sellers' cost, the lowest price at which a potential seller is willing to sell the good, and the quantity supplied at that price. Each of the five students has one book to sell and each has a different cost, as indicated in the accompanying table. At a price of $5 the quantity supplied is one (Andrew), at $15 it is two (Andrew and Betty), and so on until you reach $45, the price at which all five students are willing to sell.

Total producer surplus in a market is the sum of the individual producer surpluses of all the sellers of a good in a market.

Economists use the term **producer surplus** to refer both to individual and to total producer surplus.

As in the case of consumer surplus, we can add the individual producer surpluses of sellers to calculate the **total producer surplus,** the total net gain to all sellers in the market. Economists use the term **producer surplus** to refer to either total or individual producer surplus. Table 11-2 shows the net gain to each of the students who would sell a used book at a price of \$30: \$25 for Andrew, \$15 for Betty, and \$5 for Carlos. The total producer surplus is \$25 + \$15 + \$5 = \$45.

TABLE 11-2

Producer Surplus When the Price of a Used Textbook = \$30

Potential seller	Cost	Price received	Individual producer surplus = Price received – Price Cost
Andrew	\$ 5	\$30	\$25
Betty	15	30	15
Carlos	25	30	5
Donna	35	—	—
Engelbert	45	—	—
All sellers			**Total producer surplus = \$45**

As with consumer surplus, the producer surplus gained by those who sell books can be represented graphically. Figure 11-7 reproduces the supply curve from Figure 11-6. Each step in that supply curve is one book wide and represents one seller. The height of Andrew's step is \$5, his cost. This forms the bottom of a rectangle, with \$30, the price he actually receives for his book, forming the top. The area of this rectangle, (\$30 – \$5) × 1 = \$25, is his producer surplus. So the producer surplus Andrew gains from selling his book is the *area of the dark red rectangle* shown in the figure.

Let's assume that the campus bookstore is willing to buy all the used copies of this book that students are willing to sell at a price of \$30. Then, in addition to Andrew, Betty and Carlos will also sell their books. They will also benefit from their sales, though not as much as Andrew, because they have higher costs. Andrew, as we have

FIGURE 11-7 Producer Surplus in the Used-Textbook Market

At a price of \$30, Andrew, Betty, and Carlos each sell a book but Donna and Engelbert do not. Andrew, Betty, and Carlos get individual producer surpluses equal to the difference between the price and their cost, illustrated here by the shaded rectangles. Donna and Engelbert each have a cost that is greater than the price of \$30, so they are unwilling to sell a book and so receive zero producer surplus. The total producer surplus is given by the entire shaded area, the sum of the individual producer surpluses of Andrew, Betty, and Carlos, equal to \$25 + \$15 + \$5 = \$45.

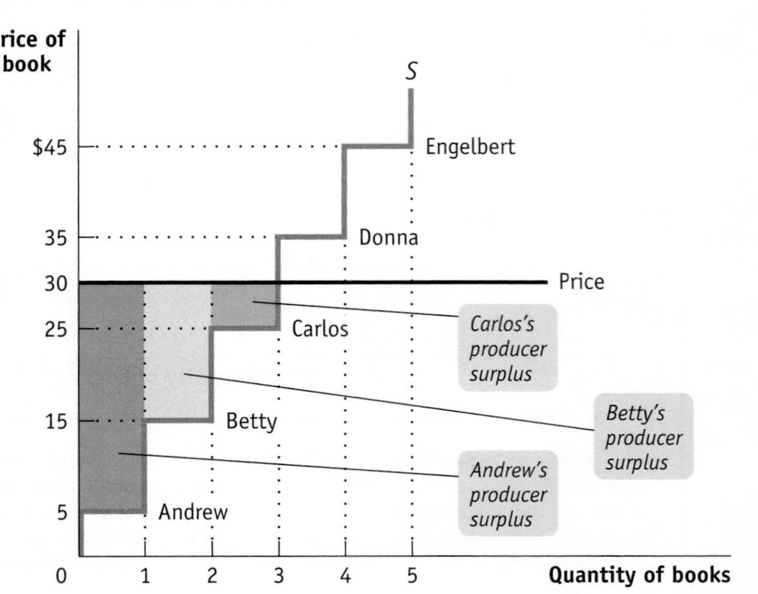

seen, gains $25. Betty gains a smaller amount: since her cost is $15, she gains only $15. Carlos gains even less, only $5.

Again, as with consumer surplus, we have a general rule for determining the total producer surplus from sales of a good: *The total producer surplus from sales of a good at a given price is the area above the supply curve but below that price.*

This rule applies both to examples like the one shown in Figure 11-7, where there are a small number of producers and a step-shaped supply curve, and to more realistic examples, where there are many producers and the supply curve is more or less smooth.

Consider, for example, the supply of wheat. Figure 11-8 shows how producer surplus depends on the price per bushel. Suppose that, as shown in the figure, the price is $5 per bushel and farmers supply 1 million bushels. What is the benefit to the farmers from selling their wheat at a price of $5? Their producer surplus is equal to the shaded area in the figure—the area above the supply curve but below the price of $5 per bushel.

FIGURE 11-8 **Producer Surplus**

Here is the supply curve for wheat. At a price of $5 per bushel, farmers supply 1 million bushels. The producer surplus at this price is equal to the shaded area: the area above the supply curve but below the price. This is the total gain to producers—farmers in this case—from supplying their product when the price is $5.

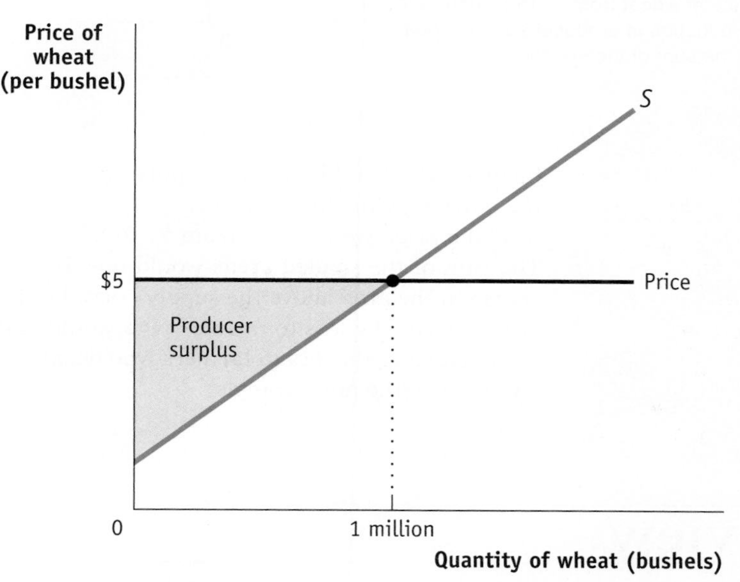

How Changing Prices Affect Producer Surplus

As in the case of consumer surplus, a change in price alters producer surplus. However, although a fall in price increases consumer surplus, it reduces producer surplus. Similarly, a rise in price reduces consumer surplus but increases producer surplus.

To see this, let's first consider a rise in the price of the good. Producers of the good will experience an increase in producer surplus, though not all producers gain the same amount. Some producers would have produced the good even at the original price; they will gain the entire price increase on every unit they produce. Other producers will enter the market because of the higher price; they will gain only the difference between the new price and their cost.

Figure 11-9 is the supply counterpart of Figure 11-5. It shows the effect on producer surplus of a rise in the price of wheat from $5 to $7 per bushel. The increase in producer surplus is the sum of the shaded areas, which consists of two parts. First, there is a red rectangle corresponding to the gains to those farmers who would have supplied wheat even at the original $5 price. Second, there is an additional pink triangle that corresponds to the gains to those

A rise in price reduces consumer surplus but increases producer surplus.

Stockbyte

FIGURE 11-9 A Rise in the Price Increases Producer Surplus

A rise in the price of wheat from $5 to $7 leads to an increase in the quantity supplied and an increase in producer surplus. The change in total producer surplus is given by the sum of the shaded areas: the total area above the supply curve but between the old and new prices. The red area represents the gain to the farmers who would have supplied 1 million bushels at the original price of $5; they each receive an increase in producer surplus of $2 for each of those bushels. The triangular pink area represents the increase in producer surplus achieved by the farmers who supply the additional 500,000 bushels because of the higher price. Similarly, a fall in the price of wheat from $7 to $5 generates a reduction in producer surplus equal to the sum of the shaded areas.

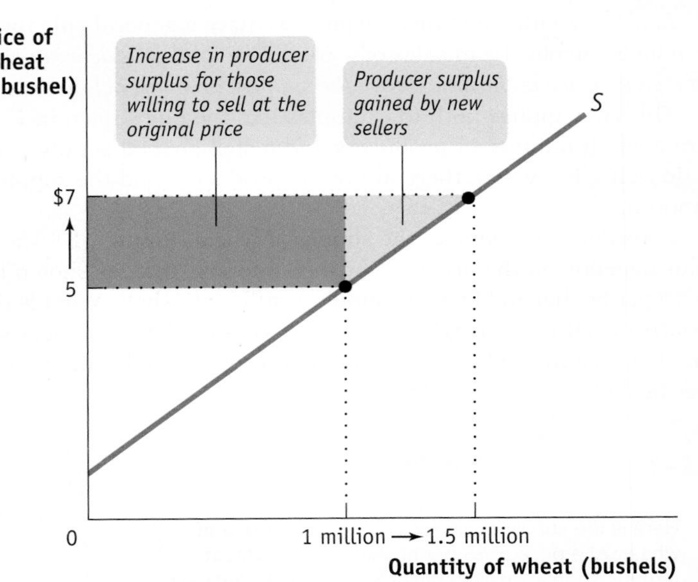

farmers who would not have supplied wheat at the original price but are drawn into the market by the higher price.

If the price were to fall from $7 to $5 per bushel, the story would run in reverse. The sum of the shaded areas would now be the decline in producer surplus, the decrease in the area above the supply curve but below the price. The loss would consist of two parts, the loss to farmers who would still grow wheat at a price of $5 (the red rectangle) and the loss to farmers who decide to no longer grow wheat because of the lower price (the pink triangle).

MODULE 11 Review

Solutions appear at the back of the book.

Check Your Understanding

1. Consider the market for cheese-stuffed jalapeno peppers. There are two consumers, Casey and Josey, and their willingness to pay for each pepper is given in the accompanying table. (Neither is willing to consume more than 4 peppers at any price.) Use the table (i) to construct the demand schedule for peppers for prices of $0.00, $0.10, and so on, up to $0.90, and (ii) to calculate the total consumer surplus when the price of a pepper is $0.40.

Quantity of peppers	Casey's willingness to pay	Josey's willingness to pay
1st pepper	$0.90	$0.80
2nd pepper	0.70	0.60
3rd pepper	0.50	0.40
4th pepper	0.30	0.30

2. Again consider the market for cheese-stuffed jalapeno peppers. There are two producers, Cara and Jamie, and their costs of producing each pepper are given in the accompanying table. (Neither is willing to produce more than 4 peppers at any price.) Use the table (i) to construct the supply schedule for peppers for prices of $0.00, $0.10, and so on, up to $0.90, and (ii) to calculate the total producer surplus when the price of a pepper is $0.70.

Quantity of peppers	Cara's cost	Jamie's cost
1st pepper	$0.10	$0.30
2nd pepper	0.10	0.50
3rd pepper	0.40	0.70
4th pepper	0.60	0.90

Multiple-Choice Questions

1. Refer to the following graph. What is the value of consumer surplus when the market price is $40?

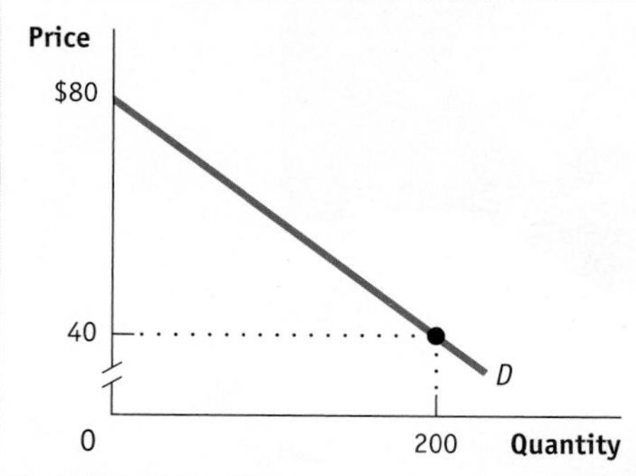

a. $400
b. $800
c. $4,000
d. $8,000
e. $16,000

2. Refer to the graph below. What is the value of producer surplus when the market price is $60?

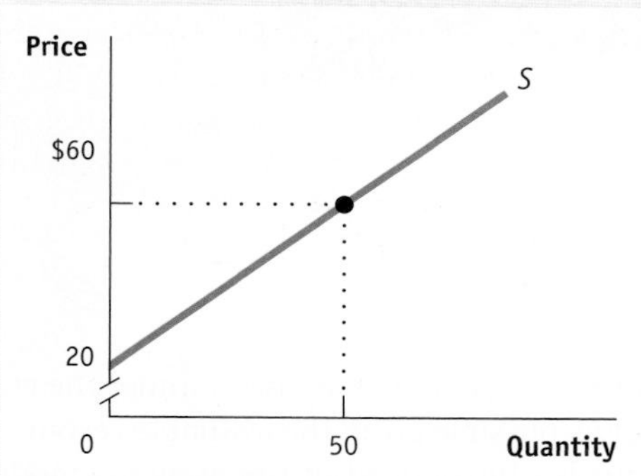

a. $100
b. $150
c. $1,000
d. $1,500
e. $3,000

3. Other things equal, a rise in price will result in which of the following?
   a. Producer surplus will rise; consumer surplus will rise.
   b. Producer surplus will fall; consumer surplus will fall.
   c. Producer surplus will rise; consumer surplus will fall.
   d. Producer surplus will fall; consumer surplus will rise.
   e. Producer surplus will not change; consumer surplus will rise.

4. Consumer surplus is found as the area
   a. above the supply curve and below the price.
   b. below the demand curve and above the price.
   c. above the demand curve and below the price.
   d. below the supply curve and above the price.
   e. below the supply curve and above the demand curve.

5. Allocating kidneys to those with the highest net benefit (where net benefit is measured as the expected increase in life span from a transplant) is an attempt to maximize
   a. consumer surplus.
   b. producer surplus.
   c. profit.
   d. equity.
   e. respect for elders.

Critical-Thinking Question

Draw a correctly labeled graph showing a competitive market in equilibrium. On your graph, clearly indicate and label the area of consumer surplus and the area of producer surplus.

MODULE 12

Efficiency and Markets

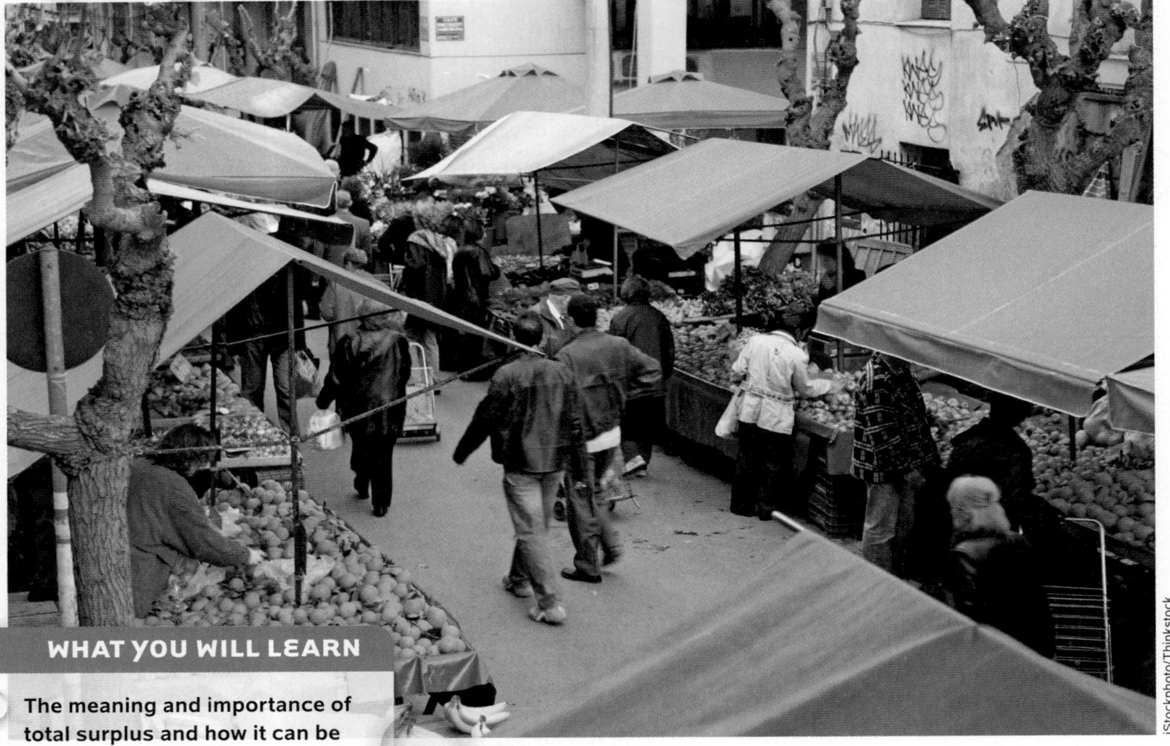

iStockphoto/Thinkstock

WHAT YOU WILL LEARN

1. The meaning and importance of total surplus and how it can be used to illustrate efficiency in markets
2. Why property rights and prices as economic signals are critical to the smooth functioning of a market
3. Why markets typically lead to efficient outcomes despite the fact that they sometimes fail

Consumer Surplus, Producer Surplus, and Efficiency

Markets are a remarkably effective way to organize economic activity: under the right conditions, they can make society as well off as possible given the available resources. The concepts of consumer and producer surplus introduced in the previous module can help us deepen our understanding of why this is so.

The Gains from Trade

Let's return to the market for used textbooks, but now consider a much bigger market—say, one at a large state university. There are many potential buyers and sellers, so the market is competitive. Let's line up incoming students who are potential buyers of a book in order of their willingness to pay, so that the entering student with the highest willingness to pay is potential buyer number 1, the student with the next highest willingness to pay is number 2, and so on. Then we can use their willingness to pay to derive a demand curve like the one in Figure 12-1.

Similarly, we can line up outgoing students, who are potential sellers of the book, in order of their cost, starting with the student with the lowest cost, then the student with the next lowest cost, and so on, to derive a supply curve like the one shown in the same figure.

As we have drawn the curves, the market reaches equilibrium at a price of $30 per book, and 1,000 books are bought and sold at that price. The two shaded triangles show the consumer surplus (blue) and the producer surplus (red) generated by this market. The sum of consumer and producer surplus is known as **total surplus.**

Total surplus is the total net gain to consumers and producers from trading in a market. It is the sum of producer and consumer surplus.

The striking thing about this picture is that both consumers and producers gain—that is, both consumers and producers are better off because there is a market for

FIGURE 12-1 Total Surplus

In the market for used textbooks, the equilibrium price is $30 and the equilibrium quantity is 1,000 books. Consumer surplus is given by the blue area, the area below the demand curve but above the price. Producer surplus is given by the red area, the area above the supply curve but below the price. The sum of the blue and the red areas is total surplus, the total benefit to society from the production and consumption of the good.

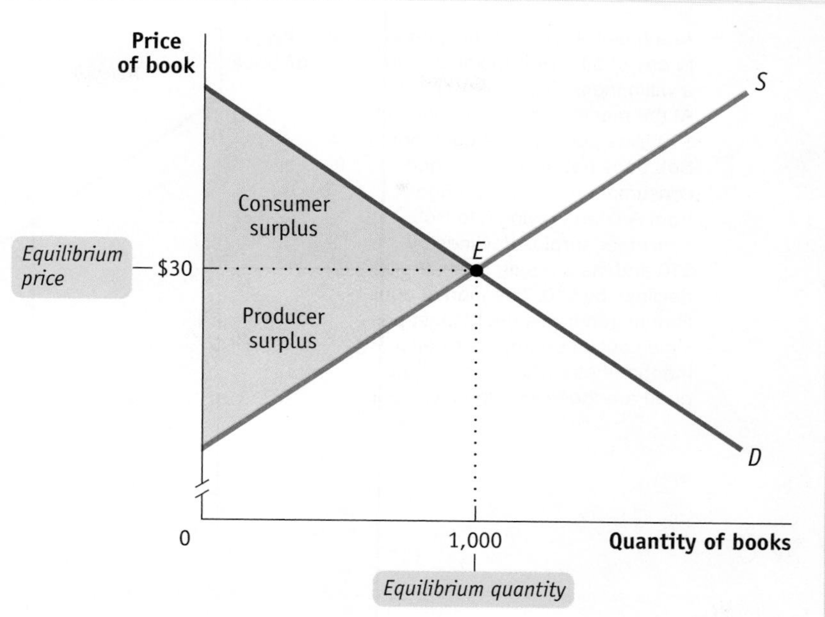

this good. But this should come as no surprise—because *there are gains from trade.* These gains from trade are the reason everyone is better off participating in a market economy than they would be if each individual tried to be self-sufficient.

But are we as well off as we could be? This brings us to the question of the efficiency of markets.

The Efficiency of Markets

A market is *efficient* if, once the market has produced its gains from trade, there is no way to make some people better off without making other people worse off. Note that market equilibrium is just *one* way of deciding who consumes a good and who sells a good. To better understand how markets promote efficiency, let's examine some alternatives.

Consider the example of kidney transplants discussed earlier in the Economics in Action in Module 11 (p. 108). There is not a market for kidneys, and available kidneys currently go to whoever has been on the waiting list the longest. Of course, those who have been waiting the longest aren't necessarily those who would benefit the most from a new kidney.

Similarly, imagine a committee charged with improving on the market equilibrium by deciding who gets and who gives up a used textbook. The committee's ultimate goal would be to bypass the market outcome and come up with another arrangement that would increase total surplus.

Let's consider three approaches the committee could take:

1. It could reallocate consumption among consumers.
2. It could reallocate sales among sellers.
3. It could change the quantity traded.

REALLOCATE CONSUMPTION AMONG CONSUMERS The committee might try to increase total surplus by selling books to different consumers. Figure 12-2 shows why this will result in lower surplus compared to the market equilibrium outcome. Points *A* and *B* show the positions on the demand curve of two potential buyers of used books, Ana and Bob. As we can see from the figure, Ana is willing to pay $35 for a

FIGURE 12-2 Reallocating Consumption Lowers Consumer Surplus

Ana (point *A*) has a willingness to pay of $35. Bob (point *B*) has a willingness to pay of only $25. At the market equilibrium price of $30, Ana purchases a book but Bob does not. If we rearrange consumption by taking a book from Ana and giving it to Bob, consumer surplus declines by $10 and, as a result, total surplus declines by $10. The market equilibrium generates the highest possible consumer surplus by ensuring that those who consume the good are those who most value it.

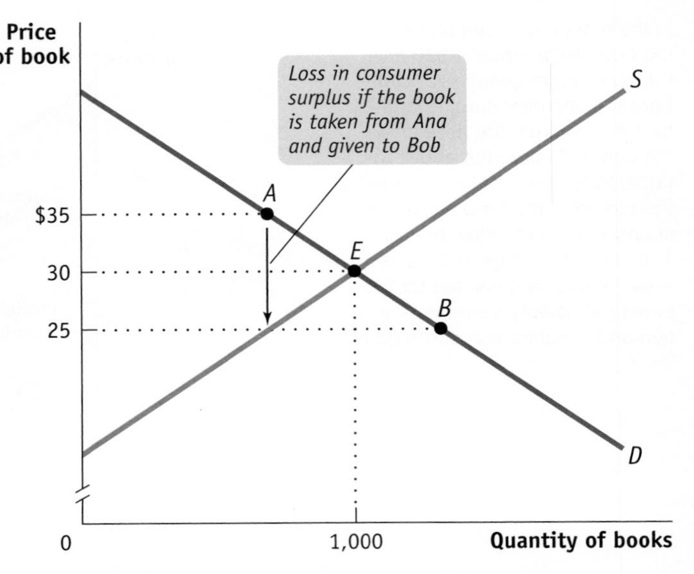

book, but Bob is willing to pay only $25. Since the market equilibrium price is $30, under the market outcome Ana gets a book and Bob does not.

Now suppose the committee reallocates consumption. This would mean taking the book away from Ana and giving it to Bob. Since the book is worth $35 to Ana but only $25 to Bob, this change *reduces total consumer surplus* by $35 – $25 = $10. Moreover, this result doesn't depend on which two students we pick. Every student who buys a book at the market equilibrium price has a willingness to pay of $30 or more, and every student who doesn't buy a book has a willingness to pay of less than $30. So reallocating the good among consumers always means taking a book away from a student who values it more and giving it to one who values it less. This necessarily reduces total consumer surplus.

REALLOCATE SALES AMONG SELLERS The committee might try to increase total surplus by altering who sells their books, taking sales away from sellers who would have sold their books in the market equilibrium and instead compelling those who would not have sold their books in the market equilibrium to sell them.

Figure 12-3 shows why this will result in lower surplus. Here points *X* and *Y* show the positions on the supply curve of Xavier, who has a cost of $25, and Yvonne, who has a cost of $35. At the equilibrium market price of $30, Xavier would sell his book but Yvonne would not sell hers. If the committee reallocated sales, forcing Xavier to keep his book and Yvonne to sell hers, total producer surplus would be reduced by $35 – $25 = $10.

Again, it doesn't matter which two students we choose. Any student who sells a book at the market equilibrium price has a lower cost than any student who keeps a book. So reallocating sales among sellers necessarily increases total cost and reduces total producer surplus.

CHANGE THE QUANTITY TRADED The committee might try to increase total surplus by compelling students to trade either more books or fewer books than the market equilibrium quantity.

Figure 12-4 shows why this will result in lower surplus. It shows all four students: potential buyers Ana and Bob, and potential sellers Xavier and Yvonne. To reduce sales, the committee will have to prevent a transaction that would have occurred in the market equilibrium—that is,

Viktor Cap/Alamy

FIGURE 12-3 **Reallocating Sales Lowers Producer Surplus**

Yvonne (point Y) has a cost of $35, $10 more than Xavier (point X), who has a cost of $25. At the market equilibrium price of $30, Xavier sells a book but Yvonne does not. If we rearrange sales by preventing Xavier from selling his book and compelling Yvonne to sell hers, producer surplus declines by $10 and, as a result, total surplus declines by $10. The market equilibrium generates the highest possible producer surplus by assuring that those who sell the good are those who most value the right to sell it.

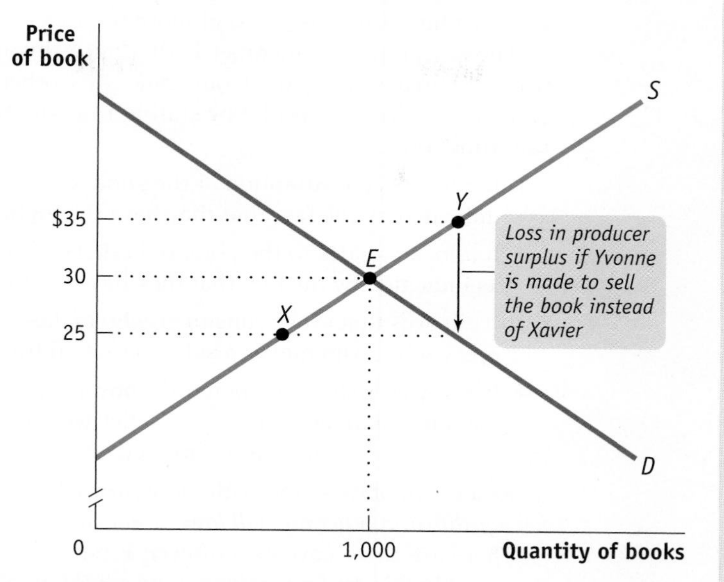

prevent Xavier from selling to Ana. Since Ana is willing to pay $35 and Xavier's cost is $25, preventing this transaction reduces total surplus by $35 – $25 = $10.

Once again, this result doesn't depend on which two students we pick: any student who would have sold the book in the market equilibrium has a cost of $30 or less, and any student who would have purchased the book in the market equilibrium has a willingness to pay of $30 or more. So preventing any sale that would have occurred in the market equilibrium necessarily reduces total surplus.

Finally, the committee might try to increase sales by forcing Yvonne, who would not have sold her book in the market equilibrium, to sell it to someone like Bob, who would not have bought a book in the market equilibrium. Because Yvonne's cost is $35, but Bob is only willing to pay $25, this transaction reduces total surplus by $10.

FIGURE 12-4 **Changing the Quantity Lowers Total Surplus**

If Xavier (point X) were prevented from selling his book to someone like Ana (point A), total surplus would fall by $10, the difference between Ana's willingness to pay ($35) and Xavier's cost ($25). This means that total surplus falls whenever fewer than 1,000 books—the equilibrium quantity—are transacted. Likewise, if Yvonne (point Y) were compelled to sell her book to someone like Bob (point B), total surplus would also fall by $10, the difference between Yvonne's cost ($35) and Bob's willingness to pay ($25). This means that total surplus falls whenever more than 1,000 books are transacted. These two examples show that at market equilibrium, all mutually beneficial transactions—and only mutually beneficial transactions—occur.

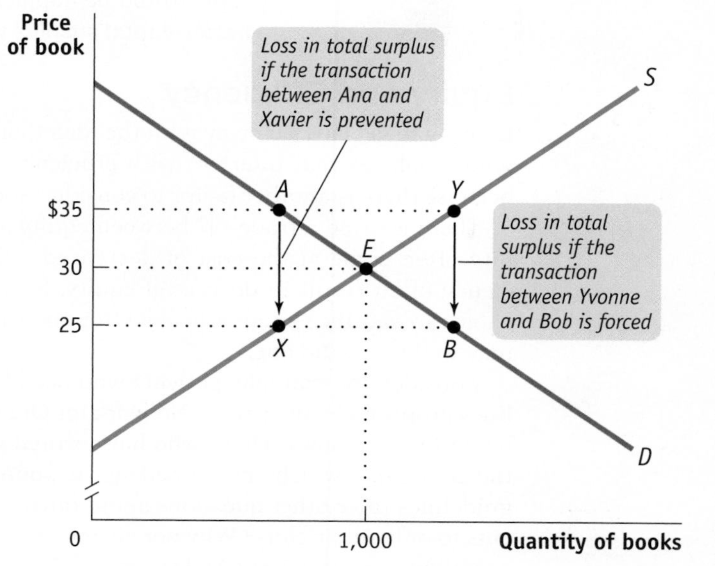

And once again it doesn't matter which two students we pick—anyone who wouldn't have bought the book has a willingness to pay of less than $30, and anyone who wouldn't have sold has a cost of more than $30.

The key point to remember is that once this market is in equilibrium, there is no way to increase the gains from trade. Any other outcome reduces total surplus. We can summarize our results by stating that an efficient market performs four important functions:

1. It allocates consumption of the good to the potential buyers who most value it, as indicated by the fact that they have the highest willingness to pay.
2. It allocates sales to the potential sellers who most value the right to sell the good, as indicated by the fact that they have the lowest cost.
3. It ensures that every consumer who makes a purchase values the good more than every seller who makes a sale, so that all transactions are mutually beneficial.
4. It ensures that every potential buyer who doesn't make a purchase values the good less than every potential seller who doesn't make a sale, so that no mutually beneficial transactions are missed.

As a result of these four functions, *any way of allocating the good other than the market equilibrium outcome will lower total surplus.*

There are three caveats, however. First, although a market may be efficient, it isn't necessarily *fair.* In fact, fairness, or *equity,* is often in conflict with efficiency. We'll discuss this next.

The second caveat is that markets sometimes *fail.* Under some well-defined conditions, markets can fail to deliver efficiency. When this occurs, markets no longer maximize total surplus. We'll take a closer look at market failures in later modules.

iStockphoto

Third, even when the market equilibrium maximizes total surplus, this does not mean that it results in the best outcome for every *individual* consumer and producer. Other things equal, each buyer would like to pay a lower price and each seller would like to receive a higher price. So if the government were to intervene in the market—say, by lowering the price below the equilibrium price to make consumers happy or by raising the price above the equilibrium price to make producers happy—the outcome would no longer be efficient. Although some people would be happier, society as a whole would be worse off because total surplus would be lower.

Equity and Efficiency

It's easy to get carried away with the idea that markets are always good and that economic policies that interfere with efficiency are bad. But that would be misguided because there is another factor to consider: society cares about equity, or what's "fair."

There is often a trade-off between equity and efficiency: policies that promote equity often come at the cost of decreased efficiency, and policies that promote efficiency often result in decreased equity. So it's important to realize that a society's choice to sacrifice some efficiency for the sake of equity, however it defines equity, may well be a valid one.

Consider, for example, patients who need kidney transplants. For them, the guidelines proposed by the United Network for Organ Sharing (UNOS), covered earlier, will be unwelcome news. Those who have waited years for a transplant will no doubt find the guidelines, which give precedence to younger patients, . . . well . . . unfair. And the guidelines raise other questions about fairness: Why limit potential transplant recipients to only Americans? Why not give precedence to those who have made recognized contributions to society? And so on.

The point is that efficiency is about *how to achieve goals, not what those goals should be.* For example, UNOS decided that its goal is to maximize the life span of kidney recipients. Some might have argued for a different goal, and efficiency does not address which goal is the best. *What efficiency does address is the best way to achieve a goal once it has been determined.*

It's important to understand that fairness, unlike efficiency, can be very hard to define. Fairness is a concept about which well-intentioned people often disagree.

Property rights are the rights of owners of valuable items, whether resources or goods, to dispose of those items as they choose.

An **economic signal** is any piece of information that helps people make better economic decisions.

A Market Economy

As we learned earlier, in a market economy decisions about production and consumption are made via markets. In fact, the economy as a whole is made up of many *interrelated markets*. Up until now, to learn how markets work, we've been examining a single market—the market for used textbooks. But in reality, consumers and producers do not make decisions in isolated markets. For example, a student's decision in the market for used textbooks might be affected by how much interest must be paid on a student loan; thus, the decision in the used-textbook market would be influenced by what is going on in the market for money.

We know that an efficient market equilibrium maximizes total surplus—the gains to buyers and sellers in that market. Is there a comparable result for an economy as a whole, an economy composed of a vast number of individual markets? The answer is yes, but with qualifications.

When each and every market in the economy maximizes total surplus, then the economy as a whole is efficient. This is a very important result: just as it is impossible to make someone better off without making other people worse off in a single market when it is efficient, the same is true when each and every market in that economy is efficient. However, it is virtually impossible to find an economy in which every market is efficient.

For now, let's examine why markets and market economies typically work so well. Once we understand why, we can then briefly address why markets sometimes get it wrong.

Why Markets Typically Work So Well

Economists have written volumes about why markets are an effective way to organize an economy. In the end, well-functioning markets owe their effectiveness to two powerful features: *property rights* and the role of prices as *economic signals*.

Property rights are a system in which valuable items in the economy have specific owners who can dispose of them as they choose. In a system of property rights, by purchasing a good you receive "ownership rights": the right to use and dispose of the good as you see fit. Property rights are what make the mutually beneficial transactions in the used-textbook market, or any market, possible.

To see why property rights are crucial, imagine that students do not have full property rights in their textbooks and are prohibited from reselling them when the semester ends. This restriction on property rights would prevent many mutually beneficial transactions. Some students would be stuck with textbooks they will never reread when they would be much happier receiving some cash instead. Other students would be forced to pay full price for brand-new books when they would be happier getting slightly battered copies at a lower price.

Once a system of well-defined property rights is in place, the second necessary feature of well-functioning markets—prices as economic signals—can operate. An **economic signal** is any piece of information that helps people make better economic

Price is the most important economic signal in a market economy.

Lifesize/Thinkstock

A market or an economy is **inefficient** if there are missed opportunities: some people could be made better off without making other people worse off.

Market failure occurs when a market fails to be efficient.

decisions. For example, business forecasters say that sales of cardboard boxes are a good early indicator of changes in industrial production: if businesses are buying lots of cardboard boxes, you can be sure that they will soon increase their production.

But prices are far and away the most important signals in a market economy, because they convey essential information about other people's costs and their willingness to pay. If the equilibrium price of used books is $30, this in effect tells everyone both that there are consumers willing to pay $30 and up and that there are potential sellers with a cost of $30 or less. The signal given by the market price ensures that total surplus is maximized by telling people whether to buy books, sell books, or do nothing at all.

This example shows that the market price "signals" to consumers with a willingness to pay equal to or more than the market price that they should buy the good, just as it signals to producers with a cost equal to or less than the market price that they should sell the good. And since, in equilibrium, the quantity demanded equals the quantity supplied, all willing consumers will find willing sellers.

Prices can sometimes fail as economic signals. Sometimes a price is not an accurate indicator of how desirable a good is. For example, you can't infer from the price alone whether a used car is good or a "lemon."

Why Markets Can Sometimes Get It Wrong

Although markets are an amazingly effective way to organize economic activity, as we've noted, markets can sometimes get it wrong—they can be *inefficient.* When markets are **inefficient,** there are missed opportunities—ways in which production or consumption can be rearranged that would make some people better off without making other people worse off. In other words, there are gains from trade that go unrealized: total surplus could be increased.

Markets can be inefficient for a number of reasons. Two of the most important are a lack of property rights and inaccuracy of prices as economic signals. When a market is inefficient, we have what is known as **market failure.** We will examine various types of market failure in later modules. For now, let's review the three main ways in which markets sometimes fall short of efficiency.

1. Markets can fail when, in an attempt to capture more surplus, one party prevents mutually beneficial trades from occurring. This situation arises, for instance, when a market contains only a single seller of a good, known as a *monopolist.* A monopolist creates inefficiency by manipulating the market price to increase profits.
2. Actions of individuals sometimes have side effects on the welfare of others that markets don't take into account. In economics, these side effects are known as *externalities*, and the best-known example is pollution. We can think of pollution as a problem of incomplete property rights; for example, existing property rights don't guarantee a right to ownership of clean air. Pollution and other externalities also give rise to inefficiency.
3. Markets for some goods fail because these goods, by their very nature, are unsuited for efficient management by markets. Falling into this category are goods for which some people possess information that others don't have. For example, the seller of a used car that is a "lemon" may have information that is unknown to potential buyers. Also in this category are goods for which there are problems limiting people's access to and consumption of the good; examples are fish in the sea and trees in the Amazonian rain forest. In these instances, markets generally fail due to incomplete property rights.

But even with these limitations, it's remarkable how well markets work at maximizing the gains from trade.

MODULE 12 Review

Solutions appear at the back of the book.

Check Your Understanding

1. Using the tables in Check Your Understanding in the preceding module, find the equilibrium price and quantity in the market for cheese-stuffed jalapeno peppers. What is the total surplus in the equilibrium in this market, and who receives it?

2. Using your answers from the previous question, show how each of the following three actions reduces total surplus:

   a. Having Josey consume one fewer pepper, and Casey one more pepper, than in the market equilibrium

   b. Having Cara produce one fewer pepper, and Jamie one more pepper, than in the market equilibrium

   c. Having Josey consume one fewer pepper, and Cara produce one fewer pepper, than in the market equilibrium

3. Suppose that in the market for used textbooks the equilibrium price is $30 but it is mistakenly announced that the equilibrium price is $300. How does this mistake affect the efficiency of the market?

Multiple-Choice Questions

1. At market equilibrium in a competitive market, which of the following is necessarily true?

   I. Consumer surplus is maximized.
   II. Producer surplus is maximized.
   III. Total surplus is maximized.

   a. I only
   b. II only
   c. III only
   d. I and II only
   e. I, II, and III

2. When a competitive market is in equilibrium, total surplus can be increased by

   I. reallocating consumption among consumers.
   II. reallocating sales among sellers.
   III. changing the quantity traded.

   a. I only
   b. II only
   c. III only
   d. I, II, and III
   e. None of the above

3. Which of the following is true regarding equity and efficiency in competitive markets?

   a. Competitive markets ensure equity and efficiency.
   b. There is often a trade-off between equity and efficiency.
   c. Competitive markets lead to neither equity nor efficiency.
   d. There is generally agreement about the level of equity and efficiency in a market.
   e. None of the above.

4. What features are essential to well-functioning markets?

   I. A system of property rights
   II. Externalities
   III. Economic signals

   a. I only
   b. II only
   c. III only
   d. I and III only
   e. I, II, and III

5. Which of the following is an example of the failure of a system of property rights to assign ownership to the appropriate party?

   I. The ability of one student to sell a used textbook to another student.
   II. The ability of some fishermen to fish as much as they wish in open waters
   III. The ability of a car salesman to make a sale to an interested buyer.

   a. I only
   b. II only
   c. I and ll only
   d. III only
   e. I, II, and III

Critical-Thinking Questions

1. Suppose UNOS alters its proposed guidelines for allocating donated kidneys to give preference to patients with young children, no longer relying solely on the concept of "net benefit." If total surplus in this case is defined as the total life span of kidney recipients, is this new guideline likely to reduce, increase, or leave total surplus unchanged? How might you justify this new guideline?

2. What is wrong with the following statement? "Markets are always the best way to organize economic activity. Any policies that interfere with markets reduce society's welfare."

BUSINESS CASE: StubHub Shows Up The Boss

Back in 1965, long before Ticketmaster, StubHub, and TicketsNow, legendary rock music promoter Bill Graham noticed that mass parties erupted wherever local rock groups played. Graham realized that fans would pay for the experience of the concert, in addition to paying for a recording of the music. He went on to create the business of rock concert promoting—booking and managing multicity tours for bands and selling lots of tickets. Those tickets were carefully rationed, a single purchaser allowed to buy only a limited number. Fans would line up at box offices, sometimes camping out the night before for popular bands.

AP Photo/Jason DeCrow

Wanting to maintain the aura of the 1960s that made rock concerts accessible to all their fans, many top bands choose to price their tickets below the market equilibrium level. For example, in 2009 Bruce Springsteen sold tickets at his concerts in New Jersey (his home state and home to his most ardent fans) for between $65 and $95. Tickets for Springsteen concerts could have sold for far more: economists Alan Krueger and Marie Connolly analyzed a 2002 Springsteen concert for which every ticket sold for $75 and concluded that The Boss forfeited about $4 million by not charging the market price, about $280 at the time.

So what was The Boss thinking? Cheap tickets can ensure that a concert sells out, making it a better experience for both band and audience. But it is believed that other factors are at work—that cheap tickets are a way for a band to reward fans' loyalty as well as a means to seem more "authentic" and less commercial. As Bruce Springsteen has said, "In some fashion, I help people hold on to their own humanity—if I'm doing my job right."

But the rise of the Internet has made things much more complicated. Now, rather than line up for tickets at the venue, fans buy tickets online, either from a direct seller like Ticketmaster (which obtains tickets directly from the concert producer) or a reseller like StubHub or TicketsNow. Resellers (otherwise known as scalpers) can—and do—make lots of money by scooping up large numbers of tickets at the box office price and reselling them at the market price. StubHub, for example, made $1 billion in the resale market for tickets in 2010.

This practice has infuriated fans as well as the bands. But resellers have cast the issue as one of the freedom to dispose of one's ticket as one chooses. In recent years, both sides—bands and their fans versus ticket resellers—have been lobbying government officials to shape ticket-reselling laws to their advantage.

Questions for Thought

1. Using the concepts of consumer surplus and producer surplus, draw a diagram to illustrate the exchange between The Boss and his fans. Explain your findings. (Hint: ticket supply is perfectly inelastic.)
2. How has the rise of Internet resellers changed the allocation of surplus between The Boss and his fans?
3. Using your diagram from the the first question, explain the effect of resellers on the allocation of consumer surplus and producer surplus in the market for concert tickets. What are the implications of the Internet for all such exchanges?

SECTION 4 REVIEW

Summary

Consumer and Producer Surplus

1. The **willingness to pay** of each individual consumer determines the shape of the demand curve. When price is less than or equal to the willingness to pay, the potential consumer purchases the good. The difference between willingness to pay and price is the net gain to the consumer, the **individual consumer surplus.**
2. **Total consumer surplus** in a market, which is the sum of all individual consumer surpluses in a market, is equal to the area below the market demand curve but above the price. A rise in the price of a good reduces consumer surplus; a fall in the price increases consumer surplus. The term **consumer surplus** is often used to refer to both individual and total consumer surplus.
3. The **cost** of each potential producer of a good, the lowest price at which he or she is willing to supply a unit of that good, determines the supply curve. If the price of a good is above a producer's cost, a sale generates a net gain to the producer, known as the **individual producer surplus.**
4. **Total producer surplus** in a market, the sum of the individual producer surpluses in a market, is equal to the area above the market supply curve but below the price. A rise in the price of a good increases producer surplus; a fall in the price reduces producer surplus. The term **producer surplus** is often used to refer to both individual and total producer surplus.

Efficiency and Markets

5. **Total surplus,** the total gain to society from the production and consumption of a good, is the sum of consumer and producer surplus.
6. Usually, markets are efficient and achieve the maximum total surplus. Any possible reallocation of consumption or sales, or change in the quantity bought and sold, reduces total surplus. However, society also cares about equity. So government intervention in a market that reduces efficiency but increases equity can be a valid choice by society.
7. An economy composed of efficient markets is also efficient, although this is virtually impossible to achieve in reality. The keys to the efficiency of a market economy are **property rights** and the operation of prices as **economic signals.**
8. Under certain conditions, **market failure** occurs, making a market **inefficient.** There are three principal sources of market failure: attempts to capture more surplus that create inefficiencies, side effects of some transactions, and problems in the nature of the good.

Key Terms

Willingness to pay, p. 103
Individual consumer surplus, p. 104
Total consumer surplus, p. 104
Consumer surplus, p. 104
Cost, p. 108
Individual producer surplus, p. 109
Total producer surplus, p. 110
Producer surplus, p. 110
Total surplus, p. 114
Property rights, p. 119
Economic signal, p. 119
Inefficiency, p. 120
Market failure, p. 120

Problems

1. Determine the amount of consumer surplus generated in each of the following situations.

   a. Leon goes to the clothing store to buy a new T-shirt, for which he is willing to pay up to $10. He picks out one he likes with a price tag of exactly $10. When he is paying for it, he learns that the T-shirt has been discounted by 50%.

   b. Alberto goes online to the iTunes store hoping to find Mumford & Son's new album, and is willing to pay up to $12. He sees that iTunes is selling the album for $11.99, so he purchases it.

   c. After soccer practice, Stacey is willing to pay $2 for a bottle of mineral water. The 7-Eleven sells mineral water for $2.25 per bottle, so she declines to purchase it.

2. Determine the amount of producer surplus generated in each of the following situations.

a. Gordon lists his old Lionel electric trains on eBay. He sets a minimum acceptable price, known as his *reserve price,* of $75. After five days of bidding, the final high bid is exactly $75. He accepts the bid.

b. So-Hee advertises her car for sale in the used-car section of the student newspaper for $2,000, but she is willing to sell the car for any price higher than $1,500. The best offer she gets is $1,200, which she declines.

c. Sanjay likes his job so much that he would be willing to do it for free. However, his annual salary is $80,000.

3. There are six potential consumers of computer games, each willing to buy only one game. Consumer 1 is willing to pay $40 for a computer game, consumer 2 is willing to pay $35, consumer 3 is willing to pay $30, consumer 4 is willing to pay $25, consumer 5 is willing to pay $20, and consumer 6 is willing to pay $15.

a. Suppose the market price is $29. What is the total consumer surplus?

b. The market price decreases to $19. What is the total consumer surplus now?

c. When the price fell from $29 to $19, how much did each consumer's individual consumer surplus change? How does total consumer surplus change?

4. You are the manager of Fun World, a small amusement park. The accompanying diagram shows the demand curve of a typical customer at Fun World.

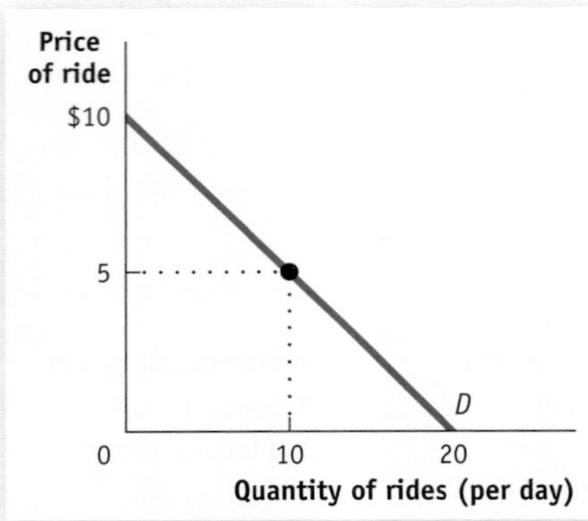

a. Suppose that the price of each ride is $5. At that price, how much consumer surplus does an individual consumer get? (Note that the area of a right triangle is ½ × the height of the triangle × the base of the triangle.)

b. Suppose that Fun World considers charging an admission fee, even though it maintains the price of each ride at $5. What is the maximum admission fee it could charge? (Assume that all potential customers have enough money to pay the fee.)

c. Suppose that Fun World lowered the price of each ride to zero. How much consumer surplus does an individual consumer get? What is the maximum admission fee Fun World could charge?

5. The accompanying diagram illustrates a taxi driver's individual supply curve (assume that each taxi ride is the same distance).

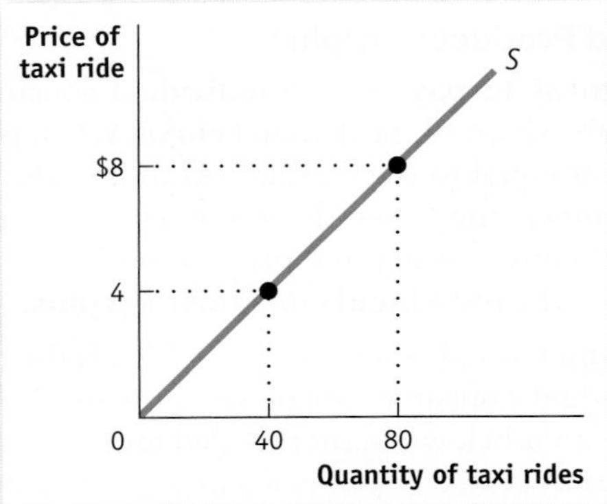

a. Suppose the city sets the price of taxi rides at $4 per ride, and at $4 the taxi driver is able to sell as many taxi rides as he desires. What is this taxi driver's producer surplus? (Note that the area of a right triangle is ½ × the height of the triangle × the base of the triangle.)

b. Suppose that the city keeps the price of a taxi ride set at $4, but it decides to charge taxi drivers a special fee. What is the maximum special fee the city could extract from this taxi driver?

c. Suppose that the city allowed the price of taxi rides to increase to $8 per ride. Again assume that, at this price, the taxi driver sells as many rides as he is willing to offer. How much producer surplus does an individual taxi driver now get? What is the maximum special fee the city could charge this taxi driver?

6. The accompanying table shows the supply and demand schedules for used copies of the second edition of this textbook. The supply schedule is derived from offers at Amazon.com. The demand schedule is hypothetical.

Price of book	Quantity of books demanded	Quantity of books supplied
$55	50	0
60	35	1
65	25	3
70	17	3
75	14	6
80	12	9
85	10	10
90	8	18
95	6	22
100	4	31
105	2	37
110	0	42

a. Calculate consumer and producer surplus at the equilibrium in this market.

b. Now the third edition of this textbook becomes available. As a result, the willingness to pay of each potential buyer for a second-hand copy of the second edition falls by $20. In a table, show the new demand schedule and again calculate consumer and producer surplus at the new equilibrium.

7. Suppose that Hollywood screenwriters negotiate a new agreement with movie producers stipulating that they will receive 10% of the revenue from every video rental of a movie they authored. They have no such agreement for movies shown on on-demand television.

a. When the new writers' agreement comes into effect, what will happen in the market for video rentals—that is, will supply or demand shift, and how? As a result, how will consumer surplus in the market for video rentals change? Illustrate with a diagram. Do you think the writers' agreement will be popular with consumers who rent videos?

b. Consumers consider video rentals and on-demand movies substitutable to some extent. When the new writers' agreement comes into effect, what will happen in the market for on-demand movies—that is, will supply or demand shift, and how? As a result, how will producer surplus in the market for on-demand movies change? Illustrate with a diagram. Do you think the writers' agreement will be popular with cable television companies that show on-demand movies?

8. A few years ago a New York district judge ruled in a copyright infringement lawsuit against the popular file-sharing website LimeWire and in favor of the 13 major record companies that had brought the lawsuit. The record companies, including Sony, Virgin, and Warner Brothers, had alleged that the file-sharing service encourages users to make illegal copies of copyrighted material. Allowing Internet users to obtain music for free limits the record companies' right to give access to their music only to those who have paid for it. In other words, it limits the record companies' property rights.

a. If everyone obtained music and video content for free from websites such as LimeWire, instead of paying the record companies, what would happen to the record companies' producer surplus from music sales? What are the implications for record companies' incentive to produce music content in the future?

b. If the record companies had lost the lawsuit and music could be freely downloaded from the Internet, what do you think would happen to mutually beneficial transactions (the producing and buying of music) in the future?

9. EAuction and EMarketplace are two competing Internet auction sites, where buyers and sellers transact goods. Each auction site earns money by charging sellers for listing their goods. Over time, because EAuction provides much better technical service than its rival, EMarketplace, buyers and sellers come to prefer EAuction. Eventually, EMarketplace closes down, leaving EAuction as the sole provider of this service (it becomes a monopolist). EAuction also owns a site that handles payments over the Internet, called PayForIt. It is competing with another Internet payment site, called PayBuddy. EAuction has now stipulated that any transaction on its auction site must use PayForIt, rather than PayBuddy, for the payment. What is the impact on market efficiency, producer surplus, and consumer surplus from EAuction's position in the market as the only provider of the service?

Module 13: Price Controls (Ceilings and Floors)
Module 14: Quantity Controls (Quotas)
Module 15: Taxes

SECTION 5

Government Policy and Taxes

BIG CITY, NOT-SO-BRIGHT IDEAS

New York City is a place where you can find almost anything—that is, almost anything, except a taxicab when you need one or a decent apartment at a rent you can afford. You might think that New York's notorious shortages of cabs and apartments are the inevitable price of big-city living. However, they are largely the product of government policies—specifically, of government policies that have, in one way or another, tried to prevail over the market forces of supply and demand.

In Section 2, we learned the principle that a market moves to equilibrium—that the market price rises or falls to the level at which the quantity of a good that people are willing to supply is equal to the quantity that other people demand.

But sometimes governments try to defy that principle. Whenever a government tries to dictate either a market price or a market quantity that's different from the equilibrium price or quantity, the market strikes back in predictable ways.

The shortages of apartments and taxicabs in New York are two examples of what happens when the logic of the market is defied. New York's housing shortage is the result of *rent control,* a law that prevents landlords from raising rents except when specifically given permission. Rent control was introduced during World War II to protect the interests of tenants, and it still remains in force. Many other American cities have had rent control at one time or another, but with the notable exceptions of New York and San Francisco, these controls have largely been done away with.

Similarly, New York's limited supply of taxis is the result of a licensing system introduced in the 1930s. New York taxi licenses are known as "medallions," and only taxis with medallions are allowed to pick up passengers. Although this system was originally intended to protect the interests of both drivers and customers, it has generated a shortage of taxis in the city.

In this section, we begin by examining what happens when governments try to control prices in a competitive market, keeping the price in a market either below its equilibrium level—a *price ceiling* such as rent control—or above it—a *price floor* such as the minimum wage paid to workers in many countries. We then turn to schemes such as taxi medallions that attempt to dictate the quantity of a good bought and sold. We conclude with a discussion of what happens when governments tax goods and services.

MODULE 13

Price Controls (Ceilings and Floors)

Thinkstock/Photodisc

WHAT YOU WILL LEARN

1. **The meaning of price controls, one way government intervenes in markets**
2. **How price controls can create problems and make a market inefficient**
3. **Why economists are often deeply skeptical of attempts to intervene in markets**
4. **Who benefits and who loses from price controls, and why they are used despite their well-known problems**

Why Governments Control Prices

As you've learned, a market moves to equilibrium—that is, the market price moves to the level at which the quantity supplied equals the quantity demanded. But this equilibrium price does not necessarily please either buyers or sellers.

After all, buyers would always like to pay less if they could, and sometimes they can make a strong moral or political case that they should pay lower prices. For example, what if the equilibrium between supply and demand for apartments in a major city leads to rental rates that an average working person can't afford? In that case, a government might well be under pressure to impose limits on the rents landlords can charge.

Sellers, however, would always like to get more money for what they sell, and sometimes they can make a strong moral or political case that they should receive higher prices. For example, consider the labor market: the price for an hour of a worker's time is the wage rate. What if the equilibrium between supply and demand for less skilled workers leads to wage rates that yield an income below the poverty level? In that case, a government might well be pressured to require employers to pay a rate no lower than some specified minimum wage.

In other words, there is often a strong political demand for governments to intervene in markets. And powerful interests can make a compelling case that a market intervention favoring them is "fair." When a government intervenes to regulate prices, we say that it imposes **price controls.** These controls typically take the form of either an upper limit, a **price ceiling,** or a lower limit, a **price floor.**

Price controls are legal restrictions on how high or low a market price may go. They can take two forms: a **price ceiling,** a maximum price sellers are allowed to charge for a good or service, or a **price floor,** a minimum price buyers are required to pay for a good or service.

Unfortunately, it's not that easy to tell a market what to do. As we will now see, when a government tries to legislate prices—whether it legislates them *down* by imposing a price ceiling or *up* by imposing a price floor—there are certain predictable and unpleasant side effects.

We make an important assumption in this module: the markets in question are efficient before price controls are imposed. Markets can sometimes be inefficient—for example, a market dominated by a monopolist, a single seller who has the power to influence the market price. When markets are inefficient, price controls don't necessarily cause problems and can potentially move the market closer to efficiency. In practice, however, price controls often *are* imposed on efficient markets—like the New York City apartment market. And so the analysis in this module applies to many important real-world situations.

Price Ceilings

Aside from rent control, there are not many price ceilings in the United States today. But at times they have been widespread. Price ceilings are typically imposed during crises—wars, harvest failures, natural disasters—because these events often lead to sudden price increases that hurt many people but produce big gains for a lucky few. The U.S. government imposed ceilings on many prices during World War II: the war sharply increased demand for raw materials, such as aluminum and steel, and price controls prevented those with access to these raw materials from earning huge profits. Price controls on oil were imposed in 1973, when an embargo by Arab oil-exporting countries seemed likely to generate huge profits for U.S. oil companies. Price controls were instituted again in 2012 by New York and New Jersey authorities in the aftermath of Hurricane Sandy, as gas shortages led to rampant price-gouging.

Rent control in New York is a legacy of World War II: it was imposed because wartime production created an economic boom, which increased demand for apartments at a time when the labor and raw materials that might have been used to build them were being used to win the war instead. Although most price controls were removed soon after the war ended, New York's rent limits were retained and gradually extended to buildings not previously covered, leading to some very strange situations.

You can rent a one-bedroom apartment in Manhattan on fairly short notice—if you are able and willing to pay several thousand dollars a month and live in a less-than-desirable area. Yet some people pay only a small fraction of this for comparable apartments, and others pay hardly more for bigger apartments in better locations.

Aside from producing great deals for some renters, however, what are the broader consequences of New York's rent-control system? To answer this question, we turn to the supply and demand model.

Modeling a Price Ceiling

To see what can go wrong when a government imposes a price ceiling on an efficient market, consider Figure 13-1, which shows a simplified model of the market for apartments in New York. For the sake of simplicity, we imagine that all apartments are exactly the same and so would rent for the same price in an unregulated market.

The table in the figure shows the demand and supply schedules; the demand and supply curves are shown on the left. We show the quantity of apartments on the horizontal axis and the monthly rent per apartment on the vertical axis. You can see that in an unregulated market the equilibrium would be at point *E:* 2 million apartments would be rented for $1,000 each per month.

Now suppose that the government imposes a price ceiling, limiting rents to a price below the equilibrium price—say, no more than $800.

Figure 13-2 shows the effect of the price ceiling, represented by the line at $800. At the enforced rental rate of $800, landlords have less incentive to offer apartments, so they won't be willing to supply as many as they would at the equilibrium rate of $1,000. They will choose point *A* on the supply curve, offering only 1.8 million apartments for rent, 200,000 fewer than in the unregulated market. At the same time, more

FIGURE 13-1 **The Market for Apartments in the Absence of Government Controls**

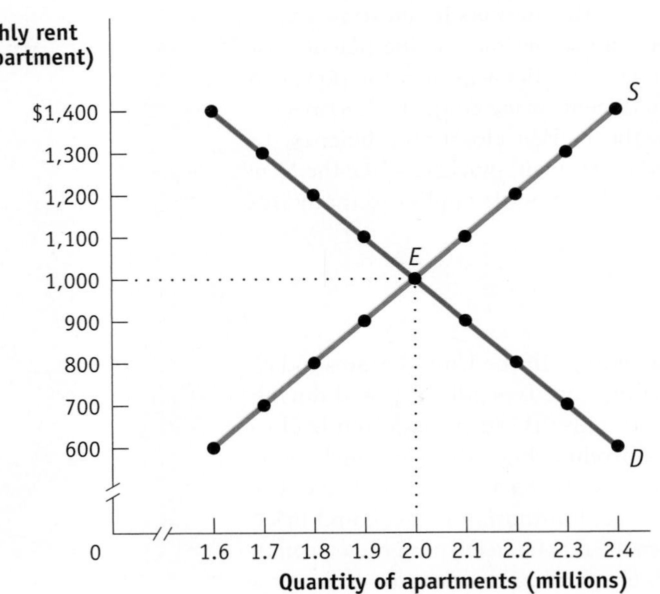

Monthly rent (per apartment)	Quantity of apartments (millions)	
	Quantity demanded	Quantity supplied
$1,400	1.6	2.4
1,300	1.7	2.3
1,200	1.8	2.2
1,100	1.9	2.1
1,000	2.0	2.0
900	2.1	1.9
800	2.2	1.8
700	2.3	1.7
600	2.4	1.6

Without government intervention, the market for apartments reaches equilibrium at point *E* with a market rent of $1,000 per month and 2 million apartments rented.

people will want to rent apartments at a price of $800 than at the equilibrium price of $1,000; as shown at point *B* on the demand curve, at a monthly rent of $800 the quantity of apartments demanded rises to 2.2 million, 200,000 more than in the unregulated market and 400,000 more than are actually available at the price of $800. So there is now a persistent shortage of rental housing: at that price, 400,000 more people want to rent than are able to find apartments.

FIGURE 13-2 **The Effects of a Price Ceiling**

The black horizontal line represents the government-imposed price ceiling on rents of $800 per month. This price ceiling reduces the quantity of apartments supplied to 1.8 million, point *A*, and increases the quantity demanded to 2.2 million, point *B*. This creates a persistent shortage of 400,000 units: 400,000 people who want apartments at the legal rent of $800 but cannot get them.

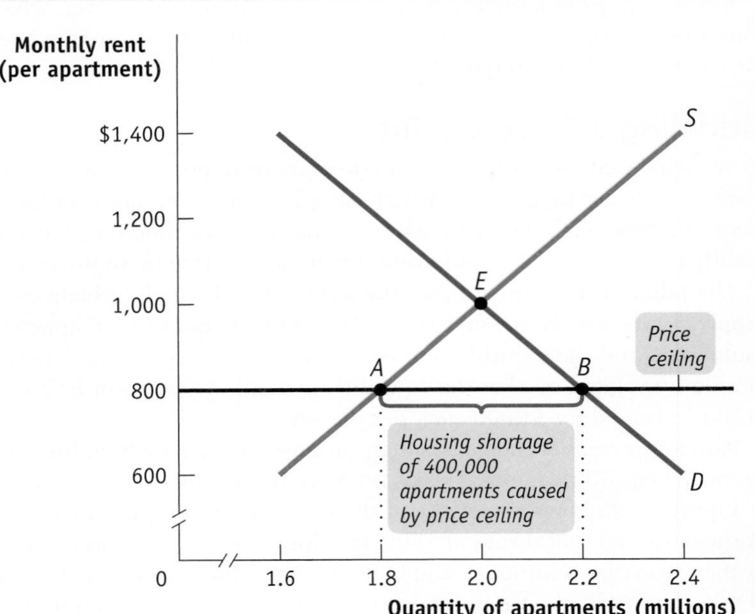

Do price ceilings always cause shortages? No. If a price ceiling is set above the equilibrium price, it won't have any effect. Suppose that the equilibrium rental rate on apartments is $1,000 per month and the city government sets a ceiling of $1,200. Who cares? In this case, the price ceiling won't be binding—it won't actually constrain market behavior—and it will have no effect.

How a Price Ceiling Causes Inefficiency

The housing shortage shown in Figure 13-2 is not merely annoying: like any shortage induced by price controls, it can be seriously harmful because it leads to inefficiency.

Rent control, like all price ceilings, creates inefficiency in at least three distinct ways. It typically leads to an inefficient allocation of apartments among would-be renters; it leads to wasted time and effort as people search for apartments; and it leads landlords to maintain apartments in inefficiently low quality or condition. In addition to inefficiency, price ceilings give rise to illegal behavior as people try to circumvent them. We should also add that price ceilings (as well as price floors) cause inefficiency in the form of *deadweight loss* by discouraging some mutually beneficial transactions from taking place. We'll learn more about deadweight loss in the upcoming two modules.

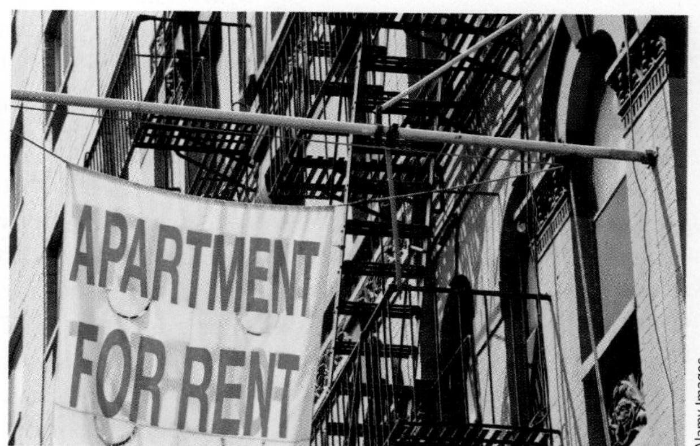

Alamy Images

Rent control often leads to the misallocation of available apartments.

INEFFICIENT ALLOCATION TO CONSUMERS Rent control doesn't just lead to too few apartments being available. It can also lead to misallocation of the apartments that are available: people who badly need a place to live may not be able to find an apartment, while some apartments may be occupied by people with much less urgent needs.

In the case shown in Figure 13-2, 2.2 million people would like to rent an apartment at $800 per month, but only 1.8 million apartments are available. Of those 2.2 million who are seeking an apartment, some want an apartment badly and are willing to pay a high price to get one. Others have a less urgent need and are only willing to pay a low price, perhaps because they have alternative housing. An efficient allocation of apartments would reflect these differences: people who really want an apartment will get one and people who aren't all that eager to find an apartment won't. In an inefficient distribution of apartments, the opposite will happen: some people who are not especially eager to find an apartment will get one and others who are very eager to find an apartment won't.

Because people usually get apartments through luck or personal connections under rent control, it generally results in an **inefficient allocation to consumers** of the few apartments available.

To see the inefficiency involved, consider the Lees, a family with young children who have no alternative housing and would be willing to pay up to $1,500 for an apartment—but are unable to find one. Also consider George, a retiree who lives most of the year in Florida but still has a lease on the New York apartment he moved into 40 years ago. George pays $800 per month for this apartment, but if the rent were even slightly more—say, $850—he would give it up and stay with his children when he is in New York.

This allocation of apartments—George has one and the Lees do not—is a missed opportunity: there is a way to make the Lees and George both better off at no additional cost. The Lees would be happy to pay George, say, $1,200 a month to sublease his apartment, which he would happily accept since the apartment is worth no more than $849 a month to him. George would prefer the money he gets from the Lees to keeping his apartment; the Lees would prefer to have the apartment rather than the money. So both would be made better off by this transaction—and nobody else would be made worse off.

Price ceilings often lead to inefficiency in the form of **inefficient allocation to consumers:** people who want the good badly and are willing to pay a high price don't get it, and those who care relatively little about the good and are only willing to pay a relatively low price do get it.

Generally, if people who really want apartments could sublease them from people who are less eager to live there, both those who gain apartments and those who trade

Price ceilings typically lead to inefficiency in the form of **wasted resources:** people expend money, effort, and time to cope with the shortages caused by the price ceiling.

Price ceilings often lead to inefficiency in that the goods being offered are of **inefficiently low quality:** sellers offer low quality goods at a low price even though buyers would prefer a higher quality at a higher price.

A **black market** is a market in which goods or services are bought and sold illegally—either because it is illegal to sell them at all or because the prices charged are legally prohibited by a price ceiling.

their occupancy for money would be better off. However, subletting is illegal under rent control because it would occur at prices above the price ceiling.

The fact that subletting is illegal doesn't mean it never happens. In fact, chasing down illegal subletting is a major business for New York private investigators, who have been known to use hidden cameras and other tricks to prove that the legal tenants in rent-controlled apartments actually live somewhere else and have sublet their apartments at two or three times the controlled rent. This subletting is a kind of illegal activity, which we will discuss shortly. For now, just notice that the aggressive pursuit of illegal subletting surely discourages the practice, so there isn't enough subletting to eliminate the inefficient allocation of apartments.

WASTED RESOURCES Another reason a price ceiling causes inefficiency is that it leads to **wasted resources:** people expend money, effort, and time to cope with the shortages caused by the price ceiling. Back in 1979, U.S. price controls on gasoline led to shortages that forced millions of Americans to spend hours each week waiting in lines at gas stations. The opportunity cost of the time spent in gas lines—the wages not earned, the leisure time not enjoyed—constituted wasted resources from the point of view of consumers and of the economy as a whole.

Because of rent control, the Lees will spend all their spare time for several months searching for an apartment, time they would rather have spent working or engaged in family activities. That is, there is an opportunity cost to the Lees' prolonged search for an apartment—the leisure or income they had to forgo. If the market for apartments worked freely, the Lees would quickly find an apartment at the equilibrium rent of $1,000, leaving them time to earn more or to enjoy themselves—an outcome that would make them better off without making anyone else worse off. Again, rent control creates missed opportunities.

INEFFICIENTLY LOW QUALITY Yet another way a price ceiling causes inefficiency is by causing goods to be of inefficiently low quality. **Inefficiently low quality** means that sellers offer low-quality goods at a low price even though buyers would rather have higher quality and are willing to pay a higher price for it.

Again, consider rent control. Landlords have no incentive to provide better conditions because they cannot raise rents to cover their repair costs but are able to find tenants easily. In many cases, tenants would be willing to pay much more for improved conditions than it would cost for the landlord to provide them—for example, the upgrade of an antiquated electrical system that cannot safely run air conditioners or computers. But any additional payment for such improvements would be legally considered a rent increase, which is prohibited. Indeed, rent-controlled apartments are notoriously badly maintained, rarely painted, subject to frequent electrical and plumbing problems, and sometimes even hazardous to inhabit.

This whole situation is a missed opportunity—some tenants would be happy to pay for better conditions, and landlords would be happy to provide them for payment. But such an exchange would occur only if the market were allowed to operate freely.

BLACK MARKETS And that leads us to a last aspect of price ceilings: the incentive they provide for illegal activities, specifically the emergence of **black markets.** We have already described one kind of black market activity—illegal subletting by tenants. But it does not stop there. Clearly, there is a temptation for a landlord to say to a potential tenant, "Look, you can have the place if you slip me an extra few hundred in cash each month"—and for the tenant to agree, if he or she is one of those people who would be willing to pay much more than the maximum legal rent.

What's wrong with black markets? In general, it's a bad thing if people break *any* law, because it encourages disrespect for the law in general. Worse yet, in this case illegal activity worsens the position of those who try to be honest. If the Lees are scrupulous about upholding the rent-control law but other people—who may need an apartment less than the Lees—are willing to bribe landlords, the Lees may *never* find an apartment.

So Why Are There Price Ceilings?

We have seen three common results of price ceilings:

- a persistent shortage of the good
- inefficiency arising from this persistent shortage in the form of inefficiently low quantity, inefficient allocation of the good to consumers, resources wasted in searching for the good, and the inefficiently low quality of the good offered for sale
- the emergence of illegal, black market activity

Given the unpleasant consequences of price ceilings, why do governments sometimes impose them?

One answer is that although price ceilings may have adverse effects, they do benefit some people. In practice, New York's rent-control rules—which are more complex than our simple model—hurt most residents but give a small minority of renters much cheaper housing than they would get in an unregulated market. And those who benefit from the controls may be better organized and more vocal than those who are harmed by them.

Also, when price ceilings have been in effect for a long time, buyers may not have a realistic idea of what would happen without them. In our previous example, the rental rate in an unregulated market (Figure 13-1) would be only 25% higher than in the regulated market (Figure 13-2): $1,000 instead of $800. But how would renters know that? Indeed, they might have heard about black market transactions at much higher prices—the Lees or some other family paying George $1,200 or more—and would not realize that these black market prices are much higher than the price that would prevail in a fully unregulated market.

A last answer is that government officials often do not understand supply and demand analysis! It is a great mistake to suppose that economic policies in the real world are always sensible or well informed.

ECONOMICS ▶ IN ACTION

HUNGER AND PRICE CONTROLS IN VENEZUELA

Something was rotten in the state of Venezuela—specifically, 30,000 tons of decomposing food in Puerto Cabello in June 2010. The discovery was particularly embarrassing for then President Hugo Chávez. He was elected in 1998 on a platform denouncing the country's economic elite and promising policies favoring the poor and working classes. Among those policies were price controls on basic foodstuffs, which led to shortages that began in 2003 and had become severe by 2006.

Generous government policies led to higher spending by consumers and sharply rising prices for goods that weren't subject to price controls or were bought on the black market. The result was a big increase in the demand for price-controlled goods. But a sharp decline in the value of Venezuela's currency led to a fall in imports of foreign food, and the result was empty shelves in the nation's food stores.

As the shortages persisted and inflation of food prices worsened (in the first five months of 2010, the prices of food and drink rose by 21%), Chávez declared "economic war" on the private sector, berating it for "hoarding and smuggling." The government expropriated farms, food manufacturers, and grocery stores, creating in their place government-owned ones, which were corrupt and inefficient. It was the government-owned food-distribution company, PDVAL, that left tens of thousands of tons of food to rot in Venezuelan ports. Food production also fell, forcing Venezuela to import 70% of its food.

Venezuela's food shortages offer a lesson in why price ceilings, however well intentioned, are usually never a good idea.

Reuters/Daniel Aguilar/Landov

The **minimum wage** is a legal floor on the wage rate, which is the market price of labor.

Not surprisingly, the shelves were far more bare in government-run grocery stores than in those still in private hands. The food shortages were so severe that they greatly diminished Chávez's popularity among working-class Venezuelans and halted his expropriation plans. As an old Venezuelan saying has it, "Love with hunger doesn't last."

Price Floors

Sometimes governments intervene to push market prices up instead of down. *Price floors* have been widely legislated for agricultural products, such as wheat and milk, as a way to support the incomes of farmers. Historically, there were also price floors on such services as trucking and air travel, although these were phased out by the U.S. government in the 1970s. If you have ever worked in a fast-food restaurant, you are likely to have encountered a price floor: governments in the United States and many other countries maintain a lower limit on the hourly wage rate of a worker's labor—that is, a floor on the price of labor—called the **minimum wage.**

Just like price ceilings, price floors are intended to help some people but generate predictable and undesirable side effects. Figure 13-3 shows hypothetical supply and demand curves for butter. Left to itself, the market would move to equilibrium at point *E*, with 10 million pounds of butter bought and sold at a price of $1 per pound.

Now suppose that the government, in order to help dairy farmers, imposes a price floor on butter of $1.20 per pound. Its effects are shown in Figure 13-4, where the line at $1.20 represents the price floor. At a price of $1.20 per pound, producers would want to supply 12 million pounds (point *B* on the supply curve) but consumers would want to buy only 9 million pounds (point *A* on the demand curve). So the price floor leads to a persistent surplus of 3 million pounds of butter.

FIGURE 13-3 The Market for Butter in the Absence of Government Controls

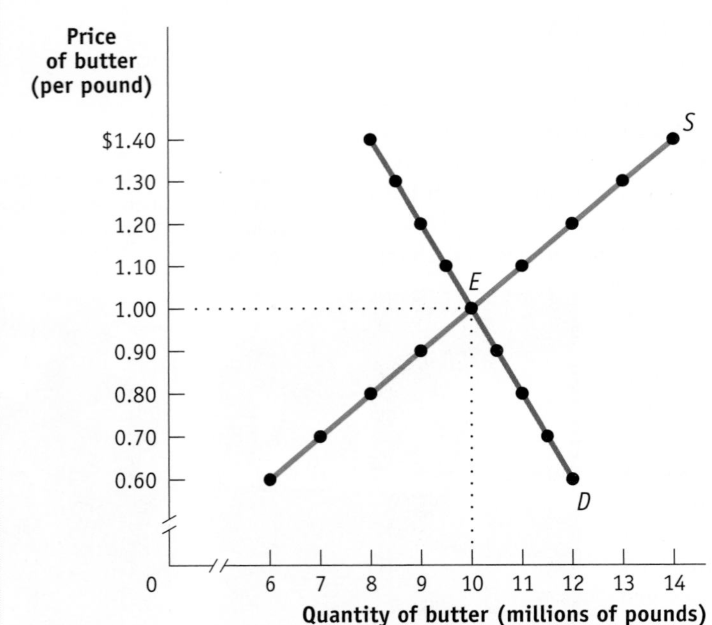

Price of butter (per pound)	Quantity of butter (millions of pounds)	
	Quantity demanded	Quantity supplied
$1.40	8.0	14.0
1.30	8.5	13.0
1.20	9.0	12.0
1.10	9.5	11.0
1.00	10.0	10.0
0.90	10.5	9.0
0.80	11.0	8.0
0.70	11.5	7.0
0.60	12.0	6.0

Without government intervention, the market for butter reaches equilibrium at a price of $1 per pound with 10 million pounds of butter bought and sold.

FIGURE 13-4 The Effects of a Price Floor

The dark horizontal line represents the government-imposed price floor of $1.20 per pound of butter. The quantity of butter demanded falls to 9 million pounds, and the quantity supplied rises to 12 million pounds, generating a persistent surplus of 3 million pounds of butter.

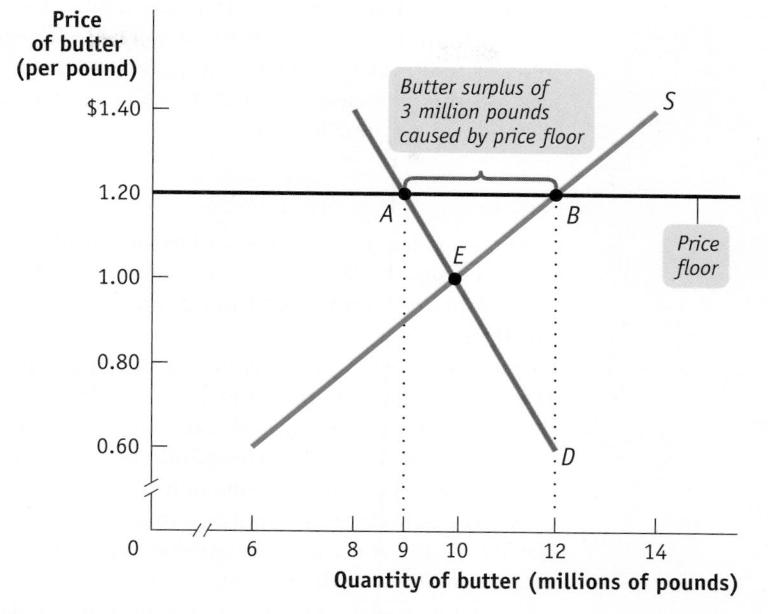

ECONOMICS IN ACTION

PRICE FLOORS AND SCHOOL LUNCHES

When you were in grade school, did your school offer free or very cheap lunches? If so, you were probably a beneficiary of price floors.

Where did all the cheap food come from? During the 1930s, when the U.S. economy was going through the Great Depression, a prolonged economic slump, prices were low and farmers were suffering severely. In an effort to help rural Americans, the U.S. government imposed price floors on a number of agricultural products. The system of agricultural price floors—officially called price support programs—continues to this day. Among the products subject to price support are sugar and various dairy products; at times grains, beef, and pork have also had a minimum price.

The big problem with any attempt to impose a price floor is that it creates a surplus. To some extent the U.S. Department of Agriculture has tried to head off surpluses by taking steps to reduce supply; for example, by paying farmers *not* to grow crops. As a last resort, however, the U.S. government has been willing to buy up the surplus, taking the excess supply off the market.

But then what? The government can't just sell the agricultural products: that would depress market prices, forcing the government to buy the stuff right back. So it has to give it away in ways that don't depress market prices. One way to do this is by giving surplus food, free, to school lunch programs. These gifts are known as "bonus foods." Along with financial aid, bonus foods allow many school districts to provide free or very cheap lunches to their students. Is this a story with a happy ending?

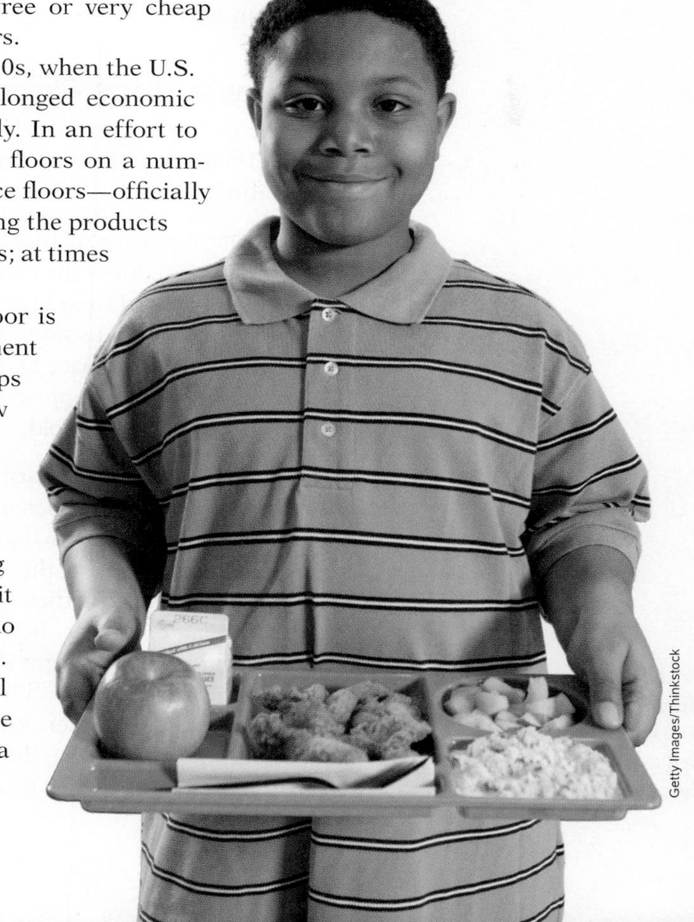

Getty Images/Thinkstock

Not really. Nutritionists, concerned about growing child obesity in the United States, place part of the blame on those bonus foods. Schools get whatever the government has too much of—and that has tended to include a lot of dairy products, beef, and corn, and not much in the way of fresh vegetables or fruit. As a result, school lunches that make extensive use of bonus foods tend to be very high in fat and calories. So this is a case in which there is such a thing as a free lunch—but this lunch may be bad for your health.

Does a price floor always lead to an unwanted surplus? No. Just as in the case of a price ceiling, the floor may not be binding—that is, it may be irrelevant. If the equilibrium price of butter is \$1 per pound but the floor is set at only \$0.80, the floor has no effect.

But suppose that a price floor *is* binding: what happens to the unwanted surplus? The answer depends on government policy. In the case of agricultural price floors, governments buy up unwanted surplus. As a result, the U.S. government has at times found itself warehousing thousands of tons of butter, cheese, and other farm products. The government then has to find a way to dispose of these unwanted goods.

Some countries pay exporters to sell products at a loss overseas; this is standard procedure for the European Union. The United States gives surplus food away to schools, which use the products in school lunches. In some cases, governments have actually destroyed the surplus production. To avoid the problem of dealing with the unwanted surplus, the U.S. government often pays farmers not to produce the products at all.

When the government is not prepared to purchase the unwanted surplus, a price floor means that would-be sellers cannot find buyers. This is what happens when there is a price floor on the wage rate paid for an hour of labor, the *minimum wage:* when the minimum wage is above the equilibrium wage rate, some people who are willing to work—that is, sell labor—cannot find buyers—that is, employers—willing to give them jobs.

How a Price Floor Causes Inefficiency

The persistent surplus that results from a price floor creates missed opportunities—inefficiencies—that resemble those created by the shortage that results from a price ceiling.

INEFFICIENTLY LOW QUANTITY Because a price floor raises the price of a good to consumers, it reduces the quantity of that good demanded; because sellers can't sell more units of a good than buyers are willing to buy, a price floor reduces the quantity of a good bought and sold below the market equilibrium quantity. Notice that this is the *same* effect as a price ceiling. You might be tempted to think that a price floor and a price ceiling have opposite effects, but both have the effect of reducing the quantity of a good bought and sold.

INEFFICIENT ALLOCATION OF SALES AMONG SELLERS Like a price ceiling, a price floor can lead to *inefficient allocation*—but in this case **inefficient allocation of sales among sellers** rather than inefficient allocation to consumers.

Price floors lead to **inefficient allocation of sales among sellers:** those who would be willing to sell the good at the lowest price are not always those who manage to sell it.

An episode from the Belgian movie *Rosetta,* a realistic fictional story, illustrates the problem of inefficient allocation of selling opportunities quite well. Like many European countries, Belgium has a high minimum wage, and jobs for young people are scarce. At one point Rosetta, a young woman who is very eager to work, loses her job at a fast-food stand because the owner of the stand replaces her with his son—a very reluctant worker. Rosetta would be willing to work for less money, and with the money he would save, the owner could give his son an allowance and let him do something else. But to hire Rosetta for less than the minimum wage would be illegal.

WASTED RESOURCES Also like a price ceiling, a price floor generates inefficiency by *wasting resources*. The most graphic examples involve government purchases of the unwanted surpluses of agricultural products caused by price floors. When the surplus production is simply destroyed, and when the stored produce goes, as officials euphemistically put it, "out of condition" and must be thrown away, it is pure waste.

Vanbeets/Dreamstime.com

Since airline deregulation in the 1970s, American passengers have seen ticket prices decrease along with the quality of in-flight service.

Price floors also lead to wasted time and effort. Consider the minimum wage. Would-be workers who spend many hours searching for jobs, or waiting in line in the hope of getting jobs, play the same role in the case of price floors as hapless families searching for apartments in the case of price ceilings.

INEFFICIENTLY HIGH QUALITY Again like price ceilings, price floors lead to inefficiency in the quality of goods produced.

We've seen that when there is a price ceiling, suppliers produce goods that are of inefficiently low quality: buyers prefer higher-quality products and are willing to pay for them, but sellers refuse to improve the quality of their products because the price ceiling prevents their being compensated for doing so. This same logic applies to price floors, but in reverse: suppliers offer goods of **inefficiently high quality.**

How can this be? Isn't high quality a good thing? Yes, but only if it is worth the cost. Suppose that suppliers spend a lot to make goods of very high quality but that this quality isn't worth much to consumers, who would rather receive the money spent on that quality in the form of a lower price. This represents a missed opportunity: suppliers and buyers could make a mutually beneficial deal in which buyers got goods of lower quality for a much lower price.

A good example of the inefficiency of excessive quality comes from the days when transatlantic airfares were set artificially high by international treaty. Forbidden to compete for customers by offering lower ticket prices, airlines instead offered expensive services, like lavish in-flight meals that went largely uneaten.

ILLEGAL ACTIVITY Finally, like price ceilings, price floors provide incentives for illegal activity. For example, in countries where the minimum wage is far above the equilibrium wage rate, workers desperate for jobs sometimes agree to work off the books for employers who conceal their employment from the government—or bribe the government inspectors. This practice, known in Europe as "black labor," is especially common in southern European countries such as Italy and Spain.

So Why Are There Price Floors?

To sum up, a price floor creates various negative side effects:

- a persistent surplus of the good
- inefficiency arising from the persistent surplus in the form of inefficiently low quantity, inefficient allocation of sales among sellers, wasted resources, and an inefficiently high level of quality offered by suppliers
- the temptation to engage in illegal activity, particularly bribery and corruption of government officials

So why do governments impose price floors when they have so many negative side effects? The reasons are similar to those for imposing price ceilings. Government officials often disregard warnings about the consequences of price floors either because they believe that the relevant market is poorly described by the supply and demand model or, more often, because they do not understand the model. Above all, just as price ceilings are often imposed because they benefit some influential buyers of a good, price floors are often imposed because they benefit some influential sellers.

Price floors often lead to inefficiency in that goods of **inefficiently high quality** are offered: sellers offer high-quality goods at a high price, even though buyers would prefer a lower quality at a lower price.

MODULE 13 Review

Solutions appear at the back of the book.

Check Your Understanding

1. On game days, homeowners near Middletown University's stadium used to rent parking spaces in their driveways to fans at a going rate of $11. A new town ordinance now sets a maximum parking fee of $7. Use the accompanying supply and demand diagram to explain how each of the following can result from the price ceiling.

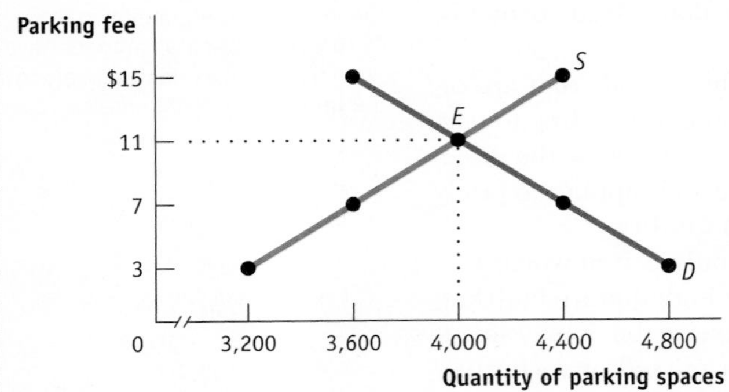

a. Some homeowners now think it's not worth the hassle to rent out spaces.

b. Some fans who used to carpool to the game now drive alone.

c. Some fans can't find parking and leave without seeing the game.

Explain how each of the following adverse effects arises from the price ceiling.

d. Some fans now arrive several hours early to find parking.

e. Friends of homeowners near the stadium regularly attend games, even if they aren't big fans. But some serious fans have given up because of the parking situation.

f. Some homeowners rent spaces for more than $7 but pretend that the buyers are nonpaying friends or family.

2. True or false? Explain your answer. A price ceiling below the equilibrium price in an otherwise efficient market does the following:

a. increases quantity supplied

b. makes some people who want to consume the good worse off

c. makes all producers worse off

3. The state legislature mandates a price floor for gasoline of P_F per gallon. Assess the following statements and illustrate your answer using the figure provided.

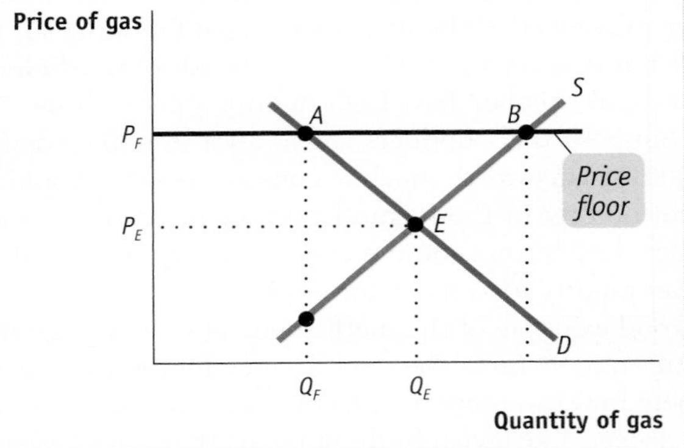

a. Proponents of the law claim it will increase the income of gas station owners. Opponents claim it will hurt gas station owners because they will lose customers.

b. Proponents claim consumers will be better off because gas stations will provide better service. Opponents claim consumers will be generally worse off because they prefer to buy gas at cheaper prices.

c. Proponents claim that they are helping gas station owners without hurting anyone else. Opponents claim that consumers are hurt and will end up doing things like buying gas in a nearby state or on the black market.

Multiple-Choice Questions

1. To be effective, a price ceiling must be set

I. above the equilibrium price.

II. in the housing market.

III. to achieve the equilibrium market quantity.

a. I

b. II

c. III

d. I, II, and III

e. None of the above

2. Refer to the graph provided. A price floor set at $5 will result in

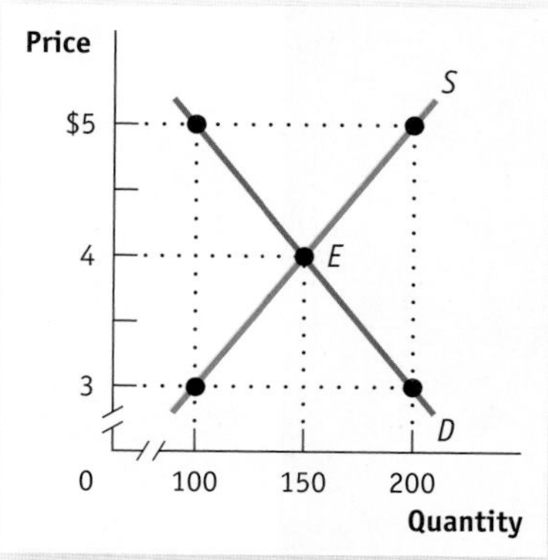

a. a shortage of 100 units.

b. a surplus of 100 units.

c. a shortage of 200 units.

d. a surplus of 200 units.

e. a surplus of 50 units.

3. Effective price ceilings are inefficient because they

a. create shortages.

b. lead to wasted resources.

c. decrease quality.

d. create black markets.

e. do all of the above.

4. Refer to the graph provided. If the government establishes a minimum wage at $10, how many workers will benefit from the higher wage?

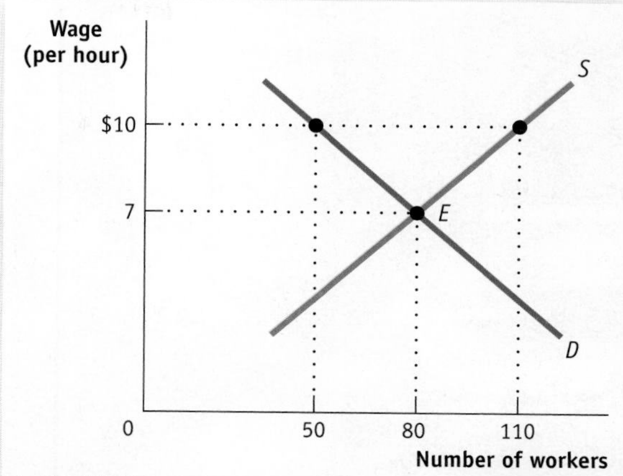

a. 30

b. 50

c. 60

d. 80

e. 110

5. Refer to the graph for question 4. With a minimum wage of $10, how many workers are unemployed (they would like to work, but are unable to find a job)?

a. 30

b. 50

c. 60

d. 80

e. 110

Critical-Thinking Question

Draw a correctly labeled graph of a housing market in equilibrium. On your graph, illustrate an effective legal limit (ceiling) on rent. Identify the quantity of housing demanded, the quantity of housing supplied, and the size of the resulting surplus or shortage.

PITFALLS

CEILINGS, FLOORS, AND QUANTITIES

? A price ceiling pushes the price of a good *down*. A price floor pushes the price of a good *up*. So it looks like we can assume that the effects of a price floor are the opposite of the effects of a price ceiling. Put another way, if a price ceiling reduces the quantity of a good bought and sold, doesn't a price floor increase the quantity?

> NO, IT DOESN'T, BECAUSE BOTH FLOORS AND CEILINGS REDUCE THE QUANTITY BOUGHT AND SOLD. Why? When the quantity of a good supplied isn't equal to the quantity demanded, the actual quantity sold is determined by the "short side" of the market—whichever quantity is less. If sellers don't want to sell as much as buyers want to buy, it's the sellers who determine the actual quantity sold, because buyers can't force unwilling sellers to sell. If buyers don't want to buy as much as sellers want to sell, it's the buyers who determine the actual quantity sold, because sellers can't force unwilling buyers to buy.

To learn more, see pp. 130–132 and 136–137, on price ceilings, floors, and inefficiency.

MODULE 14 Quantity Controls (Quotas)

Alamy Images

WHAT YOU WILL LEARN

1. The meaning of quantity controls, another way government intervenes in markets
2. How quantity controls create problems and can make a market inefficient
3. Who benefits and who loses from quantity controls, and why they are used despite their well-known problems

Controlling Quantities

In the 1930s, New York City instituted a system of licensing for taxicabs: only taxis with a "medallion" were allowed to pick up passengers. Because this system was intended to ensure quality, medallion owners were supposed to maintain certain standards, including safety and cleanliness. A total of 11,787 medallions were issued, with taxi owners paying $10 for each medallion.

In 1995, there were still only 11,787 licensed taxicabs in New York, even though the city had meanwhile become the financial capital of the world, a place where hundreds of thousands of people in a hurry tried to hail a cab every day. That same year, an additional 400 medallions were issued, and after several rounds of sales of additional medallions, today there are 13,237 medallions.

The result of this restriction on the number of taxis was that a New York City taxi medallion became very valuable. In 2012, the price of a medallion was about $700,000! If you wanted to operate a taxi in New York, you had to lease a medallion from someone else or buy one for a going price.

It turns out that this story is not unique; other cities introduced similar medallion systems in the 1930s and, like New York, have issued few new medallions since. In San Francisco and Boston, as in New York, taxi medallions trade for six-figure prices.

A taxi medallion system is a form of **quantity control,** or **quota,** by which the government regulates the quantity of a good that can be bought and sold rather than regulating the price. Typically, the government limits quantity in a market by issuing **licenses;** only people with a license can legally supply the good. A taxi medallion is just such a license. The government of New York City limits the number of taxi rides that can be sold by limiting the number of taxis to only those who hold medallions. There are many other cases of quantity controls, ranging from limits on how much

A **quantity control,** or **quota,** is an upper limit on the quantity of some good that can be bought or sold.

A **license** gives its owner the right to supply a good or service.

foreign currency (for instance, British pounds or Mexican pesos) people are allowed to buy to the quantity of clams New Jersey fishing boats are allowed to catch.

Some attempts to control quantities are undertaken for good economic reasons, some for bad ones. In many cases, as we will see, quantity controls introduced to address a temporary problem become politically hard to remove later because the beneficiaries don't want them abolished, even after the original reason for their existence is long gone. But whatever the reasons for such controls, they have certain predictable—and usually undesirable—economic consequences.

The **demand price** of a given quantity is the price at which consumers will demand that quantity.

How Quantity Controls Work

To understand why a New York taxi medallion is worth so much money, we consider a simplified version of the market for taxi rides, shown in Figure 14-1. Just as we assumed in the analysis of rent control that all apartments were the same, we now suppose that all taxi rides are the same—ignoring the real-world complication that some taxi rides are longer, and so more expensive, than others. The table in the figure shows supply and demand schedules. The equilibrium—indicated by point *E* in the figure and by the shaded entries in the table—is a fare of $5 per ride, with 10 million rides taken per year.

Ed Rooney/Alamy

The New York medallion system limits the number of taxis, but each taxi driver can offer as many rides as he or she can manage. (Now you know why New York taxi drivers are so aggressive!) To simplify our analysis, however, we will assume that a medallion system limits the number of taxi rides that can legally be given to 8 million per year.

Until now, we have derived the demand curve by answering questions of the form: "How many taxi rides will passengers want to take if the price is $5 per ride?" But it is possible to reverse the question and ask instead: "At what price will consumers want to buy 10 million rides per year?" The price at which consumers want to buy a given quantity—in this case, 10 million rides at $5 per ride—is the **demand price** of that quantity. You can see from the demand schedule in Figure 14-1 that the demand price of 6 million rides is $7 per ride, the demand price of 7 million rides is $6.50 per ride, and so on.

FIGURE 14-1 The Market for Taxi Rides in the Absence of Government Controls

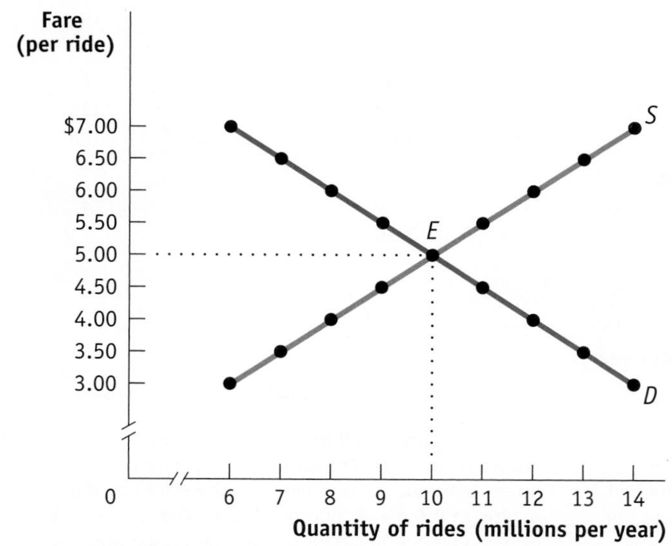

Fare (per ride)	Quantity of rides (millions per year): Quantity demanded	Quantity supplied
$7.00	6	14
6.50	7	13
6.00	8	12
5.50	9	11
5.00	10	10
4.50	11	9
4.00	12	8
3.50	13	7
3.00	14	6

Without government intervention, the market reaches equilibrium with 10 million rides taken per year at a fare of $5 per ride.

The **supply price** of a given quantity is the price at which producers will supply that quantity.

Similarly, the supply curve represents the answer to questions of the form: "How many taxi rides would taxi drivers supply at a price of $5 each?" But we can also reverse this question to ask: "At what price will producers be willing to supply 10 million rides per year?" The price at which producers will supply a given quantity—in this case, 10 million rides at $5 per ride—is the **supply price** of that quantity. We can see from the supply schedule in Figure 14-1 that the supply price of 6 million rides is $3 per ride, the supply price of 7 million rides is $3.50 per ride, and so on.

Now we are ready to analyze a quota. We have assumed that the city government limits the quantity of taxi rides to 8 million per year. Medallions, each of which carries the right to provide a certain number of taxi rides per year, are made available to selected people in such a way that a total of 8 million rides will be provided. Medallion holders may then either drive their own taxis or rent their medallions to others for a fee.

Figure 14-2 shows the resulting market for taxi rides, with the black vertical line at 8 million rides per year representing the quota. Because the quantity of rides is limited to 8 million, consumers must be at point *A* on the demand curve, corresponding to the shaded entry in the demand schedule: the demand price of 8 million rides is $6 per ride. Meanwhile, taxi drivers must be at point *B* on the supply curve, corresponding to the shaded entry in the supply schedule: the supply price of 8 million rides is $4 per ride.

But how can the price received by taxi drivers be $4 when the price paid by taxi riders is $6? The answer is that in addition to the market in taxi rides, there is also a market in medallions. Medallion-holders may not always want to drive their taxis: they may be ill or on vacation. Those who do not want to drive their own taxis will sell the right to use the medallion to someone else. So we need to consider two sets of transactions here, and so two prices: (1) the transactions in taxi rides and the price at

FIGURE 14-2 Effect of a Quota on the Market for Taxi Rides

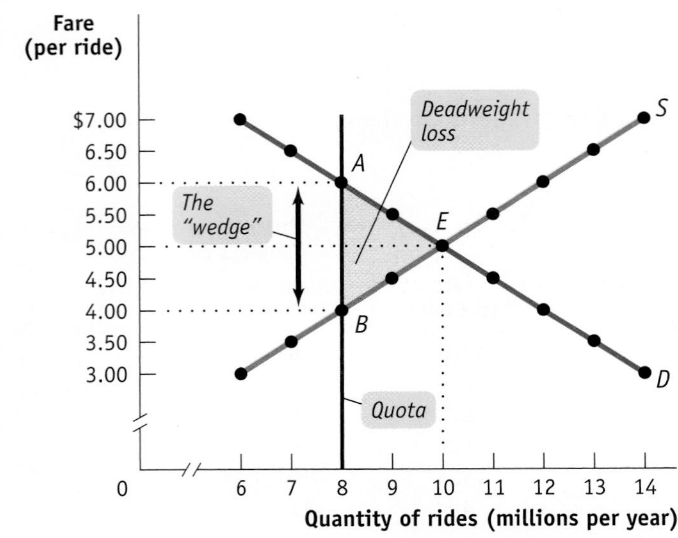

Fare (per ride)	Quantity of rides (millions per year) Quantity demanded	Quantity supplied
$7.00	6	14
6.50	7	13
6.00	8	12
5.50	9	11
5.00	10	10
4.50	11	9
4.00	12	8
3.50	13	7
3.00	14	6

The table shows the demand price and the supply price corresponding to each quantity: the price at which that quantity would be demanded and supplied, respectively. The city government imposes a quota of 8 million rides by selling enough medallions for only 8 million rides, represented by the black vertical line. The price paid by consumers rises to $6 per ride, the demand price of 8 million rides, shown by point *A*. The supply price of 8 million rides is only $4 per ride, shown by point *B*. The difference between these two prices is the quota rent per ride, the earnings that accrue to the owner of a medallion. The quota rent drives a wedge between the demand price and the supply price. Because the quota discourages mutually beneficial transactions, it creates a deadweight loss equal to the shaded triangle.

which these will occur and (2) the transactions in medallions and the price at which these will occur. It turns out that since we are looking at two markets, the $4 and $6 prices will both be right.

To see how this all works, consider two imaginary New York taxi drivers, Sunil and Harriet. Sunil has a medallion but can't use it because he's recovering from a severely sprained wrist. So he's looking to rent his medallion out to someone else. Harriet doesn't have a medallion but would like to rent one. Furthermore, at any point in time there are many other people like Harriet who would like to rent a medallion. Suppose Sunil agrees to rent his medallion to Harriet. To make things simple, assume that any driver can give only one ride per day and that Sunil is renting his medallion to Harriet for one day. What rental price will they agree on?

To answer this question, we need to look at the transactions from the viewpoints of both drivers. Once she has the medallion, Harriet knows she can make $6 per day—the demand price of a ride under the quota. And she is willing to rent the medallion only if she makes at least $4 per day—the supply price of a ride under the quota. So Sunil cannot demand a rent of more than $2—the difference between $6 and $4. And if Harriet offered Sunil less than $2—say, $1.50—there would be other eager drivers willing to offer him more, up to $2. So, in order to get the medallion, Harriet must offer Sunil at least $2. Since the rent can be no more than $2 and no less than $2, it must be exactly $2.

It is no coincidence that $2 is exactly the difference between $6, the demand price of 8 million rides, and $4, the supply price of 8 million rides. In every case in which the supply of a good is legally restricted, there is a **wedge** between the demand price of the quantity transacted and the supply price of the quantity transacted. This wedge, illustrated by the double-headed arrow in Figure 14-2, has a special name: the **quota rent.** It is the earnings that accrue to the medallion holder from ownership of a valuable commodity, the medallion. In the case of Sunil and Harriet, the quota rent of $2 goes to Sunil because he owns the medallion, and the remaining $4 from the total fare of $6 goes to Harriet.

A quantity control, or quota, drives a **wedge** between the demand price and the supply price of a good; that is, the price paid by buyers ends up being higher than that received by sellers. The difference between the demand and supply price at the quota amount is the **quota rent,** the earnings that accrue to the license-holder from ownership of the right to sell the good. It is equal to the market price of the license when the licenses are traded.

So Figure 14-2 also illustrates the quota rent in the market for New York taxi rides. The quota limits the quantity of rides to 8 million per year, a quantity at which the demand price of $6 exceeds the supply price of $4. The wedge between these two prices, $2, is the quota rent that results from the restrictions placed on the quantity of taxi rides in this market.

But wait a second. What if Sunil doesn't rent out his medallion? What if he uses it himself? Doesn't this mean that he gets a price of $6? No, not really. Even if Sunil doesn't rent out his medallion, he could have rented it out, which means that the medallion has an *opportunity cost* of $2: if Sunil decides to use his own medallion and drive his own taxi rather than renting his medallion to Harriet, the $2 represents his opportunity cost of not renting out his medallion. That is, the $2 quota rent is now the rental income he forgoes by driving his own taxi.

In effect, Sunil is in two businesses—the taxi-driving business and the medallion-renting business. He makes $4 per ride from driving his taxi and $2 per ride from renting out his medallion. It doesn't make any difference that in this particular case he has rented his medallion to himself! So regardless of whether the medallion owner uses the medallion himself or herself, or rents it to others, it is a valuable asset. And this is represented in the going price for a New York City taxi medallion.

Notice, by the way, that quotas—like price ceilings and price floors—don't always have a real effect. If the quota were set at 12 million rides—that is, above the equilibrium quantity in an unregulated market—it would have no effect because it would not be binding.

In addition to the market for taxi rides, there is also a market in taxi medallions.

Thinkstock/Getty Images

Deadweight loss is the lost gains associated with transactions that do not occur due to market intervention.

The Costs of Quantity Controls

Like price controls, quantity controls can have some predictable and undesirable side effects. The first is the by-now-familiar problem of inefficiency due to missed opportunities: quantity controls prevent mutually beneficial transactions from occurring, transactions that would benefit both buyers and sellers. Looking back at Figure 14-2, you can see that starting at the quota of 8 million rides, New Yorkers would be willing to pay at least $5.50 per ride for an additional 1 million rides and that taxi drivers would be willing to provide those rides as long as they got at least $4.50 per ride. These are rides that would have taken place if there had been no quota.

The same is true for the next 1 million rides: New Yorkers would be willing to pay at least $5 per ride when the quantity of rides is increased from 9 to 10 million, and taxi drivers would be willing to provide those rides as long as they got at least $5 per ride. Again, these rides would have occurred without the quota.

Only when the market has reached the unregulated market equilibrium quantity of 10 million rides are there no "missed-opportunity rides"—the quota of 8 million rides has caused 2 million "missed-opportunity rides." A buyer would be willing to buy the good at a price that the seller would be willing to accept, but such a transaction does not occur because it is forbidden by the quota.

Economists have a special term for the lost gains from missed opportunities such as these: **deadweight loss.** Generally, when the demand price exceeds the supply price, there is a deadweight loss. Figure 14-2 illustrates the deadweight loss with a shaded triangle between the demand and supply curves. This triangle represents the missed gains from taxi rides prevented by the quota, a loss that is experienced by both disappointed would-be riders and frustrated would-be drivers.

Because there are transactions that people would like to make but are not allowed to, quantity controls generate an incentive to evade them or even to break the law. New York's taxi industry again provides clear examples. Taxi regulation applies only to those drivers who are hailed by passengers on the street. A car service that makes prearranged pickups does not need a medallion. As a result, such hired cars provide much of the service that might otherwise be provided by taxis, as in other cities. In addition, there are substantial numbers of unlicensed cabs that simply defy the law by picking up passengers without a medallion. Because these cabs are illegal, their drivers are unregulated, and they generate a disproportionately large share of traffic accidents in New York City.

ECONOMICS IN ACTION

THE CLAMS OF THE JERSEY SHORE

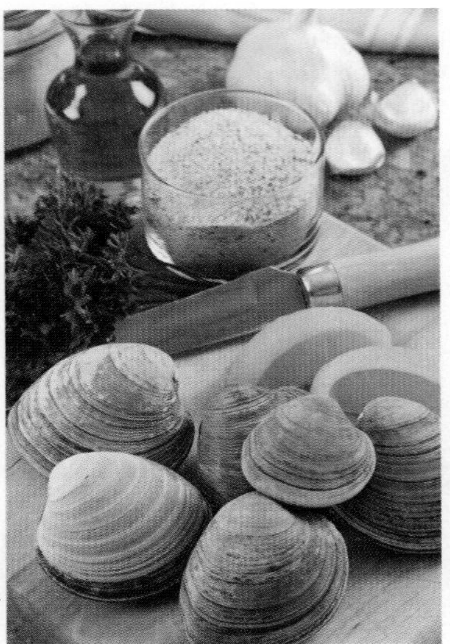

iStockphoto

Clam quotas were introduced in New Jersey to help save a threatened natural resource.

One industry that New Jersey *really* dominates is clam fishing. The Garden State typically supplies about 70% of the country's surf clams, whose tongues are used in fried-clam dinners, and about 90% of the quahogs, which are used to make clam chowder.

In the 1980s, however, excessive fishing threatened to wipe out New Jersey's clam beds. To save the resource, the U.S. government introduced a clam quota, which sets an overall limit on the number of bushels of clams that may be caught and allocates licenses to owners of fishing boats based on their historical catches.

Notice, by the way, that this is an example of a quota that is probably justified by broader economic and environmental considerations—unlike the New York taxicab quota, which has long since lost any economic rationale. Still, whatever its rationale, the New Jersey clam quota works the same way as any other quota.

Once the quota system was established, many boat owners stopped fishing for clams. They realized that rather than operate a boat part time, it was more profitable to sell or rent their licenses to someone else, who could then assemble enough licenses to operate a boat full time. Today, there are about 50 New Jersey boats fishing for clams; the license required to operate one is worth more than the boat itself.

14 Review

Solutions appear at the back of the book.

Check Your Understanding

1. Suppose that the supply and demand for taxi rides is given by Figure 14-1 and a quota is set at 6 million rides. Replicate the graph from Figure 14-1, and identify each of the following on your graph:
   a. the price of a ride
   b. the quota rent
   c. the deadweight loss resulting from the quota

   Suppose the quota on taxi rides is increased to 9 million.

   d. What happens to the quota rent and the deadweight loss?
2. Again replicate the graph from Figure 14-1. Suppose that the quota is 8 million rides and that demand decreases due to a decline in tourism. Show on your graph the smallest parallel leftward shift in demand that would result in the quota no longer having an effect on the market.

Multiple-Choice Questions

Refer to the graph provided to answer questions 1–3.

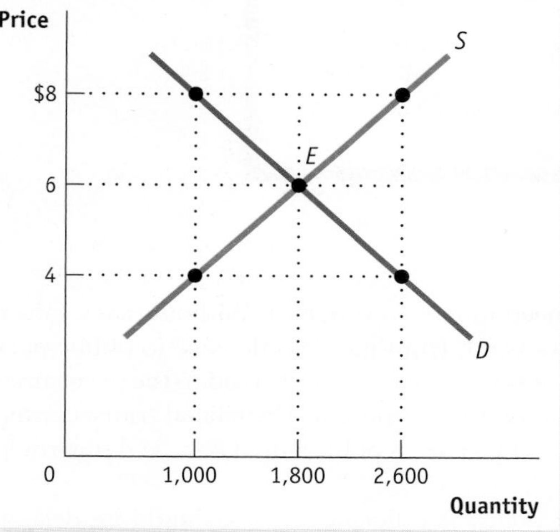

1. If the government established a quota of 1,000 in this market, the demand price would be
   a. less than $4.
   b. $4.
   c. $6.
   d. $8.
   e. more than $8.
2. If the government established a quota of 1,000 in this market, the supply price would be
   a. less than $4.
   b. $4.
   c. $6.
   d. $8.
   e. more than $8.
3. If the government established a quota of 1,000 in this market, the quota rent would be
   a. $2.
   b. $4.
   c. $6.
   d. $8.
   e. more than $8.
4. Quotas lead to which of the following?
   I. inefficiency due to missed opportunities
   II. incentives to evade or break the law
   III. a surplus in the market
   a. I
   b. II
   c. III
   d. I and II
   e. I, II, and III
5. Which of the following would decrease the effect of a quota on a market? A(n)
   a. decrease in demand
   b. increase in supply
   c. increase in demand
   d. price ceiling above the equilibrium price
   e. none of the above

Critical-Thinking Question

Draw a correctly labeled graph of the market for taxicab rides. On the graph, draw and label a vertical line showing the level of an effective quota. Label the demand price, the supply price, and the quota rent.

MODULE 15 Taxes

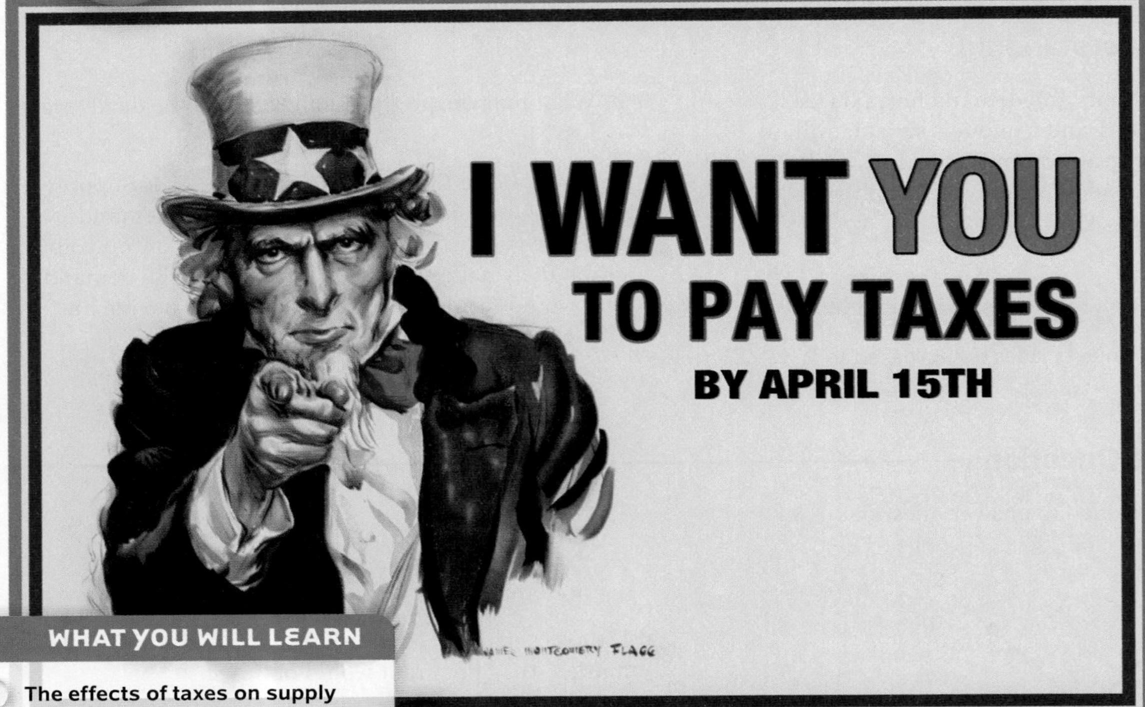

I WANT YOU
TO PAY TAXES
BY APRIL 15TH

Uncle Sam image courtesy of Library of Congress

WHAT YOU WILL LEARN

1. The effects of taxes on supply and demand
2. How taxes affect total surplus and can create deadweight loss

Taxes are necessary: all governments need money to function. Without taxes, governments could not provide the services we want, from national defense to public parks. But taxes have a cost that normally exceeds the money actually paid to the government. That's because taxes distort incentives to engage in mutually beneficial transactions.

Making tax policy isn't easy—in fact, if you are a politician, it can be dangerous to your professional health.

One principle used for guiding tax policy is efficiency: taxes should be designed to distort incentives as little as possible. But efficiency is not the only concern when designing tax rates. It's also important that a tax be seen as fair. Tax policy always involves striking a balance between the pursuit of efficiency and the pursuit of perceived fairness.

In this module, we will look at how taxes affect efficiency and fairness.

Equity, Efficiency, and Taxes

It's easy to get carried away with the idea that markets are always good and that economic policies that interfere with efficiency are bad. But that would be misguided because there is another factor to consider: society cares about equity, or what's "fair." There is often a trade-off between equity and efficiency: policies that promote equity often come at the cost of decreased efficiency, and policies that promote efficiency often result in decreased equity. Creating tax policy is no different. So it's important to realize that a society's choice to sacrifice some efficiency for the sake of equity, however it defines equity, may well be a valid one. It's important to understand that fairness, unlike efficiency, can be very hard to define, and it is a concept about which well-intentioned people often disagree.

In fact, the debate about equity and efficiency is at the core of most debates about taxation. Proponents of taxes that redistribute income from the rich to the poor often argue for the fairness of such redistributive taxes. Opponents of taxation often argue that phasing out certain taxes would make the economy more efficient.

Because taxes are ultimately paid out of income, economists classify taxes according to how they vary with the income of individuals. A tax that rises more than in proportion to income, so that high-income taxpayers pay a larger percentage of their income than low-income taxpayers, is a **progressive tax.** A tax that rises less than in proportion to income, so that high-income taxpayers pay a smaller percentage of their income than low-income taxpayers, is a **regressive tax.** A tax that rises in proportion to income, so that all taxpayers pay the same percentage of their income, is a **proportional tax.** The U.S. tax system contains a mixture of progressive and regressive taxes, though it is somewhat progressive overall.

A **progressive tax** rises more than in proportion to income. A **regressive tax** rises less than in proportion to income. A **proportional tax** rises in proportion to income.

An **excise tax** is a tax on sales of a particular good or service.

The Effects of Taxes on Total Surplus

To understand the economics of taxes, it's helpful to look at a simple type of tax known as an **excise tax**—a tax charged on each unit of a good or service that is sold. Most tax revenue in the United States comes from other kinds of taxes, but excise taxes are common. For example, there are excise taxes on gasoline, cigarettes, and foreign-made trucks, and many local governments impose excise taxes on services such as hotel room rentals. The lessons we'll learn from studying excise taxes apply to other, more complex taxes as well.

The Effect of an Excise Tax on Quantities and Prices

Suppose that the supply and demand for hotel rooms in the city of Potterville are as shown in Figure 15-1. We'll make the simplifying assumption that all hotel rooms are the same. In the absence of taxes, the equilibrium price of a room is $80 per night and the equilibrium quantity of hotel rooms rented is 10,000 per night.

Now suppose that Potterville's government imposes an excise tax of $40 per night on hotel rooms—that is, every time a room is rented for the night, the owner of the hotel must pay the city $40. For example, if a customer pays $80, $40 is collected as a

FIGURE 15-1 The Supply and Demand for Hotel Rooms in Potterville

In the absence of taxes, the equilibrium price of hotel rooms is $80 a night, and the equilibrium number of rooms rented is 10,000 per night, as shown by point *E*. The supply curve, *S*, shows the quantity supplied at any given price, pre-tax. At a price of $60 a night, hotel owners are willing to supply 5,000 rooms, as shown by point *B*. But post-tax, hotel owners are willing to supply the same quantity only at a price of $100: $60 for themselves plus $40 paid to the city as tax.

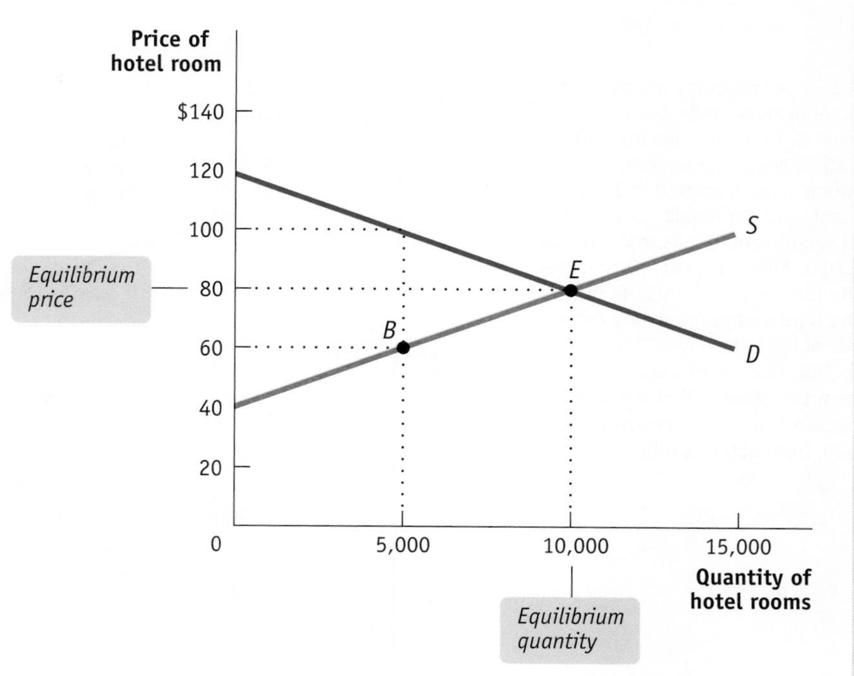

tax, leaving the hotel owner with only $40. As a result, hotel owners are less willing to supply rooms at any given price.

What does this imply about the supply curve for hotel rooms in Potterville? To answer this question, we must compare the incentives of hotel owners *pre-tax* (before the tax is levied) to their incentives *post-tax* (after the tax is levied).

From Figure 15-1 we know that pre-tax, hotel owners are willing to supply 5,000 rooms per night at a price of $60 per room. But after the $40 tax per room is levied, they are willing to supply the same amount, 5,000 rooms, only if they receive $100 per room—$60 for themselves plus $40 paid to the city as tax. In other words, in order for hotel owners to be willing to supply the same quantity post-tax as they would have pre-tax, they must receive an additional $40 per room, the amount of the tax. This implies that the post-tax supply curve shifts up by the amount of the tax compared to the pre-tax supply curve. At every quantity supplied, the supply price—the price that producers must receive to produce a given quantity—has increased by $40.

The upward shift of the supply curve caused by the tax is shown in Figure 15-2, where S_1 is the pre-tax supply curve and S_2 is the post-tax supply curve. As you can see, the market equilibrium moves from *E*, at the equilibrium price of $80 per room and 10,000 rooms rented each night, to *A*, at a market price of $100 per room and only 5,000 rooms rented each night. *A* is, of course, on both the demand curve *D* and the new supply curve S_2. In this case, $100 is the demand price of 5,000 rooms—but in effect hotel owners receive only $60, when you account for the fact that they have to pay the $40 tax. From the point of view of hotel owners, it is as if they were on their original supply curve at point *B*.

Let's check this again. How do we know that 5,000 rooms will be supplied at a price of $100? Because the price *net of tax* is $60, and according to the original supply curve, 5,000 rooms will be supplied at a price of $60, as shown by point *B* in Figure 15-2.

An excise tax *drives a wedge* between the price paid by consumers and the price received by producers. As a result of this wedge, consumers pay more and producers receive less.

In our example, consumers—people who rent hotel rooms—end up paying $100 a night, $20 more than the pre-tax price of $80. At the same time, producers—the hotel owners—receive a price net of tax of $60 per room, $20 less than the pre-tax price. In addition, the tax creates missed opportunities: 5,000 potential consumers who would

FIGURE 15-2 **An Excise Tax Imposed on Hotel Owners**

A $40 per room tax imposed on hotel owners shifts the supply curve from S_1 to S_2, an upward shift of $40. The equilibrium price of hotel rooms rises from $80 to $100 a night, and the equilibrium quantity of rooms rented falls from 10,000 to 5,000. Although hotel owners pay the tax, they actually bear only half the burden: the price they receive net of tax falls only $20, from $80 to $60. Guests who rent rooms bear the other half of the burden because the price they pay rises by $20, from $80 to $100.

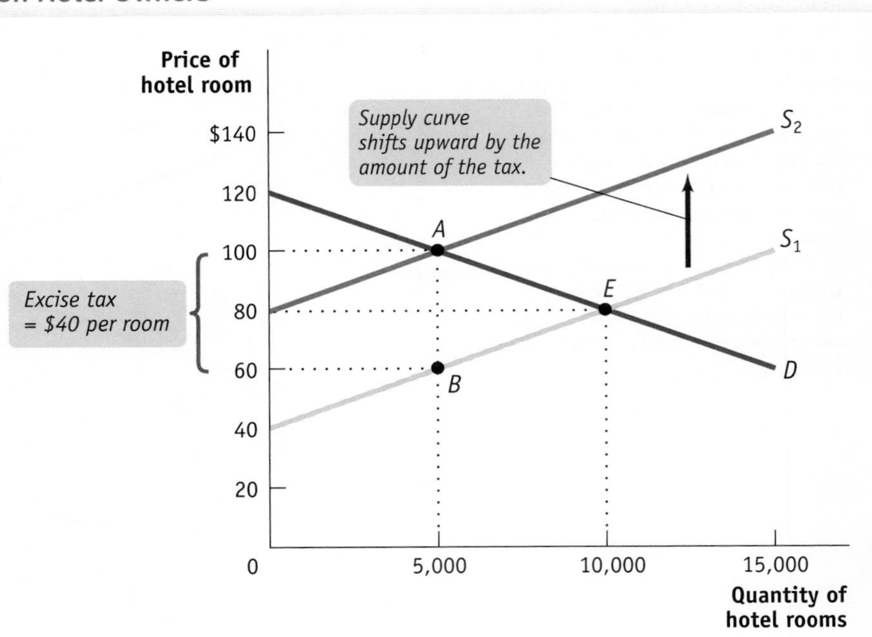

have rented hotel rooms—those willing to pay $80 but not $100 per night—are discouraged from renting rooms. Correspondingly, 5,000 rooms that would have been made available by hotel owners when they receive $80 are not offered when they receive only $60.

Like a quota on sales, discussed in Module 14, this tax leads to inefficiency by distorting incentives and creating missed opportunities for mutually beneficial transactions.

It's important to recognize that as we've described it, Potterville's hotel tax is a tax on the hotel owners, not their guests—it's a tax on the producers, not the consumers. Yet the price received by producers, net of tax, is down by only $20, half the amount of the tax, and the price paid by consumers is up by $20. In effect, half the tax is being paid by consumers.

What would happen if the city levied a tax on consumers instead of producers? That is, suppose that instead of requiring hotel owners to pay $40 a night for each room they rent, the city required hotel *guests* to pay $40 for each night they stayed in a hotel. The answer is shown in Figure 15-3. If a hotel guest must pay a tax of $40 per night, then the price for a room paid by that guest must be reduced by $40 in order for the quantity of hotel rooms demanded post-tax to be the same as that demanded pre-tax. So the demand curve shifts *downward*, from D_1 to D_2, by the amount of the tax.

At every quantity demanded, the demand price—the price that consumers must be offered to demand a given quantity—has fallen by $40. This shifts the equilibrium from *E* to *B*, where the market price of hotel rooms is $60 and 5,000 hotel rooms are bought and sold. In effect, hotel guests pay $100 when you include the tax. So from the point of view of guests, it is as if they were on their original demand curve at point *A*.

If you compare Figures 15-2 and 15-3, you will notice that the effects of the tax are the same even though different curves are shifted. In each case, consumers pay $100 per unit (including the tax, if it is their responsibility), producers receive $60 per unit (after paying the tax, if it is their responsibility), and 5,000 hotel rooms are bought and sold. *In fact, it doesn't matter who officially pays the tax—the equilibrium outcome is the same.*

This example illustrates a general principle of **tax incidence,** a measure of who really pays a tax: the burden of a tax cannot be determined by looking at who writes the check to the government. In this particular case, a $40 tax on hotel rooms brings about a $20 increase in the price paid by consumers and a $20 decrease in the price

Tax incidence is the distribution of the tax burden.

FIGURE 15-3 **An Excise Tax Imposed on Hotel Guests**

A $40 per room tax imposed on hotel guests shifts the demand curve from D_1 to D_2, a downward shift of $40. The equilibrium price of hotel rooms falls from $80 to $60 a night, and the quantity of rooms rented falls from 10,000 to 5,000. Although in this case the tax is officially paid by consumers, while in Figure 15-2 the tax was paid by producers, the outcome is the same: after taxes, hotel owners receive $60 per room but guests pay $100. This illustrates a general principle: *The incidence of an excise tax doesn't depend on whether consumers or producers officially pay the tax.*

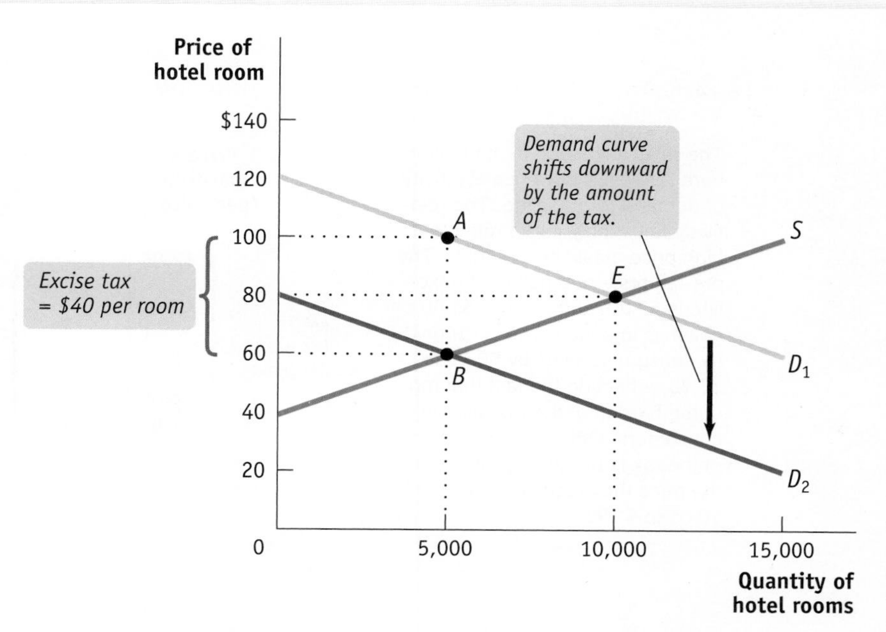

received by producers. Regardless of whether the tax is levied on consumers or producers, the incidence of the tax is the same. As we will see next, the burden of a tax depends on the price elasticities of supply and demand.

Price Elasticities and Tax Incidence

We've just learned that the incidence of an excise tax doesn't depend on who officially pays it. In the example shown in Figures 15-1 through 15-3, a tax on hotel rooms falls equally on consumers and producers, no matter on whom the tax is levied. But it's important to note that this 50–50 split between consumers and producers is a result of our assumptions in this example. In the real world, the incidence of an excise tax usually falls unevenly between consumers and producers: one group bears more of the burden than the other.

What determines how the burden of an excise tax is allocated between consumers and producers? The answer depends on the shapes of the supply and the demand curves. *More specifically, the incidence of an excise tax depends on the price elasticity of supply and the price elasticity of demand.* We can see this by looking first at a case in which consumers pay most of an excise tax, and then at a case in which producers pay most of the tax.

WHEN AN EXCISE TAX IS PAID MAINLY BY CONSUMERS Figure 15-4 shows an excise tax that falls mainly on consumers: an excise tax on gasoline, which we set at $1 per gallon. (There really is a federal excise tax on gasoline, though it is actually only about $0.18 per gallon in the United States. In addition, states impose excise taxes between $0.08 and $0.37 per gallon.) According to Figure 15-4, in the absence of the tax, gasoline would sell for $2 per gallon.

iStockphoto

Two key assumptions are reflected in the shapes of the supply and demand curves in Figure 15-4. First, the price elasticity of demand for gasoline is assumed to be very low, so the demand curve is relatively steep. Recall that a low price elasticity of demand means that the quantity demanded changes little in response to a change in price. Second, the price elasticity of supply of gasoline is assumed to be very high, so the supply curve is relatively flat. A high price elasticity of supply means that the quantity supplied changes a lot in response to a change in price.

We have just learned that an excise tax drives a wedge, equal to the size of the tax, between the price paid by consumers and the price received by producers. This wedge

FIGURE 15-4 **An Excise Tax Paid Mainly by Consumers**

The relatively steep demand curve here reflects a low price elasticity of demand for gasoline. The relatively flat supply curve reflects a high price elasticity of supply. The pre-tax price of a gallon of gasoline is $2.00, and a tax of $1.00 per gallon is imposed. The price paid by consumers rises by $0.95 to $2.95, reflecting the fact that most of the burden of the tax falls on consumers. Only a small portion of the tax is borne by producers: the price they receive falls by only $0.05 to $1.95.

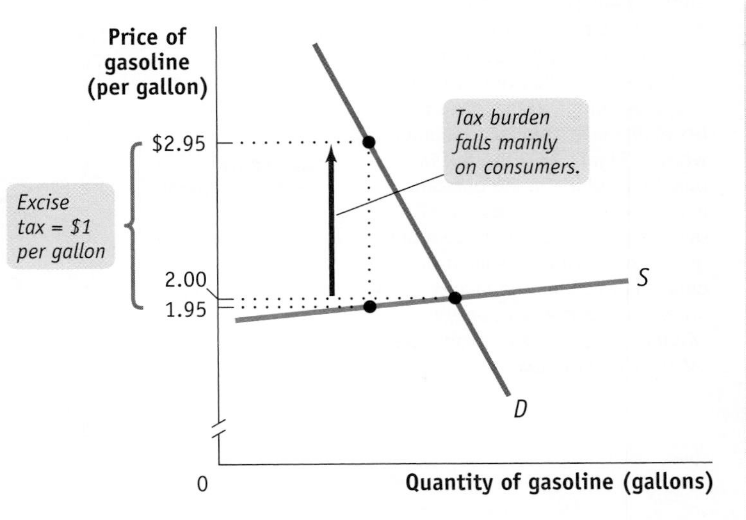

drives the price paid by consumers up and the price received by producers down. But as we can see from Figure 15-4, in this case those two effects are very unequal in size. The price received by producers falls only slightly, from $2.00 to $1.95, but the price paid by consumers rises by a lot, from $2.00 to $2.95. This means that consumers bear the greater share of the tax burden.

This example illustrates another general principle of taxation: *When the price elasticity of demand is low and the price elasticity of supply is high, the burden of an excise tax falls mainly on consumers.* Why? A low price elasticity of demand means that consumers have few substitutes and, therefore, little alternative to buying higher-priced gasoline. In contrast, a high price elasticity of supply results from the fact that producers have many production substitutes for their gasoline (that is, other uses for the crude oil from which gasoline is refined). This gives producers much greater flexibility in refusing to accept lower prices for their gasoline. And, not surprisingly, the party with the least flexibility—in this case, consumers—gets stuck paying most of the tax. This is a good description of how the burden of the most significant excise taxes actually collected in the United States today, such as those on cigarettes and alcoholic beverages, is allocated between consumers and producers.

WHEN AN EXCISE TAX IS PAID MAINLY BY PRODUCERS Figure 15-5 shows an example of an excise tax paid mainly by producers, a $5.00 per day tax on downtown parking in a small city. In the absence of the tax, the market equilibrium price of parking is $6.00 per day.

We've assumed in this case that the price elasticity of supply is very low because the lots used for parking have very few alternative uses. This makes the supply curve for parking spaces relatively steep. The price elasticity of demand, however, is assumed to be high: consumers can easily switch from the downtown spaces to other parking spaces a few minutes' walk from downtown, spaces that are not subject to the tax. This makes the demand curve relatively flat.

The tax drives a wedge between the price paid by consumers and the price received by producers. In this example, however, the tax causes the price paid by consumers to rise only slightly, from $6.00 to $6.50, but the price received by producers falls a lot, from $6.00 to $1.50. In the end, a consumer bears only $0.50 of the $5 tax burden, with a producer bearing the remaining $4.50.

Again, this example illustrates a general principle: *When the price elasticity of demand is high and the price elasticity of supply is low, the burden of an excise tax falls mainly on producers.* A real-world example is a tax on purchases of existing houses. In

FIGURE 15-5 **An Excise Tax Paid Mainly by Producers**

The relatively flat demand curve here reflects a high price elasticity of demand for downtown parking, and the relatively steep supply curve results from a low price elasticity of supply. The pre-tax price of a daily parking space is $6.00 and a tax of $5.00 is imposed. The price received by producers falls a lot, to $1.50, reflecting the fact that they bear most of the tax burden. The price paid by consumers rises a small amount, $0.50, to $6.50, so they bear very little of the burden.

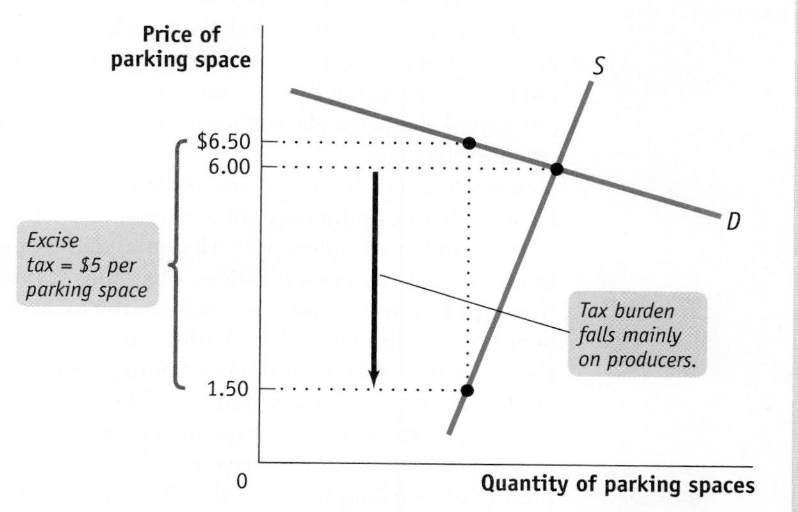

many American towns, house prices in desirable locations have risen as well-off outsiders have moved in and purchased homes from the less well-off original occupants, a phenomenon called gentrification. Some of these towns have imposed taxes on house sales intended to extract money from the new arrivals. But this ignores the fact that the price elasticity of demand for houses in a particular town is often high because potential buyers can choose to move to other towns. Furthermore, the price elasticity of supply is often low because most sellers must sell their houses due to job transfers or to provide funds for their retirement. So taxes on home purchases are actually paid mainly by the less well-off sellers—not, as town officials imagine, by wealthy buyers.

PUTTING IT ALL TOGETHER We've just seen that when the price elasticity of supply is high and the price elasticity of demand is low, an excise tax falls mainly on consumers. And when the price elasticity of supply is low and the price elasticity of demand is high, an excise tax falls mainly on producers. This leads us to the general rule: *When the price elasticity of demand is higher than the price elasticity of supply, an excise tax falls mainly on producers. When the price elasticity of supply is higher than the price elasticity of demand, an excise tax falls mainly on consumers.*

So elasticity—not who officially pays the tax—determines the incidence of an excise tax.

ECONOMICS IN ACTION

WHO PAYS THE FICA?

For 70% of Americans it's the FICA, not the income tax, that takes the biggest bite from their paychecks.

Anyone who works for an employer receives a paycheck that itemizes not only the wages paid but also the money deducted from the paycheck for various taxes. For most people, one of the big deductions is *FICA*, also known as the payroll tax. FICA, which stands for the Federal Insurance Contributions Act, pays for the Social Security and Medicare systems, federal social insurance programs that provide income and medical care to retired and disabled Americans.

In 2013, most American workers paid 7.65% of their earnings in FICA. (During 2011–2012, there was a temporary reduction in workers' tax rate to 5.65%, but that ended in 2012.) But this is literally only the half of it: each employer is required to pay an amount equal to the contributions of its employees.

How should we think about FICA? Is it really shared equally by workers and employers? We can use our previous analysis to answer that question, because FICA is like an excise tax—a tax on the sale and purchase of labor. Half of it is a tax levied on the sellers—that is, workers. The other half is a tax levied on the buyers—that is, employers.

But we already know that the incidence of a tax does not really depend on who actually makes out the check. Almost all economists agree that FICA is a tax actually paid by workers, not by their employers. The reason for this conclusion lies in a comparison of the price elasticities of the supply of labor by households and the demand for labor by firms.

Evidence indicates that the price elasticity of demand for labor is quite high, at least 3. That is, an increase in average wages of 1% would lead to at least a 3% decline in the number of hours of work demanded by employers. Labor economists believe, however, that the price elasticity of supply of labor is very low. The reason is that although a fall in the wage rate reduces the incentive to work more hours, it also makes people poorer and less able to afford leisure time. The strength of this second effect is shown in the data: the number of hours people are willing to work falls very little—if at all—when the wage per hour goes down.

Our general rule of tax incidence says that when the price elasticity of demand is much higher than the price elasticity of supply, the burden of an excise tax falls mainly on the suppliers. So the FICA falls mainly on the suppliers of labor, that is, workers—even though on paper half the tax is paid by employers. In other words, the FICA is largely borne by workers in the form of lower wages, rather than by employers in the form of lower profits.

This conclusion tells us something important about the American tax system: the FICA, rather than the much-maligned income tax, is the main tax burden on most families. For most workers, FICA is 15.3% of all wages and salaries up to $113,700 per year for 2013 (note that 7.65% + 7.65% = 15.3%). That is, the great majority of workers in the United States pay 15.3% of their wages in FICA. Only a minority of American families pay more than 15% of their income in income tax. In fact, according to estimates by the Congressional Budget Office, for more than 70% of families FICA is Uncle Sam's main bite out of their income.

The Benefits and Costs of Taxation

When a government is considering whether to impose a tax or how to design a tax system, it has to weigh the benefits of a tax against its costs. We may not think of a tax as something that provides benefits, but governments need money to provide things people want, such as streets, schools, national defense, and health care for those unable to afford it. The benefit of a tax is the revenue it raises for the government to pay for these services. Unfortunately, this benefit comes at a cost—a cost that is normally larger than the amount consumers and producers pay. Let's look first at what determines how much money a tax raises and then at the costs a tax imposes.

"What taxes would you like to see imposed on other people?"

The Revenue from an Excise Tax

How much revenue does the government collect from an excise tax? In our hotel tax example, the revenue is equal to the area of the shaded rectangle in Figure 15-6.

To see why this area represents the revenue collected by a $40 tax on hotel rooms, notice that the *height* of the rectangle is $40, equal to the tax per room. It is also, as we've seen, the size of the wedge that the tax drives between the supply price (the price received by producers) and the demand price (the price paid by consumers). Meanwhile, the *width* of the rectangle is 5,000 rooms, equal

FIGURE 15-6 The Revenue from an Excise Tax

The revenue from a $40 excise tax on hotel rooms is $200,000, equal to the tax rate, $40—the size of the wedge that the tax drives between the supply price and the demand price—multiplied by the number of rooms rented, 5,000. This is equal to the area of the shaded rectangle.

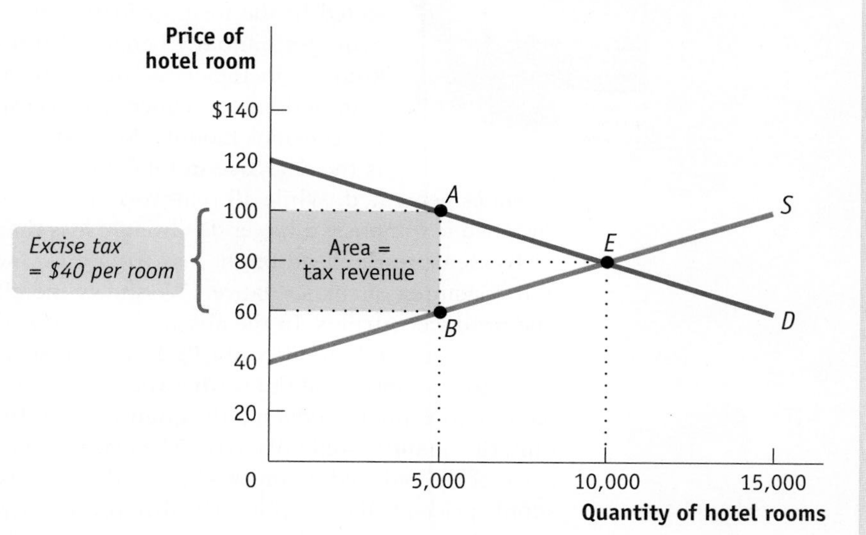

to the equilibrium quantity of rooms given the \$40 tax. With that information, we can make the following calculations.

The tax revenue collected is:

$$\text{Tax revenue} = \$40 \text{ per room} \times 5{,}000 \text{ rooms} = \$200{,}000$$

The area of the shaded rectangle is:

$$\text{Area} = \text{Height} \times \text{Width} = \$40 \text{ per room} \times 5{,}000 \text{ rooms} = \$200{,}000$$

or

$$\text{Tax revenue} = \text{Area of shaded rectangle}$$

This is a general principle: *The revenue collected by an excise tax is equal to the area of a rectangle with the height of the tax wedge between the supply price and the demand price and the width of the quantity sold under the tax.*

The Costs of Taxation

What is the cost of a tax? You might be inclined to answer that it is the amount of money taxpayers pay to the government—the tax revenue collected. But suppose the government uses the tax revenue to provide services that taxpayers want. Or suppose that the government simply hands the tax revenue back to taxpayers. Would we say in those cases that the tax didn't actually cost anything?

No—because a tax, like a quota, prevents mutually beneficial transactions from occurring. Consider Figure 15-6 once more. Here, with a \$40 tax on hotel rooms, guests pay \$100 per room but hotel owners receive only \$60 per room. Because of the wedge created by the tax, we know that some transactions didn't occur that would have occurred without the tax. More specifically, we know from the supply and demand curves that there are some potential guests who would be willing to pay up to \$90 per night and some hotel owners who would be willing to supply rooms if they received at least \$70 per night.

If these two sets of people were allowed to trade with each other without the tax, they would engage in mutually beneficial transactions—hotel rooms would be rented. But such deals would be illegal because the \$40 tax would not be paid. In our example, 5,000 potential hotel room rentals that would have occurred in the absence of the tax, to the mutual benefit of guests and hotel owners, do not take place because of the tax.

Like price controls and quantity controls, taxes create inefficiency by preventing mutually beneficial transactions from occurring.

©Visions of America, LLC/Alamy

So an excise tax imposes costs over and above the tax revenue collected in the form of inefficiency, which occurs because the tax discourages mutually beneficial transactions. The cost to society of this kind of inefficiency—the value of the forgone mutually beneficial transactions—is called *deadweight loss*, which you learned about in the previous module. More specifically, the *deadweight loss from a tax* is the decrease in total surplus resulting from the tax, minus the tax revenues generated. While all real-world taxes impose some deadweight loss, a badly designed tax imposes a larger deadweight loss than a well-designed one.

To measure the deadweight loss from a tax, we turn to the concepts of producer and consumer surplus. Figure 15-7 shows the effects of an excise tax on consumer and producer surplus. In the absence of the tax, the equilibrium is at E and the equilibrium price and quantity are P_E and Q_E, respectively. An excise tax drives a wedge equal to the amount of the tax between the price received by producers and the price paid by consumers, reducing the quantity sold. In this case, with a tax of T dollars per unit, the quantity sold falls to Q_T. The price paid by consumers rises to P_C, the demand price of the reduced quantity, Q_T, and the price received by producers falls to P_P, the supply price of that quantity. The difference between these prices, $P_C - P_P$, is equal to the excise tax, T.

FIGURE 15-7 A Tax Reduces Consumer and Producer Surplus

Before the tax, the equilibrium price and quantity are P_E and Q_E, respectively. After an excise tax of T per unit is imposed, the price to consumers rises to P_C and consumer surplus falls by the sum of the dark blue rectangle, labeled A, and the light blue triangle, labeled B. The tax also causes the price to producers to fall to P_P; producer surplus falls by the sum of the dark red rectangle, labeled C, and the light red triangle, labeled F. The government receives revenue from the tax, $Q_T \times T$, which is given by the sum of the areas A and C. Areas B and F represent the losses to consumer and producer surplus that are not collected by the government as revenue; they are the deadweight loss to society of the tax.

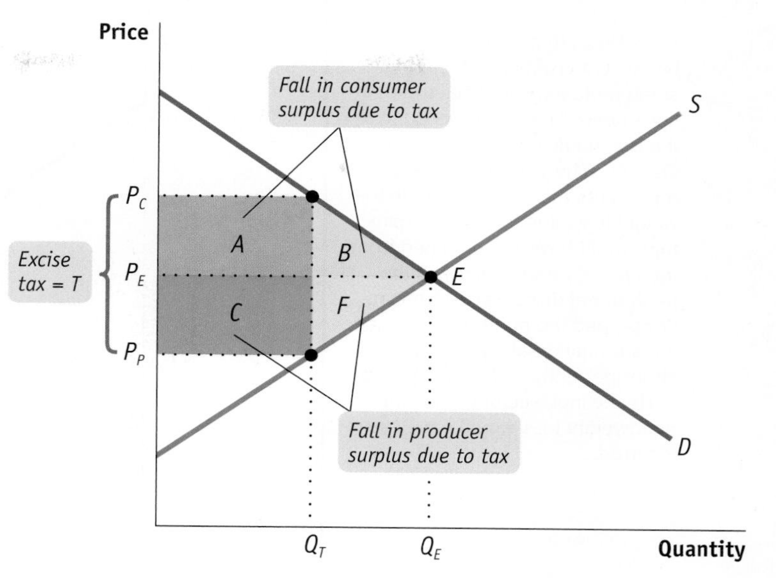

Using the concepts of producer and consumer surplus, we can show exactly how much surplus producers and consumers lose as a result of the tax. We learned previously that a fall in the price of a good generates a gain in consumer surplus that is equal to the sum of the areas of a rectangle and a triangle. Similarly, a price increase causes a loss to consumers that is represented by the sum of the areas of a rectangle and a triangle. So it's not surprising that in the case of an excise tax, the rise in the price paid by consumers causes a loss equal to the sum of the areas of a rectangle and a triangle: the dark blue rectangle labeled A and the area of the light blue triangle labeled B in Figure 15-7.

Meanwhile, the fall in the price received by producers leads to a fall in producer surplus. This, too, is equal to the sum of the areas of a rectangle and a triangle. The loss in producer surplus is the sum of the areas of the dark red rectangle labeled C and the light red triangle labeled F in Figure 15-7.

Of course, although consumers and producers are hurt by the tax, the government gains revenue. The revenue the government collects is equal to the tax per unit sold, T, multiplied by the quantity sold, Q_T. This revenue is equal to the area of a rectangle Q_T wide and T high. And we already have that rectangle in the figure: it is the sum of rectangles A and C. So the government gains part of what consumers and producers lose from an excise tax.

But a portion of the loss to producers and consumers from the tax is not offset by a gain to the government—specifically, the two triangles B and F. The deadweight loss caused by the tax is equal to the combined area of these two triangles. It represents the total surplus lost to society because of the tax—that is, the amount of surplus that would have been generated by transactions that now do not take place because of the tax.

Figure 15-8 is a version of Figure 15-7 that leaves out rectangles A (the surplus shifted from consumers to the government) and C (the surplus shifted from producers to the government) and shows only the deadweight loss, drawn here as a triangle shaded yellow. The base of that triangle is equal to the tax wedge, T; the height of the triangle is equal to the reduction in the quantity transacted due to the tax, $Q_E - Q_T$. Clearly, the larger the tax wedge and the larger the reduction in the quantity transacted, the greater the inefficiency from the tax.

But also note an important, contrasting point: if the excise tax somehow *didn't* reduce the quantity bought and sold in this market—if Q_T remained equal to Q_E after

FIGURE 15-8 **The Deadweight Loss of a Tax**

A tax leads to a deadweight loss because it creates inefficiency: some mutually beneficial transactions never take place because of the tax, namely the transactions $Q_E - Q_T$. The yellow area here represents the value of the deadweight loss: it is the total surplus that would have been gained from the $Q_E - Q_T$ transactions. If the tax had not discouraged transactions—had the number of transactions remained at Q_E because of either perfectly inelastic supply or perfectly inelastic demand—no deadweight loss would have been incurred.

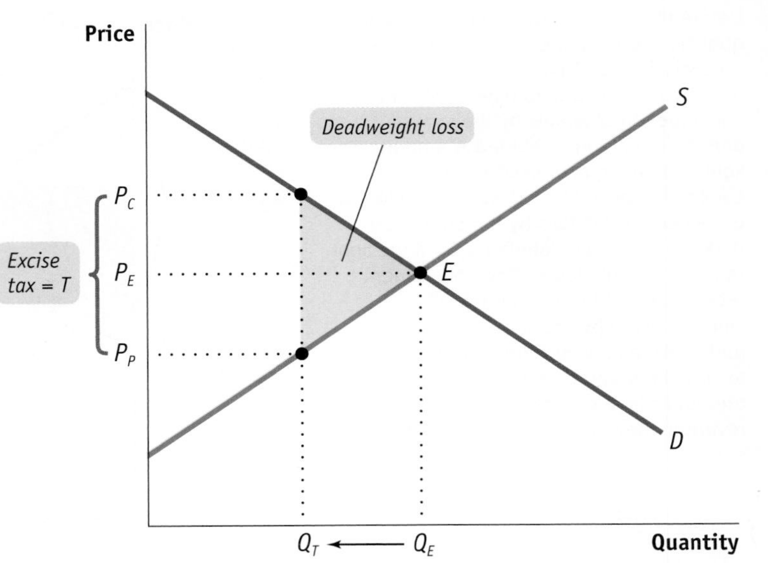

the tax was levied—the yellow triangle would disappear and the deadweight loss from the tax would be zero. So if a tax does *not* discourage transactions, which would be true if either supply or demand were perfectly inelastic, it causes no deadweight loss. In this case, the tax simply shifts surplus straight from consumers and producers to the government.

Using a triangle to measure deadweight loss is a technique used in many economic applications. For example, triangles are used to measure the deadweight loss produced by types of taxes other than excise taxes. They are also used to measure the deadweight loss produced by monopoly, another kind of market distortion. And deadweight-loss triangles are often used to evaluate the benefits and costs of public policies besides taxation—such as whether to impose stricter safety standards on a product.

In considering the total amount of inefficiency caused by a tax, we must also take into account something not shown in Figure 15-8: the resources actually used by the government to collect the tax, and by taxpayers to pay it, over and above the amount of the tax. These lost resources are called the **administrative costs** of the tax. The most familiar administrative cost of the U.S. tax system is the time individuals spend filling out their income tax forms or the money they spend on accountants to prepare their tax forms for them. (The latter is considered an inefficiency from the point of view of society because accountants could instead be performing other, non-tax-related services.)

Included in the administrative costs that taxpayers incur are resources used to evade the tax, both legally and illegally. The costs of operating the Internal Revenue Service, the arm of the federal government tasked with collecting the federal income tax, are actually quite small in comparison to the administrative costs paid by taxpayers. The total inefficiency caused by a tax is the sum of its deadweight loss and its administrative costs.

Some extreme forms of taxation, such as the *poll tax* instituted by the government of British Prime Minister Margaret Thatcher in 1989, are notably unfair but very efficient. A poll tax is an example of a **lump-sum tax,** a tax that is the same for everyone regardless of any actions people take. The poll tax in Britain was widely perceived as much less fair than the tax structure it replaced, in which local taxes were proportional to property values.

The **administrative costs** of a tax are the resources used by government to collect the tax, and by taxpayers to pay (or to evade) it, over and above the amount collected.

A **lump-sum tax** is a tax of a fixed amount paid by all taxpayers.

Under the old system, the highest local taxes were paid by the people with the most expensive houses. Because these people tended to be wealthy, they were also best able to bear the burden. But the old system definitely distorted incentives to engage in mutually beneficial transactions and created deadweight loss. People who were considering home improvements knew that such improvements, by making their property more valuable, would increase their tax bills. The result, surely, was that some home improvements that would have taken place without the tax did not take place because of it.

In contrast, a lump-sum tax does not distort incentives. Because under a lump-sum tax people have to pay the same amount of tax regardless of their actions, it does not cause them to substitute untaxed goods for a good whose price has been artificially inflated by a tax, as occurs with an excise tax. So lump-sum taxes, although unfair, are better than other taxes at promoting economic efficiency.

MODULE 15 Review

Solutions appear at the back of the book.

Check Your Understanding

1. Consider the market for butter, shown in the accompanying figure. The government imposes an excise tax of $0.30 per pound of butter. What is the price paid by consumers post-tax? What is the price received by producers post-tax? What is the quantity of butter sold? How is the incidence of the tax allocated between consumers and producers? Show this on the figure.

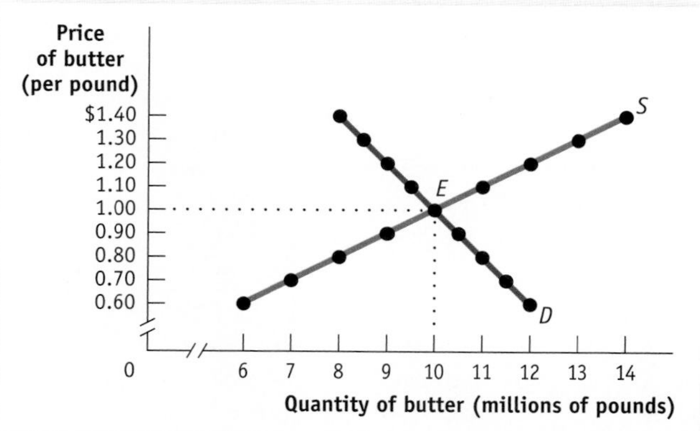

2. The accompanying table shows five consumers' willingness to pay for one can of diet soda each as well as five producers' costs of selling one can of diet soda each. Each consumer buys at most one can of soda; each producer sells at most one can of soda. The government asks your advice about the effects of an excise tax of $0.40 per can of diet soda. Assume that there are no administrative costs from the tax.

Consumer	Willingness to Pay	Producer	Cost
Ana	$0.70	Zhang	$0.10
Bernice	0.60	Yves	0.20
Chizuko	0.50	Xavier	0.30
Dagmar	0.40	Walter	0.40
Ella	0.30	Vern	0.50

a. Without the excise tax, what is the equilibrium price and the equilibrium quantity of soda?

b. The excise tax raises the price paid by consumers post-tax to $0.60 and lowers the price received by producers post-tax to $0.20. With the excise tax, what is the quantity of soda sold?

c. Without the excise tax, how much individual consumer surplus does each of the consumers gain? How much individual consumer surplus does each consumer gain with the tax? How much total consumer surplus is lost as a result of the tax?

d. Without the excise tax, how much individual producer surplus does each of the producers gain? How much individual producer surplus does each producer gain with the tax? How much total producer surplus is lost as a result of the tax?

e. How much government revenue does the excise tax create?

f. What is the deadweight loss from the imposition of this excise tax?

Multiple-Choice Questions

1. An excise tax imposed on sellers in a market will result in which of the following?
   I. an upward shift of the supply curve
   II. a downward shift of the demand curve
   III. deadweight loss
   a. I only
   b. II only
   c. III only
   d. I and III only
   e. I, II, and III

2. An excise tax will be paid mainly by producers when
   a. it is imposed on producers.
   b. it is imposed on consumers.
   c. the price elasticity of supply is low and the price elasticity of demand is high.
   d. the price elasticity of supply is high and the price elasticity of demand is low.
   e. the price elasticity of supply is perfectly elastic.

Critical-Thinking Question

Draw a correctly labeled graph of a competitive market in equilibrium. Use your graph to illustrate the effect of an excise tax imposed on consumers. Indicate each of the following on your graph:

a. the equilibrium price and quantity without the tax, labeled P_E and Q_E
b. the quantity sold in the market post-tax, labeled Q_T
c. the price paid by consumers post-tax, labeled P_C
d. the price received by producers post-tax, labeled P_P
e. the tax revenue generated by the tax, labeled "Tax revenue"
f. the deadweight loss resulting from the tax, labeled "DWL"
g. the wedge created by the tax between P_C and P_P, labeled "Excise tax"

BUSINESS CASE: Medallion Financial: Cruising Right Along

Owaki/Kulla/Corbis

Back in 1937, before New York City froze its number of taxi medallions, Andrew Murstein's immigrant grandfather bought his first one for $10. Over time, the grandfather accumulated 500 medallions, which he rented to other drivers. Those 500 taxi medallions became the foundation for Medallion Financial: the company that would eventually pass to Andrew, its current president.

With a market value of almost $300 million in early 2013, Medallion Financial has shifted its major line of business from renting out medallions to financing the purchase of new ones, lending money to those who want to buy a medallion but don't have the sizable amount of cash required to do so. Murstein believes that he is helping people who, like his Polish immigrant grandfather, want to buy a piece of the American dream.

Andrew Murstein carefully watches the value of a New York City taxi medallion: the more one costs, the more demand there is for loans from Medallion Financial, and the more interest the company makes on the loan. A loan from Medallion Financial is secured by the value of the medallion itself. If the borrower is unable to repay the loan, Medallion Financial takes possession of his or her medallion and resells it to offset the cost of the loan default. As of 2012, the value of a medallion has risen faster than stocks, oil, and gold. Since 1990, the value of a medallion rose 555% compared to only 330% for an index of stocks.

But medallion prices can fluctuate dramatically, threatening profits. During periods of a very strong economy, such as 1999 and 2001, the price of New York taxi medallions fell as drivers found jobs in other sectors. When the New York economy tanked in the aftermath of 9/11, the price of a medallion fell to $180,000, its lowest level in 12 years. In 2004, medallion owners were concerned about the impending sale by the New York City Taxi and Limousine Commission of an additional 900 medallions. As Peter Hernandez, a worried New York cabdriver who financed his medallion with a loan from Medallion Financial, said at the time: "If they pump new taxis into the industry, it devalues my medallion. It devalues my daily income, too."

Yet Murstein has always been optimistic that medallions would hold their value. He believed that a 25% fare increase would offset potential losses in their value caused by the sale of new medallions. In addition, more medallions would mean more loans for his company. As of early 2013, Murstein's optimism had been justified. Because of the financial crisis of 2007–2009, many New York companies cut back the limousine services they ordinarily provided to their employees, forcing them to take taxis instead. As a result, the price of a medallion rose to an astonishing $917,000 in March 2013. And investors have noticed the value in Medallion Financial's line of business: from March 2012 to March 2013, shares of Medallion Financial have risen 40%.

Questions for Thought

1. How does Medallion Financial benefit from the restriction on the number of New York taxi medallions?
2. What will be the effect on Medallion Financial if New York companies resume widespread use of limousine services for their employees? What is the economic motivation that prompts companies to offer this perk to their employees? (Note that it is very difficult and expensive to own a personal car in New York City.)
3. What would happen to Medallion Financial's business if New York City eliminated restrictions on the number of taxis?

SECTION 5 REVIEW

Summary

Price Controls (Ceilings and Floors)

1. Even when a market is efficient, governments often intervene to pursue greater fairness or to please a powerful interest group. Interventions can take the form of **price controls** or **quantity controls,** both of which generate predictable and undesirable side effects, consisting of various forms of inefficiency and illegal activity.
2. A **price ceiling,** a maximum market price below the equilibrium price, benefits successful buyers but creates persistent shortages. Because the price is maintained below the equilibrium price, the quantity demanded is increased and the quantity supplied is decreased compared to the equilibrium quantity. This leads to predictable problems including **inefficient allocation to consumers, wasted resources,** and **inefficiently low quality.** It also encourages illegal activity as people turn to **black markets** to get the good. Because of these problems, price ceilings have generally lost favor as an economic policy tool. But some governments continue to impose them either because they don't understand the effects or because the price ceilings benefit some influential group.
3. A **price floor,** a minimum market price above the equilibrium price, benefits successful sellers but creates a persistent surplus: because the price is maintained above the equilibrium price, the quantity demanded is decreased and the quantity supplied is increased compared to the equilibrium quantity. This leads to predictable problems: inefficiencies in the form of **inefficient allocation of sales among sellers,** wasted resources, and **inefficiently high quality.** It also encourages illegal activity such as black markets. The most well known kind of price floor is the **minimum wage,** but price floors are also commonly applied to agricultural products.

Quantity Controls (Quotas)

4. Quantity controls, or **quotas,** limit the quantity of a good that can be bought or sold. The government issues **licenses** to individuals, the right to sell a given quantity of the good. The owner of a license earns a **quota rent,** earnings that accrue from ownership of the right to sell the good. It is equal to the difference between the **demand price** at the quota amount, what consumers are willing to pay for that amount, and the **supply price** at the quota amount, what suppliers are willing to accept for that amount. Economists say that a quota drives a **wedge** between the demand price and the supply price; this wedge is equal to the quota rent. By limiting mutually beneficial transactions, quantity controls generate inefficiency. Like price controls, quantity controls lead to **deadweight loss** and encourage illegal activity.

Taxes

5. A tax that rises more than in proportion to income is a **progressive tax.** A tax that rises less than in proportion to income is a **regressive tax.** A tax that rises in proportion to income is, you guessed it, a **proportional tax.**
6. An **excise tax**—a tax on the purchase or sale of a good—raises the price paid by consumers and reduces the price received by producers, driving a wedge between the two. The **incidence** of the tax—how the burden of the tax is divided between consumers and producers—does not depend on who officially pays the tax.
7. The incidence of an excise tax depends on the price elasticities of supply and demand. If the price elasticity of demand is higher than the price elasticity of supply, the tax falls mainly on producers; if the price elasticity of supply is higher than the price elasticity of demand, the tax falls mainly on consumers.
8. The tax revenue generated by a tax depends on the **tax rate** and on the number of units sold with the tax. Excise taxes cause inefficiency in the form of deadweight loss because they discourage some mutually beneficial transactions. Taxes also impose **administrative costs:** resources used to collect the tax, to pay it (over and above the amount of the tax), and to evade it.
9. An excise tax generates revenue for the government but lowers total surplus. The loss in total surplus exceeds the tax revenue, resulting in a deadweight loss to society. This deadweight loss is represented by a triangle, the area of which equals the value of the transactions discouraged by the tax. The greater the elasticity of demand or supply, or both, the larger the deadweight loss from a tax. If either demand or supply is perfectly inelastic, there is no deadweight loss from a tax.
10. A **lump-sum tax** is a tax of a fixed amount paid by all taxpayers. Because a lump-sum tax does not depend on the behavior of taxpayers, it does not discourage mutually beneficial transactions and therefore causes no deadweight loss.

Key Terms

Price controls, p. 128
Price ceiling, p. 128
Price floor, p. 128
Inefficient allocation to consumers, p. 131
Wasted resources, p. 132
Inefficiently low quality, p. 132
Black markets, p. 132
Minimum wage, p. 134
Inefficient allocation of sales among sellers, p. 136
Inefficiently high quality, p. 137
Quantity control or quota, p. 140
License, p. 140
Demand price, p. 141
Supply price, p. 142
Wedge, p. 143
Quota rent, p. 143
Deadweight loss, p. 144
Progressive tax, p. 147
Regressive tax, p. 147
Proportional tax, p. 147
Excise tax, p. 147
Tax incidence, p. 149
Administrative costs, p. 156
Lump-sum tax, p. 156

Problems

1. Suppose it is decided that rent control in New York City will be abolished and that market rents will now prevail. Assume that all rental units are identical and are therefore offered at the same rent. To address the plight of residents who may be unable to pay the market rent, an income supplement will be paid to all low-income households equal to the difference between the old controlled rent and the new market rent.

   a. Use a diagram to show the effect on the rental market of the elimination of rent control. What will happen to the quality and quantity of rental housing supplied?

   b. Now use a second diagram to show the additional effect of the income-supplement policy on the market, namely the resulting increase in demand. What effect does it have on the market rent and quantity of rental housing supplied in comparison to your answers to part a?

   c. Are tenants better or worse off as a result of these policies? Are landlords better or worse off?

   d. From a political standpoint, why do you think cities have been more likely to resort to rent control rather than a policy of income supplements to help low-income people pay for housing?

2. In the late eighteenth century, the price of bread in New York City was controlled, set at a predetermined price above the market price.

   a. Draw a diagram showing the effect of the policy. Did the policy act as a price ceiling or a price floor?

   b. What kinds of inefficiencies were likely to have arisen when the controlled price of bread was above the market price? Explain in detail.

   One year during this period, a poor wheat harvest caused a leftward shift in the supply of bread and therefore an increase in its market price. New York bakers found that the controlled price of bread in New York was below the market price.

   c. Draw a diagram showing the effect of the price control on the market for bread during this one-year period. Did the policy act as a price ceiling or a price floor?

   d. What kinds of inefficiencies do you think occurred during this period? Explain in detail.

3. Suppose the U.S. government decides that the incomes of dairy farmers should be maintained at a level that allows the traditional family dairy farm to survive. It therefore implements a price floor of \$1 per pint by buying surplus milk until the market price is \$1 per pint. Use the accompanying diagram to answer the following questions.

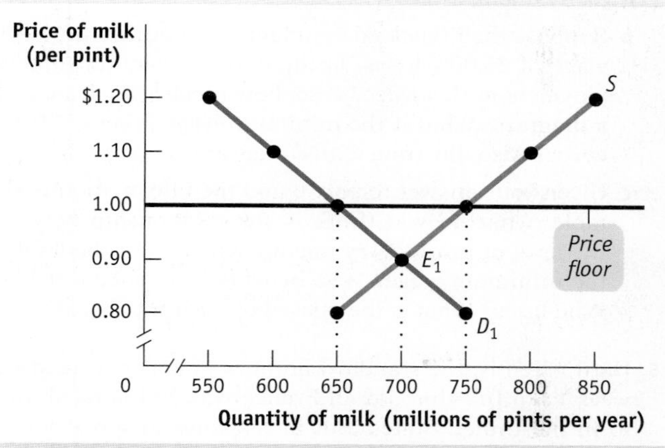

   a. How much surplus milk will be produced as a result of this policy?

   b. What will be the cost to the government of this policy?

   c. Since milk is an important source of protein and calcium, the government decides to provide the surplus milk it purchases to elementary schools at a price of only \$0.60 per pint. Assume that schools will buy any amount of milk available at this low price. But parents now reduce their purchases of milk at any price by 50 million pints per year because they know their children are getting milk at school. How much will the dairy program now cost the government?

   d. Give two examples of inefficiencies arising from wasted resources that are likely to result from this policy. What is the missed opportunity in each case?

4. European governments tend to make greater use of price controls than the U.S. government. For example, the French government sets minimum starting yearly wages for new hires who have completed *le bac,* certification

roughly equivalent to a high school diploma. The demand schedule for new hires with *le bac* and the supply schedule for similarly credentialed new job seekers are given in the accompanying table. The price here—given in euros, the currency used in France—is the same as the yearly wage.

Wage (per year)	Quantity demanded (new job offers per year)	Quantity supplied (new job seekers per year)
€45,000	200,000	325,000
40,000	220,000	320,000
35,000	250,000	310,000
30,000	290,000	290,000
25,000	370,000	200,000

a. In the absence of government interference, what is the equilibrium wage and number of graduates hired per year? Illustrate with a diagram. Will there be anyone seeking a job at the equilibrium wage who is unable to find one—that is, will there be anyone who is involuntarily unemployed?

b. Suppose the French government sets a minimum yearly wage of 35,000 euros. Is there any involuntary unemployment at this wage? If so, how much? Illustrate with a diagram. What if the minimum wage is set at 40,000 euros? Also illustrate with a diagram.

c. Given your answer to part b and the information in the table, what do you think is the relationship between the level of involuntary unemployment and the level of the minimum wage? Who benefits from such a policy? Who loses? What is the missed opportunity here?

5. Until recently, the standard number of hours worked per week for a full-time job in France was 39 hours, similar to in the United States. But in response to social unrest over high levels of involuntary unemployment, the French government instituted a 35-hour workweek—a worker could not work more than 35 hours per week even if both the worker and employer wanted it. The motivation behind this policy was that if current employees worked fewer hours, employers would be forced to hire more new workers. Assume that it is costly for employers to train new workers. French employers were greatly opposed to this policy and threatened to move their operations to neighboring countries that did not have such employment restrictions. Can you explain their attitude? Give an example of both an inefficiency and an illegal activity that are likely to arise from this policy.

6. The waters off the north Atlantic coast were once teeming with fish. Now, due to overfishing by the commercial fishing industry, the stocks of fish are seriously depleted. In 1991, the National Marine Fishery Service of the U.S. government implemented a quota to allow fish stocks to recover. The quota limited the amount of swordfish caught per year by all U.S.-licensed fishing boats to 7 million pounds. As soon as the U.S. fishing fleet had met the quota, the swordfish catch was closed down for the rest of the year. The accompanying table gives the hypothetical demand and supply schedules for swordfish caught in the United States per year.

Price of swordfish (per pound)	Quantity of swordfish (millions of pounds per year)	
	Quantity demanded	Quantity supplied
$20	6	15
18	7	13
16	8	11
14	9	9
12	10	7

a. Use a diagram to show the effect of the quota on the market for swordfish in 1991.

b. How do you think fishermen will change how they fish in response to this policy?

7. Consider the original market for pizza in Collegetown, illustrated in the accompanying table. Collegetown officials decide to impose an excise tax on pizza of $4 per pizza.

Price of pizza	Quantity of pizza demanded	Quantity of pizza supplied
10	0	6
9	1	5
8	2	4
7	3	3
6	4	2
5	5	1
4	6	0
3	7	0
2	8	0
1	9	0

a. What is the quantity of pizza bought and sold after the imposition of the tax? What is the price paid by consumers? What is the price received by producers?

b. Calculate the consumer surplus and the producer surplus after the imposition of the tax. By how much has the imposition of the tax reduced consumer surplus? By how much has it reduced producer surplus?

c. How much tax revenue does Collegetown earn from this tax?

d. Calculate the deadweight loss from this tax.

8. The state needs to raise money, and the governor has a choice of imposing an excise tax of the same amount on one of two previously untaxed goods: either restaurant meals or gasoline. Both the demand for and the supply of restaurant meals are more elastic than the demand for and the supply of gasoline. If the governor wants to minimize the deadweight loss caused by the tax, which good should be taxed? For each good, draw a diagram that illustrates the deadweight loss from taxation.

9. The U.S. government would like to help the American auto industry compete against foreign automakers that sell trucks in the United States. It can do this by imposing an excise tax on each foreign truck sold in the United States. The hypothetical pre-tax demand and supply schedules for imported trucks are given in the accompanying table.

Price of imported truck	Quantity of imported trucks (thousands)	
	Quantity demanded	Quantity supplied
$32,000	100	400
31,000	200	350
30,000	300	300
29,000	400	250
28,000	500	200
27,000	600	150

a. In the absence of government interference, what is the equilibrium price of an imported truck? The equilibrium quantity? Illustrate with a diagram.

b. Assume that the government imposes an excise tax of $3,000 per imported truck. Illustrate the effect of this excise tax in your diagram from part a. How many imported trucks are now purchased and at what price? How much does the foreign automaker receive per truck?

c. Calculate the government revenue raised by the excise tax in part b. Illustrate it on your diagram.

d. How does the excise tax on imported trucks benefit American automakers? Whom does it hurt? How does inefficiency arise from this government policy?

10. In 1990, the United States began to levy a tax on sales of luxury cars. For simplicity, assume that the tax was an excise tax of $6,000 per car. The accompanying figure shows hypothetical demand and supply curves for luxury cars.

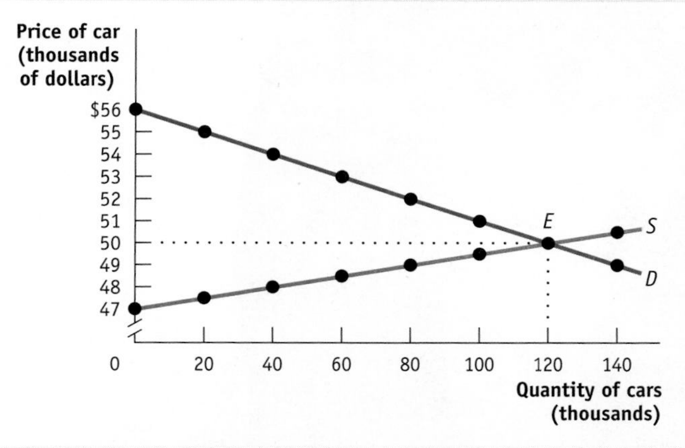

a. Under the tax, what is the price paid by consumers? What is the price received by producers? What is the government tax revenue from the excise tax?

Over time, the tax on luxury automobiles was slowly phased out (and completely eliminated in 2002). Suppose that the excise tax falls from $6,000 per car to $4,500 per car.

b. After the reduction in the excise tax from $6,000 to $4,500 per car, what is the price paid by consumers? What is the price received by producers? What is tax revenue now?

c. Compare the tax revenue created by the taxes in parts a and b. What accounts for the change in tax revenue from the reduction in the excise tax?

11. All states impose excise taxes on gasoline. According to data from the Federal Highway Administration, one year the state of California imposed an excise tax of $0.18 per gallon of gasoline. That same year, gasoline sales in California totaled 14.8 billion gallons. What was California's tax revenue from the gasoline excise tax? If California doubled the excise tax, would tax revenue double? Why or why not?

12. In each of the following cases involving taxes, explain: (i) whether the incidence of the tax falls more heavily on consumers or producers, (ii) why government revenue raised from the tax is not a good indicator of the true cost of the tax, and (iii) how deadweight loss arises as a result of the tax.

a. The government imposes an excise tax on the sale of all college textbooks. Before the tax was imposed, 1 million textbooks were sold every year at a price of $50. After the tax is imposed, 600,000 books are sold yearly; students pay $55 per book, $30 of which publishers receive.

b. The government imposes an excise tax on the sale of all airline tickets. Before the tax was imposed, 3 million airline tickets were sold every year at a price of $500. After the tax is imposed, 1.5 million tickets are sold yearly; travelers pay $550 per ticket, $450 of which the airlines receive.

c. The government imposes an excise tax on the sale of all toothbrushes. Before the tax, 2 million toothbrushes were sold every year at a price of $1.50. After the tax is imposed, 800,000 toothbrushes are sold every year; consumers pay $2 per toothbrush, $1.25 of which producers receive.

Module 16: Gains from Trade
Module 17: Supply, Demand, and International Trade

International Trade

CAR PARTS AND SUCKING SOUNDS

Stop in an auto showroom, and odds are that the majority of cars on display were produced in the United States. Even if they're Nissans, Hondas, or Volkswagens, most cars sold in this country were made here by the Big Three U.S. auto firms or by subsidiaries of foreign firms.

Although that car you're looking at may have been made in America, a significant part of what's inside was probably made elsewhere, very likely in Mexico. Since the 1980s, U.S. auto production has increasingly relied on factories in Mexico to produce *labor-intensive* auto parts, such as seat parts—products that use a relatively high amount of labor in their production.

Changes in economic policy over the years have contributed greatly to the emergence of large-scale U.S. imports of auto parts from Mexico. Until the 1980s, Mexico had a system of *trade protection*—taxes and regulations limiting imports—that kept out U.S. manufactured goods and encouraged Mexican industry to focus on selling to Mexican consumers rather than to a wider market. In 1985, however, the Mexican government began dismantling much of its trade protection, boosting trade with the United States.

A further boost came in 1993, when the United States, Mexico, and Canada signed the North American Free Trade Agreement (NAFTA), which eliminated most taxes on trade among the three nations and provided guarantees that business investments in Mexico would be protected from arbitrary changes in government policy.

NAFTA was deeply controversial when it went into effect: Mexican workers were paid only about 10% as much as their U.S. counterparts, and many expressed concern that U.S. jobs would be lost to low-wage competition. And although apocalyptic predictions about NAFTA's impact haven't come to pass, the agreement remains controversial even now.

Most economists disagreed with those who saw NAFTA as a threat to the U.S. economy. We saw in Module 4 how international trade can lead to mutual *gains from trade*. Economists, for the most part, believed that the same logic applied to NAFTA, that the treaty would make both the United States and Mexico richer. But making a nation as a whole richer isn't the same thing as improving the welfare of everyone living in a country, and there were and are reasons to believe that NAFTA hurts some U.S. citizens.

Until now, we have analyzed the economy as if it were self-sufficient, producing all the goods and services it consumes, and vice versa. This is, of course, true for the world economy as a whole. But it's not true for any individual country. Assuming self-sufficiency would have been far more accurate 50 years ago, when the United States exported only a small fraction of what it produced and imported only a small fraction of what it consumed.

Since then, however, both U.S. imports and exports have grown dramatically. Moreover, compared to the United States, other countries engage in far more foreign trade relative to the size of their economies.

To have a full picture of how national economies work, we must understand the economics of international trade, which we will examine in this section. We start by revisiting the model of comparative advantage, which, as we saw in Module 4, explains why there are gains from international trade. We then extend our study to address deeper questions about international trade, such as why some individuals can be hurt by international trade while the country, as a whole, gains. At the conclusion of the section, we'll look at the effects of policies that countries use to limit imports or promote exports. And we'll look at the challenges nations face as a result of the forward march of globalization.

MODULE 16

Gains from Trade

(left) Susana Gonzalez/Bloomberg via Getty Images • (right) Scott Olson/Getty Images

WHAT YOU WILL LEARN

1. **How comparative advantage leads to mutually beneficial international trade**
2. **The sources of international comparative advantage**
3. **Who gains and who loses from international trade, and why the gains exceed the losses**

Comparative Advantage and International Trade

The United States buys auto parts—and many other goods and services—from other countries. At the same time, it sells many goods and services to other countries. Goods and services purchased from abroad are **imports;** goods and services sold abroad are **exports.**

As illustrated by the opening story, imports and exports have taken on an increasingly important role in the U.S. economy. Over the last 50 years, both imports into and exports from the United States have grown faster than the U.S. economy as a whole. Panel (a) of Figure 16-1 shows how the values of U.S. imports and exports have grown as a percentage of gross domestic product (GDP). Panel (b) shows imports and exports as a percentage of GDP for a number of countries. It shows that foreign trade is significantly more important for many other countries than it is for the United States. (Japan is the exception.)

Goods and services purchased from other countries are **imports;** goods and services sold to other countries are **exports.**

Globalization is the phenomenon of growing economic linkages among countries.

Foreign trade isn't the only way countries interact economically. In the modern world, investors from one country often invest funds in another nation; many companies are multinational, with subsidiaries operating in several countries; and a growing number of individuals work in a country different from the one in which they were born. The growth of all these forms of economic linkages among countries is often called **globalization.**

In this module and the next, however, we'll focus mainly on international trade. To understand why international trade occurs and why economists believe it is beneficial to the economy, we will first review the concept of comparative advantage.

FIGURE 16-1 The Growing Importance of International Trade

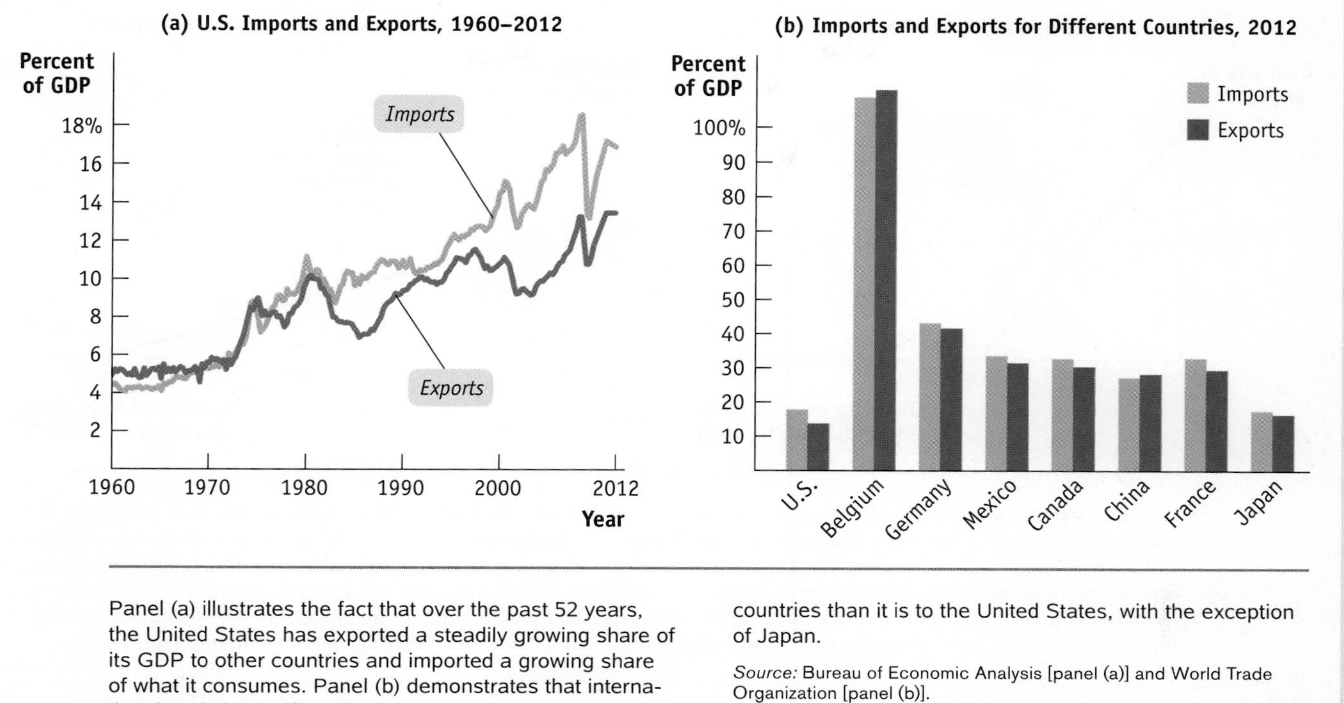

Panel (a) illustrates the fact that over the past 52 years, the United States has exported a steadily growing share of its GDP to other countries and imported a growing share of what it consumes. Panel (b) demonstrates that international trade is significantly more important to many other countries than it is to the United States, with the exception of Japan.

Source: Bureau of Economic Analysis [panel (a)] and World Trade Organization [panel (b)].

Production Possibilities and Comparative Advantage, Revisited

To produce auto parts, any country must use resources—land, labor, capital, and so on—that could have been used to produce other things. The potential production of other goods a country must forgo to produce an auto part is the opportunity cost of that part.

In some cases, it's easy to see why the opportunity cost of producing a good is especially low in a given country. In other cases, matters are a bit less obvious. It's as easy to produce auto parts in the United States as it is in Mexico, and Mexican auto parts workers are, if anything, less efficient than their U.S. counterparts. But Mexican workers are a *lot* less productive than U.S. workers in other areas, such as aircraft and chemical production. This means that diverting a Mexican worker into auto parts production reduces output of other goods less than diverting a U.S. worker into auto parts production. That is, the opportunity cost of producing auto parts in Mexico is less than it is in the United States.

So we say that Mexico has a comparative advantage in producing auto parts. Let's repeat the definition of comparative advantage from Module 4: *A country has a comparative advantage in producing a good or service if the opportunity cost of producing the good or service is lower for that country than for other countries.*

Figure 16-2 provides a hypothetical example of comparative advantage in international trade. We assume that only two goods are produced and consumed, auto parts and airplanes, and that there are only two countries in the world, the United States and Mexico. (In real life, auto parts aren't worth much without auto bodies to put them in, but let's set that issue aside). The figure shows hypothetical production possibility curves for the United States and Mexico.

FIGURE 16-2 Comparative Advantage and Production Possibilities

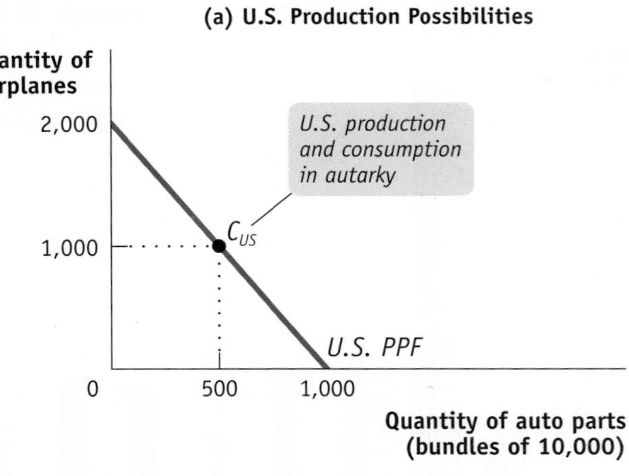

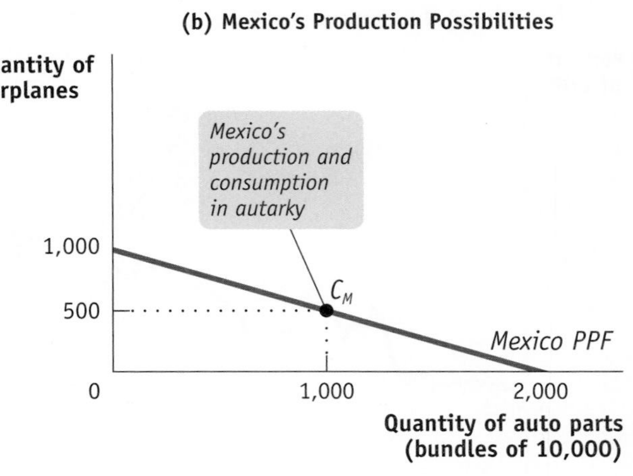

The U.S. opportunity cost of 1 bundle of auto parts in terms of airplanes is 2: for every additional bundle of auto parts, 2 airplanes must be forgone. The Mexican opportunity cost of 1 bundle of auto parts in terms of airplanes is ½: for every additional bundle of auto parts, only ½ of an airplane must be forgone. Because the opportunity cost is lower, the United States has a comparative advantage in airplane production, and Mexico has a comparative advantage in auto parts production. In autarky, each country is forced to consume only what it produces: 1,000 airplanes and 500 bundles of auto parts for the United States; 500 airplanes and 1,000 bundles of auto parts for Mexico.

In Figure 16-2 we have grouped auto parts into bundles of 10,000, so, for example, a country that produces 500 bundles of auto parts is producing 5 million individual auto parts. You can see in the figure that the United States can produce 2,000 airplanes if it produces no auto parts, or 1,000 bundles of auto parts if it produces no airplanes. Thus, the slope of the U.S. production possibility curve, or PPF, is –2,000/1,000 = –2. That is, to produce an additional bundle of auto parts, the United States must forgo the production of 2 airplanes.

Similarly, Mexico can produce 1,000 airplanes if it produces no auto parts or 2,000 bundles of auto parts if it produces no airplanes. Thus, the slope of Mexico's PPF is –1,000/2,000 = –1/2. That is, to produce an additional bundle of auto parts, Mexico must forgo the production of 1/2 an airplane.

Economists use the term **autarky** to refer to a situation in which a country does not trade with other countries. We assume that in autarky the United States chooses to produce and consume 500 bundles of auto parts and 1,000 airplanes. We also assume that in autarky Mexico produces 1,000 bundles of auto parts and 500 airplanes.

TABLE 16-1

U.S. and Mexican Opportunity Costs of Auto Parts and Airplanes

	U.S. Opportunity Cost		Mexican Opportunity Cost
1 bundle of auto parts	2 airplanes	>	1/2 airplane
1 airplane	1/2 bundle of auto parts	<	2 bundles of auto parts

The trade-offs facing the two countries when they don't trade are summarized in Table 16-1. As you can see, the United States has a comparative advantage in the production of airplanes because it has a lower opportunity cost in terms of auto parts than Mexico has: producing an airplane costs the United States only ½ a bundle of auto parts, while it costs Mexico 2 bundles of auto parts. Correspondingly, Mexico has a comparative advantage in auto parts production: 1 bundle costs it only ½ an airplane, while it costs the United States 2 airplanes.

As we've learned, each country can do better by engaging in trade than it could by not trading. A country can accomplish this by specializing in the production of the good in which it has a comparative advantage and exporting that good, while importing the good in which it has a comparative *dis*advantage. Let's see how this works.

Autarky is a situation in which a country does not trade with other countries.

The Gains from International Trade

Figure 16-3 illustrates how both countries can gain from specialization and trade, by showing a hypothetical rearrangement of production and consumption that allows *each* country to consume more of *both* goods. Again, panel (a) represents the United States and panel (b) represents Mexico. In each panel we indicate again the autarky production and consumption assumed in Figure 16-2. Once trade becomes possible, however, everything changes. With trade, each country can move to producing only the good in which it has a comparative advantage—airplanes for the United States and auto parts for Mexico. Because the world production of both goods is now higher than in autarky, trade makes it possible for each country to consume more of both goods.

FIGURE 16-3 The Gains from International Trade

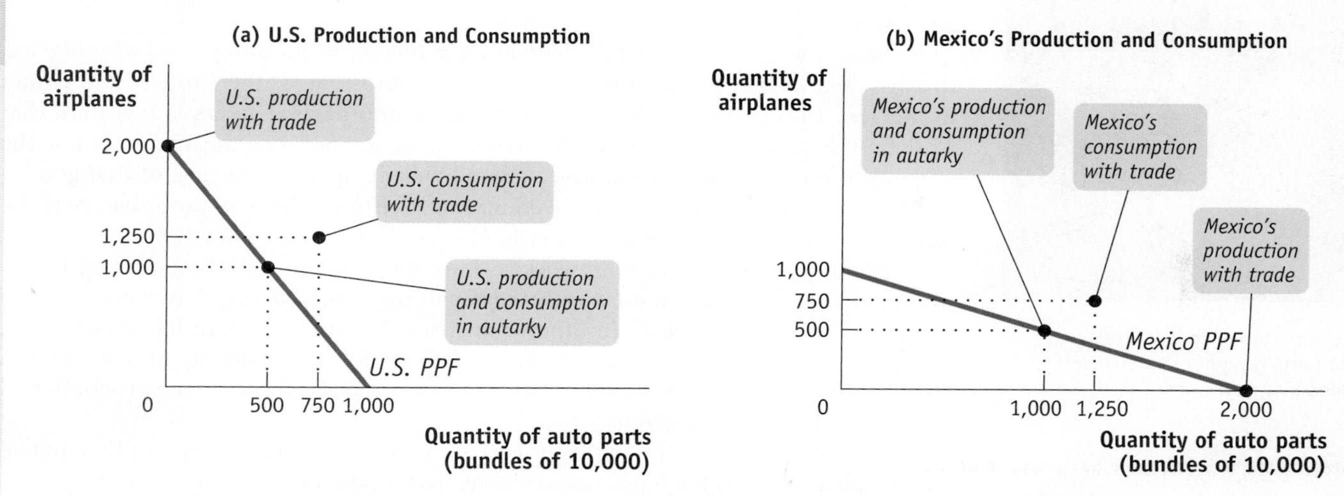

Trade increases world production of both goods, allowing both countries to consume more. Here, each country specializes its production as a result of trade: the United States concentrates on producing airplanes, and Mexico concentrates on producing auto parts. Total world production of both goods rises, which means that it is possible for both countries to consume more of both goods.

Table 16-2 sums up the changes as a result of trade and shows why both countries can gain. The left part of the table shows the autarky situation, before trade, in which each country must produce the goods it consumes. The right part of the table shows what happens as a result of trade. After trade, the United States specializes in the production of airplanes, producing 2,000 airplanes and no auto parts; Mexico specializes in the production of auto parts, producing 2,000 bundles of auto parts and no airplanes.

The result is a rise in total world production of both goods. As you can see in the Table 16-2 column at far right showing consumption with trade, the United States is able to consume both more airplanes and more auto parts than before, even though

TABLE 16-2

How the United States and Mexico Gain from Trade

		In Autarky		With Trade		
		Production	Consumption	Production	Consumption	Gains from trade
United States	**Bundles of auto parts**	500	500	0	750	+250
	Airplanes	1,000	1,000	2,000	1,250	+250
Mexico	**Bundles of auto parts**	1,000	1,000	2,000	1,250	+250
	Airplanes	500	500	0	750	+250

it no longer produces auto parts, because it can import parts from Mexico. Mexico can also consume more of both goods, even though it no longer produces airplanes, because it can import airplanes from the United States.

The key to this mutual gain is the fact that trade liberates both countries from self-sufficiency—from the need to produce the same mixes of goods they consume. Because each country can concentrate on producing the good in which it has a comparative advantage, total world production rises, making a higher standard of living possible in both nations.

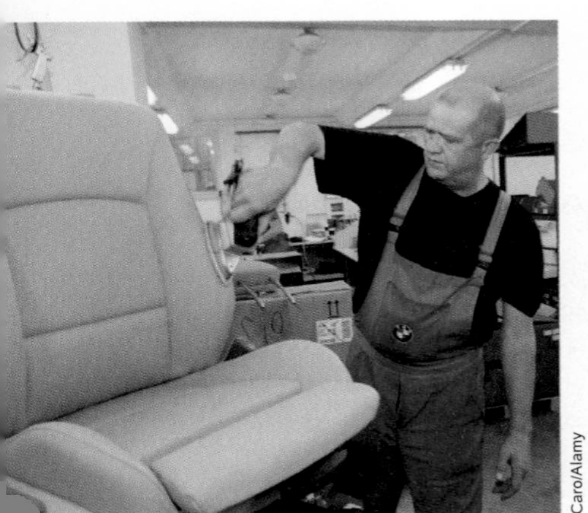

Carol/Alamy

The opportunity cost of producing auto parts is higher in the United States than in Mexico.

Comparative Advantage versus Absolute Advantage

There's nothing about Mexico's climate or resources that makes it especially good at manufacturing auto parts. In fact, it almost surely takes *fewer* hours of labor to produce an auto seat in the United States than in Mexico. Why, then, do we buy Mexican auto parts?

Because the gains from trade depend on *comparative advantage,* not *absolute advantage.* Yes, it takes less labor to produce an auto seat in the United States than in Mexico. That is, the productivity of Mexican auto parts workers is less than that of their U.S. counterparts. But what determines comparative advantage is not the amount of resources used to produce a good but the opportunity cost of that good—here, the quantity of other goods given up in order to produce an auto seat. And the opportunity cost of auto parts is lower in Mexico than in the United States.

Here's how it works: Mexican workers have low productivity compared with U.S. workers in the auto parts industry. But Mexican workers have even lower productivity compared with U.S. workers in other industries. Because Mexican labor productivity in industries other than auto parts is relatively lower, producing an auto seat in Mexico, even though it takes a lot of labor, does not require forgoing the production of large quantities of other goods.

In the United States, the opposite is true: very high productivity in other industries (such as high-technology goods) means that producing an auto seat in the United States, even though it doesn't require much labor, requires sacrificing lots of other goods. So the opportunity cost of producing auto parts is less in Mexico than in the United States. Despite its lower labor productivity, Mexico has a comparative advantage in the production of auto parts, although the United States has an absolute advantage.

Mexico's comparative advantage in auto parts is reflected in global markets by the wages Mexican workers are paid. That's because a country's wage rates, in general, reflect its labor productivity. In countries where labor is highly productive in many industries, employers are willing to pay high wages to attract workers, so competition among employers leads to an overall high wage rate. In countries where labor is less productive, competition for workers is less intense and wage rates are correspondingly lower.

The kind of trade that takes place between low-wage, low-productivity economies like Mexico and high-wage, high-productivity economies like the United States gives rise to two common misperceptions. One, the *pauper labor fallacy,* is the belief that when a country with high wages imports goods produced by workers who are paid low wages, this must hurt the standard of living of workers in the importing country. The other, the *sweatshop labor fallacy,* is the belief that trade must be bad for workers in poor exporting countries because those workers are paid very low wages by our standards.

International trade that depends on low-wage exports can raise a country's standard of living, as it has in Mexico and elsewhere.

Bloomberg via Getty Images

Both fallacies miss the nature of gains from trade: it's to the advantage of *both* countries if the poorer, lower-wage country exports goods in which it has a comparative advantage, even if its cost advantage in these goods depends on low wages. That is, both countries are able to achieve a higher standard of living through trade.

It's particularly important to understand that buying a good made by someone who is paid much lower wages than most U.S. workers doesn't necessarily imply that you're taking advantage of that person. It depends on the alternatives. Because workers in poor countries have low productivity across the board, they are offered low wages whether they produce goods exported to America or goods sold in local markets. A job that looks terrible by rich-country standards can be a step up for someone in a poor country.

International trade that depends on low-wage exports can nonetheless raise a country's standard of living. This is especially true of very-low-wage nations. For example, Bangladesh and similar countries would be much poorer than they are—their citizens might even be starving—if they weren't able to export goods such as clothing based on their low wage rates.

The **factor intensity** of production of a good is a measure of which factor is used in relatively greater quantities than other factors in production.

According to the **Heckscher–Ohlin model,** a country has a comparative advantage in a good whose production is intensive in the factors that are abundantly available in that country.

Sources of Comparative Advantage

International trade is driven by comparative advantage, but where does comparative advantage come from? Economists who study international trade have found three main sources of comparative advantage:

1. international differences in *climate*
2. international differences in *factor endowments*
3. international differences in *technology*

1. DIFFERENCES IN CLIMATE In general, differences in climate play a significant role in international trade. Tropical countries export tropical products like coffee, sugar, bananas, and shrimp. Countries in the temperate zones export crops like wheat and corn. Some trade is even driven by the difference in seasons between the northern and southern hemispheres: winter deliveries of Chilean grapes and New Zealand apples have become commonplace in U.S. and European supermarkets.

2. DIFFERENCES IN FACTOR ENDOWMENTS Canada is a major exporter of forest products—lumber and products derived from lumber, like pulp and paper—to the United States. These exports don't reflect the special skill of Canadian lumberjacks. Canada has a comparative advantage in forest products because its forested area is much greater compared to the size of its labor force than the ratio of forestland to the labor force in the United States.

Forestland, like labor and capital, is a *factor of production:* an input used to produce goods and services. (Recall that the factors of production are land, labor, physical capital, and human capital.) Due to history and geography, the mix of available factors of production differs among countries, providing an important source of comparative advantage. The relationship between comparative advantage and factor availability is found in an influential model of international trade, the *Heckscher–Ohlin model,* developed by two Swedish economists in the first half of the twentieth century.

Two key concepts in the model are *factor abundance* and *factor intensity.* Factor abundance refers to how large a country's supply of a factor is relative to its supply of other factors. Factor intensity refers to the fact that producers use different ratios of factors of production in the production of different goods. For example, oil refineries use much more capital per worker than clothing factories. Economists use the term **factor intensity** to describe this difference among goods: oil refining is capital-intensive, because it tends to use a high ratio of capital to labor, but auto seats production is labor-intensive, because it tends to use a high ratio of labor to capital.

According to the **Heckscher–Ohlin model,** *a country that has an abundant supply of a factor of production will have a comparative advantage in goods whose production is intensive in that factor.* So a country that has a relative abundance of capital will have a comparative advantage in capital-intensive industries such as oil refining, but a country that has a relative abundance of labor will have a comparative advantage in labor-intensive industries such as auto seats production.

iStockphoto

Canada's comparative advantage in forest production has little to do with the skill of its storied lumberjacks and a lot to do with the size of its forests.

The basic intuition behind this result is simple and based on opportunity cost. The opportunity cost of a given factor—the value that the factor would generate in alternative uses—is low for a country when it is relatively abundant in that factor. Relative to the United States, Mexico has an abundance of low-skilled labor. As a result, the opportunity cost of the production of low-skilled, labor-intensive goods is lower in Mexico than in the United States.

The most dramatic example of the validity of the Heckscher–Ohlin model is world trade in clothing. Clothing production is a labor-intensive activity: it doesn't take much physical capital, nor does it require a lot of human capital in the form of highly educated workers. So you would expect labor-abundant countries such as China and Bangladesh to have a comparative advantage in clothing production. And they do.

Corbis/Photolibrary

Lean production involves organizing workers and parts to ensure a smooth work flow, minimize waste, and allow for flexibility to change.

3. DIFFERENCES IN TECHNOLOGY In the 1970s and 1980s, Japan became by far the world's largest exporter of automobiles, selling large numbers to the United States and the rest of the world. Japan's comparative advantage in automobiles wasn't the result of climate. Nor can it easily be attributed to differences in factor endowments: aside from a scarcity of land, Japan's mix of available factors is quite similar to that in other advanced countries. Instead, as we discussed in the Section 1 Business Case on lean production at Toyota and Boeing, Japan's comparative advantage in automobiles was based on the superior production techniques developed by its manufacturers, which allowed them to produce more cars with a given amount of labor and capital than their American or European counterparts.

Japan's comparative advantage in automobiles was a case of comparative advantage caused by differences in technology—the techniques used in production.

ECONOMICS IN ACTION WORLD VIEW

SKILL AND COMPARATIVE ADVANTAGE

In 1953 U.S. workers were clearly better equipped with machinery than their counterparts in other countries. Most economists at the time thought that America's comparative advantage lay in capital-intensive goods. But Wassily Leontief made a surprising discovery: America's comparative advantage was in something other than capital-intensive goods. In fact, goods that the United States exported were slightly less capital-intensive than goods the country imported. This discovery came to be known as the *Leontief paradox,* and it led to a sustained effort to make sense of U.S. trade patterns.

The main resolution of this paradox, it turns out, depends on the definition of *capital.* U.S. exports aren't intensive in *physical* capital—machines and buildings. Instead, they are *skill-intensive*—that is, they are intensive in *human* capital. U.S. exporting industries use a substantially higher ratio of highly educated workers to other workers than is found in U.S. industries that compete against imports. For example, one of America's biggest export sectors is aircraft; the aircraft industry employs large numbers of engineers and other people with graduate degrees relative to the number of manual laborers. Conversely, we import a lot of clothing, which is often produced by workers with little formal education.

In general, countries with highly educated workforces tend to export skill-intensive goods, while countries with less educated workforces tend to export goods whose production requires little skilled labor.

Figure 16-4 illustrates this point by comparing the goods the United States imports from Germany, a country with a highly educated labor force, with the goods the United States imports from Bangladesh, where about half of the adult population is still illiterate. In each country industries are ranked, first, according to how skill-intensive they are. Next, for each industry, we calculate its share of U.S. imports. This allows us to plot, for each country, various industries according to their skill intensity and their share of U.S. imports.

In Figure 16-4, the horizontal axis shows a measure of the skill intensity of different industries, and the vertical axes show the share of U.S. imports in each industry coming from Germany (on the left) and Bangladesh (on the right). As you can see, each country's share of U.S. imports reflects its skill level. The curve representing Germany slopes upward: the more skill-intensive a German industry is, the higher its share of U.S. imports. In contrast, the curve representing Bangladesh slopes downward: the less skill-intensive a Bangladeshi industry is, the higher its share of U.S. imports.

FIGURE 16-4 Education, Skill Intensity, and Trade

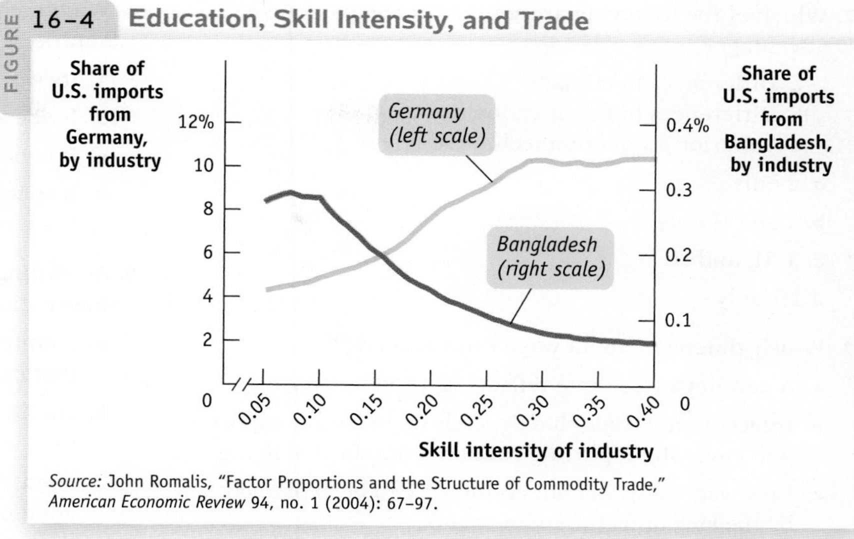

Source: John Romalis, "Factor Proportions and the Structure of Commodity Trade," *American Economic Review* 94, no. 1 (2004): 67–97.

MODULE 16 Review

Solutions appear at the back of the book.

Check Your Understanding

1. In the United States, the opportunity cost of 1 ton of corn is 50 bicycles. In China, the opportunity cost of 1 bicycle is 0.01 ton of corn.
   a. Determine the pattern of comparative advantage.
   b. In autarky, the United States can produce 200,000 bicycles if no corn is produced, and China can produce 3,000 tons of corn if no bicycles are produced. Draw each country's production possibility curve assuming constant opportunity cost, with tons of corn on the vertical axis and bicycles on the horizontal axis.
   c. With trade, each country specializes its production. The United States consumes 1,000 tons of corn and 200,000 bicycles; China consumes 3,000 tons of corn and 100,000 bicycles. Indicate the production and consumption points on your diagrams, and use them to explain the gains from trade.
2. Explain the following patterns of trade using the Heckscher–Ohlin model.
   a. France exports wine to the United States, and the United States exports movies to France.
   b. Brazil exports shoes to the United States, and the United States exports shoe-making machinery to Brazil.

Multiple-Choice Questions

1. Globalization can be defined as
   a. the growing number of multinational companies.
   b. the growth of various forms of economic linkages among countries.
   c. the value of imports and exports as a percentage of a country's GDP.
   d. the price of goods in world markets.

2. Which of the following are sources of comparative advantage?
   I. Differences in climate
   II. Differences in factor endowments
   III. Superior production techniques
   a. I only
   b. I and II only
   c. I, II, and III
   d. III only

3. Which statement about wage rates is correct?
   a. A country's wage rate reflects its productivity.
   b. International trade that depends on low-wage exports will lower the exporting country's standard of living.
   c. Low wage rates in poor countries can be explained by the lack of factor endowments.
   d. All of the above are correct.

4. Which of the following best describes a country in autarky?
   a. Its workers are highly productive in many industries.
   b. It does not trade with other countries.
   c. It benefits from trading with only one other country.
   d. It specializes in the production of goods in which it has a comparative advantage.

5. According to the Heckscher–Ohlin model of international trade,
   a. countries have a comparative advantage in the good that can be imported the most cheaply.
   b. countries have a comparative advantage in the good they want to produce.
   c. countries have a comparative advantage in the good produced with the country's most abundant resources.
   d. All of the above are true.

Critical-Thinking Question

In autarky, the equilibrium price of a good in the domestic market is $10. If the world price of the same good is $8 and the country opens up to trade, how will the domestic quantity supplied and demanded be affected? Will the country be an importer or an exporter of the good?

Supply, Demand, and International Trade

Glow Images/Superstock

WHAT YOU WILL LEARN

1. How tariffs and import quotas cause inefficiency and reduce total surplus
2. Why governments often engage in trade protection to shelter domestic industries from imports
3. About the challenges that have been created by globalization

Imports, Exports, and Wages

Simple models of comparative advantage are helpful for understanding the fundamental causes of international trade. However, to analyze the effects of international trade at a more detailed level and to understand trade policy, it helps to return to the supply and demand model. We'll start by looking at the effects of imports on domestic producers and consumers, then turn to the effects of exports.

The Effects of Imports

Figure 17-1 shows the U.S. market for auto seats, ignoring international trade for a moment. It introduces a few new concepts: the *domestic demand curve,* the *domestic supply curve,* and the domestic or autarky price.

The **domestic demand curve** shows how the quantity of a good demanded by residents of a country depends on the price of that good. Why "domestic"? Because people living in other countries may demand the good, too. Once we introduce international trade, we need to distinguish between purchases of a good by domestic consumers and purchases by foreign consumers. So the domestic demand curve reflects only the demand of residents of our own country. Similarly, the **domestic supply curve** shows how the quantity of a good supplied by producers inside our own country depends on the price of that good. Once we introduce international trade, we need to distinguish between the supply of domestic producers and foreign supply—supply brought in from abroad.

In autarky, with no international trade in auto seats, the equilibrium in this market would be determined by the intersection of the domestic demand and domestic

The **domestic demand curve** shows how the quantity of a good demanded by domestic consumers depends on the price of that good.

The **domestic supply curve** shows how the quantity of a good supplied by domestic producers depends on the price of that good.

FIGURE 17-1 Consumer and Producer Surplus in Autarky

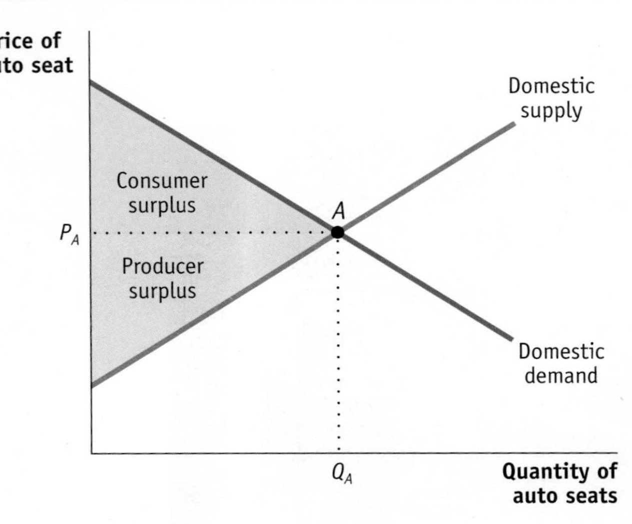

In the absence of trade, the domestic price is P_A, the autarky price at which the domestic supply curve and the domestic demand curve intersect. The quantity produced and consumed domestically is Q_A. Consumer surplus is represented by the blue-shaded area, and producer surplus is represented by the red-shaded area.

supply curves, point *A*. The equilibrium price of auto seats would be P_A, and the equilibrium quantity of auto seats produced and consumed would be Q_A. As always, both consumers and producers gain from the existence of the domestic market. In autarky, consumer surplus would be equal to the area of the blue-shaded triangle in Figure 17-1. Producer surplus would be equal to the area of the red-shaded triangle. And total surplus would be equal to the sum of these two shaded triangles.

Now let's imagine opening up this market to imports. To do this, we must make an assumption about the supply of imports. The simplest assumption, which we will adopt here, is that unlimited quantities of auto seats can be purchased from abroad at a fixed price, known as the **world price** of auto seats. Figure 17-2 shows a situation in which the world price of an auto seat, P_W, is lower than the price of an auto seat that would prevail in the domestic market in autarky, P_A.

The **world price** of a good is the price at which that good can be bought or sold abroad.

Given that the world price is below the domestic price of an auto seat, it is profitable for importers to buy auto seats abroad and resell them domestically. The imported auto seats increase the supply of auto seats in the domestic market, driving down the domestic market price. Auto seats will continue to be imported until the domestic price falls to a level equal to the world price.

The result is shown in Figure 17-2. Because of imports, the domestic price of an auto seat falls from P_A to P_W. The quantity of auto seats demanded by domestic consumers rises from Q_A to Q_D, and the quantity supplied by domestic producers falls from Q_A to Q_S. The difference between the domestic quantity demanded and the domestic quantity supplied, $Q_D - Q_S$, is filled by imports.

Now let's turn to the effects of imports on consumer surplus and producer surplus. Because imports of auto seats lead to a fall in their domestic price, consumer surplus

FIGURE 17-2 The Domestic Market with Imports

Here the world price of auto seats, P_W, is below the autarky price, P_A. When the economy is opened to international trade, imports enter the domestic market, and the domestic price falls from the autarky price, P_A, to the world price, P_W. As the price falls, the domestic quantity demanded rises from Q_A to Q_D and the domestic quantity supplied falls from Q_A to Q_S. The difference between domestic quantity demanded and domestic quantity supplied at P_W, the quantity $Q_D - Q_S$, is filled by imports.

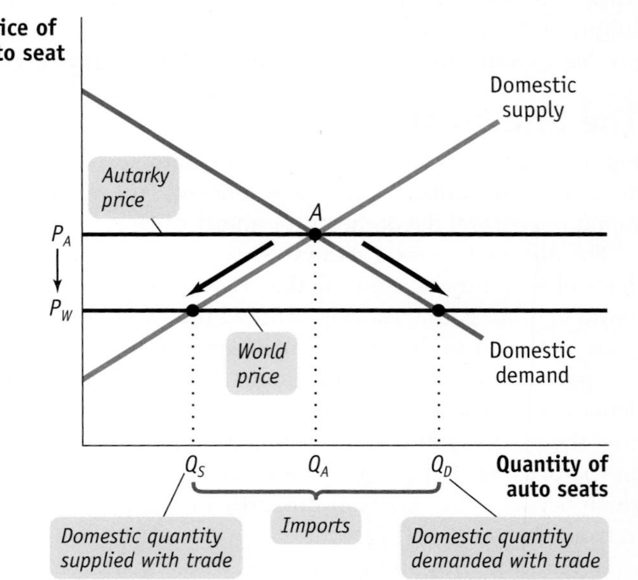

FIGURE 17-3 The Effects of Imports on Surplus

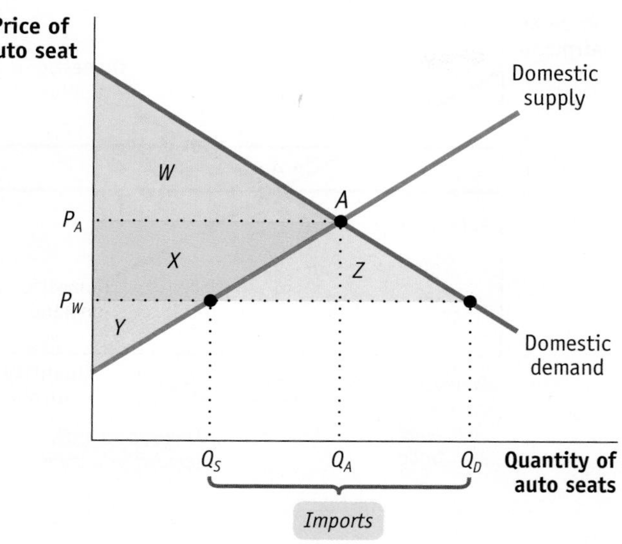

	Changes in surplus	
	Gain	Loss
Consumer surplus	$X + Z$	
Producer surplus		$-X$
Change in total surplus	$+Z$	

When the domestic price falls to P_W as a result of international trade, consumers gain additional surplus (areas $X + Z$) and producers lose surplus (area X). Because the gains to consumers outweigh the losses to producers, there is an increase in the total surplus in the economy as a whole (area Z).

rises and producer surplus falls. Figure 17-3 shows how this works. We label four areas: *W, X, Y,* and *Z*. The autarky consumer surplus we identified in Figure 17-1 corresponds to *W*, and the autarky producer surplus corresponds to the sum of *X* and *Y*. The fall in the domestic price to the world price leads to an increase in consumer surplus; it increases by *X* and *Z*, so consumer surplus now equals the sum of *W, X,* and *Z*. At the same time, producers lose *X* in surplus, so producer surplus now equals only *Y*.

The table in Figure 17-3 summarizes the changes in consumer and producer surplus when the auto seats market is opened to imports. Consumers gain surplus equal to the areas $X + Z$. Producers lose surplus equal to *X*. So the sum of producer and consumer surplus—the total surplus generated in the auto seats market—increases by *Z*. As a result of trade, consumers gain and producers lose, but the gain to consumers exceeds the loss to producers.

This is an important result. We have just shown that opening up a market to imports leads to a net gain in total surplus, which is what we should have expected given the proposition that there are gains from international trade.

However, we have also learned that although the country as a whole gains, some groups—in this case, domestic producers of auto parts—lose as a result of international trade. As we'll see shortly, the fact that international trade typically creates losers as well as winners is crucial for understanding the politics of trade policy.

We turn next to the case in which a country exports a good.

Thinkstock

Opening up a market to imports and exports leads to a net gain in total surplus, but creates losers as well as winners.

The Effects of Exports

Figure 17-4 shows the effects on a country when it exports a good, in this case airplanes. For this example, we assume that unlimited quantities of airplanes can be sold abroad at a given world price, P_W, which is higher than the price that would prevail in the domestic market in autarky, P_A.

The higher world price makes it profitable for exporters to buy airplanes domestically and sell them overseas. The purchases of domestic airplanes drive the domestic price up until it is equal to the world price. As a result, the quantity demanded by domestic consumers falls from Q_A to Q_D and the quantity supplied by domestic producers rises from Q_A to Q_S. This difference between domestic production and domestic consumption, $Q_S - Q_D$, is exported.

FIGURE 17-4 **The Domestic Market with Exports**

Here the world price, P_W, is greater than the autarky price, P_A. When the economy is opened to international trade, some of the domestic supply is now exported. The domestic price rises from the autarky price, P_A, to the world price, P_W. As the price rises, the domestic quantity demanded falls from Q_A to Q_D and the domestic quantity supplied rises from Q_A to Q_S. The portion of domestic production that is not consumed domestically, $Q_S - Q_D$, is exported.

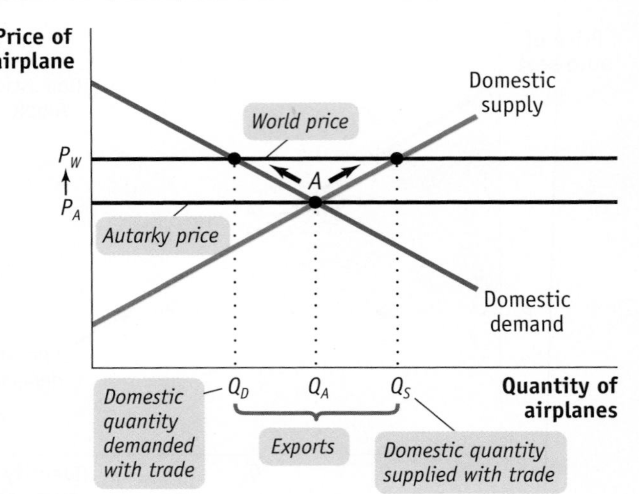

Like imports, exports lead to an overall gain in total surplus for the exporting country but also create losers as well as winners. Figure 17-5 shows the effects of airplane exports on producer and consumer surplus. In the absence of trade, the price of each airplane would be P_A. Consumer surplus in the absence of trade is the sum of areas W and X, and producer surplus is area Y. As a result of trade, price rises from P_A to P_W, consumer surplus falls to W, and producer surplus rises to $Y + X + Z$. So producers gain $X + Z$, consumers lose X, and, as shown in the table accompanying the figure, the economy as a whole gains total surplus in the amount of Z.

We have learned, then, that imports of a particular good hurt domestic producers of that good but help domestic consumers, whereas exports of a particular good hurt domestic consumers of that good but help domestic producers. In each case, the gains are larger than the losses.

International Trade and Wages

So far we have focused on the effects of international trade on producers and consumers in a particular industry. For many purposes this is a very helpful approach. How-

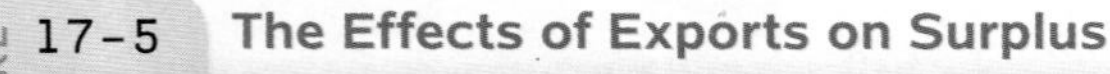

FIGURE 17-5 **The Effects of Exports on Surplus**

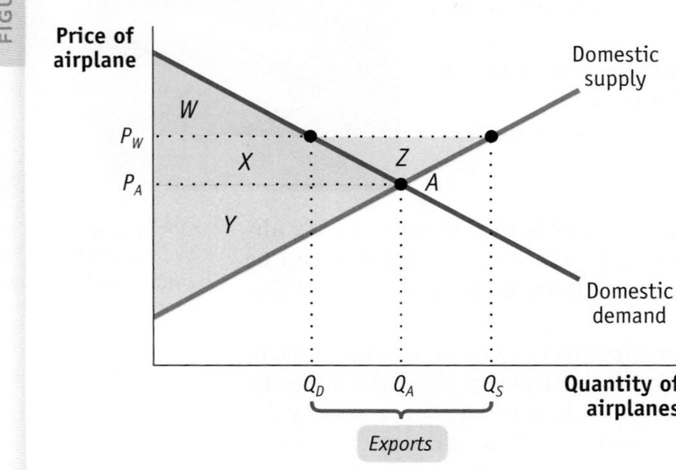

	Changes in surplus	
	Gain	**Loss**
Consumer surplus		$-X$
Producer surplus	$X + Z$	
Change in total surplus	$+Z$	

When the domestic price rises to P_W as a result of trade, producers gain additional surplus (areas $X + Z$) but consumers lose surplus (area X). Because the gains to producers outweigh the losses to consumers, there is an increase in the total surplus in the economy as a whole (area Z).

ever, producers and consumers are not the only parts of society affected by trade—so are the owners of factors of production. In particular, the owners of labor, land, and capital employed in producing goods that are exported, or goods that compete with imported goods, can be deeply affected by trade.

Moreover, the effects of trade aren't limited to just those industries that export or compete with imports because *factors of production can often move between industries.* So now we turn our attention to the long-run effects of international trade on income distribution—how a country's total income is allocated among its various factors of production.

To begin our analysis, consider the position of Maria, an accountant at Midwest Auto Parts, Inc. If the economy is opened up to imports of auto parts from Mexico, the domestic auto parts industry will contract, and it will hire fewer accountants.

But accounting is a profession with employment opportunities in many industries, and Maria might well find a better job in the aircraft industry, which expands as a result of international trade. So it may not be appropriate to think of her as a producer of auto parts who is hurt by competition from imported parts. Rather, we should think of her as an accountant who is affected by auto part imports only to the extent that these imports change the wages of accountants in the economy as a whole.

The wage rate of accountants is a *factor price*—the price employers have to pay for the services of a factor of production. One key question about international trade is how it affects factor prices—not just narrowly defined factors of production like accountants, but broadly defined factors such as capital, unskilled labor, and college-educated labor.

In the previous module we described the Heckscher–Ohlin model of trade, which states that comparative advantage is determined by a country's factor endowment. This model also suggests how international trade affects factor prices in a country: compared to autarky, international trade tends to raise the prices of factors that are abundantly available and reduce the prices of factors that are scarce.

We won't work this out in detail, but the idea is simple. The prices of factors of production, like the prices of goods and services, are determined by supply and demand. If international trade increases the demand for a factor of production, that factor's price will rise; if international trade reduces the demand for a factor of production, that factor's price will fall.

Now think of a country's industries as consisting of two kinds: **exporting industries,** which produce goods and services that are sold abroad, and **import-competing industries,** which produce goods and services that are also imported from abroad. Compared with autarky, international trade leads to higher production in exporting industries and lower production in import-competing industries. This indirectly increases the demand for the factors used by exporting industries and decreases the demand for factors used by import-competing industries.

Exporting industries produce goods and services that are sold abroad.

Import-competing industries produce goods and services that are also imported.

In addition, the Heckscher–Ohlin model says that a country tends to export goods that are intensive in its abundant factors and to import goods that are intensive in its scarce factors. So *international trade tends to increase the demand for factors that are abundant in our country compared with other countries, and to decrease the demand for factors that are scarce in our country compared with other countries.* As a result, *the prices of abundant factors tend to rise, and the prices of scarce factors tend to fall as international trade grows.* In other words, international trade tends to redistribute income toward a country's abundant factors and away from its less abundant factors.

As we've seen, U.S. exports tend to be human-capital-intensive and U.S. imports tend to be unskilled-labor-intensive. This suggests that the effect of international trade on U.S. factor markets is to raise the wage rate of highly educated American workers and reduce the wage rate of unskilled American workers.

Trade affects factor markets by raising the wages of highly educated workers and lowering them for unskilled workers.

An economy has **free trade** when the government does not attempt either to reduce or to increase the levels of exports and imports that occur naturally as a result of supply and demand.

Policies that limit imports are known as **trade protection** or simply as **protection.**

A **tariff** is a tax levied on imports.

This effect has been a source of much concern in recent years. Wage inequality—the gap between the wages of high-paid and low-paid workers—has increased substantially over the last 30 years. Some economists believe that growing international trade is an important factor in that trend. If international trade has the effects predicted by the Heckscher–Ohlin model, its growth raises the wages of highly educated American workers, who already have relatively high wages, and lowers the wages of less educated American workers, who already have relatively low wages. But keep in mind another phenomenon: trade reduces the income inequality *between* countries as poor countries improve their standard of living by exporting to rich countries.

The effects of trade on wages in the United States have generated considerable controversy in recent years. Most economists who have studied the issue agree that growing imports of labor-intensive products from newly industrializing economies, and the export of high-technology goods in return, have helped cause a widening wage gap between highly educated and less educated workers in this country. However, most economists believe that it is only one of several forces explaining the growth in American wage inequality.

The Effects of Trade Protection

Ever since the principle of comparative advantage was laid out in the early nineteenth century, most economists have advocated **free trade.** That is, they have argued that government policy should not attempt either to reduce or to increase the levels of exports and imports that occur naturally as a result of supply and demand.

Despite the free-trade arguments of economists, however, many governments use taxes and other restrictions to limit imports. Less frequently, governments offer subsidies to encourage exports. Policies that limit imports, usually with the goal of protecting domestic producers in import-competing industries from foreign competition, are known as **trade protection** or simply as **protection.**

Let's look at the two most common protectionist policies, tariffs and import quotas, then turn to the reasons governments follow these policies.

The Effects of a Tariff

A **tariff** is a form of excise tax, one that is levied only on sales of imported goods. For example, the U.S. government could declare that anyone bringing in auto seats must pay a tariff of $100 per unit. In the distant past, tariffs were an important source of government revenue because they were relatively easy to collect. But in the modern world, tariffs are usually intended to discourage imports and protect import-competing domestic producers rather than to serve as a source of government revenue.

The tariff raises both the price received by domestic producers and the price paid by domestic consumers. Suppose, for example, that our country imports auto seats, and an auto seat costs $200 on the world market. As we saw earlier, under free trade the domestic price would also be $200. But if a tariff of $100 per unit is imposed, the domestic price will rise to $300, because it won't be profitable to import auto seats unless the price in the domestic market is high enough to compensate importers for the cost of paying the tariff.

Figure 17-6 illustrates the effects of a tariff on imports of auto seats. As before, we assume that P_W is the world price of an auto seat. Before the tariff is imposed, imports have driven the domestic price down to P_W, so that pre-tariff domestic production is Q_S, pre-tariff domestic consumption is Q_D, and pre-tariff imports are $Q_D - Q_S$.

Now suppose that the government imposes a tariff on each auto seat imported. As a consequence, it is no longer profitable to import auto seats unless the domestic price received by the importer is greater than or equal to the world price *plus* the tariff. So the domestic price rises to P_T, which is equal to the world price, P_W, plus the tariff. Domestic production rises to Q_{ST}, domestic consumption falls to Q_{DT}, and imports fall to $Q_{DT} - Q_{ST}$.

FIGURE 17-6 **The Effect of a Tariff**

A tariff raises the domestic price of the good from P_W to P_T. The domestic quantity demanded shrinks from Q_D to Q_{DT}, and the domestic quantity supplied increases from Q_S to Q_{ST}. As a result, imports—which had been $Q_D - Q_S$ before the tariff was imposed—shrink to $Q_{DT} - Q_{ST}$ after the tariff is imposed.

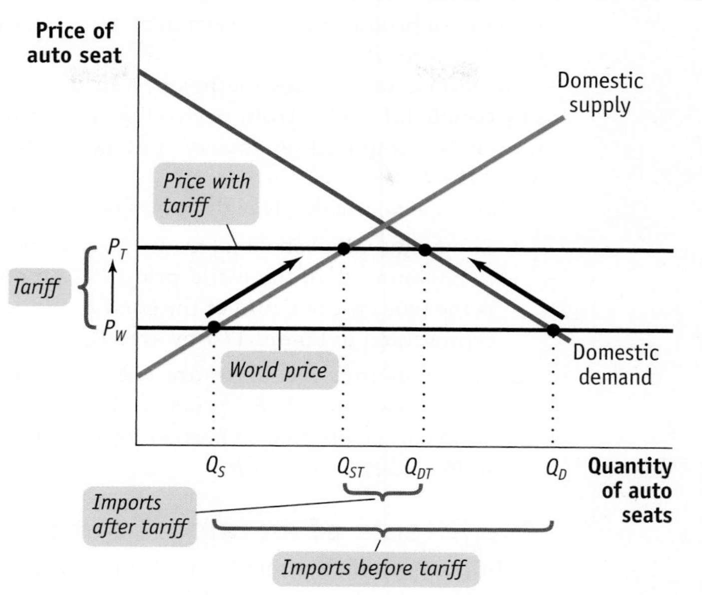

A tariff, then, raises domestic prices, leading to increased domestic production and reduced domestic consumption compared to the situation under free trade. Figure 17-7 shows the effects on surplus. There are three effects:

1. The higher domestic price increases producer surplus, a gain equal to area *A*.
2. The higher domestic price reduces consumer surplus, a reduction equal to the sum of areas *A*, *B*, *C*, and *D*.
3. The tariff yields revenue to the government. How much revenue? The government collects the tariff—which, remember, is equal to the difference between P_T and P_W on each of the $Q_{DT} - Q_{ST}$ units imported. So total revenue is $(P_T - P_W) \times (Q_{DT} - Q_{ST})$. This is equal to area *C*.

FIGURE 17-7 **A Tariff Reduces Total Surplus**

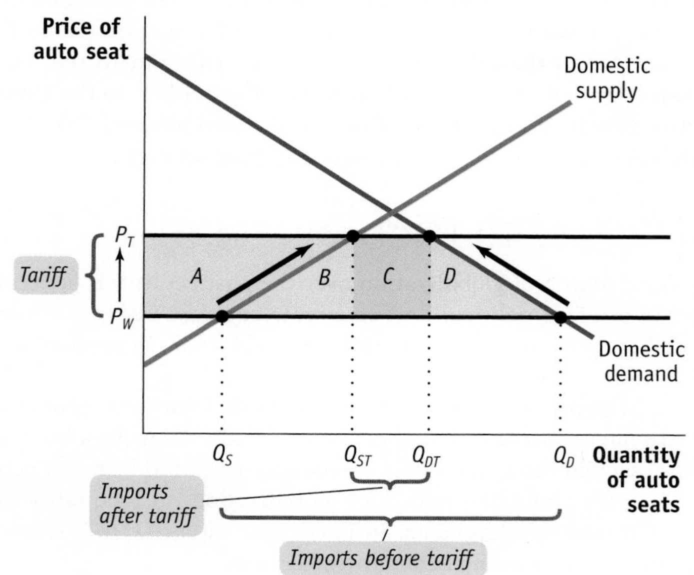

	Changes in surplus	
	Gain	**Loss**
Consumer surplus		$-(A + B + C + D)$
Producer surplus	A	
Government revenue	C	
Change in total surplus		$-(B + D)$

When the domestic price rises as a result of a tariff, producers gain additional surplus (area *A*), the government gains revenue (area *C*), and consumers lose surplus (areas $A + B + C + D$). Because the losses to consumers outweigh the gains to producers and the government, the economy as a whole loses surplus (areas $B + D$).

An **import quota** is a legal limit on the quantity of a good that can be imported.

The welfare effects of a tariff are summarized in the table in Figure 17-7. Producers gain, consumers lose, and the government gains. But consumer losses are greater than the sum of producer and government gains, leading to a net reduction in total surplus equal to areas $B + D$.

An excise tax creates inefficiency, or deadweight loss, because it prevents mutually beneficial trades from occurring. The same is true of a tariff, where the deadweight loss imposed on society is equal to the loss in total surplus represented by areas $B + D$.

Tariffs generate deadweight losses because they create inefficiencies in two ways:

1. Some mutually beneficial trades go unexploited: some consumers who are willing to pay more than the world price, P_W, do not purchase the good, even though P_W is the true cost of a unit of the good to the economy. The cost of this inefficiency is represented in Figure 17-7 by area D.
2. The economy's resources are wasted on inefficient production: some producers whose cost exceeds P_W produce the good, even though an additional unit of the good can be purchased abroad for P_W. The cost of this inefficiency is represented in Figure 17-7 by area B.

The Effects of an Import Quota

An **import quota,** another form of trade protection, is a legal limit on the quantity of a good that can be imported. For example, a U.S. import quota on Mexican auto seats might limit the quantity imported each year to 500,000 units. Import quotas are usually administered through licenses: a number of licenses are issued, each giving the license-holder the right to import a limited quantity of the good each year.

A quota on sales has the same effect as an excise tax, with one difference: the money that would otherwise have accrued to the government as tax revenue under an excise tax becomes license-holders' revenue under a quota—this revenue is also known as *quota rents.* Similarly, an import quota has the same effect as a tariff, with one difference: the money that would otherwise have been government revenue becomes quota rents to license-holders.

Look again at Figure 17-7. An import quota that limits imports to $Q_{DT} - Q_{ST}$ will raise the domestic price of auto parts by the same amount as the tariff we considered previously. That is, it will raise the domestic price from P_W to P_T. However, area C will now represent quota rents rather than government revenue.

Who receives import licenses and so collects the quota rents? In the case of U.S. import protection, the answer may surprise you: the most important import licenses—mainly for clothing, to a lesser extent for sugar—are granted to foreign governments.

Because the quota rents for most U.S. import quotas go to foreigners, the cost to the nation of such quotas is larger than that of a comparable tariff (a tariff that leads to the same level of imports). In Figure 17-7 the net loss to the United States from such an import quota would be equal to areas $B + C + D$, the difference between consumer losses and producer gains.

Economists and policy makers view growing world trade as a positive, but not everyone agrees.

© FC_Italy/Alamy

Challenges to Globalization

The forward march of globalization over the past century is generally considered a major political and economic success. Economists and policy makers alike have viewed growing world trade, in particular, as a good thing.

We would be remiss, however, if we failed to acknowledge that many people are having second thoughts about globalization. To a large extent, these second thoughts reflect two concerns shared by many economists: worries about the effects of globalization on inequality and worries that new developments, in particular the growth in *offshore outsourcing,* are increasing economic insecurity.

Globalization and Inequality

We've already mentioned the implications of international trade for factor prices, such as wages: when wealthy countries like the United States export skill-intensive products like aircraft while importing labor-intensive products like clothing, they can expect to see the wage gap between more educated and less educated domestic workers widen. Thirty years ago, this wasn't a significant concern, because most of the goods wealthy countries imported from poorer countries were raw materials or goods where comparative advantage depended on climate. Today, however, many manufactured goods are imported from relatively poor countries, with a potentially much larger effect on the distribution of income.

Trade with China, in particular, raises concerns among labor groups trying to maintain wage levels in rich countries. Although China has experienced spectacular economic growth since the economic reforms that began in the late 1970s, it remains a poor, low-wage country: wages in Chinese manufacturing are estimated to be only about 6% of U.S. wages. Meanwhile, imports from China have soared. In 1983 less than 1% of U.S. imports came from China; by 2012, the figure was 18%. There's not much question that these surging imports from China put at least some downward pressure on the wages of less educated American workers.

Outsourcing

Chinese exports to the United States overwhelmingly consist of labor-intensive manufactured goods. However, some U.S. workers have recently found themselves facing another form of international competition. *Outsourcing,* in which a company hires another company to perform some task, such as running the corporate computer system, is a long-standing business practice. Until recently, however, outsourcing was normally done locally, with a company hiring another company in the same city or country.

Now, modern telecommunications make it possible to engage in **offshore outsourcing,** in which businesses hire people in another country to perform various tasks. The classic example is a call center: the person answering the phone when you call a company's 1-800 help line may well be in India, which has taken the lead in attracting offshore outsourcing. Offshore outsourcing has also spread to fields such as software design and even health care: the radiologist examining your X-rays, like the person giving you computer help, may be on another continent.

© Image Source/Alamy

Offshore outsourcing is relatively small compared with more traditional trade.

Although offshore outsourcing has come as a shock to some U.S. workers, such as programmers whose jobs have been outsourced to India, it's still relatively small compared with more traditional trade. Some economists have warned, however, that millions or even tens of millions of workers who have never thought they could face foreign competition for their jobs may face unpleasant surprises in the not-too-distant future.

Concerns about income distribution and outsourcing, as we've said, are shared by many economists. There is also, however, widespread opposition to globalization in general, particularly among college students.

What motivates the antiglobalization movement? To some extent it's the sweatshop labor fallacy: it's easy to get outraged about the low wages paid to the person who made your shirt, and harder to appreciate how much worse off that person would be if denied the opportunity to sell goods in rich countries' markets.

Offshore outsourcing takes place when businesses hire people in another country to perform various tasks.

It's also true, however, that the movement represents a backlash against supporters of globalization who have oversold its benefits. Countries in Latin America, in particular, were promised that reducing their tariff rates would produce an economic takeoff; instead, they have experienced disappointing results.

Do these challenges to globalization undermine the argument that international trade is a good thing? The great majority of economists would argue that the gains from reducing trade protection still exceed the losses. However, it has become more important than before to make sure that the gains from international trade are widely spread. And the politics of international trade is becoming increasingly difficult as the extent of trade has grown.

ECONOMICS ▶ IN ACTION

WORLD VIEW

BEEFING UP EXPORTS

In December 2010, negotiators from the United States and South Korea reached final agreement on a free-trade deal that would phase out many of the tariffs and other restrictions on trade between the two nations. The deal also involved changes in a variety of business regulations that were expected to make it easier for U.S. companies to operate in South Korea. This was, literally, a fairly big deal: South Korea's economy is comparable in size to Mexico's, so this was the most important free-trade agreement that the United States had been party to since NAFTA. (As you'll recall, the North American Free Trade Agreement, or NAFTA, is an agreement signed in 1993 by the United States, Mexico, and Canada, that removes all barriers to trade among these three countries.)

Kyodo via AP Images

The 2010 trade agreement between South Korea and the United States was the most important free-trade deal since NAFTA.

What made this deal possible? Estimates by the U.S. International Trade Commission found that the deal would raise average American incomes, although modestly: the commission put the gains at around one-tenth of one percent. Not bad when you consider the fact that South Korea, despite its relatively large economy, is still only America's seventh-most-important trading partner.

These overall gains played little role in the politics of the deal, however, which hinged on losses and gains for particular U.S. constituencies. Some opposition to the deal came from labor, especially from autoworkers, who feared that eliminating the 8% U.S. tariff on imports of Korean automobiles would lead to job losses.

But there were also interest groups in America that badly wanted the deal, most notably the beef industry: Koreans are big beef-eaters, yet American access to that market was limited by a 38% Korean tariff.

And the Obama administration definitely wanted a deal, in part for reasons unrelated to economics: South Korea is an important U.S. ally, and military tensions with North Korea had been ratcheting up. So a trade deal was viewed in part as a symbol of U.S.–South Korean cooperation. Even labor unions weren't as opposed as they might have been.

It also helped that South Korea—unlike Mexico when NAFTA was signed—is both a fairly high-wage country and not right on the U.S. border, which meant less concern about massive shifts of manufacturing. In the end, the balance of interests was just favorable enough to make the deal politically possible.

MODULE 17 Review

Solutions appear at the back of the book.

Check Your Understanding

1. Suppose the world price of butter is $0.50 per pound and the domestic price in autarky is $1.00 per pound. Use a diagram similar to Figure 17-7 to show the following.
   a. If there is free trade, domestic butter producers want the government to impose a tariff of no less than $0.50 per pound.
   b. What happens if a tariff greater than $0.50 per pound is imposed?
2. Suppose the government imposes an import quota rather than a tariff on butter. What quota limit would generate the same quantity of imports as a tariff of $0.50 per pound?
3. Due to a strike by truckers, trade in food between the United States and Mexico is halted. In autarky, the price of Mexican grapes is lower than that of U.S. grapes. Using a diagram of the U.S. domestic demand curve and the U.S. domestic supply curve for grapes, explain the effect of these events on the following.
   a. U.S. grape consumers' surplus
   b. U.S. grape producers' surplus
   c. U.S. total surplus
4. What effect do you think the event described in question 3 will have on Mexican grape producers? Mexican grape pickers? Mexican grape consumers? U.S. grape pickers?

Multiple-Choice Questions

1. When a country imports a good,
   a. the domestic quantity supplied equals zero.
   b. the domestic quantity demanded equals zero.
   c. the domestic quantity demanded equals the quantity of imports.
   d. the domestic quantity demanded is greater than the domestic quantity supplied.
   e. the domestic quantity demanded is less than the domestic quantity supplied.
2. When a country exports a good,
   a. the domestic quantity supplied equals zero.
   b. the domestic quantity demanded equals zero.
   c. the domestic quantity supplied equals the quantity of exports.
   d. the domestic quantity demanded is greater than the domestic quantity supplied.
   e. the domestic quantity demanded is less than the domestic quantity supplied.
3. When a country opens up to trade and begins to export a particular good, the domestic quantity supplied of the good will ___________ and the wages of the workers who produce the good will ___________.
   a. increase; increase
   b. increase; decrease
   c. decrease; decrease
   d. decrease; increase
   e. remain unchanged; remain unchanged
4. If the world price is higher than the domestic autarky price, then when the economy opens up to trade, the country will become an ___________ of the good and the price in the domestic market will ___________.
   a. exporter; decrease
   b. importer; decrease
   c. importer; increase
   d. exporter; increase
   e. exporter; remain unchanged
5. A tariff or quota will increase deadweight loss because
   a. some mutually beneficial trades are unexploited.
   b. countries tend to focus on the most efficient production.
   c. countries are prevented from retaliating against each other.
   d. A and B are both correct.

Critical-Thinking Question

A few years ago, the United States imposed tariffs on steel imports, which are an input in a large number and variety of U.S. industries. Explain why political lobbying to eliminate these tariffs is more likely to be effective than political lobbying to eliminate tariffs on consumer goods such as sugar or clothing.

BUSINESS CASE: Li & Fung: From Guangzhou to You

Daniel J. Groshong/Bloomberg via Getty Images

It's a very good bet that as you read this, you're wearing something manufactured in Asia. And if you are, it's also a good bet that the Hong Kong company Li & Fung was involved in getting your garment designed, produced, and shipped to your local store. From Levi's to The Limited to Walmart, Li & Fung is a critical conduit from factories around the world to the shopping mall nearest you.

The company was founded in 1906 in Guangzhou, China. According to Victor Fung, the company's chairman, his grandfather's "value added" was that he spoke English, allowing him to serve as an interpreter in business deals between Chinese and foreigners. When Mao's Communist Party seized control in mainland China, the company moved to Hong Kong. There, as Hong Kong's market economy took off during the 1960s and 1970s, Li & Fung grew as an export broker, bringing together Hong Kong manufacturers and foreign buyers.

The real transformation of the company came, however, as Asian economies grew and changed. Hong Kong's rapid growth led to rising wages, making Li & Fung increasingly uncompetitive in garments, its main business. So the company reinvented itself: rather than being a simple broker, it became a "supply chain manager." Not only would it allocate production of a good to a manufacturer, it would also break production down, allocate production of the inputs, and then allocate final assembly of the good among its 12,000+ suppliers around the globe. Sometimes production would be done in sophisticated economies like those of Hong Kong or even Japan, where wages are high but so is quality and productivity; sometimes it would be done in less advanced locations like mainland China or Thailand, where labor is less productive but cheaper.

For example, suppose you own a U.S. retail chain and want to sell garment-washed blue jeans. Rather than simply arrange for production of the jeans, Li & Fung will work with you on their design, providing you with the latest production and style information, like what materials and colors are hot. After the design has been finalized, Li & Fung will arrange for the creation of a prototype, find the most cost-effective way to manufacture it, and then place an order on your behalf. Through Li & Fung, the yarn might be made in Korea and dyed in Taiwan, and the jeans sewn in Thailand or mainland China. And because production is taking place in so many locations, Li & Fung provides transport logistics as well as quality control.

Li & Fung has been enormously successful. In late 2013, the company had a market value of approximately $12.5 billion, with offices and distribution centers in more than 40 countries. Year after year, it continues to post sizeable profits.

Questions for Thought

1. Why do you think it was profitable for Li & Fung to go beyond brokering exports to becoming a supply chain manager, breaking down the production process and sourcing the inputs from various suppliers across many countries?
2. What principle do you think underlies Li & Fung's decisions on how to allocate production of a good's inputs and its final assembly among various countries?
3. Why do you think a retailer prefers to have Li & Fung arrange international production of its jeans rather than purchase them directly from a jeans manufacturer in mainland China?
4. What is the source of Li & Fung's success? Is it based on human capital, on ownership of a natural resource, or on ownership of capital?

SECTION 6 REVIEW

Summary

Gains from Trade

1. International trade is of growing importance to the United States and of even greater importance to most other countries. International trade, like trade among individuals, arises from comparative advantage: the opportunity cost of producing an additional unit of a good is lower in some countries than in others. Goods and services purchased abroad are **imports;** those sold abroad are **exports.** Foreign trade, like other economic linkages between countries, has been growing rapidly, a phenomenon called **globalization.**
2. There are gains from trade: two countries are better off with trade than in **autarky,** a situation in which a country does not trade with other countries.
3. In practice, comparative advantage reflects differences between countries in climate, factor endowments, and technology. The **Heckscher–Ohlin** model shows how differences in factor endowments determine comparative advantage: goods differ in **factor intensity,** and countries tend to export goods that are intensive in the factors they have in relative abundance.
4. The **domestic demand curve** and the **domestic supply curve** determine the price of a good in autarky. When international trade occurs, the domestic price is driven to equality with the **world price,** the price at which the good is bought and sold abroad.
5. If the world price is below the autarky price, a good is imported. This leads to an increase in consumer surplus, a fall in producer surplus, and a gain in total surplus. If the world price is above the autarky price, a good is exported. This leads to an increase in producer surplus, a fall in consumer surplus, and a gain in total surplus.

Supply, Demand, and International Trade

6. International trade leads to expansion in **exporting industries** and contraction in **import-competing industries.** This raises the domestic demand for abundant factors of production, reduces the demand for scarce factors, and so affects factor prices, such as wages.
7. Most economists advocate **free trade,** but in practice many governments engage in **trade protection.** The two most common forms of **protection** are tariffs and quotas. On rare occasions, export industries are subsidized.
8. A **tariff** is a tax levied on imports. It raises the domestic price above the world price, hurting consumers, benefiting domestic producers, and generating government revenue. As a result, total surplus falls. An **import quota** is a legal limit on the quantity of a good that can be imported. It has the same effects as a tariff, except that the revenue goes not to the government but to those who receive import licenses.
9. In the past few years, many concerns have been raised about the effects of globalization. One issue is the increase in income inequality due to the surge in imports from relatively poor countries over the past 20 years. Another is the increase in **offshore outsourcing,** as many jobs, once considered safe from foreign competition, have been moved abroad.

Key Terms

Problems

1. Assume Saudi Arabia and the United States face the production possibilities for oil and cars shown in the accompanying table.

   a. What is the opportunity cost of producing a car in Saudi Arabia? In the United States? What is the opportunity cost of producing a barrel of oil in Saudi Arabia? In the United States?

Saudi Arabia		United States	
Quantity of oil (millions of barrels)	Quantity of cars (millions)	Quantity of oil (millions of barrels)	Quantity of cars (millions)
0	4	0	10.0
200	3	100	7.5
400	2	200	5.0
600	1	300	2.5
800	0	400	0

b. Which country has the comparative advantage in producing oil? In producing cars?

c. Suppose that in autarky, Saudi Arabia produces 200 million barrels of oil and 3 million cars; similarly, that the United States produces 300 million barrels of oil and 2.5 million cars. Without trade, can Saudi Arabia produce more oil *and* more cars? Without trade, can the United States produce more oil *and* more cars?

2. The production possibilities for the United States and Saudi Arabia are given in Problem 1. Suppose now that each country specializes in the good in which it has the comparative advantage, and the two countries trade.

a. What is the total quantity of oil produced? What is the total quantity of cars produced?

b. Is it possible for Saudi Arabia to consume 400 million barrels of oil and 5 million cars and for the United States to consume 400 million barrels of oil and 5 million cars?

c. Suppose that, in fact, Saudi Arabia consumes 300 million barrels of oil and 4 million cars and the United States consumes 500 million barrels of oil and 6 million cars. How many barrels of oil does the United States import? How many cars does the United States export? Suppose a car costs $10,000 on the world market. How much, then, does a barrel of oil cost on the world market?

3. Both Canada and the United States produce lumber and music CDs with constant opportunity costs. The United States can produce either 10 tons of lumber and no CDs, or 1,000 CDs and no lumber, or any combination in between. Canada can produce either 8 tons of lumber and no CDs, or 400 CDs and no lumber, or any combination in between.

a. Draw the U.S. and Canadian production possibility curves in two separate diagrams, with CDs on the horizontal axis and lumber on the vertical axis.

b. In autarky, if the United States wants to consume 500 CDs, how much lumber can it consume at most? Label this point *A* in your diagram. Similarly, if Canada wants to consume 1 ton of lumber, how many CDs can it consume in autarky? Label this point *C* in your diagram.

c. Which country has the absolute advantage in lumber production?

d. Which country has the comparative advantage in lumber production?

Suppose each country specializes in the good in which it has the comparative advantage, and there is trade.

e. How many CDs does the United States produce? How much lumber does Canada produce?

f. Is it possible for the United States to consume 500 CDs and 7 tons of lumber? Label this point *B* in your diagram. Is it possible for Canada at the same time to consume 500 CDs and 1 ton of lumber? Label this point *D* in your diagram.

4. For each of the following trade relationships, explain the likely source of the comparative advantage of each of the exporting countries.

a. The United States exports software to Venezuela, and Venezuela exports oil to the United States.

b. The United States exports airplanes to China, and China exports clothing to the United States.

c. The United States exports wheat to Colombia, and Colombia exports coffee to the United States.

5. Shoes are labor-intensive and satellites are capital-intensive to produce. The United States has abundant capital. China has abundant labor. According to the Heckscher–Ohlin model, which good will China export? Which good will the United States export? In the United States, what will happen to the price of labor (the wage) and to the price of capital?

6. Before the North American Free Trade Agreement (NAFTA) gradually eliminated import tariffs on goods traded by the United States, Mexico, and Canada, the autarky price of tomatoes in Mexico was below the world price and in the United States was above the world price. Similarly, the autarky price of poultry in Mexico was above the world price and in the United States was below the world price. Draw diagrams with domestic supply and demand curves for each country and each of the two goods. As a result of NAFTA, the United States now imports tomatoes from Mexico and the United States now exports poultry to Mexico. How would you expect the following groups to be affected?

a. Mexican and U.S. consumers of tomatoes. Illustrate the effect on consumer surplus in your diagram.

b. Mexican and U.S. producers of tomatoes. Illustrate the effect on producer surplus in your diagram.

c. Mexican and U.S. tomato workers.

d. Mexican and U.S. consumers of poultry. Illustrate the effect on consumer surplus in your diagram.

e. Mexican and U.S. producers of poultry. Illustrate the effect on producer surplus in your diagram.

f. Mexican and U.S. poultry workers.

7. The accompanying table indicates the U.S. domestic demand schedule and domestic supply schedule for commercial jet airplanes. Suppose that the world price of a commercial jet airplane is $100 million.

Price of jet (millions)	Quantity of jets demanded	Quantity of jets supplied
$120	100	1,000
110	150	900
100	200	800
90	250	700
80	300	600
70	350	500
60	400	400
50	450	300
40	500	200

a. In autarky, how many commercial jet airplanes does the United States produce, and at what price are they bought and sold?

b. With trade, what will the price for commercial jet airplanes be? Will the United States import or export airplanes? How many?

8. The accompanying table shows the U.S. domestic demand schedule and domestic supply schedule for oranges. Suppose that the world price of oranges is $0.30 per orange.

Price of orange	Quantity of oranges demanded (thousands)	Quantity of oranges supplied (thousands)
$1.00	2	11
0.90	4	10
0.80	6	9
0.70	8	8
0.60	10	7
0.50	12	6
0.40	14	5
0.30	16	4
0.20	18	3

a. Draw the U.S. domestic supply curve and domestic demand curve.

b. With free trade, how many oranges will the United States import or export?

Suppose that the U.S. government imposes a tariff on oranges of $0.20 per orange.

c. How many oranges will the United States import or export after introduction of the tariff?

d. In your diagram, shade the gain or loss to the economy as a whole from the introduction of this tariff.

9. The U.S. domestic demand schedule and domestic supply schedule for oranges was given in Problem 8. Suppose that the world price of oranges is $0.30. The United States introduces an import quota of 3,000 oranges and assigns the quota rents to foreign orange exporters.

a. Draw the domestic demand and supply curves.

b. What will the domestic price of oranges be after introduction of the quota?

c. What is the value of the quota rents that foreign exporters of oranges receive?

10. The accompanying diagram illustrates the U.S. domestic demand curve and domestic supply curve for beef.

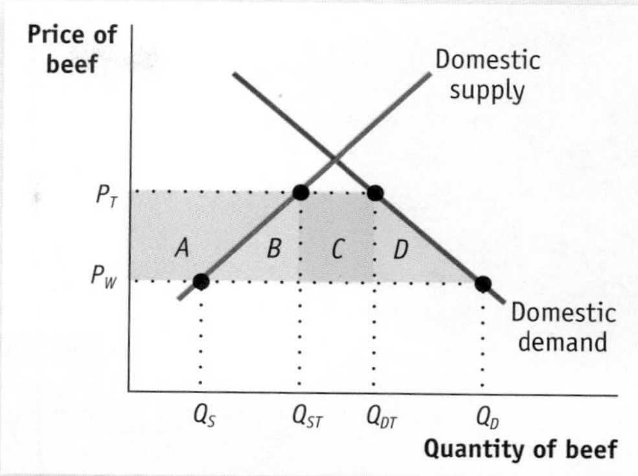

The world price of beef is P_W. The United States currently imposes an import tariff on beef, so the price of beef is P_T. Congress decides to eliminate the tariff. In terms of the areas marked in the diagram, answer the following questions.

a. What is the gain/loss in consumer surplus?

b. What is the gain/loss in producer surplus?

c. What is the gain/loss to the government?

d. What is the gain/loss to the economy as a whole?

11. As the United States has opened up to trade, it has lost many of its low-skill manufacturing jobs, but it has gained jobs in high-skill industries, such as the software industry. Explain whether the United States as a whole has been made better off by trade.

12. If a country agrees to reduce trade barriers (tariffs or quotas), is doing so a *concession* to other countries? Do you think that this terminology is appropriate?

13. Producers in import-competing industries often make the following argument: "Other countries have an advantage in production of certain goods purely because workers abroad are paid lower wages. In fact, American workers are much more productive than foreign workers. So import-competing industries need to be protected." Is this a valid argument? Explain your answer.

NORTH
This way
That

SECTION 7

Economics and Decision Making

GOING BACK TO SCHOOL

In the spring of 2010, Ashley Hildreth, a class of 2008 journalism major at the University of Oregon, was deeply frustrated. After working for 18 months in what she described as a "dead-end, part-time job" in the food industry, she decided to apply to a master's degree program in teaching.

In explaining her decision, she pointed to the many job applications she submitted without a single call back for an interview. What she hoped for was an entry-level opportunity in advertising and marketing or an administrative position with a nonprofit. What she got instead was silence or gentle rejections. After considering her options, she decided to apply for graduate school.

Hildreth was far from alone in her decision. In the spring of 2010, colleges and universities across the country were reporting a record number of applications for bachelor and associate degree programs. And as Hildreth's story illustrates, they also soared for graduate and continuing education programs.

Why did so many people make a similar choice in the spring of 2010? We'll answer that question shortly. Before we do, note that every year millions of people—just like you—face a choice about work versus continued schooling: should I continue another year (or semester, or quarter) in school, or should I get a job? That is, they are making a decision.

This section is about the economics of making decisions: how to make a decision that results in the best possible economic outcome. Economists have formulated principles of decision making that lead to the best possible—often called "optimal"—outcome, regardless of whether the decision maker is a consumer or a producer.

We start by examining three different types of economic decisions. For each of these types, there is a corresponding principle, or method, of decision making that leads to the best possible economic outcome. We'll also see why economists consider decision making to be the very essence of microeconomics.

Despite the fact that people *should* use the principles of economic decision making to achieve the best possible economic outcome, they sometimes fail to do so. In other words, people are not always rational when making decisions. For example, a shopper in pursuit of a bargain may knowingly spend more on gasoline than he or she saves. In this section, we'll learn about these tendencies when we discuss *behavioral economics,* the branch of economics that studies predictably irrational economic behavior.

The section concludes with a discussion of *utility,* a measure of satisfaction from consumption, and how individuals make consumption decisions when faced with a limited budget.

MODULE

18 Making Decisions

Vividpixel/Dreamstime

WHAT YOU WILL LEARN

1. **Why good decision making begins with accurately understanding costs and benefits**
2. **The difference between accounting profit and economic profit, and why economic profit is the correct basis for decisions**
3. **That there are three different types of economic decisions: "either–or" decisions, "how much" decisions, and decisions involving sunk costs**
4. **The principles of decision making that correspond to each type of economic decision**

Costs, Benefits, and Profits

In making any type of decision, it's critical to define the costs and benefits of that decision accurately. If you don't know the costs and benefits, it is nearly impossible to make a good decision. So that is where we begin.

An important first step is to recognize the role of *opportunity cost*, a concept we first encountered in Section 1, where we learned that opportunity costs arise because *resources are scarce*. Because resources are scarce, the true cost of anything is what you must give up to get it—its opportunity cost.

When making decisions, it is crucial to think in terms of opportunity cost, because the opportunity cost of an action is often considerably more than the cost of any outlays of money. Economists use the concepts of *explicit costs* and *implicit costs* to compare the relationship between monetary outlays and opportunity costs. We'll discuss these two concepts first. Then we'll define the concepts of *accounting profit* and *economic profit,* which are *ways of measuring whether the benefit of an action is greater than the cost.* Armed with these concepts for assessing costs and benefits, we will be in a position to consider three principles of economic decision making.

Explicit versus Implicit Costs

Suppose that, after graduating from college, you have two options: to go to school for an additional year to get an advanced degree or to take a job immediately. You would like to enroll in the extra year in school but are concerned about the cost.

What exactly is the cost of that additional year of school? Here is where it is important to remember the concept of opportunity cost: the cost of the year spent getting an advanced degree includes what you forgo by not taking a job for that year. The opportunity cost of an additional year of school, like any cost, can be broken into two parts: the *explicit* cost of the year's schooling and the *implicit* cost.

An **explicit cost** is a cost that requires an outlay of money.

An **implicit cost** does not require an outlay of money; it is measured by the value, in dollar terms, of benefits that are forgone.

Accounting profit is equal to revenue minus explicit cost.

An **explicit cost** is a cost that requires an outlay of money. For example, the explicit cost of the additional year of schooling includes tuition. An **implicit cost,** though, does not involve an outlay of money; instead, it is measured by the value, in dollar terms, of the benefits that are forgone. For example, the implicit cost of the year spent in school includes the income you would have earned if you had taken a job instead.

A common mistake, both in economic analysis and in life—whether individual or business—is to ignore implicit costs and focus exclusively on explicit costs. But often the implicit cost of an activity is quite substantial—indeed, sometimes it is much larger than the explicit cost.

Table 18-1 gives a breakdown of hypothetical explicit and implicit costs associated with spending an additional year in school instead of taking a job. The explicit cost consists of tuition, books, supplies, and a computer for doing assignments—all of which require you to spend money. The implicit cost is the salary you would have earned if you had taken a job instead. As you can see, the total cost of attending an additional year of schooling is $44,500, the sum of the total implicit cost—$35,000 in forgone salary, and the total explicit cost—$9,500 in outlays on tuition, supplies, and computer. Because the implicit cost is more than three times as much as the explicit cost, ignoring the implicit cost would lead to a seriously misguided decision.

TABLE 18-1

Opportunity Cost of an Additional Year of School

Explicit cost		Implicit cost	
Tuition	$7,000	Forgone salary	$35,000
Books and supplies	1,000		
Computer	1,500		
Total explicit cost	**9,500**	**Total implicit cost**	**35,000**
Total opportunity cost = Total explicit cost + Total implicit cost = $44,500			

A slightly different way of looking at the implicit cost in this example can deepen our understanding of opportunity cost. The forgone salary is the cost of using your own resources—your time—in going to school rather than working. The use of your time for more schooling, despite the fact that you don't have to spend any money on it, is still costly to you. This illustrates an important aspect of opportunity cost: in considering the cost of an activity, you should include the cost of using any of your own resources for that activity. You can calculate the cost of using your own resources by determining what they would have earned in their next best use.

Accounting Profit versus Economic Profit

Let's return to Ashley Hildreth. Assume that Ashley faces the choice of either completing a two-year full-time graduate program in teaching or spending those two years working in her original field of advertising. We'll also assume that in order to be certified as a teacher, she must complete the entire two years of the graduate program. Which choice should she make?

To get started, let's consider what Ashley gains by getting the teaching degree—what we might call her *revenue* from the teaching degree. Once she has completed her degree two years from now, she will receive earnings from her degree valued at $600,000 over the rest of her lifetime. In contrast, if she doesn't get the degree and stays in advertising, two years from now her future lifetime earnings will be valued at $500,000. The cost of the tuition for her teaching degree program is $40,000, which she pays for with a student loan that costs her $4,000 in interest.

At this point, what she should do might seem obvious: if she chooses the teaching degree, she gets a lifetime increase in the value of her earnings of $600,000 – $500,000 = $100,000, and she pays $40,000 in tuition plus $4,000 in interest. Doesn't that mean she makes a profit of $100,000 – $40,000 – $4,000 = $56,000 by getting her teaching degree? This $56,000 is Ashley's **accounting profit** from obtaining her teaching degree: her revenue minus her explicit cost. In this example her explicit cost of getting the degree is $44,000, the amount of her tuition plus student loan interest.

Although accounting profit is a useful measure, it would be misleading for Ashley to use it alone in making her decision. To make the right decision, the one that leads to the best possible economic outcome for her, she

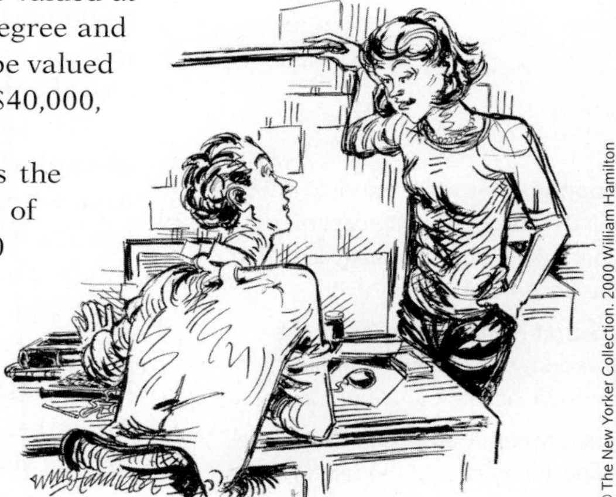

© The New Yorker Collection. 2000 William Hamilton from cartoonbank.com. All Rights Reserved

"I've done the numbers, and I will marry you."

needs to calculate her **economic profit**—the revenue she receives from the teaching degree minus her opportunity cost of staying in school (which is equal to her explicit cost *plus* her implicit cost). In general, the economic profit of a given project will be less than the accounting profit because there are almost always implicit costs in addition to explicit costs.

When economists use the term *profit*, they are referring to *economic* profit, not *accounting* profit. This will be our convention in the rest of the book: when we use the term *profit*, we mean economic profit.

How does Ashley's economic profit from staying in school differ from her accounting profit? We've already encountered one source of the difference: her two years of forgone job earnings. This is an implicit cost of going to school full time for two years. We assume that Ashley's total forgone earnings for the two years is $57,000.

TABLE 18-2

Ashley's Economic Profit from Acquiring a Teaching Degree

Value of increase in lifetime earnings	$100,000
Explicit cost:	
Tuition	−40,000
Interest paid on student loan	− 4,000
Accounting Profit	**56,000**
Implicit cost:	
Income forgone during 2 years spent in school	−57,000
Economic Profit	**−1,000**

Once we factor in implicit costs and calculate her economic profit, we see that she is better off not getting a teaching degree. You can see this in Table 18-2: her economic profit from getting the teaching degree is −$1,000. In other words, she incurs an *economic loss* of $1,000 if she gets the degree. Clearly, she is better off sticking to advertising and going to work now.

To make sure that the concepts of opportunity costs and economic profit are well understood, let's consider a slightly different scenario. Let's suppose that Ashley does not have to take out $40,000 in student loans to pay her tuition. Instead, she can pay for it with an inheritance from her grandmother. As a result, she doesn't have to pay $4,000 in interest. In this case, her accounting profit is $60,000 rather than $56,000. Would the right decision now be for her to get the teaching degree? Wouldn't the economic profit of the degree now be $60,000 − $57,000 = $3,000?

The answer is no, because Ashley is using her own *capital* to finance her education, and the use of that capital has an opportunity cost even when she owns it. **Capital** is the total value of the assets of an individual or a firm. An individual's capital usually consists of cash in the bank, stocks, bonds, and the ownership value of real estate such as a house. In the case of a business, capital also includes its equipment, its tools, and its inventory of unsold goods and used parts. (Economists like to distinguish between *financial assets,* such as cash, stocks, and bonds, and *physical assets,* such as buildings, equipment, tools, and inventory.)

The point is that even if Ashley owns the $40,000, using it to pay tuition incurs an opportunity cost—what she forgoes in the next best use of that $40,000. If she hadn't used the money to pay her tuition, her next best use of the money would have been to deposit it in a bank to earn interest. To keep things simple, let's assume that she earns $4,000 on that $40,000 once it is deposited in a bank. Now, rather than pay $4,000 in explicit costs in the form of student loan interest, Ashley incurs $4,000 in implicit costs from the forgone interest she could have earned.

This $4,000 in forgone interest earnings is what economists call the **implicit cost of capital**—the income the owner of the capital could have earned if the capital had been employed in its next best alternative use. The net effect is that it makes no difference whether Ashley finances her tuition with a student loan or by using her own funds. This comparison reinforces how carefully you must keep track of opportunity costs when making a decision.

Economic profit is equal to revenue minus the opportunity cost of resources used. It is usually less than the accounting profit.

Capital is the total value of assets owned by an individual or firm—physical assets plus financial assets.

The **implicit cost of capital** is the opportunity cost of the use of one's own capital—the income earned if the capital had been employed in its next best alternative use.

Making "Either–Or" Decisions

An "either–or" decision is one in which you must choose between two activities. That's in contrast to a "how much" decision, which requires you to choose how much of a given activity to undertake. For example, Ashley faced an "either–or" decision: to spend two years in graduate school to obtain a teaching degree, or to work. In contrast, a "how much" decision would be deciding how many hours to study or how many hours to work at a job. Table 18-3 contrasts a variety of "either–or" and "how much" decisions.

In making economic decisions, as we have already emphasized, it is vitally important to calculate opportunity costs correctly. The best way to make an "either–or" decision, the method that leads to the best possible economic outcome, is the straightforward **principle of "either–or" decision making.** According to this principle, *when making an "either–or" choice between two activities, choose the one with the positive economic profit.*

TABLE 18-3

"How Much" versus "Either–Or" Decisions

"Either–or" decisions	"How much" decisions
Do the laundry with Tide or Cheer?	How many days before you do your laundry?
Buy a car or not?	How many miles do you go before an oil change in your car?
An order of nachos or a sandwich?	How many jalapeños on your nachos?
Run your own business or work for someone else?	How many workers should you hire in your company?
Prescribe drug A or drug B for your patients?	How much should a patient take of a drug that generates side effects?
Graduate school or not?	How many hours to study?

Let's examine Ashley's dilemma from a different angle to understand how this principle works. If she continues with advertising and goes to work immediately, the total value of her lifetime earnings is $57,000 (her earnings over the next two years) + $500,000 (the value of her lifetime earnings thereafter) = $557,000. If she gets her teaching degree instead and works as a teacher, the total value of her lifetime earnings is $600,000 (value of her lifetime earnings after two years in school) – $40,000 (tuition) – $4,000 (interest payments) = $556,000. The economic profit from continuing in advertising versus becoming a teacher is $557,000 – $556,000 = $1,000.

So the right choice for Ashley is to begin work in advertising immediately, which gives her an economic profit of $1,000, rather than become a teacher, which would give her an economic profit of –$1,000. In other words, by becoming a teacher she loses the $1,000 economic profit she would have gained by working in advertising immediately.

In making "either–or" decisions, mistakes most commonly arise when people or businesses use their own assets in projects rather than rent or borrow assets. That's because they fail to account for the implicit cost of using self-owned capital. In contrast, when they rent or borrow assets, these rental or borrowing costs show up as explicit costs. If, for example, a restaurant owns its equipment and tools, it would have to compute its implicit cost of capital by calculating how much the equipment could be sold for and how much could be earned by using those funds in the next best alternative project. In addition, businesses run by the owner (an *entrepreneur)* often fail to calculate the opportunity cost of the owner's time in running the business. In that way, small businesses often underestimate their opportunity costs and overestimate their economic profit of staying in business.

Making "How Much" Decisions: The Role of Marginal Analysis

Although many decisions in economics are "either–or," many others are "how much." Not many people will give up their cars if the price of gasoline goes up, but many people will drive less. How much less? A rise in corn prices won't necessarily persuade a lot of people to take up farming for the first time, but it will persuade farmers who are already growing corn to plant more. How much more?

To understand "how much" decisions, we will use an approach known as **marginal analysis.** Marginal analysis involves comparing the benefit of doing a little bit more of some activity with the cost of doing a little bit more of that activity. The benefit of doing a little bit more of something is what economists call its *marginal benefit,* and the cost of doing a little bit more of something is its *marginal cost.*

Why is this called "marginal" analysis? A margin is an edge; what you do in marginal analysis is push out the edge a bit and see whether that is a good move. We will study marginal analysis by considering a hypothetical decision of how many years of school to complete. We'll consider the case of Alex, who studies computer

According to the **principle of "either–or" decision making,** when faced with an "either–or" choice between two activities, choose the one with the positive economic profit.

Marginal analysis involves comparing the benefit of doing a little bit more of some activity with the cost of doing a little bit more of that activity.

Wavebreakmedia/Shutterstock

To make his decision, Alex will need to compare the benefit of additional years of schooling with the cost of spending more time in school.

programming and design. Since there are many computer languages, app design methods, and graphics programs that can be learned one year at a time, each year Alex can decide whether to continue his studies or not.

Unlike Ashley, who faced an "either–or" decision of whether to get a teaching degree, Alex faces a "how much" decision of how many years to study computer programming and design. For example, he could study one more year, or five more years, or any number of years in between. We'll begin our analysis of Alex's decision problem by defining Alex's *marginal cost* of another year of study.

Marginal Cost

We'll assume that each additional year of schooling costs Alex $10,000 in explicit costs—tuition, interest on a student loan, and so on. In addition to the explicit costs, he also has implicit costs—the income forgone by spending one more year in school. Unlike Alex's explicit costs, which are constant (that is, the same each year), Alex's implicit cost changes each year. That's because each year he spends in school leaves him better trained than the year before; and the better trained he is, the higher the salary he can command. Consequently, the income he forgoes by not working rises each additional year he stays in school.

Table 18-4 contains the data on how Alex's cost of an additional year of schooling changes as he completes more years. The second column shows how his total cost of schooling changes as the number of years he has completed increases. For example, Alex's first year has a total cost of $30,000: $10,000 in explicit costs of tuition and the like as well as $20,000 in forgone salary.

TABLE 18-4

Alex's Marginal Cost of Additional Years in School

Quantity of schooling (years)	Total cost	Marginal cost
0	$0	
		$30,000
1	30,000	
		40,000
2	70,000	
		60,000
3	130,000	
		90,000
4	220,000	
		130,000
5	350,000	

The second column also shows that the total cost of attending two years is $70,000: $30,000 for his first year plus $40,000 for his second year. During his second year in school, his explicit costs have stayed the same ($10,000) but his implicit cost of forgone salary has gone up to $30,000. That's because he's a more valuable worker with one year of schooling under his belt than with no schooling. Likewise, the total cost of three years of schooling is $130,000: $30,000 in explicit cost for three years of tuition (at $10,000 per year), plus $100,000 in implicit cost of three years of forgone salary. The total cost of attending four years is $220,000, and $350,000 for five years.

The change in Alex's total cost of schooling when he goes to school an additional year is his *marginal cost* of the one-year increase in years of schooling. In general, the **marginal cost** of producing a good or service (in this case, producing one's own education) is the additional cost incurred by producing one more unit of that good or service. The arrows, which zigzag between the total costs in the second column and the marginal costs in the third column, are there to help you to see how marginal cost is calculated from total cost, and vice versa.

The **marginal cost** of producing a good or service is the additional cost incurred by producing one more unit of that good or service.

Production of a good or service has **increasing marginal cost** when each additional unit costs more to produce than the previous one.

The **marginal cost curve** shows how the cost of producing one more unit depends on the quantity that has already been produced.

Production of a good or service has **constant marginal cost** when each additional unit costs the same to produce as the previous one.

Alex's marginal costs of more years of schooling have a clear pattern: they are increasing. They go from $30,000, to $40,000, to $60,000, to $90,000, and finally to $130,000 for the fifth year of schooling. That's because each year of schooling would make Alex a more valuable and highly paid employee if he were to work. As a result, forgoing a job becomes more and more costly as he becomes more educated. This is an example of what economists call **increasing marginal cost,** which occurs when each unit of a good costs more to produce than the previous unit.

Figure 18-1 shows a **marginal cost curve,** a graphic representation of Alex's marginal costs. The height of each shaded bar corresponds to the marginal cost of a given year of schooling. The red line connecting the dots at the midpoint of the top of each bar is Alex's marginal cost curve. Alex has an upward-sloping marginal cost curve because he has increasing marginal cost of additional years of schooling.

Although increasing marginal cost is a frequent phenomenon in real life, it's not the only possibility. **Constant marginal cost** occurs when the cost of producing an

FIGURE 18-1 Marginal Cost

The height of each shaded bar corresponds to Alex's marginal cost of an additional year of schooling. The height of each bar is higher than the preceding one because each year of schooling costs more than the previous years. As a result, Alex has increasing marginal cost and the marginal cost curve, the line connecting the midpoints at the top of each bar, is upward sloping.

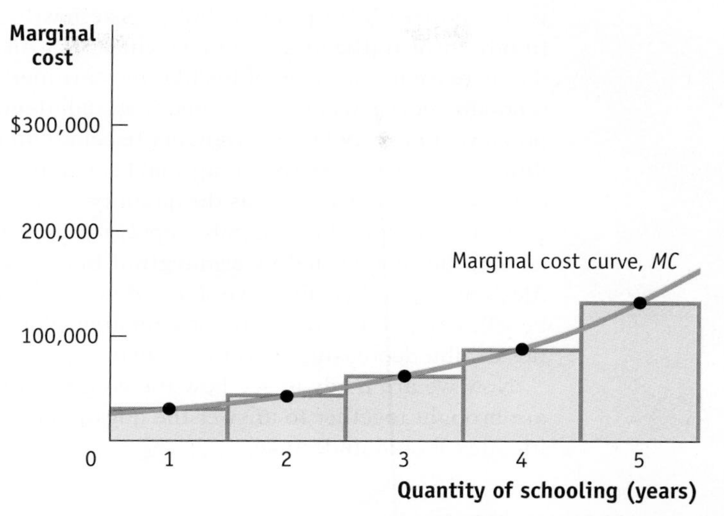

additional unit is the same as the cost of producing the previous unit. Plant nurseries, for example, typically have constant marginal cost—the cost of growing one more plant is the same, regardless of how many plants have already been produced. With constant marginal cost, the marginal cost curve is a horizontal line.

There can also be **decreasing marginal cost,** which occurs when marginal cost falls as the number of units produced increases. With decreasing marginal cost, the marginal cost line is downward sloping. Decreasing marginal cost is often due to *learning effects* in production: for complicated tasks, such as assembling a new model of a car, workers are often slow and mistake-prone when assembling the earliest units, making for higher marginal cost on those units. But as workers gain experience, assembly time and the rate of mistakes fall, generating lower marginal cost for later units. As a result, overall production has decreasing marginal cost.

Finally, for the production of some goods and services the shape of the marginal cost curve changes as the number of units produced increases. For example, auto production is likely to have decreasing marginal costs for the first batch of cars produced as workers iron out kinks and mistakes in production. Then production has constant marginal costs for the next batch of cars as workers settle into a predictable pace. But at some point, as workers produce more and more cars, marginal cost begins to increase as they run out of factory floor space and the auto company incurs costly overtime wages. This gives rise to what we call a "swoosh"-shaped marginal cost curve—a topic we will discuss in more detail in the next section. For now, we'll stick to the simpler example of an increasing marginal cost curve.

Production of a good or service has **decreasing marginal cost** when each additional unit costs less to produce than the previous one.

The **marginal benefit** of a good or service is the additional benefit derived from producing one more unit of that good or service.

Marginal Benefit

Alex benefits from higher lifetime earnings as he completes more years of school. Exactly how much he benefits is shown in Table 18-5. Column 2 shows Alex's total benefit according to the number of years of school completed, expressed as the value of the increase in lifetime earnings. The third column shows Alex's *marginal benefit* from an additional year of schooling. In general, the **marginal benefit** of producing a good or service is the additional benefit earned from producing one more unit.

As in Table 18-4, the data in the third column of Table 18-5 show a clear pattern. However, this time the numbers are decreasing rather than increasing. The first year of schooling gives

TABLE 18-5

Alex's Marginal Benefit of Additional Years in School

Quantity of schooling (years)	Total benefit	Marginal benefit
0	$0	
		$300,000
1	300,000	
		150,000
2	450,000	
		90,000
3	540,000	
		60,000
4	600,000	
		50,000
5	650,000	

Alex a $300,000 increase in the value of his lifetime earnings. The second year also gives him a positive return, but the size of that return has fallen to $150,000; the third year's return is also positive, but its size has fallen yet again to $90,000; and so on. In other words, the more years of school that Alex has already completed, the smaller the increase in the value of his lifetime earnings from attending one more year. Alex's schooling decision has what economists call **decreasing marginal benefit:** each additional year of school yields a smaller benefit than the previous year. Or, to put it slightly differently, with decreasing marginal benefit, the benefit from producing one more unit of the good or service falls as the quantity already produced rises.

Just as marginal cost can be represented by a marginal cost curve, marginal benefit can be represented by a **marginal benefit curve,** shown in blue in Figure 18-2. Alex's marginal benefit curve slopes downward because he faces decreasing marginal benefit from additional years of schooling. Note, however that not all goods or activities exhibit decreasing marginal benefit.

Now we are ready to see how the concepts of marginal benefit and marginal cost are brought together to answer the question of how many years of additional schooling Alex should undertake.

FIGURE 18-2 Marginal Benefit

The height of each shaded bar corresponds to Alex's marginal benefit of an additional year of schooling. The height of each bar is lower than the one preceding it because an additional year of schooling has decreasing marginal benefit. As a result, Alex's marginal benefit curve, the curve connecting the midpoints at the top of each bar, is downward sloping.

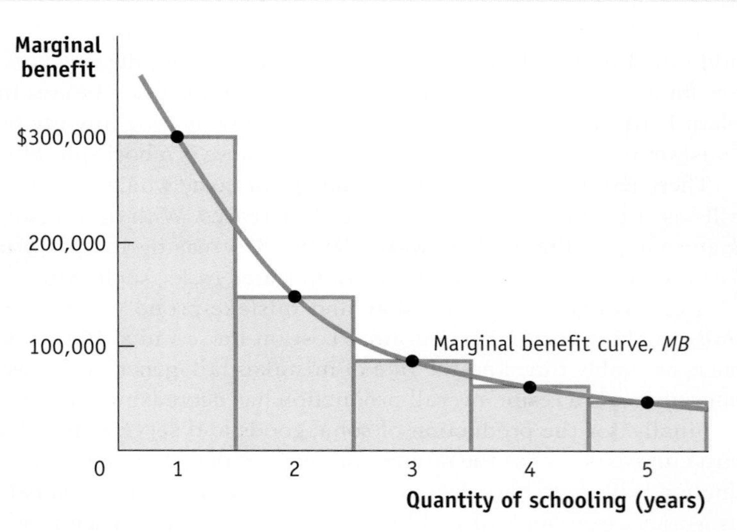

Marginal Analysis

Table 18-6 shows the marginal cost and marginal benefit numbers from Tables 18-4 and 18-5. It also adds an another column: the additional profit to Alex from staying in school one more year, equal to the difference between the marginal benefit and the marginal cost of that additional year in school. (Remember that it is Alex's economic profit that we care about, not his accounting profit.) We can now use Table 18-6 to determine how many additional years of schooling Alex should undertake in order to maximize his total profit.

There is **decreasing marginal benefit** from an activity when each additional unit of the activity yields less benefit than the previous unit.

The **marginal benefit curve** shows how the benefit from producing one more unit depends on the quantity that has already been produced.

First, imagine that Alex chooses not to attend any additional years of school. We can see from column 4 that this is a mistake if Alex wants to achieve the highest total profit from his schooling—the sum of the additional profits generated by another year of schooling. If he attends one additional year of school, he increases the value of his lifetime earnings by $270,000, the profit from the first additional year attended.

Now, let's consider whether Alex should attend the second year of school. The additional profit from the second year is $110,000, so Alex should attend the second year as well. What about the third year? The additional profit from that year is $30,000; so, yes, Alex should attend the third year as well. What about a fourth year? In this case, the additional profit is negative: it is –$30,000. Clearly, Alex is worse off by attending the fourth additional year rather than taking a job. And the same is true for the fifth year as well: it has a negative additional profit of –$80,000.

TABLE 18-6

Alex's Profit from Additional Years of Schooling

Quantity of schooling (years)	Marginal benefit	Marginal cost	Additional profit
0			
	$300,000	$30,000	$270,000
1			
	150,000	40,000	110,000
2			
	90,000	60,000	30,000
3			
	60,000	90,000	–30,000
4			
	50,000	130,000	–80,000
5			

What have we learned? That Alex should attend three additional years of school and stop at that point. Although the first, second, and third years of additional schooling increase the value of his lifetime earnings, the fourth and fifth years diminish it. So three years of additional schooling lead to the quantity that generates the maximum possible total profit. It is what economists call the **optimal quantity**—the quantity that generates the maximum possible total profit.

Figure 18-3 shows how the optimal quantity can be determined graphically. Alex's marginal benefit and marginal cost curves are shown together. If Alex chooses fewer than three additional years (that is, years 0, 1, or 2), he will choose a level of schooling at which his marginal benefit curve lies *above* his marginal cost curve. He can make himself better off by staying in school. If instead he chooses more than three additional years (years 4 or 5), he will choose a level of schooling at which his marginal benefit curve lies *below* his marginal cost curve. He can make himself better off by not attending the additional year of school and taking a job instead.

The table in Figure 18-3 confirms our result. The second column repeats information from Table 18-6, showing Alex's marginal benefit minus marginal cost—the additional profit per additional year of schooling. The third column shows Alex's total

The **optimal quantity** is the quantity that generates the highest possible total profit.

FIGURE 18-3 Alex's Optimal Quantity of Years of Schooling

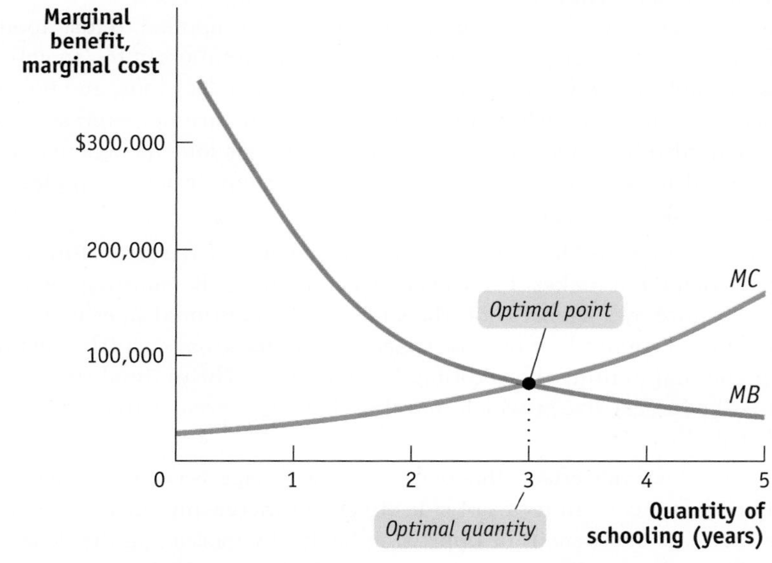

Quantity of schooling (years)	Additional profit	Total profit
0		$0
	$270,000	
1		270,000
	110,000	
2		380,000
	30,000	
3		410,000
	–30,000	
4		380,000
	–80,000	
5		300,000

The optimal quantity is the quantity that generates the highest possible total profit. It is the quantity at which marginal benefit is greater than or equal to marginal cost. Equivalently, it is the quantity at which the marginal benefit and marginal cost curves intersect. Here, they intersect at 3 additional years of schooling. The table confirms that 3 is indeed the optimal quantity: it leads to the maximum total profit of $410,000.

profit for different years of schooling. The total profit, for each possible year of schooling is simply the sum of numbers in the second column up to and including that year. For example, Alex's profit from additional years of schooling is $270,000 for the first year and $110,000 for the second year. So the total profit for two additional years of schooling is $270,000 + $110,000 = $380,000. Similarly, the total profit for three additional years is $270,000 + $110,000 + $30,000 = $410,000. Our claim that three years is the optimal quantity for Alex is confirmed by the data in the table in Figure 18-3: at three years of additional schooling, Alex reaps the greatest total profit, $410,000.

Purestock/Thinkstock

How many years of schooling will maximize your total profit?

Alex's decision problem illustrates how you go about finding the optimal quantity when the choice involves a small number of quantities. (In this example, one through five years.) With small quantities, the rule for choosing the optimal quantity is: *increase the quantity as long as the marginal benefit from one more unit is greater than the marginal cost, but stop before the marginal benefit becomes less than the marginal cost.*

In contrast, when a "how much" decision involves relatively large quantities, the rule for choosing the optimal quantity simplifies to this: *The optimal quantity is the quantity at which marginal benefit is equal to marginal cost.*

With very large quantities, increasing output by one unit will produce very small changes in marginal benefit and marginal cost. To see why this is so, consider the example of a farmer who finds that her optimal quantity of wheat produced is 5,000 bushels. Typically, she will find that in going from 4,999 to 5,000 bushels, her marginal benefit is only very slightly greater than her marginal cost—that is, the difference between marginal benefit and marginal cost is close to zero. Similarly, in going from 5,000 to 5,001 bushels, her marginal cost is only very slightly greater than her marginal benefit—again, the difference between marginal cost and marginal benefit is very close to zero. So a simple rule in choosing the optimal quantity is to produce the quantity at which the difference between marginal benefit and marginal cost is approximately zero—that is, the quantity at which marginal benefit equals marginal cost.

Now we are ready to state the general rule for choosing the optimal quantity—one that applies for decisions involving either small quantities or large quantities. This general rule is known as the **profit-maximizing principle of marginal analysis:** *When making a profit-maximizing "how much" decision, the optimal quantity is the largest quantity at which marginal benefit is greater than or equal to marginal cost.*

According to the **profit-maximizing principle of marginal analysis,** when faced with a profit-maximizing "how much" decision, the optimal quantity is the largest quantity at which marginal benefit is greater than or equal to marginal cost.

The profit-maximizing principle of marginal analysis can be applied to just about any "how much" decision in which you want to maximize the total profit for an activity. It is equally applicable to production decisions, consumption decisions, and policy decisions. Furthermore, decisions where the benefits and costs are not expressed in dollars and cents can also be made using marginal analysis, as long as benefits and costs can be measured in some type of common units. Here are a few examples of decisions that are suitable for marginal analysis:

- A producer, the retailer PalMart, must decide on the size of the new store it is constructing in Beijing. It makes this decision by comparing the marginal benefit of enlarging the store by 1 square foot (the value of the additional sales it makes from that additional square foot of floor space) to the marginal cost (the cost of constructing and maintaining the additional square foot). The optimal store size for PalMart is the largest size at which marginal benefit is greater than or equal to marginal cost.
- Many useful drugs have side effects that depend on the dosage. So a physician must consider the marginal cost, in terms of side effects, of increasing the dosage of a drug versus the marginal benefit of improving health by increasing the dosage. The optimal dosage level is the largest level at which the marginal benefit of disease amelioration is greater than or equal to the marginal cost of side effects.
- A farmer must decide how much fertilizer to apply. More fertilizer increases crop yield but also costs more. The optimal amount of fertilizer is the largest quantity at which the marginal benefit of higher crop yield is greater than or equal to the marginal cost of purchasing and applying more fertilizer.

ECONOMICS IN ACTION 

THE COST OF A LIFE

What's the marginal benefit to society of saving a human life? You might be tempted to answer that human life is infinitely precious. If in the real world resources are scarce, then we must decide how much to spend on saving lives since we cannot spend infinite amounts. After all, we could surely reduce highway deaths by dropping the speed limit on interstates to 40 miles per hour, but the cost of such a lower speed limit—in time and money—is more than most people are willing to pay.

Generally, people are reluctant to talk in a straightforward way about comparing the marginal cost of a life saved with the marginal benefit—it sounds too callous. Sometimes, however, the question becomes unavoidable.

For example, the cost of saving a life became an object of intense discussion in the United Kingdom after a horrible train crash near London's Paddington Station killed 31 people. There were accusations that the British government was spending too little on rail safety. However, the government estimated that improving rail safety would cost an additional $4.5 million per life saved.

But if that amount were worth spending—that is, if the estimated marginal benefit of saving a life exceeded $4.5 million—then the implication was that the British government was spending far too little on traffic safety. In contrast, the estimated marginal cost per life saved through highway improvements was only $1.5 million, making it a much better deal than saving lives through greater rail safety.

Sunk Costs

When making decisions, knowing what to ignore can be as important as what to include. Although we have devoted much attention in this module to costs that are important to take into account when making a decision, some costs should be ignored when doing so. Let's now look at the kinds of costs that people should ignore when making decisions—what economists call *sunk costs*—and why they should be ignored.

To gain some intuition, consider the following scenario. You own a car that is a few years old, and you have just replaced the brake pads at a cost of $250. But then you find out that the entire brake system is defective and also must be replaced. This will cost you an additional $1,500. Alternatively, you could sell the car and buy another of comparable quality, but with no brake defects, by spending an additional $1,600. What should you do: fix your old car, or sell it and buy another?

Daniel Grill/Getty Images

The $250 you already spent on brake pads is irrelevant because it is a sunk cost.

Some might say that you should take the latter option. After all, this line of reasoning goes, if you repair your car, you will end up having spent $1,750: $1,500 for the brake system and $250 for the brake pads. If instead you sell your old car and buy another, you would spend only $1,600.

But this reasoning, although it sounds plausible, is wrong. It is wrong because it ignores the fact that you have *already* spent $250 on brake pads, and that $250 cannot be recovered. Therefore, it should be ignored and should have no effect on your decision whether or not to repair your car and keep it. From a rational viewpoint, the real cost at this time of repairing and keeping your car is $1,500, not $1,750. So the correct decision is to repair your car and keep it rather than spend $1,600 on a new car.

In this example, the $250 that has already been spent and cannot be recovered is what economists call a **sunk cost.** Sunk costs should be ignored in making decisions about future actions because they have no influence on their actual costs and benefits. It's like the old saying, "There's no use crying over spilled milk": once something can't be recovered, it is irrelevant in making decisions about what to do in the future.

A **sunk cost** is a cost that has already been incurred and is nonrecoverable. A sunk cost should be ignored in decisions about future actions.

It is often psychologically hard to ignore sunk costs. And if, in fact, you haven't yet incurred the costs, then you should take them into consideration. That is, if you had known at the beginning that it would cost $1,750 to repair your car, then the right choice at that time would have been to replace the car for $1,600. But once you have already paid the $250 for brake pads, you should no longer include it in your decision making about your next actions. It may be hard to accept that "bygones are bygones," but it is the right way to make a decision.

MODULE 18 Review

Solutions appear at the back of the book.

Check Your Understanding

1. Karma and Don run a furniture-refinishing business from their home. Which of the following represent an explicit cost of the business and which represent an implicit cost?
   a. Supplies such as paint stripper, varnish, polish, sandpaper, and so on
   b. Basement space that has been converted into a workroom
   c. Wages paid to a part-time helper
   d. A van that they inherited and use only for transporting furniture
   e. The job at a larger furniture restorer that Karma gave up in order to run the business

2. Ashley Hildreth faced the choice of either completing a two-year graduate program in teaching or working at a job in advertising. Assume that she has a third alternative to consider: entering a two-year apprenticeship program for skilled machinists that would, upon completion, make her a licensed machinist. During the apprenticeship, she earns a reduced salary of $15,000 per year. At the end of the apprenticeship, the value of her lifetime earnings is $725,000. What is Ashley's best career choice?

3. Suppose you have three alternatives—A, B, and C—and you can undertake only one of them. In comparing A versus B, you find that B has an economic profit and A yields an economic loss. But in comparing A versus C, you find that C has an economic profit and A yields an economic loss. How do you decide what to do?

4. For each of the "how much" decisions listed in Table 18-3, describe the nature of the marginal cost and of the marginal benefit.

5. Suppose that Alex's school charges a fixed fee of $70,000 for four years of schooling. If Alex drops out before he finishes those four years, he still has to pay the $70,000. Alex's total cost for different years of schooling is now given by the data in the accompanying table. Assume that Alex's total benefit and marginal benefit remain as reported in Table 18-5.

   Use this information to calculate (i) Alex's new marginal cost, (ii) his new profit, and (iii) his new optimal years of schooling. What kind of marginal cost does Alex now have—constant, increasing, or decreasing?

Quantity of schooling (years)	Total cost
0	$0
1	90,000
2	120,000
3	170,000
4	250,000
5	370,000

6. You have decided to go into the ice-cream business and have bought a used ice-cream truck for $8,000. Now you are reconsidering. What is your sunk cost in the following scenarios?
   a. The truck cannot be resold.
   b. The truck can be resold, but only at a 50% discount.

7. You have gone through two years of medical school but are suddenly wondering whether you wouldn't be happier as a musician. Which of the following statements are potentially valid arguments and which are not?
   a. "I can't give up now, after all the time and money I've put in."
   b. "If I had thought about it from the beginning, I never would have gone to med school, so I should give it up now."
   c. "I wasted two years, but never mind—let's start from here."
   d. "My parents would kill me if I stopped now." (*Hint:* We're discussing your decision-making ability, not your parents'.)

Multiple-Choice Questions

1. Which of the following is NOT considered an explicit cost of attending college?
   a. Tuition
   b. Room and board
   c. Lab and student fees
   d. Lost income from a job you had to quit

2. Suppose that at your current level of consumption, marginal benefit of the most recent unit is 6, and marginal cost is 5. Which of the following is true?
   a. You must be maximizing economic profit.
   b. If possible, you should consume more units until marginal benefit equals marginal cost.
   c. If possible, you should consume more units until marginal benefits are less than marginal cost.
   d. You must reduce consumption until the difference between marginal benefit and marginal cost is greatest.

3. In her previous job, Mei was earning $38,000 a year. She now has a new job where she is paid an annual salary of $42,000. What was Mei's economic profit when she switched jobs?
   a. $42,000
   b. $38,000
   c. $4,000
   d. $0

4. Which of the following is true about accounting profit and economic profit?
   a. Accounting profit considers both explicit and implicit costs.
   b. Accounting profit considers only implicit costs.
   c. Economic profit considers only explicit costs.
   d. Economic profit considers both explicit and implicit costs.

5. Which of the following is an example of increasing marginal cost?
   a. On-the-job training makes it easier for workers to produce.
   b. Planting a second field with crops costs the same as planting the first field.
   c. The further Steven goes in his education, the more difficult the schoolwork becomes.
   d. Learning a new production technique allows workers to produce more than they ever could in the past.

Critical-Thinking Question

You and your friend are at the stadium watching your favorite football team. But they are losing so badly that you can't bear to watch anymore and want to leave. Your friend, however, says, "But we paid $100 for these seats. Shouldn't we stay and get our money's worth?" How do you respond?

PITFALLS

MUDDLED AT THE MARGIN

? The idea of setting marginal benefit equal to marginal cost sometimes confuses people. Aren't we trying to maximize the *difference* between benefits and costs? And don't we wipe out our gains by setting benefits and costs equal to each other?

> THE ANSWER TO BOTH QUESTIONS IS YES. BUT THIS IS NOT WHAT WE ARE DOING. RATHER, WHAT WE ARE DOING IS SETTING *MARGINAL*, NOT *TOTAL*, BENEFIT AND COST EQUAL TO EACH OTHER. Once again, the point is to maximize the total profit from an activity. If the marginal benefit from the activity is greater than the marginal cost, doing a bit more will increase that profit. If the marginal benefit is less than the marginal cost, doing a bit less will increase the total profit. So only when the *marginal* benefit and *marginal* cost are equal is the difference between *total* benefit and *total* cost at a maximum.

To learn more about the idea of setting marginal benefit equal to marginal cost, see pages 198–200 on marginal analysis, and Figure 18-3.

MODULE 19 Behavioral Economics

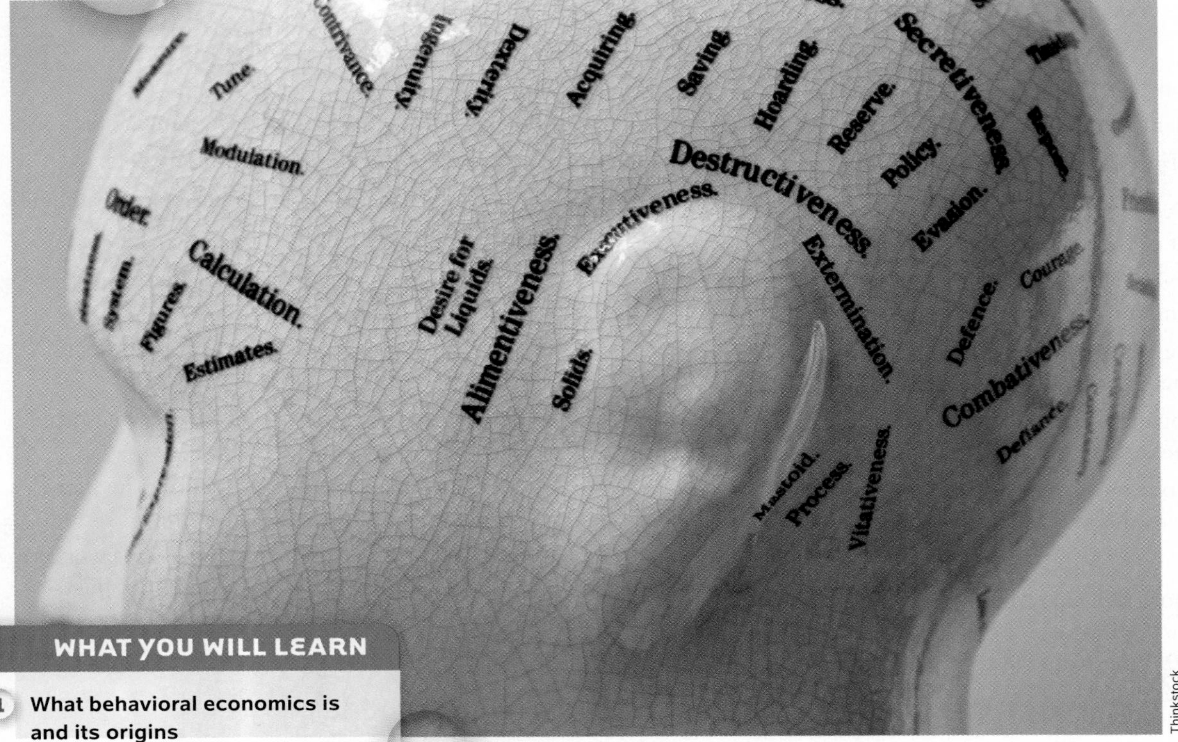

Thinkstock

WHAT YOU WILL LEARN

1. What behavioral economics is and its origins
2. What economists consider to be rational and irrational behavior
3. Why people sometimes behave irrationally in predictable ways

How People Make Economic Choices

Most economic models assume that people make choices based on achieving the best possible economic outcome for themselves. Human behavior, however, is often not so simple. Rather than acting like economic computing machines, people often make choices that fall short—sometimes far short—of the greatest possible economic outcome, or payoff. Why people sometimes make less-than-perfect choices is the subject of behavioral economics, a branch of economics that combines economic modeling with insights from human psychology. Behavioral economics grew out of economists' and psychologists' attempts to understand how people actually make economic choices in real life (instead of in theory).

It's well documented that people consistently engage in *irrational* behavior, choosing an option that leaves them worse off than other available options. Yet, as we'll soon learn, sometimes it's entirely *rational* for people to make a choice that is different from the one that generates the highest possible profit for themselves. For example, Ashley Hildreth, who we read about in Module 18, may decide to earn a teaching degree because she enjoys teaching more than advertising, even though the profit from the teaching degree is less than that from continuing with advertising.

The study of irrational economic behavior was largely pioneered by Daniel Kahneman and Amos Tversky. Kahneman won the 2002 Nobel Prize in economics for his work integrating insights from the psychology of human judgment and decision making into economics. Their work and the insights of others into why people often behave irrationally are having a significant influence on how economists analyze financial markets, labor markets, and other economic concerns.

Rational, but Human, Too

If you are **rational,** you will choose the available option that leads to the outcome you most prefer. But is the outcome you most prefer always the same as the one that gives you the best possible economic payoff? No. It can be entirely rational to choose an option that gives you a worse economic payoff because you care about something other than the size of the economic payoff. There are three principal reasons why people might prefer a worse economic payoff: concerns about fairness, bounded rationality, and risk aversion.

A **rational** decision maker chooses the available option that leads to the outcome he or she most prefers.

A decision maker operating with **bounded rationality** makes a choice that is close to but not exactly the one that leads to the best possible economic outcome.

Risk aversion is the willingness to sacrifice some economic payoff in order to avoid a potential loss.

An **irrational** decision maker chooses an option that leaves him or her worse off than choosing another available option.

CONCERNS ABOUT FAIRNESS In social situations, people often care about fairness as well as about the economic payoff to themselves. For example, no law requires you to tip a waiter or waitress. But concern for fairness leads most people to leave a tip (unless they've had outrageously bad service) because a tip is seen as fair compensation for good service according to society's norms. Tippers are reducing their own economic payoff in order to be fair to waiters and waitresses.

BOUNDED RATIONALITY Being an economic computing machine—choosing the option that gives you the best economic payoff—can require a fair amount of work: sizing up the options, computing the opportunity costs, calculating the marginal amounts, and so on. The mental effort required has its own opportunity cost. This realization led economists to the concept of **bounded rationality**—making a choice that is close to but not exactly the one that leads to the highest possible profit because the effort of finding the best payoff is too costly. In other words, bounded rationality is the "good enough" method of decision making.

Retailers are particularly good at exploiting their customers' tendency to engage in bounded rationality. For example, pricing items in units ending in 99¢ takes advantage of shoppers' tendency to interpret an item that costs, say, $2.99 as significantly cheaper than one that costs $3.00. Bounded rationality leads them to give more weight to the $2 part of the price (the first number they see) than the 99¢ part.

RISK AVERSION Because life is uncertain and the future unknown, sometimes a choice comes with significant risk. Although you may receive a high payoff if things turn out well, the possibility also exists that things may turn out badly and leave you worse off. So even if you think a choice will give you the best payoff of all your available options, you may forgo it because you find the possibility that things could turn out badly too, well, risky. This is called **risk aversion**—the willingness to sacrifice some potential economic payoff in order to avoid a potential loss. Because risk makes most people uncomfortable, it's rational for them to give up some potential economic gain in order to avoid it.

Irrationality: An Economist's View

Sometimes, though, instead of being rational, people are **irrational**—they make choices that leave them worse off in terms of economic payoff *and* other considerations like fairness than if they had chosen another available option. Is there anything systematic that economists and psychologists can say about economically irrational behavior? Yes, because most people are irrational in predictable ways. People's irrational behavior *typically* stems from six mistakes they make when thinking about economic decisions. The mistakes are listed in Table 19-1, and we will discuss each in turn.

TABLE 19-1

Six Common Mistakes in Economic Decision Making

1.	Misperceiving opportunity costs
2.	Being overconfident
3.	Having unrealistic expectations about future behavior
4.	Counting dollars unequally
5.	Being loss-averse
6.	Having a bias toward the status quo

MISPERCEPTIONS OF OPPORTUNITY COSTS As we've seen, people tend to ignore nonmonetary opportunity costs also known as *implicit costs.* These are opportunity costs that don't involve an outlay of cash. Likewise,

Mental accounting is the habit of mentally assigning dollars to different accounts so that some dollars are worth more than others.

a misperception of what exactly constitutes an opportunity cost (and what does not) is at the root of the tendency to count sunk costs in one's decision making. In this case, someone takes an opportunity cost into account when none actually exists.

OVERCONFIDENCE It's a function of ego: we tend to think we know more than we actually do. And even if alerted to how widespread overconfidence is, people tend to think that it's someone else's problem, not theirs. (Certainly not yours or mine!) For example, a 1994 study asked students to estimate how long it would take them to complete their thesis "if everything went as well as it possibly could" and "if everything went as poorly as it possibly could." The results: the typical student thought it would take him or her 33.9 days to finish, with an average estimate of 27.4 days if everything went well and 48.6 days if everything went poorly. In fact, the average time it took to complete a thesis was much longer, 55.5 days. Students were, on average, from 14% to 102% more confident than they should have been about the time it would take to complete their theses.

Jack Watts/Alamy

Overconfidence can be bad for your financial health.

Overconfidence can cause trouble by having a strong adverse effect on people's financial health. Overconfidence often persuades people that they are in better financial shape than they actually are. It can also lead to bad investment and spending decisions. For example, nonprofessional investors who engage in a lot of speculative investing—such as quickly buying and selling stocks—on average have significantly worse results than professional brokers because of their misguided faith in their ability to spot a winner. Similarly, overconfidence can lead people to make a large spending decision, such as buying a car, without doing research on the pros and cons, relying instead on anecdotal evidence. Even worse, people tend to remain overconfident because they remember their successes and explain away or forget their failures.

UNREALISTIC EXPECTATIONS ABOUT FUTURE BEHAVIOR Another form of overconfidence is being overly optimistic about your future behavior: tomorrow you'll study, tomorrow you'll give up ice cream, tomorrow you'll spend less and save more, and so on. Of course, as we all know, when tomorrow arrives, it's still just as hard to study or give up something that you like as it is right now.

Strategies that keep a person on the straight-and-narrow over time are often, at their root, ways to deal with the problem of unrealistic expectations about one's future behavior. Examples are automatic payroll deduction savings plans, diet plans with prepackaged foods, and mandatory attendance at study groups. By providing a way for someone to commit today to an action tomorrow, such plans counteract the habit of pushing difficult actions off into the future.

COUNTING DOLLARS UNEQUALLY If you tend to spend more when you pay with a credit card than when you pay with cash, particularly if you tend to splurge, then you are very likely engaging in **mental accounting.** This is the habit of mentally assigning dollars to different accounts, making some dollars worth more than others. By spending more with a credit card, you are in effect treating dollars in your wallet as more valuable than dollars on your credit card balance, although in reality they count equally in your budget.

A dollar is a dollar, whether it's in your wallet or on your credit card balance.

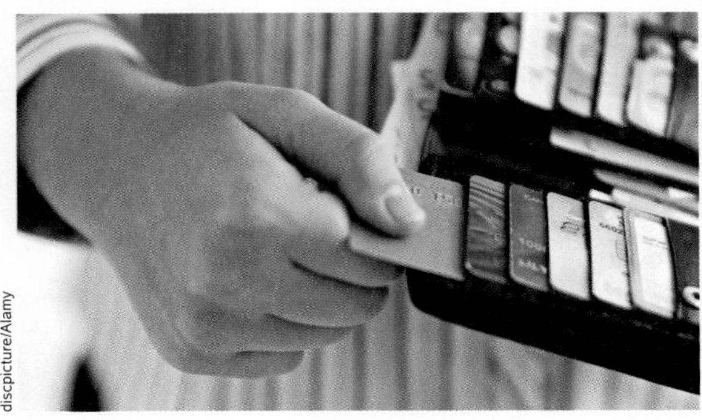

discpicture/Alamy

Credit card overuse is the most recognizable form of mental accounting. However, there are other forms as well, such as splurging after receiving a windfall, like an unexpected inheritance, or overspending at sales, buying something that seemed like a great bargain at the time whose purchase you later regretted. It's the failure to understand that, regardless of the form it comes in, a dollar is a dollar.

LOSS AVERSION An oversensitivity to loss, leading to an unwillingness to recognize a loss and move on, is called **loss aversion.** In fact, in the lingo of the financial markets, "selling discipline"—being able and willing to quickly acknowledge when a stock you've bought is a loser and sell it—is a highly desirable trait to have. Many investors, though, are reluctant to acknowledge that they've lost money on a stock and won't make it back.

Loss aversion is an oversensitivity to loss, leading to unwillingness to recognize a loss and move on.

The **status quo bias** is the tendency to avoid making a decision and stick with existing conditions.

Although it's rational to sell the stock at that point and redeploy the remaining funds, most people find it so painful to admit a loss that they avoid selling for much longer than they should. According to Daniel Kahneman and Amos Tversky, most people feel the misery of losing $100 about twice as keenly as they feel the pleasure of gaining $100.

Loss aversion can help explain why sunk costs are so hard to ignore: ignoring a sunk cost means recognizing that the money you spent is unrecoverable and therefore lost.

STATUS QUO BIAS Another irrational behavior is **status quo bias,** the tendency to avoid making a decision altogether. A well-known example is the way that employees make decisions about investing in their employer-directed retirement accounts, known as 401(k)s. With a 401(k), employees can, through payroll deductions, set aside part of their salary tax-free, a practice that saves a significant amount of money every year in taxes. Some companies operate on an opt-in basis: employees have to actively choose to participate in a 401(k). Other companies operate on an opt-out basis: employees are automatically enrolled in a 401(k) unless they choose to opt out.

If everyone behaved rationally, then the proportion of employees enrolled in 401(k) accounts at opt-in companies would be roughly equal to the proportion enrolled at opt-out companies. In other words, your decision about whether to participate in a 401(k) should be independent of the default choice at your company. But, in reality, when companies switch to automatic enrollment and an opt-out system, employee enrollment rises dramatically. Clearly, people tend to just go with the status quo.

Why do people exhibit status quo bias? Some claim it's a form of "decision paralysis": when given many options, people find it harder to make a decision. Others claim it's due to loss aversion and the fear of regret, to thinking that "if I do nothing, then I won't have to regret my choice." Irrational, yes. But not altogether surprising. However, rational people know that, in the end, the act of not making a choice is still a choice.

Rational Models for Irrational People?

So why do economists still use models based on rational behavior when people are at times manifestly irrational? For one thing, models based on rational behavior still provide mostly accurate predictions about how people behave in most markets. For example, the great majority of farmers will use less fertilizer when it becomes more expensive—a result consistent with rational behavior.

Another explanation is that sometimes market forces can compel people to behave more rationally over time. For example, if you are a small-business owner who exaggerates your abilities or refuses to acknowledge that your favorite line of items is a loser, then sooner or later you will be out of business unless you learn to correct your mistakes. As a result, it is reasonable to assume that when people are disciplined for their mistakes, as happens in most markets, rationality will win out over time.

Finally, economists depend on the assumption of rationality for the simple but fundamental reason that it makes modeling so much simpler. Remember that models are built on generalizations, and it's much harder to extrapolate from messy, irrational behavior. Even behavioral economists, in their research, search for *predictably* irrational behavior in an attempt to build better models of how people behave. Clearly, there is an ongoing dialogue between behavioral economists and the rest of the economics profession, and economics itself has been irrevocably changed by it.

ECONOMICS ▶ IN ACTION

"THE JINGLE MAIL BLUES"

It's called jingle mail—when a homeowner seals the keys to his or her house in an envelope and leaves them with the bank that holds the mortgage on the house. (A mortgage is a loan taken out to buy a house.) By leaving the keys with the bank, the homeowner is walking away not only from the house but also from the obligation to continue paying the mortgage. And to their great consternation, banks have lately been flooded with jingle mail.

To default on a mortgage—that is, to walk away from one's obligation to repay the loan and lose the house to the bank in the process—used to be a fairly rare phenomenon. For decades, continually rising home values made homeownership a good investment for the typical household.

"Officer, that couple is just walking away from their mortgage!"

© Tom Cheney/The New Yorker Collection/www.cartoonbank.com

In recent years, though, an entirely different phenomenon—called "strategic default"—has appeared. In a strategic default, a homeowner who is financially capable of paying the mortgage instead chooses not to, voluntarily walking away. Strategic defaults account for a significant proportion of jingle mail; in March 2010, they accounted for 31% of all foreclosures, up from 22% in 2009. And there is little indication that number will change dramatically: in the spring of 2011, strategic defaults still accounted for 30% of all defaults.

What happened? The Great American Housing Bust happened. After decades of huge increases, house prices began a precipitous fall in 2008. Prices dropped so much that a significant proportion of homeowners found their homes "underwater"—they owed more on their homes than the homes were worth. And with house prices projected to stay depressed for several years, possibly a decade, there appeared to be little chance that an underwater house would recover its value enough in the foreseeable future to move "abovewater."

Many homeowners suffered a major loss. They lost their down payment, money spent on repairs and renovation, moving expenses, and so on. And because they were paying a mortgage that was greater than the house was now worth, they found they could rent a comparable dwelling for less than their monthly mortgage payments. In the words of Benjamin Koellmann, who paid $215,000 for an apartment in Miami where similar units were now selling for $90,000, "There is no financial sense in staying."

Realizing their losses were sunk costs, underwater homeowners walked away. Perhaps they hadn't made the best economic decision when purchasing their houses, but in leaving them they showed impeccable economic logic.

MODULE 19 Review

Solutions appear at the back of the book.

Check Your Understanding

1. Which of the types of irrational behavior are suggested by the following events?
   a. Although the housing market has fallen and Jenny wants to move, she refuses to sell her house for any amount less than what she paid for it.
   b. Dan worked more overtime hours last week than he had expected. Although he is strapped for cash, he spends his unexpected overtime earnings on a weekend getaway rather than trying to pay down his student loan.
   c. Carol has just started her first job and deliberately decided to opt out of the company's savings plan. Her reasoning is that she is very young and there is plenty of time in the future to start saving. Why not enjoy life now?
   d. Jeremy's company requires employees to download and fill out a form if they want to participate in the company-sponsored savings plan. One year after starting the job, Jeremy had still not submitted the form needed to participate in the plan.

Multiple-Choice Questions

1. Kookie's friends give her gift cards that she forgets to use before they expire. However, she is very careful about how she spends her cash. Kookie has made which of the following mistakes in economic decision making?
   a. Status quo bias
   b. Unrealistic expectations about future behavior
   c. Counting dollars unequally
   d. Loss aversion

2. Why would decision makers choose an option that doesn't give them the best possible economic payoff?
   a. Concerns about fairness
   b. Concerns about taking risks
   c. Because the effort to find the best possible payoff is too costly
   d. All of [illegible]he above

3. Which [illegible]e following is unlikely to lead to an irratio[illegible]ecision?
   a. Counting sunk costs
   b. Overconfidence
   c. Committing today to an action tomorrow
   d. Splurging after winning the lottery

4. Despite the fact that some people are irrational, why do economists continue to assume that people behave rationally?
   a. Because economists want everyone to behave rationally
   b. Because markets don't require rationality
   c. Because people will behave rationally in most markets
   d. Because models of rationality are much more complex and reflect the real world

5. Which of the following would be an example of irrational behavior?
   a. Ignoring opportunity cost in your calculation of economic cost
   b. Not being overconfident, even when others around you encourage you to be overconfident
   c. Treating your credit card in the same way you do cash
   d. Considering sunk costs as irrelevant for decision making

Critical-Thinking Question

How would you determine whether a decision you made was rational or irrational?

20 Maximizing Utility

craftvision/Getty Images

WHAT YOU WILL LEARN

1. Why consumers' general goal is to maximize utility
2. Why the principle of diminishing marginal utility applies to the consumption of most goods and services
3. How to use marginal analysis to find the optimal consumption bundle

Earlier in this section we learned about principles for rational economic decision making that lead to the best possible outcomes. In this module, we will show how economists analyze the decisions of rational consumers, those who know what they want and make the most of available opportunities. We begin with the concept of utility—a measure of consumer satisfaction.

Utility: It's All About Getting Satisfaction

When analyzing consumer behavior, we're looking into how people pursue their needs and wants and the subjective feelings that motivate purchases. Yet there is no simple way to measure subjective feelings. How much satisfaction do I get from my third cookie? Is it less or more than the satisfaction you receive from your first cookie? Does it even make sense to ask that question?

Luckily, we don't need to make comparisons between your feelings and mine. An analysis of consumer behavior requires only the assumption that individuals try to maximize some personal measure of the satisfaction gained from consumption. That measure of satisfaction is known as **utility,** a concept we use to understand behavior but don't expect to measure in practice.

Utility and Consumption

We can think of consumers as using consumption to "produce" utility, much in the same way that producers use inputs to produce output. As consumers, we do not make explicit calculations of the utility generated by consumption choices, but we must make choices, and we usually base them on at least a rough attempt to achieve greater satisfaction. I can have either soup or salad with my dinner. Which will I enjoy more? I can go to Disney World this year or put the money toward buying a new

Utility is a measure of personal satisfaction.

car. Which will make me happier? These are the types of questions that go into utility maximization.

A **util** is a hypothetical unit of utility.

The concept of utility offers a way to study choices that are made in a more or less rational way.

How do we measure utility? For the sake of simplicity, it is useful to suppose that we can measure utility in hypothetical units called—what else?—**utils.** A *utility function* shows the relationship between a consumer's utility and the combination of goods and services—the *consumption bundle*—he or she consumes.

Figure 20-1 illustrates a utility function. It shows the total utility that Cassie, who likes fried clams, gets from an all-you-can-eat clam dinner. We suppose that her consumption bundle consists of a side of coleslaw, which comes with the meal, plus a number of clams to be determined. The table that accompanies the figure shows how Cassie's total utility depends on the number of clams; the curve in panel (a) of the figure shows that same information graphically.

FIGURE 20-1 Cassie's Total Utility and Marginal Utility

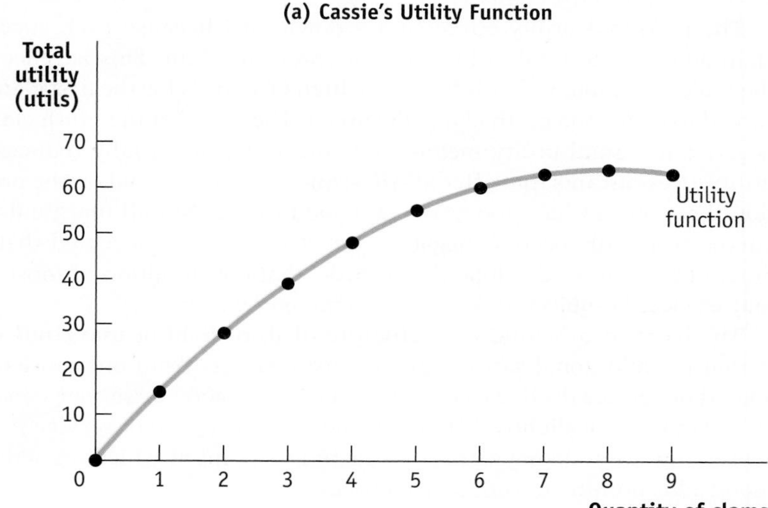

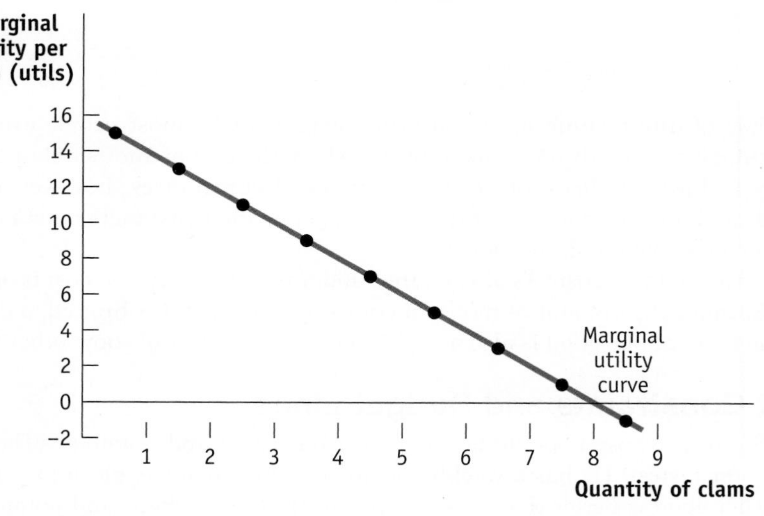

Quantity of clams	Total utility (utils)	Marginal utility per clam (utils)
0	0	
		15
1	15	
		13
2	28	
		11
3	39	
		9
4	48	
		7
5	55	
		5
6	60	
		3
7	63	
		1
8	64	
		−1
9	63	

Panel (a) shows how Cassie's total utility depends on her consumption of fried clams. It increases until it reaches its maximum utility level of 64 utils at 8 clams consumed and decreases after that. Marginal utility is calculated in the table. Panel (b) shows the marginal utility curve, which slopes downward due to diminishing marginal utility. That is, each additional clam gives Cassie less utility than the previous clam.

Cassie's utility function slopes upward over most of the range shown, but it gets flatter as the number of clams consumed increases. And in this example it eventually turns downward. According to the information in the table in Figure 20-1, nine clams is a clam too many. Adding that additional clam actually makes Cassie worse off: it would lower her total utility. If she's rational, of course, Cassie will realize that and not consume the ninth clam.

So when Cassie chooses how many clams to consume, she will make this decision by considering the *change* in her total utility from consuming one more clam. This illustrates the general point: to maximize *total* utility, consumers must focus on *marginal* utility.

The Principle of Diminishing Marginal Utility

In addition to showing how Cassie's total utility depends on the number of clams she consumes, the table in Figure 20-1 also shows the **marginal utility** generated by consuming each additional clam—that is, the *change* in total utility from consuming one additional clam. The **marginal utility curve** is constructed by plotting points at the midpoint between the numbered quantities since marginal utility is found as consumption levels change. For example, when consumption rises from 1 to 2 clams, marginal utility is 13. Therefore, we place the point corresponding to marginal utility of 13 halfway between 1 and 2 clams.

iStockphoto

When is more of a good thing too much?

The marginal utility curve slopes downward because each successive clam adds less to total utility than the previous clam. This is reflected in the table: marginal utility falls from a high of 15 utils for the first clam consumed to –1 for the ninth clam consumed. The fact that the ninth clam has negative marginal utility means that consuming it actually reduces total utility. (Restaurants that offer all-you-can-eat meals depend on the proposition that you can have too much of a good thing.) Not all marginal utility curves eventually become negative. But it is generally accepted that marginal utility curves do slope downward—that consumption of most goods and services is subject to *diminishing marginal utility*.

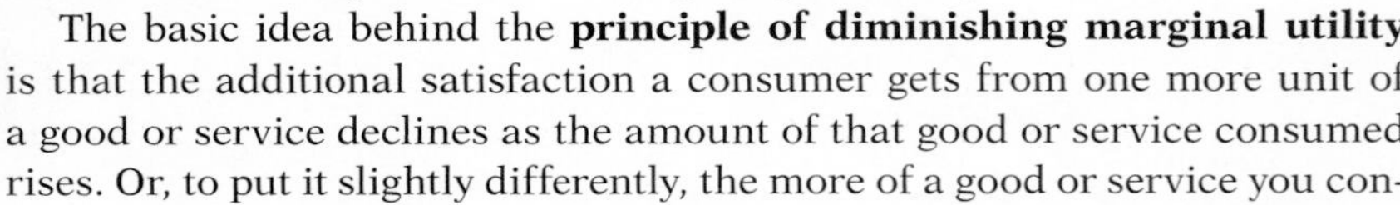

The basic idea behind the **principle of diminishing marginal utility** is that the additional satisfaction a consumer gets from one more unit of a good or service declines as the amount of that good or service consumed rises. Or, to put it slightly differently, the more of a good or service you consume, the closer you are to being satiated—reaching a point at which an additional unit of the good adds nothing to your satisfaction.

The principle of diminishing marginal utility doesn't always apply, but it does apply in the great majority of cases, enough to serve as a foundation for our analysis of consumer behavior.

Budgets and Optimal Consumption

The **marginal utility** of a good or service is the change in total utility generated by consuming one additional unit of that good or service.

The **marginal utility curve** shows how marginal utility depends on the quantity of a good or service consumed.

According to the **principle of diminishing marginal utility**, each successive unit of a good or service consumed adds less to total utility than does the previous unit.

The principle of diminishing marginal utility explains why most people eventually reach a limit, even at an all-you-can-eat buffet where the cost of another clam is measured only in future indigestion. Under ordinary circumstances, however, it costs some additional resources to consume more of a good, and consumers must take that cost into account when making choices.

What do we mean by cost? As always, the fundamental measure of cost is *opportunity cost*. Because the amount of money a consumer can spend is limited, a decision to consume more of one good is also a decision to consume less of some other good.

Budget Constraints and Budget Lines

Consider Sammy, whose appetite is exclusively for clams and potatoes. (There's no accounting for tastes.) He has a weekly income of $20 and since, given his appetite, more of either good is better than less, he spends all of it on clams and potatoes. We will assume that clams cost $4 per pound and potatoes cost $2 per pound. What are his possible choices?

Whatever Sammy chooses, we know that the cost of his consumption bundle cannot exceed the amount of money he has to spend. That is,

(20-1) *Expenditure on clams + Expenditure on potatoes ≤ Total income*

Consumers always have limited income, which constrains how much they can consume. So the requirement illustrated by Equation 20-1—that a consumer must choose a consumption bundle that costs no more than his or her income—is known as the consumer's **budget constraint.** It's a simple way of saying that a consumer can't spend more than the total amount of income available to him or her. We call the set of all of Sammy's affordable consumption bundles his **consumption possibilities.** In general, whether or not a particular consumption bundle is included in a consumer's consumption possibilities depends on the consumer's income and the prices of goods and services.

A **budget constraint** limits the cost of a consumer's consumption bundle to no more than the consumer's income.

A consumer's **consumption possibilities** is the set of all consumption bundles that are affordable, given the consumer's income and prevailing prices.

Figure 20-2 shows Sammy's consumption possibilities. The quantity of clams in his consumption bundle is measured on the horizontal axis and the quantity of potatoes on the vertical axis. The downward-sloping line connecting points *A* through *F* shows which consumption bundles are affordable and which are not. Every bundle on or inside this line (the shaded area) is affordable; every bundle outside this line is unaffordable.

As an example of one of the points, let's look at point *C*, representing 2 pounds of clams and 6 pounds of potatoes, and check whether it satisfies Sammy's budget constraint. The cost of bundle *C* is 6 pounds of potatoes × $2 per pound + 2 pounds of clams × $4 per pound = $12 + $8 = $20. So bundle *C* does indeed satisfy Sammy's budget constraint: it costs no more than his weekly income of $20. In fact, bundle *C* costs exactly as much as Sammy's income. By doing the arithmetic, you can check

FIGURE 20-2 **The Budget Line**

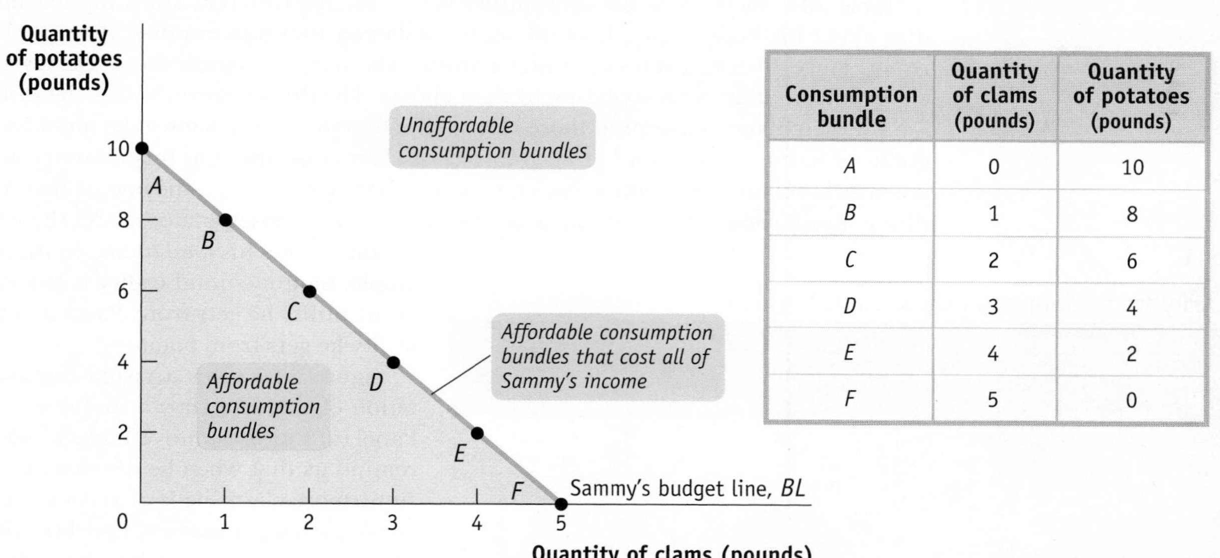

Consumption bundle	Quantity of clams (pounds)	Quantity of potatoes (pounds)
A	0	10
B	1	8
C	2	6
D	3	4
E	4	2
F	5	0

The *budget line* represents all the possible combinations of quantities of potatoes and clams that Sammy can purchase if he spends all of his income. Also, it is the boundary between the set of affordable consumption bundles (the *consumption possibilities*) and the unaffordable ones. Given that clams cost $4 per pound and potatoes cost $2 per pound, if Sammy spends all of his income on clams (bundle *F*), he can purchase 5 pounds of clams. If he spends all of his income on potatoes (bundle *A*), he can purchase 10 pounds of potatoes.

A consumer's **budget line** shows the consumption bundles available to a consumer who spends all of his or her income.

A consumer's **optimal consumption bundle** is the consumption bundle that maximizes the consumer's total utility given his or her budget constraint.

that all the other points lying on the downward-sloping line are also bundles on which Sammy spends all of his income.

The downward-sloping line has a special name, the **budget line.** It shows all the consumption bundles available to Sammy when he spends all of his income. It's downward-sloping because when Sammy is spending all of his income, say by consuming at point *A* on the budget line, then in order to consume more clams he must consume fewer potatoes—that is, he must move to a point like *B*. In other words, when Sammy is on his budget line, the opportunity cost of consuming more clams is consuming fewer potatoes, and vice versa. As Figure 20-2 indicates, any consumption bundle that lies above the budget line is unaffordable.

Do we need to consider the other bundles in Sammy's consumption possibilities, the ones that lie *within* the shaded region in Figure 20-2 bounded by the budget line? The answer is, for all practical situations, no: as long as Sammy doesn't get satiated—that is, as long as his marginal utility from consuming either good is always positive—then he will always choose to consume a bundle that lies on his budget line.

Given his $20 per week budget, which point on his budget line will Sammy choose?

The Optimal Consumption Bundle

Because Sammy's budget constrains him to a consumption bundle somewhere along the budget line, a choice to consume a given quantity of clams also determines his potato consumption, and vice versa. We want to find the consumption bundle—represented by a point on the budget line—that maximizes Sammy's total utility. This bundle is Sammy's **optimal consumption bundle.**

Table 20-1 shows how much utility Sammy gets from different levels of consumption of clams and potatoes, respectively. According to the table, Sammy has a healthy appetite; the more of either good he consumes, the higher his utility.

But because he has a limited budget, he must make a trade-off: the more pounds of clams he consumes, the fewer pounds of potatoes, and vice versa. That is, he must choose a point on his budget line.

Table 20-2 shows how his total utility varies for the different consumption bundles along his budget line. Each of six possible consumption bundles, *A* through *F* from Figure 20-2, is given in the first column. The second column shows the level of clam consumption corresponding to each choice. The third column shows the utility Sammy gets from consuming those clams. The fourth column shows the quantity of potatoes Sammy can afford *given* the level of clam consumption; this quantity goes down as his clam consumption goes up because he is sliding down the budget line. The fifth column shows the utility he gets from consuming those potatoes. And the final column shows his *total utility*. In this example, Sammy's total utility is the sum of the utility he gets from clams and the utility he gets from potatoes.

Figure 20-3 gives a visual representation of the data shown in Table 20-2. Panel (a) shows Sammy's budget line, to remind us that when he decides to consume more clams he is also deciding to consume fewer potatoes. Panel (b) then shows how his total utility depends on that choice. The horizontal axis in panel (b) has two sets of labels: it shows both the quantity of clams, increasing from left to right, and the quantity of potatoes, increasing from right to left. The reason we can use the same axis to represent consumption of both goods is, of course, that he is constrained by

TABLE 20-1

Sammy's Utility from Clam and Potato Consumption

Utility from clam consumption		Utility from potato consumption	
Quantity of clams (pounds)	Utility from clams (utils)	Quantity of potatoes (pounds)	Utility from potatoes (utils)
0	0	0	0
1	15	1	11.5
2	25	2	21.4
3	31	3	29.8
4	34	4	36.8
5	36	5	42.5
		6	47.0
		7	50.5
		8	53.2
		9	55.2
		10	56.7

TABLE 20-2

Sammy's Budget and Total Utility

Consumption bundle	Quantity of clams (pounds)	Utility from clams (utils)	Quantity of potatoes (pounds)	Utility from potatoes (utils)	Total utility (utils)
A	0	0	10	56.7	56.7
B	1	15	8	53.2	68.2
C	2	25	6	47.0	72.0
D	3	31	4	36.8	67.8
E	4	34	2	21.4	55.4
F	5	36	0	0	36.0

FIGURE 20-3 Optimal Consumption Bundle

Panel (a) shows Sammy's budget line and his six possible consumption bundles. Panel (b) shows how his total utility is affected by his consumption bundle, which must lie on his budget line. The quantity of clams is measured from left to right on the horizontal axis, and the quantity of potatoes is measured from right to left. His total utility is maximized at bundle *C*, where he consumes 2 pounds of clams and 6 pounds of potatoes. This is Sammy's *optimal consumption bundle.*

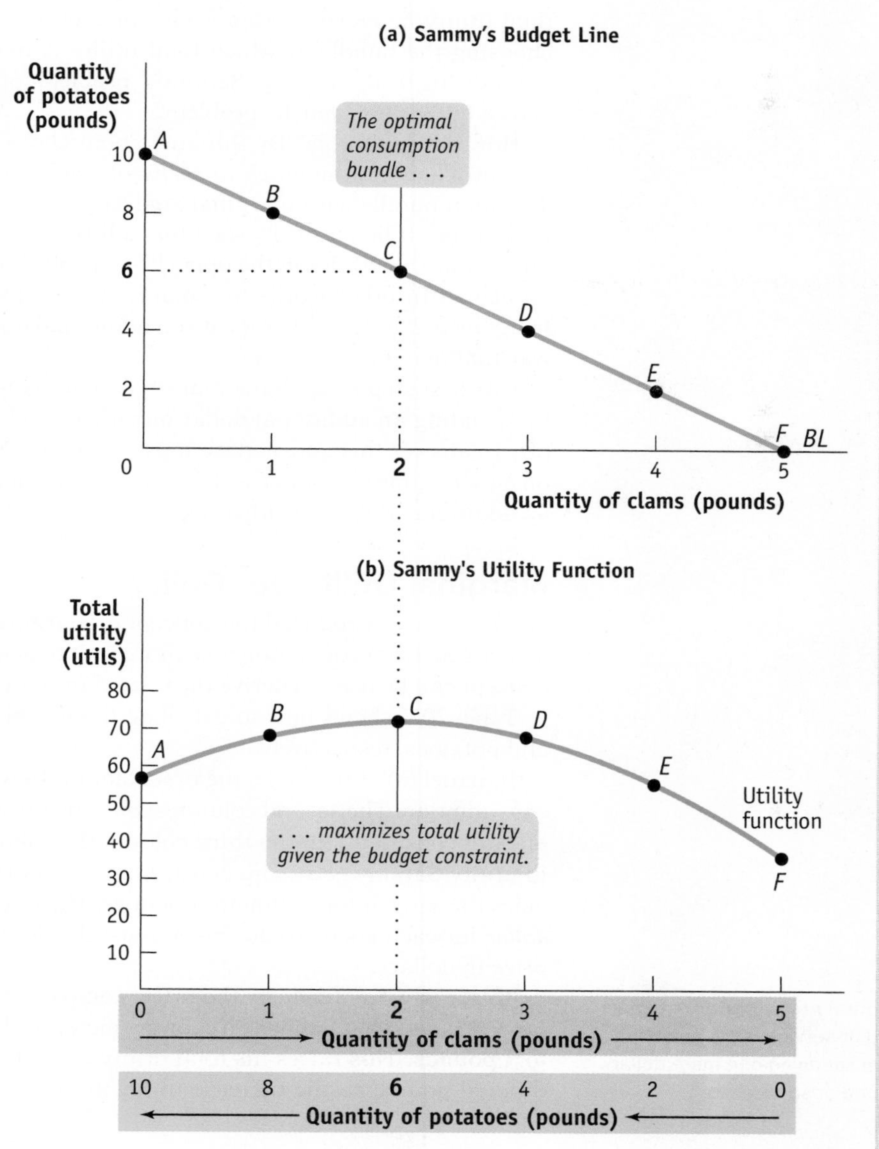

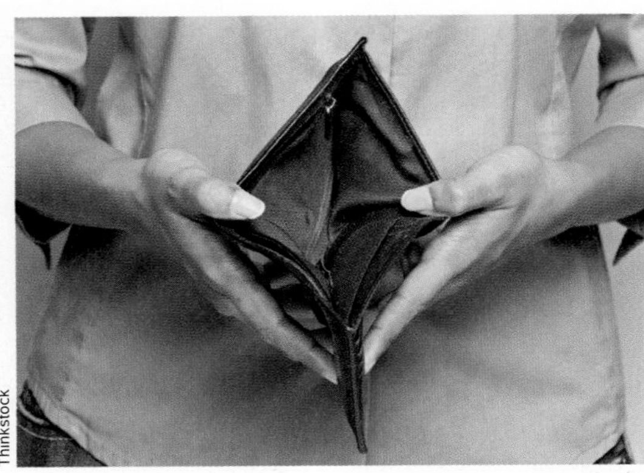

Budget constraints limit our spending to no more than our total available income.

the budget line: the more pounds of clams Sammy consumes, the fewer pounds of potatoes he can afford, and vice versa.

Clearly, the consumption bundle that makes the best of the trade-off between clam consumption and potato consumption, the optimal consumption bundle, is the one that maximizes Sammy's total utility. That is, Sammy's optimal consumption bundle puts him at the top of the total utility curve.

As always, we can find the top of the curve by direct observation. We can see from Figure 20-3 that Sammy's total utility is maximized at point *C*—that his optimal consumption bundle contains 2 pounds of clams and 6 pounds of potatoes. But we know that we usually gain more insight into "how much" problems when we use *marginal analysis*. So in the next section we turn to representing and solving the optimal consumption choice problem with marginal analysis.

Spending the Marginal Dollar

As we've just seen, we can find Sammy's optimal consumption choice by finding the total utility he receives from each consumption bundle on his budget line and then choosing the bundle at which total utility is maximized. But we can use marginal analysis instead, turning Sammy's problem of finding his optimal consumption choice into a "how much" problem.

How do we do this? By thinking about choosing an optimal consumption bundle as a problem of *how much to spend on each good*. That is, to find the optimal consumption bundle with marginal analysis we ask the question of whether Sammy can make himself better off by spending a little bit more of his income on clams and less on potatoes, or by doing the opposite—spending a little bit more on potatoes and less on clams. In other words, the marginal decision is a question of how to *spend the marginal dollar*—how to allocate an additional dollar between clams and potatoes in a way that maximizes utility.

Our first step in applying marginal analysis is to ask if Sammy is made better off by spending an additional dollar on either good; and if so, by how much is he better off. To answer this question we must calculate the **marginal utility per dollar** spent on either clams or potatoes—how much additional utility Sammy gets from spending an additional dollar on either good.

Marginal Utility per Dollar

We've already introduced the concept of marginal utility, the additional utility a consumer gets from consuming one more unit of a good or service; now let's see how this concept can be used to derive the related measure of marginal utility per dollar.

Table 20-3 shows how to calculate the marginal utility per dollar spent on clams and potatoes, respectively.

In panel (a) of the table, the first column shows different possible amounts of clam consumption. The second column shows the utility Sammy derives from each amount of clam consumption; the third column then shows the marginal utility, the increase in utility Sammy gets from consuming an additional pound of clams. Panel (b) provides the same information for potatoes. The next step is to derive marginal utility *per dollar* for each good. To do this, we just divide the marginal utility of the good by its price in dollars.

The **marginal utility per dollar** spent on a good or service is the additional utility from spending one more dollar on that good or service.

To see why we divide by the price, compare the third and fourth columns of panel (a). Consider what happens if Sammy increases his clam consumption from 2 pounds to 3 pounds. This raises his total utility by 6 utils. But he must spend $4 for that additional pound, so the increase in his utility per additional dollar spent on clams is

TABLE 20-3

Sammy's Marginal Utility per Dollar

(a) Clams (price of clams = $4 per pound)

Quantity of clams (pounds)	Utility from clams (utils)	Marginal utility per pound of clams (utils)	Marginal utility per dollar (utils)
0	0		
		15	3.75
1	15		
		10	2.50
2	25		
		6	1.50
3	31		
		3	0.75
4	34		
		2	0.50
5	36		

(b) Potatoes (price of potatoes = $2 per pound)

Quantity of potatoes (pounds)	Utility from potatoes (utils)	Marginal utility per pound of potatoes (utils)	Marginal utility per dollar (utils)
0	0		
		11.5	5.75
1	11.5		
		9.9	4.95
2	21.4		
		8.4	4.20
3	29.8		
		7.0	3.50
4	36.8		
		5.7	2.85
5	42.5		
		4.5	2.25
6	47.0		
		3.5	1.75
7	50.5		
		2.7	1.35
8	53.2		
		2.0	1.00
9	55.2		
		1.5	0.75
10	56.7		

6 utils/$4 = 1.5 utils per dollar. Similarly, if he increases his clam consumption from 3 pounds to 4 pounds, his marginal utility is 3 utils but his marginal utility per dollar is 3 utils/$4 = 0.75 utils per dollar.

Notice that because of diminishing marginal utility, Sammy's marginal utility per pound of clams falls as the quantity of clams he consumes rises. As a result, his marginal utility per dollar spent on clams also falls as the quantity of clams he consumes rises.

So the last column of panel (a) shows how Sammy's marginal utility per dollar spent on clams depends on the quantity of clams he consumes. Similarly, the last column of panel (b) shows how his marginal utility per dollar spent on potatoes depends on the quantity of potatoes he consumes. Again, marginal utility per dollar spent on each good declines as the quantity of that good consumed rises because of diminishing marginal utility.

We will use the symbols MU_C and MU_P to represent the marginal utility per pound of clams and potatoes, respectively. And we will use the symbols P_C and P_P to represent the price of clams (per pound) and the price of potatoes (per pound). Then the marginal utility per dollar spent on clams is MU_C/P_C and the marginal utility per dollar spent on potatoes is MU_P/P_P. In general, the additional utility generated from an additional dollar spent on a good is equal to:

(20-2) *Marginal utility per dollar spent on a good*
= Marginal utility of one unit of the good/Price of one unit of the good
$= MU_{good}/P_{good}$

Next we'll see how this concept helps us determine a consumer's optimal consumption bundle using marginal analysis.

Optimal Consumption

Let's consider Figure 20-4. As in Figure 20-3, we can measure both the quantity of clams and the quantity of potatoes on the horizontal axis due to the budget constraint. Along the horizontal axis of Figure 20-4—also as in Figure 20-3—the quantity of clams increases as you move from left to right, and the quantity of potatoes increases as you move from right to left. The curve labeled MU_C/P_C in Figure 20-4 shows Sammy's marginal utility per dollar spent on clams as derived in Table 20-3. Likewise, the curve labeled MU_P/P_P shows his marginal utility per dollar spent on potatoes. Notice that the two curves, MU_C/P_C and MU_P/P_P, cross at the optimal consumption bundle, point *C*, consisting of 2 pounds of clams and 6 pounds of potatoes. Moreover, Figure 20-4 illustrates an important feature of Sammy's optimal consumption bundle: when Sammy consumes 2 pounds of clams and 6 pounds of potatoes, his marginal utility per dollar spent is the same, 2, for both goods. That is, at the optimal consumption bundle, $MU_C/P_C = MU_P/P_P = 2$.

This isn't an accident. Consider another one of Sammy's possible consumption bundles—say, *B* in Figure 20-3, at which he consumes 1 pound of clams and 8 pounds of potatoes. The marginal utility per dollar spent on each good is shown by points B_C and B_P in Figure 20-4. At that consumption bundle, Sammy's marginal utility per dollar spent on clams would be approximately 3, but his marginal utility per dollar spent on potatoes would be only approximately 1. This shows that he has made a mistake: he is consuming too many potatoes and not enough clams.

FIGURE 20-4 **Marginal Utility per Dollar**

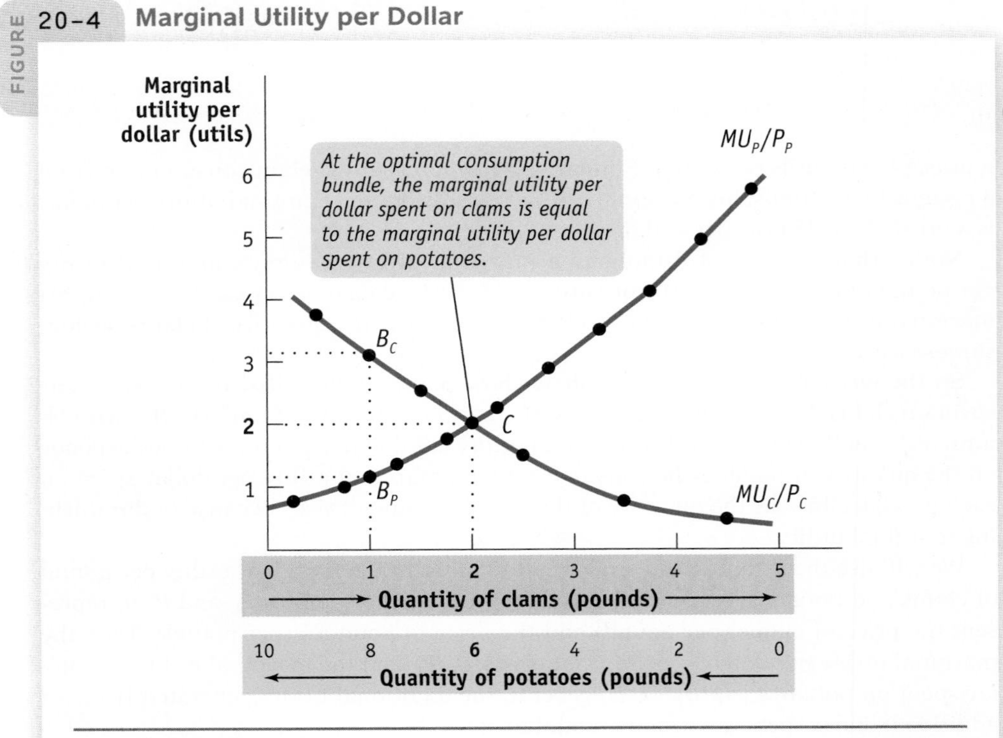

Sammy's optimal consumption bundle is at point *C*, where his marginal utility per dollar spent on clams, MU_C/P_C, is equal to his marginal utility per dollar spent on potatoes, MU_P/P_P. This illustrates the optimal consumption rule: *at the optimal consumption bundle, the marginal utility per dollar spent on each good and service is the same.* At any other consumption bundle on Sammy's budget line, such as bundle *B* in Figure 20-3, represented here by points B_C and B_P, consumption is not optimal: Sammy can increase his utility at no additional cost by reallocating his spending.

How do we know this? If Sammy's marginal utility per dollar spent on clams is higher than his marginal utility per dollar spent on potatoes, he has a simple way to make himself better off while staying within his budget: spend $1 less on potatoes and $1 more on clams. By spending an additional dollar on clams, he adds about 3 utils to his total utility; meanwhile, by spending $1 less on potatoes, he subtracts only about 1 util from his total utility.

The **optimal consumption rule** says that in order to maximize utility, a consumer must equate the marginal utility per dollar spent on each good and service in the consumption bundle.

Because his marginal utility per dollar spent is higher for clams than for potatoes, reallocating his spending toward clams and away from potatoes would increase his total utility. On the other hand, if his marginal utility per dollar spent on potatoes is higher, he can increase his utility by spending less on clams and more on potatoes. So if Sammy has in fact chosen his optimal consumption bundle, his marginal utility per dollar spent on clams and potatoes must be equal.

This is a general principle, known as the **optimal consumption rule:** *when a consumer maximizes utility in the face of a budget constraint, the marginal utility per dollar spent on each good or service in the consumption bundle is the same.* That is, for any two goods *C* and *P*, the optimal consumption rule says that at the optimal consumption bundle

$$\textbf{(20-3)} \quad \frac{MU_C}{P_C} = \frac{MU_P}{P_P}$$

It's easiest to understand this rule using examples in which the consumption bundle contains only two goods, but it applies no matter how many goods or services a consumer buys: the marginal utilities per dollar spent for each and every good or service in the optimal consumption bundle are equal.

The main reason for studying consumer behavior is to look behind the market demand curve. We learned in Section 3 how the *substitution effect* leads consumers to buy less of a good when its price increases. We used the substitution effect to explain, in general, why the individual demand curve obeys the law of demand. Marginal analysis adds clarity to the utility-maximizing behavior of individuals and explains more precisely how an increase in price leads to less marginal utility per dollar and therefore a decrease in the quantity demanded.

ECONOMICS IN ACTION

BUYING YOUR WAY OUT OF TEMPTATION

It might seem odd to pay more to get less. But snack food companies have discovered that consumers are indeed willing to pay more for smaller portions, and exploiting this trend is a recipe for success.

Over the last few years, sales of 100-calorie packs of crackers, chips, cookies, and candy have passed the $20 million-a-year mark, growing much more quickly than the rest of the snack industry. A company executive explained why small packages are popular—they help consumers eat less without having to count calories themselves. "The irony," said David Adelman, a food industry analyst, "is if you take Wheat Thins or Goldfish, buy a large-size box, count out the items and put them in a Ziploc bag, you'd have essentially the same product." He estimates that snack packs are about 20% more profitable for snack makers than larger packages.

Worth Publishers

For many consumers, paying extra for portion control is worth it.

It's clear that in this case consumers are making a calculation: the extra utility gained from not having to worry about whether they've eaten too much is worth the extra cost. As one shopper said, "They're pretty expensive, but they're worth it. It's individually packaged for the amount I need, so I don't go overboard." So it's clear that consumers aren't being irrational here. Rather, they're being entirely rational: in addition to their snack, they're buying a little hand-to-mouth restraint.

MODULE 20 Review

Solutions appear at the back of the book.

Check Your Understanding

1. Explain why a rational consumer who has diminishing marginal utility for a good would not consume an additional unit when it generates negative marginal utility, even when that unit is free.

2. In the following two examples, find all the consumption bundles that lie on the consumer's budget line. Illustrate these consumption possibilities in a diagram, and draw the budget line through them.

   a. The consumption bundle consists of movie tickets and buckets of popcorn. The price of each ticket is $10.00, the price of each bucket of popcorn is $5.00, and the consumer's income is $20.00. In your diagram, put movie tickets on the vertical axis and buckets of popcorn on the horizontal axis.

   b. The consumption bundle consists of underwear and socks. The price of each pair of underwear is $4.00, the price of each pair of socks is $2.00, and the consumer's income is $12.00. In your diagram, put pairs of socks on the vertical axis and pairs of underwear on the horizontal axis.

3. In Table 20-3 you can see that the marginal utility per dollar spent on clams and the marginal utility per dollar spent on potatoes are equal when Sammy increases his consumption of clams from 3 pounds to 4 pounds and his consumption of potatoes from 9 pounds to 10 pounds. Explain why this is not Sammy's optimal consumption bundle. Illustrate your answer using a budget line like the one in Figure 20-3.

Multiple-Choice Questions

1. Generally, each successive unit of a good consumed will cause marginal utility to

   a. increase at an increasing rate.

   b. increase at a decreasing rate.

   c. increase at a constant rate.

   d. decrease.

   e. either increase or decrease.

2. Assume there are two goods, good *X* and good *Y*. Good *X* costs $5 and good *Y* costs $10. If your income is $200, which of the following combinations of good *X* and good *Y* is on your budget line?

   a. 0 units of good *X* and 18 units of good *Y*

   b. 0 units of good *X* and 20 units of good *Y*

   c. 20 units of good *X* and 0 units of good *Y*

   d. 10 units of good *X* and 12 units of good *Y*

   e. all of the above

3. The optimal consumption rule states that total utility is maximized when all income is spent and

   a. *MU*/*P* is equal for all goods.

   b. *MU* is equal for all goods.

   c. *P*/*MU* is equal for all goods.

   d. *MU* is as high as possible for all goods.

   e. the amount spent on each good is equal.

4. A consumer is spending all of her income and receiving 100 utils from the last unit of good A and 80 utils from the last unit of good B. If the price of good A is $2 and the price of good B is $1, to maximize total utility the consumer should buy

   a. more of good A.

   b. more of good B.

   c. less of good B.

   d. more of both goods.

   e. less of both goods.

5. The optimal consumption bundle is always represented by a point

   a. inside the consumer's budget line.

   b. outside the consumer's budget line.

   c. at the highest point on the consumer's budget line.

   d. on the consumer's budget line.

   e. at the horizontal intercept of the consumer's budget line.

Critical-Thinking Questions

Assume you have an income of $100. The price of good X is $5, and the price of good Y is $20.

1. Draw a correctly labeled budget line with "Quantity of good X" on the horizontal axis and "Quantity of good Y" on the vertical axis. Be sure to correctly label the horizontal and vertical intercepts.
2. With your current consumption bundle, you receive 100 utils from consuming your last unit of good X and 400 utils from consuming your last unit of good Y. Are you maximizing your total utility? Explain.
3. What will happen to the total and marginal utility you receive from consuming good X if you decide to consume another unit of good X? Explain.

PITFALLS

THE RIGHT MARGINAL COMPARISON

? Marginal analysis solves "how much" decisions by weighing costs and benefits at the margin: the *benefit* of doing a little bit more versus the *cost* of doing a little bit more. But, as we saw in the previous module, the *form* of the marginal analysis can differ, depending upon whether you are making a production decision or a consumption decision. How do these two forms of marginal analysis differ?

> THE FORM OF MARGINAL ANALYSIS DIFFERS DEPENDING UPON WHETHER YOU ARE MAKING A PRODUCTION DECISION THAT MAXIMIZES PROFITS OR A CONSUMPTION DECISION THAT MAXIMIZES UTILITY. In Module 18, Alex's decision was a production decision because the problem he faced was maximizing the profit from years of schooling. The optimal quantity of years that maximized his profit was found using marginal analysis: at the optimal quantity, the marginal benefit of another year of schooling was equal to its marginal cost. Alex did not face a budget constraint because he could always borrow to finance another year of school.

But if you were to extend the way we solved Alex's production problem to the consumption problem Sammy faced in Module 20, without any change in form, you might be tempted to say that Sammy's optimal consumption bundle is the one at which the marginal utility of clams is equal to the marginal utility of potatoes, or that the marginal utility of clams was equal to the price of clams. But both of those statements would be wrong because they don't properly account for the budget constraint and the fact that consuming more of one good requires consuming less of another. In a consumption decision, your objective is to maximize the utility that your limited budget can deliver. And the right way to find the optimal consumption bundle is to set the *marginal utility per dollar* equal for each good in the consumption bundle. When this condition is satisfied, the "bang per buck" is the same across all the goods and services you consume. Only then is there no way to rearrange your consumption and get more utility from your budget.

To learn more, reread "Spending the Marginal Dollar," on pages 216–219, including Figure 20-4.

BUSINESS CASE • Citi Puts Card Holders "inControl"

The Photo Works

In late 2010, Citi, a global financial services company with 200 million customers in 160 countries, became the first American company to introduce MasterCards with a special set of features known as *inControl.* Previously introduced in the United Kingdom by Barclays Bank, inControl cards contain budgeting and alert features that help credit card holders stay within their spending limits and prevent credit card fraud. With inControl, card holders can do the following:

- Set up and manage spending limits
- Set up budgets for particular types of spending
- Manage where, when, how, and for what types of purchases their credit cards can be used
- Receive alerts, via text or e-mail, to safeguard against overspending and fraud

Users can customize their cards, choosing to receive alerts only when they are exceeding their limits or to have a card declined when a limit is breached. So, for example, if you choose the latter and have set a monthly limit on restaurant meals, your card will be rejected for restaurant bills above your pre-set cap. Card holders can also arrange to have their credit cards shut off once a limit is reached that corresponds to monthly disposable income.

inControl is not the first product that alerts card holders when they have exceeded their limit. Mint.com offers such a service, but you have to log into your bank's website to retrieve updates, and those sites are updated only every 24 hours. In contrast, alerts from inControl happen in real time. Until inControl was introduced, no other product allowed you to completely cut off certain types of spending. "The personalization of consumer products has reached far deeper than it ever has before," says Ed McLaughlin, chief payments officer of MasterCard.

But what about the obvious question of whether credit card companies are hurting or helping themselves by introducing this product? After all, if consumers get serious about budgeting and place caps on their credit card spending, won't that reduce the interest that credit card companies profit from? In answer to this question, McLaughlin replied, "I think anyone knows that having a superior offering wins out in the long run."

The service, though, is not ironclad—having hit the self-imposed limit, a customer can turn the card back on with a phone call or text message. The thinking goes, however, that having your card rejected will make a significant enough impression to put a damper on your urge to splurge.

In the end, how well inControl does, and whether something like it is adopted by competitors like VISA, depends on whether customers actually use the service *and* how much customers' newfound discipline hurts credit card companies' bottom lines.

Questions for Thought

1. What aspects of decision making does the inControl card address? Be specific.
2. Consider credit scores, the scores assigned to individuals by credit-rating agencies, based on whether you pay your bills on time, how many credit cards you have (too many is a bad sign), whether you have ever declared bankruptcy, and so on. Now consider people who choose inControl cards and those who don't. Which group do you think has better credit scores *before* they adopt the inControl cards? After adopting the inControl cards? Explain.
3. What do you think explains Ed McLaughlin's optimism that his company will profit from the introduction of inControl?

SECTION 7 REVIEW

Summary

Making Decisions

1. All economic decisions involve the allocation of scarce resources. Some decisions are "either–or" decisions, in which the question is whether or not to do something. Other decisions are "how much" decisions, in which the question is how much of a resource to put into a given activity.
2. The cost of using a resource for a particular activity is the opportunity cost of that resource. Some opportunity costs are **explicit costs;** they involve a direct outlay of money. Other opportunity costs, however, are **implicit costs;** they involve no outlay of money but are measured by the dollar value of the benefits that are forgone. Both explicit and implicit costs should be taken into account in making decisions. Many decisions involve the use of **capital** and time, for both individuals and firms. So they should base decisions on **economic profit,** which takes into account implicit costs such as the opportunity cost of time and the **implicit cost of capital.** Making decisions based on **accounting profit** can be misleading. It is often considerably larger than the economic profit because it includes only explicit costs and not implicit costs.
3. According to the **principle of "either–or" decision making,** when faced with an "either–or" choice between two activities, one should choose the activity with the positive economic profit.
4. A **"how much" decision** is made using marginal analysis, which involves comparing the benefit to the cost of doing an additional unit of an activity. The **marginal cost** of producing a good or service is the additional cost incurred by producing one more unit of that good or service. The **marginal benefit** of producing a good or service is the additional benefit earned by producing one more unit. The **marginal cost curve** is the graphical illustration of marginal cost, and the **marginal benefit curve** is the graphical illustration of marginal benefit.
5. In the case of **constant marginal cost,** each additional unit costs the same amount to produce as the previous unit. However, marginal cost and marginal benefit typically depend on how much of the activity has already been done. With **increasing marginal cost,** each unit costs more to produce than the previous unit and is represented by an upward-sloping marginal cost curve. With **decreasing marginal cost,** each unit costs less to produce than the previous unit, leading to a downward-sloping marginal cost curve. In the case of **decreasing marginal benefit,** each additional unit produces a smaller benefit than the unit before.
6. The **optimal quantity** is the quantity that generates the highest possible total profit. According to the **profit-maximizing principle of marginal analysis,** the optimal quantity is the highest quantity at which marginal benefit is greater than or equal to marginal cost. It is the quantity at which the marginal cost curve and the marginal benefit curve intersect.
7. A cost that has already been incurred and that is nonrecoverable is a **sunk cost.** Sunk costs should be ignored in decisions about future actions because they have no effect on future benefits and costs.

Behavioral Economics

8. With **rational** behavior, individuals will choose the available option that leads to the outcome they most prefer. **Bounded rationality** occurs because the effort needed to find the best economic payoff is costly. **Risk aversion** causes individuals to sacrifice some economic payoff in order to avoid a potential loss. People might also prefer outcomes with worse economic payoffs because they are concerned about fairness.
9. An **irrational** choice leaves someone worse off than if they had chosen another available option. It takes the form of misperceptions of opportunity cost; overconfidence; unrealistic expectations about future behavior; **mental accounting,** in which dollars are valued unequally; **loss aversion,** an oversensitivity to loss; and **status quo bias,** avoiding a decision by sticking with the status quo.

Maximizing Utility

10. Consumers maximize a measure of satisfaction called **utility.** We measure utility in hypothetical units called **utils.**
11. A good's or service's **marginal utility** is the additional utility generated by consuming one more unit of the good or service. We usually assume that the **principle of diminishing marginal utility** holds: consumption of another unit of a good or service yields less additional utility than the previous unit. As a result, the **marginal utility curve** slopes downward.
12. A **budget constraint** limits a consumer's spending to no more than his or her income. It defines the consumer's **consumption possibilities,** the set of all affordable consumption bundles. A consumer who spends all of his or her income will choose a consumption bundle on the **budget line.** An individual chooses the consumption bundle that maximizes total utility, the **optimal consumption bundle.**

13. We use marginal analysis to find the optimal consumption bundle by analyzing how to allocate the marginal dollar. According to the **optimal consumption rule,** with the optimal consumption bundle, the **marginal utility per dollar** spent on each good and service—the marginal utility of a good divided by its price—is the same.

Key Terms

Problems

1. Hiro owns and operates a small business that provides economic consulting services. During the year he spends $57,000 on travel to clients and other expenses. In addition, he owns a computer that he uses for business. If he didn't use the computer, he could sell it and earn yearly interest of $100 on the money created through this sale. Hiro's total revenue for the year is $100,000. Instead of working as a consultant for the year, he could teach economics at a small local college and make a salary of $50,000.

   a. What is Hiro's accounting profit?

   b. What is Hiro's economic profit?

   c. Should Hiro continue working as a consultant, or should he teach economics instead?

2. Jackie owns and operates a web-design business. To keep up with new technology, she spends $5,000 per year upgrading her computer equipment. She runs the business out of a room in her home. If she didn't use the room as her business office, she could rent it out for $2,000 per year. Jackie knows that if she didn't run her own business, she could return to her previous job at a large software company that would pay her a salary of $60,000 per year. Jackie has no other expenses.

   a. How much total revenue does Jackie need to make in order to break even in the eyes of her accountant? That is, how much total revenue would give Jackie an accounting profit of just zero?

   b. How much total revenue does Jackie need to make in order for her to want to remain self-employed? That is, how much total revenue would give Jackie an economic profit of just zero?

3. You own and operate a bike store. Each year, you receive revenue of $200,000 from your bike sales, and it costs you $100,000 to obtain the bikes. In addition, you pay $20,000 for electricity, taxes, and other expenses per year. Instead of running the bike store, you could become an accountant and receive a yearly salary of $40,000. A large clothing retail chain wants to expand and offers to rent the store from you for $50,000 per year. How do you explain to your friends that despite making a profit, it is too costly for you to continue running your store?

4. Suppose you have just paid a nonrefundable fee of $1,000 for your meal plan for this academic term. This allows you to eat dinner in the cafeteria every evening.

   a. You are offered a part-time job in a restaurant where you can eat for free each evening. Your parents say that you should eat dinner in the cafeteria anyway, since you have already paid for those meals. Are your parents right? Explain why or why not.

   b. You are offered a part-time job in a different restaurant where, rather than being able to eat for free, you receive only a large discount on your meals. Each meal there will cost you $2; if you eat there each evening this semester, it will add up to $200. Your roommate says that you should eat in the restaurant since it costs less than the $1,000 that you paid for the meal plan. Is your roommate right? Explain why or why not.

5. You have bought a $10 ticket in advance for the college soccer game, a ticket that cannot be resold. You know that going to the soccer game will give you a benefit equal to $20. After you have bought the ticket, you hear that there will be a professional baseball post-season game at the same time. Tickets to the baseball game cost $20, and you know that going to the baseball game will give you a benefit equal to $35. You tell your friends the following: "If I had known about the baseball game before buying the ticket to the soccer game, I would have gone to the baseball game instead. But now that I already have the ticket to the soccer game, it's better for me to just go to the soccer game." Are you making the correct decision? Justify your answer by calculating the benefits and costs of your decision.

6. Amy, Bill, and Carla all mow lawns for money. Each of them operates a different lawn mower. The accompanying table shows the total cost to Amy, Bill, and Carla of mowing lawns.

Quantity of lawns mowed	Amy's total cost	Bill's total cost	Carla's total cost
0	$0	$0	$0
1	20	10	2
2	35	20	7
3	45	30	17
4	50	40	32
5	52	50	52
6	53	60	82

a. Calculate Amy's, Bill's, and Carla's marginal costs, and draw each of their marginal cost curves.

b. Who has increasing marginal cost, who has decreasing marginal cost, and who has constant marginal cost?

7. You are the manager of a gym, and you have to decide how many customers to admit each hour. Assume that each customer stays exactly one hour. Customers are costly to admit because they inflict wear and tear on the exercise equipment. Moreover, each additional customer generates more wear and tear than the customer before. As a result, the gym faces increasing marginal cost. The accompanying table shows the marginal costs associated with each number of customers per hour.

Quantity of customers per hour	Marginal cost of customer
0	
	$14.00
1	
	14.50
2	
	15.00
3	
	15.50
4	
	16.00
5	
	16.50
6	
	17.00
7	

a. Suppose that each customer pays $15.25 for a one-hour workout. Use the profit-maximizing principle of marginal analysis to find the optimal number of customers that you should admit per hour.

b. You increase the price of a one-hour workout to $16.25. What is the optimal number of customers per hour that you should admit now?

8. Georgia and Lauren are economics students who go to a karate class together. Both have to choose how many classes to go to per week. Each class costs $20. The accompanying table shows Georgia's and Lauren's estimates of the marginal benefit that each of them gets from each class per week.

Quantity of classes	Lauren's marginal benefit of each class	Georgia's marginal benefit of each class
0		
	$23	$28
1		
	19	22
2		
	14	15
3		
	8	7
4		

a. Use marginal analysis to find Lauren's optimal number of karate classes per week. Explain your answer.

b. Use marginal analysis to find Georgia's optimal number of karate classes per week. Explain your answer.

9. The Centers for Disease Control and Prevention (CDC) recommended against vaccinating the whole population against the smallpox virus because the vaccination has undesirable, and sometimes fatal, side effects. Suppose the accompanying table gives the data that are available about the effects of a smallpox vaccination program.

Percent of population vaccinated	Deaths due to smallpox	Deaths due to vaccination side effects
0%	200	0
10	180	4
20	160	10
30	140	18
40	120	33
50	100	50
60	80	74

a. Calculate the marginal benefit (in terms of lives saved) and the marginal cost (in terms of lives lost) of each 10% increment of smallpox vaccination. Calculate the net increase in human lives for each 10% increment in population vaccinated.

b. Using marginal analysis, determine the optimal percentage of the population that should be vaccinated.

10. Patty delivers pizza using her own car, and she is paid according to the number of pizzas she delivers. The accompanying table shows Patty's total benefit and total cost when she works a specific number of hours.

Quantity of hours worked	Total benefit	Total cost
0	$0	$0
1	30	10
2	55	21
3	75	34
4	90	50
5	100	70

a. Use marginal analysis to determine Patty's optimal number of hours worked.

b. Calculate the total profit to Patty from working 0 hours, 1 hour, 2 hours, and so on. Now suppose Patty chooses to work for 1 hour. Compare her total profit from working for 1 hour with her total profit from working the optimal number of hours. How much would she lose by working for only 1 hour?

11. Assume De Beers is the sole producer of diamonds. When it wants to sell more diamonds, it must lower its price in order to induce shoppers to buy more. Furthermore, each additional diamond that is produced costs more than the previous one due to the difficulty of mining for diamonds. De Beers's total benefit schedule is given in the accompanying table, along with its total cost schedule.

Quantity of diamonds	Total benefit	Total cost
0	$0	$0
1	1,000	50
2	1,900	100
3	2,700	200
4	3,400	400
5	4,000	800
6	4,500	1,500
7	4,900	2,500
8	5,200	3,800

a. Draw the marginal cost curve and the marginal benefit curve and, from your diagram, graphically derive the optimal quantity of diamonds to produce.

b. Calculate the total profit to De Beers from producing each quantity of diamonds. Which quantity gives De Beers the highest total profit?

12. In each of the following examples, explain whether the decision is rational or irrational. Describe the type of behavior exhibited.

a. Rick has just gotten his teaching degree and has two job offers. One job, replacing a teacher who has gone on leave, will last only two years. It is at a prestigious high school, and he will be paid $35,000 per year. He thinks he will probably be able to find another good job in the area after the two years are up but isn't sure. The other job, also at a high school, pays $25,000 per year and is virtually guaranteed for five years; after those five years, he will be evaluated for a permanent teaching position at the school. About 75% of the teachers who start at the school are hired for permanent positions. Rick takes the five-year position at $25,000 per year.

b. Kimora has planned a trip to Florida during spring break in March. She has several school projects due after her return. Rather than do them in February, she figures she can take her books with her to Florida and complete her projects there.

c. Sahir overpaid when buying a used car that has turned out to be a lemon. He could sell it for parts, but instead he lets it sit in his garage and deteriorate.

d. Barry considers himself an excellent investor in stocks. He selects new stocks by finding ones with characteristics similar to those of his previous winning stocks. He chocks up losing trades to ups and downs in the macroeconomy.

13. You have been hired as a consultant by a company to develop the company's retirement plan, taking into account different types of predictably irrational behavior commonly displayed by employees. State at least two types of irrational behavior employees might display with regard to the retirement plan and the steps you would take to forestall such behavior.

14. For each of the following situations, decide whether Al has increasing, constant, or diminishing marginal utility.

a. The more economics classes Al takes, the more he enjoys the subject. And the more classes he takes, the easier each one gets, making him enjoy each additional class even more than the one before.

b. Al likes loud music. In fact, according to him, "the louder, the better." Each time he turns the volume up a notch, he adds 5 utils to his total utility.

c. Al enjoys watching reruns of the old sitcom *Friends*. He claims that these episodes are always funny, but he does admit that the more times he sees an episode, the less funny it gets.

d. Al loves toasted marshmallows. The more he eats, however, the fuller he gets and the less he enjoys each additional marshmallow. And there is a point at which he becomes satiated: beyond that point, more marshmallows actually make him feel worse rather than better.

15. Use the concept of marginal utility to explain the following: Newspaper vending machines are designed so that once you have paid for one paper, you could take more than one paper at a time. But soda vending machines, once you have paid for one soda, dispense only one soda at a time.

16. Brenda likes to have bagels and coffee for breakfast. The accompanying table shows Brenda's total utility from various consumption bundles of bagels and coffee.

Consumption bundle		
Quantity of bagels	Quantity of coffee (cups)	Total utility (utils)
0	0	0
0	2	28
0	4	40
1	2	48
1	3	54
2	0	28
2	2	56
3	1	54
3	2	62
4	0	40
4	2	66

Suppose Brenda knows she will consume 2 cups of coffee for sure. However, she can choose to consume different quantities of bagels: she can choose either 0, 1, 2, 3, or 4 bagels.

a. Calculate Brenda's marginal utility from bagels as she goes from consuming 0 bagel to 1 bagel, from 1 bagel to 2 bagels, from 2 bagels to 3 bagels, and from 3 bagels to 4 bagels.

b. Draw Brenda's marginal utility curve of bagels. Does Brenda have increasing, diminishing, or constant marginal utility of bagels?

17. Bernie loves notebooks and Beyoncé CDs. The accompanying table shows the utility Bernie receives from each product.

Quantity of notebooks	Utility from notebooks (utils)	Quantity of CDs	Utility from CDs (utils)
0	0	0	0
2	70	1	80
4	130	2	150
6	180	3	210
8	220	4	260
10	250	5	300

The price of a notebook is $5, the price of a CD is $10, and Bernie has $50 of income to spend.

a. Which consumption bundles of notebooks and CDs can Bernie consume if he spends all his income? Illustrate Bernie's budget line with a diagram, putting notebooks on the horizontal axis and CDs on the vertical axis.

b. Calculate the marginal utility of each notebook and the marginal utility of each CD. Then calculate the marginal utility per dollar spent on notebooks and the marginal utility per dollar spent on CDs.

c. Draw a diagram like Figure 20-4 in which both the marginal utility per dollar spent on notebooks and the marginal utility per dollar spent on CDs are illustrated. Using this diagram and the optimal consumption rule, predict which bundle—from all the bundles on his budget line—Bernie will choose.

18. For each of the following situations, decide whether the bundle Lakshani is considering is optimal or not. If it is not optimal, how could Lakshani improve her overall level of utility? That is, determine which good she should spend more on and which good she should spend less on.

a. Lakshani has $200 to spend on sneakers and sweaters. Sneakers cost $50 per pair, and sweaters cost $20 each. She is thinking about buying 2 pairs of sneakers and 5 sweaters. She tells her friend that the additional utility she would get from the second pair of sneakers is the same as the additional utility she would get from the fifth sweater.

b. Lakshani has $5 to spend on pens and pencils. Each pen costs $0.50 and each pencil costs $0.10. She is thinking about buying 6 pens and 20 pencils. The last pen would add five times as much to her total utility as the last pencil.

c. Lakshani has $50 per season to spend on tickets to football games and tickets to soccer games. Each football ticket costs $10, and each soccer ticket costs $5. She is thinking about buying 3 football tickets and 2 soccer tickets. Her marginal utility from the third football ticket is twice as much as her marginal utility from the second soccer ticket.

Production and Costs

THE FARMER'S MARGIN

"O Beautiful for spacious skies, for amber waves of grain." So begins the song "America the Beautiful." And those amber waves of grain are for real: though farmers are now only a small minority of America's population, our agricultural industry is immensely productive and feeds much of the world.

If you look at agricultural statistics, however, something may seem a bit surprising: when it comes to yield per acre, U.S. farmers are often nowhere near the top. For example, farmers in Western European countries grow about three times as much wheat per acre as their U.S. counterparts. Are the Europeans better at growing wheat than we are?

No: European farmers are very skillful, but no more so than Americans. They produce more wheat per acre because they employ more inputs—more fertilizer and, especially, more labor—per acre. Of course, this means that European farmers have higher costs than their American counterparts. But because of government policies, European farmers receive a much higher price for their wheat than American farmers. This gives them an incentive to use more inputs and to expend more effort at the margin to increase the crop yield per acre.

Notice our use of the phrase "at the margin." Like most decisions that involve a comparison of benefits and costs, decisions about inputs and production involve a comparison of marginal quantities—the marginal cost versus the marginal benefit of producing a bit more from each acre.

In Module 18 we considered the case of Alex, who had to choose the number of years of schooling that maximized his profit from schooling. There we used the profit-maximizing principle of marginal analysis to find the optimal quantity of years of schooling. In this chapter, we will encounter producers who have to make similar "how much" decisions: choosing the quantity of output produced to maximize profit.

In this section, we will show how marginal analysis can be used to understand these output decisions—decisions that lie behind the supply curve.

The first step in this analysis is to show how the relationship between a firm's inputs and its output—its *production function*—determines its *cost curves,* the relationship between cost and quantity of output produced. That is what we do in Module 21. In Modules 22 and 23, we will use our understanding of the firm's cost curves to derive the individual and the market supply curves.

MODULE 21 The Production Function

© Terrance Klassen/AgeFotostock

WHAT YOU WILL LEARN

1. The importance of the firm's production function, the relationship between the quantity of inputs and the quantity of output
2. Why production is often subject to diminishing returns to inputs

The Production Function

A *firm* produces goods or services for sale. To do this, it must transform inputs into output. The quantity of output a firm produces depends on the quantity of inputs; this relationship is known as the firm's **production function.** As we'll see, a firm's production function underlies its *cost curves*. As a first step, let's look at the characteristics of a hypothetical production function.

Inputs and Output

To understand the concept of a production function, let's consider a farm that we assume, for the sake of simplicity, produces only one output, wheat, and uses only two inputs, land and labor. This particular farm is owned by a couple named George and Martha. They hire workers to do the actual physical labor on the farm. Moreover, we will assume that all potential workers are of the same quality—they are all equally knowledgeable and capable of performing farmwork.

A **production function** is the relationship between the quantity of inputs a firm uses and the quantity of output it produces.

A **fixed input** is an input whose quantity is fixed for a period of time and cannot be varied.

A **variable input** is an input whose quantity the firm can vary at any time.

The **long run** is the time period in which all inputs can be varied.

The **short run** is the time period in which at least one input is fixed.

George and Martha's farm sits on 10 acres of land; no more acres are available to them, and they are currently unable to either increase or decrease the size of their farm by selling, buying, or leasing acreage. Land here is what economists call a **fixed input**—an input whose quantity is fixed for a period of time and cannot be varied. George and Martha are, however, free to decide how many workers to hire. The labor provided by these workers is called a **variable input**—an input whose quantity the firm can vary at any time.

In reality, whether or not the quantity of an input is really fixed depends on the time horizon. In the **long run**—that is, given that a long enough period of time has elapsed—firms can adjust the quantity of any input. So there are no fixed inputs in the long run. In contrast, the **short run** is defined as the time period during which at least one input is fixed. Later, we'll look more carefully at the distinction between the short run and the long run. But for now, we will restrict our attention to the short run and assume that at least one input (land) is fixed.

George and Martha know that the quantity of wheat they produce depends on the number of workers they hire. Using modern farming techniques, one worker can cultivate the 10-acre farm, albeit not very intensively. When an additional worker is added, the land is divided equally among all the workers: each worker has 5 acres to cultivate when 2 workers are employed, each cultivates 3⅓ acres when 3 are employed, and so on. So as additional workers are employed, the 10 acres of land are cultivated more intensively and more bushels of wheat are produced.

The relationship between the quantity of labor and the quantity of output, for a given amount of the fixed input, constitutes the farm's production function. The production function for George and Martha's farm, where land is the fixed input and labor is the variable input, is shown in the first two columns of the table in Figure 21-1; the diagram there depicts the same information graphically. The curve in Figure 21-1 shows how the quantity of output depends on the quantity of the variable input for a given quantity of the fixed input; it is called the farm's **total product curve.** The physical quantity of output, bushels of wheat, is measured on the vertical axis; the quantity of the variable input, labor (that is, the number of workers employed), is measured on the horizontal axis. The total product curve here slopes upward, reflecting the fact that more bushels of wheat are produced as more workers are employed.

Although the total product curve in Figure 21-1 slopes upward along its entire length, the slope isn't constant: as you move up the curve to the right, it flattens out. To understand this changing slope, look at the third column of the table in Figure 21-1, which shows the *change in the quantity of output* generated by adding one more worker. That is, it shows the **marginal product** of labor, or *MPL*: the additional quantity of output from using one more unit of labor (one more worker).

The **total product curve** shows how the quantity of output depends on the quantity of the variable input, for a given quantity of the fixed input.

The **marginal product** of an input is the additional quantity of output produced by using one more unit of that input.

FIGURE 21-1 **Production Function and Total Product Curve for George and Martha's Farm**

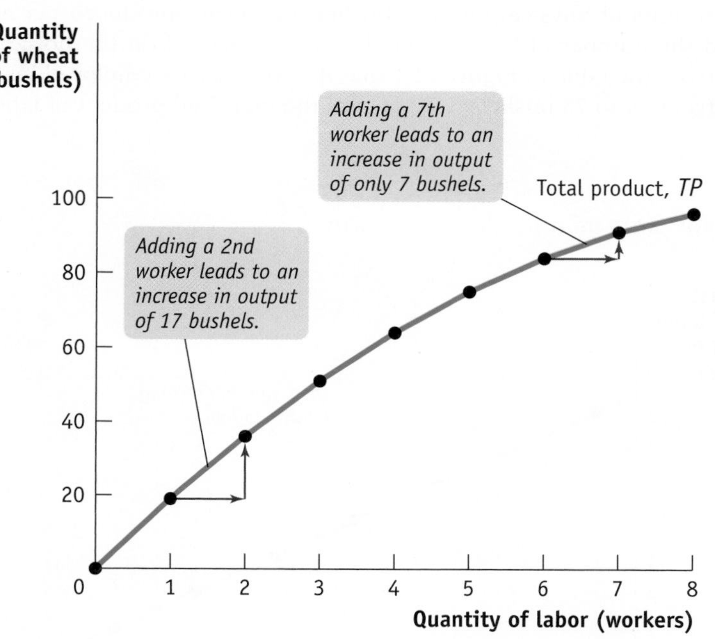

Quantity of labor *L* (workers)	Quantity of wheat *Q* (bushels)	Marginal product of labor $MPL = \Delta Q/\Delta L$ (bushels per worker)
0	0	
		19
1	19	
		17
2	36	
		15
3	51	
		13
4	64	
		11
5	75	
		9
6	84	
		7
7	91	
		5
8	96	

The table shows the production function, the relationship between the quantity of the variable input (labor, measured in number of workers) and the quantity of output (wheat, measured in bushels) for a given quantity of the fixed input. It also shows the marginal product of labor on George and Martha's farm. The total product curve shows the production function graphically. It slopes upward because more wheat is produced as more workers are employed. It also becomes flatter because the marginal product of labor declines as more and more workers are employed.

In this example, we have data at intervals of 1 worker—that is, we have information on the quantity of output when there are 3 workers, 4 workers, and so on. Sometimes data aren't available in increments of 1 unit—for example, you might have information on the quantity of output only when there are 40 workers and when there are 50 workers. In this case, you can use the following equation to calculate the marginal product of labor:

$$\text{(21-1)}\quad \begin{array}{l}\text{Marginal}\\ \text{product}\\ \text{of labor}\end{array} = \begin{array}{l}\text{Change in quantity of}\\ \text{output produced by one}\\ \text{additional unit of labor}\end{array} = \frac{\text{Change in quantity of output}}{\text{Change in quantity of labor}}$$

or

$$MPL = \frac{\Delta Q}{\Delta L}$$

Note that Δ, the Greek uppercase delta, represents the change in a variable.

Now we can explain the significance of the slope of the total product curve: it is equal to the marginal product of labor. The slope of a line is equal to "rise" over "run." This implies that the slope of the total product curve is the change in the quantity of output (the "rise") divided by the change in the quantity of labor (the "run"). And this, as we can see from Equation 21-1, is simply the marginal product of labor. So in Figure 21-1, the fact that the marginal product of the first worker is 19 also means that the slope of the total product curve in going from 0 to 1 worker is 19. Similarly, the slope of the total product curve in going from 1 to 2 workers is the same as the marginal product of the second worker, 17, and so on.

In this example, the marginal product of labor steadily declines as more workers are hired—that is, each successive worker adds less to output than the previous worker. So as employment increases, the total product curve gets flatter.

Figure 21-2 shows how the marginal product of labor depends on the number of workers employed on the farm. The marginal product of labor, *MPL,* is measured on the vertical axis in units of physical output—bushels of wheat—produced per additional worker, and the number of workers employed is measured on the horizontal axis. You can see from the table in Figure 21-1 that if 5 workers are employed instead of 4, output rises from 64 to 75 bushels; in this case the marginal product of labor is

FIGURE 21-2 Marginal Product of Labor Curve for George and Martha's Farm

The marginal product of labor curve plots each worker's marginal product, the increase in the quantity of output generated by each additional worker. The change in the quantity of output is measured on the vertical axis and the number of workers employed on the horizontal axis. The first worker employed generates an increase in output of 19 bushels, the second worker generates an increase of 17 bushels, and so on. The curve slopes downward due to diminishing returns to labor.

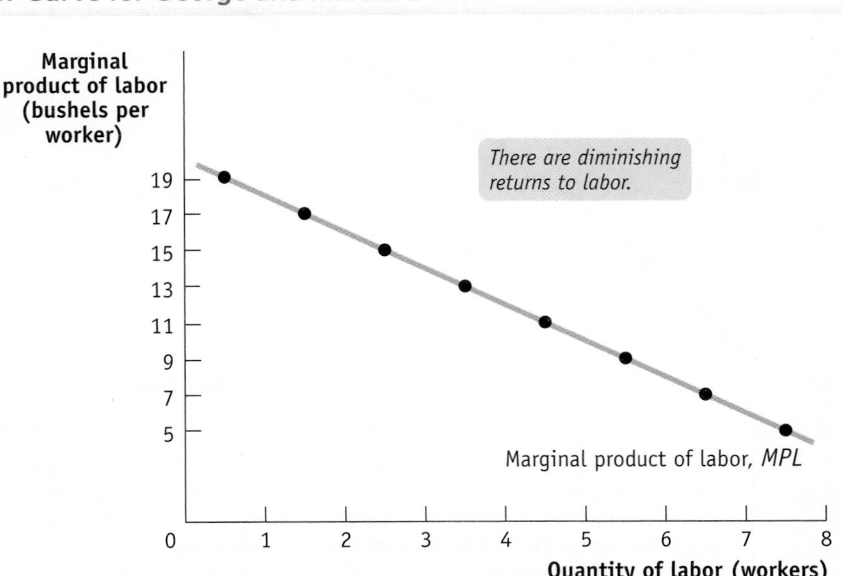

11 bushels—the same number found in Figure 21-2. To indicate that 11 bushels is the marginal product when employment rises from 4 to 5, we place the point corresponding to that information halfway between 4 and 5 workers.

In this example the marginal product of labor falls as the number of workers increases. That is, there are *diminishing returns to labor* on George and Martha's farm. In general, there are **diminishing returns to an input** when an increase in the quantity of that input, holding the quantity of all other inputs fixed, reduces that input's marginal product. Due to diminishing returns to labor, the *MPL* curve is negatively sloped.

There are **diminishing returns to an input** when an increase in the quantity of that input, holding the levels of all other inputs fixed, leads to a decline in the marginal product of that input.

To grasp why diminishing returns can occur, think about what happens as George and Martha add more and more workers without increasing the number of acres. As the number of workers increases, the land is farmed more intensively and the number of bushels increases. But each additional worker is working with a smaller share of the 10 acres—the fixed input—than the previous worker. As a result, the additional worker cannot produce as much output as the previous worker. So it's not surprising that the marginal product of the additional worker falls.

Cultura Limited/Superstock

As more workers are added to a fixed amount of land, each worker adds less to total output than the previous worker.

The crucial point to emphasize about diminishing returns is that, like many propositions in economics, it is an "other things equal" proposition: each successive unit of an input will raise production by less than the last *if the quantity of all other inputs is held fixed.*

What would happen if the levels of other inputs were allowed to change? You can see the answer illustrated in Figure 21-3. Panel (a) shows two total product curves, TP_{10} and TP_{20}. TP_{10} is the farm's total product curve when its total area is 10 acres (the same curve as in Figure 21-1). TP_{20} is the total product curve when the farm's area

FIGURE 21-3 Total Product, Marginal Product, and the Fixed Input

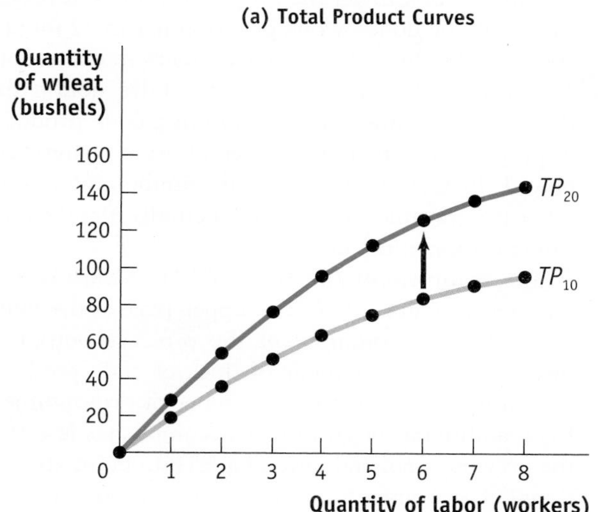

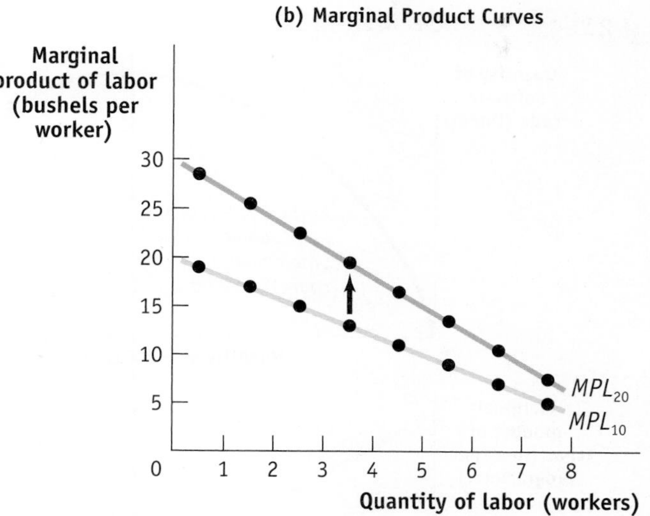

This figure shows how the quantity of output—illustrated by the total product curve—and marginal product depend on the level of the fixed input. Panel (a) shows two total product curves for George and Martha's farm, TP_{10} when their farm is 10 acres and TP_{20} when it is 20 acres. With more land, each worker can produce more wheat. So an increase in the fixed input shifts the total product curve up from TP_{10} to TP_{20}. This also implies that the marginal product of each worker is higher when the farm is 20 acres than when it is 10 acres. As a result, an increase in acreage also shifts the marginal product of labor curve up from MPL_{10} to MPL_{20}. Panel (b) shows the marginal product of labor curves. Note that both marginal product of labor curves still slope downward due to diminishing returns to labor.

has increased to 20 acres. Except when 0 workers are employed, TP_{20} lies everywhere above TP_{10} because with more acres available, any given number of workers produces more output. Panel (b) shows the corresponding marginal product of labor curves. MPL_{10} is the marginal product of labor curve given 10 acres to cultivate (the same curve as in Figure 21-2), and MPL_{20} is the marginal product of labor curve given 20 acres. Both curves slope downward because, in each case, the amount of land is fixed, although at different levels. But MPL_{20} lies everywhere above MPL_{10}, reflecting the fact that the marginal product of the same worker is higher when he or she has more of the fixed input to work with.

Figure 21-3 demonstrates a general result: the position of the total product curve depends on the quantities of other inputs. If you change the quantities of the other inputs, both the total product curve and the marginal product curve of the remaining input will shift.

ECONOMICS IN ACTION

THE MYTHICAL MAN-MONTH

The concept of diminishing returns to an input was first formulated by economists during the late eighteenth century. These economists, notably including Thomas Malthus, drew their inspiration from agricultural examples. Although still valid, examples drawn from agriculture can seem somewhat musty and old-fashioned in our modern economy.

However, the idea of diminishing returns to an input applies with equal force to the most modern of economic activities—such as, say, the design of software. In 1975 Frederick P. Brooks Jr., a project manager at IBM during the days when it dominated the computer business, published a book titled *The Mythical Man-Month* that soon became a classic.

The chapter that gave its title to the book is basically about diminishing returns to labor in the writing of software. Brooks observed that multiplying the number of programmers assigned to a project did not produce a proportionate reduction in the time it took to get the program written. A project that could be done by one programmer in 12 months could *not* be done by 12 programmers in one month. The "mythical man-month" is the false notion that the number of lines of programming code produced is proportional to the number of code writers employed. In fact, above a certain number, adding another programmer on a project actually *increased* the time to completion.

FIGURE 21-4 Mythical Man-Month

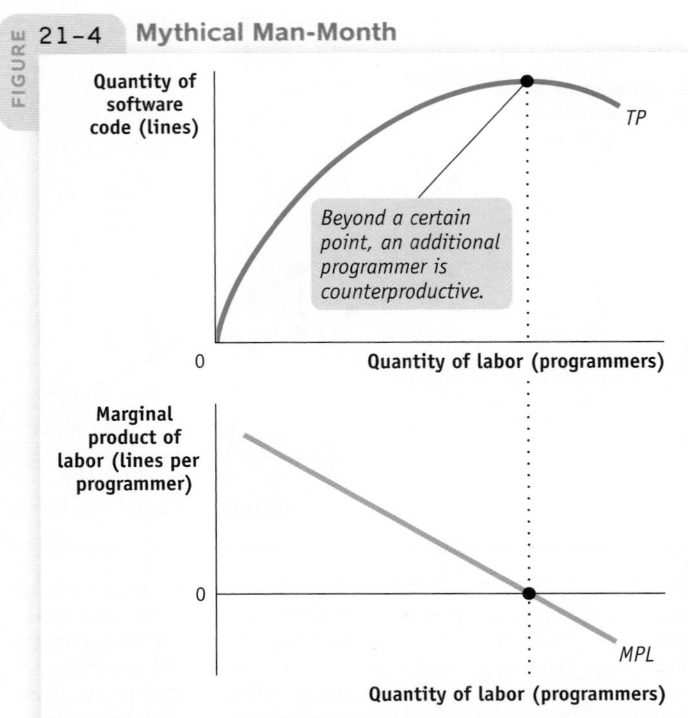

The argument of *The Mythical Man-Month* is summarized in Figure 21-4. The upper part of the figure shows how the quantity of the project's output, as measured by the number of lines of code produced per month, varies with the number of programmers. Each additional programmer accomplishes less than the previous one, and beyond a certain point an additional programmer is actually counterproductive. The lower part of the figure shows the marginal product of each successive programmer, which falls as more programmers are employed and eventually becomes negative.

In other words, programming is subject to diminishing returns so severe that at some point more programmers actually have negative marginal product.

The source of the diminishing returns lies in the nature of the production function for a programming project: each programmer must coordinate his or her work with that of all the other programmers on the project, leading to each person spending more time communicating with others—exchanging e-mails, devising project plans, attending meetings, and so on. In other words, other things equal, there are diminishing returns to labor. It is likely, however, that if fixed inputs devoted to programming projects are increased—say, installing a faster *Wiki system*—the problem of diminishing returns for additional programmers can be mitigated.

MODULE 21 Review

Solutions appear at the back of the book.

Check Your Understanding

1. Bernie's ice-making company produces ice cubes using a 10-ton machine and electricity (along with water, which we will ignore as an input for simplicity). The quantity of output, measured in pounds of ice, is given in the accompanying table.
   a. What is the fixed input? What is the variable input?
   b. Construct a table showing the marginal product of the variable input. Does it show diminishing returns?
   c. Suppose a 50% increase in the size of the fixed input increases output by 100% for any given amount of the variable input. What is the fixed input now? Construct a table showing the quantity of output and the marginal product in this case.

Quantity of electricity (kilowatts)	Quantity of ice (pounds)
0	0
1	1,000
2	1,800
3	2,400
4	2,800

Multiple-Choice Questions

1. A production function shows the relationship between inputs and
   a. fixed costs.
   b. variable costs.
   c. total revenue.
   d. output.
   e. profit.

2. Which of the following defines the short run?
   a. less than a year
   b. when all inputs are fixed
   c. when no inputs are variable
   d. when only one input is variable
   e. when at least one input is fixed

3. The slope of the total product curve is also known as
   a. marginal product.
   b. marginal cost.
   c. average product.
   d. average revenue.
   e. profit.

4. Diminishing returns to an input means that as a firm continues to produce, the total product curve will have what kind of slope?
   a. negative decreasing
   b. positive decreasing
   c. negative increasing
   d. positive increasing
   e. positive constant

5. Historically, the limits imposed by diminishing returns have been alleviated by
   a. investment in capital.
   b. increases in the population.
   c. discovery of more land.
   d. Thomas Malthus.
   e. economic models.

Critical-Thinking Question

Use the data in the table below to graph the production function and the marginal product of labor. Do the data illustrate diminishing returns to labor? Explain.

Quantity of labor	Quantity of output
L	*Q*
0	0
1	19
2	36
3	51
4	64
5	75
6	84
7	91
8	96

PITFALLS

WHAT ARE THE RIGHT UNITS TO USE?

? The marginal product of labor (or any other input) is defined as the increase in the quantity of output when you increase the quantity of that input by one unit. But when we say a "unit" of labor, do we mean an additional hour of labor, an additional week, or a person-year?

> IT DOESN'T MATTER, *AS LONG AS YOU ARE CONSISTENT*. WHATEVER UNITS YOU USE, ALWAYS BE CAREFUL THAT YOU USE THE SAME UNITS THROUGHOUT YOUR ANALYSIS OF ANY PROBLEM. One common source of error in economics is getting units confused—say, comparing the output added by an additional *hour* of labor with the cost of employing a worker for a *week*.

To learn more, review the definition of marginal product of labor *on pages 231–232.*

Firm Costs

©Ilene MacDonald/Alamy

WHAT YOU WILL LEARN

1. The various types of cost a firm faces, including fixed cost, variable cost, and total cost
2. How a firm's costs generate marginal cost curves and average cost curves

From the Production Function to Cost Curves

Now that we have learned about the firm's production function, we can use that knowledge to develop its cost curves. To see how a firm's production function is related to its cost curves, let's turn once again to George and Martha's farm.

Once George and Martha know their production function, they know the relationship between inputs of labor and land and output of wheat. But if they want to maximize their profits, they need to translate this knowledge into information about the relationship between the quantity of output and cost. Let's see how they can do this.

To translate information about a firm's production function into information about its cost, we need to know how much the firm must pay for its inputs. We will assume that George and Martha face either an explicit or an implicit cost of $400 for the use of the land. As we learned previously, it is irrelevant whether George and Martha must rent the land for $400 from someone else or whether they own the land themselves and forgo earning $400 from renting it to someone else. Either way, they pay an opportunity cost of $400 by using the land to grow wheat. Moreover, since the land is a fixed input for which George and Martha pay $400 whether they grow one bushel of wheat or one hundred, its cost is a **fixed cost,** denoted by *FC*—a cost that does not depend on the quantity of output produced. In business, a fixed cost is often referred to as an *overhead cost*.

A **fixed cost** is a cost that does not depend on the quantity of output produced. It is the cost of the fixed input.

We also assume that George and Martha must pay each worker $200. Using their production function, George and Martha know that the number of workers they must hire depends on the amount of wheat they intend to produce. So the cost of labor, which is equal to the number of workers multiplied by $200, is a **variable cost,** denoted by *VC*—a cost that depends on the quantity of output produced. Adding the fixed cost and the variable cost of a given quantity of output gives the **total cost,** or

A **variable cost** is a cost that depends on the quantity of output produced. It is the cost of the variable input.

The **total cost** of producing a given quantity of output is the sum of the fixed cost and the variable cost of producing that quantity of output.

The **total cost curve** shows how total cost depends on the quantity of output.

TC, of that quantity of output. We can express the relationship among fixed cost, variable cost, and total cost as an equation:

$$\textbf{(22-1)} \text{ Total cost} = \text{Fixed cost} + \text{Variable cost}$$

or

$$TC = FC + VC$$

The table in Figure 22-1 shows how total cost is calculated for George and Martha's farm. The second column shows the number of workers employed, *L*. The third column shows the corresponding level of output, *Q*, taken from the table in Figure 22-1. The fourth column shows the variable cost, *VC*, equal to the number of workers multiplied by $200. The fifth column shows the fixed cost, *FC*, which is $400 regardless of the quantity of wheat produced. The sixth column shows the total cost of output, *TC*, which is the variable cost plus the fixed cost.

The first column labels each row of the table with a letter, from *A* to *I*. These labels will be helpful in understanding our next step: drawing the **total cost curve,** a curve that shows how total cost depends on the quantity of output.

George and Martha's total cost curve is shown in the diagram in Figure 22-1, where the horizontal axis measures the quantity of output in bushels of wheat and the vertical axis measures total cost in dollars. Each point on the curve corresponds to one

FIGURE 22-1 **Total Cost Curve for George and Martha's Farm**

The table shows the variable cost, fixed cost, and total cost for various output quantities on George and Martha's 10-acre farm. The total cost curve shows how total cost (measured on the vertical axis) depends on the quantity of output (measured on the horizontal axis). The labeled points on the curve correspond to the rows of the table. The total cost curve slopes upward because the number of workers employed, and hence total cost, increases as the quantity of output increases. The curve gets steeper as output increases due to diminishing returns to labor.

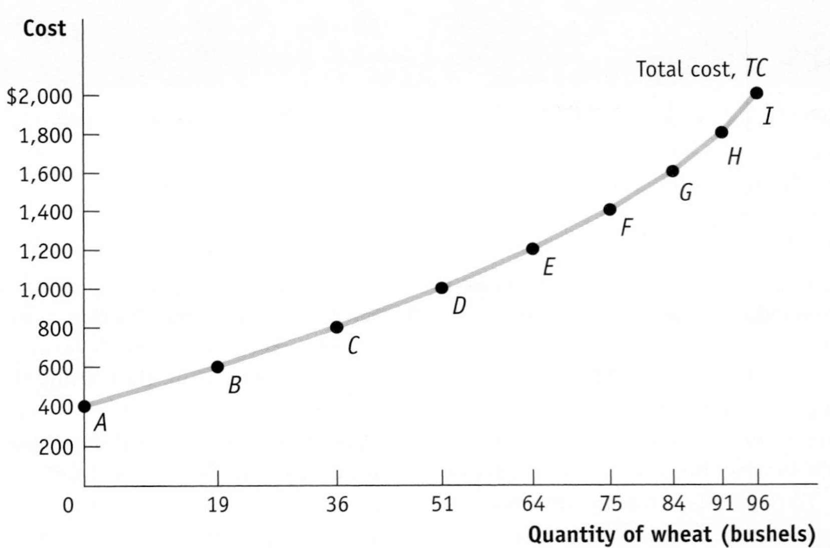

Point on graph	Quantity of labor *L* (workers)	Quantity of wheat *Q* (bushels)	Variable cost *VC*	Fixed cost *FC*	Total cost *TC = FC + VC*
A	0	0	$0	$400	$400
B	1	19	200	400	600
C	2	36	400	400	800
D	3	51	600	400	1,000
E	4	64	800	400	1,200
F	5	75	1,000	400	1,400
G	6	84	1,200	400	1,600
H	7	91	1,400	400	1,800
I	8	96	1,600	400	2,000

row of the table in Figure 22-1. For example, point *A* shows the situation when 0 workers are employed: output is 0, and total cost is equal to fixed cost, $400. Similarly, point *B* shows the situation when 1 worker is employed: output is 19 bushels, and total cost is $600, equal to the sum of $400 in fixed cost and $200 in variable cost.

Like the total product curve, the total cost curve slopes upward: due to the increasing variable cost, the more output produced, the higher the farm's total cost. But unlike the total product curve, which gets flatter as employment rises, the total cost curve gets *steeper*. That is, the slope of the total cost curve is greater as the amount of output produced increases. As we will soon see, the steepening of the total cost curve is also due to diminishing returns to the variable input. Before we can see why, we must first look at the relationships among several useful measures of cost.

Two Key Concepts: Marginal Cost and Average Cost

We've just learned how to derive a firm's total cost curve from its production function. Our next step is to take a deeper look at total cost by deriving two extremely useful measures: *marginal cost* and *average cost*. As we'll see, these two measures of the cost of production have a somewhat surprising relationship to each other. Moreover, they will prove to be vitally important in later modules, where we will use them to analyze the firm's output decision and the market supply curve.

Marginal Cost

Marginal cost is the added cost of doing something one more time. In the context of production, marginal cost is the change in total cost generated by producing one more unit of output. We've already seen that marginal product is easiest to calculate if data on output are available in increments of one unit of input. Similarly, marginal cost is easiest to calculate if data on total cost are available in increments of one unit of output because the increase in total cost for each unit is clear. When the data come in less convenient increments, it's still possible to calculate marginal cost over each interval. But for the sake of simplicity, let's work with an example in which the data come in convenient one-unit increments.

Selena's Gourmet Salsas produces bottled salsa; Table 22-1 shows how its costs per day depend on the number of cases of salsa it produces per day. The firm has a fixed cost of $108 per day, shown in the second column, which is the daily rental cost of its food-preparation equipment. The third column shows the variable cost, and the fourth column shows the total cost. Panel (a) of Figure 22-2 plots the total cost curve. Like the total cost curve for George and Martha's farm in Figure 22-1, this curve slopes upward, getting steeper as quantity increases.

iStockphoto

The significance of the slope of the total cost curve is shown by the fifth column of Table 22-1, which indicates marginal cost—the additional cost of each additional unit. The general formula for marginal cost is:

$$\textbf{(22-2)}\quad \text{Marginal cost} = \begin{array}{l}\text{Change in total}\\ \text{cost generated}\\ \text{by one additional}\\ \text{unit of output}\end{array} = \frac{\text{Change in total cost}}{\text{Change in quantity of output}}$$

or

$$MC = \frac{\Delta TC}{\Delta Q}$$

As in the case of marginal product, marginal cost is equal to "rise" (the increase in total cost) divided by "run" (the increase in the quantity of output). So just as marginal product is equal to the slope of the total product curve, marginal cost is equal to the slope of the total cost curve.

TABLE 22-1

Costs at Selena's Gourmet Salsas

Quantity of salsa Q (cases)	Fixed cost FC	Variable cost VC	Total cost $TC = FC + VC$	Marginal cost of case $MC = \Delta TC/\Delta Q$
0	$108	$0	$108	
				$12
1	108	12	120	
				36
2	108	48	156	
				60
3	108	108	216	
				84
4	108	192	300	
				108
5	108	300	408	
				132
6	108	432	540	
				156
7	108	588	696	
				180
8	108	768	876	
				204
9	108	972	1,080	
				228
10	108	1,200	1,308	

Now we can understand why the total cost curve gets steeper as it increases from left to right: as you can see in Table 22-1, marginal cost at Selena's Gourmet Salsas rises as output increases. And because marginal cost equals the slope of the total cost curve, a higher marginal cost means a steeper slope. Panel (b) of Figure 22-2 shows the marginal cost curve corresponding to the data in Table 22-1. Notice that we plot the marginal cost for increasing output from 0 to 1 case of salsa halfway between 0

FIGURE 22-2 Total Cost and Marginal Cost Curves for Selena's Gourmet Salsas

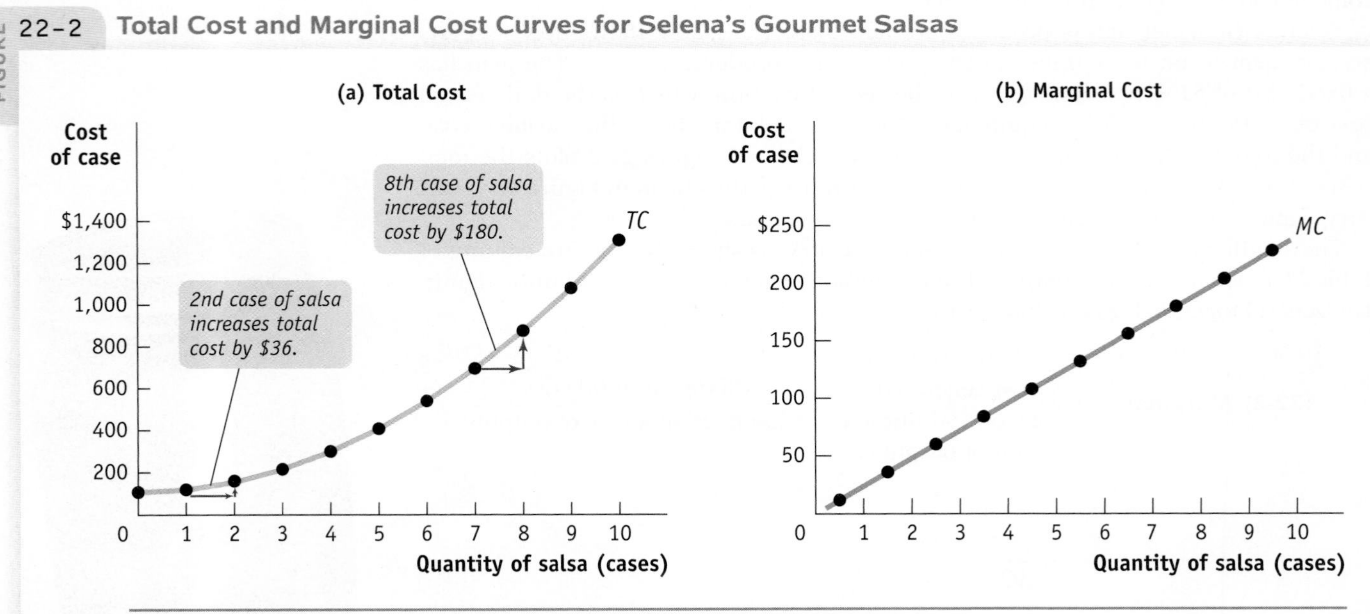

Panel (a) shows the total cost curve from Table 22-1. Like the total cost curve in Figure 22-1, it slopes upward and gets steeper as we move up it to the right. Panel (b) shows the marginal cost curve. It also slopes upward, reflecting diminishing returns to the variable input.

and 1, the marginal cost for increasing output from 1 to 2 cases of salsa halfway between 1 and 2, and so on.

Why does the marginal cost curve slope upward? Because there are diminishing returns to inputs in this example. As output increases, the marginal product of the variable input declines. This implies that more and more of the variable input must be used to produce each additional unit of output as the amount of output already produced rises. And since each unit of the variable input must be paid for, the additional cost per additional unit of output also rises.

Recall that the flattening of the total product curve is also due to diminishing returns: if the quantities of other inputs are fixed, the marginal product of an input falls as more of that input is used. The flattening of the total product curve as output increases and the steepening of the total cost curve as output increases are just flip-sides of the same phenomenon. That is, as output increases, the marginal cost of output also increases because the marginal product of the variable input decreases. Our next step is to introduce another measure of cost: *average cost.*

Average total cost, often referred to simply as **average cost,** is total cost divided by quantity of output produced.

Average Total Cost

In addition to total cost and marginal cost, it's useful to calculate **average total cost,** often simply called **average cost.** The average total cost is total cost divided by the quantity of output produced; that is, it is equal to total cost per unit of output. If we let *ATC* denote average total cost, the equation looks like this:

$$\textbf{(22-3)}\quad ATC = \frac{\text{Total cost}}{\text{Quantity of output}} = \frac{TC}{Q}$$

Average total cost is important because it tells the producer how much the *average* or *typical* unit of output costs to produce. Marginal cost, meanwhile, tells the producer how much *one more* unit of output costs to produce. Although they may look very similar, these two measures of cost typically differ. And confusion between them is a major source of error in economics, both in the classroom and in real life.

Table 22-2 uses data from Selena's Gourmet Salsas to calculate average total cost. For example, the total cost of producing 4 cases of salsa is $300, consisting of $108 in fixed cost and $192 in variable cost (from Table 22-1 So the average total cost of producing 4 cases of salsa is $300/4 = $75. You can see from Table 22-2 that as the quantity of output increases, average total cost first falls, then rises.

Alamy

Average total cost tells producers how much the *typical* unit of output costs to produce; marginal cost tells them how much *one more unit* of output costs to produce.

TABLE 22-2

Average Costs for Selena's Gourmet Salsas

Quantity of salsa *Q* (cases)	Total cost *TC*	Average total cost of case *ATC = TC/Q*	Average fixed cost of case *AFC = FC/Q*	Average variable cost of case *AVC = VC/Q*
1	$120	$120.00	$108.00	$12.00
2	156	78.00	54.00	24.00
3	216	72.00	36.00	36.00
4	300	75.00	27.00	48.00
5	408	81.60	21.60	60.00
6	540	90.00	18.00	72.00
7	696	99.43	15.43	84.00
8	876	109.50	13.50	96.00
9	1,080	120.00	12.00	108.00
10	1,308	130.80	10.80	120.00

FIGURE 22-3 Average Total Cost Curve for Selena's Gourmet Salsas

The average total cost curve at Selena's Gourmet Salsas is U-shaped. At low levels of output, average total cost falls because the "spreading effect" of falling average fixed cost dominates the "diminishing returns effect" of rising average variable cost. At higher levels of output, the opposite is true and average total cost rises. At point *M*, corresponding to an output of three cases of salsa per day, average total cost is at its minimum level, the minimum average total cost.

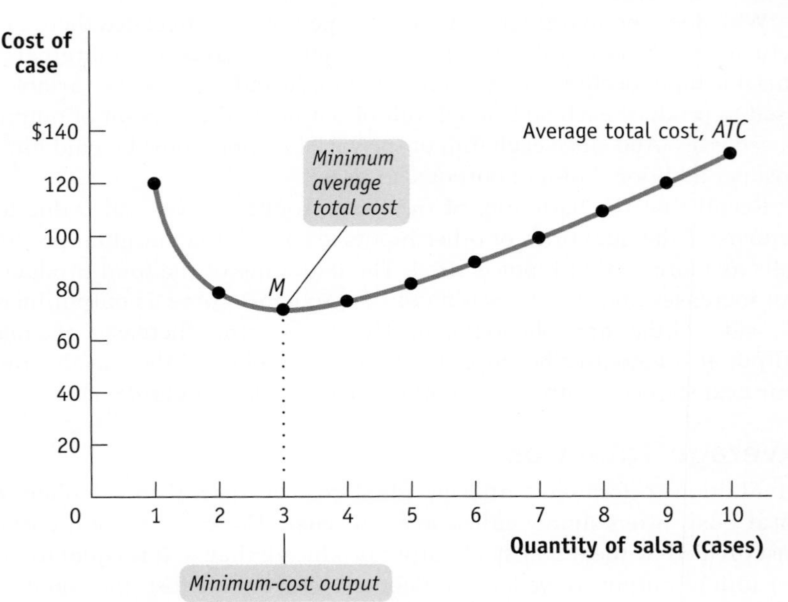

Figure 22-3 plots that data to yield the *average total cost curve,* which shows how average total cost depends on output. As before, cost in dollars is measured on the vertical axis and quantity of output is measured on the horizontal axis. The average total cost curve has a distinctive U shape that corresponds to how average total cost first falls and then rises as output increases. Economists believe that such **U-shaped average total cost curves** are the norm for firms in many industries.

To help our understanding of why the average total cost curve is U-shaped, Table 22-2 breaks average total cost into its two underlying components, *average fixed cost* and *average variable cost.* **Average fixed cost,** or *AFC,* is fixed cost divided by the quantity of output, also known as the fixed cost per unit of output. For example, if Selena's Gourmet Salsas produces 4 cases of salsa, average fixed cost is $108/4 = $27 per case. **Average variable cost,** or *AVC,* is variable cost divided by the quantity of output, also known as variable cost per unit of output. At an output of 4 cases, average variable cost is $192/4 = $48 per case. Writing these in the form of equations:

$$\textbf{(22-4)}\quad AFC = \frac{\text{Fixed cost}}{\text{Quantity of output}} = \frac{FC}{Q}$$

$$AVC = \frac{\text{Variable cost}}{\text{Quantity of output}} = \frac{VC}{Q}$$

Average total cost is the sum of average fixed cost and average variable cost; it has a U shape because these components move in opposite directions as output rises.

Average fixed cost falls as more output is produced because the numerator (the fixed cost) is a fixed number but the denominator (the quantity of output) increases as more is produced. Another way to think about this relationship is that, as more output is produced, the fixed cost is spread over more units of output; the end result is that the fixed cost *per unit of output*—the average fixed cost—falls.

You can see this effect in the fourth column of Table 22-2: average fixed cost drops continuously as output increases.

Average variable cost, however, rises as output increases. As we've seen, this reflects diminishing returns to the variable input: each additional unit of output adds more to variable cost than the previous unit because increasing amounts of the variable input are required to make another unit.

A **U-shaped average total cost curve** falls at low levels of output and then rises at higher levels.

Average fixed cost is the fixed cost per unit of output.

Average variable cost is the variable cost per unit of output.

So increasing output has two opposing effects on average total cost—the "spreading effect" and the "diminishing returns effect":

1. *The spreading effect.* The larger the output, the greater the quantity of output over which fixed cost is spread, leading to lower average fixed cost.
2. *The diminishing returns effect.* The larger the output, the greater the amount of variable input required to produce additional units, leading to higher average variable cost.

At low levels of output, the spreading effect is very powerful because even small increases in output cause large reductions in average fixed cost. So at low levels of output, the spreading effect dominates the diminishing returns effect and causes the average total cost curve to slope downward.

But when output is large, average fixed cost is already quite small, so increasing output further has only a very small spreading effect. Diminishing returns, however, usually grow increasingly important as output rises. As a result, when output is large, the diminishing returns effect dominates the spreading effect, causing the average total cost curve to slope upward.

At the bottom of the U-shaped average total cost curve, point *M* in Figure 22-3, the two effects exactly balance each other. At this point average total cost is at its minimum level, the minimum average total cost.

Figure 22-4 brings together in a single picture the four other cost curves that we have derived from the total cost curve for Selena's Gourmet Salsas: the marginal cost curve (*MC*), the average total cost curve (*ATC*), the average variable cost curve (*AVC*), and the average fixed cost curve (*AFC*). All are based on the information in Tables 22-1 and 22-2. As before, cost is measured on the vertical axis and the quantity of output is measured on the horizontal axis.

Photodisc

Let's take a moment to note some features of the various cost curves. First of all, marginal cost slopes upward—the result of diminishing returns that make an additional unit of output more costly to produce than the one before. Average variable cost also slopes upward—again, due to diminishing returns—but is flatter than the marginal cost curve. This is because the higher cost of an additional

FIGURE 22-4 **Marginal Cost and Average Cost Curves for Selena's Gourmet Salsas**

Here we have the family of cost curves for Selena's Gourmet Salsas: the marginal cost curve (*MC*), the average total cost curve (*ATC*), the average variable cost curve (*AVC*), and the average fixed cost curve (*AFC*). Note that the average total cost curve is U-shaped and the marginal cost curve crosses the average total cost curve at the bottom of the U, point *M*, corresponding to the minimum average total cost from Table 22-2 and Figure 22-3.

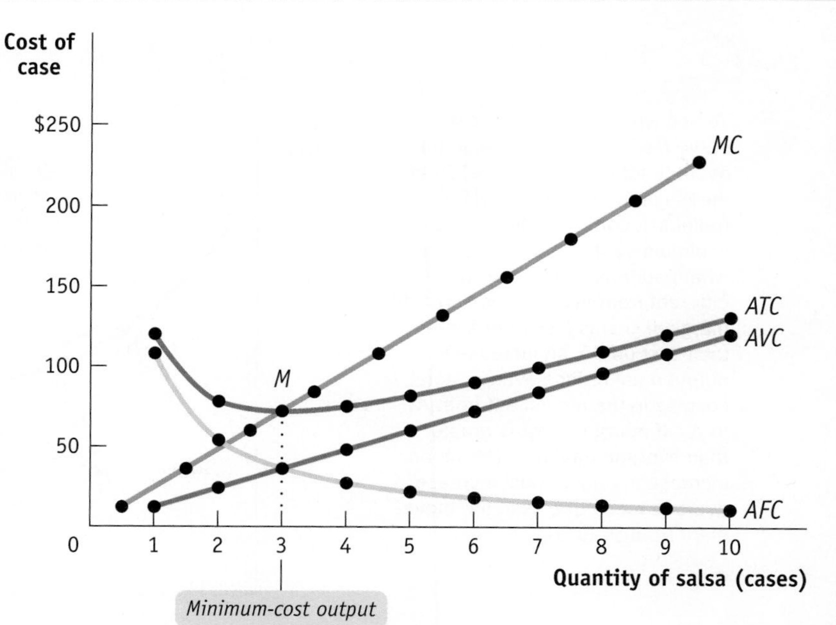

The **minimum-cost output** is the quantity of output at which average total cost is lowest—it corresponds to the bottom of the U-shaped average total cost curve.

unit of output is averaged across all units, not just the additional unit, in the average variable cost measure. Meanwhile, average fixed cost slopes downward because of the spreading effect.

Finally, notice that the marginal cost curve intersects the average total cost curve from below, crossing it at its lowest point, point M in Figure 22-4. This last feature is our next subject of study.

Minimum Average Total Cost

For a U-shaped average total cost curve, average total cost is at its minimum level at the bottom of the U. Economists call the quantity of output that corresponds to the minimum average total cost the **minimum-cost output.** In the case of Selena's Gourmet Salsas, the minimum-cost output is three cases of salsa per day.

In Figure 22-4, the bottom of the U is at the level of output at which the marginal cost curve crosses the average total cost curve from below. Is this an accident? No—it reflects three general principles that are always true about a firm's marginal cost and average total cost curves:

1. At the minimum-cost output, average total cost *is equal to* marginal cost.
2. At output less than the minimum-cost output, marginal cost *is less than* average total cost and average total cost is falling.
3. And at output greater than the minimum-cost output, marginal cost *is greater than* average total cost and average total cost is rising.

To understand these principles, think about how your grade in one course—say, a 3.0 in physics—affects your overall grade point average (GPA). If your GPA before receiving that grade was more than 3.0, the new grade lowers your average.

Similarly, if marginal cost—the cost of producing one more unit—is less than average total cost, producing that extra unit lowers average total cost. This is shown in Figure 22-5 by the movement from A_1 to A_2. In this case, the marginal cost of producing an additional unit of output is low, as indicated by the point MC_L on the marginal cost curve. When the cost of producing the next unit of output is less than average total cost, increasing production reduces average total cost. So any quantity of output at which marginal cost is less than average total cost must be on the downward-sloping segment of the U.

FIGURE 22-5 **The Relationship Between the Average Total Cost and the Marginal Cost Curves**

To see why the marginal cost curve (MC) must cut through the average total cost curve (ATC) at the minimum average total cost (point M), corresponding to the minimum-cost output, we look at what happens if marginal cost is different from average total cost. If marginal cost is *less* than average total cost (MC_L), an increase in output must reduce average total cost, as in the movement from A_1 to A_2. If marginal cost is *greater* than average total cost (MC_H), an increase in output must increase average total cost, as in the movement from B_1 to B_2.

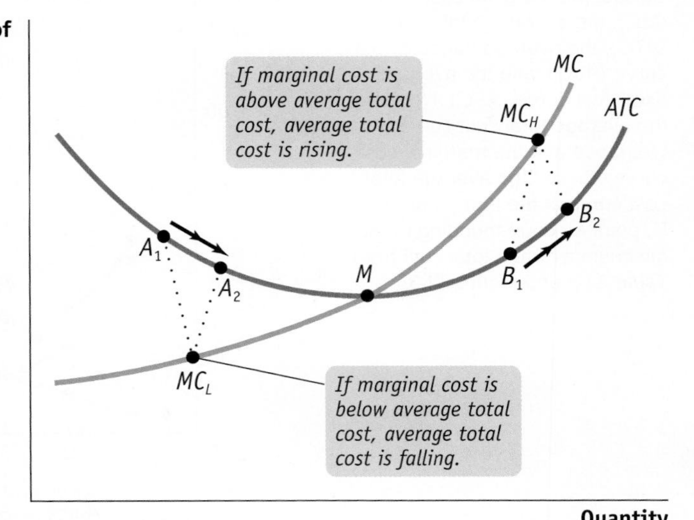

But if your grade in physics is more than the average of your previous grades, this new grade raises your GPA. Similarly, if marginal cost is greater than average total cost, producing that extra unit raises average total cost. This is illustrated by the movement from B_1 to B_2 in Figure 22-5, where the marginal cost, MC_H, is higher than average total cost. So any quantity of output at which marginal cost is greater than average total cost must be on the upward-sloping segment of the U.

Finally, if a new grade is exactly equal to your previous GPA, the additional grade neither raises nor lowers that average—it stays the same. This corresponds to point M in Figure 22-5: when marginal cost equals average total cost, we must be at the bottom of the U because only at that point is average total cost neither falling nor rising.

ECONOMICS ▶ IN ACTION

DON'T PUT OUT THE WELCOME MAT

Brand X Pictures

A new housing development leads to higher taxes for everyone in the neighborhood.

Housing developments have traditionally been considered as American as apple pie. With our abundant supply of undeveloped land, real estate developers have long found it profitable to buy big parcels of land, build a large number of homes, and create entire new communities. But what is profitable for developers is not necessarily good for the existing residents.

Of late, real estate developers have encountered increasingly stiff resistance from local residents because of the additional costs—the marginal costs—imposed on existing homeowners from new developments. Let's look at why.

In the United States, a large percentage of the funding for local services comes from taxes paid by local homeowners. In a sense, the local township authority uses those taxes to "produce" municipal services for the town. The overall level of property taxes is set to reflect the costs of providing those services. The highest service cost by far, in most communities, is the cost of public education.

The local tax rate that new homeowners pay on their new homes is the same as what existing homeowners pay on their older homes. That tax rate reflects the current total cost of services, and the taxes that an average homeowner pays reflect the average total cost of providing services to a household. The average total cost of providing services is based on the town's use of existing facilities, such as the existing school buildings, the existing number of teachers, the existing fleet of school buses, and so on.

But when a large development of homes is constructed, those facilities are no longer adequate: new schools must be built, new teachers hired, and so on. The quantity of output increases. So the *marginal cost* of providing municipal services per household associated with a new, large-scale development turns out to be much higher than the *average total cost* per household of existing homes. As a result, new developments and facilities cause everyone's local tax rate to go up, just as you would expect from Figure 22-5.

A recent study in Massachusetts estimated that a $250,000 new home with one school-age child imposed an additional cost to the community of $5,527 per year over and above the taxes paid by the new homeowners. As a result, in many towns across America, potential new housing developments and newcomers are now facing a distinctly chilly reception.

Does the Marginal Cost Curve Always Slope Upward?

Up to this point, we have emphasized the importance of diminishing returns, which lead to a marginal product curve that always slopes downward and a marginal cost curve that always slopes upward. In practice, however, economists believe that marginal cost curves often slope *downward* as a firm increases its production from zero

FIGURE 22-6 More Realistic Cost Curves

A realistic marginal cost curve has a "swoosh" shape. Starting from a very low output level, marginal cost often falls as the firm increases output. That's because hiring additional workers allows for specialization of their tasks and leads to increasing returns. Once specialization is achieved, however, diminishing returns to additional workers set in and marginal cost rises. The corresponding average variable cost curve is now U-shaped, like the average total cost curve.

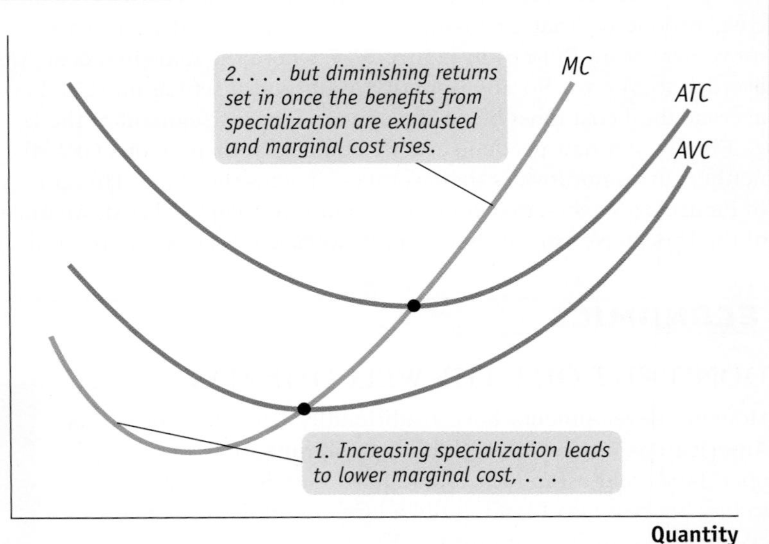

up to some low level, sloping upward only at higher levels of production: marginal cost curves look like the curve labeled *MC* in Figure 22-6.

This initial downward slope occurs because a firm often finds that, when it starts with only a very small number of workers, employing more workers and expanding output allows its workers to specialize in various tasks. This, in turn, lowers the firm's marginal cost as it expands output. For example, one individual producing salsa would have to perform all the tasks involved: selecting and preparing the ingredients, mixing the salsa, bottling and labeling it, packing it into cases, and so on.

As more workers are employed, they can divide the tasks, with each worker specializing in one or a few aspects of salsa-making. This specialization leads to *increasing returns* to the hiring of additional workers and results in a marginal cost curve that initially slopes downward. But once there are enough workers to have completely exhausted the benefits of further specialization, diminishing returns to labor set in and the marginal cost curve changes direction and slopes upward. So typical marginal cost curves actually have the "swoosh" shape shown by *MC* in Figure 22-6. For the same reason, average variable cost curves typically look like *AVC* in Figure 22-6: they are U-shaped rather than strictly upward sloping.

However, as Figure 22-6 also shows, the key features we saw from the example of Selena's Gourmet Salsas remain true: the average total cost curve is U-shaped, and the marginal cost curve passes through the point of minimum average total cost.

MODULE 22 Review

Solutions appear at the back of the book.

Check Your Understanding

1. Alicia's Apple Pies is a roadside business. Alicia must pay \$9.00 in rent each day. In addition, it costs her \$1.00 to produce the first pie of the day, and each subsequent pie costs 50% more to produce than the one before. For example, the second pie costs \$1.00 × 1.5 = \$1.50 to produce, and so on.

   a. Calculate Alicia's marginal cost, variable cost, average fixed cost, average variable cost, and average total cost as her daily pie output rises from 0 to 6. (*Hint:* The variable cost of two pies is just the marginal cost of the first pie, plus the marginal cost of the second, and so on.)

b. Indicate the range of pies for which the spreading effect dominates and the range for which the diminishing returns effect dominates.

c. What is Alicia's minimum-cost output? Explain why making one more pie lowers Alicia's average total cost when output is lower than the minimum-cost output. Similarly, explain why making one more pie raises Alicia's average total cost when output is greater than the minimum-cost output.

Multiple-Choice Questions

1. When a firm is producing zero output, total cost equals
   a. zero.
   b. variable cost.
   c. fixed cost.
   d. average total cost.
   e. marginal cost.

2. Which of the following statements is true?
   I. Marginal cost is the change in total cost generated by one additional unit of output.
   II. Marginal cost is the change in variable cost generated by one additional unit of output.
   III. The marginal cost curve must cross the minimum of the average total cost curve.
   a. I only
   b. II only
   c. III only
   d. I and II only
   e. I, II, and III

3. Which of the following is correct?
   a. AVC is the change in total cost generated by one additional unit of output.
   b. MC = TC/Q
   c. The average cost curve crosses at the minimum of the marginal cost curve.
   d. The AFC curve slopes upward.
   e. AVC = ATC – AFC

4. The slope of the total cost curve equals
   a. variable cost.
   b. average variable cost.
   c. average total cost.
   d. average fixed cost.
   e. marginal cost.

5. On the basis of the data in the table, what is the marginal cost of the third unit of output?

Q	*VC*	*TC*
0	$0	$40
1	20	60
2	50	90
3	90	130
4	140	180
5	200	240

   a. 40
   b. 50
   c. 60
   d. 90
   e. 130

Critical-Thinking Question

Draw a correctly labeled graph showing a firm with an upward sloping *MC* curve and typically shaped *ATC, AVC,* and *AFC* curves.

Long-Run Costs and Economies of Scale

iStockphoto

WHAT YOU WILL LEARN

1. Why a firm's costs may differ in the short run versus the long run
2. How the firm's technology of production can generate increasing returns to scale

Up to this point, we have treated fixed cost as completely outside the control of a firm because we have focused on the short run. But all inputs are variable in the long run: this means that in the long run, even "fixed cost" may change. *In the long run, in other words, a firm's fixed cost becomes a variable it can choose.* For example, given time, Selena's Gourmet Salsas can acquire additional food-preparation equipment or dispose of some of its existing equipment. In this module, we will examine how a firm's costs behave in the short run and in the long run. We will also see that the firm will choose its fixed cost in the long run based on the level of output it expects to produce.

Short-Run versus Long-Run Costs

Let's begin by supposing that Selena's Gourmet Salsas is considering whether to acquire additional food-preparation equipment. Acquiring additional machinery will affect its total cost in two ways. First, the firm will have to rent or buy the additional equipment; either way, that will mean a higher fixed cost in the short run. Second, if the workers have more equipment, they will be more productive: fewer workers will be needed to produce any given output, so variable cost for any given output level will be reduced.

The table in Figure 23-1 shows how acquiring an additional machine affects costs. In our original example, we assumed that Selena's Gourmet Salsas had a fixed cost of \$108. The left half of the table shows variable cost as well as total cost and average total cost assuming a fixed cost of \$108. The average total cost curve for this level of fixed cost is given by ATC_1 in Figure 23-1. Let's compare that to a situation in which the firm buys additional food-preparation equipment, doubling its fixed cost to \$216 but reducing its variable cost at any given level of output. The right half of the table shows the firm's variable cost, total cost, and average total cost with this higher level of fixed cost. The average total cost curve corresponding to \$216 in fixed cost is given by ATC_2 in Figure 23-1.

From the figure you can see that when output is small, 4 cases of salsa per day or fewer, average total cost is smaller when Selena forgoes the additional equipment and maintains the lower fixed cost of \$108: ATC_1 lies below ATC_2. For example, at 3 cases per day, average total cost is \$72 without the additional machinery and \$90 with the additional machinery. But as output increases beyond 4 cases per day, the firm's average total cost is lower if it acquires the additional equipment, raising its fixed cost to \$216. For example, at 9 cases of salsa per day, average total cost is \$120 when fixed cost is \$108 but only \$78 when fixed cost is \$216.

Why does average total cost change like this when fixed cost increases? When output is low, the increase in fixed cost from the additional equipment outweighs the reduction in variable cost from higher worker productivity—that is, there are too few units of output over which to spread the additional fixed cost. So if Selena plans to produce 4 or fewer cases per day, she would be better off choosing the lower level of fixed cost, \$108, to achieve a lower average total cost of production. When planned output is high, however, she should acquire the additional machinery.

In general, for each output level there is some choice of fixed cost that minimizes the firm's average total cost for that output level. So when the firm has a desired output level that it expects to maintain over time, it should choose the optimal fixed cost for that level—that is, the level of fixed cost that minimizes its average total cost.

Now that we are studying a situation in which fixed cost can change, we need to take *time* into account when discussing average total cost. All of the average total cost curves we have considered until now are defined for a given level of fixed cost—that is, they are defined for the short run, the period of time over which fixed cost doesn't

FIGURE 23-1 **Choosing the Level of Fixed Cost for Selena's Gourmet Salsas**

There is a trade-off between higher fixed cost and lower variable cost for any given output level, and vice versa. ATC_1 is the average total cost curve corresponding to a fixed cost of \$108; it leads to lower fixed cost and higher variable cost. ATC_2 is the average total cost curve corresponding to a higher fixed cost of \$216 but lower variable cost. At low output levels, at 4 or fewer cases of salsa per day, ATC_1 lies below ATC_2: average total cost is lower with only \$108 in fixed cost. But as output goes up, average total cost is lower with the higher amount of fixed cost, \$216: at more than 4 cases of salsa per day, ATC_2 lies below ATC_1.

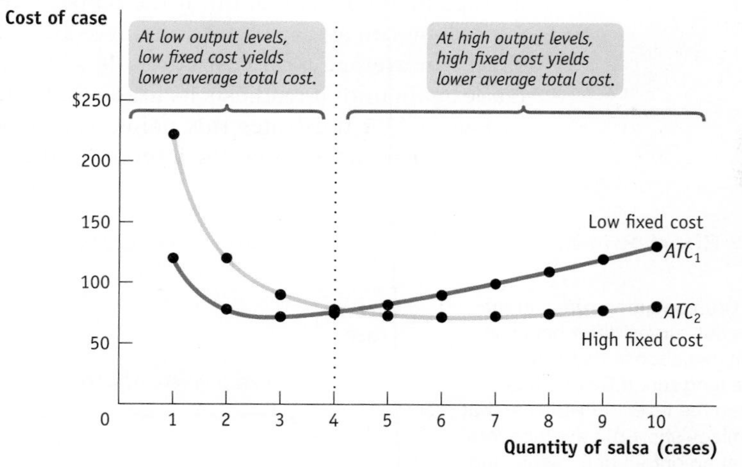

Quantity of salsa (cases)	Low fixed cost (*FC* = \$108) High variable cost	Total cost	Average total cost of case ATC_1	High fixed cost (*FC* = \$216) Low variable cost	Total cost	Average total cost of case ATC_2
1	\$12	\$120	\$120.00	\$6	\$222	\$222.00
2	48	156	78.00	24	240	120.00
3	108	216	72.00	54	270	90.00
4	192	300	75.00	96	312	78.00
5	300	408	81.60	150	366	73.20
6	432	540	90.00	216	432	72.00
7	588	696	99.43	294	510	72.86
8	768	876	109.50	384	600	75.00
9	972	1,080	120.00	486	702	78.00
10	1,200	1,308	130.80	600	816	81.60

The **long-run average total cost curve** shows the relationship between output and average total cost when fixed cost has been chosen to minimize average total cost for each level of output.

vary. To reinforce that distinction, for the rest of this module we will refer to these average total cost curves as "short-run average total cost curves."

For most firms, it is realistic to assume that there are many possible choices of fixed cost, not just two. The implication: for such a firm, many possible short-run average total cost curves will exist, each corresponding to a different choice of fixed cost and so giving rise to what is called a firm's "family" of short-run average total cost curves.

At any given time, a firm will find itself on one of its short-run cost curves, the one corresponding to its current level of fixed cost; a change in output will cause it to move along that curve. If the firm expects that change in output level to be long-standing, then it is likely that the firm's current level of fixed cost is no longer optimal. Given sufficient time, it will want to adjust its fixed cost to a new level that minimizes average total cost for its new output level. For example, if Selena had been producing 2 cases of salsa per day with a fixed cost of $108 but found herself increasing her output to 8 cases per day for the foreseeable future, then in the long run she should purchase more equipment and increase her fixed cost to a level that minimizes average total cost at the 8-cases-per-day output level.

Suppose we do a thought experiment and calculate the lowest possible average total cost that can be achieved for each output level if the firm were to choose its fixed cost for each output level. Economists have given this thought experiment a name: the *long-run average total cost curve*. Specifically, the **long-run average total cost curve,** or *LRATC,* is the relationship between output and average total cost when fixed cost has been chosen to minimize average total cost *for each level of output*. If there are many possible choices of fixed cost, the long-run average total cost curve will have the familiar, smooth U shape, as shown by *LRATC* in Figure 23-2.

We can now draw the distinction between the short run and the long run more fully. In the long run, when a producer has had time to choose the fixed cost appropriate for its desired level of output, that producer will be at some point on the long-run average total cost curve. But if the output level is altered, the firm will no longer be on its long-run average total cost curve and will instead be moving along its current short-run average total cost curve. It will not be on its long-run average total cost curve again until it readjusts its fixed cost for its new output level.

Figure 23-2 illustrates this point. The curve ATC_3 shows short-run average total cost if Selena has chosen the level of fixed cost that minimizes average total cost at

FIGURE 23-2 **Short-Run and Long-Run Average Total Cost Curves**

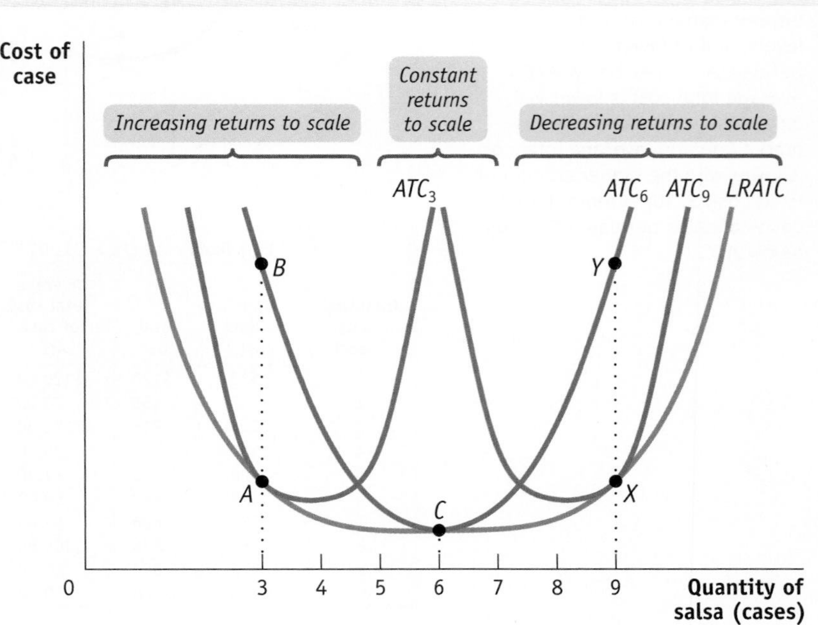

Short-run and long-run average total cost curves differ because a firm can choose its fixed cost in the long run. If Selena has chosen the level of fixed cost that minimizes short-run average total cost at an output of 6 cases, and actually produces 6 cases, then she will be at point *C* on *LRATC* and ATC_6. But if she produces only 3 cases, she will move to point *B*. If she expects to produce only 3 cases for a long time, in the long run she will reduce her fixed cost and move to point *A* on ATC_3. Likewise, if she produces 9 cases (putting her at point *Y*) and expects to continue this for a long time, she will increase her fixed cost in the long run and move to point *X*.

an output of 3 cases of salsa per day. This is confirmed by the fact that at 3 cases per day, ATC_3 touches $LRATC$, the long-run average total cost curve. Similarly, ATC_6 shows short-run average total cost if Selena has chosen the level of fixed cost that minimizes average total cost if her output is 6 cases per day. It touches $LRATC$ at 6 cases per day. And ATC_9 shows short-run average total cost if Selena has chosen the level of fixed cost that minimizes average total cost if her output is 9 cases per day. It touches $LRATC$ at 9 cases per day.

Suppose that Selena initially chose to be on ATC_6. If she actually produces 6 cases of salsa per day, her firm will be at point C on both its short-run and long-run average total cost curves. Suppose, however, that Selena ends up producing only 3 cases of salsa per day. In the short run, her average total cost is indicated by point B on ATC_6; it is no longer on $LRATC$. If Selena had known that she would be producing only 3 cases per day, she would have been better off choosing a lower level of fixed cost, the one corresponding to ATC_3, thereby achieving a lower average total cost. Then her firm would have found itself at point A on the long-run average total cost curve, which lies below point B.

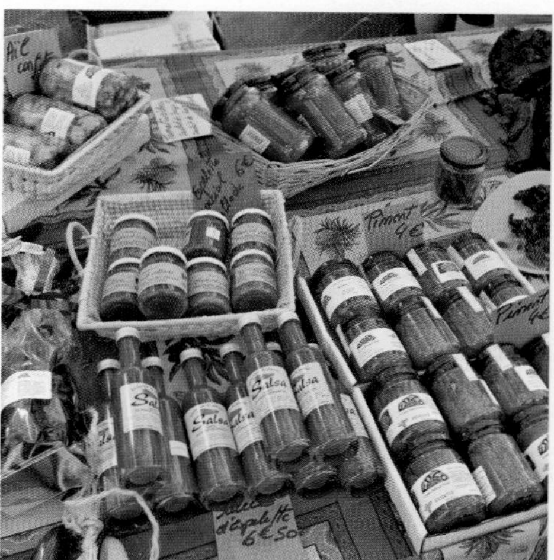
Egmont Strigl/Westend61/Superstock

To understand how firms operate over time, be sure to distinguish between short-run and long-run average total costs.

Suppose, conversely, that Selena ends up producing 9 cases per day even though she initially chose to be on ATC_6. In the short run her average total cost is indicated by point Y on ATC_6. But she would be better off purchasing more equipment and incurring a higher fixed cost in order to reduce her variable cost and move to ATC_9. This would allow her to reach point X on the long-run average total cost curve, which lies below Y.

The distinction between short-run and long-run average total costs is extremely important in making sense of how real firms operate over time. A company that has to increase output suddenly to meet a surge in demand will typically find that in the short run its average total cost rises sharply because it is hard to get extra production out of existing facilities. But given time to build new factories or add machinery, short-run average total cost falls.

Returns to Scale

What determines the shape of the long-run average total cost curve? It is the influence of *scale,* the size of a firm's operations, on its long-run average total cost of production. Firms that experience *scale effects* in production find that their long-run average total cost changes substantially depending on the quantity of output they produce.

There are **increasing returns to scale** (also known as *economies of scale*) when long-run average total cost declines as output increases. As you can see in Figure 23-2, Selena's Gourmet Salsas experiences increasing returns to scale over output levels ranging from 0 up to 5 cases of salsa per day—the output levels over which the long-run average total cost curve is declining. In contrast, there are **decreasing returns to scale** (also known as *diseconomies of scale*) when long-run average total cost increases as output increases.

For Selena's Gourmet Salsas, decreasing returns to scale occur at output levels greater than 7 cases, the output levels over which its long-run average total cost curve is rising. There is also a third possible relationship between long-run average total cost and scale: firms experience **constant returns to scale** when long-run average total cost is constant as output increases. In this case, the firm's long-run average total cost curve is horizontal over the output levels for which there are constant returns to scale. As you can see in Figure 23-2, Selena's Gourmet Salsas has constant returns to scale when it produces anywhere from 5 to 7 cases of salsa per day.

There are **increasing returns to scale** when long-run average total cost declines as output increases.

There are **decreasing returns to scale** when long-run average total cost increases as output increases.

There are **constant returns to scale** when long-run average total cost is constant as output increases.

What explains these scale effects in production? The answer ultimately lies in the firm's technology of production. Economies of scale often arise from the increased *specialization* that larger output levels allow—a larger scale of operation means that individual workers can limit themselves to more specialized tasks, becoming more skilled and efficient at doing them. Another source of economies of scale is a very large initial setup cost; in some industries—such as auto manufacturing, electricity generating, and petroleum refining—it is necessary to pay a high fixed cost in the form of plant and equipment before producing any output. A third source of economies of scale, found in certain high-tech industries such as software development, is *network externalities,* a topic covered in a later module. As we'll see when we study monopoly, increasing returns have very important implications for how firms and industries behave and interact.

ECONOMICS IN ACTION

THERE'S NO BUSINESS LIKE SNOW BUSINESS

iStockphoto/Thinkstock

A lesson in returns to scale: cities with higher average annual snowfall maintain larger snowplow fleets.

Anyone who has lived both in a snowy city, like Chicago, and in a city that only occasionally experiences significant snowfall, like Washington, D.C., is aware of the differences in total cost that arise from making different choices about fixed cost.

In Washington, even a minor snowfall—say, an inch or two overnight—is enough to create chaos during the next morning's commute. The same snowfall in Chicago has hardly any effect at all. The reason is not that Washingtonians are wimps and Chicagoans are made of sterner stuff; it is that Washington, where it rarely snows, has only a fraction as many snowplows and other snow-clearing equipment as cities where heavy snow is a fact of life.

In this sense Washington and Chicago are like two producers who expect to produce different levels of output, where the "output" is snow removal. Washington, which rarely has significant snow, has chosen a low level of fixed cost in the form of snow-clearing equipment. This makes sense under normal circumstances but leaves the city unprepared when major snow does fall. Chicago, which knows that it will face lots of snow, chooses to accept the higher fixed cost that leaves it in a position to respond effectively.

Diseconomies of scale—the opposite scenario—typically arise in large firms due to problems of coordination and communication: as a firm grows in size, it becomes ever more difficult and therefore costly to communicate and to organize activities. Although economies of scale induce firms to grow larger, diseconomies of scale tend to limit their size.

And when there are constant returns to scale, scale has no effect on a firm's long-run average total cost: it is the same regardless of whether the firm produces one unit or 100,000 units.

Summing Up Costs: The Short and Long of It

If a firm is to make the best decisions about how much to produce, it has to understand how its costs relate to the quantity of output it chooses to produce. Table 23-1 provides a quick summary of the concepts and measures of cost you have learned about.

TABLE 23-1

Concepts and Measures of Cost

	Measurement	Definition	Mathematical term
Short run	Fixed cost	Cost that does not depend on the quantity of output produced	*FC*
	Average fixed cost	Fixed cost per unit of output	$AFC = FC/Q$
Short run and long run	Variable cost	Cost that depends on the quantity of output produced	*VC*
	Average variable cost	Variable cost per unit of output	$AVC = VC/Q$
	Total cost	The sum of fixed cost (short run) and variable cost	$TC = FC$ (short run) $+ VC$
	Average total cost (average cost)	Total cost per unit of output	$ATC = TC/Q$
	Marginal cost	The change in total cost generated by producing one more unit of output	$MC = \Delta TC/\Delta Q$
Long run	Long-run average total cost	Average total cost when fixed cost has been chosen to minimize average total cost for each level of output	*LRATC*

MODULE 23 Review

Solutions appear at the back of the book.

Check Your Understanding

1. The accompanying table shows three possible combinations of fixed cost and average variable cost. Average variable cost is constant in this example. (It does not vary with the quantity of output produced.)

Choice	Fixed cost	Average variable cost
1	$8,000	$1.00
2	12,000	0.75
3	24,000	0.25

   a. For each of the three choices, calculate the average total cost of producing 12,000, 22,000, and 30,000 units. For each of these quantities, which choice results in the lowest average total cost?

   b. Suppose that the firm, which has historically produced 12,000 units, experiences a sharp, permanent increase in demand that leads it to produce 22,000 units. Explain how its average total cost will change in the short run and in the long run.

   c. Explain what the firm should do instead if it believes the change in demand is temporary.

2. In each of the following cases, explain whether the firm is likely to experience economies of scale or diseconomies of scale and why.

   a. an interior design firm in which design projects are based on the expertise of the firm's owner

   b. a diamond-mining company

Multiple-Choice Questions

1. In the long run,
   a. all inputs are variable.
   b. all inputs are fixed.
   c. some inputs are variable and others are fixed.
   d. a firm will go out of business.
   e. firms increase in size.

2. Which of the following is always considered the long run?
   a. 1 month
   b. 1 year
   c. 5 years
   d. 10 years
   e. none of the above

3. Which of the following statements is generally correct?
   I. The long-run average total cost curve is U-shaped.
   II. The short-run average total cost curve is U-shaped.
   III. Firms tend to experience economies of scale at low levels of production and diseconomies of scale at high levels of production.
   a. I only
   b. II only
   c. III only
   d. I and II only
   e. I, II, and III

4. A firm is at the minimum of its short run average cost curve, but also experiencing diseconomies of scale. A permanent increase in output will:
   a. lower the number of units produced.
   b. lower average total cost in the short run.
   c. lower average total cost in the long run.
   d. increase average total cost in the long run.
   e. not change average total cost in the long run.

5. Economies of scale will allow which of the following types of cities to lower their average total cost of clearing snow by investing in larger snow plow fleets? Cities with
   a. more people.
   b. more existing snow plows.
   c. less snowfall.
   d. larger budgets.
   e. more snowfall.

Critical-Thinking Question

Draw a correctly labeled graph showing a short-run average total cost curve and the corresponding long-run average total cost curve. On your graph, identify the areas of economies and diseconomies of scale.

BUSINESS CASE • Kiva Systems' Robots versus Humans: The Challenge of Holiday Order Fulfillment

For those who like to procrastinate when it comes to holiday shopping, the rise of e-commerce has been a welcome phenomenon. Amazon.com boasts that in 2012, customers living in 11 cities in the United States could receive same-day delivery for orders placed on the day before Christmas.

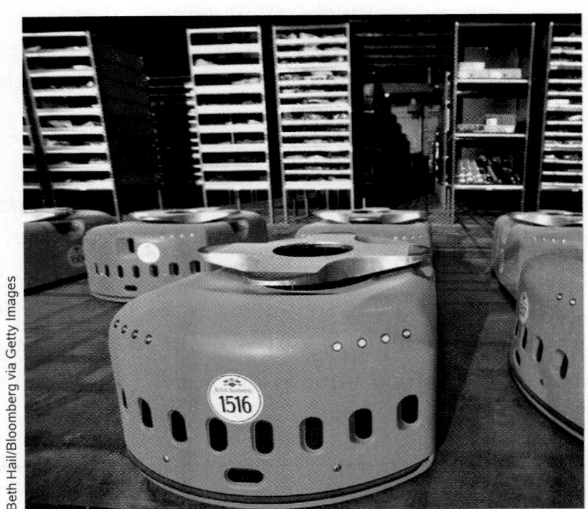

Beth Hall/Bloomberg via Getty Images

E-commerce retailers like Amazon.com and Crateand-Barrel.com can see their sales quadruple for the holidays. With advances in order fulfillment technology that get customers' orders to them quickly, e-commerce sellers have been able to capture an ever-greater share of sales from brick-and-mortar retailers. Holiday sales at e-commerce sites grew by over 13% from 2011 to 2012.

Behind these technological advances, however, lies an intense debate: people versus robots. Amazon has relied on a large staff of temporary workers to get it through the previous holiday seasons, often quadrupling its staff and operating 24 hours a day. In contrast, Crate and Barrel only doubled its workforce, thanks to a cadre of orange robots that allows each worker to do the work of six people.

But, Amazon is set to increase its robotic work force in the future. In May of 2012, Amazon bought Kiva Systems, the leader in order fulfillment robotics, for $775 million, with the hope of tailoring Kiva's systems to best fit Amazon's warehouse and fulfillment needs.

Although many retailers—Staples, Gap, Saks Fifth Avenue, and Walgreens, for example—also use Kiva equipment, installation of a robotic system can be expensive, with some installations costing as much as $20 million. Yet hiring workers has a cost, too: during the 2010 holiday season, before it had installed an extensive robotic system, Amazon hired some 12,500 temporary workers at its 20 distribution centers around the United States.

As one industry analyst noted, an obstacle to the purchase of a robotic system for many e-commerce retailers is that it often doesn't make economic sense: it's too expensive to buy sufficient robots for the busiest time of the year because they would be idle at other times. Before Amazon's purchase, Kiva was testing a program to rent out its robots seasonally so that retailers could "hire" enough robots to handle their holiday orders just like Amazon used to hire more humans.

Questions for Thought

1. Assume that a firm can sell a robot, but that the sale takes time and the firm is likely to get less than what it paid. Other things equal, which system, human-based or robotic, will have a higher fixed cost? Which will have a higher variable cost? Explain.
2. What pattern of off-holiday sales versus holiday sales would induce a retailer to keep a human-based system? What pattern would induce a retailer to move to a robotic system?
3. How would a "robot-for-hire" program affect your answer to Question 2? Explain.

SECTION 8 REVIEW

Summary

The Production Function

1. The relationship between inputs and output is represented by a firm's **production function.** In the **short run,** the quantity of a **fixed input** cannot be varied but the quantity of a **variable input,** by definition, can. In the **long run,** the quantities of all inputs can be varied. For a given amount of the fixed input, the **total product curve** shows how the quantity of output changes as the quantity of the variable input changes. The **marginal product** of an input is the increase in output that results from using one more unit of that input.
2. There are **diminishing returns to an input** when its marginal product declines as more of the input is used, holding the quantity of all other inputs fixed.

Firm Costs

3. **Total cost,** represented by the **total cost curve,** is equal to the sum of **fixed cost,** which does not depend on output, and **variable cost,** which does depend on output. Due to diminishing returns, marginal cost, the increase in total cost generated by producing one more unit of output, normally increases as output increases.
4. **Average total cost** (also known as **average cost**) is the total cost divided by the quantity of output. Economists believe that **U-shaped average total cost curves** are typical because average total cost consists of two parts: **average fixed cost,** which falls when output increases (the spreading effect), and **average variable cost,** which rises with output (the diminishing returns effect).
5. When average total cost is U-shaped, the bottom of the U is the level of output at which average total cost is minimized, the point of **minimum-cost output.** This is also the point at which the **marginal cost curve** crosses the average total cost curve from below. Due to gains from specialization, the marginal cost curve may slope downward initially before sloping upward, giving it a "swoosh" shape.

Long-Run Costs and Economies of Scale

6. In the long run, a firm can change its fixed input and its level of fixed cost. By accepting higher fixed cost, a firm can lower its variable cost for any given output level, and vice versa. The **long-run average total cost curve** shows the relationship between output and average total cost when fixed cost has been chosen to minimize average total cost at each level of output. A firm moves along its short-run average total cost curve as it changes the quantity of output, and it returns to a point on both its short-run and long-run average total cost curves once it has adjusted fixed cost to its new output level.
7. As output increases, long-run average total cost changes. There are **increasing returns to scale** if long-run average total cost falls as output rises; **decreasing returns to scale** if long-run average cost rises as output rises; and **constant returns to scale** if long-run average total cost does not change as output rises.

Key Terms

Production function, p. 230
Fixed input, p. 230
Variable input, p. 230
Long run, p. 230
Short run, p. 230
Total product curve, p. 231
Marginal product, p. 231
Diminishing returns to an input, p. 233
Fixed cost, p. 237
Variable cost, p. 237
Total cost, p. 237
Total cost curve, p. 238
Average total cost, p. 241
Average cost, p. 241
U-shaped average total cost curve, p. 242
Average fixed cost, p. 242
Average variable cost, p. 242
Minimum-cost output, p. 244
Long-run average total cost curve, p. 250
Increasing returns to scale, p. 251
Decreasing returns to scale, p. 251
Constant returns to scale, p. 251

Problems

1. Changes in the prices of key commodities can have a significant impact on a company's bottom line. According to an article in the *Wall Street Journal,* "Now, with oil, gas and electricity prices soaring, companies are beginning to realize that saving energy can translate into dramatically lower costs." Another *Wall Street Journal* article states, "Higher grain prices are taking an increasing financial toll." Energy is an input into virtually all types of production; corn is an input into the production of beef, chicken, high-fructose corn syrup, and ethanol (the gasoline substitute fuel).

   a. Explain how the cost of energy can be both a fixed cost and a variable cost for a company.

b. Suppose energy is a fixed cost and energy prices rise. What happens to the company's average total cost curve? What happens to its marginal cost curve? Illustrate your answer with a diagram.

c. Explain why the cost of corn is a variable cost but not a fixed cost for an ethanol producer.

d. When the cost of corn goes up, what happens to the average total cost curve of an ethanol producer? What happens to its marginal cost curve? Illustrate your answer with a diagram.

2. Marty's Frozen Yogurt is a small shop that sells cups of frozen yogurt in a university town. Marty owns three frozen-yogurt machines. His other inputs are refrigerators, frozen-yogurt mix, cups, sprinkle toppings, and, of course, workers. He estimates that his daily production function when he varies the number of workers employed (and at the same time, of course, yogurt mix, cups, and so on) is as shown in the accompanying table.

Quantity of labor (workers)	Quantity of frozen yogurt (cups)
0	0
1	110
2	200
3	270
4	300
5	320
6	330

a. What are the fixed inputs and variable inputs in the production of cups of frozen yogurt?

b. Draw the total product curve. Put the quantity of labor on the horizontal axis and the quantity of frozen yogurt on the vertical axis.

c. What is the marginal product of the first worker? The second worker? The third worker? Why does marginal product decline as the number of workers increases?

3. The production function for Marty's Frozen Yogurt is given in Problem 2. Marty pays each of his workers \$80 per day. The cost of his other variable inputs is \$0.50 per cup of yogurt. His fixed cost is \$100 per day.

a. What is Marty's variable cost and total cost when he produces 110 cups of yogurt? 200 cups? Calculate variable and total cost for every level of output given in Problem 2.

b. Draw Marty's variable cost curve. On the same diagram, draw his total cost curve.

c. What is the marginal cost per cup for the first 110 cups of yogurt? For the next 90 cups? Calculate the marginal cost for all remaining levels of output.

4. The production function for Marty's Frozen Yogurt is given in Problem 2. The costs are given in Problem 3.

a. For each of the given levels of output, calculate the average fixed cost (*AFC*), average variable cost (*AVC*), and average total cost (*ATC*) per cup of frozen yogurt.

b. On one diagram, draw the *AFC*, *AVC*, and *ATC* curves.

c. What principle explains why the *AFC* declines as output increases? What principle explains why the *AVC* increases as output increases? Explain your answers.

d. How many cups of frozen yogurt are produced when average total cost is minimized?

5. The accompanying table shows a car manufacturer's total cost of producing cars.

Quantity of cars	*TC*
0	\$500,000
1	540,000
2	560,000
3	570,000
4	590,000
5	620,000
6	660,000
7	720,000
8	800,000
9	920,000
10	1,100,000

a. What is this manufacturer's fixed cost?

b. For each level of output, calculate the variable cost (*VC*). For each level of output except zero, calculate the average variable cost (*AVC*), average total cost (*ATC*), and average fixed cost (*AFC*). What is the minimum-cost output?

c. For each level of output, calculate this manufacturer's marginal cost (*MC*).

d. On one diagram, draw the manufacturer's *AVC*, *ATC*, and *MC* curves.

6. Labor costs represent a large percentage of total costs for many firms. Assume that in September 2013 U.S. labor costs were up 0.9% during the preceding three months and 0.8% over the three months preceding those.

a. When labor costs increase, what happens to average total cost and marginal cost? Consider a case in which labor costs are only variable costs and a case in which they are both variable and fixed costs.

An increase in labor productivity means each worker can produce more output. Recent data on productivity show that labor productivity in the U.S. nonfarm business sector grew 2% for each of the years 2011, 2012, and 2013. Annual growth in labor productivity averaged 1.5% from the mid-1970s to mid-1990s, 2.6% in the past decade, and 4% for a couple of years in the early 2000s.

b. When productivity growth is positive, what happens to the total product curve and the marginal product of labor curve? Illustrate your answer with a diagram.

c. When productivity growth is positive, what happens to the marginal cost curve and the average total cost curve? Illustrate your answer with a diagram.

d. If labor costs are rising over time on average, why would a company want to adopt equipment and methods that increase labor productivity?

7. Magnificent Blooms is a florist specializing in floral arrangements for weddings, graduations, and other events. The firm has a fixed cost associated with space and equipment of \$100 per day. Each worker is paid \$50 per day. The daily production function for Magnificent Blooms is shown in the accompanying table.

Quantity of labor (workers)	Quantity of floral arrangements
0	0
1	5
2	9
3	12
4	14
5	15

a. Calculate the marginal product of each worker. What principle explains why the marginal product per worker declines as the number of workers employed increases?

b. Calculate the marginal cost of each level of output. What principle explains why the marginal cost per floral arrangement increases as the number of arrangements increases?

8. You have the information shown in the accompanying table about a firm's costs. Complete the missing data.

Quantity	*TC*	*MC*	*ATC*	*AVC*
0	\$20		—	—
		\$20		
1	?		?	?
		10		
2	?		?	?
		16		
3	?		?	?
		20		
4	?		?	?
		24		
5	?		?	?

9. Evaluate each of the following statements. If a statement is true, explain why; if it is false, identify the mistake and try to correct it.

a. A decreasing marginal product tells us that marginal cost must be rising.

b. An increase in fixed cost increases the minimum-cost output.

c. An increase in fixed cost increases marginal cost.

d. When marginal cost is above average total cost, average total cost must be falling.

10. Mark and Jeff operate a small company that produces souvenir footballs. Their fixed cost is \$2,000 per month. They can hire workers for \$1,000 per worker per month. Their monthly production function for footballs is as given in the accompanying table.

Quantity of labor (workers)	Quantity of footballs
0	0
1	300
2	800
3	1,200
4	1,400
5	1,500

a. For each quantity of labor, calculate average variable cost (*AVC*), average fixed cost (*AFC*), average total cost (*ATC*), and marginal cost (*MC*).

b. On one diagram, draw the *AVC*, *ATC*, and *MC* curves.

c. At what level of output is Mark and Jeff's average total cost minimized?

11. You produce widgets. Currently you produce four widgets at a total cost of \$40.

a. What is your average total cost?

b. Suppose you could produce one more (the fifth) widget at a marginal cost of \$5. If you do produce that fifth widget, what will your average total cost be? Has your average total cost increased or decreased? Why?

c. Suppose instead that you could produce one more (the fifth) widget at a marginal cost of \$20. If you do produce that fifth widget, what will your average total cost be? Has your average total cost increased or decreased? Why?

Coca-Cola
pepsi
ORGANIC!
TOMATOES!
FIRST OF SEASON

SECTION 9

Market Structure and Perfect Competition

DOING WHAT COMES NATURALLY

Food consumers in the United States are concerned about health issues. Demand for natural foods and beverages, such as bottled water and organically grown fruits and vegetables, increased rapidly over the past 25 years at an average growth rate of about 20% per year. The small group of farmers who had pioneered organic farming techniques prospered thanks to higher prices.

But everyone knew that the high prices of organic produce were unlikely to persist even if the new, higher demand for naturally grown food continued: the supply of organic food, although relatively price-inelastic in the short run, was surely price-elastic in the long run. Over time, farms already producing organically would increase their capacity, and conventional farmers would enter the organic food business. So the increase in the quantity supplied in response to the increase in price would be much larger in the long run than in the short run.

Where does the market supply curve come from? Why is there a difference between the short-run and the long-run supply curve? In this section we will use our understanding of costs, developed in Section 8, as the basis for an analysis of the market supply curve. As we'll see, this will require that we understand the behavior both of individual firms and of an entire industry, composed of these many individual firms.

Our analysis in this section assumes that the industry in question is characterized by *perfect competition.* We begin with an introduction to *market structures,* a system economists use to classify markets and industries according to two main dimensions. Perfect competition is actually one particular type of market structure, along with monopoly, oligopoly, and monopolistic competition (we will look at these three other types of market structures in upcoming sections). We continue by explaining the concept of perfect competition, providing a brief introduction to the conditions that give rise to a perfectly competitive industry. Then we show how a producer under perfect competition decides how much to produce. Finally, we use the cost curves of the individual producers to derive the *industry supply curve* under perfect competition.

By analyzing the way a competitive industry evolves over time, we will come to understand the distinction between the short-run and long-run effects of changes in demand on a competitive industry—for example, the effect of America's new taste for organic food on the organic farming industry. We conclude with a more in-depth discussion of the conditions necessary for an industry to be perfectly competitive.

MODULE

24 Introduction to Market Structure

Richard B. Levine/Alamy

WHAT YOU WILL LEARN

1. **The meaning and dimensions of market structure**
2. **The four principal types of market structure—perfect competition, monopoly, oligopoly, and monopolistic competition**

To discuss the supply curve in a market, we need to identify the type of market we are looking at. In this module we will learn about the basic characteristics of the four major types of markets in the economy.

Types of Market Structure

The real world holds a mind-boggling array of different markets. Patterns of firm behavior vary as widely as the markets themselves: in some markets firms are extremely competitive; in others, they seem somehow to coordinate their actions to limit competition; and some markets are monopolies in which there is no competition at all.

In order to develop principles and make predictions about markets and firm behavior, economists have developed four primary models of market structure: *perfect competition, monopoly, oligopoly,* and *monopolistic competition*. This system of market structure is based on two dimensions:

1. the number of firms in the market (one, few, or many)
2. whether the goods offered are identical or *differentiated*.

Differentiated goods are goods that are different but considered at least somewhat substitutable by consumers—think Coke versus Pepsi.

Figure 24-1 provides a simple visual summary of the types of market structure classified according to the two dimensions. In *perfect competition* many firms each sell an identical product. In *monopoly,* a single firm sells a single, undifferentiated product. In *oligopoly,* a few firms—more than one but not a large number—sell products that may be either identical or differentiated. And in *monopolistic competition,* many firms each sell a differentiated product—think of producers of economics textbooks.

FIGURE 24-1 Types of Market Structure

The behavior of any given firm and the market it occupies are analyzed using one of four models of market structure—monopoly, oligopoly, perfect competition, or monopolistic competition. This system for categorizing market structure is based on two dimensions: (1) whether products are differentiated or identical and (2) the number of firms in the industry—one, a few, or many.

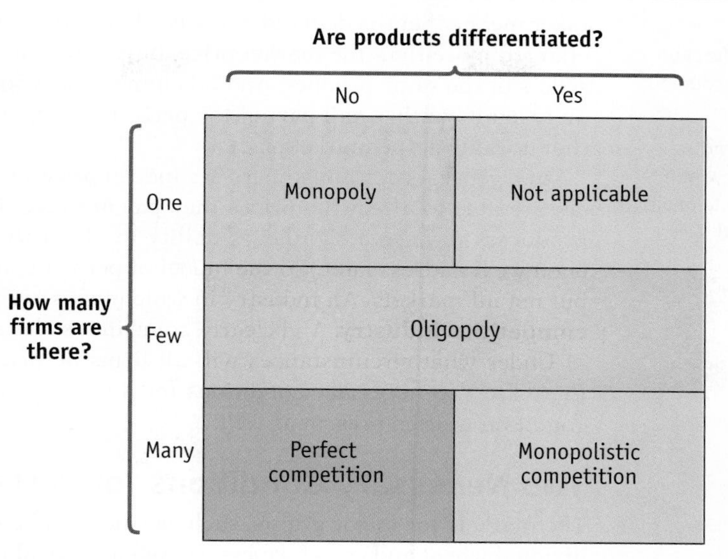

Perfect Competition

Suppose that Yves and Zoe are neighboring farmers, both of whom grow organic tomatoes. Both sell their output to the same grocery store chains that carry organic foods; so, in a real sense, Yves and Zoe compete with each other.

Does this mean that Yves should try to stop Zoe from growing tomatoes or that Yves and Zoe should form an agreement to grow fewer? Almost certainly not: there are hundreds or thousands of organic tomato farmers, and Yves and Zoe are competing with all those other growers as well as with each other. Because so many farmers sell organic tomatoes, if any one of them produced more or fewer, there would be no measurable effect on market prices.

When people talk about business competition, they often imagine a situation in which two or three rival firms are struggling for advantage. But economists know that when a business focuses on a few main competitors, it's actually a sign that competition is fairly limited. As the example of organic tomatoes suggests, when the number of competitors is large, it doesn't even make sense to identify rivals and engage in aggressive competition because each firm is too small within the scope of the market to make a significant difference.

We can put it another way: Yves and Zoe are *price-takers*. A firm or producer is a **price-taker** when its actions cannot affect the market price of the good or service it sells. As a result, a price-taking firm takes the market price as given. When there is enough competition—when competition is what economists call "perfect"—then every firm is a price-taker. There is a similar definition for consumers: a **price-taking consumer** is a consumer who cannot influence the market price of the good or service by his or her actions. That is, the market price is unaffected by how much or how little of the good the consumer buys.

The actions of a **price-taking firm** have no effect on the market price of the good or service it sells.

A **price-taking consumer** is a consumer whose actions have no effect on the market price of the good or service he or she buys.

A **perfectly competitive market** is a market in which all market participants are price-takers.

Defining Perfect Competition

In a **perfectly competitive market,** all market participants, both consumers and producers, are price-takers. That is, neither consumption decisions by individual consumers nor production decisions by individual producers affect the market price of the good.

The supply and demand model is a model of a perfectly competitive market. It depends fundamentally on the assumption that no individual buyer or seller of a good,

A **perfectly competitive industry** is an industry in which firms are price-takers.

A firm's **market share** is the fraction of the total industry output accounted for by that firm's output.

A good is a **standardized product**, also known as a **commodity**, when consumers regard the products of different firms as the same good.

such as raw cotton or organic tomatoes, believes that it is possible to individually affect the price at which he or she can buy or sell the good. For a firm, being a price-taker means that the demand curve is a horizontal line at the market price. If the firm charged more than the market price, buyers would go to any of the many alternative sellers of the same product. And it is unnecessary to charge a lower price because, as an insignificantly small part of the perfectly competitive market, the firm can sell all that it wants at the market price.

As a general rule, consumers are indeed price-takers. Instances in which consumers are able to affect the prices they pay are rare. It is, however, quite common for producers to have a significant ability to affect the prices they receive, a phenomenon we'll address later. So the model of perfect competition is appropriate for some but not all markets. An industry in which firms are price-takers is called a **perfectly competitive industry.** And clearly, some industries aren't perfectly competitive.

Under what circumstances will all firms be price-takers? As we'll discover next, there are two necessary conditions for a perfectly competitive industry and a third condition is often present as well.

Two Necessary Conditions for Perfect Competition

The markets for major grains, such as wheat and corn, are perfectly competitive: individual wheat and corn farmers, as well as individual buyers of wheat and corn, take market prices as given. In contrast, the markets for some of the food items made from these grains—in particular, breakfast cereals—are by no means perfectly competitive. There is intense competition among cereal brands, but not *perfect* competition. To understand the difference between the market for wheat and the market for shredded wheat cereal is to understand the two necessary conditions for perfect competition.

1. AN INDUSTRY MUST CONTAIN MANY FIRMS, EACH HAVING A SMALL MARKET SHARE For an industry to be perfectly competitive, it must contain many firms, none of whom have a large **market share.** A firm's market share is the fraction of the total industry output accounted for by that firm's output.

The distribution of market share constitutes a major difference between the grain industry and the breakfast cereal industry. There are thousands of wheat farmers, none of whom account for more than a tiny fraction of total wheat sales. The breakfast cereal industry, however, is dominated by four firms: Kellogg's, General Mills, Post, and Quaker Foods. Kellogg's alone accounts for about one-third of all cereal sales. Kellogg's executives know that if they try to sell more corn flakes, they are likely to drive down the market price of corn flakes. That is, they know that their actions influence market prices—due to their tremendous size, changes in their production will significantly affect the overall quantity supplied. It makes sense to assume that firms are price-takers only when they are numerous and relatively small.

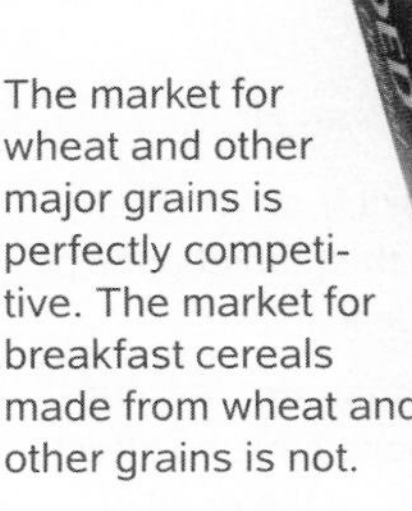

The market for wheat and other major grains is perfectly competitive. The market for breakfast cereals made from wheat and other grains is not.

The Photo Works

2. THE INDUSTRY MUST PRODUCE A STANDARDIZED PRODUCT An industry can be perfectly competitive only if consumers regard the products of all firms as equivalent. This clearly isn't true in the breakfast cereal market: consumers don't consider Cap'n Crunch to be a good substitute for Shredded Wheat. As a result, the maker of Shredded Wheat has some ability to increase its price without fear that it will lose all its customers to the maker of Cap'n Crunch.

Contrast this with the case of a **standardized product,** sometimes known as a **commodity,** which is a product that consumers regard as the same good even when it comes from different firms. Because wheat is a standardized product, consumers regard the output of one wheat producer as a perfect substitute for that of another producer. Consequently, one farmer cannot increase the price for his or her wheat without losing all sales to other wheat farmers. So the second necessary condition for a perfectly competitive industry is that the industry output is a standardized product. (See the upcoming Economics in Action.)

ECONOMICS ▶ IN ACTION

WHAT'S A STANDARDIZED PRODUCT?

A perfectly competitive industry must produce a standardized product. But is it enough for the products of different firms actually to be the same? No: people must also *think* that they are the same. And producers often go to great lengths to convince consumers that they have a distinctive, or *differentiated,* product, even when they don't.

Consider, for example, champagne—not the super-expensive premium champagnes, but the more ordinary stuff. Most people cannot tell the difference between champagne actually produced in the Champagne region of France, where the product originated, and similar products from Spain or California. But the French government has sought and obtained legal protection for the winemakers of Champagne, ensuring that around the world only bubbly wine from that region can be called champagne. If it's from someplace else, all the seller can do is say that it was produced using the *méthode Champenoise.* This creates a differentiation in the minds of consumers and lets the champagne producers of Champagne charge higher prices.

Similarly, Korean producers of *kimchi,* the spicy fermented cabbage that is the Korean national side dish, are doing their best to convince consumers that the same product packaged by Japanese firms is just not the real thing. The purpose is, of course, to ensure higher prices for Korean *kimchi.*

© Gabriel Pent/Dreamstime.com

In the end, only discerning *kimchi* eaters can tell you if there is truly a difference between Korean-produced *kimchi* and the Japanese-produced variety.

So is an industry perfectly competitive if it sells products that are indistinguishable except in name but that consumers, for whatever reason, don't think are standardized? No. When it comes to defining the nature of competition, the consumer is always right.

Free Entry and Exit

Most perfectly competitive industries are also characterized by one more feature: it is easy for new firms to enter the industry or for firms that are currently in the industry to leave. That is, no obstacles in the form of government regulations or limited access to key resources prevent new firms from entering the market. And no additional costs are associated with shutting down a company and leaving the industry. Economists refer to the arrival of new firms into an industry as *entry;* they refer to the departure of firms from an industry as *exit.* When there are no obstacles to entry into or exit from an industry, we say that the industry has **free entry and exit.**

Free entry and exit is not strictly necessary for perfect competition. However, it ensures that the number of firms in an industry can adjust to changing market conditions. And, in particular, it ensures that firms in an industry cannot act to keep other firms out.

To sum up, then, perfect competition depends on two necessary conditions. First, the industry must contain many firms, each having a small market share. Second, the industry must produce a standardized product. In addition, perfectly competitive industries are normally characterized by free entry and exit.

Monopoly

The De Beers diamond monopoly of South Africa was created in the 1880s by Cecil Rhodes, a British businessman. By 1880, mines in South Africa already dominated the world's supply of diamonds. There were, however, many mining companies, all competing with each other. During the 1880s Rhodes bought the great majority of those

An industry has **free entry and exit** when new firms can easily enter into the industry and existing firms can easily leave the industry.

A **monopolist** is the only producer of a good that has no close substitutes. An industry controlled by a monopolist is known as a **monopoly.**

To earn economic profits, a monopolist must be protected by a **barrier to entry**—something that prevents other firms from entering the industry.

A **natural monopoly** exists when economies of scale provide a large cost advantage to a single firm that produces all of an industry's output.

mines and consolidated them into a single company, De Beers. By 1889, De Beers controlled almost all of the world's diamond production.

De Beers, in other words, became a *monopolist*. But what does it mean to be a monopolist? And what do monopolists do?

Defining Monopoly

As we mentioned earlier, the supply and demand model of a market is not universally valid. Instead, it's a model of perfect competition, which is only one of several types of market structure. A market will be perfectly competitive only if there are many firms, all of which produce the same good. Monopoly is the most extreme departure from perfect competition.

A **monopolist** is a firm that is the only producer of a good that has no close substitutes. An industry controlled by a monopolist is known as a **monopoly.**

In practice, true monopolies are hard to find in the modern American economy, partly because of legal obstacles. A contemporary entrepreneur who tried to consolidate all the firms in an industry the way Rhodes did would soon find himself in court, accused of breaking *antitrust* laws, which are intended to prevent monopolies from emerging. Monopolies do, however, play an important role in some sectors of the economy.

Why Do Monopolies Exist?

A monopolist making profits will not go unnoticed by others. (Recall that we mean "economic profit," revenue over and above the opportunity costs of the firm's resources.) But won't other firms crash the party, grab a piece of the action, and drive down prices and profits in the long run?

If possible, yes, they will. For a profitable monopoly to persist, something must keep others from going into the same business; that "something" is known as a **barrier to entry.** There are four principal types of barriers to entry: control of a scarce resource or input, economies of scale, technological superiority, and government-created barriers.

CONTROL OF A SCARCE RESOURCE OR INPUT A monopolist that controls a resource or input crucial to an industry can prevent other firms from entering its market. Cecil Rhodes made De Beers into a monopolist by establishing control over the mines that produced the bulk of the world's diamonds.

ECONOMIES OF SCALE Many Americans have natural gas piped into their homes for cooking and heating. Invariably, the local gas company is a monopolist. But why don't rival companies compete to provide gas?

In the early nineteenth century, when the gas industry was just starting up, companies did compete for local customers. But this competition didn't last long; soon local gas companies became monopolists in almost every town because of the large fixed cost of providing a town with gas lines. The cost of laying gas lines didn't depend on how much gas a company sold, so a firm with a larger volume of sales had a cost advantage: because it was able to spread the fixed cost over a larger volume, it had a lower average total cost than smaller firms.

The natural gas industry is one in which average total cost falls as output increases, resulting in economies of scale and encouraging firms to grow larger. In an industry characterized by economies of scale, larger firms are more profitable and drive out smaller ones. For the same reason, established firms have a cost advantage over any potential entrant—a potent barrier to entry. So economies of scale can both give rise to and sustain a monopoly.

A monopoly created and sustained by economies of scale is called a **natural monopoly.** The defining characteristic of a natural monopoly is that it possesses economies of scale over the range of output that is relevant for the industry. The source of this condition is large fixed costs: when large fixed costs are required to operate, a given quantity of output is produced at lower average total cost by one large firm than by two or more smaller firms.

The most visible natural monopolies in the modern economy are local utilities—water, gas, electricity, local land line phone service, and, in most locations, cable television. As we'll see later, natural monopolies pose a special challenge to public policy.

TECHNOLOGICAL SUPERIORITY A firm that maintains a consistent technological advantage over potential competitors can establish itself as a monopolist. For example, from the 1970s through the 1990s, the chip manufacturer Intel was able to maintain a consistent advantage over potential competitors in both the design and production of microprocessors, the chips that run computers. But technological superiority is typically not a barrier to entry over the longer term: over time competitors will invest in upgrading their technology to match that of the technology leader. In fact, in the last few years Intel found its technological superiority eroded by a competitor, Advanced Micro Devices (also known as AMD), which was able to produce chips approximately as fast and as powerful as Intel chips.

We should note, however, that in certain high-tech industries, technological superiority is not a guarantee of success against competitors. Some high-tech industries are characterized by *network externalities,* a condition that arises when the value of a good to a consumer rises as the number of other people who also use the good rises. In these industries, the firm possessing the largest network—the largest number of consumers currently using its product—has an advantage over its competitors in attracting new customers. For example, think about the number of people who use Facebook. What value would Facebook have to consumers if only a few people had pages instead of the current 1 billion users worldwide? Users are attracted to Facebook precisely because so many other people are using it as well. Facebook has been cited as an example of a company with the potential to gain significant monopoly power in its industry through the phenomenon of network externalities.

Stephanie Pilick/picture-alliance/dpa/AP Images

Top social-media sites like Twitter (500 million users) and Tumblr (over 200 million users) have an advantage over their competition in attracting new customers.

GOVERNMENT-CREATED BARRIERS In 1998 the pharmaceutical company Merck introduced Propecia, a drug effective against baldness. Despite the fact that Propecia was very profitable and other drug companies had the know-how to produce it, no other firms challenged Merck's monopoly. That's because the U.S. government had given Merck the sole legal right to produce the drug in the United States. Propecia is an example of a monopoly protected by government-created barriers.

The most important legally created monopolies today arise from *patents* and *copyrights.* A **patent** gives an inventor the sole right to make, use, or sell that invention for a period that in most countries lasts between 16 and 20 years. Patents are given to the creators of new products, such as drugs or mechanical devices. Similarly, a **copyright** gives the creator of a literary or artistic work the sole right to profit from that work, usually for a period equal to the creator's lifetime plus 70 years.

The justification for patents and copyrights is a matter of incentives. If inventors were not protected by patents, they would gain little reward from their efforts: as soon as a valuable invention was made public, others would copy it and sell products based on it. And if inventors could not expect to profit from their inventions, then there would be no incentive to incur the costs of invention in the first place. Likewise for the creators of literary or artistic works. So the law allows a monopoly to exist temporarily by granting property rights that encourage invention and creation.

Patents and copyrights are temporary because the law strikes a compromise. The higher price for the good that holds while the legal protection is in effect compensates inventors for the cost of invention; conversely, the lower price that results once the legal protection lapses benefits consumers.

A **patent** gives an inventor a temporary monopoly in the use or sale of an invention.

A **copyright** gives the creator of a literary or artistic work the sole right to profit from that work.

An **oligopoly** is an industry with only a small number of firms. A producer in such an industry is known as an **oligopolist.**

When no one firm has a monopoly, but producers nonetheless realize that they can affect market prices, an industry is characterized by **imperfect competition.**

Because the lifetime of the temporary monopoly cannot be tailored to specific cases, this system is imperfect and leads to some missed opportunities. In some cases there can be significant welfare issues. For example, the violation of American drug patents by pharmaceutical companies in poor countries has been a major source of controversy, pitting the needs of poor patients who cannot afford to pay retail drug prices against the interests of drug manufacturers who have incurred high research costs to discover these drugs. To solve this problem, some American drug companies and poor countries have negotiated deals in which the patents are honored but the American companies sell their drugs at deeply discounted prices. (This is an example of *price discrimination,* which we'll learn more about in the next section.)

Oligopoly

An industry with only a few firms is known as an **oligopoly;** a producer in such an industry is known as an **oligopolist.**

Oligopolists compete with each other for sales. But oligopolists aren't like producers in a perfectly competitive industry, who take the market as given. Oligopolists know their decisions about how much to produce will affect the market price. That is, like monopolists, oligopolists have some *market power.*

Economists refer to a situation in which firms compete but also possess market power—which enables them to affect market prices—as **imperfect competition.** There are two important forms of imperfect competition: oligopoly and *monopolistic competition.* Of these, oligopoly is probably the more important in practice.

Many familiar goods and services are supplied by only a few competing sellers, which means the industries in question are oligopolies. For example, most air routes are served by only two or three airlines: in recent years, regularly scheduled shuttle service between New York and either Boston or Washington, D.C., has been provided only by Delta and US Airways. Three firms—Chiquita, Dole, and Del Monte, which own huge banana plantations in Central America—control 65% of world banana exports. Most cola beverages are sold by Coca-Cola and Pepsi. This list could go on for many pages.

© Colin Underhill/Alamy

Oligopolies supply familiar goods and services in a market with only a few competing sellers.

It's important to realize that an oligopoly isn't necessarily made up of large firms. What matters isn't size per se; the question is how many competitors there are. When a small town has only two grocery stores, grocery service there is just as much an oligopoly as air shuttle service between New York and Washington.

Why are oligopolies so prevalent? Essentially, an oligopoly is the result of the same factors that sometimes produce a monopoly, but in somewhat weaker form. Probably the most important source of oligopolies is the existence of economies of scale, which give bigger firms a cost advantage over smaller ones. When these effects are very strong, as we have seen, they lead to a monopoly; when they are not that strong, they lead to an industry with a small number of firms. For example, larger grocery stores typically have lower costs than smaller stores. But the advantages of large scale taper off once grocery stores are reasonably large, which is why two or three stores often survive in small towns.

Is It an Oligopoly or Not?

In practice, it is not always easy to determine an industry's market structure just by looking at the number of sellers. Many oligopolistic industries contain a number of small "niche" firms, which don't really compete with the major players. For example, the U.S. airline industry includes a number of regional airlines such as New Mexico Airlines, which flies propeller planes between Albuquerque and Carlsbad, New Mexico; if you count these carriers, the U.S. airline industry contains nearly one hundred firms, which doesn't sound like competition among a small group. But there are only a handful of national competitors like American and United, and on many routes, as we've seen, there are only two or three competitors.

To get a better picture of market structure, economists often use a measure called the **Herfindahl–Hirschman Index,** or HHI. The HHI for an industry is the square of each firm's share of market sales summed over the firms in the industry. The HHI takes into account the distribution of market sales among the top firms by squaring each firm's market share, thereby giving more weight to larger firms. For example, if an industry contains only 3 firms and their market shares are 60%, 25%, and 15%, then the HHI for the industry is:

Herfindahl–Hirschman Index, or HHI, is the square of each firm's share of market sales summed over the industry. It gives a picture of the industry market structure.

$$\text{HHI} = 60^2 + 25^2 + 15^2 = 4{,}450$$

By squaring each market share, the HHI calculation produces numbers that are much larger when a larger share of an industry output is dominated by fewer firms. So it's a better measure of just how concentrated the industry is. This is confirmed by the data in Table 24-1. Here, the indices for industries dominated by a small number of firms, like the personal computer operating systems industry or the wide-body aircraft industry, are many times larger than the index for the retail grocery industry, which has numerous firms of approximately equal size.

TABLE 24-1

The HHI for Some Oligopolistic Industries

Industry	HHI	Largest firms
PC operating systems	9,182	Microsoft, Linux
Wide-body aircraft	5,098	Boeing, Airbus
Diamond mining	2,338	De Beers, Alrosa, Rio Tinto
Automobiles	1,432	GM, Ford, Chrysler, Toyota, Honda, Nissan, VW
Movie distributors	1,096	Buena Vista, Sony Pictures, 20th Century Fox, Warner Bros., Universal, Paramount, Lionsgate
Internet service providers	750	SBC, Comcast, AOL, Verizon, Road Runner, Earthlink, Charter, Qwest
Retail grocers	321	Walmart, Kroger, Sears, Target, Costco, Walgreens, Ahold, Albertsons

Sources: Canadian Government; Diamond Facts 2006; www.w3counter.com; Planet retail; Autodata; Reuters; ISP Planet; Swivel. Data cover 2006–2007.

Monopolistic Competition

Leo manages the Wonderful Wok stand in the food court of a big shopping mall. He offers the only Chinese food there, but there are more than a dozen alternatives, from Bodacious Burgers to Pizza Paradise. When deciding what to charge for a meal, Leo knows that he must take those alternatives into account: even people who normally prefer stir-fry won't order a \$15 lunch from Leo when they can get a burger, fries, and drink for \$4.

But Leo also knows that he won't lose all his business even if his lunches cost a bit more than the alternatives. Chinese food isn't the same thing as burgers or pizza. Some people will really be in the mood for Chinese that day, and they will buy from Leo even if they could have dined more cheaply on burgers. Of course, the reverse is also true: even if Chinese is a bit cheaper, some people will choose burgers instead. In other words, Leo does have some market power: he has *some* ability to set his own price.

So how would you describe Leo's situation? He definitely isn't a price-taker, so he isn't in a situation of perfect competition. But you wouldn't exactly call him a monopolist, either. Although he's the only seller of Chinese food in that food court, he does face competition from other food vendors.

Yet it would also be wrong to call him an oligopolist. Oligopoly, remember, involves competition among a small number of interdependent firms in an industry protected

Monopolistic competition is a market structure in which there are many competing firms in an industry, each firm sells a differentiated product, and there is free entry into and exit from the industry in the long run.

by some—albeit limited—barriers to entry and whose profits are highly interdependent. Because their profits are highly interdependent, oligopolists have an incentive to collude, tacitly or explicitly. But in Leo's case there are *lots* of vendors in the shopping mall, too many to make tacit collusion feasible.

Defining Monopolistic Competition

Economists describe Leo's situation as one of **monopolistic competition.** Monopolistic competition is particularly common in service industries such as the restaurant and gas station industries, but it also exists in some manufacturing industries. It involves three conditions:

1. a large number of competing firms,
2. differentiated products, and
3. free entry into and exit from the industry in the long run.

In a monopolistically competitive industry, each producer has some ability to set the price of her differentiated product. But exactly how high she can set it is limited by the competition she faces from other existing and potential firms that produce close, but not identical, products.

LARGE NUMBERS In a monopolistically competitive industry there are many firms. Such an industry does not look either like a monopoly, where the firm faces no competition, or like an oligopoly, where each firm has only a few rivals. Instead, each seller has many competitors. For example, there are many vendors in a big food court, many gas stations along a major highway, and many hotels at a popular beach resort.

DIFFERENTIATED PRODUCTS In a monopolistically competitive industry, each firm has a product that consumers view as somewhat distinct from the products of competing firms. Such product differentiation can come in the form of different styles or types, different locations, or different levels of quality. At the same time, though, consumers see these competing products as close substitutes. If Leo's food court contained 15 vendors selling exactly the same kind and quality of food, there would be perfect competition: any seller who tried to charge a higher price would have no customers. But suppose that Wonderful Wok is the only Chinese food vendor, Bodacious Burgers is the only hamburger stand, and so on. The result of this differentiation is that each vendor has some ability to set his or her own price: each firm has some—albeit limited—market power.

© imac/Alamy

You'll find monopolistic competition in action in any food court, where restaurants like Burger King, TCBY, Popeyes, and others vie for your food dollar.

FREE ENTRY AND EXIT IN THE LONG RUN In monopolistically competitive industries, new firms, with their own distinct products, can enter the industry freely in the long run. For example, other food vendors would open outlets in the food court if they thought it would be profitable to do so. In addition, firms will exit the industry if they find they are not covering their costs in the long run.

Monopolistic competition, then, differs from the three market structures we have examined so far. It's not the same as perfect competition: firms have some power to set prices. It's not pure monopoly: firms face some competition. And it's not the same as oligopoly: there are many firms and free entry, which eliminates the potential for collusion that is so important in oligopoly. As we'll see in a later section, competition among the sellers of differentiated products is the key to understanding how monopolistic competition works.

Now that we have introduced the idea of market structure and presented the four principal models of market structure, we can proceed to explain and predict firm behavior (e.g., price and quantity determination) and analyze individual markets.

Module 24 Review

Solutions appear at the back of the book.

Check Your Understanding

1. In each of the following situations, what type of market structure do you think the industry represents?
   a. There are three producers of aluminum in the world, a good sold in many places.
   b. There are thousands of farms that produce indistinguishable soybeans to thousands of buyers.
   c. Many designers sell high-fashion clothes. Each designer has a distinctive style and a somewhat loyal clientele.
   d. A small town in the middle of Alaska has one bicycle shop.

Multiple-Choice Questions

1. Which of the following is true for a perfectly competitive industry?
   I. There are many firms, each with a large market share.
   II. The firms in the industry produce a standardized product.
   III. There are barriers to entry and exit.
   a. I only
   b. II only
   c. III only
   d. I and II only
   e. I, II, and III

2. Which of the following is true for a monopoly?
   I. There is only one firm.
   II. The firm produces a product with many close substitutes.
   III. The industry has free entry and exit.
   a. I only
   b. II only
   c. III only
   d. I and II only
   e. I, II, and III

3. Which of the following is true for an oligopoly?
   I. There are a few firms, each with a large market share.
   II. The firms in the industry are interdependent.
   III. The industry experiences diseconomies of scale.
   a. I only
   b. II only
   c. III only
   d. I and II only
   e. I, II, and III

4. Which of the following is true for a monopolistically competitive industry?
   I. There are many firms, each with a small market share.
   II. The firms in the industry produce a standardized product.
   III. Firms are price-takers.
   a. I only
   b. II only
   c. III only
   d. I and II only
   e. I, II, and III

5. Which of the following is an example of differentiated products?
   a. Coke and Pepsi
   b. automobiles and bicycles
   c. trucks and gasoline
   d. stocks and bonds
   e. gold and silver

Critical-Thinking Questions

1. Draw a correctly labeled graph of a perfectly competitive firm's demand curve if the market price is $10.
2. What does the firm's marginal revenue equal any time it sells one more unit of its output?

MODULE 25 Perfect Competition

iStockphoto

WHAT YOU WILL LEARN

1. **How a price-taking firm determines its profit-maximizing quantity of output**
2. **How to assess whether or not a competitive firm is profitable**

Recall the example of the market for organic tomatoes from the previous module. There, Yves and Zoe run organic tomato farms. But many other organic tomato farmers sell their output to the same grocery store chains. Since organic tomatoes are a standardized product, consumers don't care which farmer produces the organic tomatoes they buy. And because so many farmers sell organic tomatoes, no individual farmer has a large market share, which means that no individual farmer can have a measurable effect on market prices. These farmers are price-takers and their customers are price-taking consumers. The market for organic tomatoes meets the two necessary conditions for perfect competition: there are many producers each with a small market share, and the firms produce a standardized product. In this module we learn how to determine the quantity of output that would maximize a producer's profit as we build the model of perfect competition and use it to look at a representative firm in the market.

Production and Profits

Let's now consider Jennifer and Jason, who, like Yves and Zoe, run an organic tomato farm. Suppose that the market price of organic tomatoes is $18 per bushel and that Jennifer and Jason can sell as many as they would like at that price. We can use the data in Table 25-1 to find their profit-maximizing level of output.

The first column shows the quantity of output in bushels, and the second column shows Jennifer and Jason's total revenue from their output: the market value of their output. Total revenue, TR, is equal to the market price multiplied by the quantity of output:

(25-1) $TR = P \times Q$

TABLE 25-1

Profit for Jennifer and Jason's Farm When the Market Price Is $18

Quantity of tomatoes *Q* (bushels)	Total revenue *TR*	Total cost *TC*	Profit *TR* − *TC*
0	$0	$14	−$14
1	18	30	−12
2	36	36	0
3	54	44	10
4	72	56	16
5	90	72	18
6	108	92	16
7	126	116	10

In this example, total revenue is equal to $18 per bushel times the quantity of output in bushels.

The third column of Table 25-1 shows Jennifer and Jason's total cost, *TC*. The fourth column shows their profit, equal to total revenue minus total cost:

(25-2) $\text{Profit} = TR - TC$

As indicated by the numbers in the table, profit is maximized at an output of five bushels, where profit is equal to $18. But we can gain more insight into the profit-maximizing choice of output by viewing it as a problem of marginal analysis, a task we'll dive into next.

Using Marginal Analysis to Choose the Profit-Maximizing Quantity of Output

Recall from Module 18 the *profit-maximizing principle of marginal analysis:* the optimal amount of an activity is the level at which marginal benefit equals marginal cost. To apply this principle, consider the effect on a producer's profit of increasing output by one unit. The marginal benefit of that unit is the additional revenue generated by selling it; this measure has a name—it is called the **marginal revenue** of that unit of output. The general formula for marginal revenue is:

(25-3) $$\text{Marginal revenue} = \begin{array}{l}\text{Change in total}\\ \text{revenue generated}\\ \text{by one additional}\\ \text{unit of output}\end{array} = \frac{\text{Change in total revenue}}{\text{Change in quantity of output}}$$

or

$$MR = \Delta TR/\Delta Q$$

In this equation, the Greek uppercase delta (the triangular symbol) represents the change in a variable.

So Jennifer and Jason maximize their profit by producing bushels up to the point at which marginal revenue is equal to marginal cost. We can summarize this result as the producer's **optimal output rule,** which states that profit is maximized by producing the quantity at which the marginal revenue of the last unit produced is equal to its marginal cost. That is, $MR = MC$ at the optimal quantity of output.

Note that there may not be any particular quantity at which marginal revenue exactly equals marginal cost. In this case the producer should produce until one more unit would cause marginal benefit to fall below marginal cost. As a common simplification, we can think of marginal cost as rising steadily, rather than jumping from

Marginal revenue is the change in total revenue generated by an additional unit of output.

The **optimal output rule** says that profit is maximized by producing the quantity of output at which the marginal revenue of the last unit produced is equal to its marginal cost.

TABLE 25-2

Short-Run Costs for Jennifer and Jason's Farm

Quantity of tomatoes Q (bushels)	Total cost TC	Marginal cost of bushel $MC = \Delta TC/\Delta Q$	Marginal revenue of bushel MR	Net gain of bushel = $MR - MC$
0	$14			
		$16	$18	$2
1	30			
		6	18	12
2	36			
		8	18	10
3	44			
		12	18	6
4	56			
		16	18	2
5	72			
		20	18	−2
6	92			
		24	18	−6
7	116			

one level at one quantity to a different level at the next quantity. This ensures that marginal cost will equal marginal revenue at some quantity. We will now employ this simplified approach.

Consider Table 25-2, which provides cost and revenue data for Jennifer and Jason's farm. The second column contains the farm's total cost of output. The third column shows their marginal cost. Notice that, in this example, marginal cost initially falls as output rises but then begins to increase, so that the marginal cost curve has a "swoosh" shape. (Later you will see that this shape has important implications for short-run production decisions.)

The fourth column contains the farm's marginal revenue, which has an important feature: Jennifer and Jason's marginal revenue is assumed to be constant at $18 for every output level. The fifth and final column shows the calculation of the net gain per bushel of tomatoes, which is equal to marginal revenue minus marginal cost. As you can see, it is positive for the first through fifth bushels; producing each of these bushels raises Jennifer and Jason's profit. For the sixth and seventh bushels, however, net gain is negative: producing them would decrease, not increase, profit. (You can verify this by reexamining Table 25-1.) So five bushels are Jennifer and Jason's profit-maximizing output; it is the level of output at which marginal cost is equal to the market price, $18.

This example, in fact, illustrates an application of the optimal output rule to the particular case of a price-taking firm—the price-taking firm's optimal output rule, which says that a price-taking firm's profit is maximized by producing the quantity of output at which the market price is equal to the marginal cost of the last unit produced. That is, *$P = MC$ at the price-taking firm's optimal quantity of output.*

iStockphoto/Thinkstock

In fact, the price-taking firm's optimal output rule is just an application of the optimal output rule to the particular case of a price-taking firm. Why? Because *in the case of a price-taking firm, marginal revenue is equal to the market price.*

A price-taking firm cannot influence the market price by its actions. It always takes the market price as given because it cannot lower the market price by selling more or raise the market price by selling less. So, for a price-taking firm, the additional revenue generated by producing one more unit is always the market price. We will need to keep this fact in mind when we turn to Sections 10 and 11, where we will learn that marginal revenue is not equal to the market price if the industry is not perfectly competitive. As a result, firms are not price-takers when an industry is not perfectly competitive.

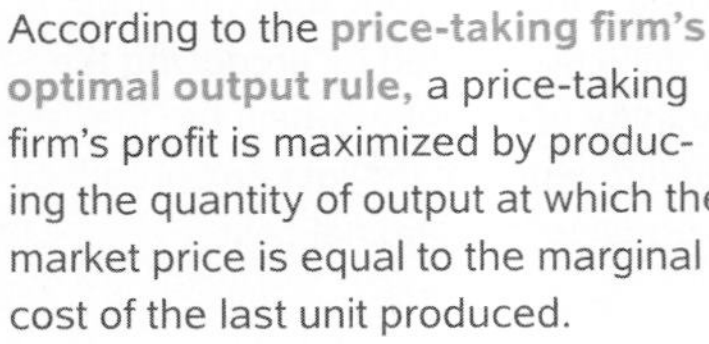

According to the **price-taking firm's optimal output rule,** a price-taking firm's profit is maximized by producing the quantity of output at which the market price is equal to the marginal cost of the last unit produced.

FIGURE 25-1 The Firm's Profit-Maximizing Quantity of Output

At the profit-maximizing quantity of output, marginal revenue is equal to marginal cost. It is located at the point where the marginal cost curve crosses the marginal revenue curve, which is a horizontal line at the market price. Here, the profit-maximizing point is at an output of 5 bushels of tomatoes, the output quantity at point *E*.

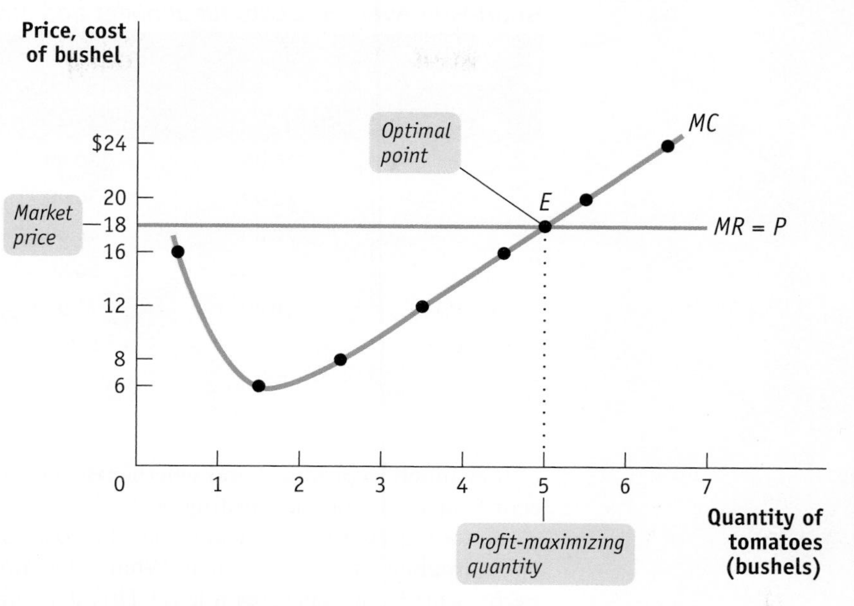

Figure 25-1 shows that Jennifer and Jason's profit-maximizing quantity of output is, indeed, the number of bushels at which the marginal cost of production is equal to price. The figure shows the *marginal cost curve, MC,* drawn from the data in the third column of Table 25-2. Recall that the marginal cost curve shows how the cost of producing one more unit depends on the quantity that has already been produced.

The **marginal revenue curve** shows how marginal revenue varies as output varies.

We plot the marginal cost of increasing output from one to two bushels halfway between one and two, and so on. The horizontal line at $18 is Jennifer and Jason's **marginal revenue curve,** which shows how marginal revenue varies as output varies. Note that marginal revenue stays the same regardless of how much Jennifer and Jason sell because we have assumed marginal revenue is constant.

Does this mean that the firm's production decision can be entirely summed up as "produce up to the point where the marginal cost of production is equal to the price"? No, not quite. Before applying the price-taking firm's optimal output rule to determine how much to produce, a potential producer must, as a first step, answer an "either–or" question: Should I produce at all? If the answer to that question is yes, the producer then proceeds to the second step—a "how much" decision: maximizing profit by choosing the quantity of output at which marginal cost is equal to price.

To understand why the first step in the production decision involves an "either–or" question, we need to ask how we determine whether it is profitable or unprofitable to produce at all.

When Is Production Profitable?

Remember that firms make their production decisions with the goal of maximizing *economic profit*—a measure based on the opportunity cost of resources used by the firm. In the calculation of economic profit, a firm's total cost incorporates the *implicit cost*—the benefits forgone in the next best use of the firm's resources—as well as the *explicit cost* in the form of actual cash outlays.

In contrast, *accounting profit* is profit calculated using only the explicit costs incurred by the firm. This means that economic profit incorporates all of the opportunity cost of resources owned by the firm and used in the production of output, while accounting profit does not.

A firm may make positive accounting profit while making zero or even negative economic profit. It's important to understand that a firm's decisions

iStockphoto

TABLE 25-3

Short-Run Average Costs for Jennifer and Jason's Farm

Quantity of tomatoes *Q* (bushels)	Variable cost *VC*	Total cost *TC*	Short-run average variable cost of bushel *AVC* = *VC*/*Q*	Short-run average total cost of bushel *ATC* = *TC*/*Q*
1	$16.00	$30.00	$16.00	$30.00
2	22.00	36.00	11.00	18.00
3	30.00	44.00	10.00	14.67
4	42.00	56.00	10.50	14.00
5	58.00	72.00	11.60	14.40
6	78.00	92.00	13.00	15.33
7	102.00	116.00	14.57	16.57

of how much to produce, and whether or not to stay in business, should be based on economic profit, not accounting profit.

So we will assume, as usual, that the cost numbers given in Table 25-1 include all costs, implicit as well as explicit. What determines whether Jennifer and Jason's farm earns a profit or generates a loss? This depends on the market price of tomatoes—specifically, *whether the market price is more or less than the farm's minimum average total cost.*

In Table 25-3 we calculate short-run average variable cost and short-run average total cost for Jennifer and Jason's farm. These are short-run values because we take fixed cost as given. (We'll turn to the effects of changing fixed cost shortly.) The short-run average total cost curve, *ATC*, is shown in Figure 25-2, along with the marginal cost curve, *MC*, from Figure 25-1. As you can see, average total cost is minimized at point *C*, corresponding to an output of 4 bushels—the *minimum-cost output*—and an average total cost of $14 per bushel.

To see how these curves can be used to decide whether production is profitable or unprofitable, recall that profit is equal to total revenue minus total cost, $TR - TC$. This means:

- If the firm produces a quantity at which $TR > TC$, the firm is profitable.
- If the firm produces a quantity at which $TR = TC$, the firm earns neither a profit nor a loss—it *breaks even.*
- If the firm produces a quantity at which $TR < TC$, the firm incurs a loss.

We can also express this idea in terms of revenue and cost per unit of output. If we divide profit by the number of units of output, *Q*, we obtain the following expression for profit per unit of output:

(25-4) $\text{Profit}/Q = TR/Q - TC/Q$

TR/Q is average revenue, which is the market price. TC/Q is average total cost. So a firm is profitable if the market price for its product is more than the average total cost of the quantity the firm produces; a firm experiences losses if the market price is less than the average total cost of the quantity the firm produces. This means:

- If the firm produces a quantity at which $P > ATC$, the firm is profitable.
- If the firm produces a quantity at which $P = ATC$, the firm earns neither a profit nor a loss—it breaks even.
- If the firm produces a quantity at which $P < ATC$, the firm incurs a loss.

In summary, in the short run a firm will maximize profit by producing the quantity of output at which $MC = MR$. A perfectly competitive firm is a price-taker, so it can sell

FIGURE 25-2 Costs and Production in the Short Run

This figure shows the marginal cost curve, *MC*, and the short-run average total cost curve, *ATC*. When the market price is $14, output will be 4 bushels of tomatoes (the minimum-cost output), represented by point *C*. The price of $14 is equal to the firm's minimum average total cost, so at this price the firm earns neither a profit nor a loss (it breaks even).

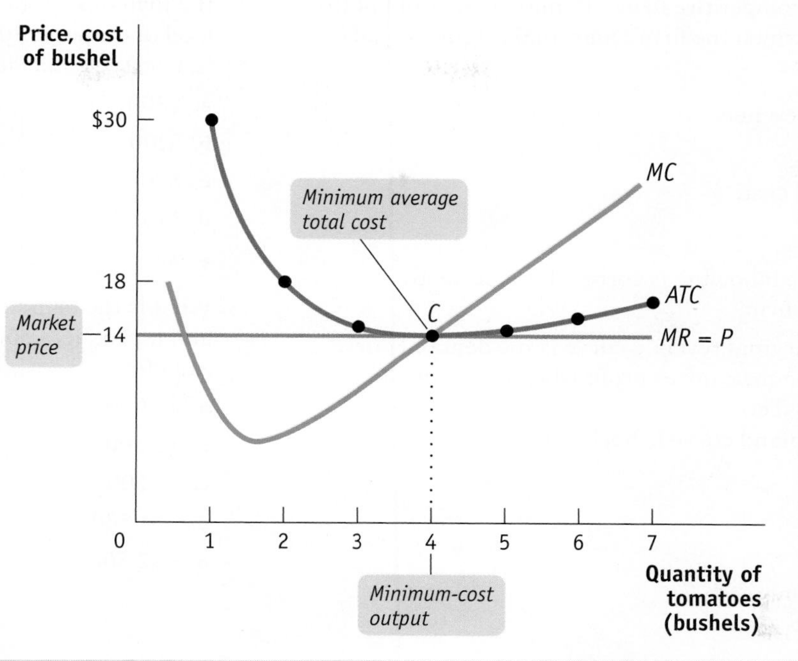

as many units of output as it would like at the market price. For a perfectly competitive firm then, it is always true that $MR = P$. The firm is profitable, or breaks even, as long as the market price is greater than, or equal to, average total cost. In the next module, we develop the perfect competition model using graphs to analyze the firm's level of profit.

MODULE 25 Review

Solutions appear at the back of the book.

Check Your Understanding

1. Refer to the graph provided to answer the questions that follow.

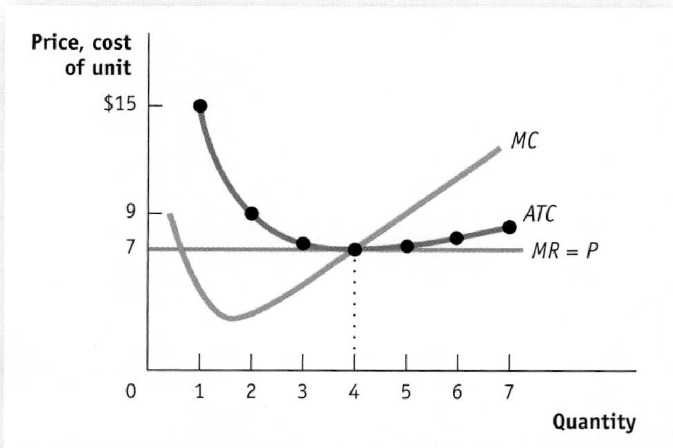

a. At what level of output does the firm maximize profit? Explain how you know.

b. At the profit-maximizing quantity of output, is the firm profitable, does it just break even, or does it earn a loss? Explain.

2. If a firm has a total cost of $500 at a quantity of 50 units, and it is at that quantity that average total cost is minimized for the firm, what is the lowest price that would allow the firm to break even? Explain.

Multiple-Choice Questions

1. A perfectly competitive firm will maximize profit at the quantity at which the firm's marginal revenue equals
   a. price.
   b. average revenue.
   c. total cost.
   d. marginal cost.
   e. demand.

2. Which of the following is correct for a perfectly competitive firm?
   I. The marginal revenue curve is the demand curve.
   II. The firm maximizes profit when price equals marginal cost.
   III. The demand curve is horizontal.
   a. I only
   b. II only
   c. III only
   d. I and II only
   e. I, II, and III

3. A firm is profitable if
   a. $TR < TC$.
   b. $AR < ATC$.
   c. $MC < ATC$.
   d. $ATC < P$.
   e. $ATC > MC$.

4. If a firm has a total cost of $200, its profit-maximizing level of output is 10 units, and it is breaking even (that is, earning a normal profit), what is the market price?
   a. $200
   b. $100
   c. $20
   d. $10
   e. $2

5. What is the firm's profit if the price of its product is $5 and it produces 500 units of output at a total cost of $1,000?
   a. $5,000
   b. $2,500
   c. $1,500
   d. −$1,500
   e. −$2,500

Critical-Thinking Questions

The table provided presents the short-run costs for Jennifer and Jason's farm. Price is equal to $14. Using the table:

1. calculate the firm's marginal cost at each quantity.
2. determine the firm's profit-maximizing level of output.
3. calculate the firm's profit at the profit-maximizing level of output.

Quantity of tomatoes *Q* (bushels)	Variable cost *VC*	Total cost *TC*
0	$0	$14
1	16	30
2	22	36
3	30	44
4	42	56
5	58	72
6	78	92
7	102	116

PITFALLS

WHAT'S A FIRM TO DO?

? The optimal output rule says that to maximize profit, a firm should produce the quantity at which marginal revenue is equal to marginal cost. But what should a firm do if there is no output level at which marginal revenue equals marginal cost?

> IN THIS CASE, A FIRM WOULD PRODUCE THE LARGEST QUANTITY FOR WHICH MARGINAL REVENUE EXCEEDS MARGINAL COST. This is the case in Table 25-2 at an output of 5 bushels. However, a simpler version of the optimal output rule applies when production involves much larger numbers, such as hundreds or thousands of units. In such cases, marginal cost comes in small increments, and there is always a level of output at which marginal cost almost exactly equals marginal revenue.

To learn more, see pages 271–273, and Table 25-2.

Graphing Perfect Competition

iStockphoto

WHAT YOU WILL LEARN

1. How to evaluate a perfectly competitive firm's situation using a graph
2. How to determine a perfect competitor's profit or loss
3. How a firm decides whether to produce or shut down in the short run

In the previous module we learned how to compare market price and average total cost to determine whether or not a competitive firm is profitable. Now we can evaluate the profitability of perfectly competitive firms in a variety of situations.

Interpreting Perfect Competition Graphs

Figure 26-1 illustrates how the market price determines whether a firm is profitable. It also shows how profits are depicted graphically. Each panel shows the marginal cost curve, *MC*, and the short-run average total cost curve, *ATC*. Average total cost is minimized at point *C*. Panel (a) shows the case in which the market price of tomatoes is \$18 per bushel. Panel (b) shows the case in which the market price of tomatoes is lower, \$10 per bushel.

In panel (a), we see that at a price of \$18 per bushel the profit-maximizing quantity of output is 5 bushels, indicated by point *E*, where the marginal cost curve, *MC*, intersects the marginal revenue curve, *MR*—which for a price-taking firm is a horizontal line at the market price. At that quantity of output, average total cost is \$14.40 per bushel, indicated by point *Z*. Since the price per bushel exceeds the average total cost per bushel, Jennifer and Jason's farm is profitable.

Jennifer and Jason's total profit when the market price is \$18 is represented by the area of the shaded rectangle in panel (a). To see why, notice that total profit can be expressed in terms of profit per unit:

(26-1) $\text{Profit} = TR - TC = (TR/Q - TC/Q) \times Q$

FIGURE 26-1 **Profitability and the Market Price**

In panel (a) the market price is \$18. The farm is profitable because price exceeds minimum average total cost, the break-even price, \$14. The farm's optimal output choice is indicated by point *E*, corresponding to an output of 5 bushels. The average total cost of producing 5 bushels is indicated by point *Z* on the *ATC* curve, corresponding to an amount of \$14.40. The vertical distance between *E* and *Z* corresponds to the farm's per-unit profit, \$18.00 – \$14.40 = \$3.60. Total profit is given by the area of the shaded rectangle, 5 × \$3.60 = \$18.00. In panel (b) the market price is \$10; the farm is unprofitable because the price falls below the minimum average total cost, \$14. The farm's optimal output choice when producing is indicated by point *A*, corresponding to an output of 3 bushels. The farm's per-unit loss, \$14.67 – \$10.00 = \$4.67, is represented by the vertical distance between *A* and *Y*. The farm's total loss is represented by the shaded rectangle, 3 × \$4.67 = \$14.00 (adjusted for rounding error).

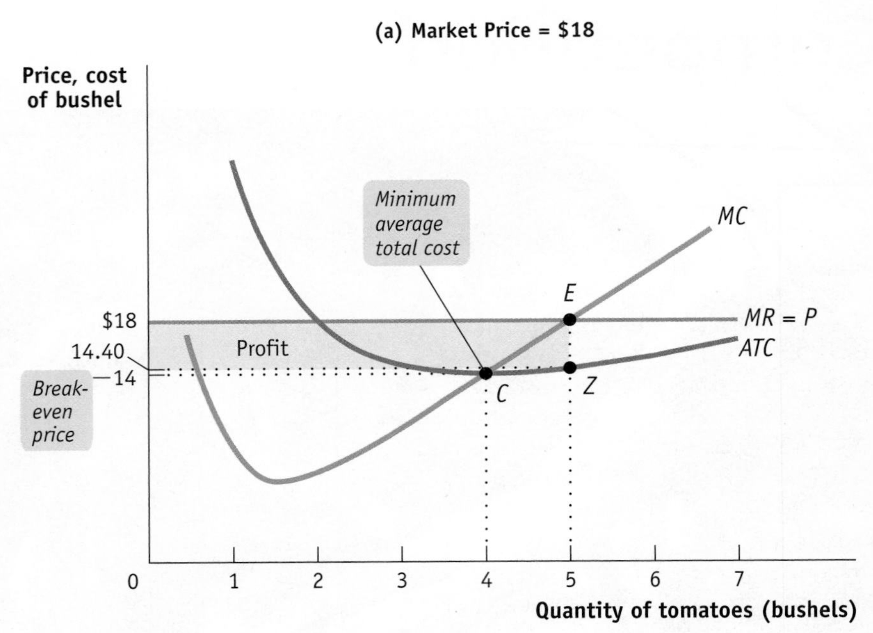

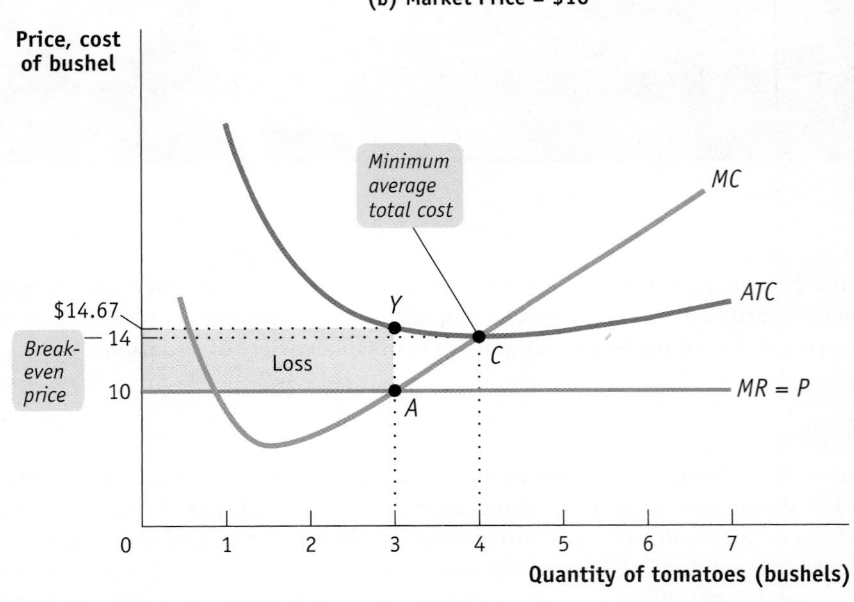

or, equivalently, because P is equal to TR/Q and ATC is equal to TC/Q,

$$\text{Profit} = (P - ATC) \times Q$$

The height of the shaded rectangle in panel (a) corresponds to the vertical distance between points *E* and *Z*. It is equal to $P - ATC$ = \$18.00 – \$14.40 = \$3.60 per bushel. The shaded rectangle has a width equal to the output: Q = 5 bushels. So the area of that rectangle is equal to Jennifer and Jason's profit: 5 bushels × \$3.60 profit per bushel = \$18.

What about the situation illustrated in panel (b)? Here the market price of tomatoes is $10 per bushel. Producing until price equals marginal cost leads to a profit-maximizing output of 3 bushels, indicated by point *A*. At this output, Jennifer and Jason have an average total cost of $14.67 per bushel, indicated by point *Y*. At their profit-maximizing output quantity—3 bushels—average total cost exceeds the market price. This means that Jennifer and Jason's farm generates a loss, not a profit.

How much do they lose by producing when the market price is $10? On each bushel they lose $ATC - P$ = $14.67 – $10.00 = $4.67, an amount corresponding to the vertical distance between points *A* and *Y*. And they produce 3 bushels, which corresponds to the width of the shaded rectangle. So the total value of the losses is $4.67 × 3 = $14.00 (adjusted for rounding error), an amount that corresponds to the area of the shaded rectangle in panel (b).

But how does a producer know, in general, whether or not its business will be profitable? It turns out that the crucial test lies in a comparison of the market price to the firm's *minimum average total cost.* On Jennifer and Jason's farm, average total cost reaches its minimum, $14, at an output of 4 bushels, indicated by point *C*. Whenever the market price exceeds the minimum average total cost, there are output levels for which the average total cost is less than the market price. In other words, the producer can find a level of output at which the firm makes a profit. So Jennifer and Jason's farm will be profitable whenever the market price exceeds $14. And they will achieve the highest possible profit by producing the quantity at which marginal cost equals price.

Conversely, if the market price is less than the minimum average total cost, there is no output level at which price exceeds average total cost. As a result, the firm will be unprofitable at any quantity of output. As we saw, at a price of $10—an amount less than the minimum average total cost—Jennifer and Jason did indeed lose money. By producing the quantity at which marginal cost equaled price, Jennifer and Jason did the best they could, but the best they could do was a loss of $14. Any other quantity would have increased the size of their loss.

Thinkstock

A firm will earn positive profit when the market price is above the break-even price.

The minimum average total cost of a price-taking firm is called its **break-even price,** the market price at which it earns zero economic profit. A firm will earn positive profit when the market price is above the break-even price, and it will suffer losses when the market price is below the break-even price. Jennifer and Jason's break-even price of $14 is the price at point *C* in Figure 26-1.

So the rule for determining whether a firm is profitable depends on a comparison of the market price of the good to the firm's break-even price—its minimum average total cost:

- Whenever the market price exceeds the minimum average total cost, the producer is profitable.
- Whenever the market price equals the minimum average total cost, the producer breaks even.
- Whenever the market price is less than the minimum average total cost, the producer is unprofitable.

The Short-Run Production Decision

You might be tempted to say that if a firm is unprofitable because the market price is below its minimum average total cost, it shouldn't produce any output. In the short run, however, this conclusion isn't right. In the short run, sometimes the firm should produce even if price falls below minimum average total cost. The reason is that total cost includes *fixed cost*—cost that does not depend on the amount of output produced and can be altered only in the long run. In the short run, fixed cost must still be paid,

The **break-even price** of a price-taking firm is the market price at which it earns zero economic profit.

regardless of whether or not a firm produces. For example, if Jennifer and Jason have rented a tractor for the year, they have to pay the rent on the tractor regardless of whether they produce any tomatoes. *Since it cannot be changed in the short run, their fixed cost is irrelevant to their decision about whether to produce or shut down in the short run.*

Although fixed cost should play no role in the decision about whether to produce in the short run, another type of cost—variable cost—does matter. Part of the variable cost for Jennifer and Jason is the wage cost of workers who must be hired to help with planting and harvesting. Variable cost can be eliminated by *not* producing, which makes it a critical consideration when determining whether or not to produce in the short run.

Let's turn to Figure 26-2: it shows both the short-run average total cost curve, *ATC*, and the short-run average variable cost curve, *AVC*, drawn from the information in Table 25-3. Recall that the difference between the two curves—the vertical distance between them—represents average fixed cost, the fixed cost per unit of output, *FC/Q*. Because the marginal cost curve has a "swoosh" shape—falling at first before rising—the short-run average variable cost curve is U-shaped: the initial fall in marginal cost causes average variable cost to fall as well, and then the rise in marginal cost eventually pulls average variable cost up again. The short-run average variable cost curve reaches its minimum value of $10 at point *A*, at an output of 3 bushels.

26-2 The Short-Run Individual Supply Curve

When the market price equals or exceeds Jennifer and Jason's *shut-down price* of $10, the minimum average variable cost indicated by point *A*, they will produce the output quantity at which marginal cost is equal to price. So at any price equal to or above the minimum average *variable* cost, the short-run individual supply curve is the firm's marginal cost curve; this corresponds to the upward-sloping segment of the individual supply curve. When market price falls below minimum average variable cost, the firm ceases operation in the short run. This corresponds to the vertical segment of the individual supply curve along the vertical axis.

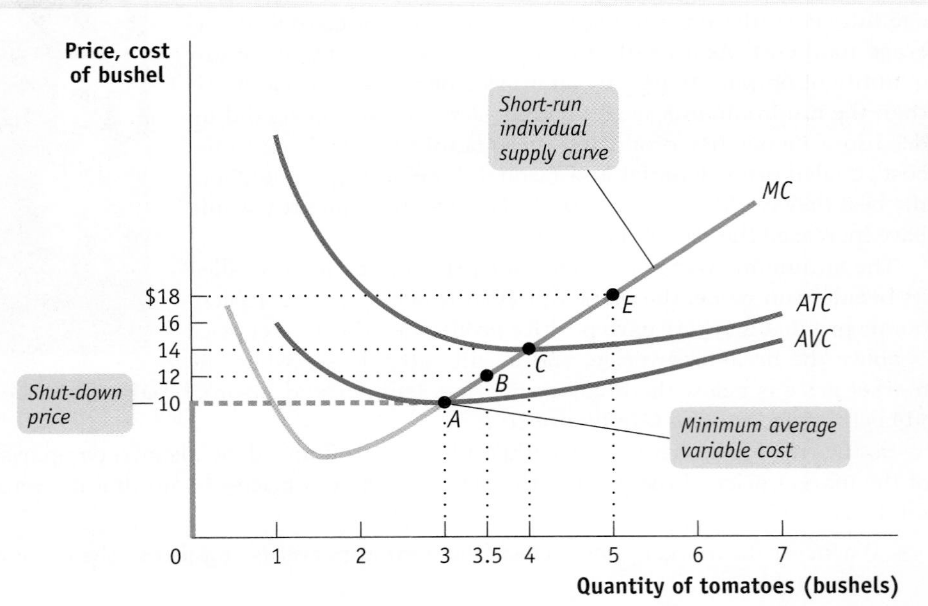

The Shut-Down Price

We are now prepared to analyze the optimal production decision in the short run. We have two cases to consider:

- When the market price is below the minimum average *variable* cost
- When the market price is greater than or equal to the minimum average *variable* cost

When the market price is below the minimum average variable cost, the price the firm receives per unit is not covering its variable cost per unit. A firm in this situation should cease production immediately. Why? Because there is no level of output at which the firm's total revenue covers its variable cost—the cost it can avoid by not operating. In this case the firm maximizes its profit by not producing at all—by, in effect, minimizing its loss. It will still incur a fixed cost in the short run, but it will no longer incur any variable cost. This means that the minimum average variable cost determines the **shut-down price,** the price at which the firm ceases production in the short run.

A firm will cease production in the short run if the market price falls below the **shut-down price,** which is equal to minimum average variable cost.

When price is greater than minimum average variable cost, however, the firm should produce in the short run. In this case, the firm maximizes profit—or minimizes loss—by choosing the output level at which its marginal cost is equal to the market price. For example, if the market price of tomatoes is $18 per bushel, Jennifer and Jason should produce at point *E* in Figure 26-2, corresponding to an output of 5 bushels. Note that point *C* in Figure 26-2 corresponds to the farm's break-even price of $14 per bushel. Since *E* lies above *C*, Jennifer and Jason's farm will be profitable; they will generate a per-bushel profit of $18.00 – $14.40 = $3.60 when the market price is $18.

But what if the market price lies between the shut-down price and the break-even price—that is, between the minimum average *variable* cost and the minimum average *total* cost? In the case of Jennifer and Jason's farm, this corresponds to prices anywhere between $10 and $14—say, a market price of $12. At $12, Jennifer and Jason's farm is not profitable; since the market price is below the minimum average total cost, the farm is losing (on average) the difference between price and average total cost on every unit produced. Yet even though the market price isn't covering Jennifer and Jason's average total cost, it is covering their average variable cost and some—but not all—of the average fixed cost. If a firm in this situation shuts down, it will incur no variable cost but it will incur the *full* fixed cost. As a result, shutting down will generate an even greater loss than continuing to operate.

This means that whenever price falls between minimum average total cost and minimum average variable cost, the firm is better off producing some output in the short run. The reason is that by producing, it can cover its variable cost and at least some of its fixed cost, even though it is incurring a loss. In this case, the firm maximizes profit—that is, minimizes loss—by choosing the quantity of output at which its marginal cost is equal to the market price. So if Jennifer and Jason face a market price of $12 per bushel, their profit-maximizing output is given by point *B* in Figure 26-2, corresponding to an output of 3.5 bushels.

Anthony Masterson/Digital Vision/Getty Images

In the short-run production decision, a firm's fixed cost is essentially a sunk cost.

It's worth noting that the decision to produce when the firm is covering its variable cost but not all of its fixed cost is similar to the decision to ignore a *sunk cost,* a concept we studied previously. You may recall that a sunk cost is a cost that has already been incurred and cannot be recouped; and because it cannot be changed, it should have no effect on any current decision. In the short-run production decision, fixed cost is, in effect, like a sunk cost—it has been spent, and it can't be recovered in the short run. This comparison also illustrates why variable cost does indeed matter in the short run: it can be avoided by not producing.

And what happens if the market price is exactly equal to the shut-down price, the minimum average variable cost? In this instance, the firm is indifferent between producing 3 units or 0 units. As we'll see shortly, this is an important point when looking at the behavior of an industry as a whole. For the sake of clarity, we'll assume that the firm, although indifferent, does indeed produce output when price is equal to the shut-down price.

Putting everything together, we can now draw the *short-run individual supply curve* of Jennifer and Jason's farm, the red line in Figure 26-2; it shows how the profit-maximizing quantity of output in the short run depends on the price. As you can see, the curve is in two segments. The upward-sloping red segment starting at point *A* shows the short-run profit-maximizing output when market price is equal to or above the shut-down price of $10 per bushel.

As long as the market price is equal to or above the shut-down price, Jennifer and Jason will produce the quantity of output at which marginal cost is equal to the market price. So at market prices equal to or above the shut-down price, the firm's short-run supply curve corresponds to its marginal cost curve. But at any market price below the minimum average variable cost, in this case, $10 per bushel—the firm shuts down and output drops to zero in the short run. This corresponds to the vertical segment of the curve that lies on top of the vertical axis.

V.e.r.i.k/Dreamstime.com

Some firms shut down temporarily without going out of business.

Do firms sometimes shut down temporarily without going out of business? Yes. In fact, in some industries temporary shut-downs are routine. The most common examples are industries in which demand is highly seasonal, like outdoor amusement parks in climates with cold winters. Such parks would have to offer very low prices to entice customers during the colder months—prices so low that the owners would not cover their variable cost (principally wages and electricity). The wiser choice economically is to shut down until warm weather brings enough customers who are willing to pay a higher price.

Changing Fixed Cost

Although fixed cost cannot be altered in the short run, in the long run firms can acquire or get rid of machines, buildings, and so on. In the long run the level of fixed cost is a matter of choice, and a firm will choose the level of fixed cost that minimizes the average total cost for its desired output level. Now we will focus on an even bigger question facing a firm when choosing its fixed cost: whether to incur *any* fixed cost at all by continuing to operate.

In the long run, a firm can always eliminate fixed cost by selling off its plant and equipment. If it does so, of course, it can't produce any output—it has exited the industry. In contrast, a new firm can take on some fixed cost by acquiring machines and other resources, which puts it in a position to produce—it can enter the industry. In most perfectly competitive industries the set of firms, although fixed in the short run, changes in the long run as some firms enter or exit the industry.

Consider Jennifer and Jason's farm once again. In order to simplify our analysis, we will sidestep the issue of choosing among several possible levels of fixed cost. Instead, we will assume that if they operate at all, Jennifer and Jason have only one possible choice of fixed cost: $14. Alternatively, they can choose a fixed cost of zero if they exit the industry. It is changes in fixed cost that cause short-run average total cost curves to differ from long-run average total cost curves, so with this assumption, Jennifer and Jason's short-run and long-run average total cost curves are one and the same.

Suppose that the market price of organic tomatoes is consistently less than the break-even price of $14 over an extended period of time. In that case, Jennifer and Jason never fully cover their total cost: their business runs at a persistent loss. In the long run, then, they can do better by closing their business and leaving the industry. In other words, *in the long run* firms will exit an industry if the market price is consistently less than their break-even price—their minimum average total cost.

Conversely, suppose that the price of organic tomatoes is consistently above the break-even price, $14, for an extended period of time. Because their farm is profitable, Jennifer and Jason will remain in the industry and continue producing.

But things won't stop there. The organic tomato industry meets the criterion of *free entry*: there are many potential organic tomato producers because the necessary inputs are easy to obtain. And the cost curves of those potential producers are likely to be similar to those of Jennifer and Jason, since the technology used by other producers is likely to be very similar to that used by Jennifer and Jason. If the price is high enough to generate profits for existing producers, it will also attract some of these potential producers into the industry. So *in the long run* a price in excess of $14 should lead to entry: new producers will come into the organic tomato industry.

As we will see shortly, exit and entry lead to an important distinction between the *short-run industry supply curve* and the *long-run industry supply curve.*

ECONOMICS IN ACTION

PRICES ARE UP . . . BUT SO ARE COSTS

Because of the Energy Policy Act of 2005, 7.5 billion gallons of alternative fuel, mostly corn-based ethanol, was added to the American fuel supply to help reduce gasoline consumption. The unsurprising result of this mandate: the demand for corn skyrocketed, along with its price. In August 2012, a bushel of corn hit a high of $8.32, nearly quadruple the January 2005 price of $2.09.

This sharp rise in the price of corn caught the eye of American farmers like Ronnie Gerik of Aquilla, Texas, who, in response to surging corn prices, reduced the size of his cotton crop and increased his corn acreage by 40%. He was not alone; overall, the U.S. corn acreage planted in 2011 was 9% more than the average planted over the previous decade. And 4% more was planted in 2012.

Although this sounds like a sure way to make a profit, Gerik was actually taking a big gamble: even though the price of corn increased, so did the cost of the raw materials needed to grow it—by 20%. Consider the cost of just two inputs: fertilizer and fuel. Corn requires more fertilizer than other crops and, with more farmers planting corn, the increased demand for fertilizer led to a price increase.

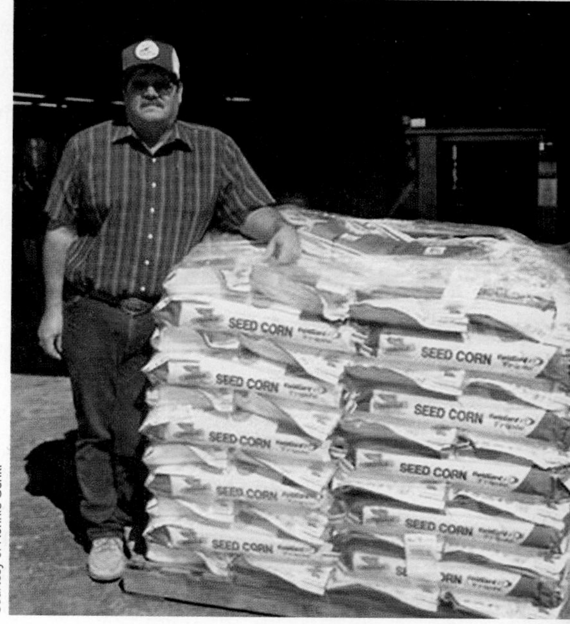

Courtesy of Ronnie Gerik.

Although Gerik was taking a big gamble when he cut the size of his cotton crop to plant more corn, his decision made good economic sense.

Moreover, corn is much more sensitive to the amount of rainfall than a crop like cotton. So farmers who plant corn in drought-prone places like Texas are increasing their risk of loss. Gerik had to incorporate into his calculations his best guess of what a dry spell would cost him.

Despite all of this, what Gerik did made complete economic sense. By planting more corn, he was moving up his individual short-run supply curve for corn production. And because his individual supply curve is his marginal cost curve, his costs also went up because he had to use more inputs—inputs that had become more expensive to obtain.

So the moral of this story is that farmers will increase their corn acreage until the marginal cost of producing corn is approximately equal to the market price of corn—which shouldn't come as a surprise because corn production satisfies all the requirements of a perfectly competitive industry.

Summing Up: The Perfectly Competitive Firm's Profitability and Production Conditions

In this module we've studied what's behind the supply curve for a perfectly competitive, price-taking firm. A perfectly competitive firm maximizes profit, or minimizes loss, by producing the quantity that equates price and marginal cost. The exception is if price is below minimum average variable cost in the short run, or below minimum average total cost in the long run, in which case the firm is better off shutting down. Table 26-1 summarizes the perfectly competitive firm's profitability and production conditions. It also relates them to entry into and exit from the industry in the long run. Now that we understand how a perfectly competitive *firm* makes its decisions, we can go on to look at the supply curve for a perfectly competitive *market* and the long-run market equilibrium in perfect competition.

TABLE 26-1

Summary of the Perfectly Competitive Firm's Profitability and Production Conditions

Profitability condition (minimum *ATC* = break-even price)	Result
P > minimum *ATC*	Firm profitable. Entry into industry in the long run.
P = minimum *ATC*	Firm breaks even. No entry into or exit from industry in the long run.
P < minimum *ATC*	Firm unprofitable. Exit from industry in the long run.
Production condition (minimum *AVC* = shut-down price)	**Result**
P > minimum *AVC*	Firm produces in the short run. If *P* < minimum *ATC*, firm covers variable cost and some but not all of fixed cost. If *P* > minimum *ATC*, firm covers all variable cost and fixed cost.
P = minimum *AVC*	Firm indifferent between producing in the short run or not. Just covers variable cost.
P < minimum *AVC*	Firm shuts down in the short run. It cannot cover variable cost.

MODULE 26 Review

Solutions appear at the back of the book.

Check Your Understanding

1. Draw a short-run diagram showing a U-shaped average total cost curve, a U-shaped average variable cost curve, and a "swoosh"-shaped marginal cost curve. On it, indicate the range of prices for which the following actions are optimal. Explain your answers.
   - a. The firm shuts down immediately.
   - b. The firm operates in the short run despite sustaining a loss.
   - c. The firm operates while making a profit.

2. The state of Maine has a very active lobster industry, which harvests lobsters during the summer months. During the rest of the year, lobsters can be obtained by restaurants from producers in other parts of the world, but at a much higher price. Maine is also full of "lobster shacks," roadside restaurants serving lobster dishes that are open only during the summer. Supposing that the market demand for lobster dishes remains the same throughout the year, explain why it is optimal for lobster shacks to operate only during the summer.

Multiple-Choice Questions

To answer questions 1–3, refer to the graph provided.

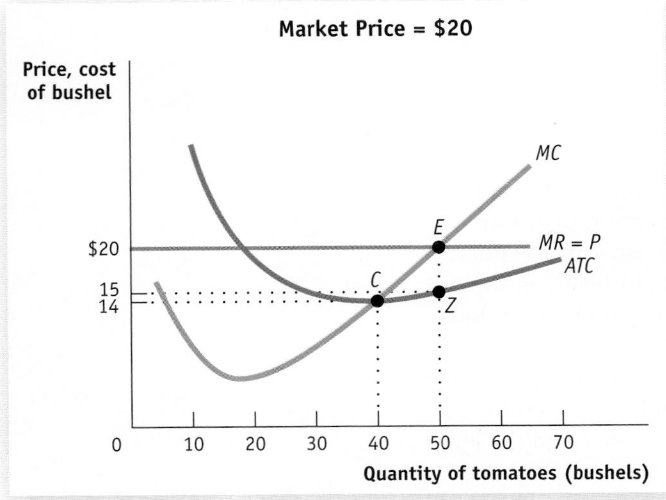

1. The firm's total revenue is equal to
   - a. $14.
   - b. $20.
   - c. $560.
   - d. $750.
   - e. $1,000.

2. The firm's total cost is equal to
   - a. $14.
   - b. $15.
   - c. $560.
   - d. $750.
   - e. $1,000.

3. The firm is earning a
   - a. profit equal to $5.
   - b. profit equal to $250.
   - c. loss equal to $15.
   - d. loss equal to $750.
   - e. loss equal to $250.

4. A firm should continue to produce in the short run as long as price is at least equal to
   a. *MR*.
   b. *MC*.
   c. minimum *ATC*.
   d. minimum *AVC*.
   e. *AFC*.

5. At prices that motivate the firm to produce at all, the short-run supply curve for a perfect competitor corresponds to which curve?
   a. the *ATC* curve
   b. the *AVC* curve
   c. the *MC* curve
   d. the *AFC* curve
   e. the *MR* curve

Critical-Thinking Questions

Refer to the graph provided to answer the questions that follow.

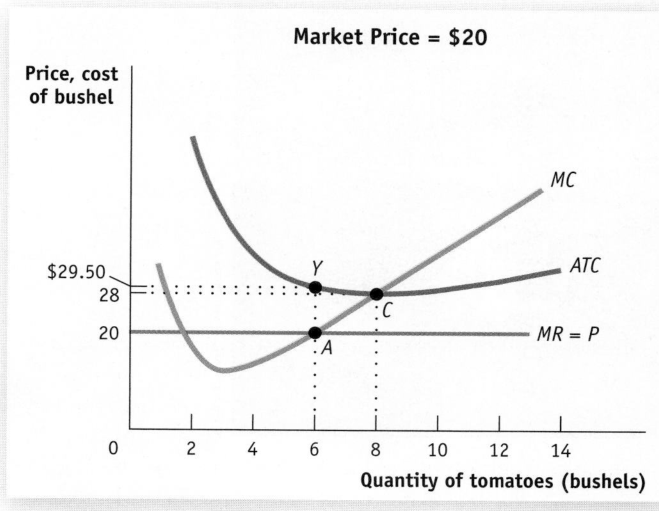

1. Assuming it is appropriate for the firm to produce in the short run, what is the firm's profit-maximizing level of output?
2. Calculate the firm's total revenue.
3. Calculate the firm's total cost.
4. Calculate the firm's profit or loss.
5. If *AVC* were $22 at the profit-maximizing level of output, would the firm produce in the short run? Explain why or why not.

MODULE 27 Long-Run Outcomes in Perfect Competition

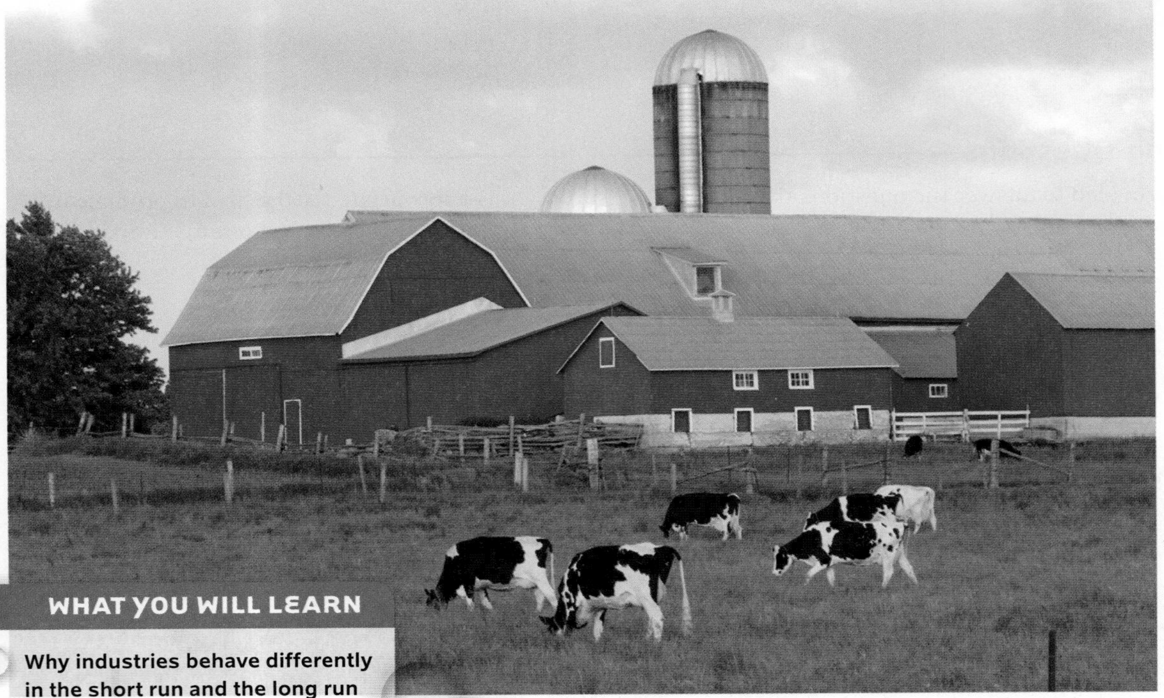

© George Kroll | Dreamstime.com

WHAT YOU WILL LEARN

1. Why industries behave differently in the short run and the long run
2. What determines the industry supply curve in both the short run and the long run

Up to this point we have been discussing the perfectly competitive firm's short-run situation—whether to produce or not, and if so, whether the firm earns a positive profit, breaks even, or takes a loss. In this module, we look at the long-run situation in a perfectly competitive market. We will see that perfect competition leads to some interesting and desirable market outcomes. In upcoming sections, we will contrast these outcomes with the outcomes in monopolistic and imperfectly competitive markets.

The Industry Supply Curve

Why will an increase in the demand for organic tomatoes lead to a large price increase at first but a much smaller increase in the long run? The answer lies in the behavior of the **industry supply curve**—the relationship between the price and the total output of an industry as a whole. The industry supply curve is what we referred to in earlier modules as the supply curve or the market supply curve. But here we take some extra care to distinguish between the *individual supply curve* of a single firm and the supply curve of the industry as a whole.

As you might guess from the previous module, the industry supply curve must be analyzed in somewhat different ways for the short run and the long run. Let's start with the short run.

The **industry supply curve** shows the relationship between the price of a good and the total output of the industry as a whole.

The Short-Run Industry Supply Curve

Recall that in the short run the number of firms in an industry is fixed—there is no entry or exit. And you may also remember from Section 2 that the market supply

FIGURE 27-1 The Short-Run Individual Supply Curve

When the market price equals or exceeds Jennifer and Jason's *shut-down price* of $10, the minimum average variable cost indicated by point *A*, they will produce the output quantity at which marginal cost is equal to price. So at any price equal to or above the minimum average *variable* cost, the short-run individual supply curve is the firm's marginal cost curve; this corresponds to the upward-sloping segment of the individual supply curve. When market price falls below minimum average variable cost, the firm ceases operation in the short run. This corresponds to the vertical segment of the individual supply curve along the vertical axis.

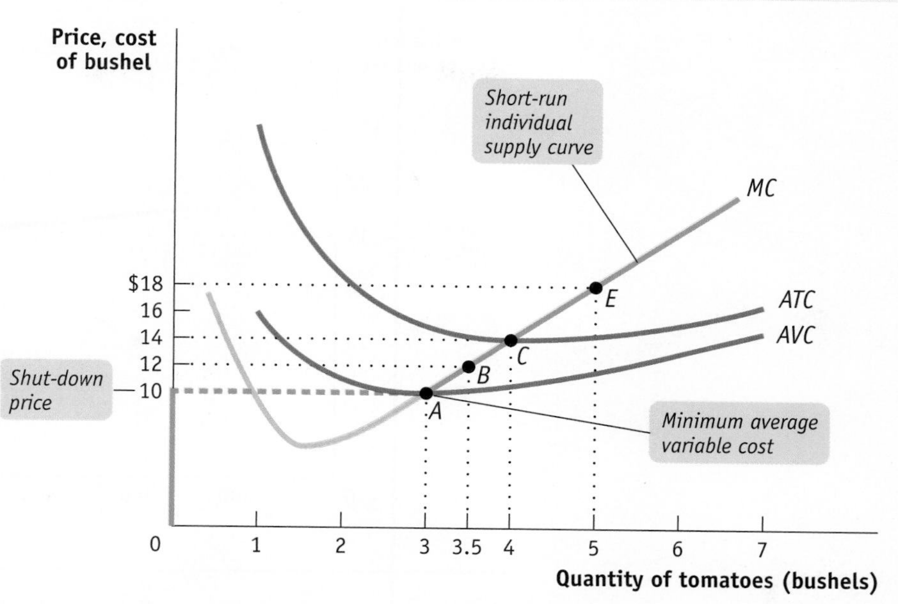

curve is the horizontal sum of the individual supply curves of all firms—you find it by summing the total output across all suppliers at every given price. We will do that exercise here under the assumption that all the firms are alike—an assumption that makes the derivation particularly simple. So let's assume that there are 100 organic tomato farms, each with the same costs as Jennifer and Jason's farm.

Each of these 100 farms will have an individual short-run supply curve like the one in Figure 26-2 from the previous module, which appears again here, as Figure 27-1 for your convenience.

At a price below $10, no farms will produce. At a price of more than $10, each farm will produce the quantity of output at which its marginal cost is equal to the market price. As you can see from Figure 27-1, this will lead each farm to produce 4 bushels if the price is $14 per bushel, 5 bushels if the price is $18, and so on.

So if there are 100 organic tomato farms and the price of organic tomatoes is $18 per bushel, the industry as a whole will produce 500 bushels, corresponding to 100 farms × 5 bushels per farm. The result is the **short-run industry supply curve,** shown as *S* in Figure 27-2. This curve shows the quantity that producers will supply at each price, *taking the number of farms as given.*

The market demand curve, labeled *D* in Figure 27-2, crosses the short-run industry supply curve at E_{MKT}, corresponding to a price of $18 and a quantity of 500 bushels. Point E_{MKT} is a **short-run market equilibrium:** the quantity supplied equals the quantity demanded, taking the number of farms as given. But the long run may look quite different because in the long run farms may enter or exit the industry.

The **short-run industry supply curve** shows how the quantity supplied by an industry depends on the market price, given a fixed number of firms.

There is a **short-run market equilibrium** when the quantity supplied equals the quantity demanded, taking the number of producers as given.

The Long-Run Industry Supply Curve

Suppose that in addition to the 100 farms currently in the organic tomato business, there are many other potential organic tomato farms. Suppose also that each of these potential farms would have the same cost curves as existing farms, like the one owned by Jennifer and Jason, upon entering the industry.

When will additional farms enter the industry? Whenever existing farms are making a profit—that is, whenever the market price is above the break-even price of $14

FIGURE 27-2 **The Short-Run Market Equilibrium**

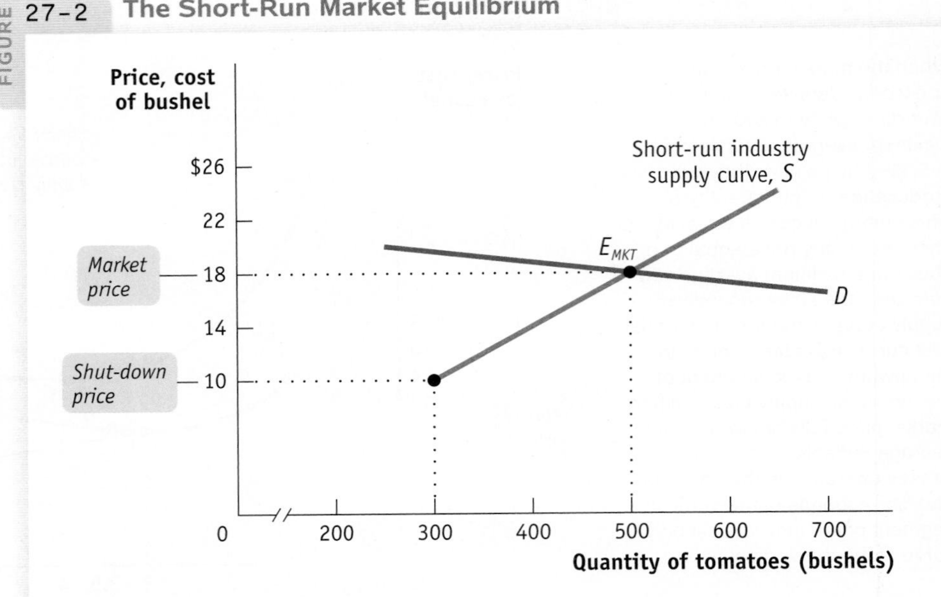

The short-run industry supply curve, *S*, is the industry supply curve taking the number of producers—here, 100—as given. It is generated by adding together the individual supply curves of the 100 producers. Below the shut-down price of $10, no producer wants to produce in the short run. Above $10, the short-run industry supply curve slopes upward, as each producer increases output as price increases. It intersects the demand curve, *D*, at point E_{MKT}, the point of short-run market equilibrium, corresponding to a market price of $18 and a quantity of 500 bushels.

per bushel, the minimum average total cost of production. For example, at a price of $18 per bushel, new farms will enter the industry.

What will happen as additional farms enter the industry? Clearly, the quantity supplied at any given price will increase. The short-run industry supply curve will shift to the right. This will, in turn, alter the market equilibrium and result in a lower market price. Existing farms will respond to the lower market price by reducing their output, but the total industry output will increase because of the larger number of farms in the industry.

Figure 27-3 illustrates the effects of this chain of events on an existing farm and on the market; panel (a) shows how the market responds to entry, and panel (b) shows how an individual existing farm responds to entry. (Note that these two graphs have been rescaled in comparison to Figures 27-1 and 27-2 to better illustrate how profit changes in response to price.) In panel (a), S_1 is the initial short-run industry supply curve, based on the existence of 100 producers. The initial short-run market equilibrium is at E_{MKT}, with an equilibrium market price of $18 and a quantity of 500 bushels. At this price existing farms are profitable, which is reflected in panel (b): an existing farm makes a total profit represented by the green shaded rectangle labeled A when the market price is $18.

These profits will induce new producers to enter the industry, shifting the short-run industry supply curve to the right. For example, the short-run industry supply curve when the number of farms has increased to 167 is S_2. Corresponding to this supply curve is a new short-run market equilibrium labeled D_{MKT}, with a market price of $16 and a quantity of 750 bushels. At $16, each farm produces 4.5 bushels, so that industry output is $167 \times 4.5 = 750$ bushels (rounded). From panel (b) you can see the

FIGURE 27-3 The Long-Run Market Equilibrium

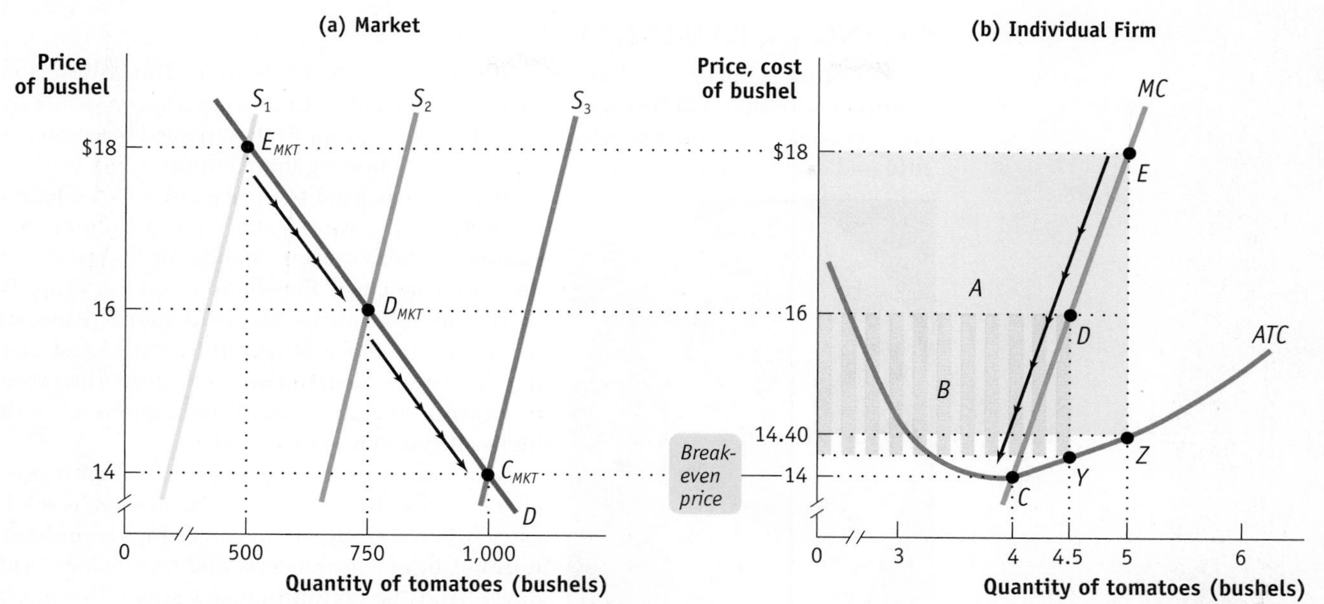

Point E_{MKT} of panel (a) shows the initial short-run market equilibrium. Each of the 100 existing producers makes an economic profit, illustrated in panel (b) by the green rectangle labeled *A*, the profit of an existing firm. Profits induce entry by additional producers, shifting the short-run industry supply curve outward from S_1 to S_2 in panel (a), resulting in a new short-run equilibrium at point D_{MKT}, at a lower market price of $16 and higher industry output. Existing firms reduce output and profit falls to the area given by the striped rectangle labeled *B* in panel (b). Entry continues to shift out the short-run industry supply curve, as price falls and industry output increases yet again. Entry ceases at point C_{MKT} on supply curve S_3 in panel (a). Here market price is equal to the break-even price; existing producers make zero economic profits and there is no incentive for entry or exit. Therefore C_{MKT} is also a long-run market equilibrium.

effect of the entry of 67 new farms on an existing farm: the fall in price causes it to reduce its output, and its profit falls to the area represented by the striped rectangle labeled *B*.

Although diminished, the profit of existing farms at D_{MKT} means that entry will continue and the number of farms will continue to rise. If the number of farms rises to 250, the short-run industry supply curve shifts out again to S_3, and the market equilibrium is at C_{MKT}, with a quantity supplied and demanded of 1,000 bushels and a market price of $14 per bushel.

Like E_{MKT} and D_{MKT}, C_{MKT} is a short-run equilibrium. But it is also something more. Because the price of $14 is each farm's break-even price, an existing producer makes zero economic profit—neither a profit nor a loss, earning only the opportunity cost of the resources used in production—when producing its profit-maximizing output of 4 bushels. At this price there is no incentive either for potential producers to enter or for existing producers to exit the industry. So C_{MKT} corresponds to a **long-run market equilibrium**—a situation in which the quantity supplied equals the quantity demanded, given that sufficient time has elapsed for producers to either enter or exit the industry. In a long-run market equilibrium, all existing and potential producers have fully adjusted to their optimal long-run choices; as a result, no producer has an incentive to either enter or exit the industry.

A market is in **long-run market equilibrium** when the quantity supplied equals the quantity demanded, given that sufficient time has elapsed for entry into and exit from the industry to occur.

ECONOMICS ▶ IN ACTION

WORLD VIEW

BALING IN, BAILING OUT

"King Cotton is back," proclaimed a 2010 article in the *Los Angeles Times*, describing a cotton boom that had "turned great swaths of Central California a snowy white during harvest season." Cotton prices were soaring: they more than tripled between early 2010 and early 2011. And farmers responded by planting more cotton.

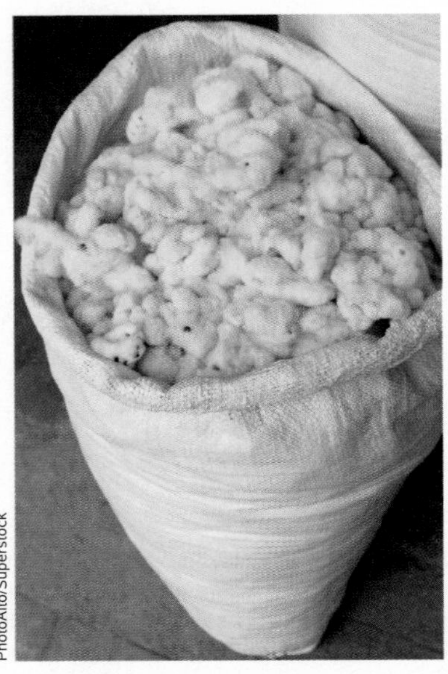

PhotoAlto/Superstock

King Cotton's reign will inevitably end as new producers enter the market and bring prices down.

What was behind the price rise? As we learned in Section 2, it was partly caused by temporary factors, notably severe floods in Pakistan that destroyed much of that nation's cotton crop. But there was also a big rise in demand, especially from China, whose burgeoning textile and clothing industries demanded ever more raw cotton to weave into cloth. And all indications were that higher demand was here to stay.

So is cotton farming going to be a highly profitable business from now on? The answer is no, because when an industry becomes highly profitable, it draws in new producers, and that brings prices down. And the cotton industry was following the standard script.

For it wasn't just the Central Valley of California that had turned "snowy white." Farmers around the world were moving into cotton growing. "This summer, cotton will stretch from Queensland through northern NSW [New South Wales] all the way down to the Murrumbidgee valley in southern NSW," declared an Australian report.

And by 2012, the entry of all these new producers had a big effect. By the summer of 2012, cotton prices were only about a third of their peak in early 2011. It was clear that the cotton boom had reached its limit—and that at some point in the not too distant future some of the farmers who had rushed into the industry would leave it again.

To explore further the difference between short-run and long-run equilibrium, consider the effect of an increase in demand on an industry with free entry that is initially in long-run equilibrium. Panel (b) in Figure 27-4 shows the market adjustment; panels (a) and (c) show how an existing individual firm behaves during the process.

In panel (b) of Figure 27-4, D_1 is the initial demand curve and S_1 is the initial short-run industry supply curve. Their intersection at point X_{MKT} is both a short-run and a long-run market equilibrium because the equilibrium price of \$14 leads to zero economic profit—and therefore neither entry nor exit. It corresponds to point X in panel (a), where an individual existing firm is operating at the minimum of its average total cost curve.

Now suppose that the demand curve shifts out for some reason to D_2. As shown in panel (b), in the short run, industry output moves along the short-run industry supply curve, S_1, to the new short-run market equilibrium at Y_{MKT}, the intersection of S_1 and D_2. The market price rises to \$18 per bushel, and industry output increases from Q_X to Q_Y. This corresponds to an existing firm's movement from X to Y in panel (a) as the firm increases its output in response to the rise in the market price.

But we know that Y_{MKT} is not a long-run equilibrium because \$18 is higher than minimum average total cost, so existing firms are making economic profits. This will lead additional firms to enter the industry. Over time entry will cause the short-run industry supply curve to shift to the right. In the long run, the short-run industry

FIGURE 27-4 The Effect of an Increase in Demand in the Short Run and the Long Run

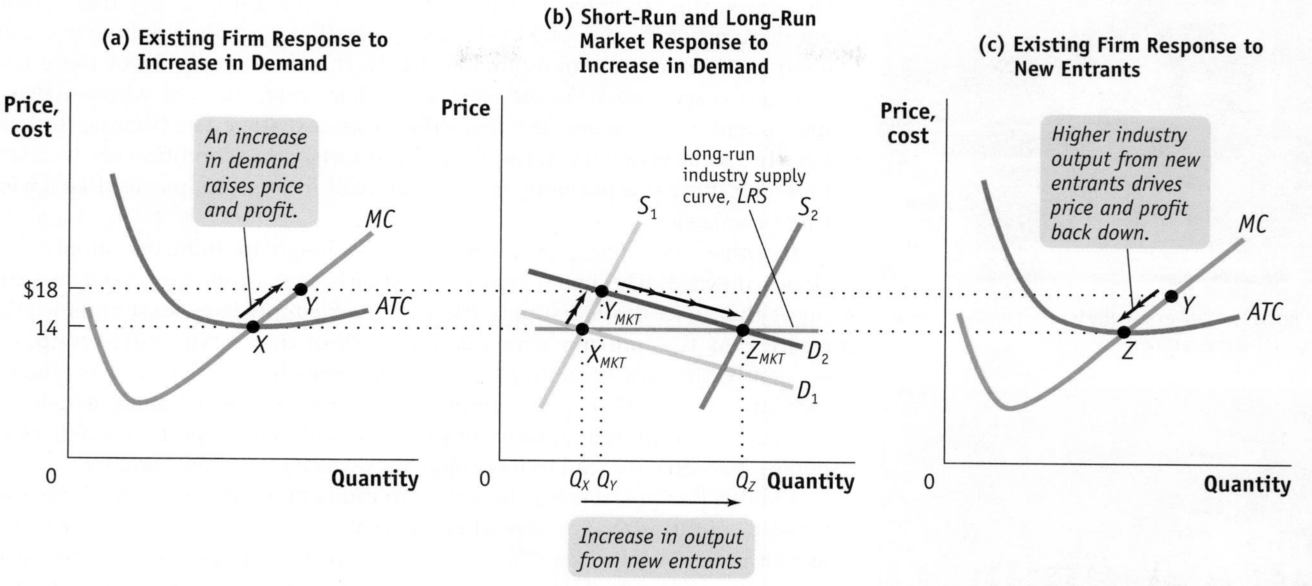

Panel (b) shows how an industry adjusts in the short and long run to an increase in demand; panels (a) and (c) show the corresponding adjustments by an existing firm. Initially the market is at point X_{MKT} in panel (b), a short-run and long-run equilibrium at a price of $14 and industry output of Q_X. An existing firm makes zero economic profit, operating at point X in panel (a) at minimum average total cost. Demand increases as D_1 shifts rightward to D_2, in panel (b), raising the market price to $18. Existing firms increase their output, and industry output moves along the short-run industry supply curve S_1 to a short-run equilibrium at Y_{MKT}. Correspondingly, the existing firm in panel (a) moves from point X to point Y. But at a price of $18 existing firms are profitable. As shown in panel (b), in the long run new entrants arrive and the short-run industry supply curve shifts rightward, from S_1 to S_2. There is a new equilibrium at point Z_{MKT}, at a lower price of $14 and higher industry output of Q_Z. An existing firm responds by moving from Y to Z in panel (c), returning to its initial output level and zero economic profit. Production by new entrants accounts for the total increase in industry output, $Q_Z - Q_X$. Like X_{MKT}, Z_{MKT} is also a short-run and long-run equilibrium: with existing firms earning zero economic profit, there is no incentive for any firms to enter or exit the industry. The horizontal line passing through X_{MKT} and Z_{MKT}, LRS, is the *long-run industry supply curve:* at the break-even price of $14, producers will produce any amount that consumers demand in the long run.

supply curve will have shifted out to S_2, and the equilibrium will be at Z_{MKT}—with the price falling back to $14 per bushel and industry output increasing yet again, from Q_Y to Q_Z. Like X_{MKT} before the increase in demand, Z_{MKT} is both a short-run and a long-run market equilibrium.

The effect of entry on an existing firm is illustrated in panel (c), in the movement from Y to Z along the firm's individual supply curve. The firm reduces its output in response to the fall in the market price, ultimately arriving back at its original output quantity, corresponding to the minimum of its average total cost curve. In fact, every firm that is now in the industry—the initial set of firms and the new entrants—will operate at the minimum of its average total cost curve, at point Z. This means that the entire increase in industry output, from Q_X to Q_Z, comes from production by new entrants.

The line LRS that passes through X_{MKT} and Z_{MKT} in panel (b) is the **long-run industry supply curve.** It shows how the quantity supplied by an industry responds to the price, given that firms have had time to enter or exit the industry.

The **long-run industry supply curve** shows how the quantity supplied responds to the price once producers have had time to enter or exit the industry.

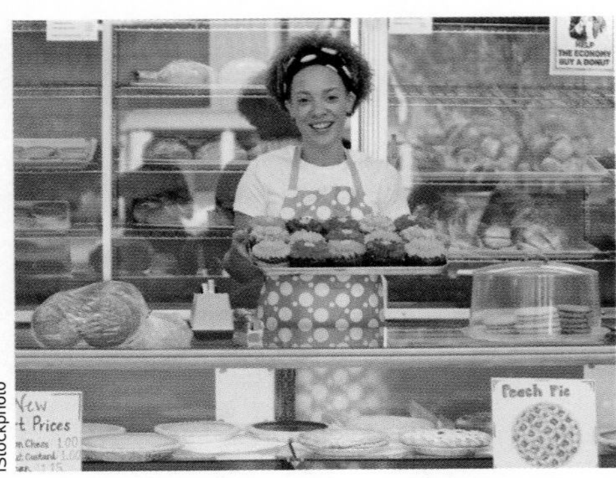
iStockphoto

For firms like bakeries, there are constant costs across the industry.

iStockphoto

Firms like beachfront resorts face increasing costs across the industry.

Simon Turner/Alamy

Firms producing electric cars enjoy decreasing costs across the industry.

In this particular case, the long-run industry supply curve is horizontal at $14. In other words, in this industry supply is *perfectly elastic* in the long run: given time to enter or exit, firms will supply any quantity that consumers demand at a price of $14. Perfectly elastic long-run supply is actually a good assumption for many industries. In this case we speak of there being *constant costs across the industry*: each firm, regardless of whether it is an incumbent or a new entrant, faces the same cost structure (that is, they each have the same cost curve). Industries that satisfy this condition are industries in which there is a perfectly elastic supply of inputs—industries like agriculture or bakeries.

In other industries, however, even the long-run industry supply curve slopes upward. The usual reason for this is that producers must use some input that is in limited supply (that is, their supply is at least somewhat inelastic). As the industry expands, the price of that input is driven up. Consequently, the cost structure for firms becomes higher than it was when the industry was smaller. An example is beachfront resort hotels, which must compete for a limited quantity of prime beachfront property. Industries that behave like this are said to have *increasing costs across the industry*.

Finally, it is possible for the long-run industry supply curve to slope downward, a condition that occurs when the cost structure for firms becomes lower as the industry expands. This is the case in industries such as the electric car industry, in which increased output allows for economies of scale in the production of lithium batteries and other specialized inputs, and thus lower input prices. A downward-sloping industry supply curve indicates *decreasing costs across the industry*.

Regardless of whether the long-run industry supply curve is horizontal, upward sloping, or downward sloping, the long-run price elasticity of supply is *higher* than the short-run price elasticity whenever there is free entry and exit. As shown in Figure 27-5, the long-run industry supply curve is always flatter than the short-run industry supply curve. The reason is entry and exit: a high price caused by an increase in demand attracts entry by new firms, resulting in a rise in industry output and an eventual fall in price; a low price caused by a decrease in demand induces existing firms to exit, leading to a fall in industry output and an eventual increase in price.

The distinction between the short-run industry supply curve and the long-run industry supply curve is very important in practice. We often see a sequence of events like that shown in Figure 27-4: an increase in demand initially leads to a large price increase, but prices return to their initial level once new firms have entered the industry. Or we see the sequence in reverse: a fall in demand reduces prices in the short run, but they return to their initial level as producers exit the industry.

The Cost of Production and Efficiency in Long-Run Equilibrium

Our analysis leads us to three conclusions about the cost of production and efficiency in the long-run equilibrium of a perfectly competitive industry. These results will be important in our upcoming discussion of how monopoly gives rise to inefficiency.

First, in a perfectly competitive industry in equilibrium, the value of marginal cost is the same for all firms. That's because all firms produce the quantity of output at which marginal cost equals the market price, and as price-takers they all face the same market price.

Second, in a perfectly competitive industry with free entry and exit, each firm will have zero economic profit in the long-run equilibrium. Each firm produces the quantity of output that minimizes its average total cost—corresponding to point *Z* in panel (c) of Figure 27-4. So the total cost of producing the industry's output is minimized in a perfectly competitive industry.

FIGURE 27-5 **Comparing the Short-Run and Long-Run Industry Supply Curves**

The long-run industry supply curve may slope upward, but it is always flatter—more elastic—than the short-run industry supply curve. This is because of entry and exit: a higher price attracts new entrants in the long run, resulting in a rise in industry output and a fall in price; a lower price induces existing producers to exit in the long run, generating a fall in industry output and a rise in price.

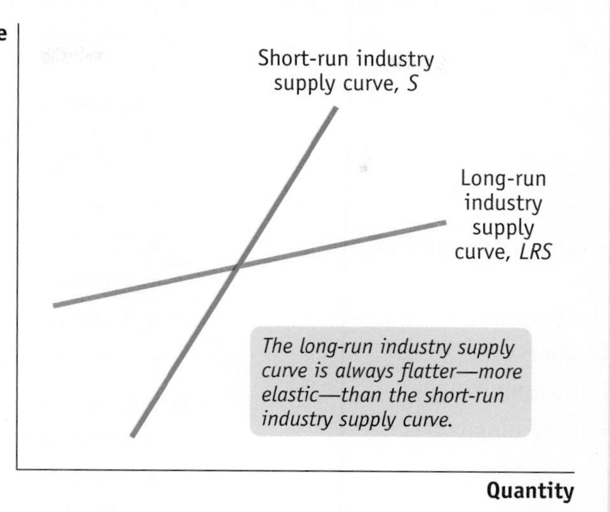

The third and final conclusion is that the long-run market equilibrium of a perfectly competitive industry is efficient: no mutually beneficial transactions go unexploited. To understand this, recall a fundamental requirement for efficiency: all consumers who are willing to pay an amount greater than or equal to the sellers' cost actually get the good. We also learned that when a market is efficient (except under certain, well-defined conditions), the market price matches all consumers willing to pay at least the market price with all sellers who have a cost of production that is less than or equal to the market price.

So in the long-run equilibrium of a perfectly competitive industry, production is efficient: costs are minimized and no resources are wasted. In addition, the allocation of goods to consumers is efficient: every consumer willing to pay the cost of producing the good gets it. Indeed, no mutually beneficial transaction is left unexploited. Moreover, this condition tends to persist over time as the environment changes: the force of competition makes producers responsive to changes in consumers' desires and to changes in technology.

MODULE 27 Review

Solutions appear at the back of the book.

Check Your Understanding

1. Which of the following events will induce firms to enter an industry? Which will induce firms to exit? When will entry or exit cease? Explain your answer.
   a. A technological advance lowers the fixed cost of production of every firm in the industry.
   b. The wages paid to workers in the industry go up for an extended period of time.
   c. A permanent change in consumer tastes increases demand for the good.
   d. The price of a key input rises due to a long-term shortage of that input.
2. Assume that the egg industry is perfectly competitive and is in long-run equilibrium with a perfectly elastic long-run industry supply curve. Health concerns about cholesterol then lead to a decrease in demand. Construct a figure similar to Figure 27-4, showing the short-run behavior of the industry and how long-run equilibrium is reestablished.

Multiple-Choice Questions

1. In the long run, a perfectly competitive firm will earn
   a. a negative market return.
   b. a positive profit.
   c. a loss.
   d. zero economic profit.
   e. excess profit.

2. With perfect competition, efficiency is generally attained in
   a. the short run but not the long run.
   b. the long run but not the short run.
   c. both the short run and the long run.
   d. neither the short run nor the long run.
   e. specific firms only.

3. Compared to the short-run industry supply curve, the long-run industry supply curve will be more
   a. elastic.
   b. inelastic.
   c. steeply sloped.
   d. profitable.
   e. accurate.

4. Which of the following is generally true for perfect competition?
   I. There is free entry and exit.
   II. Long-run market equilibrium is efficient.
   III. Firms maximize profits at the output level where $P = MC$.
   a. I only
   b. II only
   c. III only
   d. I and II only
   e. I, II, and III

5. Which of the following will happen if perfectly competitive firms are earning positive economic profit?
   a. Firms will exit the industry.
   b. The short-run industry supply curve will shift right.
   c. The short-run industry supply curve will shift left.
   d. Firm output will increase.
   e. Market price will increase.

Critical-Thinking Question

Draw correctly labeled side-by-side graphs to show the long-run adjustment that would take place if perfectly competitive firms were earning a profit.

BUSINESS CASE • TheFind Finds the Cheapest Price

Courtesy of The Find, Inc.

In Sunnyvale, California, Tri Trang walked into a Best Buy and found the perfect gift for his girlfriend, a $184.85 Garmin GPS system. A year earlier, he would have put the item in his cart and purchased it. Instead, he whipped out his Android phone; using an app that instantly compared Best Buy's price to those of other retailers, he found the same item on Amazon.com for $106.75, with no shipping charges and no sales tax. Trang proceeded to buy it from Amazon, right there on the spot.

It doesn't stop there. TheFind, the most popular of the price-comparison sites, will also provide users with a map to the store with the best price, coupon codes and shipping deals, and other tools to help organize purchases. *Terror* has been the word used to describe the reaction of brick-and-mortar retailers.

Before the advent of apps like TheFind's, a retailer could lure customers into its store with enticing specials, and reasonably expect them to buy other, more profitable things, too—with some prompting from salespeople. But those days are disappearing. According to one study, 73% of customers with mobile devices prefer to shop by phone rather than talk to a salesperson. Best Buy recently settled a lawsuit alleging that it posted web prices at in-store kiosks faster than the ones customers saw on their home computers, a maneuver that would have been quickly discovered by users of TheFind's app.

Not surprisingly, use of TheFind's app has increased at an extremely fast clip. The number of people making purchases on their phones nearly doubled between 2011 and 2012. Indeed, retailers are expecting even more shoppers to use their phones to make purchases in the coming years. The accompanying figure illustrates their projections for dramatic growth in cell phone sales through 2016. On TheFind, the most frequently searched items in stores are iPhones, iPads, video games, and other electronics.

Expected Growth in Cell Phone Purchases in the United States, 2010–2016

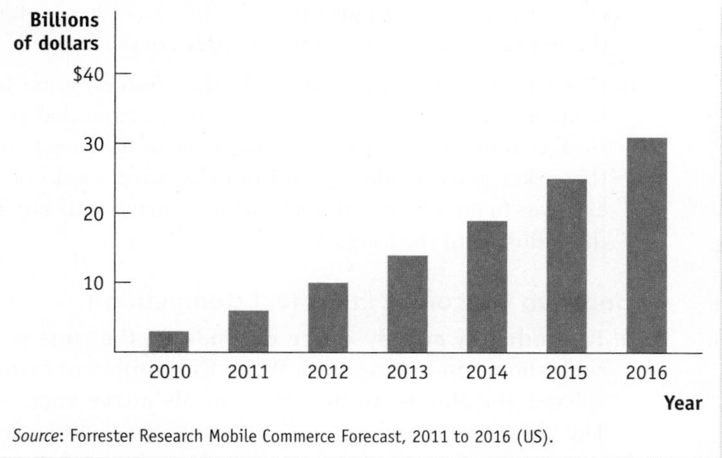

Source: Forrester Research Mobile Commerce Forecast, 2011 to 2016 (US).

According to e-commerce experts, U.S. retailers have begun to alter their selling strategies in response. One strategy involves stocking products that manufacturers have slightly modified for the retailer, which allows the retailer to be their exclusive seller. In addition, when confronted by an in-store customer wielding a lower price on a mobile device, some retailers will lower their price to avoid losing the sale.

Yet retailers are clearly frightened. As one analyst said, "Only a couple of retailers can play the lowest-price game. This is going to accelerate the demise of retailers who do not have either competitive pricing or stand-out store experience."

Questions for Thought

1. What do the details in the case suggest about whether or not the retail market for electronics was perfectly competitive before the advent of mobile-device comparison shopping?
2. What effect will the introduction of TheFind's and similar apps have on competition in the retail market for electronics? On the profitability of brick-and-mortar retailers like Best Buy? What, on average, will be the effect on the consumer surplus of purchasers of these items?
3. Why are some retailers responding by having manufacturers make exclusive versions of products for them? Is this trend likely to increase or diminish?

SECTION 9 REVIEW

Summary

Introduction to Market Structure

1. There are four main types of market structure based on the number of firms in the industry and product differentiation: perfect competition, monopoly, oligopoly, and monopolistic competition.
2. In a **perfectly competitive market** all firms are **price-taking firms** and all consumers are **price-taking consumers**—no one's actions can influence the market price. Consumers are normally price-takers, but firms often are not. In a **perfectly competitive industry,** every firm in the industry is a price-taker.
3. A **monopolist** is a producer who is the sole supplier of a good without close substitutes. An industry controlled by a monopolist is a **monopoly.**
4. To persist, a monopoly must be protected by a **barrier to entry.** This can take the form of control of a natural resource or input, increasing returns to scale that give rise to a **natural monopoly,** technological superiority, or government rules that prevent entry by other firms, such as **patents** or **copyrights.**
5. There are two necessary conditions for a perfectly competitive industry: there are many firms, none of which has a large **market share,** and the industry produces a **standardized product** or **commodity**—goods that consumers regard as equivalent. A third condition is often satisfied as well: **free entry and exit** into and from the industry.
6. Many industries are **oligopolies:** there are only a few sellers, called **oligopolists.** Oligopolies exist for more or less the same reasons that monopolies exist, but in weaker form. They are characterized by **imperfect competition:** firms compete but possess some market power.
7. **Monopolistic competition** is a market structure in which there are many competing firms, each producing a differentiated product, and there is free entry and exit in the long run. Product differentiation takes three main forms: by style or type, by location, and by quality. The extent of imperfect competition can be measured by the **Herfindahl–Hirschman Index.**

Perfect Competition

8. A producer chooses output according to the **optimal output rule:** produce the quantity at which **marginal revenue** equals marginal cost. For a price-taking firm, marginal revenue is equal to price and its **marginal revenue curve** is a horizontal line at the market price. It chooses output according to the **price-taking firm's optimal output rule:** produce the quantity at which price equals marginal cost. However, a firm that produces the optimal quantity may not be profitable.

Graphing Perfect Competition

9. A firm is profitable if total revenue exceeds total cost or, equivalently, if the market price exceeds its **break-even price**—minimum average total cost. If market price exceeds the break-even price, the firm is profitable. If market price is less than minimum average total cost, the firm is unprofitable. If market price is equal to minimum average total cost, the firm breaks even. When profitable, the firm's per-unit profit is $P - ATC$; when unprofitable, its per-unit loss is $ATC - P$.
10. Fixed cost is irrelevant to the firm's optimal short-run production decision. The short-run production decision depends on the firm's **shut-down price**—its minimum average variable cost—and the market price. When the market price is equal to or exceeds the shut-down price, the firm produces the output quantity at which marginal cost equals the market price. When the market price falls below the shut-down price, the firm ceases production in the short run. This decision to produce or shut down generates the firm's *short-run individual supply curve.*
11. Fixed cost matters over time. If the market price is below minimum average total cost for an extended period of time, firms will exit the industry in the long run. If market price is above minimum average total cost, existing firms are profitable and new firms will enter the industry in the long run.

Long-Run Outcomes in Perfect Competition

12. The **industry supply curve** depends on the time period (short run or long run). When the number of firms is fixed, the **short-run industry supply curve** applies. The **short-run market equilibrium** occurs where the short-run industry supply curve and the demand curve intersect.
13. With sufficient time for entry into and exit from an industry, the **long-run industry supply curve** applies. The **long-run market equilibrium** occurs at the intersection of the long-run industry supply curve and the demand curve. At this point, no producer has an incentive to enter or exit. The long-run industry supply curve is often horizontal. It may slope upward if there is limited supply of an input, resulting in increasing costs across the industry. It may even slope downward, as in the case of decreasing costs across the industry. But the long-run industry supply curve is always more elastic than the short-run industry supply curve.

14. In the long-run market equilibrium of a competitive industry, profit maximization leads each firm to produce at the same marginal cost, which is equal to the market price. Free entry and exit means that each firm earns zero economic profit—producing the output corresponding to its minimum average total cost. So the total cost of production of an industry's output is minimized. The outcome is efficient because every consumer with willingness to pay greater than or equal to marginal cost gets the good.

Key Terms

Problems

1. For each of the following, is the industry perfectly competitive? Referring to market share, standardization of the product, and/or free entry and exit, explain your answers.

   a. aspirin

   b. Alicia Keys concerts

   c. SUVs

2. Kate's Katering provides catered meals, and the catered meals industry is perfectly competitive. Kate's machinery costs $100 per day and is the only fixed input. Her variable cost consists of the wages paid to the cooks and the food ingredients. The variable cost per day associated with each level of output is given in the accompanying table.

Quantity of meals	*VC*
0	$0
10	200
20	300
30	480
40	700
50	1,000

   a. Calculate the total cost, the average variable cost, the average total cost, and the marginal cost for each quantity of output.

   b. What is the break-even price? What is the shut-down price?

   c. Suppose that the price at which Kate can sell catered meals is $21 per meal. In the short run, will Kate earn a profit? In the short run, should she produce or shut down?

   d. Suppose that the price at which Kate can sell catered meals is $17 per meal. In the short run, will Kate earn a profit? In the short run, should she produce or shut down?

   e. Suppose that the price at which Kate can sell catered meals is $13 per meal. In the short run, will Kate earn a profit? In the short run, should she produce or shut down?

3. Bob produces DVD movies for sale, which requires a building and a machine that copies the original movie onto a DVD. Bob rents a building for $30,000 per month and rents a machine for $20,000 a month. Those are his fixed costs. His variable costs per month are given in the accompanying table.

Quantity of DVDs	*VC*
0	$0
1,000	5,000
2,000	8,000
3,000	9,000
4,000	14,000
5,000	20,000
6,000	33,000
7,000	49,000
8,000	72,000
9,000	99,000
10,000	150,000

   a. Calculate Bob's average variable cost, average total cost, and marginal cost for each quantity of output.

   b. There is free entry into the industry, and anyone who enters will face the same costs as Bob. Suppose that currently the price of a DVD is $25. What will Bob's profit be? Is this a long-run equilibrium? If not, what will the price of DVD movies be in the long run?

4. Consider Bob's DVD company described in Problem 3. Assume that DVD production is a perfectly competitive industry. For each of the following questions, explain your answers.

   a. What is Bob's break-even price? What is his shut-down price?

   b. Suppose the price of a DVD is $2. What should Bob do in the short run?

   c. Suppose the price of a DVD is $7. What is the profit-maximizing quantity of DVDs that Bob should produce? What will his total profit be? Will he produce or shut down in the short run? Will he stay in the industry or exit in the long run?

   d. Suppose instead that the price of DVDs is $20. Now what is the profit-maximizing quantity of DVDs that Bob should produce? What will his total profit be now? Will he produce or shut down in the short run? Will he stay in the industry or exit in the long run?

5. Consider again Bob's DVD company described in Problem 3.

   a. Draw Bob's marginal cost curve.

   b. Over what range of prices will Bob produce no DVDs in the short run?

   c. Draw Bob's individual supply curve.

6. a. A profit-maximizing business incurs an economic loss of $10,000 per year. Its fixed cost is $15,000 per year. Should it produce or shut down in the short run? Should it stay in the industry or exit in the long run?

   b. Suppose instead that this business has a fixed cost of $6,000 per year. Should it produce or shut down in the short run? Should it stay in the industry or exit in the long run?

7. The first sushi restaurant opens in town. Initially, people are very cautious about eating tiny portions of raw fish, as this is a town where large portions of grilled meat have always been popular. Soon, however, an influential health report warns consumers against grilled meat and suggests that they increase their consumption of fish, especially raw fish. The sushi restaurant becomes very popular and its profit increases.

   a. What will happen to the short-run profit of the sushi restaurant? What will happen to the number of sushi restaurants in town in the long run? Will the first sushi restaurant be able to sustain its short-run profit over the long run? Explain your answers.

   b. Local steakhouses suffer from the popularity of sushi and start incurring losses. What will happen to the number of steakhouses in town in the long run? Explain your answer.

8. A perfectly competitive firm has the following short-run total costs:

Quantity	*TC*
0	$5
1	10
2	13
3	18
4	25
5	34
6	45

Market demand for the firm's product is given by the following market demand schedule:

Price	Quantity demanded
$12	300
10	500
8	800
6	1,200
4	1,800

   a. Calculate this firm's marginal cost and, for all output levels except zero, the firm's average variable cost and average total cost.

   b. There are 100 firms in this industry that all have costs identical to those of this firm. Draw the short-run industry supply curve. In the same diagram, draw the market demand curve.

   c. What is the market price, and how much profit will each firm make?

9. A new vaccine against a deadly disease has just been discovered. Presently, 55 people die from the disease each year. The new vaccine will save lives, but it is not completely safe. Some recipients of the shots will die from adverse reactions. The projected effects of the inoculation are given in the accompanying table:

Percent of population inoculated	Total deaths due to disease	Total deaths due to inoculation	Marginal benefit of inoculation	Marginal cost of inoculation	"Profit" of inoculation
0	55	0			
			___	___	___
10	45	0			
			___	___	___
20	36	1			
			___	___	___
30	28	3			
			___	___	___
40	21	6			
			___	___	___
50	15	10			
			___	___	___
60	10	15			
			___	___	___
70	6	20			
			___	___	___
80	3	25			
			___	___	___
90	1	30			
			___	___	___
100	0	35			

a. What are the interpretations of "marginal benefit" and "marginal cost" here? Calculate marginal benefit and marginal cost per each 10% increase in the rate of inoculation. Write your answers in the table.

b. What proportion of the population should optimally be inoculated?

c. What is the interpretation of "profit" here? Calculate the profit for all levels of inoculation.

10. The production of agricultural products like wheat is one of the few examples of a perfectly competitive industry. In this question, we analyze results from a hypothetical study about wheat production in the United States in 2001 and make some comparisons to wheat production in 2013.

a. The average variable cost per acre planted with wheat was $107 per acre. Assuming a yield of 50 bushels per acre, calculate the average variable cost per bushel of wheat.

b. The average price of wheat received by a farmer in 1998 was $2.65 per bushel. Do you think the average farm would have shut down in the short run? Explain.

c. With a yield of 50 bushels of wheat per acre, the average total cost per farm was $3.80 per bushel. The harvested acreage for rye (a type of wheat) in the United States fell from 418,000 acres in 1998 to 250,000 in 2010. Using the information on prices and costs here and in parts a and b, explain why this might have happened.

d. Using the above information, do you think the price of wheat was higher or lower than $2.65 per bushel prior to 1998? Why?

M0-M1-M2
M3-M4-M5

SECTION 10 Monopoly

EVERYBODY MUST GET STONES

A few years back De Beers, the world's main supplier of diamonds, ran an ad urging men to buy their wives diamond jewelry. "She married you for richer, for poorer," read the ad. "Let her know how it's going."

Crass? Yes. Effective? No question. For generations diamonds have been a symbol of luxury, valued not only for their appearance but also for their rarity.

But geologists will tell you that diamonds aren't all that rare. In fact, according to the *Dow Jones-Irwin Guide to Fine Gems and Jewelry,* diamonds are "more common than any other gem-quality colored stone. They only seem rarer . . ."

Why do diamonds seem rarer than other gems? Part of the answer is a brilliant marketing campaign. But mainly diamonds seem rare because De Beers *makes* them rare: the company controls most of the world's diamond mines and limits the quantity of diamonds supplied to the market.

In the previous section we concentrated on perfectly competitive markets—those in which the producers are perfect competitors. But De Beers isn't like the producers we've studied so far: it is a *monopolist,* the sole (or almost sole) producer of a good.

Monopolists behave differently from producers in perfectly competitive industries: whereas perfect competitors take the price at which they can sell their output as given, monopolists know that their actions affect market prices and take that effect into account when deciding how much to produce.

In this section we examine how monopolies function and differ from industries in perfect competition. We'll also look at the policies governments adopt in response to monopoly behavior. We conclude with a discussion of how monopolists use *price discrimination*—charging different types of consumers different prices for the same good—to increase profits.

MODULE 28

Monopoly in Practice

iStockphoto

WHAT YOU WILL LEARN

1. How a monopolist determines the profit-maximizing price and quantity
2. How to determine whether a monopoly is earning a profit or a loss

In this module we turn to monopoly, the market structure at the opposite end of the spectrum from perfect competition. A monopolist's profit-maximizing decision is subtly different from that of a price-taking producer, yet it has large implications for the output produced and the welfare created. We will see the crucial role that market demand plays in leading a monopolist to behave differently from a firm in a perfectly competitive industry.

The Monopolist's Demand Curve and Marginal Revenue

Recall the firm's *optimal output rule:* a profit-maximizing firm produces the quantity of output at which the marginal cost of producing the last unit of output equals marginal revenue—the change in total revenue generated by the last unit of output. That is, $MR = MC$ at the profit-maximizing quantity of output.

Although the optimal output rule holds for *all* firms, decisions about price and the quantity of output differ between monopolies and perfectly competitive industries due to differences in the demand curves faced by monopolists and perfectly competitive firms.

We have learned that even though the *market* demand curve always slopes downward, each of the firms that make up a perfectly competitive industry faces a horizontal, *perfectly elastic* demand curve, like D_C in panel (a) of Figure 28-1. Any attempt by an individual firm in a perfectly competitive industry to charge more than the going market price will cause the firm to lose all its sales. It can, however, sell as much as it likes at the market price.

FIGURE 28-1 **Comparing the Demand Curves of a Perfectly Competitive Producer and a Monopolist**

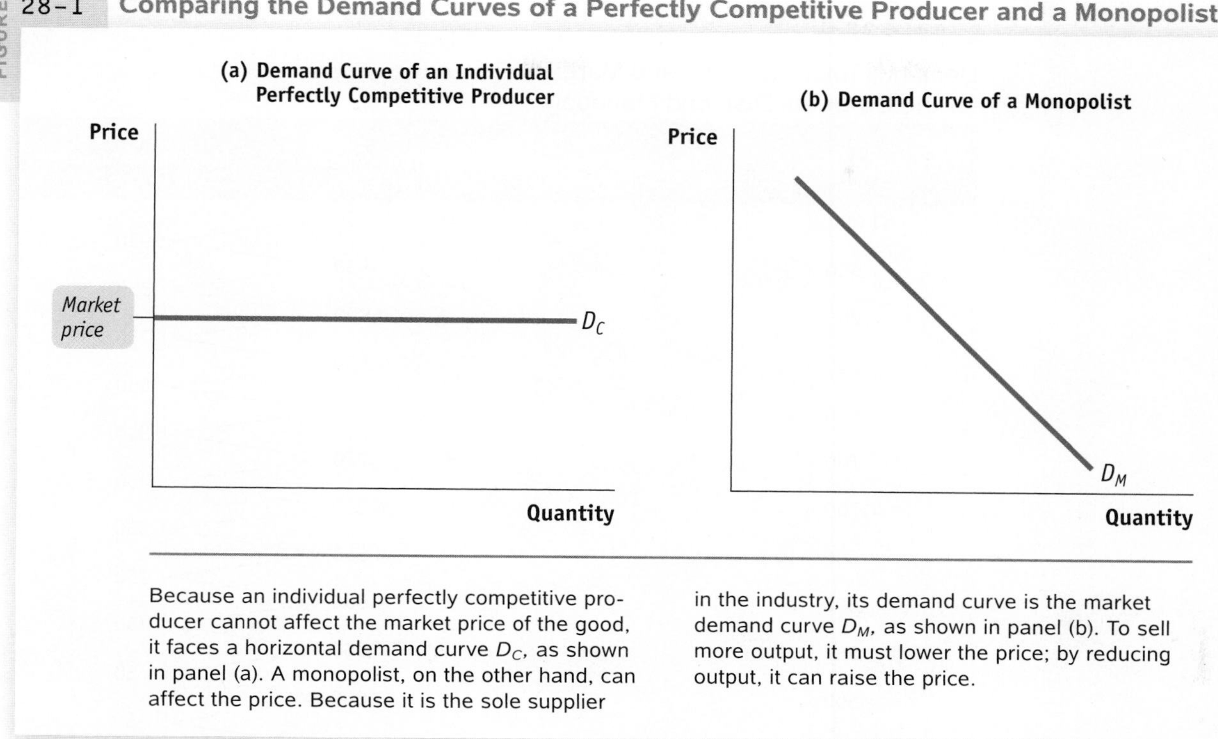

Because an individual perfectly competitive producer cannot affect the market price of the good, it faces a horizontal demand curve D_C, as shown in panel (a). A monopolist, on the other hand, can affect the price. Because it is the sole supplier in the industry, its demand curve is the market demand curve D_M, as shown in panel (b). To sell more output, it must lower the price; by reducing output, it can raise the price.

We saw that the marginal revenue of a perfectly competitive firm is simply the market price. As a result, the price-taking firm's optimal output rule is to produce the output level at which the marginal cost of the last unit produced is equal to the market price.

A monopolist, in contrast, is the sole supplier of its good. So its demand curve is simply the market demand curve, which slopes downward, like D_M in panel (b) of Figure 28-1. This downward slope creates a "wedge" between the price of the good and the marginal revenue of the good.

Table 28-1 shows how this wedge develops. The first two columns of Table 28-1 show a hypothetical demand schedule for De Beers diamonds. For the sake of simplicity, we assume that all diamonds are exactly alike. And to make the arithmetic easy, we suppose that the number of diamonds sold is far smaller than is actually the case. For instance, at a price of $500 per diamond, we assume that only 10 diamonds are sold. The demand curve implied by this schedule is shown in panel (a) of Figure 28-2.

The third column of Table 28-1 shows De Beers's total revenue from selling each quantity of diamonds—the price per diamond multiplied by the number of diamonds sold. The last column shows marginal revenue, the change in total revenue from producing and selling another diamond.

Clearly, after the first diamond, the marginal revenue a monopolist receives from selling one more unit is less than the price at which that unit is sold. For example, if De Beers sells 10 diamonds, the price at which the 10th diamond is sold is $500. But the marginal revenue—the change in total revenue in going from 9 to 10 diamonds—is only $50.

Why is the marginal revenue from that 10th diamond less than the price? Because an increase in production by a monopolist has two opposing effects on revenue:

1. *A quantity effect.* One more unit is sold, increasing total revenue by the price at which the unit is sold (in this case, +$500).
2. *A price effect.* In order to sell that last unit, the monopolist must cut the market price on *all* units sold. This decreases total revenue (in this case, by $9 \times (-\$50) = -\$450$).

TABLE 28-1

Demand, Total Revenue, and Marginal Revenue for the De Beers Diamond Monopoly

Price of diamond P	Quantity of diamonds demanded Q	Total revenue $TR = P \times Q$	Marginal revenue $MR = \Delta TR/\Delta Q$
$1,000	0	$0	
			$950
950	1	950	
			850
900	2	1,800	
			750
850	3	2,550	
			650
800	4	3,200	
			550
750	5	3,750	
			450
700	6	4,200	
			350
650	7	4,550	
			250
600	8	4,800	
			150
550	9	4,950	
			50
500	10	5,000	
			−50
450	11	4,950	
			−150
400	12	4,800	
			−250
350	13	4,550	
			−350
300	14	4,200	
			−450
250	15	3,750	
			−550
200	16	3,200	
			−650
150	17	2,550	
			−750
100	18	1,800	
			−850
50	19	950	
			−950
0	20	0	

The quantity effect and the price effect are illustrated by the two shaded areas in panel (a) of Figure 28-2. Increasing diamond sales from 9 to 10 means moving down the demand curve from *A* to *B,* reducing the price per diamond from $550 to $500. The green-shaded area represents the quantity effect: De Beers sells the 10th diamond at a price of $500. This is offset, however, by the price effect, represented by the orange-shaded area. In order to sell that 10th diamond, De Beers must reduce the price on all its diamonds from $550 to $500. So it loses 9 × $50 = $450 in revenue, the orange-shaded area. So, as point *C* indicates, the total effect on revenue of selling one more diamond—the marginal revenue—derived from an increase in diamond sales from 9 to 10 is only $50.

Point *C* lies on the monopolist's marginal revenue curve, labeled *MR* in panel (a) of Figure 28-2 and taken from the last column of Table 28-1. The crucial point about the monopolist's marginal revenue curve is that it is always *below* the demand curve. That's because of the price effect, which means that a monopolist's marginal revenue from selling an additional unit is always less than the price the monopolist receives

FIGURE 28-2 A Monopolist's Demand, Total Revenue, and Marginal Revenue Curves

Panel (a) shows the monopolist's demand and marginal revenue curves for diamonds from Table 28-1. The marginal revenue curve lies below the demand curve. To see why, consider point *A* on the demand curve, where 9 diamonds are sold at $550 each, generating total revenue of $4,950. To sell a 10th diamond, the price on all 10 diamonds must be cut to $500, as shown by point *B*. As a result, total revenue increases by the green area (the quantity effect: +$500) but decreases by the orange area (the price effect: –$450). So the marginal revenue from the 10th diamond is $50 (the difference between the green and orange areas), which is much lower than its price, $500. Panel (b) shows the monopolist's total revenue curve for diamonds. As output goes from 0 to 10 diamonds, total revenue increases. It reaches its maximum at 10 diamonds—the level at which marginal revenue is equal to 0—and declines thereafter. When the quantity effect dominates the price effect, total revenue rises. When the price effect dominates the quantity effect, total revenue falls.

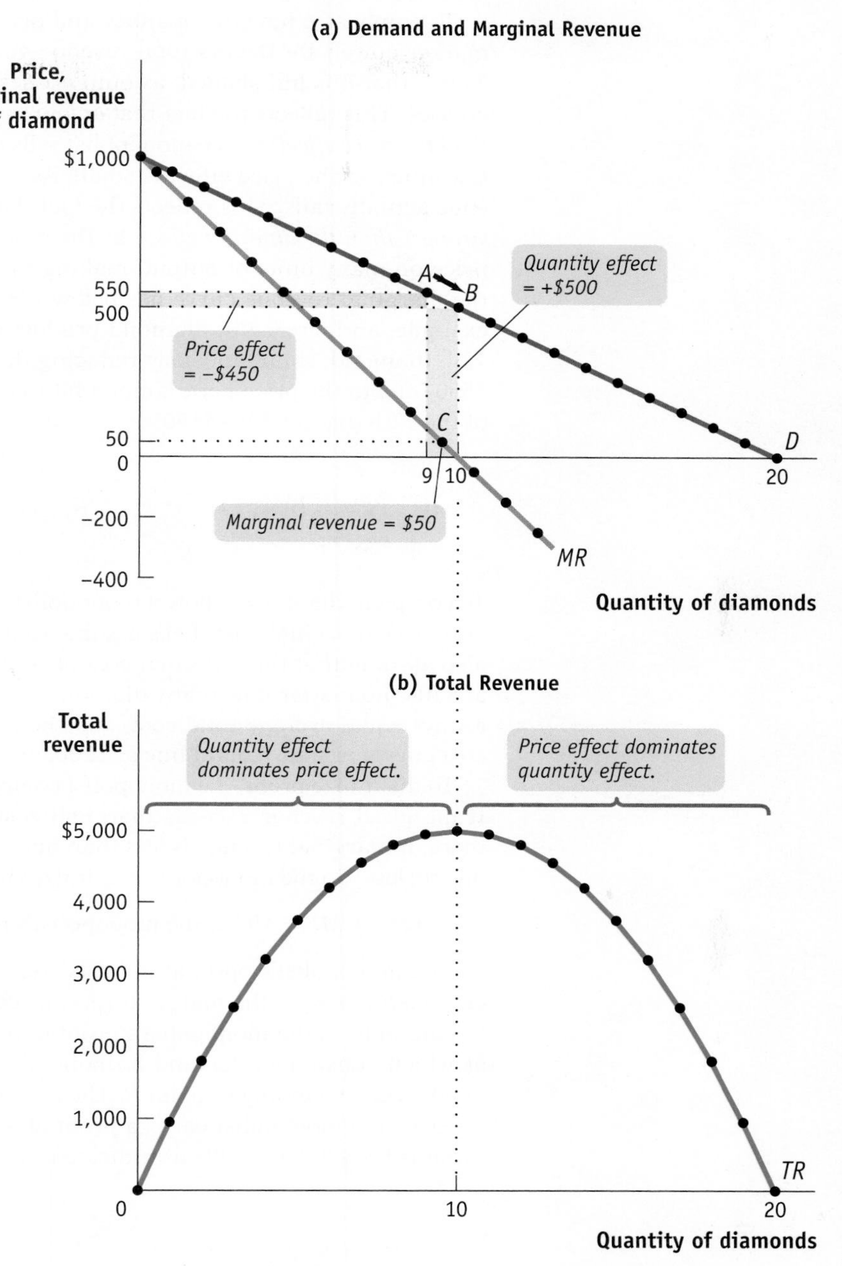

for that unit. It is the price effect that creates the wedge between the monopolist's marginal revenue curve and the demand curve: in order to sell an additional diamond, De Beers must cut the market price on all units sold.

In fact, this wedge exists for any firm that possesses market power, such as an oligopolist. Having market power means that the firm faces a downward-sloping demand curve. As a result, there will always be a price effect from an increase in output for a firm with market power that charges every customer the same price. So for such a firm, the marginal revenue curve always lies below the demand curve.

Take a moment to compare the monopolist's marginal revenue curve with the marginal revenue curve for a perfectly competitive firm, which has no market power. For such a firm there is no price effect from an increase in output: its marginal revenue curve is simply its horizontal demand curve. So for a perfectly competitive firm, market price and marginal revenue are always equal.

To emphasize how the quantity and price effects offset each other for a firm with market power, De Beers's total revenue curve is shown in panel (b) of Figure 28-2. Notice that it is hill-shaped: as output rises from 0 to 10 diamonds, total revenue increases. This reflects the fact that *at low levels of output, the quantity effect is stronger than the price effect:* as the monopolist sells more, it has to lower the price on only very few units, so the price effect is small. As output rises beyond 10 diamonds, total revenue actually falls. This reflects the fact that *at high levels of output, the price effect is stronger than the quantity effect:* as the monopolist sells more, it now has to lower the price on many units of output, making the price effect very large. Correspondingly, the marginal revenue curve lies below zero at output levels above 10 diamonds. For example, an increase in diamond production from 11 to 12 yields only $400 for the 12th diamond, simultaneously reducing the revenue from diamonds 1 through 11 by $550 (due to the price per diamond falling by $50). As a result, the marginal revenue of the 12th diamond is –$150.

The Monopolist's Profit-Maximizing Output and Price

To complete the story of how a monopolist maximizes profit, we now bring in the monopolist's marginal cost. Let's assume that there is no fixed cost of production; we'll also assume that the marginal cost of producing an additional diamond is constant at $200, no matter how many diamonds De Beers produces. Then marginal cost will always equal average total cost, and the marginal cost curve (and the average total cost curve) is a horizontal line at $200, as shown in Figure 28-3.

To maximize profit, the monopolist compares marginal cost with marginal revenue. If marginal revenue exceeds marginal cost, De Beers increases profit by producing more; if marginal revenue is less than marginal cost, De Beers increases profit by producing less. So the monopolist maximizes its profit by using the optimal output rule:

(28-1) $MR = MC$ at the monopolist's profit-maximizing quantity of output

The monopolist's optimal point is shown in Figure 28-3. At *A,* the marginal cost curve, *MC,* crosses the marginal revenue curve, *MR.* The corresponding output level, 8 diamonds, is the monopolist's profit-maximizing quantity of output, Q_M. The price at which consumers demand 8 diamonds is $600, so the monopolist's price, P_M, is $600—corresponding to point *B.* The average total cost of producing each diamond is $200, so the monopolist earns a profit of $600 – $200 = $400 per diamond, and total profit is 8 × $400 = $3,200, as indicated by the shaded area.

Monopoly versus Perfect Competition

In the 1880s, when Cecil Rhodes consolidated many independent diamond producers into the company he founded, De Beers, he converted a perfectly competitive industry into a monopoly. We can now use our analysis to see the effects of such a consolidation.

Let's look again at Figure 28-3 and ask how this same market would work if, instead of being a monopoly, the industry were perfectly competitive. We will continue to assume that there is no fixed cost and that marginal cost is constant, so average total cost and marginal cost are equal.

If the diamond industry consists of many perfectly competitive firms, each of those producers takes the market price as given. That is, each producer acts as if its marginal revenue is equal to the market price. So each firm within the industry uses the price-taking firm's optimal output rule:

(28-2) $P = MC$ at the perfectly competitive firm's profit-maximizing quantity of output.

FIGURE 28-3 The Monopolist's Profit-Maximizing Output and Price

This figure shows the demand, marginal revenue, and marginal cost curves. Marginal cost per diamond is constant at $200, so the marginal cost curve is horizontal at $200. According to the optimal output rule, the profit-maximizing quantity of output for the monopolist is at $MR = MC$, shown by point A, where the marginal cost and marginal revenue curves cross at an output of 8 diamonds. The price De Beers can charge per diamond is found by going to the point on the demand curve directly above point A, which is point B here—a price of $600 per diamond. It makes a profit of $400 × 8 = $3,200. A perfectly competitive industry produces the output level at which $P = MC$, given by point C, where the demand curve and marginal cost curves cross. So a competitive industry produces 16 diamonds, sells at a price of $200, and makes zero economic profit.

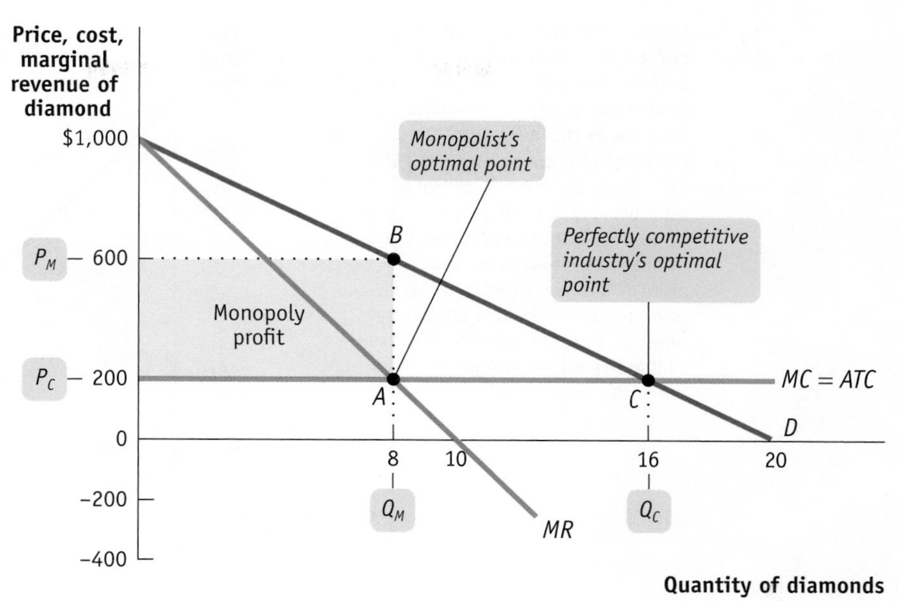

In Figure 28-3, this would correspond to producing at C, where the price per diamond, P_C, is $200, equal to the marginal cost of production. So the profit-maximizing output of an industry under perfect competition, Q_C, is 16 diamonds.

But does the perfectly competitive industry earn any profit at C? No: the price of $200 is equal to the average total cost per diamond. So there is no economic profit for this industry when it produces at the perfectly competitive output level.

We've already seen that once the industry is consolidated into a monopoly, the result is very different. The monopolist's marginal revenue is influenced by the price effect, so that marginal revenue is less than the price. That is,

(28-3) $P > MR = MC$ at the monopolist's profit-maximizing quantity of output

As shown in Figure 28-3, the monopolist produces less than the competitive industry—8 diamonds rather than 16. The price under monopoly is $600, compared with only $200 under perfect competition. The monopolist earns a positive profit, but the competitive industry does not.

So, we can see that compared with a competitive industry, a monopolist does the following:

- produces a smaller quantity: $Q_M < Q_C$
- charges a higher price: $P_M > P_C$
- earns a profit

Compared with competitive firms, monopolies produce less, charge more, and earn a profit.

Monopoly: The General Picture

Figure 28-3 involved specific numbers and assumed that marginal cost was constant, there was no fixed cost, and therefore, that the average total cost curve was a horizontal line. Figure 28-4 shows a more general picture of monopoly in action: D is the market demand curve; MR, the marginal revenue curve; MC, the marginal cost curve; and ATC, the average total cost curve. Here we return to the usual assumption

FIGURE 28-4 The Monopolist's Profit

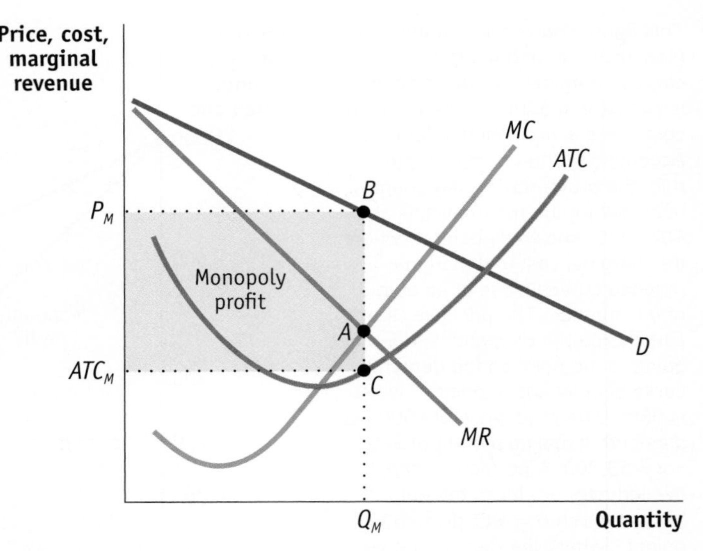

In this case, the marginal cost curve has a "swoosh" shape and the average total cost curve is U-shaped. The monopolist maximizes profit by producing the level of output at which $MR = MC$, given by point A, generating quantity Q_M. It finds its monopoly price, P_M, from the point on the demand curve directly above point A, point B here. The average total cost of Q_M is shown by point C. Profit is given by the area of the shaded rectangle.

that the marginal cost curve has a "swoosh" shape and the average total cost curve is U-shaped.

Applying the optimal output rule, we see that the profit-maximizing level of output, identified as the quantity at which marginal revenue and marginal cost intersect (see point A), is Q_M. The monopolist charges the highest price possible for this quantity, P_M, found at the height of the demand curve at Q_M (see point B). At the profit-maximizing level of output, the monopolist's average total cost is ATC_M (see point C).

Profit is equal to the difference between total revenue and total cost. So we have

$$\textbf{(28-4)}\quad \text{Profit} = TR - TC$$
$$= (P_M \times Q_M) - (ATC_M \times Q_M)$$
$$= (P_M - ATC_M) \times Q_M$$

Profit is equal to the area of the shaded rectangle in Figure 28-4, with a height of $P_M - ATC_M$ and a width of Q_M.

We learned that a perfectly competitive industry can have profits *in the short run but not in the long run*. In the short run, price can exceed average total cost, allowing a perfectly competitive firm to make a profit. But we also know that this cannot persist. In the long run, any profit in a perfectly competitive industry will be competed away as new firms enter the market. In contrast, while a monopoly can earn a profit or a loss in the short run, barriers to entry make it possible for a monopolist to make positive profits in the long run.

ECONOMICS ▶ IN ACTION

SHOCKED BY THE HIGH PRICE OF ELECTRICITY

Historically, electric utilities were recognized as natural monopolies. As you'll recall, these are monopolies that are created and sustained by economies of scale. A utility serviced a defined geographical area, owning the plants that generated electricity as well as the transmission lines that delivered it to retail customers. The rates charged customers were regulated by the government, set at a level to cover the utility's cost of operation plus a modest return on capital to its shareholders.

In the late 1990s, however, there was a move toward deregulation, based on the belief that competition would result in lower retail electricity prices. Competition was introduced at two junctures in the channel from power generation to retail customers: (1) distributors would compete to sell electricity to retail customers, and (2) power generators would compete to supply power to the distributors.

That was the theory, at least. According to one detailed report, 92% of households in states claiming to have retail choice actually cannot choose an alternative supplier of electricity because their wholesale market is still dominated by one power generator.

What proponents of deregulation failed to realize is that the bulk of power generation still entails large up-front fixed costs. Although many small, gas-fired power generators have been built in the last decade, massive, coal-fired plants are still the cheapest and most plentiful form of electricity generation.

In addition, deregulation and the lack of genuine competition enabled power generators to engage in market manipulation—intentionally reducing the amount of power they supplied to distributors in order to drive up prices.

Brand X Pictures

Although electric utilities were deregulated in the 1990s, there's been a trend toward reregulating them.

The most shocking case occurred during the California energy crisis of 2000–2001 that brought blackouts and billions of dollars in electricity surcharges to homes and businesses. On audiotapes later acquired by regulators, workers could be heard discussing plans to shut down power plants during times of peak energy demand, joking about how they were "stealing" more than $1 million a day from California.

According to a Michigan State University study, from 2002 to 2006, average retail electricity prices rose 21% in regulated states versus 36% in fully deregulated states. Another study found that from 1999 to 2007, the difference between prices charged to industrial retail customers in deregulated states and regulated states tripled. And data through 2011 indicate that customers in deregulated states continue to pay more for electricity than those in regulated states.

Angry customers have prompted several states to change the way they regulate their industries, slow down the process of deregulation, or move to reregulate their industries. California has gone so far as to mandate that its electricity distributors reacquire their generation plants (and has plans to reregulate the industry). In addition, regulators continue to be on the lookout for price manipulation in energy markets.

MODULE 28 Review

Solutions appear at the back of the book.

Check Your Understanding

1. Use the accompanying total revenue schedule of Emerald, Inc., a monopoly producer of 10-carat emeralds, to calculate the items listed in parts a–d. Then answer part e.

Quantity of emeralds demanded	Total revenue
1	$100
2	186
3	252
4	280
5	250

a. the demand schedule (Hint: the average revenue at each quantity indicates the price at which that quantity would be demanded.)

b. the marginal revenue schedule

c. the quantity effect component of marginal revenue at each output level

d. the price effect component of marginal revenue at each output level

e. What additional information is needed to determine Emerald, Inc.'s profit-maximizing output?

2. Using the price, quantity, and marginal revenue information from Table 28-1, and a marginal cost of $200, replicate Figure 28-3. Let the marginal cost of diamond production rise to $400. On your graph, show what happens to each of the following:
   a. the marginal cost curve
   b. the profit-maximizing price and quantity
   c. the profit of the monopolist
   d. the quantity that would be produced if the diamond industry were perfectly competitive, and the associated profit

Multiple-Choice Questions

Refer to the graph provided for questions 1–4.

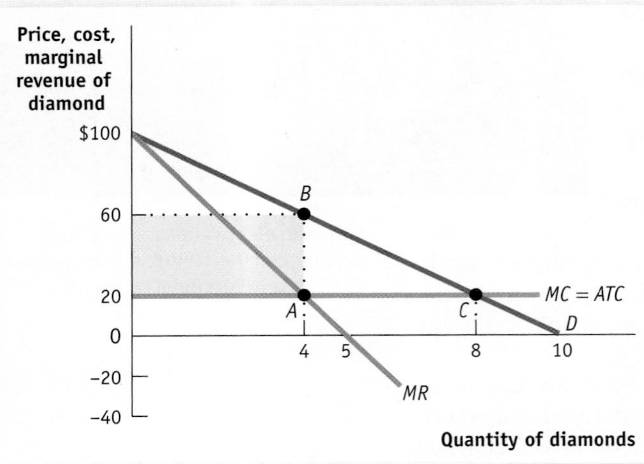

1. The monopolist's profit-maximizing output is
   a. 0.
   b. 4.
   c. 5.
   d. 8.
   e. 10.

2. The monopolist's total revenue equals
   a. $80.
   b. $160.
   c. $240.
   d. $300.
   e. $480.

3. The monopolist's total cost equals
   a. $20.
   b. $80.
   c. $160.
   d. $240.
   e. $480.

4. The monopolist is earning a profit equal to
   a. $0.
   b. $40.
   c. $80.
   d. $160.
   e. $240.

5. How does a monopoly differ from a perfectly competitive industry with the same costs?
   I. It produces a smaller quantity.
   II. It charges a higher price.
   III. It earns zero economic profit in the long run.
   a. I only
   b. II only
   c. III only
   d. I and II only
   e. I, II, and III

Critical-Thinking Questions

1. Draw a graph showing a monopoly earning zero economic profit in the short run.

2. Can a monopoly earn zero economic profit in the long run? Explain.

PITFALLS

IS THERE A MONOPOLY SUPPLY CURVE?

? Given that a monopolist applies its optimal output rule in the same way as a perfectly competitive industry, can we then conclude that a monopolist's supply curve can be calculated in the same way as the supply curve for the industry in perfect competition?

> No, *BECAUSE MONOPOLISTS DON'T HAVE SUPPLY CURVES!* Remember that a supply curve shows the quantity that producers are willing to supply for any given market price. A monopolist, however, does not take the price as given; it chooses a profit-maximizing quantity, taking into account its own ability to influence the price.

To learn more, see pages 302–306.

Monopoly and Public Policy

Shutterstock/YuryZap

WHAT YOU WILL LEARN

1. The effects of the difference between perfect competition and monopoly on society's welfare
2. How policy makers address the problems posed by monopoly

It's good to be a monopolist, but it's not so good to be a monopolist's customer. A monopolist, by reducing output and raising prices, benefits at the expense of consumers. But buyers and sellers always have conflicting interests. Is the conflict of interest under monopoly any different from what it is under perfect competition?

The answer is yes, because monopoly is a source of inefficiency: the losses to consumers from monopoly behavior are larger than the gains to the monopolist. Because monopoly leads to net losses for the economy, governments often try to adopt policies that either prevent the emergence of monopolies or limit their effects. In this module, we will see why monopoly leads to inefficiency and examine the policies governments turn to in response.

Welfare Effects of Monopoly

By holding output below the level at which marginal cost is equal to the market price, a monopolist increases its profit but hurts consumers. To assess whether this is a net benefit or loss to society, we must compare the monopolist's gain in profit to the consumers' loss. And what we learn is that the consumers' loss is larger than the monopolist's gain. Monopoly causes a net loss for society.

To see why, let's return to the case in which the marginal cost curve is horizontal, as shown in the two panels of Figure 29-1. Here the marginal cost curve is MC, the demand curve is D, and, in panel (b), the marginal revenue curve is MR.

Panel (a) shows what happens if this industry is perfectly competitive. Equilibrium output is Q_C; the price of the good, P_C, is equal to marginal cost, and marginal cost is also equal to average total cost because there is no fixed cost and marginal cost is constant. Each firm is earning exactly its average total cost per unit of output, so there is no producer surplus in this equilibrium. The consumer surplus generated by the market is equal to the area of the blue-shaded triangle CS_C shown in panel (a). Since there

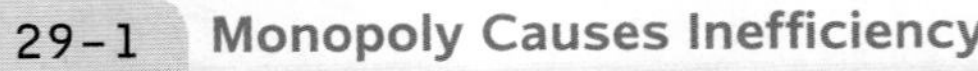

FIGURE 29-1 Monopoly Causes Inefficiency

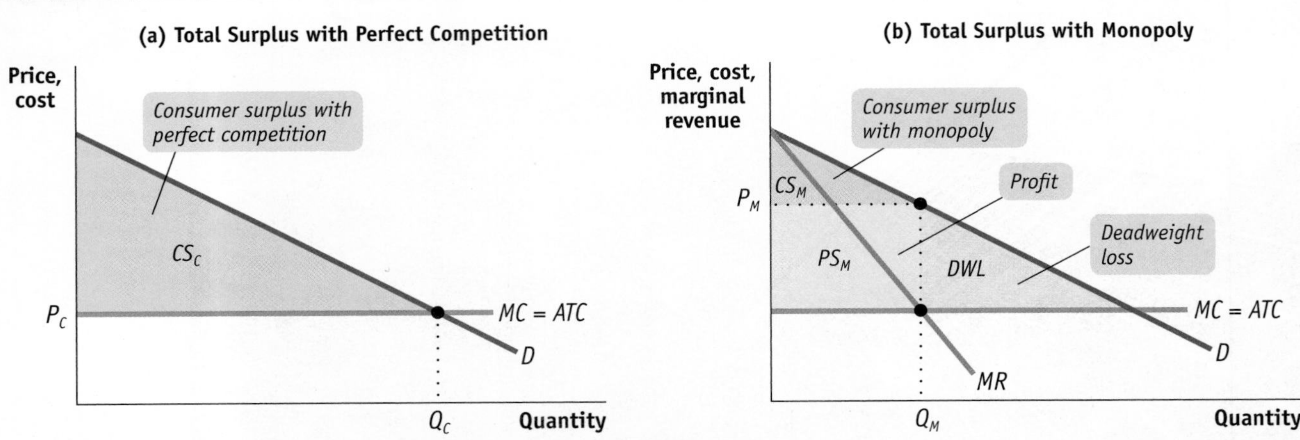

Panel (a) depicts a perfectly competitive industry: output is Q_C, and market price, P_C, is equal to *MC*. Since price is exactly equal to each producer's average total cost of production, there is no producer surplus. So total surplus is equal to consumer surplus, the entire shaded area. Panel (b) depicts the industry under monopoly: the monopolist decreases output to Q_M and charges P_M. Consumer surplus (blue area) has shrunk: a portion of it has been captured as profit (green area), and a portion of it has been lost to deadweight loss (yellow area), the value of mutually beneficial transactions that do not occur because of monopoly behavior. As a result, total surplus falls.

is no producer surplus when the industry is perfectly competitive, CS_C also represents the total surplus.

Panel (b) shows the results for the same market, but this time assuming that the industry is a monopoly. The monopolist produces the level of output, Q_M, at which marginal cost is equal to marginal revenue, and it charges the price, P_M. The industry now earns profit—which is also the producer surplus in this case—equal to the area of the green rectangle, PS_M. Note that this profit is part of what was consumer surplus in the perfectly competitive market, and consumer surplus with the monopoly shrinks to the area of the blue triangle, CS_M.

By comparing panels (a) and (b), we see that in addition to the redistribution of surplus from consumers to the monopolist, another important change has occurred: the sum of profit and consumer surplus—total surplus—is *smaller* under monopoly than under perfect competition. That is, the sum of CS_M and PS_M in panel (b) is less than the area CS_C in panel (a).

Previously, we analyzed how taxes could cause *deadweight loss* for society. Here we show that a monopoly creates deadweight loss equal to the area of the yellow triangle, *DWL*. So monopoly produces a net loss for society.

This net loss arises because some mutually beneficial transactions do not occur. There are people for whom an additional unit of the good is worth more than the marginal cost of producing it but who don't consume it because they are not willing to pay the monopoly price, P_M. Indeed, by driving a wedge between price and marginal cost, a monopoly acts much like a tax on consumers and produces the same kind of inefficiency.

So monopoly power detracts from the welfare of society as a whole and is a source of market failure. Is there anything government policy can do about it?

Preventing Monopoly

Policy toward monopolies depends crucially on whether or not the industry in question is a natural monopoly. As you know, a *natural monopoly* is one in which increasing returns to scale ensure that a bigger producer has lower average total cost. If the industry is *not* a natural monopoly, the best policy is to prevent a monopoly from arising or break it up if it already exists.

Dealing with a Natural Monopoly

Breaking up a monopoly that isn't natural is clearly a good idea: the gains to consumers outweigh the loss to the producer. But it's not so clear whether a natural monopoly, one in which large producers have lower average total costs than small producers, should be broken up, because this would raise average total cost. For example, a town government that tried to prevent a single company from dominating local gas supply—which, as we've discussed, is almost surely a natural monopoly—would raise the cost of providing gas to its residents.

Yet even in the case of a natural monopoly, a profit-maximizing monopolist acts in a way that causes inefficiency—it charges consumers a price that is higher than marginal cost and, by doing so, prevents some potentially beneficial transactions. Also, it can seem unfair that a firm that has managed to establish a monopoly position earns a large profit at the expense of consumers.

What can public policy do about this? There are two common answers:

1. Public ownership
2. Regulation

Public Ownership

In many countries, the preferred answer to the problem of natural monopoly has been **public ownership.** Instead of allowing a private monopolist to control an industry, the government establishes a public agency to provide the good and protect consumers' interests.

There are some examples of public ownership in the United States. Passenger rail service is provided by the public company Amtrak; regular mail delivery is provided by the U.S. Postal Service; some cities, including Los Angeles, have publicly owned electric power companies.

Richard Elliot/AA World Travel/Topfoto/The Image Works

Amtrak, a public company, has provided train service, at a loss, to destinations that attract few passengers.

The advantage of public ownership, in principle, is that a publicly owned natural monopoly can set prices based on the criterion of efficiency rather than profit maximization. In a perfectly competitive industry, profit-maximizing behavior *is* efficient because producers set price equal to marginal cost; that is why there is no economic argument for public ownership of, say, wheat farms.

Experience suggests, however, that public ownership as a solution to the problem of natural monopoly often works badly in practice. One reason is that publicly owned firms are often less eager than private companies to keep costs down or offer high-quality products. Another is that publicly owned companies all too often end up serving political interests—providing contracts or jobs to people with the right connections.

Regulation

In the United States, the more common answer to the existence of natural monopolies has been to leave the industry in private hands but subject it to regulation. In particular, most local utilities, like electricity, telephone service, natural gas, and so on, are covered by **price regulation** that limits the prices they can charge.

Figure 29-2 shows an example of price regulation of a natural monopoly—a highly simplified version of a local gas company. The company faces a demand curve, D, with an associated marginal revenue curve, MR. For simplicity, we assume that the firm's total cost consists of two parts: a fixed cost and a variable cost that is the same for every unit. So marginal cost is constant in this case, and the marginal cost curve (which here is also the average variable cost curve) is the horizontal line MC. The average total cost curve is the downward-sloping curve ATC; it slopes downward because the higher the output, the lower the average fixed cost (the fixed cost per unit of

In **public ownership** of a monopoly, the good is supplied by the government or by a firm owned by the government.

Price regulation limits the price that a monopolist is allowed to charge.

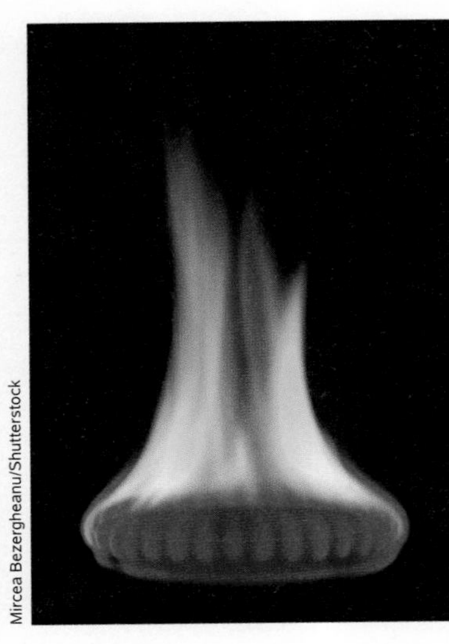
Mircea Bezergheanu/Shutterstock

output). Because average total cost slopes downward over the range of output relevant for market demand, this is a natural monopoly.

Panel (a) illustrates a case of natural monopoly without regulation. The unregulated natural monopolist chooses the monopoly output Q_M and charges the price P_M. Since the monopolist receives a price greater than average total cost, it earns a profit, represented by the green-shaded rectangle in panel (a). Consumer surplus is given by the blue-shaded triangle.

Now suppose that regulators impose a price ceiling on local gas deliveries—one that falls below the monopoly price P_M but above average total cost, say, at P_R in panel (a). At that price the quantity demanded is Q_R.

Does the company have an incentive to produce that quantity? Yes. If the price the monopolist can charge is fixed at P_R by regulators, the firm can sell any quantity between zero and Q_R for the same price, P_R. Because it doesn't have to lower its price to sell more (up to Q_R), there is no price effect to bring marginal revenue below price, so the regulated price becomes the marginal revenue for the monopoly just like the market price is the marginal revenue for a perfectly competitive firm. With marginal revenue being above marginal cost and price exceeding average cost, the firm expands output to meet the quantity demanded, Q_R. This policy has appeal because at the regulated price, the monopolist produces more at a lower price.

Of course, the monopolist will not be willing to produce at all in the long run if the regulated price means producing at a loss. That is, the price ceiling has to be set high enough to allow the firm to cover its average total cost. Panel (b) shows a situation in which regulators have pushed the price down as far as possible, at the level where the average total cost curve crosses the demand curve. At any lower price the firm loses money. The price here, P_R^*, is the best regulated price: the monopolist is just willing to operate because profits are zero and produces Q_R^*, the quantity demanded at that price. Consumers and society gain as a result.

The welfare effects of this regulation can be seen by comparing the shaded areas in the two panels of Figure 29-2. Consumer surplus is increased by the regulation, with the gains coming from two sources. First, profits are eliminated and added instead

FIGURE 29-2 **Unregulated and Regulated Natural Monopoly**

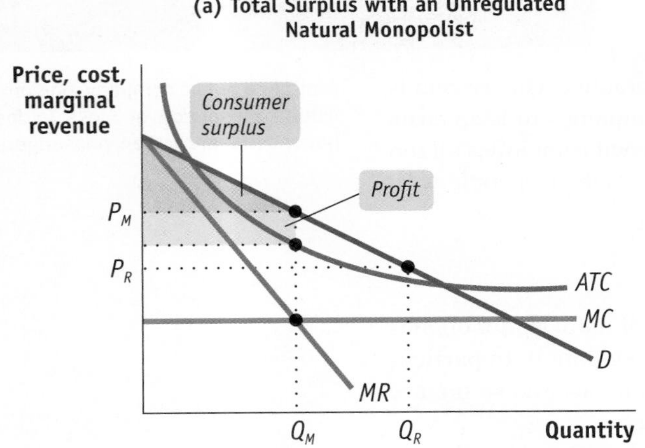

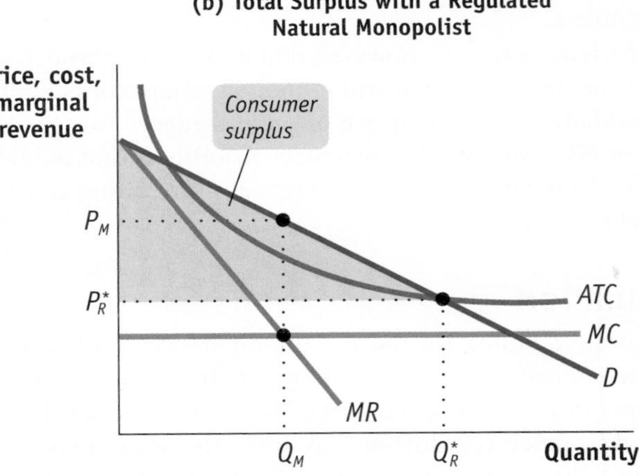

This figure shows the case of a natural monopolist. In panel (a), if the monopolist is allowed to charge P_M, it makes a profit, shown by the green area; consumer surplus is shown by the blue area. If it is regulated and must charge the lower price, P_R, output increases from Q_M to Q_R, profit falls, and consumer surplus increases.

Panel (b) shows what happens when the monopolist must charge a price equal to average total cost, the price P_R^*. Output expands to Q_R^*, and consumer surplus is now the entire blue area. The monopolist makes zero profit. This is the greatest total surplus possible without the monopoly incurring losses.

to consumer surplus. Second, the larger output and lower price leads to an overall welfare gain—an increase in total surplus. In fact, panel (b) illustrates the largest total surplus possible.

Must Monopoly Be Controlled?

Sometimes the cure is worse than the disease. Some economists have argued that the best solution, even in the case of a natural monopoly, may be to live with it. The case for doing nothing is that attempts to control monopoly will, one way or another, do more harm than good.

The following Economics in Action describes the case of cable television, a natural monopoly that has been alternately regulated and deregulated as politicians change their minds about the appropriate policy.

ECONOMICS ▶ IN ACTION

CHAINED BY YOUR CABLE

PhotoAlto/Alamy

Cable prices have increased by around 3% every year, an amount that exceeds the rate of inflation.

The old saying "you can't escape death and taxes" now has a modern twist: "you can't escape death, taxes, and *cable price increases*." Over the last 10 years consumers have seen their cable prices increase by around 3% every year, an amount exceeding the rate of inflation.

Until 1984, cable prices were regulated locally. Because running a cable through a town entailed large fixed costs, cable TV was considered a natural monopoly. However, in 1984 Congress passed a law prohibiting most local governments from regulating cable prices. The result: prices increased sharply, and in 1992 the ensuing consumer backlash led to a new law that once again allowed local governments to set limits on cable prices. But cable operators found ways to circumvent the restrictions.

What went wrong? One possible explanation is that the 1992 law applied only to "basic" packages, and those prices did indeed level off. In response, cable operators began offering fewer channels in the basic package and charging more for premium channels like HBO.

Cable operators have defended their pricing policies, claiming they have been forced to pay higher prices to content providers for popular shows. For example, Time Warner Cable and the Fox network fought fiercely when their contract ended in late 2009, with Fox demanding to be paid $1 per subscriber to their content. When a deal was reached, it was reported that Time Warner had agreed to pay Fox more than 50 cents per subscriber.

Yet critics counter that this defense is largely invalid because about 40% of the channels that command the highest prices are owned in whole or in part by the cable operators themselves. So in paying high prices for content, cable operators are actually profiting.

Cable operators also claim they need to raise prices to pay for system upgrades. Critics, however, once again dismiss the claim, asserting that upgrades pay for themselves through premium pricing and so should not have any effect on the price of non-upgraded services.

Critics also point to evidence that cable operators are exploiting their monopoly power. For example, a study by the Federal Communications Commission showed that cable operators have increased their take per subscriber by over 30% after factoring out all operating costs, including the cost of content. Similarly, the General Accounting Office found that prices are on average 17% lower in communities with two cable operators compared to one.

TV-watchers should not give up hope just yet. Telephone companies Verizon and AT&T are increasingly using their fiber-optic networks to compete with cable operators in many communities. And technological advances in streaming video services are beginning to make a dent in cable's subscriber base. Stay tuned.

MODULE 29 Review

Solutions appear at the back of the book.

Check Your Understanding

1. What policy should the government adopt in the following cases? Explain.
   a. Internet service in Anytown, OH, is provided by cable. Customers feel they are being overcharged, but the cable company claims it must charge prices that let it recover the costs of laying cable.
   b. The only two airlines that currently fly to Alaska need government approval to merge. Other airlines wish to fly to Alaska but need government-allocated landing slots to do so.
2. True or false? Explain your answer.
   a. Society's welfare is lower under monopoly because some consumer surplus is transformed into profit for the monopolist.
   b. A monopolist causes inefficiency because there are consumers who are willing to pay a price greater than or equal to marginal cost but less than the monopoly price.
3. Suppose a monopolist mistakenly believes that its marginal revenue is always equal to the market price. Assuming constant marginal cost and no fixed cost, draw a diagram comparing the level of profit, consumer surplus, total surplus, and deadweight loss for this misguided monopolist compared to a smart monopolist. Explain your findings.

Multiple-Choice Questions

1. Which of the following statements is true of a monopoly as compared to a perfectly competitive market with the same costs?
   I. Consumer surplus is smaller.
   II. Profit is smaller.
   III. Deadweight loss is smaller.
   a. I only
   b. II only
   c. III only
   d. I and II only
   e. I, II, and III
2. Which of the following is true of a natural monopoly?
   a. It experiences diseconomies of scale.
   b. *ATC* is lower if there is a single firm in the market.
   c. It occurs in a market that relies on natural resources for its production.
   d. There are decreasing returns to scale in the industry.
   e. The government must provide the good or service to achieve efficiency.
3. Which of the following government actions is the most common for a natural monopoly in the United States?
   a. prevent its formation
   b. break it up using antitrust laws
   c. use price regulation
   d. public ownership
   e. elimination of the market
4. Which of the following markets is an example of a regulated natural monopoly?
   a. local cable TV
   b. gasoline
   c. cell phone service
   d. organic tomatoes
   e. diamonds
5. Which of the following is most likely to be higher for a regulated natural monopoly than for an unregulated natural monopoly?
   a. product variety
   b. quantity
   c. price
   d. profit
   e. deadweight loss

Critical-Thinking Question

Draw a correctly labeled graph of a natural monopoly. Use your graph to identify each of the following:

a. consumer surplus if the market were somehow able to operate as a perfectly competitive market
b. consumer surplus with the monopoly
c. monopoly profit
d. deadweight loss with the monopoly

Price Discrimination

Exactostock/Superstock

WHAT YOU WILL LEARN

1. The meaning of price discrimination
2. Why price discrimination is so prevalent when producers have market power

Up to this point, we have considered only the case of a monopolist who charges all consumers the same price. However, monopolists want to maximize their profits and often they do so by charging different prices for the same product. In this module we look at how monopolists increase their profits by engaging in *price discrimination*.

Price Discrimination Defined

A monopolist that charges everyone the same price is known as a **single-price monopolist.** As the term suggests, not all monopolists do this. In fact, many monopolists find that they can increase their profits by selling the same good to different customers for different prices: they practice **price discrimination.**

An example of price discrimination that travelers encounter regularly involves airline tickets. Although there are a number of airlines, most routes in the United States are serviced by only one or two carriers, which, as a result, have market power and can influence prices. So any regular airline passenger quickly becomes aware that the simple question "How much will it cost me to fly there?" rarely has a simple answer.

If you are willing to buy a nonrefundable ticket a month in advance and stay over a Saturday night, the round trip may cost only $150—or less if you are a senior citizen or a student. But if you have to go on a business trip tomorrow, which happens to be Tuesday, and want to come back on Wednesday, the same round trip might cost $550. Yet the business traveler and the visiting grandparent receive the same product.

You might object that airlines are not usually monopolies—that in most flight markets the airline industry is an oligopoly. In fact, price discrimination takes place under oligopoly and monopolistic competition as well as monopoly. But it doesn't happen under perfect competition. And once we've seen why monopolists sometimes price-discriminate, we'll be in a good position to understand why it happens in other cases, too.

A **single-price monopolist** charges all consumers the same price.

Sellers engage in **price discrimination** when they charge different prices to different consumers for the same good.

The Logic of Price Discrimination

To get a preliminary view of why price discrimination might be more profitable than charging all consumers the same price, imagine that Air Sunshine offers the only nonstop flights between Bismarck, North Dakota, and Ft. Lauderdale, Florida. Assume that there are no capacity problems—the airline can fly as many planes as the number of passengers warrants. Also assume that there is no fixed cost. The marginal cost to the airline of providing a seat is $125 however many passengers it carries.

Further assume that the airline knows there are two kinds of potential passengers. First, there are business travelers, 2,000 of whom want to travel between the destinations each week. Second, there are high school students, 2,000 of whom also want to travel each week.

Will potential passengers take the flight? It depends on the price. The business travelers, it turns out, really need to fly; they will take the plane as long as the price is no more than $550. Since they are flying purely for business, we assume that cutting the price below $550 will not lead to any increase in business travel. The students, however, have less money and more time; if the price goes above $150, they will take the bus. The implied demand curve is shown in Figure 30-1.

So what should the airline do? If it has to charge everyone the same price, its options are limited. It could charge $550; that way it would get as much as possible out of the business travelers but lose the student market. Or it could charge only $150; that way it would get both types of travelers but would make significantly less money from sales to business travelers.

We can quickly calculate the profits from each of these alternatives. If the airline charged $550, it would sell 2,000 tickets to the business travelers, earning a total revenue of 2,000 × $550 = $1.1 million and incurring costs of 2,000 × $125 = $250,000; so its profit would be $850,000, illustrated by the shaded area B in Figure 30-1. If the airline charged only $150, it would sell 4,000 tickets, receiving revenue of 4,000 × $150 = $600,000 and incurring costs of 4,000 × $125 = $500,000; so its profit would be $100,000. If the airline must charge everyone the same price, charging the higher price and forgoing sales to students is clearly more profitable.

What the airline would really like to do, however, is charge the business travelers the full $550 but offer $150 tickets to the students. That's a lot less than the price paid by business travelers, but it's still above marginal cost; so if the airline could sell those

FIGURE 30-1 Two Types of Airline Customers

Air Sunshine has two types of customers, business travelers willing to pay at most $550 per ticket and students willing to pay at most $150 per ticket. There are 2,000 of each kind of customer. Air Sunshine has constant marginal cost of $125 per seat. If Air Sunshine could charge these two types of customers different prices, it would maximize its profit by charging business travelers $550 and students $150 per ticket. It would capture all of the consumer surplus as profit.

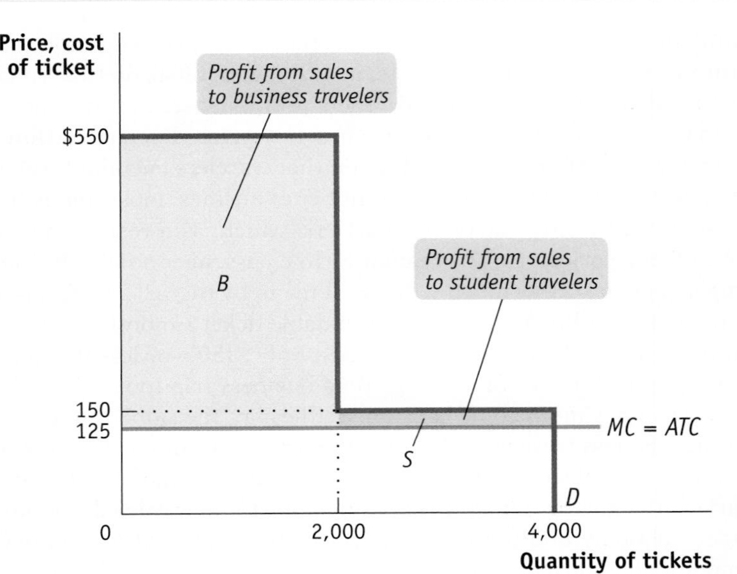

extra 2,000 tickets to students, it would make an additional $50,000 in profit. That is, it would make a profit equal to the areas *B* plus *S* in Figure 30-1.

It would be more realistic to suppose that there is some "give" in the demand of each group: at a price below $550, there would be some increase in business travel; and at a price above $150, some students would still purchase tickets. But this, it turns out, does not do away with the argument for price discrimination. The important point is that the two groups of consumers differ in their *sensitivity to price*—that a high price has a larger effect in discouraging purchases by students than by business travelers. As long as different groups of customers respond differently to the price, a monopolist will find that it can capture more consumer surplus and increase its profit by charging them different prices.

Price Discrimination and Elasticity

A more realistic description of the demand that airlines face would not specify particular prices at which different types of travelers would choose to fly. Instead, it would distinguish between the groups on the basis of their sensitivity to the price—their price elasticity of demand.

Suppose that a company sells its product to two easily identifiable groups of people—business travelers and students. It just so happens that business travelers are very insensitive to the price: there is a certain amount of the product they just have to have whatever the price, but they cannot be persuaded to buy much more than that no matter how cheap it is. Students, though, are more flexible: offer a good enough price and they will buy quite a lot, but raise the price too high and they will switch to something else. What should the company do?

The answer is the one already suggested by our simplified example: the company should charge business travelers, with their low price elasticity of demand, a higher price than it charges students, with their high price elasticity of demand.

The actual situation of the airlines is very much like this hypothetical example. Business travelers typically place a high priority on being in the right place at the right time and are not very sensitive to the price. But leisure travelers are fairly sensitive to the price: faced with a high price, they might take the bus, drive to another airport to get a lower fare, or skip the trip altogether.

So why doesn't an airline simply announce different prices for business and leisure customers? First, this would probably be illegal. (U.S. law places some limits on the ability of companies to practice blatant price discrimination.) Second, even if it were legal, it would be a hard policy to enforce: business travelers might be willing to wear casual clothing and claim they were visiting family in Ft. Lauderdale in order to save $400.

So what the airlines do—quite successfully—is impose rules that indirectly have the effect of charging business and leisure travelers different fares. Business travelers usually travel during the week and want to be home on the weekend, so the round-trip fare is much higher if you don't stay over a Saturday night. The requirement of a weekend stay for a cheap ticket effectively separates business travelers from leisure travelers. Similarly, business travelers often visit several cities in succession rather than make a simple round trip; so round-trip fares are much lower than twice the one-way fare. Many business trips are scheduled on short notice, so fares are much lower if you book far in advance. Fares are also lower if you travel standby, taking your chances on whether you actually get a seat—business travelers have to make it to that meeting; people visiting their relatives don't.

Ostill/Shutterstock

On many airline routes, the fare you pay depends on the type of traveler you are.

Because customers must show their ID at check-in, airlines make sure there are no resales of tickets between the two groups that would undermine their ability to price-discriminate—students can't buy cheap tickets and resell them to business travelers. Look at the rules that govern ticket pricing, and you will see an ingenious implementation of profit-maximizing price discrimination.

Perfect price discrimination takes place when a monopolist charges each consumer his or her willingness to pay—the maximum that the consumer is willing to pay.

Perfect Price Discrimination

Let's return to the example of business travelers and students traveling between Bismarck and Ft. Lauderdale, illustrated in Figure 30-1, and ask what would happen if the airline could distinguish between the two groups of customers in order to charge each a different price.

Clearly, the airline would charge each group its *willingness to pay*—that is, the maximum that each group is willing to pay. For business travelers, the willingness to pay is $550; for students, it is $150. As we have assumed, the marginal cost is $125 and does not depend on output, making the marginal cost curve a horizontal line. And as we noted earlier, we can easily determine the airline's profit: it is the sum of the areas of rectangle *B* and rectangle *S*.

In this case, the consumers do not get any consumer surplus! The entire surplus is captured by the monopolist in the form of profit. When a monopolist is able to capture the entire surplus in this way, we say that the monopolist achieves **perfect price discrimination.**

Fernando Jose V. Soares/ Shutterstock

Perfect price discrimination is almost impossible to achieve in practice.

In general, the greater the number of different prices charged, the closer the monopolist is to perfect price discrimination. Figure 30-2 shows a monopolist facing a downward-sloping demand curve, a monopolist who we assume is able to charge different prices to different groups of consumers, with the consumers who are willing to pay the most being charged the most. In panel (a) the monopolist charges two different prices; in panel (b) the monopolist charges three different prices. Two things are apparent:

- The greater the number of prices the monopolist charges, the lower the lowest price—that is, some consumers will pay prices that approach marginal cost.
- The greater the number of prices the monopolist charges, the more surplus extracted from consumers.

With a very large number of different prices, the picture would look like panel (c), a case of perfect price discrimination. Here, every consumer pays the most he or she is willing to pay, and the entire consumer surplus is extracted as profit.

Both our airline example and the example in Figure 30-2 can be used to make another point: a monopolist that can engage in perfect price discrimination doesn't cause any inefficiency! The reason is that the source of inefficiency is eliminated: all potential consumers who are willing to purchase the good at a price equal to or above marginal cost are able to do so. The perfectly price-discriminating monopolist manages to "scoop up" all consumers by offering some of them lower prices than others.

Perfect price discrimination is almost never possible in practice. At a fundamental level, the inability to achieve perfect price discrimination is a problem of prices as economic signals. When prices work as economic signals, they convey the information needed to ensure that all mutually beneficial transactions will indeed occur: the market price signals the seller's cost, and a consumer signals willingness to pay by purchasing the good whenever that willingness to pay is at least as high as the market price.

The problem in reality, however, is that prices are often not perfect signals: a consumer's true willingness to pay can be disguised, as by a business traveler who claims to be a student when buying a ticket in order to obtain a lower fare. When such disguises work, a monopolist cannot achieve perfect price discrimination.

However, monopolists do try to move in the direction of perfect price discrimination through a variety of pricing strategies. Common techniques for price discrimination include the following:

- *Advance purchase restrictions.* Prices are lower for those who purchase well in advance (or in some cases for those who purchase at the last minute). This separates those who are likely to shop for better prices from those who won't.
- *Volume discounts.* Often the price is lower if you buy a large quantity. For a consumer who plans to consume a lot of a good, the cost of the last unit—the marginal cost to the consumer—is considerably less than the average price. This

separates those who plan to buy a lot, and so are likely to be more sensitive to price, from those who don't.

- *Two-part tariffs.* In a discount club like Costco or Sam's Club (which are not monopolists but monopolistic competitors), you pay an annual fee (the first part of the tariff) in addition to the price of the item(s) you purchase (the second part of the tariff). So the full price of the first item you buy is in effect much higher than that of subsequent items, making the two-part tariff behave like a volume discount.

Our discussion also helps explain why government policies on monopoly typically focus on preventing deadweight loss, not preventing price discrimination—unless it causes serious issues of equity. Compared to a single-price monopolist, price discrimination—even when it is not perfect—can increase the efficiency of the market.

Consider the case of consumers formerly priced out of the market who can now purchase the good at a lower price. If they generate enough surplus to offset the loss in surplus to those facing a higher price and no longer buying the good, then total surplus will increase when price discrimination is introduced.

FIGURE 30-2 Price Discrimination

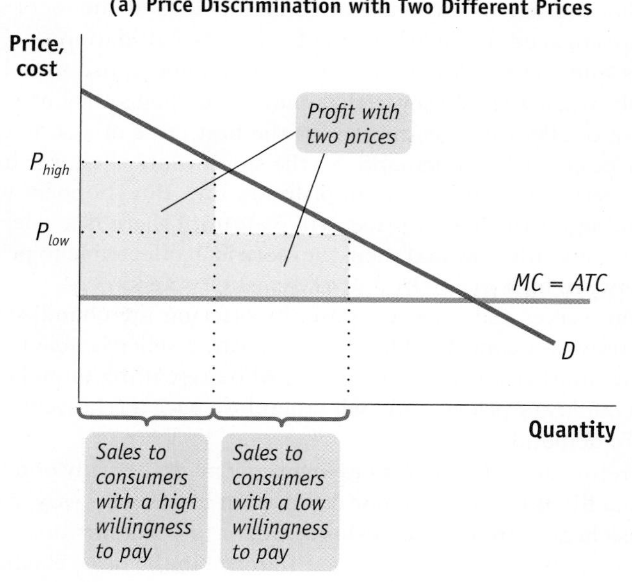

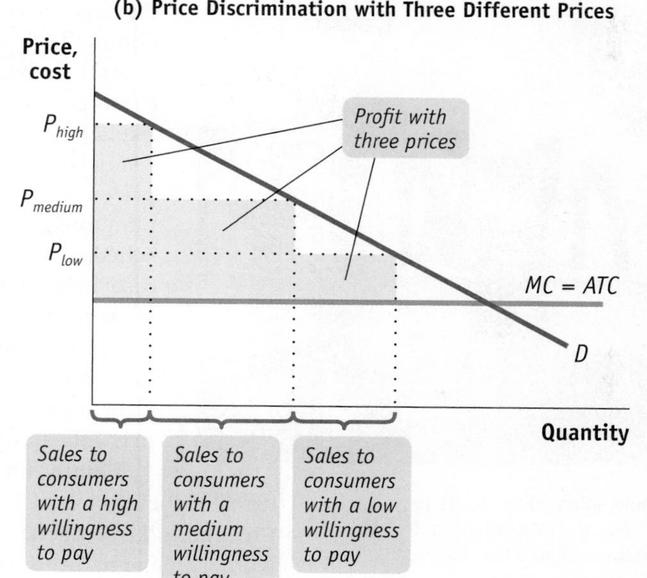

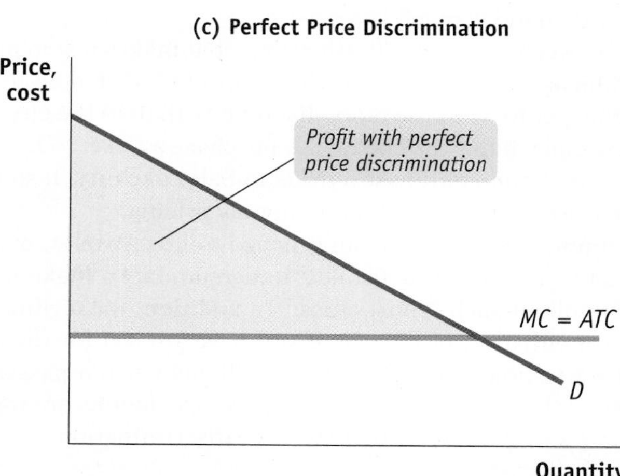

Panel (a) shows a monopolist that charges two different prices; its profit is shown by the shaded area. Panel (b) shows a monopolist that charges three different prices; its profit, too, is shown by the shaded area. It is able to capture more of the consumer surplus and to increase its profit. That is, by increasing the number of different prices charged, the monopolist captures more of the consumer surplus and makes a larger profit. Panel (c) shows the case of perfect price discrimination, where a monopolist charges each consumer his or her willingness to pay; the monopolist's profit is given by the shaded triangle.

Consider the example of a drug that is disproportionately prescribed to senior citizens, who are often on fixed incomes and so are very sensitive to price. A policy that allows a drug company to charge senior citizens a low price and everyone else a high price will serve more consumers and create more total surplus than a situation in which everyone is charged the same price.

But price discrimination that creates serious concerns about equity is likely to be prohibited—for example, an ambulance service that charges patients based on the severity of their emergency.

ECONOMICS IN ACTION

SALES, FACTORY OUTLETS, AND GHOST CITIES

Have you ever wondered why department stores occasionally hold sales, offering their merchandise for considerably less than the usual prices? Or why, driving along America's highways, you sometimes encounter clusters of "factory outlet" stores, often a couple of hours' drive from the nearest city?

These familiar features of the economic landscape are actually rather peculiar if you think about them: why should sheets and towels be cheaper for a week each winter, or raincoats be offered for less in Freeport, Maine, than in Boston? In each case the answer is that the sellers—who are often oligopolists or monopolistic competitors—are engaged in a subtle form of price discrimination.

Periodic sales allow stores to price-discriminate between their high-elasticity and low-elasticity customers.

As for sheets and towels, stores are aware that some consumers buy these goods only when they discover that they need them; they are not likely to put a lot of effort into searching for the best price and so have a relatively low price elasticity of demand. So the store wants to charge high prices for customers who come in on an ordinary day. But shoppers who plan ahead, looking for the lowest price, will wait until there is a sale. By scheduling such sales only now and then, the store is in effect able to price-discriminate between high-elasticity and low-elasticity customers.

An outlet store serves the same purpose: by offering merchandise for low prices, but only at a considerable distance away, a seller is able to establish a separate market for those customers who are willing to make an effort to search out lower prices—and who therefore have a relatively high price elasticity of demand.

Finally, let's return to airline tickets to mention one of the truly odd features of their prices. Often a flight from one major destination to another—say, from Chicago to Los Angeles—is cheaper than a much shorter flight to a smaller city—say, from Chicago to Salt Lake City. Again, the reason is a difference in the price elasticity of demand: customers have a choice of many airlines between Chicago and Los Angeles, so the demand for any one flight is quite elastic; customers have very little choice in flights to a small city, so the demand is much less elastic.

But often there is a flight between two major destinations that makes a stop along the way—say, a flight from Chicago to Los Angeles with a stop in Salt Lake City. In these cases, it is sometimes cheaper to fly to the more distant city than to the city that is a stop along the way. For example, it may be cheaper to purchase a ticket to Los Angeles and get off in Salt Lake City than to purchase a ticket to Salt Lake City! It sounds ridiculous but makes perfect sense given the logic of monopoly pricing.

So why don't passengers simply buy a ticket from Chicago to Los Angeles, but get off at Salt Lake City? Well, some do—but the airlines, understandably, make it difficult for customers to find out about such "ghost cities." In addition, the airline will not allow you to check baggage only part of the way if you have a ticket for the final destination. And airlines refuse to honor tickets for return flights when a passenger has not completed all the legs of the outbound flight. All these restrictions are meant to enforce the separation of markets necessary to allow price discrimination.

MODULE 30 Review

Solutions appear at the back of the book.

Check Your Understanding

1. True or false? Explain your answer.
   a. A single-price monopolist sells to some customers that would not find the product affordable if purchasing from a price-discriminating monopolist.
   b. A price-discriminating monopolist creates more inefficiency than a single-price monopolist because it captures more of the consumer surplus.
   c. Under price discrimination, a customer with highly elastic demand will pay a lower price than a customer with inelastic demand.

2. Which of the following are cases of price discrimination and which are not? In the cases of price discrimination, identify the consumers with high price elasticity of demand and those with low price elasticity of demand.
   a. Damaged merchandise is marked down.
   b. Restaurants have senior citizen discounts.
   c. Food manufacturers place discount coupons for their merchandise in newspapers.
   d. Airline tickets cost more during the summer peak flying season.

Multiple-Choice Questions

1. Which of the following characteristics is necessary for a firm to price-discriminate?
   a. free entry and exit
   b. differentiated product
   c. many sellers
   d. some control over price
   e. horizontal demand curve

2. Price discrimination
   a. is the opposite of volume discounts.
   b. is a practice limited to movie theaters and the airline industry.
   c. can lead to increased efficiency in the market.
   d. rarely occurs in the real world.
   e. helps to increase the profits of perfect competitors.

3. With perfect price discrimination, consumer surplus
   a. is maximized.
   b. equals zero.
   c. is increased.
   d. cannot be determined.
   e. is the area below the demand curve above *MC*.

4. Which of the following is a technique used by price discriminating monopolists?
   I. advance purchase restrictions
   II. two-part tariffs
   III. volume discounts
   a. I only
   b. II only
   c. III only
   d. I and II only
   e. I, II, and III

5. A price discriminating monopolist will charge a higher price to consumers with
   a. a more inelastic demand.
   b. a less inelastic demand.
   c. higher income.
   d. lower willingness to pay.
   e. less experience in the market.

Critical-Thinking Question

Draw a correctly labeled graph showing a monopoly practicing perfect price discrimination. On your graph, identify the monopoly's profit. What does consumer surplus equal in this case? Explain.

BUSINESS CASE: Newly Emerging Markets: A Diamond Monopolist's Best Friend

Daniel Acker/Bloomberg via Getty Images

When Cecil Rhodes created the De Beers monopoly in 1888, it was a particularly opportune moment. The new diamond mines in South Africa dwarfed all previous sources, so almost all of the world's diamond production was concentrated in a few square miles.

For almost a century, De Beers was able to extend its control of resources even as new mines opened. De Beers either bought out new producers or entered into agreements with local governments that controlled some of the new mines, effectively making them part of the De Beers monopoly. The most remarkable of these was an agreement with the former Soviet Union, which ensured that Russian diamonds would be marketed through De Beers, preserving its ability to control retail prices. De Beers also went so far as to stockpile a year's supply of diamonds in its London vaults so that when demand dropped, newly mined stones would be stored rather than sold, restricting retail supply until demand and prices recovered.

However, the De Beers monopoly has been under assault. Until the 1980s, De Beers accounted for 90% of all rough diamond sales. Today, that share has dropped to about 40%, courtesy of dramatic changes in the industry.

Government regulators have forced De Beers to loosen its control of the market. For the first time, De Beers has competition: a number of independent companies have begun mining for diamonds in other African countries, including Alrosa, a Russian-based mining company, BHP Billiton of Australia, and Anglo-Australian mining group Rio Tinto. The growing market share of these companies has helped to erode De Beers's dominance. In addition, high-quality, inexpensive synthetic diamonds have become an alternative to real gems, eating into De Beers's profits. So does this mean an end to high diamond prices and De Beers's high profits?

Not really. Although today's De Beers is more of a "near-monopolist" than a true monopolist, it still mines more of the world's supply of diamonds than any other single producer. And it has been benefiting from newly emerging markets. Consumer demand for diamonds has soared in countries like China and India, leading to price increases.

Although the economic crisis of 2009 put a serious dent in worldwide demand for diamonds, forcing De Beers to cut production by 20% (compared to 2008), affluent Chinese continue to be heavy buyers of diamonds. In fact, in 2011, China surpassed Japan to become the biggest diamond-consuming nation behind the United States. Buyers in China and India made up about 20% of global demand in 2011, and estimates are that number will rise to 28% in 2016. De Beers is anticipating that Asian demand will accelerate the depletion of the world's existing diamond mines. As a result, diamond analysts predict rough diamond prices to rise by at least 6% per year through 2020.

In the end, although a diamond monopoly may not be forever, a near-monopoly with rising demand in newly emerging markets may be just as profitable.

Questions for Thought

1. What will happen to the demand for De Beers's diamonds when consumers start seeing high-quality, inexpensive synthetic diamonds as a substitute? Explain.
2. Using the concept of monopoly profits, explain what would happen if demand for De Beers's diamonds decreases. Also explain what would happen to the market price and market quantity of De Beers's diamonds.
3. What effect will the market entry of other diamond-mining firms have on the extent of De Beers's market power?
4. Given that the depletion of existing diamond mines will make it more costly to produce (mine) diamonds, draw a graph to illustrate the effects of this development on De Beers's prices and quantities. Explain your findings.

SECTION 10 REVIEW

Summary

Monopoly in Practice

1. The key difference between a monopoly and a perfectly competitive industry is that a single, perfectly competitive firm faces a horizontal demand curve but a monopolist faces a downward-sloping demand curve. This gives the monopolist market power, the ability to raise the market price by reducing output.
2. The marginal revenue of a monopolist is composed of a quantity effect (the price received from the additional unit) and a price effect (the reduction in the price at which all units are sold). Because of the price effect, a monopolist's marginal revenue is always less than the market price, and the marginal revenue curve lies below the demand curve.
3. At the monopolist's profit-maximizing output level, marginal cost equals marginal revenue, which is less than market price. At the perfectly competitive firm's profit-maximizing output level, marginal cost equals the market price. So in comparison to perfectly competitive industries, monopolies produce less, charge higher prices, and can earn profits in both the short run and the long run.

Monopoly and Public Policy

4. A monopoly creates deadweight losses by charging a price above marginal cost: the loss in consumer surplus exceeds the monopolist's profit. This makes monopolies a source of market failure and governments often make policies to prevent or end them.
5. Natural monopolies also cause deadweight losses. To limit these losses, governments sometimes impose **public ownership** and at other times impose **price regulation.** A price ceiling on a monopolist, as opposed to a perfectly competitive industry, need not cause shortages and can increase total surplus.

Price Discrimination

6. Not all monopolists are **single-price monopolists.** Monopolists, as well as oligopolists and monopolistic competitors, often engage in **price discrimination** to make higher profits, using various techniques to differentiate consumers based on their sensitivity to price and charging those with less elastic demand higher prices. A monopolist that achieves **perfect price discrimination** charges each consumer a price equal to his or her willingness to pay and captures the total surplus in the market. Although perfect price discrimination creates no inefficiency, it is practically impossible to implement.

Key Terms

Public ownership, p. 313
Price regulation, p. 313
Single-price monopolist, p. 317
Price discrimination, p. 317
Perfect price discrimination, p. 320

Problems

1. Skyscraper City has a subway system for which a one-way fare is \$1.50. There is pressure on the mayor to reduce the fare by one-third, to \$1.00. The mayor is dismayed, thinking that this will mean Skyscraper City is losing one-third of its revenue from sales of subway tickets. The mayor's economic adviser reminds her that she is focusing only on the price effect and ignoring the quantity effect. Explain why the mayor's estimate of a one-third loss of revenue is likely to be an overestimate. Illustrate with a diagram.

2. Consider an industry with the demand curve (*D*) and marginal cost curve (*MC*) shown in the accompanying diagram. There is no fixed cost. If the industry is a single-price monopoly, the monopolist's marginal revenue curve would be *MR*. Answer the following questions by naming the appropriate points or areas.

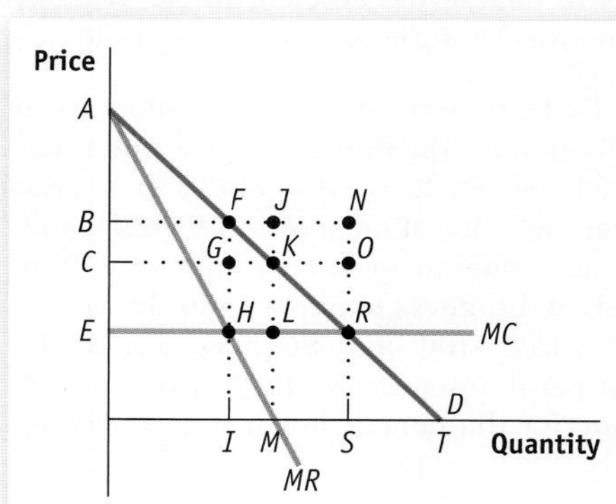

a. If the industry is perfectly competitive, what will be the total quantity produced? At what price?

b. Which area reflects consumer surplus under perfect competition?

c. If the industry is a single-price monopoly, what quantity will the monopolist produce? Which price will it charge?

d. Which area reflects the single-price monopolist's profit?

e. Which area reflects consumer surplus under single-price monopoly?

f. Which area reflects the deadweight loss to society from single-price monopoly?

g. If the monopolist can price-discriminate perfectly, what quantity will the perfectly price-discriminating monopolist produce?

3. Bob, Bill, Ben, and Brad Baxter have just made a documentary movie about their basketball team. They are thinking about making the movie available for download on the Internet, and they can act as a single-price monopolist if they choose to. Each time the movie is downloaded, their Internet service provider charges them a fee of $4. The Baxter brothers are arguing about which price to charge customers per download. The accompanying table shows the demand schedule for their film.

Price of download	Quantity of downloads demanded
$10	0
8	1
6	3
4	6
2	10
0	15

a. Calculate the total revenue and the marginal revenue per download.

b. Bob is proud of the film and wants as many people as possible to download it. Which price would he choose? How many downloads would be sold?

c. Bill wants as much total revenue as possible. Which price would he choose? How many downloads would be sold?

d. Ben wants to maximize profit. Which price would he choose? How many downloads would be sold?

e. Brad wants to charge the efficient price. Which price would he choose? How many downloads would be sold?

4. Suppose that De Beers is a single-price monopolist in the market for diamonds. De Beers has five potential customers: Raquel, Jackie, Joan, Mia, and Sophia. Each of these customers will buy at most one diamond—and only if the price is just equal to, or lower than, her willingness to pay. Raquel's willingness to pay is $400; Jackie's, $300; Joan's, $200; Mia's, $100; and Sophia's, $0. De Beers's marginal cost per diamond is $100. This leads to the demand schedule for diamonds shown in the accompanying table.

Price of diamond	Quantity of diamonds demanded
$500	0
400	1
300	2
200	3
100	4
0	5

a. Calculate De Beers's total revenue and its marginal revenue. From your calculation, draw the demand curve and the marginal revenue curve.

b. Explain why De Beers faces a downward-sloping demand curve.

c. Explain why the marginal revenue from an additional diamond sale is less than the price of the diamond.

d. Suppose De Beers currently charges $200 for its diamonds. If it lowers the price to $100, how large is the price effect? How large is the quantity effect?

e. Add the marginal cost curve to your diagram from part a, and determine which quantity maximizes the company's profit and which price De Beers will charge.

5. Use the demand schedule for diamonds given in Problem 4. The marginal cost of producing diamonds is constant at $100. There is no fixed cost.

a. If De Beers charges the monopoly price, how large is the individual consumer surplus that each buyer experiences? Calculate total consumer surplus by summing the individual consumer surpluses. How large is producer surplus?

b. Suppose that upstart Russian and Asian producers enter the market and the market becomes perfectly competitive. What is the perfectly competitive price? What quantity will be sold in this perfectly competitive market?

c. At the competitive price and quantity, how large is the consumer surplus that each buyer experiences? How large is total consumer surplus? How large is producer surplus?

d. Compare your answer to part c to your answer to part a. How large is the deadweight loss associated with monopoly in this case?

6. Use the demand schedule for diamonds given in Problem 4. De Beers is a monopolist, but it can now price-discriminate perfectly among all five of its potential customers. De Beers's marginal cost is constant at $100. There is no fixed cost.

a. If De Beers can price-discriminate perfectly, to which customers will it sell diamonds and at what prices?

b. How large is each individual consumer surplus? How large is total consumer surplus? Calculate producer surplus by summing the producer surplus generated by each sale.

7. Download Records decides to release an album by the group Mary and the Little Lamb. It produces the album with no fixed cost, but the total cost of downloading an album to a CD and paying Mary her royalty is \$6 per album. Download Records can act as a single-price monopolist. Its marketing division finds that the demand schedule for the album is as shown in the accompanying table.

Price of album	Quantity of albums demanded
\$22	0
20	1,000
18	2,000
16	3,000
14	4,000
12	5,000
10	6,000
8	7,000

a. Calculate the total revenue and the marginal revenue per album.

b. The marginal cost of producing each album is constant at \$6. To maximize profit, what level of output should Download Records choose, and which price should it charge for each album?

c. Mary renegotiates her contract and now needs to be paid a higher royalty per album. So the marginal cost rises to be constant at \$14. To maximize profit, what level of output should Download Records now choose, and which price should it charge for each album?

8. The accompanying diagram illustrates your local electricity company's natural monopoly. The diagram shows the demand curve for kilowatt-hours (kWh) of electricity, the company's marginal revenue (*MR*) curve, its marginal cost (*MC*) curve, and its average total cost (*ATC*) curve. The government wants to regulate the monopolist by imposing a price ceiling.

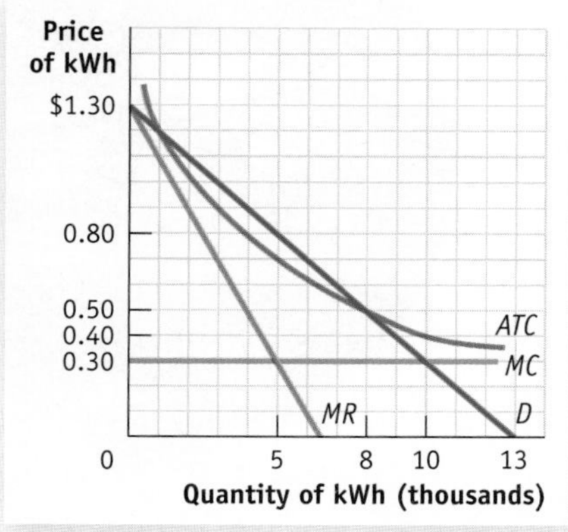

a. If the government does not regulate this monopolist, which price will the monopolist charge? Illustrate the inefficiency this creates by shading the deadweight loss from monopoly.

b. If the government imposes a price ceiling equal to the marginal cost, \$0.30, will the monopolist make a profit or lose money? Shade the area of profit (or loss) for the monopolist. If the government does impose this price ceiling, do you think the firm will continue to produce in the long run?

c. If the government imposes a price ceiling of \$0.50, will the monopolist make a profit, lose money, or break even?

9. The movie theater in Collegetown serves two kinds of customers: students and professors. There are 900 students and 100 professors in Collegetown. Each student's willingness to pay for a movie ticket is \$5. Each professor's willingness to pay for a movie ticket is \$10. Each will buy at most one ticket. The movie theater's marginal cost per ticket is constant at \$3, and there is no fixed cost.

a. Suppose the movie theater cannot price-discriminate and needs to charge both students and professors the same price per ticket. If the movie theater charges \$5, who will buy tickets and what will the movie theater's profit be? How large is consumer surplus?

b. If the movie theater charges \$10, who will buy movie tickets and what will the movie theater's profit be? How large is consumer surplus?

c. Now suppose that, if it chooses to, the movie theater can price-discriminate between students and professors by requiring students to show their student ID. If the movie theater charges students \$5 and professors \$10, how much profit will the movie theater make? How large is consumer surplus?

10. A monopolist knows that in order to expand the quantity of output it produces from 8 to 9 units, it must lower the price of its output from \$2 to \$1. Calculate the quantity effect and the price effect. Use these results to calculate the monopolist's marginal revenue of producing the 9th unit. The marginal cost of producing the 9th unit is positive. Is it a good idea for the monopolist to produce the 9th unit?

Mobil
3.59
3.99
EXXON
359
369
chili's
CALIFORNIA PIZZA KITCHEN
Carvel
STARBUCKS COFFEE
CINNABON

Imperfect Competition

ILLEGAL AND LEGAL PRACTICES

The agricultural products company Archer Daniels Midland (also known as ADM) has often described itself as "supermarket to the world." Its name is familiar to many Americans not only because of its important role in the economy but also because of its advertising and sponsorship of public television programs. But in 1993, ADM itself was on camera as executives from ADM and its Japanese competitor Ajinomoto met to discuss the market for lysine, an additive used in animal feed. In this and subsequent meetings, the two companies joined with several other producers to set targets for the price of lysine, behavior known as *price-fixing*. Each company agreed to limit its production to achieve the price targets, with the goal of raising industry profits.

But what the companies were doing was illegal, and the FBI had bugged the meeting room with a camera hidden in a lamp. Over the past few years, there have been numerous investigations and some convictions for price-fixing in a variety of industries, from insurance to college education to computer chips. Despite its illegality, some firms continue to attempt to fix the price of their products.

In the fast-food market, it is the legal practice of *product differentiation* that occupies the minds of marketing executives. Fast-food producers go to great lengths to convince you they have something special to offer beyond the ordinary burger: it's flame broiled or 100% beef or super-thick or lathered with special sauce. Or maybe they offer chicken or fish or roast beef. And the differentiation dance goes on in the pizza industry as well. Domino's offers their never-frozen handmade pan pizza. At Pizza Hut they "make it great." Papa John's claims "better ingredients." The slogans and logos for fast-food restaurants often seem to differ more than the food itself.

To understand why ADM engaged in illegal price-fixing and why fast-food restaurants go to great lengths to differentiate their patties and pizzas, we need to understand the two market structures in between perfect competition and monopoly in the spectrum of market power: *oligopoly* and *monopolistic competition*. The models of these two market structures are at the same time more complicated and more realistic than those we studied previously. Indeed, they describe the behavior of most firms in the real world.

MODULE 31

Oligopoly

Martin Barraud/Getty Images

WHAT YOU WILL LEARN

1. Why oligopolists have an incentive to act in ways that reduce their combined profit
2. Why oligopolies can benefit from collusion

Although much that we have learned about both perfect competition and monopoly is relevant to oligopoly, oligopoly also raises some entirely new issues. Among other things, firms in an oligopoly are often tempted to engage in the kind of behavior that got ADM, Ajinomoto, and other lysine producers into trouble with the law. We will devote three modules to the study of oligopoly, beginning here, where we examine what oligopoly is and why it is so important.

Interdependence and Oligopoly

Earlier we learned that an oligopoly is an industry with only a few sellers. But what number constitutes a "few"? There is no universal answer, and it is not always easy to determine an industry's market structure just by looking at the number of sellers. Economists use various measures to gain a better picture of market structure, such as the *Herfindahl–Hirschman Index,* as explained in Module 24.

In addition to having a small number of sellers in the industry, an oligopoly is characterized by **interdependence,** a relationship in which the outcome (profit) of each firm depends on the actions of the other firms in the market. This is not true for monopolies because, by definition, they have no other firms to consider. And competitive markets contain so many firms that no one firm has a significant effect on the outcome of the others.

However, in an oligopoly, an industry with few sellers, the outcome for each seller depends on the behavior of the others. Interdependence makes studying a market much more interesting because firms must observe and predict the behavior of other firms. But it is also more complicated. To understand the strategies of oligopolists, we must do more than find the point where the *MC* and *MR* curves intersect!

Firms are **interdependent** when the outcome (profit) of each firm depends on the actions of the other firms in the market.

Understanding Oligopoly

How much will a firm produce? Up to this point, we have always answered: the quantity that maximizes its profit. When a firm is a perfect competitor or a monopolist, we can assume that the firm will use its cost curves to determine its profit-maximizing output. When it comes to oligopoly, however, we run into some difficulties. In fact, economists often describe the behavior of oligopolistic firms as a "puzzle."

An oligopoly consisting of only two firms is a **duopoly.** Each firm is known as a **duopolist.**

Sellers engage in **collusion** when they cooperate to raise their joint profits. A **cartel** is a group of producers that agree to restrict output in order to increase prices and their joint profits.

A Duopoly Example

Let's begin looking at the puzzle of oligopoly with the simplest version, an industry in which there are only two firms—a **duopoly**—and each is known as a **duopolist.**

Going back to our opening story, imagine that ADM and Ajinomoto are the only two producers of lysine. To make things even simpler, suppose that once a company has incurred the fixed cost needed to produce lysine, the marginal cost of producing another pound is zero. So the companies are concerned only with the revenue they receive from sales.

Table 31-1 shows a hypothetical demand schedule for lysine and the total revenue of the industry at each price–quantity combination.

TABLE 31-1

Demand Schedule for Lysine

Price of lysine (per pound)	Quantity of lysine demanded (millions of pounds)	Total revenue (millions)
$12	0	$0
11	10	110
10	20	200
9	30	270
8	40	320
7	50	350
6	60	360
5	70	350
4	80	320
3	90	270
2	100	200
1	110	110
0	120	0

If this were a perfectly competitive industry, each firm would have an incentive to produce more as long as the market price was above marginal cost. Since the marginal cost is assumed to be zero, this would mean that at equilibrium, lysine would be provided for free. Firms would produce until price equals zero, yielding a total output of 120 million pounds and zero revenue for both firms.

However, surely the firms would not be foolish enough to allow price and revenue to plummet to zero. Each would realize that by producing more, it drives down the market price. So each firm would, like a monopolist, see that profits would be higher if it and its rival limited their production.

So how much will the two firms produce?

One possibility is that the two companies will engage in **collusion**—they will cooperate to raise their joint profits. The strongest form of collusion is a **cartel,** a group of producers with an agreement to work together to limit output and increase price, and therefore profit. The world's most famous cartel is the Organization of Petroleum Exporting Countries (OPEC), whose members routinely meet to try to set targets for oil production.

As its name indicates, OPEC is actually a cartel made up of governments rather than firms. There's a reason for this: cartels among firms are illegal in the United States and many other jurisdictions. But let's ignore the law for a moment (which is, of course, what ADM and Ajinomoto did in real life—to their own detriment).

It is in OPEC's interest to keep oil prices high and output low.

Suppose that ADM and Ajinomoto were to form a cartel and that this cartel decided to act as if it were a monopolist, maximizing total industry profits. We can see from Table 31-1 that in order to maximize the combined profits of the firms, this cartel should set total industry output at 60 million pounds of lysine, which would sell at a price of $6 per pound, leading to revenue of $360 million, the maximum possible. Then the only question would be how much of that 60 million pounds each firm gets to produce. A "fair" solution might be for each firm to produce 30 million pounds and receive revenues of $180 million.

But even if the two firms agreed on such a deal, they might have a problem: each of the firms would have an incentive to break its word and produce more than the agreed-upon quantity.

When firms ignore the effects of their actions on each other's profits, they engage in **noncooperative behavior.**

Collusion and Competition

Suppose that the presidents of ADM and Ajinomoto were to agree that each would produce 30 million pounds of lysine over the next year. Both would understand that this plan maximizes their combined profits. And both would have an incentive to cheat.

To see why, consider what would happen if Ajinomoto honored its agreement, producing only 30 million pounds, but ADM ignored its promise and produced 40 million pounds. This increase in total output would drive the price down from \$6 to \$5 per pound, the price at which 70 million pounds are demanded. The industry's total revenue would fall from \$360 million (\$6 × 60 million pounds) to \$350 million (\$5 × 70 million pounds). However, ADM's revenue would *rise*, from \$180 million to \$200 million. Since we are assuming a marginal cost of zero, this would mean a \$20 million increase in ADM's profits.

But Ajinomoto's president might make exactly the same calculation. And if *both* firms were to produce 40 million pounds of lysine, the price would drop to \$4 per pound. So each firm's profits would fall, from \$180 million to \$160 million.

The incentive to cheat motivates ADM and Ajinomoto to produce more than the quantity that maximizes their joint profits rather than limiting output as a true monopolist would. We know that a profit-maximizing monopolist sets marginal cost (which in this case is zero) equal to marginal revenue. But what is marginal revenue? Recall that producing an additional unit of a good has two effects:

1. A positive *quantity* effect: one more unit is sold, increasing total revenue by the price at which that unit is sold.
2. A negative *price* effect: in order to sell one more unit, the monopolist must cut the market price on *all* units sold.

The negative price effect is the reason marginal revenue for a monopolist is less than the market price. But when considering the effect of increasing production, a firm is concerned only with the price effect on its *own* units of output, not on those of its fellow oligopolists. Both ADM and Ajinomoto suffer a negative price effect if ADM decides to produce extra lysine and so drives down the price. But ADM cares only about the negative price effect on the units it produces, not about the loss to Ajinomoto.

This tells us that an individual firm in an oligopolistic industry faces a smaller price effect from an additional unit of output than a monopolist; therefore, the marginal revenue that such a firm calculates is higher. So it will seem to be profitable for any one firm in an oligopoly to increase production, even if that increase reduces the profits of the industry as a whole. But if everyone thinks that way, the result is that everyone earns a lower profit!

Because collusion is more profitable than noncooperative behavior, firms have an incentive to collude if they can.

Until now, we have been able to analyze producer behavior by asking what a producer should do to maximize profits. But even if our duopolists, ADM and Ajinomoto, are both trying to maximize profits, what does this predict about their behavior? Will they engage in collusion, reaching and holding to an agreement that maximizes their combined profits? Or will they engage in **noncooperative behavior,** with each firm acting in its own self-interest, even though this has the effect of driving down everyone's profits? Both strategies can be carried out with a goal of profit maximization. Which will actually describe their behavior?

Moodboard/Alamy

Now you see why oligopoly presents a puzzle: there are only a small number of players, making collusion a real possibility. If there were dozens or hundreds of firms, it would be safe to assume they would behave noncooperatively. Yet, when there are only a handful of firms in an industry, it's hard to determine whether collusion will actually occur.

Since collusion is ultimately more profitable than noncooperative behavior, firms have an incentive to collude if they can. One way to do so is to formalize it—sign an agreement (maybe even make a legal contract) or establish some financial incentives for the companies to set their prices high. But in the United States and many other nations, firms can't do that—at least not legally. A contract among firms to keep prices high would be unenforceable, and it could be a one-way ticket to jail. The same goes for an informal agreement.

In fact, executives from rival firms rarely meet without lawyers present, who make sure that the conversation does not stray into inappropriate territory. Even hinting at how nice it would be if prices were higher can bring an unwelcome interview with the Justice Department or the Federal Trade Commission. For example, in 2003 the Justice Department launched a price-fixing case against Monsanto and other large producers of genetically modified seed. The Justice Department was alerted by a series of meetings held between Monsanto and Pioneer Hi-Bred International, two companies that account for 60% of the U.S. market in maize and soybean seed. These companies, parties to a licensing agreement involving genetically modified seed, claimed that no illegal discussions of price-fixing occurred in those meetings. But the fact that the two firms discussed prices as part of the licensing agreement was enough to trigger action by the Justice Department.

ECONOMICS IN ACTION

WORLD VIEW

BITTER CHOCOLATE?

Millions of chocolate lovers around the world have been spending more to satisfy their cravings, and regulators in Germany, Canada, and the United States have become suspicious. They have been investigating whether the seven leading chocolate companies—including Mars, Kraft Foods, Nestlé, Hershey, and Cadbury—have been colluding to raise prices. The amount of money involved could well run into the billions of dollars.

iStockphoto/Thinkstock

Are chocolate makers engaging in price-fixing?

Many of the nation's largest grocery stores and snack retailers are convinced that they have been the victims of collusion. They claim that the chocolate industry has responded to stagnant consumer sales by price-fixing, an allegation the chocolate makers have vigorously denied.

In 2010, one of those stores, Supervalu, filed a lawsuit against Mars, Hershey, Nestlé, and Cadbury, who together control about 76% of the U.S. chocolate market. Supervalu claimed that the confectioners had been fixing prices since 2002, regularly increasing prices by mid-single to double-digit amounts. Supervalu also claimed that grocers who resisted or refused to raise prices were systematically penalized with delayed or insufficient product deliveries.

What's clear is that chocolate candy prices have been soaring while sales fell. Chocolate makers defend their actions, contending that they were simply passing on increases in their costs.

But, as antitrust experts point out, price collusion is often very difficult to prove because it is not illegal for businesses to increase their prices at the same time. To prove collusion, there must be some evidence of conversations or written agreements.

Such evidence did emerge in our chocolate case. According to the Canadian press, 13 Cadbury executives voluntarily provided information to the courts about contacts between the companies. And, according to affidavits submitted to a Canadian court, top executives at Hershey, Mars, and Nestlé met secretly in coffee shops, in restaurants, and at conventions to set prices.

More recently, in 2013, Nestlé, Mars, and others were accused of conspiring to fix the prices of popular chocolate bars in Canada. This episode came not too long after similar charges were filed against chocolate sellers in Germany, including Nestlé and Mars, that resulted in multi-million-dollar fines for the companies involved.

Critics of the chocolate makers may get some sweet vindication in the end.

MODULE 31 Review

Solutions appear at the back of the book.

Check Your Understanding

1. Explain whether each of the following factors will increase or decrease the likelihood that a firm will collude with other firms in an oligopoly to restrict output.
   a. The firm's initial market share is small. (Hint: think about the price effect.)
   b. The firm has a cost advantage over its rivals.
   c. The firm's customers face additional costs when they switch from one firm's product to another firm's product.
   d. The firm and its rivals are currently operating at maximum production capacity, which cannot be altered in the short run.

Multiple-Choice Questions

1. When firms cooperate to raise their joint profits, they are necessarily
   a. colluding.
   b. in a cartel.
   c. a monopoly.
   d. in a duopoly.
   e. in a competitive industry.

2. Use the information in the accompanying table on market shares in the search engine industry and measures of market power (defined in Module 24) to determine which of the following statements are correct.

Search engine	Market share
Google	44%
Yahoo	29
MSN	13
AOL	6
Ask	5
Other	3

   I. The Herfindahl–Hirschman Index is 3,016.
   II. The industry is likely to be an oligopoly.

   a. I only
   b. II only
   c. Both I and II
   d. Neither I nor II

3. An agreement among several producers to restrict output and increase profit is necessary for
   a. cooperation.
   b. collusion.
   c. monopolization.
   d. a cartel.
   e. competition.

4. Oligopolists engage in which of the following types of behavior?
   I. quantity competition
   II. price competition
   III. cooperative behavior

   a. I only
   b. II only
   c. III only
   d. I and II only
   e. I, II, and III

5. Which of the following will make it easier for firms in an industry to maintain positive economic profit?
   a. a ban on cartels
   b. a small number of firms in the industry
   c. a lack of product differentiation
   d. low start-up costs for new firms
   e. the assumption by firms that other firms have variable output levels

Critical-Thinking Question

What are the two major reasons we don't see cartels among oligopolistic industries in the United States today?

Game Theory

Photosindia/Getty Images

WHAT YOU WILL LEARN

1. How our understanding of oligopoly can be enhanced by using game theory
2. The concept of the prisoners' dilemma
3. How repeated interactions among oligopolists can result in collusion in the absence of any formal agreement

Games Oligopolists Play

In our duopoly example (from the previous module) and in real life, each oligopolistic firm realizes both that its profit depends on what its competitor does and that its competitor's profit depends on what it does. That is, the two firms are in a situation of *interdependence,* whereby each firm's decision significantly affects the profit of the other firm (or firms, in the case of more than two).

In effect, the two firms are playing a "game" in which the profit of each player depends not only on its own actions but on those of the other player (or players). In order to understand more fully how oligopolists behave, economists, along with mathematicians, developed the area of study of such games, known as **game theory.** It has many applications, not just to economics but also to military strategy, politics, and other social sciences.

Let's see how game theory helps us understand how oligopolies behave.

The Prisoners' Dilemma

Game theory deals with any situation in which the reward to any one player—the **payoff**—depends not only on his or her own actions but also on those of other players in the game. In the case of oligopolistic firms, the payoff is simply the firm's profit.

When there are only two players, as in a lysine duopoly, the interdependence between the players can be represented with a **payoff matrix** like that shown in Figure 32-1. Each row corresponds to an action by one player (in this case, ADM); each column corresponds to an action by the other (in this case, Ajinomoto). For simplicity, let's assume that each of our firms can pick only one of two alternatives: produce 30 million pounds of lysine or produce 40 million pounds.

The matrix contains four boxes, each divided by a diagonal line. Each box shows the payoff to the two firms that results from a pair of choices; the number below the diagonal shows ADM's profits, the number above the diagonal shows Ajinomoto's profits.

The study of behavior in situations of interdependence is known as **game theory.**

The reward received by a player in a game, such as the profit earned by an oligopolist, is that player's **payoff.**

A **payoff matrix** shows how the payoff to each of the participants in a two-player game depends on the actions of both. Such a matrix helps us analyze situations of interdependence.

FIGURE 32-1 A Payoff Matrix

Two firms, ADM and Ajinomoto, must decide how much lysine to produce. The profits of the two firms are *interdependent:* each firm's profit depends not only on its own decision but also on the other's decision. Each row represents an action by ADM, each column, one by Ajinomoto. Both firms will be better off if they both choose the lower output, but it is in each firm's individual interest to choose the higher output.

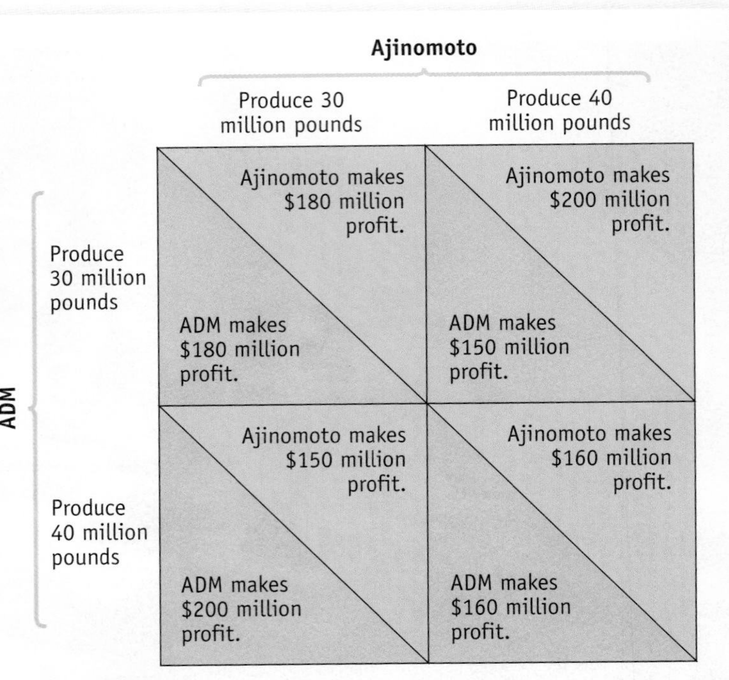

These payoffs show what we concluded from our earlier analysis: the combined profit of the two firms is maximized if they each produce 30 million pounds. Either firm can, however, increase its own profits by producing 40 million pounds if the other produces only 30 million pounds. But if both produce the larger quantity, both will have lower profits than if they had both held their output down.

The particular situation shown here is a version of a famous—and paradoxical—case of interdependence that appears in many contexts. Known as the **prisoners' dilemma,** it is a type of game in which the payoff matrix implies the following:

- Each player has an incentive, regardless of what the other player does, to cheat—to take an action that benefits it at the other's expense.
- When both players cheat, both are worse off than they would have been if neither had cheated.

The original illustration of the prisoners' dilemma occurred in a fictional story about two accomplices in crime—let's call them Thelma and Louise—who have been caught by the police. The police have enough evidence to put them behind bars for 5 years. They also know that the pair have committed a more serious crime, one that carries a 20-year sentence; unfortunately, they don't have enough evidence to convict the women on that charge. To do so, they would need each of the prisoners to implicate the other in the second crime.

So the police put the miscreants in separate cells and say the following to each: "Here's the deal: if neither of you confesses, you know that we'll send you to jail for 5 years. If you confess and implicate your partner, and she doesn't do the same, we reduce your sentence from 5 years to 2. But if your partner confesses and you don't, you'll get the maximum 20 years. And if both of you confess, we'll give you both 15 years."

The **prisoners' dilemma** is a game based on two premises: (1) Each player has an incentive to choose an action that benefits itself at the other player's expense; and (2) When both players act in this way, both are worse off than if they had acted cooperatively.

Figure 32-2 shows the payoffs that face the prisoners, depending on the decision of each to remain silent or to confess. (Usually the payoff matrix reflects the players' payoffs, and higher payoffs are better than lower payoffs. This case is an exception: a higher number of years in prison is bad, not good!) Let's assume that the prisoners have no way to communicate and that they have not sworn an oath not to harm each other or anything of that sort. So each acts in her own self-interest. What will they do?

FIGURE 32-2 The Prisoners' Dilemma

Each of two prisoners, held in separate cells, is offered a deal by the police—a light sentence if she confesses and implicates her accomplice but her accomplice does not do the same, a heavy sentence if she does not confess but her accomplice does, and so on. It is in the joint interest of both prisoners not to confess; it is in each one's individual interest to confess.

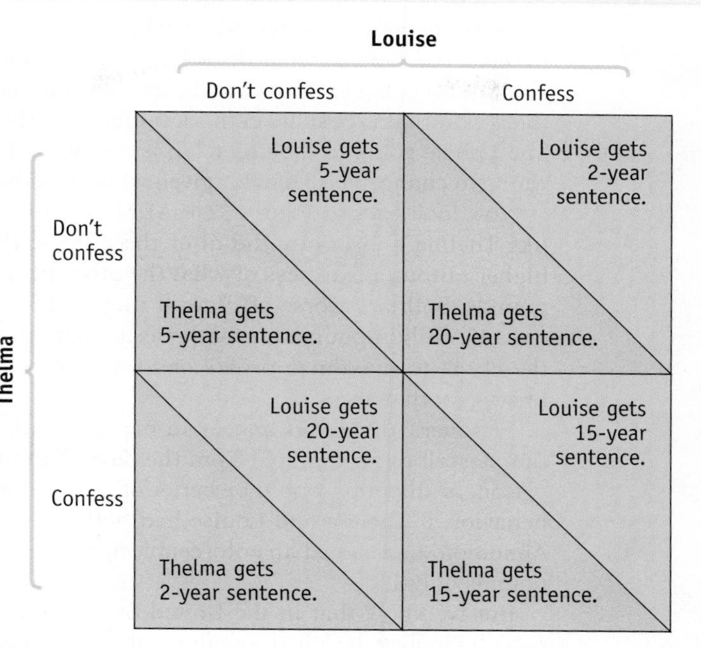
Louise
Don't confess
Confess
Thelma
Don't confess
Confess
Louise gets 5-year sentence.
Thelma gets 5-year sentence.
Louise gets 2-year sentence.
Thelma gets 20-year sentence.
Louise gets 20-year sentence.
Thelma gets 2-year sentence.
Louise gets 15-year sentence.
Thelma gets 15-year sentence.

The answer is clear: both will confess. Look at it first from Thelma's point of view: she is better off confessing, regardless of what Louise does. If Louise doesn't confess, Thelma's confession reduces her own sentence from 5 years to 2. If Louise *does* confess, Thelma's confession reduces her sentence from 20 to 15 years. Either way, it's clearly in Thelma's interest to confess. And because she faces the same incentives, it's clearly in Louise's interest to confess, too. To confess in this situation is a type of action that economists call a *dominant strategy*. An action is a **dominant strategy** when it is the player's best action regardless of the action taken by the other player.

It's important to note that not all games have a dominant strategy—it depends on the structure of payoffs in the game. But in the case of Thelma and Louise, it is clearly in the interest of the police to structure the payoffs so that confessing is a dominant strategy for each person. As long as the two prisoners have no way to make an enforceable agreement that neither will confess (something they can't do if they can't communicate, and the police certainly won't allow them to do so because the police want to compel each one to confess), the dominant strategy exists as the best alternative.

So if each prisoner acts rationally in her own interest, both will confess. Yet if neither of them had confessed, both would have received a much lighter sentence! In a prisoners' dilemma, each player has a clear incentive to act in a way that hurts the other player—but when both make that choice, it leaves both of them worse off.

When Thelma and Louise both confess, they reach an *equilibrium* of the game. We have used the concept of equilibrium many times in this book; it is an outcome in which no individual or firm has any incentive to change his or her action. In game theory, this kind of equilibrium, in which each player takes the action that is best for her, given the actions taken by other players, is known as a **Nash equilibrium,** after the mathematician and Nobel Laureate John Nash. Because the players in a Nash equilibrium do not take into account the effect of their actions on others, this is also known as a **noncooperative equilibrium.**

An action is a **dominant strategy** when it is a player's best action regardless of the action taken by the other player.

A **Nash equilibrium,** also known as a **noncooperative equilibrium,** is the result when each player in a game chooses the action that maximizes his or her payoff, given the actions of other players.

In the prisoners' dilemma, the Nash equilibrium happens to be an equilibrium of two dominant strategies—a *dominant strategy equilibrium*—but Nash equilibria can exist when there is no dominant strategy at all. For example, suppose that after serving time in jail, Thelma and Louise are disheartened by the mutual distrust that led them to confess, and each wants nothing more than to avoid seeing the other. On a Saturday night, they might each have to choose between going to the nightclub and going to the movie theater. Neither has a dominant strategy because the best strategy for each depends on what the other is doing. However, Thelma going to the nightclub and Louise going to the movie theater is a Nash equilibrium because each player takes the action that is best given the action of the other. Thelma going to the movie theater and Louise going to the nightclub is also a Nash equilibrium, because again, neither wants to change her behavior given what the other is doing.

Now look back at Figure 32-1: ADM and Ajinomoto face a prisoners' dilemma just like Thelma and Louise did after the crimes. Each firm is better off producing the higher output, regardless of what the other firm does. Yet if both produce 40 million pounds, both are worse off than if they had followed their agreement and produced only 30 million pounds. In both cases, then, the pursuit of individual self-interest—the effort to maximize profits or to minimize jail time—has the perverse effect of hurting both players.

Prisoners' dilemmas appear in many situations. The following Economics in Action describes an example from the days of the Cold War. Clearly, the players in any prisoners' dilemma would be better off if they had some way of enforcing cooperative behavior: if Thelma and Louise had both sworn to a code of silence, or if ADM and Ajinomoto had signed an enforceable agreement not to produce more than 30 million pounds of lysine.

But we know that in the United States an agreement setting the output levels of two oligopolists isn't just unenforceable, it's illegal. So it seems that a noncooperative equilibrium is the only possible outcome. Or is it?

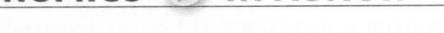

PRISONERS OF THE ARMS RACE

TASS/Sovfoto

Caught in the prisoners' dilemma: heavy military spending hastened the collapse of the Soviet Union.

Between World War II and the late 1980s, the United States and the Soviet Union were locked in a seemingly endless struggle that never broke out into open war. During this Cold War, both countries spent huge sums on arms, sums that were a significant drain on the U.S. economy and eventually proved a crippling burden for the Soviet Union, whose underlying economic base was much weaker. Yet neither country was ever able to achieve a decisive military advantage.

As many people pointed out, both nations would have been better off if they had both spent less on arms. Yet the arms race continued for 40 years.

Why? As political scientists were quick to notice, one way to explain the arms race was to suppose that the two countries were locked in a classic prisoners' dilemma. Each government would have liked to achieve decisive military superiority, and each feared military inferiority. But both would have preferred a stalemate with low military spending to one with high spending. However, each government rationally chose to engage in high spending. If its rival did not spend heavily, this would lead to military superiority; not spending heavily would lead to inferiority if the other government continued its arms buildup. So the countries were trapped.

The answer to this trap could have been an agreement not to spend as much; indeed, the two sides tried repeatedly to negotiate limits on some kinds of weapons. But these agreements weren't very effective. In the end the issue was resolved as heavy military spending hastened the collapse of the Soviet Union in 1991.

Unfortunately, the logic of an arms race has not disappeared. A nuclear arms race has developed between Pakistan and India, neighboring countries with a history of mutual antagonism. In 1998 the two countries confirmed the unrelenting logic of the prisoners' dilemma: both publicly tested their nuclear weapons in a tit-for-tat sequence, each seeking to prove to the other that it could inflict just as much damage as its rival.

Overcoming the Prisoners' Dilemma: Repeated Interaction and Tacit Collusion

A firm engages in **strategic behavior** when it attempts to influence the future behavior of other firms.

A strategy of **tit for tat** involves playing cooperatively at first, then doing whatever the other player did in the previous period.

Thelma and Louise are playing what is known as a *one-shot* game—they play the game with each other only once. They get to choose once and for all whether to confess or deny, and that's it. However, most of the games that oligopolists play aren't one-shot games; instead, the players expect to play the game repeatedly with the same rivals. An oligopolist usually expects to be in business for many years, and knows that a decision today about whether to cheat is likely to affect the decisions of other firms in the future. So a smart oligopolist doesn't just decide what to do based on the effect on profit in the short run. Instead, it engages in **strategic behavior,** taking into account the effects of its action on the future actions of other players. And under some conditions oligopolists that behave strategically can manage to behave as if they had a formal agreement to collude.

Suppose that ADM and Ajinomoto expect to be in the lysine business for many years and therefore expect to play the game of cheat versus collude shown in Figure 32-1 many times. Would they really betray each other time and again?

Probably not. Suppose that ADM considers two strategies. In one strategy it always cheats, producing 40 million pounds of lysine each year, regardless of what Ajinomoto does. In the other strategy, it starts with good behavior, producing only 30 million pounds in the first year, and watches to see what its rival does. If Ajinomoto also keeps its production down, ADM will stay cooperative, producing 30 million pounds again for the next year. But if Ajinomoto produces 40 million pounds, ADM will take the gloves off and also produce 40 million pounds next year. This latter strategy—start by behaving cooperatively, but thereafter do whatever the other player did in the previous period—is generally known as **tit for tat.**

Tit for tat is a form of strategic behavior because it is intended to influence the future actions of other players. The tit-for-tat strategy offers a reward to the other player for cooperative behavior—if you behave cooperatively, so will I. It also provides a punishment for cheating—if you cheat, don't expect me to be nice in the future.

The payoff to ADM of each of these strategies would depend on which strategy Ajinomoto chooses. Consider the four possibilities, shown in Figure 32-3:

1. If ADM plays tit for tat and so does Ajinomoto, both firms will make a profit of $180 million each year.
2. If ADM plays always cheat but Ajinomoto plays tit for tat, ADM makes a profit of $200 million the first year but only $160 million per year thereafter.
3. If ADM plays tit for tat but Ajinomoto plays always cheat, ADM makes a profit of only $150 million in the first year but $160 million per year thereafter.
4. If ADM plays always cheat and Ajinomoto does the same, both firms will make a profit of $160 million each year.

Which strategy is better? In the first year, ADM does better playing always cheat, whatever its rival's strategy: it assures itself that it will get either $200 million or $160 million. (Which of the two payoffs it actually receives depends on whether Ajinomoto plays tit for tat or always cheat.) This is better than what it would get in the first year if it played tit for tat: either $180 million or $150 million. But by the second year, a strategy of always cheat gains ADM only $160 million per year for the second and all subsequent years, regardless of Ajinomoto's actions.

Over time, the total amount gained by ADM by playing always cheat is less than the amount gained by playing tit for tat: for the second and all subsequent years, it would never get any less than $160 million and would get as much as $180 million if Ajinomoto played tit for tat as well. Which strategy, always cheat or tit for tat, is more profitable depends on two things: how many years ADM expects to play the game and what strategy Ajinomoto follows.

FIGURE 32-3 **How Repeated Interaction Can Support Collusion**

A strategy of tit for tat involves playing cooperatively at first, then following the other player's move. This rewards good behavior and punishes bad behavior. If the other player cheats, playing tit for tat will lead to only a short-term loss in comparison to playing always cheat. But if the other player plays tit for tat, also playing tit for tat leads to a long-term gain. So a firm that expects other firms to play tit for tat may well choose to do the same, leading to successful tacit collusion.

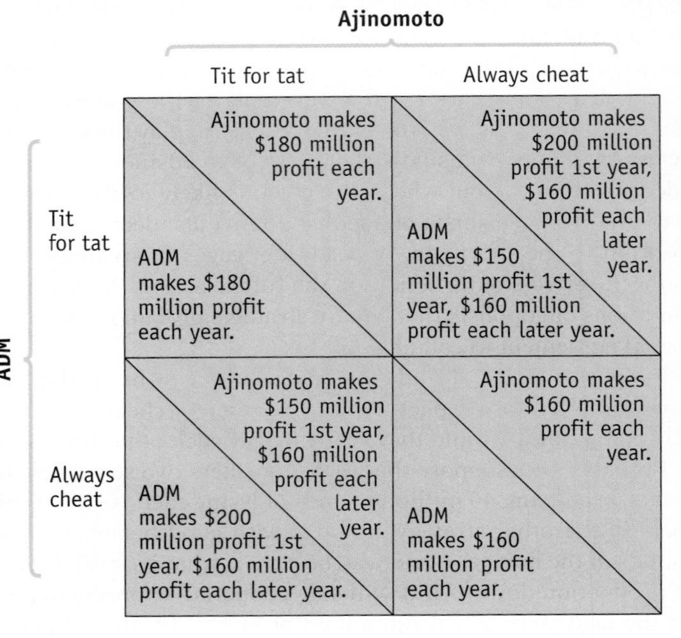

ADM \ Ajinomoto	Tit for tat	Always cheat
Tit for tat	Ajinomoto makes $180 million profit each year. ADM makes $180 million profit each year.	Ajinomoto makes $200 million profit 1st year, $160 million profit each later year. ADM makes $150 million profit 1st year, $160 million profit each later year.
Always cheat	Ajinomoto makes $150 million profit 1st year, $160 million profit each later year. ADM makes $200 million profit 1st year, $160 million profit each later year.	Ajinomoto makes $160 million profit each year. ADM makes $160 million profit each year.

When firms limit production and raise prices in a way that raises each other's profits, even though they have not made any formal agreement, they are engaged in **tacit collusion.**

If ADM expects the lysine business to end in the near future, it is in effect playing a one-shot game. So it might as well cheat and grab what it can. Even if ADM expects to remain in the lysine business for many years (therefore to find itself repeatedly playing this game with Ajinomoto) and, for some reason, expects Ajinomoto will always cheat, it should also always cheat. That is, ADM should follow the old rule, "Do unto others before they do unto you."

But if ADM expects to be in the business for a long time and thinks Ajinomoto is likely to play tit for tat, it will make more profits over the long run by playing tit for tat, too. It could have made some extra short-term profit by cheating at the beginning, but this would provoke Ajinomoto into cheating, too, and would, in the end, mean less profit.

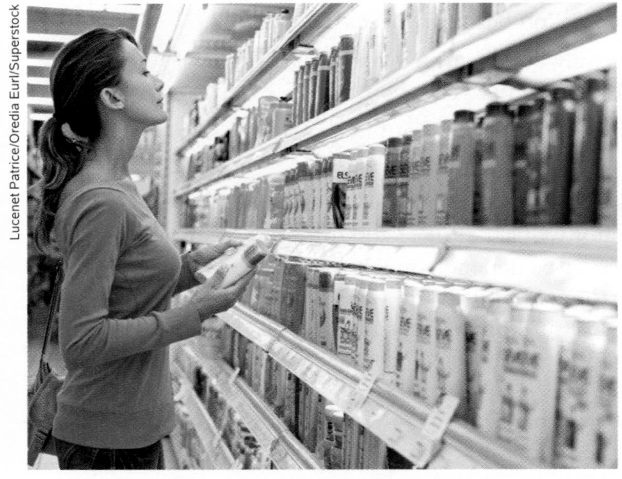

Lucenet Patrice/Oredia Eurl/Superstock

Oligopolists engage in unspoken agreements that limit output and raise prices.

The lesson of this story is that when oligopolists expect to compete with each other over an extended period of time, each individual firm will often conclude that it is in its own best interest to be helpful to the other firms in the industry. So it will restrict its output in a way that raises the profit of the other firms, expecting them to return the favor. Despite the fact that firms have no way of making an enforceable agreement to limit output and raise prices (and are in legal jeopardy if they even discuss prices), they manage to act "as if" they had such an agreement. When this type of unspoken agreement comes about, we say that the firms are engaging in **tacit collusion.**

MODULE 32 Review

Solutions appear at the back of the book.

Check Your Understanding

1. Suppose world leaders Nikita and Margaret are engaged in an arms race and face the decision of whether to build a missile. Answer the following questions using the information in the payoff matrix below, which shows how each set of actions will affect the utility, a measure of personal satisfaction, of the players (the numbers represent utils gained or lost).

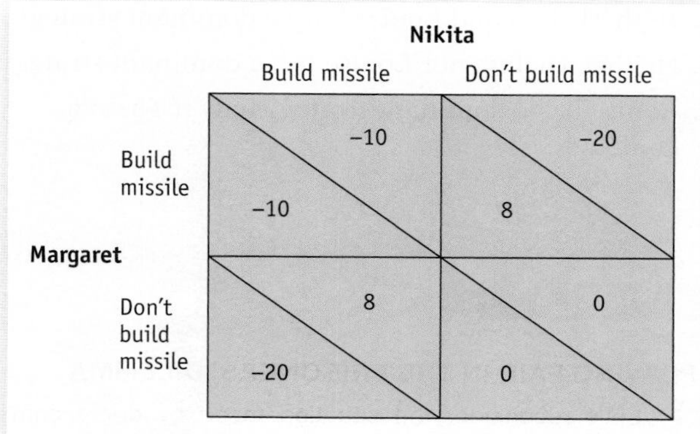

   a. Identify any Nash equilibria that exist in this game, and explain why they exist.

   b. Which set of actions maximizes the total payoff for Nikita and Margaret?

   c. Why is it unlikely that they will choose the payoff-maximizing set of actions without some communication?

2. Which of the following factors make it more likely that oligopolists will play noncooperatively? Which make it more likely that they will engage in tacit collusion? Explain.

   a. Each oligopolist expects several new firms to enter the market in the future.

   b. It is very difficult for a firm to detect whether another firm has raised output.

   c. The firms have coexisted while maintaining high prices for a long time.

Multiple-Choice Questions

1. Each player has an incentive to choose an action that, when both players choose it, makes them both worse off. This situation describes

   a. a dominant strategy.
   b. the prisoners' dilemma.
   c. interdependence.
   d. Nash equilibrium.
   e. tit for tat.

2. Which of the following types of oligopoly behavior is/are illegal?

   I. tacit collusion
   II. cartel formation
   III. tit for tat

   a. I only
   b. II only
   c. III only
   d. I and II only
   e. I, II, and III

3. A situation in which each player in a game chooses the action that maximizes his or her payoff, given the actions of the other players, ignoring the effects of his or her action on the payoffs received by others, is known as a

   a. dominant strategy.
   b. cooperative equilibrium.
   c. Nash equilibrium.
   d. strategic situation.
   e. prisoners' dilemma.

4. In the context of the Thelma and Louise story in the module, suppose that Louise discovers Thelma's action (confess or don't confess) before choosing her own action.

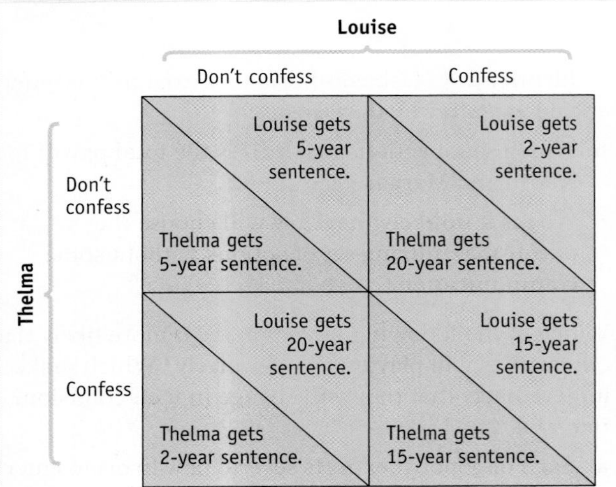

Louise
Don't confess
Confess
Thelma
Don't confess
Confess
Louise gets 5-year sentence.
Thelma gets 5-year sentence.
Louise gets 2-year sentence.
Thelma gets 20-year sentence.
Louise gets 20-year sentence.
Thelma gets 2-year sentence.
Louise gets 15-year sentence.
Thelma gets 15-year sentence.

Based on the payoff matrix provided, Louise will

a. confess whether or not Thelma confessed.
b. not confess only if Thelma confessed.
c. not confess only if Thelma didn't confess.
d. not confess regardless of whether or not Thelma confessed.
e. confess only if Thelma did not confess.

5. Which of the following is true on the basis of the payoff matrix provided in Question 4?

a. Louise has no dominant strategy, but Thelma does.
b. Thelma has no dominant strategy, but Louise does.
c. Both Thelma and Louise have a dominant strategy.
d. Neither Thelma nor Louise has a dominant strategy.
e. Louise has a dominant strategy only if Thelma confesses.

Critical-Thinking Question

Draw a clearly labeled payoff matrix illustrating the following situation. There are two firms, "Firm A" and "Firm B." Each firm must decide whether to charge a high price or a low price. If one firm charges a high price and the other a low price, the firm charging the high price will earn low profits while the firm charging the low price will earn high profits. If both firms charge a high price, both earn high profits and if both firms charge low prices, both earn low profits.

PITFALLS

PLAYING FAIR IN THE PRISONERS' DILEMMA

? Let's reconsider the situation faced by our accomplices in crime, Thelma and Louise. Is it rational for them to confess in the prisoners' dilemma? They are both criminals, after all, and it's not unreasonable to think that they would keep their mouths shut out of fear that the other would take revenge for a confession.

> YES, IT IS RATIONAL FOR BOTH OF THEM TO CONFESS. TO UNDERSTAND THE DILEMMA, YOU HAVE TO PLAY FAIR AND IMAGINE PRISONERS WHO CARE *ONLY* ABOUT THE LENGTH OF THEIR SENTENCES. YOU CANNOT CHANGE THE PAYOFFS IN THE PAYOFF MATRIX! Doing so is a little bit like cheating. Luckily, when it comes to oligopoly, it's a lot easier to believe that the firms care only about their profits. There is no indication that anyone at ADM felt either fear of or affection for Ajinomoto, or vice versa; it was strictly about business.

To learn more, see pp. 335–336, especially Figure 32-1.

Oligopoly in Practice

(L) Tim Sloan/AFP/Getty Images/Newscom (R) AP Photo/Steven Senne

WHAT YOU WILL LEARN

1. The legal constraints of antitrust policy
2. The factors that limit tacit collusion
3. The cause and effect of product differentiation and price leadership
4. The importance of oligopoly in the real world

How do oligopolies usually work in practice? The answer depends both on the legal framework that limits what firms can do and on the underlying ability of firms in a given industry to cooperate without formal agreements. In this module we will explore a variety of oligopoly behaviors and how antitrust laws limit oligopolists' attempts to maximize their profits.

The Legal Framework

To understand oligopoly pricing in practice, we must be familiar with the legal constraints under which oligopolistic firms operate. In the United States, oligopoly first became an issue during the second half of the nineteenth century, when the growth of railroads—themselves an oligopolistic industry—created a national market for many goods. Large firms producing oil, steel, and many other products soon emerged. The industrialists quickly realized that profits would be higher if they could limit price competition. So many industries formed cartels—that is, they signed formal agreements to limit production and raise prices. Until 1890, when the first federal legislation against such cartels was passed, this was perfectly legal.

However, although these cartels were legal, their agreements weren't legally *enforceable*—members of a cartel couldn't ask the courts to force a firm that was violating its agreement to reduce its production. And firms often did violate their agreements, for the reason already suggested by our duopoly example in the two previous modules: there is always a temptation for each firm in a cartel to produce more than it is supposed to.

In 1881 clever lawyers at John D. Rockefeller's Standard Oil Company came up with a solution—the so-called *trust*. In a trust, shareholders of all the major companies in an industry placed their shares in the hands of a board of trustees who controlled the companies. This, in effect, merged the companies into a single firm that could then engage in monopoly pricing. In this way, the Standard Oil Trust established what was

HARD COAL TRUST
BEEF TRUST
STANDARD OIL TRUST
NO LACK OF BIG GAME
The President Seems to Have Scared Up Quite a Bunch of Octop

Library of Congress Prints and Photographs Division Washington, D.C. [LC-USZ62-8664]

The Sherman Antitrust Act went mostly unenforced until Theodore Roosevelt's presidency (1901–1909).

essentially a monopoly of the oil industry, and it was soon followed by trusts in sugar, whiskey, lead, cottonseed oil, and linseed oil.

Eventually, there was a public backlash, driven partly by concern about the economic effects of the trust movement and partly by fear that the owners of the trusts were simply becoming too powerful. The result was the Sherman Antitrust Act of 1890, which was intended both to prevent the creation of more monopolies and to break up existing ones. At first this law went largely unenforced. But over the decades that followed, the federal government became increasingly committed to making it difficult for oligopolistic industries either to become monopolies or to behave like them. Such efforts are known to this day as **antitrust policy.**

One of the most striking early actions of antitrust policy was the breakup of Standard Oil in 1911. Its components formed the nuclei of many of today's large oil companies—Standard Oil of New Jersey became Exxon, Standard Oil of New York became Mobil, and so on. In the 1980s a long-running case led to the breakup of Bell Telephone, which once had a monopoly on both local and long-distance phone service in the United States. As we mentioned earlier, the Justice Department reviews proposed mergers between companies in the same industry and will bar mergers that it believes will reduce competition.

Among advanced countries, the United States is unique in its long tradition of antitrust policy. Until recently, other advanced countries did not have policies against price-fixing, and some even supported the creation of cartels, believing that it would help their own firms compete against foreign rivals. But the situation has changed radically over the past 20 years, as the European Union (EU)—an international body with the duty of enforcing antitrust policy for its member countries—has converged toward U.S. practices. Today, EU and U.S. regulators often target the same firms because price-fixing has "gone global" as international trade has expanded.

During the early 1990s, the United States instituted an amnesty program in which a price-fixer receives a much-reduced penalty if it provides information on its co-conspirators. In addition, Congress substantially increased maximum fines levied upon conviction. These two new policies clearly made informing on cartel partners a dominant strategy, and it has paid off: in recent years, executives from Belgium, Britain, Canada, France, Germany, Italy, Mexico, the Netherlands, South Korea, and Switzerland, as well as from the United States, have been convicted in U.S. courts of cartel crimes. As one lawyer commented, "You get a race to the courthouse" as each conspirator seeks to be the first to come clean. (For an example out of the United Kingdom, see the Business Case at the end of the section.)

Life has gotten much tougher over the past few years if you want to operate a cartel. So what's an oligopolist to do?

Tacit Collusion and Price Wars

If real life were as simple as our lysine story, it probably wouldn't be necessary for the company presidents to meet or do anything that could land them in jail. Both firms would realize that it was in their mutual interest to restrict output to 30 million pounds each and that any short-term gains to either firm from producing more would be much less than the later losses as the other firm retaliated. So even without any explicit agreement, the firms would probably have achieved the tacit collusion needed to maximize their combined profits.

Real industries are nowhere near that simple; nonetheless, in most oligopolistic industries, most of the time, the sellers do appear to succeed in keeping prices above their noncooperative level. Tacit collusion, in other words, is the normal state of oligopoly.

Antitrust policy involves efforts by the government to prevent oligopolistic industries from becoming or behaving like monopolies.

Although tacit collusion is common, it rarely allows an industry to push prices all the way up to their monopoly level; collusion is usually far from perfect. Four factors make it hard for an industry to coordinate on high prices.

1. LARGE NUMBERS Suppose that there were three instead of two firms in the lysine industry and that each was currently producing only 20 million pounds. In that case any one firm that decided to produce an extra 10 million pounds would gain more in short-term profits—and lose less once another firm responded in kind—than in our original example because it has fewer units on which to feel the price effect. The general point is that the more firms there are in an oligopoly, the less is the incentive for any one firm to behave cooperatively, taking into account the impact of its actions on the profits of the other firms. Large numbers of firms, also known as less concentration in an industry, also make the monitoring of price and output levels more difficult, and typically indicate low barriers to entry.

2. COMPLEX PRODUCTS AND PRICING SCHEMES In our simplified lysine example the two firms produce only one product. In reality, however, oligopolists often sell thousands or even tens of thousands of different products. In these circumstances, as when there are a large number of firms, keeping track of what other firms are producing and what prices they are charging is difficult. This makes it hard to determine whether a firm is cheating on the tacit agreement.

3. DIFFERENCES IN INTERESTS In the lysine example, a tacit agreement for the firms to split the market equally is a natural outcome, probably acceptable to both firms. In other situations, however, firms often differ both in their perceptions about what is fair and in their real interests.

For example, suppose that Ajinomoto was a long-established lysine producer and ADM a more recent entrant into the industry. Ajinomoto might feel that it deserved to continue producing more than ADM, but ADM might feel that it was entitled to 50% of the business.

Alternatively, suppose that ADM's marginal costs were lower than Ajinomoto's. Even if they could agree on market shares, they would then disagree about the profit-maximizing level of output.

4. BARGAINING POWER OF BUYERS Often oligopolists sell not to individual consumers but to large buyers—other industrial enterprises, nationwide chains of stores, and so on. These large buyers are in a position to bargain for lower prices from the oligopolists: they can ask for a discount from an oligopolist, and warn that they will go to a competitor if they don't get it. An important reason large retailers like Walmart are able to offer lower prices to customers than small retailers is precisely their ability to use their size to extract lower prices from their suppliers.

These difficulties in enforcing tacit collusion have sometimes led companies to defy the law and create illegal cartels. We've already examined the cases of the lysine industry and the chocolate industry. An older, classic example was the U.S. electrical equipment conspiracy of the 1950s, which led to the indictment of and jail sentences for some executives. The industry was one in which tacit collusion was especially difficult because of all the reasons just mentioned. There were many firms—40 companies were indicted. They produced a very complex array of products, often more or less custom-built for particular clients. They differed greatly in size, from giants like General Electric to family firms with only a few dozen employees. And the customers in many cases were large buyers like electrical utilities, which would normally try to force suppliers to compete for their business. Tacit collusion just didn't seem practical—so executives met secretly and illegally to decide who would bid what price for which contract.

Because tacit collusion is often hard to achieve, most oligopolies charge prices that are well below what the same industry would charge if it were controlled by a monopolist—or what they would charge if they were able to collude explicitly. In addition, sometimes tacit collusion breaks down and aggressive price competition amounts to a **price war.** A price war sometimes precipitates a collapse of prices to their noncooperative level, or even lower, as sellers try to put each other out of business or at least punish what they regard as cheating.

A **price war** occurs when tacit collusion breaks down and aggressive price competition causes prices to collapse.

ECONOMICS IN ACTION

THE PRICE WARS OF CHRISTMAS

During the last several holiday seasons, the toy aisles of American retailers have been the scene of cutthroat competition: Target priced the latest Elmo doll at 89 cents less than Walmart (for those with a coupon), and $6 less than Toys "R" Us. So extreme is the price-cutting that since 2003 three toy retailers—KB Toys, FAO Schwarz, and Zany Brainy—have been forced into bankruptcy. Due to aggressive price-cutting by competitors, the market share of Toys "R" Us has fallen from first to third.

What is happening? The turmoil can be traced back to trouble in the toy industry itself as well as to changes in toy retailing. Every year for several years, overall toy sales have fallen a few percentage points as children increasingly turn to video games and the Internet. There have also been new entrants into the toy business: Walmart and Target have expanded their numbers of stores and have been aggressive price-cutters.

The result is much like a story of tacit collusion sustained by repeated interaction run in reverse: because the overall industry is in a state of decline and there are new entrants, the future payoff from collusion is shrinking. The predictable outcome is a price war.

Bloomberg via Getty Images

The price wars of Christmas now arrive earlier each year.

Since retailers depend on holiday sales for nearly half of their annual sales, the holidays are a time of intense price-cutting. Traditionally, the biggest shopping day of the year has been the day after Thanksgiving. But in an effort to expand sales and undercut rivals, retailers—particularly Walmart—have begun slashing prices earlier in the fall, well before Thanksgiving. In fact, in 2010, Walmart slashed its toy prices in early November to within a few cents of Target's prices. Target then placed about half of its toys on sale. Toys "R" Us instead relied on a selection of exclusive toys to avoid direct price competition.

With other retailers feeling as if they have no choice but to follow this pattern, we have the phenomenon known as "creeping Christmas": the price wars of Christmas arrive earlier each year.

Product Differentiation and Price Leadership

Lysine is lysine: there was no question in anyone's mind that ADM and Ajinomoto were producing the same good and that consumers would make their decision about which company's lysine to buy based on the price. In many oligopolies, however, firms produce products that consumers regard as similar but not identical. A $10 difference in the price won't make many customers switch from a Ford to a Chrysler, or vice versa. Sometimes the differences between products are real, like differences between Froot Loops and Wheaties; sometimes, they exist mainly in the minds of consumers, like differences between brands of vodka (which is *supposed* to be tasteless). Either way, the effect is to reduce the intensity of competition among the firms: consumers will not all rush to buy whichever product is cheapest.

As you might imagine, oligopolists welcome the extra market power that comes when consumers think that their product is different from that of competitors. So in many oligopolistic industries, firms make considerable efforts to create the perception that their product is different—that is, they engage in **product differentiation.**

Product differentiation is an attempt by a firm to convince buyers that its product is different from the products of other firms in the industry.

A firm that tries to differentiate its product may do so by altering what it actually produces, adding "extras," or choosing a different design. It may also use advertising and marketing campaigns to create a differentiation in the minds of consumers, even though its product is more or less identical to the products of rivals.

A classic case of how products may be perceived as different even when they are really pretty much the same is over-the-counter medication. For many years there were only three widely sold pain relievers—aspirin, ibuprofen, and acetaminophen. Yet each of these generic pain relievers was marketed under a number of brand names. And each brand used a marketing campaign implying some special superiority.

Whatever the nature of product differentiation, oligopolists producing differentiated products often reach a tacit understanding not to compete on price. For example, during the years when the great majority of cars sold in the United States were produced by the Big Three auto companies (General Motors, Ford, and Chrysler), there was an unwritten rule that none of the three companies would try to gain market share by making its cars noticeably cheaper than those of the other two.

But then who would decide on the overall price of cars? The answer was normally General Motors: as the biggest of the three, it would announce its prices for the year first; and the other companies would adopt similar prices. This pattern of behavior, in which one company tacitly sets prices for the industry as a whole, is known as **price leadership.**

Interestingly, firms that have a tacit agreement not to compete on price often engage in vigorous **nonprice competition**—adding new features to their products, spending large sums on ads that proclaim the inferiority of their rivals' offerings, and so on.

BW Folsom/ Shutterstock

Oligopolists enjoy extra market power when consumers view their product as superior to the competition.

Perhaps the best way to understand the mix of cooperation and competition in such industries is with a political analogy. During the long Cold War between the United States and the Soviet Union, the two countries engaged in intense rivalry for global influence. They not only provided financial and military aid to their allies; they sometimes supported forces trying to overthrow governments allied with their rival (as the Soviet Union did in Vietnam in the 1960s and early 1970s, and as the United States did in Afghanistan from 1979 until the collapse of the Soviet Union in 1991). They even sent their own soldiers to support allied governments against rebels (as the United States did in Vietnam and the Soviet Union did in Afghanistan). But they did not get into direct military confrontations with each other; open warfare between the two superpowers was regarded by both as too dangerous—and tacitly avoided.

Price wars aren't as serious as shooting wars, but the principle is the same.

How Important Is Oligopoly?

We have seen that, across industries, oligopoly is far more common than either perfect competition or monopoly. When we try to analyze oligopoly, the economist's usual way of thinking—asking how self-interested individuals would behave, then analyzing their interaction—does not work as well as we might hope because we do not know whether rival firms will engage in noncooperative behavior or manage to engage in some kind of collusion. Given the prevalence of oligopoly, then, is the analysis we developed in earlier modules, which was based on perfect competition, still useful?

The conclusion of the great majority of economists is yes. For one thing, important parts of the economy are fairly well described by perfect competition. And even though many industries are oligopolistic, in many cases the limits to collusion keep prices relatively close to marginal costs—in other words, the industry behaves "almost" as if it were perfectly competitive.

It is also true that predictions from supply and demand analysis are often valid for oligopolies. For example, we saw that price controls will produce shortages. Strictly speaking, this conclusion is certain only for perfectly competitive industries. But in the 1970s, when the U.S. government imposed price controls on the definitely oligopolistic oil industry, the result was indeed to produce shortages and lines at the gas pumps.

So how important is it to take account of oligopoly? Most economists adopt a pragmatic approach. As we have seen here, the analysis of oligopoly is far more difficult and messy than that of perfect competition; so in situations where they do not expect the complications associated with oligopoly to be crucial, economists prefer to adopt the working assumption of perfectly competitive markets. They always keep in mind the possibility that oligopoly might be important; they recognize that there are important issues, from antitrust policies to price wars, that make trying to understand oligopolistic behavior crucial.

In **price leadership,** one firm sets its price first, and other firms then follow.

Firms that have a tacit understanding not to compete on price often engage in intense **nonprice competition,** using advertising and other means to try to increase their sales.

MODULE 33 Review

Solutions appear at the back of the book.

Check Your Understanding

1. For each of the following industry practices, explain whether the practice supports the conclusion that there is tacit collusion in this industry.
   a. For many years the price in the industry has changed infrequently, and all the firms in the industry charge the same price. The largest firm publishes a catalog containing a "suggested" retail price. Changes in price coincide with changes in the catalog.
   b. There has been considerable variation in the market shares of the firms in the industry over time.
   c. Firms in the industry build into their products unnecessary features that make it hard for consumers to switch from one company's products to another's.
   d. Firms meet yearly to discuss their annual sales forecasts.
   e. Firms tend to adjust their prices upward at the same times.

Multiple-Choice Questions

1. Having which of the following makes it easier for oligopolies to coordinate on raising prices?
   a. a large number of firms
   b. differentiated products
   c. buyers with bargaining power
   d. identical perceptions of fairness
   e. complex pricing schemes
2. Which of the following led to the passage of the first antitrust laws?
   I. growth of the railroad industry
   II. the emergence of the Standard Oil Company
   III. increased competition in agricultural industries
   a. I only
   b. II only
   c. III only
   d. I and II only
   e. I, II, and III
3. When was the first federal legislation against cartels passed?
   a. 1776
   b. 1800
   c. 1890
   d. 1900
   e. 1980
4. Based on your reading about oligopoly in this section, firms in which of the following industries have been prosecuted for creating an illegal cartel?
   a. the lysine industry
   b. top firms in the chocolate industry
   c. the U.S. electrical equipment industry
   d. none of the above
   e. all of the above
5. Oligopolists engage in tacit collusion in order to
   a. raise prices.
   b. increase output.
   c. share profits.
   d. increase market share.
   e. all of the above

Critical-Thinking Question

List four factors that make it difficult for firms to form a cartel. Explain each.

Monopolistic Competition

iStockphoto

WHAT YOU WILL LEARN

1. How prices and profits are determined in monopolistic competition, both in the short run and in the long run
2. How monopolistic competition can lead to inefficiency and excess capacity

Understanding Monopolistic Competition

Suppose an industry is monopolistically competitive: it consists of many producers, all competing for the same consumers but offering differentiated products. There is also free entry into and exit from the industry in the long run. How does such an industry behave?

As the term *monopolistic competition* suggests, this market structure combines some features typical of monopoly with others typical of perfect competition. Because each firm is offering a distinct product, it is in a way like a monopolist: it faces a downward-sloping demand curve and has some market power—the ability within limits to determine the price of its product.

However, unlike a pure monopolist, a monopolistically competitive firm does face competition: the amount of its product it can sell depends on the prices and products offered by other firms in the industry.

The same, of course, is true of an oligopoly. In a monopolistically competitive industry, however, there are *many* producers, as opposed to the small number that defines an oligopoly. This means that the "puzzle" of oligopoly—whether firms will collude or behave noncooperatively—does not arise in the case of monopolistically competitive industries. True, if all the gas stations or all the restaurants in a town could agree—explicitly or tacitly—to raise prices, it would be in their mutual interest to do so. But such collusion is virtually impossible when the number of firms is large and, by implication, there are no barriers to entry.

So in situations of monopolistic competition, we can safely assume that firms behave noncooperatively and ignore the potential for collusion.

Monopolistic Competition in the Short Run

We introduced the distinction between short-run and long-run equilibrium when we studied perfect competition. The short-run equilibrium of an industry takes the number of firms as given. The long-run equilibrium, by contrast, is reached only after enough time has elapsed for firms to enter or exit the industry. To analyze monopolistic competition, we focus first on the short run and then on how an industry moves from the short run to the long run.

Panels (a) and (b) of Figure 34-1 show two possible situations that a typical firm in a monopolistically competitive industry might face in the short run. In each case, the firm looks like any monopolist: it faces a downward-sloping demand curve, which implies a downward-sloping marginal revenue curve.

We assume that every firm has an upward-sloping marginal cost curve but that it also faces some fixed costs, so that its average total cost curve is U-shaped. This assumption doesn't matter in the short run; but, as we'll see shortly, it is crucial to understanding the long-run equilibrium.

In each case the firm, in order to maximize profit, sets marginal revenue equal to marginal cost. So how do these two figures differ? In panel (a) the firm is profitable; in panel (b) it is unprofitable. (Recall that we are referring always to economic profit and not accounting profit—that is, a profit given that all factors of production are earning their opportunity costs.)

In panel (a) the firm faces the demand curve D_P and the marginal revenue curve MR_P. It produces the profit-maximizing output Q_P, the quantity at which marginal

FIGURE 34-1 **The Monopolistically Competitive Firm in the Short Run**

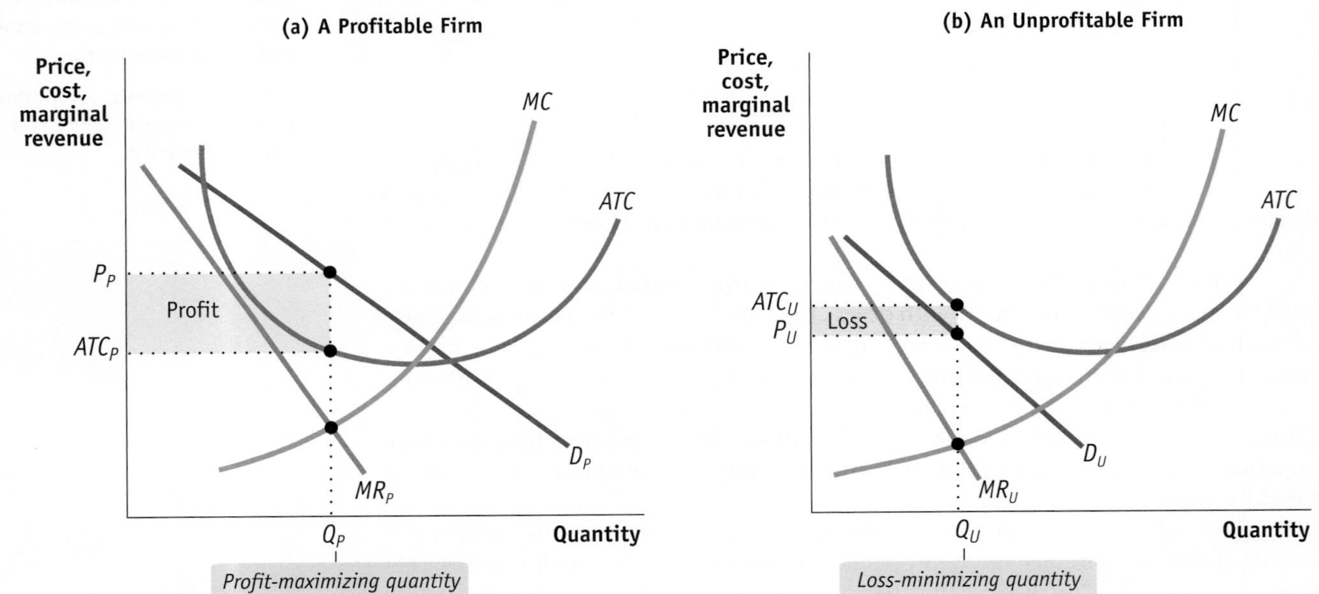

The firm in panel (a) can be profitable for some output quantities: the quantities for which its average total cost curve, *ATC*, lies below its demand curve, D_P. The profit-maximizing output quantity is Q_P, the output at which marginal revenue, MR_P, is equal to marginal cost, *MC*. The firm charges price P_P and earns a profit, represented by the area of the green shaded rectangle. The firm in panel (b), however, can never be profitable because its average total cost curve lies above its demand curve, D_U, for every output quantity. The best that it can do if it produces at all is to produce quantity Q_U and charge price P_U. This generates a loss, indicated by the area of the yellow shaded rectangle. Any other output quantity results in a greater loss.

revenue is equal to marginal cost, and sells it at the price P_P. This price is above the average total cost at this output, ATC_P. The firm's profit is indicated by the area of the shaded rectangle.

In panel (b) the firm faces the demand curve D_U and the marginal revenue curve MR_U. It chooses the quantity Q_U at which marginal revenue is equal to marginal cost. However, in this case the price P_U is *below* the average total cost ATC_U; so at this quantity the firm loses money. Its loss is equal to the area of the shaded rectangle. Since Q_U is the profit-maximizing quantity—which means, in this case, the loss-minimizing quantity—there is no way for a firm in this situation to make a profit. We can confirm this by noting that at any quantity of output, the average total cost curve in panel (b) lies above the demand curve D_U. Because $ATC > P$ at all quantities of output, this firm always suffers a loss.

As this comparison suggests, the key to whether a firm with market power is profitable or unprofitable in the short run lies in the relationship between its demand curve and its average total cost curve. In panel (a) the demand curve D_P crosses the average total cost curve, meaning that some of the demand curve lies above the average total cost curve. So there are some price–quantity combinations available at which price is higher than average total cost, indicating that the firm can choose a quantity at which it makes positive profit.

In panel (b), by contrast, the demand curve D_U does not cross the average total cost curve—it always lies below it. So the price corresponding to each quantity demanded is always less than the average total cost of producing that quantity. There is no quantity at which the firm can avoid losing money.

These figures, showing firms facing downward-sloping demand curves and their associated marginal revenue curves, look just like ordinary monopoly graphs. The "competition" aspect of monopolistic competition comes into play, however, when we move from the short run to the long run.

Monopolistic Competition in the Long Run

Obviously, an industry in which existing firms are losing money, like the one in panel (b) of Figure 34-1, is not in long-run equilibrium. When existing firms are losing money, some firms will *exit* the industry. The industry will not be in long-run equilibrium until the persistent losses have been eliminated by the exit of some firms.

It may be less obvious that an industry in which existing firms are earning profits, like the one in panel (a) of Figure 34-1, is also not in long-run equilibrium. Given there is *free entry* into the industry, persistent profits earned by the existing firms will lead to the entry of additional producers. The industry will not be in long-run equilibrium until the persistent profits have been eliminated by the entry of new producers.

©Brooke Becker/Dreamstime.com

In the long run, profit lures new firms to enter an industry.

How will entry or exit by other firms affect the profit of a typical existing firm? Because the differentiated products offered by firms in a monopolistically competitive industry are available to the same set of customers, entry or exit by other firms will affect the demand curve facing every existing producer.

If new gas stations open along a highway, each of the existing gas stations will no longer be able to sell as much gas as before at any given price. So, as illustrated in

FIGURE 34-2 Entry and Exit Shift Existing Firms' Demand Curves and Marginal Revenue Curves

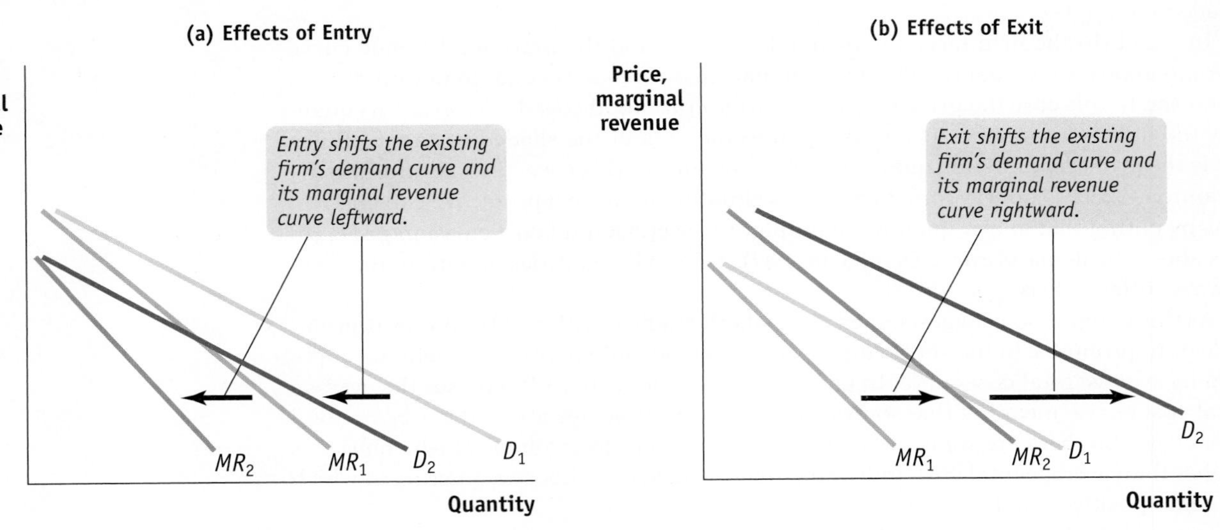

Entry will occur in the long run when existing firms are profitable. In panel (a), entry causes each existing firm's demand curve and marginal revenue curve to shift to the left. The firm receives a lower price for every unit it sells, and its profit falls. Entry will cease when firms make zero profit. Exit will occur in the long run when existing firms are unprofitable. In panel (b), exit from the industry shifts each remaining firm's demand curve and marginal revenue curve to the right. The firm receives a higher price for every unit it sells, and profit rises. Exit will cease when the remaining firms make zero profit.

panel (a) of Figure 34-2, entry of additional producers into a monopolistically competitive industry will lead to a *leftward* shift of the demand curve and the marginal revenue curve facing a typical existing producer.

Conversely, suppose that some of the gas stations along the highway close. Then each of the remaining stations will be able to sell more gasoline at any given price. So as illustrated in panel (b), exit of firms from an industry leads to a *rightward* shift of the demand curve and marginal revenue curve facing a typical remaining producer.

The industry will be in long-run equilibrium when there is neither entry nor exit. This will occur only when every firm earns zero profit. So in the long run, a monopolistically competitive industry will end up in **zero-profit equilibrium,** in which firms just manage to cover their costs at their profit-maximizing output quantities.

We have seen that a firm facing a downward-sloping demand curve will earn positive profit if any part of that demand curve lies above its average total cost curve; it will incur a loss if its entire demand curve lies below its average total cost curve. So in zero-profit equilibrium, the firm must be in a borderline position between these two cases; its demand curve must just touch its average total cost curve. That is, the demand curve must be just *tangent* to the average total cost curve (meaning it just touches the curve) at the firm's profit-maximizing output quantity—the output quantity at which marginal revenue equals marginal cost.

If this is not the case, the firm operating at its profit-maximizing quantity will find itself making either a profit or loss, as illustrated in the panels of Figure 34-1. But we also know that free entry and exit means that this cannot be a long-run equilibrium. Why?

In the long run, a monopolistically competitive industry ends up in **zero-profit equilibrium:** each firm makes zero profit at its profit-maximizing quantity.

In the case of a profit, new firms will enter the industry, shifting the demand curve of every existing firm leftward until all profit is eliminated. In the case of a loss, some existing firms exit and so shift the demand curve of every remaining firm to the right until all losses are eliminated. All entry and exit ceases only when every existing firm makes zero profit at its profit-maximizing quantity of output.

FIGURE 34-3 The Long-Run Zero-Profit Equilibrium

If existing firms are profitable, entry will occur and shift each existing firm's demand curve leftward. If existing firms are unprofitable, each remaining firm's demand curve shifts rightward as some firms exit the industry. Entry and exit will cease when every existing firm makes zero profit at its profit-maximizing quantity. So, in long-run zero-profit equilibrium, the demand curve of each firm is tangent to its average total cost curve at its profit-maximizing quantity: at the profit-maximizing quantity, Q_{MC}, price, P_{MC}, equals average total cost, ATC_{MC}. A monopolistically competitive firm is like a monopolist without monopoly profits.

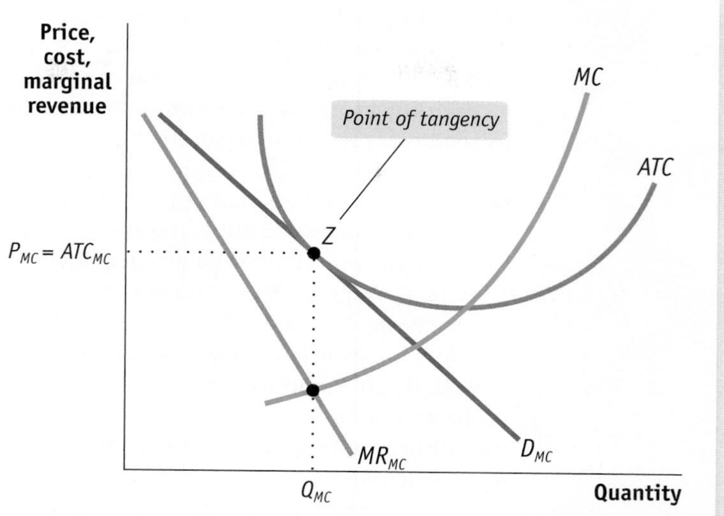

Figure 34-3 shows a typical monopolistically competitive firm in such a zero-profit equilibrium. The firm produces Q_{MC}, the output at which $MR_{MC} = MC$, and charges price P_{MC}. At this price and quantity, represented by point Z, the demand curve is just tangent to its average total cost curve. The firm earns zero profit because price, P_{MC}, is equal to average total cost, ATC_{MC}.

The normal long-run condition of a monopolistically competitive industry, then, is that each producer is in the situation shown in Figure 34-3. Each producer acts like a monopolist, facing a downward-sloping demand curve and setting marginal cost equal to marginal revenue so as to maximize profit. But this is just enough to achieve zero economic profit. The producers in the industry are like monopolists without monopoly profit.

ECONOMICS IN ACTION

THE HOUSING BUST AND THE DEMISE OF THE 6% COMMISSION

The vast majority of home sales in the United States are transacted with the use of real estate agents. A homeowner looking to sell hires an agent, who lists the house for sale and shows it to interested buyers. Correspondingly, prospective home buyers hire their own agent to arrange inspections of available houses.

Traditionally, agents were paid by the seller: a commission equal to 6% of the sales price of the house, which the seller's agent and the buyer's agent would split equally. If a house sold for \$300,000, for example, the seller's agent and the buyer's agent each received \$9,000 (equal to 3% of \$300,000).

The real estate brokerage industry fits the model of monopolistic competition quite well: in any given local market, there are many real estate agents, all competing with one another, but the agents are differentiated by location and personality as well as by the type of home they sell (whether condominiums, very expensive homes, and so on). And the industry has free entry: it's relatively easy for someone to become a real estate agent (take a course and then pass a test to obtain a license).

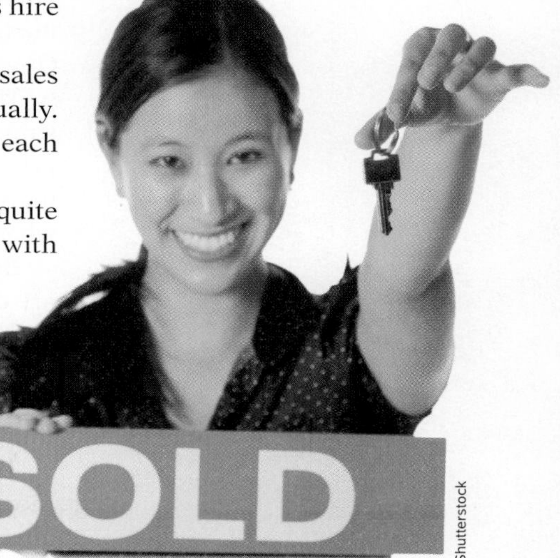

Shutterstock

But for a long time there was one feature that didn't fit the model of monopolistic competition: the fixed 6% commission that had not changed over time and was unaffected by the ups and downs of the housing market.

You may wonder how agents were able to maintain the 6% commission. Why didn't new agents enter the market and drive the commission down to the zero-profit level? One tactic used by agents was their control of the Multiple Listing Service, or MLS, which lists nearly all the homes for sale in a community. Traditionally, only sellers who agreed to the 6% commission were allowed to list their homes on the MLS.

But protecting the 6% commission was always an iffy endeavor because any action by the brokerage industry to fix the commission rate at a given percentage would run afoul of antitrust laws. And by the early to mid-2000s, as the housing boom intensified, discount brokers had appeared on the scene. But traditional agents refused to work with them. So in 2005, the Justice Department sued the National Association of Realtors, the powerful trade group of agents.

In fact, oversight by regulators and the housing market bust which began in 2006 hastened the demise of the non-negotiable 6% commission. With sellers forced to accept less for their houses than often anticipated, agents were pressured to accept less as well. By 2009, the average commission fell to 5.36%, and agents were offering to list properties on broker databases for as little as a few hundred dollars. As Steve Murray, the editor of a trade publication, said in 2011, "The standard 6 percent went out the window a long time ago."

Monopolistic Competition versus Perfect Competition

In a way, long-run equilibrium in a monopolistically competitive industry looks a lot like long-run equilibrium in a perfectly competitive industry. In both cases, there are many firms; in both cases, profits have been competed away; in both cases, the price received by every firm is equal to the average total cost of production.

However, the two versions of long-run equilibrium are different—in ways that are economically significant.

Price, Marginal Cost, and Average Total Cost

Figure 34-4 compares the long-run equilibrium of a typical firm in a perfectly competitive industry with that of a typical firm in a monopolistically competitive industry. Panel (a) shows a perfectly competitive firm facing a market price equal to its minimum average total cost; panel (b) reproduces Figure 34-3. Comparing the panels, we see two important differences.

First, in the case of the perfectly competitive firm shown in panel (a), the price, P_{PC}, received by the firm at the profit-maximizing quantity, Q_{PC}, is equal to the firm's marginal cost of production, MC_{PC}, at that quantity of output. By contrast, at the profit-maximizing quantity chosen by the monopolistically competitive firm in panel (b), Q_{MC}, the price, P_{MC}, is *higher* than the marginal cost of production, MC_{MC}.

This difference translates into a difference in the attitude of firms toward consumers. A wheat farmer, who can sell as much wheat as he likes at the going market price, would not get particularly excited if you offered to buy some more wheat at the market price. Since he has no desire to produce more at that price and can sell the wheat to someone else, you are not doing him a favor.

But if you decide to fill up your tank at Jamil's gas station rather than at Katy's, you are doing Jamil a favor. He is not willing to cut his price to get more customers—he's already made the best of that trade-off. But if he gets a few more customers than he expected at the *posted* price, that's good news: an additional sale at the posted price increases his revenue more than it increases his cost because the posted price exceeds marginal cost.

The fact that monopolistic competitors, unlike perfect competitors, want to sell more at the going price is crucial to understanding why they engage in activities like advertising that help increase sales.

FIGURE 34-4 Comparing Long-Run Equilibrium in Perfect Competition and Monopolistic Competition

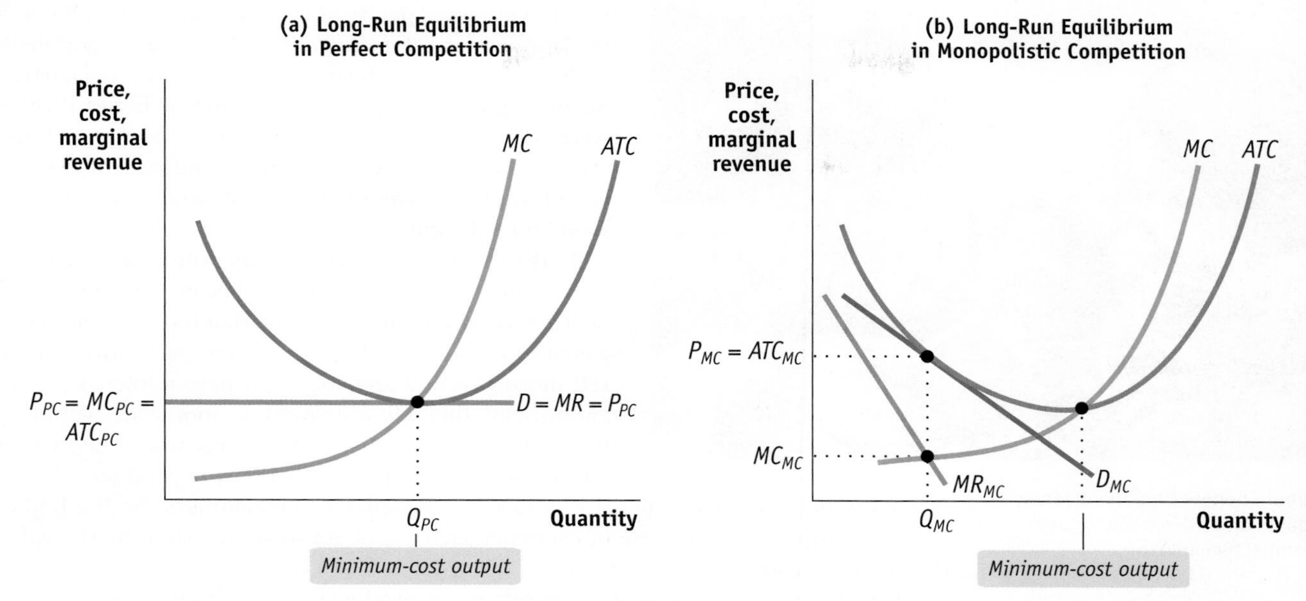

Panel (a) shows the situation of the typical firm in long-run equilibrium in a perfectly competitive industry. The firm operates at the minimum-cost output Q_{PC}, sells at the competitive market price P_{PC}, and makes zero profit. It is indifferent to selling another unit of output because P_{PC} is equal to its marginal cost, MC_{PC}. Panel (b) shows the situation of the typical firm in long-run equilibrium in a monopolistically competitive industry. At Q_{MC} it makes zero profit because its price, P_{MC}, just equals average total cost, ATC_{MC}. At Q_{MC} the firm would like to sell another unit at price P_{MC} since P_{MC} exceeds marginal cost, MC_{MC}. But it is unwilling to lower price to make more sales. It therefore operates to the left of the minimum-cost output level and has excess capacity.

The other difference between monopolistic competition and perfect competition that is visible in Figure 34-4 involves the position of each firm on its average total cost curve. In panel (a), the perfectly competitive firm produces at point Q_{PC}, at the bottom of the U-shaped *ATC* curve. That is, each firm produces the quantity at which average total cost is minimized—the *minimum-cost output*. As a consequence, the total cost of industry output is also minimized.

Under monopolistic competition, in panel (b), the firm produces at Q_{MC}, on the *downward-sloping* part of the U-shaped *ATC* curve: it produces less than the quantity that would minimize average total cost. This failure to produce enough to minimize average total cost is sometimes described as the **excess capacity** issue. The typical vendor in a food court or a gas station along a road is not big enough to take maximum advantage of available cost savings. So the total cost of industry output is not minimized in the case of a monopolistically competitive industry.

Some people have argued that, because every monopolistic competitor has excess capacity, monopolistically competitive industries are inefficient. But the issue of efficiency under monopolistic competition turns out to be a subtle one that does not have a clear answer.

Is Monopolistic Competition Inefficient?

A monopolistic competitor, like a monopolist, charges a price that is above marginal cost. As a result, some people who are willing to pay at least as much for an egg roll at Wonderful Wok as it costs to produce it are deterred from doing so. In monopolistic competition, some mutually beneficial transactions go unexploited.

Firms in a monopolistically competitive industry have **excess capacity:** they produce less than the output at which average total cost is minimized.

iStockphoto

Consumers benefit from the diversity of products offered in a monopolistically competitive industry.

Furthermore, it is often argued that monopolistic competition is subject to a further kind of inefficiency: that the excess capacity of every monopolistic competitor implies *wasteful duplication* because monopolistically competitive industries offer too many varieties. According to this argument, it would be better if there were only two or three vendors in the food court, not six or seven. If there were fewer vendors, they would each have lower average total costs and so could offer food more cheaply.

Is this argument against monopolistic competition right—that it lowers total surplus by causing inefficiency? Not necessarily. It's true that if there were fewer gas stations along a highway, each gas station would sell more gasoline and so would have a lower cost per gallon. But there is a drawback: motorists would be inconvenienced because gas stations would be farther apart. The point is that the diversity of products offered in a monopolistically competitive industry is beneficial to consumers. So the higher price consumers pay because of excess capacity is offset to some extent by the value they receive from greater diversity.

There is, in other words, a trade-off: more producers mean higher average total costs but also greater product diversity. Does a monopolistically competitive industry arrive at the socially optimal point in this trade-off? Probably not—but it is hard to say whether there are too many firms or too few! Most economists now believe that duplication of effort and excess capacity in monopolistically competitive industries are not large problems in practice.

MODULE 34 Review

Solutions appear at the back of the book.

Check Your Understanding

1. Suppose a monopolistically competitive industry composed of firms with U-shaped average total cost curves is in long-run equilibrium. For each of the following changes, explain how the industry is affected in the short run and how it adjusts to a new long-run equilibrium.
   a. a technological change that increases fixed cost for every firm in the industry
   b. a technological change that decreases marginal cost for every firm in the industry
2. Why is it impossible for firms in a monopolistically competitive industry to join together to form a monopoly that is capable of maintaining positive economic profit in the long run?
3. Are the following statements true or false? Explain your answers.
   a. Like a firm in a perfectly competitive industry, a firm in a monopolistically competitive industry is willing to sell a good at any price that equals or exceeds marginal cost.
   b. Suppose there is a monopolistically competitive industry in long-run equilibrium that possesses excess capacity. All the firms in the industry would be better off if they merged into a single firm and produced a single product, but whether consumers would be made better off by this is ambiguous.
   c. Fads and fashions are more likely to arise in industries characterized by monopolistic competition or oligopoly than in those characterized by perfect competition or monopoly.

Multiple-Choice Questions

1. Which of the following is a characteristic of monopolistic competition?
   a. a standardized product
   b. many sellers
   c. barriers to entry
   d. positive long-run profits
   e. a perfectly elastic demand curve

2. Which of the following results is possible for a monopolistic competitor in the short run?
   I. positive economic profit
   II. normal profit
   III. loss
   a. I only
   b. II only
   c. III only
   d. I and II only
   e. I, II, and III

3. Which of the following results is possible for a monopolistic competitor in the long run?
   I. positive economic profit
   II. normal profit
   III. loss
   a. I only
   b. II only
   c. III only
   d. I and II only
   e. I, II, and III

4. Which of the following best describes a monopolistic competitor's demand curve?
   a. upward sloping
   b. downward sloping
   c. U-shaped
   d. horizontal
   e. vertical

5. The long-run outcome in a monopolistically competitive industry results in
   a. inefficiency because firms earn positive economic profits.
   b. efficiency due to excess capacity.
   c. inefficiency due to product diversity.
   d. efficiency because price exceeds marginal cost.
   e. a trade-off between higher average total cost and more product diversity.

Critical-Thinking Question

Draw a correctly labeled graph for a monopolistically competitive firm in long-run equilibrium. Label the distance on the quantity axis that represents excess capacity.

Product Differentiation and Advertising

Andrew Moore/Gallery Stock

WHAT YOU WILL LEARN

1. **Why oligopolists and monopolistic competitors differentiate their products**
2. **The economic significance of advertising and brand names**

In previous modules we learned that product differentiation often plays an important role in oligopolistic industries. In such industries, product differentiation reduces the intensity of competition between firms when tacit collusion cannot be achieved. It plays an even more crucial role in monopolistically competitive industries. Because tacit collusion is virtually impossible when there are many producers, product differentiation is the only way monopolistically competitive firms can acquire some market power.

In this module, we look at how oligopolists and monopolistic competitors differentiate their products in order to maximize profits.

How Firms Differentiate Their Products

How do firms in the same industry—such as fast-food vendors, gas stations, or chocolate makers—differentiate their products? Sometimes the difference is mainly in the minds of consumers rather than in the products themselves. We'll discuss the role of advertising and the importance of brand names in achieving this kind of product differentiation later. But, in general, firms differentiate their products by—surprise!—actually making them different.

The key to product differentiation is that consumers have different preferences and are willing to pay somewhat more to satisfy those preferences. Each producer can carve out a market niche by producing something that caters to the particular preferences of some group of consumers better than the products of other firms. There are three important forms of product differentiation:

- differentiation by style or type
- differentiation by location
- differentiation by quality.

Differentiation by Style or Type

Recall our discussion of Leo's Wonderful Wok in an earlier module. The sellers in Leo's food court offer different types of fast food: hamburgers, pizza, Chinese food, Mexican food, and so on. Each consumer arrives at the food court with some preference for one or another of these offerings. This preference may depend on the consumer's mood, her diet, or what she has already eaten that day. These preferences will not make consumers indifferent to price: if Wonderful Wok were to charge $15 for an egg roll, everybody would go to Bodacious Burgers or Pizza Paradise instead. But some people will choose a more expensive meal if that type of food is closer to their preference. So the products of the different vendors are substitutes, but they aren't *perfect* substitutes—they are *imperfect substitutes.*

Vendors in a food court or the restaurant chains in Times Square (shown in the photo at left) aren't the only sellers who differentiate their offerings by type. Clothing stores concentrate on women's or men's clothes, on business attire or sportswear, on trendy or classic styles, and so on. Auto manufacturers offer sedans, minivans, sport-utility vehicles, and sports cars, each type aimed at drivers with different needs and tastes.

Books offer yet another example of differentiation by type and style. Mysteries are differentiated from romances; among mysteries, we can differentiate among hard-boiled detective stories, whodunits, and police procedurals. And no two writers of hard-boiled detective stories are exactly alike: Raymond Chandler and Sue Grafton each have devoted fans.

In fact, product differentiation is characteristic of most consumer goods. As long as people differ in their tastes, producers find it possible and profitable to offer variety.

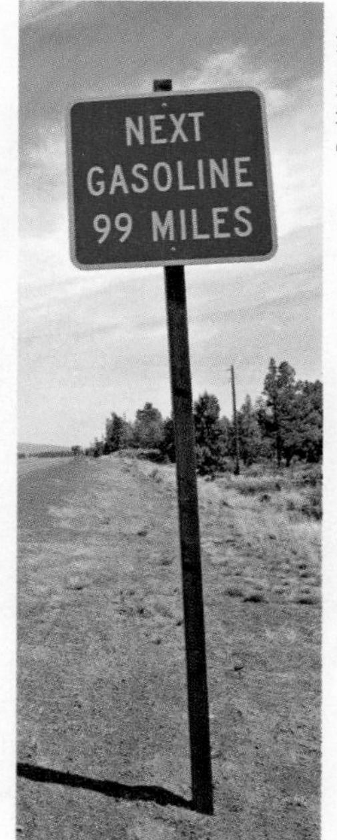

Buddy Mays/Alamy

For industries that differentiate by location, proximity is everything.

Differentiation by Location

Gas stations along a road offer differentiated products. True, the gas may be exactly the same. But the location of the stations is different, and location matters to consumers: it's more convenient to stop for gas near your home, near your workplace, or near wherever you are when the gas gauge gets low.

In fact, many monopolistically competitive industries supply goods differentiated by location. This is especially true in service industries, from dry cleaners to hairdressers, where customers often choose the seller who is closest rather than cheapest.

Differentiation by Quality

Do you have a craving for chocolate? How much are you willing to spend on it? You see, there's chocolate and then there's chocolate: although ordinary chocolate may not be very expensive, gourmet chocolate can cost several dollars per bite.

With chocolate, as with many goods, there is a range of possible qualities. You can get a usable bicycle for less than $100; you can get a much fancier bicycle for 10 times as much. It all depends on how much the additional quality matters to you and how much you will miss the other things you could have purchased with that money.

Because consumers vary in what they are willing to pay for higher quality, producers can differentiate their products by quality—some offering lower-quality, inexpensive products and others offering higher-quality products at a higher price.

iStockphoto

Chocolate lovers know that there's ordinary chocolate and then there's *extraordinary* chocolate.

Product differentiation, then, can take several forms. Whatever form it takes, however, there are two important features of industries with differentiated products: *competition among sellers* and *value in diversity.*

Competition among sellers means that even though sellers of differentiated products are not offering identical goods, they are to some extent competing for a limited market. If more businesses enter the market, each will find that it sells a lower quantity at any given price. For example, as we saw in the previous chapter, if a new gas station opens along a road, each of the existing gas stations will sell a bit less.

Value in diversity refers to the gain to consumers from the proliferation of differentiated products. A food court with eight vendors makes consumers happier than one with only six vendors, even if the prices are the same, because some customers will get a meal that is closer to what they had in mind. A road on which there is a gas station every two miles is more convenient for motorists than a road where gas stations are five miles apart. When a product is available in many different qualities, fewer people are forced to pay for more quality than they need or to settle for lower quality than they want. There are, in other words, benefits to consumers from a greater diversity of available products.

ECONOMICS IN ACTION

Science and Society/Superstock

ANY COLOR, SO LONG AS IT'S BLACK

The early history of the auto industry offers a classic illustration of the power of product differentiation.

The modern automobile industry was created by Henry Ford, who first introduced assembly-line production. This technique made it possible for him to offer the famous Model T at a far lower price than anyone else was charging for a car; by 1920, Ford dominated the automobile business.

Ford's strategy was to offer just one style of car, which maximized his economies of scale in production but made no concessions to differences in consumers' tastes. He supposedly declared that customers could get the Model T in "any color, so long as it's black."

This strategy was challenged by Alfred P. Sloan, who had merged a number of smaller automobile companies into General Motors. Sloan's strategy was to offer a range of car types, differentiated by quality and price. Chevrolets were basic cars that directly challenged the Model T, Buicks were bigger and more expensive, and so on up to Cadillacs. And you could get each model in several different colors.

By the 1930s the verdict was clear: customers preferred a range of styles, and General Motors, not Ford, became the dominant auto manufacturer for the rest of the twentieth century.

Controversies About Product Differentiation

Up to this point, we have assumed that products are differentiated in a way that corresponds to some real desire of consumers. There is real convenience in having a gas station in your neighborhood; Chinese food and Mexican food are really different from each other.

In the real world, however, some instances of product differentiation can seem puzzling if you think about them. What is the real difference between Crest and Colgate toothpaste? Between Energizer and Duracell batteries? Or a Marriott and a Hilton hotel room? Most people would be hard-pressed to answer any of these questions. Yet the producers of these goods make considerable efforts to convince consumers that their products are different from and better than those of their competitors.

This example illustrates one rationale for the welfare state: *alleviating income inequality.* Because a marginal dollar is worth more to a poor person than a rich one, modest transfers from the rich to the poor will do the rich little harm but benefit the poor a lot. So, according to this argument, a government that plays Robin Hood, taking from the rich to give to the poor, does more good than harm. Programs that are designed to aid the poor are known as **poverty programs.**

2. ALLEVIATING ECONOMIC INSECURITY Another rationale for the welfare state is *alleviating economic insecurity.* Imagine ten families, each of which expect an income next year of $50,000 if nothing goes wrong. But suppose the odds are that something *will* go wrong for one of the families, although nobody knows which one. For example, suppose each of the families has a one in ten chance of experiencing a sharp drop in income because a family member is laid off or incurs large medical bills. And assume that this produces severe hardship for the family.

Now suppose there's a government program that provides aid to families in distress, paying for that aid by taxing families that are having a good year. Arguably, this program will make all the families better off, because even families not currently receiving aid might need it at some point in the future. Each family will therefore feel safer knowing that the government stands ready to help when disaster strikes. Programs designed to provide protection against unpredictable financial distress are known as **social insurance programs.**

3. REDUCING POVERTY AND PROVIDING ACCESS TO HEALTH CARE The final rationale for the welfare state involves *the social benefits of poverty reduction and access to health care,* especially when applied to children of poor households. Researchers have documented that such children, on average, suffer lifelong disadvantages. Even after adjusting for ability, children from disadvantaged backgrounds are more likely to be underemployed or unemployed, to engage in crime, and to suffer chronic health problems—all of which impose significant social costs. So, according to the evidence, programs that help to alleviate poverty and provide access to health care generate external benefits to society.

But while some political philosophers argue that principles of social justice demand that society take care of the poor and unlucky, others disagree, arguing that welfare state programs go beyond the proper role of government. To an important extent, the difference between those two positions defines what we mean in politics by "liberalism" and "conservatism."

But before we get carried away, it's important to realize that things aren't so cut and dried. Even conservatives who believe in limited government typically support some welfare state programs. And even economists who support the goals of the welfare state are concerned about the effects of large-scale aid to the poor and unlucky on their incentives to work and save. Like taxes, welfare state programs can create substantial deadweight losses, so their true economic costs can be considerably larger than the direct monetary cost. We'll soon look at the costs and benefits of the welfare state. First, however, let's examine the problems the welfare state is supposed to address.

The Problem of Poverty

What, exactly, do we mean by *poverty?* Any definition is somewhat arbitrary. Since 1965, however, the U.S. government has maintained an official definition of the **poverty threshold,** a minimum annual income that is considered adequate to purchase the necessities of life. Families whose incomes fall below the poverty threshold are considered poor.

The official poverty threshold depends on the size and composition of a family. In 2012 the poverty threshold for an adult living alone was $11,945; for a household consisting of two adults and two children, it was $23,283.

TRENDS IN POVERTY Contrary to popular misconceptions, although the official poverty threshold is adjusted each year to reflect changes in the cost of living, it has *not*

A **poverty program** is a government program designed to aid the poor.

A **social insurance program** is a government program designed to provide protection against unpredictable financial distress.

The **poverty threshold** is the annual income below which a family is officially considered poor.

The **poverty rate** is the percentage of the population with incomes below the poverty threshold.

been adjusted upward over time to reflect the long-term rise in the standard of living of the average American family. As a result, as the economy grows and becomes more prosperous, and average incomes rise, you might expect the percentage of the population living below the poverty threshold to steadily decline.

Somewhat surprisingly, however, this hasn't happened. Figure 39-1 shows the U.S. **poverty rate**—the percentage of the population living below the poverty threshold—from 1960 to 2011. As you can see, the poverty rate fell steeply during the 1960s and early 1970s. Since then, however, it has fluctuated up and down, with no clear trend. In fact, in 2011 the poverty rate was higher than it was in 1969.

WHO ARE THE POOR? Many Americans probably hold a stereotyped image of poverty: an African-American or Hispanic family with no husband present and the female head of the household unemployed at least part of the time. This picture isn't completely off-base: poverty is disproportionately high among African-Americans and Hispanics as well as among female-headed households. But a majority of the poor don't fit the stereotype.

iStockphoto

In 2011, about 43.2 million Americans were in poverty—15% of the population. About one-quarter of the poor were African-American, substantially exceeding their share of the overall population (only about 13% of the population is African-American). The average poverty rate among the group was 27.6%. Hispanics were also more likely than the average American to be poor, with a poverty rate of 25.3%. But there was also widespread poverty among non-Hispanic Whites, who made up more than half the ranks of the poor.

There is also a correlation between family makeup and poverty. Female-headed families had a very high poverty rate: 31.2%. Married couples were much less likely to be poor, with a poverty rate of only 6.2%; still, about one-third of the poor were in married families with both spouses present.

What really stands out in the data, however, is the association between poverty and inadequate employment. Adults who work full time are very unlikely to be poor: only 2.8% of full-time workers were poor in 2011.

Many industries, particularly in the retail and service sectors, now rely primarily on part-time workers. Part-time work typically lacks benefits such as health plans,

FIGURE 39-1 **Trends in the U.S. Poverty Rate, 1960–2011**

The poverty rate fell sharply from the 1960s to the early 1970s but has not shown a clear trend since then.
Source: U.S. Census Bureau.

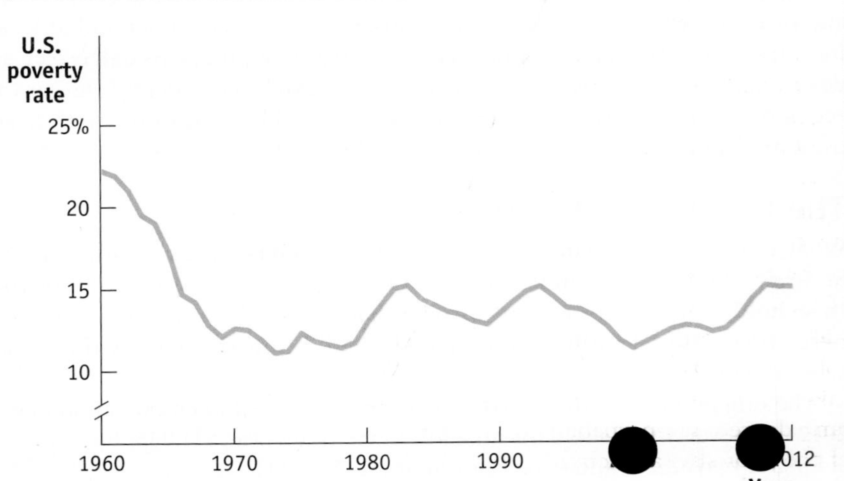

paid vacation days, andretirement benefits, and it also usually pays a lower hourly wage than comparable full-time work. As a result, many of the poor are members of what analysts call the *working poor:* workers whose income falls at or below the poverty threshold.

WHAT CAUSES POVERTY? Poverty is often blamed on lack of education, and educational attainment clearly has a strong positive effect on income level—those with more education earn, on average, higher incomes than those with less education. For example, in 1979 the average hourly wage of men with a college degree was 38% higher than that of men with only a high school diploma; by 2011, the "college premium" had increased to 82%.

Lack of proficiency in English is also a barrier to higher income. For example, Mexican-born male workers in the United States—two-thirds of whom have not graduated from high school and many of whom have poor English skills—earn less than half of what native-born men earn.

And it's important not to overlook the role of racial and gender discrimination; although less pervasive today than 50 years ago, discrimination still creates formidable barriers to advancement for many Americans. Non-Whites earn less and are less likely to be employed than Whites with comparable levels of education. Studies find that African-American males suffer persistent discrimination by employers in favor of Whites, African-American women, and Hispanic immigrants. Women earn lower incomes than men with similar qualifications.

In addition, one important source of poverty that should not be overlooked is bad luck. Many families find themselves impoverished when a wage-earner loses a job or a family member falls seriously ill.

iStockphoto

Poverty tends to be self-perpetuating.

CONSEQUENCES OF POVERTY The consequences of poverty are often severe, particularly for children. In 2012, 22% of children in the United States lived in poverty. Poverty is often associated with a lack of access to health care, which can lead to further health problems that erode the ability to attend school and work later in life. Affordable housing is also frequently a problem, leading poor families to move often, disrupting school and work schedules. Recent medical studies have shown that children raised in severe poverty tend to suffer from lifelong learning disabilities. As a result, American children growing up in or near poverty don't have an equal chance at the starting line: they tend to be at a disadvantage throughout their lives.

Table 39-1 shows the results of a long-term survey conducted by the U.S. Department of Education, which tracked a group of students who were in eighth grade in 1988. That year, the students took a mathematics test that the study used as an indicator of their innate ability; the study also scored students by the socioeconomic status of their families, a measure that took into account their parents' income and employment.

As you can see, the results were disturbing: only 29% of students who were in the highest-scoring 25% on the test but whose parents were of low status finished college. By contrast, the equally talented children of high-status parents had a 74% chance of finishing college—and children of high-status parents had a 30% chance of finishing college even if they had low test scores. What this tells us is that poverty is, to an important degree, self-perpetuating: the children of the poor start with a disadvantage relative to other Americans that it's very hard for them to achieve a better life.

TABLE 39-1

Percent of Eighth-Graders Finishing College, 1988

	Mathematics test score in bottom quartile	Mathematics test score in top quartile
Parents in bottom quartile	3%	29%
Parents in top quartile	30	74

Source: National Center for Education Statistics, *The Condition of Education 2003*, p. 47.

Mean household income is the average income across all households.

Median household income is the income of the household lying at the exact middle of the income distribution.

Economic Inequality

The United States is a rich country. In 2007, before the recession hit, the average U.S. household had an income of $67,609, far exceeding the poverty threshold. Even after a devastating recession, average household income in 2012 was slightly higher at $69,677. How is it possible, then, that so many Americans still live in poverty? The answer is that income is unequally distributed, with many households earning much less than the average and others earning much more.

Table 39-2 shows the distribution of pre-tax income—income before federal income taxes are paid—among U.S. families in 2011, as estimated by the Census Bureau. Households are grouped into *quintiles*, each containing 20%, or one-fifth, of the population. The first, or bottom, quintile contains households whose income put them below the 20th percentile in income, the second quintile contains households whose income put them between the 20th and 40th percentiles, and so on.

For each group, Table 39-2 shows three numbers. The second column shows the income ranges that define the group. For example, in 2011, the bottom quintile consisted of households with annual incomes of less than $20,262, the next quintile of households had incomes between $20,262 and $38,520, and so on. The third column shows the average income in each group, ranging from $11,239 for the bottom fifth to $311,444 for the top 5%. The fourth column shows the percentage of total U.S. income received by each group.

TABLE 39-2

U.S. Income Distribution in 2011

Income group	Income range	Average income	Percent of total income
Bottom quintile	Less than $20,262	$11,239	3.2%
Second quintile	$20,262 to $38,520	29,204	8.4
Third quintile	$38,520 to $62,434	49,842	[illegible]
Fourth quintile	$62,434 to $101,582	80,080	23.0
Top quintile	More than $101,582	178,020	51.1
Top 5%	More than $186,000	311,444	22.3
Mean income = $69,677		Median income = $50,054	

Source: U.S. Census Bureau.

MEAN VERSUS MEDIAN HOUSEHOLD INCOME At the bottom of Table 39-2 are two useful numbers for thinking about the incomes of American households. **Mean household income,** also called average household income, is the total income of all U.S. households divided by the number of households. **Median household income** is the income of a household in the exact middle of the income distribution—the level of income at which half of all households have lower income and half have higher income. It's very important to realize that these two numbers do not measure the same thing.

Economists often illustrate the difference by asking people first to imagine a room containing several dozen more or less ordinary wage-earners, then to think about what happens to the mean and median incomes of the people in the room if a Wall Street tycoon, some of whom earn more than a billion dollars a year, walks in. The mean income soars, because the tycoon's income pulls up the average, but median income hardly rises at all.

This example helps explain why economists generally regard median income as a better guide to the economic status of typical American families than mean income: mean income is strongly affected by the incomes of a relatively small number of very-high-income Americans, who are not representative of the population as a whole; median income is not.

What we learn from Table 39-2 is that income in the United States is quite unequally distributed. The average income of the poorest fifth of families is less than a quarter of the average income of families in the middle, and the richest fifth have an average income more than three times that of families in the middle. The incomes of the richest fifth of the population are, on average, about 15 times as high as those of the poorest fifth. In fact, the distribution of income in America has become more unequal since 1980, rising to a level that has made it a significant political issue.

The **Gini coefficient** is a number that summarizes a country's level of income inequality based on how unequally income is distributed across quintiles.

THE GINI COEFFICIENT It's often convenient to have a single number that summarizes a country's level of income inequality. The **Gini coefficient,** the most widely used measure of inequality, is based on how disparately income is distributed across the quintiles. A country with a perfectly equal distribution of income—that is, one in which the bottom 20% of the population received 20% of the income, the bottom 40% of the population received 40% of the income, and so on—would have a Gini coefficient of 0. At the other extreme, the highest possible value for the Gini coefficient is 1—the level it would attain if all a country's income went to just one person.

One way to get a sense of what Gini coefficients mean in practice is to look at international comparisons. Figure 39-2 shows the most recent estimates of the Gini coefficient for many of the world's countries. Aside from a few countries in Africa, the highest levels of income inequality are found in Latin America, especially Colombia; countries with a high degree of inequality have Gini coefficients close to 0.6. The most equal distributions of income are in Europe, especially in Scandinavia; countries with very equal income distributions, such as Sweden, have Gini coefficients around 0.25. Compared to other wealthy countries, the United States, with a Gini coefficient of 0.41, has unusually high inequality, though it isn't as unequal as in Latin America.

How serious an issue is income inequality? In a direct sense, high income inequality means that some people don't share in a nation's overall prosperity. As we've seen, rising inequality explains how it's possible that the U.S. poverty rate has failed to fall for the past 40 years even though the country as a whole has become considerably richer. Also, extreme inequality, as found in Latin America, is often associated with political instability because of tension between a wealthy minority and the rest of the population.

FIGURE 39-2 **Income Inequality Around the World**

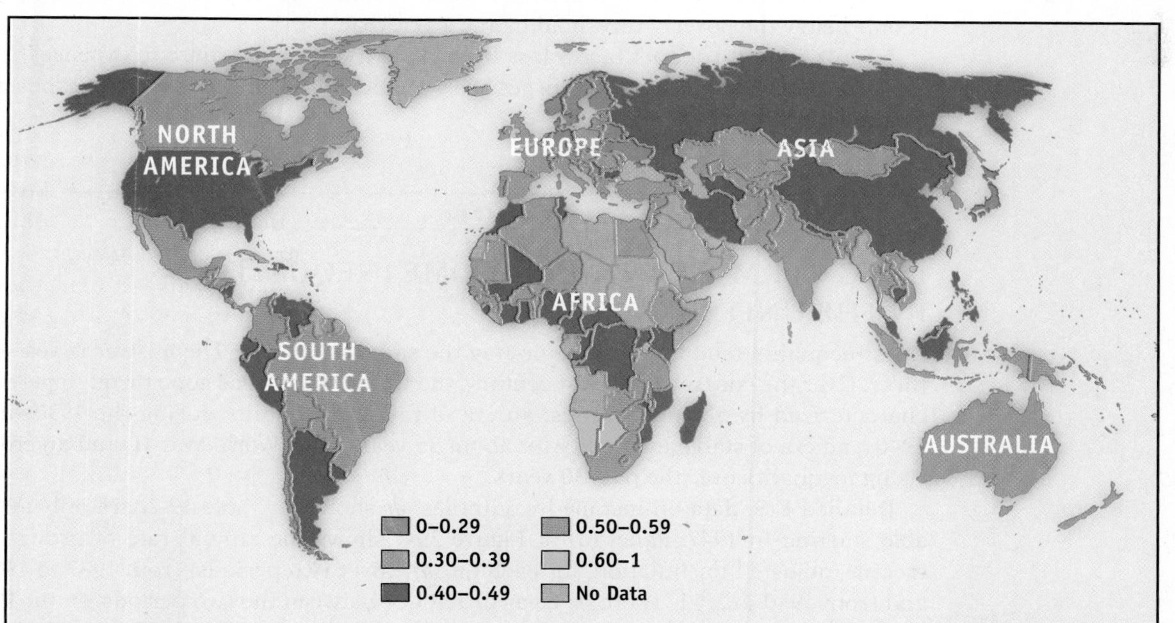

The highest levels of income inequality are found in Africa and Latin America. The most equal distributions of income are in Europe, especially in Scandinavia. Compared to other wealthy countries, the United States, with a Gini coefficient of 0.41, has unusually high inequality.
Source: World Bank, *World Development Indicators* 2010.

AgeFotostock/Superstock

It's important to realize, however, that the data shown in Table 39-2 overstate the true degree of inequality in America, for several reasons. One is that the data represent a snapshot for a single year, whereas the incomes of many individual families fluctuate over time. That is, many of those near the bottom in any given year are having an unusually bad year and many of those at the top are having an unusually good one. Over time, their incomes will revert to a more normal level. So a table showing average incomes within quintiles over a longer period, such as a decade, would not show as much inequality.

Furthermore, a family's income tends to vary over its life cycle: most people earn considerably less in their early working years than they will later in life, then experience a considerable drop in income when they retire. Consequently, the numbers in Table 39-2, which combine young workers, mature workers, and retirees, show more inequality than would a table that compares families of similar ages.

Despite these qualifications, there is a considerable amount of genuine inequality in the United States. In fact, inequality not only persists for long periods of time for individuals, it extends across generations—a situation that is unique to the United States compared to other rich countries.

Economic Insecurity

As we stated earlier, although the rationale for the welfare state rests in part on the social benefits of reducing poverty and inequality, it also rests in part on the benefits of reducing economic insecurity, which afflicts even relatively well-off families.

One form economic insecurity takes is the risk of a sudden loss of income, which usually happens when a family member loses a job and either spends an extended period without work or is forced to take a new job that pays considerably less.

In a given year, according to recent estimates, about one in six American families will see their income cut in half from the previous year. Related estimates show that the percentage of people who find themselves below the poverty threshold for at least one year over the course of a decade is several times higher than the percentage of people below the poverty threshold in any given year.

Even if a family doesn't face a loss in income, it can face a surge in expenses. The most common reasons for such surges are a medical problem that requires expensive treatment or the loss of a job.

ECONOMICS ▶ IN ACTION

LONG-TERM TRENDS IN INCOME INEQUALITY IN THE UNITED STATES

Does inequality tend to rise, fall, or stay the same over time? The answer is yes—all three. Over the course of the past century, the United States has gone through periods characterized by all three trends: an era of falling inequality during the 1930s and 1940s, an era of stable inequality for about 35 years after World War II, and an era of rising inequality over the past 30 years.

Detailed U.S. data on income by quintiles, as shown in Table 39-2, are only available starting in 1947. Panel (a) of Figure 39-3 shows the annual rate of growth of income, adjusted for inflation, for each quintile over two periods: from 1947 to 1980, and from 1980 to 2011. There's a clear difference between the two periods. In the first period, income within each group grew at about the same rate—that is, there wasn't much change in the inequality of income, just growing incomes across the board. After 1980, however, incomes grew much more quickly at the top than in the middle, and more quickly in the middle than near the bottom. So inequality has increased substantially since 1980. Overall, inflation-adjusted income for families in the top quintile rose 47% between 1980 and 2011, while almost holding constant for families in the bottom quintile.

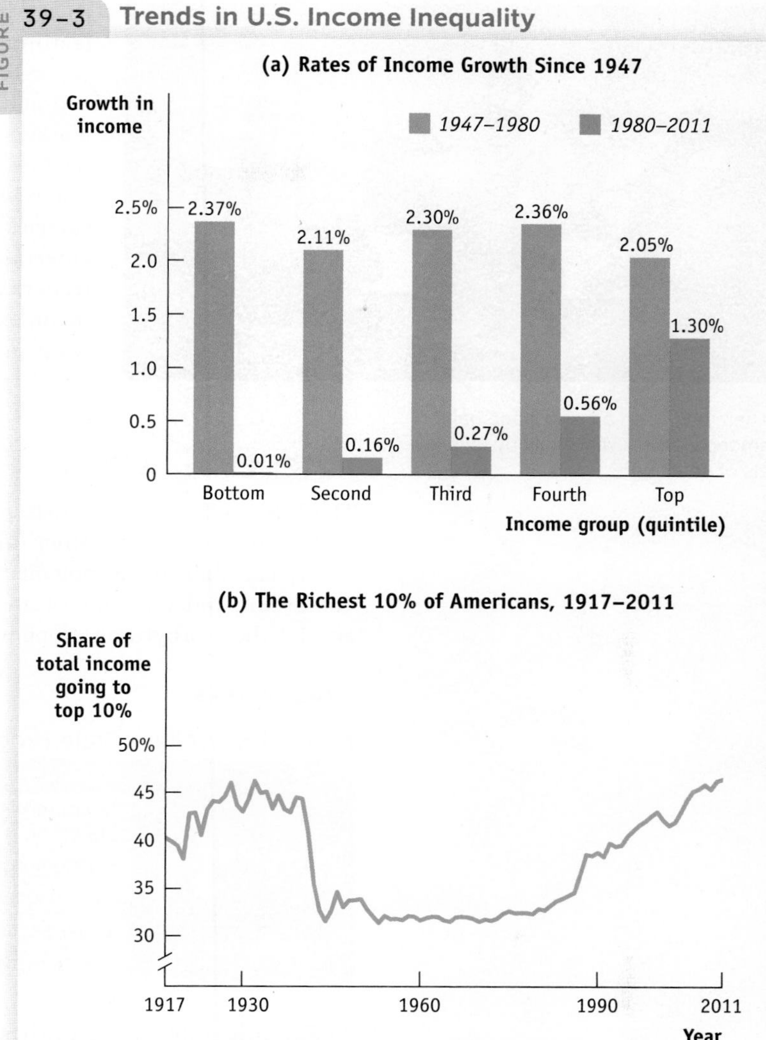

FIGURE 39-3 Trends in U.S. Income Inequality

Sources: U.S. Census Bureau (panel (a)). Emmanuel Saez, "Striking It Richer: The Evolution of Top Incomes in the United States," University of California, Berkeley, discussion paper, 2008 (updated January 2013) (panel (b)).

Although detailed data on income distribution aren't available before 1947, economists have instead used other information like income tax data to estimate the share of income going to the top 10% of the population all the way back to 1917. Panel (b) of Figure 39-3 shows this measure from 1917 to 2011. These data, like the more detailed data available since 1947, show that American inequality was more or less stable between 1947 and the late 1970s but has risen substantially since. The longer-term data also show, however, that the relatively equal distribution of 1947 was something new. In the late nineteenth century, often referred to as the Gilded Age, American income was very unequally distributed. This high level of inequality persisted into the 1930s. But inequality declined sharply between the late 1930s and the end of World War II. In a famous paper, Claudia Goldin and Robert Margo, two economic historians, dubbed this narrowing of income inequality "the Great Compression."

The Great Compression roughly coincided with World War II, a period during which the U.S. government imposed special controls on wages and prices. Evidence indicates that these controls were applied in ways that reduced inequality—for example, it was much easier for employers to get approval to increase the wages of their lowest-paid employees than to increase executive salaries. What remains puzzling is that the equality imposed by wartime controls lasted for decades after those controls were lifted in 1946.

Since the 1970s, as we've already seen, inequality has increased substantially. In fact, pre-tax income appears to be as unequally distributed in America today as it was in the 1920s, prompting many commentators to describe the current state of the nation as a new Gilded Age—albeit one in which the effects of inequality are moderated by taxes and the existence of the welfare state.

There is intense debate about the causes of this widening inequality. These are a few explanations economists offer for the dramatic rise in inequality:

- The most popular explanation is rapid technological change, which has increased the demand for highly skilled or talented workers more rapidly than the demand for other workers, leading to a rise in the wage gap between the highly skilled and other workers.
- Growing international trade may also have contributed by allowing the United States to import labor-intensive products from low-wage countries rather than making them domestically, reducing the demand for less skilled American workers and depressing their wages.
- Rising immigration may be yet another source. On average, immigrants have lower education levels than native-born workers and increase the supply of low-skilled labor while depressing low-skilled wages.

Photodisc

There has been a rising wage gap among workers with similarly high levels of education.

All these explanations, however, fail to account for one key feature: much of the rise in inequality doesn't reflect a rising gap between highly educated workers and those with less education but rather growing differences among highly educated workers themselves. For example, schoolteachers and top business executives have similarly high levels of education, but executive paychecks have risen dramatically and teachers' salaries have not. For some reason, a few superstars in the entertainment world, but also such groups as Wall Street traders and top corporate executives, now earn much higher incomes than was the case a generation ago. It's still unclear what caused the change.

The U.S. Welfare State

The U.S. welfare state consists of three huge programs—Social Security, Medicare, and Medicaid—several other fairly big programs, including Temporary Assistance for Needy Families, the Supplemental Nutrition Assistance Program, the Earned Income Tax Credit, and a number of smaller programs. Table 39-3 shows one useful way to categorize these programs, along with the amount spent on each listed program in 2011.

TABLE 39-3

Major U.S. Welfare State Programs, 2011

	Monetary transfers	In-kind
Means-tested	Temporary Assistance for Needy Families: $15 billion Supplemental Security Income: $50 billion Earned Income Tax Credit: $56 billion	Supplemental Nutrition Assistance Program: $78 billion Medicaid: $275 billion
Not means-tested	Social Security: $725 billion Unemployment insurance: $129 billion	Medicare: $555 billion

First, the table distinguishes between programs that are **means-tested** and those that are not. In means-tested programs, benefits are available only to families or individuals whose income and/or wealth falls below some minimum. Basically, means-tested programs are poverty programs designed to help only those with low incomes. By contrast, non-means-tested programs provide their benefits to everyone, although, as we'll see, they tend in practice to reduce income inequality by increasing the incomes of the poor by a larger proportion than the incomes of the rich.

Second, the table distinguishes between programs that provide monetary transfers that beneficiaries can spend as they choose and those that provide **in-kind benefits,** which are given in the form of goods or services rather than money. As the numbers suggest, in-kind benefits are dominated by Medicare and Medicaid, which pay for health care.

Means-Tested Programs

When people use the term *welfare,* they're often referring to monetary aid to poor families. The main source of such monetary aid in the United States is Temporary Assistance for Needy Families, or TANF. This program does not aid everyone who is poor; it is available only to poor families with children and only for a limited period of time.

A **means-tested** program is available only to individuals or families whose incomes fall below a certain level.

An **in-kind benefit** is a benefit given in the form of goods or services.

TANF was introduced in the 1990s to replace a highly controversial program known as Aid to Families with Dependent Children, or AFDC. The older program was widely accused of creating perverse incentives for the poor, including encouraging family breakup. Partly as a result of the change in programs, the benefits of modern "welfare" are considerably less generous than those available a generation ago, once the data

Spencer Platt/Getty Images

The Supplemental Nutrition Assistance Program (SNAP) helps those with low incomes put food on the table.

are adjusted for inflation. Also, TANF contains time limits, so welfare recipients—even single parents—must eventually seek work. As you can see from Table 39-3, TANF is a relatively small part of the modern U.S. welfare state.

Other means-tested programs, though more expensive, are less controversial. The Supplemental Security Income program aids disabled Americans who are unable to work and have no other source of income. The Supplemental Nutrition Assistance Program (SNAP), formerly known as food stamps, helps low-income families and individuals buy food staples.

Finally, economists use the term **negative income tax** for a program that supplements the earnings of low-income workers. For example, in the United States, the Earned Income Tax Credit (EITC) provides additional income to millions of workers. It has become more generous as traditional welfare has become less generous. As an incentive to work, only workers who earn income are eligible for the EITC. And as an incentive to work more, over a certain range of incomes, the more a worker earns, the higher the amount of EITC received. That is, the EITC acts as a negative income tax for low-wage workers. In 2011, married couples who had two children and earned less than $13,660 per year received EITC payments equal to 40% of their earnings. Payments were slightly lower for single-parent families or workers without children. At higher incomes, the EITC is phased out, disappearing at an income of $46,044 for married couples with two children in 2011.

Social Security and Unemployment Insurance

Social Security, the largest program in the U.S. welfare state, is a non-means-tested program that guarantees retirement income to qualifying older Americans. It also provides benefits to workers who become disabled and "survivor benefits" to family members of workers who die.

Social Security is supported by a dedicated tax on wages: the Social Security portion of the payroll tax pays for Social Security benefits. The benefits workers receive on retirement depend on their taxable earnings during their working years: the more you earn up to the maximum amount subject to Social Security taxes ($113,700 in 2013), the more you receive in retirement. Benefits are not, however, strictly proportional to earnings. Instead, they're determined by a formula that gives high earners more than low earners, but with a sliding scale that makes the program relatively more generous for low earners.

Because most senior citizens don't receive pensions from their former employers, and most don't own enough assets to live off the income from their assets, Social Security benefits are an enormously important source of income for them. Fully 60% of Americans 65 and older rely on Social Security for more than half their income, and 20% have no income at all except for Social Security.

Unemployment insurance, although a much smaller amount of government transfers than Social Security, is another key social insurance program. It provides workers who lose their jobs with about 35% of their previous salary until they find a new job or until 26 weeks have passed. This period is sometimes extended when the economy is in a slump. For example, in response to the severe recession of 2007–2009, some unemployed workers received benefits for as long as 99 weeks.

Unemployment insurance is financed by a tax on employers. Like Social Security, unemployment insurance is not means-tested.

The Effects of the Welfare State on Poverty and Inequality

Because the people who receive government transfers tend to be different from those who are taxed to pay for those transfers, the U.S. welfare state has the effect of redistributing income from some people to others.

A **negative income tax** is a program that supplements the income of low-income workers.

TABLE 39-4

Effects of Taxes and Transfers on the Poverty Rate, 2009

Group (by age)	Poverty rate without taxes and transfers	Poverty rate with taxes and transfers
All	23.7%	13.1%
Under 18	24.7	16.6
18 to 64	17.5	11.7
65 and over	48.0	9.8

Source: U.S. Census Bureau.

TABLE 39-5

Effects of Taxes and Transfers on Income Distribution, 2009

Quintiles	Share of aggregate income without taxes and transfers	Share of aggregate income with taxes and transfers
Bottom quintile	0.7%	3.7%
Second quintile	6.9	9.8
Third quintile	14.0	15.9
Fourth quintile	24.1	24.2
Top quintile	54.3	46.4

Source: U.S. Census Bureau.

Each year the Census Bureau estimates the effect of this redistribution in a report titled "The Effects of Government Taxes and Transfers on Income and Poverty." The report calculates only the *direct* effects of taxes and transfers, without taking into account changes in behavior that the taxes and transfers might cause. For example, the report doesn't try to estimate how many older Americans who are now retired would still be working if they weren't receiving Social Security checks. As a result, the estimates are only a partial indicator of the true effects of the welfare state. Nonetheless, the results are striking.

Table 39-4 shows how taxes and government transfers affected the poverty threshold for the population as a whole and for different age groups in 2009. It shows two numbers for each group: the percentage of the group that *would have had* incomes below the poverty threshold if the government neither collected taxes nor made transfers, and the percentage that actually fell below the poverty threshold once taxes and transfers were taken into account. (For technical reasons, the second number is somewhat lower than the standard measure of the poverty rate.)

Overall, the combined effect of taxes and transfers was to cut the U.S. poverty rate nearly in half. The elderly derived the greatest benefits from redistribution, which reduced their potential poverty [illegible] of 48.0% to an actual poverty rate of 9.8%.

Table 39-5 shows the effects of taxes and transfers on the share of aggregate income going to each quintile of the income distribution in 2009. Like Table 39-4, it shows both what the distribution of income *would have been* if there were no taxes or government transfers and the actual distribution of income taking into account both taxes and transfers. The effect of government programs was to increase the share of income going to the poorest 80% of the population, especially the share going to the poorest 20%, while reducing the share of income going to the richest 20%.

FIGURE 39-4 Who Paid for U.S. Health Care in 2011?

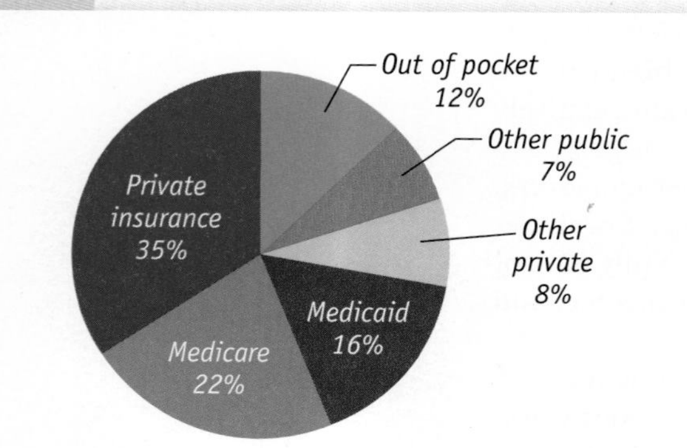

In the United States in 2011, insurance paid for 73% of health care consumption costs: the sum of 35% (private insurance), 22% (Medicare), and 16% (Medicaid). The percentage paid for by private insurance, 35%, was a uniquely high number among advanced countries. Even so, substantially more U.S. health care was paid for by Medicare, Medicaid, and other government programs than by other means.

Source: Department of Health and Human Services Centers for Medicare and Medicaid Services.

Health Care in the United States

A large part of the welfare state, in both the United States and other wealthy countries, is devoted to paying for health care. In most wealthy countries, the government pays between 70% and 80% of all medical costs. The private sector plays a larger role in the U.S. health care system. Yet even in America the government pays almost half of all health care costs; furthermore, it indirectly subsidizes private health insurance through the federal tax code.

Figure 39-4 shows who paid for U.S. health care in 2011. Only 12% of health care consumption spending (that is, all spending on health care except investment in health care buildings and facilities) was expenses "out of pocket"—that is, paid directly by individuals. Most health care spending, [illegible], was pa[illegible]or by some kind of insurance. Of this 73%, considerably less than half was private insurance; the rest was some kind of government insurance, mainly Medicare and Medicaid.

The Need for Health Insurance

In 2011, U.S. personal health care expenses were $7,326 per person—17.9% of gross domestic product. This did not, however, mean that the typical American spent more than $7,000 on medical treatment. In fact, in any given year half the population incurs only minor medical expenses. But a small percentage of the population faces huge medical bills, with 10% of the population typically accounting for almost two-thirds of medical costs.

Is it possible to predict who will have high medical costs? To a limited extent, yes: there are broad patterns to illness. For example, the elderly are more likely to need expensive surgery and/or drugs than the young. But the fact is that anyone can suddenly find himself or herself needing very expensive medical treatment, costing many thousands of dollars in a very short time—far beyond what most families can easily afford. Yet nobody wants to be unable to afford such treatment if it becomes necessary.

Medicare and Medicaid

Table 39-6 shows the breakdown of health insurance coverage across the U.S. population in 2011. A majority of Americans, more than 170 million people, received health insurance through their employers. The majority of those who didn't have private insurance were covered by two government programs, Medicare and Medicaid.

TABLE 39-6

Number of Americans Covered by Health Insurance, 2011 (thousands)

Covered by private health insurance	197,323
Employment-based	170,102
Direct purchase	30,244
Covered by government	99,497
Medicaid	50,835
Medicare	46,922
Military health care	13,712
Not covered	48,613

Source: U.S. Census Bureau.

Medicare, financed by payroll taxes, is available to all Americans 65 and older, regardless of their income and wealth. It began in 1966 as a program to cover the cost of hospitalization but has since been expanded to cover a number of other medical expenses. At the beginning of 2006, there was a major expansion of Medicare to cover the cost of prescription drugs.

Unlike Medicare, Medicaid is a means-tested program, paid for with federal and state government revenues. There's no simple way to summarize the criteria for eligibility because it is partly paid for by state governments and each state sets its own rules. Of the 51 million Americans covered by Medicaid in 2011, 26 million were children under the age of 18 and many of the rest were parents of children under the age of 18. Most of the cost of Medicaid, however, is accounted for by a small number of older Americans, especially those needing long-term care.

The U.S. health care system, then, offers most Americans a mix of private insurance, mainly from employers, and public insurance of various forms. However, in 2011 almost 49 million people in America, 15.7% of the population, had no health insurance at all.

The Kaiser Family Foundation, an independent nonpartisan group that studies health care issues, offers this summary of who is uninsured in America: "The uninsured are largely low-income adult workers for whom coverage is unaffordable or unavailable."

Medicare provides health insurance to 47 million Americans—38.5 million are age 65 and older and 8.5 million are younger people with disabilities.

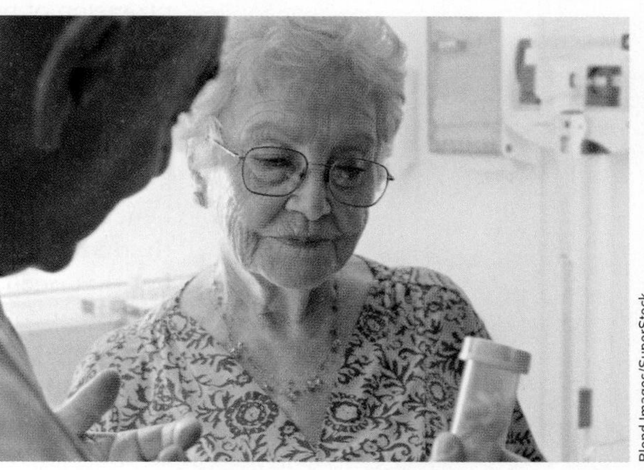

Blend Images/SuperStock

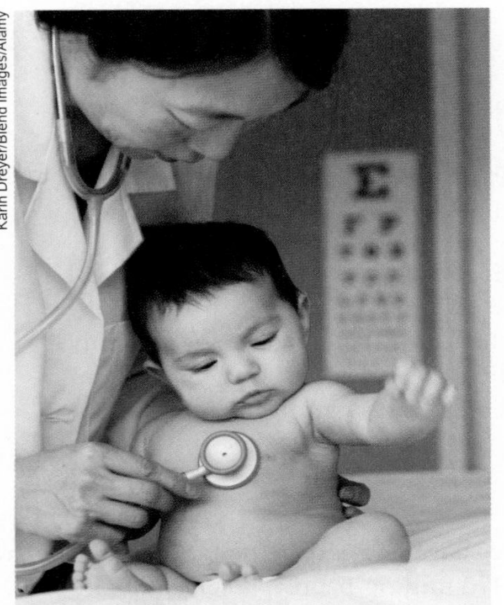
Karin Dreyer/Blend Images/Alamy

Medicaid has been shown to make a big difference in the well-being of recipients.

The reason the uninsured are primarily adults is that Medicaid, supplemented by SCHIP (which provides health care for children in families that are above the poverty threshold but still have relatively low income), covers many, though not all, low-income children but is much less likely to provide coverage to adults, especially if they do not have children.

Because of the rising number of uninsured individuals and rising health care costs, there have been many calls for health care reform in the United States. And in 2010, Congress passed comprehensive health care reform legislation, officially known as the Patient Protection and Affordable Care Act (PPACA), or ACA for short. ACA, which takes full effect in 2014, is the largest expansion of the U.S. welfare state since the creation of Medicare and Medicaid in 1965. The two main goals of ACA are to cover the uninsured, especially adults who have been denied heath insurance because of preexisting medial conditions, and to help control rising health care costs in a variety of ways, including stricter oversight of reimbursements to medical providers.

The Debate over the Welfare State

The goals of the welfare state seem laudable: to help the poor, protect everyone from financial risk, and ensure that people can afford essential health care. But good intentions don't always make for good policy.

There is an intense debate about how large the welfare state should be, a debate that partly reflects differences in philosophy but also reflects concern about the possibly counterproductive effects of incentives from welfare state programs. Disputes about the size of the welfare state are also one of the defining issues of modern American politics.

Problems with the Welfare State

There are two different lines of argument against the welfare state. One is based on philosophical concerns about the proper role of government. Some political theorists believe that redistributing income is not a legitimate role of government—that government's role should be limited to maintaining the rule of law, providing public goods, and managing externalities.

The more conventional argument against the welfare state involves the trade-off between efficiency and equity. A government with a large welfare state requires more revenue, and thus higher marginal tax rates, than one that limits itself mainly to the provision of public goods such as national defense.

The trade-off between welfare state programs and high marginal tax rates seems to suggest that we should try to hold down the cost of these programs. One way to do this is to means-test benefits: make them available only to those who need them.

But means-testing, it turns out, creates a different kind of trade-off between equity and efficiency. Consider the following example: Suppose there is some means-tested benefit, worth $2,000 per year, that is available only to families with incomes of less than $20,000 per year. Now suppose that a family currently has an income of $19,500 but that one family member is deciding whether to take a new job that will raise the family's income to $20,500. Well, taking that job will actually make the family worse off because it will gain $1,000 in earnings but lose the $2,000 government benefit.

This situation, in which earning more actually leaves a family worse off through lost benefits, is known as a *notch*. It is a well-known problem with programs that aid the poor and behaves much like a high marginal tax rate on income.

Most welfare state programs are designed to avoid creating a notch. This is typically done by setting a sliding scale for benefits such that they fall off gradually as the recipient's income rises. As long as benefits are reduced by less than a dollar for every additional dollar earned, there is an incentive to work more if possible. However, current programs are not always successful in providing incentives for work.

The Politics of the Welfare State

In 1791, in the early phase of the French Revolution, France had a sort of congress, the National Assembly, in which representatives were seated according to social class: nobles, who pretty much liked the way things were, sat on the right; commoners, who wanted big changes, sat on the left. Ever since, it has been common in political discourse to talk about politicians as being on the "right" (more conservative) or on the "left" (more liberal).

But what do modern politicians on the left and right disagree about? In the modern United States, they mainly disagree about the appropriate size of the welfare state. The debate over the Affordable Care Act was a case in point, with the vote on the bill breaking down entirely according to party lines—Democrats (on the left) in favor of ACA and Republicans (on the right) opposed.

You might think that saying that political debate is really about just one thing—how big to make the welfare state—is a huge oversimplification. But political scientists have found that once you carefully rank members of Congress from right to left, a congressperson's position in that ranking does a very good job of predicting his or her votes on proposed legislation.

The same studies that show a strong left–right spectrum in U.S. politics also show strong polarization between the major parties on this spectrum. Forty years ago there was a substantial overlap between the parties: some Democrats were to the right of some Republicans, or, if you prefer, some Republicans were to the left of some Democrats. Today, however, the rightmost Democrats appear to be to the left of the leftmost Republicans. There's nothing necessarily wrong with this. Although it's common to decry "partisanship," it's hard to see why members of different political parties shouldn't have different views about policy.

Can economic analysis help resolve this political conflict? Only up to a point.

Some of the political controversy over the welfare state involves differences in opinion about the trade-offs we have just discussed: if you believe that the disincentive effects of generous benefits and high taxes are very large, you're likely to look less favorably on welfare state programs than if you believe they're fairly small. Economic analysis, by improving our knowledge of the facts, can help resolve some of these differences.

To an important extent, however, differences of opinion on the welfare state reflect differences in values and philosophy. And those are differences economics can't resolve.

MODULE 39 Review

Solutions appear at the back of the book.

Check Your Understanding

1. Indicate whether each of the following programs is a poverty program or a social insurance program.
   - **a.** a pension guarantee program, which provides pensions for retirees if they have lost their employment-based pension due to their employer's bankruptcy
   - **b.** the federal program known as SCHIP, which provides health care for children in families that are above the poverty threshold but still have relatively low income
   - **c.** the Section 8 housing program, which provides housing subsidies for low-income households
   - **d.** the federal flood program, which provides financial help to communities hit by major floods

2. Recall that the poverty threshold is not adjusted to reflect changes in the standard of living. As a result, is the poverty threshold a relative or an absolute measure of poverty? That is, does it define poverty according to how poor someone is relative to others or according to some fixed measure that doesn't change over time? Explain.

3. The accompanying table gives the distribution of income for a very small economy.

	Income
Sephora	$39,000
Kelly	17,500
Raul	900,000
Vijay	15,000
Oskar	28,000

   a. What is the mean income? What is the median income? Which measure is more representative of the income of the average person in the economy? Why?

   b. What income range defines the first quintile? The third quintile?

4. Which of the following statements more accurately reflects the principal source of rising inequality in the United States today?

   a. The salary of the manager of the local branch of Sunrise Bank has risen relative to the salary of the neighborhood gas station attendant.

   b. The salary of the CEO of Sunrise Bank has risen relative to the salary of the local branch bank manager; these two individuals have similar education levels.

5. Explain how the negative income tax avoids the disincentive to work that characterizes poverty programs that simply give benefits based on low income.

6. According to Table 39-4, what effect does the U.S. welfare state have on the overall poverty rate? On the poverty rate for those aged 65 and over?

7. Over the past 40 years, has the polarization in Congress increased, decreased, or stayed the same?

Multiple-Choice Questions

1. Which of the following is true of the U.S. poverty rate?
   a. It fell in the 1960s.
   b. There has been a clear upward trend since 1973.
   c. It was lower in 2009 than in 1973.
   d. It has remained unchanged since the mid-1970s.
   e. It has been steadily decreasing since 1959.

2. In 2011, approximately what percentage of the U.S. population lived in poverty?
   a. 2%
   b. 15%
   c. 20%
   d. 26%
   e. 32%

3. Average household income in the United States in 2012 was approximately
   a. $12,000.
   b. $22,000.
   c. $33,000.
   d. $48,201.
   e. $70,000.

4. Programs designed to help only those with low incomes are called
   a. welfare programs.
   b. in-kind programs.
   c. means-tested programs.
   d. income maintenance programs.
   e. social programs.

5. If a country has a perfectly equal distribution of income, its Gini coefficient equals
   a. 0.
   b. 1.
   c. 10.
   d. 50.
   e. 100.

Critical-Thinking Question

In your opinion, what are the strongest arguments for and against government programs to redistribute income? To what extent can economics be used to resolve the debate?

BUSINESS CASE • A Tale of Two Research Clusters

Courtesy Silicon Maps

Silicon Valley in California and Route 128 in Massachusetts are the preeminent high-tech clusters in the world. Silicon Valley dates back to the early 1930s, when Stanford University encouraged its electrical engineering graduates to stay in the area and start companies.

In the early 1950s Stanford created the Stanford Industrial Park, leasing university land to high-tech companies that worked closely with its engineering school. In the mid-1950s, defense contractors such as Lockheed brought dollars to the area. Soon after, a critical mass of talent had accumulated. For example, in 1968, eight young engineers left their employer over a disagreement; over the next 20 years, they founded 65 new companies, including Intel, which later created the microprocessor chip, the brain of personal computers.

This pattern repeated: one researcher estimated that in small and medium-sized firms, 35% of the workforce would, on average, turn over in a year. Silicon Valley became a fertile location for startups, with dozens sprouting every year—everything from firms specializing in hardware and software to network firms like eBay, Facebook, and Google. It also became home to investors who specialize in financing new high-tech companies. Silicon Valley's compact geographical location allowed people to form close social and research bonds even while working for rival firms.

On the other side of the country, a high-tech cluster known as Route 128 came into being on a 65-mile highway surrounding Boston and Cambridge. It owes its start to the Massachusetts Institute of Technology (MIT), the top engineering university in the world, as well as funding from the U.S. military, NASA, and the National Science Foundation. In the 1950s Route 128 dominated Silicon Valley, with three times the number of employees.

But early on, Route 128 differed from Silicon Valley in significant ways. It was much more spread out and its firms were larger, reflecting the needs of defense contractors during the Cold War. And MIT extended little help to Route 128 firms.

Another major difference between the two clusters was in how firms were organized. Route 128 firms tended to be "vertically integrated," combining the entire chain of production from research to design to production in the same firm. Silicon Valley firms focused exclusively on research and design, contracting production out to specialized firms to achieve economies of scale. In contrast to the fluidity of employees and ideas across companies in Silicon Valley, Route 128 firms emphasized a commitment to lifetime employment and closely guarded their innovations.

The 1970s and 1980s were harsh for Route 128. Military spending dried up, and it lost its edge in minicomputers when Apollo Computers lost its preeminence to an aggressive Silicon Valley firm, Sun Microsystems. By 1980, electronics employment in Silicon Valley was three times that of Route 128. Over time, Route 128 ceded the advantage to Silicon Valley in electronics and networking. Today its niche is in biotechnology, genetics, materials engineering, and finance.

Questions for Thought

1. What positive externalities were common to both Silicon Valley and Route 128? What positive externalities were not common to both? Explain.
2. What factors made Silicon Valley such a fertile place for startups? How did these factors interact with one another? What inhibited startups in Route 128?
3. In hindsight, what could Apollo Computers have done to maintain its advantage in minicomputers? What does this tell you generally about research clusters?

SECTION 12 REVIEW

Summary

Externalities

1. When pollution can be directly observed and controlled, government policies should be geared directly to producing the **socially optimal quantity of pollution,** the quantity at which the **marginal social cost of pollution** is equal to the **marginal social benefit of pollution.** In the absence of government intervention, a market produces too much pollution because polluters take only their benefit from polluting into account, not the costs imposed on others.
2. The cost to society of pollution from a power plant is an example of an **external cost;** the benefit to neighbors of beautiful flowers planted in your yard is an example of an **external benefit.** External costs and benefits are jointly known as **externalities,** with external costs called **negative externalities** and external benefits called **positive externalities.**
3. According to the **Coase theorem,** when externalities exist, bargaining will cause individuals to **internalize the externalities,** making government intervention unnecessary, as long as property rights are clearly defined and **transaction costs**—the costs of making a deal—are sufficiently low. However, in many cases transaction costs are too high to permit such deals.

Externalities and Public Policy

4. Governments often deal with pollution by imposing **environmental standards,** an approach, economists argue, that is usually inefficient. Two efficient (cost-minimizing) methods for reducing pollution are **emissions taxes,** a form of **Pigouvian tax,** and **tradable emissions permits.** The optimal Pigouvian tax on pollution is equal to its marginal social cost at the socially optimal quantity of pollution. These methods also provide incentives for the creation and adoption of production technologies that cause less pollution.
5. When a good or activity yields external benefits, or positive externalities, such as **technology spillovers,** then an optimal **Pigouvian subsidy** to producers moves the market to the socially optimal quantity of production.
6. High-technology goods are frequently subject to **network externalities,** which arise when the value of the good to an individual is greater when a large number of people use the good. Such goods are likely to be subject to **positive feedback:** if large numbers of people buy the good, other people are more likely to buy it, too. So success breeds greater success and failure breeds failure: the good with the larger network will eventually dominate, and competing products will disappear.

Public Goods and Common Resources

7. Goods may be classified according to whether or not they are **excludable,** meaning that people can be prevented from consuming them, and whether or not they are **rival in consumption,** meaning that one person's consumption of them affects another person's consumption of them.
8. Free markets can deliver efficient levels of production and consumption for **private goods,** which are both excludable and rival in consumption. When goods are nonexcludable, nonrival in consumption, or both, free markets cannot achieve efficient outcomes.
9. When goods are **nonexcludable,** there is a **free-rider problem:** consumers will not pay for the good, leading to inefficiently low production. When goods are **nonrival in consumption,** any positive price leads to inefficiently low consumption.
10. A **public good** is nonexcludable and nonrival in consumption. In most cases a public good must be supplied by the government. The marginal social benefit of a public good is equal to the sum of the marginal benefits to each consumer. The efficient quantity of a public good is the quantity at which marginal social benefit equals the marginal social cost of providing the good. As with a positive externality, the marginal social benefit is greater than any one individual's marginal benefit, so no individual is willing to provide the efficient quantity.
11. A **common resource** is rival in consumption but nonexcludable. It is subject to **overuse,** because an individual does not take into account the fact that his or her use depletes the amount available for others. This is similar to the problem with a negative externality: the marginal social cost of an individual's use of a common resource is always higher than his or her individual marginal cost. Pigouvian taxes, the creation of a system of tradable licenses, and the assignment of property rights are possible solutions.
12. **Artificially scarce goods** are excludable but nonrival in consumption. Because no marginal cost arises from allowing another individual to consume the good, the efficient price is zero. A positive price compensates the producer for the cost of production but leads to inefficiently low consumption.

The Economics of the Welfare State

13. The **welfare state** absorbs a large share of government spending in all wealthy countries. **Government transfers** are the payments made by the government to individuals and families. **Poverty programs** alleviate

No discussion of product differentiation is complete without spending at least a bit of time on the two related issues—and puzzles—of *advertising* and *brand names*.

The Role of Advertising

Wheat farmers don't advertise their wares on TV, but car dealers do. That's not because farmers are shy and car dealers are outgoing; it's because advertising is worthwhile only in industries in which firms have at least some market power.

The purpose of advertisements is to persuade people to buy more of a seller's product at the going price. A perfectly competitive firm, which can sell as much as it likes at the going market price, has no incentive to spend money persuading consumers to buy more. Only a firm that has some market power, and which therefore charges a price that is above marginal cost, can gain from advertising. Some industries that are more or less perfectly competitive, like the milk industry, do advertise—but these ads are sponsored by an association on behalf of the industry as a whole, not on behalf of a particular farm.

Given that advertising "works," it's not hard to see why firms with market power would spend money on it. But the big question about advertising is, *why* does it work? A related question is whether advertising is, from society's point of view, a waste of resources.

Not all advertising poses a puzzle. Much of it is straightforward: it's a way for sellers to inform potential buyers about what they have to offer (or, occasionally, for buyers to inform potential sellers about what they want). Nor is there much controversy about the economic usefulness of ads that provide information: the real estate ad that declares "sunny, charming, 2 bedrooms, 1 bath, a/c" tells you things you need to know (even if a few euphemisms are involved—"charming," of course, means "small").

But what information is being conveyed when a TV actress proclaims the virtues of one or another toothpaste or a sports hero declares that some company's batteries are better than those inside that pink mechanical rabbit? Surely nobody believes that the sports star is an expert on batteries—or that he chose the company that he personally believes makes the best batteries, as opposed to the company that offered to pay him the most. Yet companies believe, with good reason, that money spent on such promotions increases their sales—and that they would be in big trouble if they stopped advertising but their competitors continued to do so.

Why are consumers influenced by ads that do not really provide any information about the product? One answer is that consumers are not as rational as economists typically assume. Perhaps consumers' judgments, or even their tastes, can be influenced by things that economists think ought to be irrelevant, such as which company has hired the most charismatic celebrity to endorse its product. And there is surely some truth to this. Consumer rationality is a useful working assumption; it is not an absolute truth.

However, another answer is that consumer response to advertising is not entirely irrational because ads can serve as indirect "signals" in a world where consumers don't have good information about products. Suppose, to take a common example, that you need to avail yourself of some local service that you don't use regularly—body work on your car, say, or furniture moving. You can go online, as many of us do, or turn to the Yellow Pages, where you see a number of small listings and several large display ads. You know that those display ads are large because the firms paid extra for them; still, it may be quite rational to call one of the firms with a big display ad. After all, the big ad probably means that it's a relatively large, successful company—otherwise, the company wouldn't have found it worth spending the money for the larger ad.

The same principle may partly explain why ads feature celebrities. You don't really believe that the supermodel prefers that watch; but the fact that the watch manufacturer is willing and able to pay her fee tells you that it is a major company that is likely

A **brand name** is a name owned by a particular firm that distinguishes its products from those of other firms.

to stand behind its product. According to this reasoning, an expensive advertisement serves to establish the quality of a firm's products in the eyes of consumers.

The possibility that it is rational for consumers to respond to advertising also has some bearing on the question of whether advertising is a waste of resources. If ads work by manipulating only the weak-minded, the $140 billion U.S. businesses spent on advertising in 2013 would have been an economic waste—except to the extent that ads sometimes provide entertainment. To the extent that advertising conveys important information, however, it is an economically productive activity after all.

Brand Names

You've been driving all day, and you decide that it's time to find a place to sleep. On your right, you see a sign for the Bates Motel; on your left, you see a sign for a Motel 6, or a Best Western, or some other national chain. Which one do you choose?

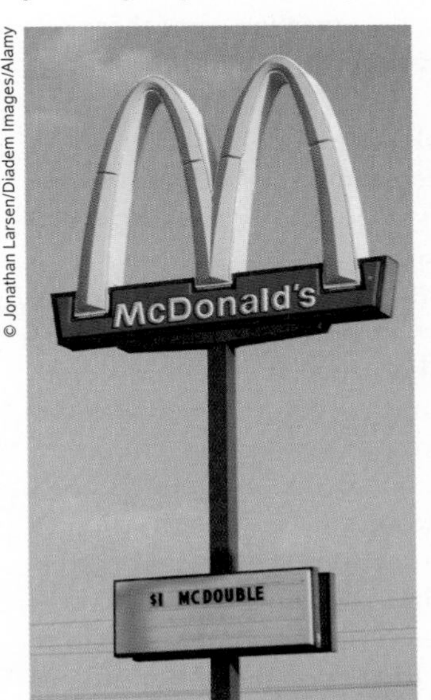

© Jonathan Larsen/Diadem Images/Alamy

Unless they were familiar with the area, most people would head for the chain. In fact, most motels in the United States are members of major chains; the same is true of most fast-food restaurants and many, if not most, stores in shopping malls.

Motel chains and fast-food restaurants are only one aspect of a broader phenomenon: the role of **brand names,** names owned by particular companies that differentiate their products in the minds of consumers. In many cases, a company's brand name is the most important asset it possesses: clearly, McDonald's is worth far more than the sum of the deep-fat fryers and hamburger grills the company owns.

Advertising and brand names that provide useful information can be valuable to consumers.

In fact, companies often go to considerable lengths to defend their brand names, suing anyone else who uses them without permission. You may talk about blowing your nose on a kleenex or googling data for a research project, but unless the product in question comes from Kleenex or Google, legally the seller must describe it as a facial tissue or a search engine.

As with advertising, with which they are closely linked, the social usefulness of brand names is a source of dispute. Does the preference of consumers for known brands reflect consumer irrationality? Or do brand names convey real information? That is, do brand names create unnecessary market power, or do they serve a real purpose?

As in the case of advertising, the answer is probably some of both. On the one hand, brand names often do create unjustified market power. Consumers often pay more for brand-name goods in the supermarket even though consumer experts assure us that the cheaper store brands are equally good. Similarly, many common medicines, like aspirin, are cheaper—with no loss of quality—in their generic form.

On the other hand, for many products the brand name does convey information. A traveler arriving in a strange town can be sure of what awaits in a Holiday Inn or a McDonald's; a tired and hungry traveler may find this preferable to trying an independent hotel or restaurant that might be better—but might be worse.

In addition, brand names offer some assurance that the seller is engaged in repeated interaction with its customers and so has a reputation to protect. If a traveler eats a bad meal at a restaurant in a tourist trap and vows never to eat there again, the restaurant owner may not care, since the chance is small that the traveler will be in the same area again in the future. But if that traveler eats a bad meal at McDonald's and vows never to eat at a McDonald's again, that matters to the company. This gives McDonald's an incentive to provide consistent quality, thereby assuring travelers that quality controls are in place.

MODULE 35 Review

Solutions appear at the back of the book.

Check Your Understanding

1. Each of the following goods and services is a differentiated product. Which are differentiated as a result of monopolistic competition and which are not? Explain your answers.
   a. ladders
   b. soft drinks
   c. department stores
   d. steel
2. You must determine which of two types of market structure better describes an industry, but you are allowed to ask only one question about the industry. What question should you ask to determine if an industry is
   a. perfectly competitive or monopolistically competitive?
   b. a monopoly or monopolistically competitive?
3. For each of the following types of advertising, explain whether it is likely to be useful or wasteful from the standpoint of consumers.
   a. advertisements explaining the benefits of aspirin
   b. advertisements for Bayer aspirin
   c. advertisements that state how long a plumber or an electrician has been in business
4. Some industry analysts have stated that a successful brand name is like a barrier to entry. Explain why this might be true.

Multiple-Choice Questions

1. Which of the following is a form of product differentiation?
   I. style or type
   II. location
   III. quality
   a. I only
   b. II only
   c. III only
   d. I and II only
   e. I, II, and III
2. In which of the following market structures will individual firms advertise?
   I. perfect competition
   II. oligopoly
   III. monopolistic competition
   a. I only
   b. II only
   c. III only
   d. II and III only
   e. I, II, and III
3. Advertising is an attempt to affect which of the following?
   a. consumer tastes and preferences
   b. consumer income
   c. the price of complements
   d. the price of substitutes
   e. input prices
4. Brand names generally serve to
   a. waste resources.
   b. decrease firm profits.
   c. confuse consumers.
   d. decrease information.
   e. signal quality.
5. Which of the following is true of advertising expenditures in monopolistic competition? Monopolistic competitors
   a. will not advertise.
   b. use only informational advertising.
   c. waste resources on advertising.
   d. attempt to create popular brand names.
   e. earn long-run profits through advertising.

Critical-Thinking Question

When is product differentiation socially efficient? Explain. When is it not socially efficient? Explain.

BUSINESS CASE: Virgin Atlantic Blows the Whistle . . . or Blows It?

Ian Waldie/Getty Images

The United Kingdom is home to two long-haul airline carriers (carriers that fly between continents): British Airways and its rival, Virgin Atlantic. Although British Airways is the dominant company, with a market share generally between 50% and 100% on routes between London and various American cities, Virgin has been a tenacious competitor.

The rivalry between the two has ranged from relatively peaceable to openly hostile over the years. In the 1990s, British Airways lost a court case alleging it had engaged in "dirty tricks" to drive Virgin out of business. In April 2010, however, British Airways may well have wondered if the tables had been turned.

It all began in mid-July 2004, when oil prices were rising (long-haul airlines are especially vulnerable to oil price hikes). British prosecutors alleged that the two airlines had plotted to levy fuel surcharges on passengers. For the next two years, according to the prosecutors, the rivals had established a cartel through which they coordinated increases in surcharges. British Airways first introduced a £5 ($8.25) surcharge on long-haul flights when a barrel of oil traded at about $38. It increased the surcharge six times, so that by 2006, when oil was trading at about $69 a barrel, the surcharge was £70 ($115). At the same time, Virgin Atlantic also levied a £70 fee. These surcharges increased within days of each other.

Eventually, three Virgin executives decided to blow the whistle in exchange for immunity from prosecution. British Airways immediately suspended its executives under suspicion and paid fines of nearly $500 million to U.S. and U.K. authorities. And in 2010 four British Airways executives were prosecuted by British authorities for their alleged role in the conspiracy.

The lawyers for the executives argued that although the two airlines had swapped information, this was not proof of a criminal conspiracy. In fact, they argued, Virgin so feared American regulators that it had admitted to criminal behavior before confirming that it had committed an offense. One of the defense lawyers, Clare Montgomery, argued that because U.S. laws against anti-competitive behavior are much tougher than those in the United Kingdom, companies may be compelled to blow the whistle to avoid investigation. "It's a race," she said. "If you don't get to them and confess first, you can't get immunity. The only way to protect yourself is to go to the authorities, even if you haven't [done anything]." The result was that Virgin executives were given immunity in both the United States and the United Kingdom, but British Airways executives were subject to prosecution (and possible multiyear jail terms) in both countries.

In late 2011 the case came to a shocking end. Citing e-mails that Virgin had finally been forced by the court to turn over, the judge found insufficient evidence that there had ever been a conspiracy between the two airlines. The court was incensed enough to threaten to rescind the immunity granted to the three Virgin executives.

Questions for Thought

1. Explain why Virgin Atlantic and British Airlines might collude in response to increased oil prices. Was the market conducive to collusion or not?
2. How would you determine whether illegal behavior actually occurred? What might explain these events other than illegal behavior?
3. Did these two airlines and their individual executives face a prisoners' dilemma? Explain your answer.

SECTION 11 REVIEW

Summary

Oligopoly

1. Many industries are oligopolies, characterized by a small number of sellers. The smallest type of oligopoly, a **duopoly,** has only two sellers. Oligopolies exist for more or less the same reasons that monopolies exist, but in weaker form. They are characterized by imperfect competition: firms compete but possess market power.
2. Predicting the behavior of oligopolists poses something of a puzzle. The firms in an oligopoly could maximize their combined profits by acting as a **cartel,** setting output levels for each firm as if they were a single monopolist; to the extent that firms manage to do this, they engage in **collusion.** But each individual firm has an incentive to produce more than the agreed upon quantity of output—to engage in **noncooperative behavior.** Informal collusion is likely to be easier to achieve in industries in which firms face capacity constraints.

Game Theory

3. The situation of **interdependence,** in which each firm's profit depends noticeably on what other firms do, is the subject of **game theory.** In the case of a game with two players, the **payoff** of each player depends on both its own actions and on the actions of the other; this interdependence can be shown in a **payoff matrix.** Depending on the structure of payoffs in the payoff matrix, a player may have a **dominant strategy**—an action that is always the best regardless of the other player's actions.
4. Some **duopolists** face a particular type of game known as a **prisoners' dilemma;** if each acts independently in its own interest, the resulting **Nash equilibrium** or **noncooperative equilibrium** will be bad for both. However, firms that expect to play a game repeatedly tend to engage in **strategic behavior,** trying to influence each other's future actions. A particular strategy that seems to work well in such situations is **tit for tat,** which often leads to **tacit collusion.**

Oligopoly in Practice

5. In order to limit the ability of oligopolists to collude and act like monopolists, most governments pursue **antitrust policy** designed to make collusion more difficult. In practice, however, tacit collusion is widespread.
6. A variety of factors make tacit collusion difficult: a large numbers of firms, complex products and pricing, differences in interests, and buyers with bargaining power. When tacit collusion breaks down, there can be a **price war.** Oligopolists try to avoid price wars in various ways, such as through **product differentiation** and through **price leadership,** in which one firm sets prices for the industry. Another approach is **nonprice competition,** such as advertising.

Monopolistic Competition

7. Monopolistic competition is a market structure in which there are many competing producers, each producing a differentiated product, and there is free entry and exit in the long run.
8. Short-run profits will attract the entry of new firms in the long run. This reduces the quantity each existing producer sells at any given price and shifts its demand curve to the left. Short-run losses will induce exit by some firms in the long run. This shifts the demand curve of each remaining firm to the right.
9. In the long run, a monopolistically competitive industry is in **zero-profit equilibrium:** at its profit-maximizing quantity, the demand curve for each existing firm is tangent to its average total cost curve. There are zero profits in the industry and no entry or exit.
10. In long-run equilibrium, firms in a monopolistically competitive industry sell at a price greater than marginal cost. They also have **excess capacity** because they produce less than the minimum-cost output; as a result, they have higher costs than firms in a perfectly competitive industry. Whether or not monopolistic competition is inefficient is ambiguous because consumers value the product diversity that it creates.

Product Differentiation and Advertising

11. Product differentiation takes three main forms: style or type, location, and quality. Firms will engage in advertising to increase demand for their products and enhance their market power. Advertising and **brand names** that provide useful information to consumers are valuable to society. Advertisements can be wasteful from a societal standpoint when their only purpose is to create market power.

Key Terms

Interdependence, p. 330
Duopoly, p. 331
Duopolist, p. 331
Collusion, p. 331
Cartel, p. 331
Noncooperative behavior, p. 332
Game theory, p. 335
Payoff, p. 335
Payoff matrix, p. 335
Prisoners' dilemma, p. 336
Dominant strategy, p. 337
Nash equilibrium, p. 337
Noncooperative equilibrium, p. 337
Strategic behavior, p. 339
Tit for tat, p. 339
Tacit collusion, p. 340
Antitrust policy, p. 344
Price war, p. 345
Product differentiation, p. 346
Price leadership, p. 347
Nonprice competition, p. 347
Zero-profit equilibrium, p. 352
Excess capacity, p. 355
Brand name, p. 362

Problems

1. The accompanying table shows the demand schedule for vitamin D. Suppose that the marginal cost of producing vitamin D is zero.

Price of vitamin D (per ton)	Quantity of vitamin D demanded (tons)
$8	0
7	10
6	20
5	30
4	40
3	50
2	60
1	70

a. Assume that BASF is the only producer of vitamin D and acts as a monopolist. It currently produces 40 tons of vitamin D at $4 per ton. If BASF were to produce 10 more tons, what would be the price effect for BASF? What would be the quantity effect? Would BASF have an incentive to produce those 10 additional tons?

b. Now assume that Roche enters the market by also producing vitamin D and the market is now a duopoly. BASF and Roche agree to produce 40 tons of vitamin D in total, 20 tons each. BASF cannot be punished for deviating from the agreement with Roche. If BASF, on its own, were to deviate from that agreement and produce 10 more tons, what would be the price effect for BASF? What would be the quantity effect for BASF? Would BASF have an incentive to produce those 10 additional tons?

2. The market for olive oil in New York City is controlled by two families, the Sopranos and the Contraltos. Both families will ruthlessly eliminate any other family that attempts to enter the New York City olive oil market. The marginal cost of producing olive oil is constant and equal to $40 per gallon. There is no fixed cost. The accompanying table gives the market demand schedule for olive oil.

Price of olive oil (per gallon)	Quantity of olive oil demanded (gallons)
$100	1,000
90	1,500
80	2,000
70	2,500
60	3,000
50	3,500
40	4,000
30	4,500
20	5,000
10	5,500

a. Suppose the Sopranos and the Contraltos form a cartel. For each of the quantities given in the table, calculate the total revenue for their cartel and the marginal revenue for each additional gallon. How many gallons of olive oil would the cartel sell in total and at what price? The two families share the market equally (each produces half of the total output of the cartel). How much profit does each family make?

b. Uncle Junior, the head of the Soprano family, breaks the agreement and sells 500 more gallons of olive oil than under the cartel agreement. Assuming the Contraltos maintain the agreement, how does this affect the price for olive oil and the profits earned by each family?

c. Anthony Contralto, the head of the Contralto family, decides to punish Uncle Junior by increasing his sales by 500 gallons as well. How much profit does each family earn now?

3. In France, the market for bottled water is controlled by two large firms, Perrier and Evian. Each firm has a fixed cost of €1 million and a constant marginal cost of €2 per liter of bottled water (€1 = 1 euro). The following table gives the market demand schedule for bottled water in France.

Price of bottled water (per liter)	Quantity of bottled water demanded (millions of liters)
€10	0
9	1
8	2
7	3
6	4
5	5
4	6
3	7
2	8
1	9

a. Suppose the two firms form a cartel and act as a monopolist. Calculate marginal revenue for the cartel. What will the monopoly price and output be? Assuming the firms divided the output evenly, how much will each produce and what will each firm's profits be?

b. Now suppose Perrier decides to increase production by 1 million liters. Evian doesn't change its production. What will the new market price and output be? What is Perrier's profit? What is Evian's profit?

c. What if Perrier increases production by 3 million liters? Evian doesn't change its production. What would its output and profits be relative to those in part b?

d. What do your results tell you about the likelihood of cheating on such agreements?

4. To preserve the North Atlantic fish stocks, it is decided that only two fishing fleets, one from the United States and the other from the European Union (EU), can fish in those waters. The accompanying table shows the market demand schedule per week for fish from these waters. The only costs are fixed costs, so fishing fleets maximize profit by maximizing revenue.

Price of fish (per pound)	Quantity of fish demanded (pounds)
$17	1,800
16	2,000
15	2,100
14	2,200
12	2,300

a. If both fishing fleets collude, what is the revenue-maximizing output for the North Atlantic fishery? What price will a pound of fish sell for?

b. If both fishing fleets collude and share the output equally, what is the revenue to the EU fleet? To the U.S. fleet?

c. Suppose the EU fleet cheats by expanding its own catch by 100 pounds per week. The U.S. fleet doesn't change its catch. What is the revenue to the U.S. fleet? To the EU fleet?

d. In retaliation for the cheating by the EU fleet, the U.S. fleet also expands its catch by 100 pounds per week. What is the revenue to the U.S. fleet? To the EU fleet?

5. Suppose that the fisheries agreement in Problem 4 breaks down, so that the fleets behave noncooperatively. Assume that the United States and the EU each can send out either one or two fleets. The more fleets in the area, the more fish they catch in total but the lower the catch of each fleet. The accompanying matrix shows the profit (in dollars) per week earned by the two sides.

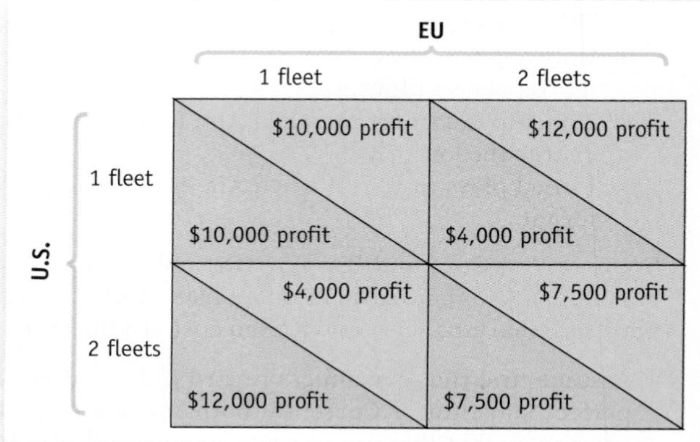

a. What is the noncooperative Nash equilibrium? Will each side choose to send out one or two fleets?

b. Suppose that the fish stocks are being depleted. Each region considers the future and comes to a tit-for-tat agreement whereby each side will send only one fleet out as long as the other does the same. If either of them breaks the agreement and sends out a second fleet, the other will also send out two and will continue to do so until its competitor sends out only one fleet. If both play this tit-for-tat strategy, how much profit will each make every week?

6. Untied and Air "R" Us are the only two airlines operating flights between Collegeville and Bigtown. That is, they operate in a duopoly. Each airline can charge either a high price or a low price for a ticket. The accompanying matrix shows their payoffs, in profits per seat (in dollars), for any choice that the two airlines can make.

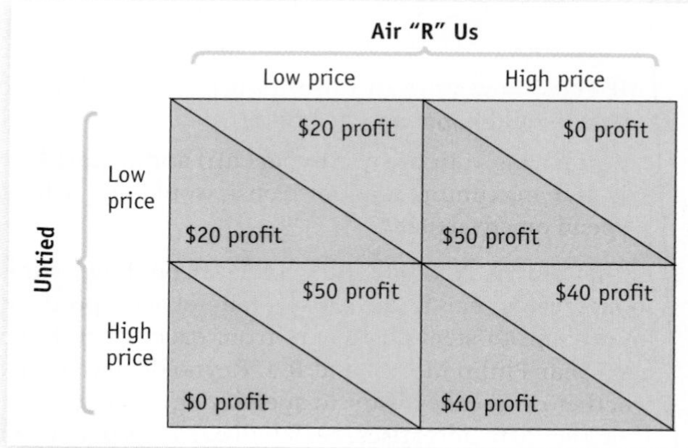

a. Suppose the two airlines play a one-shot game—that is, they interact only once and never again. What will be the Nash equilibrium in this one-shot game?

b. Now suppose the two airlines play this game twice. And suppose each airline can play one of two strategies: it can play either "always charge the low price" or "tit for tat"—that is, start off charging the high price in the first period, and then in the second period do whatever the other airline did in the previous period. Write down the payoffs to Untied from the following four possibilities:

i. Untied plays always charge the low price when Air "R" Us also plays always charge the low price.

ii. Untied plays always charge the low price when Air "R" Us plays tit for tat.

iii. Untied plays tit for tat when Air "R" Us plays always charge the low price.

iv. Untied plays tit for tat when Air "R" Us also plays tit for tat.

7. Suppose that Coke and Pepsi are the only two producers of cola drinks, making them duopolists. Both companies have zero marginal cost and a fixed cost of $100,000.

a. Assume first that consumers regard Coke and Pepsi as perfect substitutes. Currently both are sold for $0.20 per can, and at that price each company sells 4 million cans per day.

i. How large is Pepsi's profit?

ii. If Pepsi were to raise its price to $0.30 cents per can, and Coke did not respond, what would happen to Pepsi's profit?

b. Now suppose that each company advertises to differentiate its product from the other company's. As a result of advertising, Pepsi realizes that if it raises or lowers its price, it will sell less or more of its product, as shown by the demand schedule in the accompanying table.

Price of Pepsi (per can)	Quantity of Pepsi demanded (millions of cans)
$0.10	5
0.20	4
0.30	3
0.40	2
0.50	1

If Pepsi now were to raise its price to $0.30 per can, what would happen to its profit?

c. Comparing your answer to part a(i) and to part b, what is the maximum amount Pepsi would be willing to spend on advertising?

8. Philip Morris and R.J. Reynolds spend huge sums of money each year to advertise their tobacco products in an attempt to steal customers from each other. Suppose each year Philip Morris and R.J. Reynolds have to decide whether or not they want to spend money on advertising. If neither firm advertises, each will earn a profit of $2 million. If they both advertise, each will earn a profit of $1.5 million. If one firm advertises and the other does not, the firm that advertises will earn a profit of $2.8 million and the other firm will earn $1 million.

a. Use a payoff matrix to depict this problem.

b. Suppose Philip Morris and R.J. Reynolds can write an enforceable contract about what they will do. What is the cooperative solution to this game?

c. What is the Nash equilibrium without an enforceable contract? Explain why this is the likely outcome.

9. Use the three conditions for monopolistic competition discussed in this section to decide which of the following firms are likely to be operating as monopolistic competitors. If they are not monopolistically competitive firms, are they monopolists, oligopolists, or perfectly competitive firms?

a. a local band that plays for weddings, parties, and so on

b. Minute Maid, a producer of individual-serving juice boxes

c. a dry cleaner in a large metropolitan area

d. a farmer who produces soybeans

10. You are thinking of setting up a coffee shop. The market structure for coffee shops is monopolistic competition. There are three Starbucks shops, and two other coffee shops very much like Starbucks, in your town already. In order for you to have some degree of market power, you may want to differentiate your coffee shop. Thinking about the three different ways in which products can be differentiated, explain how you would decide whether you should copy Starbucks or whether you should sell coffee in a completely different way.

11. The restaurant business in town is a monopolistically competitive industry in long-run equilibrium. One restaurant owner asks for your advice. She tells you that, each night, not all tables in her restaurant are full. She also tells you that if she lowered the prices on her menu, she would attract more customers and that doing so would lower her average total cost. Should she lower her prices? Draw a diagram showing the demand curve, marginal revenue curve, marginal cost curve, and average total cost curve for this restaurant to explain your advice. Show in your diagram what would happen to the restaurant owner's profit if she were to lower the price so that she sells the minimum-cost output.

12. The local hairdresser industry has the market structure of monopolistic competition. Your hairdresser boasts that he is making a profit and that if he continues to do so, he will be able to retire in five years. Use a diagram to illustrate your hairdresser's current situation. Do you expect this to last? In a separate diagram, draw what you expect to happen in the long run. Explain your reasoning.

13. Magnificent Blooms is a florist in a monopolistically competitive industry. It is a successful operation, producing the quantity that minimizes its average total cost and making a profit. The owner also says that at its current level of output, its marginal cost is above marginal revenue. Illustrate the current situation of Magnificent Blooms in a diagram. Answer the following questions by illustrating with a diagram.

a. In the short run, could Magnificent Blooms increase its profit?

b. In the long run, could Magnificent Blooms increase its profit?

14. "In both the short run and in the long run, the typical firm in monopolistic competition and a monopolist each make a profit." Do you agree with this statement? Explain your reasoning.

15. The market for clothes has the structure of monopolistic competition. What impact will fewer firms in this industry have on you as a consumer? Address the following issues:

a. variety of clothes

b. differences in quality of service

c. price

16. For each of the following situations, decide whether advertising is directly informative about the product or simply an indirect signal of its quality. Explain your reasoning.

a. Star quarterback Peyton Manning drives a Buick in a TV commercial and claims that he prefers it to any other car.

b. A newspaper ad states, "For sale: 2006 Honda Civic, 160,000 miles, new transmission."

c. McDonald's spends millions of dollars on an advertising campaign that proclaims: "I'm lovin' it."

d. Subway advertises one of its sandwiches by claiming that it contains 6 grams of fat and fewer than 300 calories.

17. In each of the following cases, explain how the advertisement functions as a signal to a potential buyer. Explain what information the buyer lacks that is being supplied by the advertisement and how the information supplied by the advertisement is likely to affect the buyer's willingness to buy the good.

a. "Looking for work. Excellent references from previous employers available."

b. "Electronic equipment for sale. All merchandise carries a one-year, no-questions-asked warranty."

c. "Car for sale by original owner. All repair and maintenance records available."

clothes
shoes

Module 36: Externalities
Module 37: Externalities and Public Policy
Module 38: Public Goods and Common Resources
Module 39: The Economics of the Welfare State

SECTION 12

Market Failure and the Role of Government

WHO'LL STOP THE RAIN?

For many people in the northeastern United States, there is no better way to relax than to fish in one of the region's thousands of lakes. But in the 1960s, avid fishermen noticed something alarming: lakes that had formerly teemed with fish were now almost empty. What had happened?

The answer was acid rain, caused mainly by coal-burning power plants. When coal is burned, it releases sulfur dioxide and nitric oxide into the atmosphere; these gases react with water, producing sulfuric acid and nitric acid. The result in the Northeast, downwind from the nation's industrial heartland, was rain sometimes as acidic as lemon juice. Acid rain didn't just kill fish; it also damaged trees and crops, and in time even began to dissolve limestone buildings.

You'll be glad to hear that the acid rain problem today is much less serious than it was in the 1960s. Power plants have reduced their emissions by switching to low-sulfur coal and installing scrubbers in their smokestacks. But they didn't do this out of the goodness of their hearts; they did it in response to government policy. Without such government intervention, power companies would have had no incentive to take the environmental effects of their actions into account.

We've already seen that inefficiency can arise from market power, which allows monopolists and colluding oligopolists to charge prices above marginal cost, thereby preventing mutually beneficial transactions from occurring.

In this section we will consider other reasons for market failure. First we will see that inefficiency can arise from *externalities,* like pollution, which result from the side effects of actions. Then we will focus on how the characteristics of goods often determine whether markets can deliver them efficiently. We'll look at goods that are public, private, common resources, and artificially scarce. This investigation of sources of inefficiency will deepen our understanding of why markets sometimes don't work well and how government can take actions that reduce economic insecurity, address income inequality (to some degree), and increase society's welfare.

MODULE 36 Externalities

iStockphoto/Thinkstock

WHAT YOU WILL LEARN

1. What externalities are and why they can lead to inefficiency
2. Why externalities often require government intervention
3. The difference between negative and positive externalities
4. The importance of the Coase theorem, which explains how private individuals can sometimes remedy externalities

Externalities: An Overview

When individuals or firms take actions that impose costs on or provide benefits for others but don't have an economic incentive to take those costs or benefits into account, economists say that *externalities* are generated. One of the principal sources of market failure is actions that create *side effects* that are not properly taken into account—that is, externalities.

Externalities, then, arise from the side effects of actions. We begin this module by looking at the case of pollution, which generates a *negative externality*—a side effect that imposes costs on others. Whenever a side effect can be directly observed and quantified, it can be regulated: by imposing direct controls on it, by taxing it, or by subsidizing it (as we will see in the next module, where we examine policy). Other activities generate *positive externalities,* side effects that generate benefits for others—for example, preserving farmland instead of developing it.

In the case of both positive and negative externalities, achieving the best solution takes place at the margin, setting the benefit of doing a little bit more of something equal to the cost of doing that little bit more, as we'll see.

The Economics of Pollution

Pollution is a bad thing. Yet most pollution is a side effect of activities that provide us with good things: our air is polluted by power plants generating the electricity that lights our cities, and our rivers are sullied by fertilizer runoff from farms that grow our food. Why shouldn't we accept a certain amount of pollution as the cost of a good life?

Actually, we do. Even highly committed environmentalists don't think that we can or should completely eliminate pollution—even an environmentally conscious society would accept *some* pollution as the cost of producing useful goods and services. What

environmentalists argue is that unless there is a strong and effective environmental policy, our society will generate *too much* pollution—too much of a bad thing. And the great majority of economists agree.

To see why, we need a framework that lets us think about how much pollution a society *should* have. We'll then be able to see why a market economy, left to itself, will produce more pollution than it should. We'll start by adopting a framework to study the problem under the simplifying assumption that the amount of pollution emitted by a polluter is directly observable and controllable.

The **marginal social cost of pollution** is the additional cost imposed on society as a whole by an additional unit of pollution.

The **marginal social benefit of pollution** is the additional gain to society as a whole from an additional unit of pollution.

The **socially optimal quantity of pollution** is the quantity of pollution that society would choose if all the costs and benefits of pollution were fully accounted for.

Costs and Benefits of Pollution

How much pollution should society allow? We learned previously that "how much" decisions always involve comparing the marginal benefit from an additional unit of something with the marginal cost of that additional unit. The same is true of pollution.

The **marginal social cost of pollution** is the additional cost imposed on society as a whole by an additional unit of pollution. For example, acid rain harms fisheries, crops, and forests; and each additional ton of sulfur dioxide released into the atmosphere increases the harm.

The **marginal social benefit of pollution** is the additional benefit to society from an additional unit of pollution. This concept may seem counterintuitive—what's good about pollution? However, pollution avoidance requires the use of money and inputs that could otherwise be used for other purposes. For example, to reduce the quantity of sulfur dioxide they emit, power companies must either buy expensive low-sulfur coal or install special scrubbers to remove sulfur from their emissions. The more sulfur dioxide they are allowed to emit, the lower are these avoidance costs. If we calculated how much money the power industry would save if it were allowed to emit an additional ton of sulfur dioxide, that savings would be the marginal benefit to society of emitting that ton of sulfur dioxide.

Using hypothetical numbers, Figure 36-1 shows how we can determine the **socially optimal quantity of pollution**—the quantity of pollution that makes society as well off as possible, taking all costs and benefits into account. The upward-sloping marginal

FIGURE 36-1 **The Socially Optimal Quantity of Pollution**

Pollution yields both costs and benefits. Here the curve *MSC* shows how the marginal cost to society as a whole from emitting one more ton of pollution emissions depends on the quantity of emissions. The curve *MSB* shows how the marginal benefit to society as a whole of emitting an additional ton of pollution emissions depends on the quantity of pollution emissions. The socially optimal quantity of pollution is Q_{OPT}; at that quantity, the marginal social benefit of pollution is equal to the marginal social cost, corresponding to $200.

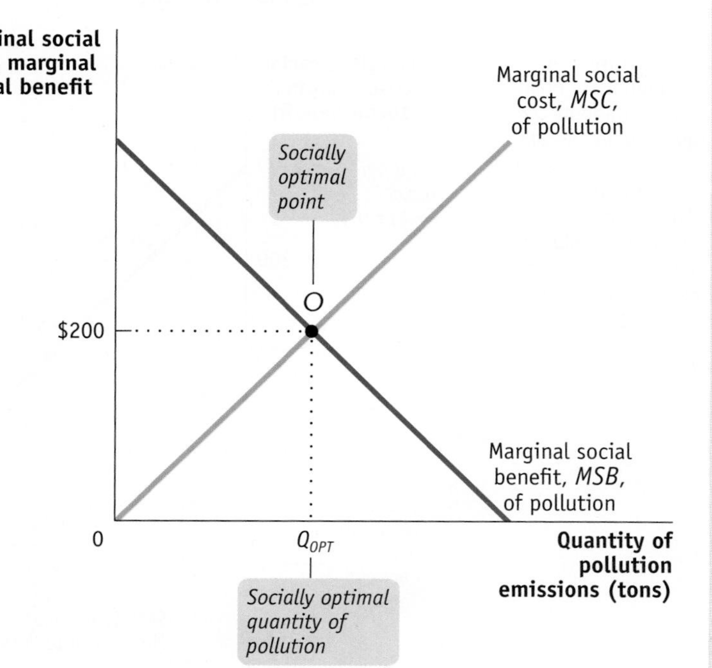

social cost curve, labeled *MSC,* shows how the marginal cost to society of an additional ton of pollution emissions varies with the quantity of emissions. (An upward slope is likely because nature can often safely handle low levels of pollution but is increasingly harmed as pollution reaches high levels.) The marginal social benefit curve, labeled *MSB,* is downward sloping because it is progressively harder, and therefore more expensive, to achieve a further reduction in pollution as the total amount of pollution falls—increasingly more expensive technology must be used. As a result, as pollution falls, the cost savings to a polluter of being allowed to emit one more ton rises.

The socially optimal quantity of pollution in this example isn't zero. It's Q_{OPT}, the quantity corresponding to point *O,* where the marginal social benefit curve crosses the marginal social cost curve. At Q_{OPT}, the marginal social benefit from an additional ton of emissions and its marginal social cost are equalized at $200.

But will a market economy, left to itself, arrive at the socially optimal quantity of pollution? No, it won't.

Pollution: An External Cost

Pollution yields both benefits and costs to society. But in a market economy without government intervention, those who benefit from pollution—like the owners of power companies—decide how much pollution occurs. They have no incentive to take into account the costs of pollution that they impose on others.

To see why, remember the nature of the benefits and costs from pollution. For polluters, the benefits take the form of monetary savings: by emitting an extra ton of sulfur dioxide, any given polluter saves the cost of buying expensive, low-sulfur coal or installing pollution-control equipment. So the benefits of pollution accrue directly to the polluters.

The costs of pollution, though, fall on people who have no say in the decision about how much pollution takes place: for example, people who fish in northeastern lakes do not control the decisions of power plants.

Figure 36-2 shows the result of this asymmetry between who reaps the benefits and who pays the costs. In a market economy without government intervention to protect the environment, only the benefits of pollution are taken into account in choosing the quantity of pollution. So the quantity of emissions won't be the socially optimal

FIGURE 36-2 **Why a Market Economy Produces Too Much Pollution**

In the absence of government intervention, the quantity of pollution will be Q_{MKT}, the quantity at which the marginal social benefit of pollution equals the price polluters pay for each unit of pollution they emit: $0. This is an inefficiently high quantity of pollution because the marginal social cost, $400, greatly exceeds the marginal social benefit, $0.

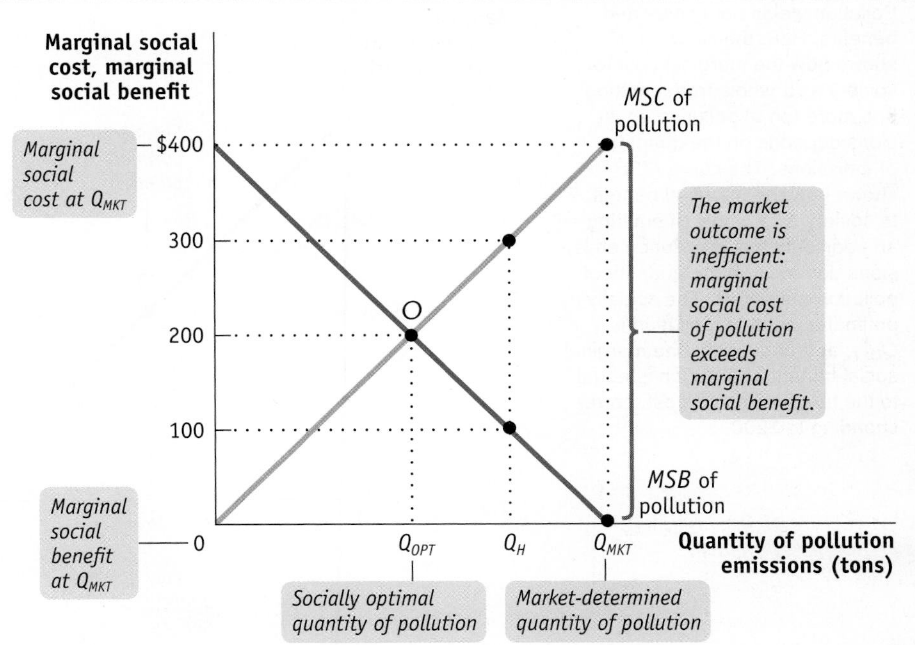

quantity Q_{OPT}; it will be Q_{MKT}, the quantity at which the marginal social benefit of an additional ton of pollution is zero, but the marginal social cost of that additional ton is much larger—$400. The quantity of pollution in a market economy without government intervention will be higher than its socially optimal quantity.

The reason is that in the absence of government intervention, those who derive the benefit from pollution—the owners of polluting firms—don't have to compensate those who bear the cost. So the marginal cost of pollution to any given polluter is zero (the assumption being that the polluter isn't also the pollution victim): polluters have no incentive to limit the amount of emissions. For example, before the Clean Air Act of 1970, midwestern power plants used the cheapest type of coal available, despite the fact that cheap coal generated more pollution, and they did nothing to scrub their emissions.

An **external cost** is an uncompensated cost that an individual or firm imposes on others.

An **external benefit** is a benefit that an individual or firm confers on others without receiving compensation.

External costs and benefits are known as **externalities.**

External costs are **negative externalities,** and external benefits are **positive externalities.**

The environmental cost of pollution is perhaps the best-known and most important example of an **external cost**—an uncompensated cost that an individual or firm imposes on others. There are many other examples of external costs besides pollution. Another important, and certainly familiar, external cost is traffic congestion—an individual who chooses to drive during rush hour increases congestion and so increases the travel time of other drivers.

We'll see in the next module that there are also important examples of **external benefits,** benefits that individuals or firms confer on others without receiving compensation. External costs and external benefits are jointly known as **externalities.** External costs are called **negative externalities** and external benefits are called **positive externalities.**

As we've already suggested, externalities can lead to individual decisions that are not optimal for society as a whole. Let's take a closer look at why, focusing on the case of pollution.

ECONOMICS IN ACTION

TALKING, TEXTING, AND DRIVING

Why is that woman in the car in front of us driving so erratically? Is she drunk? No, she's talking on her cell phone or texting.

Traffic safety experts take the risks posed by driving while using a cell phone very seriously: a recent study found a six-fold increase in accidents caused by driving while distracted.

In 2010, the National Safety Council estimated that 28% of traffic accidents were attributable to cell phone use. Of the annual 1.4 million traffic accidents in the United States, 200,000 are blamed on texting while driving.

And using hands-free, voice-activated phones to make a call doesn't improve driver safety on the road because the main danger is distraction. As one traffic consultant put it, "It's not where your eyes are; it's where your head is."

Pawel Gaul/Getty Images

"It's not where your eyes are; it's where your head is."

The National Safety Council urges people not to use phones while driving. Most states have some restrictions on talking on a cell phone while driving. But in response to a growing number of accidents, several states have banned cell phone use behind the wheel altogether. In 41 states and the District of Columbia, it is illegal to text and drive. Cell phone use while driving is illegal in many other countries as well, including Japan and Israel.

Why not leave the decision up to the driver? Because the risk posed by driving while using a cell phone isn't just a risk to the driver; it's also a safety risk to others—to a driver's passengers, pedestrians, and people in other cars. Even if you decide that the benefit to you of using your cell phone while driving is worth the cost, you aren't taking into account the cost to other people. Driving while using a cell phone, in other words, generates a serious—and sometimes fatal—negative externality.

The Inefficiency of Excess Pollution

We have just shown that in the absence of government action, the quantity of pollution will be *inefficient:* polluters will pollute up to the point at which the marginal social benefit of pollution is zero, as shown by quantity Q_{MKT} in Figure 36-2. Recall that an outcome is inefficient if some people could be made better off without making others worse off. We have already seen why the equilibrium quantity in a perfectly competitive market with no externalities is the efficient quantity of the good, the quantity that maximizes total surplus. Here, we can use a variation of that analysis to show how the presence of a negative externality upsets that result.

Because the marginal social benefit of pollution is zero at Q_{MKT}, reducing the quantity of pollution by one ton would subtract very little from the total social benefit from pollution. In other words, the benefit to polluters from that last unit of pollution is very low—virtually zero. Meanwhile, the marginal social cost imposed on the rest of society of that last ton of pollution at Q_{MKT} is quite high—$400. In other words, by reducing the quantity of pollution at Q_{MKT} by one ton, the total social cost of pollution falls by $400, but total social benefit falls by virtually zero. So total surplus rises by approximately $400 if the quantity of pollution at Q_{MKT} is reduced by one ton.

If the quantity of pollution is reduced further, there will be more gains in total surplus, though they will be smaller. For example, if the quantity of pollution is Q_H in Figure 36-2, the marginal social benefit of a ton of pollution is $100, but the marginal social cost is still much higher at $300. This means that reducing the quantity of pollution by one ton leads to a net gain in total surplus of approximately $300 – $100 = $200. Thus Q_H is still an inefficiently high quantity of pollution. Only if the quantity of pollution is reduced to Q_{OPT}, where the marginal social cost and the marginal social benefit of an additional ton of pollution are both $200, is the outcome efficient.

Private Solutions to Externalities

Can the private sector solve the problem of externalities without government intervention? Bear in mind that when an outcome is inefficient, there is potentially a deal that makes people better off. Why don't individuals find a way to make that deal?

In an influential 1960 article, economist and Nobel laureate Ronald Coase pointed out that in an ideal world the private sector could indeed deal with all externalities. According to the **Coase theorem,** even in the presence of externalities, an economy can reach an efficient solution, provided that the legal rights of the parties are clearly defined and the costs of making a deal are sufficiently low. In some cases it takes a lot of time, or even money, to bring the relevant parties together, negotiate a deal, and carry out the terms of the deal. The costs of making a deal are known as **transaction costs.**

To get a sense of Coase's argument, imagine two neighbors, Mick and Christina, who both like to barbecue in their backyards on summer afternoons. Mick likes to play classic rock while barbecuing, but this annoys Christina, who can't stand that kind of music.

Who prevails? You might think it depends on the legal rights involved in the case: if the law says that Mick has the right to play whatever music he wants, Christina just has to suffer; if the law says that Mick needs Christina's consent to play music in his backyard, Mick has to live without his favorite music while barbecuing.

But as Coase pointed out, the outcome need not be determined by legal rights, because Christina and Mick can make a private deal as long as the legal rights are clearly defined. Even if Mick has the right to play his music, Christina could pay him not to. Even if Mick can't play the music without an OK from Christina, he can offer to pay her to give that OK. These payments allow them to reach an efficient solution, regardless of who has the legal upper hand. If the benefit of the music to Mick exceeds its cost to Christina, the music will go on; if the benefit to Mick is less than the cost to Christina, there will be silence.

According to the **Coase theorem,** even in the presence of externalities, an economy can always reach an efficient solution as long as **transaction costs**—the costs to individuals of making a deal—are sufficiently low. When individuals take external costs or benefits into account, they **internalize the externalities.**

The implication of Coase's analysis is that externalities need not lead to inefficiency because individuals have an incentive to make mutually beneficial deals—deals that lead them to take externalities into account when making decisions.

When individuals *do* take externalities into account when making decisions, economists say that they **internalize the externalities.** If externalities are fully internalized, as when Mick must forgo a payment from Christina *equal to the external cost he imposes on her* in order to play music, the outcome is efficient even without government intervention.

Why can't individuals always internalize externalities? Our barbecue example implicitly assumes the transaction costs are low enough for Mick and Christina to be able to make a deal. In many situations involving externalities, however, transaction costs prevent individuals from making efficient deals. Examples of transaction costs include the following:

- *The costs of communication among the interested parties.* Such costs may be very high if many people are involved.
- *The costs of making legally binding agreements.* Such costs may be high if expensive legal services are required.
- *Costly delays involved in bargaining.* Even if there is a potentially beneficial deal, both sides may hold out in an effort to extract more favorable terms, leading to increased effort and forgone utility.

Let's make a deal that takes externalities into account.

In some cases, transaction costs are low enough to allow individuals to resolve externality problems. For example, while filming *A League of Their Own* on location in a neighborhood ballpark, director Penny Marshall paid a man $100 to stop using his noisy chainsaw nearby. But in many other cases, transaction costs are too high to make it possible to deal with externalities through private action. For example, tens of millions of people are adversely affected by acid rain. It would be prohibitively expensive to try to make a deal among all those people and all those power companies.

When transaction costs prevent the private sector from dealing with externalities, it is time to look for government solutions—the subject of the next module.

MODULE 36 Review

Solutions appear at the back of the book.

Check Your Understanding

1. Wastewater runoff from large poultry farms adversely affects residents in neighboring homes. Explain the following:
   a. why this is considered an externality problem
   b. the efficiency of the outcome with neither government intervention nor a private deal
   c. how the socially optimal outcome is determined and how it compares with the no-intervention, no-deal outcome

2. According to Yasmin, any student who borrows a book from the university library and fails to return it on time imposes a negative externality on other students. She claims that rather than charging a modest fine for late returns, the library should charge a huge fine, so that borrowers will never return a book late. Is Yasmin's economic reasoning correct?

Multiple-Choice Questions

1. The socially optimal level of pollution is
   a. less than that created by the market, but not zero.
   b. more than that created by the market.
   c. whatever the market creates.
   d. determined by firms.
   e. zero.

2. Which of the following is a source of negative externalities?
   a. loud conversations in a library
   b. smokestack scrubbers
   c. a beautiful view
   d. national defense
   e. a decision to purchase dressy but uncomfortable shoes.

3. Inefficiencies created by externalities can be dealt with through
   a. government actions only.
   b. private actions only.
   c. market outcomes only.
   d. either private or government actions.
   e. neither private nor government actions.

4. The Coase theorem asserts that, in the right circumstances, inefficiencies created by externalities can be dealt with through
   a. lawsuits.
   b. private bargaining.
   c. vigilante actions.
   d. government policies.
   e. mediation.

5. Which of the following makes it more likely that private solutions to externality problems will succeed?
   a. high transaction costs
   b. high prices for legal services
   c. delays in the bargaining process
   d. a small number of affected parties
   e. loosely defined legal rights

Critical-Thinking Questions

1. Define the marginal social cost of pollution.
2. Define the marginal social benefit of pollution, and explain why polluting more can provide benefits to a firm even when it could produce the same quantity of output without polluting as much.
3. Define the socially optimal level of pollution.

Externalities and Public Policy

© Accent Alaska.com/Alamy

WHAT YOU WILL LEARN

1. How external benefits and costs cause inefficiency in the markets for goods
2. Why some government policies to deal with externalities are efficient, while others are not

Policies Toward Pollution

Before 1970 there were no rules governing the amount of sulfur dioxide that power plants in the United States could emit—which is why acid rain got to be such a problem. In 1970, the Clean Air Act set rules about sulfur dioxide emissions; thereafter, the acidity of rainfall declined significantly. Economists argued, however, that a more flexible system of rules that exploited the effectiveness of markets could achieve lower pollution levels at a lower cost. In 1990 this theory was put into effect with a modified version of the Clean Air Act. And guess what? The economists were right!

In this module we'll look at the three types of policies governments typically use to deal with pollution:

1. Environmental standards
2. Emissions taxes
3. Tradable emissions permits

We'll also see how economic analysis has been used to improve those policies.

Environmental Standards

Because the economy, and life itself, depends on a viable environment, external costs that threaten the environment—air pollution, water pollution, habitat destruction, and so on, are worthy of attention. Protection of the environment has become a major focus of government in every advanced nation. In the United States, the Environmental Protection Agency is the principal enforcer of environmental policies at the national level and is supported by the actions of state and local governments.

How does a country protect its environment? At present the main policy tools are **environmental standards,** rules that protect the environment by specifying actions by producers and consumers. A familiar example is the law that requires almost all

Environmental standards are rules that protect the environment by specifying limits or actions for producers and consumers.

An **emissions tax** is a tax that depends on the amount of pollution a firm produces.

vehicles to have catalytic converters, which reduce the emission of chemicals that can cause smog and lead to health problems. Other rules require communities to treat their sewage, factories to limit their pollution emissions, and homes to be painted with lead-free paint, among many other examples.

Environmental standards came into widespread use in the 1960s and 1970s with considerable success. Since the United States passed the Clean Air Act in 1970, for example, the emission of air pollutants has fallen by more than a third, even though the population has grown by a third and the size of the economy has more than doubled. Even in Los Angeles, still famous for its smog, the air has improved dramatically: in 1976 ozone levels in the South Coast Air Basin exceeded federal standards on 194 days; in 2010, on only 7 days. Improvements have continued in 2013.

iStockphoto

Environmental standards have helped reduce the Los Angeles smog and improve air quality.

Despite these successes, economists believe that when regulators can control a polluter's emissions directly, there are more efficient ways than environmental standards to deal with pollution. By using methods grounded in economic analysis, society can achieve a cleaner environment at lower cost.

Most current environmental standards are inflexible and don't allow reductions in pollution to be achieved at the lowest possible cost. For example, two power plants—plant A and plant B—might be ordered to reduce pollution by the same percentage, even if their costs of achieving that objective are very different.

How does economic theory suggest that pollution should be controlled? We'll examine two approaches: taxes and tradable permits. As we'll see, either approach can achieve the efficient outcome at the minimum feasible cost.

Emissions Taxes

One way to deal with pollution directly is to charge polluters an **emissions tax.** Emissions taxes depend on the amount of pollution a firm produces. For example, power plants might be charged $200 for every ton of sulfur dioxide they emit.

Consider the socially optimal quantity of pollution, Q_{OPT}, shown in Figure 37-1. At that quantity of pollution, the marginal social benefit and the marginal social cost of

FIGURE 37-1 **In Pursuit of the Efficient Quantity of Pollution**

The market determined quantity of pollution, Q_{MKT}, is too high because polluters don't pay the marginal social cost, and thus pollute beyond the socially optimal quantity, Q_{OPT}, at which marginal social cost equals marginal social benefit. A Pigouvian tax of $200—the value of the marginal social cost of pollution when it equals the marginal social benefit of pollution—gives polluters the incentive to emit only the socially optimal quantity of pollution. Another solution is to provide permits for only the socially optimal quantity of pollution.

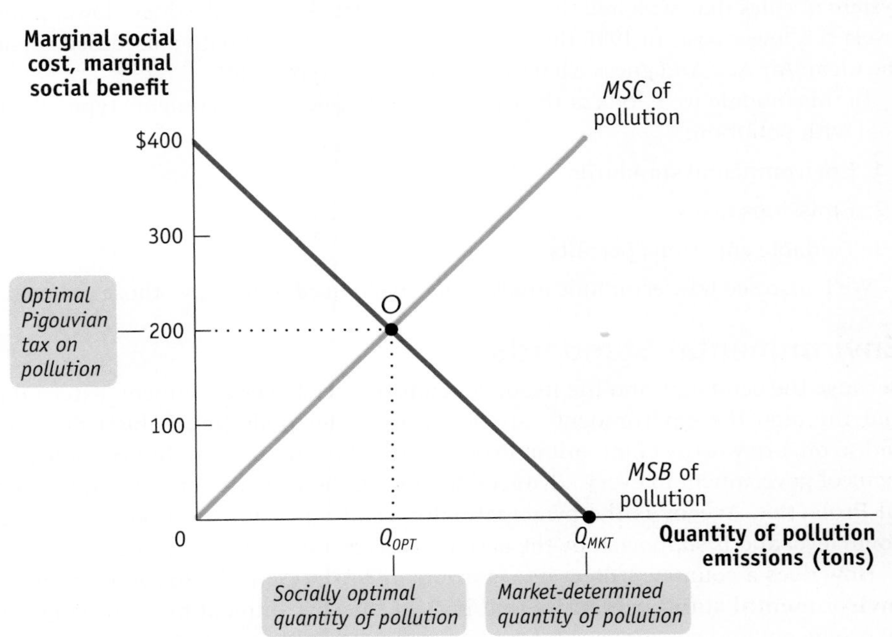

an additional ton of emissions are equal at $200. But in the absence of government intervention, power companies have no incentive to limit pollution to the socially optimal quantity Q_{OPT}; instead, they will push pollution up to the quantity Q_{MKT}, at which the marginal social benefit is zero.

It's now easy to see how an emissions tax can solve the problem. If power companies are required to pay a tax of $200 per ton of emissions, they face a marginal cost of $200 per ton and have an incentive to reduce emissions to Q_{OPT}, the socially optimal quantity. This illustrates a general result: an emissions tax equal to the marginal social cost at the socially optimal quantity of pollution induces polluters to internalize the externality—to take into account the true cost to society of their actions. (The Pigouvian tax noted in Figure 37-1 will be explained shortly.)

Why is an emissions tax an efficient way (that is, a cost-minimizing way) to reduce pollution but environmental standards generally are not? Because an emissions tax ensures that the marginal benefit of pollution is equal for all sources of pollution, but an environmental standard does not.

Figure 37-2 shows a hypothetical industry consisting of only two plants, plant A and plant B. We'll assume that plant A uses newer technology than plant B and so has a lower cost of reducing pollution. Reflecting this difference in costs, plant A's marginal benefit of pollution curve, MB_A, lies below plant B's marginal benefit of pollution curve, MB_B. Because it is more costly for plant B to reduce its pollution at any output quantity, an additional ton of pollution is worth more to plant B than to plant A.

FIGURE 37-2 Environmental Standards versus Emissions Taxes

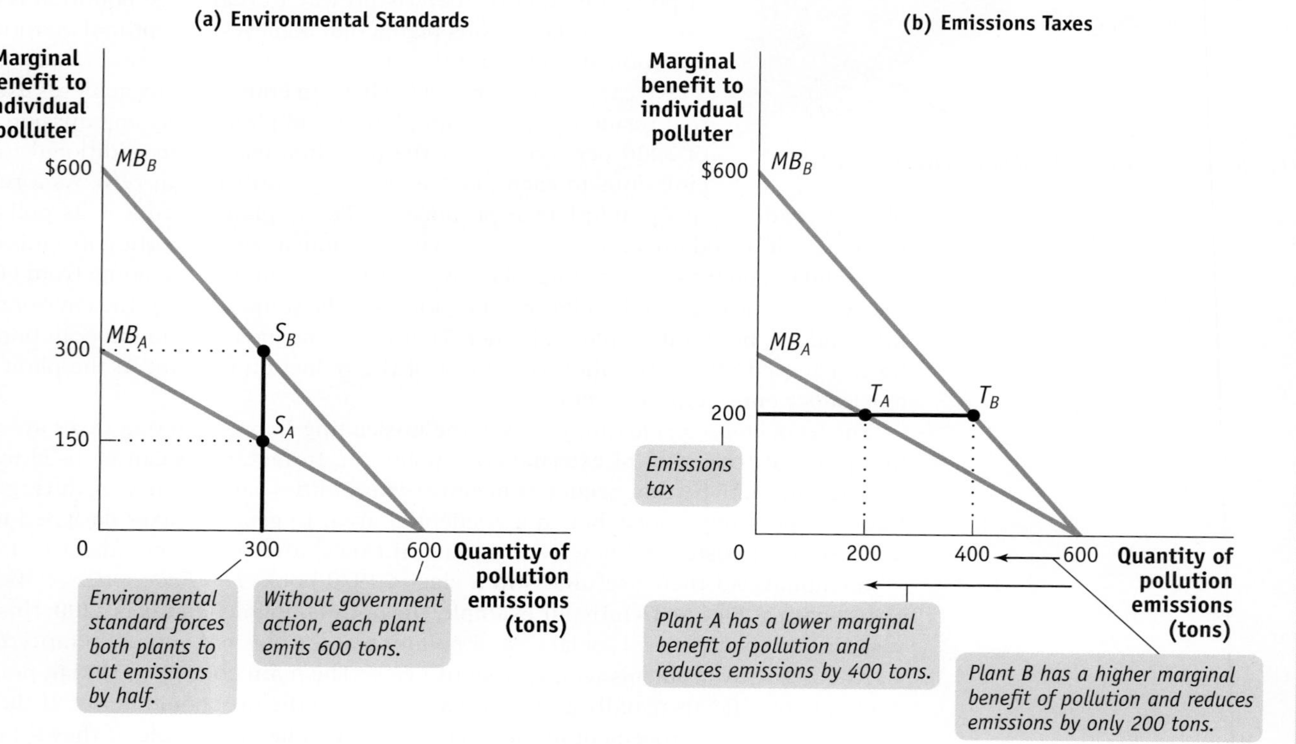

In both panels, MB_A shows the marginal benefit of pollution to plant A and MB_B shows the marginal benefit of pollution to plant B. In the absence of government intervention, each plant would emit 600 tons. However, the cost of reducing emissions is lower for plant A, as shown by the fact that MB_A lies below MB_B. Panel (a) shows the result of an environmental standard that requires both plants to cut emissions in half; this is inefficient, because it leaves the marginal benefit of pollution higher for plant B than for plant A. Panel (b) shows that an emissions tax achieves the same quantity of overall pollution efficiently: faced with an emissions tax of $200 per ton, both plants reduce pollution to the point where its marginal benefit is $200.

In the absence of government action, polluters will pollute until the marginal social benefit of an additional unit of emissions is equal to zero. Recall that the marginal social benefit of pollution is the cost savings, at the margin, to polluters of an additional unit of pollution. As a result, without government intervention each plant will pollute until its own marginal benefit of pollution is equal to zero. This corresponds to an emissions quantity of 600 tons each for plants A and B—the quantity of pollution at which MB_A and MB_B are each equal to zero. So although plant A and plant B value a ton of emissions differently, without government action they will each choose to emit the same amount of pollution.

Now suppose that the government decides that overall pollution from this industry should be cut in half, from 1,200 tons to 600 tons. Panel (a) of Figure 37-2 shows how this might be achieved with an environmental standard that requires each plant to cut its emissions in half, from 600 to 300 tons. The standard has the desired effect of reducing overall emissions from 1,200 to 600 tons but accomplishes it in an inefficient way. As you can see from panel (a), the environmental standard leads plant A to produce at point S_A, where its marginal benefit of pollution is $150, but plant B produces at point S_B, where its marginal benefit of pollution is twice as high, $300.

© Mischa Richter/The New Yorker Collection/www.cartoonbank.com

"They have very strict anti-pollution laws in this state."

This difference in marginal benefits between the two plants tells us that the same quantity of pollution can be achieved at lower total cost by allowing plant B to pollute more than 300 tons but inducing plant A to pollute less. In fact, the efficient way to reduce pollution is to ensure that at the industry-wide outcome, the marginal benefit of pollution is the same for all plants. When each plant values a unit of pollution equally, there is no way to rearrange pollution reduction among the various plants that achieves the optimal quantity of pollution at a lower total cost.

We can see from panel (b) how an emissions tax achieves exactly that result. Suppose both plant A and plant B pay an emissions tax of $200 per ton so that the marginal cost of an additional ton of emissions to each plant is now $200 rather than zero. As a result, plant A produces at T_A and plant B produces at T_B. So plant A reduces its pollution more than it would under an inflexible environmental standard, cutting its emissions from 600 to 200 tons; meanwhile, plant B reduces its pollution less, going from 600 to 400 tons. In the end, total pollution—600 tons—is the same as under the environmental standard, but total surplus is higher. That's because the reduction in pollution has been achieved efficiently, allocating most of the reduction to plant A, the plant that can reduce emissions at lower cost.

The term *emissions tax* may convey the misleading impression that taxes are a solution to only one kind of external cost, pollution. In fact, taxes can be used to discourage any activity that generates negative externalities, such as driving during rush hour or operating a noisy bar in a residential area. In general, taxes designed to reduce external costs are known as **Pigouvian taxes,** after the economist A.C. Pigou, who emphasized their usefulness in a classic 1920 book, *The Economics of Welfare*. Look again at Figure 37-1. In our example, the optimal Pigouvian tax is $200; this corresponds to the marginal social cost of pollution at the optimal output quantity, Q_{OPT}.

Are there any problems with emissions taxes? The main concern is that in practice government officials usually aren't sure at what level the tax should be set. If they set the tax too low, improvement in the environment will be inadequate; if they set it too high, emissions will be reduced by more than is efficient. This uncertainty cannot be eliminated, but the nature of the risks can be changed by using an alternative strategy, issuing tradable emissions permits.

Taxes designed to reduce external costs are known as **Pigouvian taxes.**

Tradable emissions permits are licenses to emit limited quantities of pollutants that can be bought and sold by polluters.

Tradable Emissions Permits

Tradable emissions permits are licenses to emit limited quantities of pollutants that can be bought and sold by polluters. They are usually issued to polluting firms accord-

ing to some formula reflecting their history. For example, each power plant might be issued permits equal to 50% of its emissions before the system went into effect. The more important point, however, is that these permits are *tradable*. Firms with differing costs of reducing pollution can now engage in mutually beneficial transactions: those that find it easier to reduce pollution will sell some of their permits to those that find it more difficult.

In other words, firms will use transactions in permits to reallocate pollution reduction among themselves, so that in the end those with the lowest cost will reduce their pollution the most and those with the highest cost will reduce their pollution the least. Assume that the government issues 300 permits each to plant A and plant B, where one permit allows the emission of one ton of pollution. Under a system of tradable emissions permits, commonly known as a *cap and trade program*, plant A will find it profitable to sell 100 of its 300 government-issued permits to plant B. The effect of a cap and trade program is to create a market in rights to pollute.

Just like emissions taxes, tradable permits provide polluters with an incentive to take the marginal social cost of pollution into account. To see why, suppose that the market price of a permit to emit one ton of sulfur dioxide is $200. Then every plant has an incentive to limit its emissions of sulfur dioxide to the point where its marginal benefit of emitting another ton of pollution is $200. This is obvious for plants that buy rights to pollute: if a plant must pay $200 for the right to emit an additional ton of sulfur dioxide, it faces the same incentives as a plant facing an emissions tax of $200 per ton.

But it's equally true for plants that have more permits than they plan to use: by *not* emitting a ton of sulfur dioxide, a plant frees up a permit that it can sell for $200, so the opportunity cost of a ton of emissions to the plant's owner is $200.

In short, tradable emissions permits have the same cost-minimizing advantage as emissions taxes over environmental standards: either system ensures that those who can reduce pollution most cheaply are the ones who do so. The socially optimal quantity of pollution shown in Figure 37-1 could be efficiently achieved either way: by imposing an emissions tax of $200 per ton of pollution or by issuing tradable permits to emit Q_{OPT} tons of pollution. If regulators choose to issue Q_{OPT} permits, where one permit allows the release of one ton of emissions, then the equilibrium market price of a permit among polluters will indeed be $200. Why? You can see from Figure 37-1 that at Q_{OPT}, only polluters with a marginal benefit of pollution of $200 or more will buy a permit. And the last polluter who buys—who has a marginal benefit of exactly $200—sets the market price.

It's important to realize that emissions taxes and tradable permits do more than induce polluting industries to reduce their output. Unlike rigid environmental standards, emissions taxes and tradable permits provide incentives to create and use technology that emits less pollution—new technology that lowers the socially optimal level of pollution. The main effect of the permit system for sulfur dioxide has been to change *how* electricity is produced rather than to reduce the nation's electricity output. For example, power companies have shifted to the use of alternative fuels such as low-sulfur coal and natural gas; they have also installed scrubbers that take much of the sulfur dioxide out of a power plant's emissions.

The main problem with tradable emissions permits is the flip-side of the problem with emissions taxes: because it is difficult to determine the optimal quantity of pollution, governments can find themselves either issuing too many permits (that is, they don't reduce pollution enough) or issuing too few (that is, they reduce pollution too much).

After first relying on environmental standards, the U.S. government has turned to a system of tradable permits to control acid rain. Current proposals would extend the system to other major sources of pollution. And in 2005 the European Union created an emissions-trading scheme with the purpose of controlling emissions of carbon dioxide, a greenhouse gas. The European Union scheme is part of a larger global market for the trading of greenhouse gas permits. The Economics in Action that follows describes these two systems in greater detail.

ECONOMICS IN ACTION WORLD VIEW

CAP AND TRADE

The tradable emissions permit systems for both acid rain in the United States and greenhouse gases in the European Union are examples of *cap and trade systems:* the government sets a *cap* (a maximum amount of pollutant that can be emitted), issues tradable emissions permits, and enforces a yearly rule that a polluter must hold a number of permits equal to the amount of pollutant emitted. The goal is to set the cap low enough to generate environmental benefits, while giving polluters flexibility in meeting environmental standards and motivating them to adopt new technologies that will lower the cost of reducing pollution.

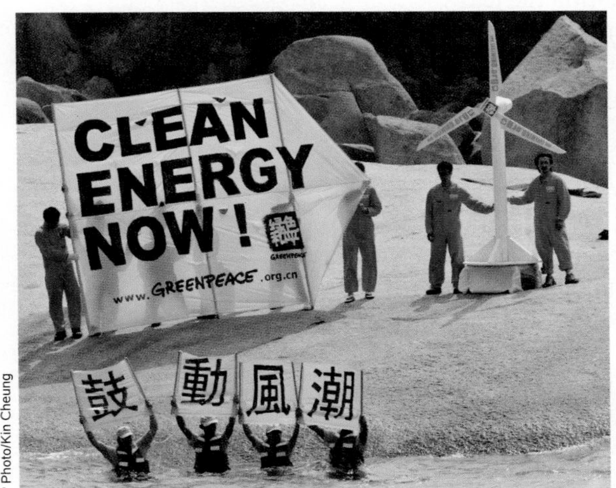

AP Photo/Kin Cheung

Cap and trade systems can benefit the environment, but they are not a silver bullet against pollution.

In 1994 the United States began a cap and trade system for the sulfur dioxide emissions that cause acid rain by issuing permits to power plants based on their historical consumption of coal. Thanks to the system, air pollutants in the United States decreased by more than 40% from 1990 to 2008, and 2010 acid rain levels dropped to approximately 50% of their 1980 levels and they continue to drop.

Economists who have analyzed the sulfur dioxide cap and trade system point to another reason for its success: it would have been a lot more expensive—80% more to be exact—to reduce emissions by this much using a non-market-based regulatory policy.

The EU cap and trade scheme, covering all 28 member nations of the European Union (plus Iceland, Liechtenstein, and Norway), is the world's only mandatory trading scheme for greenhouse gases. It is scheduled to achieve a 21% reduction in greenhouse gases by 2020 compared to 2005 levels.

Despite all this good news, however, cap and trade systems are not silver bullets for the world's pollution problems for these reasons:

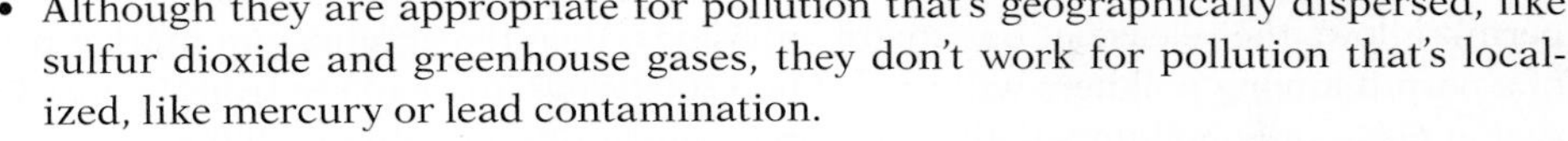

- Although they are appropriate for pollution that's geographically dispersed, like sulfur dioxide and greenhouse gases, they don't work for pollution that's localized, like mercury or lead contamination.
- The amount of overall reduction in pollution depends on the level of the cap. Under industry pressure, regulators run the risk of issuing too many permits, effectively eliminating the cap.
- There must be vigilant monitoring of compliance if the system is to work. Without oversight of a polluter's emissions, there is no way to know for sure that the rules are being followed.

Positive Externalities

New Jersey is the most densely populated state in the country, lying along the northeastern corridor, an area of almost continuous development stretching from Washington, D.C., to Boston. Yet a drive through New Jersey reveals a surprising feature: acre upon acre of farmland, growing everything from corn to pumpkins to the famous Jersey tomatoes. This situation is no accident: starting in 1961, New Jerseyans have voted in a series of measures that subsidize farmers to permanently preserve their farmland rather than sell it to developers.

Why have New Jersey citizens voted to raise their own taxes to subsidize the preservation of farmland? Because they believe that preserved farmland in an already heavily developed state provides external benefits, such as natural beauty, access to fresh food, and the conservation of wild bird populations. In addition, preservation alleviates the external costs that come with more development, such as pressure on roads, water supplies, and municipal services—and, inevitably, more pollution.

In this section we'll explore the topics of external benefits and positive externalities. They are, in many ways, the mirror images of external costs and negative externalities. Left on its own, the market will produce too little of a good (in this case, preserved New Jersey farmland) that confers external benefits on others. But society as a whole is better off when policies are adopted that increase the supply of such a good.

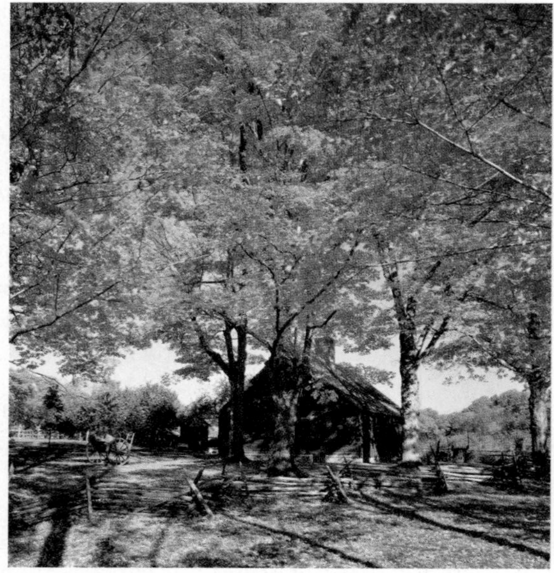
© Gene Ahrens/Alamy

Preserved farmland provides external benefits to an entire community.

Preserved Farmland: An External Benefit

Preserved farmland yields both benefits and costs to society. In the absence of government intervention, the farmer who wants to sell his land incurs all the costs of preservation—namely, the forgone profit to be made from selling the farmland to a developer. But the benefits of preserved farmland accrue not to the farmer but to neighboring residents, who have no right to influence how the farmland is disposed of.

Figure 37-3 illustrates society's problem. The marginal social cost of preserved farmland, shown by the *MSC* curve, is the additional cost imposed on society by an additional acre of such farmland. This represents the forgone profits that would have accrued to farmers if they had sold their land. The line is upward-sloping because when very few acres are preserved and there is plenty of land available for development, the profit that could be made from selling an acre to a developer is small. But as the number of preserved acres increases and few are left for development, the amount a developer is willing to pay for them, and therefore the forgone profit, increases as well.

The *MSB* curve represents the marginal social benefit of preserved farmland. It is the additional benefit that accrues to society—in this case, the farmer's neighbors—when an additional acre of farmland is preserved. The curve is downward sloping because as more farmland is preserved, the benefit to society of preserving another acre falls. As Figure 37-3 shows, the socially optimal point, *O*, occurs when the marginal social cost and the marginal social benefit are equalized—here, at a price of $10,000 per acre. At the socially optimum point, Q_{OPT} acres of farmland are preserved.

FIGURE 37-3 Why a Market Economy Preserves Too Little Farmland

Without government intervention, the quantity of preserved farmland will be zero, the level at which the marginal social cost of preservation is zero. This is an inefficiently low quantity of preserved farmland: the marginal social benefit is $20,000, but the marginal social cost is zero. An optimal Pigouvian subsidy of $10,000, the value of the marginal social benefit of preservation when it equals the marginal social cost, can move the market to the socially optimal level of preservation, Q_{OPT}.

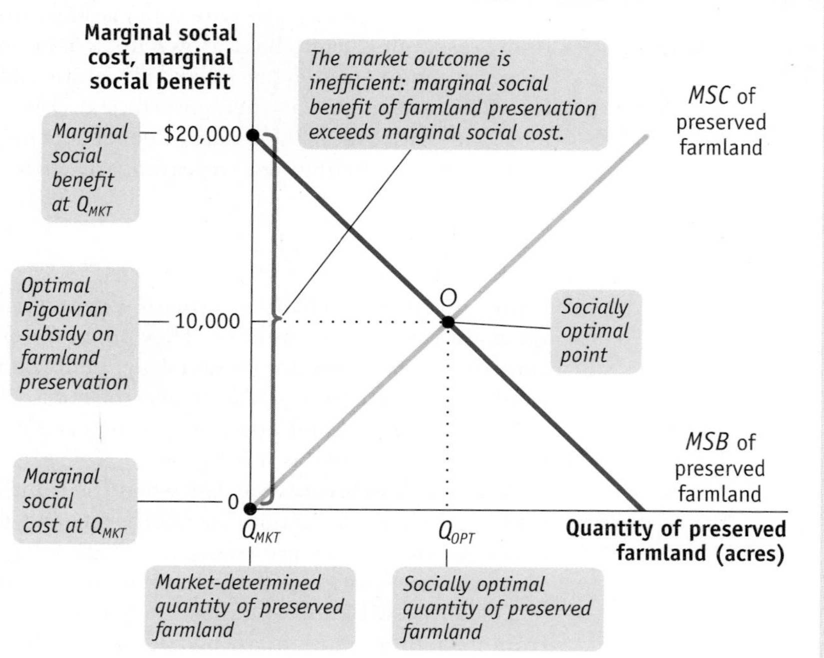

A **Pigouvian subsidy** is a payment designed to encourage activities that yield external benefits.

A **technology spillover** is an external benefit that results when knowledge spreads among individuals and firms.

A good is subject to a **network externality** when the value of the good to an individual is greater when other people also use the good.

The market alone will not provide Q_{OPT} acres of preserved farmland. Instead, in the market outcome no acres will be preserved; the level of preserved farmland, Q_{MKT}, is equal to zero. That's because farmers will set the marginal social cost of preservation—their forgone profits—at zero and sell all their acres to developers. Because farmers bear the entire cost of preservation but gain none of the benefits, an inefficiently low quantity of acres will be preserved in the market outcome.

This is clearly inefficient because at zero acres preserved, the marginal social benefit of preserving an acre of farmland is $20,000. So how can the economy be induced to produce Q_{OPT} acres of preserved farmland, the socially optimal level? The answer is a **Pigouvian subsidy:** a payment designed to encourage activities that yield external benefits. The optimal Pigouvian subsidy, as shown in Figure 37-3, is equal to the marginal social benefit of preserved farmland at the socially optimal level, Q_{OPT}—that is, $10,000 per acre.

So New Jersey voters are indeed implementing the right policy to raise their social welfare—taxing themselves in order to provide subsidies for farmland preservation.

Positive Externalities in the Modern Economy

In the overall U.S. economy, the most important single source of external benefits is the creation of knowledge. In high-tech industries such as semiconductors, software design, green technology, and bioengineering, innovations by one firm are quickly emulated and improved upon by rival firms. Such spreading of knowledge across individuals and firms is known as a **technology spillover.** In the modern economy, the greatest sources of technology spillovers are major universities and research institutes.

Creatista/Shutterstock

Informal interactions can lead to technological innovation.

In technologically advanced countries such as the United States, Japan, the United Kingdom, Germany, France, and Israel, there is an ongoing exchange of people and ideas among private industries, major universities, and research institutes located in close proximity. The dynamic interplay that occurs in these *research clusters* spurs innovation and competition, theoretical advances, and practical applications. (See the Business Case at the end of the section for more on research clusters.) Ultimately, these areas of technology spillover increase the economy's productivity and raise living standards.

But research clusters don't appear out of thin air. Except in a few instances in which firms have funded basic research on a long-term basis, research clusters have grown up around major universities. And like farmland preservation in New Jersey, major universities and their research activities are subsidized by government. In fact, government policy makers in advanced countries have long understood that the external benefits generated by knowledge, stemming from basic education to high-tech research, are key to the economy's growth over time.

Network Externalities

Unlike positive externalities, *network externalities* have no inherently favorable or adverse effect on society at large. They do, however, affect other users of the associated good or service. Consider Facebook again: if you were the only user of Facebook, what would it be worth to you? The answer, of course, is nothing. Facebook derives its value only from the fact that other people also use it. And the more people who use Facebook, the more valuable it is to you.

A **network externality** exists when the value of a good or service to an individual is greater when a large number of other people also use the good or service. Although network externalities are common in technology-driven sectors of the economy, the phenomenon is much more widespread than that.

For all network externalities, the value of the good or service is derived entirely from its ability to link many people possessing the same good or service. As a result,

the marginal benefit of the good or service to any one individual depends on the number of other individuals who use it.

Although most network externalities involve methods of communication—the Internet and cell phones, for example—they can exist when other users are not strictly necessary for the use of a good, as long as they enhance its usefulness. For example, a scheduled flight between two airports becomes more valuable if one or both of those airports is a hub with connections to other places.

Even your choice of a car is influenced by a form of network externality. Most people would be reluctant to switch to a car that runs on natural gas because fueling the car would be difficult: very few gas stations offer natural gas. And the reason service stations do not offer natural gas is, of course, that few people drive anything other than gasoline-powered cars.

When a good or service is subject to a network externality, it exhibits **positive feedback:** if large numbers of people buy it, other people become more likely to buy it, too. If people *don't* buy the good or service, others become less likely to buy it. So both success and failure tend to be self-reinforcing. Producers of products that are subject to network externalities are aware of this problem, understanding that of two competing products, it's the one with the largest network—not necessarily the one that's the better product—that will win in the end. That is, the product with the largest network will eventually dominate the market, and competing products will eventually disappear.

A good is subject to **positive feedback** when success breeds greater success and failure breeds further failure.

Review

Solutions appear at the back of the book.

Check Your Understanding

1. Some opponents of tradable emissions permits object to them on the grounds that polluters that sell their permits benefit monetarily from their involvement in polluting the environment. Assess this argument.
2. In 2010, the U.S. Department of Education spent almost $35 billion on college student aid. Explain why this can be an optimal policy to encourage the creation of knowledge.
3. For each of the following cases, explain whether an external cost or an external benefit is created and identify an appropriate policy response.
   a. Trees planted in urban areas improve air quality and lower summer temperatures.
   b. Water-saving toilets reduce the need to pump water from rivers and aquifers. The cost of a gallon of water to homeowners is virtually zero.
   c. Old computer monitors contain toxic materials that pollute the environment when improperly disposed of.

Multiple-Choice Questions

1. Which of the following policy tools is inefficient even when correctly administered?
   a. environmental standards
   b. emissions taxes
   c. tradable emissions permits
   d. Pigouvian taxes
   e. cap and trade programs
2. An efficient Pigouvian subsidy for a good is set equal to the good's
   a. external cost.
   b. external benefit.
   c. marginal external cost.
   d. price at which $MSC = MSB$.

3. Which of the following is true in the case of a positive externality?
   a. The optimal amount of the good is reached without government intervention.
   b. Society would prefer more of the good to be produced.
   c. Markets provide too much of the external benefit.
   d. The government can increase production with a Pigouvian tax.
   e. All of the above.

4. One example of a source of external benefits is
   a. technology spillover.
   b. traffic congestion.
   c. pollution.
   d. subsidies for polluters.
   e. taxes on environmental conservation.

5. Which of the following goods provides network externalities to users?
   I. Facebook
   II. Twitter
   III. Alternative sources of energy
   a. I only
   b. II only
   c. III only
   d. I and II
   e. I, II, and III

Critical-Thinking Question

The use of plastic water bottles creates a negative externality by increasing pollution and the amount of material sent into a landfill. Suppose we imposed a tax of $0.50 for each water bottle purchased in the United States. Would that be an efficient Pigouvian tax? Why or why not?

Public Goods and Common Resources

Telekhovskyi/Shutterstock

WHAT YOU WILL LEARN

1. How public goods are characterized and why markets fail to supply efficient quantities of them
2. What common resources are and why they are overused
3. What artificially scarce goods are and why they are underconsumed

In this module, we take a somewhat different approach to the question of why markets sometimes fail. Here we focus on how the characteristics of goods often determine whether markets can deliver them efficiently. When goods have the "wrong" characteristics, the resulting market failures resemble those associated with externalities or market power.

This alternative way of looking at sources of inefficiency deepens our understanding of why markets sometimes don't work well and how government can take actions that improve the welfare of society.

Private Goods—and Others

What's the difference between installing a new bathroom in a house and building a municipal sewage system? What's the difference between growing wheat and fishing in the open ocean?

These aren't trick questions. In each case there is a basic difference in the characteristics of the goods involved. Bathroom appliances and wheat have the characteristics necessary to allow markets to work efficiently. Public sewage systems and fish in the sea do not.

Let's look at these crucial characteristics and why they matter.

Characteristics of Goods

Goods like bathroom fixtures and wheat have two characteristics that are essential if a good is to be provided in efficient quantities by a market economy.

A good is **excludable** if the supplier of that good can prevent people who do not pay from consuming it.

A good is **rival in consumption** if the same unit of the good cannot be consumed by more than one person at the same time.

A good that is both excludable and rival in consumption is a **private good.**

When a good is **nonexcludable,** the supplier cannot prevent consumption by people who do not pay for it.

A good is **nonrival in consumption** if more than one person can consume the same unit of the good at the same time.

- They are **excludable:** suppliers of the good can prevent people who don't pay from consuming it.
- They are **rival in consumption:** the same unit of the good cannot be consumed by more than one person at the same time.

When a good is both excludable and rival in consumption, it is called a **private good.** Wheat is an example of a private good. It is *excludable:* the farmer can sell a bushel to one consumer without having to provide wheat to everyone in the county. And it is *rival in consumption:* if I eat bread baked with a farmer's wheat, that wheat cannot be consumed by someone else.

But not all goods possess these two characteristics. Some goods are **nonexcludable**—the supplier cannot prevent consumption of the good by people who do not pay for it. Fire protection is one example: a fire department that puts out fires before they spread protects the whole city, not just people who have made contributions to the Firemen's Benevolent Association. An improved environment is another: pollution can't be ended for some users of a river while leaving the river foul for others.

Nor are all goods rival in consumption. Goods are **nonrival in consumption** if more than one person can consume the same unit of the good at the same time. TV programs are nonrival in consumption: your decision to watch a show does not prevent other people from watching the same show.

Because goods can be either excludable or nonexcludable, and either rival or nonrival in consumption, there are four types of goods, illustrated by the matrix in Figure 38-1:

- *Private goods,* which are excludable and rival in consumption, like wheat
- *Public goods,* which are nonexcludable and nonrival in consumption, like a public sewer system
- *Common resources,* which are nonexcludable but rival in consumption, like clean water in a river
- *Artificially scarce goods,* which are excludable but nonrival in consumption, like on-demand movies on satellite TV

FIGURE 38-1 Four Types of Goods

There are four types of goods. The type of a good depends on (1) whether or not it is excludable—whether a producer can prevent someone from consuming it; and (2) whether or not it is rival in consumption—whether it is impossible for the same unit of a good to be consumed by more than one person at the same time.

	Rival in consumption	Nonrival in consumption
Excludable	**Private goods** • Wheat • Bathroom fixtures	**Artificially scarce goods** • Pay-per-view movies • Computer software
Non-excludable	**Common resources** • Clean water • Biodiversity	**Public goods** • Public sanitation • National defense

There are, of course, many other characteristics that distinguish between types of goods—necessities versus luxuries, normal versus inferior, and so on. Why focus on whether goods are excludable and rival in consumption?

Why Markets Can Supply Only Private Goods Efficiently

As we learned in earlier modules, markets are typically the best means for a society to deliver goods and services to its members; that is, markets are efficient except in the case of market power, externalities, or other instances of market failure. One source

of market failure is rooted in the nature of the good itself: markets cannot supply goods and services efficiently unless they are private goods—excludable and rival in consumption.

Goods that are nonexcludable suffer from the **free-rider problem:** individuals have no incentive to pay for their own consumption and instead will take a "free ride" on anyone who does pay.

To see why excludability is crucial, suppose that a farmer had only two choices: either produce no wheat or provide a bushel of wheat to every resident of the county who wants it, whether or not that resident pays for it. It seems unlikely that anyone would grow wheat under those conditions.

Yet the operator of a public sewage system faces pretty much the same problem as our hypothetical farmer. A sewage system makes the whole city cleaner and healthier—but that benefit accrues to all the city's residents, whether or not they pay the system operator.

The general point is that if a good is nonexcludable, rational consumers won't be willing to pay for it—they will take a "free ride" on anyone who *does* pay. So there is a **free-rider problem.** Examples of the free-rider problem are familiar from daily life. One example you may have encountered happens when students are required to do a group project. There is often a tendency of some group members to shirk their responsibilities, relying on others in the group to get the work done. The shirkers *free-ride* on someone else's effort.

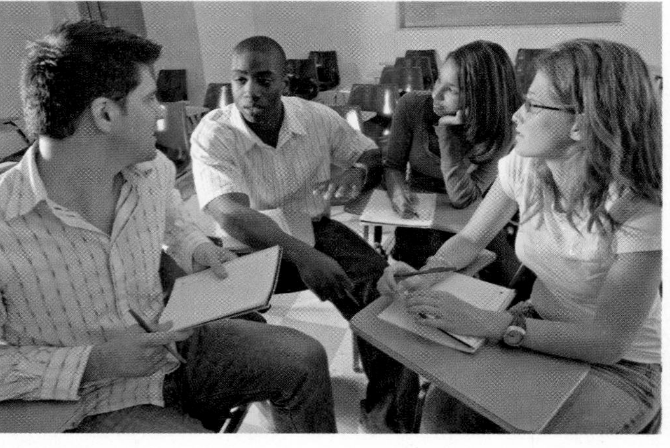
Purestock/Thinkstock

When the benefits from a group project are nonexcludable, there is a temptation to free-ride on the efforts of others.

Because of the free-rider problem, the forces of self-interest alone do not lead to an efficient level of production for a nonexcludable good. Even though consumers would benefit from increased production of the good, no one individual is willing to pay for more, and so no producer is willing to supply it. The result is that nonexcludable goods suffer from *inefficiently low production* in a market economy. In fact, in the face of the free-rider problem, self-interest may not ensure that any amount of the good—let alone the efficient quantity—is produced.

Goods that are excludable and nonrival in consumption, like pay-per-view movies, suffer from a different kind of inefficiency. As long as a good is excludable, it is possible to earn a profit by making it available only to those who pay. Therefore, producers are willing to supply an excludable good. But the marginal cost of letting an additional viewer watch a pay-per-view movie is zero because it is nonrival in consumption. So the efficient price to the consumer is also zero—or, to put it another way, individuals should watch pay-per-view movies up to the point where their marginal benefit is zero.

But if a satellite TV provider actually charges viewers $4, viewers will consume the good only up to the point where their marginal benefit is $4. When consumers must pay a price greater than zero for a good that is nonrival in consumption, the price they pay is higher than the marginal cost of allowing them to consume that good, which is zero. So in a market economy goods that are nonrival in consumption suffer from *inefficiently low consumption.*

Now we can see why private goods are the only goods that will be produced and consumed in efficient quantities in a competitive market. (That is, a private good will be produced and consumed in efficient quantities in a market free of market power, externalities, and other sources of market failure.) Because private goods are excludable, producers can charge for them and so have an incentive to produce them. And because they are also rival in consumption, it is efficient for consumers to pay a positive price—a price equal to the marginal cost of production. If one or both of these characteristics are lacking, a market economy will lack the incentives to bring about efficient quantities of the good.

Fortunately for the market system, most goods are private goods. Food, clothing, shelter, and most other desirable things in life are excludable and rival in consumption, so markets can provide us with most things. Yet there are crucial goods that don't meet these criteria—and in most cases, that means that the government must step in.

A **public good** is both nonexcludable and nonrival in consumption.

Public Goods

A **public good** is the exact opposite of a private good: it is both nonexcludable and nonrival in consumption. A public sewage system is an example of a public good: you can't keep a river clean without making it clean for everyone who lives near its banks, and my protection from sewage contamination does not prevent my neighbor from being protected as well.

Here are some other examples of public goods:

- *Disease prevention.* When a disease is stamped out, no one can be excluded from the benefit, and one person's health doesn't prevent others from being healthy.
- *National defense.* A strong military protects all citizens.
- *Scientific research.* In many cases new findings provide widespread benefits that are not excludable or rival.

Because these goods are nonexcludable, they suffer from the free-rider problem, so private firms would produce inefficiently low quantities of them. And because they are nonrival in consumption, it would be inefficient to charge people for consuming them. As a result, society must find nonmarket methods for providing these goods.

Providing Public Goods

Public goods are provided in a variety of ways. The government doesn't always get involved—in many cases a nongovernmental solution has been found for the free-rider problem. But these solutions are usually imperfect in some way.

Some public goods are supplied through voluntary contributions. For example, private donations help support public radio and a considerable amount of scientific research. But private donations are insufficient to finance large programs of great importance, such as the Centers for Disease Control and Prevention and national defense.

Some public goods are supplied by self-interested individuals or firms because those who produce them are able to make money in an indirect way. The classic example is broadcast television, which in the United States is supported entirely by advertising. The downside of such indirect funding is that it skews the nature and quantity of the public goods that are supplied, while imposing additional costs on consumers. TV stations show the programs that yield the most advertising revenue (that is, programs best suited for selling antacids, hair-loss remedies, antihistamines, and the like to the segment of the population that buys them), which are not necessarily the programs people most want to see. And viewers must endure many commercials.

Government provides public goods like national defense and the legal system.

Oleg Zabielin/Shutterstock

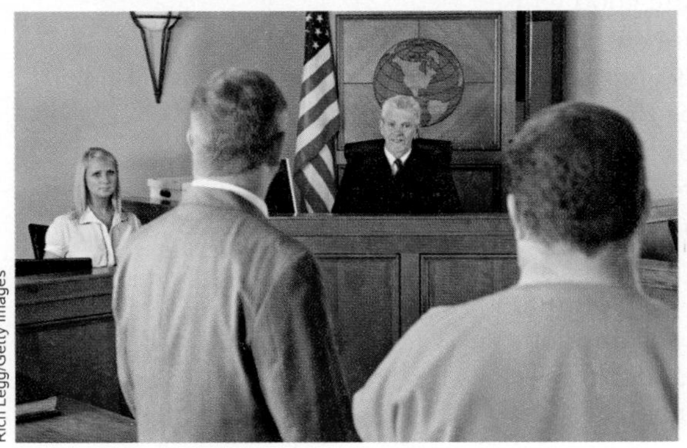

Rich Legg/Getty Images

Some potentially public goods are deliberately made excludable and therefore subject to charge, like pay-per-view movies. However, as noted earlier, when suppliers charge a price greater than zero for a nonrival good, consumers will consume an inefficiently low quantity of that good.

In small communities, a high level of social encouragement or pressure can be brought to bear on people to contribute money or time to provide the efficient level of a public good. Volunteer fire departments, which depend both on the volunteered services of the firefighters themselves and on contributions from local residents, are a good example. But as communities grow larger and more anonymous, social pressure is increasingly difficult to apply, compelling larger towns and cities to tax residents and depend on salaried firefighters for fire protection services.

As this last example suggests, when other solutions fail, it is up to the government to provide public goods. Indeed, the most important public goods—national defense, the legal system, disease control, fire protection in large cities, and so on—are provided by government and paid for by taxes. Economic theory tells us that the provision of public goods is one of the crucial roles of government.

How Much of a Public Good Should Be Provided?

In some cases, the provision of a public good is an "either–or" decision: a city can either have a sewage system—or not. But in most cases, governments must decide not only whether to provide a public good but also *how much* of that public good to provide. For example, street cleaning is a public good—but how often should the streets be cleaned? Once a month? Twice a month? Every other day?

Imagine a city with only two residents, Ted and Alice. Assume that the public good in question is street cleaning and that Ted and Alice truthfully tell the government how much they value a unit of the public good, one unit being one street cleaning per month. Specifically, each of them tells the government his or her *willingness to pay* for another unit of the public good supplied—an amount that corresponds to that *individual's marginal benefit* from another unit of the public good.

Using this information along with information on the cost of providing the good, the government can use marginal analysis to find the efficient level of providing the public good: the level at which the *marginal social benefit* of the public good is equal to the marginal social cost of producing it. Recall that the marginal social benefit of a good is the benefit that accrues to society as a whole from the consumption of one additional unit of the good.

But what is the marginal social benefit of another unit of a public good—a unit that generates utility for *all* consumers, not just one consumer, because it is nonexcludable and nonrival in consumption?

This question leads us to an important principle: *In the special case of a public good, the marginal social benefit of a unit of the good is equal to the sum of the individual marginal benefits enjoyed by all consumers of that unit.* Or to consider it from a slightly different angle, if a consumer could be compelled to pay for a unit before consuming it (the good is made excludable), then the marginal social benefit of a unit is equal to the *sum* of each consumer's willingness to pay for that unit. Using this principle, the marginal social benefit of an additional street cleaning per month is equal to Ted's individual marginal benefit from that additional cleaning *plus* Alice's individual marginal benefit.

Why? Because a public good is nonrival in consumption—Ted's benefit from a cleaner street does not diminish Alice's benefit from that same clean street, and vice versa. Because people can simultaneously consume the same unit of street cleaning, the marginal social benefit is the *sum* of their individual marginal benefits. And the efficient quantity of a public good is the quantity at which the marginal social benefit is equal to the marginal social cost of providing it.

© a-ts/Alamy

We all benefit when someone else does the cleaning up.

Figure 38-2 illustrates the efficient provision of a public good, showing three marginal benefit curves. Panel (a) shows Ted's individual marginal benefit curve from street cleaning, MB_T: he would be willing to pay \$25 for the city to clean its streets once a month, an additional \$18 to have it done a second time, and so on. Panel (b) shows Alice's individual marginal benefit curve from street cleaning, MB_A. Panel (c) shows the marginal social benefit curve from street cleaning, *MSB*: it is the vertical sum of Ted's and Alice's individual marginal benefit curves, MB_T and MB_A.

To maximize society's welfare, the government should increase the quantity of street cleanings until the marginal social benefit of an additional cleaning would fall below the marginal social cost. Suppose that the marginal social cost is \$6 per cleaning. Then the city should clean its streets 5 times per month, because the marginal social benefit of each of the first 5 cleanings is more than \$6, but going from 5 to 6 cleanings would yield a marginal social benefit of only \$2, which is less than the marginal social cost.

One basic rationale for the existence of government is that it provides a way for citizens to tax themselves in order to provide public goods—particularly a vital public good like national defense. Responsible governments try to estimate both the social

FIGURE 38-2 A Public Good

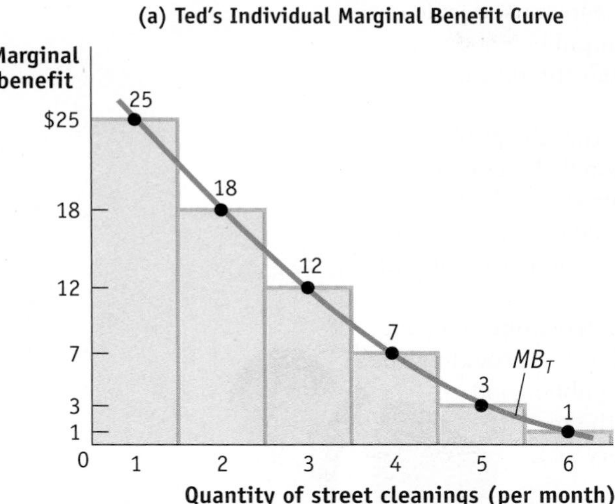

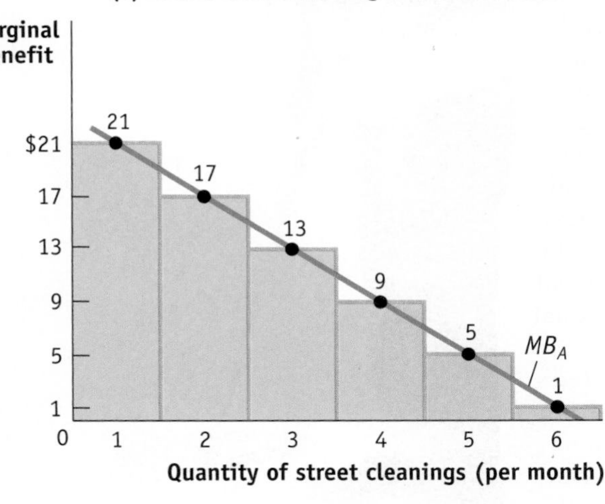

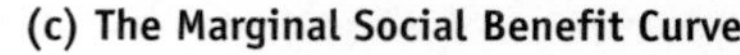

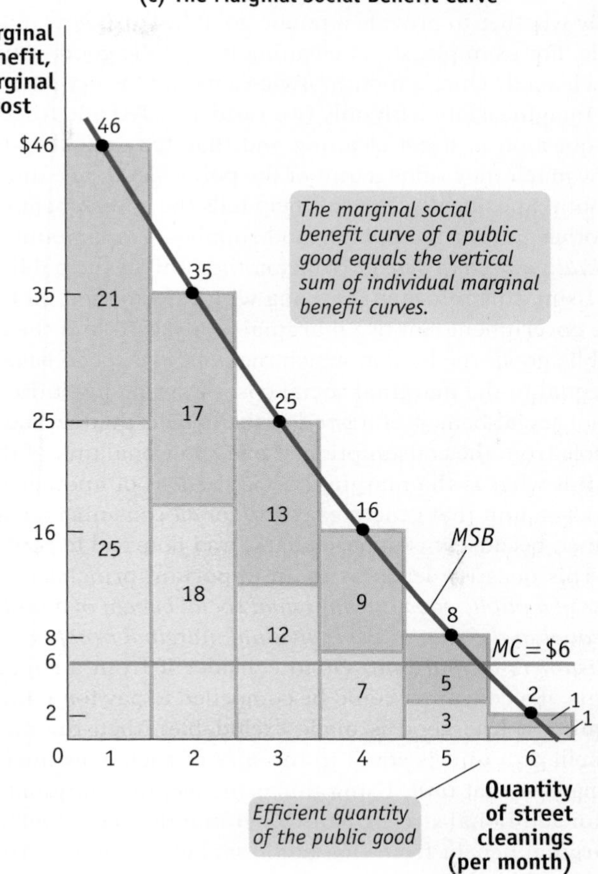

Panel (a) shows Ted's individual marginal benefit curve of street cleanings per month, MB_T, and panel (b) shows Alice's individual marginal benefit curve, MB_A. Panel (c) shows the marginal social benefit of the public good, equal to the sum of the individual marginal benefits to all consumers (in this case, Ted and Alice). The marginal social benefit curve, *MSB*, is the vertical sum of the individual marginal benefit curves MB_T and MB_A. At a constant marginal social cost of $6, there should be 5 street cleanings per month, because the marginal social benefit of going from 4 to 5 cleanings is $8 ($3 for Ted plus $5 for Alice), but the marginal social benefit of going from 5 to 6 cleanings is only $2.

benefits and the social costs of providing a public good, a process known as *cost-benefit analysis*.

Of course, if society really consisted of only two individuals, they would probably manage to strike a deal to provide the good. But imagine a city with a million residents, each of whose marginal benefit from a good is only a tiny fraction of the marginal social benefit. It would be impossible for people to reach a voluntary agreement to pay for the efficient level of a good like street cleaning—the potential for free-riding would make it too difficult to make and enforce an agreement among so many people. But they could and would vote to tax themselves to pay for a citywide sanitation department.

ECONOMICS IN ACTION

VOTING AS A PUBLIC GOOD

It's a sad fact that many Americans who are eligible to vote don't bother to. As a result, their interests tend to be ignored by politicians. But what's even sadder is that this self-defeating behavior may be completely rational.

As the economist Mancur Olson pointed out in a famous book titled *The Logic of Collective Action,* voting is a public good, one that suffers from severe free-rider problems.

Imagine that you are one of a million people who would stand to gain the equivalent of $100 each if some plan is passed in a statewide referendum—say, a plan to improve public schools. And suppose that the opportunity cost of the time it would take you to vote is $10. Will you be sure to go to the polls and vote for the referendum?

If you are rational, the answer is no! The reason is that it is very unlikely that your vote will decide the issue, either way. If the measure passes, you benefit, even if you didn't bother to vote—the benefits are nonexcludable. If the measure doesn't pass, your vote would not have changed the outcome. Either way, by not voting—by free-riding on those who do vote—you save $10.

Of course, many people do vote out of a sense of civic duty. But because political action is a public good, in general people devote too little effort to defending their own interests.

The result, Olson pointed out, is that when a large group of people share a common political interest, they are likely to exert too little effort promoting their cause and so will be ignored. Conversely, small, well-organized interest groups that act on issues narrowly targeted in their favor tend to have disproportionate power.

Is this a reason to distrust democracy? Winston Churchill said it best: "Democracy is the worst form of government, except for all the other forms that have been tried."

YOUR VOTE COUNTS

iStockphoto

Common Resources

A **common resource** is a good that is nonexcludable but is rival in consumption. An example is the stock of fish in a fishing area, like the fisheries off the coast of New England. Traditionally, anyone who had a boat could go out to sea and catch fish—fish in the sea were a nonexcludable good. Yet the total number of fish is limited: the fish that one person catches are no longer available to be caught by someone else. So fish in the sea are rival in consumption.

Other examples of common resources include clean air, water, and the diversity of animal and plant species on the planet (biodiversity). In each of these cases the fact that the good is rival in consumption, and yet nonexcludable, poses a serious problem.

The Problem of Overuse

Because common resources are nonexcludable, individuals cannot be charged for their use. But the resources are rival in consumption, so an individual who uses a unit depletes the resource by making that unit unavailable to others. As a result, a common resource is subject to **overuse:** an individual will continue to use it until his or her marginal benefit is equal to his or her individual marginal cost, ignoring the cost that this action inflicts on society as a whole.

Fish are a classic example of a common resource. Particularly in heavily fished waters, my fishing imposes a cost on others by reducing the fish population and making it harder for others to catch fish. But I have no personal incentive to take this cost into account, since I cannot be charged for fishing. As a result, from society's point of view, I catch too many fish.

A **common resource** is nonexcludable and rival in consumption: you can't stop me from consuming the good, and more consumption by me means less of the good available for you.

Overuse is the depletion of a common resource that occurs when individuals ignore the fact that their use depletes the amount of the resource remaining for others.

Traffic congestion is another example of overuse of a common resource. A major highway during rush hour can accommodate only a certain number of vehicles per hour. If I decide to drive to work alone rather than carpool or work at home, I cause many other people to have a longer commute; but I have no incentive to take these consequences into account.

In the case of a common resource, the *marginal social cost* of my use of that resource is higher than my *individual marginal cost,* the cost to me of using an additional unit of the good. Figure 38-3 illustrates this point. It shows the demand curve for fish, which measures the marginal benefit of fish (as well as the marginal social benefit because there are no external benefits from catching and consuming fish).

FIGURE 38-3 **A Common Resource**

The supply curve *S*, which shows the individual marginal cost of production of the fishing industry, is composed of the individual supply curves of the individual fishermen. But each fisherman's individual marginal cost does not include the cost that his or her actions impose on others: the depletion of the common resource. As a result, the marginal social cost curve, *MSC*, lies above the supply curve; in an unregulated market, the quantity of the common resource used, Q_{MKT}, exceeds the efficient quantity of use, Q_{OPT}.

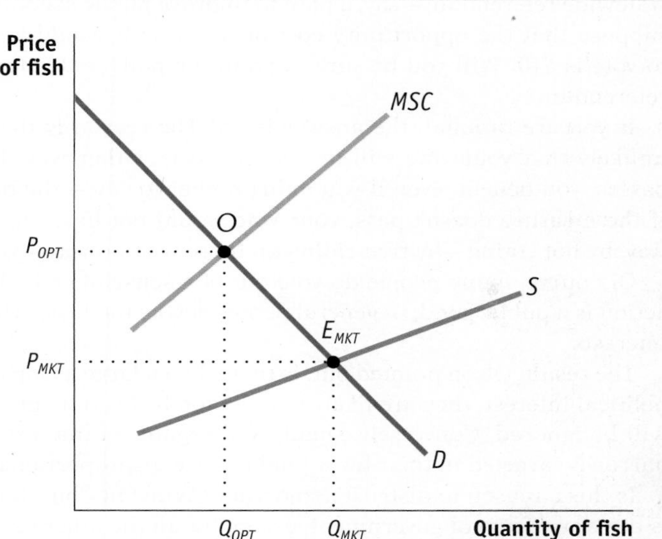

The figure also shows the supply curve for fish, which measures the marginal cost of production of the fishing industry. We know that the industry supply curve is the horizontal sum of each individual fisherman's supply curve—equivalent to his or her individual marginal cost curve. The fishing industry supplies the quantity Q_{MKT} at which its marginal cost equals the price. But the efficient quantity is Q_{OPT}, the quantity of fish that equates the marginal social benefit (as reflected by the demand curve) to the marginal social cost, not to the fishing industry's marginal cost of production. Thus, the market outcome results in overuse of the common resource.

As we noted, there is a close parallel between the problem of managing a common resource and the problem posed by negative externalities. In the case of an activity that generates a negative externality, the marginal social cost of production is greater than the marginal cost of production, the difference being the marginal external cost imposed on society. Here, the loss to society arising from a fisher's depletion of the common resource plays the same role as the external cost when there is a negative externality. In fact, many negative externalities (such as pollution) can be thought of as involving common resources (such as clean air).

The Efficient Use and Maintenance of a Common Resource

Because common resources pose problems similar to those created by negative externalities, the solutions are also similar. To ensure efficient use of a common resource, society must find a way to get individual users of the resource to take into account the costs they impose on others. This is the same principle as that of getting individuals to internalize a negative externality that arises from their actions.

There are three principal ways to induce people who use common resources to internalize the costs they impose on others:

1. Tax or otherwise regulate the use of the common resource
2. Create a system of tradable licenses for the right to use the common resource
3. Make the common resource excludable and assign property rights to some individuals

If it weren't for fees and restrictions, some common resources would be overrun.

TAX AND REGULATE Like activities that generate negative externalities, use of a common resource can be reduced to the efficient quantity by imposing a Pigouvian tax. For example, some countries have imposed "congestion charges" on those who drive during rush hour, in effect charging them for the use of highway space, a common resource. Likewise, visitors to national parks in the United States must pay an entry fee that is essentially a Pigouvian tax.

CREATE A SYSTEM OF TRADABLE LICENSES Another way to correct the problem of overuse is to create a system of tradable licenses for the use of the common resource, much like the systems designed to address negative externalities. The policy maker issues the number of licenses that corresponds to the efficient level of use of the good. Making the licenses tradable ensures that the right to use the good is allocated efficiently—that is, those who end up using the good (those willing to pay the most for a license) are those who gain the most from its use.

ASSIGN PROPERTY RIGHTS But when it comes to common resources, often the most natural solution is simply to assign property rights. At a fundamental level, common resources are subject to overuse because *nobody owns them.* The essence of ownership of a good—the *property right* over the good—is that you can limit who can and cannot use the good as well as how much of it can be used.

When a good is nonexcludable, in a very real sense no one owns it because a property right cannot be enforced—and consequently no one has an incentive to use it efficiently. So one way to correct the problem of overuse is to make the good excludable and assign property rights over it to someone. The good now has an owner who has an incentive to protect the value of the good—to use it efficiently rather than overuse it. This solution is applicable when currently nonexcludable goods can be made excludable, as with the privatization of parks and even roads, but it cannot be applied to resources that are inherently nonexcludable, including the air and flowing water.

Artificially Scarce Goods

An **artificially scarce good** is a good that is excludable but nonrival in consumption. As we've already seen, pay-per-view movies are a familiar example. The marginal cost to society of allowing an individual to watch a movie is zero because one person's viewing doesn't interfere with other people's viewing. Yet satellite TV providers prevent an individual from seeing a movie if he or she hasn't paid. Goods like computer software and audio files, which are valued for the information they embody (and are sometimes called *information goods*), are also artificially scarce.

Markets will supply artificially scarce goods because their excludability allows firms to charge people for them. However, since the efficient price is equal to the marginal cost of zero and the actual price is something higher than that, the good is "artificially scarce" and consumption is inefficiently low. The problem is that, unless the producer can somehow earn revenue from producing and selling the good, none will be produced, which is likely to be worse than a positive but inefficiently low quantity.

We have seen that, in the cases of public goods, common resources, and artificially scarce goods, a market economy will not provide adequate incentives for efficient levels of production and consumption. Fortunately for the sake of market efficiency, most goods are private goods. Food, clothing, shelter, and most other desirable things in life are excludable and rival in consumption, so the types of market failure discussed in this module are important exceptions rather than the norm.

An **artificially scarce good** is a good that is excludable but nonrival in consumption.

MODULE 38 Review

Solutions appear at the back of the book.

Check Your Understanding

1. For each of the following goods, indicate whether it is excludable, whether it is rival in consumption, and what kind of good it is.
   a. a public space such as a park
   b. a cheese burrito
   c. information from a website that is password-protected
   d. publicly announced information about the path of an incoming hurricane
2. Which of the goods in Question 1 will be provided by a private producer without government intervention? Which will not be? Explain your answer.
3. The town of Centreville, population 16, has two types of residents, Homebodies and Revelers. Using the accompanying table, the town must decide how much to spend on its New Year's Eve party. No individual resident expects to directly bear the cost of the party.
   a. Suppose there are 10 Homebodies and 6 Revelers. Determine the marginal social benefit schedule of money spent on the party. What is the efficient level of spending?
   b. Suppose there are 6 Homebodies and 10 Revelers. How do your answers to part a change? Explain.
   c. Suppose that the individual marginal benefit schedules are known but no one knows the true proportion of Homebodies versus Revelers. Individuals are asked their preferences. What is the likely outcome if each person assumes that others will pay for any additional amount of the public good? Why is it likely to result in an inefficiently high level of spending? Explain.

Money spent on party	Individual marginal benefit of additional $1 spent on party: Homebody	Reveler
$0		
	$0.05	$0.13
1		
	0.04	0.11
2		
	0.03	0.09
3		
	0.02	0.07
4		

4. Rocky Mountain Forest is a government-owned forest in which private citizens were allowed in the past to harvest as much timber as they wanted free of charge. State in economic terms why this is problematic from society's point of view.
5. You are the new Forest Service Commissioner and have been instructed to come up with ways to preserve the Rocky Mountain Forest for the general public. Name three different methods you could use to maintain the efficient level of tree harvesting and explain how each would work. For each method, what information would you need to know in order to achieve an efficient outcome?

Multiple-Choice Questions

1. Which of the following types of goods are always nonrival in consumption?
   a. public goods
   b. private goods
   c. common resources
   d. inferior goods
   e. goods provided by the government
2. The free-rider problem occurs in the case of
   a. private goods.
   b. common resources.
   c. artificially scarce goods.
   d. motorcycles.
   e. all of the above.
3. Public goods are sometimes provided through which of the following means?
   I. voluntary contributions
   II. individual self-interest
   III. the government
   a. I only
   b. II only
   c. III only
   d. I and III only
   e. I, II, and III
4. Market provision of a public good will lead to
   a. the efficient quantity.
   b. the efficient price.

c. inefficiently high production of the good.
d. inefficiently low production of the good.
e. none of the good being provided.

5. The overuse of a common resource can be reduced by which of the following?
   a. a Pigouvian tax
   b. government regulations
   c. tradable licenses
   d. the assignment of property rights
   e. all of the above

Critical-Thinking Questions

1. Identify and explain the two characteristics shared by every public good.
2. Suppose a new resident moves to a community that purchases a public good for the benefit of every member of the community. What is the additional cost of providing the public good to the new community member? Explain.

PITFALLS

THE MARGINAL COST OF WHAT EXACTLY?

? When we consider the marginal cost of a good that is nonrival in consumption, what exactly are we thinking about? What about a good that is rival in consumption?

> IN THE CASE OF A GOOD THAT IS NONRIVAL IN CONSUMPTION, WE COULD CONSIDER EITHER THE MARGINAL COST OF *PRODUCING* A UNIT OF THE GOOD OR THE MARGINAL COST OF *ALLOWING* A UNIT OF THE GOOD *TO BE CONSUMED*. It is easy to confuse the two, but try not to. To help clarify the distinction, consider this example: the satellite TV provider DirecTV incurs a marginal cost in making a movie available to its subscribers that is equal to the cost of the resources it uses to produce and broadcast that movie. However, *once that movie is being broadcast,* no marginal cost is incurred by letting an additional family watch it. In other words, no costly resources are "used up" when one more family consumes a movie that has already been produced and is being broadcast.

This complication does not arise, however, when a good is rival in consumption. In this case, the resources used to produce a unit of the good are "used up" by a person's consumption of it—they are no longer available to satisfy someone else's consumption. So when a good is rival in consumption, the marginal cost to society of allowing an individual to consume a unit is equal to the resource cost of producing that unit—that is, equal to the marginal cost of producing it.

39 The Economics of the Welfare State

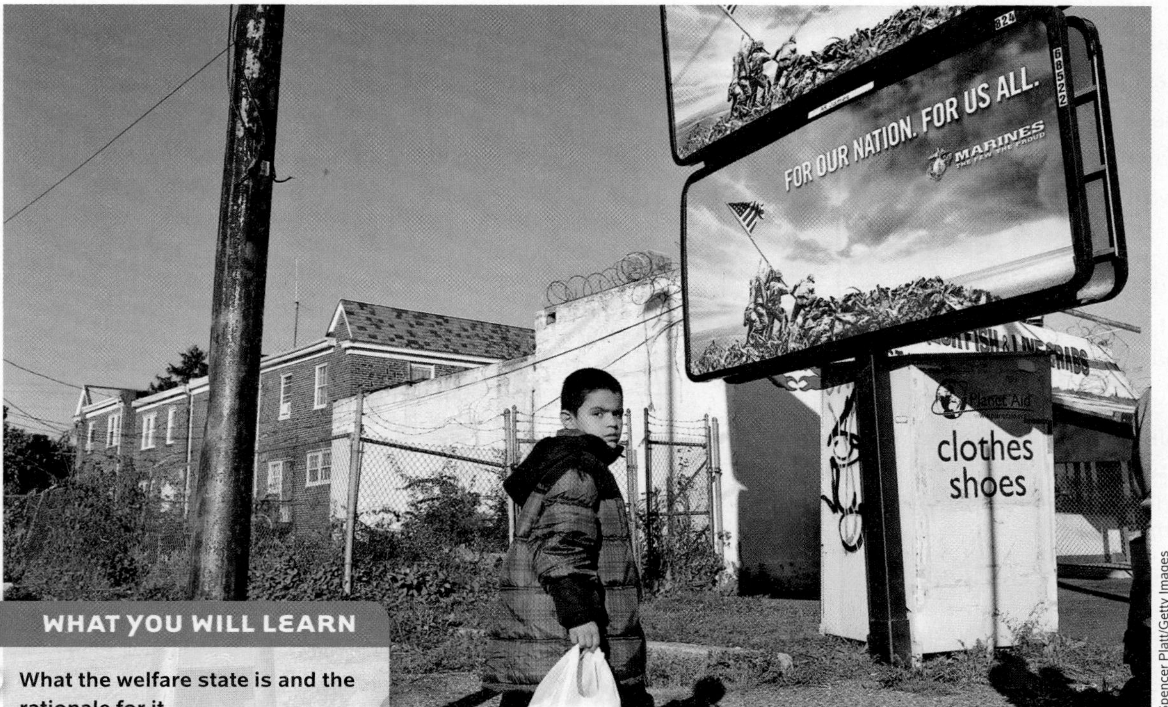

Spencer Platt/Getty Images

WHAT YOU WILL LEARN

1. What the welfare state is and the rationale for it
2. What defines poverty, what causes poverty, and the consequences of poverty
3. How income inequality in America has changed over time
4. How programs like Social Security, Medicare, and Medicaid affect poverty and income inequality
5. Why there are political differences and debate over the size of the welfare state

Poverty, Inequality, and Public Policy

The term **welfare state** has come to refer to the collection of government programs that are designed to alleviate economic hardship. A large share of the government spending of all wealthy countries consists of **government transfers**—payments by the government to individuals and families—that provide financial aid to the poor, assistance to unemployed workers, guaranteed income for the elderly, and assistance in paying medical bills for those with large health care expenses.

In this module, we discuss the underlying rationale for welfare state programs. We'll look at the the two main kinds of programs operating in the United States: income support programs, of which Social Security is by far the largest, and health care programs, dominated by Medicare and Medicaid. We conclude by evaluating the effectiveness of these programs.

The Logic of the Welfare State

There are three major economic rationales for the creation of the welfare state. We'll turn now to a discussion of each.

1. ALLEVIATING INCOME INEQUALITY Suppose that the Taylor family, which has an income of only $15,000 a year, received a government check for $1,500. This check might allow the Taylors to afford a better place to live, eat a more nutritious diet, or in other ways significantly improve their quality of life. Also suppose that the Fisher family, which has an income of $300,000 a year, faced an extra tax of $1,500. This probably wouldn't make much difference to their quality of life: at worst, they might have to give up a few minor luxuries.

The **welfare state** is the collection of government programs designed to alleviate economic hardship.

A **government transfer** is a government payment to an individual or a family.

income inequality by helping the poor; **social insurance programs** alleviate economic insecurity. Welfare state programs also deliver external benefits to society through poverty reduction and improved access to health care, particularly for children.

14. Despite the fact that the **poverty threshold** is adjusted according to the cost of living but not according to the standard of living, and that the average American income has risen substantially over the last 30 years, the **poverty rate,** the percentage of the population with an income below the poverty threshold, is no lower than it was 30 years ago. There are various causes of poverty: lack of education, the legacy of discrimination, and bad luck. The consequences of poverty are particularly harmful for children.

15. **Median household income,** the income of a family at the center of the income distribution, is a better indicator of the income of the typical household than **mean household income** because it is not distorted by the inclusion of a small number of very wealthy households. The **Gini coefficient,** a number that summarizes a country's level of income inequality based on how unequally income is distributed across quintiles, is used to compare income inequality across countries.

16. Both **means-tested** and non-means-tested programs reduce poverty. The major **in-kind benefits** programs are Medicare and Medicaid, which pay for medical care. Due to concerns about the effects on incentives to work and on family cohesion, aid to poor families has become significantly less generous even as the **negative income tax** has become more generous. Social Security, the largest U.S. welfare state program, has significantly reduced poverty among the elderly. Unemployment insurance is also a key social insurance program.

17. Most Americans are covered by employment-based private health insurance; the majority of the remaining are covered by Medicare (for those over 65) or Medicaid (for those with low incomes). The Patient Protection and Affordable Care Act (ACA) was passed in 2010 with the objectives of reducing the number of uninsured and reducing the rate of growth of health care costs.

18. Debates over the size of the welfare state are based on philosophical and equity-versus-efficiency considerations. Although high marginal tax rates to finance an extensive welfare state can reduce the incentive to work, means-testing of programs in order to reduce the cost of the welfare state can also reduce the incentive to work unless carefully designed to avoid notches.

19. Politicians on the left tend to favor a bigger welfare state and those on the right to oppose it. This left–right distinction is central to today's politics.

Key Terms

Problems

1. What type of externality (positive or negative) is present in each of the following examples? Is the marginal social benefit of the activity greater than or equal to the marginal benefit to the individual? Is the marginal social cost of the activity greater than or equal to the marginal cost to the individual? Without intervention, will there be too little or too much (relative to what would be socially optimal) of this activity?

   a. Mr. Chau plants lots of colorful flowers in his front yard.

   b. Your next-door neighbor likes to build bonfires in his backyard, and sparks often drift onto your house.

   c. Maija, who lives next to an apple orchard, decides to keep bees to produce honey.

   d. Justine buys a large SUV that consumes a lot of gasoline.

2. The loud music coming from the sorority next to your dorm is a negative externality that can be directly quantified. The accompanying table shows the marginal social benefit and the marginal social cost per decibel (dB, a measure of volume) of music.

Volume of music (dB)	Marginal social benefit of dB	Marginal social cost of dB
90		
	$36	$0
91		
	30	2
92		
	24	4
93		
	18	6
94		
	12	8
95		
	6	10
96		
	0	12
97		

 a. Draw the marginal social benefit curve and the marginal social cost curve. Use your diagram to determine the socially optimal volume of music.

 b. Only the members of the sorority benefit from the music and they bear none of the cost. Which volume of music will they choose?

 c. The college imposes a Pigouvian tax of $3 per decibel of music played. From your diagram, determine the volume of music the sorority will now choose.

3. Many dairy farmers in California are adopting a new technology that allows them to produce their own electricity from methane gas captured from animal wastes. (One cow can produce up to 2 kilowatts a day.) This practice reduces the amount of methane gas released into the atmosphere. In addition to reducing their own utility bills, the farmers are allowed to sell any electricity they produce at favorable rates.

 a. Explain how the ability to earn money from capturing and transforming methane gas behaves like a Pigouvian tax on methane gas pollution and can lead dairy farmers to emit the efficient amount of methane gas pollution.

 b. Suppose some dairy farmers have lower costs of transforming methane into electricity than others. Explain how this system leads to an efficient allocation of emissions reduction among farmers.

4. According to a report from the U.S. Census Bureau, "the average [lifetime] earnings of a full-time, year round worker with a high school education are about $1.2 million compared with $2.1 million for a college graduate." This indicates that there is a considerable benefit to a graduate from investing in his or her own education. Tuition at most state universities covers only about two-thirds to three-quarters of the cost, so the state applies a Pigouvian subsidy to college education.

 If a Pigouvian subsidy is appropriate, is the externality created by a college education a positive or a negative externality? What does this imply about the differences between the costs and benefits to students compared to social costs and benefits? What are some reasons for the differences?

5. The city of Falls Church, Virginia, subsidizes trees planted in homeowners' front yards when they are within 15 feet of the street.

 a. Using concepts from this section, explain why a municipality would subsidize trees planted on private property, but near the street.

 b. Draw a diagram similar to Figure 37-3 that shows the marginal social benefit, the marginal social cost, and the optimal Pigouvian subsidy on trees.

6. Smoking produces a negative externality because it imposes a health risk on others who inhale second-hand smoke. Cigarette smoking also causes productivity losses to the economy due to the shorter expected life span of a smoker. The U.S. Centers for Disease Control and Prevention (CDC) has estimated the average social cost of smoking a single pack of cigarettes for different states by taking these negative externalities into account. Assume that the accompanying table provides the price of cigarettes and the estimated average social cost of smoking in five states.

State	Cigarette retail price with taxes (per pack)	CDC estimate of smoking cost in 2013 (per pack)
California	$4.40	$15.10
New York	5.82	21.91
Florida	3.80	10.14
Texas	4.76	9.94
Ohio	4.60	9.19

 a. At the current level of consumption, what is the optimal retail price of a pack of cigarettes in the different states? Is the current price below or above this optimal price? Does this suggest that the current level of consumption is too high or too low? Explain your answer.

 b. In order to deal with negative externalities, state governments currently impose excise taxes on cigarettes. Are current taxes set at the optimal level? Justify your answer.

 c. What is the correct size of an additional Pigouvian tax on cigarette sales in the different states if the CDC's estimate for smoking cost does not change with an increase in the retail price of cigarettes?

7. Fishing for sablefish has been so intensive that sablefish were threatened with extinction. After several years of banning such fishing, the government is now proposing to introduce tradable vouchers, each of which entitles its holder to a catch of a certain size. Explain how fishing generates a negative externality and how the voucher scheme may overcome the inefficiency created by this externality.

8. Which of the following are characterized by network externalities? Which are not? Explain.

 a. the choice between installing 110-volt electrical current in structures rather than 220-volt

b. the choice between purchasing a Toyota versus a Ford

c. the choice of a printer, where each printer requires its own specific type of ink cartridge

d. the choice of whether to purchase an iPod Touch or an iPod Nano.

9. The government is involved in providing many goods and services. For each of the goods or services listed, determine whether it is rival or nonrival in consumption and whether it is excludable or nonexcludable. What type of good is it? Without government involvement, would the quantity provided be efficient, inefficiently low, or inefficiently high?

a. street signs

b. Amtrak rail service

c. regulations limiting pollution

d. an interstate highway without tolls

e. a lighthouse on the coast

10. A residential community has 100 residents who are concerned about security. The accompanying table gives the total cost of hiring a 24-hour security service as well as each individual resident's total benefit.

Quantity of security guards	Total cost	Total individual benefit to each resident
0	$ 0	$ 0
1	150	10
2	300	16
3	450	18
4	600	19

a. Explain why the security service is a public good for the residents of the community.

b. Calculate the marginal cost, the individual marginal benefit for each resident, and the marginal social benefit.

c. If an individual resident were to decide about hiring and paying for security guards on his or her own, how many guards would that resident hire?

d. If the residents act together, how many security guards will they hire?

11. The accompanying table shows Tanisha's and Ari's individual marginal benefit of different numbers of street cleanings per month. Suppose that the marginal cost of street cleanings is constant at $9 each.

Quantity of street cleanings per month	Tanisha's individual marginal benefit	Ari's individual marginal benefit
0		
	$10	$8
1		
	6	4
2		
	2	1
3		

a. If Tanisha had to pay for street cleaning on her own, how many street cleanings would there be?

b. Calculate the marginal social benefit of street cleaning. What is the optimal number of street cleanings?

c. Consider the optimal number of street cleanings. The last street cleaning of that number costs $9. Is Tanisha willing to pay for that last cleaning on her own? Is Ari willing to pay for that last cleaning on his own?

12. Anyone with a radio receiver can listen to public radio, which is funded largely by donations.

a. Is public radio excludable or nonexcludable? Is it rival in consumption or nonrival? What type of good is it?

b. Should the government support public radio? Explain your reasoning.

c. In order to finance itself, public radio decides to transmit only to satellite radios, for which users have to pay a fee. What type of good is public radio then? Will the quantity of radio listening be efficient? Why or why not?

13. Your economics teacher assigns a group project for the course. Describe the free-rider problem that can lead to a suboptimal outcome for your group. To combat this problem, the instructor asks you to evaluate the contribution of your peers in a confidential report. Will this evaluation have the desired effects?

14. The accompanying table shows six consumers' willingness to pay (his or her individual marginal benefit) for one MP3 file copy of a Jay-Z album. The marginal cost of making the file accessible to one additional consumer is constant, at zero.

Consumer	Individual marginal benefit
Adriana	$ 2
Bhagesh	15
Chizuko	1
Denzel	10
Emma	5
Frank	4

a. What would be the efficient price to charge for a download of the file?

b. All six consumers are able to download the file for free from a file-sharing service, Pantster. Which consumers will download the file? What will be the total consumer surplus to those consumers?

c. Pantster is shut down for copyright law infringement. In order to download the file, consumers now have to pay $4.99 at a commercial music site. Which consumers will download the file? What will be the total consumer surplus to those consumers? How much producer surplus accrues to the commercial music site? What is the total surplus? What is the deadweight loss from the new pricing policy?

15. Software has historically been an artificially scarce good—it is nonrival because the cost of replication is negligible once the investment to write the code is made, but software companies make it excludable by charging for

user licenses. Recently, however, open-source software has emerged, most of which is free to download and can be modified and maintained by anyone.

a. Discuss the free-rider problem that might exist in the development of open-source software. What effect might this have on quality? Why does this problem not exist for proprietary software, such as the products of a company like Microsoft or Adobe?

b. Some argue that open-source software serves an unsatisfied market demand that proprietary software ignores. Draw a typical diagram that illustrates how proprietary software may be underproduced. Put the price and marginal cost of software on the vertical axis and the quantity of software on the horizontal axis. Draw a typical demand curve and a marginal cost curve (*MC*) that is always equal to zero. Assume that the software company charges a positive price, *P*, for the software. Label the equilibrium point and the efficient point.

16. The two dry-cleaning companies in Collegetown, College Cleaners and Big Green Cleaners, are a major source of air pollution. Together they currently produce 350 units of air pollution, which the town wants to reduce to 200 units. The accompanying table shows the current pollution level produced by each company and each company's marginal cost of reducing its pollution. The marginal cost is constant.

Company	Initial pollution level (units)	Marginal cost of reducing pollution (per unit)
College Cleaners	230	$5
Big Green Cleaners	120	2

a. Suppose that Collegetown passes an environmental standards law that limits each company to 100 units of pollution. What would be the total cost to the two companies of each reducing its pollution emissions to 100 units?

Suppose instead that Collegetown issues 100 pollution vouchers to each company, each entitling the company to one unit of pollution, and that these vouchers can be traded.

b. How much is each pollution voucher worth to College Cleaners? to Big Green Cleaners? (That is, how much would each company, at most, be willing to pay for one more voucher?)

c. Who will sell vouchers and who will buy them? How many vouchers will be traded?

d. What is the total cost to the two companies of the pollution controls under this voucher system?

17. Ronald owns a cattle farm at the source of a long river. His cattle's waste flows into the river and down many miles to where Carla lives. Carla gets her drinking water from the river. By allowing his cattle's waste to flow into the river, Ronald imposes a negative externality on Carla. In each of the two following cases, do you think that through negotiation, Ronald and Carla can find an efficient solution? What might this solution look like?

a. There are no telephones, and for Carla to talk to Ronald, she has to travel for two days on a rocky road.

b. Carla and Ronald both have e-mail access, making it costless for them to communicate.

18. In the city of Metropolis, there are 100 residents, each of whom lives until age 75. Residents of Metropolis have the following incomes over their lifetime: Through age 14, they earn nothing. From age 15 until age 29, they earn 200 metros (the currency of Metropolis) per year. From age 30 to age 49, they earn 400 metros. From age 50 to age 64, they earn 300 metros. Finally, at age 65 they retire and are paid a pension of 100 metros per year until they die at age 75. Each year, everyone consumes whatever their income is that year (that is, there is no saving and no borrowing). Currently, 20 residents are 10 years old, 20 residents are 20 years old, 20 residents are 40 years old, 20 residents are 60 years old, and 20 residents are 70 years old.

a. Study the income distribution among all residents of Metropolis. Split the population into quintiles according to their income. How much income does a resident in the lowest quintile have? In the second, third, fourth, and top quintiles? What share of total income of all residents goes to the residents in each quintile? Construct a table showing the share of total income that goes to each quintile. Does this income distribution show inequality?

b. Now look only at the 20 residents of Metropolis who are currently 40 years old, and study the income distribution among only those residents. Split those 20 residents into quintiles according to their income. How much income does a resident in the lowest quintile have? In the second, third, fourth, and top quintiles? What share of total income of all 40-year-olds goes to the residents in each quintile? Does this income distribution show inequality?

c. What is the relevance of these examples for assessing data on the distribution of income in any country?

19. The accompanying table presents data from the U.S. Census Bureau on median and mean income of male workers for the years 1972 and 2009. The income figures are adjusted to eliminate the effect of inflation.

Year	Median income (in 2009 dollars)	Mean income (in 2009 dollars)
1972	$34,159	$39,593
2009	32,184	46,800

Source: U.S. Census Bureau.

a. By what percentage has median income changed over this period? By what percentage has mean income changed over this period?

b. Between 1972 and 2009, has the income distribution become less or more unequal? Explain.

20. There are 100 households in the economy of Equalor. Initially, 99 of them have an income of $10,000 each, and one household has an income of $1,010,000.

a. What is the median income in this economy? What is the mean income?

Through its poverty programs, the government of Equalor now redistributes income: it takes $990,000 away from the richest household and distributes it equally among the remaining 99 households.

b. What is the median income in this economy now? What is the mean income? Has the median income changed? Has the mean income changed? Which indicator (mean or median household income) is a better indicator of the typical Equalorian household's income? Explain.

21. The tax system in Taxilvania includes a negative income tax. For all incomes below $10,000, individuals pay an income tax of –40% (that is, they receive a payment of 40% of their income). For any income above the $10,000 threshold, the tax rate on that additional income is 10%. For the first three scenarios below, calculate the amount of income tax to be paid and after-tax income.

a. Lowani earns income of $8,000.

b. Midram earns income of $40,000.

c. Hi-Wan earns income of $100,000.

d. Can you find a notch in this tax system? That is, can you find a situation where earning more pre-tax income actually results in less after-tax income?

22. In the city of Notchingham, each worker is paid a wage rate of $10 per hour. Notchingham administers its own unemployment benefit, which is structured as follows: If you are unemployed (that is, if you do not work at all), you get unemployment benefits (a transfer from the government) of $50 per day. As soon as you work for only one hour, the unemployment benefit is completely withdrawn. That is, there is a notch in the benefit system.

a. How much income does an unemployed person have per day? How much daily income does an individual who works four hours per day have? How many hours do you need to work to earn just the same as if you were unemployed?

b. Will anyone ever accept a part-time job that requires working four hours per day, rather than being unemployed?

c. Suppose that Notchingham now changes the way in which the unemployment benefit is withdrawn. For each additional dollar an individual earns, $0.50 of the unemployment benefit is withdrawn. How much daily income does an individual who works four hours per day now have? Is there an incentive now to work four hours per day rather than being unemployed?

23. The accompanying table shows data on the total number of people in the United States and the number of all people who were uninsured, for selected years from 1999 to 2009. It also shows data on the total number of poor children in the United States—those under 18 and below the poverty threshold—and the number of poor children who were uninsured.

Year	Total people	Uninsured people	Total poor children	Uninsured poor children
	(millions)			
1999	276.8	38.8	12.3	2.8
2001	282.1	39.8	11.7	2.4
2003	288.3	43.4	12.9	2.4
2005	293.8	44.8	12.9	2.4
2007	299.1	45.7	13.3	2.3
2009	304.3	50.7	15.5	2.3

Source: U.S. Census Bureau.

For each year, calculate the percentage of all people who were uninsured and the percentage of poor children who were uninsured. How have these percentages changed over time? What is a possible explanation for the change in the percentage of uninsured poor children?

24. The American National Election Studies conducts periodic research on the opinions of U.S. voters. The accompanying table shows the percentage of people, in selected years from 1952 to 2008, who agreed with the statement "There are important differences in what the Republicans and Democrats stand for."

Year	Agree with statement
1952	50%
1972	46
1992	60
2004	76
2008	78

Source: American National Election Studies.

What do these data say about the degree of partisanship in U.S. politics over time?

Module 40: Factor Markets
Module 41: Marginal Productivity Theory
Module 42: The Market for Labor

SECTION 13

Factor Markets and the Distribution of Income

THE VALUE OF A DEGREE

Does higher education pay? Yes, it does: in the modern economy, employers are willing to pay a premium for workers with more education. And the size of that premium has increased a lot over the last few decades. Back in 1973 workers with advanced degrees, such as law degrees or MBAs, earned only 76% more than those who had only graduated from high school. By 2011, the premium for an advanced degree had risen to over 225%.

Who decided that the wages of workers with advanced degrees would rise so much compared with those of high school grads? The answer, of course, is that nobody decided it. Wage rates are prices, the prices of different kinds of labor; and they are decided, like other prices, by supply and demand.

Still, there is a qualitative difference between the wage rate of high school grads and the price of used textbooks: the wage rate isn't the price of a *good,* it's the price of a *factor of production.* And although markets for factors of production are in many ways similar to those for goods, there are also some important differences.

In this section, we examine *factor markets,* the markets in which the factors of production such as labor, land, and capital are traded. Factor markets, like markets for goods and services, play a crucial role in the economy: they allocate productive resources to producers and help ensure those resources are used efficiently.

This section begins by describing the major factors of production. Then we consider the demand for factors of production, which leads us to a crucial insight: the *marginal productivity theory of income distribution.* We then consider some challenges to the marginal productivity theory. The section concludes with a discussion of the supply of the most important factor, labor.

MODULE

40 Factor Markets

iStockphoto/Thinkstock

Comstock/Thinkstock

iStockphoto/Thinkstock

iStockphoto/Thinkstock

WHAT YOU WILL LEARN

1. **How factors of production are traded in factor markets**
2. **How factor markets determine the factor distribution of income**
3. **How the demand for a factor of production is determined**

The Economy's Factors of Production

You may recall that we have already defined a factor of production in the context of the circular-flow diagram; it is any resource that is used by firms to produce goods and services, items that are consumed by households. The markets in which factors of production are bought and sold are called *factor markets,* and the prices in factor markets are known as *factor prices.*

What are these factors of production, and why do factor prices matter?

The Factors of Production

Economists divide factors of production into four principal classes. The first is *labor,* the work done by human beings. The second is *land,* which encompasses resources provided by nature. The third is *physical capital*—often referred to simply as "capital"—which consists of manufactured resources such as equipment, buildings, tools, and machines. The fourth and final factor of production is *human capital,* the improvement in labor created by education and knowledge, and embodied in the workforce.

Technological progress has boosted the importance of human capital and made technical sophistication essential to many jobs, thus helping to create the premium for workers with advanced degrees.

The demand for a factor is a **derived demand.** It results from (that is, it is derived from) the demand for the output being produced.

The **factor distribution of income** is the division of total income among land, labor, physical capital, and human capital.

Why Factor Prices Matter: The Allocation of Resources

The factor prices determined in factor markets play a vital role in the important process of allocating resources among firms.

Consider the example of Mississippi and Louisiana in the aftermath of Hurricane Katrina, the costliest hurricane ever to hit the U.S. mainland. The states had an urgent need for workers in the building trades—everything from excavation to roofing—to repair or replace damaged structures.

What ensured that those needed workers actually came? The factor market: the high demand for workers drove up wages. During 2005, the average U.S. wage grew at a rate of around 6%. But in areas heavily affected by Katrina, the average wage during the fall of 2005 grew by 30% more than the national rate, and some areas saw twice that rate of increase. Over time, these higher wages led large numbers of workers with the right skills to move temporarily to these states to do the work.

In other words, the market for a factor of production—construction workers—allocated that factor of production to where it was needed.

In this sense factor markets are similar to goods markets, which allocate goods among consumers. But there are two features that make factor markets special. Unlike in a goods market, demand in a factor market is what we call **derived demand.** That is, demand for the factor is derived from demand for the firm's output. The second feature is that factor markets are where most of us get the largest shares of our income (government transfers being the next largest source of income in the economy).

Media Bakery

After major hurricanes like Katrina in 2005 and Sandy in 2012, home repair becomes a profitable line of work for those with the right skills.

Factor Incomes and the Distribution of Income

Most American families get most of their income in the form of wages and salaries—that is, they get their income by selling labor. Some people, however, get most of their income from physical capital: when you own stock in a company, what you really own is a share of that company's physical capital. Some people get much of their income from rents earned on land they own. And successful business owners earn income in the form of profits.

Obviously, then, the prices of factors of production have a major impact on how the economic "pie" is sliced among different groups. For example, a higher wage rate, other things equal, means that a larger proportion of the total income in the economy goes to people who derive their income from labor and less goes to those who derive their income from physical capital, land, or human capital. Economists refer to how the economic pie is sliced as the "distribution of income." Specifically, factor prices determine the **factor distribution of income**—how the total income of the economy is divided among labor, land, physical capital, and human capital.

As the following Economics in Action explains, the factor distribution of income in the United States has been quite stable over the past few decades. In other times and places, however, large changes have taken place in the factor distribution. One notable example: during the Industrial Revolution, the share of total income earned by landowners fell sharply, while the share earned by physical capital owners rose.

ECONOMICS IN ACTION

THE FACTOR DISTRIBUTION OF INCOME IN THE UNITED STATES

When we talk about the factor distribution of income, what are we talking about in practice?

In the United States, as in all advanced economies, payments to labor account for most of the economy's total income. Figure 40-1 shows the factor distribution of income in the United States in 2012: in that year, 71% of total income in the economy took the form of "compensation of employees"—a number that includes both wages and benefits such as health insurance. This number is in line with historical standards (it was 72.2% in 1972 and 70.4% in 2007), and reflects the fact that the economy has begun to rebound from the high unemployment and reduced wages for many American employees in the recent recession.

However, measured wages and benefits don't capture the full income of "labor" because a significant fraction of total income in the United States (usually 7 to 10%) is "proprietors' income"—the earnings of people who own their own businesses. Part of that income should be

FIGURE 40-1 Factor Distribution of Income in the United States in 2012

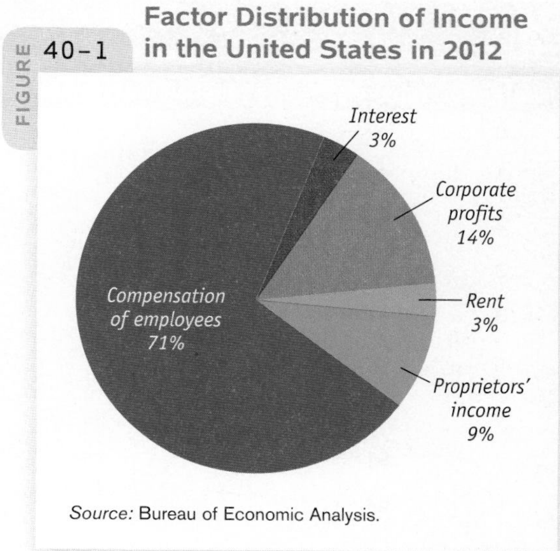

Source: Bureau of Economic Analysis.

considered wages these business owners pay themselves. So the true share of labor in the economy is probably a few percentage points higher than the reported "compensation of employees" share.

But much of what we call compensation of employees is really a return on human capital. A surgeon isn't just supplying the services of a pair of ordinary hands (at least the patient hopes not!): that individual is also supplying the result of many years and hundreds of thousands of dollars invested in training and experience. We can't directly measure what fraction of wages is really a payment for education and training, but many economists believe that human capital has become *the* most important factor of production in modern economies.

Marginal Productivity and Factor Demand

All economic decisions are about comparing costs and benefits—and usually about comparing marginal costs and marginal benefits. This goes both for a consumer, deciding whether to buy more goods or services, and for a firm, deciding whether to hire an additional worker.

Although there are some important exceptions, most factor markets in the modern American economy are perfectly competitive. This means that most buyers and sellers of factors are price-takers because they are too small relative to the market to do anything but accept the market price. And in a competitive labor market, it's clear how to define the marginal cost an employer pays for a worker: it is simply the worker's wage rate. But what is the marginal benefit of that worker? To answer that question, we return to the production function, which relates inputs to output. For now we assume that all firms are price-takers in their output markets—that is, they operate in a perfectly competitive industry.

Value of the Marginal Product

Figure 40-2 reproduces Figures 21-1 and 21-2, which show the production function for wheat on George and Martha's farm. Panel (a) of Figure 40-2 uses the total product curve to show how total wheat production depends on the number of workers employed on the farm; panel (b) shows how the *marginal product of labor,* the increase in output from employing one more worker, depends on the number of workers employed. Table 40-1 shows the numbers behind the figure. Note: sometimes the marginal product (*MP*) is called the marginal product of labor, or *MPL.*

TABLE 40-1

Employment and Output for George and Martha's Farm

Quantity of labor L (workers)	Quantity of wheat Q (bushels)	Marginal product of labor $MPL = \frac{\Delta Q}{\Delta L}$ (bushels per worker)
0	0	
		19
1	19	
		17
2	36	
		15
3	51	
		13
4	64	
		11
5	75	
		9
6	84	
		7
7	91	
		5
8	96	

If workers are paid $200 each and wheat sells for $20 per bushel, how many workers should George and Martha employ to maximize profit?

Earlier we showed how to answer this question in several steps. First, we used information from the production function to derive the firm's total cost and its marginal cost. Then we used the *price-taking firm's optimal output rule:* a price-taking firm's profit is maximized by producing the quantity of output at which the marginal cost is equal to the market price. Having determined the optimal quantity of output, we went back to the production function to find the optimal number of workers—which was simply the number of workers needed to produce the optimal quantity of output.

As you might have guessed, marginal analysis provides a more direct way to find the number of workers that maximizes a firm's profit. This alternative approach is just a different way of looking at the same thing. But it gives us more insight into the demand for factors as opposed to the supply of goods.

To see how this alternative approach works, suppose that George and Martha are deciding whether to employ another worker. The increase in *cost* from employing another worker is the wage rate, *W.*

FIGURE 40-2 The Production Function for George and Martha's Farm

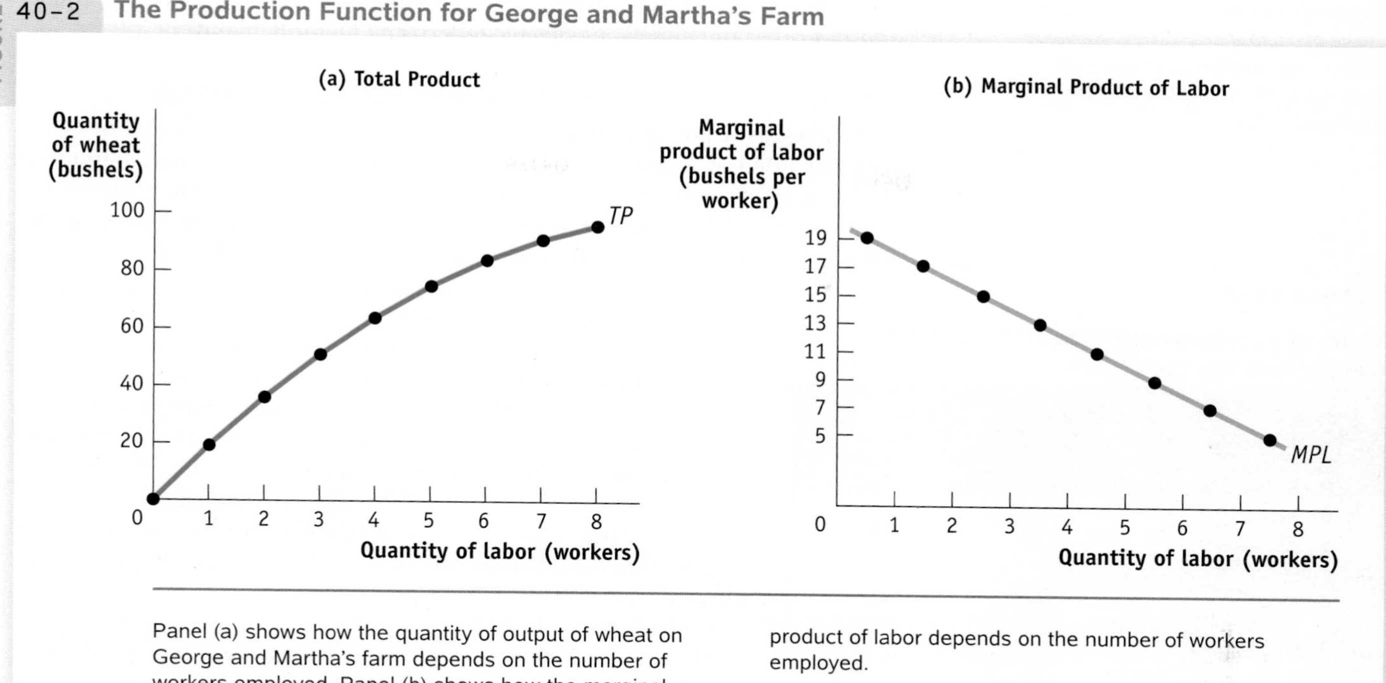

Panel (a) shows how the quantity of output of wheat on George and Martha's farm depends on the number of workers employed. Panel (b) shows how the marginal product of labor depends on the number of workers employed.

The *benefit* to George and Martha from employing another worker is the value of the extra output that worker can produce. What is this value? It is the marginal product of labor, *MPL*, multiplied by the price per unit of output, *P*. This amount—the extra value of output generated by employing one more unit of labor—is known as the **value of the marginal product** of labor, or *VMPL*:

(40-1) Value of the marginal product of labor = $VMPL = P \times MPL$

So should George and Martha hire another worker? Yes, if the value of the extra output is more than the cost of the additional worker—that is, if $VMPL > W$. Otherwise, they should not.

The hiring decision is made using marginal analysis, by comparing the marginal benefit from hiring another worker (*VMPL*) with the marginal cost (*W*). And as with any decision that is made on the margin, the optimal choice is made by equating marginal benefit with marginal cost (or if they're never equal, by continuing to hire until the marginal cost of one more unit would exceed the marginal benefit). That is, to maximize profit, George and Martha will employ workers up to the point at which, for the last worker employed,

A firm should hire another worker if the value of the extra output is more than the cost of the additional worker.

(40-2) $VMPL = W$ *at the profit-maximizing level of employment*

This rule doesn't apply only to labor; it applies to any factor of production. The value of the marginal product of any factor is its marginal product times the price of the good it produces. The general rule is that a *profit-maximizing price-taking producer employs each factor of production up to the point at which the value of the marginal product of the last unit of the factor employed is equal to that factor's price.*

This rule is consistent with our previous analysis. We saw that a profit-maximizing firm chooses the level of output at which the price of the good it produces equals the marginal cost of producing that good. It turns out that if the level of output is chosen so that price equals marginal cost, then it is also true that with the amount of labor required to produce that output level, the value of the marginal product of labor will equal the wage rate.

The **value of the marginal product** of a factor is the value of the additional output generated by employing one more unit of that factor.

The **value of the marginal product curve** of a factor shows how the value of the marginal product of that factor depends on the quantity of the factor employed.

Now let's look more closely at why choosing the level of employment to equate *VMPL* and *W* works, and at how it helps us understand factor demand.

Value of the Marginal Product and Factor Demand

Table 40-2 shows the value of the marginal product of labor on George and Martha's farm when the price of wheat is $20 per bushel. In Figure 40-3, the horizontal axis shows the number of workers employed; the vertical axis measures the value of the marginal product of labor *and* the wage rate. The curve shown is the **value of the marginal product curve** of labor. This curve, like the marginal product of labor curve, slopes downward because of diminishing returns to labor in production. That is, the value of the marginal product of each worker is less than that of the preceding worker because the marginal product of each worker is less than that of the preceding worker.

TABLE 40-2

Value of the Marginal Product of Labor for George and Martha's Farm

Quantity of labor *L* (workers)	Marginal product of labor *MPL* (bushels per worker)	Value of the marginal product of labor *VMPL* = *P* × *MPL*
0		
	19	$380
1		
	17	340
2		
	15	300
3		
	13	260
4		
	11	220
5		
	9	180
6		
	7	140
7		
	5	100
8		

We have just seen that to maximize profit, George and Martha hire workers until the wage rate is equal to the value of the marginal product of the last worker employed. Let's use the example to see how this principle really works. Assume that George and Martha currently employ 3 workers and that these workers must be paid the market wage rate of $200. Should they employ an additional worker?

Looking at Table 40-2, we see that if George and Martha currently employ 3 workers, the value of the marginal product of an additional worker is $260. So if they employ an additional worker, they will increase the value of their production by $260 but increase their cost by only $200, yielding an increased profit of $60. In fact, a firm can always increase profit by employing one more unit of a factor of production as long as the value of the marginal product produced by that unit exceeds the factor price.

Alternatively, suppose that George and Martha employ 8 workers. By reducing the number of workers to 7, they can save $200 in wages. In addition, the value of the marginal product of the 8th worker is only $100. So, by reducing employment by one worker, they can increase profit by $200 – $100 = $100. In other words, a firm can always increase profit by employing one less unit of a factor of production as long as the value of the marginal product produced by that unit is less than the factor price.

Using this method, we can see from Table 40-2 that the profit-maximizing employment level is 5 workers, given a wage rate of $200. The value of the marginal product of the 5th worker is $220, so adding the 5th worker results in $20 of additional profit.

Firms keep hiring more workers until the value of the marginal product of labor equals the wage rate.

© Ilene MacDonald/Alamy

But George and Martha should not hire more than 5 workers: the value of the marginal product of the 6th worker is only $180, $20 less than the cost of that worker. So, to maximize profit, George and Martha should employ workers up to but not beyond the point at which the value of the marginal product of the last worker employed is equal to the wage rate.

Now look again at the value of the marginal product curve in Figure 40-3. To determine the profit-maximizing level of employment, we set the value of the marginal product of labor equal to the price of labor—a wage rate of $200 per worker. This means that the profit-maximizing level of employment is at point *A*, corresponding to an employment level of 5 workers. If the wage rate were higher, we would simply move up the curve and decrease the number of workers employed: if the wage rate were lower than $200, we would move down the curve and increase the number of workers employed.

In this example, George and Martha have a small farm in which the potential employment level varies from 0 to 8 workers, and they hire workers up to the point at which the value of the marginal product of another worker would fall below the wage rate.

FIGURE 40-3 The Value of the Marginal Product Curve

This curve shows how the value of the marginal product of labor depends on the number of workers employed. It slopes downward because of diminishing returns to labor in production. To maximize profit, George and Martha choose the level of employment at which the value of the marginal product of labor is equal to the market wage rate. For example, at a wage rate of $200 the profit-maximizing level of employment is 5 workers, shown by point *A*. The value of the marginal product curve of a factor is the producer's individual demand curve for that factor.

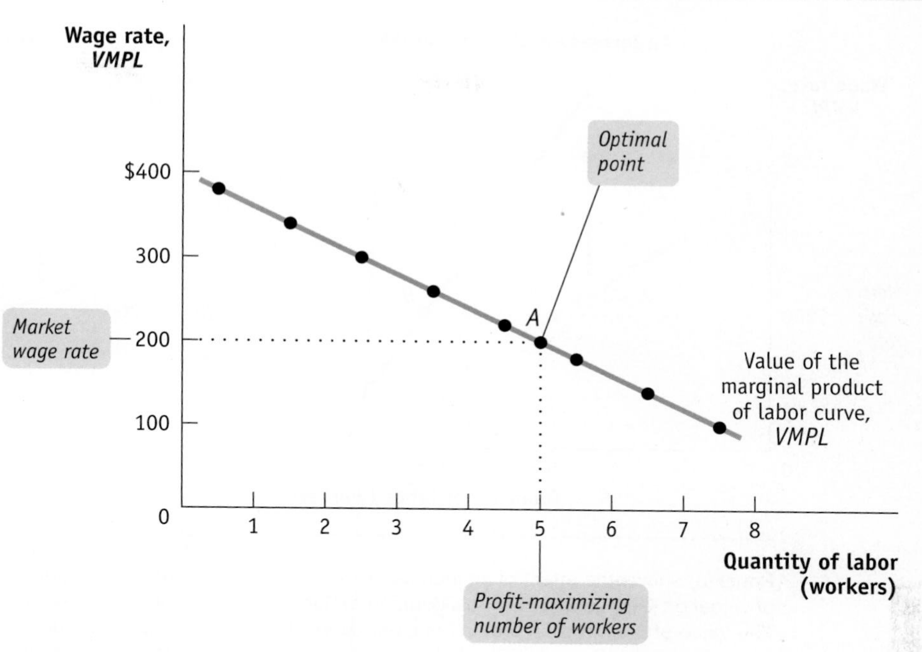

For a larger farm with many employees, the value of the marginal product of labor falls only slightly when an additional worker is employed. As a result, there will be some worker whose value of the marginal product almost exactly equals the wage rate. (In keeping with the George and Martha example, this means that some worker generates a value of the marginal product of approximately $200.) In this case, the firm maximizes profit by choosing a level of employment at which the value of the marginal product of the last worker hired *equals* (to a very good approximation) the wage rate.

In the interest of simplicity, we will assume from now on that firms use this rule to determine the profit-maximizing level of employment. *This means that the value of the marginal product of labor curve is the individual firm's labor demand curve.* And in general, a firm's value of the marginal product curve for any factor of production is that firm's individual demand curve for that factor of production.

Shifts of the Factor Demand Curve

As in the case of ordinary demand curves, it is important to distinguish between movements along the factor demand curve and shifts of the factor demand curve. What causes factor demand curves to shift? There are three main causes:

1. Changes in the prices of goods
2. Changes in the supply of other factors
3. Changes in technology

1. CHANGES IN THE PRICES OF GOODS Remember that factor demand is *derived demand:* if the price of the good that is produced with a factor changes, so will the value of the marginal product of the factor. That is, in the case of labor demand, if P changes, $VMPL = P \times MPL$ will change at any given level of employment.

Figure 40-4 illustrates the effects of changes in the price of wheat, assuming that $200 is the current wage rate. Panel (a) shows the effect of an *increase* in the price of wheat. This shifts the value of the marginal product of labor curve upward because *VMPL* rises at any given level of employment. If the wage rate remains unchanged at $200, the optimal point moves from point *A* to point *B*: the profit-maximizing level of employment rises.

FIGURE 40-4 Shifts of the Value of the Marginal Product Curve

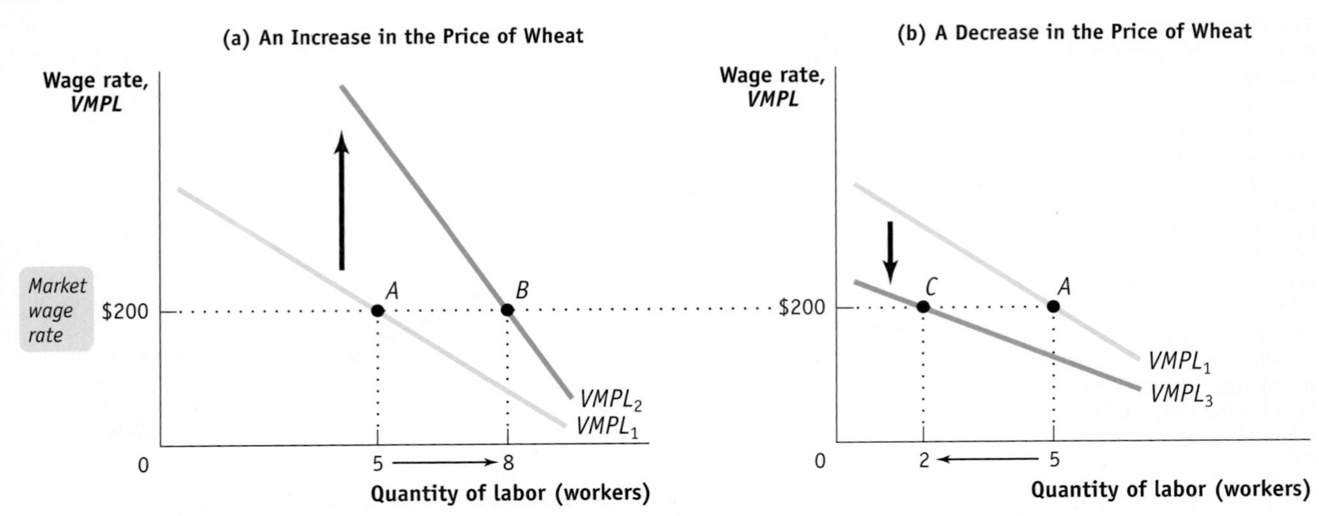

Panel (a) shows the effect of an increase in the price of wheat on George and Martha's demand for labor. The value of the marginal product of labor curve shifts upward, from $VMPL_1$ to $VMPL_2$. If the market wage rate remains at $200, profit-maximizing employment rises from 5 workers to 8 workers, shown by the movement from point *A* to point *B*. Panel (b) shows the effect of a decrease in the price of wheat. The value of the marginal product of labor curve shifts downward, from $VMPL_1$ to $VMPL_3$. At the market wage rate of $200, profit-maximizing employment falls from 5 workers to 2 workers, shown by the movement from point *A* to point *C*.

Panel (b) shows the effect of a *decrease* in the price of wheat. This shifts the value of the marginal product of labor curve downward. If the wage rate remains unchanged at $200, the optimal point moves from point *A* to point *C*: the profit-maximizing level of employment falls.

2. CHANGES IN THE SUPPLY OF OTHER FACTORS Suppose that George and Martha acquire more land to cultivate—say, by clearing a woodland on their property. Each worker now produces more wheat because each one has more land to work with. As a result, the marginal product of labor on the farm rises at any given level of employment. This has the same effect as an increase in the price of wheat, which is illustrated in panel (a) of Figure 40-4: the value of the marginal product of labor curve shifts upward, and at any given wage rate the profit-maximizing level of employment rises. Similarly, suppose George and Martha cultivate less land. This leads to a fall in the marginal product of labor at any given employment level. Each worker produces less wheat because each has less land to work with. As a result, the value of the marginal product of labor curve shifts downward—as in panel (b) of Figure 40-4—and the profit-maximizing level of employment falls.

3. CHANGES IN TECHNOLOGY In general, the effect of technological progress on the demand for any given factor can go either way: improved technology can either increase or decrease the demand for a given factor of production.

How can technological progress decrease factor demand? Consider horses, which were once an important factor of production. The development of substitutes for horse power, such as automobiles and tractors, greatly reduced the demand for horses.

The usual effect of technological progress, however, is to increase the demand for a given factor, often because it raises the marginal product of the factor. In particular, although there have been persistent fears that machinery would reduce the demand for labor, over the long run the U.S. economy has seen both large wage increases and large increases in employment, suggesting that technological progress has greatly increased labor demand.

MODULE 40 Review

Solutions appear at the back of the book.

Check Your Understanding

1. Suppose that the government places price controls on the market for college professors, imposing a wage that is lower than the market wage. Describe the effect of this policy on the production of college degrees. What sectors of the economy do you think would be adversely affected by this policy? What sectors of the economy might benefit?

2. a. Suppose service industries, such as retailing and banking, experience an increase in demand. These industries use relatively more labor than nonservice industries. Does the demand curve for labor shift to the right, shift to the left, or remain unchanged?
   b. Suppose diminishing fish populations off the coast of Maine lead to policies restricting the use of the most productive types of nets in that area. The result is a decrease in the number of fish caught per day by commercial fishers in Maine. The price of fish is unaffected. Does the demand curve for fishers in Maine shift to the right, shift to the left, or remain unchanged?

Multiple-Choice Questions

1. Which of the following is an example of *physical* capital?
   a. manual labor
   b. welding equipment
   c. farm land
   d. coal
   e. education

2. Which of the following can shift the factor demand curve to the right?
   I. an increase in the price of the good being produced
   II. an increase in the factor's marginal productivity
   III. a technological advance
   a. I only
   b. II only
   c. III only
   d. I and II only
   e. I, II, and III

3. Factor market demand is called a *derived* demand because it
   a. derives its name from the Latin *factorus*.
   b. is derived from the market wage received by workers.
   c. is derived from the productivity of workers.
   d. is derived from the product market.
   e. derives its shape from the price of the factor.

4. Which factor of production receives the largest portion of income in the United States?
   a. land
   b. labor
   c. physical capital
   d. human capital
   e. interest

5. The individual firm's demand curve for labor is
   a. the *VMPL* curve.
   b. upward sloping.
   c. horizontal at the level of the product price.
   d. vertical.
   e. equal to the *MPL* curve.

Critical-Thinking Question

Draw three separate, correctly labeled graphs illustrating the effect of each of the following changes on the demand for labor. Adopt the usual *ceteris paribus* assumption that all else remains unchanged in each case.

a. The price of the product being produced decreases.
b. Worker productivity increases.
c. Firms invest in more capital to be used by workers.

PITFALLS

WHAT IS A FACTOR, ANYWAY?

? Imagine a business that produces shirts. The business will make use of workers and machines—that is, of labor and capital. But it will also use other inputs, such as electricity and cloth. Are all of these inputs factors of production?

> NO: LABOR AND PHYSICAL CAPITAL ARE FACTORS OF PRODUCTION, BUT CLOTH AND ELECTRICITY ARE NOT. THE KEY DISTINCTION IS THAT A FACTOR OF PRODUCTION EARNS INCOME FROM THE SELLING OF ITS SERVICES OVER AND OVER AGAIN BUT AN INPUT CANNOT. For example, a worker earns income over time from repeatedly selling his or her efforts; the owner of a machine earns income over time from repeatedly selling the use of that machine. So a factor of production, such as labor and physical capital, represents an enduring source of income. An input like electricity or cloth, however, is used up in the production process. Once exhausted, it cannot be a source of future income for its owner.

To learn more, see the discussion on pages 424–425.

MODULE 41 Marginal Productivity Theory

Kurhan/Shutterstock

WHAT YOU WILL LEARN

1. Labor market applications of the marginal productivity theory of income distribution
2. Sources of wage disparities and the role of discrimination

In the previous module we introduced the factor distribution of income. In this module, we will go a step further and explain how the *marginal productivity theory of income distribution* helps to explain how income is divided among factors of production in an economy. We will consider how the markets for factors of production are broken down. There are different markets for different types of factors. For example, there are different labor markets for different types of labor, such as for computer programmers, pastry chefs, and economists. Then, we look at the marginal productivity theory of income distribution and the extent to which it explains wage disparities between workers.

The Marginal Productivity Theory of Income Distribution

The **marginal productivity theory of income distribution** sums up what we have learned about payments to factors when goods markets and factor markets are perfectly competitive. According to this theory, each factor is paid the value of the output generated by the last unit of that factor employed in the factor market as a whole—its **equilibrium value of the marginal product.**

According to the **marginal productivity theory of income distribution,** every factor of production is paid the equilibrium value of its marginal product.

The **equilibrium value of the marginal product** of a factor is the additional value produced by the last unit of that factor employed in the factor market as a whole.

To understand why the marginal productivity theory of income distribution is important, look back at Figure 40-1, which shows the factor distribution of income in the United States in 2012, and ask yourself this question: who or what determined that labor would get 71% of total U.S. income? Why not 90% or 50%?

The answer, according to this theory, is that the division of income among the economy's factors of production isn't arbitrary: in the economy-wide factor market, the price paid for each factor is equal to the increase in the value of output generated by the last unit of that factor employed in the market. Therefore, if a unit of labor is paid more than a unit of capital, it is because at the equilibrium quantity of each factor, the value of the marginal product of labor exceeds the value of the marginal product of capital.

So far we have treated factor markets as if every unit of each factor were identical. That is, as if all land were identical, all labor were identical, and all capital were identical. But in reality factors differ considerably with respect to productivity. For instance, land resources differ in their ability to produce crops and workers have different skills and abilities.

Rather than thinking of one land market for all land resources in an economy, and similarly one capital market and one labor market, we can instead think of different markets for different types of land, physical capital, human capital, and labor. For example, the market for computer programmers is different from the market for pastry chefs.

When we consider that there are separate factor markets for different types of factors, the marginal productivity theory of income distribution still holds. That is, when the labor market for computer programmers is in equilibrium, the wage rate earned by all computer programmers is equal to the market's equilibrium value of the marginal product—the value of the marginal product of the last computer programmer hired in that market.

The marginal productivity theory can explain the distribution of income among different types of land, labor, physical capital, and human capital as well as the distribution of income among the factors of production. Next we look more closely at the distribution of income between different types of labor and the extent to which the marginal productivity theory of income distribution explains differences in workers' wages.

ECONOMICS ▶ IN ACTION

HELP WANTED!

Hamill Manufacturing of Pennsylvania makes precision components for military helicopters and nuclear submarines. Their highly skilled senior machinists are well paid compared to other workers in manufacturing, earning nearly $70,000 in 2011, excluding benefits. Like most skilled machinists in the United States, Hamill's machinists are very productive: according to the U.S. Census Annual Survey of Manufacturers, in 2010 the average skilled machinist generated approximately $137,000 in value added.

Fatihhoca/Getty Images

The marginal productivity theory of income distribution holds for skilled machinists at Hamill Manufacturing.

But there is a $67,000 difference between the salary paid to Hamill machinists and the value added they generate. Does this mean that the marginal productivity theory of income distribution doesn't hold? Doesn't the theory imply that machinists should be paid $137,000, the average value added that each one generates?

The answer is no, for two reasons. First, the $137,000 figure is averaged over *all machinists currently employed.* The theory says that machinists will be paid the value of the marginal product of the *last machinist hired,* and due to diminishing returns to labor, that value will be lower than the average over all machinists currently employed. Second, a worker's equilibrium wage rate includes other costs, such as employee benefits, that have to be added to the $70,000 salary. The marginal productivity theory of income distribution says that workers are paid a wage rate, *including all benefits,* equal to the value of the marginal product.

You can see all these costs are present at Hamill. There the machinists have good benefits and job security, which add to their salary. Including these benefits, machinists' total compensation will be equal to the value of the marginal product of the last machinist employed.

In Hamill's case, there is yet another factor that explains the $67,000 gap: there are not enough machinists at the current wage rate. Although the company increased the number of employees from 85 in 2004 to 125 in 2011, they would like to hire more.

Why doesn't Hamill raise its wages in order to attract more skilled machinists? The problem is that the work they do is so specialized that it is hard to hire from the outside, even when the company raises wages as an inducement. To address this problem, Hamill has spent a significant amount of money training each new hire, approximately $125,000 plus the cost of benefits per trainee. In the end, it does appear that the marginal productivity theory of income distribution holds.

Is the Marginal Productivity Theory of Income Distribution Really True?

Although the marginal productivity theory of income distribution is a well-established part of economic theory, closely linked to the analysis of markets in general, it is a source of some controversy. There are two main objections to it.

First, in the real world we see large disparities in income between factors of production that, in the eyes of some observers, should receive the same payment. Perhaps the most conspicuous examples in the United States are the large differences in the average wages between women and men and among various racial and ethnic groups. Do these wage differences really reflect differences in marginal productivity, or is something else going on?

Second, many people wrongly believe that the marginal productivity theory of income distribution gives a *moral* justification for the distribution of income, implying that the existing distribution is fair and appropriate. This misconception sometimes leads other people, who believe that the current distribution of income is unfair, to reject marginal productivity theory.

To address these controversies, we'll start by looking at income disparities across gender and ethnic groups. Then we'll ask what factors might account for these disparities and whether these explanations are consistent with the marginal productivity theory of income distribution.

Wage Disparities in Practice

Wage rates in the United States cover a very wide range. In 2012, hundreds of thousands of workers received the legal federal minimum of $7.25 per hour. At the other extreme, the chief executives of several companies were paid more than $100 million, which works out to $20,000 per hour even if they worked 100-hour weeks. Even leaving out these extremes, there is a huge range of wage rates. Are people really that different in their marginal productivities?

A particular source of concern is the existence of systematic wage differences across gender and ethnicity. Figure 41-1 compares annual median earnings in 2011 of workers age 25 or older classified by gender and ethnicity. As a group, White males had the highest earnings. Other data show that women (averaging across all ethnicities) earned only about 69% as much; African-American workers (male and female combined), only 69% as much; Hispanic workers (again, male and female combined), only 59% as much.

We are a nation founded on the belief that all men are created equal—and if the Constitution were rewritten today, we would say that *all people* are created equal. So why do they receive such unequal pay? Let's start with the marginal productivity explanations, then look at other influences.

Marginal Productivity and Wage Inequality

A large part of the observed inequality in wages can be explained by considerations that are consistent with the marginal productivity theory of income distribution. In particular, there are three well-understood sources of wage differences across occupations and individuals.

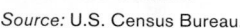

FIGURE 41-1 **Median Earnings by Gender and Ethnicity, 2011**

The U.S. labor market continues to show large differences across workers according to gender and ethnicity. Women are paid substantially less than men; African-American and Hispanic workers are paid substantially less than White male workers.
Source: U.S. Census Bureau.

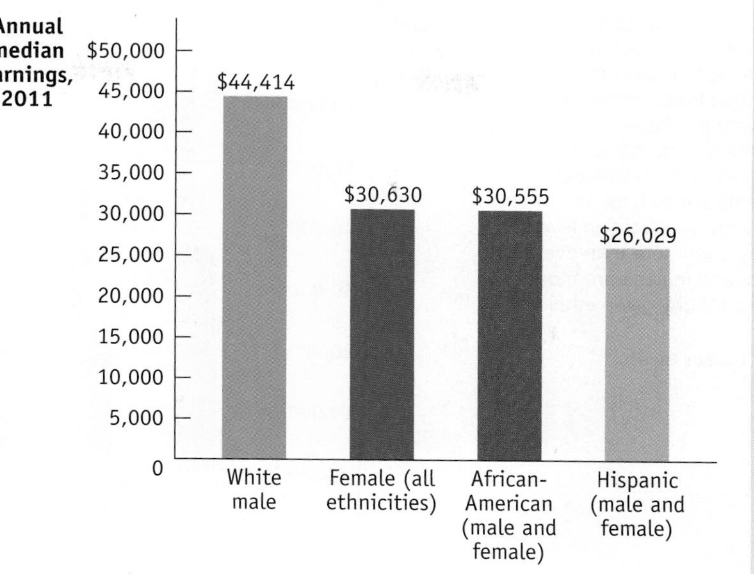

First is the existence of **compensating differentials:** across different types of jobs, wages are often higher or lower depending on how attractive or unattractive the job is. Workers with unpleasant or dangerous jobs demand a higher wage in comparison to workers with jobs that require the same skill and effort but lack the unpleasant or dangerous qualities. For example, truckers who haul hazardous loads are paid more than truckers who haul non-hazardous loads. But for any *given* job, the marginal productivity theory of income distribution generally holds true. For example, hazardous-load truckers are paid a wage equal to the equilibrium value of the marginal product of the last person employed in the labor market for hazardous-load truckers.

A second reason for wage inequality that is clearly consistent with marginal productivity theory is differences in talent. People differ in their abilities: a higher-ability person, by producing a better product that commands a higher price compared to a lower-ability person, generates a higher value of the marginal product. And these differences in the value of the marginal product translate into differences in earning potential. We all know that this is true in sports: practice is important, but 99.99% (at least) of the population just doesn't have what it takes to throw passes like Tom Brady or hit tennis balls like Roger Federer. The same is true, though less obvious, in other fields of endeavor.

A third and very important reason for wage differences is differences in the quantity of *human capital.* Recall that human capital—education and training—is at least as important in the modern economy as physical capital in the form of buildings and machines. Different people "embody" quite different quantities of human capital, and a person with a higher quantity of human capital typically generates a higher value of the marginal product by producing a product that commands a higher price. So differences in human capital account for substantial differences in wages. People with high levels of human capital, such as skilled surgeons or engineers, generally receive high wages.

The most direct way to see the effect of human capital on wages is to look at the relationship between educational levels and earnings. Figure 41-2 shows earnings differentials by gender, ethnicity, and three educational levels for people age 25 or older in 2010. As you can see, regardless of gender or ethnicity, higher education is associated with higher median earnings. For example, in 2010 White females with 9 to 12 years of schooling but without a high school diploma had median earnings 32%

Compensating differentials are wage differences across jobs that reflect the fact that some jobs are less pleasant than others.

FIGURE 41-2 Earnings Differentials by Education, Gender, and Ethnicity, 2010

It is clear that, regardless of gender or ethnicity, education pays: those with a high school diploma earn more than those without one, and those with a college degree earn substantially more than those with only a high school diploma. Other patterns are evident as well: for any given education level, White males earn more than every other group, and males earn more than females for any given ethnic group.

Source: U.S. Census Bureau.

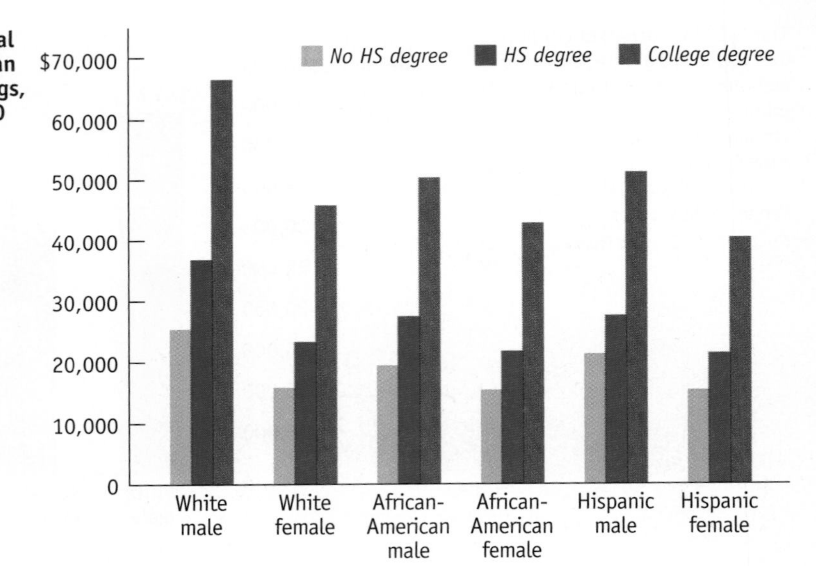

less than those with a high school diploma and 65% less than those with a college degree—and similar patterns exist for the other five groups. Additional data show that surgeons—an occupation that requires steady hands and many years of formal training—earned an average of $225,390 in 2010.

Because even now men typically have had more years of education than women and Whites more years than non-Whites, differences in level of education are part of the explanation for the earnings differences shown in Figure 41-1.

It's also important to realize that formal education is not the only source of human capital; on-the-job training and experience are also very important. Differences in job tenure and experience can partly explain one notable aspect of Figure 41-2: across all ethnicities, women's median earnings are less than men's median earnings for any given education level.

But it's also important to emphasize that earnings differences arising from differences in human capital are not necessarily "fair." A society in which non-White children typically receive a poor education because they live in underfunded school districts, then go on to earn low wages because they are poorly educated, may have labor markets that are well described by marginal productivity theory (and would be consistent with the earnings differentials across ethnic groups shown in Figure 41-1). Yet many people would still consider the resulting distribution of income unfair.

Still, many observers think that actual wage differentials cannot be entirely explained by compensating differentials, differences in talent, and differences in human capital. They believe that market power, efficiency wages, and discrimination also play an important role. We will examine these forces next.

Market Power

The marginal productivity theory of income distribution is based on the assumption that factor markets are perfectly competitive. In such markets we can expect workers to be paid the equilibrium value of their marginal product, regardless of who they are. But how valid is this assumption?

Unions are organizations of workers that try to raise wages and improve working conditions for their members by bargaining collectively with employers.

We studied markets that are *not* perfectly competitive; now let's touch briefly on the ways in which labor markets may deviate from the competitive assumption.

One undoubted source of differences in wages between otherwise similar workers is the role of **unions**—organizations that try to raise wages and improve working conditions for their members. Labor unions, when they are successful, replace one-on-one wage deals between workers and employers with collective bargaining, in which the employer must negotiate wages with union representatives. Without question, this leads to higher wages for those workers who are represented by unions. In 2012 the median weekly earnings of union members in the United States were $943, compared with $742 for workers not represented by unions—a 27% difference.

AP Photo/Rick Bowner

Unions today have a fairly minor impact on wages compared to several decades ago.

Just as workers can sometimes organize to extract higher wages than they would otherwise receive, employers can sometimes organize to pay *lower* wages than would result from competition. For example, health care workers—doctors, nurses, and so on—sometimes argue that health maintenance organizations (HMOs) are engaged in a collective effort to hold down their wages.

How much does collective action, either by workers or by employers, affect wages in the modern United States? Several decades ago, when around 30% of American workers were union members, unions probably had a significant upward effect on wages. Today, however, most economists think unions exert a fairly minor influence. Union membership in the United States is relatively limited: in 2012, only 6.6% of the employees of private businesses were represented by unions.

Efficiency Wages

A second source of wage inequality is the phenomenon of *efficiency wages*—a type of incentive scheme used by employers to motivate workers to work hard and to reduce turnover. Suppose a worker performs a job that is extremely important but that the employer can observe how well the job is being performed only at infrequent intervals—say, serving as a caregiver for the employer's child. Then it often makes sense for the employer to pay more than the worker could earn in an alternative job—that is, more than the equilibrium wage. Why? Because earning a premium makes losing this job and having to take the alternative job quite costly for the worker.

So a worker who happens to be observed performing poorly and is therefore fired is now worse off for having to accept a lower-paying job. The threat of losing a job that pays a premium motivates the worker to perform well and avoid being fired. Likewise, paying a premium also reduces worker turnover—the frequency with which an employee leaves a job voluntarily.

The **efficiency-wage model** explains why we might observe wages offered above their equilibrium level. Like the price floors we studied in an earlier module—and, in particular, much like the minimum wage—this phenomenon leads to a surplus of labor in labor markets that are characterized by the efficiency-wage model. This surplus of labor translates into unemployment—some workers are actively searching for a high-paying efficiency-wage job but are unable to get one, and other more fortunate but no more deserving workers are able to acquire one.

As a result, two workers with exactly the same profile—the same skills and same job history—may earn unequal wages: the worker who is lucky enough to get an efficiency-wage job earns more than the worker who gets a standard job (or who remains unemployed while searching for a higher-paying job). Efficiency wages are a response to a type of market failure that arises from the fact that some employees don't always perform as well as they should and are able to hide that fact. As a result, employers use nonequilibrium wages in order to motivate their employees, leading to an inefficient outcome.

According to the **efficiency-wage model**, some employers pay an above-equilibrium wage as an incentive for better performance.

Discrimination

It is a real and ugly fact that throughout history there has been discrimination against workers who are considered to be of the wrong race, ethnicity, gender, or other characteristics. How does this fit into our economic models?

The main insight economic analysis offers is that discrimination is *not* a natural consequence of market competition. On the contrary, market forces tend to work against discrimination. To see why, consider the incentives that would exist if social convention dictated that women be paid, say, 30% less than men with equivalent qualifications and experience. A company whose management was itself unbiased would then be able to reduce its costs by hiring women rather than men—and such companies would have an advantage over other companies that hired men despite their higher cost. The result would be to create an excess demand for female workers, which would tend to drive up their wages.

But if market competition works against discrimination, how is it that so much discrimination has taken place? The answer is twofold. First, when labor markets don't work well, employers may have the ability to discriminate without hurting their profits. For example, market interferences (such as unions or minimum-wage laws) or market failures (such as efficiency wages) can lead to wages that are above their equilibrium levels. In these cases, there are more job applicants than there are jobs, leaving employers free to discriminate among applicants. In 2011, with unemployment over 9%, the Equal Employment Opportunity Commission, the federal agency tasked with investigating employment discrimination charges, reported that the complaints from workers and job-seekers had hit an all-time high, the most logged in the agency's 46-year history.

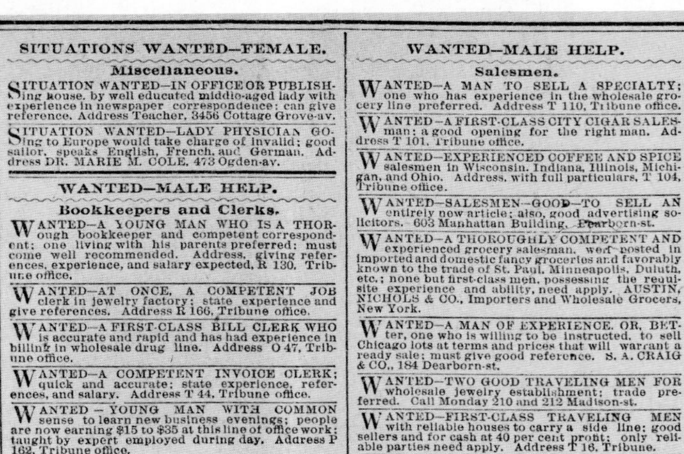

SITUATIONS WANTED—FEMALE.

Miscellaneous.

SITUATION WANTED—IN OFFICE OR PUBLISHING house, by well educated middle-aged lady with experience in newspaper correspondence; can give reference. Address Teacher, 3456 Cottage Grove-av.

SITUATION WANTED—LADY PHYSICIAN GOING to Europe would take charge of invalid; good sailor, speaks English, French, and German. Address DR. MARIE M. COLE, 473 Ogden-av.

WANTED—MALE HELP.

Bookkeepers and Clerks.

WANTED—A YOUNG MAN WHO IS A THOROUGH bookkeeper and competent correspondent; one living with his parents preferred; must come well recommended. Address, giving references, experience, and salary expected, R 130, Tribune office.

WANTED—AT ONCE, A COMPETENT JOB clerk in jewelry factory; state experience and give references. Address R 166, Tribune office.

WANTED—A FIRST-CLASS BILL CLERK WHO is accurate and rapid and has had experience in billing in wholesale drug line. Address O 47, Tribune office.

WANTED—A COMPETENT INVOICE CLERK; quick and accurate; state experience, references, and salary. Address T 44, Tribune office.

WANTED — YOUNG MAN WITH COMMON sense to learn new business evenings; people are now earning $15 to $35 at this line of office work; taught by expert employed during day. Address P 162, Tribune office.

WANTED—MALE HELP.

Salesmen.

WANTED—A MAN TO SELL A SPECIALTY; one who has experience in the wholesale grocery line preferred. Address T 110, Tribune office.

WANTED—A FIRST-CLASS CITY CIGAR SALESman; a good opening for the right man. Address T 101, Tribune office.

WANTED—EXPERIENCED COFFEE AND SPICE salesmen in Wisconsin, Indiana, Illinois, Michigan, and Ohio. Address, with full particulars, T 104, Tribune office.

WANTED—SALESMEN—GOOD—TO SELL AN entirely new article; also, good advertising solicitors. 603 Manhattan Building, Dearborn-st.

WANTED—A THOROUGHLY COMPETENT AND experienced grocery salesman, well posted in imported and domestic fancy groceries and favorably known to the trade of St. Paul, Minneapolis, Duluth, etc.; none but first-class men, possessing the requisite experience and ability, need apply. AUSTIN, NICHOLS & CO., Importers and Wholesale Grocers, New York.

WANTED—A MAN OF EXPERIENCE, OR, BETter, one who is willing to be instructed, to sell Chicago lots at terms and prices that will warrant a ready sale; must give good reference. S. A. CRAIG & CO., 184 Dearborn-st.

WANTED—TWO GOOD TRAVELING MEN FOR wholesale jewelry establishment; trade preferred. Call Monday 210 and 212 Madison-st.

WANTED—FIRST-CLASS TRAVELING MEN with reliable houses to carry a side line; good sellers and for cash at 40 per cent profit; only reliable parties need apply. Address T 16, Tribune.

Library of Congress Prints and Photographs Division, Washington DC (LCDIG-ppmsca-02927

In the past, newspapers separated help-wanted ads by gender, as in this case, and by race.

Second, discrimination has sometimes been institutionalized in government policy. This institutionalization of discrimination has made it easier to maintain it against market pressure, and historically it is the form that discrimination has typically taken. For example, at one time in the United States, African-Americans were barred from attending "Whites-only" public schools and universities in many parts of the country and forced to attend inferior schools. Although market competition tends to work against *current* discrimination, it is not a remedy for past discrimination, which typically has had an impact on the education and experience of its victims and thereby reduces their income.

So Does Marginal Productivity Theory Work?

The main conclusion you should draw from this discussion is that the marginal productivity theory of income distribution is not a perfect description of how factor incomes are determined but that it works pretty well. The deviations are important. But, by and large, in a modern economy with well-functioning labor markets, factors of production are paid the equilibrium value of the marginal product—the value of the marginal product of the last unit employed in the market as a whole.

It's important to emphasize, once again, that this does not mean that the factor distribution of income is morally justified.

MODULE 41 Review

Solutions appear at the back of the book.

Check Your Understanding

1. Assess each of the following statements. Do you think they are true, false, or ambiguous? Explain.
   a. The marginal productivity theory of income distribution is inconsistent with the presence of income disparities associated with gender, race, or ethnicity.
   b. Companies that engage in workplace discrimination but whose competitors do not are likely to earn less profit as a result of their actions.
   c. Workers who are paid less because they have less experience are not the victims of discrimination.

Multiple-Choice Questions

1. Which group of U.S. workers had the highest median earnings in 2011?
   a. white males
   b. females (all ethnicities)
   c. African-Americans (males and female)
   d. Hispanics
   e. African-American males

2. Which of the following sources of wage differences is/are consistent with the marginal productivity theory of income distribution?
   I. talent
   II. discrimination
   III. efficiency wages
   a. I only
   b. II only
   c. III only
   d. I and II only
   e. I, II, and III

3. Compensating differentials mean that which of the following leads to higher wages for some jobs?
   a. danger
   b. discrimination
   c. marginal productivity
   d. market power
   e. a surplus of labor

4. Which of the following is a result in the efficiency-wage model?
   a. compensating differentials
   b. surpluses of labor
   c. shortages of labor
   d. discrimination
   e. increased productivity

5. Which of the following statements regarding the marginal productivity theory of income distribution is correct?
   a. Each worker should earn a wage based on his or her marginal productivity.
   b. Substantial differences in human capital do not account for substantial differences in wages.
   c. Workers with higher marginal products always receive a higher wage than workers with lower marginal products.
   d. The factor distribution of income is morally justified.
   e. With well-functioning labor markets, each factor is paid the equilibrium value of the marginal product of that factor.

Critical-Thinking Question

List three different economic concepts that explain wage differences when the marginal productivity theory of income distribution does not. Explain each.

PITFALLS

GETTING MARGINAL PRODUCTIVITY THEORY RIGHT

? According to the marginal productivity theory, are workers paid a wage equal to the value of their own marginal product of labor?

\> NO, THEY ARE NOT. REMEMBER WHAT THE MARGINAL PRODUCTIVITY THEORY OF INCOME DISTRIBUTION SAYS: *ALL UNITS OF A FACTOR GET PAID THE FACTOR'S EQUILIBRIUM VALUE OF THE MARGINAL PRODUCT*—THE ADDITIONAL VALUE PRODUCED BY THE *LAST* UNIT OF THE FACTOR EMPLOYED. A COMMON SOURCE OF ERROR IS TO FORGET THAT THE RELEVANT VALUE OF THE MARGINAL PRODUCT IS THE *EQUILIBRIUM VALUE, NOT THE VALUE OF THE MARGINAL PRODUCTS YOU CALCULATE ON THE WAY TO EQUILIBRIUM.* For an example, look back at Table 40-2 on p. 428. There, the first worker has a value of the marginal product of $380. It's tempting to conclude that because that worker has a value of the marginal product of $380, he or she is paid $380 in equilibrium. But, that's not the case. If the equilibrium value of the marginal product in the labor market is equal to $200, then *all* workers receive $200.

To learn more, see pages 432–433 and 436–437.

MODULE

42 The Market for Labor

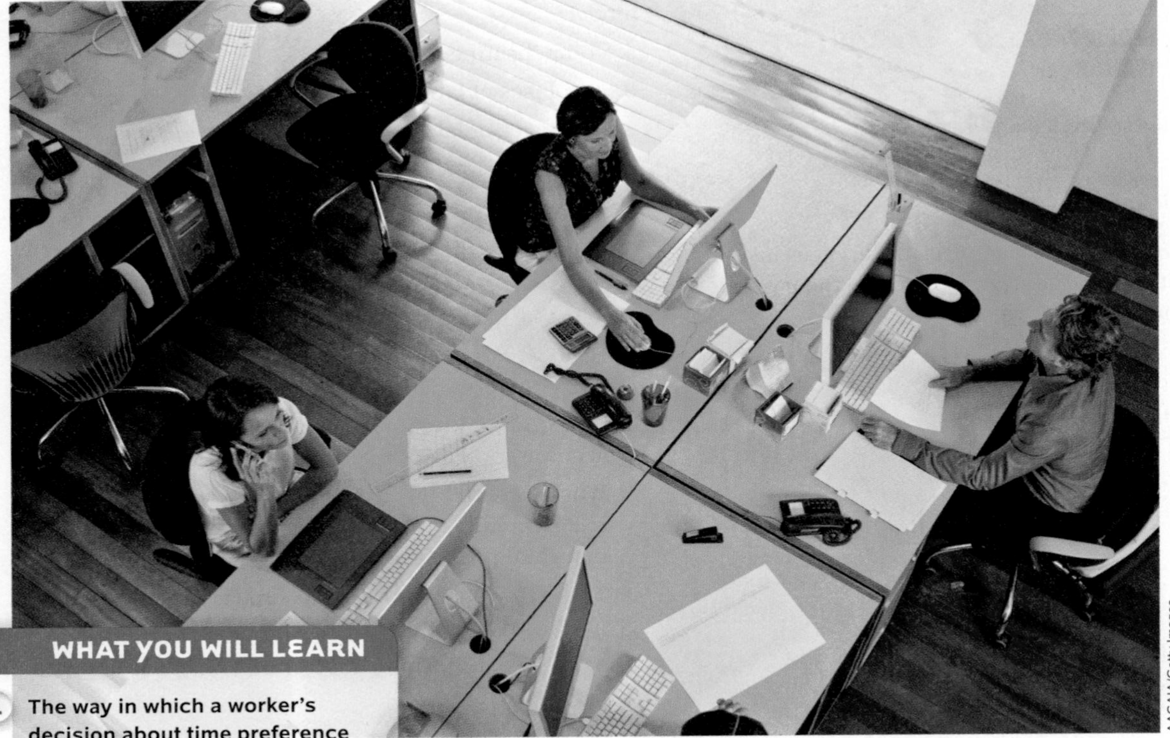
AAGAIA/Getty Images

WHAT YOU WILL LEARN

1. The way in which a worker's decision about time preference gives rise to labor supply
2. How to find equilibrium in the labor market

So far in this section we've focused on the demand for factors, which determines the quantities demanded of labor, capital, or land by producers as a function of their factor prices. But what about the supply of factors? In this module we focus exclusively on the supply of labor. Labor is the most important factor of production in the modern U.S. economy, accounting for most of factor income. We will look at how labor supply arises from a worker's decision about time allocation and explore the determination of equilibrium wage and quantity in the labor market.

The Supply of Labor

There are only 24 hours in a day, so to supply labor is to give up leisure, which presents a dilemma of sorts. For this and other reasons, as we'll see, the labor market looks different from markets for goods and services.

Work versus Leisure

In the labor market, the roles of firms and households are the reverse of what they are in markets for goods and services. A good such as wheat is supplied by firms and demanded by households; labor, though, is demanded by firms and supplied by households. How do people decide how much labor to supply?

As a practical matter, most people have limited control over their work hours: sometimes a worker has little choice but to take a job for a set number of hours per week. However, there is often flexibility to choose among different careers and employment situations that involve varying numbers of work hours. There is a range of part-time and full-time jobs; some are strictly 9:00 A.M. to 5:00 P.M., and others have much longer or shorter work hours. Some people work two jobs; others don't work at all. And self-employed people have many work-hour options. To simplify our study of labor supply, we will imagine an individual who can choose to work as many or as few hours as he or she likes.

Why wouldn't such an individual work as many hours as possible? Because workers are human beings, too, and have other uses for their time. An hour spent on the job is an hour not spent on other, presumably more pleasant, activities. So the decision about how much labor to supply involves making a decision about **time allocation**—how many hours to spend on different activities.

By working, people earn income that they can use to buy goods. The more hours an individual works, the more goods he or she can afford to buy. But this increased purchasing power comes at the expense of a reduction in **leisure,** the time spent not working. (Leisure doesn't necessarily mean time goofing off. It could mean time spent with one's family, pursuing hobbies, exercising, and so on.) And though purchased goods yield utility, so does leisure. Indeed, we can think of leisure itself as a normal good, which most people would like to consume more of as their incomes increase.

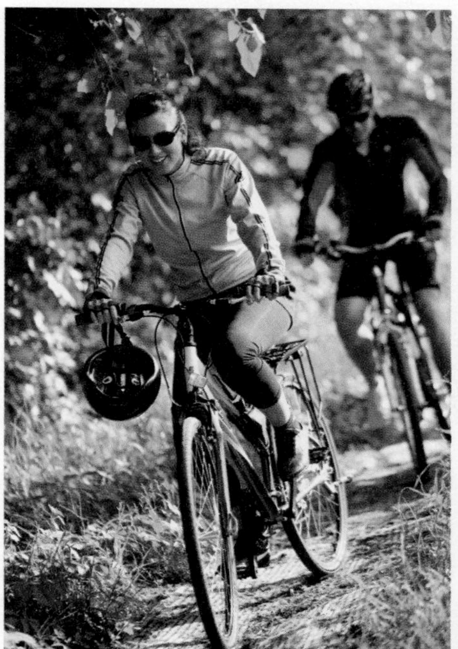

iStockphoto

Every worker faces a trade-off between leisure and work.

How does a rational individual decide how much leisure to consume? By making a marginal comparison, of course. In analyzing consumer choice, we asked how a utility-maximizing consumer uses a marginal *dollar.* In analyzing labor supply, we ask how an individual uses a marginal *hour.*

Consider Clive, an individual who likes both leisure and the goods money can buy. Suppose that his wage rate is $10 per hour. In deciding how many hours he wants to work, he must compare the marginal utility of an additional hour of leisure with the additional utility he gets from $10 worth of goods. If $10 worth of goods adds more to his total utility than an additional hour of leisure, he can increase his total utility by giving up an hour of leisure in order to work an additional hour. If an extra hour of leisure adds more to his total utility than $10 worth of goods, he can increase his total utility by working one fewer hour in order to gain an hour of leisure.

At Clive's optimal level of labor supply, then, the marginal utility he receives from one hour of leisure is equal to the marginal utility he receives from the goods that his hourly wage can purchase. This is very similar to the *optimal consumption rule* we encountered previously, except that it is a rule about time rather than money.

Our next step is to ask how Clive's decision about time allocation is affected when his wage rate changes.

Wages and Labor Supply

Suppose that Clive's wage rate doubles, from $10 to $20 per hour. How will he change his time allocation?

You could argue that Clive will work longer hours because his incentive to work has increased: by giving up an hour of leisure, he can now gain twice as much money as before. But you could equally well argue that he will work less because he doesn't need to work as many hours to generate the income required to pay for the goods he wants.

As these opposing arguments suggest, the quantity of labor Clive supplies can either rise or fall when his wage rate rises. To understand why, let's recall the distinction between *substitution effects* and *income effects*. We have seen that a price change affects consumer choice in two ways: by changing the opportunity cost of a good in terms of other goods (the substitution effect) and by making the consumer richer or poorer (the income effect).

Now think about how a rise in Clive's wage rate affects his demand for leisure. The opportunity cost of leisure—the amount of money he gives up by taking an hour off instead of working—rises. That substitution effect gives him an incentive, other things equal, to consume less leisure and work longer hours. Conversely, a higher wage rate makes Clive richer—and this income effect leads him, other things equal, to want to consume *more* leisure and supply less labor because leisure is a normal good.

So in the case of labor supply, the substitution effect and the income effect work in opposite directions. If the substitution effect is so powerful that it dominates the income effect, an increase in Clive's wage rate leads him to supply *more* hours of labor.

Decisions about labor supply result from decisions about **time allocation:** how many hours to spend on different activities.

Leisure is time available for purposes other than earning money to buy marketed goods.

The **individual labor supply curve** shows how the quantity of labor supplied by an individual depends on that individual's wage rate.

If the income effect is so powerful that it dominates the substitution effect, an increase in the wage rate leads him to supply *fewer* hours of labor.

We see, then, that the **individual labor supply curve**—the relationship between the wage rate and the number of hours of labor supplied by an individual worker—does not necessarily slope upward. If the income effect dominates, a higher wage rate will reduce the quantity of labor supplied.

Figure 42-1 illustrates the two possibilities for labor supply. If the substitution effect dominates the income effect, the individual labor supply curve slopes upward; panel (a) shows an increase in the wage rate from $10 to $20 per hour leading to a *rise* in the number of hours worked from 40 to 50. However, if the income effect dominates, the quantity of labor supplied goes down when the wage rate increases. Panel (b) shows the same rise in the wage rate leading to a *fall* in the number of hours worked from 40 to 30.

Economists refer to an individual labor supply curve that contains both upward-sloping and downward-sloping segments as a "backward-bending labor supply curve." At lower wage rates, the substitution effect dominates the income effect. At higher wage rates, the income effect eventually dominates the substitution effect.

Is a backward-bending labor supply curve a real possibility? Yes: many labor economists believe that income effects on the supply of labor may be somewhat stronger than substitution effects at high wage rates.

The most compelling piece of evidence for this belief comes from Americans' increasing consumption of leisure over the past century. At the end of the nineteenth century, wages adjusted for inflation were only about one-eighth what they are today; the typical work week was 70 hours, and very few workers retired at age 65. Today the typical work week is less than 40 hours, and most people retire at age 65 or earlier. So it seems that Americans have chosen to take advantage of higher wages in part by consuming more leisure.

FIGURE 42-1 The Individual Labor Supply Curve

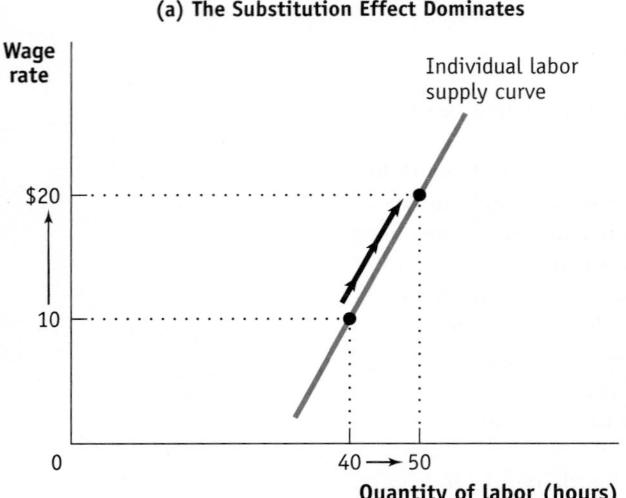

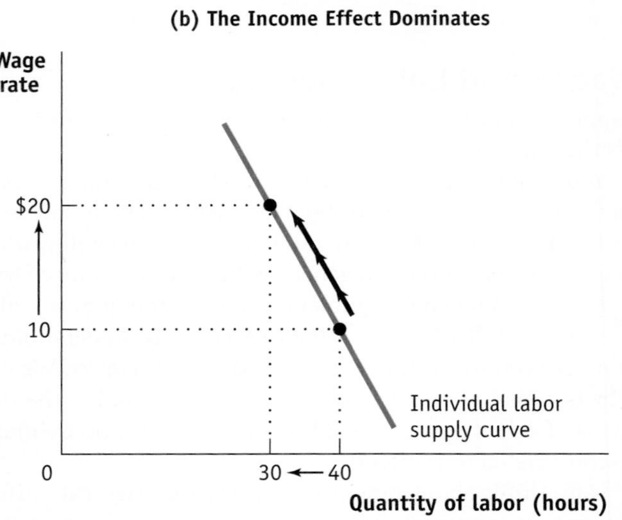

When the substitution effect of a wage increase dominates the income effect, the individual labor supply curve slopes upward, as in panel (a). Here a rise in the wage rate from $10 to $20 per hour increases the number of hours worked from 40 to 50. But when the income effect of a wage increase dominates the substitution effect, the individual labor supply curve slopes downward, as in panel (b). Here the same rise in the wage rate reduces the number of hours worked from 40 to 30. The individual labor supply curve shows how the quantity of labor supplied by an individual depends on that individual's wage rate.

Shifts of the Labor Supply Curve

Now that we have examined how income and substitution effects shape the individual labor supply curve, we can turn to the market labor supply curve. In any labor market, the market supply curve is the horizontal sum of the individual labor supply curves of all workers in that market. A change in any factor *other than the wage* that alters workers' willingness to supply labor causes a shift of the labor supply curve. A variety of factors can lead to such shifts, including changes in preferences and social norms, changes in population, changes in opportunities, and changes in wealth.

Kurhan/Shutterstock

When factors other than wages alter the willingness of workers to supply labor, the labor supply curve will shift.

CHANGES IN PREFERENCES AND SOCIAL NORMS Changes in preferences and social norms can lead workers to increase or decrease their willingness to work at any given wage. A striking example of this phenomenon is the large increase in the number of employed women—particularly married, employed women—that has occurred in the United States since the 1960s. Until that time, women who could afford to largely avoided working outside the home.

Changes in preferences and norms in post–World War II America (helped along by the invention of labor-saving home appliances such as washing machines, the trend for more people to live in cities, and higher female education levels) have induced large numbers of American women to join the workforce—a phenomenon often observed in other countries that experience similar social and technological changes.

CHANGES IN POPULATION Changes in the population size generally lead to shifts of the labor supply curve. A larger population tends to shift the labor supply curve rightward as more workers are available at any given wage; a smaller population tends to shift the labor supply curve leftward due to fewer available workers. Currently the size of the U.S. labor force grows by approximately 1% per year, a result of immigration and, in comparison to other developed countries, a relatively high birth rate, shifting the U.S. labor supply curve to the right. Of course, from 2008 to 2010, due to the Great Recession and despite continued population growth, the size of the labor force began to shrink as workers disillusioned by bad job prospects left the labor force. The result: during that time, the U.S. labor supply curve shifted leftward.

CHANGES IN OPPORTUNITIES At one time, teaching was the only occupation considered suitable for well-educated women. However, as opportunities in other professions opened up to women starting in the 1960s, many women left teaching and chose other careers. This generated a leftward shift of the supply curve for teachers, reflecting a fall in the willingness to work at any given wage and forcing school districts to pay more to maintain an adequate teaching staff.

These events illustrate a general result: when superior alternatives arise for workers in another labor market, the supply curve in the original labor market shifts leftward as workers move to the new opportunities.

Similarly, when opportunities diminish in one labor market—say, layoffs in the manufacturing industry due to increased foreign competition—the supply in alternative labor markets increases as workers move to these other markets.

CHANGES IN WEALTH A person whose wealth increases will buy more normal goods, including leisure. So when a class of workers experiences a general increase in wealth—say, due to a stock market boom—the income effect from the wealth increase will shift the labor supply curve associated with those workers leftward as workers consume more leisure and work less. Note that *the income effect caused by a change in wealth shifts the labor supply curve,* but *the income effect from a wage rate increase*—as we discussed in the case of the individual labor supply curve—*is a movement along the labor supply curve.*

ECONOMICS ▶ IN ACTION

THE OVERWORKED AMERICAN?

Americans today may work less than they did a hundred years ago, but they still work more than workers in any other industrialized country.

Figure 42-2 compares average annual hours worked in the United States with those worked in other industrialized countries. The differences result from a combination of Americans' longer workweeks and shorter vacations. For example, the great majority of full-time American workers put in at least 40 hours per week. Until recently, however, a government mandate limited most French workers to a 35-hour workweek; collective bargaining has achieved a similar reduction in the workweek for many German workers.

FIGURE 42-2 The Average Number of Hours Worked Annually for Select Industrialized Countries, 2012

Country	Average annual number of hours worked
Germany	1,397
France	1,479
Sweden	1,621
United Kingdom	1,654
Canada	1,710
Australia	1,728
Japan	1,745
United States	1,790

Source: OECD.

In 2012, American workers got, on average, ten paid vacation days, but 23% of American workers got none at all. In contrast, German workers are guaranteed six weeks of paid vacation a year. Also, American workers use fewer of the vacation days they are entitled to than do workers in other industrialized countries. A 2011 survey found that only 57% of American workers use all the vacation days they are entitled to, compared to 89% in France.

Why do Americans work so much more than others? Unlike their counterparts in other industrialized countries, Americans are not legally entitled to paid vacation days; as a result, the average American worker gets fewer of them. Moreover, anecdotal evidence suggests that during the recent recession, with its high rates of unemployment, American workers became more reluctant to use the vacation days they were entitled to.

Equilibrium in the Labor Market

Now that we have discussed the labor supply curve, we can use the supply and demand curves for labor to determine the equilibrium wage and level of employment in the labor market.

Figure 42-3 illustrates the labor market as a whole. The *market labor demand curve,* like the market demand curve for a good, is the horizontal sum of all the individual labor demand curves of all the firms that hire labor. And recall that a price-taking firm's labor demand curve is the same as its value of the marginal product of labor curve.

The equilibrium wage rate is the wage rate at which the quantity of labor supplied is equal to the quantity of labor demanded. In Figure 42-3, this leads to an equilibrium wage rate of W^* and the corresponding equilibrium employment level of L^*. (The equilibrium wage rate is also known as the market wage rate.)

When the Product Market Is Not Perfectly Competitive

When the product market is perfectly competitive, the wage rate is equal to the value of the marginal product of labor at equilibrium. In other market structures this is not the case. For example, in a monopoly, the demand curve for the product faced by the monopolist slopes downward. This means that to sell an additional unit of output, the monopolist must lower the price. As a result, the additional revenue received from selling one more unit for a monopolist is not simply the price like it was for a perfect competitor. It is less than the price by the amount of the *price effect* explained previously—the decreased revenue on units that could have been sold at a higher price if the price hadn't been lowered to sell another unit. How does this affect hiring? To

FIGURE 42-3 **Equilibrium in the Labor Market**

The market labor demand curve is the horizontal sum of the individual labor demand curves of all producers. Here the equilibrium wage rate is W^*, the equilibrium employment level is L^*, and every producer hires labor up to the point at which $VMPL = W^*$. So labor is paid its equilibrium value of the marginal product, that is, the value of the marginal product of the last worker hired in the labor market as a whole.

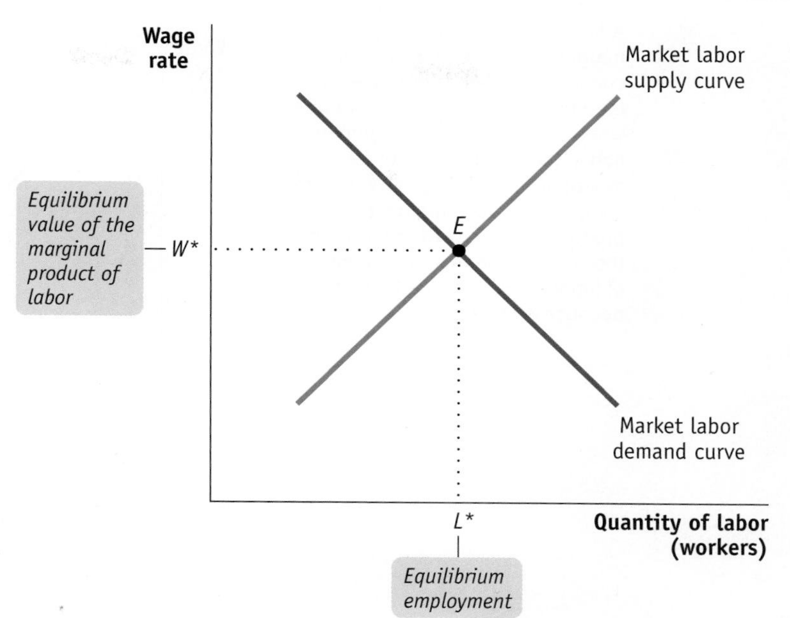

determine its demand for workers, the monopolist must multiply the marginal product of labor by the *marginal revenue* received from selling the additional output. This is called the **marginal revenue product of labor** or ***MRPL***.

(42-1) $MRPL = MPL \times MR$

Table 42-1 shows the calculation of a firm's marginal revenue product of labor.

For a perfectly competitive firm, marginal revenue equals price, so *VMPL* and *MRPL* are equivalent. The two concepts measure the same thing: the value to the firm of hiring an additional worker. The term *MRPL* is a more general term that applies to firms in both perfect competition and imperfect competition. The general rule is that *a profit-maximizing firm in an imperfectly competitive product market employs each factor of production up to the point at which the marginal revenue product of the last unit of the factor employed is equal to that factor's cost.*

The demand curve for labor for a firm operating in an imperfectly competitive product market is the **marginal revenue product of labor (*MRPL*)**. It is equal to the marginal product of labor times the marginal revenue received from selling the additional output. The marginal revenue product of land and the marginal revenue product of capital are equivalent concepts.

TABLE 42-1

Marginal Revenue Product of Labor with Imperfect Competition in the Product Market

Quantity of labor (L)	Quantity of output (Q)	Marginal product of labor (MPL)	Product price (P)	Total revenue (TR) = $P \times Q$	Marginal revenue (MR) = $\Delta TR / \Delta Q$	Marginal revenue product of labor ($MRPL$) = $MPL \times MR$
0	0			$0.00		
		10			$10.00	$100.00
1	10		$10.00	100.00		
		9			9.58	86.20
2	19		9.80	186.20		
		8			9.13	73.00
3	27		9.60	259.20		
		7			8.63	60.40
4	34		9.40	319.60		
		6			8.07	48.40
5	40		9.20	368.00		

FIGURE 42-4 Firm Labor Demand with Imperfect Competition

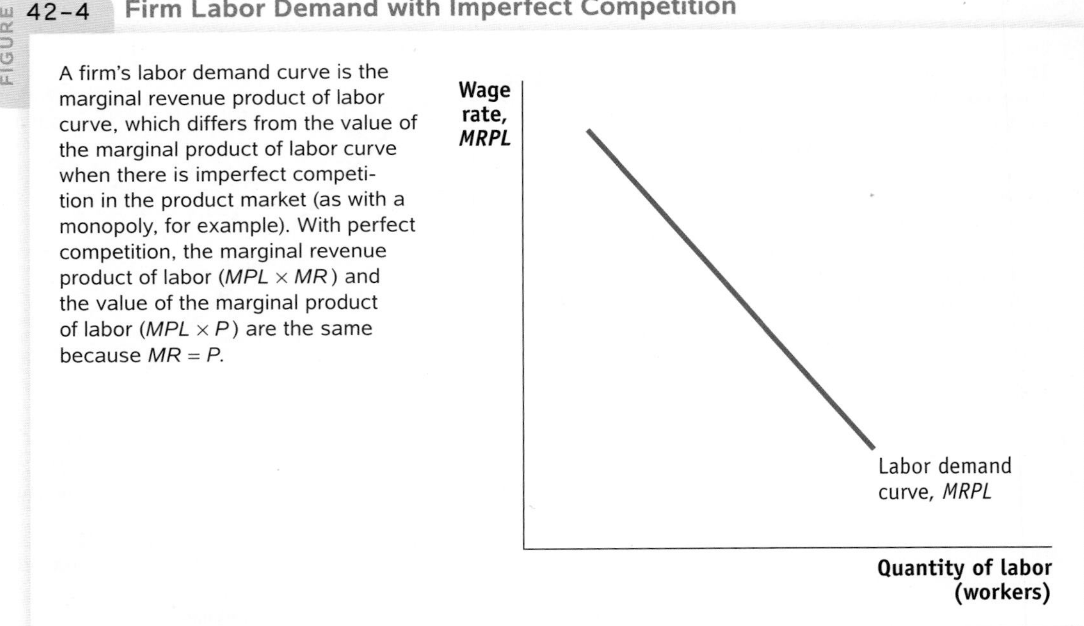

A firm's labor demand curve is the marginal revenue product of labor curve, which differs from the value of the marginal product of labor curve when there is imperfect competition in the product market (as with a monopoly, for example). With perfect competition, the marginal revenue product of labor ($MPL \times MR$) and the value of the marginal product of labor ($MPL \times P$) are the same because $MR = P$.

In the case of a firm operating in an imperfectly competitive product market, the demand curve for a factor is the marginal revenue product curve, as shown in Figure 42-4.

When the Labor Market Is Not Perfectly Competitive

There are also important differences when considering the labor demand curve for a firm in an imperfectly competitive *labor* market rather than in a perfectly competitive labor market. With perfect competition in the labor market, each firm is so small that it can hire as much labor as it wants at the market wage. The firm's hiring decision will not affect the market. In contrast, a firm in an imperfectly competitive labor market is large enough to affect the market wage. A labor market in which there is only one firm hiring labor is called a **monopsony.** A **monopsonist** is the single buyer of a factor. Perhaps you've seen a small town where one firm, such as a meatpacking company or a lumber mill, hires most of the labor—that's an example of a monopsony. Since the firm already hires most of the available labor in the town, if it wants to hire more workers, it has to offer higher wages to attract them.

A **monopsonist** is a single buyer in a factor market. A market in which there is a monopsonist is a **monopsony.**

MODULE 42 Review

Solutions appear at the back of the book.

Check Your Understanding

1. Formerly, Clive was free to work as many or as few hours per week as he wanted. But a new law limits the maximum number of hours he can work per week to 35. Explain under what circumstances, if any, he is made
   a. worse off.
   b. equally well off.
   c. better off.

2. Explain in terms of the income and substitution effects how a fall in Clive's wage rate can induce him to work more hours than before.

Multiple-Choice Questions

1. Which of the following is necessarily true if you work more when your wage rate increases?
   a. The income effect is large.
   b. The substitution effect is small.
   c. The income effect dominates the substitution effect.
   d. The substitution effect dominates the income effect.
   e. The income effect equals the substitution effect.

2. Which of the following will cause you to work more as your wage rate decreases?
   I. the income effect
   II. the substitution effect
   III. a desire for leisure
   a. I only
   b. II only
   c. III only
   d. I and II only
   e. I, II, and III

3. Which of the following will shift the supply curve for labor to the right?
   a. a decrease in the labor force participation rate of women
   b. a decrease in population
   c. an increase in wealth
   d. a decrease in the opportunity cost of leisure
   e. an increase in labor market opportunities for women

4. An increase in the wage rate will
   a. shift the labor supply curve to the right.
   b. shift the labor supply curve to the left.
   c. cause an upward movement along the labor supply curve.
   d. cause a downward movement along the labor supply curve.
   e. have no effect on the quantity of labor supplied.

5. Which of the following statements about the U.S. labor force since World War II is incorrect?
   a. Increases in population have shifted the labor supply curve to the right.
   b. Increases in immigration have shifted the labor supply curve to the right.
   c. Increases in educational opportunities for women have shifted the labor supply curve to the right.
   d. Decreases in work opportunities in foreign markets have shifted the labor supply curve to the right.
   e. Disillusionment with the state of the job market during a recession has shifted the labor supply curve to the left.

Critical-Thinking Questions

1. Draw a correctly labeled graph showing a perfectly competitive labor market in equilibrium. On your graph, label the labor demand curve, the labor supply curve, marginal revenue product of labor, the equilibrium wage (W^*), and the equilibrium quantity of labor (L^*).

2. Then, on the same graph, illustrate how a decrease in the price of the product made by the firm would affect the equilibrium wage and quantity of labor. Label the resulting wage rate W_2 and the resulting quantity of labor L_2.

BUSINESS CASE • Alta Gracia: Can Fair Trade Work?

Check out a T-shirt or sweatshirt emblazoned with your school's logo at your campus bookstore, and the odds are very good that it was made by Alta Gracia, the leading supplier of college-logo apparel to American universities. Alta Gracia is owned by Knights Apparel, a company based in Spartanburg, South Carolina, that manufactures apparel in 30 factories around the world. The Alta Gracia factory is located in the Dominican Republic, where 120 employees turn out T-shirts and sweats.

Julian Eales/Alamy

Workers at Alta Gracia consider themselves lucky because the company pays what it considers a "living wage"—sufficient to feed and shelter a family of four—and allows workers to join a union. Seamstress Santa Castillo, for example, earns $500 a month, three times the average monthly pay of $147 earned by apparel workers in the Dominican Republic, where a loaf of bread costs $1.

Workers at the factory have not always been so fortunate. When the factory was owned by another company, BJ&B, which made baseball caps for Nike and Reebok, workers were paid the prevailing wage and were fired if they complained about working conditions or tried to form a union. Eventually, BJ&B moved its operations to lower-wage Bangladesh, where the minimum wage is 15 cents an hour, compared to 85 cents an hour in the Dominican Republic. In contrast, Alta Gracia pays $2.83 an hour.

Joe Bozich started Knights Apparel in 2000; through scores of deals he has made with universities, his company has surpassed Nike as the number-one college supplier. He works closely with the Worker Rights Consortium, a group of 186 universities that press college-logo apparel manufacturers to improve workers' welfare. The consortium is part of the "Fair Trade Movement," an organization dedicated to improving the welfare of workers in developing countries, principally by raising wages. In 2011, $6.6 billion of Fair Trade–approved goods were sold globally, up 12% from 2010.

Alta Gracia was conceived by Bozich as a model factory to show that an apparel manufacturer could pay its workers a living wage and still succeed when competitors are paying their workers much less. Its production cost for a T-shirt is $4.80—80 cents, or 20%, higher than if it paid minimum wage. Knights Apparel accepts a lower profit margin so it doesn't have to ask retailers to pay a higher wholesale price for its merchandise.

Some observers, though, are skeptical because Alta Gracia merchandise is sold alongside products made by Nike and Adidas, at approximately the same premium price these well-known brands command. "It's a noble effort, but it is an experiment," says Andrew Jassin, an industry analyst. "There are consumers who really care and will buy this apparel at a premium price, and there are those who say they care, but just want value."

Kellie McElhaney, a professor of corporate social responsibility at the University of California at Berkeley, is less skeptical: "A lot of college students would much rather pay for a brand that shows workers are treated well."

Questions for Thought

1. Use the marginal productivity theory of income distribution to explain how the prevailing wage for apparel workers can fall below a living wage in the Dominican Republic.
2. From the point of view of Knights Apparel, what are the pros and cons of paying the Alta Gracia workers a living wage? What are the pros and cons from the point of view of workers generally?
3. What factors does the success or failure of Alta Gracia depend on? What should Knights Apparel do to improve its chances of success?

SECTION 13 REVIEW

Summary

Factor Markets

1. Just as there are markets for goods and services, there are markets for factors of production, including labor, land, and both *physical capital* and *human capital.* These markets determine the **factor distribution of income.**

2. A profit-maximizing, price-taking firm will keep employing more units of a factor until the factor's price is equal to the **value of the marginal product**—the marginal product of the factor multiplied by the price of the output it produces. The **value of the marginal product curve** is therefore the price-taking firm's demand curve for a factor. Factor demand is often referred to as a **derived demand** because it is derived from the demand for the producer's output.

3. The market demand curve for labor is the horizontal sum of the individual demand curves of firms in that market. It shifts for three main reasons: changes in the prices of goods, changes in the supply of other factors, and technological changes.

Marginal Productivity Theory

4. According to the **marginal productivity theory of income distribution,** each factor is paid the value of the marginal product of the last unit of that factor employed in the factor market as a whole—its **equilibrium value of the marginal product.**

5. Large disparities in wages raise questions about the validity of the marginal productivity theory of income distribution. Many disparities can be explained by **compensating differentials** and by differences in talent, job experience, and human capital across workers. Market interference in the forms of **unions** and collective action by employers also creates wage disparities. The **efficiency-wage model,** which arises from a type of market failure, shows how wage disparities can result from employers' attempts to increase worker performance. Free markets tend to diminish discrimination, but discrimination remains a real source of wage disparity. Discrimination is typically maintained either through problems in labor markets or (historically) through institutionalization in government policies.

The Market for Labor

6. Labor supply is the result of decisions about **time allocation,** with each worker facing a trade-off between **leisure** and work. An increase in the hourly wage rate tends to increase work hours via the substitution effect but decrease work hours via the income effect. If the net result is that a worker increases the quantity of labor supplied in response to a higher wage, the **individual labor supply curve** slopes upward. If the net result is that a worker decreases work hours, the individual labor supply curve—unlike supply curves for goods and services—slopes downward.

7. The market labor supply curve is the horizontal sum of the individual labor supply curves of all workers in that market. It shifts for four main reasons: changes in preferences and social norms, changes in population, changes in opportunities, and changes in wealth.

8. When a firm is not a price-taker in a factor market, the firm will consider the **marginal revenue product** when determining how much of a factor to hire. This concept is equivalent to the value of the marginal product in a perfectly competitive market.

9. A **monopsonist** is the single buyer of a factor. A market in which there is a monopsonist is a **monopsony.**

Key Terms

Problems

1. Assume that in 2012 national income in the United States was $11,186.9 billion. In the same year, 137 million workers were employed, at an average wage of $57,526 per worker per year.

   a. How much compensation of employees was paid in the United States in 2012?

   b. Analyze the factor distribution of income. What percentage of national income was received in the form of compensation to employees in 2012?

   c. Suppose the supply of labor rises due to an increase in the retirement age. What happens to the percentage of national income received in the form of compensation of employees?

2. Marty's Frozen Yogurt has the production function per day shown in the accompanying table. The equilibrium wage rate for a worker is $80 per day. Each cup of frozen yogurt sells for $2.

Quantity of labor (workers)	Quantity of frozen yogurt (cups)
0	0
1	110
2	200
3	270
4	300
5	320
6	330

   a. Calculate the marginal product of labor for each worker and the value of the marginal product of labor per worker.

   b. How many workers should Marty employ?

3. Patty's Pizza Parlor has the production function per hour shown in the accompanying table. The hourly wage rate for each worker is $10. Each pizza sells for $2.

Quantity of labor (workers)	Quantity of pizza
0	0
1	9
2	15
3	19
4	22
5	24

   a. Calculate the marginal product of labor for each worker and the value of the marginal product of labor per worker.

   b. Draw the value of the marginal product of labor curve. Use your diagram to determine how many workers Patty should employ.

   c. Now the price of pizza increases to $4. Calculate the value of the marginal product of labor per worker, and draw the new value of the marginal product of labor curve in your diagram. Use your diagram to determine how many workers Patty should employ now.

4. The production function for Patty's Pizza Parlor is given in the table in Problem 3. The price of pizza is $2, but the hourly wage rate rises from $10 to $15. Use a diagram to determine how Patty's demand for workers responds as a result of this wage rate increase.

5. Patty's Pizza Parlor initially had the production function given in the table in Problem 3. A worker's hourly wage rate was $10, and pizza sold for $2. Now Patty buys a new high-tech pizza oven that allows her workers to become twice as productive as before. That is, the first worker now produces 18 pizzas per hour instead of 9, and so on.

   a. Calculate the new marginal product of labor and the new value of the marginal product of labor.

   b. Use a diagram to determine how Patty's hiring decision responds to this increase in the productivity of her workforce.

6. Jameel runs a driver education school. The more driving instructors he hires, the more driving lessons he can sell. But because he owns a limited number of training automobiles, each additional driving instructor adds less to Jameel's output of driving lessons. The accompanying table shows Jameel's production function per day. Each driving lesson can be sold at $35 per hour.

Quantity of labor (driving instructors)	Quantity of driving lessons (hours)
0	0
1	8
2	15
3	21
4	26
5	30
6	33

Determine Jameel's labor demand schedule (his demand schedule for driving instructors) for each of the following daily wage rates for driving instructors: $160, $180, $200, $220, $240, and $260.

7. Dale and Dana work at a self-service gas station and convenience store. Dale opens up every day, and Dana arrives later to help stock the store. They are both paid the current market wage of $9.50 per hour. But Dale feels he should be paid much more because the revenue generated from the gas pumps he turns on every morning is much higher than the revenue generated by the items that Dana stocks. Assess this argument.

8. Your local newspaper publishes an article stating that the wage of farmworkers in Mexico is $11 an hour but the wage of immigrant Mexican farmworkers in California is $9 an hour.

a. Assume that the output sells for the same price in the two countries. Does this imply that the marginal product of labor of farmworkers is higher in Mexico or in California? Explain your answer, and illustrate with a diagram that shows the demand and supply curves for labor in the respective markets. In your diagram, assume that the quantity supplied of labor for any given wage rate is the same for Mexican farmworkers as it is for immigrant Mexican farmworkers in California.

b. Now suppose that farmwork in Mexico is more arduous and more dangerous than farmwork in California. As a result, the quantity supplied of labor for any given wage rate is not the same for Mexican farmworkers as it is for immigrant Mexican farmworkers in California. How does this change your answer to part a? What concept best accounts for the difference between wage rates between Mexican farmworkers and immigrant Mexican farmworkers in California?

c. Illustrate your answer to part b with a diagram. In this diagram, assume that the quantity of labor demanded for any given wage rate is the same for Mexican employers as it is for Californian employers.

9. Research consistently finds that despite nondiscrimination policies, African-American workers on average receive lower wages than White workers do. What are the possible reasons for this? Are these reasons consistent with marginal productivity theory?

10. Wendy works at a fast-food restaurant. When her wage rate was $5 per hour, she worked 30 hours per week. When her wage rate rose to $6 per hour, she decided to work 40 hours. But when her wage rate rose further to $7, she decided to work only 35 hours.

a. Draw Wendy's individual labor supply curve.

b. Is Wendy's behavior irrational, or can you find a rational explanation? Explain your answer.

11. You are the governor's economic policy adviser. The governor wants to put in place policies that encourage employed people to work more hours at their jobs and that encourage unemployed people to find and take jobs. Assess each of the following policies in terms of reaching that goal. Explain your reasoning in terms of income and substitution effects, and indicate when the impact of the policy may be ambiguous.

a. The state income tax rate is lowered, which has the effect of increasing workers' after-tax wage rate.

b. The state income tax rate is increased, which has the effect of decreasing workers' after-tax wage rate.

c. The state property tax rate is increased, which reduces workers' after-tax income.

12. A study by economists at the Federal Reserve Bank of Boston found that between 1965 and 2003 the average American's leisure time increased by between 4 and 8 hours a week. The study claims that this increase is primarily driven by a rise in wage rates.

a. Use the income and substitution effects to describe the labor supply for the average American. Which effect dominates?

b. The study also found an increase in female labor force participation—more women were choosing to hold jobs rather than exclusively perform household tasks. For the average woman who had newly entered the labor force, which effect dominates?

c. Draw typical individual labor supply curves that illustrate your answers to part a and part b above.

Module 43: The Cost-Minimizing Input Combination
Module 44: The Economics of Information

SECTION 14

Additional Topics in Microeconomics

This section includes two modules devoted to additional topics in microeconomics. The modules cover the cost-minimizing input combination and the economics of information, topics which are an important part of contemporary economic theory. These modules complement some of what you've learned in earlier sections. And if you continue your study of economics, you will see these topics again in future courses.

The Cost-Minimizing Input Combination

(left) Beth Hail/Bloomberg via Getty Images; (right) iStockphoto

WHAT YOU WILL LEARN

1. How firms determine the optimal input mix
2. The cost-minimizing rule for hiring inputs

In the previous section we discussed the markets for factors of production and how firms determine the optimal quantity of each factor to hire. But firms don't determine how much of each input to hire separately. Production requires multiple inputs, and firms must decide what *combination* of inputs to use to produce their output. In this module, we will look at how firms decide the optimal combination of factors for producing the desired level of output.

Alternative Input Combinations

In many instances a firm can choose among a number of alternative combinations of inputs that will produce a given level of output. For example, on George and Martha's wheat farm, the decision might involve labor and capital. To produce their optimal quantity of wheat, they could choose to have a relatively *capital-intensive* operation by investing in several tractors and other mechanized farm equipment and hiring relatively little labor. Alternatively, they could have a more *labor-intensive* operation by hiring a lot of workers to do much of the planting and harvesting by hand.

The same amount of wheat can be produced using many different combinations of capital and labor. George and Martha must determine which combination of inputs will maximize their profits.

To begin our study of the optimal combination of inputs, we'll look at the relationship between the inputs used for production. Depending on the situation, inputs can be either substitutes or complements.

Substitutes and Complements in Factor Markets

Early in this book we discussed substitutes and complements in the context of the supply and demand model. Two goods are *substitutes* if a rise in the price of one good makes consumers more willing to buy the other good. For example, an increase in the price of oranges will cause some buyers to switch from purchasing oranges to purchasing tangerines.

When buyers tend to consume two goods together, the goods are known as *complements*. For example, cereal and milk are considered complements because many people consume them together. If the price of cereal increases, people will buy less cereal and therefore need less milk. The decision about how much of a good to buy is influenced by the prices of related goods.

iStockphoto

ATMs can substitute for bank tellers.

The concepts of substitutes and complements also apply to a firm's purchase of inputs. And just as the price of related goods affects consumers' purchasing decisions, the price of other inputs can affect a firm's decision about how much of an input it will use. In some situations, capital and labor are substitutes. For example, George and Martha can produce the same amount of wheat by substituting more tractors for fewer farm workers. Likewise, ATM machines can substitute for bank tellers.

Capital and labor can also be complements when more of one increases the marginal product of the other. For example, a farm worker is more productive when George and Martha buy a tractor, and each tractor requires a worker to drive it. Office workers are more productive when they can use faster computers, and doctors are more productive with modern X-ray machines. In these cases the quantity and quality of capital available affect the marginal product of labor, and thus the demand for labor.

Given the relationship between inputs, how does a firm determine which of the possible combinations to use?

Determining the Optimal Input Mix

If several alternative input combinations can be used to produce the optimal level of output, a profit-maximizing firm will select the input combination with the lowest cost. This process is known as cost minimization.

Cost Minimization

How does a firm determine the combination of inputs that maximizes profits? Let's consider this question using an example.

Imagine you manage a grocery store chain and you need to decide the right combination of self-checkout stations and cashiers at a new store. Table 43-1 shows the alternative combinations of capital (self-checkout stations) and labor (cashiers) you can hire to check out customers shopping at the store. If the store puts in 20 self-checkout stations, you will need to hire 1 cashier to monitor every 5 stations for a total of 4 cashiers. However, trained cashiers are faster than customers at scanning goods, so the store could check out the same number of customers using 10 cashiers and only 10 self-checkout stations.

If you can check out the same number of customers using either of these combinations of capital and labor, how do you decide which combination of inputs to use? By finding the input combination that costs the least—the cost-minimizing input combination.

TABLE 43-1

Cashiers and Self-Checkout Stations

	Capital (self-checkout stations)	Labor (cashiers)
	Rental rate = $1,000/month	Wage rate = $1,600/month
a.	20	4
b.	10	10

Assume that the cost to rent, operate, and maintain a self-checkout station for a month is $1,000 and hiring a cashier costs $1,600 per month. The cost of each input combination from Table 43-1 is shown below.

a. Cost of capital	$20 \times \$1{,}000 =$	$20,000
Cost of labor	$4 \times \$1{,}600 =$	$ 6,400
Total		**$26,400**
b. Cost of capital	$10 \times \$1{,}000 =$	$10,000
Cost of labor	$10 \times \$1{,}600 =$	$16,000
Total		**$26,000**

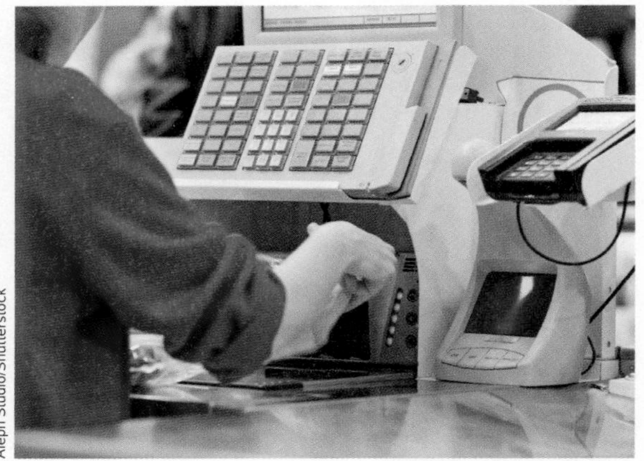

Aleph Studio/Shutterstock

What is the right combination of cashiers and self-checkout stations?

Clearly, your firm would choose the lower cost combination, combination b, and hire 10 cashiers and put in 10 self-checkout stations.

When firms must choose between alternative combinations of inputs, they evaluate the cost of each combination and select the one that minimizes the cost of production. This can be done by calculating the total cost of each alternative combination of inputs, as shown in this example. However, because the number of possible combinations can be very large, it is more practical to use marginal analysis to find the cost-minimizing level of output—which brings us to the cost-minimization rule.

The Cost-Minimization Rule

We already know that the additional output that results from hiring an additional unit of an input is the marginal product (*MP*) of that input. Firms want to receive the highest possible marginal product from each dollar spent on inputs. To do this, firms adjust their hiring of inputs until the marginal product per dollar is equal for all inputs. This is the **cost-minimization rule.** When the inputs are labor and capital, this amounts to equating the marginal product of labor (*MPL*) per dollar spent on wages to the marginal product of capital (*MPK*) per dollar spent to rent capital:

(43-1) $MPL/\text{Wage} = MPK/\text{Rental rate}$

To understand why cost minimization occurs when the marginal product per dollar is equal for all inputs, let's start by looking at two counterexamples. Consider a situation in which the marginal product of labor per dollar is greater than the marginal product of capital per dollar. This situation is described by Equation 43-2:

(43-2) $MPL/\text{Wage} > MPK/\text{Rental rate}$

Suppose the marginal product of labor is 20 units and the marginal product of capital is 100 units. If the wage is $10 and the rental rate for capital is $100, then the marginal product per dollar will be 20/$10 = 2 units of output per dollar for labor and 100/$100 = 1 unit of output per dollar for capital. The firm is receiving 2 additional units of output for each dollar spent on labor and only 1 additional unit of output for each dollar spent on capital. In this case, the firm gets more additional output for its money by hiring labor, so it should hire more labor and less capital.

Because of diminishing returns, as the firm hires more labor, the marginal product of labor falls and as it hires less capital, the marginal product of capital rises. The firm will continue to substitute labor for capital until the falling marginal product of labor per dollar meets the rising marginal product of capital per dollar and the two are equivalent. That is, the firm will adjust its hiring of capital and labor until the marginal product per dollar spent on each input is equal, as in Equation 43-1.

A firm determines the cost-minimizing combination of inputs using the **cost-minimization rule:** hire factors so that the marginal product per dollar spent on each factor is the same.

Next, consider a situation in which the marginal product of capital per dollar is greater than the marginal product of labor per dollar. This situation is described by Equation 43-3:

(43-3) $MPL/\text{Wage} < MPK/\text{Rental rate}$

Let's continue with the assumption that the marginal product of labor for the last unit of labor hired is 20 units and the marginal product of capital for the last unit of capital hired is 100 units. If the wage is \$10 and the rental rate for capital is \$25, then the marginal product per dollar will be 20/\$10 = 2 units of output per dollar for labor and 100/\$25 = 4 units of output per dollar for capital. The firm is receiving 4 additional units of output for each dollar spent on capital and only 2 additional units of output for each dollar spent on labor. In this case, the firm gets more additional output for its money by hiring capital, so it should hire more capital and less labor.

Because of diminishing returns, as the firm hires more capital, the marginal product of capital falls, and as it hires less labor, the marginal product of labor rises. The firm will continue to hire more capital and less labor until the falling marginal product of capital per dollar meets the rising marginal product of labor per dollar to satisfy the cost-minimization rule. That is, the firm will adjust its hiring of capital and labor until the marginal product per dollar spent on each input is equal.

The cost-minimization rule is analogous to the optimal consumption rule (introduced in the module on maximizing utility): consumers maximize their utility by choosing the combination of goods so that the marginal utility per dollar is equal for all goods.

MODULE 43 Review

Solutions appear at the back of the book.

Check Your Understanding

1. A firm produces its output using only capital and labor. Labor costs \$100 per worker per day and capital costs \$200 per unit per day. If the marginal product of the last worker employed is 500 and the marginal product of the last unit of capital employed is 1,000, is the firm employing the cost-minimizing combination of inputs? Explain.

Multiple-Choice Questions

1. An automobile factory employs either assembly-line workers or robotic arms to produce automobile engines. In this case, labor and capital are considered
   a. independent.
   b. complements.
   c. substitutes.
   d. supplements.
   e. human capital.

2. If an increase in the amount of capital employed by a firm leads to an increase in the marginal product of labor, labor and capital are considered
   a. independent.
   b. complements.
   c. substitutes.
   d. supplements.
   e. human capital.

3. If the marginal product of labor per dollar is greater than the marginal product of capital per dollar, which of the following is true? The firm should
   a. not change its employment of capital and labor.
   b. hire more capital.
   c. hire more labor.
   d. hire less labor.
   e. hire more capital and labor.

4. The cost-minimization rule states that costs are minimized when
   a. *MP* per dollar is equal for all factors.
   b. ($MP \times P$) is equal for all factors.
   c. each factor's *MP* is the same.
   d. consumers maximize their utility.
   e. *MPL* falls.

5. A firm currently produces its desired level of output. Its marginal product of labor is 400, its marginal product of capital is 1,000, the wage rate is $20 and the rental rate of capital is $100. In that case, the firm should
   a. employ more capital and more labor.
   b. employ less labor and less capital.
   c. employ less labor and more capital.
   d. employ less capital and more labor.
   e. not change its allocation of capital and labor.

Critical-Thinking Questions

Refer to the accompanying table to answer the questions. Assume that the wage is $10 per day and the price of pencils is $1.

Quantity of labor (workers)	Quantity produced (pencils)
0	0
1	40
2	90
3	120
4	140
5	150
6	160
7	166

1. What is the *MPL* of the 4th worker?
2. What is the *MPL* per dollar of the 5th worker?
3. How many workers would the firm hire if it hired every worker for whom the marginal product per dollar is greater than or equal to 1 pencil per dollar?
4. If the marginal product per dollar spent on labor is 1 pencil per dollar, the marginal product of the last unit of capital hired is 100 pencils per dollar, and the rental rate is $50 per day, is the firm minimizing its cost? Explain.

The Economics of Information

iStockphoto

WHAT YOU WILL LEARN

1. The special problems posed by private information—situations in which some people know things that other people do not
2. How situations of private information can lead to the problem of adverse selection
3. How firms deal with the need for information by using screening and signaling
4. How situations of private information can lead to the problem of moral hazard

Private Information: What You Don't Know Can Hurt You

Markets do very well at dealing with situations in which nobody knows what is going to happen. However, markets have much more trouble with situations in which *some people know things that other people don't know*—situations of **private information.** (Sometimes economists use the term *asymmetric information* rather than *private information,* but the terms are equivalent.) As we will see, private information can distort economic decisions and sometimes prevent mutually beneficial economic transactions from taking place.

Why is some information private? The most important reason is that people generally know more about themselves than other people do. For example, you know whether or not you are a careful driver; but unless you have already been in several accidents, your auto insurance company does not. You are more likely to have a better estimate than your health insurance company of whether or not you will need an expensive medical procedure. And if you are selling me your used car, you are more likely to be aware of any problems with it than I am.

But why should such differences in who knows what be a problem? It turns out that there are two distinct sources of trouble: *adverse selection,* which arises from having private information about the way things are, and *moral hazard,* which arises from having private information about what people do.

Private information is information that some people have that others do not.

Adverse Selection: The Economics of Lemons

Suppose that someone offers to sell you an almost brand-new car—purchased just three months ago, with only 2,000 miles on the odometer and no dents or scratches. Will you be willing to pay almost the same for it as for a car direct from the dealer?

Probably not, for one main reason: you cannot help but wonder why this car is being sold. Is it because the owner has discovered that something is wrong with it—that it is a "lemon"? Having driven the car for a while, the owner knows more about it than you do—and people are more likely to sell cars that give them trouble.

You might think that the fact that sellers of used cars know more about them than buyers do represents an advantage to the sellers. But potential buyers know that potential sellers are likely to offer them lemons—they just don't know exactly which car is a lemon. Because potential buyers of a used car know that potential sellers are more likely to sell lemons than good cars, buyers will offer a lower price than they would if they had a guarantee of the car's quality. Worse yet, this poor opinion of used cars tends to be self-reinforcing, precisely because it depresses the prices that buyers offer. Used cars sell at a discount because buyers expect a disproportionate share of those cars to be lemons. Even a used car that is not a lemon would sell only at a large discount because buyers don't know whether it's a lemon or not.

Oleksiy Maksymenko/Alamy

But potential sellers who have good cars are unwilling to sell them at a deep discount, except under exceptional circumstances. So good used cars are rarely offered for sale, and used cars that are offered for sale have a strong tendency to be lemons. (This is why people who have a compelling reason to sell a car, such as moving overseas, make a point of revealing that information to potential buyers—as if to say "This car is not a lemon!")

The end result, then, is not only that used cars sell for low prices but also that there are a large number of used cars with hidden problems. Equally important, many potentially beneficial transactions—sales of good cars by people who would like to get rid of them to people who would like to buy them—end up being frustrated by the inability of potential sellers to convince potential buyers that their cars are actually worth the higher price demanded. So some mutually beneficial trades between those who want to sell used cars and those who want to buy them go unexploited.

Although economists sometimes refer to situations like this as the "lemons problem" (the issue was introduced in a famous 1970 paper by economist and Nobel laureate George Akerlof entitled "The Market for Lemons"), the more formal name of the problem is **adverse selection.** The reason for the name is obvious: because the potential sellers know more about the quality of what they are selling than the potential buyers, they have an incentive to select the worst things to sell.

Adverse selection does not apply only to used cars. It is a problem for many parts of the economy—notably for insurance companies, and most notably for health insurance companies.

Suppose that a health insurance company were to offer a standard policy to everyone with the same premium. The premium would reflect the *average* risk of incurring a medical expense. But that would make the policy look very expensive to healthy people, who know that they are less likely than the average person to incur medical expenses. So healthy people would be less likely than less healthy people to buy the policy, leaving the health insurance company with exactly the customers it doesn't want: people with a higher-than-average risk of needing medical care, who would find the premium to be a good deal.

Adverse selection occurs when one person knows more about the way things are than other people do. Adverse selection exists, for example, when sellers offer items of particularly low (hidden) quality for sale, and when the people with the greatest need for insurance are those most likely to purchase it.

In order to cover its expected losses from this sicker customer pool, the health insurance company is compelled to raise premiums, driving away more of the remaining healthier customers, and so on. Because the insurance company can't determine who is healthy and who is not, it must charge everyone the same premium, thereby discouraging healthy people from purchasing policies and encouraging unhealthy people to buy policies.

Adverse selection can be reduced through **screening:** using observable information about people to make inferences about their private information.

Adverse selection can be diminished by people **signaling** their private information through actions that credibly reveal what they know.

A long-term **reputation** allows an individual to assure others that he or she isn't concealing adverse private information.

Adverse selection can lead to a phenomenon called an *adverse selection death spiral* as the market for health insurance collapses: insurance companies refuse to offer policies because there is no premium at which the company can cover its losses. Because of the severe adverse selection problems, governments in many advanced countries assume the role of providing health insurance to their citizens. The U.S. government, through its various health insurance programs including Medicare, Medicaid, and the State Children's Health Insurance Program (SCHIP), now disburses more than half the total payments for medical care in the United States.

People or firms faced with the problem of adverse selection have three well-established strategies for dealing with it: *screening, signaling,* and establishing a good *reputation*.

SCREENING The first strategy, **screening,** involves using observable information to make inferences about private information. If you apply to purchase health insurance, you'll find that the insurance company will demand documentation of your health status in an attempt to "screen out" sicker applicants, whom they will refuse to insure or will insure only at very high premiums.

Auto insurance also provides a very good example. An insurance company may not know whether you are a careful driver, but it has statistical data on the accident rates of people who resemble your profile—and it uses those data in setting premiums. A 19-year-old male who drives a sports car and has already had a fender-bender is likely to pay a very high premium. A 40-year-old female who drives a minivan and has never had an accident is likely to pay much less. In some cases, this may be quite unfair: some adolescent males are very careful drivers, and some mature women drive their minivans as if they were F-16s. But nobody can deny that the insurance companies are right on average.

SIGNALING The second strategy is for people who are good prospects to somehow *signal* their private information. **Signaling** involves taking some action that wouldn't be worth taking unless they were indeed good prospects. Reputable used-car dealers often offer warranties—promises to repair any problems with the cars they sell that arise within a given amount of time. This isn't just a way of insuring their customers against possible expenses; it's a way of credibly showing that they are not selling lemons. As a result, more sales occur and dealers can command higher prices for their used cars.

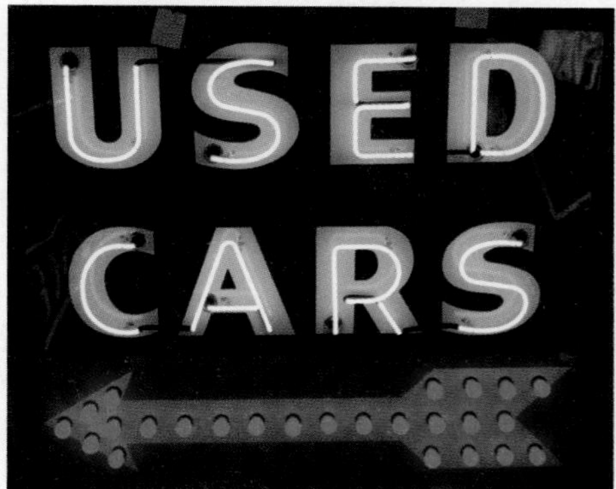

Thinkstock

REPUTATION In the face of adverse selection, it can be very valuable to establish a good **reputation,** our third strategy. A used-car dealership will often advertise how long it has been in business to show that it has continued to satisfy its customers. As a result, new customers will be willing to purchase cars and to pay more for that dealer's cars.

Moral Hazard

In the late 1970s, New York and other major cities experienced an epidemic of suspicious fires—fires that appeared to be deliberately set. Some of the fires were probably started by teenagers on a lark, others by gang members struggling over turf. But investigators eventually became aware of patterns in a number of the fires. Particular landlords who owned several buildings seemed to have an unusually large number of their buildings burn down. Although it was difficult to prove, police had few doubts that most of these fire-prone landlords were hiring professional arsonists to torch their own properties.

Why burn your own buildings? These buildings were typically in declining neighborhoods, where rising crime and middle-class flight had led to a decline in property values. But the insurance policies on the buildings were written to compensate owners based on historical property values, and so would pay the owner of a destroyed building more than the building was worth in the current market. For an unscrupulous landlord who knew the right people, this presented a profitable opportunity.

The arson epidemic became less severe during the 1980s, partly because insurance companies began making it difficult to over-insure properties and partly because a boom in real estate values made many previously arson-threatened buildings worth more unburned.

The arson episodes make it clear that it is a bad idea for insurance companies to let customers insure buildings for more than their value—it gives the customers some destructive incentives. You might think, however, that the incentive problem would go away as long as the insurance is no more than 100% of the value of what is being insured.

©Tetra Images/Alamy

Franchise owners have an incentive to work hard because of their personal stake in the businesses they run.

But, unfortunately, anything close to 100% insurance still distorts incentives—it induces policyholders to behave differently from how they would in the absence of insurance. The reason is that preventing fires requires effort and cost on the part of a building's owner. Fire alarms and sprinkler systems have to be kept in good repair, fire safety rules have to be strictly enforced, and so on. All of this takes time and money—time and money that the owner may not find worth spending if the insurance policy will provide close to full compensation for any losses.

Of course, the insurance company could specify in the policy that it won't pay if basic safety precautions have not been taken. But it isn't always easy to tell how careful a building's owner has been—the owner knows, but the insurance company does not.

The point is that the building's owner has private information about his or her own actions; the owner knows whether he or she has really taken all appropriate precautions. As a result, the insurance company is likely to face greater claims than if it were able to determine exactly how much effort a building owner exerts to prevent a loss. The problem of distorted incentives arises when an individual has private information about his or her own actions but someone else bears the costs of a lack of care or effort. This is known as **moral hazard.**

To deal with moral hazard, it is necessary to give individuals with private information some personal stake in what happens, a stake that gives them a reason to exert effort even if others cannot verify that they have done so. Moral hazard is the reason salespeople in many stores receive a commission on sales: it's hard for managers to be sure how hard the salespeople are really working, and if they were paid only straight salary, they would not have an incentive to exert effort to make those sales. Similar logic explains why many stores and restaurants, even if they are part of national chains, are actually franchises, licensed outlets owned by the people who run them.

Insurance companies deal with moral hazard by requiring a **deductible:** they compensate for losses only above a certain amount, so that coverage is always less than 100%. The insurance on your car, for example, may pay for repairs only after the first $500 in loss. This means that a careless driver who gets into a fender-bender will end up paying $500 for repairs even if he is insured, which provides at least some incentive to be careful and reduces moral hazard.

Moral hazard occurs when an individual knows more about his or her own actions than other people do. This leads to a distortion of incentives to take care or to exert effort when someone else bears the costs of the lack of care or effort.

A **deductible** is a sum specified in an insurance policy that the insured individuals must pay before being compensated for a claim; deductibles reduce *moral hazard*.

In addition to reducing moral hazard, deductibles provide a partial solution to the problem of adverse selection. Your insurance premium often drops substantially if you are willing to accept a large deductible. This is an attractive option to people who know they are low-risk customers; it is less attractive to people who know they are high-risk—and so are likely to have an accident and end up paying the deductible. By offering a menu of policies with different premiums and deductibles, insurance companies can screen their customers, inducing them to sort themselves out on the basis of their private information.

As the example of deductibles suggests, moral hazard limits the ability of the economy to allocate risks efficiently. You generally can't get full (100%) insurance on your home or car, even though you would like to buy full insurance, and you bear the risk of large deductibles, even though you would prefer not to.

MODULE 44 Review

Solutions appear at the back of the book.

Check Your Understanding

1. Your car insurance premiums are lower if you have had no moving violations for several years. Explain how this feature tends to decrease the potential inefficiency caused by adverse selection.

2. A common feature of home construction contracts is that when it costs more to construct a building than was originally estimated, the contractor must absorb the additional cost. Explain how this feature reduces the problem of moral hazard but also forces the contractor to bear more risk than she would like.

3. True or false? Explain your answer, stating what concept analyzed in this module accounts for the feature.

   People with higher deductibles on their auto insurance

   a. generally drive more carefully.

   b. pay lower premiums.

Multiple-Choice Questions

1. Which of the following is true about private information?

   I. It has value.
   II. Everyone has access to it.
   III. It can distort economic decisions.

   a. I only
   b. II only
   c. III only
   d. I and III only
   e. I, II, and III

2. Due to adverse selection,

   a mutually beneficial trades go unexploited.
   b. people buy lemons rather than other fruit.
   c. sick people buy less insurance.
   d. private information is available to all.
   e. public information is available to no one.

3. When colleges use grade point averages to make admissions decisions, they are employing which strategy?

   a. signaling
   b. screening
   c. profit maximization
   d. marginal analysis
   e. adverse selection

4. Moral hazard is the result of

   a. private information.
   b. signaling.
   c. toxic waste.
   d. adverse selection.
   e. public information.

5. A deductible is used by insurance companies to

   a. allow customers to pay for insurance premiums using payroll deduction.
   b. deal with moral hazard.
   c. make public information private.
   d. compensate policyholders fully for their losses.
   e. avoid all payments to policyholders.

Critical-Thinking Questions

Individuals or corporations (for example home-buyers or banks) believe that the government will "bail them out" in the event that their decisions lead to a financial collapse.

1. This is an example of what problem created by private information?

2. How does this situation lead to inefficiency?

3. What is a possible remedy for the problem?

SECTION 14 REVIEW

Summary

The Cost-Minimizing Input Combination

1. Firms will determine the optimal input combination using the **cost-minimization rule:** When a firm uses the cost-minimizing combination of inputs, the marginal product of labor divided by the wage rate is equal to the marginal product of capital divided by the rental rate.

The Economics of Information

2. **Private information** can cause inefficiency by distorting economic decisions and preventing mutually beneficial transactions from taking place. One problem is **adverse selection,** private information about the way things are. It creates the "lemons problem" in used-car markets, where sellers of high-quality cars drop out of the market. Adverse selection can be limited in several ways—through **screening** of individuals, through the **signaling** that people use to reveal their private information, and through the building of a **reputation.**
3. A related problem is **moral hazard:** individuals have private information about their actions, which distorts their incentives to exert effort or care when someone else bears the costs of that lack of effort or care. It limits the ability of markets to allocate risk efficiently. Insurance companies try to limit moral hazard by imposing **deductibles,** placing more risk on the insured.

Key Terms

Problems

1. You are considering buying a second-hand Volkswagen. From reading car magazines, you know that half of all Volkswagens have problems of some kind (they are "lemons") and the other half run just fine (they are "plums"). If you knew that you were getting a plum, you would be willing to pay $10,000 for it: this is how much a plum is worth to you. You would also be willing to buy a lemon, but only if its price were no more than $4,000: this is how much a lemon is worth to you. And someone who owns a plum would be willing to sell it at any price above $8,000. Someone who owns a lemon would be willing to sell it for any price above $2,000.
   a. For now, suppose that you can immediately tell whether the car that you are being offered is a lemon or a plum. Suppose someone offers you a plum. Will there be trade?

   Now suppose that the seller has private information about the car she is selling: the seller knows whether she has a lemon or a plum. But when the seller offers you a Volkswagen, you do not know whether it is a lemon or a plum. So this is a situation of adverse selection.

   b. Since you do not know whether you are being offered a plum or a lemon, what is the most you are willing to pay for your vehicle? Why?
2. For each of the following situations describe whether it is a situation of moral hazard or of adverse selection. Then explain what inefficiency can arise from this situation and explain how the proposed solution reduces the inefficiency.
   a. When you buy a second-hand car, you do not know whether it is a lemon (low quality) or a plum (high quality), but the seller knows. A solution is for sellers to offer a warranty with the car that pays for repair costs.
   b. Some people are prone to see doctors unnecessarily for minor complaints like headaches, and health maintenance organizations do not know how urgently you need a doctor. A solution is for insurees to have to make

a co-payment of a certain dollar amount (for example, $10) each time they visit a health care provider.

c. When airlines sell tickets, they do not know whether a buyer is a business traveler (who is willing to pay a lot for a seat) or a leisure traveler (who has a low willingness to pay). A solution for a profit-maximizing airline is to offer an expensive ticket that is very flexible (it allows date and route changes) and a cheap ticket that is very inflexible (it has to be booked in advance and cannot be changed).

d. When making a decision about hiring you, prospective employers do not know whether you are a productive or unproductive worker. A solution is for productive workers to provide potential employers with references from previous employers.

SECTION 15

Macroeconomic Measurement

THE NEW #2

"China Passes Japan as Second-Largest Economy." That was the headline in the *New York Times* on August 15, 2010. Citing economic data suggesting that Japan's economy was weakening while China's was roaring ahead, the article predicted—correctly, as it turned out—that 2010 would mark the first year in which the surging Chinese economy finally overtook Japan's, taking second place to the United States on the world economic stage.

"The milestone," wrote the *Times,* "though anticipated for some time, is the most striking evidence yet that China's ascendance is for real and that the rest of the world will have to reckon with a new economic superpower."

But wait a minute—what does it mean to say that China's economy is larger than Japan's? The two economies are, after all, producing very different mixes of goods. Despite its rapid advance, China is still a fairly poor country whose greatest strength is in relatively low-tech production. Japan, by contrast, is very much a high-tech nation, and it dominates world output of some sophisticated goods, like electronic sensors for automobiles. That's why the 2011 earthquake in northeastern Japan, which put many factories out of action, temporarily caused major production disruptions for auto factories around the world.

How can you compare the sizes of two economies when they aren't producing the same things?

The answer is that comparisons of national economies are based on the *value* of their production. When news reports declared that China's economy had overtaken Japan's, they meant that China's *gross domestic product,* or *GDP*—a measure of the overall value of goods and services produced—had surpassed Japan's GDP.

GDP is one of the most important measures used to track the macroeconomy—that is, to quantify movements in the overall level of output and prices. Measures like GDP and the rates of unemployment and inflation play an important role in formulating economic policy, since policy makers need to know what's going on, and anecdotes are no substitute for hard data. The data are also important for business decisions (for an example, see the business case at the end of this section, on page 496).

In this section we start with a general description of some of the field's major concerns. Then we explain how macroeconomists measure key aspects of the economy. We will explore ways to measure the economy's total output and total income using the circular-flow diagram. We then formally define GDP and explain how to calculate it. We also learn about the value of real GDP and how it is calculated.

Introduction to Macroeconomics

American Stock/Getty Images

WHAT YOU WILL LEARN

1. What a business cycle is and why diminishing the severity of business cycles is a goal for policy makers
2. How long-run economic growth determines a country's standard of living
3. The meaning of inflation and deflation and why price stability is preferred
4. The importance of open-economy macroeconomics and how economies interact through trade deficits and trade surpluses

Today many people enjoy walking through New York's beautiful Central Park. But in 1932 there were many people living there in squalor in one of the many "Hoovervilles"—the shantytowns that had sprung up across America as a result of a catastrophic economic slump that started in 1929. Millions of people were out of work and unable to feed, clothe, and house themselves and their families. Beginning in 1933, the U.S. economy would stage a partial recovery. But joblessness stayed high throughout the 1930s—a period that came to be known as the Great Depression.

These shantytowns were named after Herbert Hoover, who had been elected president in 1928. When the Depression struck, people blamed Hoover who, along with his economic advisers, didn't seem to understand the crisis and had no idea what to do about it.

At the time of the Great Depression, *microeconomics,* which is concerned with the consumption and production decisions of individual consumers and producers and with the allocation of scarce resources among industries, was already a well-developed branch of economics. *Macroeconomics,* which focuses on the behavior of the economy as a whole, was still in its infancy.

But macroeconomics came into its own during the Depression. Economists realized that they needed to understand the nature of the catastrophe that had overtaken the United States and much of the rest of the world in order to learn how to avoid such events in the future. To this day, the effort to understand economic slumps and find ways to prevent them is at the core of macroeconomics.

In this module we will begin to explore the key features of macroeconomic analysis. We will look at some of the field's major concerns, including

- Business cycles
- Economic growth
- Price stability
- Trade imbalances

The Business Cycle

Figure 45-1 shows a stylized representation of the way the economy evolves over time. The vertical axis shows either employment or an indicator of how much the economy is producing, such as *real gross domestic product (real GDP),* a measure of the economy's overall output that we'll learn about in the next module

A broad-based downturn, in which output and employment fall in many industries, is called a **recession** (sometimes referred to as a *contraction*). Recessions, as officially declared by the National Bureau of Economic Research, or NBER, are indicated by the shaded areas in Figure 45-1. When the economy isn't in a recession, when most economic numbers are following their normal upward trend, the economy is said to be in an **expansion** (sometimes referred to as a *recovery*). The alternation between recessions and expansions is known as the **business cycle.** The point in time at which the economy shifts from expansion to recession is known as a **business-cycle peak;** the point at which the economy shifts from recession to expansion is known as a **business-cycle trough.**

Recessions, or contractions, are periods of economic downturn when output and employment are falling.

Expansions, or recoveries, are periods of economic upturn when output and employment are rising.

The **business cycle** is the short-run alternation between recessions and expansions.

The point at which the economy turns from expansion to recession is a **business-cycle peak.**

The point at which the economy turns from recession to expansion is a **business-cycle trough.**

FIGURE 45-1 The Business Cycle

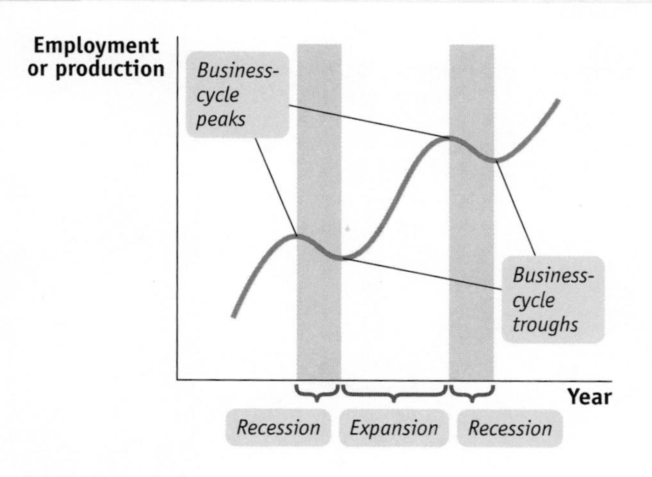

This is a stylized picture of the business cycle. The vertical axis measures either employment or total output in the economy. Periods when these two variables turn down are *recessions;* periods when they turn up are *expansions.* The point at which the economy turns down is a *business-cycle peak;* the point at which it turns up again is a *business-cycle trough.*

TABLE 45-1

The History of the Business Cycle

Business-Cycle Peak	Business-Cycle Trough
no prior data available	December 1854
June 1857	December 1858
October 1860	June 1861
April 1865	December 1867
June 1869	December 1870
October 1873	March 1879
March 1882	May 1885
March 1887	April 1888
July 1890	May 1891
January 1893	June 1894
December 1895	June 1897
June 1899	December 1900
September 1902	August 1904
May 1907	June 1908
January 1910	January 1912
January 1913	December 1914
August 1918	March 1919
January 1920	July 1921
May 1923	July 1924
October 1926	November 1927
August 1929	March 1933
May 1937	June 1938
February 1945	October 1945
November 1948	October 1949
July 1953	May 1954
August 1957	April 1958
April 1960	February 1961
December 1969	November 1970
November 1973	March 1975
January 1980	July 1980
July 1981	November 1982
July 1990	March 1991
March 2001	November 2001
December 2007	June 2009

Source: National Bureau of Economic Research.

The business cycle is an enduring feature of the economy. Table 45-1 shows the official list of business-cycle peaks and troughs. As you can see, there have been recessions and expansions for at least the past 155 years. Whenever there is a prolonged expansion, as there was in the 1960s and again in the 1990s, books and articles come out proclaiming the end of the business cycle. Such proclamations have always proved wrong: the cycle always comes back. But why does it matter?

The Pain of Recession

Not many people complain about the business cycle when the economy is expanding. Recessions, however, create a great deal of pain.

The most important effect of a recession is its impact on the ability of workers to find and hold jobs. The most widely used indicator of conditions in the labor market

"I can't move in with my parents. They moved in with my grandparents."

is the *unemployment rate*. We'll explain how that rate is calculated in the next section, but for now it's enough to say that a high unemployment rate tells us that jobs are scarce and a low unemployment rate tells us that jobs are easy to find. Figure 45-2 shows the unemployment rate from 1988 to 2013. As you can see, the U.S. unemployment rate surged during and after each recession but eventually fell during periods of expansion. The rising unemployment rate in 2008 was a sign that a new recession might be under way, which was later confirmed by the NBER to have begun in December 2007.

Because recessions cause many people to lose their jobs and also make it hard to find new ones, recessions hurt the standard of living of many families. Recessions are usually associated with a rise in the number of people living below the poverty line, an increase in the number of people who lose their houses because they can't afford the mortgage payments, and a fall in the percentage of Americans with health insurance coverage.

You should not think, however, that workers are the only group that suffers during a recession. Recessions are also bad for firms: like employment and wages, profits suffer during recessions, with many small businesses failing.

All in all, then, recessions are bad for almost everyone. Can anything be done to reduce their frequency and severity?

FIGURE 45-2 The U.S. Unemployment Rate, 1988–2013

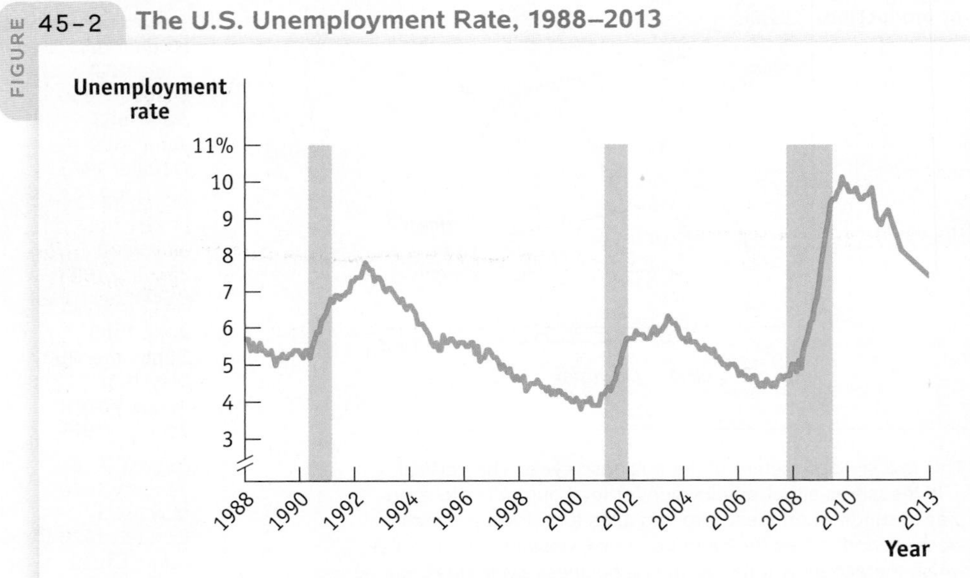

The unemployment rate, a measure of joblessness, rises sharply during recessions and usually falls during expansions. The shaded areas indicate periods of recession.
Source: Bureau of Labor Statistics.

ECONOMICS ▶ IN ACTION

DEFINING RECESSIONS AND EXPANSIONS

How exactly are recessions and expansions defined? The answer is that there is no exact definition!

In many countries, economists adopt the rule that a recession is a period of at least two consecutive quarters (a quarter is three months) during which the total output of the economy shrinks. The two-consecutive-quarters requirement is designed to avoid classifying brief hiccups in the economy's performance, with no lasting significance, as recessions.

Sometimes, however, this definition seems too strict. For example, an economy that has three months of sharply declining output, then three months of slightly positive growth, then another three months of rapid decline, should surely be considered to have endured a nine-month recession.

In the United States, we try to avoid such misclassifications by assigning the task of determining when a recession begins and ends to an independent panel of experts at the National Bureau of Economic Research (NBER). This panel looks at a variety of economic indicators, with the main focus on employment and production, and then makes a judgment call.

Sometimes this judgment is controversial. In fact, there is lingering controversy over the 2001 recession. According to the NBER, that recession began in March 2001 and ended in November 2001 when output began rising. Some critics argue, however, that the recession really began several months earlier, when industrial production began falling. Other critics argue that the recession didn't really end in 2001 because employment continued to fall and the job market remained weak for another year and a half.

Taming the Business Cycle

Modern macroeconomics largely came into being as a response to the worst recession in history—the 43-month downturn that began in 1929 and continued into 1933, ushering in the Great Depression. The havoc wreaked by the 1929–1933 recession spurred economists to search both for understanding and for solutions: they wanted to know how such things could happen and how to prevent them.

Corbis

Modern macroeconomics came into being as a response to the Great Depression of 1929–1933.

The work of the British economist John Maynard Keynes, published during the Great Depression, suggested that a depressed economy results from inadequate spending, and that using *monetary policy* (changing the quantity of money to alter interest rates, which in turn affect overall spending) and *fiscal policy* (changing taxes and government spending to affect overall spending) can mitigate the effect of recessions. To this day, governments turn to these policies, known as *Keynesian Economics,* when recession strikes. Later work, notably that of another great macroeconomist, Milton Friedman, led to a consensus that it's important to rein in booms as well as to fight slumps.

So modern policy makers try to "smooth out" the business cycle. They haven't been completely successful, as a look at Table 45-1 makes clear. It's widely believed, however, that policy guided by macroeconomic analysis has helped make the economy more stable.

Although the business cycle is one of the main concerns of macroeconomics and historically played a crucial role in fostering the development of the field, macroeconomists are also concerned with other issues, such as the question of long-run growth.

ECONOMICS IN ACTION

COMPARING RECESSIONS

The alternation of recessions and expansions seems to be an enduring feature of economic life. However, not all business cycles are created equal. In particular, some recessions have been much worse than others.

FIGURE 45-3 Two Recessions

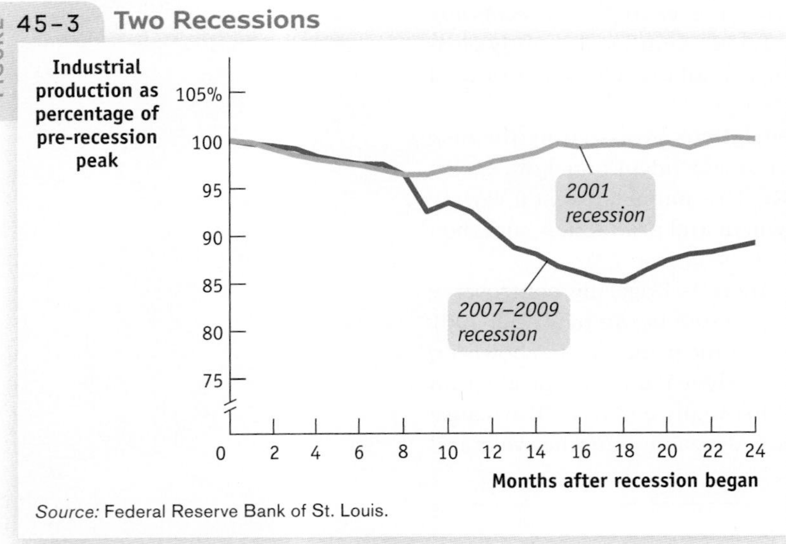

Source: Federal Reserve Bank of St. Louis.

Let's compare the two most recent recessions: the 2001 recession and the Great Recession of 2007–2009. These recessions differed in duration: the first lasted only eight months, the second more than twice as long. Even more important, however, they differed greatly in depth.

In Figure 45-3 we compare the depth of the recessions by looking at what happened to industrial production over the months after the recession began. In each case, production is measured as a percentage of its level at the recession's start. Thus the line for the 2007–2009 recession shows that industrial production eventually fell to about 85% of its initial level.

Clearly, the 2007–2009 recession hit the economy vastly harder than the 2001 recession. Indeed, by comparison to many recessions, the 2001 slump was very mild.

Of course, this was no consolation to the millions of American workers who lost their jobs, even in that mild recession.

Long-Run Economic Growth

In 1955, Americans were delighted with the nation's prosperity. The economy was expanding, consumer goods that had been rationed during World War II were available for everyone to buy, and most Americans believed, rightly, that they were better off than the citizens of any other nation, past or present.

Yet by today's standards, Americans were quite poor in 1955. Figure 45-4 shows the percentage of American homes equipped with a variety of appliances in 1905, 1955, and 2005: in 1955 only 37% of American homes contained washing machines

FIGURE 45-4 The Fruits of Long-Run Growth in America

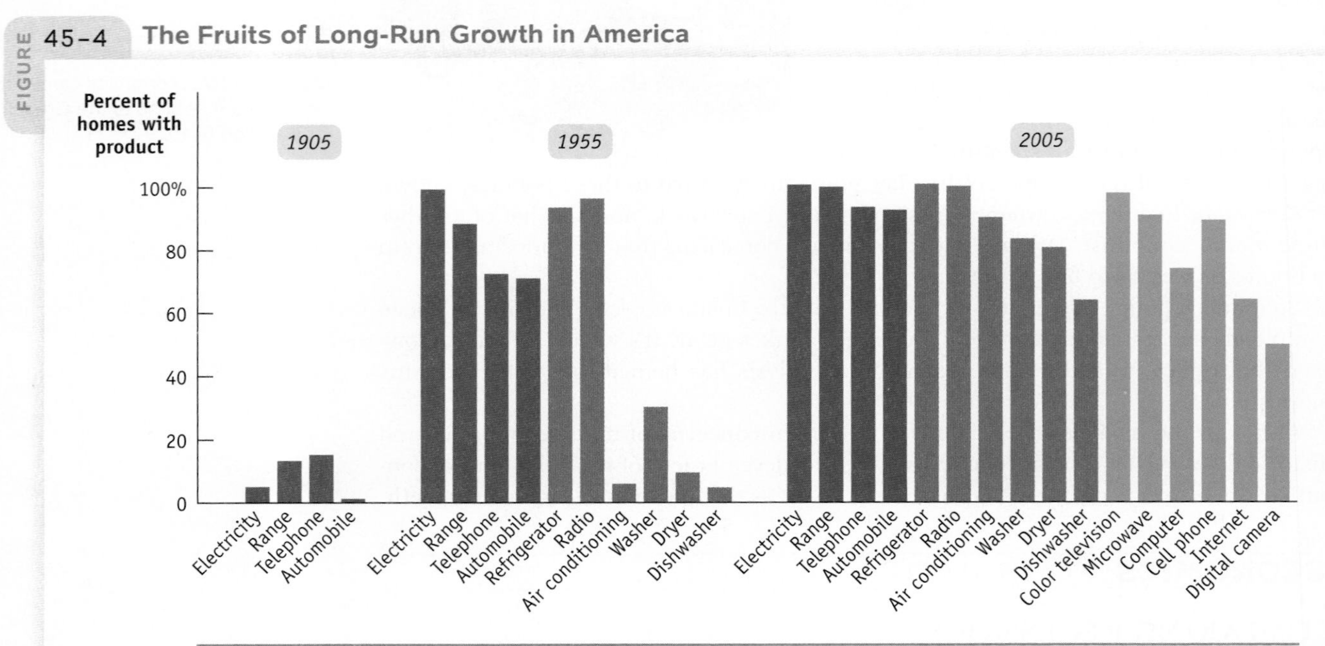

Americans have become able to afford many more material goods over time thanks to long-run economic growth.

Source: W. Michael Cox and Richard Alm, "How Are We Doing?" *The American* (July/August 2008). http://www.american.com/archive/2008/july-august-magazine-contents/how-are-we-doing

and hardly anyone had air conditioning. And if we turn the clock back another half-century, to 1905, we find that life for many Americans was startlingly primitive by today's standards.

Long-run economic growth is the sustained upward trend in the economy's output over time.

Why are the vast majority of Americans today able to afford conveniences that many Americans lacked in 1955? The answer is **long-run economic growth,** the sustained rise in the quantity of goods and services the economy produces. Figure 45-5 shows the growth since 1900 in real GDP per capita, a measure of total output per person in the economy. The severe recession of 1929–1933 stands out, but business cycles between World War II and 2007 are almost invisible, dwarfed by the strong upward trend.

FIGURE 45-5 **Growth, the Long View**

Over the long run, growth in real GDP per capita has dwarfed the ups and downs of the business cycle. Except for the recession that began the Great Depression, recessions are almost invisible until 2007.

Sources: Angus Maddison, *Statistics on World Population, GDP, and Per Capita GDP, 1–2008AD*, http://www.ggdc.net/MADDISON/oriindex.htm; Bureau of Economic Analysis.

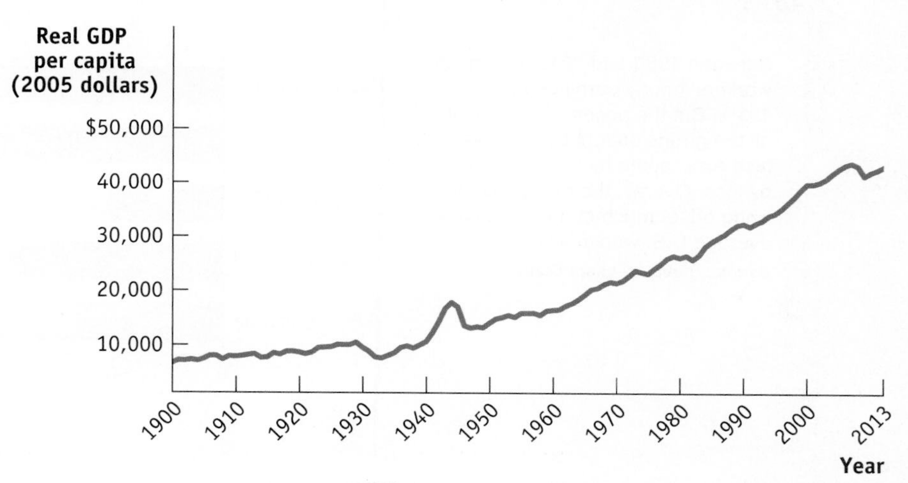

Part of the long-run increase in output is accounted for by the fact that we have a growing population and workforce. But the economy's overall production has increased by much more than the population. On average, in 2013 the U.S. economy produced about $43,000 worth of goods and services per person, about twice as much as in 1971, about three times as much as in 1951, and almost eight times as much as in 1900.

Long-run economic growth is fundamental to many of the most pressing economic questions today. Responses to key policy questions, like the country's ability to bear the future costs of government programs such as Social Security and Medicare, depend in part on how fast the U.S. economy grows over the next few decades. More broadly, the public's sense that the country is making progress depends crucially on success in achieving long-run growth.

When growth slows, as it did in the 1970s, it can help feed a national mood of pessimism. In particular, *long-run growth per capita*—a sustained upward trend in output per person—is the key to higher wages and a rising standard of living. A major concern of macroeconomics is trying to understand the forces behind long-run growth.

Long-run growth is an even more urgent concern in poorer, less developed countries which would like to achieve a higher standard of living. In these cases, the central concern of economic policy is how to accelerate long-run growth.

Thinkstock

Long-run growth is the key to higher living standards in the poorer, less developed countries of the world.

Inflation and Deflation

In January 1980 the average production worker in the United States was paid $6.57 an hour. By December 2013, the average hourly earnings for such a worker had risen to $19.40 an hour. Three cheers for economic progress!

But wait. American workers were paid much more in 2013, but they also faced a much higher cost of living. In early 1980, a dozen eggs cost only about $0.88; by December 2013, that was up to $2.00. The price of a loaf of white bread went from about $0.50 to $1.39. And the price of a gallon of gasoline rose from just $1.11 to $3.33.

Figure 45-6 compares the percentage increase in hourly earnings between 1980 and 2013 with the increases in the prices of some standard items: the average worker's paycheck went further in terms of some goods, but less far in terms of others. Overall, the rise in the cost of living wiped out many, if not all, of the wage gains of the typical worker from 1980 to 2013. In other words, once changes in prices are taken into account, the living standard of the typical U.S. worker has stagnated from 1980 to the present.

FIGURE 45-6 Rising Prices

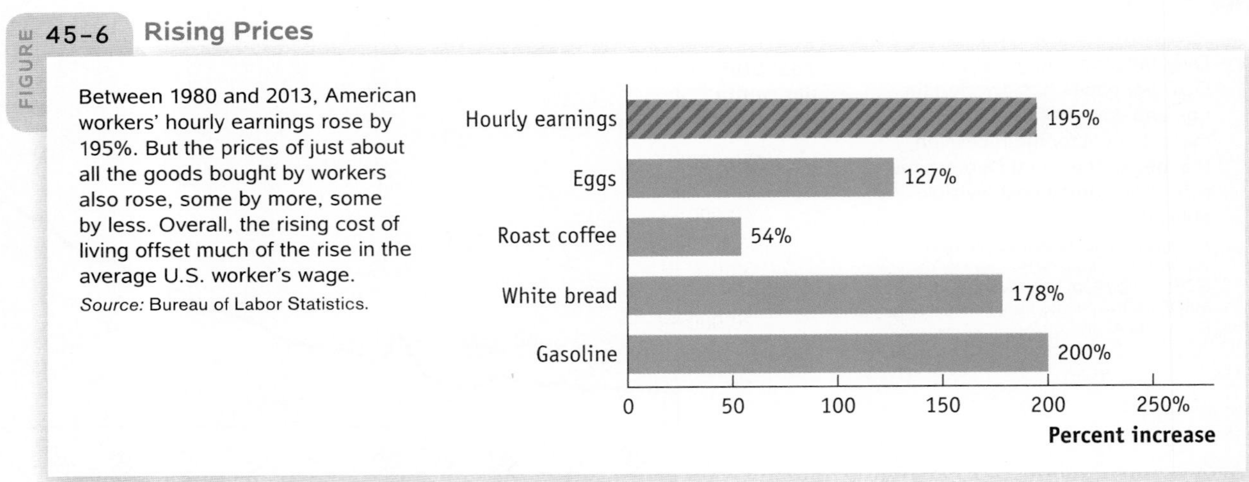

Between 1980 and 2013, American workers' hourly earnings rose by 195%. But the prices of just about all the goods bought by workers also rose, some by more, some by less. Overall, the rising cost of living offset much of the rise in the average U.S. worker's wage.

Source: Bureau of Labor Statistics.

The point is that between 1980 and 2013 the economy experienced substantial **inflation:** a rise in the overall level of prices. Understanding the causes of inflation and its opposite, **deflation**—a fall in the overall level of prices—is another main concern of macroeconomics because both inflation and deflation can pose problems for the economy. Here are two examples:

- Inflation discourages people from holding onto cash, because cash loses value over time if the overall price level is rising. That is, the amount of goods and services you can buy with a given amount of cash falls. In extreme cases, people stop holding cash altogether and turn to barter.
- Deflation can cause the reverse problem. If the price level is falling, cash gains value over time. In other words, the amount of goods and services you can buy with a given amount of cash increases. So holding on to it can become more attractive than investing in new factories and other productive assets. This can deepen a recession.

We'll describe other costs of inflation and deflation in a later section. For now, let's just note that, in general, economists regard **price stability**—in which the overall level of prices is changing, if at all, only slowly—as a desirable goal. Price stability is a goal that seemed far out of reach for much of the post–World War II period but was achieved to most macroeconomists' satisfaction in the 1990s.

A rising overall level of prices is **inflation**.

A falling overall level of prices is **deflation**.

The economy has **price stability** when the overall level of prices changes slowly or not at all.

An **open economy** is an economy that trades goods and services with other countries.

International Imbalances

The United States is an **open economy** that trades goods and services with other countries. There have been times when that trade was more or less balanced—when the United States sold about as much to the rest of the world as it bought. But this isn't one of those times.

In 2012, the United States ran a big **trade deficit**—that is, the value of the goods and services U.S. residents bought from the rest of the world was a lot larger than the value of the goods and services American producers sold to customers abroad.

A country runs a **trade deficit** when the value of goods and services bought from foreigners is more than the value of goods and services it sells to them. It runs a **trade surplus** when the value of goods and services bought from foreigners is less than the value of the goods and services it sells to them.

Meanwhile, some other countries were in the opposite position, selling much more to foreigners than they bought. Figure 45-7 shows the exports and imports of goods and services for several important economies in 2012. As you can see, the United States imported much more than it exported, but Germany, China, and Saudi Arabia did the reverse: they each ran a **trade surplus.**

A country runs a trade surplus when the value of the goods and services it buys from the rest of the world is smaller than the value of the goods and services it sells abroad. Was America's trade deficit a sign that something was wrong with our economy—that we weren't able to make things that people in other countries wanted to buy?

No, not really. Trade deficits and their opposite, trade surpluses, are macroeconomic phenomena. They're the result of situations in which the whole is very different from the sum of its parts. You might think that countries with highly productive workers or widely desired products and services to sell run trade surpluses while countries with unproductive workers or poor-quality products and services run deficits. But the reality is that there's no simple relationship between the success of an economy and whether it runs trade surpluses or deficits.

EvrenKalinbacak/Shutterstock

There isn't an obvious relationship between the success of an economy and whether it runs trade surpluses or deficits.

Microeconomic analysis tells us why countries trade but not why they run trade surpluses or deficits. Earlier we learned that international trade is the result of comparative advantage: countries export goods they're relatively good at producing and import goods they're not as good at producing. That's why the United States exports wheat and imports coffee. One important question the concept of comparative advantage doesn't answer, however, is why the value of a country's imports is sometimes much larger than the value of its exports, or vice versa.

So what does determine whether a country runs a trade surplus or a trade deficit? Later on we'll learn the surprising answer: the determinants of the overall balance between exports and imports lie in decisions about savings and investment spending—spending on goods like machinery and factories that are in turn used to produce goods and services for consumers. Countries with high investment spending relative to savings run trade deficits; countries with low investment spending relative to savings run trade surpluses.

FIGURE 45-7 **Unbalanced Trade**

In 2012, the goods and services the United States bought from other countries were worth considerably more than the goods and services sold abroad. Germany, China, and Saudi Arabia were in the reverse position. Trade deficits and trade surpluses reflect macroeconomic forces, especially differences in savings and investment spending.
Source: World Trade Organization.

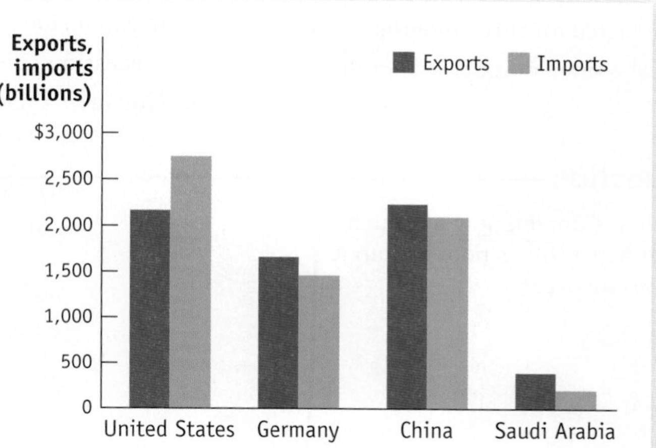

MODULE 45 Review

Solutions appear at the back of the book.

Check Your Understanding

1. Why do we talk about business cycles for the economy as a whole, rather than just talking about the ups and downs of particular industries?

2. Many poor countries have high rates of population growth. What does this imply about the long-run growth rates of overall output that they must achieve in order to generate a higher standard of living per person?

3. Which of these sound like inflation, which sound like deflation, and which are ambiguous?
   a. Gasoline prices are up 10%, food prices are down 20%, and the prices of most services are up 1%–2%.
   b. Gas prices have doubled, food prices are up 50%, and prices of most services seem to be up 5% or 10%.
   c. Gas prices haven't changed, food prices are way down, and services have gotten cheaper, too.

Multiple-Choice Questions

1. During the recession phase of a business cycle, which of the following is likely to increase?
   a. the unemployment rate
   b. the price level
   c. economic growth rates
   d. the production of goods and services
   e. wages

2. Based on the data below, which of the following is true about the period from 1990–2009?

Business-Cycle Peak	Business-Cycle Trough
July 1990	March 1991
March 2001	November 2001
December 2007	June 2009

   a. The economy spent more years in recession than expansion.
   b. Each of the recessions during this period lasted for less than a year.
   c. The longest expansion in this period lasted for 10 years.
   d. The shortest recession lasted for three months.
   e. Each recession lasted the same number of months.

3. A sustained increase in aggregate output over several decades represents
   a. an expansion.
   b. a recovery.
   c. a recession.
   d. a depression.
   e. economic growth.

4. Which of the following is the most likely result of inflation?
   a. falling employment
   b. a dollar buys more than it did before
   c. people are discouraged from holding cash
   d. price stability
   e. low aggregate output per capita

5. If the value of goods and services bought from other countries is more than the value of goods and services sold to other countries, this is called
   a. a trade deficit.
   b. a trade surplus.
   c. an expansion.
   d. a recession.
   e. a business cycle.

Critical-Thinking Question

Argentina used to be as rich as Canada; now it's much poorer. Does this mean that Argentina is poorer than it was in the past? Explain your answer.

The Circular-Flow Diagram and the National Accounts

SFC/Shutterstock

WHAT YOU WILL LEARN

1. How economists use aggregate measures to track the performance of the economy
2. How the circular-flow diagram of the economy helps with an understanding of the national accounts

The National Accounts

Almost all countries calculate a set of numbers known as the *national income and product accounts*. In fact, the accuracy of a country's accounts is a remarkably reliable indicator of its state of economic development—in general, the more reliable the accounts, the more economically advanced the country. When international economic agencies seek to help a less developed country, typically the first order of business is to send a team of experts to audit and improve the country's accounts.

In the United States, these numbers are calculated by the Bureau of Economic Analysis (BEA), a division of the U.S. government's Department of Commerce. The **national income and product accounts,** often referred to simply as the **national accounts,** keep track of the spending of consumers, sales of producers, business investment spending, government purchases, and a variety of other flows of money among different sectors of the economy. Let's see how they work.

The Circular-Flow Diagram

To understand the principles behind the national accounts, it helps to look at a graphic called a **circular-flow diagram.** Some of you have already encountered a version of this diagram in your study of microeconomics.

The circular-flow diagram is a simplified representation of the economy that shows the flows of money, goods and services, and factors of production through the economy. It allows us to visualize the key concepts behind the national accounts. The underlying principle is that the flow of money into each market or sector is equal to the flow of money coming out of that market or sector.

National income and product accounts, or **national accounts,** keep track of spending and the flows of money between different sectors of the economy.

The **circular-flow diagram** illustrates the flows of money, goods and services, and factors of production in an economy.

The Simple Circular-Flow Diagram

The U.S. economy is incredibly complex, with more than a hundred million workers employed by millions of companies, producing millions of different goods and services. Yet you can learn some very important things about the economy by considering Figure 46-1. This simple diagram represents the transactions that take place by two kinds of flows around a circle: flows of physical things such as goods, services, labor, or raw materials in one direction, and flows of money that pay for these things in the opposite direction. In this case, the physical flows are shown in yellow, the money flows in green.

FIGURE 46-1 **The Simple Circular-Flow Diagram**

This diagram represents the flows of money and of goods and services in the economy. In the markets for goods and services, households purchase goods and services from firms, generating a flow of money to the firms and a flow of goods and services to the households. The money flows back to households as firms purchase factors of production from the households in factor markets.

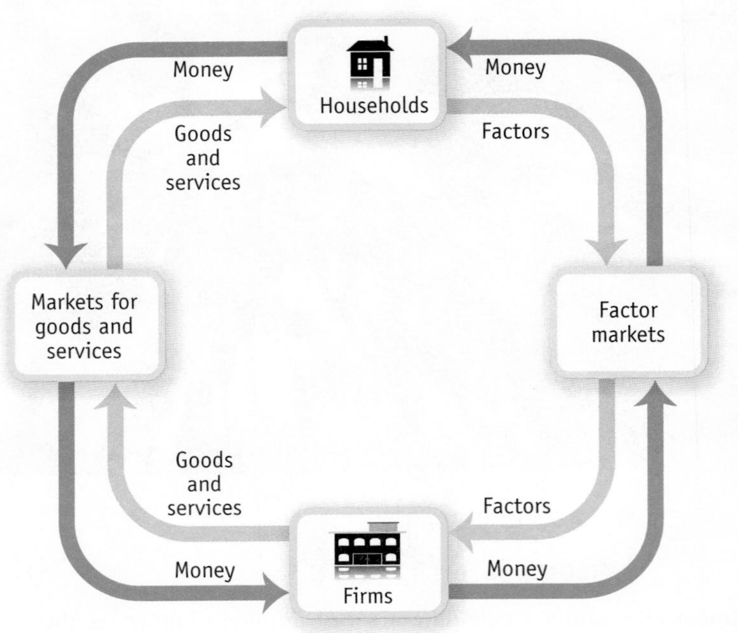

The simplest circular-flow diagram illustrates an economy that contains only two kinds of "inhabitants": households and firms. A **household** consists of either an individual or a group of people who share their income. A **firm** is an organization that produces goods and services for sale—and that employs members of households.

As you can see in Figure 46-1, there are two kinds of markets in this simple economy. On one side (here the left side) there are markets for goods and services (also known as **product markets**) in which households buy the goods and services they want from firms. This produces a flow of goods and services to the households and a return flow of money to firms.

On the other side (at right) there are **factor markets** in which firms buy the resources they need to produce goods and services. The best known factor market is the *labor market,* in which workers are paid for their time. Besides labor, we can think of households as owning and selling the other factors of production to firms.

This simple circular-flow diagram omits a number of real-world complications in the interest of simplicity. It does not offer a complete picture of participants in the economy and the flows that take place among them. But, it is a useful aid to thinking about the economy. And, we will use the simple diagram as the starting point for developing a more realistic (and therefore more detailed and complicated) circular-flow diagram.

A **household** is a person or group of people who share income.

A **firm** is an organization that produces goods and services for sale.

Product markets are where goods and services are bought and sold.

Factor markets are where resources, especially capital and labor, are bought and sold.

The Expanded Circular-Flow Diagram

Figure 46-2 is a revised and expanded circular-flow diagram. This diagram shows only the flows of money in the economy, but is expanded to include extra elements that were ignored in the interest of simplicity in the simple circular-flow diagram. The underlying principle that the inflow of money into each market or sector must equal the outflow of money coming from that market or sector still applies in this diagram.

In Figure 46-2, the circular flow of money between households and firms illustrated in Figure 46-1 remains. In the product markets, households engage in **consumer spending,** buying goods and services from domestic firms and from firms in the rest

Consumer spending is household spending on goods and services.

FIGURE 46-2 **An Expanded Circular-Flow Diagram: The Flows of Money Through the Economy**

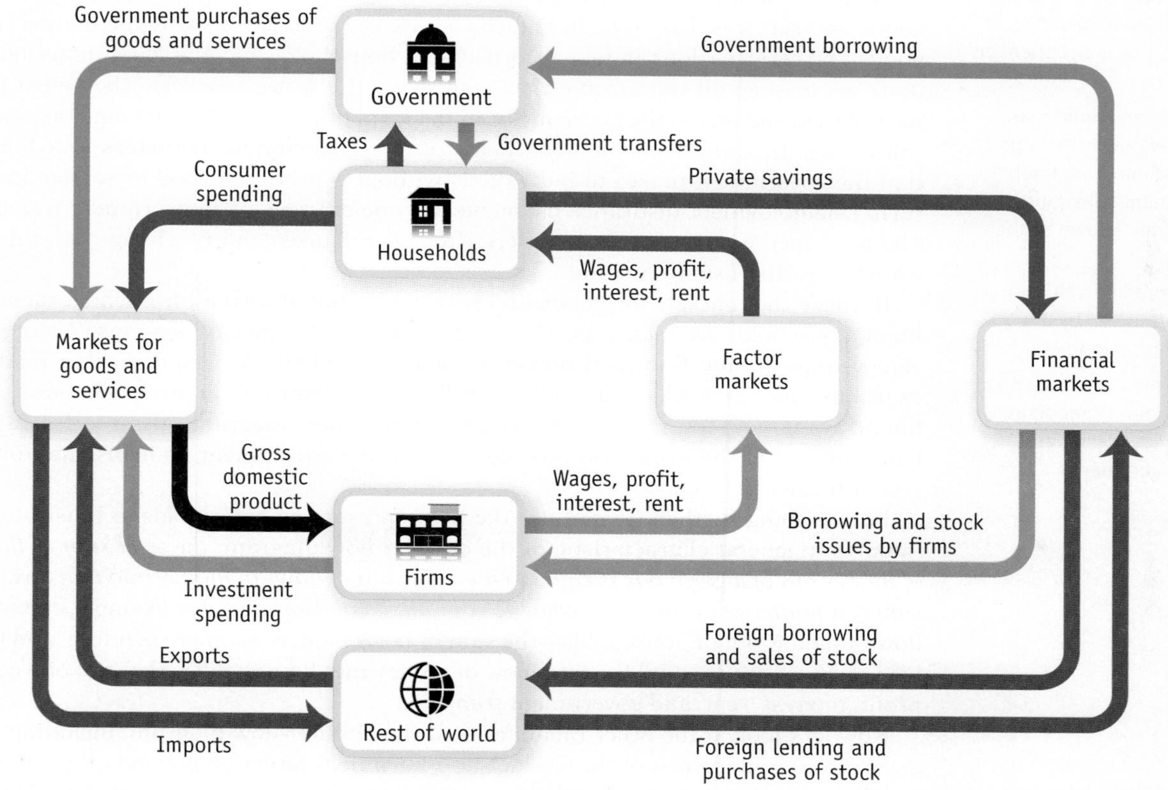

A circular flow of funds connects the four sectors of the economy—households, firms, government, and the rest of the world—via three types of markets: the factor markets, the markets for goods and services, and the *financial markets*.

- Funds flow from firms to households in the form of wages, profit, interest, and rent through the factor markets. After paying taxes to the government and receiving *government transfers,* households allocate the remaining income—*disposable income*—to private savings and consumer spending.
- Via the financial markets, *private savings* and funds from the rest of the world are channeled into investment spending by firms, government borrowing, foreign borrowing and lending, and foreign transactions of stocks.
- In turn, funds flow from the government and households to firms to pay for purchases of goods and services.
- Finally, exports to the rest of the world generate a flow of funds into the economy and imports lead to a flow of funds out of the economy.

If we add up consumer spending on goods and services, investment spending by firms, government purchases of goods and services, and exports, then subtract the value of imports, the total flow of funds represented by this calculation is total spending on final goods and services produced in the United States. Equivalently, it's the value of all the final goods and services produced in the United States—that is, the *gross domestic product* of the economy.

A **stock** is a share in the ownership of a company held by a shareholder.

A **bond** is a loan in the form of an IOU that pays interest.

Government transfers are payments that the government makes to individuals without expecting a good or service in return.

Disposable income, equal to income plus government transfers minus taxes, is the total amount of household income available to spend on consumption and to save.

Private savings, equal to disposable income minus consumer spending, is disposable income that is not spent on consumption.

The banking, stock, and bond markets, which channel private savings and foreign lending into investment spending, government borrowing, and foreign borrowing, are known as the **financial markets**.

Government borrowing is the amount of funds borrowed by the government in the financial markets.

Government purchases of goods and services are total expenditures on goods and services by federal, state, and local governments.

of the world. Households also own factors of production—land, labor, and capital. They sell the use of these factors of production to firms, receiving rent, wages, and interest payments in return. Firms buy, and pay households for, the use of those factors of production in factor markets, represented to the right of center in the diagram. Most households derive the bulk of their income from wages earned by selling labor.

Some households derive additional income from their indirect ownership of the physical capital used by firms, mainly in the form of **stocks**—shares in the ownership of a company—and **bonds**—loans to firms in the form of an IOU that pays interest. In other words, the income households receive from the factor markets includes profit distributed to company shareholders and the interest payments on any bonds that they hold. Households also receive rent from firms in exchange for the use of land or structures that the households own. So in factor markets, households receive income in the form of wages, profit, interest, and rent via factor markets.

Households spend most of the income received from factors of production on goods and services. However, in Figure 46-2 we see two reasons why the markets for goods and services don't in fact absorb *all* of a household's income. First, households don't get to keep all the income they receive via the factor markets. They must pay part of their income to the government in the form of taxes, such as income taxes and sales taxes. In addition, some households receive **government transfers**—payments that the government makes to individuals without expecting a good or service in return. Unemployment insurance payments are one example of a government transfer. The total income households have left after paying taxes and receiving government transfers is **disposable income.**

Because the markets for goods and services do not absorb all household income, many households set aside a portion of their income for **private savings.** These private savings go into **financial markets** where individuals, banks, and other institutions buy and sell stocks and bonds as well as make loans. As Figure 46-2 shows, the financial markets (on the far right of the circular flow diagram) also receive funds from the rest of the world and provide funds to the government, to firms, and to the rest of the world.

Before going further, we can use the box representing households to illustrate an important general characteristic of the circular-flow diagram: *the total sum of flows of money out of a given box is equal to the total sum of flows of money into that box. It's simply a matter of accounting: what goes in must come out.* So, for example, the total flow of money out of households—the sum of taxes paid, consumer spending, and private savings—must equal the total flow of money into households—the sum of wages, profit, interest, rent, and government transfers.

Now let's look at the other inhabitants in the circular-flow diagram, including the government and the rest of the world. The government returns a portion of the money it collects from taxes to households in the form of government transfers. However, it uses much of its tax revenue, plus additional funds borrowed in the financial markets through **government borrowing,** to buy goods and services. **Government purchases of goods and services,** the total of purchases made by federal, state, and local governments, includes everything from military spending on ammunition to your local public school's spending on chalk, erasers, and teacher salaries.

Shutterstock

Thinkstock

The rest of the world participates in the U.S. economy in three ways. First, some of the goods and services produced in the United States are sold to residents of other countries. For example, more than half of America's annual wheat and cotton crops are sold abroad. Goods and services sold to other countries are known as *exports*. Export sales lead to a flow of funds from the rest of the world into the United States to pay for them.

Second, some of the goods and services purchased by residents of the United States are produced abroad. For example, many consumer goods are now made in China. Goods and services purchased from residents of other countries are known as *imports*. Import purchases lead to a flow of funds out of the United States to pay for them.

Third, foreigners can participate in U.S. financial markets. Foreign lending—lending by foreigners to borrowers in the United States and purchases by foreigners of shares of stock in American companies—generates a flow of funds into the United States from the rest of the world. Conversely, foreign borrowing—borrowing by foreigners from U.S. lenders and purchases by Americans of stock in foreign companies—leads to a flow of funds out of the United States to the rest of the world.

Inventories are stocks of goods and raw materials held to facilitate business operations.

Investment spending is spending on new productive physical capital, such as machinery and structures, and on changes in inventories.

Note that like households, firms also buy goods and services in our economy. An automobile company that is building a new factory will buy investment goods—machinery like stamping presses and welding robots—from companies that manufacture these items. It will also accumulate an inventory of finished cars in preparation for shipment to dealers. **Inventories,** then, are goods and raw materials that firms hold to facilitate their operations. The national accounts count this **investment spending**—spending on new productive physical capital, such as machinery and buildings, and on changes in *inventories*—as part of total spending on goods and services.

Richard Peterson/ Shutterstock

You might ask why changes in inventories are included in investment spending—finished cars aren't, after all, used to produce more cars. Changes in inventories of finished goods are counted as investment spending because, like machinery, they change the ability of a firm to make future sales. So spending on additions to inventories is a form of investment spending by a firm. Conversely, a drawing-down of inventories is counted as a fall in investment spending because it leads to lower future sales.

It's also important to understand that investment spending includes spending on the construction of any structure, regardless of whether it is an assembly plant or a new house. Why include the construction of homes? Because, like a plant, a new house produces a future stream of output—housing services for its occupants.

Suppose we add up consumer spending on goods and services, investment spending, government purchases of goods and services, and the value of exports, then subtract the value of imports. This gives us a measure of the overall market value of the goods and services the economy produces. That measure has a name: it's a country's *gross domestic product,* which is the topic of the next module.

ECONOMICS IN ACTION

CREATING THE NATIONAL ACCOUNTS

The national accounts, like modern macroeconomics, owe their creation to the Great Depression. As the economy plunged into depression, government officials found their ability to respond crippled not only by the lack of adequate economic theories but also by the lack of adequate information. All they had were scattered statistics: railroad freight car loadings, stock prices, and incomplete indexes of industrial production. They could only guess at what was happening to the economy as a whole.

National income accounting is a tool of economic analysis and policy making used around the world.

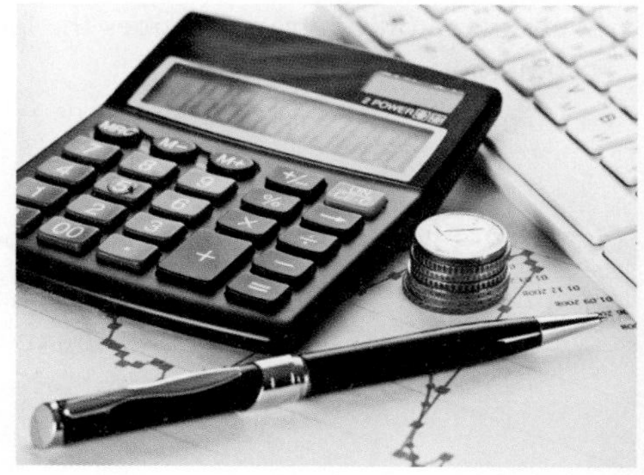

Thinkstock

In response to this perceived lack of information, the Department of Commerce commissioned Simon Kuznets, a young Russian-born economist, to develop a set of national income accounts. (Kuznets later won the Nobel Prize in economics for his work.) The first version of these accounts was presented to Congress in 1937 and in a research report titled *National Income, 1929–35.*

Kuznets's initial estimates fell short of the full modern set of accounts because they focused on income, not production. The push to complete the national accounts came during World War II, when policy makers were in need of comprehensive measures of the economy's performance. The federal government began issuing estimates of gross domestic product and gross national product in 1942.

In January 2000, in the *Survey of Current Business,* the Department of Commerce ran an article titled "GDP: One of the Great Inventions of the 20th Century." This may seem a bit over the top, but national income accounting, invented in the United States, has since become a tool of economic analysis and policy making around the world.

MODULE 46 Review

Solutions appear at the back of the book.

Check Your Understanding

1. How does a circular-flow diagram of the economy explain the connection between the following sectors, in terms of the flows that occur between the sectors?
   - a. households and firms
   - b. households and government
   - c. households and the rest of the world
2. Define the four different types of income received by households from firms via the factor markets. What is this income used for?

Multiple-Choice Questions

1. The government uses the ___________ to keep track of the flows of money between different sectors of the economy.
   - a. national income and product accounts
   - b. circular-flow diagram
   - c. production possibilities frontier
   - d. financial market
   - e. factor market
2. Markets in which labor and capital are bought and sold are called ___________ markets.
   - a. consumer
   - b. factor
   - c. product
   - d. investment
   - e. money
3. A circular-flow diagram assumes the factors of production are owned by
   - a. firms.
   - b. the government.
   - c. foreigners.
   - d. firms and the government.
   - e. households.
4. In a circular-flow diagram, funds that flow between households and the government are
   - a. taxes and government spending.
   - b. wages, taxes, and transfers.
   - c. taxes and transfers.
   - d. taxes, transfers, and profit.
   - e. taxes, transfers, and government spending.
5. The bank, stock, and money markets are collectively known as the ___________ market.
   - a. investment
   - b. savings
   - c. money
   - d. financial
   - e. factor

Critical-Thinking Question

Explain the difference between the market for goods and services, the factor market, and the financial market.

Gross Domestic Product (GDP)

Shutterstock

WHAT YOU WILL LEARN

1. An exact definition for gross domestic product, or GDP
2. Three different ways to calculate GDP

In the previous module we used the circular-flow diagram to show that adding up consumer spending, investment spending, government spending, and the value of exports minus the value of imports would give us a measure of a country's gross domestic product.

In this module we will formally define *gross domestic product,* or *GDP,* and then look at how it is calculated.

Gross Domestic Product Defined

A consumer's purchase of a new car from a dealer is one example of a sale of **final goods and services:** goods and services sold to the final, or end, user. But an automobile manufacturer's purchase of steel from a steel foundry or glass from a glassmaker is an example of a sale of **intermediate goods and services:** goods and services that are inputs into the production of final goods and services. In the case of intermediate goods and services, the purchaser—another firm—is *not* the final user.

Gross domestic product, or **GDP,** is the total value of all *final goods and services* produced in an economy during a given period, usually a year. In 2013 the GDP of the United States was $16,803 billion, or about $53,086 per person.

Final goods and services are goods and services sold to the final, or end, user.

Intermediate goods and services are goods and services bought from one firm by another firm to be used as inputs into the production of final goods and services.

Gross domestic product, or **GDP,** is the total value of all final goods and services produced in the economy during a given year.

Aggregate spending—the total spending on domestically produced final goods and services in the economy—is the sum of consumer spending (C), investment spending (I), government purchases of goods and services (G), and exports minus imports ($X - IM$).

Calculating GDP

Government statisticians use three methods to calculate GDP:

1. Survey and add up the total value of the production of final goods and services.
2. Add up **aggregate spending** on domestically produced final goods and services in the economy—the sum of consumer spending, investment spending, government purchases of goods and services, and exports minus imports.
3. Sum the total factor income earned by households from firms in the economy.

The **value added** of a producer is the value of its sales minus the value of its purchases of inputs.

To illustrate how the methods of calculating GDP work, we will consider a hypothetical economy, shown in Figure 47-1. This economy consists of three firms—American Motors, Inc., which produces one car per year; American Steel, Inc., which produces the steel that goes into the car; and American Ore, Inc., which mines the iron ore that goes into the steel. GDP in this economy is $21,500, the value of the one car per year the economy produces. Let's look at how the three different methods of calculating GDP yield the same result.

Mircea Bezergheanu/Shutterstock

Steel is an intermediate good because it is sold to other product manufacturers like automakers or refrigerator makers, and rarely to final buyers, such as consumers.

MEASURING GDP AS THE VALUE OF PRODUCTION OF FINAL GOODS AND SERVICES

The first method for calculating GDP is to add up the value of all the final goods and services produced in the economy—a calculation that excludes the value of intermediate goods and services. Why are intermediate goods and services excluded? After all, don't they represent a very large and valuable portion of the economy?

To understand why only final goods and services are included in GDP, look at the simplified economy described in Figure 47-1. Should we measure the GDP of this economy by adding up the total sales of the iron ore producer, the steel producer, and the auto producer?

If we did, we would in effect be counting the value of the steel twice—once when it is sold by the steel plant to the auto plant and again when the steel auto body is sold to a consumer as a finished car. And we would be counting the value of the iron ore *three* times—once when it is mined and sold to the steel company, a second time when it is made into steel and sold to the auto producer, and a third time when the steel is made into a car and sold to the consumer. So counting the full value of each producer's sales would cause us to count the same items several times and artificially inflate the calculation of GDP.

In Figure 47-1, the total value of all sales, intermediate and final, is $34,700: $21,500 from the sale of the car, plus $9,000 from the sale of the steel, plus $4,200 from the sale of the iron ore. Yet we know that GDP—the total value of all final goods and services in a given year—is only $21,500.

To avoid double-counting, we count only each producer's **value added** in the calculation of GDP: the difference between the value of its sales and the value of the inputs it purchases from other businesses. That is, at each stage of the production process we subtract the cost of inputs—the intermediate goods—at that stage. In this case, the

FIGURE 47-1 Calculating GDP

In this hypothetical economy consisting of three firms, GDP can be calculated in three different ways: 1) measuring GDP as the value of production of final goods and services, by summing each firm's value added; 2) measuring GDP as aggregate spending on domestically produced final goods and services; and 3) measuring GDP as factor income earned by households from firms in the economy.

2. Aggregate spending on domestically produced final goods and services = $21,500

	American Ore, Inc.	American Steel, Inc.	American Motors, Inc.	Total factor income
Value of sales	$4,200 (ore)	$9,000 (steel)	$21,500 (car)	
Intermediate goods	0	4,200 (iron ore)	9,000 (steel)	
Wages	2,000	3,700	10,000	$15,700
Interest payments	1,000	600	1,000	2,600
Rent	200	300	500	1,000
Profit	1,000	200	1,000	2,200
Total expenditure by firm	4,200	9,000	21,500	
Value added per firm = Value of sales − Cost of intermediate goods	4,200	4,800	12,500	

3. Total payments to factors = $21,500

1. Value of production of final goods and services, sum of value added = $21,500

value added of the auto producer is the dollar value of the cars it manufactures *minus* the cost of the steel it buys, or $12,500. The value added of the steel producer is the dollar value of the steel it produces *minus* the cost of the ore it buys, or $4,800.

Only the ore producer, who we have assumed doesn't buy any inputs, has value added equal to its total sales, $4,200. The sum of the three producers' value added is $21,500, equal to GDP.

Net exports are the difference between the value of exports and the value of imports ($X - IM$).

MEASURING GDP AS SPENDING ON DOMESTICALLY PRODUCED FINAL GOODS AND SERVICES Another way to calculate GDP is by adding up aggregate spending on domestically produced final goods and services. That is, GDP can be measured by the flow of funds into firms. Like the method that estimates GDP as the value of domestic production of final goods and services, this measurement must be carried out in a way that avoids double-counting.

In terms of our steel and auto example, we don't want to count both consumer spending on a car (represented in Figure 47-1 by the sales price of the car) and the auto producer's spending on steel (represented in Figure 47-1 by the price of a car's worth of steel). If we counted both, we would be counting the steel embodied in the car twice.

We solve this problem by counting only the value of sales to *final buyers,* such as consumers, firms that purchase investment goods, the government, or foreign buyers. In other words, in order to avoid the double-counting of spending, we omit sales of inputs from one business to another when estimating GDP using spending data. You can see from Figure 47-1 that aggregate spending on final goods and services—the finished car—is $21,500.

As we've already pointed out, the national accounts *do* include investment spending by firms as a part of final spending. That is, an auto company's purchase of steel to make a car isn't considered a part of final spending, but the company's purchase of new machinery for its factory *is* considered a part of final spending. What's the difference? Steel is an input that is used up in production; machinery will last for a number of years. Since purchases of capital goods that will last for a considerable time aren't closely tied to current production, the national accounts consider such purchases a form of final sales.

What types of spending make up GDP? Look again at Figure 46-2 of the circular-flow diagram (page 473), and you will see that one source of sales revenue for firms is consumer spending. Let's denote consumer spending with the symbol C. Figure 46-2 shows three other components of sales: sales of investment goods to other businesses, or investment spending, which we will denote by I; government purchases of goods and services, which we will denote by G; and sales to foreigners—that is, exports—which we will denote by X.

In reality, not all of this final spending goes toward domestically produced goods and services. We must take account of spending on imports, which we will denote by IM. Income spent on imports is income not spent on domestic goods and services—it is income that has "leaked" across national borders. So to calculate domestic production using spending data, we must subtract spending on imports. Putting this all together gives us the following equation, which breaks GDP down by the four sources of aggregate spending:

$$\textbf{(47-1)} \quad \text{GDP} = C + I + G + X - IM$$

where C = consumer spending, I = investment spending, G = government purchases of goods and services, X = sales to foreigners, or exports, and IM = spending on imports. Note that the value of $X - IM$—the difference between the value of exports and the value of imports—is known as **net exports.** We'll be seeing a lot of Equation 47-1 in later modules!

Lisa Thornberg/Getty Images

MEASURING GDP AS FACTOR INCOME EARNED FROM FIRMS IN THE ECONOMY A final way to calculate GDP is to add up all the income earned by factors of production in the economy—the wages earned by labor; the interest earned by those who lend their savings to firms and the government; the rent earned by those who lease their land or structures to firms; and the profit earned by the shareholders, the owners of the firms' physical capital. This is a valid measure because the money firms earn by selling goods and services must go somewhere; whatever isn't paid as wages, interest, or rent is profit. And part of profit is paid out to shareholders as *dividends*.

Figure 47-1 shows how this calculation works for our simplified economy. The shaded column at the far right shows the total wages, interest, and rent paid by all these firms as well as their total profit. Summing up all of these yields a total factor income of $21,500—again, equal to GDP.

We won't emphasize the income method as much as the other two methods of calculating GDP. It's important to keep in mind, however, that all the money spent on domestically produced goods and services generates factor income to households—that is, there really is a circular flow.

The Components of GDP

Now that we know how GDP is calculated in principle, let's see what it looks like in practice.

Figure 47-2 shows the first two methods of calculating GDP side by side. The height of each bar above the horizontal axis represents the GDP of the U.S. economy in 2013: $16,803 billion. Each bar is divided to show the breakdown of that total in terms of where the value was added and how the money was spent.

In the left bar in Figure 47-2, we see the breakdown of GDP by value added according to sector, the first method of calculating GDP. Of the $16,803 billion, $12,688 billion consisted of value added by businesses. Another $2,036 billion consisted of value added by government, in the form of military, education, and other government services. Finally, $2,079 billion of value added was added by households and institutions. For example, the value added by households includes the value of work performed in homes by professional gardeners, maids, and cooks.

FIGURE 47-2 U.S. GDP in 2013: Two Methods of Calculating GDP

The two bars show two equivalent ways of calculating GDP. The height of each bar above the horizontal axis represents $16,803 billion, U.S. GDP in 2013. The left bar shows the breakdown of GDP according to the value added of each sector of the economy. The right bar shows the breakdown of GDP according to the four types of aggregate spending: $C + I + G + X - IM$. The right bar has a total length of $16,803 billion + $494 billion = $17,297 billion. The $494 billion, shown as the area extending below the horizontal axis, is the amount of total spending absorbed by net imports (negative net exports) in 2013.

Source: Bureau of Economic Analysis.

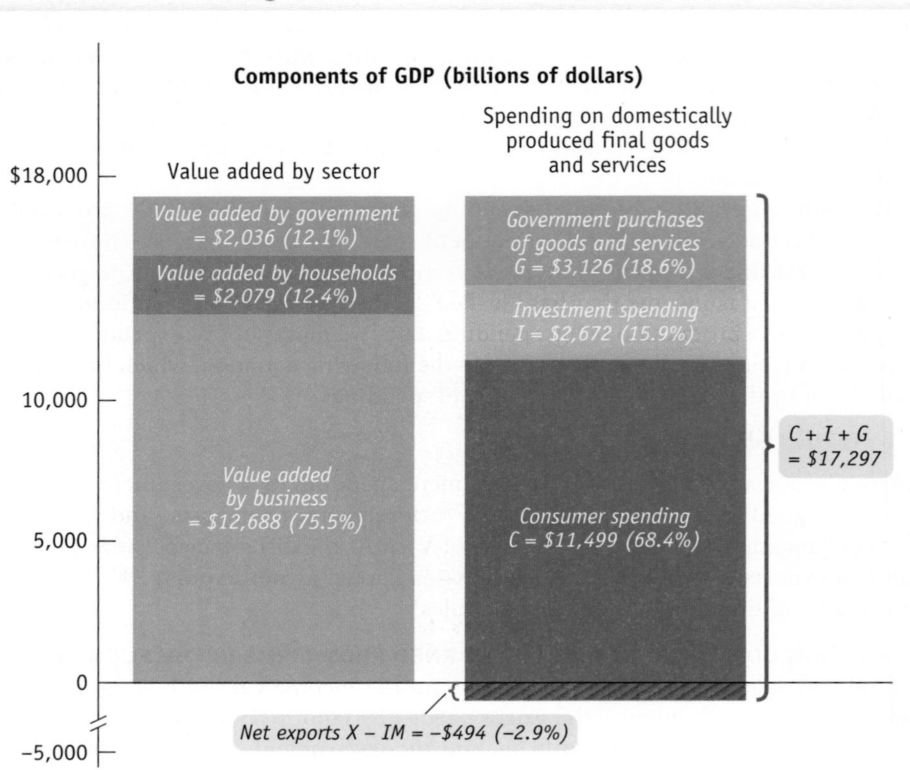

The right bar in Figure 47-2 corresponds to the second method of calculating GDP, showing the breakdown by the four types of aggregate spending. The total length of the right bar is longer than the total length of the left bar, a difference of $494 billion (which, as you can see, extends below the horizontal axis). That's because the total length of the right bar represents total spending in the economy, spending on both domestically produced and foreign-produced—imported—final goods and services.

Within the bar at right, consumer spending (C), which is 68.4% of GDP, dominates the picture. But some of that spending was absorbed by foreign-produced goods and services. In 2013, the value of net exports, the difference between the value of exports and the value of imports ($X - IM$ in Equation 47-1), was negative—the United States was a net importer of foreign goods and services. The 2013 value of $X - IM$ was –$494 billion, or –2.9% of GDP. Thus, a portion of the right bar extends below the horizontal axis by $494 billion to represent the amount of total spending that was absorbed by net imports and so did not lead to higher U.S. GDP. Investment spending (I) constituted 15.9% of GDP; government purchases of goods and services (G) constituted 18.6% of GDP.

GDP: What's In and What's Out?

It's easy to confuse what is included and what isn't included in GDP. So let's stop here and make sure the distinction is clear.

Be sure not to confuse investment spending with spending on inputs. Investment spending—spending on productive physical capital, the construction of structures (residential as well as commercial), and changes to inventories—is included in GDP. But spending on inputs is not. Why the difference?

Recall the distinction between resources that are *used up* and those that are *not used up* in production. An input, like steel, is used up in production. A metal-stamping machine, an investment good, is not. It will last for many years and will be used repeatedly to make many cars. Since spending on productive physical capital—investment goods—and the construction of structures is not directly tied to current output, economists consider such spending to be spending on final goods. Spending on changes to inventories is considered a part of investment spending so it is also included in GDP. Why? Because, like a machine, additional inventory is an investment in future sales. And when a good is released for sale from inventories, its value is subtracted from the value of inventories and so from GDP.

Liu Zheng/Color China Photo/AP Images

The United States is a net importer of goods and services, such as computers from China, which is, by far, the biggest exporter to the United States.

Used goods are not included in GDP because, as with inputs, to include them would be to double-count: counting them once when sold as new and again when sold as used.

Also, financial assets such as stocks and bonds are not included in GDP because they don't represent either the production or the sale of final goods and services. Rather, a bond represents a promise to repay with interest, and a stock represents a proof of ownership. And for obvious reasons, foreign-produced goods and services are not included in calculations of gross *domestic* product.

Here is a summary of what's included and not included in GDP:

Included

- Domestically produced final goods and services, including capital goods, new construction of structures, and changes to inventories

Not Included

- Intermediate goods and services
- Inputs
- Used goods
- Financial assets such as stocks and bonds
- Foreign-produced goods and services

ECONOMICS IN ACTION

OUR IMPUTED LIVES

An old line says that when a person marries the household cook, GDP falls. And it's true: when someone provides services for pay, those services are counted as a part of GDP. But the services family members provide to each other are not. Some economists have produced alternative measures that try to "impute" the value of household work—that is, assign an estimate of what the market value of that work would have been if it had been paid for. But the standard measure of GDP doesn't contain that imputation.

The value of the services that family members provide to each other is not counted as part of GDP.

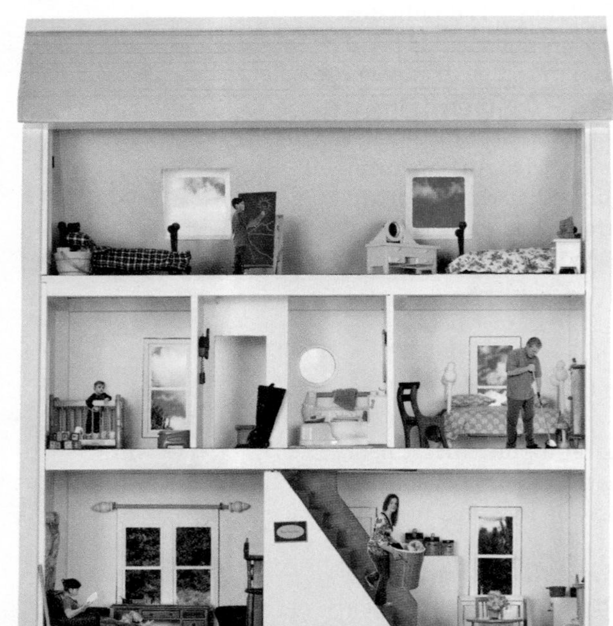

Shutterstock

GDP estimates do, however, include an imputation for the value of "owner-occupied housing." That is, if you buy the home you were formerly renting, GDP does not go down. It's true that because you no longer pay rent to your landlord, the landlord no longer sells a service to you—namely, use of the house or apartment. But the statisticians make an estimate of what you would have paid if you rented whatever you live in, whether it's an apartment or a house. For the purposes of the statistics, it's as if you were renting your dwelling from yourself.

If you think about it, this makes a lot of sense. In a homeowning country like the United States, the pleasure we derive from our houses is an important part of the standard of living. So to be accurate, estimates of GDP must take into account the value of housing that is occupied by owners as well as the value of rental housing.

MODULE 47 Review

Solutions appear at the back of the book.

Check Your Understanding

1. Explain why the three methods of calculating GDP produce the same estimate of GDP.
2. What does the investment spending category of GDP measure?
3. Consider Figure 47-1. Explain why it would be incorrect to calculate total value added as $30,500, the sum of the sales price of a car and a car's worth of steel.

Multiple-Choice Questions

1. GDP is equal to
   - a. the total value of all goods and services produced in an economy during a given period.
   - b. the sum of the spending by consumers and firms.
   - c. the total value of the intermediate and final goods produced during a given period.
   - d. the profit earned by the firms producing new goods and services.
   - e. the income earned by the factors of production.
2. Which of the following is included in GDP?
   - a. changes to inventories
   - b. intermediate goods
   - c. used goods
   - d. financial assets such as stocks and bonds
   - e. foreign-produced goods
3. Value added is best defined as
   - a. the profit earned by firms.

b. the value of a firm's sales.

c. the value of a firm's sales minus the value of purchased intermediate goods and services.

d. the increase in aggregate income during a given period.

e. the value of investment spending in the economy during a given period.

4. Which of the following is *not* included in GDP?

a. capital goods such as machinery

b. imports

c. the value of domestically produced services

d. government purchases of goods and services

e. the construction of structures

5. Which of the following components make up the largest percentage of GDP measured by aggregate spending?

a. consumer spending

b. investment spending

c. government purchases of goods and services

d. exports

e. imports

Critical-Thinking Questions

1. Explain why the government cannot simply add up the total value of new goods and services produced in the economy during a given time period to come up with an estimate of GDP.

2. How does the concept of value added help the government obtain a more accurate measure of GDP?

48 Interpreting Real Gross Domestic Product

Corbis/Superstock

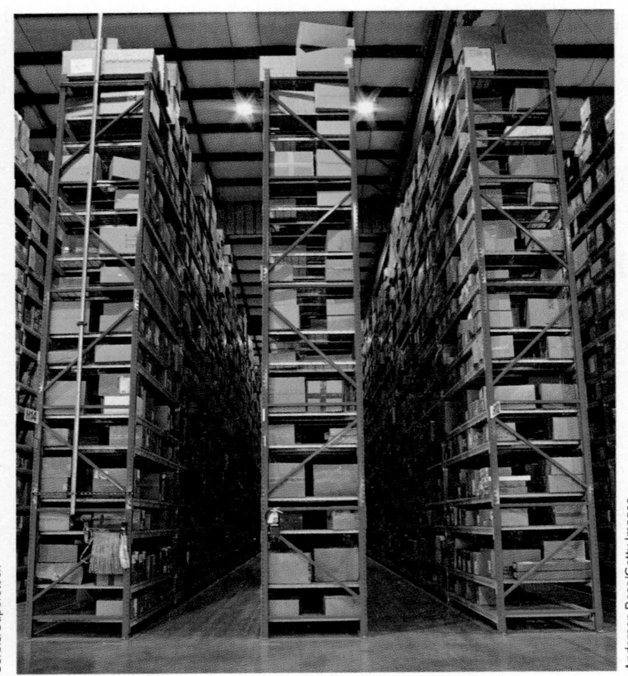

Andersen Ross/Getty Images

WHAT YOU WILL LEARN

1. **The difference between real GDP and nominal GDP**
2. **Why real GDP is the appropriate measure of real economic activity**

What GDP Tells Us

We now know what gross domestic product (GDP) is and how it's calculated. But what does the measurement of GDP tell us?

The most important use of GDP is as a measure of the size of the economy, providing us a scale against which to compare the economic performance of other years or other countries. For example, in 2013, U.S. GDP was $16,803 billion, China's GDP was $9,272 billion, and the combined GDP of the 28 countries that make up the European Union was $17,267 billion. This comparison tells us that China, although it has the world's second-largest national economy, carries considerably less economic weight than does the United States. When taken in aggregate, Europe's economy is larger than the U.S. economy.

Still, one must be careful when using GDP numbers, especially when making comparisons over time. That's because part of the increase in the value of GDP over time represents *increases in the prices* of goods and services rather than an increase in output. For example, U.S. GDP was $7,085 billion in 1994 and had approximately doubled to $14,990 billion by 2011. But U.S. production didn't actually double over that period. To measure actual changes in aggregate output, we need a modified version of GDP that is adjusted for price changes, known as *real GDP.* We'll see how real GDP is calculated next.

Real GDP: A Measure of Aggregate Output

In the section-opening story, we described how China passed Japan as the world's second-largest economy in 2010. At the time, Japan's economy was weakening: during the second quarter of 2010, output declined by an annual rate of 6.3%. Oddly, however, GDP was up. In fact, Japan's GDP measured in yen, its national currency, rose by an annual rate of 4.8% during the quarter. How was that possible? The answer is that Japan was experiencing inflation at the time. As a result, the yen value of Japan's GDP rose although output actually fell.

The moral of this story is that the commonly cited GDP number is an interesting and useful statistic, one that provides a good way to compare the size of different economies, but *it's not a good measure of the economy's growth over time.* GDP can grow because the economy grows, but it can also grow simply because of inflation. Even if an economy's output doesn't change, GDP will go up if the prices of the goods and services the economy produces increase. Likewise, GDP can fall either because the economy is producing less or because prices have fallen.

To measure the economy's growth with accuracy, we need a measure of **aggregate output:** the total quantity of final goods and services the economy produces. The measure that is used for this purpose is known as *real GDP.* By tracking real GDP over time, we avoid the problem of changes in prices distorting the value of changes in production over time. Let's look first at how real GDP is calculated and then at what it means.

Aggregate output is the total quantity of final goods and services produced within an economy.

Real GDP is the total value of all final goods and services produced in the economy during a given year, calculated using the prices of a selected base year.

Nominal GDP is the total value of all final goods and services produced in the economy during a given year, calculated with the prices current in the year in which the output is produced.

Calculating Real GDP

To understand how real GDP is calculated, imagine an economy in which only two goods, apples and oranges, are produced and in which both goods are sold only to final consumers. The outputs and prices of the two fruits for two consecutive years are shown in Table 48-1.

The first thing we can say about these data is that the value of sales increased from year 1 to year 2. In the first year, the total value of sales was (2,000 billion × $0.25) + (1,000 billion × $0.50) = $1,000 billion; in the second, it was (2,200 billion × $0.30) + (1,200 billion × $0.70) = $1,500 billion, which is 50% larger. But it is also clear from the table that this increase in the dollar value of GDP overstates the real growth in the economy. Although the quantities of both apples and oranges increased, the prices of both apples and oranges also rose. So part of the 50% increase in the dollar value of GDP simply reflects higher prices, not higher production of output.

TABLE 48-1

Calculating GDP and Real GDP in a Simple Economy

	Year 1	Year 2
Quantity of apples (billions)	2,000	2,200
Price of an apple	$0.25	$0.30
Quantity of oranges (billions)	1,000	1,200
Price of an orange	$0.50	$0.70
GDP (billions of dollars)	$1,000	$1,500
Real GDP (billions of year 1 dollars)	$1,000	$1,150

To estimate the true increase in aggregate output produced, we have to ask the following question: How much would GDP have gone up if prices had *not* changed? To answer this question, we need to find the value of output in year 2 expressed in year 1 prices. In year 1, the price of apples was $0.25 each and the price of oranges $0.50 each. So year 2 output *at year 1 prices* is (2,200 billion × $0.25) + (1,200 billion × $0.50) = $1,150 billion. And output in year 1 at year 1 prices was $1,000 billion. So in this example, GDP measured in year 1 prices rose 15%—from $1,000 billion to $1,150 billion.

Now we can define **real GDP:** it is the total value of final goods and services produced in the economy during a year, calculated as if prices had stayed constant at the level of some given base year. A real GDP number always comes with information about what the base year is. A GDP number that has not been adjusted for changes in prices is calculated using the prices in the year in which the output is produced. Economists call this measure **nominal GDP,** GDP at current prices. If we had used nominal GDP to measure the true change in output from year 1 to year 2 in our apples and oranges example, we would have overstated the true growth in output: we would have claimed it to be 50%, when in fact it was only 15%. By comparing output in the two years using a common

Lee Avison/Alamy

Chained dollars is the method of calculating changes in real GDP using the average between the growth rate calculated using an early base year and the growth rate calculated using a late base year.

set of prices—the year 1 prices in this example—we are able to focus solely on changes in the quantity of output by eliminating the influence of changes in prices.

Table 48-2 shows a real-life version of our apples and oranges example. The second column shows nominal GDP in 2001, 2005, and 2012. The third column shows real GDP for each year in 2005 dollars (that is, using the value of the dollar in the year 2005). For 2005 the nominal GDP and the real GDP are the same. But real GDP in 2001 expressed in 2005 dollars was higher than nominal GDP in 2001, reflecting the fact that prices were in general higher in 2005 than in 2001. Real GDP in 2012 expressed in 2005 dollars, however, was less than nominal GDP in 2012 because prices in 2005 were lower than in 2012.

TABLE 48-2

Nominal versus Real GDP in 2001, 2005, and 2012

	Nominal GDP (billions of current dollars)	Real GDP (billions of 2005 dollars)
2001	$10,286	$11,347
2005	12,683	12,638
2012	15,829	13,648

Source: Bureau of Economic Analysis.

You might have noticed that there is an alternative way to calculate real GDP using the data in Table 48-1. Why not measure it using the prices of year 2 rather than year 1 as the base-year prices? This procedure seems equally valid. According to that calculation, real GDP in year 1 at year 2 prices is (2,000 billion × $0.30) + (1,000 billion × $0.70) = $1,300 billion; real GDP in year 2 at year 2 prices is $1,500 billion, the same as nominal GDP in year 2. So using year 2 prices as the base year, the growth rate of real GDP is equal to ($1,500 billion − $1,300 billion)/$1,300 billion = 0.154, or 15.4%. This is slightly higher than the figure we got from the previous calculation, in which year 1 prices were the base-year prices. In that calculation, we found that real GDP increased by 15%. Neither answer, 15.4% versus 15%, is more "correct" than the other.

In reality, the government economists who put together the U.S. national accounts have adopted a method to measure the change in real GDP known as chain linking, which uses the average between the GDP growth rate calculated using an early base year and the GDP growth rate calculated using a late base year. As a result, U.S. statistics on real GDP are always expressed in **chained dollars.**

ECONOMICS IN ACTION

MIRACLE IN VENEZUELA?

FIGURE 48-1 Real Versus Nominal GDP in Venezuela

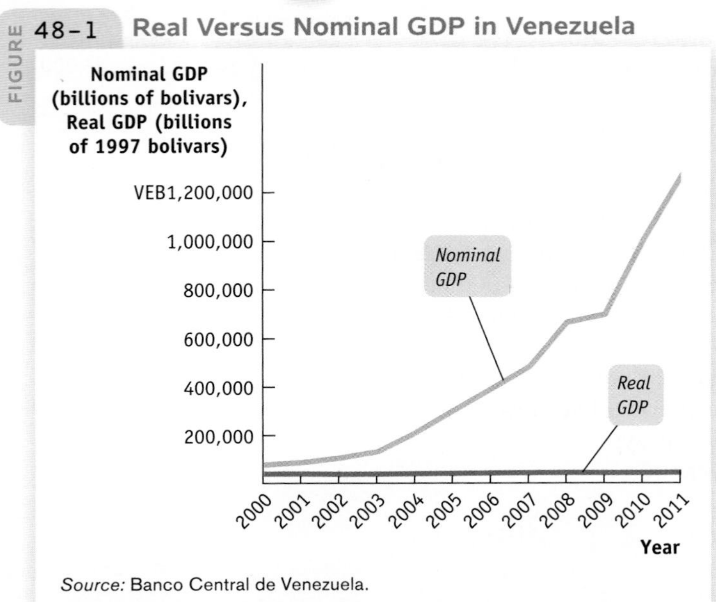

Source: Banco Central de Venezuela.

The South American nation of Venezuela has a distinction that may surprise you: in recent years, it has had one of the world's fastest-growing nominal GDPs. Between 2000 and 2011, Venezuelan nominal GDP grew by an average of 29% each year—much faster than nominal GDP in the United States or even in booming economies like China.

So is Venezuela experiencing an economic miracle? No, it's just suffering from unusually high inflation. Figure 48-1 shows Venezuela's nominal and real GDP from 2000 to 2011, with real GDP measured in 1997 prices. Real GDP did grow over the period, but at an annual rate of only 3%. That's about twice the U.S. growth rate over the same period, but it is far short of China's 10% growth.

What Real GDP Doesn't Measure

GDP is a measure of a country's aggregate output. Other things equal, a country with a larger population will have higher GDP simply because there are more people working. So if we want to compare GDP across countries but want to eliminate the effect of differences in population size, we use the measure **GDP per capita**—GDP divided by the size of the population, equivalent to the average GDP per person. Correspondingly, **real GDP per capita** is the average real GDP per person.

GDP per capita is GDP divided by the size of the population; it is equivalent to the average GDP per person.

Real GDP per capita is the average real GDP per person.

Real GDP per capita can be a useful measure in some circumstances, such as in a comparison of labor productivity between two countries. However, despite the fact that it is a rough measure of the average real output per person, real GDP per capita has well-known limitations as a measure of a country's living standards.

Every once in a while economists are accused of believing that growth in real GDP per capita is the only thing that matters—that is, thinking that increasing real GDP per capita is a goal in itself. In fact, economists rarely make that mistake; the idea that economists care only about real GDP per capita is a sort of urban legend. Let's take a moment to be clear about why a country's real GDP per capita is not a sufficient measure of human welfare in that country and why growth in real GDP per capita is not an appropriate policy goal in itself.

Real GDP does not include many of the things that contribute to happiness, such as leisure time, volunteerism, housework, and natural beauty. And real GDP increases with expenditures on some things that make people unhappy, including disease, divorce, crime, and natural disasters.

Real GDP per capita is a measure of an economy's average aggregate output per person—and so of what it *can* do. A country with a high real GDP can afford to be healthy, to be well educated, and in general to have a good quality of life. But there is not a one-to-one match between real GDP and the quality of life. Real GDP doesn't address how a country uses that output to affect living standards, it doesn't include some sources of well-being, and it does include some things that are detriments to well-being.

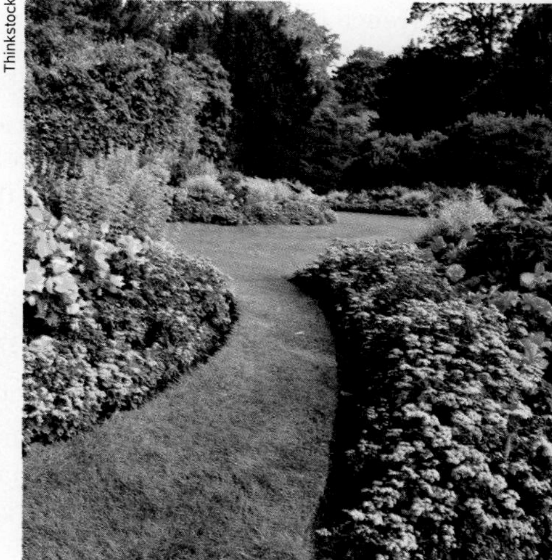

Thinkstock

Real GDP doesn't include many of the things that contribute to quality of life and happiness.

ECONOMICS IN ACTION — WORLD VIEW

GDP AND THE MEANING OF LIFE

"I've been rich and I've been poor," the actress Mae West famously declared. "Believe me, rich is better." But is the same true for countries?

This figure shows two pieces of information for a number of countries: how rich they are, as measured by GDP per capita, and how people assess their well-being. Well-being was measured by a Gallup world survey that asked people to rate their lives at the current time and their expectations for the next five years. The graph shows the percentage of people who rated their well-being as "thriving."

The figure seems to tell us three things:

1. *Rich is better.* Richer countries on average have higher well-being than poor countries.
2. *Money matters less as you grow richer.* The gain in life satisfaction as you go from GDP per capita of $20,000 to $30,000 is greater than the gain as you go from $40,000 to $50,000.
3. *Money isn't everything.* Israelis, though rich by world standards, are poorer than Americans—but they seem more satisfied with their lives. Japan is richer than most other nations, but by and large, quite miserable.

FIGURE 48-2 Percentage of Population for Select Countries That Rate Their Well-Being as Thriving

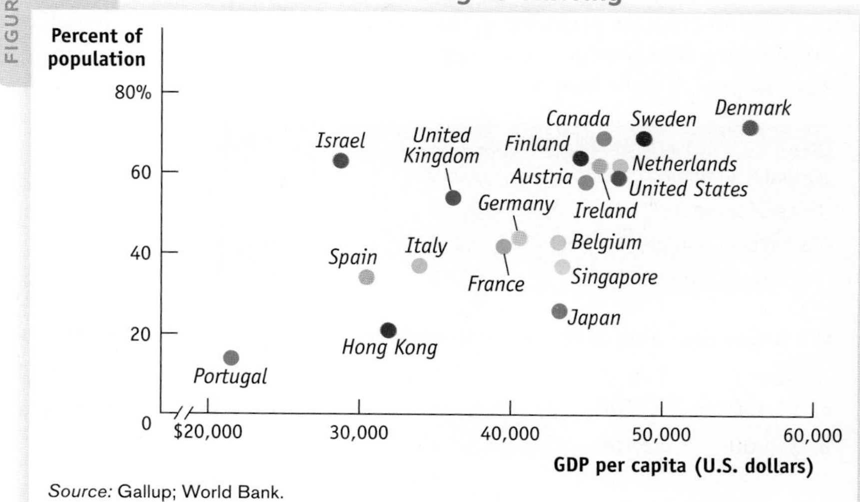

Source: Gallup; World Bank.

These results are consistent with the observation that high GDP per capita makes it easier to achieve a good life but that countries aren't equally successful in taking advantage of that possibility.

MODULE 48 Review

Solutions appear at the back of the book.

Check Your Understanding

1. Assume there are only two goods in the economy, french fries and onion rings. In 2012, 1,000,000 servings of french fries were sold for $0.40 each and 800,000 servings of onion rings were sold for $0.60 each. From 2012 to 2013, the price of french fries rose to $0.50 and the servings sold fell to 900,000; the price of onion rings fell to $0.51 and the servings sold rose to 840,000.
   - a. Calculate nominal GDP in 2012 and 2013. Calculate real GDP in 2013 using 2012 prices.
   - b. Why would an assessment of growth using nominal GDP be misguided?

2. From 1990 to 2000 the price of housing rose dramatically. What are the implications of this in deciding whether to use 1990 or 2000 as the base year in calculating 2010 real GDP?

Multiple-Choice Questions

1. Which of the following is true of real GDP?
   - I. It is adjusted for changes in prices.
   - II. It is always equal to nominal GDP.
   - III. It increases whenever aggregate output increases.
   - a. I only
   - b. II only
   - c. III only
   - d. I and III
   - e. I, II, and III

2. The best measure for comparing a country's aggregate output over time is
   - a. nominal GDP.
   - b. real GDP.
   - c. nominal GDP per capita.
   - d. real GDP per capita.
   - e. average GDP per capita.

3. Use the information provided in the table below for an economy that produces only apples and oranges. Assume year 1 is the base year.

	Year 1	Year 2
Quantity of apples	3,000	4,000
Price of an apple	$0.20	$0.30
Quantity of oranges	2,000	3,000
Price of an orange	$0.40	$0.50

What was the value of real GDP in each year?

	Year 1	*Year 2*
a.	$1,400	$2,700
b.	$1,900	$2,700
c.	$1,400	$2,000
d.	$1,900	$2,000
e.	$1,400	$1,900

4. Real GDP per capita is an imperfect measure of the quality of life in part because it
   - a. includes the value of leisure time.
   - b. excludes expenditures on education.
   - c. includes expenditures on natural disasters.
   - d. excludes expenditures on entertainment.
   - e. includes the value of housework.

5. Refer to the 2011 data in the following table.

	Nominal GDP in billions of dollars
United States	$14,990
China	7,318
European Union	17,570

Which of the following must be true?
   - I. Residents of China were worse off than residents of the United States or the European Union.
   - II. The European Union had a higher nominal GDP per capita than the United States.
   - III. The European Union had a larger economy than the United States.
   - a. I only
   - b. II only
   - c. III only
   - d. II and III
   - e. I, II, and III

Critical-Thinking Questions

Use the information in the accompanying table to answer the following questions.

	Year	Nominal GDP	Price Level	Population
Country A	2008	$2,000	$100	10
	2013	4,000	100	20
Country B	2008	$2,000	$100	10
	2013	6,000	200	15

1. Calculate the percent increase in nominal GDP between 2008 and 2013 for each country.
2. What happened to the price level in each country between 2008 and 2013?
3. Calculate real GDP in each country in 2013, using 2008 as the base year.
4. Calculate the percent increase in real GDP between 2008 and 2013 for each country.
5. Compare the two countries' real GDP per capita in 2013 using 2008 as the base year.

BUSINESS CASE: Getting a Jump on GDP

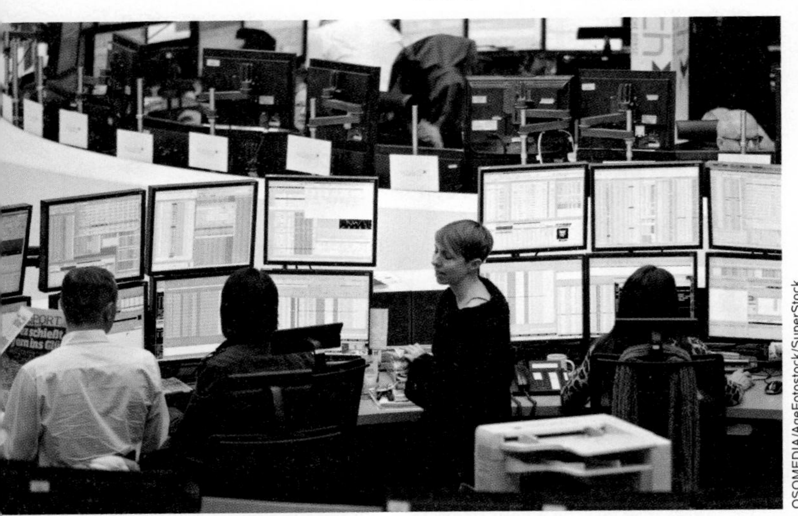
OSOMEDIA/AgeFotostock/SuperStock

GDP matters. Investors and business leaders are always eager to get the latest numbers. When the Bureau of Economic Analysis releases its first estimate of each quarter's GDP, normally on the 27th or 28th day of the month after the quarter ends, it's invariably a big news story.

In fact, many companies and other players in the economy are so eager to know what's happening to GDP that they don't want to wait for the official estimate. So a number of organizations produce numbers that can be used to predict what the official GDP number will say. Let's talk about two of those organizations, the economic consulting firm Macroeconomic Advisers and the nonprofit Institute of Supply Management.

Macroeconomic Advisers takes a direct approach: it produces its own estimates of GDP based on raw data from the U.S. government. But whereas the Bureau of Economic Analysis estimates GDP only on a quarterly basis, Macroeconomic Advisers produces monthly estimates. This means that clients can, for example, look at the estimates for January and February and make a pretty good guess at what first-quarter GDP, which also includes March, will turn out to be. The monthly estimates are derived by looking at a number of monthly measures that track purchases, such as car and truck sales, new housing construction, and exports.

The Institute for Supply Management (ISM) takes a very different approach. It relies on monthly surveys of purchasing managers—that is, executives in charge of buying supplies—who are basically asked whether their companies are increasing or reducing production. (We say "basically" because the ISM asks a longer list of questions.)

Responses to the surveys are released in the form of indexes showing the percentage of companies that are expanding. Obviously, these indexes don't directly tell you what is happening to GDP. But historically, the ISM indexes have been strongly correlated with the rate of growth of GDP, and this historical relationship can be used to translate ISM data into "early warning" GDP estimates.

So if you just can't wait for those quarterly GDP numbers, you're not alone. The private sector has responded to demand, and you can get your data fix every month.

Questions for Thought

1. Why do businesses care about GDP to such an extent that they want early estimates?
2. How do the methods of Macroeconomic Advisers and the Institute of Supply Management fit into the three different ways to calculate GDP?
3. If private firms are producing GDP estimates, why do we need the Bureau of Economic Analysis?

SECTION 15 REVIEW

Summary

Introduction to Macroeconomics

1. One key concern of macroeconomics is the **business cycle,** the short-run alternation between **recessions,** periods of falling employment and output, and **expansions,** periods of rising employment and output.
2. The point at which expansion turns to recession is a **business-cycle peak.** The point at which recession turns to expansion is a **business-cycle trough.**
3. Another key area of macroeconomic study is **long-run economic growth,** the sustained upward trend in the economy's output over time. Long-run economic growth is the force behind long-term increases in living standards and is important for financing some economic programs. It is especially important for poorer countries.
4. When the prices of most goods and services are rising, so that the overall level of prices is going up, the economy experiences **inflation.** When the overall level of prices is going down, the economy experiences **deflation.**
5. In the short run, inflation and deflation are closely related to the business cycle. In the long run, prices tend to reflect changes in the overall quantity of money. Because both inflation and deflation can cause problems, economists and policy makers generally aim for **price stability.**
6. Although comparative advantage explains why **open economies** export some things and import others, macroeconomic analysis is needed to explain why countries run **trade surpluses** or **trade deficits.** The determinants of the overall balance between exports and imports lie in decisions about savings and investment spending.

The Circular-Flow Diagram and the National Accounts

7. Economists keep track of the flows of money between sectors with the **national income and product accounts,** or **national accounts.** To understand the principles behind the national accounts, it helps to look at a **circular-flow diagram,** a simplified representation of the economy showing the flows of money, goods and services, and factors of production through the economy.
8. Households earn income via the factor markets from wages, interest on **bonds,** profit accruing to owners of **stocks,** and rent on land. In addition, they receive **government transfers** from the government. **Disposable income,** total household income minus taxes plus government transfers, is allocated to **consumer spending** (C) and **private savings.**
9. Via the **financial markets,** private savings and foreign lending are channeled to **investment spending** (I), government borrowing, and foreign borrowing.
10. **Government purchases of goods and services** (G) are paid for by tax revenues and any **government borrowing.**
11. Exports (X) generate an inflow of funds into the country from the rest of the world, but imports (IM) lead to an outflow of funds to the rest of the world. Foreigners can also buy stocks and bonds in the U.S. financial markets.

Gross Domestic Product (GDP)

12. **Gross domestic product,** or **GDP,** measures the value of all **final goods and services** produced in the economy. It does not include the value of **intermediate goods and services,** but it does include **inventories** and **net exports** (X – IM).
13. GDP can be calculated in three ways: add up the **value added** by all producers; add up all spending on domestically produced final goods and services, leading to the equation GDP = C + I + G + X – IM, also known as **aggregate spending;** or add up all the income paid by domestic firms to factors of production.
14. The three methods of calculating GDP are equivalent, because in the economy as a whole, total income paid by domestic firms to factors of production must equal total spending on domestically produced final goods and services.

Interpreting Real Gross Domestic Product

15. **Real GDP** is the value of the final goods and services produced calculated using the prices of a selected base year. Except in the base year, real GDP is usually not the same as **nominal GDP,** the value of **aggregate output** calculated using current prices.
16. Analysis of the growth rate of aggregate output must use real GDP because doing so eliminates any change in the value of aggregate output due solely to price changes. U.S. statistics on real GDP are always expressed in **chained dollars.**
17. **Real GDP per capita** is a measure of average aggregate output per person but is not in itself an appropriate policy goal.

Key Terms

Problems

1. How do economists in the United States determine when a recession begins and when it ends? How do other countries determine whether or not a recession is occurring?

2. The U.S. Department of Labor reports statistics on employment and earnings that are used as key indicators by many economists to gauge the health of the economy. Figure 45-2 in the text plots historical data on the unemployment rate each month. Noticeably, the numbers were high during the recessions in the early 1990s, in 2001, and in 2007–2009.

a. Locate the latest data on the national unemployment rate. (*Hint:* Go to the website of the Bureau of Labor Statistics, www.bls.gov, and locate the latest release of the Employment Situation.)

b. Compare the current numbers with the recessions in the early 1990s, in 2001, and in 2007–2009 as well as with the periods of relatively high economic growth just before the recessions. Are the current numbers indicative of a recessionary trend?

3. The accompanying figure shows the annual rate of growth in employment for the United Kingdom and Japan from 1991 to 2010. (The annual growth rate is the percent change in each year's employment over the previous year.) Comment on the business cycles of these two economies. Are their business cycles similar or dissimilar?

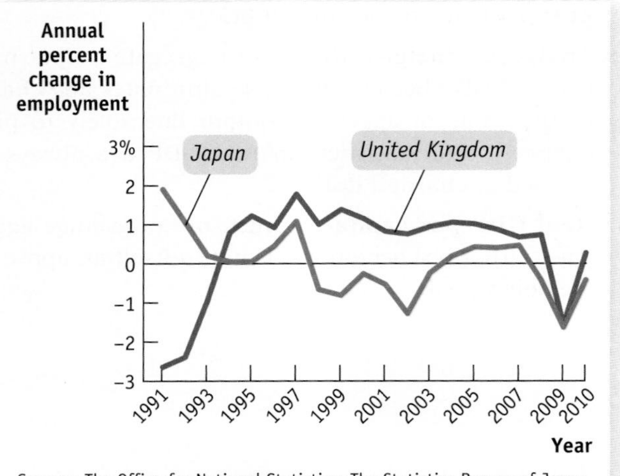

Sources: The Office for National Statistics; The Statistics Bureau of Japan.

4. a. What three measures of the economy tend to move together during the business cycle? Which way do they move during an upturn? During a downturn?

b. Who in the economy is hurt during a recession? How?

c. How did Milton Friedman alter the consensus that had developed in the aftermath of the Great Depression on how the economy should be managed? What is the current goal of policy makers in managing the economy?

5. Why do we consider a business-cycle expansion different from long-run economic growth? Why do we care about the size of the long-run growth rate of real GDP versus the size of the growth rate of the population?

6. College tuition has risen significantly in the last few decades. From the 1979–1980 academic year to the 2009–2010 academic year, total tuition, room, and board paid by full-time undergraduate students went from $2,327 to $15,041 at public institutions and from $5,013 to $35,061 at private institutions. This is an average annual tuition increase of 6.4% at public institutions and 6.7% at private institutions. Over the same time, average personal income after taxes rose from $7,956 to $35,088 per year, which is an average annual rate of growth of personal income of 5.0%. Have these tuition increases made it more difficult for the average student to afford college tuition?

7. Each year, *The Economist* publishes data on the price of the Big Mac in different countries and exchange rates. The accompanying table shows some data used for the index from 2007 and 2011. Use this information to answer the following questions.

Country	2007 Price of Big Mac (in local currrency)	2007 Price of Big Mac (in U.S. dollars)	2011 Price of Big Mac (in local currency)	2011 Price of Big Mac (in U.S. dollars)
Argentina	peso8.25	$2.65	peso20.0	$4.84
Canada	C$3.63	$3.08	C$4.73	$5.00
Euro area	€2.94	$3.82	€3.44	$4.93
Japan	¥280	$2.31	¥320	$4.08
United States	$3.22	$3.22	$4.07	$4.07

a. Where was it cheapest to buy a Big Mac in U.S. dollars in 2007?

b. Where was it cheapest to buy a Big Mac in U.S. dollars in 2011?

c. Using the increase in the local currency price of the Big Mac in each country to measure the percent change in the overall price level from 2007 to 2011, which nation experienced the most inflation? Did any of the nations experience deflation?

8. The accompanying figure illustrates the trade deficit of the United States since 1992. The United States has been consistently and, on the whole, increasingly importing more goods than it has been exporting. One of the countries it runs a trade deficit with is China. Which of the following statements are valid possible explanations of this fact? Explain.

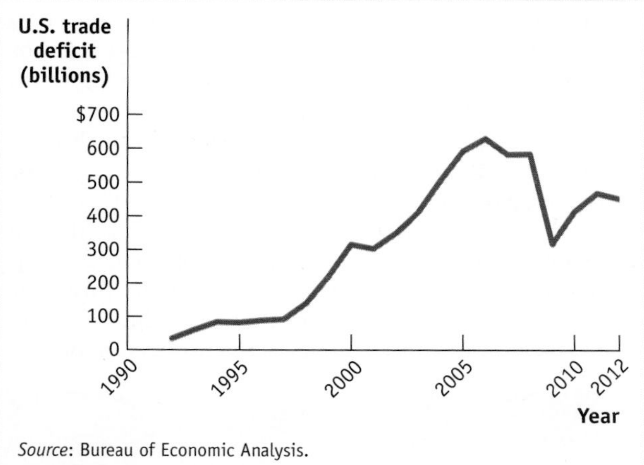

Source: Bureau of Economic Analysis.

a. Many products, such as televisions, that were formerly manufactured in the United States are now manufactured in China.

b. The wages of the average Chinese worker are far lower than the wages of the average American worker.

c. Investment spending in the United States is high relative to its level of savings.

9. Following is a simplified circular-flow diagram for the economy of Micronia. (Note that there is no investment in Micronia.)

a. What is the value of GDP in Micronia?

b. What is the value of net exports?

c. What is the value of disposable income?

d. Does the total flow of money out of households—the sum of taxes paid and consumer spending—equal the total flow of money into households?

e. How does the government of Micronia finance its purchases of goods and services?

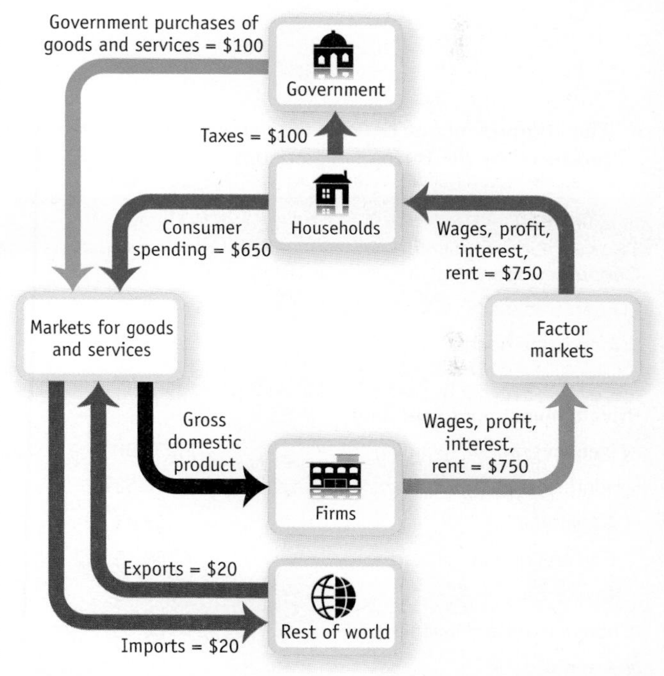

10. A more complex circular-flow diagram for the economy of Macronia is shown at right. (Note that Macronia has investment and financial markets.)

a. What is the value of GDP in Macronia?

b. What is the value of net exports?

c. What is the value of disposable income?

d. Does the total flow of money out of households—the sum of taxes paid, consumer spending, and private savings—equal the total flow of money into households?

e. How does the government finance its spending?

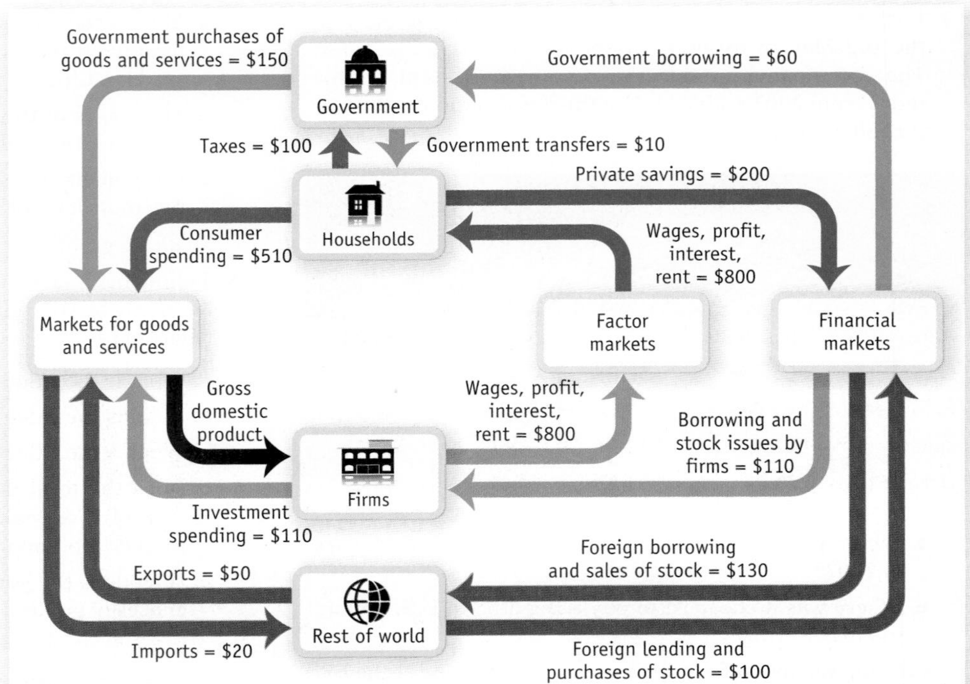

11. The components of GDP in the accompanying table were produced by the Bureau of Economic Analysis.

Category	Components of GDP in 2012 (billions of dollars)
Consumer spending	
Durable goods	$1,218.80
Nondurable goods	2,563.00
Services	7,337.68
Private investment spending	
Fixed investment spending	1,998.98
Nonresidential	1,616.58
Structures	458.48
Equipment and software	1,158.13
Residential	382.38
Change in private inventories	60.63
Net exports	
Exports	2,179.70
Imports	2,746.35
Government purchases of goods and services and investment spending	
Federal	1,214.23
National defense	809.10
Nondefense	405.10
State and local	1,849.40

a. Calculate 2012 consumer spending.

b. Calculate 2012 private investment spending.

c. Calculate 2012 net exports.

d. Calculate 2012 government purchases of goods and services and investment spending.

e. Calculate 2012 gross domestic product.

f. Calculate consumer spending on services as a percentage of total consumer spending.

g. Calculate 2012 exports as a percentage of imports.

h. Calculate 2012 government purchases on national defense as a percentage of federal government purchases of goods and services.

12. The small economy of Pizzania produces three goods (bread, cheese, and pizza), each produced by a separate company. The bread and cheese companies produce all the inputs they need to make bread and cheese, respectively. The pizza company uses the bread and cheese from the other companies to make its pizzas. All three companies employ labor to help produce their goods, and the difference between the value of goods sold and the sum of labor and input costs is the firm's profit. The accompanying table summarizes the activities of the three companies when all the bread and cheese produced are sold to the pizza company as inputs in the production of pizzas.

	Bread company	Cheese company	Pizza company
Cost of inputs	$0	$0	$50 (bread) 35 (cheese)
Wages	15	20	75
Value of output	50	35	200

a. Calculate GDP as the value added in production.

b. Calculate GDP as spending on final goods and services.

c. Calculate GDP as factor income.

13. In the economy of Pizzania (from Problem 13), bread and cheese produced are sold both to the pizza company for inputs in the production of pizzas and to consumers as final goods. The accompanying table summarizes the activities of the three companies.

	Bread company	Cheese company	Pizza company
Cost of inputs	$0	$0	$50 (bread) 35 (cheese)
Wages	25	30	75
Value of output	100	60	200

a. Calculate GDP as the value added in production.

b. Calculate GDP as spending on final goods and services.

c. Calculate GDP as factor income.

14. Which of the following transactions will be included in GDP for the United States?

a. Coca-Cola builds a new bottling plant in the United States.

b. Delta sells one of its existing airplanes to Korean Air.

c. Ms. Moneybags buys an existing share of Disney stock.

d. A California winery produces a bottle of Chardonnay and sells it to a customer in Montreal, Canada.

e. An American buys a bottle of French perfume in Paris.

f. A book publisher produces too many copies of a new book; the books don't sell this year, so the publisher adds the surplus books to inventories.

15. The economy of Britannica produces three goods: computers, DVDs, and pizza. The accompanying table shows the prices and output of the three goods for the years 2010, 2011, and 2012.

	Computers		DVDs		Pizzas	
Year	Price	Quantity	Price	Quantity	Price	Quantity
2010	$900	10	$10	100	$15	2
2011	1,000	10.5	12	105	16	2
2012	1,050	12	14	110	17	3

a. What is the percent change in production of each of the goods from 2010 to 2011 and from 2011 to 2012?

b. What is the percent change in prices of each of the goods from 2010 to 2011 and from 2011 to 2012?

c. Calculate nominal GDP in Britannica for each of the three years. What is the percent change in nominal GDP from 2010 to 2011 and from 2011 to 2012?

d. Calculate real GDP in Britannica using 2010 prices for each of the three years. What is the percent change in real GDP from 2010 to 2011 and from 2011 to 2012?

16. The accompanying table shows data on nominal GDP (in billions of dollars), real GDP (in billions of 2005 dollars), and population (in thousands) of the United States in 1960, 1970, 1980, 1990, 2000, and 2010. The U.S. price level rose consistently over the period 1960–2010.

Year	Nominal GDP (billions of dollars)	Real GDP (billions of 2005 dollars)	Population (thousands)
1960	$526.4	$2,828.5	180,760
1970	1,038.5	4,266.3	205,089
1980	2,788.1	5,834.0	227,726
1990	5,800.5	8,027.1	250,181
2000	9,951.5	11,216.4	282,418
2010	14,526.5	13,088.0	310,106

a. Why is real GDP greater than nominal GDP for all years until 2000 and lower for 2010?

b. Calculate the percent change in real GDP from 1960 to 1970, 1970 to 1980, 1980 to 1990, 1990 to 2000, and 2000 to 2010. Which period had the highest growth rate?

c. Calculate real GDP per capita for each of the years in the table.

d. Calculate the percent change in real GDP per capita from 1960 to 1970, 1970 to 1980, 1980 to 1990, 1990 to 2000, and 2000 to 2010. Which period had the highest growth rate?

e. How do the percent change in real GDP and the percent change in real GDP per capita compare? Which is larger? Do we expect them to have this relationship?

HIRE ME
GAS GOING UP
TOMORROW
BUY
TODAY!

SECTION 16

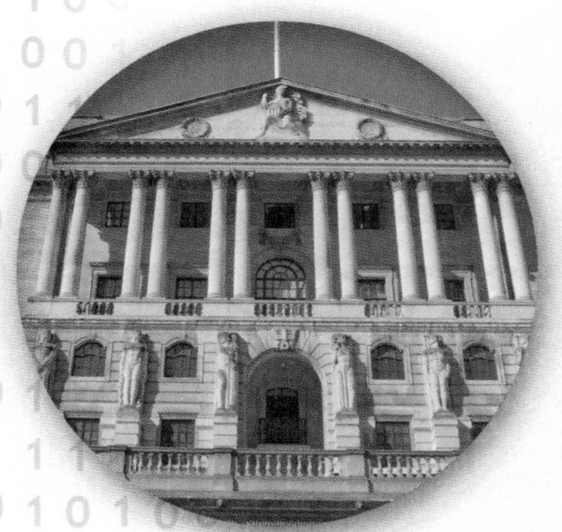

Unemployment and Inflation

A VERY BRITISH DILEMMA

The Bank of England is a venerable institution—so venerable that it makes the Federal Reserve, its American counterpart, look like a youthful upstart. The Old Lady of Threadneedle Street, as the Bank is sometimes known, has been managing Great Britain's money supply for three centuries—pumping up the money supply when the economy needs a boost, putting on the brakes when inflation looms.

But in early 2011, it wasn't at all clear what the Bank should do. British inflation was rising: consumer prices were 4.4 percent higher than they had been a year earlier, a rate of increase far above the Bank's comfort level. At the same time, the British economy was still suffering the aftereffects of a severe recession, and unemployment, especially among young people, was disturbingly high. So should the Bank have focused on fighting inflation, or should it have kept trying to bring down unemployment?

Opinion was sharply divided. The Bank faced "a genuine problem of credibility," declared Patrick Minford, a professor at Cardiff University, who urged the Bank to fight inflation by raising interest rates. The rise in inflation reflected temporary factors and would soon reverse course, countered Adam Posen, a member of the Bank's Policy Committee, who argued that any tightening would risk putting Britain into a prolonged slump.

Whoever was right, the dispute highlighted the key concerns of macroeconomic policy. Unemployment and inflation are the two great evils of macroeconomics. So the two principal goals of macroeconomic policy are low unemployment and price stability, usually defined as a low but positive rate of inflation.

Unfortunately, those goals sometimes appear to be in conflict with each other: economists often warn that policies intended to fight unemployment run the risk of increasing inflation; conversely, policies intended to bring down inflation can raise unemployment.

We look at the nature of the trade-off between low unemployment and price stability in Section 24. In this section we will provide an overview of the basic facts about unemployment and inflation: how they're measured, how they affect consumers and firms, and how they change over time.

Defining Unemployment

Frances Roberts/Alamy

WHAT YOU WILL LEARN

1. How unemployment is measured
2. How the unemployment rate is calculated
3. The significance of the unemployment rate for the economy
4. The relationship between the unemployment rate and economic growth

The Unemployment Rate

One of the most important issues in both the 2008 and 2012 presidential elections was the high unemployment rate. Figure 49-1 shows the U.S. unemployment rate from 1948 to 2013. As you can see, the labor market hit a difficult patch starting in mid-2008, with the unemployment rate rising from 4.8% in February 2008 to 10.1% in October 2009. What did the rise in the unemployment rate during the Great Recesssion mean, and why was it such a big factor in people's lives? To understand why policy makers pay so much attention to employment and unemployment, we need to understand how both are defined and measured.

Defining and Measuring Unemployment

It's easy to define employment: you're **employed** if and only if you have a job.

Unemployment, however, is a more subtle concept. Just because a person isn't working doesn't mean that we consider that person unemployed. For example, in November 2013 there were 42 million retired workers in the United States receiving Social Security checks. Most of them were probably happy that they were no longer working, so we wouldn't consider someone who has settled into a comfortable, well-earned retirement to be unemployed. There were also 14 million disabled U.S. workers receiving benefits because they were unable to work. Again, although they weren't working, we wouldn't normally consider them to be unemployed.

The U.S. Census Bureau, the federal agency that collects data on unemployment, considers the unemployed to be those who are "jobless, looking for jobs, and available for work." Retired people don't count because they aren't looking for jobs; the disabled don't count because they aren't available for work. More specifically, an individual is considered unemployed if he or she doesn't currently have a job and has been actively seeking a job during the past four weeks. So the **unemployed** are people who are actively looking for work but aren't currently employed.

Employed people are currently holding a job in the economy, either full time or part time.

Unemployed people are actively looking for work but aren't currently employed.

FIGURE 49-1 The U.S. Unemployment Rate, 1948–2013

The unemployment rate has fluctuated widely over time. It always rises during recessions, which are shown by the shaded bars. It usually, but not always, falls during periods of economic expansion.

Source: Bureau of Labor Statistics; National Bureau of Economic Research.

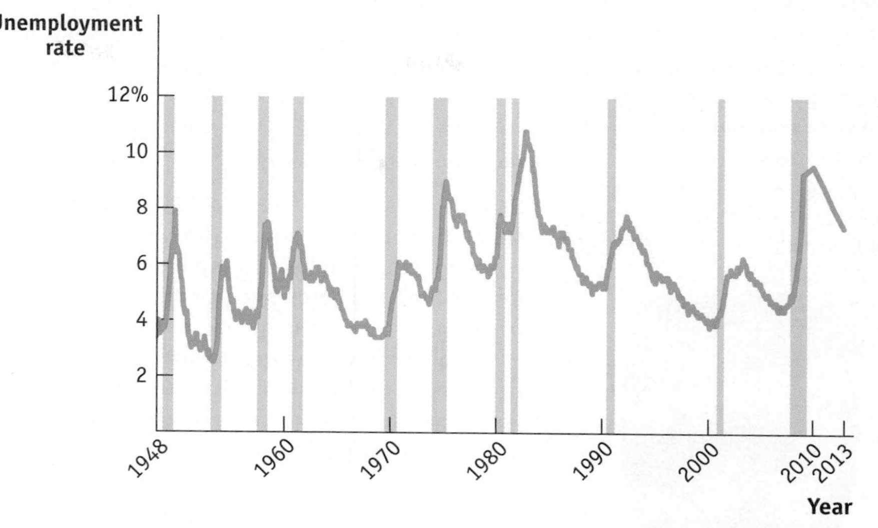

A country's **labor force** is the sum of the employed and the unemployed—that is, the people who are currently working and the people who are currently looking for work. The **labor force participation rate,** defined as the share of the working-age population that is in the labor force, is calculated as follows:

The **labor force** is equal to the sum of the employed and the unemployed.

The **labor force participation rate** is the percentage of the population aged 16 or older that is in the labor force.

The **unemployment rate** is the percentage of the total number of people in the labor force who are unemployed.

$$\textbf{(49-1)}\ \text{Labor force participation rate} = \frac{\text{Labor force}}{\text{Population age 16 and older}} \times 100$$

The **unemployment rate,** defined as the percentage of the total number of people in the labor force who are unemployed, is calculated as follows:

$$\textbf{(49-2)}\ \text{Unemployment rate} = \frac{\text{Number of unemployed workers}}{\text{Labor force}} \times 100$$

To estimate the numbers that go into calculating the unemployment rate, the U.S. Census Bureau carries out a monthly survey called the Current Population Survey, which involves interviewing a random sample of 60,000 American families. People are asked whether they are currently employed. If they are not employed, they are asked whether they have been looking for a job during the past four weeks. The results are then scaled up, using estimates of the total population, to estimate the total number of employed and unemployed Americans.

AP Photo/Bob Child

Only those without a job and actively seeking work are considered to be unemployed.

The Significance of the Unemployment Rate

In general, the unemployment rate is a good indicator of how easy or difficult it is to find a job given the current state of the economy. When the unemployment rate is low, nearly everyone who wants a job can find one. In 2000, when the unemployment rate averaged 4%, jobs were so abundant that employers spoke of a "mirror test" for getting a job: if you were breathing (therefore, your breath would fog a mirror), you could find work. By contrast, in 2009, the unemployment rate in 17 states rose to over 10% (over 15% in Michigan). Even in 2013, with the unemployment rate averaging 7.4%, it was difficult to find work. More than three times as many Americans were looking for work as there were job openings.

Although the unemployment rate is a good indicator of current labor market conditions, it is not a perfect measure. It has been known to overstate or understate the true level of unemployment.

Discouraged workers are nonworking people who are capable of working but have given up looking for a job due to the state of the job market.

Marginally attached workers would like to be employed and have looked for a job in the recent past but are not currently looking for work.

The **underemployed** are people who work part time because they cannot find full-time jobs.

People who would like to work but have given up searching for a job are not counted as unemployed.

HOW THE UNEMPLOYMENT RATE CAN OVERSTATE THE TRUE LEVEL OF UNEMPLOYMENT If you are searching for work, it's normal to take at least a few weeks to find a suitable job. Yet a worker who is quite confident of finding a job, but has not yet accepted a position, is counted as unemployed. As a consequence, the unemployment rate never falls to zero, even in boom times when jobs are plentiful. Even in the buoyant labor market of 2000, when it was easy to find work, the unemployment rate was still 4%. Later, we'll discuss in greater depth the reasons that measured unemployment persists even when jobs are abundant.

HOW THE UNEMPLOYMENT RATE CAN UNDERSTATE THE TRUE LEVEL OF UNEMPLOYMENT Frequently, people who would like to work but aren't working still don't get counted as unemployed. In particular, an individual who has given up looking for a job for the time being because there are no jobs available isn't counted as unemployed because he or she has not been searching for a job during the previous four weeks.

Individuals who want to work but aren't currently searching because they see little prospect of finding a job given the state of the job market are known as **discouraged workers.** Because it does not count discouraged workers, the measured unemployment rate may understate the percentage of people who want to work but are unable to find jobs.

Discouraged workers are part of a larger group known as **marginally attached workers.** These are people who say they would like to have a job and have looked for work in the recent past but are not currently looking for work. They are also not included when calculating the unemployment rate.

Finally, another category of workers who are frustrated in their ability to find work but aren't counted as unemployed are the **underemployed:** workers who would like to find full-time jobs but are currently working part time "for economic reasons"—that is, they can't find a full-time job. Again, they aren't counted in the unemployment rate.

The Bureau of Labor Statistics is the federal agency that calculates the official unemployment rate. It also calculates broader "measures of labor underutilization" that include the three categories of frustrated workers. Figure 49-2 shows what happens to the measured unemployment rate once marginally attached workers (including discouraged workers) and the underemployed are counted.

The broadest measure of unemployment and underemployment, known as *U6,* is the sum of these three measures plus the unemployed; it is substantially higher than the rate usually quoted by the news media. But U6 and the unemployment rate move very much in parallel, so changes in the unemployment rate remain a good guide to what's happening in the overall labor market.

FIGURE 49-2 **Alternative Measures of Unemployment, 1994–2013**

The unemployment number usually quoted in the news media counts someone as unemployed only if he or she has been looking for work during the past four weeks. Broader measures also count discouraged workers, marginally attached workers, and the underemployed. These broader measures show a higher unemployment rate, but they move closely in parallel with the standard rate.

Source: Bureau of Labor Statistics.

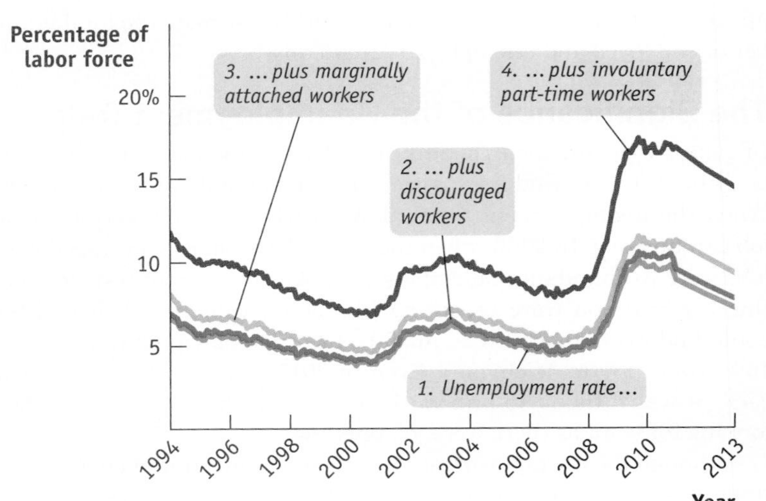

Finally, it's important to realize that the unemployment rate varies greatly among demographic groups. Other things equal, jobs are generally easier to find for more experienced workers and for workers during their "prime" working years, from ages 25 to 54. For younger workers, as well as workers nearing retirement age, jobs are typically harder to find, other things equal.

Figure 49-3 shows unemployment rates for different groups in December 2007, when the overall unemployment rate of 5.0% was low by historical standards. As you can see, in December 2007 the unemployment rate for African-American workers was much higher than the national average; the unemployment rate for White teenagers (ages 16–19) was more than three times the national average; and the unemployment rate for African-American teenagers, at 33.1%, was over six times the national average. (Bear in mind that a teenager isn't considered unemployed, even if he or she isn't working, unless that teenager is looking for work but can't find it.) So even at a time when the overall unemployment rate was relatively low, jobs were hard to find for some groups.

So although the unemployment rate is not an exact, literal measure of the percentage of people unable to find jobs, it is a good indicator of overall labor market conditions. The ups and downs of the unemployment rate closely reflect economic changes that have a significant impact on people's lives. Let's turn now to the causes of these fluctuations.

FIGURE 49-3 Unemployment Rates of Different Groups, 2007

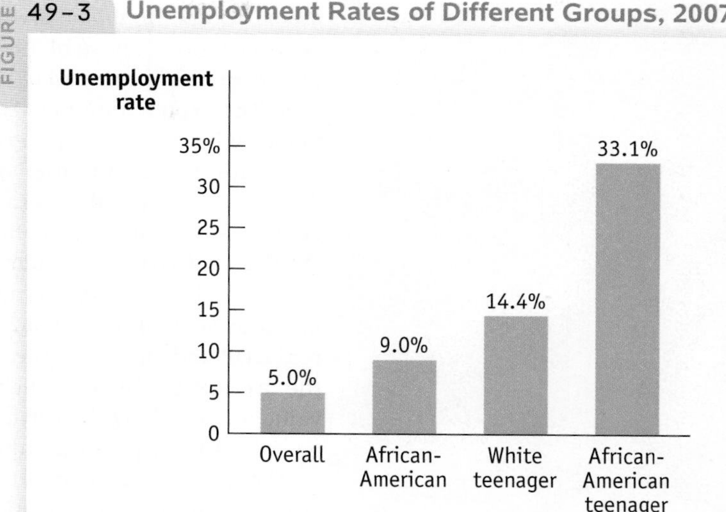

Unemployment rates vary greatly among different demographic groups. For example, although the overall unemployment rate in December 2007 was 5.0%, the unemployment rate among African-American teenagers was 33.1%. As a result, even during periods of low overall unemployment, unemployment remains a serious problem for some groups.

Source: Bureau of Labor Statistics.

Growth and Unemployment

Compared to Figure 49-1, Figure 49-4 shows the U.S. unemployment rate over a somewhat shorter period, the 35 years from 1978 to 2013. The shaded bars represent periods of recession. As you can see, during every recession, without exception, the unemployment rate rose. The severe recession of 2007–2009, like the earlier one of 1981–1982, led to a huge rise in unemployment.

FIGURE 49-4 Unemployment and Recessions, 1978–2013

This figure shows a close-up of the unemployment rate for the past three decades, with the shaded bars indicating recessions. It's clear that unemployment always rises during recessions and *usually* falls during expansions. But in both the early 1990s and the early 2000s, unemployment continued to rise for some time after the recession was officially declared over.

Source: Bureau of Labor Statistics.

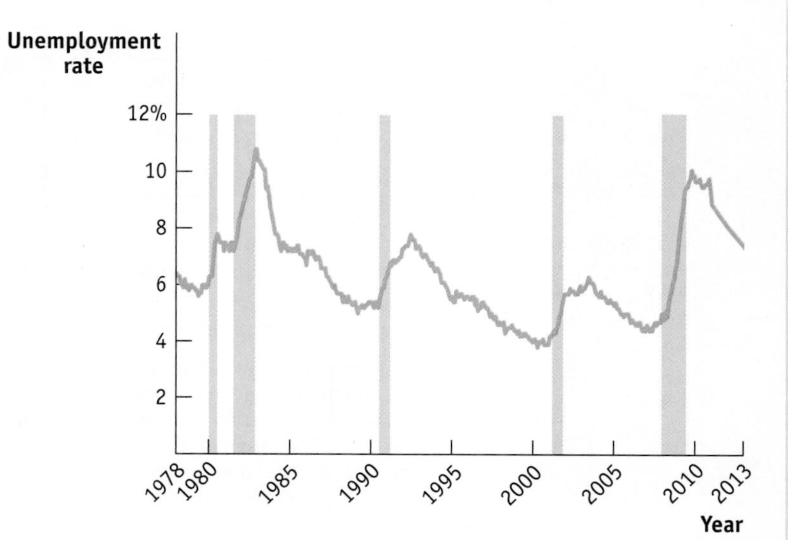

Correspondingly, during periods of economic expansion the unemployment rate usually falls. The long economic expansion of the 1990s eventually brought the unemployment rate below 4%, and the expansion of the mid-2000s brought the rate down to 4.7%. However, it's important to recognize that *economic expansions aren't always periods of falling unemployment.* Look at the periods immediately following two recent recessions, those of 1990–1991 and 2001 in Figure 49-4. In each case the unemployment rate continued to rise for more than a year after the recession was officially over. The explanation in both cases is that although the economy was growing, it was not growing fast enough to reduce the unemployment rate.

Figure 49-5 is a scatter diagram showing U.S. data for the period from 1949 to 2012. The horizontal axis measures the annual rate of growth in real GDP—the percent by which each year's real GDP changed compared to the previous year's real GDP. (Notice that there were ten years in which growth was negative—that is, real GDP shrank.) The vertical axis measures the *change* in the unemployment rate over the previous year in percentage points. Each dot represents the observed growth rate of real GDP and change in the unemployment rate for a given year. For example, in 2000 the average unemployment rate fell to 4.0% from 4.2% in 1999; this is shown as a value of −0.2 along the vertical axis for the year 2000. Over the same period, real GDP grew by 4.1%; this is the value shown along the horizontal axis for the year 2000.

The downward trend of the scatter points in Figure 49-5 shows that there is a generally strong negative relationship between growth in the economy and the rate of unemployment. Years of high growth in real GDP were also years in which the unemployment rate fell, and years of low or negative growth in real GDP were years in which the unemployment rate rose.

The green vertical line in Figure 49-5 at the value of 3.19% indicates the average growth rate of real GDP over the period from 1949 to 2012. Points lying to the right of the vertical line are years of above-average growth. In these years, the value on the

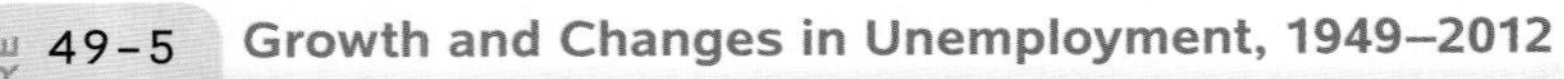

FIGURE 49-5 Growth and Changes in Unemployment, 1949–2012

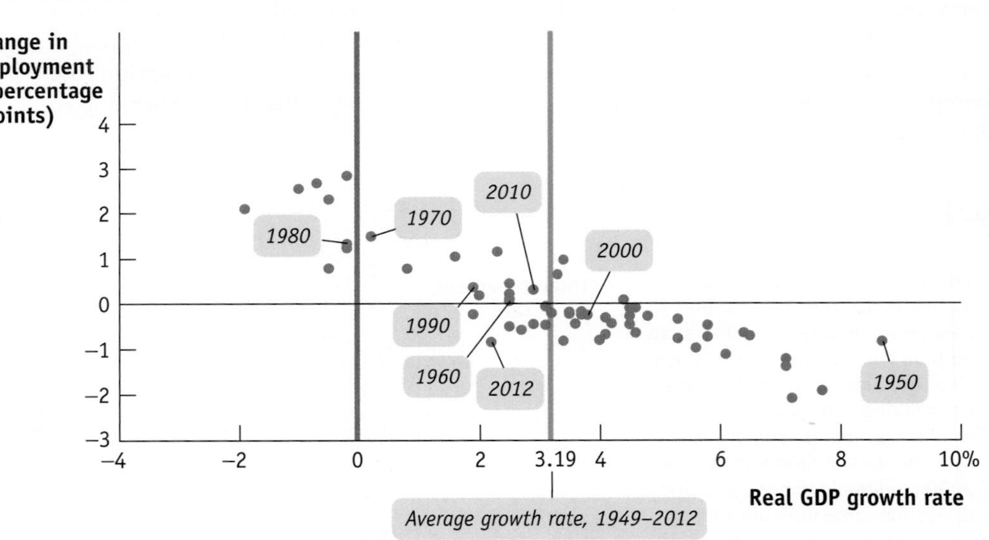

Each dot shows the growth rate of the economy and the change in the unemployment rate for a specific year between 1949 and 2012. For example, in 2000 the economy grew 4.1% and the unemployment rate fell 0.2 percentage point, from 4.2% to 4.0%. In general, the unemployment rate fell when growth was above its average rate of 3.19% a year and rose when growth was below average. Unemployment always rose when real GDP fell.

Sources: Bureau of Labor Statistics; Bureau of Economic Analysis.

vertical axis is usually negative, meaning that the unemployment rate fell. That is, years of above-average growth were usually years in which the unemployment rate was falling. Conversely, points lying to the left of the vertical line were years of below-average growth. In these years, the value on the purple vertical line is usually positive, meaning that the unemployment rate rose. That is, years of below-average growth were usually years in which the unemployment rate was rising.

A **jobless recovery** is a period in which the GDP growth rate is positive but the unemployment rate is still rising.

A period in which GDP is growing at a below-average rate and unemployment is rising is called a **jobless recovery** or a "growth recession." Since 1990, there have been three recessions, in 1990–1991, 2001, and 2007–2009, all of which have been followed by jobless recoveries.

But true recessions, periods when real GDP falls, are especially painful for workers. As illustrated by the points to the left of the purple vertical line in Figure 49-5 (representing years in which the real GDP growth rate is negative), falling real GDP is always associated with a rising rate of unemployment, causing a great deal of hardship to families.

ECONOMICS IN ACTION

FAILURE TO LAUNCH

In March 2010, when the U.S. job situation was near its worst, the *Harvard Law Record* published a brief note titled "Unemployed law student will work for $160K plus benefits." In a self-mocking tone, the author admitted to having graduated from Harvard Law School the previous year but not landing a job offer. "What mark on our résumé is so bad that it outweighs the crimson H?" the note asked.

Matthew Benoit/Shutterstock

The answer, of course, is that it wasn't about the résumé—it was about the economy. Times of high unemployment are especially hard on new graduates, who often find it hard to get any kind of full-time job.

How bad was it in March 2010, around the time that note was written? Researchers at the San Francisco Fed analyzed the employment experience of college graduates, ages 21–23, and their findings are in Figure 49-6.

Although the overall unemployment rate for college graduates 25 and older, even at its peak, was only about 5%, unemployment among recent graduates aged 21–23 peaked in 2010 at 10.7%. And many of those who *were* employed had been able to get only part-time jobs. In December 2007, at the beginning of the 2007–2009 recession, 83% of college graduates under the age of 24 who weren't still in school were employed full time. By December 2009, that number was down to just 72%. Quite simply, many college graduates were having a hard time getting their working lives started.

FIGURE 49-6 Unemployment Rate for College Graduates, 1995–2010

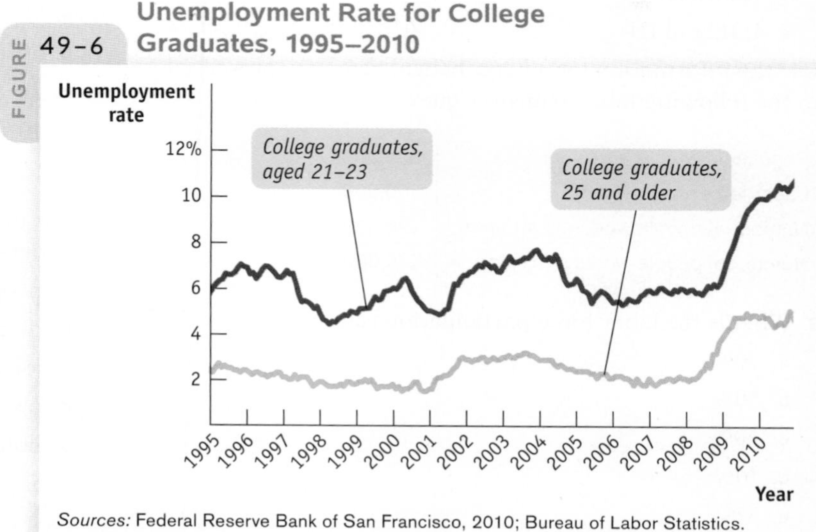

Sources: Federal Reserve Bank of San Francisco, 2010; Bureau of Labor Statistics.

The situation is improving, but slowly: by the end of 2010, 74% of recent graduates had full-time jobs and by the end of 2012 this figure was up to 81%. The rest were either unemployed or employed part time. However, even for those college graduates with jobs, 40% had landed jobs that required no college degree in 2012, up from 30% before the recession began in 2007. The U.S. labor market has a long way to go before being able to offer college graduates—and young people in general—the kinds of opportunities they deserve.

MODULE 49 Review

Solutions appear at the back of the book.

Check Your Understanding

1. Suppose that employment websites enable job-seekers to find suitable jobs more quickly. What effect will this have on the unemployment rate over time? Also suppose that these websites encourage job-seekers who had given up their searches to begin looking again. What effect will this have on the unemployment rate?

2. In which of the following cases would the worker be counted as unemployed? Explain.
   - **a.** Rosa, an older worker, has been laid off and gave up looking for work months ago.
   - **b.** Anthony, a schoolteacher, is not working during his three-month summer break.
   - **c.** Grace, an investment banker, has been laid off and is currently searching for another position.
   - **d.** Sergio, a classically trained musician, can only find work playing for local parties.
   - **e.** Natasha, a graduate student, went back to school because jobs were scarce.

3. Which of the following are consistent with the observed relationship between growth in real GDP and changes in the unemployment rate? Which are not?
   - **a.** A rise in the unemployment rate accompanies a fall in real GDP.
   - **b.** An exceptionally strong business recovery is associated with a greater percentage of the labor force being employed.
   - **c.** Negative real GDP growth is associated with a fall in the unemployment rate.

Multiple-Choice Questions

1. To be considered unemployed, a person must
   - I. not be working.
   - II. be actively seeking a job.
   - III. be available for work.

   - **a.** I only
   - **b.** II only
   - **c.** III only
   - **d.** II and III
   - **e.** I, II, and III

Use the information for a hypothetical economy presented in the following table to answer questions 2, 3, and 4.

Population age 16 and older	200,000
Labor force	100,000
Number of people working part time	20,000
Number of people working full time	70,000

2. What is the labor force participation rate?
   - **a.** 70%
   - **b.** 50%
   - **c.** 20%
   - **d.** 10%
   - **e.** 5%

3. How many people are unemployed?
   - **a.** 10,000
   - **b.** 20,000
   - **c.** 30,000
   - **d.** 100,000
   - **e.** 110,000

4. What is the unemployment rate?
   - **a.** 70%
   - **b.** 50%
   - **c.** 20%
   - **d.** 10%
   - **e.** 5%

5. The unemployment problem in an economy may be understated by the unemployment rate due to
   - **a.** people lying about seeking a job.
   - **b.** discouraged workers.
   - **c.** job candidates with one offer but waiting for more.
   - **d.** overemployed workers.
   - **e.** none of the above.

Critical-Thinking Questions

What is the labor market classification for each of the following individuals? Be as specific as possible, and explain your answer.

1. Julie has a graduate degree in mechanical engineering. She works full-time mowing lawns.
2. Jeff was laid off from his previous job. He would very much like to work at any job, but, after looking for work for a year, has stopped looking for work.
3. Ian is working 25 hours per week at a bookstore, and has no desire to work full time.
4. Raj has decided to take a year off from work to stay home with his daughter.

50 Categories of Unemployment

Lightspring/Shutterstock

WHAT YOU WILL LEARN

1. The three different types of unemployment and their causes
2. The factors that determine the natural rate of unemployment

Fast economic growth tends to reduce the unemployment rate. So how low can the unemployment rate go? You might be tempted to say zero, but that isn't feasible. Over the past half-century, the national unemployment rate has never dropped below 2.9%.

How can there be so much unemployment even when many businesses are having a hard time finding workers? To answer this question, we need to examine the nature of labor markets and why they normally lead to substantial measured unemployment even when jobs are plentiful. Our starting point is the observation that even in the best of times, jobs are constantly being created and destroyed.

Job Creation and Job Destruction

Even during good times, most Americans know someone who has lost his or her job. The U.S. unemployment rate in July 2007 was only 4.7%, relatively low by historical standards, yet in that month there were 4.5 million "job separations"—terminations of employment that occurred because a worker was either fired or quit voluntarily.

There are many reasons for such job loss. One is structural change in the economy: industries rise and fall as new technologies emerge and consumers' tastes change. For example, employment in high-tech industries such as telecommunications surged in the late 1990s but slumped severely after 2000. However, structural change also brings the creation of new jobs: since 2000, the number of jobs in the American health care sector has surged as new medical technologies have emerged and the aging of the population has increased the demand for medical care.

Poor management or bad luck at a company also leads to job loss for employees. For example, in 2005 General Motors announced plans to eliminate 30,000 jobs after several years of lagging sales, even as Japanese companies such as Toyota announced plans to open new plants in North America to meet growing demand for their cars.

Continual job creation and destruction are a feature of modern economies, making a naturally occurring amount of unemployment inevitable. Within this naturally occurring amount, there are two types of unemployment—*frictional* and *structural*.

Workers who spend time looking for employment are engaged in **job search**.

Frictional unemployment is unemployment due to the time workers spend in job search.

Frictional Unemployment

Workers who lose a job involuntarily due to job destruction often choose not to take the first new job offered. For example, suppose a skilled programmer, laid off because her software company's product line was unsuccessful, sees a help-wanted ad for clerical work online. She might respond to the ad and get the job—but that would be foolish. Instead, she should take the time to look for a job that takes advantage of her skills and pays accordingly. In addition, individual workers are constantly leaving jobs voluntarily, typically for personal reasons—family moves, dissatisfaction, and better job prospects elsewhere.

Economists say that workers who spend time looking for employment are engaged in **job search.** If all workers and all jobs were alike, job search wouldn't be necessary; if information about jobs and workers were perfect, job search would be very quick. In practice, however, it's normal for a worker who loses a job, or a young worker seeking a first job, to spend at least a few weeks searching.

Frictional unemployment is unemployment due to the time workers spend in job search. A certain amount of frictional unemployment is inevitable due to the constant process of economic change. Even in 2007, a year of low unemployment, there were 62 million "job separations," in which workers left or lost their jobs. Total employment grew because these separations were more than offset by more than 63 million hires. Inevitably, some of the workers who left or lost their jobs spent at least some time unemployed, as did some of the workers newly entering the labor force.

"At this point, I'm just happy to still have a job"

© The New Yorker Collection 2009 Christopher Weyant from cartoonbank.com. All Rights Reserved.

Figure 50-1 shows the 2007 average monthly flows of workers among three states: employed, unemployed, and not in the labor force. What the figure suggests is how much churning is constantly taking place in the labor market. An inevitable consequence of that churning is a significant number of workers who haven't yet found their next job—that is, frictional unemployment.

A limited amount of frictional unemployment is relatively harmless and may even be a good thing. The economy is more productive if workers take the time to find jobs that are well matched to their skills and workers who are unemployed for a brief

FIGURE 50-1 Labor Market Flows in an Average Month in 2007

Even in 2007, a low-unemployment year, large numbers of workers moved into and out of both employment and unemployment each month. On average, each month in 2007, 1.781 million unemployed became employed, and 1.929 million employed became unemployed.

Source: Bureau of Labor Statistics.

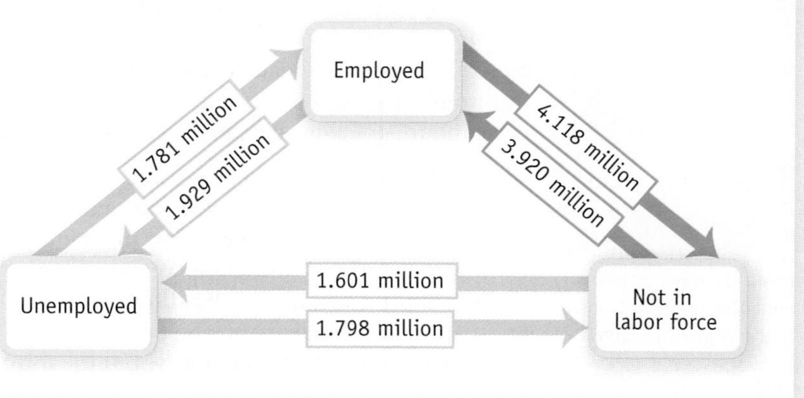

FIGURE 50-2 **Distribution of the Unemployed by Duration of Unemployment, 2007**

In years when the unemployment rate is low, most unemployed workers are unemployed for only a short period. In 2007, a year of low unemployment, 36% of the unemployed had been unemployed for less than 5 weeks and 67% for less than 15 weeks. The short duration of unemployment for most workers suggests that most unemployment in 2007 was frictional.

Source: Bureau of Labor Statistics.

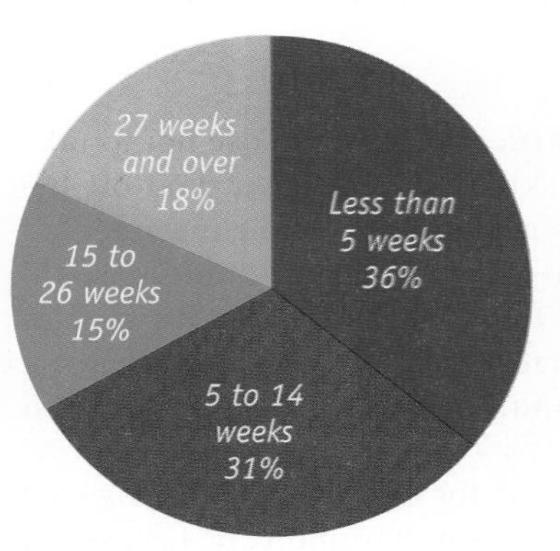

period while searching for the right job don't experience great hardship. In fact, when there is a low unemployment rate, periods of unemployment tend to be quite short, suggesting that much of the unemployment is frictional.

Figure 50-2 shows the composition of unemployment for all of 2007, when the unemployment rate was only 4.6%. Thirty-six percent of the unemployed had been unemployed for less than 5 weeks, and only 33% had been unemployed for 15 or more weeks. Only about one in six unemployed workers were considered to be "long-term unemployed"—unemployed for 27 or more weeks.

In periods of higher unemployment, however, workers tend to be jobless for longer periods of time, suggesting that a smaller share of unemployment is frictional. By 2010, the fraction of unemployed workers considered "long-term unemployed" had jumped to 43%.

Structural Unemployment

Frictional unemployment exists even when the number of people seeking jobs is equal to the number of jobs being offered—that is, the existence of frictional unemployment doesn't mean that there is a surplus of labor. Sometimes, however, there is a *persistent surplus* of job-seekers in a particular labor market, even when the economy is performing well. There may be more workers with a particular skill than there are jobs available using that skill, or there may be more workers in a particular geographic region than there are jobs available in that region. **Structural unemployment** is unemployment that results when there are more people seeking jobs in a labor market than there are jobs available at the current wage rate.

In **structural unemployment,** more people are seeking jobs in a particular labor market than there are jobs available at the current wage rate.

The supply and demand model tells us that the price of a good, service, or factor of production tends to move toward an equilibrium level that matches the quantity supplied with the quantity demanded. This is equally true, in general, of labor markets.

Figure 50-3 shows a typical market for labor. The labor demand curve indicates that when the price of labor—the wage rate—increases, employers demand less labor. The labor supply curve indicates that when the price of labor increases, more workers are willing to supply labor at the prevailing wage rate. These two forces coincide to lead to an equilibrium wage rate for any given type of labor in a particular location. That equilibrium wage rate is shown as W_E.

Even at the equilibrium wage rate, W_E, there will still be some frictional unemployment. That's because there will always be some workers engaged in job search even when the number of jobs available is equal to the number of workers seeking jobs. But there wouldn't be any structural unemployment in this labor market. *Structural unemployment occurs when the wage rate is, for some reason, persistently above* W_E. Several factors can lead to a wage rate in excess of W_E, the most important being minimum wages, labor unions, *efficiency wages,* the side effects of government policies, and mismatches between employees and employers.

MINIMUM WAGES A *minimum wage* is a government-mandated floor on the price of labor. In the United States, the national minimum wage in 2013 was $7.25 an hour. For many American workers, the minimum wage is irrelevant; the market equilibrium wage for these workers is well above this price floor. But for less-skilled workers, the minimum wage may be binding—it affects the wages that people are actually paid and can lead to structural unemployment. In countries that have higher minimum wages, the range of workers for whom the minimum wage is binding is larger.

FIGURE 50-3 The Effect of a Minimum Wage on the Labor Market

When the government sets a minimum wage, W_F, that exceeds the market equilibrium wage rate, W_E, the number of workers, Q_S, who would like to work at that minimum wage is greater than the number of workers, Q_D, demanded at that wage rate. This surplus of labor is considered structural unemployment.

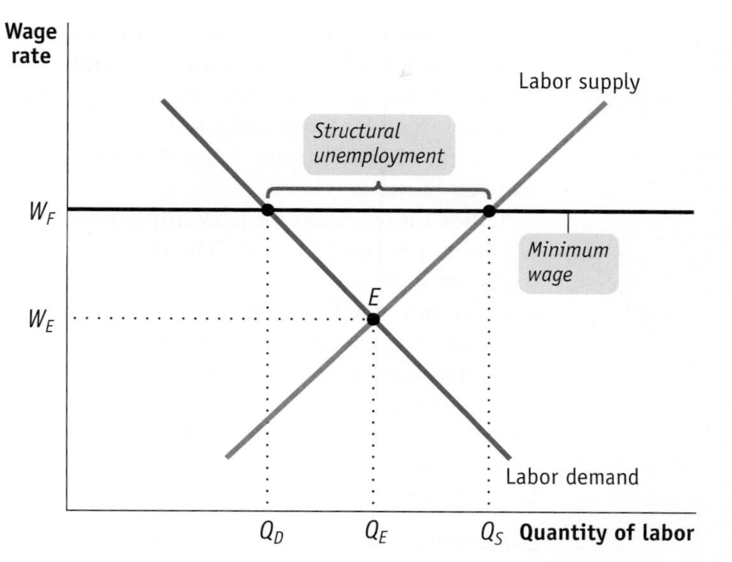

Figure 50-3 shows the effect of a binding minimum wage. In this market, there is a legal floor on wages, W_F, which is above the equilibrium wage rate, W_E. This leads to a persistent surplus in the labor market: the quantity of labor supplied, Q_S, is larger than the quantity demanded, Q_D. In other words, more people want to work than can find jobs at the minimum wage, leading to structural unemployment.

Given that minimum wages—that is, binding minimum wages—generally lead to structural unemployment, you might wonder why governments impose them. The rationale is to help ensure that people who work can earn enough income to afford at least a minimally comfortable lifestyle. However, this may come at a cost, because it may eliminate employment opportunities for some workers who would have willingly worked for lower wages. As illustrated in Figure 50-3, not only are there more sellers of labor than there are buyers, but there are also fewer people working at a minimum wage (Q_D) than there would have been with no minimum wage at all (Q_E).

Marmaduke St. John/Alamy

Minimum-wage workers advocating for a *living wage*, one that is high enough to maintain a normal standard of living.

Although economists broadly agree that a high minimum wage has the employment-reducing effects shown in Figure 50-3, there is some question about whether this is a good description of how the minimum wage actually works in the United States. The minimum wage in the United States is quite low compared with that in other wealthy countries. For three decades, from the 1970s to the mid-2000s, the U.S. minimum wage was so low that it was not binding for the vast majority of workers.

In addition, some researchers have produced evidence that increases in the minimum wage actually lead to higher employment when, as was the case in the United States at one time, the minimum wage is low compared to average wages. They argue that firms employing low-skilled workers sometimes restrict their hiring in order to keep wages low and that, as a result, the minimum wage can sometimes be increased without any loss of jobs. Most economists, however, agree that a sufficiently high minimum wage *does* lead to structural unemployment.

LABOR UNIONS The actions of *labor unions* can have effects similar to those of minimum wages, leading to structural unemployment. By bargaining collectively for all of a firm's workers, unions can win higher wages from employers than workers would have obtained by bargaining individually. This process, known as *collective bargaining*, is intended to tip the scales of bargaining power more toward workers and away from employers.

Labor unions exercise bargaining power by threatening firms with a *labor strike*, a collective refusal to work. The threat of a strike can have serious consequences for firms. In such cases, workers acting collectively can exercise more power than they could if they acted individually.

When workers have greater bargaining power, they tend to demand and push the wage that workers receive above the equilibrium wage. Consequently, there are more people willing to work at the wage being paid than there are jobs available, leading to structural unemployment. In the United States, however, because of a low level of unionization, the amount of unemployment generated by union demands is likely to be very small.

EFFICIENCY WAGES Actions by firms may also contribute to structural unemployment. Firms may choose to pay **efficiency wages**—wages that employers set above the equilibrium wage rate as an incentive for their workers to deliver better performance.

Employers may feel the need for such incentives for several reasons. For example, employers often have difficulty observing directly how hard an employee works. They can, however, elicit more work effort by paying above-market wages: employees receiving these higher wages are more likely to work harder to ensure that they aren't fired, which would cause them to lose their higher wages.

When many firms pay efficiency wages, the result is a pool of workers who want jobs but can't find them. So the use of efficiency wages by firms leads to structural unemployment.

SIDE EFFECTS OF GOVERNMENT POLICIES In addition, government policies designed to help workers who lose their jobs can lead to structural unemployment as an unintended side effect. Most economically advanced countries provide benefits to laid-off workers as a way to tide them over until they find a new job. In the United States, these benefits typically replace only a small fraction of a worker's income and expire after 26 weeks. This was extended in some cases to 99 weeks during the period of high unemployment that began in 2009. Although the extension expired at the end of 2013, at the time of this writing, Congress was considering whether to once again extend the benefits.

In other countries, particularly in Europe, benefits are more generous and last longer. The drawback to this generosity is that it reduces the incentive to quickly find a new job, and by keeping more people searching for longer, the benefits increase structural and frictional unemployment. Generous unemployment benefits in some European countries are widely believed to be one of the main causes of "Eurosclerosis," the persistent high unemployment that afflicts a number of European economies.

MISMATCHES BETWEEN EMPLOYEES AND EMPLOYERS It takes time for workers and firms to adjust to shifts in the economy. The result can be a mismatch between what employees have to offer and what employers are looking for. A skills mismatch is one form; for example, in the aftermath of the housing bust of 2009, there were more construction workers looking for jobs than jobs available. Another form is geographic, as in Michigan, which has had a long-standing surplus of workers since its auto industry went into decline.

Until the mismatch is resolved through a fall in wages for surplus workers that is big enough to induce retraining or relocation, there will be structural unemployment.

Efficiency wages are wages that employers set above the equilibrium wage rate as an incentive for better employee performance.

The Natural Rate of Unemployment

Because some frictional unemployment is inevitable and because many economies also suffer from structural unemployment, a certain amount of unemployment is normal, or "natural." Actual unemployment fluctuates around this normal level.

The **natural rate of unemployment** is the normal unemployment rate around which the actual unemployment rate fluctuates. It is the rate of unemployment that arises from the effects of frictional plus structural unemployment. **Cyclical unemployment** is the deviation of the actual rate of unemployment from the natural rate; that is, it is the difference between the actual and natural rates of unemployment. As the name suggests, cyclical unemployment is the share of unemployment that arises from the business cycle. Later we'll see that government policy cannot keep the unemployment rate persistently below the natural rate without leading to accelerating inflation.

The **natural rate of unemployment** is the unemployment rate that arises from the effects of frictional plus structural unemployment.

Cyclical unemployment is the deviation of the actual rate of unemployment from the natural rate.

We can summarize the relationships between the various types of unemployment as follows:

(50-1) Natural unemployment =
Frictional unemployment + Structural unemployment

(50-2) Actual unemployment =
Natural unemployment + Cyclical unemployment

Perhaps because of its name, people often imagine that the natural rate of unemployment is a constant that doesn't change over time and can't be affected by policy. Neither proposition is true. Let's take a moment to stress two facts: the natural rate of unemployment changes over time, and it can be affected by economic policies.

Changes in the Natural Rate of Unemployment

Private-sector economists and government agencies need estimates of the natural rate of unemployment to make forecasts and conduct policy analyses. Almost all these estimates show that the U.S. natural rate rises and falls over time. For example, the Congressional Budget Office, the independent agency that conducts budget and economic analyses for Congress, believes that the U.S. natural rate of unemployment was 5.3% in 1950, rose to 6.3% by the end of the 1970s, but has fallen to 5.5% today. European countries have experienced even larger swings in their natural rates of unemployment.

What causes the natural rate of unemployment to change? The most important factors are

- Changes in the characteristics of the labor force
- Changes in labor market institutions
- Changes in government policies.

CHANGES IN LABOR FORCE CHARACTERISTICS In December 2013 the overall rate of unemployment in the United States was 6.7%. Young workers, however, had much higher unemployment rates: 20.2% for teenagers and 11.1% for workers aged 20 to 24. Workers aged 25 to 54 had an unemployment rate of only 5.8%.

In general, unemployment rates tend to be lower for experienced than for inexperienced workers. Because experienced workers tend to stay in a given job longer, they have lower frictional unemployment. Also, because older workers are more likely than young workers to be family breadwinners, they have a stronger incentive to find and keep jobs.

One reason the natural rate of unemployment rose during the 1970s was a large rise in the number of new workers—children

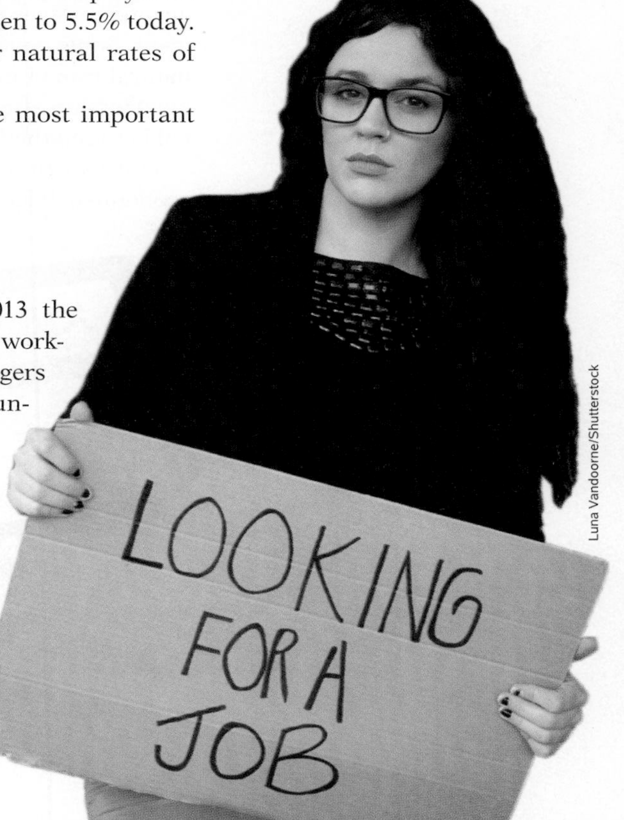

Luna Vandoorne/Shutterstock

FIGURE 50-4 The Changing Makeup of the U.S. Labor Force, 1948–2013

In the 1970s the percentage of the labor force consisting of women rose rapidly, as did the percentage under age 25. These changes reflected the entry of large numbers of women into the paid labor force for the first time and the fact that baby boomers were reaching working age. The natural rate of unemployment may have risen because many of these workers were relatively inexperienced. Today, the labor force is much more experienced, which is one possible reason the natural rate has fallen since the 1970s.

Source: Bureau of Labor Statistics.

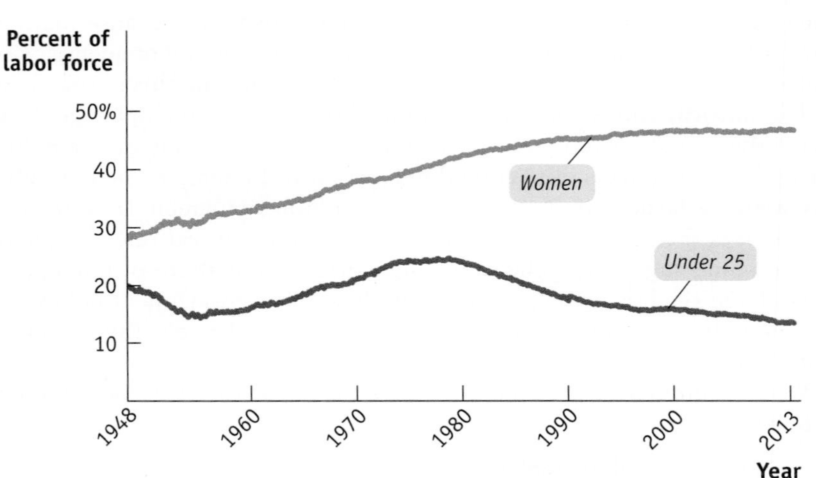

of the post–World War II baby boom entered the labor force, as did a rising percentage of married women.

As Figure 50-4 shows, both the percentage of the labor force less than 25 years old and the percentage of women in the labor force surged in the 1970s. By the end of the 1990s, however, the share of women in the labor force had leveled off and the percentage of workers under 25 had fallen sharply. As a result, the labor force as a whole is more experienced today than it was in the 1970s, one likely reason that the natural rate of unemployment is lower today than in the 1970s.

CHANGES IN LABOR MARKET INSTITUTIONS As we pointed out earlier, unions that negotiate wages above the equilibrium level can be a source of structural unemployment. Some economists believe that strong labor unions are one reason for the high natural rate of unemployment in Europe. In the United States, a sharp fall in union membership after 1980 may have been one reason the natural rate of unemployment fell between the 1970s and the 1990s.

Other institutional changes may also have been at work. For example, some labor economists believe that temporary employment agencies, which have proliferated in recent years, have reduced frictional unemployment by helping match workers to jobs. And, of course, job-search websites such as Monster.com may have reduced frictional unemployment.

YinYang/Getty Images

Technological change, coupled with labor market institutions, can also affect the natural rate of unemployment. Technological change probably leads to an increase in the demand for skilled workers who are familiar with the relevant technology and a reduction in the demand for unskilled workers. Economic theory predicts that wages should increase for skilled workers and decrease for unskilled workers.

But if wages for unskilled workers cannot go down—say, due to a binding minimum wage—increased structural unemployment, and therefore a higher natural rate of unemployment, will result.

CHANGES IN GOVERNMENT POLICIES A high minimum wage can cause structural unemployment and generous unemployment benefits can increase both structural and frictional unemployment. So government policies intended to help workers can have the undesirable side effect of raising the natural rate of unemployment.

Some government policies, however, may reduce the natural rate. Two examples are job training and employment subsidies. Job-training programs are supposed to provide unemployed workers with skills that widen the range of jobs they can perform. Employment subsidies are payments either to workers or to employers that provide a financial incentive to accept or offer jobs.

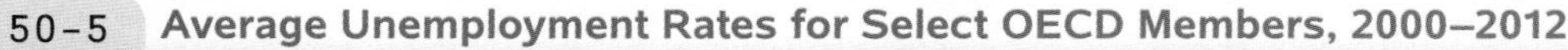

NATURAL UNEMPLOYMENT AROUND THE OECD

The Organization for Economic Co-operation and Development (OECD) is an association of relatively wealthy countries, in Europe and North America but also including Japan, Korea, New Zealand, and Australia. Among other activities, the OECD collects data on unemployment rates for member nations. Figure 50-5 shows average unemployment, which is a rough estimate of the natural rate of unemployment, for select OECD members, from 2000–2012. The purple bar in the middle shows the average across all the OECD countries.

FIGURE 50-5 Average Unemployment Rates for Select OECD Members, 2000–2012

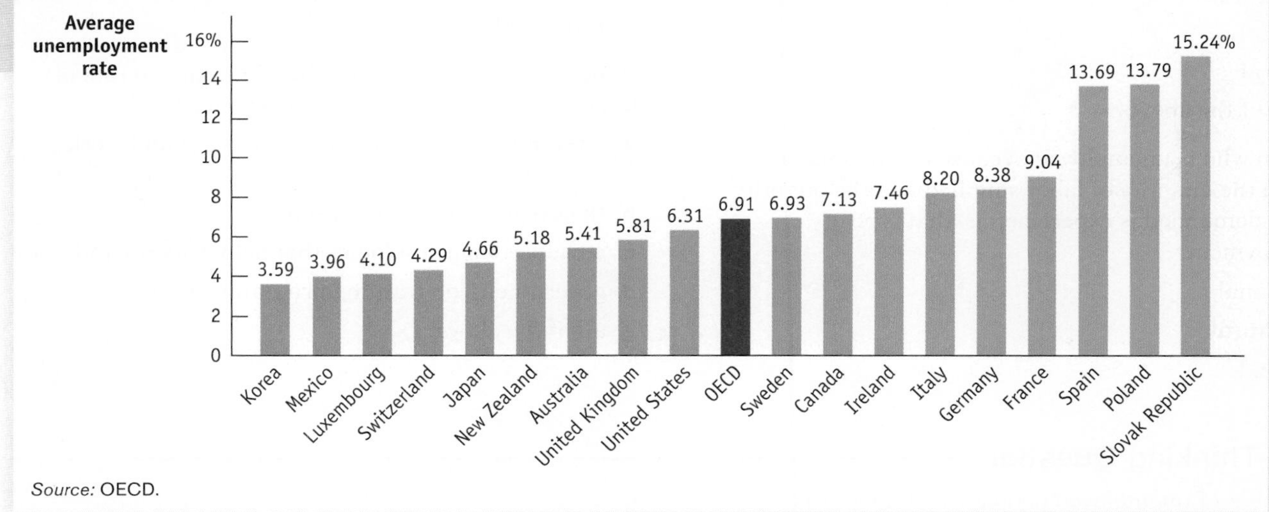

Source: OECD.

The U.S. natural rate of unemployment appears to be somewhat below average; those of many European countries (including the major economies of Germany, Italy, and France) are above average. Many economists think that persistently high European unemployment rates are the result of government policies, such as high minimum wages and generous unemployment benefits, which discourage employers from offering jobs and discourage workers from accepting jobs, leading to high rates of structural unemployment.

MODULE 50 Review

Solutions appear at the back of the book.

Check Your Understanding

1. Explain the following.
   a. Frictional unemployment always exists.
   b. Frictional unemployment accounts for a larger share of total unemployment when the unemployment rate is low.

2. Why does collective bargaining have the same general effect on unemployment as a minimum wage? Illustrate your answer with a diagram.

3. Suppose the United States dramatically increases benefits for unemployed workers. Explain what will happen to the natural rate of unemployment.

Multiple-Choice Questions

1. A person who moved to a new state and took two months to find a new job experienced which type of unemployment?
   a. frictional
   b. structural
   c. cyclical
   d. natural
   e. none of the above

2. What type of unemployment is created by a recession?
   a. frictional
   b. structural
   c. cyclical
   d. natural
   e. none of the above

3. A person who is unemployed because of a mismatch between the quantity of labor supplied and the quantity of labor demanded is experiencing what type of unemployment?
   a. frictional
   b. structural
   c. cyclical
   d. natural
   e. none of the above

4. Which of the following is true of the natural rate of unemployment?
   I. It includes frictional unemployment.
   II. It includes structural unemployment.
   III. It is equal to 0%.
   a. I only
   b. II only
   c. III only
   d. I and II
   e. I, II, and III

5. Which of the following can affect the natural rate of unemployment in an economy over time?
   a. labor force characteristics such as age and work experience
   b. the existence of labor unions
   c. advances in technologies that help workers find jobs
   d. government job training programs
   e. all of the above

Critical-Thinking Question

If the number of unemployed people who find jobs is greater than the number of employed people who lose their jobs in a given month then the unemployment rate will decrease. Is this statement true or false? Explain.

The Costs of Inflation

AP Photo/Paul Sakuma

WHAT YOU WILL LEARN

1. The economic costs of inflation
2. How inflation creates winners and losers
3. The difference between real and nominal values of income, wages, and interest rates
4. The problems of deflation and disinflation

The Inflation Rate

Why do policy makers get anxious when they see the inflation rate moving upward? Why is inflation something to worry about? The answer to both questions is that inflation can impose costs on the economy—but not in the way most people think. In this module we will look at these costs, including the related problems of deflation and disinflation.

The Level of Prices Doesn't Matter . . .

The most common complaint about *inflation,* an increase in the price level, is that it makes everyone poorer—after all, a given amount of money buys less. But inflation does *not* make everyone poorer. To see why, it's helpful to imagine what would happen if the United States did something other countries have done from time to time—replaced the dollar with a new currency.

An example of this kind of currency conversion happened in 2002, when France, like a number of other European countries, replaced its national currency, the franc, with the new Pan-European currency, the euro. People turned in their franc coins and notes, and received euro coins and notes in exchange, at a rate of precisely 6.55957 francs per euro. At the same time, all contracts were restated in euros at the same rate of exchange. For example, if a French citizen had a home mortgage debt of 500,000 francs, this became a debt of 500,000/6.55957 = 76,224.51 euros. If a worker's contract specified that he or she should be paid 100 francs per hour, it became a contract specifying a wage of 100/6.55957 = 15.2449 euros per hour, and so on.

You could imagine doing the same thing here, replacing the dollar with a "new dollar" at a rate of exchange of, say, 7 to 1. If you owed $140,000 on your home, that would become a debt of 20,000 new dollars. If you had a wage rate of $14 an hour, it

The **real wage** is the wage rate divided by the price level.

Real income is income divided by the price level.

The **inflation rate** is the percent change per year in a price index—typically the consumer price index.

would become 2 new dollars an hour, and so on. This would bring the overall U.S. price level back to about what it was when John F. Kennedy was president.

So would everyone be richer as a result because prices would be only one-seventh as high? Of course not. Prices would be lower, but so would wages and incomes in general. If you cut a worker's wage to one-seventh of its previous value, but also cut all prices to one-seventh of their previous level, the worker's **real wage**—the wage rate divided by the price level—doesn't change. In fact, bringing the overall price level back to what it was during the Kennedy administration would have no effect on overall purchasing power, because doing so would reduce income exactly as much as it reduced prices.

Conversely, the rise in prices that has actually taken place since the early 1960s hasn't made America poorer, because it has also raised incomes by the same amount: **real income**—income divided by the price level—hasn't been affected by the rise in overall prices.

The moral of this story is that the *level* of prices doesn't matter: the United States would be no richer than it is now if the overall level of prices were still as low as it was in 1961; conversely, the rise in prices over the past 50 years hasn't made us poorer.

. . . But the Rate of Change of Prices Does

The conclusion that the level of prices doesn't matter might seem to imply that the inflation rate doesn't matter either. But that's not true.

To see why, it's crucial to distinguish between the *level of prices* and the *inflation rate*. In the next module, we will discuss precisely how the level of prices in the economy is measured using price indexes such as the consumer price index. For now, let's look at the **inflation rate,** the percent increase in the overall level of prices per year. The inflation rate is calculated as follows:

$$\text{Inflation rate} = \frac{\text{Price level in year 2} - \text{Price level in year 1}}{\text{Price level in year 1}} \times 100$$

Figure 51-1 highlights the difference between the price level and the inflation rate in the United States since 1960, with the price level measured along the left vertical axis

FIGURE 51-1 The Price Level versus the Inflation Rate, 1960–2013

With the exception of 2009, over the past half-century the consumer price index has continuously increased. But the *inflation rate*—the rate at which consumer prices are rising—has had both ups and downs. And in 2009, the inflation rate briefly turned negative, a phenomenon called *deflation*.

Source: Bureau of Labor Statistics.

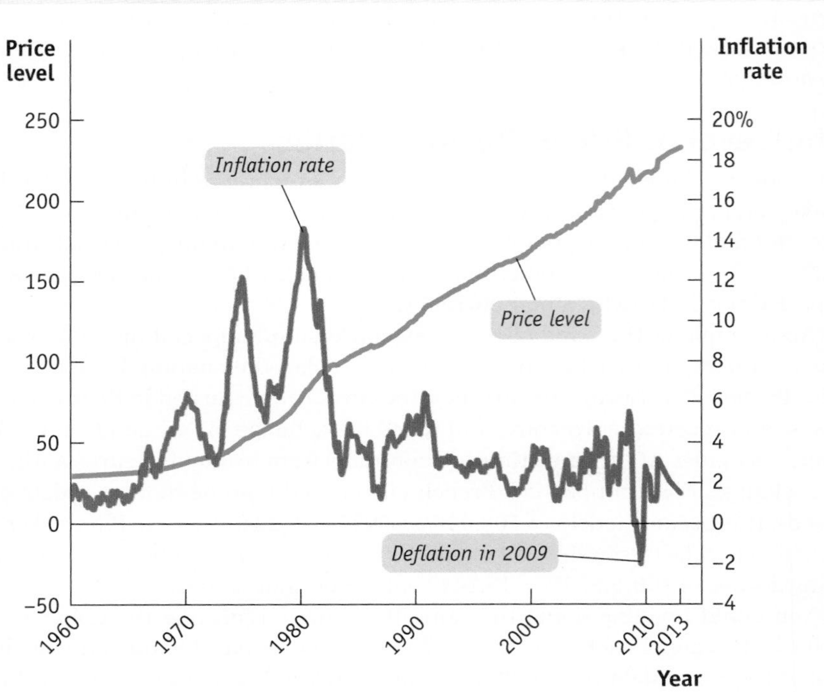

and the inflation rate measured along the right vertical axis. In the 2000s, the overall level of prices in the United States was much higher than it was in 1960—but that, as we've learned, didn't matter. The inflation rate in the 2000s, however, was much lower than in the 1970s—and that almost certainly made the economy richer than it would have been if high inflation had continued.

Shoe-leather costs are the increased costs of transactions caused by inflation.

The Economic Costs of High Inflation

Economists believe that high rates of inflation impose significant economic costs. The most important of these costs are *shoe-leather costs, menu costs,* and *unit-of-account costs.*

SHOE-LEATHER COSTS People hold money—cash in their wallets and bank deposits on which they can write checks—for convenience in making transactions. A high inflation rate, however, discourages people from holding money, because the purchasing power of the cash in your wallet and the funds in your bank account steadily erodes as the overall level of prices rises. This leads people to search for ways to reduce the amount of money they hold, often at considerable economic cost.

During the most famous of all inflations, the German *hyperinflation* of 1921–1923, merchants employed runners to take their cash to the bank many times a day to convert it into something that would hold its value, such as a stable foreign currency. In an effort to avoid having the purchasing power of their money eroded, people used up valuable resources—the time and labor of the runners—that could have been used productively elsewhere. During the German hyperinflation, so many banking transactions were taking place that the number of employees at German banks nearly quadrupled—from around 100,000 in 1913 to 375,000 in 1923.

In addition, Brazil experienced hyperinflation during the early 1990s; during that episode, the Brazilian banking sector grew so large that it accounted for 15% of GDP, more than twice the size of the financial sector in the United States measured as a share of GDP. The large increase in the Brazilian banking sector that was needed to cope with the consequences of inflation represented a loss of real resources to its society.

Increased costs of transactions caused by inflation are known as **shoe-leather costs,** an allusion to the wear and tear caused by the extra running around that takes place when people are trying to avoid holding money. Shoe-leather costs are substantial in economies with very high inflation rates, as anyone who has lived in such an economy—say, one suffering inflation of 100% or more per year—can attest. Most estimates suggest, however, that the shoe-leather costs of inflation at the rates seen in the United States—which in peacetime has never had inflation above 15%—are quite small.

ECONOMICS ▶ IN ACTION

ISRAEL'S EXPERIENCE WITH INFLATION

It's hard to see the costs of inflation clearly because serious inflation is often associated with other problems that disrupt the economy and life in general, notably war or political instability (or both). In the mid-1980s, however, Israel experienced a "clean" inflation: there was no war, the government was stable, and there was order in the streets. Yet a series of policy errors led to very high inflation, with prices often rising more than 10% a month.

As it happens, one of the authors spent a month visiting Tel Aviv University at the height of the inflation, so we can give a first-hand account of the effects.

First, the shoe-leather costs of inflation were substantial. At the time, Israelis spent a lot of time in lines at the bank, moving

An inflation rate of 500% came with very high costs for Israeli citizens.

Ricki Rosen/Corbis Saba

Menu costs are the real costs of changing listed prices.

money in and out of accounts that provided high enough interest rates to offset inflation. People walked around with very little cash in their wallets; they had to go to the bank whenever they needed to make even a moderately large cash payment. Banks responded by opening a lot of branches, a costly business expense.

Second, although menu costs weren't that visible to a visitor, what you could see were the efforts businesses made to minimize them. For example, restaurant menus often didn't list prices. Instead, they listed numbers that you had to multiply by another number, written on a chalkboard and changed every day, to figure out the price of a dish.

Finally, it was hard to make decisions because prices changed so much and so often. It was a common experience to walk out of a store because prices were 25% higher than at one's usual shopping destination, only to discover that prices had just been increased 25% there, too.

MENU COSTS In a modern economy, most of the things we buy have a listed price. There's a price listed under each item on a supermarket shelf, a price printed on the front page of your newspaper, a price listed for each dish on a restaurant's menu. Changing a listed price has a real cost, called a **menu cost.** For example, to change a price in a supermarket may require a clerk to change the price listed under the item on the shelf and a worker to change the price associated with the item's UPC code in the store's computer. In the face of inflation, of course, firms are forced to change prices more often than they would if the price level were more or less stable. This means higher costs for the economy as a whole.

In times of very high inflation rates, menu costs can be substantial. During the Brazilian inflation of the early 1990s, for instance, supermarket workers reportedly spent half of their time replacing old price stickers with new ones. When the inflation rate is high, merchants may decide to stop listing prices in terms of the local currency and use either an artificial unit—in effect, measuring prices relative to one another—or a more stable currency, such as the U.S. dollar. This is exactly what the Israeli real estate market began doing in the mid-1980s: prices were quoted in U.S. dollars, even though payment was made in Israeli shekels. And this is what happened in Zimbabwe, in 2008, as official estimates of the inflation rate reached 1,694,000%. By 2009, the government suspended the Zimbabwean dollar altogether.

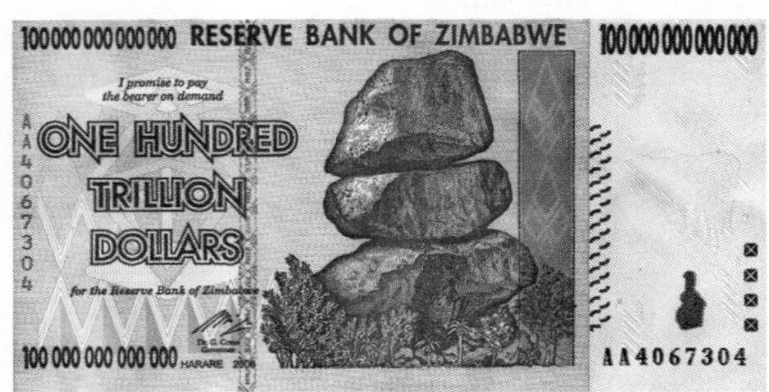

Menu costs are also present in low-inflation economies, but they are not severe. In low-inflation economies, businesses might update their prices only sporadically—not daily or even more frequently, as is the case in high-inflation or hyperinflation economies. Also, with technological advances, menu costs are becoming less important, since prices can be changed electronically and fewer merchants attach price stickers to merchandise.

UNIT-OF-ACCOUNT COSTS In the Middle Ages, contracts were often specified "in kind": a tenant might, for example, be obliged to provide his landlord with a certain number of cattle each year (the phrase *in kind* actually comes from an ancient word for *cattle*). This may have made sense at the time, but it would be an awkward way to conduct modern business. Instead, we state contracts in monetary terms: a renter owes a certain number of dollars per month, a company that issues a bond promises to pay the bondholder the dollar value of the bond when it comes due, and so on. We also tend to make our economic calculations in dollars: a family planning its budget, or a small business owner trying to figure out how well the business is doing, makes estimates of the amount of money coming in and going out.

This role of the dollar as a basis for contracts and calculation is called the *unit-of-account* role of money. It's an important aspect of the modern economy. Yet it's a role that can be degraded by inflation, which causes the purchasing power of a dollar to change over time—a dollar next year is worth less than a dollar this year. The effect, many economists argue, is to reduce the quality of economic decisions: the economy as a whole makes less efficient use of its resources because of the uncertainty caused by changes in the unit of account, the dollar. The **unit-of-account costs** of inflation are the costs arising from the way inflation makes money a less reliable unit of measurement.

"*Of course I know the value of a dollar . . . that's why I'm asking if I can borrow your credit card*"

©Marty Bucella/CartoonStock.com

Unit-of-account costs may be particularly important in the tax system, because inflation can distort the measures of income on which taxes are collected. Here's an example: Assume that the inflation rate is 10%, so that the overall level of prices rises 10% each year. Suppose that a business buys an asset, such as a piece of land, for \$100,000 and then resells it a year later at a price of \$110,000. In a fundamental sense, the business didn't make a profit on the deal: in real terms, it got no more for the land than it paid for it, because the \$110,000 would purchase no more goods than the \$100,000 would have a year earlier. But U.S. tax law would say that the business made a capital gain of \$10,000, and it would have to pay taxes on that phantom gain.

During the 1970s, when the United States had a relatively high inflation rate, the distorting effects of inflation on the tax system were a serious problem. Some businesses were discouraged from productive investment spending because they found themselves paying taxes on phantom gains. Meanwhile, some unproductive investments became attractive because they led to phantom losses that reduced tax bills. When the inflation rate fell in the 1980s—and tax rates were reduced—these problems became much less important.

Winners and Losers from Inflation

As we've just learned, a high inflation rate imposes overall costs on the economy. In addition, inflation can produce winners and losers within the economy. The main reason inflation sometimes helps some people while hurting others is that economic transactions, such as loans, often involve contracts that extend over a period of time and these contracts are normally specified in nominal—that is, in dollar—terms.

In the case of a loan, the borrower receives a certain amount of funds at the beginning, and the loan contract specifies how much he or she must repay at some future date. But what that dollar repayment is worth in real terms—that is, in terms of purchasing power—depends greatly on the rate of inflation over the intervening years of the loan.

The *interest rate* on a loan is the percentage of the loan amount that the borrower must pay to the lender, typically on an annual basis, in addition to the repayment of the loan amount itself. Economists summarize the effect of inflation on borrowers and lenders by distinguishing between *nominal* interest rates and *real* interest rates.

The **nominal interest rate** is the interest rate that is actually paid for a loan, unadjusted for the effects of inflation. For example, the interest rates advertised on student loans and every interest rate you see listed by a bank is a nominal rate. The **real interest rate** is the nominal interest rate adjusted for inflation. This adjustment is achieved by simply subtracting the inflation rate from the nominal interest rate. For example, if a loan carries a nominal interest rate of 8%, but the inflation rate is 5%, the real interest rate is 8% − 5% = 3%.

When a borrower and a lender enter into a loan contract, the contract normally specifies a nominal interest rate. But each party has an expectation about the future

Unit-of-account costs arise from the way inflation makes money a less reliable unit of measurement.

The **nominal interest rate** is the interest rate actually paid for a loan.

The **real interest rate** is the nominal interest rate minus the rate of inflation.

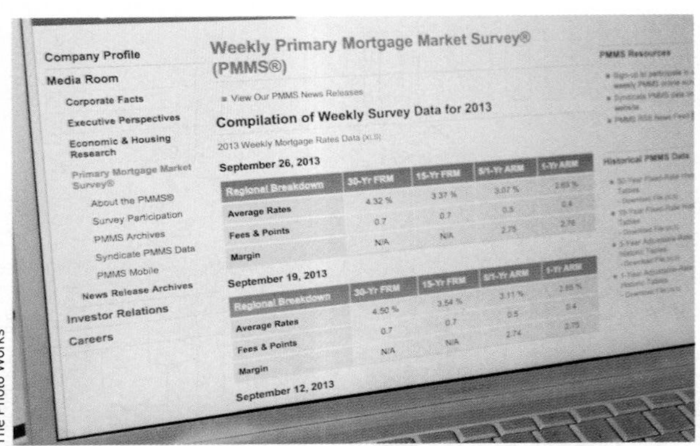

The Photo Works

When inflation is higher than expected, borrowers gain at the expense of lenders; but when inflation is lower than expected, lenders come out ahead.

rate of inflation and therefore an expectation about the real interest rate on the loan. If the actual inflation rate is *higher* than expected, borrowers gain at the expense of lenders: borrowers will repay their loans with funds that have a lower real value than had been expected—they can purchase fewer goods and services than expected due to the surprisingly high inflation rate. Conversely, if the inflation rate is *lower* than expected, lenders will gain at the expense of borrowers: borrowers must repay their loans with funds that have a higher real value than had been expected.

Historically, the fact that inflation creates winners and losers has sometimes been a major source of political controversy. In 1896 William Jennings Bryan electrified the Democratic presidential convention with a speech in which he declared, "You shall not crucify mankind on a cross of gold." What he was actually demanding was an inflationary policy. At the time, the U.S. dollar had a fixed value in terms of gold. Bryan wanted the U.S. government to abandon the gold standard and print more money, which would have raised the level of prices and, he believed, helped the nation's farmers who were deeply in debt.

In modern America, home mortgages (loans for the purchase of homes) are the most important source of gains and losses from inflation. Americans who took out mortgages in the early 1970s quickly found their real payments reduced by higher-than-expected inflation: by 1983, the purchasing power of a dollar was only 45% of what it had been in 1973. Those who took out mortgages in the early 1990s were not so lucky, because the inflation rate fell to lower-than-expected levels in the following years: in 2003 the purchasing power of a dollar was 78% of what it had been in 1993.

Because gains for some and losses for others result from inflation that is either higher or lower than expected, yet another problem arises: uncertainty about the future inflation rate discourages people from entering into any form of long-term contract. This is an additional cost of high inflation, because high rates of inflation are usually unpredictable, too. In countries with high and uncertain inflation, long-term loans are rare. This, in turn, makes it difficult for people to commit to long-term investments.

One last point: unexpected **deflation**—a surprise fall in the price level—creates winners and losers, too. Between 1929 and 1933, as the U.S. economy plunged into the Great Depression, the price level fell by 35%. This meant that debtors, including many farmers and homeowners, saw a sharp rise in the real value of their debts, which led to widespread bankruptcy and helped create a banking crisis, as lenders found their customers unable to pay back their loans.

Inflation Is Easy; Disinflation Is Hard

There is not much evidence that a rise in the inflation rate from, say, 2% to 5% would do a great deal of harm to the economy. Still, policy makers generally move forcefully to bring inflation back down when it creeps above 2% or 3%. Why? Because experience shows that bringing the inflation rate down—a process called **disinflation—**is very difficult and costly once a higher rate of inflation has become well established in the economy.

A falling overall level of prices is **deflation**.

Disinflation is the process of bringing the inflation rate down.

Figure 51-2 shows what happened during two major episodes of disinflation in the United States, in the mid-1970s and in the early 1980s. The horizontal axis shows the unemployment rate. The vertical axis shows "core" inflation over the previous year, a measure that excludes volatile food and energy prices and is widely considered a better measure of underlying inflation than overall consumer prices. Each marker represents the inflation rate and the unemployment rate for one month. In each episode, unemployment and inflation followed a sort of clockwise spiral, with high inflation gradually falling in the face of an extended period of very high unemployment.

FIGURE 51-2 The Cost of Disinflation

There were two major periods of disinflation in modern U.S. history, in the mid-1970s and the early 1980s. This figure shows the track of the unemployment rate and the "core" inflation rate, which excludes food and energy, during these two episodes. In each case bringing inflation down required a temporary but very large increase in the unemployment rate, demonstrating the high cost of disinflation.

Source: Bureau of Labor Statistics.

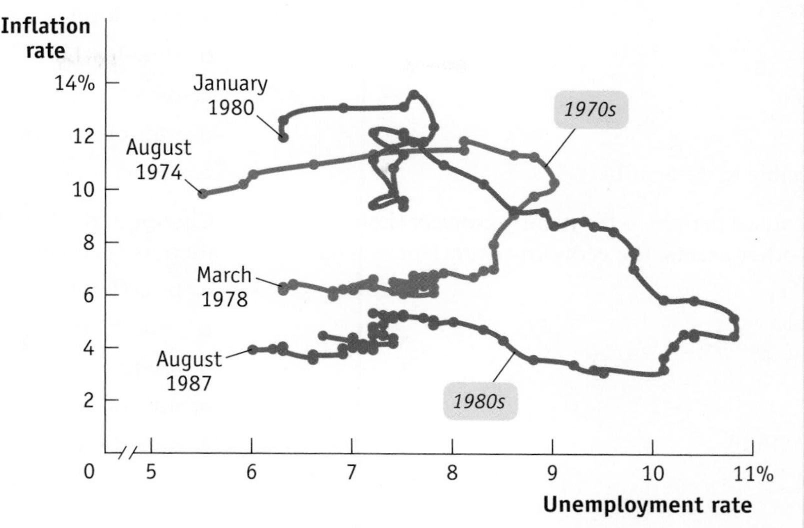

Many economists believe that these periods of high unemployment are necessary, because they are the only way to reduce inflation that has become deeply embedded in the economy. The best way to avoid having to put the economy through a wringer to reduce inflation, however, is to avoid having a serious inflation problem in the first place. So, policy makers respond forcefully to signs that inflation may be accelerating as a form of preventive medicine for the economy.

MODULE 51 Review

Solutions appear at the back of the book.

Check Your Understanding

1. The widespread use of technology has revolutionized the banking industry, making it much easier for customers to access and manage their assets. Does this mean that the shoe-leather costs of inflation are higher or lower than they used to be? Explain.

2. Most Americans have grown accustomed to a modest inflation rate of around 2–3%. Who would gain and who would lose if inflation came to a complete stop for several years? Explain.

Multiple-Choice Questions

1. Which of the following is true regarding prices in an economy?
   - I. An increase in the price level is called inflation.
   - II. The level of prices doesn't matter.
   - III. The rate of change in prices matters.

   a. I only
   b. II only
   c. III only
   d. II and III only
   e. I, II, and III

2. If your nominal wage doubles at the same time as prices double, your real wage will
   a. increase.
   b. decrease
   c. not change.
   d. double.
   e. be impossible to determine.

3. If inflation causes people to frequently convert their dollars into other assets, the economy experiences what type of cost?
   a. price level
   b. shoe-leather
   c. menu
   d. unit-of-account
   e. monetary

4. Because dollars are used as the basis for contracts, inflation leads to which type of cost?
   a. price level
   b. shoe-leather
   c. menu
   d. unit-of-account
   e. monetary

5. Changing the listed price when inflation leads to a price increase is an example of which type of cost?
   a. price level
   b. shoe-leather
   c. menu
   d. unit-of-account
   e. monetary

Critical-Thinking Questions

You borrow $1,000 for one year at 5% interest to buy a couch. Although you did not anticipate any inflation, there is unexpected inflation of 5% over the life of your loan.

1. What was the real interest rate on your loan?
2. Explain how you gained from the inflation.
3. Who lost as a result of the situation described? Explain.

Measuring Inflation

Oleg Doroshin/Shutterstock

WHAT YOU WILL LEARN

1. How the inflation rate is measured
2. What a price index is and how it is calculated
3. The importance of the consumer price index and other price indexes

The Aggregate Price Level

In the fall of 2012, Americans were facing sticker shock at the gas pump: the price of a gallon of regular gasoline had risen from about \$3.40 that spring, to \$3.90—an increase of 15%. For consumers, that meant paying \$5.00 more for every 10 gallons of gas purchased. Food prices were also up, rising about 3% per year for each of the last five years. Some prices, though, were falling: housing prices had dropped dramatically since 2008, and most electronics were getting cheaper. Yet practically everyone felt that the overall cost of living seemed to be rising. But how fast?

Clearly there is a need for a single number summarizing what happens to consumer prices. Just as macroeconomists find it useful to have a single number to represent the overall level of output, they also find it useful to have a single number to represent the overall level of prices: the **aggregate price level.** Yet a huge variety of goods and services are produced and consumed in the economy. How can we summarize the prices of all these goods and services with a single number? The answer lies in the concept of a *price index*—a concept best introduced with an example.

Market Baskets and Price Indexes

Suppose that a frost in Florida destroys most of the citrus harvest. As a result, the price of oranges rises from \$0.20 each to \$0.40 each, the price of grapefruit rises from \$0.60 to \$1.00, and the price of lemons rises from \$0.25 to \$0.45. How much has the price of citrus fruit increased?

One way to answer that question is to state three numbers—the changes in prices for oranges, grapefruit, and lemons. But this is a very cumbersome method. Rather than having to recite three numbers in an effort to track changes in the prices of

The **aggregate price level** is a measure of the overall level of prices in the economy.

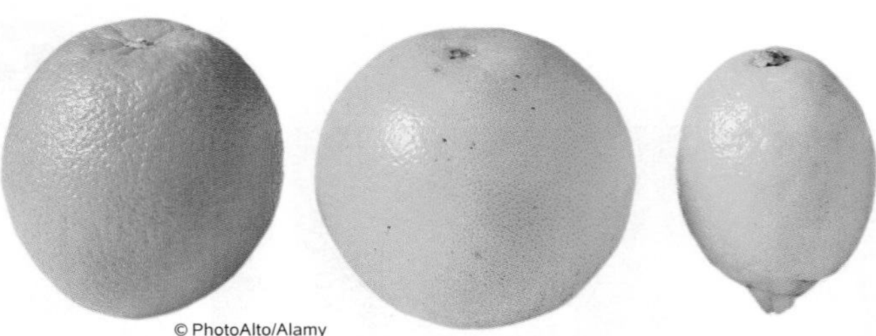
© PhotoAlto/Alamy

citrus fruit, we would prefer to have some kind of overall measure of the *average* price change.

To measure average price changes for consumer goods and services, economists track changes in the cost of a typical consumer's *consumption bundle*—the typical basket of goods and services purchased before the price changes. A hypothetical consumption bundle, used to measure changes in the overall price level, is known as a **market basket.** For our market basket in this example we will suppose that, before the frost, a typical consumer bought 200 oranges, 50 grapefruit, and 100 lemons over the course of a year.

Table 52-1 shows the pre-frost and post-frost costs of this market basket. Before the frost, it cost \$95; after the frost, the same basket of goods cost \$175. Since \$175/\$95 = 1.842, the post-frost basket costs 1.842 times the cost of the pre-frost basket, a cost increase of 84.2%. In this example, the average price of citrus fruit has increased 84.2% since the base year as a result of the frost, where the base year is the initial year used in the measurement of the price change.

TABLE 52-1

Calculating the Cost of a Market Basket

	Pre-frost	Post-frost
Price of orange	\$0.20	\$0.40
Price of grapefruit	0.60	1.00
Price of lemon	0.25	0.45
Cost of market basket (200 oranges, 50 grapefruit, 100 lemons)	(200 × \$0.20) + (50 × \$0.60) + (100 × \$0.25) = \$95.00	(200 × \$0.40) + (50 × \$1.00) + (100 × \$0.45) = \$175.00

Economists use the same method to measure changes in the overall price level: they track changes in the cost of buying a given market basket. Working with a market basket and a base year, we obtain what is known as a **price index,** a measure of the overall price level. It is always cited along with the year for which the aggregate price level is being measured and the base year. A price index can be calculated using the following formula:

$$\textbf{(52-1)}\ \text{Price index in a given year} = \frac{\text{Cost of market basket in a given year}}{\text{Cost of market basket in base year}} \times 100$$

In our example, the citrus fruit market basket cost \$95 in the base year, the year before the frost. So by applying Equation 52-1, we define the price index for citrus fruit as (cost of market basket in the current year/\$95) × 100, yielding an index of 100 for the period before the frost and 184.2 after the frost.

You should note that applying Equation 52-1 to calculate the price index for the base year always results in a price index of (cost of market basket in base year/cost of market basket in base year) × 100 = 100. Choosing a price index formula that always normalizes the index value to 100 in the base year avoids the need to keep track of the cost of the market basket, for example, \$95, in such and such a year.

The price index makes it clear that the average price of citrus has risen 84.2% as a consequence of the frost. Because of its simplicity and intuitive appeal, the method we've just described is used to calculate a variety of price indexes to track average price changes among a variety of different groups of goods and services. Examples include the *consumer price index* and the *producer price index,* which we'll discuss shortly.

A **market basket** is a hypothetical set of consumer purchases of goods and services.

A **price index** measures the cost of purchasing a given market basket in a given year. The index value is normalized so that it is equal to 100 in the selected base year.

Price indexes are also the basis for measuring inflation. The price level mentioned in the inflation rate formula in the previous module is simply a price index value, and the inflation rate is determined as the annual percent change in an official price index. The inflation rate from year 1 to year 2 is thus calculated using the following formula, with year 1 and year 2 being consecutive years.

The **consumer price index,** or **CPI,** measures the cost of the market basket of a typical urban American family.

$$\textbf{(52-2)}\ \text{Inflation rate} = \frac{\text{Price index in year 2} - \text{Price index in year 1}}{\text{Price index in year 1}} \times 100$$

Typically, a news report that cites "the inflation rate" is referring to the annual percent change in the consumer price index.

The Consumer Price Index

The most widely used measure of the overall price level in the United States is the **consumer price index** (often referred to simply as the **CPI**), which is intended to show how the cost of all purchases by a typical urban family has changed over time. It is calculated by surveying market prices for a market basket that is constructed to represent the consumption of a typical family of four living in a typical American city. The base period for the index is currently 1982–1984, that is, the index is calculated so that the average of consumer prices in 1982–1984 is 100.

Ivan Smuk/Shutterstock

The CPI measures the changes in price level for a representative basket of goods and services purchased by a typical household.

The market basket used to calculate the CPI is far more complex than the three-fruit market basket we just described. In fact, to calculate the CPI, the Bureau of Labor Statistics sends its employees out to survey supermarkets, gas stations, hardware stores, and so on—some 23,000 retail outlets in 87 cities. Every month it tabulates about 80,000 prices, on everything from romaine lettuce to movie rentals. Figure 52-1 shows the weight of major categories in the consumer price index as of December 2012. For example, motor fuel, mainly gasoline, accounted for 5% of the CPI in December 2012.

Every few years the Bureau of Labor Statistics updates the market basket used to calculate the CPI to reflect changes in the monthly purchases of the typical urban family of four. For example, food and beverages are now a smaller percentage of the basket, having gone from 21% in 1978 to 15% in 2012. In addition, as technology has changed over time, new goods are added to the basket, such as smart phones and tablets like the iPad.

Figure 52-2 shows how the CPI has changed since measurement began in 1913. Since 1940, the CPI has risen steadily, although the annual percent increases in recent years have been much smaller than those of the 1970s and early 1980s. A logarithmic scale is used so that equal percent changes in the CPI appear the same.

Nearly every country in the world calculates a consumer price index. As you might expect, the market baskets that make up these indexes differ quite a lot

FIGURE 52-1 The Makeup of the Consumer Price Index in 2012

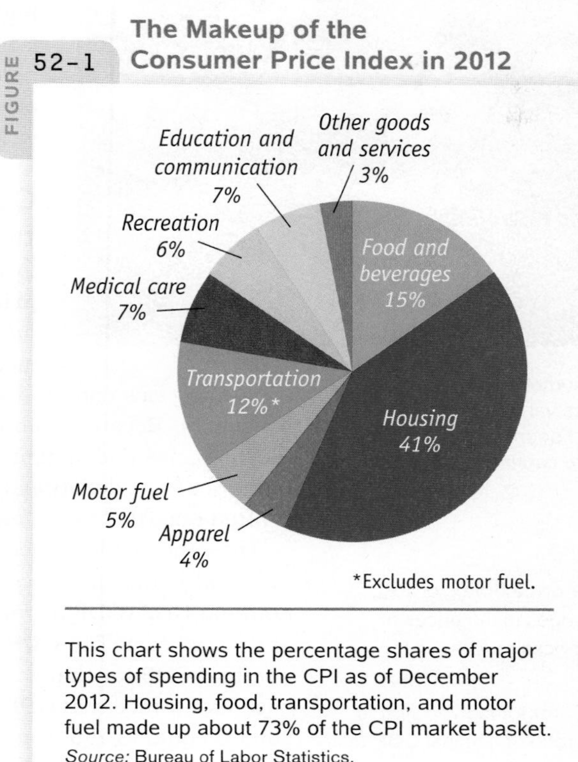

This chart shows the percentage shares of major types of spending in the CPI as of December 2012. Housing, food, transportation, and motor fuel made up about 73% of the CPI market basket.
Source: Bureau of Labor Statistics.

FIGURE 52-2 The CPI, 1913–2013

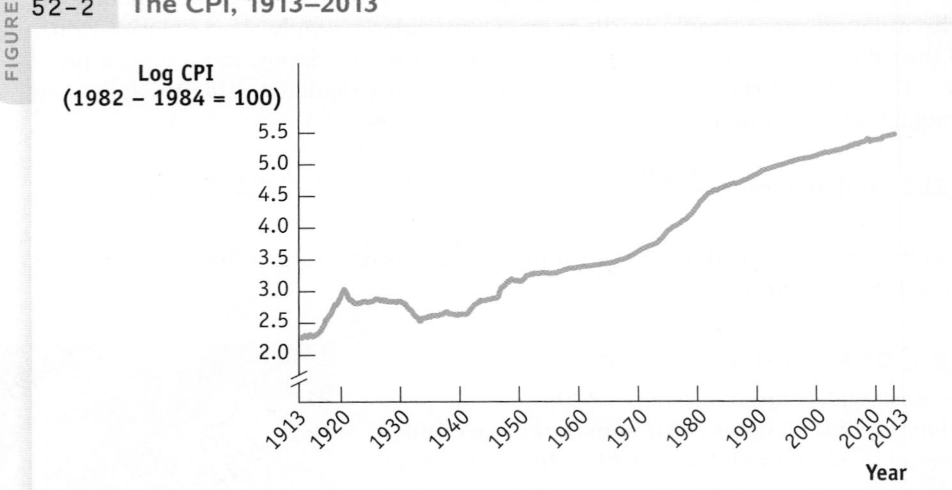

Since 1940, the CPI has risen steadily. But the annual percent increases in recent years have been much smaller than those of the 1970s and early 1980s. (The vertical axis is measured on a logarithmic scale so that equal percent changes in the CPI have the same slope.)

Source: Bureau of Labor Statistics.

© Michael Dwyer/Alamy

Because consumption patterns vary, market baskets vary dramatically between rich and poor counties and then from country to country.

from country to country. In poor countries, where people must spend a high proportion of their income just to feed themselves, food makes up a large share of the price index. Among high-income countries, differences in consumption patterns lead to differences in the price indexes: the Japanese price index puts a larger weight on raw fish and a smaller weight on beef than ours does, and the French price index puts a larger weight on wine.

Other Price Measures

There are two other price measures that are also widely used to track economy-wide price changes. One is the **producer price index** (or **PPI,** which used to be known as the *wholesale price index*). As its name suggests, the producer price index measures the cost of a typical basket of goods and services—containing raw commodities such as steel, electricity, coal, and so on—purchased by producers. Because commodity producers are relatively quick to raise prices when they perceive a change in overall demand for their goods, the PPI often responds to inflationary or deflationary pressures more quickly than the CPI. As a result, the PPI is often regarded as an "early warning signal" of changes in the inflation rate.

The **producer price index,** or **PPI,** measures changes in the prices of goods and services purchased by producers.

The **GDP deflator** for a given year is 100 times the ratio of nominal GDP to real GDP in that year.

The other widely used price measure is the *GDP deflator;* it isn't exactly a price index, although it serves the same purpose. Recall how we distinguished between nominal GDP (GDP in current prices) and real GDP (GDP calculated using the prices of a base year). The **GDP deflator** for a given year is equal to 100 times the ratio of nominal GDP for that year to real GDP for that year expressed in prices of a selected base year. Since real GDP is currently expressed in 2005 dollars, the GDP deflator for 2005 is equal to 100. If nominal GDP doubles but real GDP does not change, the GDP deflator indicates that the aggregate price level doubled.

Perhaps the most important point about the different inflation rates generated by these three measures of prices is that they usually move closely together (although the producer price index tends to fluctuate more than either of the other two measures). Figure 52-3 shows the annual percent changes in the three indexes since 1930. By all three measures, the U.S. economy experienced deflation during the early years of the Great Depression, inflation during World War II, accelerating inflation during the 1970s, and a return to relative price stability in the 1990s.

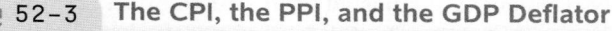

FIGURE 52-3 **The CPI, the PPI, and the GDP Deflator**

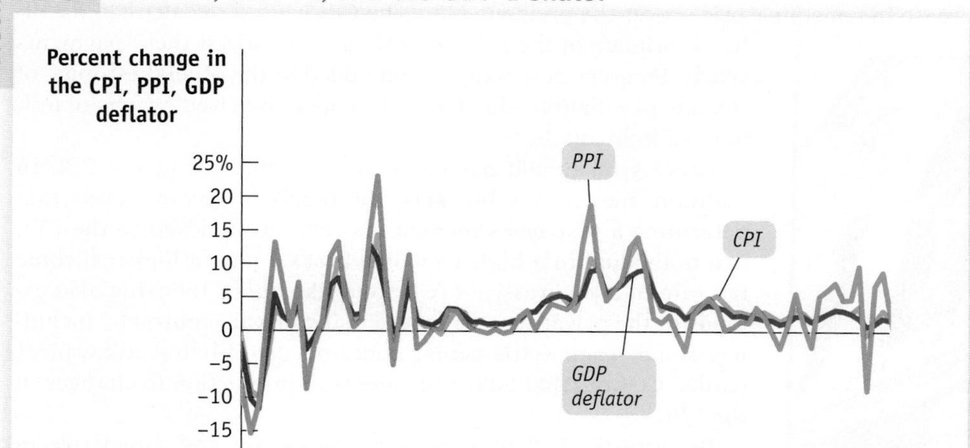

As the figure shows, the three different measures of inflation, the PPI (orange), the CPI (green), and the GDP deflator (purple), usually move closely together. Each reveals a drastic acceleration of inflation during the 1970s and a return to relative price stability in the 1990s.

Sources: Bureau of Labor Statistics; Bureau of Economic Analysis.

Notice, by the way, the dramatic ups and downs in producer prices from 2000 through 2012 shown in Figure 52-3. This roller-coaster ride in prices reflects large changes in energy and food prices, which play a much bigger role in the PPI than they do in either the CPI or the GDP deflator.

ECONOMICS ▶ IN ACTION

INDEXING TO THE CPI

Although GDP is a very important number for shaping economic policy, official statistics on GDP don't have a direct effect on people's lives. The CPI, by contrast, has a direct and immediate impact on millions of Americans. The reason is that many payments are tied, or "indexed," to the CPI—the amount paid rises or falls when the CPI rises or falls.

The practice of indexing payments to consumer prices goes back to the dawn of the United States as a nation. In 1780 the Massachusetts State Legislature recognized that the pay of its soldiers fighting the British needed to be increased because of inflation that occurred during the Revolutionary War. The legislature adopted a formula that made a soldier's pay proportional to the cost of a market basket consisting of 5 bushels of corn, 68⁴⁄₇ pounds of beef, 10 pounds of sheep's wool, and 16 pounds of sole leather.

Today, over 56 million people, most of them old or disabled, receive checks from Social Security, a national retirement program that accounts for almost a quarter of current total federal spending—more than the defense budget. The amount of an individual's check is determined by a formula that reflects his or her previous payments into the system as well as other factors.

In addition, all Social Security payments are adjusted each year to offset any increase in consumer prices over the previous year. The CPI is used to calculate the official estimate of the inflation rate used to adjust these payments yearly. So every percentage point added to the official estimate of the rate of inflation adds 1% to the checks received by tens of millions of individuals.

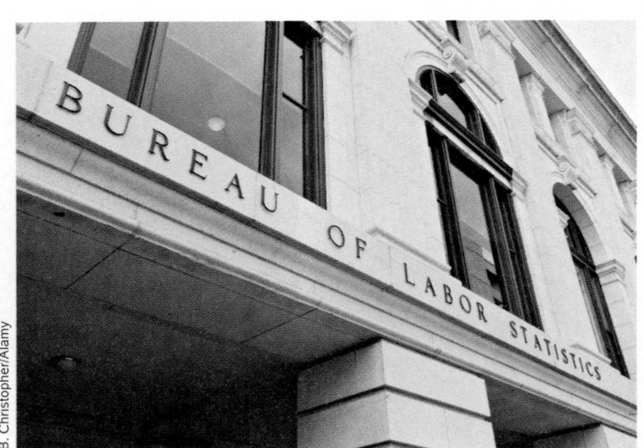

B. Christopher/Alamy

The Bureau of Labor Statistics calculates the CPI by collecting and interpreting price and consumption data.

Other government payments are also indexed to the CPI. In addition, income tax brackets, the bands of income levels that determine a taxpayer's income tax rate, are indexed to the CPI. (An individual in a higher income bracket pays a higher income tax rate in a progressive tax system like ours.) Indexing also extends to the private sector, where many private contracts, including some wage settlements, contain cost-of-living allowances (called COLAs) that adjust payments in proportion to changes in the CPI.

Because the CPI plays such an important and direct role in people's lives, it's a politically sensitive number. The Bureau of Labor Statistics, which calculates the CPI, takes great care in collecting and interpreting price and consumption data. It uses a complex method in which households are surveyed to determine what they buy and where they shop, and a carefully selected sample of stores are surveyed to get representative prices.

MODULE 52 Review

Solutions appear at the back of the book.

Check Your Understanding

1. Consider Table 52-1 but suppose that the market basket is composed of 100 oranges, 50 grapefruit, and 200 lemons. How does this change the pre-frost and post-frost consumer price indexes? Explain. Generalize your answer to explain how the construction of the market basket affects the CPI.

2. For each of the following events, explain how the use of a 10-year-old market basket would bias measurements of price changes over the past decade.
   a. A typical family owns more cars than it would have a decade ago. Over that time, the average price of a car has increased more than the average prices of other goods.
   b. Virtually no households had Internet access a decade ago. Now many households have it, and the price has been falling.

3. The consumer price index in the United States (base period 1982–1984) was 224.9 in 2011 and 229.6 in 2012. Calculate the inflation rate from 2011 to 2012.

Multiple-Choice Questions

1. If the cost of a market basket of goods increases from \$100 in year 1 to \$108 in year 2, what is the consumer price index in year 2 if year 1 is the base year?
   a. 8
   b. 10
   c. 100
   d. 108
   e. 110

2. If the consumer price index increases from 80 to 120 from one year to the next, the inflation rate over that time period was
   a. 20%.
   b. 40%.
   c. 50%.
   d. 80%.
   e. 120%.

3. Which of the following is true of the CPI?
   I. It is the most common measure of the price level.
   II. It measures the price of a typical market basket of goods.
   III. It currently uses a base period of 1982–1984.
   a. I only
   b. II only
   c. III only
   d. I and II only
   e. I, II, and III

4. The value of a price index in the base year is
   a. 0.
   b. 100.
   c. 200.
   d. the inflation rate.
   e. the average cost of a market basket of goods.

5. If your wage doubles at the same time as the consumer price index goes from 100 to 300, your real wage
   a. doubles.
   b. falls.
   c. increases.
   d. stays the same.
   e. cannot be determined.

Critical-Thinking Question

The accompanying table contains the values of two price indexes for the years 2010, 2011, and 2012: the GDP deflator and the CPI. For each price index, calculate the inflation rate from 2010 to 2011 and from 2011 to 2012.

Year	GDP deflator	CPI
2010	111.0	218.1
2011	113.4	224.9
2012	115.4	229.6

BUSINESS CASE • A Monster Slump

NetPhotos/Alamy

The 1990s were famously an era of business hype, a decade when numerous online companies were created, then sold their stock at incredibly high prices, and, in the end, went bust. Some of the dot-coms, however, turned out to have workable business models and have endured. Among them is Monster.com, a job-search company that, along with its competitors, has helped replace traditional help-wanted ads in newspapers with online listings.

Monster Worldwide (the company's current name) and its competitors sell services to both employers seeking workers and workers seeking jobs. The employers place job listings, to which workers can respond; in addition to responding to these listings, job-seekers can pay for premium services such as résumé-writing and priority listing of their résumés.

The growing importance of online job listings was brought home in 2007 when The Conference Board, a business group that has long tracked the economy by producing an index of help-wanted ads, added an index of online help-wanted ads. As the figure shows, a plunge in online help-wanted ads heralded the surge in unemployment in 2008–2009; when online ads began to recover, unemployment stabilized and began a slow decline.

A Plunge in Online Help-Wanted Ads Heralds a Surge in Unemployment, 2008–2009

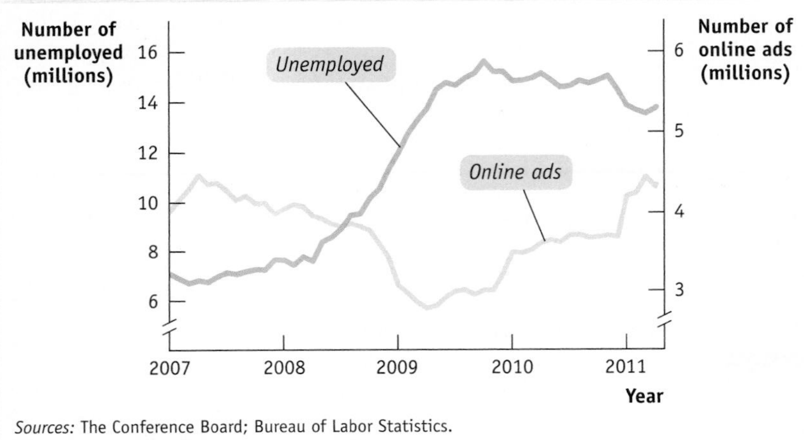

Sources: The Conference Board; Bureau of Labor Statistics.

In the late 1990s, when the U.S. economy was experiencing unusually low unemployment, some economists suggested that Monster Worldwide and other online job services might be partly responsible, by making it easier for workers to get new jobs without a prolonged intervening period of unemployment. The evidence for this effect is, however, inconclusive.

You might have thought that the 2007–2009 recession, in which many laid-off workers were desperately seeking new jobs, would have been good for Monster Worldwide. And the company did, in fact, receive a lot more business from workers wanting to post their résumés. But the company makes much more money from employer job listings, and these were sharply lower during the slump, hurting their bottom line.

By late 2010, the economy seemed to be on the road to recovery, and so was Monster Worldwide, with one caveat: by 2010, online job listings, which were cutting-edge a decade earlier, were losing ground to Twitter and social-networking sites like LinkedIn—a trend that continues.

Questions for Thought

1. How is the existence of services such as Monster.com likely to affect frictional and structural unemployment?
2. In light of our discussion of the determinants of the unemployment rate, how could improved matching of job-seekers and employers through online job listings help?
3. What does the fact that Monster Worldwide did badly during the 2008–2009 surge in unemployment suggest about the nature of that surge?

SECTION 16 REVIEW

Summary

Defining Unemployment

1. **Employed** people currently hold a part-time or full-time job; **unemployed** people do not hold a job but are actively looking for work. Their sum is equal to the **labor force,** and the **labor force participation rate** is the percentage of the population age 16 or older that is in the labor force.
2. The **unemployment rate,** the percentage of the labor force that is unemployed and actively looking for work, can overstate or understate the true level of unemployment. It can overstate because it counts as unemployed those who are continuing to search for a job despite having been offered one (that is, workers who are frictionally unemployed). It can understate because it ignores frustrated workers, such as **discouraged workers, marginally attached workers,** and the **underemployed.** In addition, the unemployment rate varies greatly among different groups in the population; it is typically higher for younger workers and for workers near retirement age than for workers in their prime working years.
3. The unemployment rate is affected by the business cycle. The unemployment rate generally falls when the growth rate of real GDP is above average and generally rises when the growth rate of real GDP is below average. In a **jobless recovery** the GDP growth rate is positive but the unemployment rate is still rising.

Categories of Unemployment

4. Job creation and destruction, as well as voluntary job separations, lead to **job search** and **frictional unemployment.** In addition, a variety of factors such as minimum wages, unions, **efficiency wages,** and government policies designed to help laid-off workers result in a situation in which there is a surplus of labor at the market wage rate, creating **structural unemployment.** As a result, the **natural rate of unemployment,** the sum of frictional and structural unemployment, is well above zero, even when jobs are plentiful.
5. The actual unemployment rate is equal to the natural rate of unemployment, the share of unemployment that is independent of the business cycle, plus **cyclical unemployment,** the share of unemployment that depends on fluctuations in the business cycle.
6. The natural rate of unemployment changes over time, largely in response to changes in labor force characteristics, labor market institutions, and government policies.

The Costs of Inflation

7. Inflation does not, as many assume, make everyone poorer by raising the level of prices. That's because if wages and incomes are adjusted to take into account a rising price level, **real wages** and **real income** remain unchanged. However, a high inflation rate imposes overall costs on the economy: **shoe-leather costs, menu costs,** and **unit-of-account costs.**
8. Inflation can produce winners and losers within the economy, because long-term contracts are generally written in dollar terms. Loans typically specify a **nominal interest rate,** which differs from the **real interest rate** due to inflation. A higher-than-expected inflation rate is good for borrowers and bad for lenders. A lower-than-expected inflation rate is good for lenders and bad for borrowers.
9. It is very costly to create **disinflation,** so policy makers try to prevent inflation from becoming excessive in the first place.

Measuring Inflation

10. To measure the **aggregate price level,** economists calculate the cost of purchasing a **market basket.** A **price index** is the ratio of the current cost of that market basket to the cost in a selected base year, multiplied by 100.
11. The **inflation rate** is the yearly percent change in a price index, typically based on the **consumer price index,** or **CPI,** the most common measure of the aggregate price level. A similar index for goods and services purchased by firms is the **producer price index,** or **PPI.** Finally, economists also use the **GDP deflator,** which measures the price level by calculating the ratio of nominal to real GDP times 100.

Key Terms

Employed, p. 504
Unemployed, p. 504
Labor force, p. 505
Labor force participation rate, p. 505
Unemployment rate, p. 505
Discouraged workers, p. 506
Marginally attached workers, p. 506
Underemployed, p. 506
Jobless recovery, p. 509
Job search, p. 513
Frictional unemployment, p. 513

Problems

1. Each month, usually on the first Friday of the month, the Bureau of Labor Statistics releases the Employment Situation Summary for the previous month. Go to www.bls.gov and find the latest report. (On the Bureau of Labor Statistics home page, at the top of the page, select the "Subject" tab, find "Unemployment," and select "National Unemployment Rate." You will find the Employment Situation Summary on the middle of the page under "CPS News Releases" by selecting "Employment Situation.") How does the unemployment rate compare to the rate one month earlier? How does the unemployment rate compare to the rate one year earlier?

2. In general, how do changes in the unemployment rate vary with changes in real GDP? After several quarters of a severe recession, explain why we might observe a decrease in the official unemployment rate. Explain why we could see an increase in the official unemployment rate after several quarters of a strong expansion.

3. In each of the following situations, what type of unemployment is Melanie facing?

   a. After completing a complex programming project, Melanie is laid off. Her prospects for a new job requiring similar skills are good, and she has signed up with a programmer placement service. She has passed up offers for low-paying jobs.

   b. When Melanie and her co-workers refused to accept pay cuts, her employer outsourced their programming tasks to workers in another country. This phenomenon is occurring throughout the programming industry.

   c. Due to the current slump, Melanie has been laid off from her programming job. Her employer promises to rehire her when business picks up.

4. Part of the information released in the Employment Situation Summary concerns how long individuals have been unemployed. Go to www.bls.gov to find the latest report. Use the same technique as in Problem 1 to find the Employment Situation Summary. Near the end of the Employment Situation, click on Table A-12, titled "Unemployed persons by duration of unemployment." Use the seasonally adjusted numbers to answer the following questions.

   a. How many workers were unemployed less than 5 weeks? What percentage of all unemployed workers do these workers represent? How do these numbers compare to the previous month's data?

   b. How many workers were unemployed for 27 or more weeks? What percentage of all unemployed workers do these workers represent? How do these numbers compare to the previous month's data?

   c. How long has the average worker been unemployed (average duration, in weeks)? How does this compare to the average for the previous month's data?

   d. Comparing the latest month for which there are data with the previous month, has the problem of long-term unemployment improved or deteriorated?

5. There is only one labor market in Profunctia. All workers have the same skills, and all firms hire workers with these skills. Use the accompanying diagram, which shows the supply of and demand for labor, to answer the following questions. Illustrate each answer with a diagram.

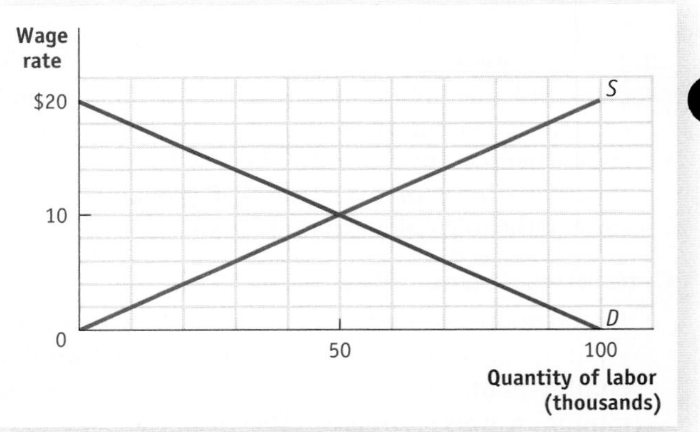

   a. What is the equilibrium wage rate in Profunctia? At this wage rate, what are the level of employment, the size of the labor force, and the unemployment rate?

   b. If the government of Profunctia sets a minimum wage equal to $12, what will be the level of employment, the size of the labor force, and the unemployment rate?

   c. If unions bargain with the firms in Profunctia and set a wage rate equal to $14, what will be the level of employment, the size of the labor force, and the unemployment rate?

   d. If the concern for retaining workers and encouraging high-quality work leads firms to set a wage rate equal to $16, what will be the level of employment, the size of the labor force, and the unemployment rate?

6. A country's labor force is the sum of the number of employed and unemployed workers. The accompanying table provides data on the size of the labor force and the number of unemployed workers for different regions of the United States.

Region	Labor force (thousands)		Unemployed (thousands)	
	Dec 2011	Dec 2012	Dec 2011	Dec 2012
Northeast	28,241.8	28,492.7	2,245.5	2,310.5
South	56,378.0	56,732.4	4,713.8	4,064.8
Midwest	34,352.0	34,260.3	2,710.8	2,439.6
West	35,964.7	35,876.0	3,534.2	3,102.1

Source: Bureau of Labor Statistics.

a. Calculate the number of workers employed in each of the regions in December 2011 and December 2012. Use your answers to calculate the change in the total number of workers employed between December 2011 and December 2012.

b. For each region, calculate the growth in the labor force from December 2011 and December 2012.

c. Compute unemployment rates in the different regions of the country in December 2011 and December 2012.

d. What can you infer about the fall in unemployment rates over this period? Was it caused by a net gain in the number of jobs or by a large fall in the number of people seeking jobs?

7. In which of the following cases is it more likely for efficiency wages to exist? Why?

a. Jane and her boss work as a team selling ice cream.

b. Jane sells ice cream without any direct supervision by her boss.

c. Jane speaks Korean and sells ice cream in a neighborhood in which Korean is the primary language. It is difficult to find another worker who speaks Korean.

8. How will the following changes affect the natural rate of unemployment?

a. The government reduces the time during which an unemployed worker can receive unemployment benefits.

b. More teenagers focus on their studies and do not look for jobs until after college.

c. Greater access to the Internet leads both potential employers and potential employees to use the Internet to list and find jobs.

d. Union membership declines.

9. With its tradition of a job for life for most citizens, Japan once had a much lower unemployment rate than that of the United States; from 1960 to 1995, the unemployment rate in Japan exceeded 3% only once. However, since the crash of its stock market in 1989 and slow economic growth in the 1990s, the job-for-life system has broken down and unemployment rose to more than 5% in 2003.

a. Explain the likely effect of the breakdown of the job-for-life system in Japan on the Japanese natural rate of unemployment.

b. As the accompanying diagram shows, the rate of growth of real GDP picked up in Japan after 2001 and before the global economic crisis of 2007–2009. Explain the likely effect of this increase in real GDP growth on the unemployment rate. Was the likely cause of the change in the unemployment rate during this period a change in the natural rate of unemployment or a change in the cyclical unemployment rate?

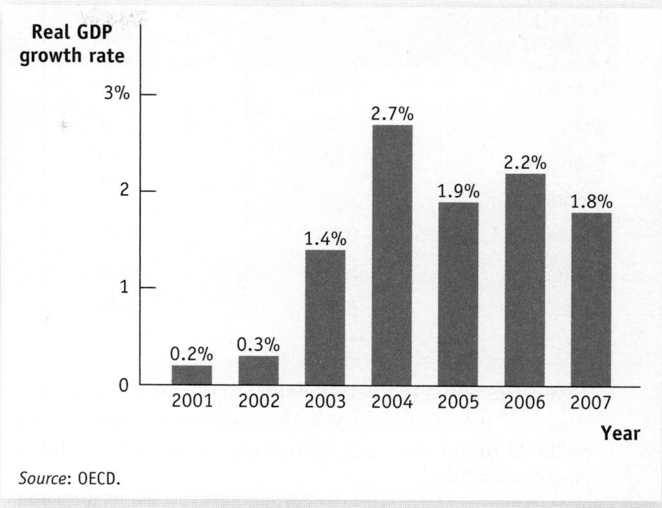

Source: OECD.

10. In the following examples, is inflation creating winners and losers at no net cost to the economy or is inflation imposing a net cost on the economy? If a net cost is being imposed, which type of cost is involved?

a. When inflation is expected to be high, workers get paid more frequently and make more trips to the bank.

b. Lanwei is reimbursed by her company for her work-related travel expenses. Sometimes, however, the company takes a long time to reimburse her. So when inflation is high, she is less willing to travel for her job.

c. Hector Homeowner has a mortgage with a fixed nominal 6% interest rate that he took out five years ago. Over the years, the inflation rate has crept up unexpectedly to its present level of 7%.

d. In response to unexpectedly high inflation, the manager of Cozy Cottages of Cape Cod must reprint and resend expensive color brochures correcting the price of rentals this season.

11. The accompanying diagram shows the interest rate on one-year loans and inflation during 1995–2010 in the economy of Albernia. When would one-year loans have been especially attractive and why?

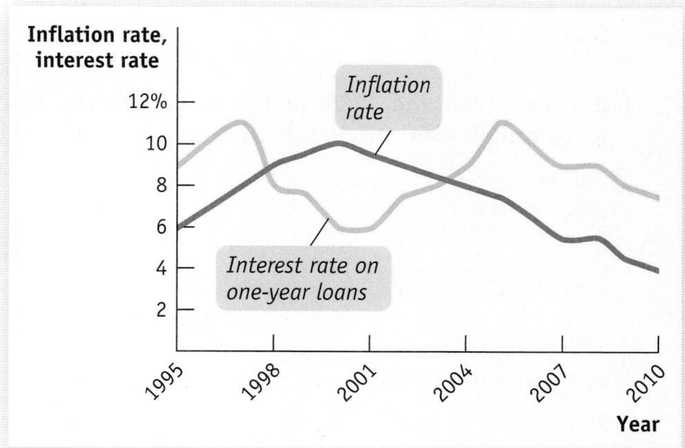

12. The accompanying table provides the inflation rate in the year 2000 and the average inflation rate over the period 2001–2010 for seven different countries.

Country	Inflation rate in 2000	Average inflation rate in 2001–2010
Brazil	7.06%	6.70%
China	0.4	2.16
France	1.83	1.86
Indonesia	3.77	8.55
Japan	−0.78	−0.25
Turkey	55.03	18.51
United States	3.37	2.40

Source: IMF.

a. Given the expected relationship between average inflation and menu costs, rank the countries in descending order of menu costs using average inflation over the period 2001–2010.

b. Rank the countries in order of inflation rates that most favored borrowers with ten-year loans that were taken out in 2000. Assume that the loans were agreed upon with the expectation that the inflation rate for 2001 to 2010 would be the same as the inflation rate in 2000.

c. Did borrowers who took out ten-year loans in Japan gain or lose overall versus lenders? Explain.

13. The accompanying diagram shows the inflation rate in the United Kingdom from 1980 to 2010.

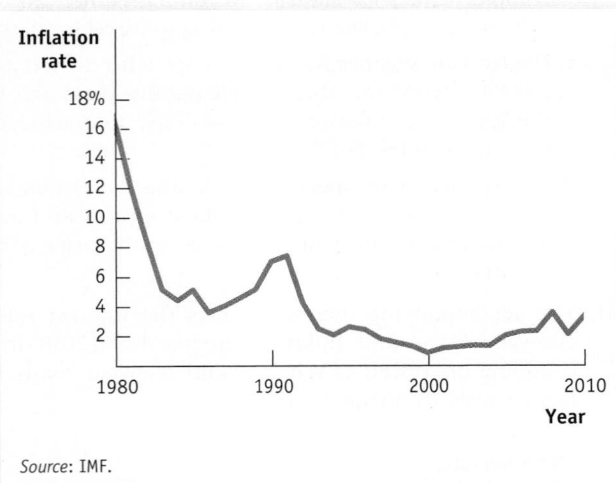

Source: IMF.

a. Between 1980 and 1985, policy makers in the United Kingdom worked to lower the inflation rate. What would you predict happened to unemployment between 1980 and 1985?

b. Policy makers in the United Kingdom react forcefully when the inflation rate rises above a target rate of 2%. Why would it be harmful if inflation rose from 3.4% (the level in 2010) to, say, a level of 5%?

14. Eastland College is concerned about the rising price of textbooks that students must purchase. To better identify the increase in the price of textbooks, the dean asks you, the Economics Department's star student, to create an index of textbook prices. The average student purchases three English, two math, and four economics textbooks per year. The prices of these books are given in the accompanying table.

	2010	2011	2012
English textbook	$50	$55	$57
Math textbook	70	72	74
Economics textbook	80	90	100

a. What is the percent change in the price of an English textbook from 2010 to 2012?

b. What is the percent change in the price of a math textbook from 2010 to 2012?

c. What is the percent change in the price of an economics textbook from 2010 to 2012?

d. Using 2010 as a base year, create a price index for these books for all years.

e. What is the percent change in the price index from 2010 to 2012?

15. The consumer price index, or CPI, measures the cost of living for a typical urban household by multiplying the price for each category of expenditure (housing, food, and so on) times a measure of the importance of that expenditure in the average consumer's market basket and summing over all categories. However, using data from the consumer price index, we can see that changes in the cost of living for different types of consumers can vary a great deal. Let's compare the cost of living for a hypothetical retired person and a hypothetical college student. Let's assume that the market basket of a retired person is allocated in the following way: 10% on housing, 15% on food, 5% on transportation, 60% on medical care, 0% on education, and 10% on recreation. The college student's market basket is allocated as follows: 5% on housing, 15% on food, 20% on transportation, 0% on medical care, 40% on education, and 20% on recreation. The accompanying table shows the December 2012 CPI for each of the relevant categories.

	CPI December 2012
Housing	235.2
Food	224.0
Transportation	211.9
Medical care	418.7
Education	134.7
Recreation	114.4

Calculate the overall CPI for the retired person and for the college student by multiplying the CPI for each of the categories by the relative importance of that category to the individual and then summing each of the categories. The CPI for all items in December 2012 was 229.6. How do your calculations for a CPI for the retired person and the college student compare to the overall CPI?

16. Each month the Bureau of Labor Statistics releases the Consumer Price Index Summary for the previous month. Go to the Bureau of Labor Statistics home page at www.bls.gov. Place the cursor over the "Data Tools" tab and then click on "Top Picks." On that page, scroll down to "Price Indexes" and select the "CPI for all urban consumers," for base year 1982–84, to retrieve the data. What was the CPI last month? How did it change from the previous month? How does the CPI compare to the same month one year ago?

17. The accompanying table provides the annual real GDP (in billions of 2005 dollars) and nominal GDP (in billions of dollars) for the United States.

	2008	2009	2010	2011	2012
Real GDP (billions of 2005 dollars)	13,161.9	12,757.9	13,063.0	13,299.1	13,588.8
Nominal GDP (billions of dollars)	14,291.5	13,973.7	14,498.9	15,075.7	15,676.0

a. Calculate the GDP deflator for each year.

b. Use the GDP deflator to calculate the inflation rate for all years except 2008.

18. The cost of a college education in the United States is rising at a rate faster than inflation. The following table shows the average cost of a college education in the United States during the academic year that began in 2009 and the academic year that began in 2010 for public and private colleges. Assume the costs listed in the table are the only costs experienced by the various college students in a single year.

a. Calculate the cost of living for an average college student in each category for 2009 and 2010.

b. Calculate an inflation rate for each type of college student between 2009 and 2010.

	Cost of college education during academic year beginning 2009 (averages in 2009 dollars)				
	Tuition and fees	Room and board	Books and supplies	Transportation	Other expenses
Two-year public college: commuter	$2,544	$7,202	$1,098	$1,445	$1,996
Four-year public college: in-state, on-campus	7,020	8,193	1,122	1,079	1,974
Four-year public college: out-of-state, on-campus	18,548	8,193	1,122	1,079	1,974
Four-year private college: on-campus	26,273	9,363	1,116	849	1,427
	Cost of college education during academic year beginning 2010 (averages in 2010 dollars)				
	Tuition and fees	Room and board	Books and supplies	Transportation	Other expenses
Two-year public college: commuter	$2,713	$7,259	$1,133	$1,491	$2,041
Four-year public college: in-state, on-campus	7,605	8,535	1,137	1,073	1,989
Four-year public college: out-of-state, on-campus	19,595	8,535	1,137	1,073	1,989
Four-year private college: on-campus	27,293	9,700	1,181	862	1,440

Module 53: Sources of Long-Run Economic Growth
Module 54: Productivity and Growth
Module 55: Long-Run Growth Policy

SECTION 17

Long-Run Economic Growth

TALL TALES

China is growing—and so are the Chinese. According to official statistics, children in China are almost 2½ inches taller now than they were 30 years ago. The average Chinese citizen is still a lot shorter than the average American, but at the current rate of growth the difference may be largely gone in a couple of generations.

If that does happen, China will be following in Japan's footsteps. Older Americans tend to think of the Japanese as short, but today young Japanese men are more than 5 inches taller on average than they were in 1900, which makes them almost as tall as their American counterparts.

There's no mystery about why the Japanese grew taller—it's because they grew richer. In the early twentieth century, Japan was a relatively poor country in which many families couldn't afford to give their children adequate nutrition. As a result, their children grew up to be short adults. However, since World War II, Japan has become an economic powerhouse in which food is ample and young adults are much taller than before.

The same phenomenon is now happening in China. Although it continues to be a relatively poor country, China has made great economic strides over the past 30 years. Its recent history is probably the world's most dramatic example of economic growth—a sustained increase in output per capita. Yet despite its impressive performance, China is currently playing catch-up with economically advanced countries like the United States and Japan. It's still relatively poor because these other nations began their own processes of economic growth many decades ago—and in the case of the United States and European countries, more than a century ago.

Many economists have argued that long-run economic growth—why it happens and how to achieve it—is the single most important issue in macroeconomics. In this section, we present some facts about long-run growth, look at the factors that economists believe determine the pace at which long-run growth takes place, examine how government policies can help or hinder growth, and address questions about the environmental sustainability of long-run growth.

53 Sources of Long-Run Economic Growth

Prisma/UIG via Getty Images

Kaband/Shutterstock

WHAT YOU WILL LEARN

1. How to measure long-run economic growth
2. How real GDP has changed over time and how it varies across countries
3. The sources of long-run economic growth

Comparing Economies Across Time and Space

Before we analyze the sources of long-run economic growth, it's useful to have a sense of just how much the U.S. economy has grown over time and how large the gaps are between wealthy countries like the United States and countries that have yet to achieve comparable growth. So let's take a look at the numbers.

Real GDP per Capita

The key statistic used to track economic growth is *real GDP per capita*—real GDP divided by the population size. We focus on GDP because, as we learned, GDP measures the total value of an economy's production of final goods and services as well as the income earned in that economy in a given year. We use *real* GDP because we want to separate changes in the quantity of goods and services from the effects of a rising price level. We focus on real GDP *per capita* because we want to isolate the effect of changes in the population. For example, other things equal, an increase in the population lowers the standard of living for the average person—there are now more people to share a given amount of real GDP. An increase in real GDP that only matches an increase in population leaves the average standard of living unchanged.

Although we also learned that growth in real GDP per capita should not be a policy goal in and of itself, it does serve as a very useful summary measure of a country's economic progress over time. Figure 53-1 shows real GDP per capita for the United States, India, and China, measured in 1990 dollars, from 1900 to 2010. The vertical axis is drawn on a logarithmic scale so that equal percent changes in real GDP per capita across countries are the same size in the graph.

FIGURE 53-1 Economic Growth in the United States, India, and China over the Past Century

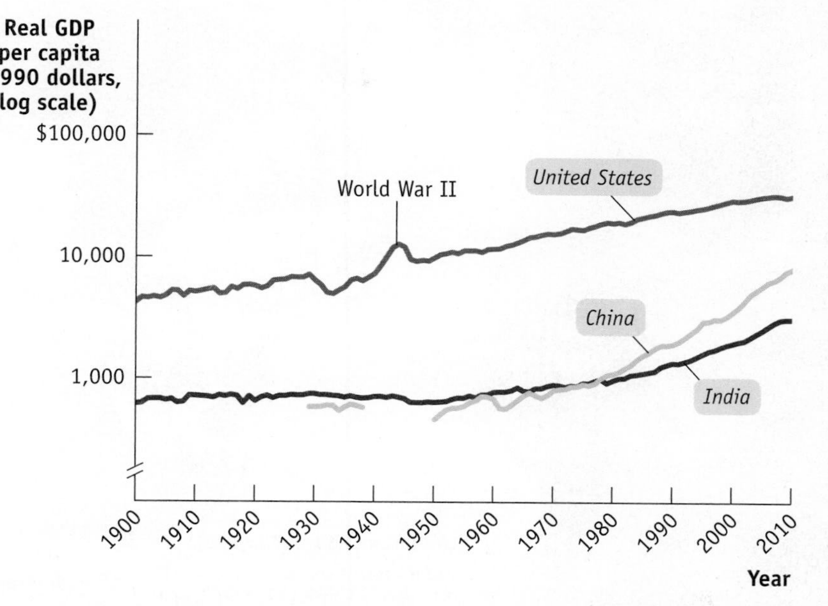

Real GDP per capita from 1900 to 2010, measured in 1990 dollars, is shown for the United States, India, and China. Equal percent changes in real GDP per capita are drawn the same size. As the steeper slopes of the lines representing China and India show, since 1980 India and China had a much higher growth rate than the United States. In 2000, China attained the standard of living achieved in the United States in 1900. In 2010, India was still poorer than the United States was in 1900. (The break in the China data from 1940 to 1950 is due to war.)

Source: Maddison Project, http://www.ggdc.net/maddison.

To give a sense of how much the U.S. economy grew during the last century, Table 53-1 shows real GDP per capita at selected years, expressed two ways: as a percentage of the 1900 level and as a percentage of the 2010 level. In 1920, the U.S. economy already produced 136% as much per person as it did in 1900. In 2010, it produced 745% as much per person as it did in 1900, a more than sevenfold increase. Alternatively, in 1900 the U.S. economy produced only 13% as much per person as it did in 2010.

TABLE 53-1

U.S. Real GDP per Capita

Year	Percentage of 1900 real GDP per capita	Percentage of 2010 real GDP per capita
1900	100%	13%
1920	136	18
1940	171	23
1980	454	61
2000	701	94
2010	745	100

Source: Maddison Project, http://www.ggdc.net/maddison.

The income of the typical family normally grows more or less in proportion to per capita income. For example, a 1% increase in real GDP per capita corresponds, roughly, to a 1% increase in the income of the median or typical family—a family at the center of the income distribution. In 2010, the median American household had an income of about $50,000. Since Table 53-1 tells us that real GDP per capita in 1900 was only 13% of its 2010 level, a typical family in 1900 probably had a purchasing power only 13% as large as the purchasing power of a typical family in 2010. That's around $6,100 in today's dollars, representing a standard of living that we would now consider severe poverty. Today's typical American family, if transported back to the United States of 1900, would feel quite a lot of deprivation.

Yet about 50% of the world's people live in countries with a lower standard of living than the United States had a century ago. That's the message about China and India in Figure 53-1: despite dramatic economic growth in China over the last three decades and the less dramatic acceleration of economic growth in India, China has only recently exceeded the standard of living that the United States enjoyed in the early twentieth century, while India is still poorer than the United States was at that time. And much of the world today is poorer than China or India.

You can get a sense of how poor much of the world remains by looking at Figure 53-2, a map of the world in which countries are classified according to their 2010 levels of GDP per capita, in U.S. dollars. As you can see, large parts of the world have very low incomes. Generally speaking, the countries of Europe and North America, as well as a few in the Pacific, have high incomes. The rest of the world, containing most of its population, is dominated by countries with GDP less than $3,976 per capita—and often much less.

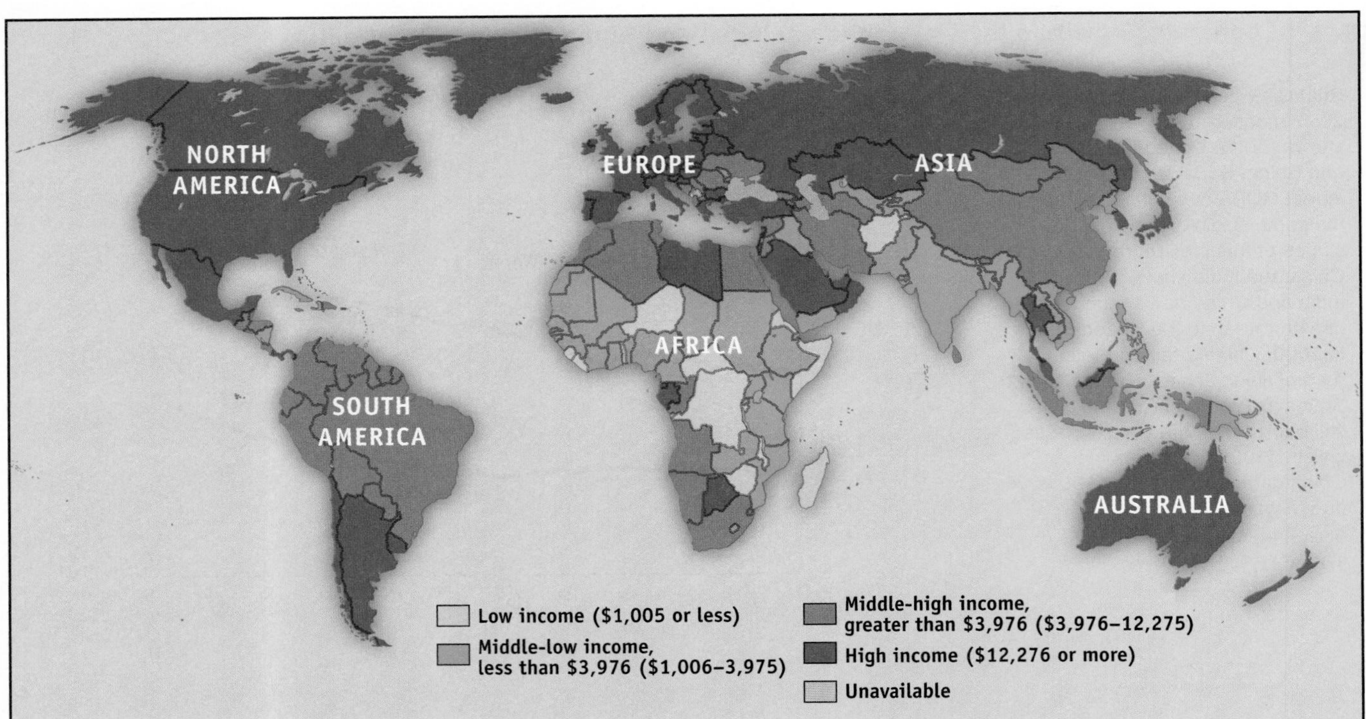

FIGURE 53-2 Per Capita Income Around the World, 2010 Although the countries of Europe and North America—along with a few in the Pacific—have high incomes, much of the world is still very poor. Today, about 50% of the world's population lives in countries with a lower standard of living than the United States had a century ago. *Source:* International Monetary Fund.

Growth Rates

How did the United States manage to produce over seven times as much per person in 2010 than in 1900? The answer is a little bit at a time. Long-run economic growth is normally a gradual process in which real GDP per capita grows at most a few percent per year. From 1900 to 2010, real GDP per capita in the United States increased an average of 1.9% each year.

To have a sense of the relationship between the annual growth rate of real GDP per capita and the long-run change in real GDP per capita, it's helpful to keep in mind the **Rule of 70,** a mathematical formula that tells us how long it takes real GDP per capita, or any other variable that grows gradually over time, to double. The approximate answer is:

$$\textbf{(53-1)}\ \text{Number of years for variable to double} = \frac{70}{\text{Annual growth rate of variable}}$$

(Note that the Rule of 70 can only be applied to a positive growth rate.) So if real GDP per capita grows at 1% per year, it will take 70 years to double. If it grows at 2% per year, it will take only 35 years to double.

In fact, U.S. real GDP per capita rose on average 1.9% per year over the last century. Applying the Rule of 70 to this information implies that it should have taken 37 years for real GDP per capita to double; it would have taken 111 years—three periods of 37 years each—for U.S. real GDP per capita to double three times. That is, the Rule of 70 implies that over the course of 111 years, U.S. real GDP per capita should have increased by a factor of $2 \times 2 \times 2 = 8$. And this does turn out to be a pretty good approximation of reality. Between 1899 and 2010—a period of 111 years—real GDP per capita rose just about eightfold.

According to the **Rule of 70,** the time it takes a variable that grows gradually over time to double is approximately 70 divided by that variable's annual growth rate.

Figure 53-3 shows the average annual rate of growth of real GDP per capita for selected countries from 1980 to 2010. Some countries were notable success stories: for example, China, though still quite a poor country, has made spectacular progress. India, although not matching China's performance, has also achieved impressive growth, as discussed in the following Economics in Action.

FIGURE 53-3 Comparing Recent Growth Rates

The average annual rate of growth of real GDP per capita from 1980 to 2010 is shown here for selected countries. China and, to a lesser extent, India and Ireland achieved impressive growth. The United States and France had moderate growth. Once considered an economically advanced country, Argentina had more sluggish growth. Still others, such as Zimbabwe, slid backward.

Source: International Monetary Fund.

*Data for Zimbabwe is average annual growth rate 2000–2010 due to data limitations.

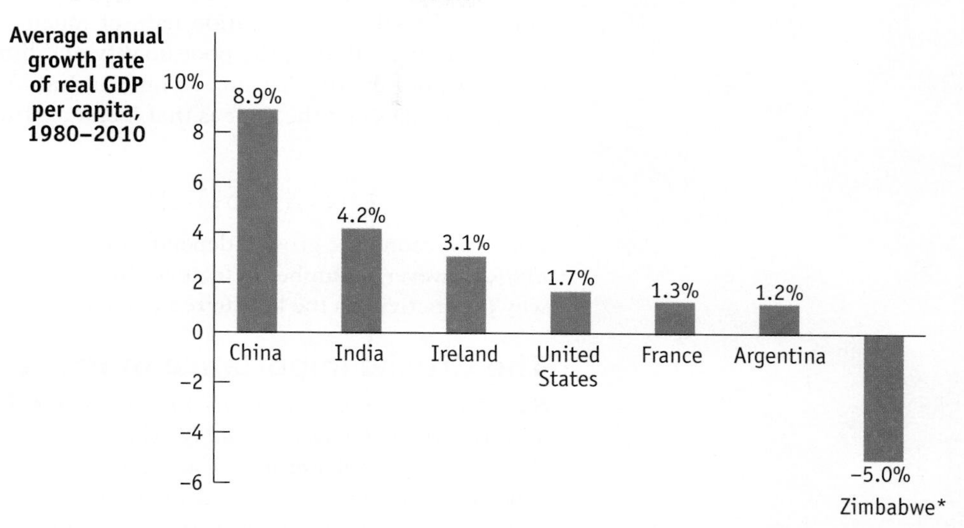

Some countries, though, have had very disappointing growth. Argentina was once considered a wealthy nation. In the early years of the twentieth century, it was in the same league as the United States and Canada. But since then it has lagged far behind more dynamic economies. And still others, like Zimbabwe, have slid backward.

What explains these differences in growth rates? To answer that question, we need to examine the sources of long-run economic growth.

ECONOMICS ▶ IN ACTION

WORLD VIEW

INDIA TAKES OFF

India achieved independence from Great Britain in 1947, becoming the world's most populous democracy—a status it has maintained to this day. For more than three decades after independence, however, this happy political story was partly overshadowed by economic disappointment. Despite ambitious economic development plans, India's performance was consistently sluggish. In 1980, India's real GDP per capita was only about 50% higher than it had been in 1947; the gap between Indian living standards and those in wealthy countries like the United States had been growing rather than shrinking.

Lionel Derimais/Alamy

India's high rate of economic growth has raised living standards and led to the emergence of a rapidly growing middle class.

Since then, however, India has done much better. As Figure 53-3 shows, real GDP per capita has grown at an average rate of 4.2% a year, more than tripling between 1980 and 2010. India now has a large and rapidly growing middle class. And yes, the well-fed children of that middle class are much taller than their parents.

What went right in India after 1980? Many economists point to policy reforms. For decades after independence, India had a tightly controlled, highly regulated economy. Today, things are very different: a series of reforms opened the economy to international trade and freed up domestic competition. Some economists, however, argue that this can't be the main story because the big policy reforms weren't adopted until 1991, yet growth accelerated around 1980.

Regardless of the explanation, India's economic rise has transformed it into a major new economic power—and allowed hundreds of millions of people to have a much better life, better than their grandparents could have dreamed.

The big question now is whether this growth can continue. Skeptics argue that there are bottlenecks in the Indian economy that may constrain future growth. They point to the still low education level of much of India's population and inadequate infrastructure—that is, the poor quality and limited capacity of the country's roads, railroads, power supplies, and so on. But India's economy has defied the skeptics for several decades and the hope is that it can continue doing so.

What Are the Sources of Long-Run Growth?

Long-run economic growth depends almost entirely on one ingredient: rising *productivity*. However, a number of factors affect the growth of productivity. Let's look first at why productivity is the key ingredient and then examine what affects it.

The Crucial Importance of Productivity

Sustained economic growth occurs only when the amount of output produced by the average worker increases steadily. The term **labor productivity,** or **productivity** for short, is used to refer either to output per worker or, in some cases, to output per hour. (The number of hours worked by an average worker differs to some extent across countries, although this isn't an important factor in the difference between living standards in, say, India and the United States.)

In this book we'll focus on output per worker. For the economy as a whole, productivity—output per worker—is simply real GDP divided by the number of people working.

You might wonder why we say that higher productivity is the only source of long-run growth. Can't an economy also increase its real GDP per capita by putting more of the population to work? The answer is, yes, but . . . . For short periods of time, an economy can experience a burst of growth in output per capita by putting a higher percentage of the population to work.

That happened in the United States during World War II, when millions of women who previously worked only in the home entered the paid workforce. The percentage of adult civilians employed outside the home rose from 50% in 1941 to 58% in 1944, and you can see the resulting bump in real GDP per capita during those years in Figure 53-1.

Over the longer run, however, the rate of employment growth is never very different from the rate of population growth. Over the course of the twentieth century, for example, the population of the United States rose at an average rate of 1.3% per year and employment rose 1.5% per year. Real GDP per capita rose 1.9% per year; of that, 1.7%—that is, almost 90% of the total—was the result of rising productivity. In general, overall real GDP can grow because of population growth, but any large increase in real GDP *per capita* must be the result of increased output *per worker.* That is, it must be due to higher productivity.

So increased productivity is the key to long-run economic growth. But what leads to higher productivity?

Explaining Growth in Productivity

There are three main reasons why the average U.S. worker today produces far more than his or her counterpart a century ago. First, the modern worker has far more *physical capital,* such as machinery and office space, to work with. Second, the modern worker is much better educated and so possesses much more *human capital.* Finally, modern firms have the advantage of a century's accumulation of technical advancements reflecting a great deal of *technological progress.*

Let's look at each of these factors in turn.

Labor productivity, often referred to simply as **productivity,** is output per worker.

Physical capital consists of human-made resources such as buildings and machines.

INCREASE IN PHYSICAL CAPITAL Economists define **physical capital** as manufactured resources such as buildings and machines. Physical capital makes workers more productive. For example, a worker operating a backhoe can dig a lot more feet of trench per day than one equipped only with a shovel.

The average U.S. private-sector worker today is backed up by more than $150,000 worth of physical capital—far more than a U.S. worker had 100 years ago and far more than the average worker in most other countries has today.

Human capital is the improvement in labor created by the education and knowledge embodied in the workforce.

Technological progress is an advance in the technical means of the production of goods and services.

INCREASE IN HUMAN CAPITAL It's not enough for a worker to have good equipment—he or she must also know what to do with it. **Human capital** refers to the improvement in labor created by the education and knowledge embodied in the workforce.

The human capital of the United States has increased dramatically over the past century. A century ago, although most Americans were able to read and write, very few had an extensive education. In 1910, only 13.5% of Americans over 25 had graduated from high school and only 3% had four-year-college degrees. By 2010, the percentages were 87% and 30%, respectively. It would be impossible to run today's economy with a population as poorly educated as that of a century ago.

Analyses based on *growth accounting*, described in the next module, suggest that education—and its effect on productivity—is an even more important determinant of growth than increases in physical capital.

TECHNOLOGICAL PROGRESS Probably the most important driver of productivity growth is **technological progress,** which is broadly defined as an advance in the technical means of the production of goods and services. We'll see shortly how economists measure the impact of technology on growth.

Workers today are able to produce more than those in the past, even with the same amount of physical and human capital, because technology has advanced over time. It's important to realize that economically important technological progress need not be flashy or rely on cutting-edge science. Historians have noted that past economic growth has been driven not only by major inventions, such as the railroad or the semiconductor chip, but also by thousands of modest innovations, such as the flat-bottomed paper bag, patented in 1870, which made packing groceries and many other goods much easier, and the Post-it® note, introduced in 1981, which has had surprisingly large benefits for office productivity. Experts attribute much of the productivity surge that took place in the United States late in the twentieth century to new technology adopted by retail companies like Walmart rather than to high-technology companies.

Marty Bucella/Cartoonstock

MODULE 53 Review

Solutions appear at the back of the book.

Check Your Understanding

1. Why do economists focus on real GDP per capita as a measure of economic progress rather than on some other measure, such as nominal GDP per capita or real GDP?
2. Apply the Rule of 70 to the data in Figure 53.3 to determine how long it will take each of the countries listed there to double its real GDP per capita. Would India's real GDP per capita exceed that of the United States in the future if growth rates remained the same? Why or why not?
3. Although China and India currently have growth rates much higher than the U.S. growth rate, the typical Chinese or Indian household is far poorer than the typical American household. Explain why.

Multiple-Choice Questions

1. Which of the following is true regarding growth rates for countries around the world compared to the United States?
   - I. Fifty percent of the world's people live in countries with a lower standard of living than the U.S. in 1900.
   - II. The U.S. growth rate is six times the growth rate in the rest of the world.
   - III. China has only just attained the same standard of living the U.S. had in 1900.

   a. I only
   b. II only
   c. III only
   d. I and III only
   e. I, II, and III

2. Which of the following is the key statistic used to track economic growth?

   a. GDP
   b. real GDP
   c. real GDP per capita
   d. median real GDP
   e. median real GDP per capita

3. According to the Rule of 70, if a country's real GDP per capita grows at a rate of 2% per year, it will take how many years for real GDP per capita to double?

   a. 3.5
   b. 20
   c. 35
   d. 70
   e. It will never double at that rate.

4. If a country's real GDP per capita doubles in 10 years, what was its average annual rate of growth of real GDP per capita?

   a. 3.5%
   b. 7%
   c. 10%
   d. 70%
   e. 700%

5. Long-run economic growth depends almost entirely on

   a. technological change.
   b. rising productivity.
   c. increased labor force participation.
   d. rising real GDP per capita.
   e. population growth.

Critical-Thinking Question

Increases in real GDP per capita result mostly from changes in what variable? Define that variable. What other factor could also lead to increased real GDP per capita? Why is this other factor not as significant?

PITFALLS

CHANGE IN LEVEL VERSUS RATE OF CHANGE

? What's the difference between a *change in the level of real GDP* and a *change in the growth rate*?

\> WHEN YOU HEAR THAT REAL GDP "GREW," IT MEANS THAT THE *LEVEL* OF REAL GDP INCREASED. WHEN YOU HEAR STATEMENTS ABOUT ECONOMIC GROWTH OVER A PERIOD OF YEARS, YOU ARE ALMOST ALWAYS HEARING ABOUT *CHANGES IN THE GROWTH RATE*. Consider this example. We might say that U.S. real GDP grew during 2010 by $385 billion. If we knew the level of U.S. real GDP in 2009, we could also represent the amount of 2010 growth in terms of a rate of change. So, if U.S. real GDP in 2009 was $12,703 billion, then U.S. real GDP in 2010 was $12,703 billion + $385 billion = $13,088 billion. We could calculate the rate of change, or the growth rate, of U.S. real GDP during 2010 as: ($13,088 billion − $12,703 billion)/$12,703 billion) × 100 = ($385 billion/$12,703 billion) × 100 = 3.03%.

When talking about growth or growth rates, economists often use phrases that appear to mix the two concepts. Admittedly, this can be confusing. For example, when economists say that "U.S. growth fell during the 1970s," they are really saying that the U.S. growth rate of real GDP was lower in the 1970s in comparison to the 1960s. When they say that "growth accelerated during the early 1990s," what they mean is that the growth rate increased year after year in the early 1990s—for example, going from 3% to 3.5% to 4%.

To learn more, see pages 546 and 547.

Productivity and Growth

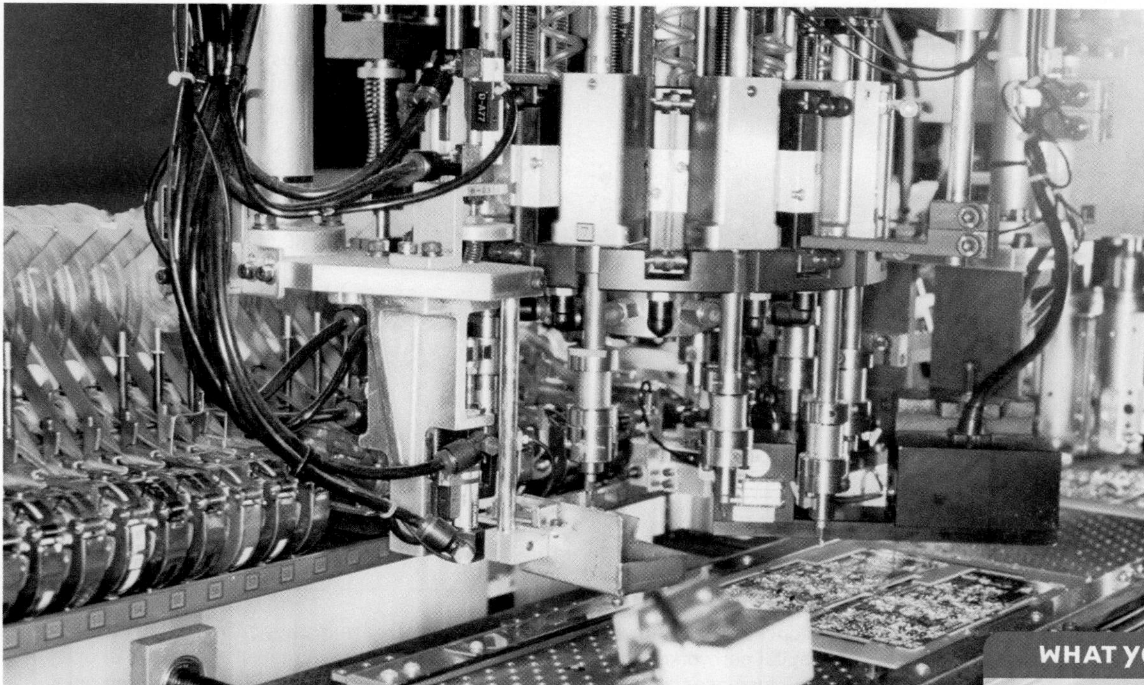

Kim Steele/Getty Images

WHAT YOU WILL LEARN

1. How changes in productivity are illustrated using an aggregate production function
2. About challenges to growth posed by limited natural resources and efforts to make growth sustainable

The Aggregate Production Function

Productivity is higher, other things equal, when workers are equipped with more physical capital, more human capital, better technology, or any combination of the three. But can we put numbers to these effects? To do this, economists make use of the **aggregate production function,** which shows how productivity depends on the quantities of physical capital per worker and human capital per worker as well as the state of technology. In general, all three factors tend to rise over time, as workers are equipped with more machinery, receive more education, and benefit from technological advances.

In analyzing historical economic growth, economists have discovered a crucial fact about the estimated aggregate production function: it exhibits **diminishing returns to physical capital.** That is, when the amount of human capital per worker and the state of technology are held fixed, each successive increase in the amount of physical capital per worker leads to a smaller increase in productivity. Figure 54-1 and the accompanying table give a hypothetical example of how the level of physical capital per worker might affect the level of real GDP per worker, holding human capital per worker and the state of technology fixed. In this example, we measure the quantity of physical capital in dollars.

The **aggregate production function** is a hypothetical function that shows how productivity (real GDP per worker) depends on the quantities of physical capital per worker and human capital per worker as well as the state of technology.

An aggregate production function exhibits **diminishing returns to physical capital** when, holding the amount of human capital per worker and the state of technology fixed, each successive increase in the amount of physical capital per worker leads to a smaller increase in productivity.

To see why the relationship between physical capital per worker and productivity exhibits diminishing returns, think about how having farm equipment affects the productivity of farmworkers. A little bit of equipment makes a big difference: a worker equipped with a tractor can do much more than a worker without one. And a worker using more expensive equipment will, other things equal, be more productive: a worker with a \$40,000 tractor will normally be able to cultivate more farmland in a given amount of time than a worker with a \$20,000 tractor because the more expensive machine will be more powerful, perform more tasks, or both.

FIGURE 54-1 Physical Capital and Productivity

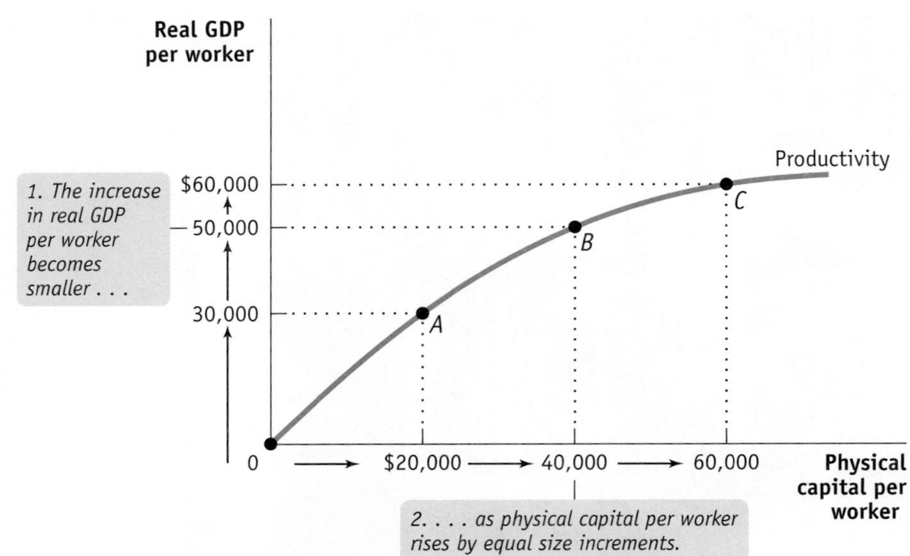

Physical capital per worker	Real GDP per worker
$ 0	$ 0
20,000	30,000
40,000	50,000
60,000	60,000

The aggregate production function shows how, in this case holding human capital per worker and technology fixed, productivity increases as physical capital per worker rises. Other things equal, a greater quantity of physical capital per worker leads to higher real GDP per worker but is subject to diminishing returns: each successive addition to physical capital per worker produces a smaller increase in productivity. Starting at the origin, 0, a $20,000 increase in physical capital per worker leads to an increase in real GDP per worker of $30,000, indicated by point *A*. Starting from point *A*, another $20,000 increase in physical capital per worker leads to an increase in real GDP per worker but only of $20,000, indicated by point *B*. Finally, a third $20,000 increase in physical capital per worker leads to only a $10,000 increase in real GDP per worker, indicated by point *C*.

But will a worker with a $40,000 tractor, holding human capital and technology constant, be twice as productive as a worker with a $20,000 tractor? Probably not: there's a huge difference between not having a tractor at all and having even an inexpensive tractor; there's much less difference between having an inexpensive tractor and having a better tractor. And we can be sure that a worker with a $200,000 tractor won't be 10 times as productive: a tractor can be improved only so much. Because the same is true of other kinds of equipment, the aggregate production function shows diminishing returns to physical capital.

Diminishing returns to physical capital imply a relationship between physical capital per worker and output per worker like the one shown in Figure 54-1. As the productivity curve for physical capital and the accompanying table illustrate, more physical capital per worker leads to more output per worker. But each $20,000 increment in physical capital per worker adds less to productivity.

As you can see from the table, there is a big payoff for the first $20,000 of physical capital: real GDP per worker rises by $30,000. The second $20,000 of physical capital also raises productivity, but not by as much: real GDP per worker goes up by only $20,000. The third $20,000 of physical capital raises real GDP per worker by only $10,000.

By comparing points along the curve you can also see that as physical capital per worker rises, output per worker also rises—but at a diminishing rate. Going from the origin at 0 to point *A*, a $20,000 increase in physical capital per worker, leads to an increase of $30,000 in real GDP per worker. Going from point *A* to point *B*, a second $20,000 increase in physical capital per worker, leads to an increase of only $20,000 in real GDP per worker. And from point *B* to point *C*, a $20,000 increase in physical capital per worker increased real GDP per worker by only $10,000.

It's important to realize that diminishing returns to physical capital is an "other things equal" phenomenon: additional amounts of physical capital are less productive *when the amount of human capital per worker and the technology are held fixed.* Diminishing returns may disappear if we increase the amount of human capital per worker, or improve the technology, or both at the same time the amount of physical capital per worker is increased.

For example, a worker with a $40,000 tractor who has also been trained in the most advanced cultivation techniques may in fact be more than twice as productive as a worker with only a $20,000 tractor and no additional human capital. But diminishing returns to any one input—regardless of whether it is physical capital, human capital, or number of workers—is a pervasive characteristic of production.

Growth accounting estimates the contribution of each major factor in the aggregate production function to economic growth.

Total factor productivity is the amount of output that can be achieved with a given amount of factor inputs.

Growth Accounting

In practice, all the factors contributing to higher productivity rise during the course of economic growth: both physical capital and human capital per worker increase, and technology advances as well. To disentangle the effects of these factors, economists use **growth accounting,** which estimates the contribution of each major factor in the aggregate production function to economic growth. For example, suppose the following are true:

- The amount of physical capital per worker grows 3% a year.
- Each 1% rise in physical capital per worker, holding human capital and technology constant, raises output per worker by one-third of 1%, or 0.33%.

In that case, we would estimate that growing physical capital per worker is responsible for 3% × 0.33 = 1 percentage point of productivity growth per year. A similar but more complex procedure is used to estimate the effects of growing human capital. The procedure is more complex because there aren't simple dollar measures of the quantity of human capital.

Growth accounting allows us to calculate the effects of greater physical and human capital on economic growth. But how can we estimate the effects of technological progress? We do so by estimating what is left over after the effects of physical and human capital have been taken into account. For example, let's imagine that there was no increase in human capital per worker so that we can focus on changes in physical capital and in technology.

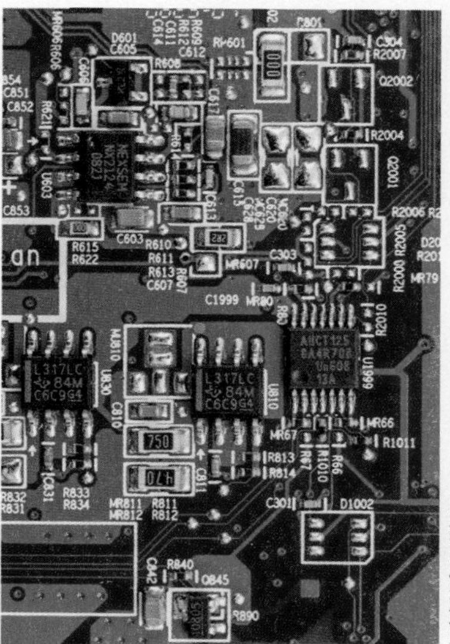

Radek Hofman/Alamy

Technological progress is central to economic growth.

In Figure 54-2, the lower curve shows the same hypothetical relationship between physical capital per worker and output per worker shown in Figure 54-1. Let's assume that this was the relationship given the technology available in 1942. The upper curve also shows a relationship between physical capital per worker and productivity, but this time given the technology available in 2012. (We've chosen a 70-year stretch to allow us to use the Rule of 70.) The 2012 curve is shifted up compared to the 1942 curve because technologies developed over the previous 70 years made it possible to produce more output for a given amount of physical capital per worker than was possible with the technology available in 1942. (Note that the two curves are measured in constant dollars.)

Let's assume that between 1942 and 2012 the amount of physical capital per worker rose from $20,000 to $60,000. If this increase in physical capital per worker had taken place without any technological progress, the economy would have moved from *A* to *C:* output per worker would have risen, but only from $30,000 to $60,000, or 1% per year (using the Rule of 70 tells us that a 1% growth rate over 70 years doubles output). In fact, however, the economy moved from *A* to *D:* output rose from $30,000 to $120,000, or 2% per year. There was an increase in both physical capital per worker and technological progress, which shifted the aggregate production function.

In this case, 50% of the annual 2% increase in productivity—that is, 1% in annual productivity growth—is due to higher **total factor productivity,** the amount of output that can be produced with a given amount of factor inputs. So when total factor

FIGURE 54-2 Technological Progress and Productivity Growth

Technological progress raises productivity at any given level of physical capital per worker, and therefore shifts the aggregate production function upward. Here we hold human capital per worker fixed. We assume that the lower curve (the same curve as in Figure 54-1) reflects technology in 1942 and the upper curve reflects technology in 2012. Holding technology and human capital fixed, tripling physical capital per worker from $20,000 to $60,000 leads to a doubling of real GDP per worker, from $30,000 to $60,000. This is shown by the movement from point *A* to point *C*, reflecting an approximately 1% per year rise in real GDP per worker. In reality, technological progress raised productivity at any given level of physical capital—shown here by the upward shift of the curve—and the actual rise in real GDP per worker is shown by the movement from point *A* to point *D*. Real GDP per worker grew 2% per year, leading to a quadrupling during the period. The extra 1% in growth of real GDP per worker is due to higher total factor productivity.

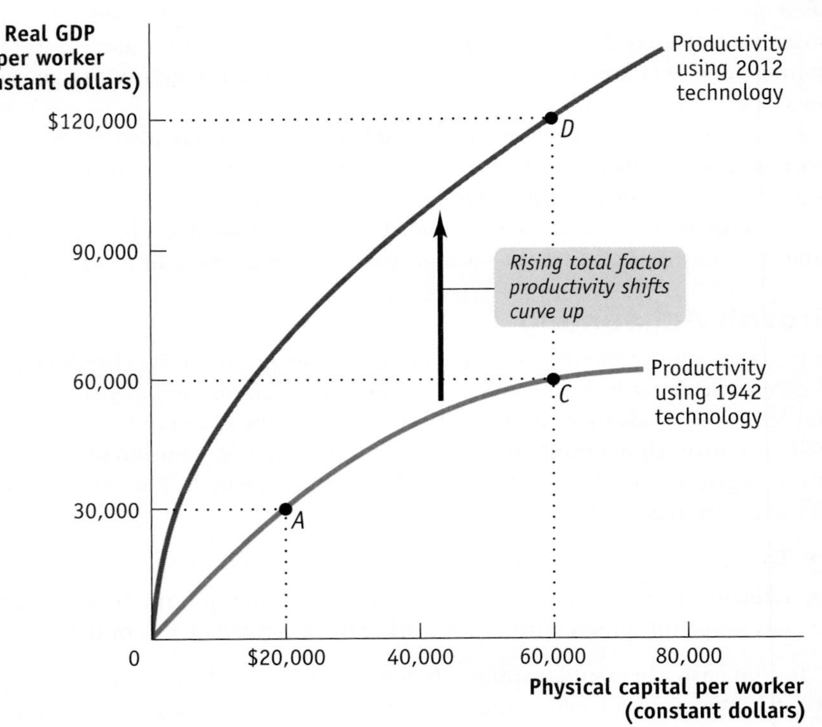

productivity increases, the economy can produce more output with the same quantity of physical capital, human capital, and labor.

Most estimates find that increases in total factor productivity are central to a country's economic growth. We believe that observed increases in total factor productivity in fact measure the economic effects of technological progress. All of this implies that technological change is crucial to economic growth. The Bureau of Labor Statistics estimates the growth rate of both labor productivity and total factor productivity for nonfarm business in the United States. According to the Bureau's estimates, during the past 70 years, only about half of the productivity in the economy is explained by increases in physical and human capital per worker; the rest is explained by rising total factor productivity—that is, by technological progress.

ECONOMICS IN ACTION

THE INFORMATION TECHNOLOGY PARADOX

From the early 1970s through the mid-1990s, the United States went through a slump in total factor productivity growth. Figure 54-3 shows Bureau of Labor Statistics estimates of annual total factor productivity growth, averaged for each 10-year period from 1948 to 2010. As you can see, there was a large fall in the total factor productivity growth rate beginning in the early 1970s. Because higher total factor productivity plays such a key role in long-run growth, the economy's overall growth was also disappointing, leading to a widespread sense that economic progress had ground to a halt.

Many economists were puzzled by the slowdown in total factor productivity growth after 1973, since in other ways the era seemed to be one of rapid technological progress. Modern information technology really began with the development of the first microprocessor—a computer on a chip—in 1971. In the 25 years that followed, a series of inventions that seemed revolutionary became standard equipment in the business world: computers, the Internet, cell phones, and e-mail.

Yet the rate of growth of total factor productivity remained stagnant. In a famous remark, MIT economics professor and Nobel laureate Robert Solow, a pioneer in the analysis of economic growth, declared that the information technology revolution could be seen everywhere except in the economic statistics. Why didn't information technology show large rewards?

Paul David, a Stanford University economic historian, offered a theory and a prediction. He pointed out that 100 years earlier another miracle technology—electric power—had spread through the economy, again with surprisingly little impact on productivity growth at first. The reason, he suggested, was that a new technology doesn't yield its full potential if you use it in old ways.

For example, a traditional factory around 1900 was a multistory building, with the machinery tightly crowded together and designed to be powered by a steam engine in the basement. This design had problems: it was very difficult to move people and materials around. Yet owners who electrified their factories initially maintained the multistory, tightly packed layout. Only with the switch to spread-out, one-story factories that took advantage of the flexibility of electric power—most famously Henry Ford's auto assembly line—did productivity take off.

FIGURE 54-3 The U.S. Productivity Growth Slowdown and Recovery

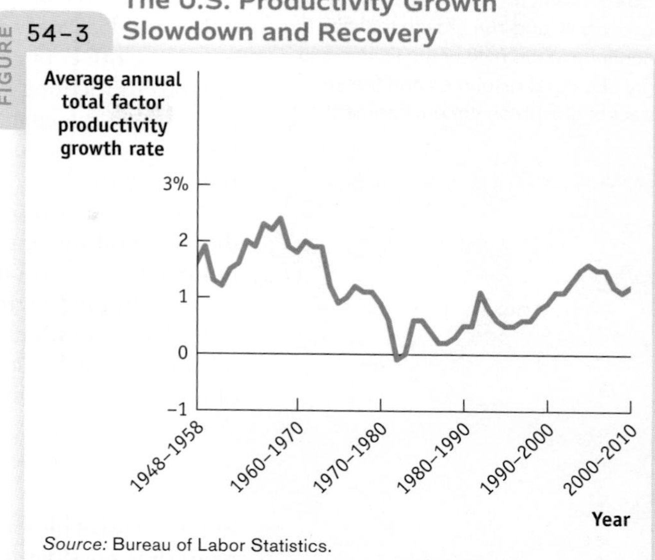

Source: Bureau of Labor Statistics.

David suggested that the same phenomenon was happening with information technology. Productivity, he predicted, would take off when people really changed their way of doing business to take advantage of the new technology—such as replacing letters and phone calls with e-mail. Sure enough, productivity growth accelerated dramatically in the second half of the 1990s as companies discovered how to effectively use information technology. (The business case at the end of the section details Walmart's innovative practices.)

What About Natural Resources?

In our discussion so far, we haven't mentioned natural resources, which certainly have an effect on productivity. Other things equal, countries that are abundant in valuable natural resources, such as highly fertile land or rich mineral deposits, have higher real GDP per capita than less fortunate countries. The most obvious modern example is the Middle East, where enormous oil deposits have made a few sparsely populated countries very rich. For example, Kuwait has about the same level of real GDP per capita as Germany, but Kuwait's wealth is based on oil, not manufacturing, the source of Germany's high output per worker.

But other things are often not equal. In the modern world, natural resources are a much less important determinant of productivity than human or physical capital for the great majority of countries. For example, some nations with very high real GDP per capita, such as Japan, have very few natural resources. Some resource-rich nations, such as Nigeria (which has sizable oil deposits), are very poor.

Historically, natural resources played a much more prominent role in determining productivity. In the nineteenth century, the countries with the highest real GDP per capita were those abundant in rich farmland and mineral deposits: the United States, Canada, Argentina, and Australia. As a consequence, natural resources figured prominently in the development of economic thought.

In a famous book published in 1798, *An Essay on the Principle of Population,* the English economist Thomas Malthus made the fixed quantity of land in the world the basis of a pessimistic prediction about future productivity. As population grew, he pointed out, the amount of land per worker would decline. And this, other things equal, would cause productivity to fall.

Sustainable long-run economic growth is long-run growth that can continue in the face of the limited supply of natural resources and the impact of growth on the environment.

His view, in fact, was that improvements in technology or increases in physical capital would lead only to temporary improvements in productivity because they would always be offset by the pressure of rising population and more workers on the supply of land. In the long run, he concluded, the great majority of people were condemned to living on the edge of starvation. Only then would death rates be high enough and birth rates low enough to prevent rapid population growth from outstripping productivity growth.

It hasn't turned out that way, although many historians believe that Malthus's prediction of falling or stagnant productivity was valid for much of human history. Population pressure probably did prevent large productivity increases until the eighteenth century. But in the time since Malthus wrote his book, any negative effects on productivity from population growth have been far outweighed by other, positive factors—advances in technology, increases in human and physical capital, and the opening up of enormous amounts of cultivatable land in the New World.

Is World Growth Sustainable?

Some skeptics have expressed doubt about whether **sustainable long-run economic growth** is possible—whether it can continue in the face of the limited supply of natural resources and the impact of growth on the environment.

In 1972 a group of scientists made a big splash with a book titled *The Limits to Growth,* which argued that long-run economic growth wasn't sustainable due to limited supplies of nonrenewable resources such as oil and natural gas.

These concerns at first seemed to be validated by a sharp rise in resource prices in the 1970s, then came to seem foolish when resource prices fell sharply in the 1980s. After 2005, however, resource prices rose sharply again, leading to renewed concern about resource limitations to growth. Figure 54-4 shows the real price of oil—the price of oil adjusted for inflation in the rest of the economy. The rise, fall, and rise of concern about resource-based limits to growth have more or less followed the rise, fall, and rise of oil prices shown in the figure.

FIGURE 54-4 The Real Price of Oil, 1950–2012

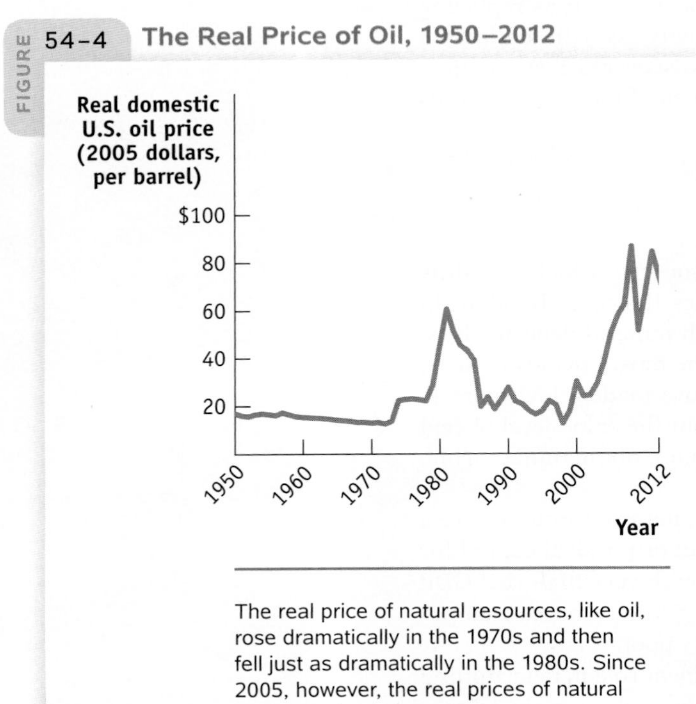

The real price of natural resources, like oil, rose dramatically in the 1970s and then fell just as dramatically in the 1980s. Since 2005, however, the real prices of natural resources have soared.

Sources: Energy Information Administration; Bureau of Labor Statistics.

Differing views about the impact of limited natural resources on long-run economic growth turn on the answers to the following three questions:

1. **HOW LARGE ARE THE SUPPLIES OF KEY NATURAL RESOURCES?** It's mainly up to geologists to answer this question. And the response changes as new technologies, such as hydraulic fracking, are developed, allowing access to previously inaccessible oil and natural gas resources. Unfortunately, there's wide disagreement among the experts, especially about the prospects for future oil production.

Some analysts believe that there is enough untapped oil in the ground that world oil production can continue to rise for several decades. Others, including a number of oil company executives, believe that the growing difficulty of finding new oil fields will cause oil production to plateau—that is, stop growing and eventually begin a gradual decline—in the fairly near future. Some analysts believe that we have already reached that plateau.

2. **HOW EFFECTIVE WILL TECHNOLOGY BE AT FINDING ALTERNATIVES TO NATURAL RESOURCES?** This question will have to be answered by engineers. There's no question that there are many alternatives to the natural resources currently being depleted, some of which are already being exploited. For example, oil extracted from

Canadian tar sands is making a significant contribution to world oil supplies, and the amount of electricity generated by wind and solar power continues to grow.

3. CAN LONG-RUN ECONOMIC GROWTH CONTINUE IN THE FACE OF RESOURCE SCARCITY? This is mainly a question for economists. And most, though not all, economists are optimistic: they believe that modern economies can find ways to work around limits in the supply of natural resources. One reason for this optimism is the fact that resource scarcity leads to high resource prices. These high prices in turn provide strong incentives to conserve the scarce resource and to find alternatives.

For example, after the sharp oil price increases of the 1970s, American consumers turned to smaller, more fuel-efficient cars, and U.S. industry also greatly intensified its efforts to reduce energy bills. The result is shown in Figure 54-5, which compares U.S. real GDP per capita and oil consumption before and after the 1970s energy crisis. In the United States before 1973, there seemed to be a more or less one-to-one relationship between economic growth and oil consumption.

FIGURE 54-5 U.S. Oil Consumption and Growth over Time

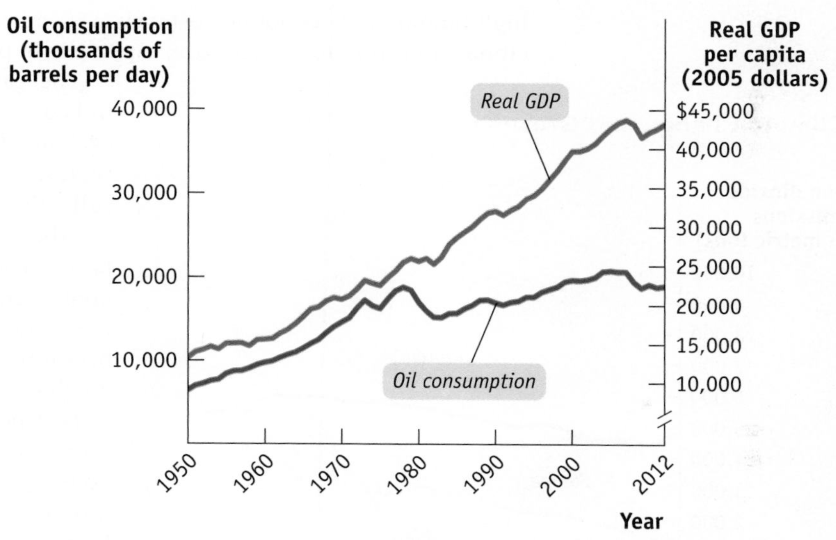

Until 1973, the real price of oil was relatively cheap and there was a more or less one-to-one relationship between economic growth and oil consumption. Conservation efforts increased sharply after the spike in the real price of oil in the mid-1970s. Yet the U.S. economy was still able to deliver growth despite cutting back on oil consumption.

Sources: Energy Information Administration; Bureau of Economic Analysis.

However, after 1973 the U.S. economy continued to deliver growth in real GDP per capita even as it substantially reduced the use of oil. This move toward conservation paused after 1990, as low real oil prices encouraged consumers to shift back to gas-guzzling larger cars and SUVs. But a sharp rise in oil prices since 2005 encouraged renewed shifts toward oil conservation.

Given such responses to prices, economists generally tend to see resource scarcity as a problem that modern economies handle fairly well, and so not as a fundamental limit to long-run economic growth. Environmental issues, however, pose a more difficult problem because dealing with them requires effective political action.

David Benton/Alamy

One response to resource scarcity.

Economic Growth and the Environment

Economic growth, other things equal, tends to increase the human impact on the environment. For example, China's spectacular economic growth has also brought a spectacular increase in air pollution in that nation's cities. But again, other things aren't necessarily equal: countries can and do take action to protect their environments.

In fact, air and water quality in today's advanced countries is generally much better than it was a few decades ago. London's famous "fog"—actually a form of air pollution, which killed more than 4,000 people during a two-week episode in 1952—is gone, thanks to regulations that virtually eliminated the use of coal heat. The equally famous smog of Los Angeles, although not extinguished, is far less severe than it was in the 1960s and early 1970s, again thanks to pollution regulations.

Despite these past environmental success stories, there is widespread concern today about the environmental impacts of continuing economic growth, reflecting a change in the scale of the problem. Environmental success stories have mainly involved dealing with *local* impacts of economic growth, such as the effect of widespread car ownership on air quality in the Los Angeles basin. Today, however, we are faced with *global* environmental issues—the adverse impacts on the environment of the Earth as a whole by worldwide economic growth.

The biggest of these issues involves the impact of fossil-fuel consumption on the world's climate. Burning coal and oil releases carbon dioxide into the atmosphere. There is broad scientific consensus that rising levels of carbon dioxide and other gases are causing a greenhouse effect on the Earth, trapping more of the sun's energy and raising the planet's overall average temperature. And rising temperatures may impose high human and economic costs: rising sea levels may flood coastal areas; changing climate may disrupt agriculture, especially in poor countries; and so on.

FIGURE 54-6 Climate Change and Growth

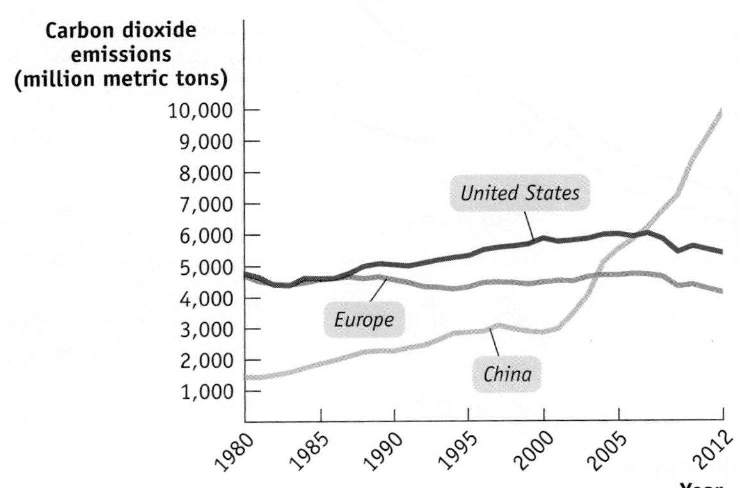

Greenhouse gas emissions are positively related to growth. As shown here by the United States and Europe, wealthy countries have historically been responsible for the great bulk of greenhouse gas emissions because of their richer and faster-growing economies. As China and other emerging economies have grown, they have begun to emit much more carbon dioxide.

Source: Energy Information Administration.

The problem of climate change is clearly linked to economic growth. Figure 54-6 shows carbon dioxide emissions from the United States, Europe, and China since 1980. Historically, the wealthy nations have been responsible for the bulk of these emissions because they have consumed far more energy per person than poorer countries. As China and other emerging economies have grown, however, they have begun to consume much more energy and emit much more carbon dioxide.

Is it possible to continue long-run economic growth while curbing the emissions of greenhouse gases? The answer, according to most economists who have studied the issue, is yes. It should be possible to reduce greenhouse gas emissions in a wide variety of ways, ranging from the use of non-fossil-fuel energy sources such as wind, solar, and nuclear power, to preventive measures such as capturing the carbon dioxide from power plants and storing it, to simpler things like designing buildings so that they're easier to keep warm in winter and cool in summer. Such measures would impose costs on the economy, but the best available estimates suggest that even a large reduction in greenhouse gas emissions over the next few decades would only modestly dent the long-term rise in real GDP per capita.

The big question is how to make all of this happen. Unlike resource scarcity, environmental problems don't automatically provide incentives for changed behavior. Pollution is an example of a *negative externality,* a cost that individuals or firms impose on others without having to offer compensation. In the absence of government intervention, individuals and firms have no incentive to reduce negative externalities, which is why it took regulation to reduce air pollution in America's cities.

So there is a broad consensus among economists—although there are some dissenters—that government action is needed to deal with climate change. There is also broad consensus that this action should take the form of market-based incentives, either in the form of a carbon tax—a tax per unit of carbon emitted—or a cap and trade system in which the total amount of emissions is capped, and producers must buy licenses to emit greenhouse gases. There is, however, considerable dispute about how to proceed.

ChinaFotoPress/Getty Images

Emissions from coal-fired municipal heating systems contribute to the heavy smog that has become a problem in many Chinese cities.

There are also several aspects of the climate change problem that make it much more difficult to deal with than, say, smog in Los Angeles. One is the problem of taking the long view. The impact of greenhouse gas emissions on the climate is very gradual: carbon dioxide put into the atmosphere today won't have its full effect on the climate for several generations. As a result, there is the political problem of persuading voters to accept pain today in return for gains that will benefit future generations.

There is also a difficult problem of international burden sharing. As Figure 54-6 shows, rich economies have historically been responsible for most greenhouse gas emissions, but newly emerging economies like China are responsible for most of the recent growth. Inevitably, rich countries are reluctant to pay the price of reducing emissions only to have their efforts frustrated by rapidly growing emissions from new players. At the same time, countries like China, which are still relatively poor, consider it unfair that they should be expected to bear the burden of protecting an environment threatened by the past actions of rich nations.

The general moral of this story is that it is possible to reconcile long-run economic growth with protecting the environment. The main question is one of getting political consensus around the necessary policies.

MODULE 54 Review

Solutions appear at the back of the book.

Check Your Understanding

1. Explain the effect of each of the following on the growth rate of productivity.
   a. The amounts of physical and human capital per worker are unchanged, but there is significant technological progress.
   b. The amount of physical capital per worker grows, but the level of human capital per worker and technology are unchanged.

2. The economy of Erehwon has grown 3% per year over the past 30 years. The labor force has grown at 1% per year, and the quantity of physical capital has grown at 4% per year. The average education level hasn't changed. Estimates by economists say that each 1% increase in physical capital per worker, other things equal, raises productivity by 0.3%.
   a. How fast has productivity in Erehwon grown?
   b. How fast has physical capital per worker grown?
   c. How much has growing physical capital per worker contributed to productivity growth? What percentage of total productivity growth is that?
   d. How much has technological progress contributed to productivity growth? What percentage of total productivity growth is that?

3. Multinomics, Inc., is a large company with many offices around the country. It has just adopted a new computer system that will affect virtually every function performed within the company. Why might a period of time pass before employees' productivity is improved by the new computer system? Why might there be a temporary decrease in employees' productivity?

4. What is the link between greenhouse gas emissions and growth? What is the expected effect on growth from emissions reduction? Why is international burden sharing of greenhouse gas emissions reduction a contentious problem?

Multiple-Choice Questions

1. Which of the following is a source of increased productivity growth?
   I. increased physical capital
   II. increased human capital
   III. technological progress
   a. I only
   b. II only
   c. III only
   d. I and II only
   e. I, II, and III

2. Which of the following is an example of physical capital?
   a. machinery
   b. healthcare
   c. education
   d. money
   e. all of the above

3. Which of the following is true of sustainable long-run economic growth?
   a. Long-run growth can continue in the face of the limited supply of natural resources.
   b. It was predicted by Thomas Malthus.
   c. Modern economies handle resource scarcity problems poorly.
   d. It is less likely when we find alternatives to natural resources.
   e. All of the above are true.

4. Which of the following statements is true of environmental quality?
   a. It is typically not affected by government policy.
   b. Other things equal, it tends to improve with economic growth.
   c. There is broad scientific consensus that rising levels of carbon dioxide and other gases are raising the planet's overall temperature.
   d. Most economists believe it is not possible to reduce greenhouse gas emissions while economic growth continues.
   e. Most environmental success stories involve dealing with global, rather than local, impacts.

5. When economists talk about *diminishing returns to physical capital,* they mean that
   a. an increase in physical capital per worker will cause a reduction in real GDP per worker.
   b. an increase in physical capital per worker will lead to smaller and smaller increases in real GDP per worker.
   c. over time physical capital wears out.
   d. increasing physical capital per worker has no effect on real GDP per worker.
   e. increasing physical capital is not a source of economic growth.

Critical-Thinking Questions

Assume that between 1942 and 2012:

- The amount of physical capital per worker grows at 2% per year.
- Each 1% rise in physical capital per worker (holding human capital and technology constant) raises output per worker by ½ of a percent, or 0.5%.
- There is no growth in human capital.
- Real GDP per capita rises from $30,000 to $60,000.

1. Growing physical capital per worker is responsible for how much productivity growth per year? Show your calculation.
2. By how much did total factor productivity grow over the time period? Explain.

PITFALLS

IT MAY BE DIMINISHED . . . BUT IT'S STILL POSITIVE

? If there are diminishing returns to physical capital per worker, does it mean that GDP per worker is falling?

> No, it does not. An increase in physical capital per worker will never reduce productivity. But due to diminishing returns, at some point increasing the amount of physical capital per worker will no longer produce an economic payoff: at that point, the increase in output will be so small that it won't be worth the cost of the additional physical capital. To answer the question, keep in mind what diminishing returns to physical capital per worker means and what it doesn't mean. As we've seen, it is an "other things equal" statement: holding the amount of human capital per worker and the technology fixed, each successive increase in the amount of physical capital per worker results in a smaller increase in real GDP per worker. But this doesn't mean that real GDP per worker eventually falls as more and more physical capital is added. It's just that the increase in real GDP per worker gets smaller and smaller, while remaining at or above zero.

To learn more, see pages 551–553.

Long-Run Growth Policy

FocusJapan/Alamy

WHAT YOU WILL LEARN

1. **Why growth rates vary in different regions of the world**
2. **What the convergence hypothesis predicts**

Why Growth Rates Differ

In 1820, Mexico had somewhat higher real GDP per capita than Japan. Today, Japan has higher real GDP per capita than most European nations and Mexico is a poor country, though by no means among the poorest. The difference? Over the long run—since 1820—real GDP per capita grew at 1.9% per year in Japan but at only 1.3% per year in Mexico.

As this example illustrates, even small differences in growth rates have large consequences over the long run. So why do growth rates differ across countries and across periods of time?

Explaining Differences in Growth Rates

As one might expect, economies with rapid growth tend to add physical capital, increase their human capital, or experience rapid technological progress. Striking economic success stories, like Japan in the 1950s and 1960s or China today, tend to be countries that do all three:

1. Rapidly add to their physical capital through high savings and investment spending
2. Upgrade their educational level
3. Make fast technological progress.

Evidence also points to the importance of government policies, property rights, political stability, and good governance in fostering the sources of growth.

SAVINGS AND INVESTMENT SPENDING One reason for differences in growth rates between countries is that some countries are increasing their stock of physical capital much more rapidly than others, through high rates of investment spending. In the 1960s, Japan was the fastest-growing major economy; it also spent a much higher share of its GDP on investment goods than did other major economies.

Today, China is the fastest-growing major economy, and it similarly spends a very large share of its GDP on investment goods. In 2010, investment spending was 38% of China's GDP, compared with only 16% in the United States.

FIGURE 55-1 China's Students Are Catching Up

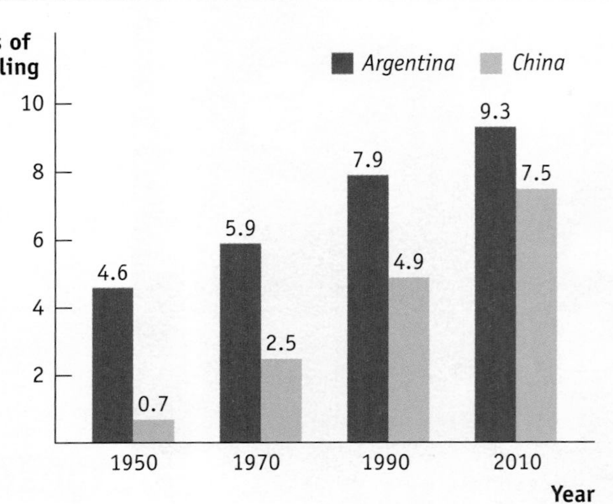

In both China and Argentina, the average educational level—measured by the number of years the average adult aged 25 or older has spent in school—has risen over time. Although China is still lagging behind Argentina, it is catching up—and China's success at adding human capital is one key to its spectacular long-run growth.

Source: Robert Barro and Jong-Wha Lee, "A New Data Set of Educational Attainment in the World, 1950–2010," NBER Working Paper No. 15902 (April 2010).

Where does the money for high investment spending come from? From savings. Investment spending must be paid for either out of savings from domestic households or by savings from foreign households—that is, an inflow of foreign capital.

Foreign capital has played an important role in the long-run economic growth of some countries, including the United States, which relied heavily on foreign funds during its early industrialization. For the most part, however, countries that invest a large share of their GDP are able to do so because they have high domestic savings. In fact, China in 2012 saved an even higher percentage of its GDP than it invested at home. The extra savings were invested abroad, largely in the United States.

EDUCATION Just as countries differ substantially in the rate at which they add to their physical capital, there have been large differences in the rate at which countries add to their human capital through education.

A case in point is the comparison between Argentina and China. In both countries the average educational level has risen steadily over time, but it has risen much faster in China. Figure 55-1 shows the average years of education of adults in China, which we have highlighted as a spectacular example of long-run growth, and in Argentina, a country whose growth has been disappointing. Compared to China, sixty years ago, Argentina had a much more educated population, while many Chinese were still illiterate.

As of 2010, the average educational level in China was still slightly below that in Argentina—but that's mainly because there are still many elderly adults who never received basic education. In terms of secondary and tertiary education, China has outstripped once-rich Argentina.

Dennis MacDonald/Alamy

Thomas Edison (shown here), is known as the inventor of R&D because he was first to form an organization devoted solely to creating new products and processes for business.

RESEARCH AND DEVELOPMENT The advance of technology is a key force behind economic growth. What drives technological progress?

Scientific advances make new technologies possible. To take the most spectacular example in today's world, the semiconductor chip—which is the basis for all modern information technology—could not have been developed without the theory of quantum mechanics in physics.

But science alone is not enough: scientific knowledge must be translated into useful products and processes. And that often requires devoting a lot of resources to **research and development,** or **R&D,** spending to create new technologies and apply them to practical use.

Although some research and development is conducted by governments, much R&D is paid for by the private sector. The United States became the world's leading economy in large part because American businesses were among the first to make systematic research and development a part of their operations.

Research and development, or **R&D,** is spending to create and implement new technologies.

Roads, power lines, ports, information networks, and other underpinnings for economic activity are known as **infrastructure.**

The Role of Government in Promoting Economic Growth

Governments can play an important role in promoting—or blocking—all three sources of long-term economic growth: physical capital, human capital, and technological progress. They can either affect growth directly through subsidies to factors that enhance growth, or by creating an environment that either fosters or hinders growth.

Government policies can increase the economy's growth rate through four main channels.

1. GOVERNMENT SUBSIDIES TO INFRASTRUCTURE Governments play an important direct role in building **infrastructure:** roads, power lines, ports, information networks, and other large-scale physical capital projects that provide a foundation for economic activity. Although some infrastructure is provided by private companies, much of it is either provided by the government or requires a great deal of government regulation and support.

Ireland offers an example of the importance of government-provided infrastructure. After the government invested in an excellent telecommunications infrastructure in the 1980s, Ireland became a favored location for high-technology companies from abroad and its economy took off in the 1990s.

Poor infrastructure, such as a power grid that frequently fails and cuts off electricity, is a major obstacle to economic growth in many countries. To provide good infrastructure, an economy must not only be able to afford it, but it must also have the political discipline to maintain it.

Perhaps the most crucial infrastructure is something we, in an advanced country, rarely think about: basic public health measures in the form of a clean water supply and disease control. Poor health infrastructure is a major obstacle to economic growth in poor countries, especially those in Africa.

2. GOVERNMENT SUBSIDIES TO EDUCATION In contrast to physical capital, which is mainly created by private investment spending, much of an economy's human capital is the result of government spending on education. Government pays for the great bulk of primary and secondary education. And it pays for a significant share of higher education: 75% of students attend public colleges and universities, and government significantly subsidizes research performed at private colleges and universities. As a result, differences in the rate at which countries add to their human capital largely reflect government policy. As we saw in Figure 55-1, educational levels in China are increasing much more rapidly than in Argentina. This isn't because China is richer than Argentina; until recently, China was, on average, poorer than Argentina. Instead, it reflects the fact that the Chinese government has made education a high priority.

Ingram Publishing/Thinkstock

Economic growth depends on an educated and skilled workforce.

3. GOVERNMENT SUBSIDIES TO R&D Technological progress is largely the result of private initiative. But in the more advanced countries, important R&D is done by government agencies as well. In the upcoming Economics in Action, we describe Brazil's agricultural boom, which was made possible by government researchers who made discoveries that expanded the amount of arable land in Brazil, as well as developing new varieties of crops that flourish in Brazil's climate.

4. MAINTAINING A WELL-FUNCTIONING FINANCIAL SYSTEM Governments play an important indirect role in making high rates of private investment spending possible. Both the amount of savings and the ability of an economy to direct savings into productive investment spending depend on the economy's institutions, especially its financial system. In particular, a well-regulated and well-functioning financial system is very important for economic growth because in most countries it is the principal way in which savings are channeled into investment spending.

If a country's citizens trust their banks, they will place their savings in bank deposits, which the banks will then lend to their business customers. But if people don't trust their banks, they will hoard gold or foreign currency, keeping their savings in safe deposit boxes or under the mattress, where it cannot be turned into productive investment spending. A well-functioning financial system requires appropriate government regulation to assure depositors that their funds are protected from loss.

Governments can also create an environment that fosters economic growth by providing the following.

PROTECTION OF PROPERTY RIGHTS *Property rights* are the rights of owners of valuable items to dispose of those items as they choose. A subset, *intellectual property rights,* are the rights of an innovator to accrue the rewards of her innovation.

The state of property rights generally, and intellectual property rights in particular, are important factors in explaining differences in growth rates across economies. Why? Because no one would bother to spend the effort and resources required to innovate if someone else could appropriate that innovation and capture the rewards. So, for innovation to flourish, intellectual property rights must receive protection.

Sometimes this is accomplished by the nature of the innovation: it may be too difficult or expensive to copy. But, generally, the government has to protect intellectual property rights. A *patent* is a government-created temporary monopoly given to an innovator for the use or sale of his or her innovation. It's a temporary rather than permanent monopoly because while it's in society's interests to give an innovator an incentive to invent, it's also in society's interests to eventually encourage competition.

POLITICAL STABILITY AND GOOD GOVERNANCE There's not much point in investing in a business if rioting mobs are likely to destroy it, or saving your money if someone with political connections can steal it. Political stability and good governance (including the protection of property rights) are essential ingredients in fostering economic growth in the long run.

Long-run economic growth in successful economies, like that of the United States, has been possible because there are good laws, institutions that enforce those laws, and a stable political system that maintains those institutions. The law must state that your property is really yours so that someone else can't take it away. The courts and the police must be honest so that they can't be bribed to ignore the law. And the political system must be stable so that laws don't change capriciously.

Americans take these preconditions for granted, but they are by no means guaranteed. Aside from the disruption caused by war or revolution, many countries find that their economic growth suffers due to corruption among the government officials who should be enforcing the law.

For example, until 1991 the Indian government imposed many bureaucratic restrictions on businesses, which often had to bribe government officials to get approval for even routine activities—a tax on business, in effect. Economists have argued that a reduction in this burden of corruption is one reason Indian growth has been much faster in recent years.

Even when the government isn't corrupt, excessive government intervention can be a brake on economic growth. If large parts of the economy are supported by government subsidies, protected from imports, subject to unnecessary monopolization, or otherwise insulated from competition, productivity tends to suffer because of a lack of incentives.

ECONOMICS IN ACTION — WORLD VIEW

THE BRAZILIAN BREADBASKET

A wry Brazilian joke says that "Brazil is the country of the future—and always will be." The world's fifth most populous country has often been considered as a possible major economic power yet has never fulfilled that promise.

In recent years, however, Brazil's economy has made a better showing, especially in agriculture. This success depends on exploiting a natural resource, the tropical savanna land known as the *cerrado*. Until a quarter-century ago, the land was considered unsuitable for farming. A combination of three factors changed that: technological progress due to research and development, improved economic policies, and greater physical capital.

Fandrade/Getty Images

In Brazil, government-funded R&D has resulted in crucial agricultural technologies that turn unusable land into profitable farmland.

The Brazilian Enterprise for Agricultural and Livestock Research, a government-run agency, developed the crucial technologies. It showed that adding lime and phosphorus made *cerrado* land productive, and it developed breeds of cattle and varieties of soybeans suited for the climate.

Also, until the 1980s, Brazilian international trade policies discouraged exports, as did an overvalued exchange rate that made the country's goods more expensive to foreigners. After economic reform, investing in Brazilian agriculture became much more profitable and companies began putting in place the farm machinery, buildings, and other forms of physical capital needed to exploit the land.

What still limits Brazil's growth? Infrastructure. According to a report in the *New York Times*, Brazilian farmers are "concerned about the lack of reliable highways, railways and barge routes, which adds to the cost of doing business." Recognizing this, the Brazilian government is investing in infrastructure, and Brazilian agriculture is continuing to expand.

Success, Disappointment, and Failure

As we've seen, rates of long-run economic growth differ quite a lot around the world. Now let's look at three regions of the world that have had quite different experiences with economic growth over the last few decades.

Figure 55-2 shows trends since 1960 in real GDP per capita for three countries: Argentina, Nigeria, and South Korea. We have chosen these countries because each is a particularly striking example of what has happened in its region.

South Korea's amazing rise is part of a broad "economic miracle" in East Asia. Argentina's slow progress, interrupted by repeated setbacks, is more or less typical of the disappointing growth that has characterized much of Latin America. And Nigeria's unhappy story until very recently—with little growth in real GDP until after 2000—was, unfortunately, an experience shared by many African countries.

FIGURE 55-2 Success and Disappointment

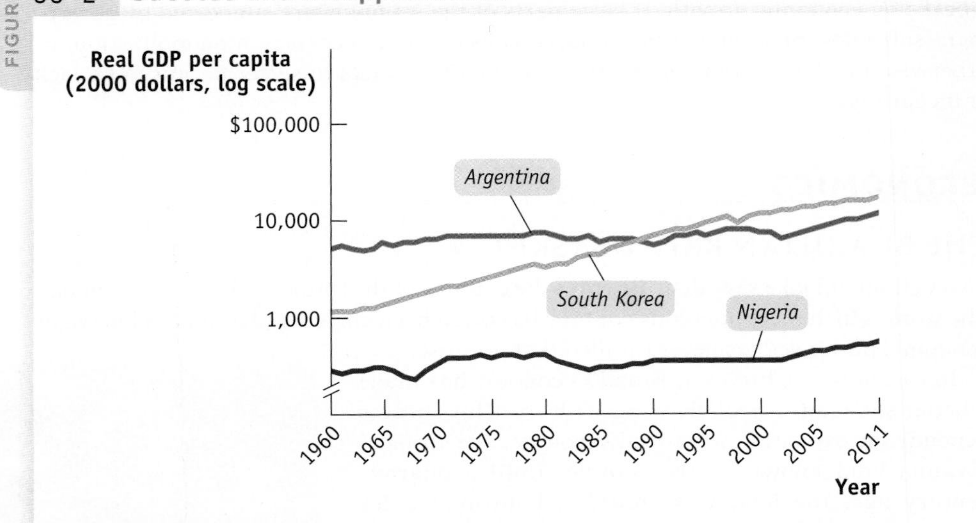

Real GDP per capita is shown for Argentina, South Korea, and Nigeria, using a logarithmic scale. South Korea and some other East Asian countries have been highly successful at achieving economic growth. Argentina, like much of Latin America, has had several setbacks, slowing its growth. Nigeria's standard of living barely budged higher over the decades, an experience shared by many African countries. Neither Argentina nor Nigeria exhibited much growth over the period either, although both have had significantly higher growth in recent years.

Source: World Bank.

East Asia's Miracle

In 1960 South Korea was a very poor country. In fact, in 1960 its real GDP per capita was lower than that of India today. But, as you can see from Figure 55-2, beginning in the early 1960s South Korea began an extremely rapid economic ascent: real GDP per capita grew about 7% per year for more than 30 years. Today South Korea, though still somewhat poorer than Europe or the United States, looks very much like an economically advanced country.

South Korea's economic growth is unprecedented in history: it took the country only 35 years to achieve growth that required centuries elsewhere. Yet South Korea is only part of a broader phenomenon, often referred to as the East Asian economic miracle. High growth rates first appeared in South Korea, Taiwan, Hong Kong, and Singapore but then spread across the region, most notably to China. Since 1975, the whole region has increased real GDP per capita by 6% per year, more than three times America's historical rate of growth.

How have the Asian countries achieved such high growth rates? The answer is that all of the sources of productivity growth have been firing on all cylinders. Very high savings rates, the percentage of GDP that is saved nationally in any given year, have allowed the countries to significantly increase the amount of physical capital per worker. Very good basic education has permitted a rapid improvement in human capital. And these countries have experienced substantial technological progress.

Why didn't any economy achieve this kind of growth in the past? Most economic analysts think that East Asia's growth spurt was possible because of its *relative* backwardness. That is, by the time that East Asian economies began to move into the modern world, they could benefit from adopting the technological advances that had been generated in technologically advanced countries such as the United States.

In 1900, the United States could not have moved quickly to a modern level of productivity because much of the technology that powers the modern economy, from jet planes to computers, hadn't been invented yet. In 1970, South Korea probably still had lower labor productivity than the United States had in 1900, but it could rapidly upgrade its productivity by adopting technology that had been developed in the United States, Europe, and Japan over the previous century. This was aided by a huge investment in human capital through widespread schooling.

According to the **convergence hypothesis**, international differences in real GDP per capita tend to narrow over time.

The East Asian experience demonstrates that economic growth can be especially fast in countries that are playing catch-up to other countries with higher GDP per capita. On this basis, many economists have suggested a general principle known as the **convergence hypothesis.** It says that differences in real GDP per capita among countries tend to narrow over time because countries that start with lower real GDP per capita tend to have higher growth rates. We'll look at the evidence on the convergence hypothesis in the Economics in Action at the end of this module.

Even before we get to that evidence, however, we can say right away that starting with a relatively low level of real GDP per capita is no guarantee of rapid growth, as the examples of Latin America and Africa demonstrate.

Latin America's Disappointment

In 1900, Latin America was not considered an economically backward region. Natural resources, including both minerals and cultivatable land, were abundant. Some countries, notably Argentina, attracted millions of immigrants from Europe in search of a better life. Measures of real GDP per capita in Argentina, Uruguay, and southern Brazil were comparable to those in economically advanced countries.

Since about 1920, however, growth in Latin America has been disappointing. As Figure 55-2 shows in the case of Argentina, growth has been disappointing for many decades, until 2000 when it finally began to increase. The fact that South Korea is now much richer than Argentina would have seemed inconceivable a few generations ago.

Why did Latin America stagnate? Comparisons with East Asian success stories suggest several factors.

- The rates of savings and investment spending in Latin America have been much lower than in East Asia, partly as a result of irresponsible government policy that has eroded savings through high inflation, bank failures, and other disruptions.
- Education—especially broad basic education—has been underemphasized: even Latin American nations rich in natural resources often failed to channel that wealth into their educational systems.
- Political instability, leading to irresponsible economic policies, has taken a toll.

In the 1980s, many economists came to believe that Latin America was suffering from excessive government intervention in markets. They recommended opening the economies to imports, selling off government-owned companies, and, in general, freeing up individual initiative. The hope was that this would produce an East Asian–type economic surge.

So far, however, only one Latin American nation, Chile, has achieved sustained rapid growth. It now seems that pulling off an economic miracle is harder than it looks. Although, in recent years Brazil and Argentina have seen their growth rates increase significantly as they exported large amounts of commodities to the advanced countries and rapidly developing China.

Africa's Troubles and Promise

Africa south of the Sahara is home to about 910 million people, more than 2 ½ times the population of the United States. On average, they are very poor, nowhere close to U.S. living standards 100 or even 200 years ago. And economic progress has been

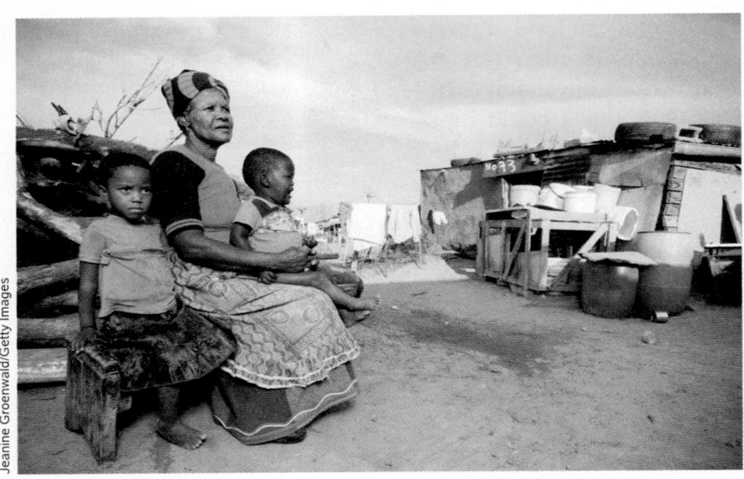

Jeanine Groenwald/Getty Images

Slow and uneven economic growth in sub-Saharan Africa has led to extreme and ongoing poverty for many of its people.

both slow and uneven, as the example of Nigeria, the most populous nation in the region, suggests.

In fact, real GDP per capita in sub-Saharan Africa actually fell 13% from 1980 to 1994, although it has recovered since then. The consequence of this poor growth performance has been intense and continuing poverty.

This is a very disheartening story. What explains it?

Several factors are probably crucial. Perhaps first and foremost is the problem of political instability. In the years since 1975, large parts of Africa have experienced savage civil wars (often with outside powers backing rival sides) that have killed millions of people and made productive investment spending impossible. The threat of war and general anarchy has also inhibited other important preconditions for growth, such as education and provision of necessary infrastructure.

Property rights are also a major problem. The lack of legal safeguards means that property owners are often subject to extortion because of government corruption, making them averse to owning property or improving it. This is especially damaging in a very poor country.

But not all economists see political instability and government corruption as the leading causes of underdevelopment in Africa; some believe the opposite. They argue that Africa is politically unstable because Africa is poor. And Africa's poverty, they go on to claim, stems from its extremely unfavorable geographic conditions—much of the continent is landlocked, hot, infested with tropical diseases, and cursed with poor soil.

They also highlight the importance of health problems in Africa. In poor countries, worker productivity is often severely hampered by malnutrition and disease. In particular, tropical diseases such as malaria can only be controlled with an effective public health infrastructure, something that is lacking in much of Africa.

Although the example of African countries represents a warning that long-run economic growth cannot be taken for granted, there are some signs of hope. As we noted in Figure 55-2, Nigeria's per capita GDP, after decades of stagnation, turned upward after 2000, achieving a 5.5% real GDP per capita growth rate in 2010. The same is true for sub-Saharan African economies as a whole.

In 2012, real GDP per capita growth rates averaged around 5.5% across sub-Saharan African countries and were projected to be nearly 6% in 2014. Rising prices for their exports are part of the reason for recent success, but there is growing optimism among development experts that a period of relative peace and better government is ushering in a new era for Africa's economies.

ECONOMICS IN ACTION

ARE ECONOMIES CONVERGING?

In the 1950s, much of Europe seemed quaint and backward to American visitors, and Japan seemed very poor. Today, a visitor to Paris or Tokyo sees a city that looks about as rich as New York. Although real GDP per capita is still somewhat higher in the United States, the differences in the standards of living among the United States, Europe, and Japan are relatively small.

Many economists have argued that this convergence in living standards is normal; the convergence hypothesis says that relatively poor countries should have higher rates of growth of real GDP per capita than relatively rich countries. And if we look at today's relatively well-off countries, the convergence hypothesis seems to be true.

FIGURE 55-3 Do Economies Converge?

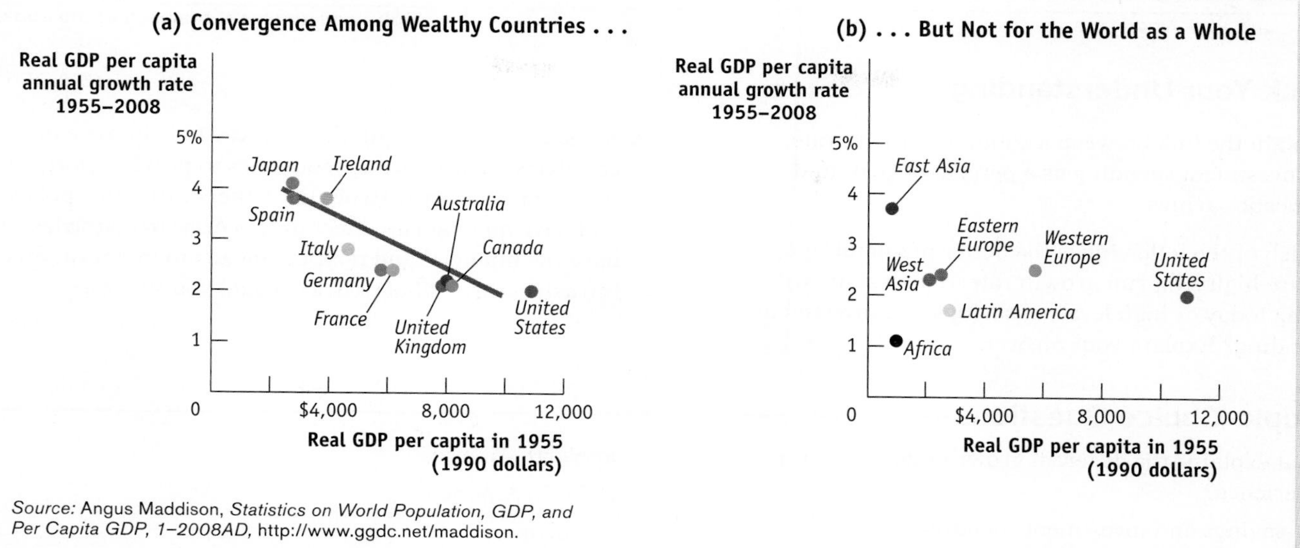

Source: Angus Maddison, *Statistics on World Population, GDP, and Per Capita GDP, 1–2008AD*, http://www.ggdc.net/maddison.

Panel (a) of Figure 55-3 shows data for a number of today's wealthy economies measured in 1990 dollars. On the horizontal axis is real GDP per capita in 1955; on the vertical axis is the average annual growth rate of real GDP per capita from 1955 to 2008. There is a clear negative relationship as can be seen from the line fitted through the points. The United States was the richest country in this group in 1955 and had the slowest rate of growth. Japan and Spain were the poorest countries in 1955 and had the fastest rates of growth. These data suggest that the convergence hypothesis is true.

But economists who looked at similar data realized that these results depend on the countries selected. If you look at successful economies that have a high standard of living today, you find that real GDP per capita has largely converged in the last half-century. But looking across the world as a whole, including countries that remain poor, there is little evidence of convergence. Panel (b) of Figure 55-3 illustrates this point using data for regions rather than individual countries (other than the United States). In 1955, East Asia and Africa were both very poor regions. Over the next 53 years, the East Asian regional economy grew quickly, as the convergence hypothesis would have predicted, but the African regional economy grew very slowly. Likewise, Western Europe had substantially higher real GDP per capita than Latin America. But, contrary to the convergence hypothesis, the Western European regional economy grew more quickly, widening the gap between the regions.

So is the convergence hypothesis all wrong? No: economists still believe that countries with relatively low real GDP per capita tend to have higher rates of growth than countries with relatively high real GDP per capita, *other things equal.* But other things—education, infrastructure, rule of law, and so on—are often not equal. Statistical studies find that when you adjust for differences in these other factors, poorer countries do tend to have higher growth rates. This result is known as *conditional convergence.*

Because other factors differ, however, there is no clear tendency toward convergence in the world economy as a whole. Western Europe, North America, and parts of Asia are becoming more similar in real GDP per capita, but the gap between these regions and the rest of the world is growing.

MODULE 55 Review

Solutions appear at the back of the book.

Check Your Understanding

1. Explain the link between a country's growth rate, its investment spending as a percent of GDP, and its domestic savings.

2. Which of the following is the better predictor of a future high long-run growth rate: a high standard of living today or high levels of savings and investment spending? Explain your answer.

3. Some economists think the best way to help African countries is for wealthier countries to provide more funds for basic infrastructure. Others think this policy will have no long-run effect unless African countries have the financial and political means to maintain this infrastructure. What policies would you suggest?

Multiple-Choice Questions

1. What explains the different growth rates economies experience?
   - I. savings and investment spending
   - II. research and development
   - III. government policies

   a. I only
   b. II only
   c. III only
   d. I and II only
   e. I, II, and III

2. Which of the following can lead to increases in physical capital in an economy?
   a. increased investment spending
   b. increased savings by domestic households
   c. increased savings from foreign households
   d. an inflow of foreign capital
   e. all of the above

3. The following statement describes which area of the world? "This area has experienced growth rates unprecedented in history and now looks like an economically advanced country."
   a. North America
   b. Latin America
   c. Europe
   d. East Asia
   e. Africa

4. Which of the following is cited as an important factor preventing long-run economic growth in Africa?
   a. political instability
   b. lack of property rights
   c. unfavorable geographic conditions
   d. poor health
   e. all of the above

5. The convergence hypothesis
   a. states that differences in real GDP per capita among countries widen over time.
   b. states that low levels of real GDP per capita are associated with higher growth rates.
   c. states that low levels of real GDP per capita are associated with lower growth rates.
   d. contradicts the Rule of 70.
   e. has been proven by evidence from around the world.

Critical-Thinking Question

Some economists think the high rates of growth of productivity achieved by many East Asian economies cannot be sustained. Why might they be right? What would have to happen for them to be wrong?

BUSINESS CASE: Big Box Boom

After 20 years of being sluggish, U.S. productivity growth accelerated sharply in the late 1990s; that is, productivity began to grow at a much faster rate than previously. What caused that acceleration? Was it the rise of the Internet?

AP Photo/Morry Gash

Not according to analysts at McKinsey and Co., the famous business consulting firm. They found that a major source of productivity improvement after 1995 was a surge in output per worker in retailing—stores were selling much more merchandise per worker.

Other analysts agree. The accompanying figure shows the result of an analysis of total factor productivity growth in France, Germany, and the United States between 1995 and 2004, the decade of the U.S. productivity surge. As you can see, the United States did considerably better than either European nation. The key to the surge was very fast growth in the productivity of the distribution sector, that is, in wholesale and retail trade.

U.S. and European Productivity Growth, 1995–2004

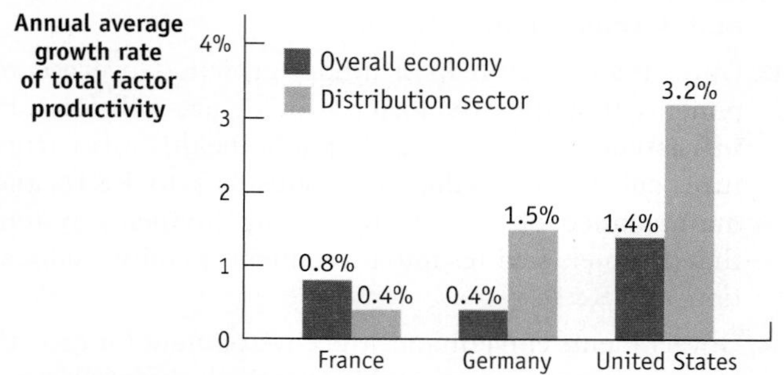

Source: Bart Van Ark, "Productivity, Sources of Growth and Potential Output in the Euro Area and the United States," *Intereconomics* 45, no. 1 (2010). Brussels: Center for European Policy Studies.

Why did productivity surge in retailing in the United States? "The reason can be explained in just two syllables: Walmart," wrote McKinsey.

Walmart is famed in the business world for its successful focus on the unglamorous but crucial area of *logistics*: getting stuff where it was needed, when it was needed. Walmart was one of the first companies to use computers to track inventory, to use bar-code scanners, to establish direct electronic links with suppliers, and so on. These practices gave it a huge advantage over competitors, leading to high profits and rapid expansion. Other firms, observing Walmart's success, have emulated its business practices, spreading productivity gains through the economy as a whole.

There are two lessons from the "Walmart effect," as McKinsey calls it. One is that how you apply a technology makes all the difference: everyone in the retail business knew about computers, but Walmart figured out what to do with them. The other is that a lot of economic growth comes from everyday improvements rather than flashy new technologies.

Questions for Thought

1. In this section we described several sources of productivity growth. Which of these sources corresponds to the "Walmart effect"?
2. How does the Walmart story relate to the "information technology paradox"?

SECTION 17 REVIEW

Summary

Sources of Long-Run Economic Growth

1. Growth is measured as changes in real GDP per capita in order to eliminate the effects of changes in the price level and changes in population size.
2. Levels of real GDP per capita vary greatly around the world: more than half of the world's population lives in countries that are still poorer than the United States was in 1900. Over the course of the twentieth century, real GDP per capita in the United States increased more than fivefold.
3. Growth rates of real GDP per capita also vary widely. According to the **Rule of 70,** the number of years it takes for real GDP per capita to double is equal to 70 divided by the annual growth rate of real GDP per capita.
4. The key to long-run economic growth is rising **labor productivity,** or just **productivity,** which is output per worker. Increases in productivity arise from increases in **physical capital** per worker and **human capital** per worker as well as **technological progress.**

Productivity and Growth

5. The **aggregate production function** shows how real GDP per worker depends on these three factors. Other things equal, there are **diminishing returns to physical capital:** holding human capital per worker and technology fixed, each successive addition to physical capital per worker yields a smaller increase in productivity than the one before. Equivalently, more physical capital per worker results in a lower, but still positive, increase in productivity.
6. **Growth accounting,** which estimates the contribution of each factor to a country's economic growth, has shown that rising **total factor productivity,** the amount of output produced from a given amount of factor inputs, is key to long-run growth. It is usually interpreted as the effect of technological progress.
7. In contrast to earlier times, natural resources are a less significant source of productivity growth in most countries today.
8. Economists generally believe that environmental issues pose a greater challenge to **sustainable long-run economic growth** than does natural resource scarcity.
9. The emission of greenhouse gases is clearly linked to growth, and limiting them will require some reduction in growth. However, the best available estimates suggest that a large reduction in emissions would require only a modest reduction in the growth rate.
10. There is broad consensus that government action to address climate change and greenhouse gases should be in the form of market-based incentives, like a carbon tax or a cap and trade system. It will also require rich and poor countries to come to some agreement on how the cost of emissions reductions will be shared.

Long-Run Growth Policy

11. The large differences in countries' growth rates are largely due to differences in their rates of accumulation of physical and human capital as well as differences in technological progress. Although inflows of foreign savings from abroad help, a prime factor is differences in domestic savings and investment spending rates, since most countries that have high investment spending in physical capital finance it by high domestic savings.
12. Technological progress is largely a result of **research and development,** or **R&D.**
13. Governments can help or hinder growth. Government policies that directly foster growth are subsidies to **infrastructure,** particularly public health infrastructure, subsidies to education, subsidies to R&D, and maintenance of a well-functioning financial system that channels savings into investment spending, education, and R&D.
14. Governments can enhance the environment for growth by protecting property rights (particularly intellectual property rights through patents), by being politically stable, and by providing good governance. Poor governance includes corruption and excessive government intervention.
15. The world economy contains examples of success and failure in the effort to achieve long-run economic growth. East Asian economies have done many things right and achieved very high growth rates. The low growth rates of Latin American and African economies over many years led economists to believe that the **convergence hypothesis,** the claim that differences in real GDP per capita across countries narrow over time, fits the data only when factors that affect growth, such as education, infrastructure, and favorable government policies and institutions, are held equal across countries. In recent years, there has been an uptick in growth among some Latin American and sub-Saharan African countries, largely due to a boom in commodity exports.

Key Terms

Rule of 70, p. 546
Labor productivity, p. 548
Productivity, p. 548
Physical capital, p. 548
Human capital, p. 549
Technological progress, p. 549
Aggregate production function, p. 551
Diminishing returns to physical capital, p. 551
Growth accounting, p. 553
Total factor productivity, p. 553
Sustainable long-run economic growth, p. 556
Research and development (R&D), p. 563
Infrastructure, p. 563
Convergence hypothesis, p. 567

Problems

1. The accompanying table shows data from the Penn World Table, Version 7.1, for real GDP per capita in 2005 U.S. dollars for Argentina, Ghana, South Korea, and the United States for 1960, 1970, 1980, 1990, 2000, and 2010.

	Argentina			Ghana			South Korea			United States		
Year	Real GDP per capita (2005 dollars)	Percentage of 1960 real GDP per capita	Percentage of 2010 real GDP per capita	Real GDP per capita (2005 dollars)	Percentage of 1960 real GDP per capita	Percentage of 2010 real GDP per capita	Real GDP per capita (2005 dollars)	Percentage of 1960 real GDP per capita	Percentage of 2010 real GDP per capita	Real GDP per capita (2005 dollars)	Percentage of 1960 real GDP per capita	Percentage of 2010 real GDP per capita
1960	$6,043	?	?	$1,286	?	?	$1,656	?	?	$15,398	?	?
1970	7,617	?	?	1,525	?	?	2,808	?	?	20,436	?	?
1980	8,496	?	?	1,295	?	?	5,179	?	?	24,952	?	?
1990	6,928	?	?	1,273	?	?	11,643	?	?	31,389	?	?
2000	8,909	?	?	1,478	?	?	18,729	?	?	36,669	?	?
2010	12,340	?	?	2,094	?	?	26,609	?	?	41,365	?	?

a. Complete the table by expressing each year's real GDP per capita as a percentage of its 1960 and 2010 levels.

b. How does the growth in living standards from 1960 to 2010 compare across these four nations? What might account for these differences?

2. The accompanying table shows the average annual growth rate in real GDP per capita for Argentina, Ghana, and South Korea using data from the Penn World Table, Version 7.1, for the past few decades.

	Average annual growth rate of real GDP per capita		
Years	Argentina	Ghana	South Korea
1960–1970	3.01%	2.08%	4.82%
1970–1980	1.21	0.68	6.35
1980–1990	−1.61	−0.47	7.19
1990–2000	2.41	1.49	5.51
2000–2010	2.97	3.66	4.00

a. For each decade and for each country, use the Rule of 70 where possible to calculate how long it would take for that country's real GDP per capita to double.

b. Suppose that the average annual growth rate that each country achieved over the period 2000–2010 continues indefinitely into the future. Starting from 2010, use the Rule of 70 to calculate the year in which a country will have doubled its real GDP per capita.

3. The accompanying table provides approximate statistics on per capita income levels and growth rates for regions defined by income levels. According to the Rule of 70, starting in 2010 the high-income countries are projected to double their per capita GDP in approximately 78 years, in 2088. Throughout this question, assume constant growth rates for each of the regions that are equal to their average value between 2000 and 2010.

Region	GDP per capita (2010)	Average annual growth rate of real GDP per capita (2000–2010)
High-income countries	$38,293	0.9%
Middle-income countries	3,980	4.8
Low-income countries	507	3.0

Source: World Bank.

a. Calculate the ratio of per capita GDP in 2010 of the following:
   i. Middle-income to high-income countries
   ii. Low-income to high-income countries
   iii. Low-income to middle-income countries

b. Calculate the number of years it will take the low-income and middle-income countries to double their per capita GDP.

c. Calculate the per capita GDP of each of the regions in 2088. (*Hint:* How many times does their per capita GDP double in 78 years, the number of years from 2010 to 2088?)

d. Repeat part a with the projected per capita GDP in 2088.

e. Compare your answers to parts a and d. Comment on the change in economic inequality between the regions.

4. You are hired as an economic consultant to the countries of Albernia and Brittania. Each country's current relationship between physical capital per worker and output per worker is given by the curve labeled "Productivity$_1$" in the accompanying diagram. Albernia is at point *A* and Brittania is at point *B*.

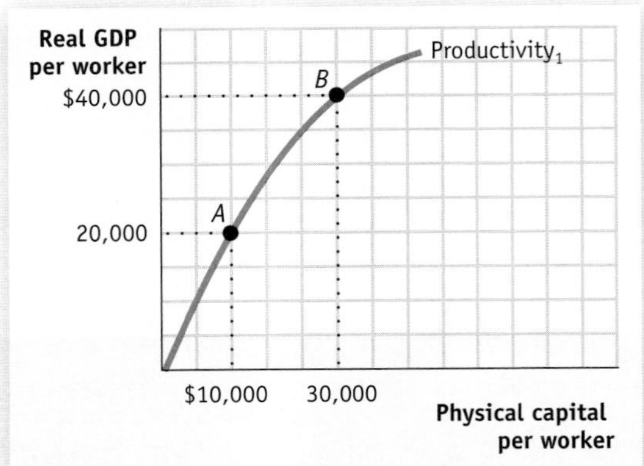

a. In the relationship depicted by the curve Productivity$_1$, what factors are held fixed? Do these countries experience diminishing returns to physical capital per worker?

b. Assuming that the amount of human capital per worker and the technology are held fixed in each country, can you recommend a policy to generate a doubling of real GDP per capita in Albernia?

c. How would your policy recommendation change if the amount of human capital per worker could be changed? Assume that an increase in human capital doubles the output per worker when physical capital per worker equals $10,000. Draw a curve on the diagram that represents this policy for Albernia.

5. The country of Androde is currently using Method 1 for its production function. By chance, scientists stumble onto a technological breakthrough that will enhance Androde's productivity. This technological breakthrough is reflected in another production function, Method 2. The accompanying table shows combinations of physical capital per worker and output per worker for both methods, assuming that human capital per worker is fixed.

Method 1		Method 2	
Physical capital per worker	Real GDP per worker	Physical capital per worker	Real GDP per worker
0	0.00	0	0.00
50	35.36	50	70.71
100	50.00	100	100.00
150	61.24	150	122.47
200	70.71	200	141.42
250	79.06	250	158.11
300	86.60	300	173.21
350	93.54	350	187.08
400	100.00	400	200.00
450	106.07	450	212.13
500	111.80	500	223.61

a. Using the data in the accompanying table, draw the two production functions in one diagram. Androde's current amount of physical capital per worker is 100. In your figure, label that point *A*.

b. Starting from point *A*, over a period of 70 years, the amount of physical capital per worker in Androde rises to 400. Assuming Androde still uses Method 1, in your diagram, label the resulting point of production *B*. Using the Rule of 70, calculate by how many percent per year output per worker has grown.

c. Now assume that, starting from point *A*, over the same period of 70 years, the amount of physical capital per worker in Androde rises to 400, but that during that time period, Androde switches to Method 2. In your diagram, label the resulting point of production *C*. Using the Rule of 70, calculate by how many percent per year output per worker has grown now.

d. As the economy of Androde moves from point *A* to point *C*, what share of the annual productivity growth is due to higher total factor productivity?

6. The Bureau of Labor Statistics regularly releases the "Productivity and Costs" report for the previous month. Go to www.bls.gov and find the latest report. (On the Bureau of Labor Statistics home page, from the tab "Subject Areas," look under the head titled "Productivity," and select the link to "Labor Productivity & Costs"; then, from the heading "LPC News Releases," find the most recent "Productivity and Costs" report.) What was the percent change in nonfarm business sector labor productivity for the previous quarter? How does the percent change in that quarter's productivity compare to data from the previous quarter?

7. What roles do physical capital, human capital, technology, and natural resources play in influencing long-run economic growth of aggregate output per capita?

8. How have U.S. policies and institutions influenced the country's long-run economic growth?

9. Over the next 100 years, real GDP per capita in Groland is expected to grow at an average annual rate of 2.0%. In Sloland, however, growth is expected to be somewhat slower, at an average annual growth rate of 1.5%. If both countries have a real GDP per capita today of $20,000, how will their real GDP per capita differ in 100 years? [*Hint:* A country that has a real GDP today of $$x$ and grows at y% per year will achieve a real GDP of $$x \times (1 + (y/100))^z$ in z years. We assume that $0 \leq y < 10$.]

10. The accompanying table shows data from the Penn World Table, Version 7.1, for real GDP per capita (2005 U.S. dollars) in France, Japan, the United Kingdom, and the United States in 1950 and 2010. Complete the table. Have these countries converged economically?

Country	1950		2010	
	Real GDP per capita (2005 dollars)	Percentage of U.S. real GDP per capita	Real GDP per capita (2005 dollars)	Percentage of U.S. real GDP per capita
France	$7,084	?	$31,299	?
Japan	2,787	?	31,447	?
United Kingdom	8,988	?	34,268	?
United States	13,069	?	41,365	?

11. The accompanying table shows data from the Penn World Table, Version 7.1, for real GDP per capita (2005 U.S. dollars) for Argentina, Ghana, South Korea, and the United States in 1960 and 2010. Complete the table. Have these countries converged economically?

Country	1960		2010	
	Real GDP per capita (2005 dollars)	Percentage of U.S. real GDP per capita	Real GDP per capita (2005 dollars)	Percentage of U.S. real GDP per capita
Argentina	$6,043	?	$12,340	?
Ghana	1,286	?	2,094	?
South Korea	1,656	?	26,609	?
United States	15,398	?	41,365	?

12. Why would you expect real GDP per capita in California and Pennsylvania to exhibit convergence but not in California and Baja California, a state of Mexico that borders the United States? What changes would allow California and Baja California to converge?

13. According to the *World Factbook*, published by the U.S. Central Intelligence Agency, the proven oil reserves existing in the world in 2012 consisted of 1,532 billion barrels. In that year, the U.S. Energy Information Administration reported that the world oil production was 88.97 million barrels a day.

a. At this rate, for how many years will the proven oil reserves last? Discuss the Malthusian view in the context of the number you just calculated.

b. In order to do the calculations in part a, what did you assume about the total quantity of oil reserves over time? About oil prices over time? Are these assumptions consistent with the Malthusian view on resource limits?

c. Discuss how market forces may affect the amount of time the proven oil reserves will last, assuming that no new oil reserves are discovered and that the demand curve for oil remains unchanged.

14. The accompanying table shows the annual growth rate for the years 2000–2009 in per capita emissions of carbon dioxide (CO_2) and the annual growth rate in real GDP per capita for selected countries.

Country	2000–2009 average annual growth rate of:	
	Real GDP per capita	CO_2 emissions per capita
Argentina	2.81%	1.01%
Bangladesh	4.17	5.47
Canada	0.68	−1.46
China	9.85	11.11
Germany	0.59	−1.23
Ireland	1.05	−2.10
Japan	0.29	−1.03
South Korea	3.48	1.68
Mexico	0.18	0.44
Nigeria	6.07	−2.46
Russia	5.22	0.52
South Africa	2.39	0.80
United Kingdom	0.88	−1.35
United States	0.58	−1.78

Sources: Energy Information Administration; International Monetary Fund.

a. Rank the countries in terms of their growth in CO_2 emissions, from highest to lowest. What five countries have the highest growth rate in emissions? What five countries have the lowest growth rate in emissions?

b. Now rank the countries in terms of their growth in real GDP per capita, from highest to lowest. What five countries have the highest growth rate? What five countries have the lowest growth rate?

c. Would you infer from your results that CO_2 emissions are linked to growth in output per capita?

d. Do high growth rates necessarily lead to high CO_2 emissions?

500
200
COMMON STOCK

Savings, Investment Spending, and the Financial System

FUNDS FOR FACEBOOK

"Facebook Is Hunting For More Money"—so read a headline in *Business Week*, which reported that the social networking site was seeking to secure a $100 million credit line. Why would a wildly successful business like Facebook need to borrow money?

Everyone knows Facebook. Founded in 2004, it has gone on to become arguably the biggest business success story of the twenty-first century—so far. Currently, Facebook has more than a billion users worldwide. How did Facebook grow so big, so fast?

In large part, of course, the answer is that the company had a good idea. Personalized web pages providing information to friends turned out to be something many people really wanted. Equally important, since advertisers wanted access to the readers of those pages, Facebook could make a lot of money selling advertising space.

But having a good idea isn't enough to build a business. Entrepreneurs need funds: you have to spend money to make money. Although businesses like Facebook seem to exist solely in the virtual world of cyberspace, free of the worldly burdens of brick-and-mortar establishments, the truth is that running such businesses requires a lot of very real and expensive hardware. Like Google, Yahoo!, and other Internet giants, Facebook maintains huge "server farms," arrays of linked computers that track and process all the information needed to provide the user experience.

So where did Facebook get the money to equip these server farms? Some of it came from investors who acquired shares in the business, but much of it was borrowed. As Facebook grew bigger, so did the amount it borrowed.

The ability of Facebook to raise large sums of money to finance its growth is, in its own way, as remarkable as the company's product. In effect, some young guy with a bright idea is able to lay his hands on hundreds of millions of dollars to build his business. It's an amazing story.

Yet this sort of thing is common in modern economies. The long-run growth we analyzed in the previous section depends crucially on a set of markets and institutions, collectively known as the *financial system,* that channels the funds of savers into productive investment spending. Without this system, businesses like Facebook would not be able to purchase the physical capital that is an important source of productivity growth. And savers would be forced to accept a lower return on their funds.

Historically, financial systems channeled funds into investment spending projects such as railroads and factories. Today, financial systems channel funds into new sources of growth such as green technology, social media, and investments in human capital. Without a well-functioning financial system, a country will suffer stunted economic growth.

In this section, we begin by focusing on the economy as a whole. We examine the relationship between savings and investment spending. Next, we look at the financial system to see how savings is transformed into investment spending, as well as the role that time plays in financial decision making. We'll also look at how the financial system works to increase the welfare of savers with funds to invest as well as those with investment spending projects to finance.

Savings and Investment Spending

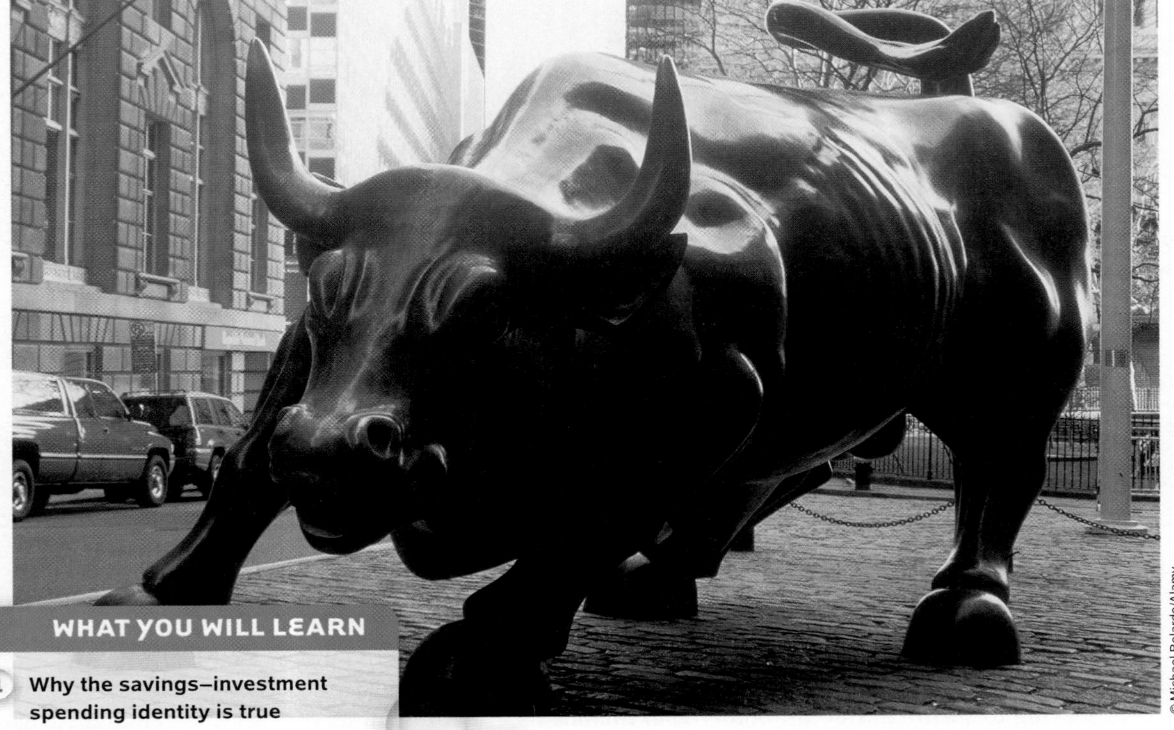
© Michael Belardo/Alamy

WHAT YOU WILL LEARN

1. Why the savings–investment spending identity is true
2. The relationship between savings and investment

Matching Up Savings and Investment Spending

We learned in the previous section that two of the essential ingredients in economic growth are increases in the economy's levels of *human capital* and *physical capital.* Human capital is largely provided by governments through public education. But physical capital, with the exception of infrastructure, is mainly created through private investment spending—that is, spending by firms rather than by the government.

Who pays for private investment spending? In some cases it's the people or corporations that actually do the spending—for example, a family that owns a business might use its own savings to buy new equipment, or a corporation might reinvest some of its profits to build a new factory. In the modern economy, however, individuals and firms that create physical capital often do it with other people's money—money that they borrow or raise by selling stock.

To understand how investment spending is financed, we need to look first at how savings and investment spending are related for the economy as a whole.

The Savings–Investment Spending Identity

According to the **savings–investment spending identity,** savings and investment spending are always equal for the economy as a whole.

The most basic point to understand about savings and investment spending is that they are always equal. This is not a theory; it's a fact of accounting called the **savings–investment spending identity.**

To see why the savings–investment spending identity must be true, let's look again at the national income accounting that we learned about earlier. Recall that GDP is equal to total spending on domestically produced final goods and services, and that we can write the following equation:

(56-1) $\text{GDP} = C + I + G + X - IM$

where C is spending by consumers, I is investment spending, G is government purchases of goods and services, X is the value of exports to other countries, and IM is spending on imports from other countries.

THE SAVINGS–INVESTMENT SPENDING IDENTITY IN A CLOSED ECONOMY In a closed economy, there are no exports or imports. So $X = 0$ and $IM = 0$, which makes Equation 56-1 simpler. As we learned, the overall income of this simplified economy would, by definition, equal total spending. Why?

Recall that one person's spending is another person's income: the only way people can earn income is by selling something to someone else, and every dollar spent in the economy creates income for somebody. This is represented by Equation 56-2: on the left, GDP represents total income earned in the economy, and on the right, $C + I + G$ represents total spending in the economy:

(56-2) $\text{GDP} = C + I + G$

Total income = Total spending

Now, what can be done with income? It can either be spent on consumption—consumer spending (C) plus government purchases of goods and service (G)—or saved (S). So it must be true that:

(56-3) $\text{GDP} = C + G + S$

Total income = Consumption spending + Savings

where S is savings. Meanwhile, as Equation 56-2 tells us, total spending consists of either consumption spending ($C + G$) or investment spending (I):

(56-4) $\text{GDP} = C + G + I$

Total income = Consumption spending + Investment spending

Putting Equations 56-3 and 56-4 together, we get:

(56-5) $C + G + S = C + G + I$

Consumption spending + Savings = Consumption Spending + Investment spending

Subtract consumption spending ($C + G$) from both sides, and we get:

(56-6) $S = I$

Savings = Investment spending

As we said, then, it's a basic accounting fact that savings equals investment spending for the economy as a whole.

Now, let's take a closer look at savings. Households are not the only parties that can save in an economy. In any given year, the government can save, too, if it collects more tax revenue than it spends. When this occurs, the difference is called a **budget surplus** and is equivalent to savings by the government.

If, alternatively, government spending exceeds tax revenue, there is a **budget deficit**—a negative budget surplus. In this case, we often say that the government is "dis-saving": by spending more than its tax revenues, the government is engaged in the opposite of savings.

We'll define the term **budget balance** to refer to both cases, with the understanding that the budget balance can be positive (a budget surplus) or negative (a budget deficit). The budget balance is defined as:

(56-7) $S_{Government} = T - G - TR$

Where T is the value of tax revenues and TR is the value of government transfers. The budget balance is equivalent to savings by government—if it's positive, the government

The **budget surplus** is the difference between tax revenue and government spending when tax revenue exceeds government spending.

The **budget deficit** is the difference between tax revenue and government spending when government spending exceeds tax revenue.

The **budget balance** is the difference between tax revenue and government spending.

National savings, the sum of private savings and the budget balance, is the total amount of savings generated within the economy.

Net capital inflow is the total inflow of funds into a country minus the total outflow of funds out of a country.

is saving; if it's negative, the government is dissaving. **National savings,** which we just called savings for short, is equal to the sum of the budget balance and private savings, where private savings is disposable income (income after taxes) minus consumption. It is given by:

$$\textbf{(56-8)} \quad S_{National} = S_{Government} + S_{Private}$$

So Equations 56-6 and 56-8 tell us that, in a closed economy, the savings–investment spending identity has the following form:

$$\textbf{(56-9)} \quad S_{National} = I$$

National savings = Investment spending

THE SAVINGS–INVESTMENT SPENDING IDENTITY IN AN OPEN ECONOMY An open economy is an economy in which goods and money can flow into and out of the country. This changes the savings–investment spending identity because savings need not be spent on investment spending projects in the same country in which the savings are generated. That's because the savings of people who live in any one country can be used to finance investment spending that takes place in other countries.

So any given country can receive *inflows* of funds—foreign savings that finance investment spending in that country. Any given country can also generate *outflows* of funds—domestic savings that finance investment spending in another country.

The net effect of international inflows and outflows of funds on the total savings available for investment spending in any given country is known as the **net capital inflow** into that country, equal to the total inflow of foreign funds minus the total outflow of domestic funds to other countries. Like the budget balance, a net capital inflow can be negative—that is, more capital can flow out of a country than flows into it.

Media Bakery

In recent years, the United States has experienced a consistent positive net capital inflow.

In recent years, the United States has experienced a consistent positive net capital inflow from foreigners, who view our economy as an attractive place to put their savings. In 2012, for example, net capital inflows into the United States were $432 billion.

It's important to note that, from a national perspective, a dollar generated by national savings and a dollar generated by capital inflow are not equivalent. Yes, they can both finance the same dollar's worth of investment spending. But any dollar borrowed from a saver must eventually be repaid with interest.

A dollar that comes from national savings is repaid with interest to someone domestically—either a private party or the government. But a dollar that comes as capital inflow must be repaid with interest to a foreigner. So a dollar of investment spending financed by a capital inflow comes at a higher *national* cost—the interest that must eventually be paid to a foreigner—than a dollar of investment spending financed by national savings.

The fact that a net capital inflow represents funds borrowed from foreigners is an important aspect of the savings–investment spending identity in an open economy. Consider an individual who spends more than his or her income; that person must borrow the difference from others.

Similarly, a country that spends more on imports than it earns from exports must borrow the difference from foreigners. And that difference, the amount of funds borrowed from foreigners, is the country's net capital inflow. This means that the net capital inflow into a country is equal to the difference between imports and exports:

$$\textbf{(56-10)} \quad NCI = IM - X$$

Net capital inflow = Imports – Exports

Re-arranging Equation 56-1 we get:

$$\textbf{(56-11)} \quad I = (\text{GDP} - C - G) + (IM - X)$$

Using Equations 56-3 and 56-9 we know that GDP – C – G is equal to national savings, so that:

$$\textbf{(56-12)}\ I = S_{National} + (IM - X) = S_{National} + NCI$$
$$\text{Investment spending} = \text{National savings} + \text{Net capital inflow}$$

So the application of the savings–investment spending identity to an economy that is open to inflows or outflows of capital means that investment spending is equal to savings, where savings is equal to national savings *plus* net capital inflow. That is, in an economy with a positive net capital inflow, some investment spending is funded by the savings of foreigners. And in an economy with a negative net capital inflow (that is, more capital is flowing out than flowing in), some portion of national savings is funding investment spending in other countries.

In the United States in 2012, investment spending totaled \$2,475 billion. Private savings totaled \$3,015 billion, offset by a government budget deficit of \$1,087 billion and supplemented by a net capital inflow of \$432 billion. Notice that these numbers don't quite add up; because data collection isn't perfect, there is a "statistical discrepancy" of \$115 billion. But we know that this is an error in the data, not in the theory, because the savings–investment spending identity must hold in reality.

It's also worth noting that 2012 was not a normal year. As we have pointed out previously, in 2008 the U.S. economy (along with the economies of many other nations) was struck by a severe financial crisis. This crisis led both to a plunge in investment spending and to large government budget deficits, effects that have continued. By using data from 2007, the last year before the crisis, we get a much better picture of what savings and investment look like in more normal times.

Figure 56-1 shows what the savings–investment spending identity looked like in 2007 for two of the world's largest economies at the time, those of the United States and Japan. To make the two economies easier to compare, we've measured savings and investment spending as percentages of GDP.

FIGURE 56-1

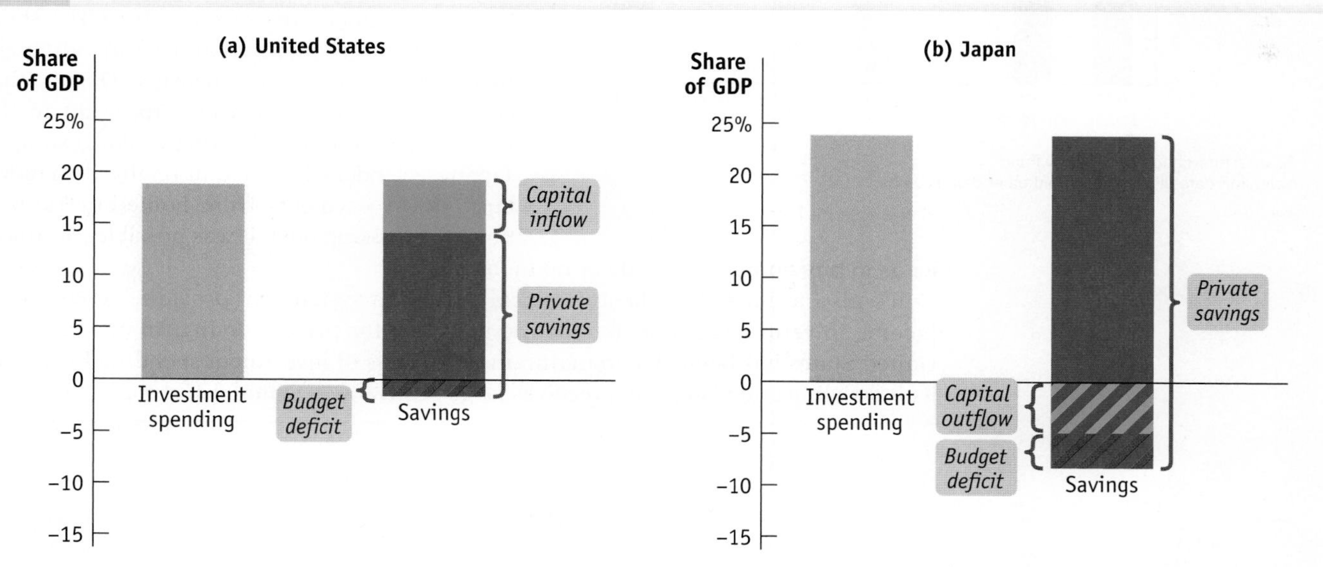

U.S. investment spending in 2007 (equal to 18.8% of GDP) was financed by a combination of private savings (15.7% of GDP) and a capital inflow (5.2% of GDP), which was partially offset by a government budget deficit (–1.6% of GDP). Japanese investment spending in 2007 was higher as a percentage of GDP (23.8%). It was financed by a higher level of private savings as a percentage of GDP (32.1%), which was offset by both a capital outflow (–4.9% of GDP) and a relatively high government budget deficit (–3.4% of GDP).
Source: Bureau of Economic Analysis; OECD.

In each panel the orange bars on the left show total investment spending and the multicolored bars on the right show the components of savings. U.S. investment spending was 18.8% of GDP, financed by a combination of private savings (15.7% of GDP) and positive net capital inflow or capital inflow (5.2% of GDP) and partly offset by a government budget deficit (–1.6% of GDP). (These numbers sum to more than 18.8% due to statistical discrepancy.)

Japanese investment spending was higher as a percentage of GDP, at 23.8%. It was financed by a higher level of private savings as a percentage of GDP (32.1%) and was offset by both a negative net capital inflow or capital outflow (–4.9% of GDP) and a budget deficit (–3.4% of GDP).

The economy's savings finance its investment spending. But how are these funds that are available for investment spending allocated among various projects? That is, what determines which projects get financed (such as Facebook's server farms) and which don't? We'll see shortly that funds get allocated to investment spending projects using a familiar method: by the market, via supply and demand.

ECONOMICS IN ACTION WORLD VIEW

AMERICA'S LOW SAVINGS

Figure 56-2 shows national savings as a percentage of GDP for seven wealthy economies in 2007. (Again, we focus on 2007 as the last pre-crisis year). The United States had the lowest savings rate, although the United Kingdom's savings were only slightly higher.

FIGURE 56-2

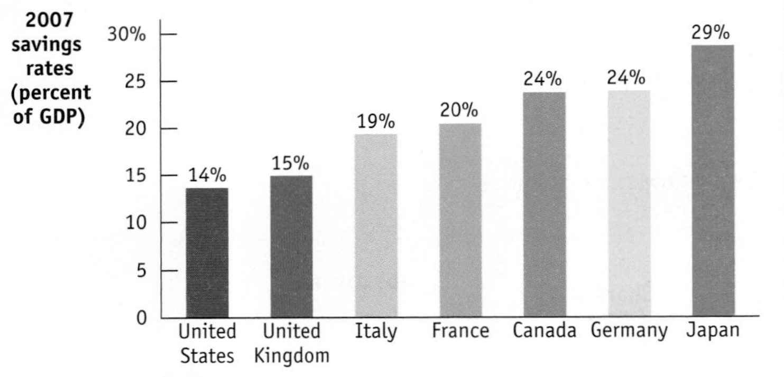

Source: International Monetary Fund.
Note: IMF data differ slightly from other data sources.

In this respect, 2007 wasn't unusual. The United States has had consistently low national savings compared with other wealthy countries since the 1980s. The main source of these international differences in national savings lies in low U.S. private savings rather than in large U.S. government budget deficits.

Why do Americans save so little? The short answer is that economists aren't sure, although there are a number of theories. One is that consumers have easier access to credit in the United States than elsewhere. For example, Japanese lenders have traditionally demanded large down payments from home-buyers; but, until the housing bust, it was possible for Americans to buy homes with little or no money down.

It's also argued that the U.S. Social Security system, by providing guaranteed income in retirement, may reduce the incentive for private saving. In any case, the United States has been able to maintain high levels of investment spending in spite of its low savings rate because it receives large positive net capital inflows.

MODULE 56 Review

Solutions appear at the back of the book.

Check Your Understanding

1. Explain whether each of the following statements is true or false for an open economy.
   a. If the budget balance has a value of zero, then private savings must be equal to investment spending.
   b. If net capital inflow is positive, then national savings must be less than investment spending.

2. Given the values in the table, find the values for investment spending, national savings, tax revenues, net capital inflow, and private savings.

	Billions of dollars
GDP	$15,851
Consumption	11,254
Government spending	3,049
Exports	2,185
Imports	2,718
Budget balance	−1,227

Multiple-Choice Questions

1. The difference between tax revenue and government spending is equal to
   a. the budget balance.
   b. national savings.
   c. net exports.
   d. the trade balance.
   e. investment spending.

2. If government savings is positive, then
   a. tax revenues exceed government spending.
   b. net exports must be positive.
   c. national savings must be greater than investment spending.
   d. there is a trade surplus.
   e. the budget balance is negative.

3. In an open economy
   a. national savings is equal to investment spending.
   b. national savings is equal to net capital inflow.
   c. net capital inflow is equal to investment spending.
   d. there is a budget deficit.
   e. investment spending is equal to national savings plus net capital inflow.

4. If national savings is less than investment spending, then
   a. net capital inflow is positive.
   b. net capital inflow is negative.
   c. there is a budget deficit.
   d. there is a budget surplus.
   e. there is a trade surplus.

5. The federal government is said to be "dissaving" when
   a. there is a budget deficit.
   b. there is a budget surplus.
   c. there is no budget surplus or deficit.
   d. savings does not equal investment spending.
   e. national savings equals private savings.

Critical-Thinking Question

Identify and describe the relationship between national savings, investment spending, and net capital inflow in an open economy.

PITFALLS

INVESTMENT VS. INVESTMENT SPENDING

? What is the difference between investment and investment spending?

> WHEN ECONOMISTS USE THE TERM *INVESTMENT SPENDING*, THEY ALMOST ALWAYS MEAN "SPENDING ON NEW PHYSICAL CAPITAL." This can be confusing, because in ordinary life we often say that someone who buys stocks or purchases an existing building is "investing." The important point to keep in mind is that only spending that adds to the economy's stock of physical capital is "investment spending." In contrast, the act of purchasing an asset such as a share of stock, a bond, or existing real estate is "making an investment."

To learn more, see pages 578–579.

MODULE 57

The Market for Loanable Funds

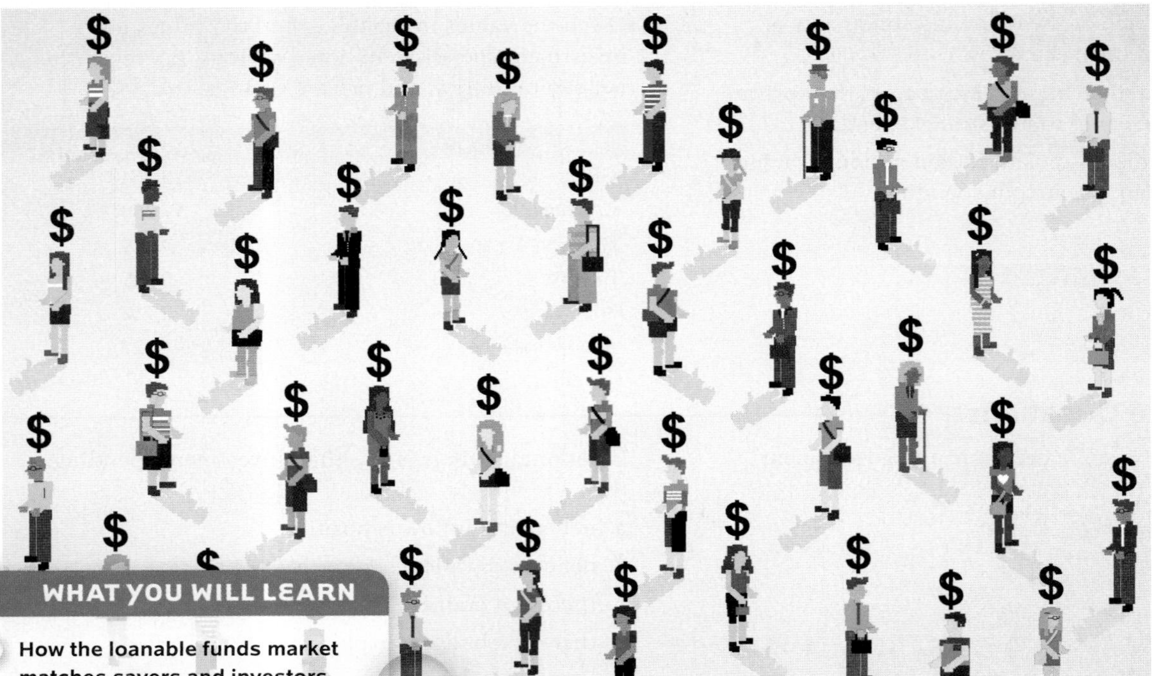
Shutterstock

WHAT YOU WILL LEARN

1. How the loanable funds market matches savers and investors
2. The determinants of supply and demand in the loanable funds market
3. How changes in the expected future inflation rate affect the nominal interest rate

The Role of the Loanable Funds Market

For the economy as a whole, savings always equals investment spending. In a closed economy, savings is equal to national savings. In an open economy, savings is equal to national savings plus capital inflow. At any given time, however, savers, the people with funds to lend, are usually not the same as borrowers, the people who want to borrow to finance their investment spending. How are savers and borrowers brought together?

Savers and borrowers are matched up with one another in much the same way producers and consumers are matched up: through markets governed by supply and demand. In Figure 46-2, the expanded circular-flow diagram on page 479, we noted that the *financial markets* channel the savings of households to businesses that want to borrow in order to purchase capital equipment. It's now time to take a look at how those financial markets work.

Although there are a large number of different financial markets in the financial system, such as the bond market and the stock market, economists often work with a simplified model in which they assume that there is just one market. The market brings together those who want to lend money (savers) and those who want to borrow (firms with investment spending projects). This hypothetical market is known as the **loanable funds market.**

The price that is determined in the loanable funds market is the interest rate, denoted by r. As we've learned, loans typically specify a nominal interest rate. So although we call r "the interest rate," it is with the understanding that r is a nominal interest rate—an interest rate that is unadjusted for inflation.

The **loanable funds market** is a hypothetical market that illustrates the market outcome of the demand for funds generated by borrowers and the supply of funds provided by lenders.

In the interest of simplicity we are also going to assume that there is only one type of loan. This, despite the fact that in reality there are many different kinds of interest rates because there are many different kinds of loans—short-term loans, long-term loans, loans made to corporate borrowers, loans made to governments, and so on.

Now we're ready to analyze how savings and investment get matched up.

The Demand for Loanable Funds

Figure 57-1 illustrates a hypothetical demand curve for loanable funds, *D*, which slopes downward. On the horizontal axis we show the quantity of loanable funds demanded. On the vertical axis we show the interest rate, which is the "price" of borrowing. But why does the demand curve for loanable funds slope downward?

To answer this question, consider what a firm is doing when it engages in investment spending—say, by buying new equipment. Investment spending means laying out money right now, expecting that this outlay will lead to higher profits at some point in the future. In fact, however, the promise of a dollar five or ten years from now is worth less than an actual dollar right now.

So an investment is worth making only if it generates a future return that is *greater* than the monetary cost of making the investment today. How much greater? To answer that, we need to take into account the *present value* of the future return the firm expects to get.

We will look at the concept of present value in more detail in the next module. For now, keep in mind that in present value calculations, we use the interest rate to determine how the value of a dollar in the future compares to the value of a dollar today. But the fact is that future dollars are worth less than a dollar today, and they are worth even less when the interest rate is higher.

The intuition behind present value calculations is simple. The interest rate measures the opportunity cost of investment spending that results in a future return: instead of spending money on an investment spending project, a company could simply put the money into the bank and earn interest on it. And the higher the interest rate, the more attractive it is to simply put money into the bank instead of investing it in an investment spending project. In other words, the higher the interest rate, the higher the opportunity cost of investment spending. And, the higher the opportunity cost of investment spending, the lower the number of investment spending projects firms want to carry out, and therefore the lower the quantity of loanable funds demanded. It is this insight that explains why the demand curve for loanable funds is downward sloping.

When firms invest in projects, they spend money today in return for an expected payoff in the future.

FIGURE 57-1 **The Demand for Loanable Funds**

The demand curve for loanable funds slopes downward: the lower the interest rate, the greater the quantity of loanable funds demanded. Here, reducing the interest rate from 12% to 4% increases the quantity of loanable funds demanded from $150 billion to $450 billion.

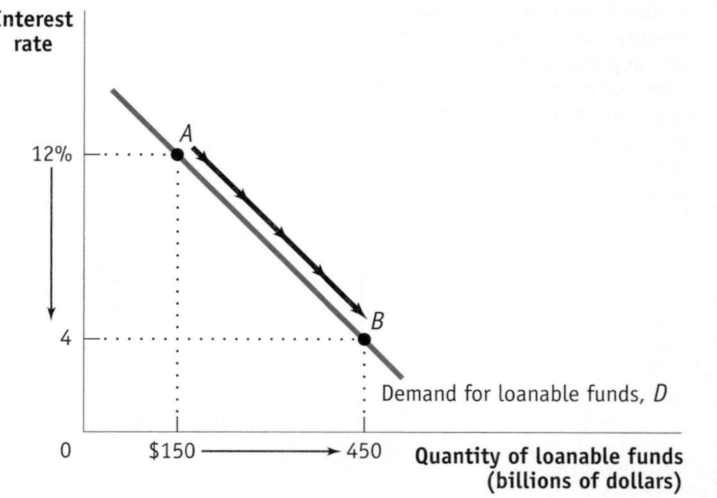

When businesses engage in investment spending, they spend money right now in return for an expected payoff in the future. So, to evaluate whether a particular investment spending project is worth undertaking, a business must compare the present value of the future payoff with the current cost of that project. If the present value of the future payoff is greater than the current cost, a project is profitable and worth investing in. If the interest rate falls, then the present value of any given project rises, so more projects pass that test. If the interest rate rises, then the present value of any given project falls, so fewer projects pass that test.

So total investment spending, and therefore the demand for loanable funds to finance that spending, is negatively related to the interest rate. Thus, the demand curve for loanable funds slopes downward. You can see this in Figure 57-1. When the interest rate falls from 12% to 4%, the quantity of loanable funds demanded rises from $150 billion (point *A*) to $450 billion (point *B*).

Savers supply loanable funds to businesses and incur an opportunity cost in doing so.

Hemera/Thinkstock

The Supply of Loanable Funds

Figure 57-2 shows a hypothetical supply curve for loanable funds, *S*. Again, the interest rate plays the same role that the price plays in ordinary supply and demand analysis. But why is this curve upward sloping?

The answer is that loanable funds are supplied by savers, and savers incur an opportunity cost when they lend to a business: the funds could instead be spent on consumption—say, a nice vacation. Whether a given saver becomes a lender by making funds available to borrowers depends on the interest rate received in return. By saving your money today and earning interest on it, you are rewarded with higher consumption in the future when the loan you made is repaid with interest.

So it is a good assumption that more people will forgo current consumption and make a loan to a borrower when the interest rate is higher. As a result, our hypothetical supply curve of loanable funds slopes upward. In Figure 57-2, lenders will supply $150 billion to the loanable funds market at an interest rate of 4% (point *X*); if the interest rate rises to 12%, the quantity of loanable funds supplied will rise to $450 billion (point *Y*).

FIGURE 57-2 The Supply of Loanable Funds

The supply curve for loanable funds slopes upward: the higher the interest rate, the greater the quantity of loanable funds supplied. Here, increasing the interest rate from 4% to 12% increases the quantity of loanable funds supplied from $150 billion to $450 billion.

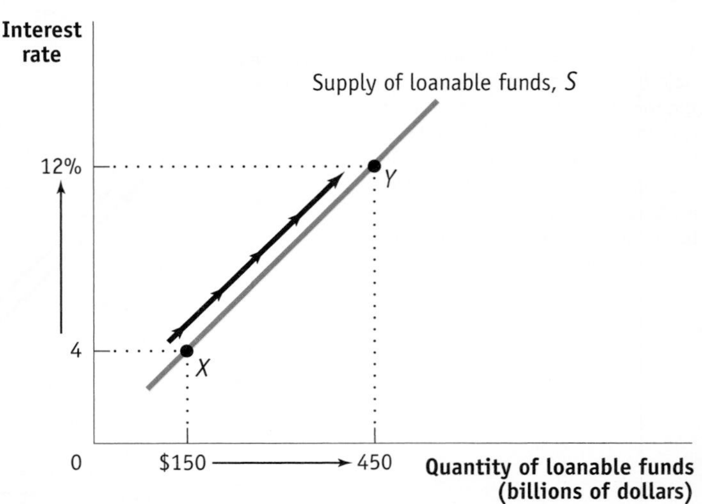

The Equilibrium Interest Rate

The interest rate at which the quantity of loanable funds supplied equals the quantity of loanable funds demanded is the *equilibrium interest rate*. As you can see in Figure 57-3, the equilibrium interest rate, r^*, and the total quantity of lending, Q^*, are determined by the intersection of the supply and demand curves, at point *E*. Here, the equilibrium interest rate is 8%, at which $300 billion is lent and borrowed. In this equilibrium, only investment spending projects that are profitable if the interest rate is 8% or higher are funded.

Projects that are profitable only when the interest rate falls below 8% are not funded. Correspondingly, only lenders who are willing to accept an interest rate of 8% or less will have their offers to lend funds accepted; lenders who demand an interest rate higher than 8% do not have their offers to lend accepted.

Figure 57-3 shows how the market for loanable funds matches up desired savings with desired investment spending: in equilibrium, the quantity of funds that savers want to lend is equal to the quantity of funds that firms want to borrow. The figure also shows that this match-up is efficient, in two senses. First, the right investments get made: the investment spending projects that are actually financed have higher payoffs (in terms of present value) than those that do not get financed. Second, the right people do the saving and lending: the savers who actually lend funds are willing to lend for lower interest rates than those who do not.

The insight that the loanable funds market leads to an efficient use of savings, although drawn from a highly simplified model, has important implications for real life: it is the reason that a well-functioning financial system increases an economy's long-run economic growth rate.

Let's look at how the market for loanable funds responds to shifts of demand and supply. As in the standard model of supply and demand, where the equilibrium price changes in response to shifts of the demand or supply curves, here the equilibrium interest rate changes when there are shifts of the demand curve for loanable funds, the supply curve for loanable funds, or both.

FIGURE 57-3 **Equilibrium in the Loanable Funds Market**

At the equilibrium interest rate, the quantity of loanable funds supplied equals the quantity of loanable funds demanded. Here, the equilibrium interest rate is 8%, with $300 billion of funds lent and borrowed. Lenders who demand an interest rate of 8% or lower have their offers of loans accepted; those who demand a higher interest rate do not. Projects that are profitable at an interest rate of 8% or higher are funded; those that are profitable only when the interest rate falls below 8% are not.

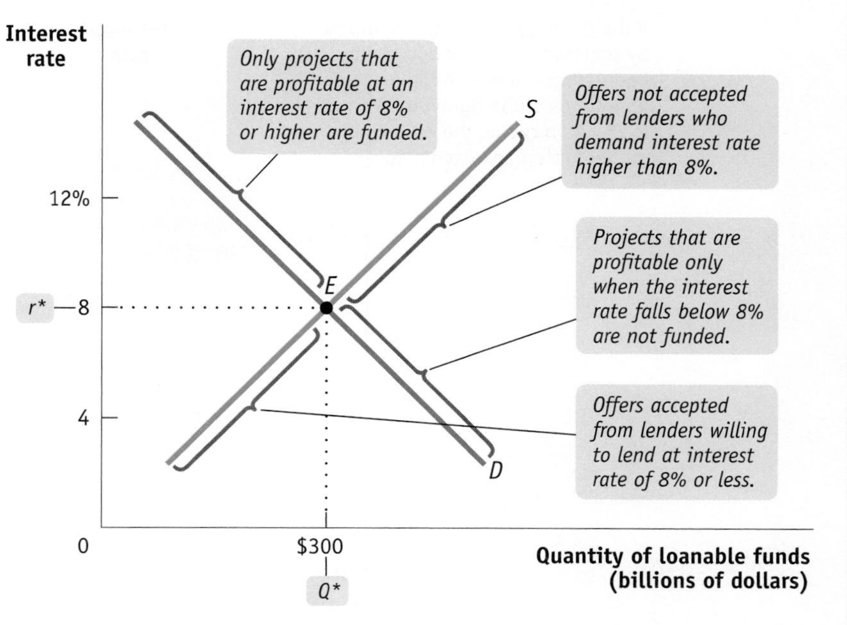
Interest rate
12%
r* —8
4
0
$300
Q*
Quantity of loanable funds (billions of dollars)
S
D
E
Only projects that are profitable at an interest rate of 8% or higher are funded.
Offers not accepted from lenders who demand interest rate higher than 8%.
Projects that are profitable only when the interest rate falls below 8% are not funded.
Offers accepted from lenders willing to lend at interest rate of 8% or less.

Shifts of the Demand for Loanable Funds

Let's start by looking at the causes and effects of changes in demand.

The factors that can cause the demand curve for loanable funds to shift include the following:

1. *Changes in perceived business opportunities.* A change in beliefs about the payoff of investment spending can increase or reduce the amount of desired spending at any given interest rate. If there is great excitement over the business possibilities created by new technology, as there was when the Internet came into wide use in the 1990s, businesses will rush to buy computer equipment, put fiber-optic cables in the ground, and so on, shifting the demand for loanable funds to the right. But if there is disillusionment with technology-related investment, as there was in 2001 when many dot-com businesses failed, the demand for loanable funds will shift back to the left.
2. *Changes in government borrowing.* A government runs a budget deficit when, in a given year, it spends more than it receives. Running budget deficits can be a major source of demand for loanable funds, with the result that changes in the government budget deficit can shift the demand curve for loanable funds. For example, between 2000 and 2003, as the U.S. federal government went from a budget surplus to a budget deficit, the government went from being a net saver that provided loanable funds to the market to being a net borrower, borrowing funds from the market. In 2000, net federal borrowing was *minus* \$189 billion, as the federal government was paying off some of its pre-existing debt. But by 2003, net federal borrowing was *plus* \$416 billion because the government had to borrow large sums to pay its bills. This change had the effect, other things equal, of shifting the demand curve for loanable funds to the right.

Figure 57-4 shows the effects of an increase in the demand for loanable funds. S is the supply of loanable funds, and D_1 is the initial demand curve. The initial equilibrium interest rate is r_1. An increase in the demand for loanable funds means that the quantity of funds demanded rises at any given interest rate, so the demand curve shifts rightward to D_2. As a result, the equilibrium interest rate rises to r_2.

FIGURE 57-4 An Increase in the Demand for Loanable Funds

If the quantity of funds demanded by borrowers rises at any given interest rate, the demand for loanable funds shifts rightward from D_1 to D_2. As a result, the equilibrium interest rate rises from r_1 to r_2.

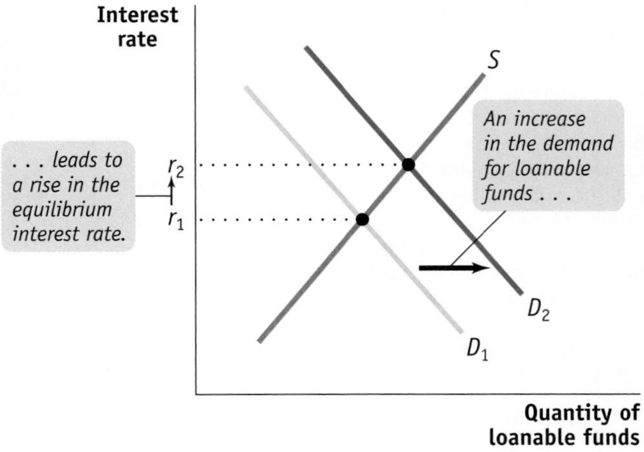

The fact that an increase in the demand for loanable funds leads, other things equal, to a rise in the interest rate has one especially important implication: it tells us that increasing or persistent government budget deficits are cause for concern because an increase in the government's deficit shifts the demand curve for loanable funds to the right, which leads to a higher interest rate. If the interest rate rises, businesses will cut back on their investment spending.

So, other things equal, a rise in the government budget deficit tends to reduce overall investment spending. Economists call the negative effect of government budget deficits on investment spending **crowding out.** Concerns about crowding out are one key reason to worry about increasing or persistent budget deficits.

Crowding out occurs when a government budget deficit drives up the interest rate and leads to reduced investment spending.

However, it's important to add a qualification here: crowding out may not occur if the economy is depressed. When the economy is operating far below full employment, government spending can lead to higher incomes; and these higher incomes lead to increased savings at any given interest rate. Higher savings allows the government to borrow without raising interest rates. Many economists believe, for example, that the large budget deficits that the U.S. government ran from 2008 to 2013, in the face of a depressed economy, caused little if any crowding out.

Shifts of the Supply of Loanable Funds

Like the demand for loanable funds, the supply of loanable funds can shift. Among the factors that can cause the supply of loanable funds to shift are the following:

1. *Changes in private savings behavior.* A number of factors can cause the level of private savings to change at any given interest rate. For example, rising home prices in the United States will make many homeowners feel richer, leading them to spend more and save less. This will have the effect of shifting the supply curve of loanable funds to the left.
2. *Changes in net capital inflows.* Capital flows into and out of a country can change as investors' perceptions of that country change. For example, Greece experienced large net capital inflows after the creation of the euro, Europe's common currency, in 1999, because investors believed that Greece's adoption of the euro as its currency had made it a safe place to put their funds. But, in the years that followed, worries about the Greek government's solvency (and the discovery that it had been understating its debt) led to a collapse in investor confidence, and the net inflow of funds dried up. The effect of shrinking capital inflows was to shift the supply curve in the Greek loanable funds market to the left.

Figure 57-5 shows the effects of an increase in the supply of loanable funds. D is the demand for loanable funds, and S_1 is the initial supply curve. The initial equilibrium interest rate is r_1. An increase in the supply of loanable funds means that the quantity of funds supplied rises at any given interest rate, so the supply curve shifts rightward to S_2. As a result, the equilibrium interest rate falls to r_2.

FIGURE 57-5 An Increase in the Supply of Loanable Funds

If the quantity of funds supplied by lenders rises at any given interest rate, the supply of loanable funds shifts rightward from S_1 to S_2. As a result, the equilibrium interest rate falls from r_1 to r_2.

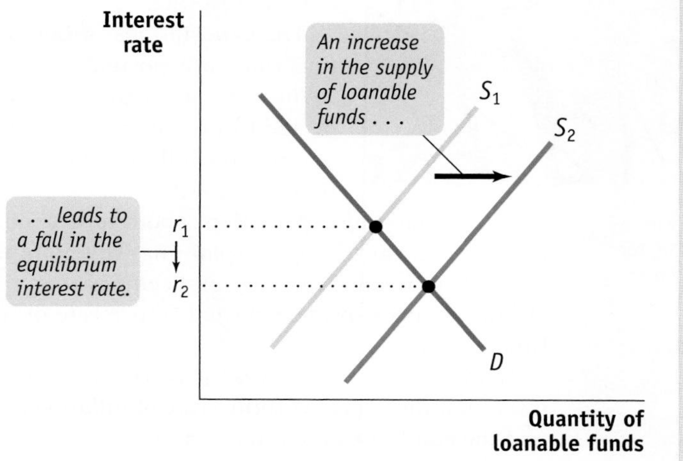
Interest rate
An increase in the supply of loanable funds . . .
S_1
S_2
. . . leads to a fall in the equilibrium interest rate.
r_1
r_2
D
Quantity of loanable funds

Inflation and Interest Rates

Anything that shifts either the supply of loanable funds curve or the demand for loanable funds curve changes the interest rate. Historically, major changes in interest rates have been driven by many factors, including changes in government policy and technological innovations that created new investment opportunities.

However, arguably the most important factor affecting interest rates over time—the reason, for example, that interest rates today are much lower than they were in the late 1970s and early 1980s—is changing expectations about future inflation, which shift both the supply and the demand for loanable funds.

To understand the effect of expected future inflation on interest rates, let's look at an example: in the 1970s and 1980s higher than expected U.S. inflation reduced the real value of homeowners' mortgages, which was good for the homeowners but bad for the banks. Economists summarize the effect of inflation on borrowers and lenders by distinguishing between the *nominal interest rate* and the *real interest rate,* where the difference is:

$$\text{Real interest rate} = \text{Nominal interest rate} - \text{Inflation rate}$$

The true cost of borrowing is the real interest rate, not the nominal interest rate.

To see why, suppose a firm borrows \$10,000 for one year at a 10% nominal interest rate. At the end of the year, it must repay \$11,000—the amount borrowed plus the interest. But suppose that over the course of the year the average level of prices increases by 10%, so that the real interest rate is zero. Then the \$11,000 repayment has the same purchasing power as the original \$10,000 loan. In real terms, the borrower has received a zero-interest loan.

Similarly, the true payoff to lending is the real interest rate, not the nominal rate. Suppose that a bank makes a \$10,000 loan for one year at a 10% nominal interest rate. At the end of the year, the bank receives an \$11,000 repayment. But if the average level of prices rises by 10% per year, the purchasing power of the money the bank gets back is no more than that of the money it lent out. In real terms, the bank has made a zero-interest loan.

Now we can add an important detail to our analysis of the loanable funds market. Figures 57-4 and 57-5 are drawn with the vertical axis measuring the *nominal interest rate for a given expected future inflation rate.* Why do we use the nominal interest rate rather than the real interest rate? Because in the real world neither borrowers nor lenders know what the future inflation rate will be when they make a deal.

Actual loan contracts therefore specify a nominal interest rate rather than a real interest rate. Because we are holding the expected future inflation rate fixed in Figures 57-4 and 57-5, however, changes in the nominal interest rate also lead to changes in the real interest rate.

The expectations of borrowers and lenders about future inflation rates are normally based on recent experience. In the late 1970s, after a decade of high inflation, borrowers and lenders expected future inflation to be high. By the late 1990s, after a decade of fairly low inflation, borrowers and lenders expected future inflation to be low.

Shutterstock

Changing expectations about future inflation is the most important factor affecting interest rates over time.

These changing expectations about future inflation had a strong effect on the nominal interest rate, largely explaining why nominal interest rates were much lower in the early years of the twenty-first century than they were in the early 1980s. Let's look at how changes in the expected future rate of inflation are reflected in the loanable funds model.

In Figure 57-6, the curves S_0 and D_0 show the supply and demand for loanable funds given that the expected future rate of inflation is 0%. In that case, equilibrium is at E_0 and the equilibrium nominal interest rate is 4%. Because expected future inflation is 0%, the equilibrium expected real interest rate over the life of the loan is also 4%.

FIGURE 57-6 The Fisher Effect

D_0 and S_0 are the demand and supply curves for loanable funds when the expected future inflation rate is 0%. At an expected inflation rate of 0%, the equilibrium nominal interest rate is 4%. An increase in expected future inflation pushes both the demand and supply curves upward by 1 percentage point for every percentage point increase in expected future inflation. D_{10} and S_{10} are the demand and supply curves for loanable funds when the expected future inflation rate is 10%. The 10 percentage point increase in expected future inflation raises the equilibrium nominal interest rate to 14%. The expected real interest rate remains at 4%, and the equilibrium quantity of loanable funds also remains unchanged.

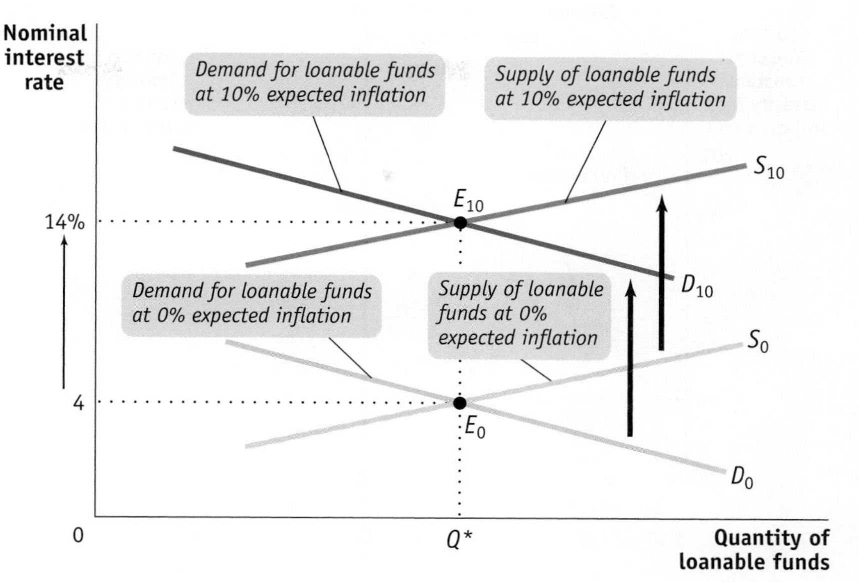

Now suppose that the expected future inflation rate rises to 10%. The demand curve for loanable funds shifts upward to D_{10}: borrowers are now willing to borrow as much at a nominal interest rate of 14% as they were previously willing to borrow at 4%. That's because with a 10% inflation rate, a 14% nominal interest rate corresponds to a 4% real interest rate.

Similarly, the supply curve of loanable funds shifts upward to S_{10}: lenders require a nominal interest rate of 14% to persuade them to lend as much as they would previously have lent at 4%. The new equilibrium is at E_{10}: the result of an expected future inflation rate of 10% is that the equilibrium nominal interest rate rises from 4% to 14%.

This situation can be summarized as a general principle, known as the **Fisher effect,** which states that *the expected real interest rate is unaffected by changes in expected future inflation.* According to the Fisher effect, an increase in expected future inflation drives up the nominal interest rate, where each additional percentage point of expected future inflation drives up the nominal interest rate by 1 percentage point.

The central point is that both lenders and borrowers base their decisions on the expected real interest rate. As a result, a change in the expected rate of inflation does not affect the equilibrium quantity of loanable funds or the expected real interest rate; all it affects is the equilibrium nominal interest rate.

ECONOMICS ▶ IN ACTION

FIFTY YEARS OF FLUCTUATIONS IN U.S. INTEREST RATES

There have been some large movements in U.S. interest rates over the past half-century. These movements clearly show how both changes in expected future inflation and changes in the expected return on investment spending move interest rates.

Panel (a) of Figure 57-7 illustrates the first effect. It shows the average interest rate on bonds issued by the U.S. government—specifically, bonds for which the government promises to repay the full amount after 10 years—from 1960 to 2012, along with the rate of consumer price inflation over the same period. As you can see, the big story about interest rates is the way they soared in the 1970s, before coming back down in the 1980s.

According to the **Fisher effect,** an increase in expected future inflation drives up the nominal interest rate, leaving the expected real interest rate unchanged.

FIGURE 57-7 Changes in U.S. Interest Rates Over Time

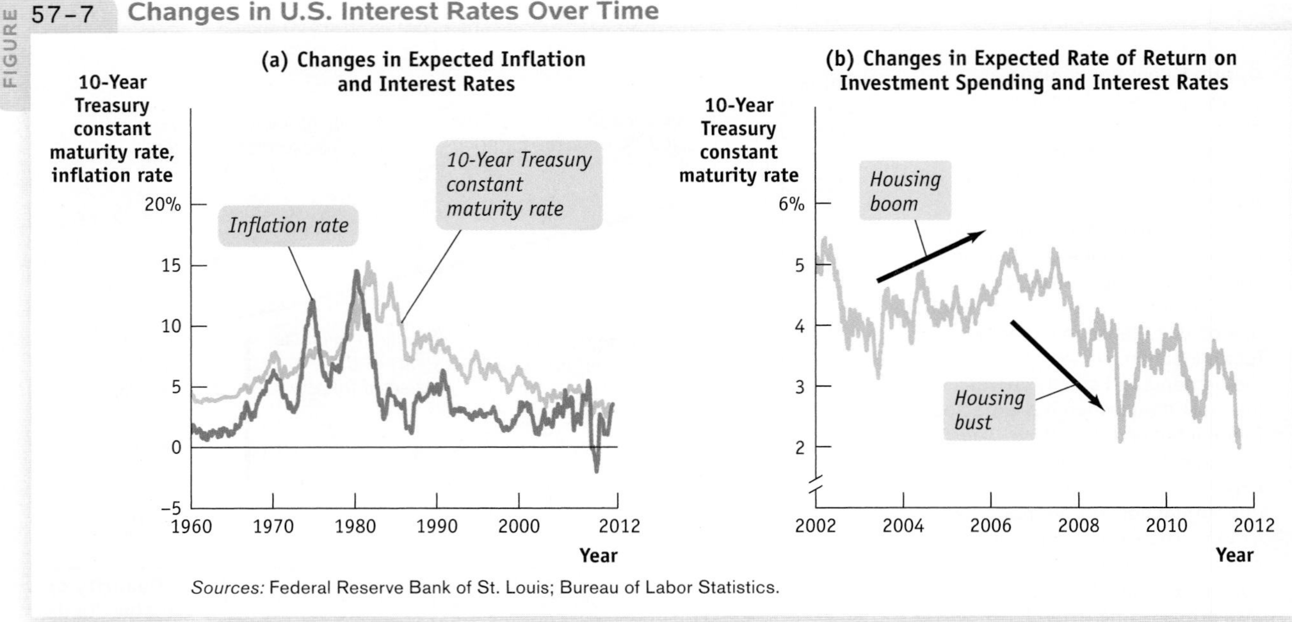

Sources: Federal Reserve Bank of St. Louis; Bureau of Labor Statistics.

It's not hard to see why that happened: inflation shot up during the 1970s, leading to widespread expectations that high inflation would continue. And as we've seen, expected inflation raises the equilibrium interest rate. As inflation came down in the 1980s, so did expectations of future inflation, and this brought interest rates down as well.

Panel (b) illustrates the second effect: changes in the expected return on investment spending and interest rates, with a "close-up" of interest rates from 2002 to 2012. Notice the rise in interest rates during the middle years of the last decade, followed by a sharp drop. We know from other evidence (such as surveys of investor opinion) that expected inflation didn't change much over those years.

What happened, instead, was the boom and bust in housing: interest rates rose as demand for housing soared, pushing the demand curve for loanable funds to the right, then fell as the housing boom collapsed, shifting the demand curve for loanable funds back to the left. Throughout this whole process, total savings was equal to total investment spending, and the rise and fall of the interest rate played a key role in matching lenders with borrowers.

MODULE 57 Review

Solutions appear at the back of the book.

Check Your Understanding

1. Use a diagram of the loanable funds market to illustrate the effect of the following events on the equilibrium interest rate and investment spending.
   a. An economy is opened to international movements of capital, and a net capital inflow occurs.
   b. Retired people generally save less than working people at any interest rate. The proportion of retired people in the population goes up.
2. Explain what is wrong with the following statement: "Savings and investment spending may not be equal in the economy as a whole because when the interest rate rises, households will want to save more money than businesses will want to invest."
3. Suppose that expected inflation rises from 3% to 6%.
   a. How will the real interest rate be affected by this change?
   b. How will the nominal interest rate be affected by this change?
   c. What will happen to the equilibrium quantity of loanable funds?

Multiple-Choice Questions

1. If the interest rate falls, then the present value of any given project ___________ and total investment spending will ___________.
   a. rises : remain unchanged
   b. rises : decrease
   c. falls : decrease
   d. falls : increase
   e. rises : increase

2. The real interest rate equals the
   a. nominal interest rate plus the inflation rate.
   b. nominal interest rate minus the inflation rate.
   c. nominal interest rate divided by the inflation rate.
   d. nominal interest rate times the inflation rate.
   e. federal funds rate.

3. Which of the following will increase the demand for loanable funds?
   a. a federal government budget surplus
   b. an increase in perceived business opportunities
   c. a decrease in the interest rate
   d. positive capital inflows
   e. decreased private saving rates

4. Which of the following will increase the supply of loanable funds?
   a. an increase in perceived business opportunities
   b. decreased government borrowing
   c. an increased private saving rate
   d. an increase in the expected inflation rate
   e. a decrease in capital inflows

5. Both lenders and borrowers base their decisions on
   a. expected real interest rates.
   b. expected nominal interest rates.
   c. real interest rates.
   d. nominal interest rates.
   e. nominal interest rates minus real interest rates.

Critical-Thinking Questions

Does each of the following affect either the supply or the demand for loanable funds, and if so, does the affected curve increase (shift to the right) or decrease (shift to the left)?

1. There is an increase in capital inflows into the economy.
2. Businesses are pessimistic about future business conditions.
3. The government increases borrowing.
4. The private savings rate decreases.

MODULE 58 The Time Value of Money

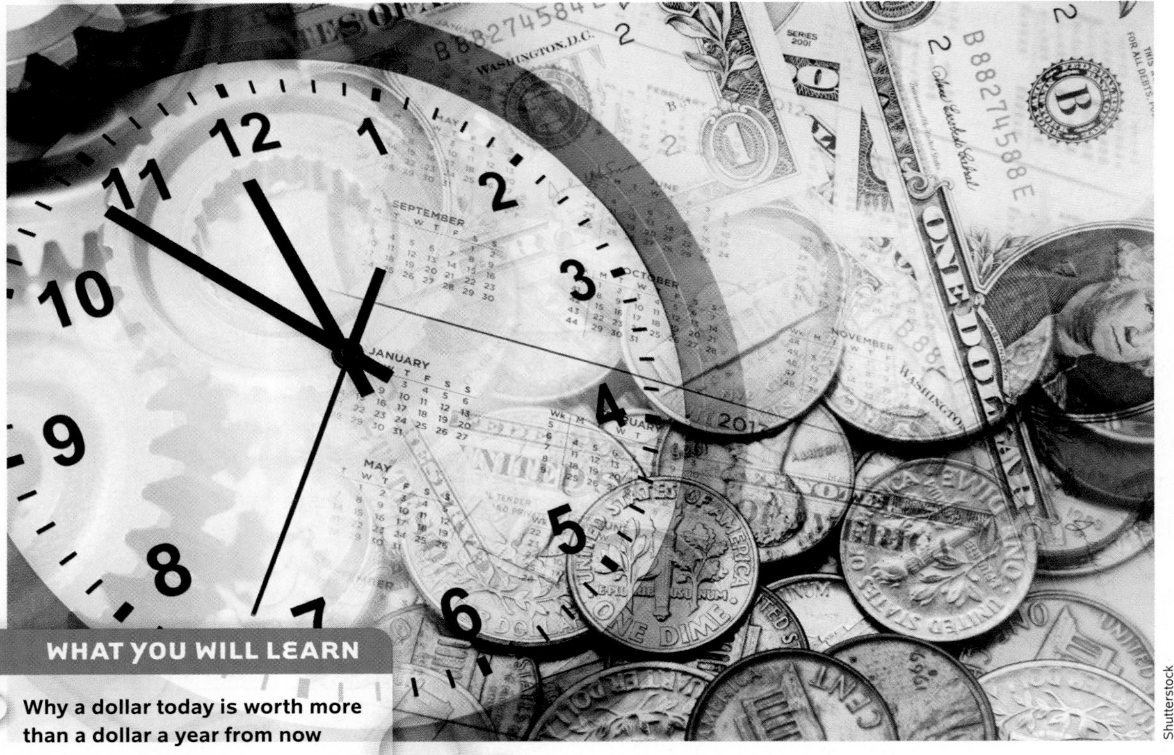
Shutterstock

WHAT YOU WILL LEARN

1. Why a dollar today is worth more than a dollar a year from now
2. How the concept of present value can help individuals and firms make decisions when costs or benefits occur in the future

In the previous module we learned that *present value* helps to explain why the demand curve for loanable funds slopes downward. In this module, we'll look more closely at present value, and consider how it is put to use by individuals and firms when making financial decisions.

The Concept of Present Value

Individuals and firms are often faced with financial decisions that will have consequences long into the future. For example, when you decided to attend college, you committed yourself to years of study, which you expect will pay off for the rest of your life. So the decision to attend college is a decision to embark on a long-term project.

The basic rule in deciding whether or not to undertake a project is that you should compare the benefits of that project with its costs, implicit as well as explicit. But making these comparisons can sometimes be difficult because the benefits and costs of a project may not arrive at the same time.

This is true of the saving and investment decisions made by individuals: these decisions also have benefits and costs that do not arrive at the same time. For example, if you save more today the benefit is that you will earn interest and have more accumulated wealth at a later date. The cost is that you have less income available for consumption today.

Likewise, when a firm decides to invest in new physical capital today, it is anticipating benefits like increased output, productivity, and profit that will come later, possibly much later. But how, specifically, is time an issue in economic decision making?

Borrowing, Lending, and Interest

In general, having a dollar today is worth more than having a dollar a year from now. To see why, let's consider two examples.

First, suppose that you get a new job that comes with a $1,000 bonus, which will be paid at the end of the first year. But you would like to spend the extra money now—say, on new clothes for work. Can you do that?

The answer is yes—you can borrow money today and use the bonus to repay the debt a year from now. But if that is your plan, you cannot borrow the full $1,000 today. You must borrow *less* than that because a year from now you will have to repay the amount borrowed *plus interest*.

Now consider a different scenario. Suppose that you are paid a bonus of $1,000 today, and you decide that you don't want to spend the money until a year from now. What do you do with it? You may decide to put it in the bank; in effect, you would be lending the $1,000 to the bank, which in turn lends it out to its customers who wish to borrow. At the end of a year, you will get *more* than $1,000 back—you will receive the $1,000 plus the interest earned.

All of this means that having $1,000 today is worth more than having $1,000 a year from now. As any borrower and lender know, this is what allows a lender to charge a borrower interest on a loan: borrowers are willing to pay interest in order to have money today rather than waiting until they acquire that money later on.

Most interest rates are stated as the percentage of the borrowed amount that must be paid to the lender for each year of the loan. Whether money is actually borrowed for 1 month or 10 years, and regardless of the amount, the same principle applies: money in your pocket today is worth more than money in your pocket tomorrow. To keep things simple in the discussions that follow, we'll restrict ourselves to examples of 1-year loans of $1.

Because the value of money depends on when it is paid or received, you can't evaluate a project by simply adding up the costs and benefits when those costs and benefits arrive at different times. You must take time into account when evaluating the project because $1 that is paid to you today is worth more than $1 that is paid to you a year from now. Similarly, $1 that you must pay today is more burdensome than $1 that you must pay next year.

Fortunately, there is a simple way to adjust for these complications so that we can correctly compare the value of dollars received and paid out at different times.

Next we'll see how the interest rate can be used to convert future benefits and costs into what economists call *present values*. By using present values when evaluating a project, you can evaluate a project *as if* all relevant costs and benefits were occurring today rather than at different times. This allows people to "factor out" the complications created by time. We'll start by defining the concept of present value.

Defining Present Value

The key to the concept of present value is to understand that the interest rate can be used to compare the value of a dollar realized today with the value of a dollar realized later. Why the interest rate? Because the interest rate correctly measures the cost of delaying the receipt of a dollar of benefit and, correspondingly, the benefit of delaying the payment of a dollar of cost.

Let's illustrate this with some examples.

Suppose that you are evaluating whether or not to take a job in which your employer promises to pay you a bonus at the end of the first year. What is the value to you today of $1 of bonus money to be paid one year in the future? A slightly different way of asking the same

Having a dollar today is worth more than having a dollar a year from now.

iStockphoto/Thinkstock

The **present value** of \$1 realized one year from now is equal to $\$1/(1 + r)$: the amount of money you must lend out today in order to have \$1 in one year. It is the value to you today of \$1 realized one year from now.

question: what amount would you be willing to accept today as a substitute for receiving \$1 one year from now?

To answer this question, begin by observing that you need *less* than \$1 today in order to be assured of having \$1 one year from now. Why? Because any money that you have today can be lent out at interest—say, by depositing it in a bank account so that the bank can then lend it out to its borrowers. This turns any amount you have today into a greater sum at the end of the year.

Let's work this out mathematically. We'll use the symbol r to represent the interest rate, expressed in decimal terms—that is, if the interest rate is 10%, then $r = 0.10$. If you lend out $\$X$, at the end of a year you will receive your $\$X$ back, plus the interest on your $\$X$, which is $\$X \times r$. Thus, at the end of the year you will receive:

(58-1) Amount received one year from now as a result of lending $\$X$ today:
$$\$X + \$X \times r = \$X \times (1 + r)$$

The next step is to find out how much you would have to lend out today to have \$1 a year from now. To do that, we just need to set Equation 58-1 equal to \$1 and solve for $\$X$. That is, we solve the following equation for $\$X$:

(58-2) Condition satisfied when \$1 is received one year from now as a result of lending $\$X$ today:
$$\$X \times (1 + r) = \$1$$

Rearranging Equation 58-2 to solve for $\$X$, the amount you need today in order to receive \$1 one year from now is:

(58-3) Amount lent today in order to receive \$1 one year from now:
$$\$X = \$1/(1 + r)$$

This means that you would be willing to accept today the amount $\$X$ defined by Equation 58-3 for every \$1 to be paid to you one year from now. The reason is that if you were to lend out $\$X$ today, you would be assured of receiving \$1 one year from now. Returning to our original question, this also means that if someone promises to pay you a sum of money one year in the future, you are willing to accept $\$X$ today in place of every \$1 to be paid one year from now.

Now let's solve Equation 58-3 for the value of $\$X$. To do this we simply need to use the actual value of r (a value determined by the financial markets). Let's assume that the actual value of r is 10%, which means that $r = 0.10$. In that case:

(58-4) Value of $\$X$ when $r = 0.10$: $\$X = \$1/(1 + 0.10) = \$1/1.10 = \$0.91$

So you would be willing to accept \$0.91 today in exchange for every \$1 to be paid to you one year from now. Economists refer to $\$X$ as the **present value** of \$1. Note that the present value of any given amount will change as the interest rate changes.

The present value of a given amount will change as the interest rate changes.

To see that this technique works for evaluating future costs as well as evaluating future benefits, consider the following example. Suppose you enter into an agreement that obliges you to pay \$1 one year from now—say, to pay off a car loan from your parents when you graduate in a year. How much money would you need today to ensure that you have \$1 in a year? The answer is $\$X$, the present value of \$1, which in our example is \$0.91.

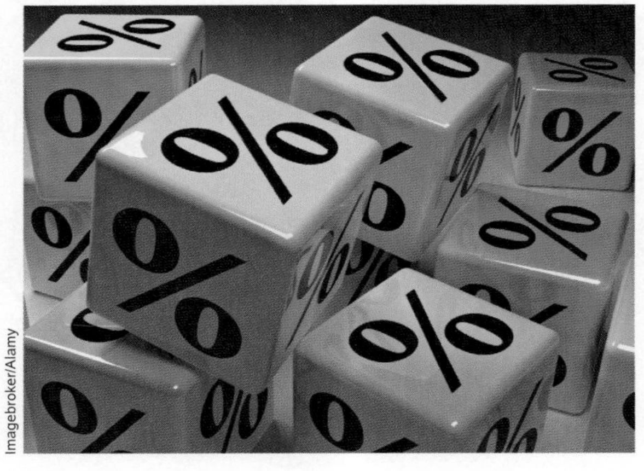
Imagebroker/Alamy

The reason \$0.91 is the right answer is that if you lend it out for one year at an interest rate of 10%, you will receive \$1 in return at the end. So if, for example, you must pay back \$5,000 one year from now, then you need to deposit $\$5,000 \times 0.91 = \$4,550$ into a bank account today earning an interest rate of 10% in order to have \$5,000 one year from now. (There is a slight discrepancy due to rounding.) In other words, today you need to have the present value of \$5,000, which equals \$4,550, in order to be assured of paying off your debt in a year.

These examples show us that the present value concept provides a way to calculate the value today of \$1 that is realized in a year—regardless of whether that \$1 is realized as a benefit (the bonus) or a cost (the car loan payback). To evaluate a project today that has benefits, costs, or both to be realized in a year, we just use the relevant interest rate to convert those future dollars into their present values. In that way we have "factored out" the complication that time creates for decision making.

Below we will use the present value concept to evaluate a project. But before we do that, it is worthwhile to note that the present value method can be used for projects in which the \$1 is realized more than a year later—say, two, three, or even more years. Let's consider a project that will pay \$1 *two* years from today. What is the value to you today of \$1 received two years into the future? We can find the answer to that question by expanding our formula for present value.

Let's call $\$V$ the amount of money that would need to be lent today at an interest rate of r in order to have \$1 in two years. So if an individual or firm lends $\$V$ today, it will receive $\$V \times (1 + r)$ in one year. And if it *relends* that sum for another year, it will receive $\$V \times (1 + r) \times (1 + r) = \$V \times (1 + r)^2$ at the end of the second year. At the end of two years, $\$V$ will be worth $\$V \times (1 + r)^2$. In other words:

(58-5) Amount received in one year from lending $\$V = \$V \times (1 + r)$

Amount received in two years from lending $\$V = \$V \times (1 + r) \times (1 + r) = \$V \times (1 + r)^2$ and so on. For example, if $r = 0.10$, then $\$V \times (1.10)^2 = \$V \times 1.21$.

Now we are ready to answer the question of what \$1 realized two years in the future is worth today. In order for the amount lent today, $\$V$, to be worth \$1 two years from now, it must satisfy this formula:

(58-6) Condition satisfied when \$1 is received two years from now as a result of lending $\$V$ today:
$\$V \times (1 + r)^2 = \$1$

Rearranging Equation 58-6, we can solve for $\$V$:

(58-7) Amount lent today in order to receive \$1 two years from now:
$\$V = \$1/(1 + r)^2$

Given $r = 0.10$ and using Equation 58-7, we arrive at $\$V = \$1/1.21 = \$0.83$. So, when the interest rate is 10%, \$1 realized two years from today is worth \$0.83 today because by lending out \$0.83 today the individual or firm can be assured of having \$1 in two years. And that means that the present value of \$1 realized two years into the future is \$0.83.

(58-8) Present value of \$1 realized two years from now:
$\$V = \$1/(1.10)^2 = \$1/1.21 = \$0.83$

From this example we can see how the present value concept can be expanded to a number of years even greater than two. If we ask what the present value is of \$1 realized any number of years, represented by N, into the future, the answer is given by a generalization of the present value formula: it is equal to $\$1/(1 + r)^N$.

Using Present Value

Suppose an individual or firm has to choose one of three hypothetical projects to undertake. Project A costs nothing and has an immediate payoff of \$100. Project B requires a payment of \$10 today in order to receive \$115 a year from now. Project C offers an immediate payoff of \$119 but requires a payment of \$20 a year from now. We'll assume that the annual interest rate is 10%—that is, $r = 0.10$.

The problem in evaluating these three projects is that their costs and benefits are realized at different times. That is, of course, where the concept of present value becomes extremely helpful: by using present value to convert any dollars realized in the future into today's value, we factor out the issue of time. Appropriate comparisons can be made using the **net present value** of a project—the present value of current and future benefits minus the present value of current and future costs. The best project to undertake is the one with the highest net present value.

The **net present value** of a project is the present value of current and future benefits minus the present value of current and future costs.

TABLE 58-1

The Net Present Value of Three Hypothetical Projects

Project	Dollars realized today	Dollars realized one year from today	Present value formula	Net present value given $r = 0.10$
A	$100	—	$100	$100.00
B	–$10	$115	–$10 + $115/(1 + *r*)	$94.55
C	$119	–$20	119 – $20/(1 + *r*)	$100.82

Table 58-1 shows how to calculate net present value for each of the three projects. The second and third columns show how many dollars are realized and when they are realized; costs are indicated by a minus sign. The fourth column shows the equations used to convert the flows of dollars into their present value, and the fifth column shows the actual amounts of the total net present value for each of the three projects.

For instance, to calculate the net present value of project B, we need to calculate the present value of $115 received in one year. The present value of $1 received in one year would be $1/(1 + *r*). So the present value of $115 is equal to 115 × $1/(1 + *r*); that is, $115/(1 + *r*). The net present value of project B is the present value of today's and future benefits minus the present value of today's and future costs: –$10 + $115/(1 + *r*).

From the fifth column, we can immediately see which is the preferred project—it is project C. That's because it has the highest net present value, $100.82, which is higher than the net present value of project A ($100) and much higher than the net present value of project B ($94.55).

This example shows how important the concept of present value is. If we had failed to use the present value calculations and instead simply added up the dollars generated by each of the three projects, we could have easily been misled into believing that project B was the best project and project C was the worst.

ECONOMICS IN ACTION

HOW BIG IS THAT JACKPOT, ANYWAY?

For a clear example of present value at work, consider the case of lottery jackpots.

On March 30, 2012, Mega Millions set a record for the largest jackpot ever in North America, with a payout of $656 million. Well, sort of. That $656 million was available only if the winner chose to take his or her winnings in the form of an "annuity," consisting of an annual payment for the next 26 years. If the winner wanted cash up front, the jackpot was only $474 million and change.

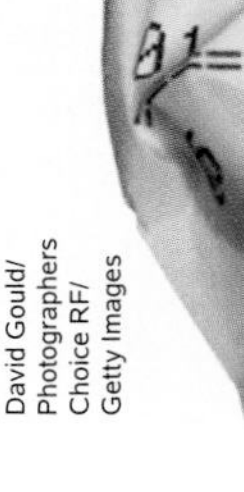

David Gould/ Photographers Choice RF/ Getty Images

Why was Mega Millions so stingy about quick payoffs? It was all a matter of present value. If the winner had been willing to take the annuity, the lottery would have invested the jackpot money, buying U.S. government bonds (in effect lending the money to the federal government). The money would have been invested in such a way that the investments would pay just enough to cover the annuity. This worked, of course, because at the interest rates prevailing at the time, the present value of a $656 million annuity spread over 26 years was just about $474 million. To put it another way, the opportunity cost to the lottery of that annuity in present value terms was $474 million.

So why didn't they just call it a $474 million jackpot? Well, $656 million sounds more impressive! But receiving $656 million over 26 years is essentially the same as receiving $474 million today.

MODULE 58 Review

Solutions appear at the back of the book.

Check Your Understanding

1. Consider the three hypothetical projects shown in Table 58-1. This time, however, suppose that the interest rate is only 2%.
   a. Calculate the net present values of the three projects. Which one is now preferred?
   b. Explain why the preferred choice with a 2% interest rate differs from one with a 10% interest rate.

Multiple-Choice Questions

1. Suppose, for simplicity, that a bank uses a single interest rate for loans and deposits, there is no inflation, and all unspent money is deposited in the bank. The interest rate measures which of the following?
   I. the cost of using a dollar today rather than a year from now
   II. the benefit of delaying the use of a dollar from today until a year from now
   III. the price of borrowing money calculated as a percentage of the amount borrowed
   a. I only
   b. II only
   c. III only
   d. I and II only
   e. I, II, and III

2. If the interest rate is zero, then the present value of a dollar received at the end of the year is
   a. more than $1.
   b. equal to $1.
   c. less than $1.
   d. zero.
   e. infinite.

3. If the interest rate is 10%, the present value of $1 paid to an individual or firm one year from now is
   a. $0.
   b. $0.89.
   c. $0.91.
   d. $1.
   e. more than $1.

4. If the interest rate is 5%, the amount received one year from now as a result of lending $100 today is
   a. $90.
   b. $95.
   c. $100.
   d. $105.
   e. $110.

5. What is the present value of $100 realized two years from now if the interest rate is 10%?
   a. $80
   b. $83
   c. $90
   d. $100
   e. $110

Critical-Thinking Questions

1. What is the amount an individual or firm will receive in three years if it lends $1,000 at 5% interest?
2. What is the present value of $1,000 received in three years if the interest rate is 5%?

MODULE

59 The Financial System

NoDerog/Getty Images

Tupungato/Thinkstock

WHAT YOU WILL LEARN

1. The purpose of the four main types of financial assets: stocks, bonds, loans, and bank deposits
2. How financial intermediaries help investors achieve diversification
3. How financial fluctuations occur in the financial system

Understanding the Financial System

A well-functioning financial system brings together the funds of investors with those looking to fund investment spending projects (making the rise of Facebook, as we saw in the section-opener, possible). Financial markets have been around for centuries. In fact, capital inflows financed the early economic development of the United States, through investment spending in mining, railroads, and canals. Let's begin by understanding exactly what is traded in financial markets.

Financial markets are where households invest their current savings and their accumulated savings, or **wealth,** by purchasing *financial assets.*

A **financial asset** is a paper claim that entitles the buyer to future income from the seller. For example, when a saver lends funds to a company, the loan is a financial asset sold by the company that entitles the lender (the buyer of the financial asset) to future income from the company.

A household can also invest its current savings or wealth by purchasing a **physical asset,** a tangible object that can be used to generate future income such as a preexisting house or preexisting piece of equipment. It gives the owner the right to dispose of the object as he or she wishes (for example, rent it or sell it).

A household's **wealth** is the value of its accumulated savings.

A **financial asset** is a paper claim that entitles the buyer to future income from the seller.

A **physical asset** is a tangible object that can be used to generate future income.

A **liability** is a requirement to pay income in the future.

If you get a loan from your local bank—say, to buy a new car—you and the bank are creating a financial asset: your loan. A *loan* is one important kind of financial asset in the real world, one that is owned by the lender—in this case, your local bank. In creating that loan, you and the bank are also creating a **liability,** a requirement to pay income in the future. So although your loan is a financial asset from the bank's point of view, it is a liability from your point of view: a requirement that you repay the loan, including any interest.

In addition to loans, there are three other important kinds of financial assets: stocks, bonds, and *bank deposits.* Because a financial asset is a claim to future income that someone has to pay, it is also someone else's liability. We'll explain in detail shortly who bears the liability for each type of financial asset.

The four types of financial assets—loans, stocks, bonds, and bank deposits—exist because the economy has developed a set of specialized markets, like the stock market and the bond market, and specialized institutions, like banks, that facilitate the flow of funds from lenders to borrowers.

Earlier, in the context of the circular-flow diagram, we defined the financial markets and institutions that make up the financial system. A well-functioning financial system encourages greater savings and investment spending and ensures that both are undertaken efficiently. To understand how these processes occur, we need to know what tasks the financial system needs to accomplish. Then we can see how the job gets done.

Three Tasks of a Financial System

Our earlier analysis of the loanable funds market ignored three important problems facing borrowers and lenders: *transaction costs, risk,* and the desire for *liquidity.* The three tasks of a financial system are to reduce these problems in a cost-effective way. Doing so enhances the efficiency of financial markets, making it more likely that lenders and borrowers will make mutually beneficial trades that make society as a whole richer.

TASK 1: REDUCING TRANSACTION COSTS The expenses involved in actually putting together and executing a deal are known as **transaction costs.** For example, arranging a loan requires spending time and money negotiating the terms of the deal, verifying the borrower's ability to pay, drawing up and executing legal documents, and so on.

Suppose a large business decided that it wanted to raise $1 billion for investment spending. No individual would be willing to lend that much. And negotiating individual loans from thousands of different people, each willing to lend a modest amount, would impose very large total costs because each individual transaction would incur a cost, with the result that the entire deal would probably be unprofitable.

Fortunately, there is another option: when large businesses want to borrow money, they either go to a bank or sell bonds in the bond market. Obtaining a loan from a bank avoids large transaction costs because it involves only a single borrower and a single lender. We'll explain more about how bonds work shortly. For now, it is enough to know that the principal reason there is a bond market is that it allows companies to borrow large sums of money without incurring large transaction costs.

TASK 2: REDUCING RISK Another problem that real-world borrowers and lenders face is **financial risk,** or simply, *risk,* uncertainty about future outcomes that involve the potential for financial losses or gains. For example, owning and driving a car entails the financial risk of a costly accident.

Most people experience the loss in welfare from losing a given amount of money more intensely than they experience the increase in welfare from gaining the same amount of money. A person who is more sensitive to a loss than to a gain of an equal dollar amount is called *risk-averse.* Most people are risk-averse, although to differing degrees. For example, people who are wealthy are typically less risk-averse than those who are not so well-off.

A well-functioning financial system helps people reduce their exposure to risk, which risk-averse people prefer to do. Suppose the owner of a business expects to make a greater profit if she buys additional capital equipment, but she isn't completely sure that this will indeed happen. She could pay for the equipment by using her savings or selling her house. But if the profit is significantly less than expected, she will have lost her savings, or her house, or both.

So, being risk-averse, this business owner wants to share the risk of purchasing new capital equipment with someone, even if that requires sharing some of the profit

Transaction costs are the expenses of negotiating and executing a deal.

Financial risk is uncertainty about future outcomes that involve financial losses or gains.

An individual can engage in **diversification** by investing in several different assets so that the possible losses are independent events.

An asset is **liquid** if it can be quickly converted into cash with relatively little loss of value.

An asset is **illiquid** if it cannot be quickly converted into cash with relatively little loss of value.

if all goes well. How can she do this? By selling shares of her company to other people and using the money she receives from selling shares, rather than money from the sale of her other assets, to finance the equipment purchase.

By selling shares in her company, she reduces her personal losses if the profit is less than expected: she won't have lost her other assets. But if things go well, the shareholders earn a share of the profit as a return on their investment.

By selling a share of her business, the owner has also achieved *diversification:* she has been able to invest in a way that lowers her total risk. She has maintained her investment in her bank account, a financial asset; in ownership of her house, a physical asset; and in ownership of the unsold portion of her business, a financial asset. These investments are likely to carry some risk of their own; for example, her bank may fail or her house may burn down (though in the United States it is likely that she is partly protected against these risks by insurance).

But even in the absence of insurance, she is better off having maintained investments in these different assets because their different risks are *unrelated,* or *independent, events.* This means that her house is no more likely to burn down if her business does poorly and that her bank is no more likely to fail if her house burns down. To put it another way, if one asset performs poorly, it is very likely that her other assets will be unaffected and, as a result, her total risk of loss has been reduced. But if she had invested all her wealth in her business, she would have faced the prospect of losing everything if the business had performed poorly. By engaging in **diversification**—investing in several assets with unrelated, or independent, risks—our business owner has lowered her total risk of loss.

The desire to reduce total risk by engaging in diversification is why we have stocks and a stock market.

TASK 3: PROVIDING LIQUIDITY Financial systems also exist to provide investors with *liquidity,* a concern that—like risk—arises because the future is uncertain. Suppose that, having made a loan, a lender suddenly finds himself in need of cash—say, to meet a medical emergency. Unfortunately, if that loan was made to a business that used it to buy new equipment, the business cannot repay the loan on short notice to satisfy the lender's need to recover his money. Knowing in advance that there is a danger of needing to get his money back before the term of the loan is up, our lender might be reluctant to lock up his money by lending it to a business.

An asset is **liquid** if it can be quickly converted into cash with relatively little loss of value, **illiquid** if it cannot. As we'll see, stocks and bonds are a partial answer to the problem of liquidity. Banks provide an additional way for individuals to hold liquid assets and still finance illiquid investment spending projects.

A loan is a financial asset to the issuer but a liability to the person taking it out.

Now that we've learned the three ways the financial system helps lenders and borrowers make mutually beneficial deals—by reducing transaction costs and risk, and by providing liquidity—we'll look at how it goes about achieving these tasks.

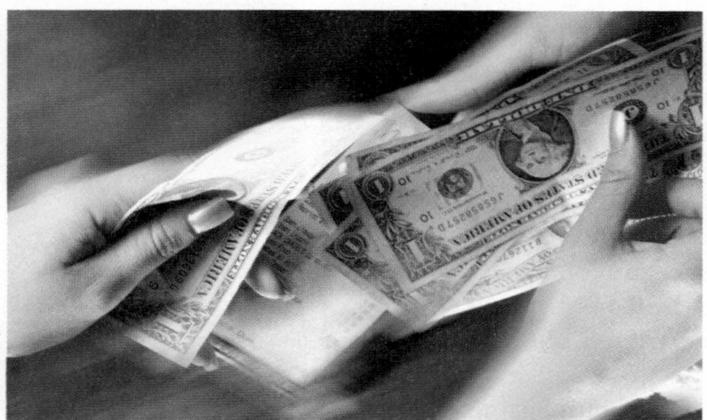
Media Bakery

Types of Financial Assets

In the modern economy there are four main types of financial assets: *loans, bonds, stocks,* and *bank deposits.* In addition, financial innovation has allowed the creation of a wide range of *loan-backed securities.* Each serves a somewhat different purpose. We'll examine loans, bonds, stocks, and loan-backed securities now. Then we'll turn to the role played by bank deposits.

LOANS A lending agreement made between an individual lender and an individual borrower is a *loan.* Individuals are likely to encounter loans in the form of a student loan or a bank loan to finance the purchase of a car or a house. Small businesses usually use bank loans to buy new equipment.

On the positive side, loans are typically tailored to the needs of the borrower. Before a small business can get a loan, it usually has to discuss its business plans, its profits, and so on with the lender. This results in a loan that meets the borrower's needs and ability to pay.

On the negative side, making a loan to an individual person or a business involves a lot of transaction costs, such as the cost of negotiating the terms of the loan, investigating the borrower's credit history and ability to repay, and so on. To minimize these costs, large borrowers such as major corporations and governments often take a more streamlined approach: they sell (or issue) bonds.

A **default** occurs when a borrower fails to make payments as specified by the loan or bond contract.

A **loan-backed security** is an asset created by pooling individual loans and selling shares in that pool.

BONDS An IOU issued by a borrower is called a *bond*. Normally, the seller of the bond promises to pay a fixed sum of interest each year and to repay the principal—the value stated on the face of the bond—to the owner of the bond on a particular date. So a bond is a financial asset from its owner's point of view and a liability from its issuer's point of view.

A bond issuer sells a number of bonds with a given interest rate and maturity date to anyone willing to buy them, a process that avoids costly negotiation of the terms of a loan with many individual lenders.

Bond purchasers can acquire information free of charge on the quality of the bond issuer, such as the bond issuer's credit history, from bond-rating agencies rather than having to incur the expense of investigating it themselves. A particular concern for investors is the possibility of **default,** the risk that the bond issuer will fail to make payments as specified by the bond contract. Once a bond's risk of default has been rated, it can be sold on the bond market as a more or less standardized product—one with clearly defined terms and quality. In general, bonds with a higher default risk must pay a higher interest rate to attract investors.

Another important advantage of bonds is that they are easy to resell. This provides liquidity to bond purchasers. Indeed, a bond will often pass through many hands before it finally comes due. Loans, in contrast, are much more difficult to resell because, unlike bonds, they are not standardized: they differ in size, quality, terms, and so on, making them a lot less liquid than bonds.

LOAN-BACKED SECURITIES **Loan-backed securities,** assets created by pooling individual loans and selling shares in that pool (a process called *securitization*), have become extremely popular over the past two decades. While mortgage-backed securities, in which thousands of individual home mortgages are pooled and then shares are sold to investors, are the best-known example, securitization has also been widely applied to student loans, credit card loans, and auto loans. These loan-backed securities are traded on financial markets like bonds; they are preferred by investors because they provide more diversification and liquidity than individual loans.

However, with so many loans packaged together, it can be difficult to assess the true quality of the asset. That difficulty came to haunt investors during the financial crisis of 2008, when the bursting of the housing bubble led to widespread defaults on mortgages and large losses for holders of "supposedly safe" mortgage-backed securities, creating pain that spread throughout the entire financial system.

STOCKS A *stock* is a share in the ownership of a company. A share of stock is a financial asset from its owner's point of view and a liability from the company's point of view. Not all companies sell shares of their stock; "privately held" companies are owned by an individual or a few partners, who get to keep all of the company's profit.

Most large companies, however, do sell stock. For example, Microsoft has over 8 billion shares outstanding; if you buy one of those shares, you are entitled to one-eight-billionth of the company's profit, as well as 1 of 8 billion votes on company decisions.

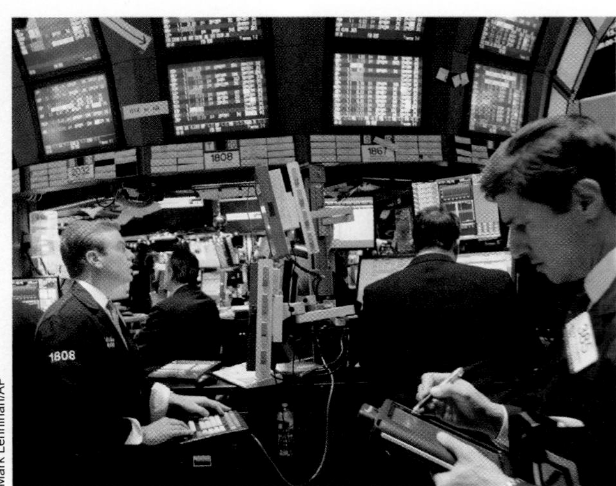
Mark Lennihan/AP

Selling stock reduces risk for business owners and benefits investors who buy the stock.

Why does Microsoft, historically a very profitable company, allow you to buy a share in its ownership? Why don't Bill Gates and Paul Allen, the two founders of Microsoft, keep complete ownership for themselves and just sell bonds for their investment spending needs? The reason is risk: few individuals are risk-tolerant enough to face the risk involved in being the sole owner of a large company.

But stocks do more than reduce the risk that business owners face. The existence of stocks improves society's welfare and improves the welfare of investors who buy stocks. Shareowners are able to enjoy the higher returns over time that stocks generally offer in comparison to bonds. Over the past century, stocks have typically yielded about 7% after adjusting for inflation; bonds have yielded only about 2%. But as investment companies warn you, "past performance is no guarantee of future performance."

And there is a downside: owning the stock of a given company is riskier than owning a bond issued by the same company. Why? Loosely speaking, a bond is a promise while a stock is a hope: by law, a company must pay what it owes its lenders before it distributes any profit to its shareholders. And if the company should fail (that is, be unable to pay its interest obligations and declare bankruptcy), its physical and financial assets go to its bondholders—its lenders—while its shareholders generally receive nothing. So although a stock generally provides a higher return to an investor than a bond, it also carries higher risk.

But the financial system has devised ways to help investors as well as business owners simultaneously manage risk and enjoy somewhat higher returns through the services of institutions known as *financial intermediaries*.

Financial Intermediaries

A **financial intermediary** is an institution that transforms funds gathered from many individuals into financial assets. The most important types of financial intermediaries are *mutual funds, pension funds, life insurance companies,* and *banks.* About three-quarters of the financial assets Americans own are held through these intermediaries rather than directly.

MUTUAL FUNDS Owning shares of a company entails accepting risk in return for a higher potential reward. But it should come as no surprise that stock investors can lower their total risk by engaging in diversification.

By owning a *diversified portfolio* of stocks—a group of stocks in which risks are unrelated to, or offset, one another—rather than concentrating investment in the shares of a single company or a group of related companies, investors can reduce their risk. In addition, financial advisers, aware that most people are risk-averse, almost always advise their clients to diversify not only their stock portfolio but also their entire wealth by holding other assets in addition to stock—assets such as bonds, real estate, and cash. (And, for good measure, to have plenty of insurance in case of accidental losses!)

However, for individuals who don't have a large amount of money to invest—say $1 million or more—building a diversified stock portfolio can incur high transaction costs (particularly fees paid to stockbrokers) because they are buying a few shares of a lot of companies. Fortunately for such investors, mutual funds help solve the problem of achieving diversification without high transaction costs.

A **financial intermediary** is an institution that transforms the funds it gathers from many individuals into financial assets.

A **mutual fund** is a financial intermediary that creates a stock portfolio and then resells shares of this portfolio to individual investors.

A **mutual fund** is a financial intermediary that creates a stock portfolio by buying and holding shares in companies and then selling shares of the stock portfolio to individual investors. By buying these shares, investors with a relatively small amount of money to invest can indirectly hold a diversified portfolio, achieving a better return for any given level of risk than they could otherwise achieve.

Many mutual funds also perform market research on the companies they invest in. This is important because there are thousands of stock-issuing U.S. companies (not to mention foreign companies), each differing in terms of its likely profitability, dividend payments, and so on. It would be extremely time-consuming and costly for an individual investor to do adequate research on even a small number of companies. Mutual funds save transaction costs by doing this research for their customers.

The mutual fund industry represents a huge portion of the modern U.S. economy, not just of the U.S. financial system. In total, U.S. mutual funds had assets of $14.8 trillion at the end of 2013.

We should mention, by the way, that mutual funds charge fees for their services. These fees are quite small for mutual funds that simply hold a diversified portfolio of stocks, without trying to pick winners. But the fees charged by mutual funds that claim to have special expertise in investing your money can be quite high.

A **pension fund** is a type of mutual fund that holds assets in order to provide retirement income to its members.

A **life insurance company** sells policies that guarantee a payment to a policyholder's beneficiaries when the policyholder dies.

A **bank deposit** is a claim on a bank that obliges the bank to give the depositor his or her cash when demanded.

A **bank** is a financial intermediary that provides liquid assets in the form of bank deposits to lenders and uses those funds to finance the illiquid investment spending needs of borrowers.

PENSION FUNDS AND LIFE INSURANCE COMPANIES In addition to mutual funds, many Americans have holdings in **pension funds,** nonprofit institutions that collect the savings of their members and invest those funds in a wide variety of assets, providing their members with income when they retire. Although pension funds are subject to some special rules and receive special treatment for tax purposes, they function much like mutual funds. They invest in a diverse array of financial assets, allowing their members to achieve more cost-effective diversification and market research than they would be able to achieve on their own.

Americans also have substantial holdings in the policies of **life insurance companies,** which guarantee a payment to the policyholder's beneficiaries (typically, the family) when the policyholder dies. By enabling policyholders to cushion their beneficiaries from financial hardship arising from their death, life insurance companies also improve welfare by reducing risk.

BANKS Recall that, other things equal, people want assets that can be readily converted into cash. Bonds and stocks are much more liquid than physical assets or loans, yet the transaction cost of selling bonds or stocks to meet a sudden expense can be large. Furthermore, for many small and moderate-sized companies, the cost of issuing bonds and stocks is too large given the modest amount of money they seek to raise. A *bank* is an institution that helps resolve the conflict between lenders' needs for liquidity and the financing needs of borrowers who don't want to use the stock or bond markets.

An increase in bank deposits in South Korea in the late 1960s allowed businesses to launch an investment spending boom that contributed to the country's spectacular economic growth.

A bank works by first accepting funds from *depositors:* when you put your money in a bank, you are essentially becoming a lender by lending the bank your money. In return, you receive credit for a **bank deposit**—a claim on the bank, which is obliged to give you your cash if and when you demand it.

So a bank deposit is a financial asset owned by the depositor and a liability of the bank that holds it.

A bank, however, keeps only a fraction of its customers' deposits in the form of ready cash. Most of its deposits are lent out to businesses, buyers of new homes, and other borrowers. These loans come with a long-term commitment by the bank to the borrower: as long as the borrower makes his or her payments on time, the loan cannot be recalled by the bank and converted into cash. So a bank enables those who wish to borrow for long lengths of time to use the funds of those who wish to lend but simultaneously want to maintain the ability to get their cash back on demand. More formally, a **bank** is a financial intermediary that provides liquid financial assets in the form of deposits to lenders and uses their funds to finance the illiquid investment spending needs of borrowers.

In essence, a bank is engaging in a kind of mismatch: lending for long periods of time while subject to the condition that its depositors could demand their funds back at any time. How can it manage that?

The bank counts on the fact that, on average, only a small fraction of its depositors will want their cash at the same time. On any given day, some people will make withdrawals and others will make new deposits; these will roughly cancel each other out. So the bank needs to keep only a limited amount of cash on hand to satisfy its depositors.

In addition, if a bank becomes financially incapable of paying its depositors, individual bank deposits are guaranteed to depositors up to $250,000 by the Federal Deposit Insurance Corporation, or FDIC, a federal agency. This reduces the risk to a depositor of holding a bank deposit, in turn reducing the incentive to withdraw funds if concerns about the financial state of the bank should arise. So, under normal conditions, banks need hold only a fraction of their depositors' cash.

By reconciling the needs of savers for liquid assets with the needs of borrowers for long-term financing, banks play a key economic role.

Financial Fluctuations and Macroeconomic Policy

We've learned that the financial system is an essential part of the economy; without stock markets, bond markets, and banks, long-run economic growth would be hard to achieve. Yet the news isn't entirely good: the financial system sometimes doesn't function well and instead is a source of instability in the short run because of asset price fluctuations. We saw this in 2008 as the economy faced a severe slump resulting from a sharp reduction in home values (a situation that we examine in detail in the upcoming Economics in Action).

How should economists and policy makers deal with the fact that asset prices fluctuate a lot and that these fluctuations can have important economic effects? This question has become one of the major problems for macroeconomic policy. On one side, policy makers are reluctant to assume that the market is wrong—that asset prices are either too high or too low. It's hard to make the general case that government officials are better judges of appropriate prices than private investors who are putting their own money on the line.

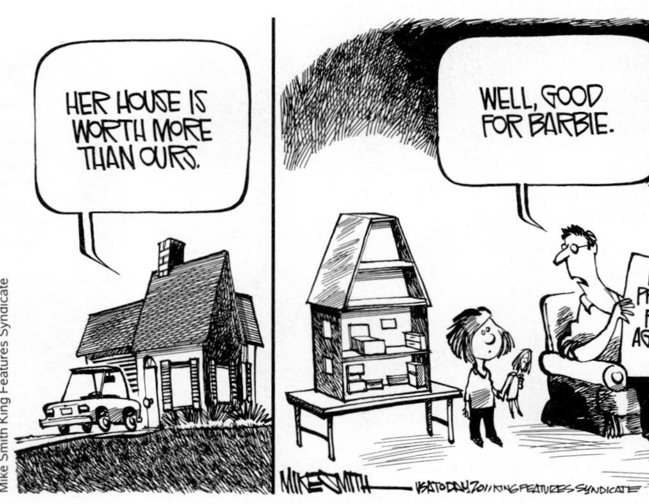

Mike Smith King Features Syndicate

On the other side, the past 15 years were marked by not one but two huge asset bubbles, each of which created major macroeconomic problems when it burst. In the late 1990s the prices of technology stocks, including but not limited to dot-com Internet firms, soared to hard-to-justify heights. When the bubble burst, these stocks lost, on average, two-thirds of their value in a short time, helping to cause the 2001 recession and a period of high unemployment. A few years later there was a major bubble in housing prices. The collapse of this bubble in 2008 triggered a severe financial crisis followed by a deep recession.

These events have led to a fierce debate among economists over whether policy makers should try to pop asset bubbles before they get too big.

ECONOMICS IN ACTION

THE GREAT AMERICAN HOUSING BUBBLE

Between 2000 and 2006, there was a huge increase in the price of houses in America. By the summer of 2006, home prices were well over twice as high as they had been in January 2000 in a number of major U.S. metropolitan areas, including Los Angeles, San Diego, San Francisco, Washington, Miami, Las Vegas, and New York. By 2004, as the increase in home prices accelerated, a number of economists (including the authors of this textbook) argued that this price increase was excessive—that it was a bubble, a rise in asset prices driven by unrealistic expectations about future prices.

It was certainly true that home prices rose much more than the cost of renting a comparable place to live. Panel (a) of Figure 59-1 compares a widely used index of U.S. housing prices with the U.S. government's index of the cost of renting, both shown as index numbers with January 2000 = 100. Home prices shot up, even though rental rates grew only gradually.

FIGURE 59-1 The Great American Housing Bubble

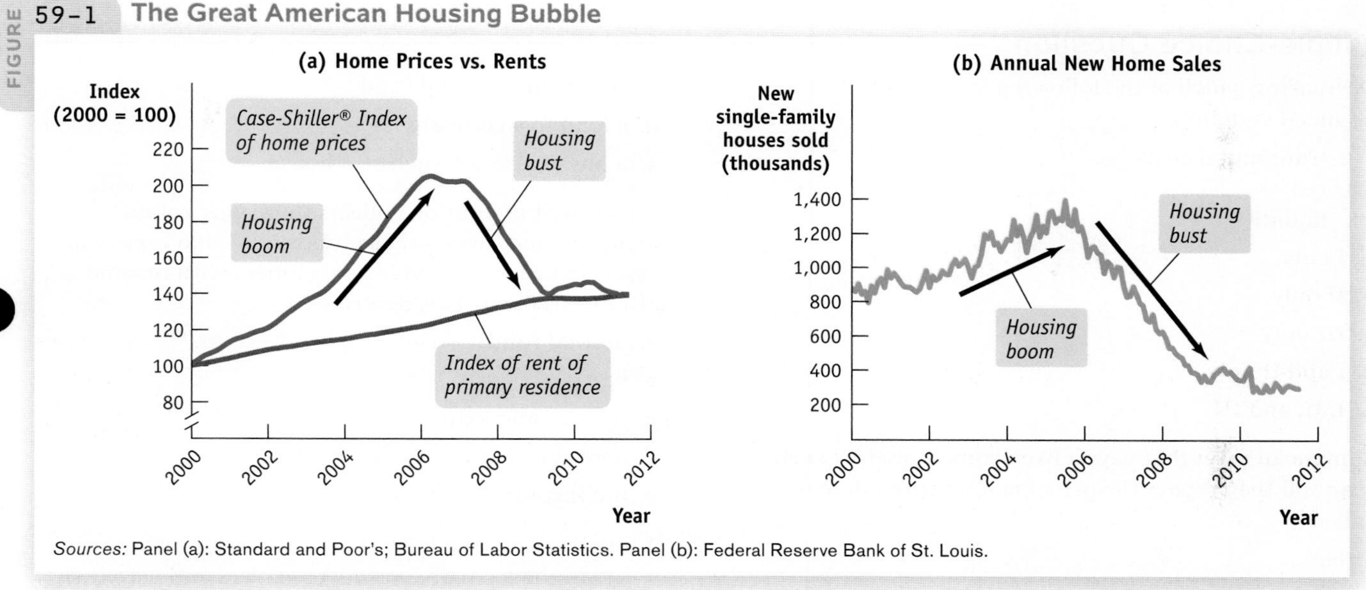

Sources: Panel (a): Standard and Poor's; Bureau of Labor Statistics. Panel (b): Federal Reserve Bank of St. Louis.

Yet there were also a number of economists who argued that the rise in housing prices was completely justified. They pointed, in particular, to interest rates that were unusually low in the years of rapid price increases, and they argued that low interest rates combined with other factors, such as growing population, explained the surge in prices. Alan Greenspan, then chairman of the Federal Reserve, conceded in 2005 that there might be some "froth" in the markets but denied that there was any national bubble.

Unfortunately, it turned out that the skeptics were right. Greenspan himself would later concede that there had, in fact, been a huge national bubble. In 2006, as home prices began to level off, it became apparent that many buyers had held unrealistic expectations about future prices. As home prices began to fall, expectations of future increases in home prices were revised downward, precipitating a sudden and dramatic collapse in prices. And with home prices falling, the demand for housing fell drastically, as illustrated by panel (b) of Figure 59-1.

The implosion in housing, in turn, created numerous economic difficulties, including severe stress on the banking system.

MODULE 59 Review

Solutions appear at the back of the book.

Check Your Understanding

1. Rank the following assets from the lowest level to the highest level of (i) transaction costs, (ii) risk, (iii) liquidity. Ties are acceptable for items that have indistinguishable rankings.
   a. a bank deposit with a guaranteed interest rate
   b. a share of a highly diversified mutual fund, which can be quickly sold
   c. a share of the family business, which can be sold only if you find a buyer and all other family members agree to the sale

2. What relationship would you expect to find between the level of development of a country's financial system and its level of economic development? Explain in terms of the country's levels of savings and investment spending.

Multiple-Choice Questions

1. Decreasing which of the following is a task of the financial system?
   I. transaction costs
   II. risk
   III. liquidity
   a. I only
   b. II only
   c. III only
   d. I and II only
   e. I, II, and III

2. A financial asset that pays a fixed sum of interest each year and then repays the principal on a given date is called a
   a. bond.
   b. stock.
   c. mutual fund.
   d. loan.
   e. loan-backed security.

3. Which of the following assets is the most diversified?
   a. stock in a company
   b. a bond issued by a company
   c. shares in a mutual fund
   d. a loan to a company
   e. a physical asset, such as a house

4. A nonprofit institution collects the savings of its members and invests those funds in a wide variety of assets in order to provide its members with income after retirement. This describes a
   a. mutual fund.
   b. bank.
   c. savings and loan.
   d. pension fund.
   e. life insurance company.

5. A financial intermediary that provides liquid financial assets in the form of deposits to lenders and uses their funds to finance the illiquid investment spending needs of borrowers is called a
   a. mutual fund.
   b. bank.
   c. corporation.
   d. pension fund.
   e. life insurance company.

Critical-Thinking Question

List and describe the four most important types of financial intermediaries.

SECTION 18 REVIEW

Summary

Savings and Investment Spending

1. Investment in physical capital is necessary for long-run economic growth. So in order for an economy to grow, it must channel savings into investment spending.
2. According to the **savings–investment spending identity,** savings and investment spending are always equal for the economy as a whole.
3. The government is a source of savings when it runs a positive **budget balance,** also known as a **budget surplus;** it is a source of dissavings when it runs a negative budget balance, also known as a **budget deficit.**
4. In a closed economy, savings is equal to **national savings,** the sum of private savings plus the budget balance. In an open economy, savings is equal to national savings plus **net capital inflow** of foreign savings. When a negative net capital inflow occurs, some portion of national savings is funding investment spending in other countries.

The Market for Loanable Funds

5. The hypothetical **loanable funds market** shows how loans from savers are allocated among borrowers with investment spending projects. By showing how gains from trade between lenders and borrowers are maximized, the loanable funds market shows why a well-functioning financial system leads to greater long-run economic growth.
6. Increasing or persistent government budget deficits can lead to **crowding out:** higher interest rates and reduced investment spending. This tells us that the demand curve for loanable funds is downward sloping. Changes in perceived business opportunities and in government borrowing shift the demand curve for loanable funds; changes in private savings and capital inflows shift the supply curve.
7. Because neither borrowers nor lenders can know the future inflation rate, loans specify a nominal interest rate rather than a real interest rate. For a given expected future inflation rate, shifts of the demand and supply curves of loanable funds result in changes in the underlying real interest rate, leading to changes in the nominal interest rate. According to the **Fisher effect,** an increase in expected future inflation raises the nominal interest rate one-to-one so that the expected real interest rate remains unchanged.

The Time Value of Money

8. The **present value** of a sum of money measures its value today.
9. The **net present value** of a project is the present value of current and future benefits minus the present value of current and future costs.

The Financial System

10. Households invest their current savings or **wealth**—their accumulated savings—by purchasing assets. Assets come in the form of either a **financial asset,** a paper claim that entitles the buyer to future income from the seller, or a **physical asset,** a tangible object that can generate future income.
11. A financial asset is also a **liability** from the point of view of its seller. There are four main types of financial assets: **loans,** bonds, stocks, and **bank deposits.** Each of them serves a different purpose in addressing the three fundamental tasks of a financial system: reducing **transaction costs**—the cost of making a deal; reducing **financial risk**—uncertainty about future outcomes that involves financial gains and losses; and providing **liquid** assets—assets that can be quickly converted into cash without much loss of value (in contrast to **illiquid** assets, which are not easily converted).
12. Although many small and moderate-sized borrowers use bank loans to fund investment spending, larger companies typically issue bonds. Bonds with a higher risk of **default** must typically pay a higher interest rate.
13. Business owners reduce their risk by selling stock. Although stocks usually generate a higher return than bonds, investors typically wish to reduce their risk by engaging in **diversification,** owning a wide range of assets whose returns are based on unrelated, or independent, events. Most people are risk-averse, more sensitive to a loss than to an equal-sized gain.
14. **Loan-backed securities,** a recent innovation, are assets created by pooling individual loans and selling shares of that pool to investors. Because they are more diversified and more liquid than individual loans, bonds are preferred by investors. It can be difficult, however, to assess a bond's quality.
15. **Financial intermediaries**—institutions such as **mutual funds, pension funds, life insurance companies,** and **banks**—are critical components of the financial system. Mutual funds and pension funds allow small investors to diversify, and life insurance companies reduce risk.
16. A bank allows individuals to hold liquid bank deposits that are then used to finance illiquid loans. Banks can perform this mismatch because on average only a small fraction of depositors withdraw their funds at any one time. A well-functioning banking sector is a key ingredient of long-run economic growth.

Key Terms

Savings–investment spending identity, p. 578
Budget surplus, p. 579
Budget deficit, p. 579
Budget balance, p. 579
National savings, p. 580
Net capital inflow, p. 580
Loanable funds market, p. 584
Crowding out, p. 589
Fisher effect, p. 591
Present value, p. 596
Net present value, p. 597
Wealth, p. 600
Financial asset, p. 600
Physical asset, p. 600
Liability, p. 600
Transaction costs, p. 601
Financial risk, p. 601
Diversification, p. 602
Liquid, p. 602
Illiquid, p. 602
Default, p. 603
Loan-backed securities, p. 603
Financial intermediary, p. 604
Mutual fund, p. 604
Pension fund, p. 605
Life insurance company, p. 605
Bank deposit, p. 605
Bank, p. 605

Problems

1. Given the following information about the closed economy of Brittania, what is the level of investment spending and private savings, and what is the budget balance? What is the relationship among the three? Is national savings equal to investment spending? There are no government transfers.

$GDP = \$1{,}000$ million $\quad T = \$50$ million
$C = \$850$ million $\quad G = \$100$ million

2. Explain how a well-functioning financial system increases savings and investment spending, holding the budget balance and any capital flows fixed.

3. Boris Borrower and Lynn Lender agree that Lynn will lend Boris $10,000 and that Boris will repay the $10,000 with interest in one year. They agree to a nominal interest rate of 8%, reflecting a real interest rate of 3% on the loan and a commonly shared expected inflation rate of 5% over the next year.

   a. If the inflation rate is actually 4% over the next year, how does that lower-than-expected inflation rate affect Boris and Lynn? Who is better off?

   b. If the actual inflation rate is 7% over the next year, how does that affect Boris and Lynn? Who is better off?

4. Explain why equilibrium in the loanable funds market maximizes efficiency.

5. Use the market for loanable funds shown in the accompanying diagram to explain what happens to private savings, private investment spending, and the interest rate if each of the following events occur. Assume that there are no capital inflows or outflows.

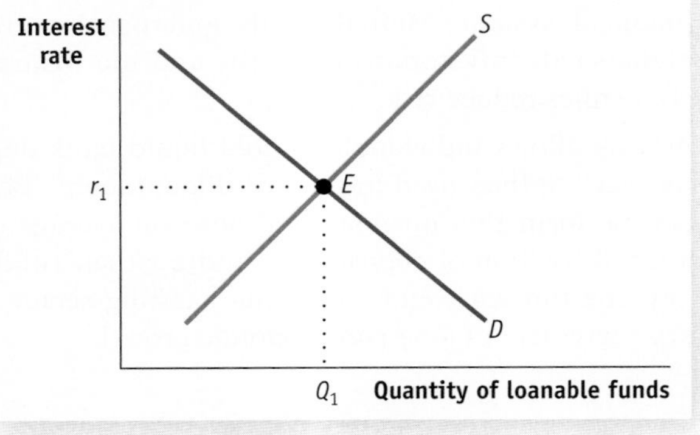

   a. The government reduces the size of its deficit to zero.

   b. At any given interest rate, consumers decide to save more. Assume the budget balance is zero.

   c. At any given interest rate, businesses become very optimistic about the future profitability of investment spending. Assume the budget balance is zero.

6. In 2010, Congress estimated that the cost of increasing the U.S. presence in Afghanistan by 30,000 troops was approximately $36 billion. The U.S. government was running a budget deficit at the time, so assume that the surge in troop levels was financed by government borrowing, which increases the demand for loanable funds without affecting supply. This question considers the likely effect of this government expenditure on the interest rate.

   a. Draw typical demand (D_1) and supply (S_1) curves for loanable funds without the cost of the surge in troop levels accounted for. Label the vertical axis "Interest rate" and the horizontal axis "Quantity of loanable funds." Label the equilibrium point (E_1) and the equilibrium interest rate (r_1).

   b. Now draw a new diagram with the cost of the surge in troop levels included in the analysis. Shift the demand curve in the appropriate direction. Label the new equilibrium point (E_2) and the new equilibrium interest rate (r_2).

   c. How does the equilibrium interest rate change in response to government expenditure on the troop surge? Explain.

7. How would you respond to a friend who claims that the government should eliminate all purchases that are financed by borrowing because such borrowing crowds out private investment spending?

8. Using the accompanying diagram, explain what will happen to the market for loanable funds when there is a fall of 2 percentage points in the expected future inflation rate. How will the change in the expected future inflation rate affect the equilibrium quantity of loanable funds?

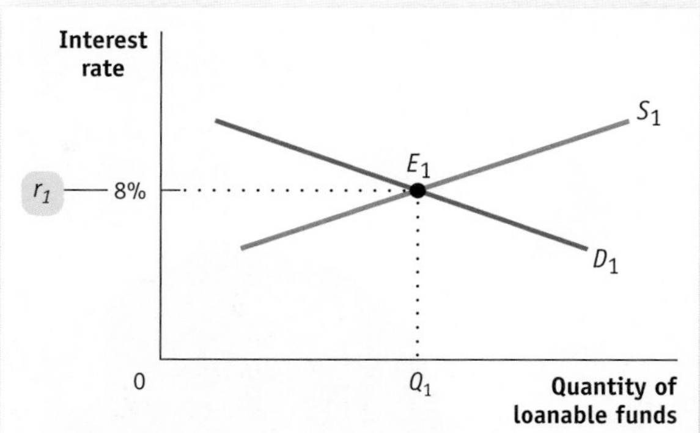

9. You have won the state lottery. There are two ways in which you can receive your prize. You can either have \$1 million in cash now, or you can have \$1.2 million that is paid out as follows: \$300,000 now, \$300,000 in one year's time, \$300,000 in two years' time, and \$300,000 in three years' time. The interest rate is 20%. How would you prefer to receive your prize?

10. The drug company Pfizer is considering whether to invest in the development of a new cancer drug. Development will require an initial investment of \$10 million now; beginning one year from now, the drug will generate annual profits of \$4 million for three years.

    a. If the interest rate is 12%, should Pfizer invest in the development of the new drug? Why or why not?

    b. If the interest rate is 8%, should Pfizer invest in the development of the new drug? Why or why not?

11. What are the important types of financial intermediaries in the U.S. economy? What are the primary assets of these intermediaries, and how do they facilitate investment spending and saving?

12. Sallie Mae is a quasi-governmental agency that packages individual student loans into pools of loans and sells shares of these pools to investors as Sallie Mae bonds.

    a. What is this process called? What effect will it have on investors compared to situations in which they could only buy and sell individual student loans?

    b. What effect do you think Sallie Mae's actions will have on the ability of students to get loans?

    c. Suppose that a very severe recession hits and, as a consequence, many graduating students cannot get jobs and default on their student loans. What effect will this have on Sallie Mae bonds? Why is it likely that investors now believe Sallie Mae bonds to be riskier than expected? What will be the effect on the availability of student loans?

13. For each of the following, is it an example of investment spending, investing in financial assets, or investing in physical assets?

    a. Rupert Moneybucks buys 100 shares of existing Coca-Cola stock.

    b. Rhonda Moviestar spends \$10 million to buy a mansion built in the 1970s.

    c. Ronald Basketballstar spends \$10 million to build a new mansion with a view of the Pacific Ocean.

    d. Rawlings builds a new plant to make catcher's mitts.

    e. Russia buys \$100 million in U.S. government bonds.

Module 60: The Multiplier
Module 61: Consumption and Investment Spending
Module 62: The Income–Expenditure Model

SECTION 19 Income and Expenditure

FROM BOOM TO BUST

Ft. Myers, Florida, was a boom town from 2003 to 2005. Jobs were plentiful: the unemployment rate in the Ft. Myers–Cape Coral metropolitan area was less than 3%. Shopping malls were humming, and new stores were opening everywhere.

But then the boom went bust. Jobs became scarce, and by the middle of 2010, the unemployment rate was above 13%. Stores had few customers, and many were closing. One new business was flourishing, however. As the local economy plunged, real estate agents began offering "foreclosure tours": visits to homes that had been seized by banks after the owners were unable to make mortgage payments—and were available at bargain prices.

What happened? Ft. Myers boomed because of a surge in home construction, fueled in part by speculators who bought houses not to live in, but to resell at much higher prices. Home construction gave jobs to construction workers, electricians, roofers, real estate agents, and others. These workers, in turn, spent money locally, creating jobs for waiters, gardeners, pool cleaners, sales people, and more. These workers, in turn, also spent money locally, creating further expansion, and so on.

The boom turned into a bust when home construction suddenly came to a virtual halt. It turned out that speculation had been feeding on itself: people were buying houses as investments, then selling them to others who were also buying houses as investments, and prices had risen to levels far beyond what people who actually wanted to live in houses were willing to pay.

The local economy then collapsed, as the process that had created the earlier boom operated in reverse. The jobs created by home construction went away, leading to a fall in local spending, leading to a loss of other local jobs, leading to further declines in spending, and so on.

The boom and bust in Ft. Myers illustrates, on a small scale, the way booms and busts happen for the economy as a whole. The business cycle is often driven by ups or downs in investment spending—either residential investment spending (that is, home construction) or nonresidential investment spending (such as the construction of office buildings, factories, and shopping malls). Changes in investment spending, in turn, indirectly lead to changes in consumer spending, which magnify—or, as economists usually say, *multiply*—the effect of the investment spending changes on the economy as a whole.

In this section we'll study how this process works, showing how *multiplier* analysis helps us understand the business cycle.

MODULE 60 The Multiplier

Thinkstock

WHAT YOU WILL LEARN

1. **The significance of the marginal propensity to consume**
2. **The nature of the multiplier, which shows how initial changes in spending lead to further changes in spending**

The Multiplier: An Informal Introduction

The story of the boom and bust in Ft. Myers that opens this section involves a sort of chain reaction in which an initial rise or fall in aggregate spending leads to changes in income, which lead to further changes in aggregate spending, and so on. Let's examine that chain reaction more closely, this time thinking through the effects of changes in aggregate spending in the economy as a whole.

For the sake of this analysis, we'll make four simplifying assumptions that we'll revisit later.

1. We assume that *producers are willing to supply additional output at a fixed price.* That is, if consumers or businesses buying investment goods decide to spend an additional $1 billion, that will translate into the production of $1 billion worth of additional goods and services without driving up the overall level of prices. As a result, *changes in aggregate spending translate into changes in aggregate output,* as measured by real GDP. As we'll learn, this assumption isn't too unrealistic in the short run, but it needs to be changed when we think about the long-run effects of changes in demand.
2. We take the interest rate as given.
3. We assume that there is no government spending and no taxes.
4. We assume that exports and imports are zero.

Given these simplifying assumptions, consider what happens if there is a change in investment spending. Specifically, imagine that for some reason home builders decide to spend an extra $100 billion on home construction over the next year.

The direct effect of this increase in investment spending will be to increase income and the value of aggregate output by the same amount. That's because each dollar spent on home construction translates into a dollar's worth of income for construction workers, suppliers of building materials, electricians, and so on. If the process stopped there, the increase in housing investment spending would raise overall income by exactly $100 billion.

But the process doesn't stop there. The increase in aggregate output leads to an increase in disposable income that flows to households in the form of profits and wages. The increase in households' disposable income leads to a rise in consumer spending, which, in turn, induces firms to increase output yet again. This generates another rise in disposable income, which leads to another round of consumer spending increases, and so on. So there are multiple rounds of increases in aggregate output.

How large is the total effect on aggregate output if we sum the effect from all these rounds of spending increases? To answer this question, we need to introduce the concept of the **marginal propensity to consume,** or ***MPC:*** the increase in consumer spending when disposable income rises by $1. When consumer spending changes because of a rise or fall in disposable income, *MPC* is the change in consumer spending divided by the change in disposable income:

The **marginal propensity to consume,** or ***MPC,*** is the increase in consumer spending when disposable income rises by $1.

The **marginal propensity to save,** or ***MPS,*** is the increase in household savings when disposable income rises by $1.

(60-1) $$MPC = \frac{\Delta \text{ Consumer spending}}{\Delta \text{ Disposable income}}$$

where the symbol Δ (delta) means "change in." For example, if consumer spending goes up by $6 billion when disposable income goes up by $10 billion, *MPC* is $6 billion/$10 billion = 0.6.

Because consumers normally spend part but not all of an additional dollar of disposable income, *MPC* is a number between 0 and 1. The additional disposable income that consumers don't spend is saved; the **marginal propensity to save,** or ***MPS,*** is the fraction of an additional dollar of disposable income that is saved. *MPS* is equal to 1 – *MPC*.

Because we assumed that there are no taxes and no international trade, each $1 increase in aggregate spending raises both real GDP and disposable income by $1. So the $100 billion increase in investment spending initially raises real GDP by $100 billion. This leads to a second-round increase in consumer spending, which raises real GDP by a further *MPC* × $100 billion. It is followed by a third-round increase in consumer spending of *MPC* × *MPC* × $100 billion, and so on. After an infinite number of rounds, the total effect on real GDP is:

$$\begin{aligned}
&\text{Increase in investment spending} &&= &&\$100 \text{ billion}\\
&+ \text{Second-round increase in consumer spending} &&= MPC &&\times \$100 \text{ billion}\\
&+ \text{Third-round increase in consumer spending} &&= MPC^2 &&\times \$100 \text{ billion}\\
&+ \text{Fourth-round increase in consumer spending} &&= MPC^3 &&\times \$100 \text{ billion}\\
& \quad\vdots && && \vdots
\end{aligned}$$

$$\text{Total increase in real GDP} = (1 + MPC + MPC^2 + MPC^3 + \ldots) \times \$100 \text{ billion}$$

So the $100 billion increase in investment spending sets off a chain reaction in the economy. The net result of this chain reaction is that a $100 billion increase in investment spending leads to a change in real GDP that is a *multiple* of the size of that initial change in spending.

How large is this multiple? It's a mathematical fact that an infinite series of the form $1 + x + x^2 + x^3 + \ldots$, where x is between 0 and 1, is equal to $1/(1 - x)$. So the total effect of a $100 billion increase in investment spending, *I*, taking into account all the subsequent increases in consumer spending (and assuming no taxes and no international trade), is given by:

(60-2) Total increase in real GDP from a $100 billion rise in *I*

$$= \frac{1}{1 - MPC} \times \$100 \text{ billion}$$

TABLE 60-1

Rounds of Increases of Real GDP When *MPC* = 0.6

	Increase in real GDP (billions)	Total increase in real GDP (billions)
First round	$100	$100
Second round	60	160
Third round	36	196
Fourth round	21.6	217.6
...	...	...
Final round	0	250

Let's consider a numerical example in which *MPC* = 0.6: each $1 in additional disposable income causes a $0.60 rise in consumer spending. In that case, a $100 billion increase in investment spending raises real GDP by $100 billion in the first round. The second-round increase in consumer spending raises real GDP by another 0.6 × $100 billion, or $60 billion. The third-round increase in consumer spending raises real GDP by another 0.6 × $60 billion, or $36 billion.

Table 60-1 shows the successive stages of increases, where ". . . " means the process goes on an infinite number of times. In the end, real GDP rises by $250 billion as a consequence of the initial $100 billion rise in investment spending:

$$\frac{1}{1-0.6} \times \$100 \text{ billion} = 2.5 \times \$100 \text{ billion} = \$250 \text{ billion}$$

Notice that even though there are an infinite number of rounds of expansion of real GDP, the total rise in real GDP is limited to $250 billion. The reason is that at each stage some of the rise in disposable income "leaks out" because it is saved. How much of an additional dollar of disposable income is saved depends on *MPS*, the marginal propensity to save.

We've described the effects of a change in investment spending, but the same analysis can be applied to any other change in aggregate spending. The important thing is to distinguish between the initial change in aggregate spending, before real GDP rises, and the additional change in aggregate spending caused by the change in real GDP as the chain reaction unfolds.

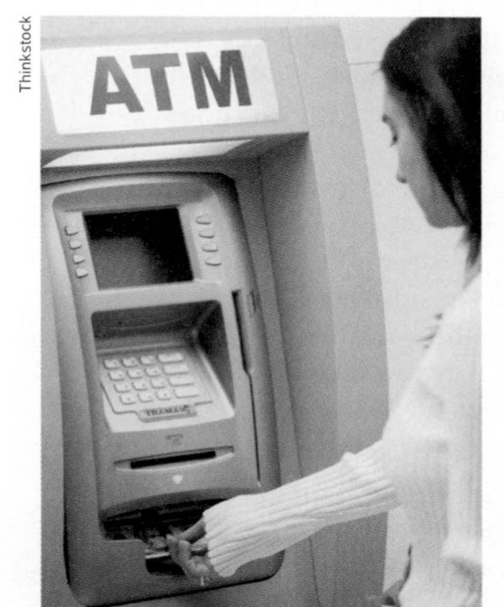

Thinkstock

Spending by one person or firm has a domino effect that leads to progressively more spending in the economy.

For example, suppose that a boom in housing prices makes consumers feel richer and that, as a result, they become willing to spend more at any given level of disposable income. This will lead to an initial rise in consumer spending, before real GDP rises. But it will also lead to second and later rounds of higher consumer spending as real GDP rises.

An initial rise or fall in aggregate spending at a given level of real GDP is called an **autonomous change in aggregate spending.** It's autonomous—which means "self-governing"—because it's the cause, not the result, of the chain reaction we've just described.

Formally, the **multiplier** is the ratio of the total change in real GDP caused by an autonomous change in aggregate spending to the size of that autonomous change. If we let ΔAAS stand for autonomous change in aggregate spending and ΔY stand for the change in real GDP, then the multiplier is equal to $\Delta Y/\Delta AAS$. And we've already seen how to find the value of the multiplier. Assuming no taxes and no trade, the change in real GDP caused by an autonomous change in spending is:

$$\textbf{(60-3)}\quad \Delta Y = \frac{1}{1-MPC} \times \Delta AAS$$

So the multiplier is:

$$\textbf{(60-4)}\quad \text{Multiplier} = \frac{\Delta Y}{\Delta AAS} = \frac{1}{1-MPC}$$

An **autonomous change in aggregate spending** is an initial change in the desired level of spending by firms, households, or government at a given level of real GDP.

The **multiplier** is the ratio of the total change in real GDP caused by an autonomous change in aggregate spending to the size of that autonomous change.

Notice that the size of the multiplier depends on *MPC*. If the marginal propensity to consume is high, so is the multiplier. This is true because the size of *MPC* determines how large each round of expansion is compared with the previous round. To put it another way, the higher *MPC* is, the less disposable income "leaks out" into savings at each round of expansion.

In later modules we'll use the concept of the multiplier to analyze the effects of fiscal and monetary policies. We'll also see that the formula for the multiplier changes when we introduce various complications, including taxes and foreign trade. First we need to look more deeply at what determines consumer spending.

ECONOMICS ▶ IN ACTION

THE MULTIPLIER AND THE GREAT DEPRESSION

The concept of the multiplier was originally devised by economists trying to understand the greatest economic disaster in history, the collapse of output and employment from 1929 to 1933, which began the Great Depression. Most economists believe that the slump from 1929 to 1933 was driven by a collapse in investment spending. But as the economy shrank, consumer spending also fell sharply, multiplying the effect on real GDP.

TABLE 60-2

Investment Spending, Consumer Spending, and Real GDP in the Great Depression (billions of 2005 dollars)

	1929	1933	Change
Investment spending	$101.4	$18.9	−$82.5
Consumer spending	736.3	600.8	−135.5
Real GDP	976.1	715.8	−260.3

Source: Bureau of Economic Analysis.

Table 60-2 shows what happened to investment spending, consumer spending, and GDP during those four terrible years. What we see is that investment spending imploded, falling by more than 80%. But consumer spending also fell drastically and actually accounted for more of the fall in real GDP. (The total fall in real GDP was larger than the combined fall in consumer and investment spending, mainly because of technical accounting issues.)

The numbers in Table 60-2 suggest that at the time of the Great Depression, the multiplier was around 3. Most current estimates put the size of the multiplier considerably lower—but there's a reason for that change. In 1929, government in the United States was very small by modern standards: taxes were low and major government programs like Social Security and Medicare had not yet come into being. In the modern U.S. economy, taxes are much higher, and so is government spending. Why does this matter? Because taxes and some government programs act as *automatic stabilizers,* reducing the size of the multiplier.

MODULE 60 Review

Solutions appear at the back of the book.

Check Your Understanding

1. Explain why a decline in investment spending caused by a change in business expectations leads to a fall in consumer spending.
2. What is the multiplier if the marginal propensity to consume is 0.5? What is it if *MPC* is 0.8?
3. As a percentage of GDP, savings accounts for a larger share of the economy in the country of Scania compared to the country of Amerigo. Which country is likely to have the larger multiplier? Explain.

Multiple-Choice Questions

1. A $100 million increase in investment spending will cause real GDP to
   a. decrease by $100 million.
   b. increase by $100 million.
   c. decrease by less than $100 million.
   d. increase by less than $100 million.
   e. increase by more than $100 million.

2. The marginal propensity to consume measures the
   a. increase in consumer spending when disposable income rises by $1.
   b. increase in consumer spending when investment spending rises by $1.
   c. increase in consumer spending when taxes rise by $1.
   d. increase in disposable income when consumer spending rises by $1.
   e. increase in disposable income when investment spending rises by $1.

3. Assuming no taxes and no trade, the multiplier is equal to:
   a. MPC
   b. $\frac{1}{1 - MPC}$
   c. $\frac{1}{1 + MPC}$
   d. $\frac{1}{MPC}$
   e. $1 - MPC$

4. If the marginal propensity to consume is 0.5, then a $100 million increase in investment spending will increase real GDP by
   a. $100 million.
   b. $200 million.
   c. $50 million.
   d. $150 million.
   e. $300 million.

5. When income is $1,000, the level of consumption spending is equal to $850. When income rises to $1,200, the level of consumption spending is equal to $1,000. In this case the value of the marginal propensity to consume is
   a. 0.85.
   b. 0.83.
   c. 0.75.
   d. 0.50.
   e. 0.80.

Critical-Thinking Question

Explain how an autonomous change in aggregate spending affects real GDP, making reference to the multiplier concept.

Consumption and Investment Spending

Monkey Business Images/Shutterstock

Johner Images/Alamy

WHAT YOU WILL LEARN

1. The meaning of the aggregate consumption function, which shows how current disposable income affects consumer spending
2. How expected future income and aggregate wealth affect consumer spending
3. The determinants of investment spending
4. Why investment spending is a leading indicator of the future state of the economy

Consumer Spending

Should you splurge on a restaurant meal or save money by eating at home? Should you buy a new car and, if so, how expensive a model? Should you redo that bathroom or live with it for another year? In the real world, households are constantly confronted with such choices—not just about the consumption mix, but also about how much to spend in total. These choices, in turn, have a powerful effect on the economy: consumer spending normally accounts for two-thirds of total spending on final goods and services. In particular, the decision about how much of an additional dollar in income to spend—the marginal propensity to consume—determines the size of the multiplier, which determines the ultimate effect on the economy of autonomous changes in spending.

But what determines how much consumers spend?

Current Disposable Income and Consumer Spending

The most important factor affecting a family's consumer spending is its current disposable income—income after taxes are paid and government transfers are received. It's obvious from daily life that people with high disposable incomes on average drive more expensive cars, live in more expensive houses, and spend more on meals and clothing than people with lower disposable incomes. And the relationship between current disposable income and spending is clear in the data.

The Bureau of Labor Statistics (BLS) collects annual data on family income and spending. Families are grouped by levels of before-tax income, and after-tax income for each group is also reported. Since the income figures include transfers from the government, what the BLS calls a household's after-tax income is equivalent to its current disposable income.

FIGURE 61-1 **Current Disposable Income and Consumer Spending for American Households in 2012**

For each income group of households, average current disposable income in 2012 is plotted versus average consumer spending in 2012. For example, the middle income group, with an annual income of \$36,134 to \$59,514, is represented by point *A*, indicating a household average current disposable income of \$46,777 and average household consumer spending of \$43,004. The data clearly show a positive relationship between current disposable income and consumer spending: families with higher current disposable income have higher consumer spending.

Source: Bureau of Labor Statistics.

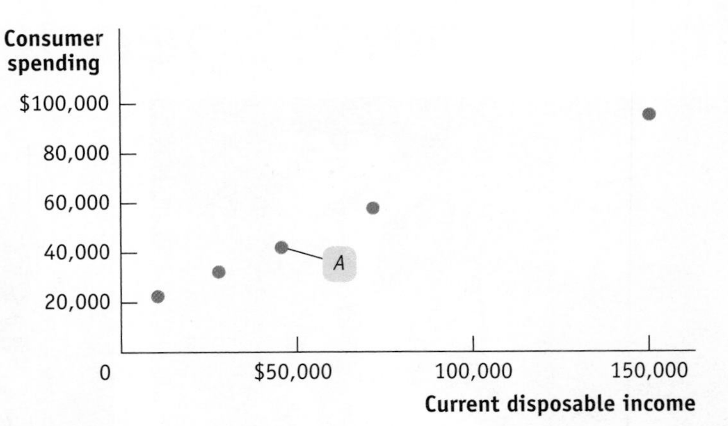

Panorama Productions Inc./Alamy

People with high disposable incomes tend to spend more than those with lower disposable incomes.

Figure 61-1 is a scatter diagram showing the relationship between household current disposable income and household consumer spending for American households by income group in 2012. For example, point *A* shows that in 2012 the middle fifth of the population had an average current disposable income of \$46,777 and average spending of \$43,004. The pattern of the dots slopes upward from left to right, making it clear that households with higher current disposable income had higher consumer spending.

It's very useful to represent the relationship between an individual household's current disposable income and its consumer spending with an equation. The **consumption function** is an equation showing how an individual household's consumer spending varies with the household's current disposable income. The simplest version of a consumption function is a linear equation:

(61-1) $c = a + MPC \times yd$

where lowercase letters indicate variables measured for an individual household.

In this equation, c is individual household consumer spending and yd is individual household current disposable income. Recall that MPC, the marginal propensity to consume, is the amount by which consumer spending rises if current disposable income rises by \$1. Finally, a is a constant term—individual household *autonomous consumer spending,* the amount of spending a household would do if it had zero disposable income. We assume that a is greater than zero because a household with zero disposable income is able to fund some consumption by borrowing or using its savings.

Notice, by the way, that we're using y for income. That's standard practice in macroeconomics, even though *income* isn't actually spelled "yncome." The reason is that I is reserved for investment spending.

Recall that we expressed MPC as the ratio of a change in consumer spending to the change in current disposable income. We've rewritten it for an individual household as Equation 61-2:

(61-2) $MPC = \Delta c / \Delta yd$

The **consumption function** is an equation showing how an individual household's consumer spending varies with the household's current disposable income.

Multiplying both sides of Equation 61-2 by Δyd, we get:

(61-3) $MPC \times \Delta yd = \Delta c$

Equation 61-3 tells us that when yd goes up by \$1, c goes up by $MPC \times \$1$.

FIGURE 61-2 **The Consumption Function**

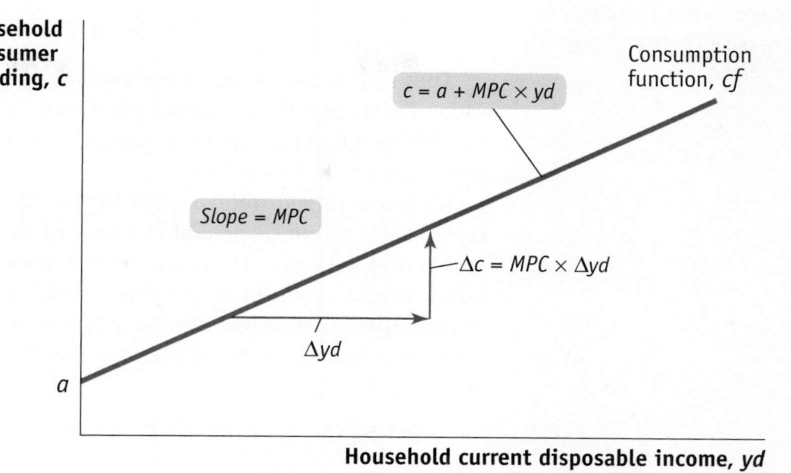

The consumption function relates a household's current disposable income to its consumer spending. The vertical intercept, *a*, is individual household autonomous consumer spending: the amount of a household's consumer spending if its current disposable income is zero. The slope of the consumption function line, *cf*, is the marginal propensity to consume, or *MPC*: of every additional $1 of current disposable income, *MPC* × $1 is spent.

Figure 61-2 shows what Equation 61-1 looks like graphically, plotting *yd* on the horizontal axis and *c* on the vertical axis. Individual household autonomous consumer spending, *a*, is the value of *c* when *yd* is zero—it is the vertical *intercept* of the consumption function, *cf*. *MPC* is the *slope* of the line, measured by rise over run. If current disposable income rises by Δyd, household consumer spending, *c*, rises by Δc. Since *MPC* is defined as $\Delta c/\Delta yd$, the slope of the consumption function is:

(61-4) Slope of consumption function
= Rise over run
= $\Delta c/\Delta yd$
= *MPC*

In reality, actual data never fit Equation 61-1 perfectly, but the fit can be pretty good. Figure 61-3 shows the data from Figure 61-1 again, together with a line drawn to fit the data as closely as possible. According to the data on households' consumer

FIGURE 61-3 **A Consumption Function Fitted to Data**

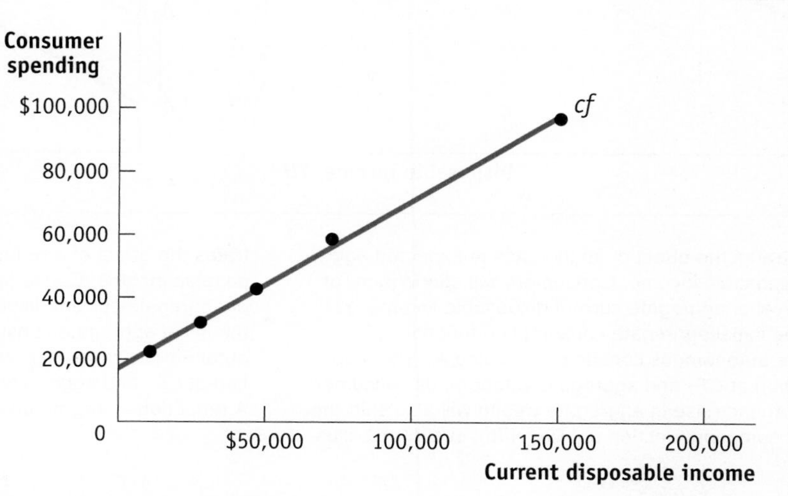

The data from Figure 61-1 are reproduced here, along with a line drawn to fit the data as closely as possible. For American households in 2012, the best estimate of the average household's autonomous consumer spending, *a*, is $18,478 and the best estimate of *MPC* is approximately 0.520.

Source: Bureau of Labor Statistics.

The **aggregate consumption function** is the relationship for the economy as a whole between aggregate current disposable income and aggregate consumer spending.

spending and current disposable income, the best estimate of a is \$18,478 and of MPC is 0.520. So the consumption function fitted to the data is:

$$c = \$18{,}478 + 0.520 \times yd$$

That is, the data suggest a marginal propensity to consume of approximately 0.52. This implies that the marginal propensity to save (MPS)—the amount of an additional \$1 of disposable income that is saved—is approximately 0.48, and the multiplier is approximately $1/0.48 = 2.08$.

It's important to realize that Figure 61-3 shows a *microeconomic* relationship between the current disposable income of individual households and their spending on goods and services. However, macroeconomists assume that a similar relationship holds *for the economy as a whole:* that there is a relationship, called the **aggregate consumption function,** between aggregate current disposable income and aggregate consumer spending. We'll assume that it has the same form as the household-level consumption function:

(61-5) $C = A + MPC \times YD$

Here, C is aggregate consumer spending (called just "consumer spending"); YD is aggregate current disposable income (called, for simplicity, just "disposable income"); and A is aggregate autonomous consumer spending, the amount of consumer spending when YD equals zero. This is the relationship represented in Figure 61-4 by CF, analogous to cf in Figure 61-3.

FIGURE 61-4 Shifts of the Aggregate Consumption Function

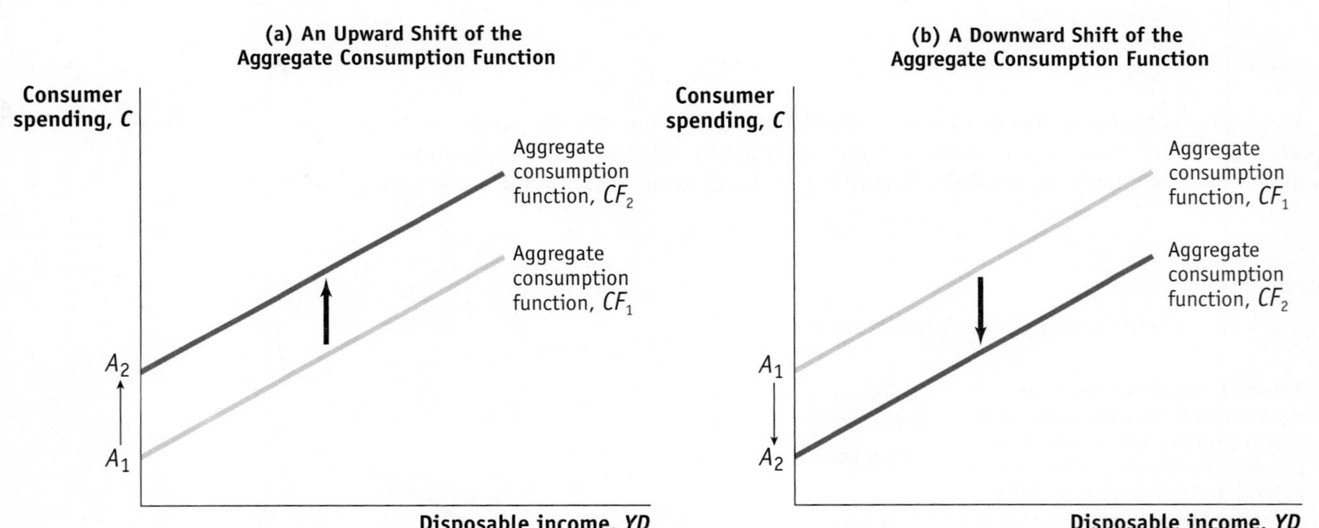

Panel (a) illustrates the effect of an increase in expected aggregate future disposable income. Consumers will spend more at every given level of aggregate current disposable income, YD. As a result, the initial aggregate consumption function CF_1, with aggregate autonomous consumer spending A_1, shifts up to a new position at CF_2 and aggregate autonomous consumer spending A_2. An increase in aggregate wealth will also shift the aggregate consumption function up. Panel (b), in contrast, illustrates the effect of a reduction in expected aggregate future disposable income. Consumers will spend less at every given level of aggregate current disposable income, YD. Consequently, the initial aggregate consumption function CF_1, with aggregate autonomous consumer spending A_1, shifts down to a new position at CF_2 and aggregate autonomous consumer spending A_2. A reduction in aggregate wealth will have the same effect.

Shifts of the Aggregate Consumption Function

The aggregate consumption function shows the relationship between disposable income and consumer spending for the economy as a whole, other things equal. When things other than disposable income change, the aggregate consumption function shifts. There are two principal causes of shifts of the aggregate consumption function: changes in expected future disposable income and changes in aggregate wealth.

CHANGES IN EXPECTED FUTURE DISPOSABLE INCOME Suppose you land a really good, well-paying job on graduating from college in May—but the job, and the paychecks, won't start until September. So your disposable income hasn't risen yet. Even so, it's likely that you will start spending more on final goods and services right away—maybe buying nicer work clothes than you originally planned—because you know that higher income is coming.

Conversely, suppose you have a good job but learn that the company is planning to downsize your division, raising the possibility that you may lose your job and have to take a lower-paying one somewhere else. Even though your disposable income hasn't gone down yet, you might well cut back on spending even while still employed, to save for a rainy day.

Both of these examples show how expectations about future disposable income can affect consumer spending. The two panels of Figure 61-4, which plot disposable income against consumer spending, show how changes in expected future disposable income affect the aggregate consumption function. In both panels, CF_1 is the initial aggregate consumption function. Panel (a) shows the effect of good news: information that leads consumers to expect higher disposable income in the future than they did before. Consumers will now spend more at any given level of current disposable income, *YD*, corresponding to an increase in *A*, aggregate autonomous consumer spending, from A_1 to A_2. The effect is to shift the aggregate consumption function up, from CF_1 to CF_2.

Panel (b) shows the effect of bad news: information that leads consumers to expect lower disposable income in the future than they did before. Consumers will now spend less at any given level of current disposable income, *YD*, corresponding to a fall in *A* from A_1 to A_2. The effect is to shift the aggregate consumption function down, from CF_1 to CF_2.

CHANGES IN AGGREGATE WEALTH Imagine two individuals, Maria and Mark, both of whom expect to earn $30,000 this year. Suppose, however, that they have different histories. Maria has been working steadily for the past 10 years, owns her own home, and has $200,000 in the bank. Mark is the same age as Maria, but he has been in and out of work, hasn't managed to buy a house, and has very little in savings. In this case, Maria has something that Mark doesn't have: wealth. Even though they have the same disposable income, other things equal, you'd expect Maria to spend more on consumption than Mark. That is, *wealth* has an effect on consumer spending.

The effect of wealth on spending is emphasized by an influential economic model of how consumers make choices about spending versus saving called the *life-cycle hypothesis*. According to this hypothesis, consumers plan their spending over a lifetime, not just in response to their current disposable income. As a result, people try to smooth their consumption over their lifetimes—they save some of their current disposable income during their years of peak earnings (typically occurring during a worker's 40s and 50s) and during their retirement live off the wealth they accumulated while working.

We won't go into the details of the life-cycle hypothesis but will simply point out that it implies an important role for wealth in determining consumer spending. For example, a middle-aged couple

Consumers tend to avoid high-priced brand-name goods and seek out less expensive alternatives when aggregate wealth declines.

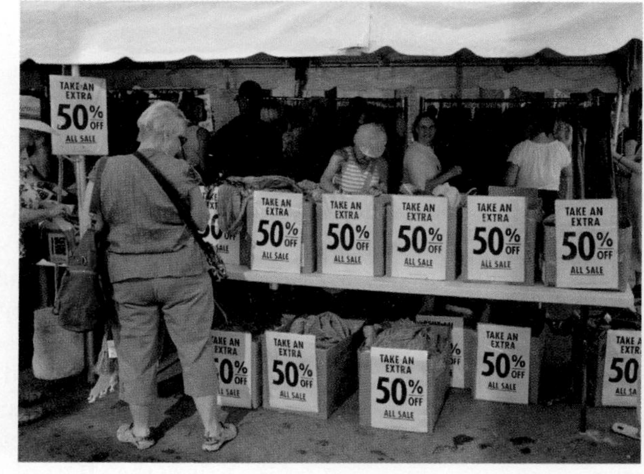

Joseph Sibilsky/Alamy

who have accumulated a lot of wealth—who have paid off the mortgage on their house and already own plenty of stocks and bonds—will, other things equal, spend more on goods and services than a couple who have the same current disposable income but still need to save for their retirement.

Because wealth affects household consumer spending, changes in wealth across the economy can shift the aggregate consumption function. A rise in aggregate wealth—say, because of a booming stock market—increases the vertical intercept A, aggregate autonomous consumer spending. This, in turn, shifts the aggregate consumption function up in the same way as does an expected increase in future disposable income. A decline in aggregate wealth—say, because of a fall in housing prices—reduces A and shifts the aggregate consumption function down.

Investment Spending

Although consumer spending is much larger than investment spending, booms and busts in investment spending tend to drive the business cycle. In fact, most recessions originate as a fall in investment spending. Figure 61-5 illustrates this point; it shows the annual percent change of investment spending and consumer spending in the United States, measured in real terms, during six recessions from 1973 to 2009. As you can see, swings in investment spending are much more dramatic than those in consumer spending. In addition, due to the multiplier process, economists believe that declines in consumer spending are usually the result of a process that begins with a slump in investment spending. Soon we'll examine in more detail how a slump in investment spending generates a fall in consumer spending through the multiplier process.

FIGURE 61-5 Fluctuations in Investment Spending and Consumer Spending

The bars illustrate the annual percent change in investment spending and consumer spending during six recent recessions. As the lengths of the bars show, swings in investment spending were much larger in percentage terms than those in consumer spending. This pattern has led economists to believe that recessions typically originate as a slump in investment spending.

Source: Bureau of Economic Analysis.

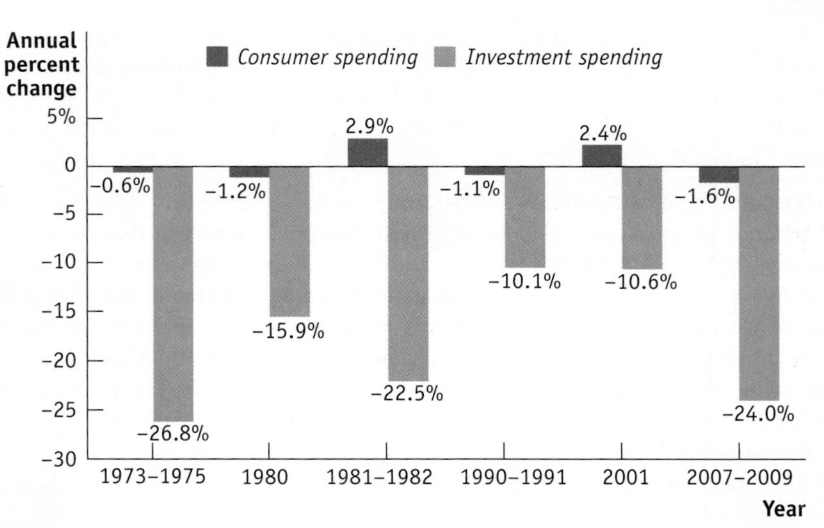

Before we do that, however, let's analyze the factors that determine investment spending, which are somewhat different from those that determine consumer spending. The most important ones are the interest rate and expected future real GDP.

Planned investment spending is the investment spending that businesses intend to undertake during a given period.

It's also important to note that the level of investment spending businesses *actually* carry out is sometimes not the same level as **planned investment spending,** the investment spending that firms *intend* to undertake during a given period. Planned investment spending depends on three principal factors: the interest rate, the expected future level of real GDP, and the current level of production capacity. First, we'll analyze the effect of the interest rate.

The Interest Rate and Investment Spending

Interest rates have their clearest effect on one particular form of investment spending: spending on residential construction—that is, on the construction of homes. The reason is straightforward: home builders only build houses they think they can sell, and houses are more affordable—and so more likely to sell—when the interest rate is low.

Consider a potential home-buying family that needs to borrow $150,000 to buy a house. At an interest rate of 7.5%, a 30-year home mortgage will mean payments of $1,048 per month. At an interest rate of 5.5%, those payments would be only $851 per month, making houses significantly more affordable. As described in the upcoming Economics in Action, lower interest rates helped set off the great housing boom described in the section-opening story.

Interest rates also affect other forms of investment spending. Firms with investment spending projects will only go ahead with a project if they expect a rate of return higher than the cost of the funds they would have to borrow to finance that project. As the interest rate rises, fewer projects will pass that test, and as a result investment spending will be lower.

Photodisc

Interest rates directly impact whether or not construction companies decide to invest in the building of new homes.

You might think that the trade-off a firm faces is different if it can fund its investment project with its past profits rather than through borrowing. Past profits used to finance investment spending are called *retained earnings*. But even if a firm pays for investment spending out of retained earnings, the trade-off it must make in deciding whether or not to fund a project remains the same because it must take into account the opportunity cost of its funds. For example, instead of purchasing new equipment, the firm could lend out the funds and earn interest. The forgone interest earned is the opportunity cost of using retained earnings to fund an investment project.

So the trade-off the firm faces when comparing a project's rate of return to the market interest rate has not changed when it uses retained earnings rather than borrowed funds, which means that regardless of whether a firm funds investment spending through borrowing or retained earnings, a rise in the market interest rate makes any given investment project less profitable. Conversely, a fall in the interest rate makes some investment projects that were unprofitable before profitable at the now lower interest rate. So some projects that had been unfunded before will be funded now.

So planned investment spending—spending on investment projects that firms voluntarily decide whether or not to undertake—is negatively related to the interest rate. Other things equal, a higher interest rate leads to a lower level of planned investment spending.

Expected Future Real GDP, Production Capacity, and Investment Spending

Suppose a firm has enough capacity to continue to produce the amount it is currently selling but doesn't expect its sales to grow in the future. Then it will engage in investment spending only to replace existing equipment and structures that wear out or are rendered obsolete by new technologies. But if, instead, the firm expects its sales to grow rapidly in the future, it will find its existing production capacity insufficient for its future production needs. So the firm will undertake investment spending to meet those needs. This implies that, other things equal, firms will undertake more investment spending when they expect their sales to grow.

Now suppose that the firm currently has considerably more capacity than necessary to meet current production needs. Even if it expects sales to grow, it won't have to undertake investment spending for a while—not until the growth in sales catches up with its excess capacity. This illustrates the fact that, other things equal, the current

According to the **accelerator principle,** a higher growth rate of real GDP leads to higher planned investment spending, but a lower growth rate of real GDP leads to lower planned investment spending.

Inventories are stocks of goods held to satisfy future sales.

Inventory investment is the value of the change in total inventories held in the economy during a given period.

Unplanned inventory investment occurs when actual sales are more or less than businesses expected, leading to unplanned changes in inventories.

Actual investment spending is the sum of planned investment spending and unplanned inventory investment.

level of productive capacity has a negative effect on investment spending: other things equal, the higher the current capacity, the lower the investment spending.

If we put together the effects on investment spending of growth in expected future sales and the size of current production capacity, we can see one situation in which we can be reasonably sure that firms will undertake high levels of investment spending: when they expect sales to grow rapidly. In that case, even excess production capacity will soon be used up, leading firms to resume investment spending.

What is an indicator of high expected growth of future sales? It's a high expected future growth rate of real GDP. A higher expected future growth rate of real GDP results in a higher level of planned investment spending, but a lower expected future growth rate of real GDP leads to lower planned investment spending. This relationship is summarized in a proposition known as the **accelerator principle.**

As we explain in the upcoming Economics in Action, when expectations of future real GDP growth turned negative, planned investment spending—and, in particular, residential investment spending—plunged, accelerating the economy's slide into recession. Generally, the effects of the accelerator principle play an important role in *investment spending slumps,* periods of low investment spending.

Inventories and Unplanned Investment Spending

Most firms maintain **inventories,** stocks of goods held to satisfy future sales. Firms hold inventories so they can quickly satisfy buyers—a consumer can purchase an item off the shelf rather than waiting for it to be manufactured. In addition, businesses often hold inventories of their inputs to be sure they have a steady supply of necessary materials and spare parts. At the end of 2012, the overall value of inventories in the U.S. economy was estimated at \$1.5 trillion, just over 10% of GDP.

A firm that increases its inventories is engaging in a form of investment spending. Suppose, for example, that the U.S. auto industry produces 800,000 cars per month but sells only 700,000. The remaining 100,000 cars are added to the inventory at auto company warehouses or car dealerships, ready to be sold in the future.

Inventory investment is the value of the change in total inventories held in the economy during a given period. Unlike other forms of investment spending, inventory investment can actually be negative. If, for example, the auto industry reduces its inventory over the course of a month, we say that it has engaged in negative inventory investment.

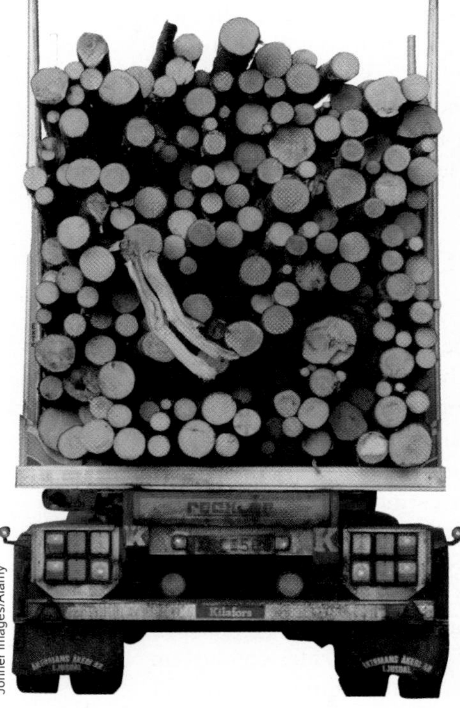

Johner Images/Alamy

Firms undertake high levels of investment spending when they expect the economy to grow rapidly. If an economic slump is expected, they do the opposite.

To understand inventory investment, think about a manager stocking the canned goods section of a supermarket. The manager tries to keep the store fully stocked so that shoppers can almost always find what they're looking for. But the manager does not want the shelves too heavily stocked because shelf space is limited and products can spoil.

Similar considerations apply to many firms and typically lead them to manage their inventories carefully. However, sales fluctuate. And because firms cannot always accurately predict sales, they often find themselves holding more or less inventories than they had intended. These unintended swings in inventories due to unforeseen changes in sales are called **unplanned inventory investment.** They represent investment spending, positive or negative, that occurred but was unplanned.

So in any given period, **actual investment spending** is equal to planned investment spending plus unplanned inventory investment. If we let $I_{Unplanned}$ represent unplanned inventory investment, $I_{Planned}$ represent planned investment spending, and I represent actual investment spending, then the relationship among all three can be represented as:

$$(61\text{-}6)\quad I = I_{Unplanned} + I_{Planned}$$

To see how unplanned inventory investment can occur, let's continue to focus on the auto industry and make the following assumptions. First, let's assume that the industry must determine each month's production volume in advance, before it knows the volume of actual sales. Second, let's assume that it anticipates selling 800,000 cars next month and that it plans neither to add to nor subtract from existing inventories. In that case, it will produce 800,000 cars to match anticipated sales.

Now imagine that next month's actual sales are less than expected, only 700,000 cars. As a result, the value of 100,000 cars will be added to investment spending as unplanned inventory investment.

The auto industry will, of course, eventually adjust to this slowdown in sales and the resulting unplanned inventory investment. It is likely that it will cut next month's production volume in order to reduce inventories. In fact, economists who study macroeconomic variables in an attempt to determine the future path of the economy pay careful attention to changes in inventory levels. Rising inventories typically indicate positive unplanned inventory investment and a slowing economy, as sales are less than had been forecast. Falling inventories typically indicate negative unplanned inventory investment and a growing economy, as sales are greater than forecast.

ECONOMICS ▶ IN ACTION

INTEREST RATES AND THE U.S. HOUSING BOOM

The housing boom in the Ft. Myers metropolitan area, described at the beginning of this section, was part of a broader housing boom in the country as a whole. There is little question that this housing boom was caused, in the first instance, by low interest rates.

Figure 61-6 shows the interest rate on 30-year home mortgages—the traditional way to borrow money for a home purchase—and the number of housing starts, the number of homes for which construction is started per month, from 1997 to early 2013, in the United States. Panel (a), which shows the mortgage rate, gives you an idea of how much interest rates fell. In the second half of the 1990s, mortgage rates

FIGURE 61-6 Interest Rates and the U.S. Housing Boom

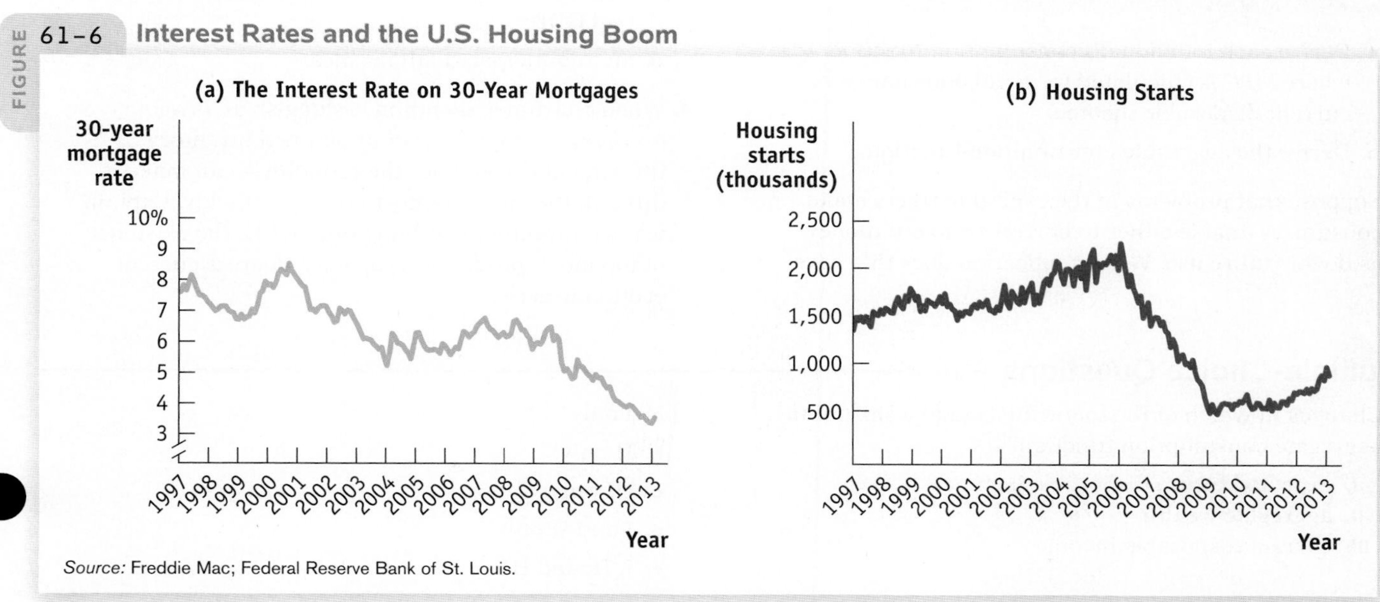

Source: Freddie Mac; Federal Reserve Bank of St. Louis.

generally fluctuated between 7% and 8%; by 2003, they were down to between 5% and 6%. These lower rates were largely the result of Federal Reserve policy: the Fed cut rates in response to the 2001 recession and continued cutting them into 2003 out of concern that the economy's recovery was too weak to generate sustained job growth.

The low interest rates led to a large increase in residential investment spending, reflected in a surge of housing starts, shown in panel (b). This rise in investment spending drove an overall economic expansion, both through its direct effects and through the multiplier process.

Unfortunately, the housing boom eventually turned into too much of a good thing. By 2006, it was clear that the U.S. housing market was experiencing a bubble: people were buying housing based on unrealistic expectations about future price increases. When the bubble burst, housing—and the U.S. economy—took a fall. The fall was so severe that even when the Fed cut rates to near zero, and mortgage rates consequently dropped to below 5% beginning in 2009, housing starts merely stabilized. It wasn't until 2012 that housing starts began to increase again.

MODULE 61 Review

Solutions appear at the back of the book.

Check Your Understanding

1. Suppose the economy consists of three people: Angelina, Felicia, and Marina. The table shows how their consumer spending varies as their current disposable income rises by $10,000.

Current disposable income	Consumer spending		
	Angelina	Felicia	Marina
$0	$8,000	$6,500	$7,250
10,000	12,000	14,500	14,250

a. Derive each individual's consumption function, where *MPC* is calculated for a $10,000 change in current disposable income.

b. Derive the aggregate consumption function.

2. Suppose that problems in the capital markets make consumers unable either to borrow or to put money aside for future use. What implication does this have for the effects of expected future disposable income on consumer spending?

3. For each event, explain whether planned investment spending or unplanned inventory investment will change and in what direction.

a. an unexpected increase in consumer spending

b. a sharp rise in the cost of business borrowing

c. a sharp increase in the economy's growth rate of real GDP

d. an unanticipated fall in sales

4. When consumer spending is sluggish an *inventory overhang*—a high level of unplanned inventory investment throughout the economy—can make it difficult for the economy to recover quickly. Explain why an inventory overhang might, like the existence of too much production capacity, depress current economic activity.

Multiple-Choice Questions

1. Changes in which of the following lead to a shift of the aggregate consumption function?

I. expected future disposable income
II. aggregate wealth
III. current disposable income

a. I only
b. II only
c. III only
d. I and II only
e. I, II, and III

2. The slope of a family's consumption function is equal to
   a. the real interest rate.
   b. the inflation rate.
   c. the marginal propensity to consume.
   d. the rate of increase in household current disposable income.
   e. the tax rate.

3. Given the consumption function $c = \$16{,}000 + 0.5\ yd$, if individual household current disposable income is \$20,000, individual household consumer spending will equal
   a. \$36,000.
   b. \$26,000.
   c. \$20,000.
   d. \$16,000.
   e. \$6,000.

4. The level of planned investment spending is negatively related to the
   a. rate of return on investment.
   b. level of consumer spending.
   c. level of actual investment spending.
   d. interest rate.
   e. all of the above.

5. Actual investment spending in any period is equal to
   a. planned investment spending + unplanned inventory investment.
   b. planned investment spending – unplanned inventory investment.
   c. planned investment spending + inventory decreases.
   d. unplanned inventory investment + inventory increases.
   e. unplanned inventory investment – inventory increases.

Critical-Thinking Question

List the three most important factors affecting planned investment spending. Explain how each is related to actual investment spending.

62 The Income–Expenditure Model

moodboard/Alamy

WHAT YOU WILL LEARN

1. **How planned aggregate spending determines income–expenditure equilibrium**
2. **How the inventory adjustment process moves the economy to a new equilibrium after a change in planned aggregate spending**

Using the Income–Expenditure Model

Earlier in this section, we described how autonomous changes in spending—such as a fall in investment spending when a housing bubble bursts—lead to a multistage process through the actions of the multiplier that magnifies the effect of these changes on real GDP. In this module, we will examine this multistage process more closely. We'll see that the multiple rounds of changes in real GDP are accomplished through changes in the amount of output produced by firms—changes that they make in response to changes in their inventories. We'll come to understand why inventories play a central role in macroeconomic models of the economy in the short run as well as why economists pay particular attention to the behavior of firms' inventories when trying to understand the likely future state of the economy.

Before we begin, let's quickly recap the assumptions underlying the multiplier process.

1. *Changes in overall spending lead to changes in aggregate output.* We assume that producers are willing to supply additional output at a fixed price level. As a result, changes in spending translate into changes in output rather than moves of the overall price level up or down. A fixed aggregate price level also implies that there is no difference between nominal GDP and real GDP. So we can use the two terms interchangeably in this module.
2. *The interest rate is fixed.* As we'll see, the model we examine here can still be used to study the effects of a change in the interest rate.
3. *Taxes, government transfers, and government purchases are all zero.*
4. *Exports and imports are both zero.*

Planned Aggregate Spending and Real GDP

In an economy with no government and no foreign trade, there are only two sources of aggregate spending: consumer spending, *C*, and investment spending, *I*. And since we assume that there are no taxes or transfers, aggregate disposable income is equal to GDP (which, since the aggregate price level is fixed, is the same as real GDP): the total value of final sales of goods and services ultimately accrues to households as income. So in this highly simplified economy, there are two basic equations of national income accounting:

(62-1) $GDP = C + I$

(62-2) $YD = GDP$

As we learned in the previous module, the aggregate consumption function shows the relationship between disposable income and consumer spending. Let's continue to assume that the aggregate consumption function is of the same form as in Equation 61-5:

(62-3) $C = A + MPC \times YD$

In our simplified model, we will also assume planned investment spending, $I_{Planned}$, is fixed.

We need one more concept before putting the model together: **planned aggregate spending,** the total amount of planned spending in the economy. Unlike firms, households don't take unintended actions like unplanned inventory investment. So planned aggregate spending is equal to the sum of consumer spending and planned investment spending. We denote planned aggregate spending by $AE_{Planned}$, so:

(62-4) $AE_{Planned} = C + I_{Planned}$

The level of planned aggregate spending in a given year depends on the level of real GDP in that year. To see why, let's look at a specific example, shown in Table 62-1. We assume that the aggregate consumption function is:

(62-5) $C = 300 + 0.6 \times YD$

Real GDP, *YD*, *C*, $I_{Planned}$, and $AE_{Planned}$ are all measured in billions of dollars, and we assume that the level of planned investment, $I_{Planned}$, is fixed at $500 billion per year. The first column shows possible levels of real GDP. The second column shows disposable income, *YD*, which in our simplified model is equal to real GDP. The third column shows consumer spending, *C*, equal to $300 billion plus 0.6 times disposable income, *YD*. The fourth column shows planned investment spending, $I_{Planned}$, which we have assumed is $500 billion regardless of the level of real GDP.

Finally, the last column shows planned aggregate spending, $AE_{Planned}$, the sum of aggregate consumer spending, *C*, and planned investment spending, $I_{Planned}$. (To economize on notation, we'll assume that it is understood from now on that all the variables in Table 62-1 are measured in billions of dollars per year.) As you can see, a higher level of real GDP leads to a higher level of disposable income: every 500 increase in real GDP raises *YD* by 500, which in turn raises *C* by $500 \times 0.6 = 300$ and $AE_{Planned}$ by 300.

TABLE 62-1

Real GDP	*YD*	*C*	$I_{Planned}$	$AE_{Planned}$
	(billions of dollars)			
$0	$0	$300	$500	$800
500	500	600	500	1,100
1,000	1,000	900	500	1,400
1,500	1,500	1,200	500	1,700
2,000	2,000	1,500	500	2,000
2,500	2,500	1,800	500	2,300
3,000	3,000	2,100	500	2,600
3,500	3,500	2,400	500	2,900

Figure 62-1 illustrates the information in Table 62-1 graphically. Real GDP is measured on the horizontal axis. *CF* is the aggregate consumption function; it shows how consumer spending depends on real GDP. $AE_{Planned}$, the planned aggregate spending line, corresponds to the aggregate consumption function shifted up by 500 (the amount of $I_{Planned}$). It shows how planned aggregate spending depends on real GDP. Both lines have a slope of 0.6, equal to *MPC*, the marginal propensity to consume.

But this isn't the end of the story. Table 62-1 reveals that real GDP equals planned aggregate spending, $AE_{Planned}$, only when the level of real GDP is at 2,000. Real GDP does not equal $AE_{Planned}$ at any other level. Is that possible? Didn't we learn from the circular-flow diagram that total spending on final goods and services in the economy

Planned aggregate spending is the total amount of planned spending in the economy.

FIGURE 62-1 The Aggregate Consumption Function and Planned Aggregate Spending

The lower line, *CF*, is the aggregate consumption function constructed from the data in Table 62-1. The upper line, $AE_{Planned}$, is the planned aggregate spending line, also constructed from the data in Table 62-1. It is equivalent to the aggregate consumption function shifted up by $500 billion, the amount of planned investment spending, $I_{Planned}$.

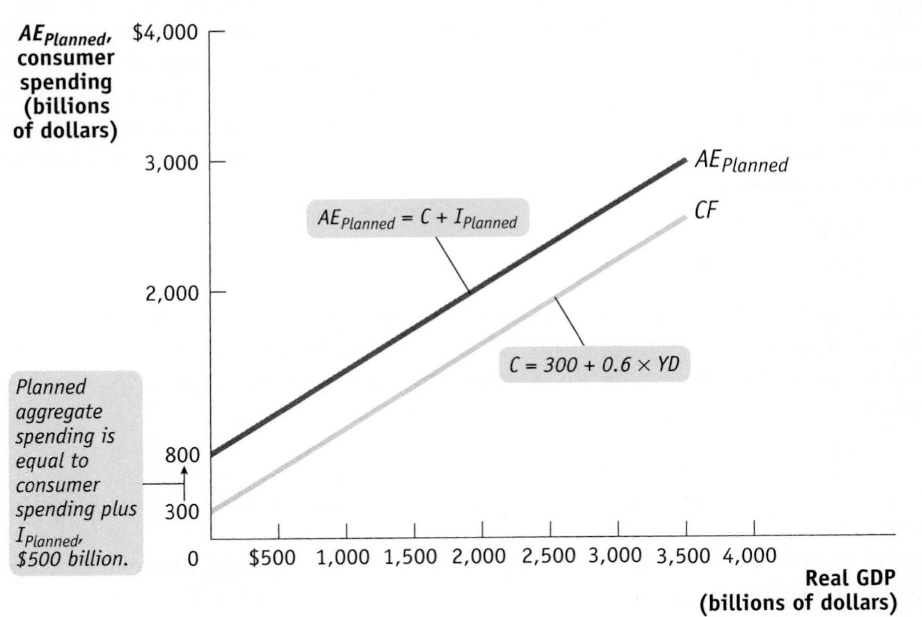

is equal to the total value of output of final goods and services? The answer is that for *brief* periods of time, planned aggregate spending can differ from real GDP because of the role of *unplanned* aggregate spending—$I_{Unplanned}$, unplanned inventory investment. But as we'll see, the economy moves over time to a situation in which there is no unplanned inventory investment, a situation called *income–expenditure equilibrium*. And when the economy is in income–expenditure equilibrium, planned aggregate spending on final goods and services equals aggregate output.

Income–Expenditure Equilibrium

For all but one value of real GDP shown in Table 62-1, real GDP is either more or less than $AE_{Planned}$, the sum of consumer spending and *planned* investment spending. For example, when real GDP is 1,000, consumer spending, *C*, is 900 and planned investment spending is 500, making planned aggregate spending 1,400. This is 400 *more* than the corresponding level of real GDP. Now consider what happens when real GDP is 2,500; consumer spending, *C*, is 1,800 and planned investment spending is 500, making planned aggregate spending only 2,300, 200 *less* than real GDP.

As we've just explained, planned aggregate spending can be different from real GDP only if there is unplanned inventory investment, $I_{Unplanned}$, in the economy. Let's examine Table 62-2, which includes the numbers for real GDP and for planned aggregate spending from Table 62-1. It also includes the levels of unplanned inventory investment, $I_{Unplanned}$, that each combination of real GDP and planned aggregate spending implies. For example, if real GDP is 2,500, planned aggregate spending is only 2,300. This 200 excess of real GDP over $AE_{Planned}$ must consist of positive unplanned inventory investment. This can happen only if firms have overestimated sales and produced too much, leading to unintended additions to inventories. More generally, any level of real GDP in excess of 2,000 corresponds to a situation in which firms are producing more than consumers and other firms want to purchase, creating an unintended increase in inventories.

Conversely, a level of real GDP below 2,000 implies that planned aggregate spending is *greater* than real GDP. For example, when real GDP is 1,000, planned aggregate

TABLE 62-2

Real GDP	$AE_{Planned}$	$I_{Unplanned}$
(billions of dollars)		
$0	$800	−$800
500	1,100	−600
1,000	1,400	−400
1,500	1,700	−200
2,000	2,000	0
2,500	2,300	200
3,000	2,600	400
3,500	2,900	600

spending is much larger, at 1,400. The 400 excess of $AE_{Planned}$ over real GDP corresponds to negative unplanned inventory investment equal to −400. More generally, any level of real GDP below 2,000 implies that firms have underestimated sales, leading to a negative level of unplanned inventory investment in the economy.

By putting together Equations 61-6, 62-1, and 62-4, we can summarize the general relationships among real GDP, planned aggregate spending, and unplanned inventory investment as follows:

(62-6) $$\begin{aligned} GDP &= C + I \\ &= C + I_{Planned} + I_{Unplanned} \\ &= AE_{Planned} + I_{Unplanned} \end{aligned}$$

So whenever real GDP exceeds $AE_{Planned}$, $I_{Unplanned}$ is positive; whenever real GDP is less than $AE_{Planned}$, $I_{Unplanned}$ is negative.

But firms will act to correct their mistakes. We've assumed that they don't change their prices, but they *can* adjust their output. Specifically, they will reduce production if they have experienced an unintended rise in inventories or increase production if they have experienced an unintended fall in inventories. And these responses will eventually eliminate the unanticipated changes in inventories and move the economy to a point at which real GDP is equal to planned aggregate spending.

Staying with our example, if real GDP is 1,000, negative unplanned inventory investment will lead firms to increase production, leading to a rise in real GDP. In fact, this will happen whenever real GDP is less than 2,000—that is, whenever real GDP is less than planned aggregate spending. Conversely, if real GDP is 2,500, positive unplanned inventory investment will lead firms to reduce production, leading to a fall in real GDP. This will happen whenever real GDP is greater than planned aggregate spending.

Monty Rakusen/Getty Images

Firms can adjust output and inventory to correct for sales projections that were too high or low, helping to move the economy back to equilibrium.

The only situation in which firms won't have an incentive to change output in the next period is when aggregate output, measured by real GDP, is equal to planned aggregate spending in the current period, an outcome known as **income–expenditure equilibrium.** In Table 62-2, income–expenditure equilibrium is achieved when real GDP is 2,000, the only level of real GDP at which unplanned inventory investment is zero. From now on, we'll denote the real GDP level at which income–expenditure equilibrium occurs as Y^* and call it the **income–expenditure equilibrium GDP.**

The economy is in **income–expenditure equilibrium** when aggregate output, measured by real GDP, is equal to planned aggregate spending.

Income–expenditure equilibrium GDP is the level of real GDP at which real GDP equals planned aggregate spending.

Figure 62-2 illustrates the concept of income–expenditure equilibrium graphically. Real GDP is on the horizontal axis and planned aggregate spending, $AE_{Planned}$, is on the vertical axis. There are two lines in the figure. The solid line is the planned aggregate spending line. It shows how $AE_{Planned}$, equal to $C + I_{Planned}$, depends on real GDP; it has a slope of 0.6, equal to the marginal propensity to consume, *MPC*, and a vertical intercept equal to $A + I_{Planned}$ (300 + 500 = 800).

The dashed line, which goes through the origin with a slope of 1 (often called a 45-degree line), shows all the possible points at which planned aggregate spending is equal to real GDP. This line allows us to easily spot the point of income–expenditure equilibrium, which must lie on both the 45-degree line and the planned aggregate spending line. So the point of income–expenditure equilibrium is at *E*, where the two lines cross. And the income–expenditure equilibrium GDP, Y^*, is 2,000—the same outcome we derived in Table 62-2.

FIGURE 62-2 Income–Expenditure Equilibrium

Income–expenditure equilibrium occurs at *E*, the point where the planned aggregate spending line, $AE_{Planned}$, crosses the 45-degree line. At *E*, the economy produces real GDP of \$2,000 billion per year, the only point at which real GDP equals planned aggregate spending, $AE_{Planned}$, and unplanned inventory investment, $I_{Unplanned}$, is zero. This is the level of income–expenditure equilibrium GDP, Y^*. At any level of real GDP less than Y^*, $AE_{Planned}$ exceeds real GDP. As a result, unplanned inventory investment, $I_{Unplanned}$, is negative and firms respond by increasing production. At any level of real GDP greater than Y^*, real GDP exceeds $AE_{Planned}$. Unplanned inventory investment, $I_{Unplanned}$, is positive and firms respond by reducing production.

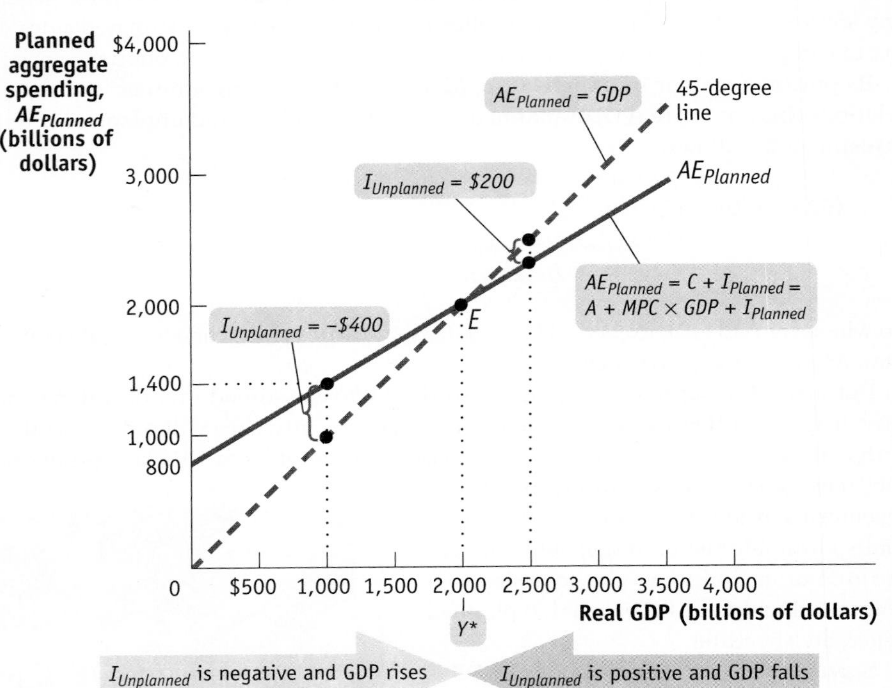

Now consider what happens if the economy isn't in income–expenditure equilibrium. We can see from Figure 62-2 that whenever real GDP is less than Y^*, the planned aggregate spending line lies above the 45-degree line and $AE_{Planned}$ exceeds real GDP. In this situation, $I_{Unplanned}$ is negative: as shown in the figure, at a real GDP of 1,000, $I_{Unplanned}$ is −400. As a consequence, real GDP will rise. In contrast, whenever real GDP is greater than Y^*, the planned aggregate expenditure line lies below the 45-degree line. Here, $I_{Unplanned}$ is positive: as shown, at a real GDP of 2,500, $I_{Unplanned}$ is 200. The unanticipated accumulation of inventory leads to a fall in real GDP.

The type of diagram shown in Figure 62-2, which identifies income–expenditure equilibrium as the point at which the planned aggregate spending line crosses the 45-degree line, has a special place in the history of economic thought. Known as the **Keynesian cross,** it was developed by Paul Samuelson, one of the greatest economists of the twentieth century (as well as a Nobel Prize winner), to explain the ideas of John Maynard Keynes, the founder of macroeconomics as we know it.

The **Keynesian cross** diagram identifies income–expenditure equilibrium as the point where the planned aggregate spending line crosses the 45-degree line.

The Multiplier Process and Inventory Adjustment

We've just learned about a very important feature of the macroeconomy: when planned spending by households and firms does not equal the current aggregate output by firms, this difference shows up in changes in inventories. The response of firms to those inventory changes moves real GDP over time to the point at which real GDP and planned aggregate spending are equal. That's why, as we mentioned earlier, changes in inventories are considered a leading indicator of future economic activity.

Now that we understand how real GDP moves to achieve income–expenditure equilibrium for a given level of planned aggregate spending, let's turn to understanding what happens when there is *a shift of the planned aggregate spending line.* How does the economy move from the initial point of income–expenditure equilibrium to a new point of income–expenditure equilibrium? And what are the possible sources of changes in planned aggregate spending?

In our simple model there are only two possible sources of a shift of the planned aggregate spending line: a change in planned investment spending, $I_{Planned}$, or a shift of the aggregate consumption function, *CF*. For example, a change in $I_{Planned}$ can occur because of a change in the interest rate. (Remember, we're assuming that the interest rate is fixed by factors that are outside the model. But we can still ask what happens when the interest rate changes.) A shift of the aggregate consumption function (that is, a change in its vertical intercept, *A*) can occur because of a change in aggregate wealth—say, due to a rise in house prices.

When the planned aggregate spending line shifts—when there is a change in the level of planned aggregate spending at any given level of real GDP—there is an autonomous change in planned aggregate spending. Recall that an autonomous change in planned aggregate spending is a change in the desired level of spending by firms, households, and government at any given level of real GDP (although we've assumed away the government for the time being). How does an autonomous change in planned aggregate spending affect real GDP in income–expenditure equilibrium?

TABLE 62-3

Real GDP	$AE_{Planned}$ before autonomous change	$AE_{Planned}$ after autonomous change
	(billions of dollars)	
$0	$800	$1,200
500	1,100	1,500
1,000	1,400	1,800
1,500	1,700	2,100
2,000	2,000	2,400
2,500	2,300	2,700
3,000	2,600	3,000
3,500	2,900	3,300
4,000	3,200	3,600

Table 62-3 and Figure 62-3 start from the same numerical example we used in Table 62-2 and Figure 62-2. They also show the effect of an autonomous increase in planned aggregate spending of 400—what happens when planned aggregate spending is 400 higher at each level of real GDP. Look first at Table 62-3. Before the autonomous increase in planned aggregate spending, the level of real GDP at which planned aggregate spending is equal to real GDP, Y^*, is 2,000. After the autonomous change, Y^* has risen to 3,000.

The same result is visible in Figure 62-3. The initial income–expenditure equilibrium is at E_1, where Y_1^* is 2,000. The autonomous rise in planned aggregate spending shifts the planned aggregate spending line up, leading to a new income–expenditure equilibrium at E_2, where Y_2^* is 3,000.

FIGURE 62-3 The Multiplier

This figure illustrates the change in Y^* caused by an autonomous increase in planned aggregate spending. The economy is initially at equilibrium point E_1 with an income–expenditure equilibrium GDP, Y_1^*, equal to 2,000. An autonomous increase in $AE_{Planned}$ of 400 shifts the planned aggregate spending line upward by 400. The economy is no longer in income–expenditure equilibrium: real GDP is equal to 2,000 but $AE_{Planned}$ is now 2,400, represented by point *X*. The vertical distance between the two planned aggregate spending lines, equal to 400, represents $I_{Unplanned}$ = −400—the negative inventory investment that the economy now experiences. Firms respond by increasing production, and the economy eventually reaches a new income–expenditure equilibrium at E_2 with a higher level of income–expenditure equilibrium GDP, Y_2^*, equal to 3,000.

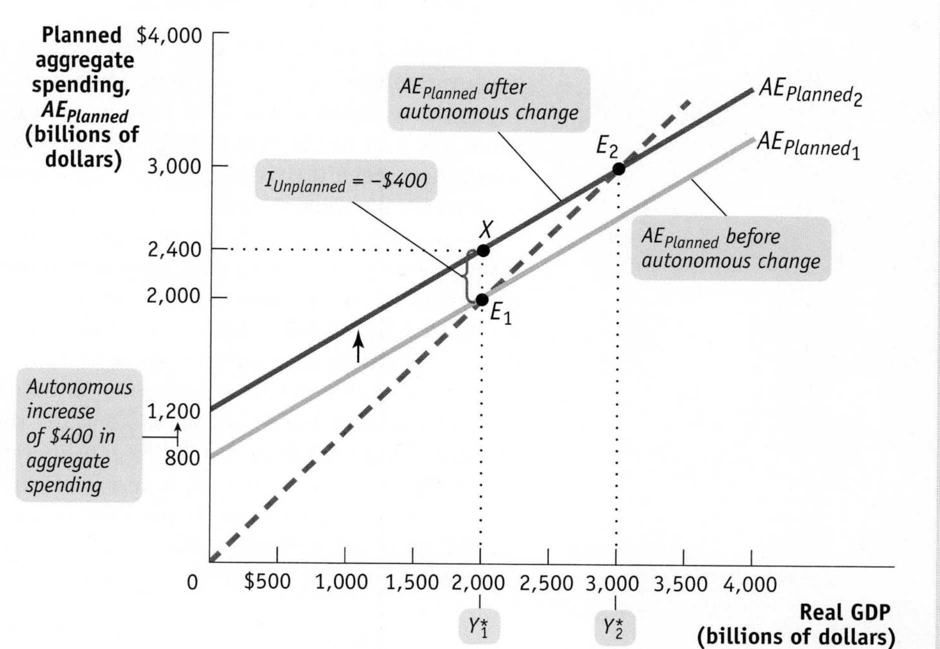

The fact that the rise in income–expenditure equilibrium GDP, from 2,000 to 3,000, is much larger than the autonomous increase in aggregate spending, which is only 400, has a familiar explanation: the multiplier process. In the specific example we have just described, an autonomous increase in planned aggregate spending of 400 leads to an increase in Y^* from 2,000 to 3,000, a rise of 1,000. So the multiplier in this example is 1,000/400 = 2.5.

We can examine in detail what underlies the multistage multiplier process by looking more closely at Figure 62-3. First, starting from E_1, the autonomous increase in planned aggregate spending leads to a gap between planned aggregate spending and real GDP. This is represented by the vertical distance between X, at 2,400, and E_1, at 2,000. This gap illustrates an unplanned fall in inventory investment: $I_{Unplanned} = -400$. Firms respond by increasing production, leading to a rise in real GDP from Y_1^*. The rise in real GDP translates into an increase in disposable income, YD.

That's the first stage in the chain reaction. But it doesn't stop there—the increase in YD leads to a rise in consumer spending, C, which sets off a second-round rise in real GDP. This in turn leads to a further rise in disposable income and consumer spending, and so on. And we could play this process in reverse: an autonomous fall in aggregate spending will lead to a chain reaction of reductions in real GDP and consumer spending.

We can summarize these results in an equation, where $\Delta AAE_{Planned}$ represents the autonomous change in $AE_{Planned}$, and $\Delta Y^* = Y_2^* - Y_1^*$, the subsequent change in income–expenditure equilibrium GDP:

$$\textbf{(62-7)}\quad \Delta Y^* = \text{Multiplier} \times \Delta AAE_{Planned} = \frac{1}{1 - MPC} \times \Delta AAE_{Planned}$$

Recalling that the multiplier, $1/(1 - MPC)$, is greater than 1, Equation 62-7 tells us that the change in income–expenditure equilibrium GDP, ΔY^*, is several times as large as the autonomous change in planned aggregate spending, $\Delta AAE_{Planned}$. It also helps us recall an important point: because the marginal propensity to consume is less than 1, each increase in disposable income and each corresponding increase in consumer spending is smaller than in the previous round. That's because at each round some of the increase in disposable income leaks out into savings. As a result, although real GDP grows at each round, the increase in real GDP diminishes from each round to the next. At some point the increase in real GDP is negligible, and the economy converges to a new income–expenditure equilibrium GDP at Y_2^*.

THE PARADOX OF THRIFT Let's now consider what happens when there is a slump in consumer spending or investment spending, or both. This causes a fall in income–expenditure equilibrium GDP that is several times larger than the original fall in spending. The fall in real GDP leaves consumers and producers worse off than they would have been if they hadn't cut their spending. Economists refer to this phenomenon as the *paradox of thrift.*

In the paradox of thrift, households and firms cut their spending in anticipation of future tough economic times. These actions depress the economy, leaving households and firms worse off than if they hadn't acted virtuously to prepare for tough times. It is called a paradox because what's usually "good" (saving for hard times) is "bad" (because it can make everyone worse off).

We've seen that declines in planned investment spending are usually the major factor causing recessions, because historically they have been the most common source of autonomous reductions in aggregate spending. Likewise, we know that consumption spending can change as a result of an increase or decrease in the aggregate wealth or expected future disposable income of individuals. But regardless of the source, there are multiplier effects in the economy that magnify the size of the initial change in aggregate spending.

ECONOMICS ▶ IN ACTION

INVENTORIES AND THE END OF A RECESSION

A very clear example of the role of inventories in the multiplier process took place in late 2001, as that year's recession came to an end.

The driving force behind the recession was a slump in business investment spending. It took several years before investment spending bounced back in the form of a housing boom. Still, the economy did start to recover in late 2001, largely because of an increase in consumer spending—especially on durable goods such as automobiles.

FIGURE 62-4 Inventories and the End of a Recession

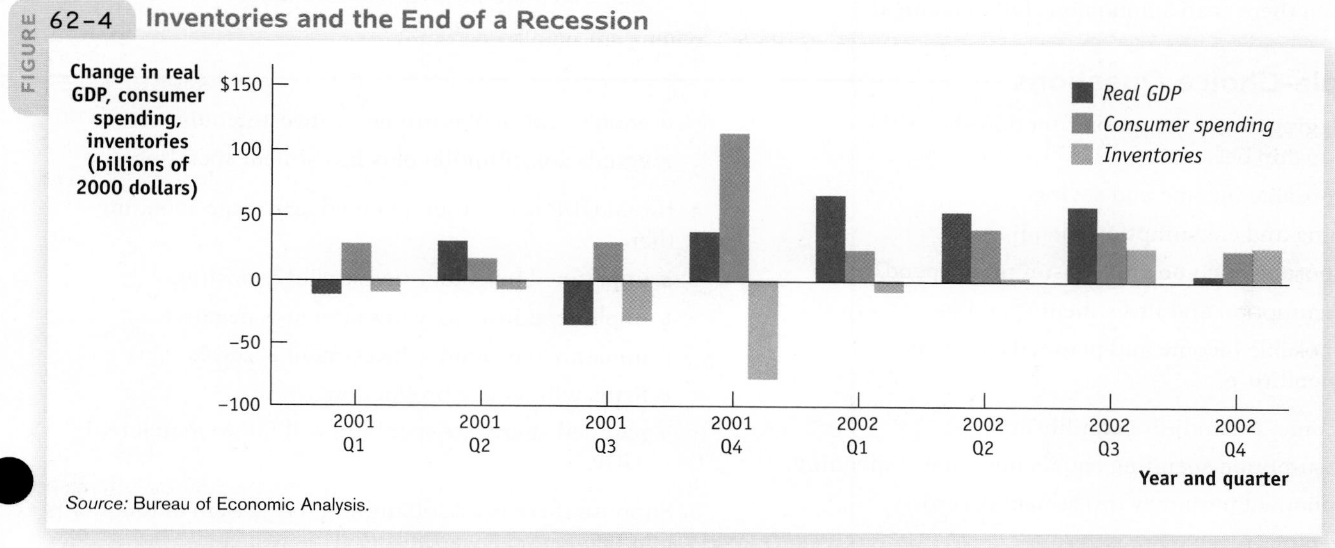

Source: Bureau of Economic Analysis.

Initially, this increase in consumer spending caught manufacturers by surprise. Figure 62-4 shows changes in real GDP, real consumer spending, and real inventories in each quarter of 2001 and 2002. Notice the surge in consumer spending in the fourth quarter of 2001. It didn't lead to a lot of GDP growth because it was offset by a plunge in inventories. But in the first quarter of 2002 producers greatly increased their production, leading to a jump in real GDP.

MODULE 62 Review

Solutions appear at the back of the book.

Check Your Understanding

1. Although economists believe that recessions typically begin as slumps in investment spending, they also believe that consumer spending eventually slumps during a recession. Explain why.

2. a. Use a diagram like Figure 62-3 to show what happens when there is an autonomous fall in planned aggregate spending. Describe how the economy adjusts to a new income–expenditure equilibrium.

   b. Suppose Y^* is originally \$500 billion, the autonomous reduction in planned aggregate spending is \$300 million (\$0.3 billion), and $MPC = 0.5$. Calculate Y^* after such a change.

Multiple-Choice Questions

1. The aggregate consumption function shows the relationship between
   - a. disposable income and saving.
   - b. saving and consumption spending.
   - c. disposable income and consumption spending.
   - d. consumption and investment spending.
   - e. disposable income and planned aggregate expenditure.

2. In income–expenditure equilibrium
   - a. consumption spending equals investment spending.
   - b. unplanned inventory investment is zero.
   - c. inventory investment is zero.
   - d. investment spending is zero.
   - e. consumption spending equals real GDP.

3. Planned aggregate spending
   - a. always equals real GDP.
   - b. never equals real GDP.
   - c. equals real GDP if unplanned inventory investment is zero.
   - d. equals real GDP if inventory investment is zero.
   - e. equals consumption plus investment spending.

4. If real GDP is less than planned aggregate spending then
   - a. unplanned inventory investment is positive.
   - b. unplanned inventory investment is negative.
   - c. unplanned inventory investment is zero.
   - d. firms will reduce production.
   - e. planned aggregate spending will fall to match real GDP.

5. Suppose there is a \$200 million increase in autonomous planned aggregate spending. This will cause the planned aggregate spending line to shift upwards by __________ and real GDP will increase by __________.
   - a. \$200 million; \$200 million
   - b. \$200 million; less than \$200 million
   - c. \$200 million; more than \$200 million
   - d. more than \$200 million; more than \$200 million
   - e. more than \$200 million; \$200 million

Critical-Thinking Question

What is the value of unplanned inventory investment in income–expenditure equilibrium? Why?

BUSINESS CASE • Making It Through in Muskegon

Thinkstock

Muskegon, Michigan, is no Ft. Myers. Unlike the Florida city whose boom and bust we described in this section's opening story, Muskegon didn't have a housing boom in the mid-2000s. And it didn't have that much of a housing bust, either.

Since real estate wasn't a big part of the local economy, the housing bubble burst couldn't do much to drag that economy down. So you might think that Muskegon-area businesses were somewhat insulated from the resulting national downturn.

However, Muskegon businesses were nonetheless hit hard by the recession. For example, Eagle Alloy—a manufacturing company that sells its products to a wide variety of industries, but not especially to the housing or construction sectors—saw its sales drop by 50%. And it wasn't only manufacturers selling to a national market that were hit.

As factories in the Muskegon–Norton Shores metropolitan area laid off workers, and the local unemployment rate increased from around 6% in 2001 to over 15% during 2010, local businesses that depended on these workers' paychecks were hurt as well; employment in retail businesses fell about 8% over the course of the recession.

This story does, however, have a somewhat happy ending.

As the U.S. economy as a whole began to recover, so did Eagle Alloy and other Muskegon-area manufacturing companies. During the recession, Eagle cut its workforce from 430 to 200, but following the recession, the workforce was back to more than 400, and the company was planning to hire another 150 workers. Eagle Alloy's president, Mark Fazakerley, was predicting a 25% increase in sales.

In the broader Muskegon–Norton Shores metropolitan area, by mid-2013, the local unemployment rate had fallen back down to under 9%. And as manufacturing for the national market revived, businesses with local sales also bounced back; the redevelopment of Muskegon's downtown, which stalled during the recession, had resumed.

Questions for Thought

1. Why did a national slump that began with housing affect companies like Eagle Alloy that didn't sell much to the construction industry?
2. Why did the troubles of Muskegon manufacturers spread to other industries, like retailing?
3. How does this story about Muskegon help explain how a slump in housing—a relatively small part of the U.S. economy—could produce such a deep national recession?

SECTION 19 REVIEW

Summary

The Multiplier

1. An **autonomous change in aggregate spending** leads to a chain reaction in which the total change in real GDP is equal to the **multiplier** times the initial change in aggregate spending.
2. The size of the multiplier, $1/(1 - MPC)$, depends on the **marginal propensity to consume, *MPC*,** the fraction of an additional dollar of disposable income spent on consumption.
3. The larger the *MPC,* the larger the multiplier and the larger the change in real GDP for any given autonomous change in aggregate spending. The **marginal propensity to save, *MPS*,** is equal to $1 - MPC$.

Consumption and Investment Spending

4. The **consumption function** shows how an individual household's consumer spending is determined by its current disposable income. The **aggregate consumption function** shows the relationship for the entire economy. According to the life-cycle hypothesis, households try to smooth their consumption over their lifetimes. As a result, the aggregate consumption function shifts in response to changes in expected future disposable income and changes in aggregate wealth.
5. **Planned investment spending** depends negatively on the interest rate and on existing production capacity; it depends positively on expected future real GDP. The **accelerator principle** says that investment spending is greatly influenced by the expected growth rate of real GDP.
6. Firms hold **inventories** of goods so that they can satisfy consumer demand quickly. **Inventory investment** is positive when firms add to their inventories, negative when they reduce them. Often, however, changes in inventories are not a deliberate decision but the result of mistakes in forecasts about sales. The result is **unplanned inventory investment,** which can be either positive or negative. **Actual investment spending** is the sum of planned investment spending and unplanned inventory investment.

The Income–Expenditure Model

7. In **income–expenditure equilibrium, planned aggregate spending,** which in a simplified model with no government and no foreign trade is the sum of consumer spending and planned investment spending, is equal to real GDP.
8. At the **income–expenditure equilibrium GDP,** or Y^*, unplanned inventory investment is zero. When planned aggregate spending is larger than Y^*, unplanned inventory investment is negative; there is an unanticipated reduction in inventories and firms increase production. When planned aggregate spending is less than Y^*, unplanned inventory investment is positive; there is an unanticipated increase in inventories and firms reduce production.
9. The **Keynesian cross** shows how the economy self-adjusts to income–expenditure equilibrium through inventory adjustments.
10. After an autonomous change in planned aggregate spending, the inventory adjustment process moves the economy to a new income–expenditure equilibrium. The change in income–expenditure equilibrium GDP arising from an autonomous change in spending is equal to $(1/(1 - MPC)) \times \Delta AAE_{Planned}$.

Key Terms

Marginal propensity to consume (*MPC*), p. 615
Marginal propensity to save (*MPS*), p. 615
Autonomous change in aggregate spending, p. 616
Multiplier, p. 616
Consumption function, p. 620
Aggregate consumption function, p. 622
Planned investment spending, p. 624
Accelerator principle, p. 626
Inventories, p. 626
Inventory investment, p. 626
Unplanned inventory investment, p. 626
Actual investment spending, p. 626
Planned aggregate spending, p. 631
Income–expenditure equilibrium, p. 633
Income–expenditure equilibrium GDP, p. 633
Keynesian cross, p. 634

Problems

1. Due to an increase in consumer wealth, there is a \$40 billion autonomous increase in consumer spending in the economies of Westlandia and Eastlandia. Assuming that the aggregate price level is constant, the interest rate is fixed in both countries, and there are no taxes and no foreign trade, complete the accompanying tables to show the various rounds of increased spending that will occur in both economies if the marginal propensity to consume is 0.5 in Westlandia and 0.75 in Eastlandia. What do your results indicate about the relationship between the size of the marginal propensity to consume and the multiplier?

Westlandia		
Rounds	Incremental change in GDP	Total change in GDP
1	$\Delta C =$ $40 billion	?
2	$MPC \times \Delta C =$?	?
3	$MPC \times MPC \times \Delta C =$?	?
4	$MPC \times MPC \times MPC \times \Delta C =$?	?
...	...	...
Total change in GDP	$(1/(1 - MPC)) \times \Delta C =$	?

Eastlandia		
Rounds	Incremental change in GDP	Total change in GDP
1	$\Delta C =$ $40 billion	?
2	$MPC \times \Delta C =$?	?
3	$MPC \times MPC \times \Delta C =$?	?
4	$MPC \times MPC \times MPC \times \Delta C =$?	?
...	...	...
Total change in GDP	$(1/(1 - MPC)) \times \Delta C =$	?

2. Assuming that the aggregate price level is constant, the interest rate is fixed, and there are no taxes and no foreign trade, what will be the change in GDP if the following events occur?

   a. There is an autonomous increase in consumer spending of $25 billion; the marginal propensity to consume is 2/3.

   b. Firms reduce investment spending by $40 billion; the marginal propensity to consume is 0.8.

   c. The government increases its purchases of military equipment by $60 billion; the marginal propensity to consume is 0.6.

3. Economists observed the only five residents of a very small economy and estimated each one's consumer spending at various levels of current disposable income. The accompanying table shows each resident's consumer spending at three income levels.

Individual consumer spending by	Individual current disposable income		
	$0	$20,000	$40,000
Andre	1,000	$15,000	29,000
Barbara	2,500	12,500	22,500
Casey	2,000	20,000	38,000
Declan	5,000	17,000	29,000
Elena	4,000	19,000	34,000

   a. What is each resident's consumption function? What is the marginal propensity to consume for each resident?

   b. What is the economy's aggregate consumption function? What is the marginal propensity to consume for the economy?

4. From 2008 to 2013, Eastlandia experienced large fluctuations in both aggregate consumer spending and disposable income, but wealth, the interest rate, and expected future disposable income did not change. The accompanying table shows the level of aggregate consumer spending and disposable income in millions of dollars for each of these years. Use this information to answer the following questions.

Year	Disposable income (millions of dollars)	Consumer spending (millions of dollars)
2008	$100	$180
2009	350	380
2010	300	340
2011	400	420
2012	375	400
2013	500	500

   a. Plot the aggregate consumption function for Eastlandia.

   b. What is the marginal propensity to consume? What is the marginal propensity to save?

   c. What is the aggregate consumption function?

5. The Bureau of Economic Analysis reported that, in real terms, overall consumer spending increased by $18.2 billion during January 2013.

   a. If the marginal propensity to consume is 0.52, by how much will real GDP change in response?

   b. If there are no other changes to autonomous spending other than the increase in consumer spending in part a, and unplanned inventory investment, $I_{Unplanned}$, decreased by $10 billion, what is the change in real GDP?

   c. GDP at the end of December 2012 was $15,851 billion. If GDP were to increase by the amount calculated in part b, what would be the percent increase in GDP?

6. During the early 2000s, the Case–Shiller U.S. Home Price Index, a measure of average home prices, rose continuously until it peaked in March 2006. From March 2006 to May 2009, the index lost 32% of its value. Meanwhile, the stock market experienced similar ups and downs. From March 2003 to October 2007, the Standard and Poor's 500 (S&P 500) stock index, a broad measure of stock market prices, almost doubled, from 800.73 to a high of 1,565.15. From that time until March 2009, the index fell by almost 60%, to a low of 676.53. How do you think the movements in home prices both influenced the growth in real GDP during the first half of the decade and added to the concern about maintaining consumer spending after the collapse in the housing market that began in 2006? To what extent did the movements in the stock market hurt or help consumer spending?

7. How will planned investment spending change as the following events occur?

   a. The interest rate falls as a result of Federal Reserve policy.

   b. The U.S. Environmental Protection Agency decrees that corporations must upgrade or replace their machinery in order to reduce their emissions of sulfur dioxide.

   c. Baby boomers begin to retire in large numbers and reduce their savings, resulting in higher interest rates.

8. Explain how each of the following actions will affect the level of planned investment spending and unplanned inventory investment. Assume the economy is initially in income–expenditure equilibrium.

   a. The Federal Reserve raises the interest rate.

   b. There is a rise in the expected growth rate of real GDP.

   c. A sizable inflow of foreign funds into the country lowers the interest rate.

9. a. The accompanying table shows GDP, disposable income (YD), consumer spending (C), and planned investment spending ($I_{Planned}$) in an economy. Assume there is no government or foreign sector in this economy. Complete the table by calculating planned aggregate spending ($AE_{Planned}$) and unplanned inventory investment ($I_{Unplanned}$).

GDP	YD	C	$I_{Planned}$	$AE_{Planned}$	$I_{Unplanned}$
(billions of dollars)					
$0	$0	$100	$300	?	?
400	400	400	300	?	?
800	800	700	300	?	?
1,200	1,200	1,000	300	?	?
1,600	1,600	1,300	300	?	?
2,000	2,000	1,600	300	?	?
2,400	2,400	1,900	300	?	?
2,800	2,800	2,200	300	?	?
3,200	3,200	2,500	300	?	?

   b. What is the aggregate consumption function?

   c. What is Y^*, income–expenditure equilibrium GDP?

   d. What is the value of the multiplier?

   e. If planned investment spending falls to $200 billion, what will be the new Y^*?

   f. If autonomous consumer spending rises to $200 billion, what will be the new Y^*?

10. In an economy with no government and no foreign sectors, autonomous consumer spending is $250 billion, planned investment spending is $350 billion, and the marginal propensity to consume is 2/3.

   a. Plot the aggregate consumption function and planned aggregate spending.

   b. What is unplanned inventory investment when real GDP equals $600 billion?

   c. What is Y^*, income–expenditure equilibrium GDP?

   d. What is the value of the multiplier?

   e. If planned investment spending rises to $450 billion, what will be the new Y^*?

11. An economy has a marginal propensity to consume of 0.5, and Y^*, income–expenditure equilibrium GDP, equals $500 billion. Given an autonomous increase in planned investment of $10 billion, show the rounds of increased spending that take place by completing the accompanying table. The first and second rows are filled in for you. In the first row, the increase of planned investment spending of $10 billion raises real GDP and YD by $10 billion, leading to an increase in consumer spending of $5 billion ($MPC \times$ change in disposable income) in row 2, raising real GDP and YD by a further $5 billion.

Rounds	Change in $I_{Planned}$ or C	Change in real GDP	Change in YD
	(billions of dollars)		
1	$\Delta I_{Planned}$ = $10.00	$10.00	$10.00
2	ΔC = $ 5.00	$ 5.00	$ 5.00
3	ΔC = ?	?	?
4	ΔC = ?	?	?
5	ΔC = ?	?	?
6	ΔC = ?	?	?
7	ΔC = ?	?	?
8	ΔC = ?	?	?
9	ΔC = ?	?	?
10	ΔC = ?	?	?

   a. What is the total change in real GDP after the 10 rounds? What is the value of the multiplier? What would you expect the total change in Y^* to be based on the multiplier formula? How do your answers to the first and third questions compare?

   b. Redo the table starting from round 2, assuming the marginal propensity to consume is 0.75. What is the total change in real GDP after 10 rounds? What is the value of the multiplier? As the marginal propensity to consume increases, what happens to the value of the multiplier?

12. Although the United States is one of the richest nations in the world, it is also the world's largest debtor nation. We often hear that the problem is the nation's low savings rate. Suppose policy makers attempt to rectify this by encouraging greater savings in the economy. What effect will their successful attempts have on real GDP?

13. The U.S. economy slowed significantly in early 2008, and policy makers were extremely concerned about growth. To boost the economy, Congress passed several relief packages that combined would deliver about $700 billion in government spending. Assume, for the sake of argument, that this spending was in the form of payments made directly to consumers. The objective was to boost the economy by increasing the disposable income of American consumers.

   a. Calculate the initial change in aggregate consumer spending as a consequence of this policy measure if the marginal propensity to consume (*MPC*) in the United States is 0.5. Then calculate the resulting change in real GDP arising from the $700 billion in payments.

   b. Illustrate the effect on real GDP with the use of a graph depicting the income–expenditure equilibrium. Label the vertical axis "Planned aggregate spending, $AE_{Planned}$" and the horizontal axis "Real GDP." Draw two planned aggregate expenditure curves ($AE_{Planned1}$ and $AE_{Planned2}$) and a 45-degree line to show the effect of the autonomous policy change on the equilibrium.

1557
379
50%
40%
30%
20%
ALL STOCK
REDUCED!

Module 63: Aggregate Demand
Module 64: Aggregate Supply
Module 65: The *AD–AS* Model

SECTION 20

Aggregate Demand and Aggregate Supply

SHOCKS TO THE SYSTEM

Sometimes it's not easy being at the helm of the Federal Reserve—the institution that sets U.S. *monetary policy,* along with regulating the financial sector. The Federal Reserve's job is to help the economy avoid the twin evils of high inflation and high unemployment. It does this, loosely speaking, either by pumping cash into the economy to fight unemployment or by pulling cash out of the economy to fight inflation.

When the U.S. economy went into a recession in 2001, the Fed, under the leadership of then chairman Alan Greenspan, rushed cash into the system. It was an easy choice: unemployment was rising, and inflation was low and falling. In fact, for much of 2002 the Fed was actually worried about the possibility of *deflation.*

For much of 2008, however, the Fed chairman at the time, Ben Bernanke, faced a much more difficult problem. In fact, he faced the problem people in his position dread most: a combination of unacceptably high inflation and rising unemployment, often referred to as *stagflation.* Stagflation was the scourge of the 1970s: the two deep recessions of 1973–1975 and 1979–1982 were both accompanied by soaring inflation. And in the first half of 2008, the threat of stagflation seemed to be back.

Why did the economic difficulties of early 2008 look so different from those of 2001? Because they had a different cause. The lesson of stagflation in the 1970s was that recessions can have different causes and that the appropriate policy response depends on the cause.

Many recessions, from the great slump of 1929–1933 to the much milder recession of 2001, have been caused by a fall in investment and consumer spending. In these recessions high inflation isn't a threat. In fact, the 1929–1933 slump was accompanied by a sharp fall in the aggregate price level. And because inflation isn't a problem in such recessions, policy makers know what they must do: pump cash in, to fight rising unemployment.

The recessions of the 1970s, however, were largely caused by events in the Middle East that led to sharp cuts in world oil production and soaring prices for oil and other fuels. Not coincidentally, soaring oil prices also contributed to the economic difficulties of early 2008. In both periods, high energy prices led to a combination of unemployment and high inflation. They also created a dilemma: should the Fed fight the slump by pumping cash *into* the economy, or should it fight inflation by pulling cash *out* of the economy?

It's worth noting, by the way, that in 2011 the Fed faced some of the same problems it faced in 2008, as rising oil and food prices led to rising inflation despite high unemployment. In 2011, however, the Fed was fairly sure that demand was the main problem.

In the previous section we developed the *income–expenditure model,* which focuses on the determinants of aggregate spending. This model is extremely useful for understanding events like the recession of 2001 and the recovery that followed. However, the income–expenditure model takes the price level as given, and is therefore much less helpful for understanding the problems policy makers faced in 2008.

In this section, we'll develop a model that shows us how to distinguish between different types of short-run economic fluctuations—*demand shocks,* like those of the Great Depression and the 2001 recession, and *supply shocks,* like those of the 1970s and 2008.

To develop this model, we'll proceed in three steps.

1. We start by developing the concept of *aggregate demand.*
2. Next we turn to the parallel concept of *aggregate supply.*
3. Then we put the two together in the *AD–AS model.*

MODULE

63 Aggregate Demand

WHAT YOU WILL LEARN

1. How the aggregate demand curve illustrates the relationship between the aggregate price level and the quantity of aggregate output demanded in the economy
2. How the wealth effect and interest rate effect explain the aggregate demand curve's negative slope
3. How the aggregate demand curve can be derived from the income–expenditure model
4. What factors can shift the aggregate demand curve

The Aggregate Demand Curve

The Great Depression, the great majority of economists agree, was the result of a massive negative demand shock. What does that mean? When economists talk about a fall in the demand for a particular good or service, they're referring to a leftward shift of the demand curve. Similarly, when economists talk about a negative demand shock to the economy as a whole, they're referring to a leftward shift of the **aggregate demand curve,** a curve that shows the relationship between the aggregate price level and the quantity of aggregate output demanded by households, firms, the government, and the rest of the world.

Figure 63-1 shows what the aggregate demand curve may have looked like in 1933, at the end of the 1929–1933 recession. The horizontal axis shows the total quantity of domestic goods and services demanded, measured in 2005 dollars. We use real GDP to measure aggregate output and will often use the two terms interchangeably. The vertical axis shows the aggregate price level, measured by the GDP deflator. With these variables on the axes, we can draw a curve, *AD,* showing how much aggregate output would have been demanded at any given aggregate price level. Since *AD* is meant to illustrate aggregate demand in 1933, one point on the curve corresponds to actual data for 1933, when the aggregate price level was 7.9 and the total quantity of domestic final goods and services purchased was $716 billion in 2005 dollars.

The **aggregate demand curve** shows the relationship between the aggregate price level and the quantity of aggregate output demanded by households, businesses, the government, and the rest of the world.

As drawn in Figure 63-1, the aggregate demand curve is downward sloping, indicating a negative relationship between the aggregate price level and the quantity of aggregate output demanded. A higher aggregate price level, other things equal, reduces the quantity of aggregate output demanded; a lower aggregate price level, other things equal, increases the quantity of aggregate output demanded. According to Figure 63-1, if the price level in 1933 had been 4.2 instead of 7.9, the total quantity of domestic

FIGURE 63-1 The Aggregate Demand Curve

The aggregate demand curve shows the relationship between the aggregate price level and the quantity of aggregate output demanded. The curve is downward sloping due to the wealth effect of a change in the aggregate price level and the interest rate effect of a change in the aggregate price level. Corresponding to the actual 1933 data, here the total quantity of goods and services demanded at an aggregate price level of 7.9 is $716 billion in 2005 dollars. According to our hypothetical curve, however, if the aggregate price level had been only 4.2, the quantity of aggregate output demanded would have risen to $1,000 billion.

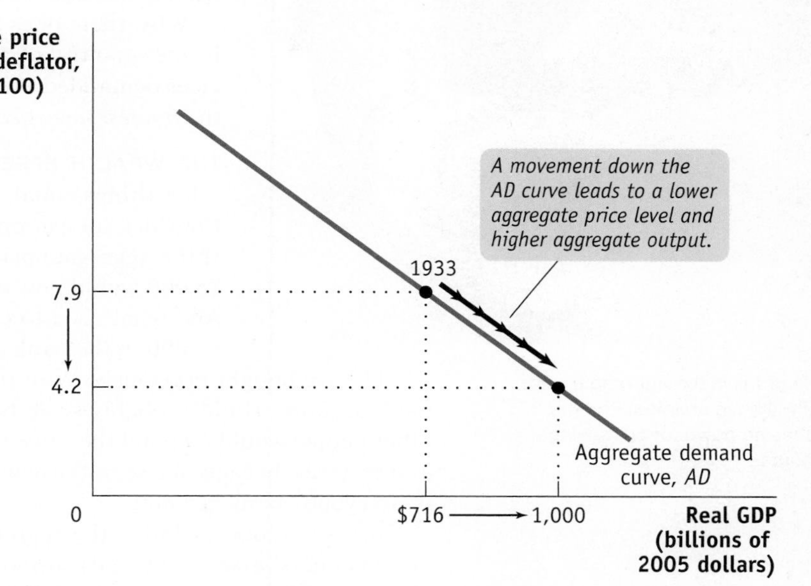

final goods and services demanded would have been $1,000 billion in 2005 dollars instead of $716 billion.

The first key question about the aggregate demand curve is: why should the curve be downward sloping?

Why Is the Aggregate Demand Curve Downward Sloping?

In Figure 63-1, the curve *AD* is downward sloping. Why? Recall the basic equation of national income accounting:

$$\textbf{(63-1)}\ \text{GDP} = C + I + G + X - IM$$

where C is consumer spending, I is investment spending, G is government purchases of goods and services, X is exports to other countries, and IM is imports. If we measure these variables in constant dollars—that is, in prices of a base year—then $C + I + G + X - IM$ is the quantity of domestically produced final goods and services demanded during a given period. G is decided by the government, but the other variables are private-sector decisions. To understand why the aggregate demand curve slopes downward, we need to understand why a rise in the aggregate price level reduces C, I, and $X - IM$.

You might think that the downward slope of the aggregate demand curve is a natural consequence of the *law of demand*. That is, since the demand curve for any one good is downward sloping, isn't it natural that the demand curve for aggregate output is also downward sloping? This turns out, however, to be a misleading parallel. The demand curve for any individual good shows how the quantity demanded depends on the price of that good, *holding the prices of other goods and services constant*. The main reason the quantity of a good demanded falls when the price of that good rises—that is, the quantity of a good demanded falls as we move up the demand curve—is that people switch their consumption to other goods and services.

But when we consider movements up or down the aggregate demand curve, we're considering *a simultaneous change in the prices of all final goods and services*. Furthermore, changes in the composition of goods and services in consumer spending aren't relevant to the aggregate demand curve: if consumers decide to buy fewer clothes

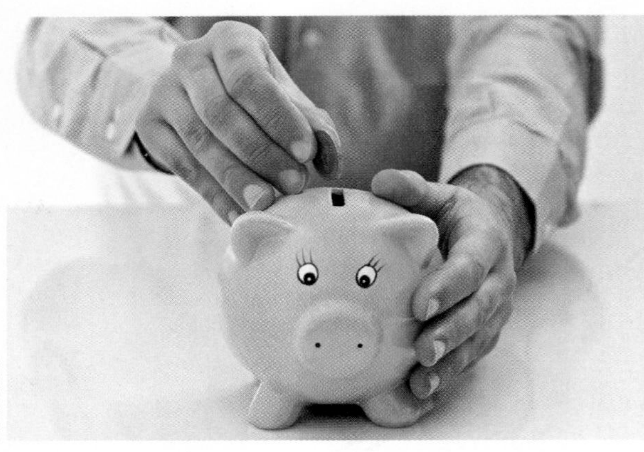

Shutterstock

A rise or fall in the aggregate price level will have an impact on the purchasing power of our savings accounts.

but more cars, this doesn't necessarily change the total quantity of final goods and services they demand.

Why, then, does a rise in the aggregate price level lead to a fall in the quantity of all domestically produced final goods and services demanded? There are two main reasons: the *wealth effect* and the *interest rate effect* of a change in the aggregate price level.

THE WEALTH EFFECT An increase in the aggregate price level, other things equal, reduces the purchasing power of many assets. Consider, for example, someone who has $5,000 in a bank account. If the aggregate price level were to rise by 25%, what used to cost $5,000 would now cost $6,250, and would no longer be affordable. And what used to cost $4,000 would now cost $5,000, so that the $5,000 in the bank account would now buy only as much as $4,000 would have bought previously. With the loss in purchasing power, the owner of that bank account would probably scale back his or her consumption plans. Millions of other people would respond the same way, leading to a fall in spending on final goods and services, because a rise in the aggregate price level reduces the purchasing power of everyone's bank account.

Correspondingly, a fall in the aggregate price level increases the purchasing power of consumers' assets and leads to more consumer demand. The **wealth effect of a change in the aggregate price level** is the effect on consumer spending caused by the effect of a change in the aggregate price level on the purchasing power of consumers' assets. Because of the wealth effect, consumer spending, *C*, falls when the aggregate price level rises, leading to a downward-sloping aggregate demand curve.

THE INTEREST RATE EFFECT Economists use the term *money* in its narrowest sense to refer to cash and bank deposits on which people can write checks. People and firms hold money because it reduces the cost and inconvenience of making transactions. An increase in the aggregate price level, other things equal, reduces the purchasing power of a given amount of money holdings. To purchase the same basket of goods and services as before, people and firms now need to hold more money. So, in response to an increase in the aggregate price level, the public tries to increase its money holdings, either by borrowing more or by selling assets such as bonds. This reduces the funds available for lending to other borrowers and drives interest rates up.

We have already learned that a rise in the interest rate reduces investment spending because it makes the cost of borrowing higher. It also reduces consumer spending because households save more of their disposable income. So a rise in the aggregate price level depresses investment spending, *I*, and consumer spending, *C*, through its effect on the purchasing power of money holdings, an effect known as the **interest rate effect of a change in the aggregate price level.** This also leads to a downward-sloping aggregate demand curve.

We'll have a lot more to say about interest rates in upcoming sections. For now, the important point to remember is that the aggregate demand curve is downward sloping due to both the wealth effect and the interest rate effect of a change in the aggregate price level.

The **wealth effect of a change in the aggregate price level** is the effect on consumer spending caused by the effect of a change in the aggregate price level on the purchasing power of consumers' assets.

The **interest rate effect of a change in the aggregate price level** is the effect on consumer spending and investment spending caused by the effect of a change in the aggregate price level on the purchasing power of consumers' and firms' money holdings.

The Aggregate Demand Curve and the Income–Expenditure Model

In the preceding section we introduced the *income–expenditure model,* which shows how the economy arrives at *income–expenditure equilibrium.* Now we've introduced the aggregate demand curve, which relates the overall demand for goods and services to the overall price level. How do these concepts fit together?

Recall that one of the assumptions of the income–expenditure model is that the aggregate price level is fixed. We now drop that assumption. We can still use the income–

expenditure model, however, to ask what aggregate spending would be *at any given aggregate price level,* which is precisely what the aggregate demand curve shows. So the *AD* curve is actually derived from the income–expenditure model. Economists sometimes say that the income–expenditure model is "embedded" in the *AD–AS* model.

Figure 63-2 shows, once again, how income–expenditure equilibrium is determined. Real GDP is on the horizontal axis; real planned aggregate spending is on the vertical axis. Other things equal, planned aggregate spending, equal to consumer spending plus planned investment spending, rises with real GDP. This is illustrated by the upward-sloping lines $AE_{Planned_1}$ and $AE_{Planned_2}$. Income–expenditure equilibrium, as you will recall, is at the point where the line representing planned aggregate spending crosses the 45-degree line. For example, if $AE_{Planned_1}$ is the relationship between real GDP and planned aggregate spending, then income–expenditure equilibrium is at point E_1, corresponding to a level of real GDP equal to Y_1.

FIGURE 63-2 **How Changes in the Aggregate Price Level Affect Income–Expenditure Equilibrium**

Income–expenditure equilibrium occurs at the point where the curve $AE_{Planned}$, which shows real aggregate planned spending, crosses the 45-degree line. A fall in the aggregate price level causes the $AE_{Planned}$ curve to shift from $AE_{Planned_1}$ to $AE_{Planned_2}$, leading to a rise in income–expenditure equilibrium GDP from Y_1 to Y_2.

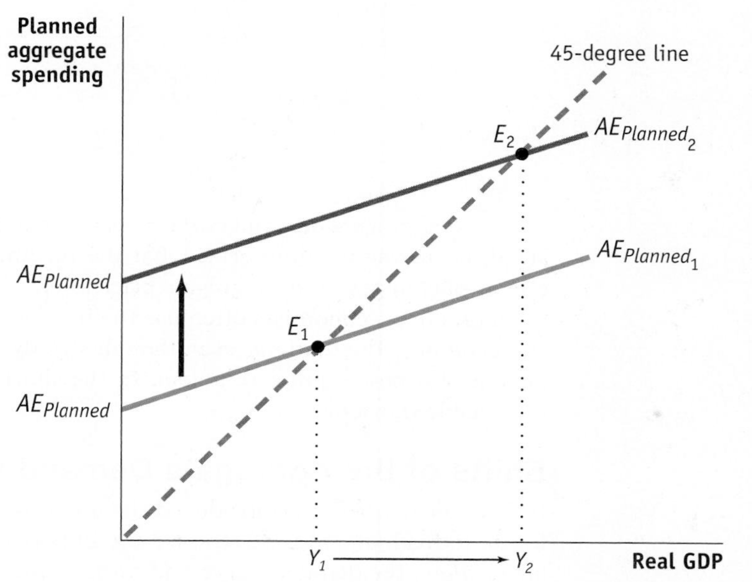

We've just seen, however, that changes in the aggregate price level change the level of planned aggregate spending *at any given level of real GDP.* This means that when the aggregate price level changes, the $AE_{Planned}$ curve shifts. For example, suppose that the aggregate price level falls. As a result of both the wealth effect and the interest rate effect, the fall in the aggregate price level will lead to higher planned aggregate spending at any given level of real GDP. So the $AE_{Planned}$ curve will shift up, as illustrated in Figure 63-2 by the shift from $AE_{Planned_1}$ to $AE_{Planned_2}$. The increase in planned aggregate spending leads to a multiplier process that moves the income–expenditure equilibrium from point E_1 to point E_2, raising real GDP from Y_1 to Y_2.

Figure 63-3 shows how this result can be used to derive the aggregate demand curve. In this figure, we show a fall in the aggregate price level from P_1 to P_2. We saw in Figure 63-2 that a fall in the aggregate price level would lead to an upward shift of the $AE_{Planned}$ curve and hence a rise in real GDP. You can see this same result in Figure 63-3 as a movement along the *AD* curve: as the aggregate price level falls, real GDP rises from Y_1 to Y_2.

FIGURE 63-3 The Income–Expenditure Model and the Aggregate Demand Curve

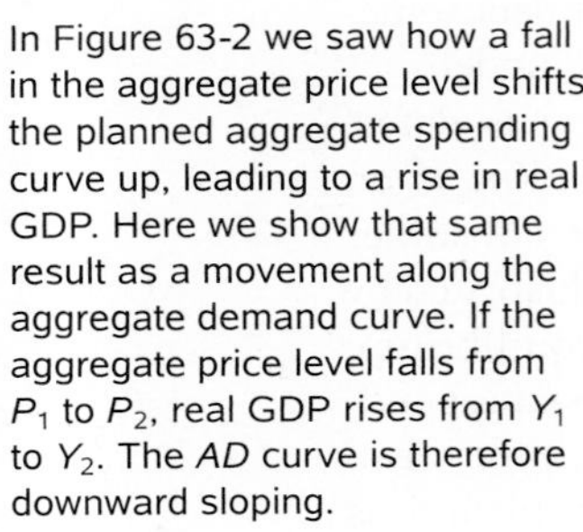

In Figure 63-2 we saw how a fall in the aggregate price level shifts the planned aggregate spending curve up, leading to a rise in real GDP. Here we show that same result as a movement along the aggregate demand curve. If the aggregate price level falls from P_1 to P_2, real GDP rises from Y_1 to Y_2. The *AD* curve is therefore downward sloping.

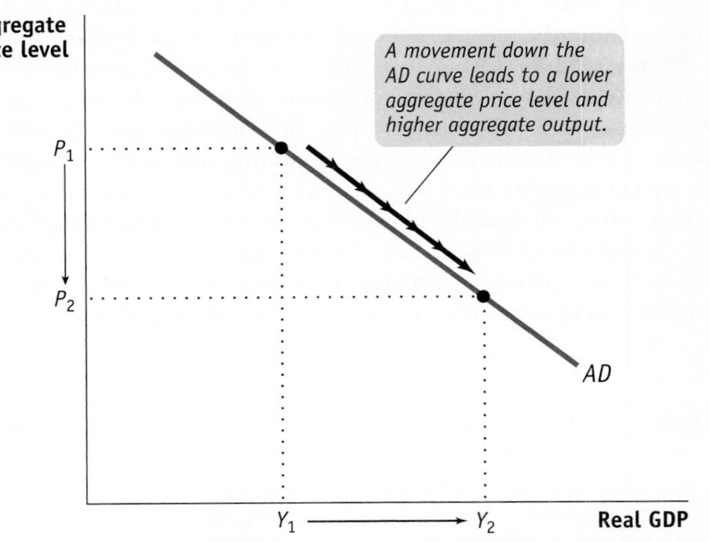
Aggregate price level
A movement down the AD curve leads to a lower aggregate price level and higher aggregate output.
P_1
P_2
AD
Y_1
Y_2
Real GDP

So the aggregate demand curve doesn't replace the income–expenditure model. Instead, it's a way to summarize what the income–expenditure model says about the effects of changes in the aggregate price level.

In practice, economists often use the income–expenditure model to analyze short-run economic fluctuations, even though strictly speaking it should be seen as a component of a more complete model. In the short run, in particular, this is usually a reasonable shortcut.

Shifts of the Aggregate Demand Curve

In Section 2, where we introduced the analysis of supply and demand in the market for an individual good, we stressed the importance of the distinction between *movements along* the demand curve and *shifts of* the demand curve. The same distinction applies to the aggregate demand curve. Figure 63-1 shows a *movement along* the aggregate demand curve, a change in the aggregate quantity of goods and services demanded as the aggregate price level changes.

But there can also be *shifts of* the aggregate demand curve, changes in the quantity of goods and services demanded at any given price level, as shown in Figure 63-4. When we talk about an increase in aggregate demand, we mean a shift of the aggregate demand curve to the right, as shown in panel (a) by the shift from AD_1 to AD_2. A rightward shift occurs when the quantity of aggregate output demanded increases at any given aggregate price level. A decrease in aggregate demand means that the *AD* curve shifts to the left, as in panel (b). A leftward shift implies that the quantity of aggregate output demanded falls at any given aggregate price level.

A number of factors can shift the aggregate demand curve. Among the most important factors are changes in expectations, changes in wealth, and the size of the existing stock of physical capital. In addition, both fiscal and monetary policy can shift the aggregate demand curve. All five factors set the multiplier process in motion. By causing an initial rise or fall in real GDP, they change disposable income, which leads to additional changes in aggregate spending, which lead to further changes in real GDP, and so on. For an overview of factors that shift the aggregate demand curve, see upcoming Table 63-1.

FIGURE 63-4 Shifts of the Aggregate Demand Curve

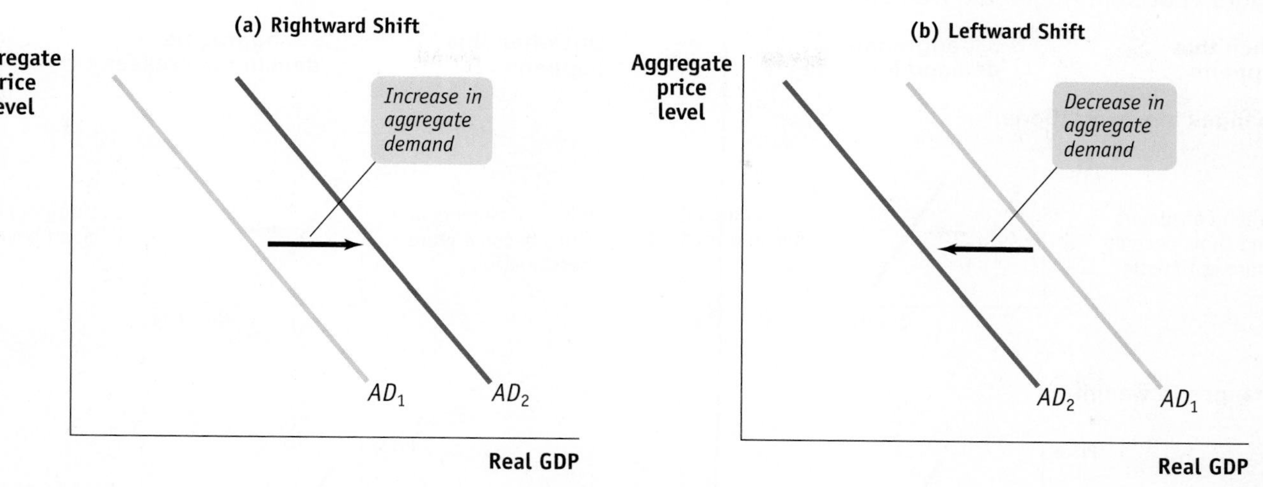

Panel (a) shows the effect of events that increase the quantity of aggregate output demanded at any given aggregate price level, such as improvements in business and consumer expectations or increased government spending. Such changes shift the aggregate demand curve to the right, from AD_1 to AD_2. Panel (b) shows the effect of events that decrease the quantity of aggregate output demanded at any given aggregate price level, such as a fall in wealth caused by a stock market decline. This shifts the aggregate demand curve leftward from AD_1 to AD_2.

CHANGES IN EXPECTATIONS As explained in the previous section, both consumer spending and planned investment spending depend in part on people's expectations about the future. Consumers base their spending not only on the income they have now but also on the income they expect to have in the future. Firms base their planned investment spending not only on current conditions but also on the sales they expect to make in the future. As a result, changes in expectations can push consumer spending and planned investment spending up or down. If consumers and firms become more optimistic, aggregate spending rises; if they become more pessimistic, aggregate spending falls. In fact, short-run economic forecasters pay careful attention to surveys of consumer and business sentiment. In particular, forecasters watch the Consumer Confidence Index, a monthly measure calculated by the Conference Board.

Harley Schwadron/Cartoonstock.com

CHANGES IN WEALTH Consumer spending depends in part on the value of household assets. When the real value of these assets rises, the purchasing power they embody also rises, leading to an increase in aggregate spending. For example, in the 1990s there was a significant rise in the stock market that increased aggregate demand. And when the real value of household assets falls—for example, because of a stock market crash—the purchasing power they embody is reduced and aggregate demand also falls. The stock market crash of 1929 was a significant factor leading to the Great Depression. Similarly, a sharp decline in real estate values was a major factor depressing consumer spending during the 2007–2009 recession.

SIZE OF THE EXISTING STOCK OF PHYSICAL CAPITAL Firms engage in planned investment spending to add to their stock of physical capital. Their incentive to spend depends in part on how much physical capital they already have: the more they have,

TABLE 63-1

Factors That Shift Aggregate Demand

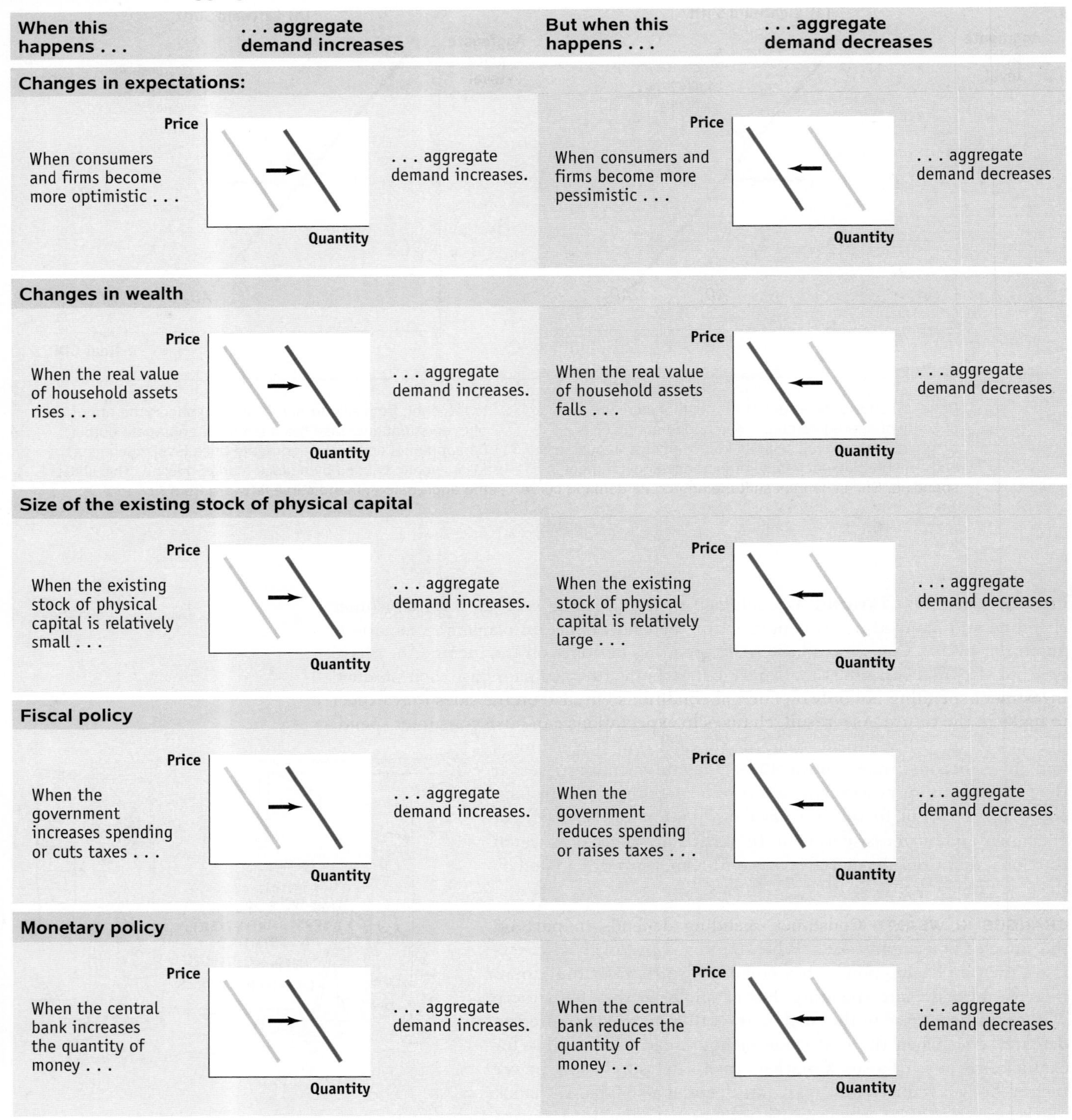

When this happens . . .	. . . aggregate demand increases	But when this happens . . .	. . . aggregate demand decreases
Changes in expectations:			
When consumers and firms become more optimistic . . .	. . . aggregate demand increases.	When consumers and firms become more pessimistic . . .	. . . aggregate demand decreases
Changes in wealth			
When the real value of household assets rises . . .	. . . aggregate demand increases.	When the real value of household assets falls . . .	. . . aggregate demand decreases
Size of the existing stock of physical capital			
When the existing stock of physical capital is relatively small . . .	. . . aggregate demand increases.	When the existing stock of physical capital is relatively large . . .	. . . aggregate demand decreases
Fiscal policy			
When the government increases spending or cuts taxes . . .	. . . aggregate demand increases.	When the government reduces spending or raises taxes . . .	. . . aggregate demand decreases
Monetary policy			
When the central bank increases the quantity of money . . .	. . . aggregate demand increases.	When the central bank reduces the quantity of money . . .	. . . aggregate demand decreases

the less they will feel a need to add more, other things equal. The same applies to other types of investment spending—for example, if a large number of houses have been built in recent years, this will depress the demand for new houses and as a result also tend to reduce residential investment spending.

In fact, that's part of the reason for the deep slump in residential investment spending that began in 2006. The housing boom of the previous few years had created an oversupply of houses: by spring 2009, the inventory of unsold houses on the market was equal to more than 14 months of sales, and prices of new homes had fallen more than 25% from their peak. This gave the construction industry little incentive to build even more homes.

FISCAL POLICY One of the key insights of macroeconomics is that the government can have a powerful influence on aggregate demand and that, in some circumstances, this influence can be used to improve economic performance.

One of the ways government can influence the aggregate demand curve is through fiscal policy, which, as we learned earlier, is the use of either government spending—government purchases of final goods and services and government transfers—or tax policy to stabilize the economy. In practice, governments often respond to recessions by increasing spending, cutting taxes, or both. They often respond to inflation by reducing spending or increasing taxes.

The effect of government purchases of final goods and services, *G*, on the aggregate demand curve is *direct* because government purchases are themselves a component of aggregate demand. So an increase in government purchases shifts the aggregate demand curve to the right and a decrease shifts it to the left. History's most dramatic example of how increased government purchases affect aggregate demand was the effect of wartime government spending during World War II. Because of the war, U.S. federal purchases surged 400%. This increase in purchases is usually credited with ending the Great Depression. Similarly, in 2009, the United States began spending more than $100 billion on infrastructure projects such as improving highways, bridges, public transportation, and more, to stimulate overall spending in the face of a slumping economy.

In contrast, changes in either tax rates or government transfers influence the economy *indirectly* through their effect on disposable income. A lower tax rate means that consumers get to keep more of what they earn, increasing their disposable income. An increase in government transfers also increases consumers' disposable income. In either case, this increases consumer spending and shifts the aggregate demand curve to the right. A higher tax rate or a reduction in transfers reduces the amount of disposable income received by consumers. This reduces consumer spending and shifts the aggregate demand curve to the left.

MONETARY POLICY Another way the government can influence the aggregate demand curve is through monetary policy. In the section-opening story we talked about the problems faced by the Federal Reserve, which controls monetary policy—the use of changes in the quantity of money or the interest rate to stabilize the economy. We've just discussed how a rise in the aggregate price level, by reducing the purchasing power of money holdings, causes a rise in the interest rate. That, in turn, reduces both investment spending and consumer spending.

But what happens if the quantity of money in the hands of households and firms changes? In modern economies, the quantity of money in circulation is largely determined by the decisions of a *central bank* created by the government. As we'll learn in upcoming sections, the Federal Reserve, the U.S. central bank, is a special institution that is neither exactly part of the government nor exactly a private institution.

When the central bank increases the quantity of money in circulation, households and firms have more money, which they are willing to lend out. The effect is to drive the interest rate down at any given aggregate price level, leading to higher investment spending and higher consumer spending. That is, increasing the quantity of money shifts the aggregate demand curve to the right. Reducing the quantity of money has the opposite effect: households and firms have less money holdings than before, leading them to borrow more and lend less. This raises the interest rate, reduces investment spending and consumer spending, and shifts the aggregate demand curve to the left.

ECONOMICS IN ACTION

MOVING ALONG THE AGGREGATE DEMAND CURVE, 1979–1980

When looking at data, it's often hard to distinguish between changes in spending that represent *movements along* the aggregate demand curve and *shifts of* the aggregate demand curve. One telling exception, however, is what happened right after the oil crisis of 1979 (which we mention in the section-opening story). Faced with a sharp increase in the aggregate price level—the rate of consumer price inflation reached 14.8% in March of 1980—the Federal Reserve stuck to a policy of increasing the quantity of money slowly. The aggregate price level was rising steeply, but the quantity of money circulating in the economy was growing slowly. The net result was that the purchasing power of the quantity of money in circulation fell.

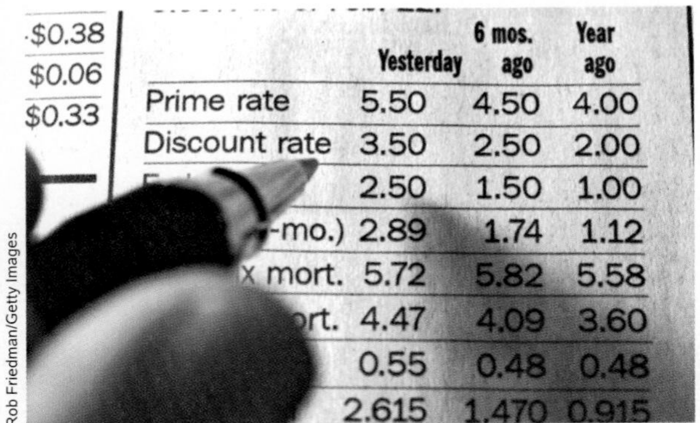

$0.38
$0.06
$0.33
Yesterday 6 mos. ago Year ago
Prime rate 5.50 4.50 4.00
Discount rate 3.50 2.50 2.00
2.50 1.50 1.00
-mo.) 2.89 1.74 1.12
x mort. 5.72 5.82 5.58
rt. 4.47 4.09 3.60
0.55 0.48 0.48
2.615 1.470 0.915

Rob Friedman/Getty Images

The interest rate effect of a rise in the aggregate price level leads to a drop in consumer and investment spending.

This led to an increase in the demand for borrowing and a surge in interest rates. The *prime rate,* which is the interest rate banks charge their best customers, climbed above 20%. High interest rates, in turn, caused both consumer spending and investment spending to fall: in 1980 purchases of durable consumer goods like cars fell by 5.3% and real investment spending fell by 8.9%.

In other words, in 1979–1980 the economy responded just as we'd expect if it were moving upward along the aggregate demand curve from right to left: due to the wealth effect and the interest rate effect of a change in the aggregate price level, the quantity of aggregate output demanded fell as the aggregate price level rose. This does not explain, of course, why the aggregate price level rose. But as we'll see in the next module, the answer to that question lies in the behavior of the *short-run aggregate supply curve.*

MODULE 63 Review

Solutions appear at the back of the book.

Check Your Understanding

1. Determine the effect on aggregate demand of each of the following events. Explain whether it represents a movement along the aggregate demand curve (up or down) or a shift of the curve (leftward or rightward).
   a. a rise in the interest rate caused by a change in monetary policy
   b. a fall in the real value of money in the economy due to a higher aggregate price level
   c. news of a worse-than-expected job market next year
   d. a fall in tax rates
   e. a rise in the real value of assets in the economy due to a lower aggregate price level
   f. a rise in the real value of assets in the economy due to a surge in real estate values

Multiple-Choice Questions

1. Which of the following explains the slope of the aggregate demand curve?
   I. the wealth effect of a change in the aggregate price level
   II. the interest rate effect of a change in the aggregate price level
   III. the product-substitution effect of a change in the aggregate price level
   a. I only
   b. II only
   c. III only
   d. I and II only
   e. I, II, and III

2. Which of the following will shift the aggregate demand curve to the right?
   a. a decrease in wealth
   b. pessimistic consumer expectations
   c. a decrease in the existing stock of capital
   d. contractionary fiscal policy
   e. a decrease in the quantity of money

3. The Consumer Confidence Index is used to measure which of the following?
   a. the level of consumer spending
   b. the rate of return on investments
   c. consumer expectations
   d. planned investment spending
   e. the level of current disposable income

4. Decreases in the stock market decrease aggregate demand by decreasing which of the following?
   a. consumer wealth
   b. the price level
   c. the stock of existing physical capital
   d. interest rates
   e. tax revenues

5. Which of the following government policies will shift the aggregate demand curve to the left?
   a. a decrease in the quantity of money
   b. an increase in government purchases of goods and services
   c. a decrease in taxes
   d. a decrease in interest rates
   e. an increase in government transfers

Critical-Thinking Question

Identify the two effects that cause the aggregate demand curve to have a downward slope. Explain each.

PITFALLS

CHANGES IN WEALTH: A MOVEMENT ALONG VERSUS A SHIFT OF THE AGGREGATE DEMAND CURVE

? Does a change in wealth move the economy along the *AD* curve or does it shift the *AD* curve?

> THE ANSWER IS THAT IT DOES BOTH, DEPENDING ON THE *SOURCE* OF THE CHANGE IN WEALTH. A movement along the *AD* curve occurs when a change in the aggregate price level changes the purchasing power of consumers' existing wealth (the real value of their assets). For example, a fall in the aggregate price level increases the purchasing power of consumers' assets and leads to a movement down the *AD* curve. In contrast, a change in wealth *independent of a change in the aggregate price level* shifts the *AD* curve. For example, a rise in the stock market or a rise in real estate values leads to an increase in the real value of consumers' assets at any given aggregate price level. In this case, the aggregate demand curve shifts to the right as consumers increase their spending due to the increase in wealth.

To learn more, see pages 648–651.

MODULE

64 Aggregate Supply

Tristan Savatier/Getty Images

WHAT YOU WILL LEARN

1. How the aggregate supply curve illustrates the relationship between the aggregate price level and the quantity of aggregate output supplied in the economy
2. What factors can shift the aggregate supply curve
3. Why the short-run aggregate supply curve is different from the long-run aggregate supply curve

The Aggregate Supply Curve

Between 1929 and 1933, there was a sharp fall in aggregate demand—a reduction in the quantity of goods and services demanded at any given price level. Consequences of the economy-wide decline in demand included:

- A fall in the prices of most goods and services. By 1933, the GDP deflator (one of the price indexes) was 26% below its 1929 level, and other indexes were down by similar amounts.
- A decline in the output of most goods and services: by 1933, real GDP was 27% below its 1929 level.
- And closely tied to the fall in real GDP was a surge in the unemployment rate from 3% to 25%.

The association between the plunge in real GDP and the plunge in prices wasn't an accident. Between 1929 and 1933, the U.S. economy was moving down its **aggregate supply curve,** which shows the relationship between the economy's aggregate price level (the overall price level of final goods and services in the economy) and the total quantity of final goods and services, or aggregate output, producers are willing to supply. (As you will recall, we use real GDP to measure aggregate output. So we'll often use the two terms interchangeably.) More specifically, between 1929 and 1933 the U.S. economy moved down its *short-run aggregate supply curve.*

The **aggregate supply curve** shows the relationship between the aggregate price level and the quantity of aggregate output supplied in the economy.

The Short-Run Aggregate Supply Curve

The period from 1929 to 1933 demonstrated that there is a positive relationship in the short run between the aggregate price level and the quantity of aggregate output supplied. That is, a rise in the aggregate price level is associated with a rise in the quantity of aggregate output supplied, other things equal; a fall in the aggregate price level is associated with a fall in the quantity of aggregate output supplied, other things equal. To understand why this positive relationship exists, consider the most basic question facing a producer: is producing a unit of output profitable or not? Let's define profit per unit:

The **nominal wage** is the dollar amount of the wage paid.

Sticky wages are nominal wages that are slow to fall even in the face of high unemployment and slow to rise even in the face of labor shortages.

(64-1) Profit per unit of output =
Price per unit of output − Production cost per unit of output

Thus, the answer to the question depends on whether the price the producer receives for a unit of output is greater or less than the cost of producing that unit of output. At any given point in time, many of the costs producers face are fixed per unit of output and can't be changed for an extended period of time. Typically, the largest source of inflexible production cost is the wages paid to workers. *Wages* here refers to all forms of worker compensation, such as employer-paid health care and retirement benefits in addition to earnings.

Wages are typically an inflexible production cost because the dollar amount of any given wage paid, called the **nominal wage,** is often determined by contracts that were signed some time ago. And even when there are no formal contracts, there are often informal agreements between management and workers, making companies reluctant to change wages in response to economic conditions. For example, companies usually will not reduce wages during poor economic times—unless the downturn has been particularly long and severe—for fear of generating worker resentment. Correspondingly, they typically won't raise wages during better economic times—until they are at risk of losing workers to competitors—because they don't want to encourage workers to routinely demand higher wages.

As a result of both formal and informal agreements, then, the economy is characterized by **sticky wages:** nominal wages that are slow to fall even in the face of high unemployment and slow to rise even in the face of labor shortages. It's important to note, however, that nominal wages cannot be sticky forever: ultimately, formal contracts and informal agreements will be renegotiated to take into account changed economic circumstances.

To understand how the fact that many costs are fixed in nominal terms gives rise to an upward-sloping short-run aggregate supply curve, it's helpful to know that prices are set somewhat differently in different kinds of markets. In *perfectly competitive markets,* producers take prices as given; in *imperfectly competitive markets,* producers have some ability to choose the prices they charge. In both kinds of markets, there is a short-run positive relationship between prices and output, but for slightly different reasons.

Nominal wages are sticky in the short run but not forever.

Let's start with the behavior of producers in perfectly competitive markets; remember, they take the price as given. Imagine that, for some reason, the aggregate price level falls, which means that the price received by the typical producer of a final good or service falls. Because many production costs are fixed in the short run, production cost per unit of output doesn't fall by the same proportion as the fall in the price of output. So the profit per unit of output declines, leading perfectly competitive producers to reduce the quantity supplied in the short run.

On the other hand, suppose that for some reason the aggregate price level rises. As a result, the typical producer receives a higher price for its final good or service. Again, many production costs are fixed in the short run, so production cost per unit of output doesn't rise by the same proportion as the rise in the price of a unit. And since the typical perfectly competitive producer takes the price as given, profit per unit of output rises and output increases.

Now consider an imperfectly competitive producer that is able to set its own price. If there is a rise in the demand for this producer's product, it will be able to sell more

The **short-run aggregate supply curve** shows the relationship between the aggregate price level and the quantity of aggregate output supplied that exists in the short run, the time period when many production costs can be taken as fixed.

at any given price. Given stronger demand for its products, it will probably choose to increase its prices as well as its output, as a way of increasing profit per unit of output. In fact, industry analysts often talk about variations in an industry's "pricing power": when demand is strong, firms with pricing power are able to raise prices—and they do.

Conversely, if there is a fall in demand, firms will normally try to limit the fall in their sales by cutting prices.

Both the responses of firms in perfectly competitive industries and those of firms in imperfectly competitive industries lead to an upward-sloping relationship between aggregate output and the aggregate price level. The positive relationship between the aggregate price level and the quantity of aggregate output producers are willing to supply during the time period when many production costs, particularly nominal wages, can be taken as fixed is illustrated by the **short-run aggregate supply curve.** The positive relationship between the aggregate price level and aggregate output in the short run gives the short-run aggregate supply curve its upward slope.

Figure 64-1 shows a hypothetical short-run aggregate supply curve, *SRAS*, which matches actual U.S. data for 1929 and 1933. On the horizontal axis is aggregate output (or, equivalently, real GDP)—the total quantity of final goods and services supplied in the economy—measured in 2005 dollars. On the vertical axis is the aggregate price level as measured by the GDP deflator, with the value for the year 2005 equal to 100. In 1929, the aggregate price level was 10.6 and real GDP was $976 billion. In 1933, the aggregate price level was 7.9 and real GDP was only $716 billion. The movement down the *SRAS* curve corresponds to the deflation and fall in aggregate output experienced over those years.

FIGURE 64-1 The Short-Run Aggregate Supply Curve

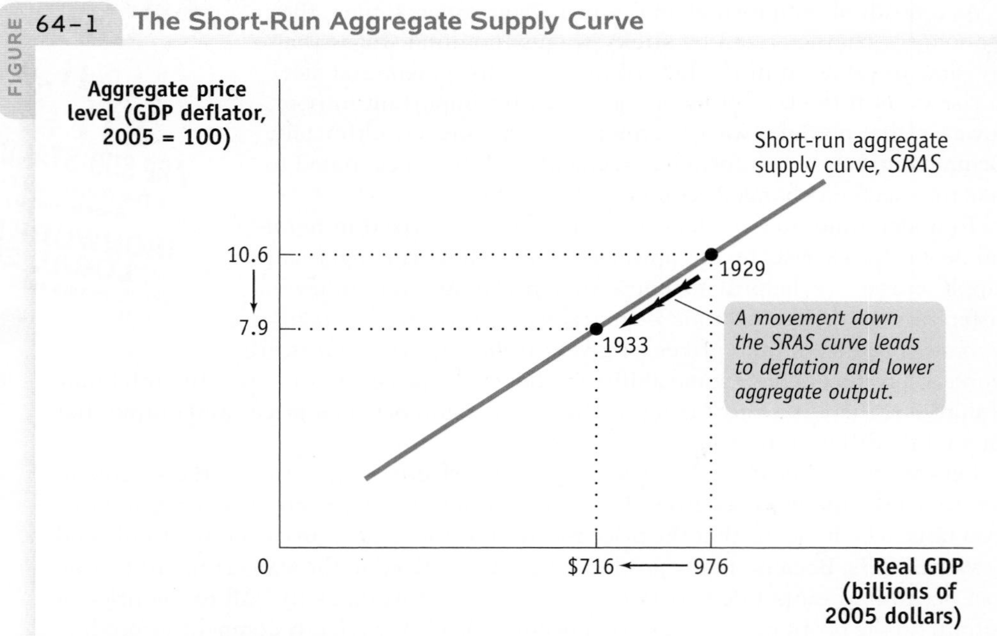

The short-run aggregate supply curve shows the relationship between the aggregate price level and the quantity of aggregate output supplied in the short run, the period in which many production costs such as nominal wages are fixed. It is upward sloping because a higher aggregate price level leads to higher profit per unit of output and higher aggregate output given fixed nominal wages. Here we show numbers corresponding to the Great Depression, from 1929 to 1933: when deflation occurred and the aggregate price level fell from 10.6 (in 1929) to 7.9 (in 1933), firms responded by reducing the quantity of aggregate output supplied from $976 billion to $716 billion measured in 2005 dollars.

Shifts of the Short-Run Aggregate Supply Curve

Figure 64-1 shows a *movement along* the short-run aggregate supply curve, as the aggregate price level and aggregate output fell from 1929 to 1933. But there can also be *shifts of* the short-run aggregate supply curve, as shown in Figure 64-2. Panel (a) shows a *decrease in short-run aggregate supply*—a leftward shift of the short-run aggregate supply curve. Aggregate supply decreases when producers reduce the quantity of aggregate output they are willing to supply at any given aggregate price level. Panel (b) shows an *increase in short-run aggregate supply*—a rightward shift of the short-run aggregate supply curve. Aggregate supply increases when producers increase the quantity of aggregate output they are willing to supply at any given aggregate price level.

To understand why the short-run aggregate supply curve can shift, it's important to recall that producers make output decisions based on their profit per unit of output. The short-run aggregate supply curve illustrates the relationship between the aggregate price level and aggregate output: because some production costs are fixed in the short run, a change in the aggregate price level leads to a change in producers' profit per unit of output and, in turn, leads to a change in aggregate output. But other factors besides the aggregate price level can affect profit per unit and, in turn, aggregate output. It is changes in these other factors that will shift the short-run aggregate supply curve.

To develop some intuition, suppose that something happens that raises production costs—say, an increase in the price of oil. At any given price of output, a producer now earns a smaller profit per unit of output. As a result, producers reduce the quantity supplied at any given aggregate price level, and the short-run aggregate supply curve shifts to the left. If, in contrast, something happens that lowers production costs—say, a fall in the nominal wage—a producer now earns a higher profit per unit of output at any given price of output. This leads producers to increase the quantity of aggregate output supplied at any given aggregate price level, and the short-run aggregate supply curve shifts to the right.

FIGURE 64-2 Shifts of the Short-Run Aggregate Supply Curve

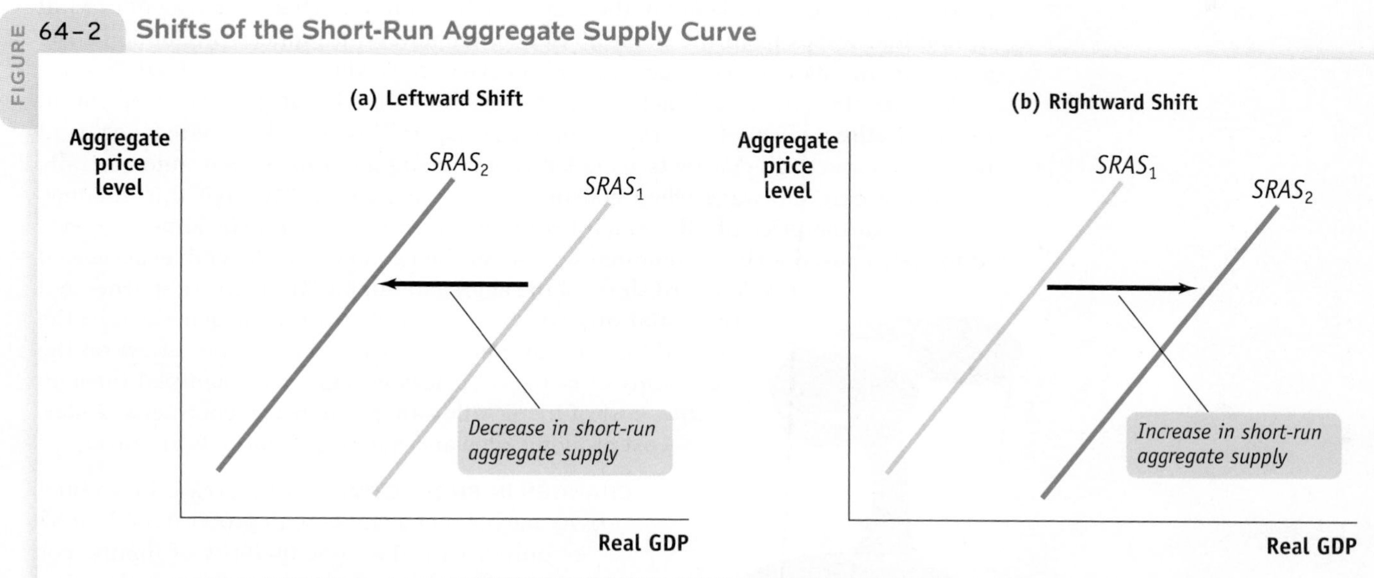

Panel (a) shows a decrease in short-run aggregate supply: the short-run aggregate supply curve shifts leftward from $SRAS_1$ to $SRAS_2$, and the quantity of aggregate output supplied at any given aggregate price level falls. Panel (b) shows an increase in short-run aggregate supply: the short-run aggregate supply curve shifts rightward from $SRAS_1$ to $SRAS_2$, and the quantity of aggregate output supplied at any given aggregate price level rises.

Now we'll discuss some of the important factors that affect producers' profit per unit and so can lead to shifts of the short-run aggregate supply curve.

CHANGES IN COMMODITY PRICES A surge in the price of oil caused problems for the U.S. economy in the 1970s, early in 2008, and again in 2011. Oil is a commodity, a standardized input bought and sold in bulk quantities. An increase in the price of a commodity—oil—raised production costs across the economy and reduced the quantity of aggregate output supplied at any given aggregate price level, shifting the short-run aggregate supply curve to the left. Conversely, a decline in commodity prices reduces production costs, leading to an increase in the quantity supplied at any given aggregate price level and a rightward shift of the short-run aggregate supply curve.

Because commodities like oil are not final goods, their prices are not included in the aggregate price level.

Why isn't the influence of commodity prices already captured by the short-run aggregate supply curve? Because commodities—unlike, say, soft drinks—are not a final good, their prices are not included in the calculation of the aggregate price level. Further, commodities represent a significant cost of production to most suppliers, just like nominal wages do. So changes in commodity prices have large impacts on production costs. And in contrast to noncommodities, the prices of commodities can sometimes change drastically due to industry-specific shocks to supply—such as wars in the Middle East or rising Chinese demand that leaves less oil for the United States.

CHANGES IN NOMINAL WAGES At any given point in time, the dollar wages of many workers are fixed because they are set by contracts or informal agreements made in the past. Nominal wages can change, however, once enough time has passed for contracts and informal agreements to be renegotiated.

Suppose, for example, that there is an economy-wide rise in the cost of health care insurance premiums paid by employers as part of employees' wages. From the employers' perspective, this is equivalent to a rise in nominal wages because it is an increase in employer-paid compensation. So this rise in nominal wages increases production costs and shifts the short-run aggregate supply curve to the left. Conversely, suppose there is an economy-wide fall in the cost of such premiums. This is equivalent to a fall in nominal wages from the point of view of employers; it reduces production costs and shifts the short-run aggregate supply curve to the right.

An important historical fact is that during the 1970s the surge in the price of oil had the indirect effect of also raising nominal wages. This "knock-on" effect occurred because many wage contracts included *cost-of-living allowances* that automatically raised the nominal wage when consumer prices increased. Through this channel, the surge in the price of oil—which led to an increase in overall consumer prices—ultimately caused a rise in nominal wages. So the economy, in the end, experienced two leftward shifts of the aggregate supply curve: the first generated by the initial surge in the price of oil, the second generated by the induced increase in nominal wages. The negative effect on the economy of rising oil prices was greatly magnified through the cost-of-living allowances in wage contracts. Today, cost-of-living allowances in wage contracts are rare.

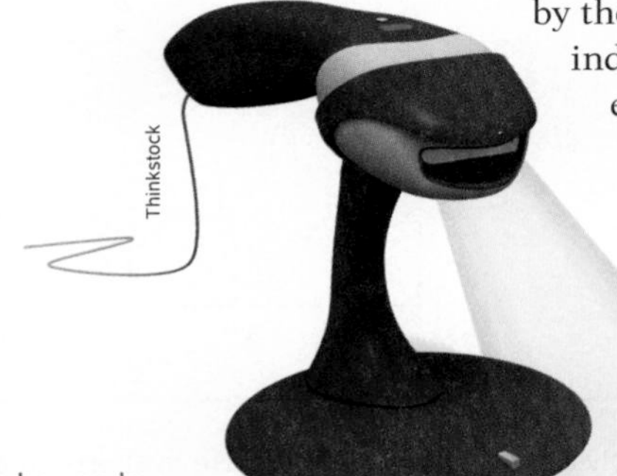

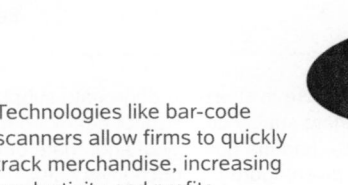

Technologies like bar-code scanners allow firms to quickly track merchandise, increasing productivity and profits.

CHANGES IN PRODUCTIVITY An increase in productivity means that a worker can produce more units of output with the same quantity of inputs. For example, the introduction of bar-code scanners in retail stores greatly increased the ability of a single worker to stock, inventory, and resupply store shelves. As a result, the cost to a store of "producing" a dollar of sales fell and profit rose. And, correspondingly, the quantity supplied increased. (Think of Walmart and the increase in the number of its stores as an increase in aggregate supply.)

So a rise in productivity, whatever the source, increases producers' profits and shifts the short-run aggregate supply curve to the right. Conversely, a fall in productivity—say, due to new regulations that require workers to spend more time filling out forms—reduces the number of units of output a worker can produce with the same quantity of inputs. Consequently, the cost per unit of output rises, profit falls, and quantity supplied falls. This shifts the short-run aggregate supply curve to the left.

For a summary of the factors that shift the short-run aggregate supply curve, see Table 64-1.

TABLE 64-1

Factors That Shift Aggregate Supply

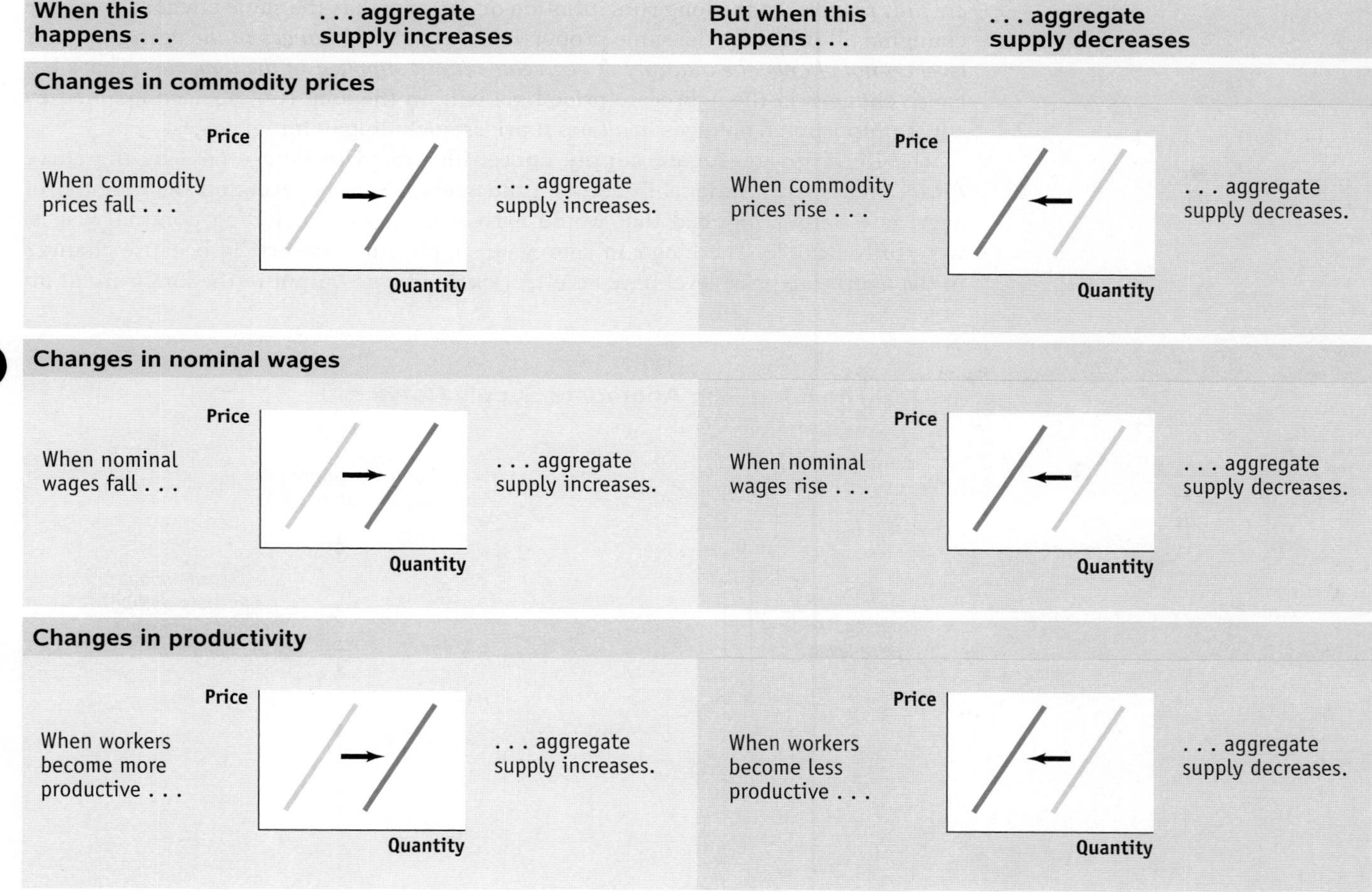

When this happens . . .	. . . aggregate supply increases	But when this happens . . .	. . . aggregate supply decreases
Changes in commodity prices			
When commodity prices fall . . .	. . . aggregate supply increases.	When commodity prices rise . . .	. . . aggregate supply decreases.
Changes in nominal wages			
When nominal wages fall . . .	. . . aggregate supply increases.	When nominal wages rise . . .	. . . aggregate supply decreases.
Changes in productivity			
When workers become more productive . . .	. . . aggregate supply increases.	When workers become less productive . . .	. . . aggregate supply decreases.

The Long-Run Aggregate Supply Curve

We've seen that in the short run a fall in the aggregate price level leads to a decline in the quantity of aggregate output supplied because nominal wages are sticky in the short run. But, as we mentioned earlier, contracts and informal agreements are renegotiated in the long run. So in the long run, nominal wages—like the aggregate price level—are flexible, not sticky. This fact greatly alters the long-run relationship between the aggregate price level and aggregate supply. In fact, in the long run the aggregate price level has *no* effect on the quantity of aggregate output supplied.

The **long-run aggregate supply curve** shows the relationship between the aggregate price level and the quantity of aggregate output supplied that would exist if all prices, including nominal wages, were fully flexible.

To see why, let's conduct a thought experiment. Imagine that you could wave a magic wand and cut *all prices* in the economy in half at the same time. By "all prices" we mean the prices of all inputs, including nominal wages, as well as the prices of final goods and services. What would happen to aggregate output, given that the aggregate price level has been halved and all input prices, including nominal wages, have been halved?

The answer is: nothing. Consider Equation 64-1 again: each producer would receive a lower price for its product, but costs would fall by the same proportion. As a result, every unit of output profitable to produce before the change in prices would still be profitable to produce after the change in prices. So a halving of *all* prices in the economy has no effect on the economy's aggregate output. In other words, changes in the aggregate price level now have no effect on the quantity of aggregate output supplied.

In reality, of course, no one can change all prices by the same proportion at the same time. But now, we'll consider the *long run, the period of time over which all prices are fully flexible.* In the long run, inflation or deflation has the same effect as someone changing all prices by the same proportion. *As a result, changes in the aggregate price level do not change the quantity of aggregate output supplied in the long run.* That's because changes in the aggregate price level will, in the long run, be accompanied by equal proportional changes in *all* input prices, including nominal wages.

The **long-run aggregate supply curve,** illustrated in Figure 64-3 by the curve *LRAS,* shows the relationship between the aggregate price level and the quantity of aggregate output supplied that would exist if all prices, including nominal wages, were fully flexible. The long-run aggregate supply curve is vertical because changes in the aggregate price level have *no* effect on aggregate output in the long run. At an

FIGURE 64-3 The Long-Run Aggregate Supply Curve

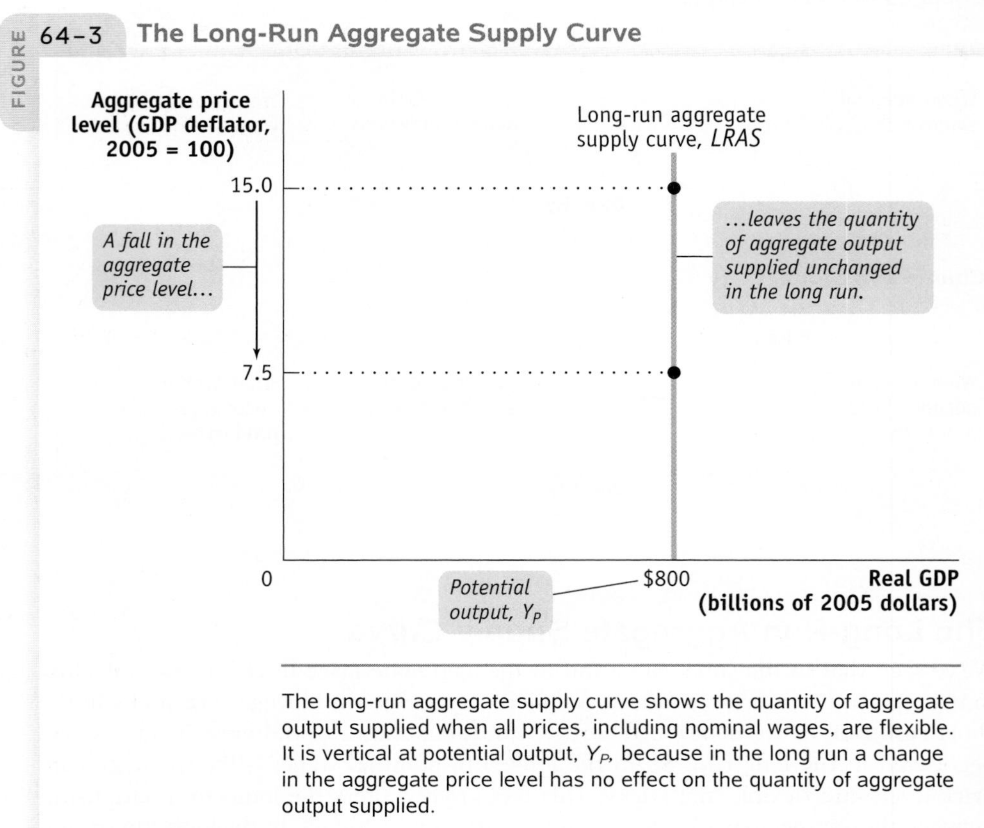

The long-run aggregate supply curve shows the quantity of aggregate output supplied when all prices, including nominal wages, are flexible. It is vertical at potential output, Y_P, because in the long run a change in the aggregate price level has no effect on the quantity of aggregate output supplied.

aggregate price level of 15.0, the quantity of aggregate output supplied is $800 billion in 2005 dollars. If the aggregate price level falls by 50% to 7.5, the quantity of aggregate output supplied is unchanged in the long run at $800 billion in 2005 dollars.

It's important to understand not only that the *LRAS* curve is vertical but also that its position along the horizontal axis represents a significant measure. The horizontal intercept in Figure 64-3, where *LRAS* touches the horizontal axis ($800 billion in 2005 dollars), is the economy's **potential output,** Y_P: the level of real GDP the economy would produce if all prices, including nominal wages, were fully flexible.

Potential output is the level of real GDP the economy would produce if all prices, including nominal wages, were fully flexible.

In reality, the actual level of real GDP is almost always either above or below potential output. We'll see why later in this section, when we discuss the *AD–AS* model. Still, an economy's potential output is an important number because it defines the trend around which actual aggregate output fluctuates from year to year.

In the United States, the Congressional Budget Office, or CBO, estimates annual potential output for the purpose of federal budget analysis. In Figure 64-4, the CBO's estimates of U.S. potential output from 1990 to 2012 are represented by the orange line and the actual values of U.S. real GDP over the same period are represented by the blue line. Years shaded purple on the horizontal axis correspond to periods in which actual aggregate output fell short of potential output, years shaded green to periods in which actual aggregate output exceeded potential output.

As you can see, U.S. potential output has risen steadily over time—implying a series of rightward shifts of the *LRAS* curve. What has caused these rightward shifts? The answer lies in the factors related to long-run growth that we discussed in Section

FIGURE 64-4 Actual and Potential Output from 1990 to 2012

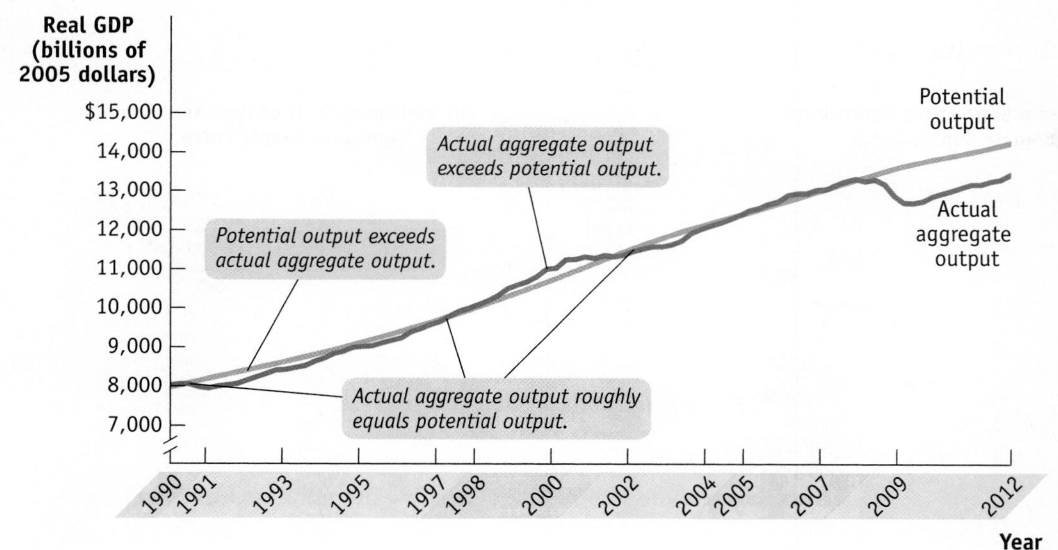

This figure shows the performance of actual and potential output in the United States from 1990 to 2012. The orange line shows estimates of U.S. potential output, produced by the Congressional Budget Office, and the blue line shows actual aggregate output. The purple-shaded years are periods in which actual aggregate output fell below potential output, and the green-shaded years are periods in which actual aggregate output exceeded potential output. As shown, significant shortfalls occurred in the recessions of the early 1990s and after 2000. Actual aggregate output was significantly above potential output in the boom of the late 1990s, and a huge shortfall occurred after the recession of 2007–2009.

Sources: Congressional Budget Office; Bureau of Economic Analysis.

17, such as increases in physical capital and human capital as well as technological progress.

Over the long run, as the size of the labor force and the productivity of labor both rise, the level of real GDP that the economy is capable of producing also rises. Indeed, one way to think about long-run economic growth is that it is the growth in the economy's potential output. We generally think of the long-run aggregate supply curve as shifting to the right over time as an economy experiences long-run growth.

From the Short Run to the Long Run

As you can see in Figure 64-4, the economy normally produces more or less than potential output: actual aggregate output was below potential output in the early 1990s, above potential output in the late 1990s, below potential output for most of the 2000s, and significantly below potential output after the recession of 2007–2009. So the economy is normally on its short-run aggregate supply curve—but not on its long-run aggregate supply curve. So why is the long-run curve relevant? Does the economy ever move from the short run to the long run? And if so, how?

The first step to answering these questions is to understand that the economy is always in one of only two states with respect to the short-run and long-run aggregate supply curves. It can be on both curves simultaneously by being at a point where the curves cross (as in the few years in Figure 64-4 in which actual aggregate output and potential output roughly coincided). Or it can be on the short-run aggregate supply curve but not the long-run aggregate supply curve (as in the years in which actual aggregate output and potential output *did not* coincide).

But that is not the end of the story. If the economy is on the short-run but not the long-run aggregate supply curve, the short-run aggregate supply curve will shift over

FIGURE 64-5 From the Short Run to the Long Run

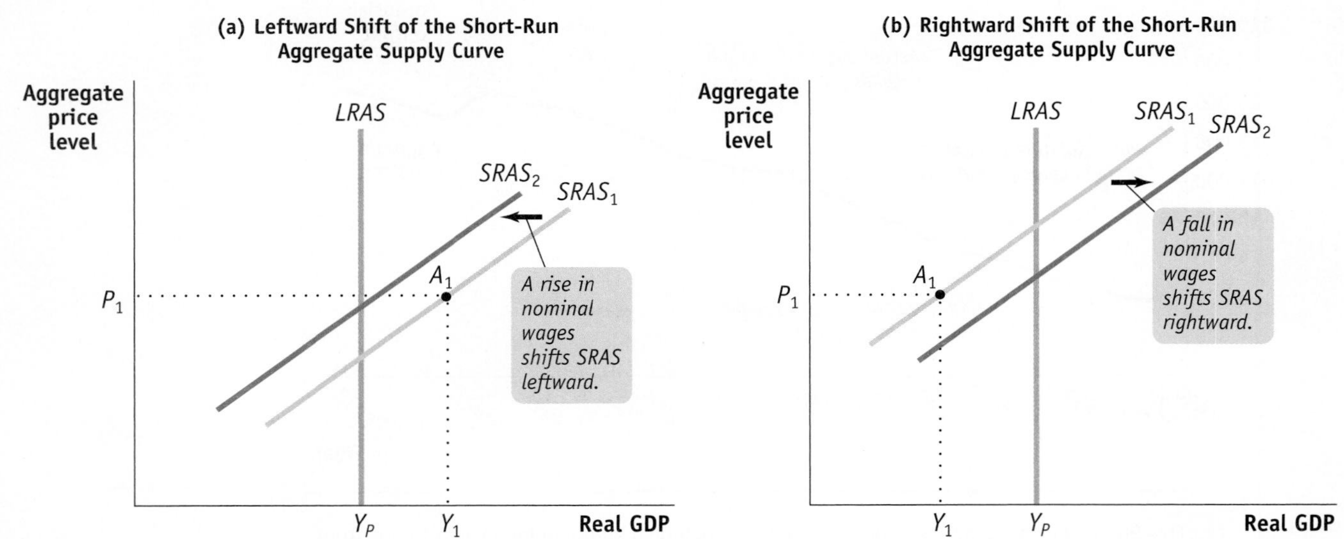

In panel (a), the initial short-run aggregate supply curve is $SRAS_1$. At the aggregate price level, P_1, the quantity of aggregate output supplied, Y_1, exceeds potential output, Y_P. Eventually, low unemployment will cause nominal wages to rise, leading to a leftward shift of the short-run aggregate supply curve from $SRAS_1$ to $SRAS_2$. In panel (b), the reverse happens: at the aggregate price level, P_1, the quantity of aggregate output supplied is less than potential output. High unemployment eventually leads to a fall in nominal wages over time and a rightward shift of the short-run aggregate supply curve.

time until the economy is at a point where both curves cross—a point where actual aggregate output is equal to potential output.

Figure 64-5 shows how this process works. In both panels *LRAS* is the long-run aggregate supply curve, $SRAS_1$ is the initial short-run aggregate supply curve, and the aggregate price level is at P_1. In panel (a) the economy starts at the initial production point, A_1, which corresponds to a quantity of aggregate output supplied, Y_1, that is higher than potential output, Y_P. Producing an aggregate output level (such as Y_1) that is higher than potential output (Y_P) is possible only because nominal wages haven't yet fully adjusted upward. Until this upward adjustment in nominal wages occurs, producers are earning high profits and producing a high level of output. But a level of aggregate output higher than potential output means a low level of unemployment. Because jobs are abundant and workers are scarce, nominal wages will rise over time, gradually shifting the short-run aggregate supply curve leftward. Eventually it will be in a new position, such as $SRAS_2$.

In panel (b), the initial production point, A_1, corresponds to an aggregate output level, Y_1, that is lower than potential output, Y_P. Producing an aggregate output level (such as Y_1) that is lower than potential output (Y_P) is possible only because nominal wages haven't yet fully adjusted downward. Until this downward adjustment occurs, producers are earning low (or negative) profits and producing a low level of output. An aggregate output level lower than potential output means high unemployment. Because workers are abundant and jobs are scarce, nominal wages will fall over time, shifting the short-run aggregate supply curve gradually to the right. Eventually it will be in a new position, such as $SRAS_2$.

We'll soon see that these shifts of the short-run aggregate supply curve will return the economy to potential output in the long run.

ECONOMICS ▶ IN ACTION

PRICES AND OUTPUT DURING THE GREAT DEPRESSION

Figure 64-6 shows the actual track of the aggregate price level, as measured by the GDP deflator and real GDP, from 1929 to 1942. As you can see, aggregate output and the aggregate price level fell together from 1929 to 1933 and rose together from 1933 to 1937. This is what we'd expect to see if the economy was moving down the short-run aggregate supply curve from 1929 to 1933 and moving up it (with a brief reversal in 1937–1938) thereafter.

But even in 1942 the aggregate price level was still lower than it was in 1929; yet real GDP was much higher. What happened?

The answer is that the short-run aggregate supply curve shifted to the right over time. This shift partly reflected rising productivity—a rightward shift of the underlying long-run aggregate supply curve. But since the U.S. economy was producing below potential output and had high unemployment during this period, the rightward shift of the short-run aggregate supply curve also reflected the adjustment process shown in panel (b) of Figure 64-5. So the change in aggregate output from 1929 to 1942 reflected both movements along and shifts of the short-run aggregate supply curve.

FIGURE 64-6 Prices and Output During the Great Depression

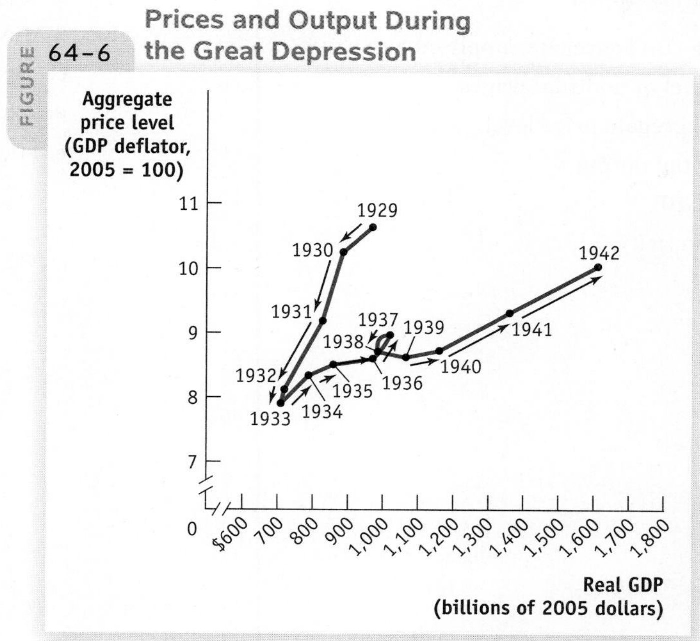

MODULE 64 Review

Solutions appear at the back of the book.

Check Your Understanding

1. Determine the effect on short-run aggregate supply of each of the following events. Explain whether it represents a movement along the *SRAS* curve or a shift of the *SRAS* curve.
   a. A rise in the consumer price index (CPI) leads producers to increase output.
   b. A fall in the price of oil leads producers to increase output.
   c. A rise in legally mandated retirement benefits paid to workers leads producers to reduce output.
2. Suppose the economy is initially at potential output and the quantity of aggregate output supplied increases. What information would you need to determine whether this was due to a movement along the *SRAS* curve or a shift of the *LRAS* curve?

Multiple-Choice Questions

1. A change in which of the following variables will cause a shift of the *SRAS* curve?
   a. profit per unit at any given price level
   b. commodity prices
   c. nominal wages
   d. productivity
   e. all of the above
2. The long-run aggregate supply curve is
   a. vertical.
   b. horizontal.
   c. fixed.
   d. negatively sloped.
   e. positively sloped.
3. The long-run aggregate supply curve shows
   a. the level of nominal wages.
   b. the aggregate price level.
   c. potential output.
   d. real GDP.
   e. productivity.
4. A decrease in which of the following will cause the short-run aggregate supply curve to shift to the left?
   a. commodity prices
   b. the cost of health care insurance premiums paid by employers
   c. nominal wages
   d. productivity
   e. the use of cost-of-living allowances in labor contracts
5. That employers are reluctant to decrease nominal wages during economic downturns and raise nominal wages during economic expansions leads nominal wages to be described as
   a. long-run.
   b. unyielding.
   c. flexible.
   d. real.
   e. sticky.

Critical-Thinking Questions

The short-run aggregate supply curve is upward sloping as a result of the price and output decisions made by firms in the short run.

1. Explain why perfectly competitive firms increase output when there is an increase in the aggregate price level.
2. Explain why imperfectly competitive firms increase both price and output when there is an increase in demand.

PITFALLS

WHAT THE LONG RUN REALLY MEANS

? You've seen the term *long run* used in two different contexts. In an earlier section, we discussed *long-run economic growth*. In this section, we introduced the *long-run aggregate supply curve*. What is the difference between the two?

> THERE IS NO DIFFERENCE! *Long-run economic growth* is growth that takes place over decades, while the *long-run aggregate supply curve* shows the economy's potential output at a particular point in time: that is, the level of aggregate output that the economy would produce if all prices, including nominal wages, were fully flexible. Because the economy always tends to return to potential output in the long run, actual aggregate output *fluctuates around* potential output. As a result, the economy's rate of growth over long periods of time is very close to the rate of growth of potential output. So this means that the "long run" of long-run growth and the "long run" of the long-run aggregate supply curve are really the same thing.

To learn more about both concepts, see pages 662–665.

MODULE 65 The *AD–AS* Model

Dorset Media Service/Alamy

WHAT YOU WILL LEARN

1. The difference between short-run and long-run macroeconomic equilibrium
2. The causes and effects of demand shocks and supply shocks
3. How to determine if an economy is experiencing a recessionary gap or an inflationary gap and how to calculate the size of output gaps
4. How monetary policy and fiscal policy can be used to stabilize the economy

Putting the Aggregate Supply Curve and the Aggregate Demand Curve Together

From 1929 to 1933, the U.S. economy moved down the short-run aggregate supply curve as the aggregate price level fell. In contrast, from 1979 to 1980, the U.S. economy moved up the aggregate demand curve as the aggregate price level rose. In each case, the cause of the movement along the curve was a shift of the other curve. In 1929–1933, it was a leftward shift of the aggregate demand curve—a major fall in consumer spending. In 1979–1980, it was a leftward shift of the short-run aggregate supply curve—a dramatic fall in short-run aggregate supply caused by the oil *price shock*.

So to understand the behavior of the economy, we must put the aggregate supply curve and the aggregate demand curve together. The result is the ***AD–AS* model,** the basic model we use to understand economic fluctuations.

In the ***AD–AS* model,** the aggregate supply curve and the aggregate demand curve are used together to analyze economic fluctuations.

The economy is in **short-run macroeconomic equilibrium** when the quantity of aggregate output supplied is equal to the quantity demanded.

The **short-run equilibrium aggregate price level** is the aggregate price level in the short-run macroeconomic equilibrium.

Short-run equilibrium aggregate output is the quantity of aggregate output produced in the short-run macroeconomic equilibrium.

Short-Run Macroeconomic Equilibrium

We'll begin our analysis by focusing on the short run. Figure 65-1 shows the aggregate demand curve and the short-run aggregate supply curve on the same diagram. The point at which the *AD* and *SRAS* curves intersect, E_{SR}, is the **short-run macroeconomic equilibrium:** the point at which the quantity of aggregate output supplied is equal to the quantity demanded by domestic households, businesses, the government, and the rest of the world. The aggregate price level at E_{SR}, P_E, is the **short-run equilibrium aggregate price level.** The level of aggregate output at E_{SR}, Y_E, is the **short-run equilibrium aggregate output.**

We have seen that a shortage of any individual good causes its market price to rise and a surplus of the good causes its market price to fall. These forces ensure that the market reaches equilibrium. The same logic applies to short-run macroeconomic

FIGURE 65-1 **The *AD–AS* Model**

The *AD–AS* model combines the aggregate demand curve and the short-run aggregate supply curve. Their point of intersection, E_{SR}, is the point of short-run macroeconomic equilibrium where the quantity of aggregate output demanded is equal to the quantity of aggregate output supplied. P_E is the short-run equilibrium aggregate price level, and Y_E is the short-run equilibrium level of aggregate output.

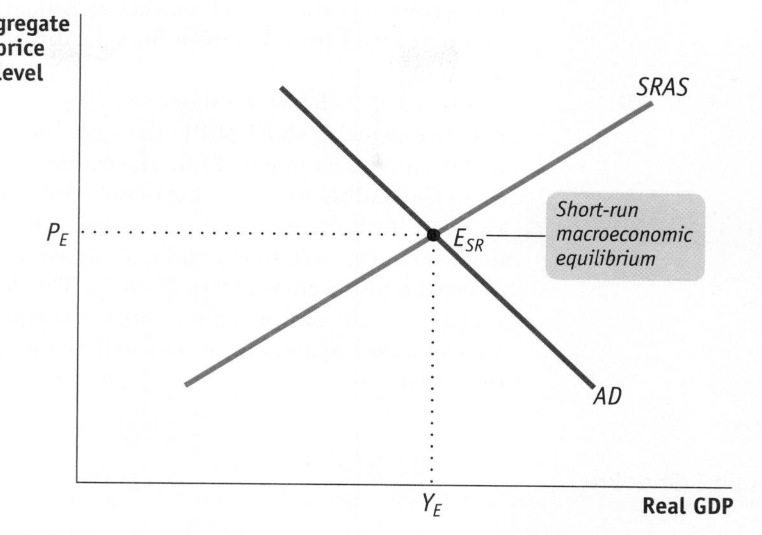

equilibrium. If the aggregate price level is above its equilibrium level, the quantity of aggregate output supplied exceeds the quantity of aggregate output demanded. This leads to a fall in the aggregate price level and pushes it toward its equilibrium level.

If the aggregate price level is below its equilibrium level, the quantity of aggregate output supplied is less than the quantity of aggregate output demanded. This leads to a rise in the aggregate price level, again pushing it toward its equilibrium level. In the discussion that follows, we'll assume that the economy is always in short-run macroeconomic equilibrium.

We'll also make another important simplification based on the observation that in reality there is a long-term upward trend in both aggregate output and the aggregate price level. We'll assume that a fall in either variable really means a fall compared to the long-run trend. For example, if the aggregate price level normally rises 4% per year, a year in which the aggregate price level rises only 3% would count, for our purposes, as a 1% decline.

In fact, since the Great Depression there have been very few years in which the aggregate price level of any major nation actually declined—Japan's period of deflation from 1995 to 2005 is one of the few exceptions. However, there have been many cases in which the aggregate price level fell relative to the long-run trend.

The short-run equilibrium aggregate output and the short-run equilibrium aggregate price level can change because of shifts of either the *AD* curve or the *SRAS* curve. Let's look at each case in turn.

Shifts of Aggregate Demand: Short-Run Effects

An event that shifts the aggregate demand curve, such as a change in expectations or wealth, the effect of the size of the existing stock of physical capital, or the use of fiscal or monetary policy, is known as a **demand shock.** The Great Depression was caused by a negative demand shock—the collapse of wealth and of business and consumer confidence that followed the stock market crash of 1929 and

An event that shifts the aggregate demand curve is a **demand shock.**

The Great Depression was caused by a negative demand shock and ended by a positive demand shock.

© Bettmann/CORBIS

the banking crises of 1930–1931. The Depression was ended by a positive demand shock—the huge increase in government purchases during World War II. In 2008, the U.S. economy experienced another significant negative demand shock as the housing market turned from boom to bust, leading consumers and firms to scale back their spending.

Figure 65-2 shows the short-run effects of negative and positive demand shocks. A negative demand shock shifts the aggregate demand curve, *AD*, to the left, from AD_1 to AD_2, as shown in panel (a). The economy moves down along the *SRAS* curve from E_1 to E_2, leading to lower short-run equilibrium aggregate output and a lower short-run equilibrium aggregate price level. A positive demand shock shifts the aggregate demand curve, *AD*, to the right, as shown in panel (b). Here, the economy moves up along the *SRAS* curve, from E_1 to E_2. This leads to higher short-run equilibrium aggregate output and a higher short-run equilibrium aggregate price level. Demand shocks cause aggregate output and the aggregate price level to move in the same direction.

FIGURE 65-2 Demand Shocks

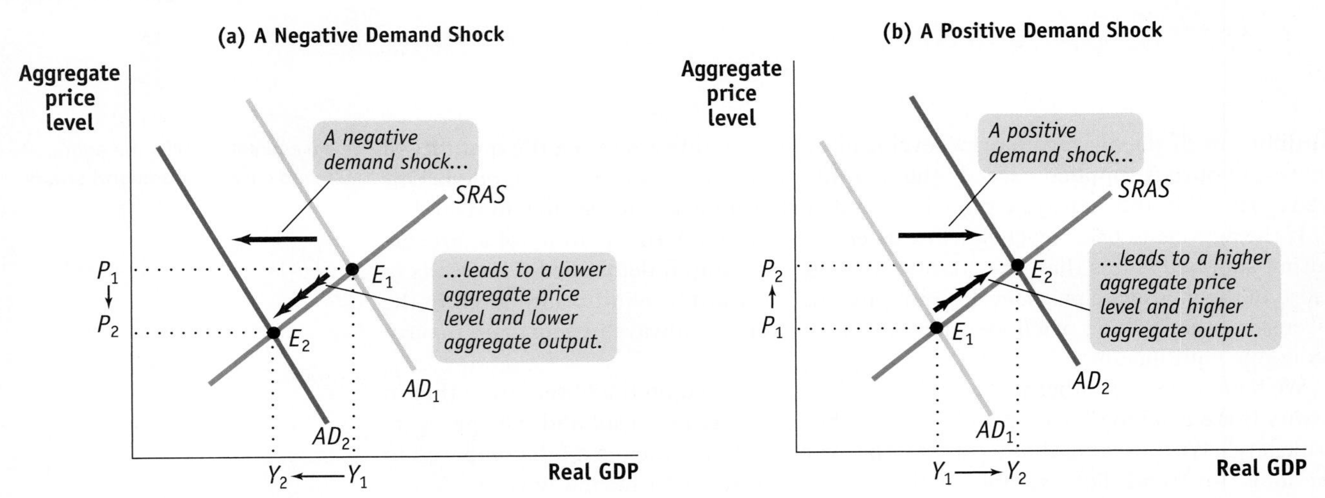

A demand shock shifts the aggregate demand curve, moving the aggregate price level and aggregate output in the same direction. In panel (a), a negative demand shock shifts the aggregate demand curve leftward from AD_1 to AD_2, reducing the aggregate price level from P_1 to P_2 and aggregate output from Y_1 to Y_2. In panel (b), a positive demand shock shifts the aggregate demand curve rightward, increasing the aggregate price level from P_1 to P_2 and aggregate output from Y_1 to Y_2.

Shifts of the *SRAS* Curve

An event that shifts the short-run aggregate supply curve, such as a change in commodity prices, nominal wages, or productivity, is known as a **supply shock.** A *negative* supply shock raises production costs and reduces the quantity producers are willing to supply at any given aggregate price level, leading to a leftward shift of the short-run aggregate supply curve. The U.S. economy experienced severe negative supply shocks following disruptions to world oil supplies in 1973 and 1979.

An event that shifts the short-run aggregate supply curve is a **supply shock**.

In contrast, a *positive* supply shock reduces production costs and increases the quantity supplied at any given aggregate price level, leading to a rightward shift of the short-run aggregate supply curve. The United States experienced a positive supply shock between 1995 and 2000, when the increasing use of the Internet and other information technologies caused productivity growth to surge.

The effects of a negative supply shock are shown in panel (a) of Figure 65-3. The initial equilibrium is at E_1, with aggregate price level P_1 and aggregate output Y_1. The disruption in the oil supply causes the short-run aggregate supply curve to shift to the left, from $SRAS_1$ to $SRAS_2$. As a consequence, aggregate output falls and the aggregate price level rises, an upward movement along the *AD* curve. At the new equilibrium, E_2, the short-run equilibrium aggregate price level, P_2, is higher, and the short-run equilibrium aggregate output level, Y_2, is lower than before.

The combination of inflation and falling aggregate output shown in panel (a) has a special name: **stagflation,** for "stagnation plus inflation." When an economy experiences stagflation, it's very unpleasant: falling aggregate output leads to rising unemployment, and people feel that their purchasing power is squeezed by rising prices. Stagflation in the 1970s led to a mood of national pessimism. It also, as we'll see shortly, poses a dilemma for policy makers.

A positive supply shock, shown in panel (b), has exactly the opposite effects. A rightward shift of the *SRAS* curve, from $SRAS_1$ to $SRAS_2$, results in a rise in aggregate output and a fall in the aggregate price level, a downward movement along the *AD* curve. The favorable supply shocks of the late 1990s led to a combination of full employment and declining inflation. That is, the aggregate price level fell compared with the long-run trend. This combination produced, for a time, a great wave of national optimism.

The distinctive feature of supply shocks, both negative and positive, is that, unlike demand shocks, they cause the aggregate price level and aggregate output to move in *opposite* directions.

Producers are vulnerable to supply shocks caused by dramatic changes in oil prices.

Stagflation is the combination of inflation and stagnating (or falling) aggregate output.

FIGURE 65-3 Supply Shocks

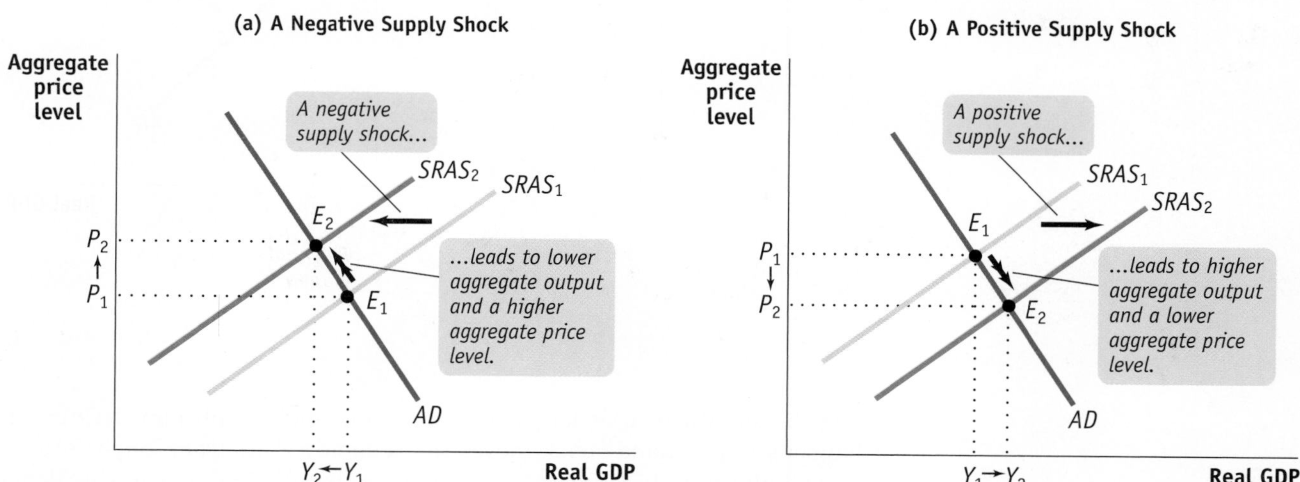

A supply shock shifts the short-run aggregate supply curve, moving the aggregate price level and aggregate output in opposite directions. Panel (a) shows a negative supply shock, which shifts the short-run aggregate supply curve leftward and causes stagflation—lower aggregate output and a higher aggregate price level. Here the short-run aggregate supply curve shifts from $SRAS_1$ to $SRAS_2$, and the economy moves from E_1 to E_2. The aggregate price level rises from P_1 to P_2, and aggregate output falls from Y_1 to Y_2. Panel (b) shows a positive supply shock, which shifts the short-run aggregate supply curve rightward, generating higher aggregate output and a lower aggregate price level. The short-run aggregate supply curve shifts from $SRAS_1$ to $SRAS_2$, and the economy moves from E_1 to E_2. The aggregate price level falls from P_1 to P_2, and aggregate output rises from Y_1 to Y_2.

The economy is in **long-run macroeconomic equilibrium** when the point of short-run macroeconomic equilibrium is on the long-run aggregate supply curve.

There's another important contrast between supply shocks and demand shocks. As we've seen, monetary policy and fiscal policy enable the government to shift the aggregate demand curve, meaning that governments are in a position to create the kinds of shocks shown in Figure 65-2. It's much harder for governments to shift the aggregate supply curve. Are there good policy reasons to shift the aggregate demand curve? We'll turn to that question soon. First, however, let's look at the difference between short-run macroeconomic equilibrium and long-run macroeconomic equilibrium.

Long-Run Macroeconomic Equilibrium

Figure 65-4 combines the aggregate demand curve with both the short-run and long-run aggregate supply curves. The aggregate demand curve, *AD*, crosses the short-run aggregate supply curve, *SRAS*, at E_{LR}. Here we assume that enough time has elapsed that the economy is also on the long-run aggregate supply curve, *LRAS*. As a result, E_{LR} is at the intersection of all three curves—*SRAS*, *LRAS*, and *AD*. So short-run equilibrium aggregate output is equal to potential output, Y_P. Such a situation, in which the point of short-run macroeconomic equilibrium is on the long-run aggregate supply curve, is known as **long-run macroeconomic equilibrium.**

FIGURE 65-4 Long-Run Macroeconomic Equilibrium

Here the point of short-run macroeconomic equilibrium also lies on the long-run aggregate supply curve, *LRAS*. As a result, short-run equilibrium aggregate output is equal to potential output, Y_P. The economy is in long-run macroeconomic equilibrium at E_{LR}.

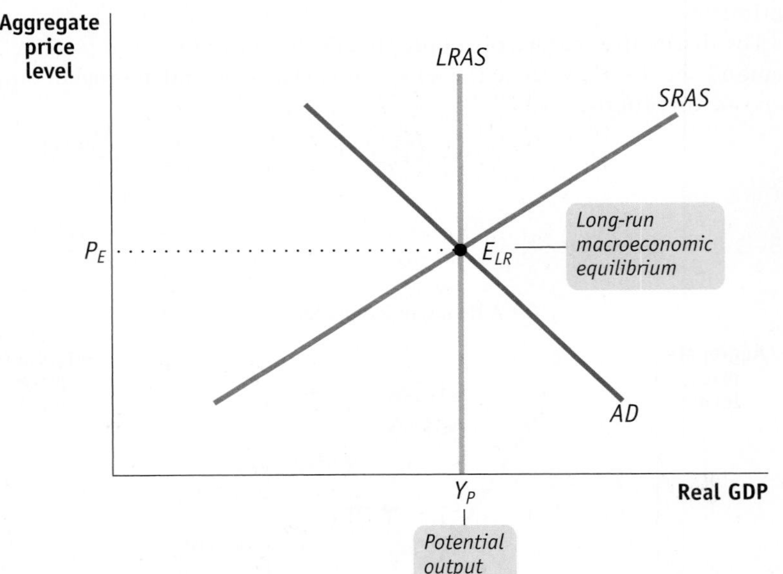

To see the significance of long-run macroeconomic equilibrium, let's consider what happens if a demand shock moves the economy away from long-run macroeconomic equilibrium. In Figure 65-5, we assume that the initial aggregate demand curve is AD_1 and the initial short-run aggregate supply curve is $SRAS_1$. So the initial macroeconomic equilibrium is at E_1, which lies on the long-run aggregate supply curve, *LRAS*. The economy, then, starts from a point of short-run and long-run macroeconomic equilibrium, and short-run equilibrium aggregate output equals potential output at Y_1.

Now suppose that for some reason—such as a sudden worsening of business and consumer expectations—aggregate demand falls and the aggregate demand curve shifts leftward to AD_2. This results in a lower equilibrium aggregate price level at P_2 and a lower equilibrium aggregate output level at Y_2 as the economy settles in the

FIGURE 65-5 **Short-Run versus Long-Run Effects of a Negative Demand Shock**

In the long run the economy is self-correcting: demand shocks have only a short-run effect on aggregate output. Starting at E_1, a negative demand shock shifts AD_1 leftward to AD_2. In the short run the economy moves to E_2 and a recessionary gap arises: the aggregate price level declines from P_1 to P_2, aggregate output declines from Y_1 to Y_2, and unemployment rises. But in the long run nominal wages fall in response to high unemployment at Y_2, and $SRAS_1$ shifts rightward to $SRAS_2$. Aggregate output rises from Y_2 to Y_1, and the aggregate price level declines again, from P_2 to P_3. Long-run macroeconomic equilibrium is eventually restored at E_3.

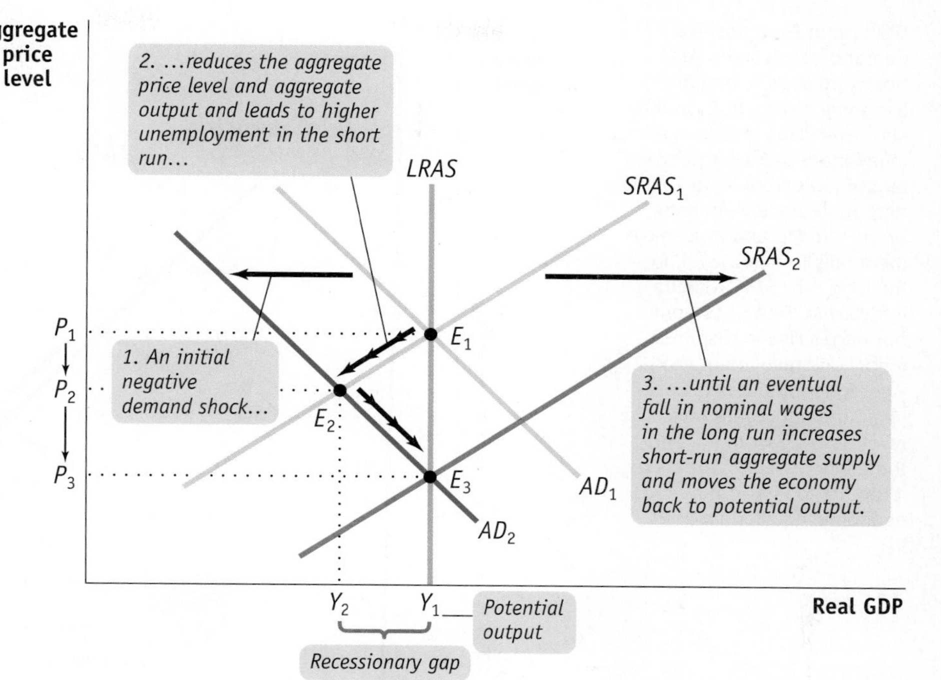

short run at E_2. The short-run effect of such a fall in aggregate demand is what the U.S. economy experienced in 1929–1933: a falling aggregate price level and falling aggregate output.

Aggregate output in this new short-run equilibrium, E_2, is below potential output. When this happens, the economy faces a **recessionary gap.** A recessionary gap inflicts a great deal of pain because it corresponds to high unemployment. The large recessionary gap that had opened up in the United States by 1933 caused intense social and political turmoil. And the devastating recessionary gap that opened up in Germany at the same time played an important role in Hitler's rise to power.

But this isn't the end of the story. In the face of high unemployment, nominal wages eventually fall, as do any other sticky prices, ultimately leading producers to increase output. As a result, a recessionary gap causes the short-run aggregate supply curve to gradually shift to the right. This process continues until $SRAS_1$ reaches its new position at $SRAS_2$, bringing the economy to equilibrium at E_3, where AD_2, $SRAS_2$, and *LRAS* all intersect. At E_3, the economy is back in long-run macroeconomic equilibrium; it is back at potential output Y_1 but at a lower aggregate price level, P_3, reflecting a long-run fall in the aggregate price level. The economy is *self-correcting* in the long run.

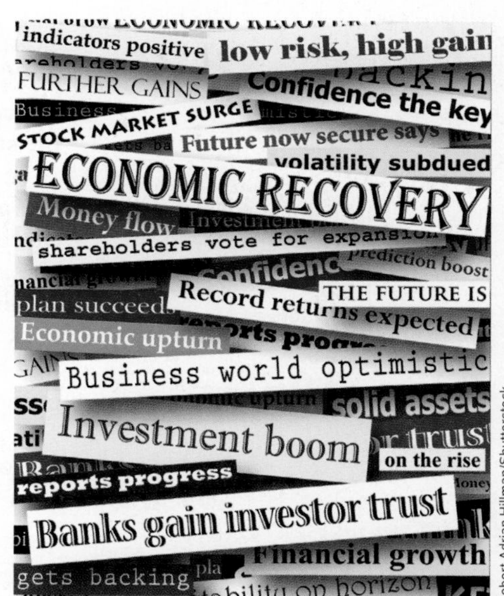

The economy is self-correcting in the long run.

What if, instead, there was an increase in aggregate demand? The results are shown in Figure 65-6, where we again assume that the initial aggregate demand curve is AD_1 and the initial short-run aggregate supply curve is $SRAS_1$, so that the initial macroeconomic equilibrium, at E_1, lies on the long-run aggregate supply curve, *LRAS*. Initially, then, the economy is in long-run macroeconomic equilibrium.

Now suppose that aggregate demand rises, and the *AD* curve shifts rightward to AD_2. This results in a higher aggregate price level, at P_2, and a higher aggregate output level, at Y_2, as the economy settles in the short run at E_2. Aggregate output in this new

There is a **recessionary gap** when aggregate output is below potential output.

FIGURE 65-6 Short-Run versus Long-Run Effects of a Positive Demand Shock

Starting at E_1, a positive demand shock shifts AD_1 rightward to AD_2, and the economy moves to E_2 in the short run. This results in an inflationary gap as aggregate output rises from Y_1 to Y_2, the aggregate price level rises from P_1 to P_2, and unemployment falls to a low level. In the long run, $SRAS_1$ shifts leftward to $SRAS_2$ as nominal wages rise in response to low unemployment at Y_2. Aggregate output falls back to Y_1, the aggregate price level rises again to P_3, and the economy self-corrects as it returns to long-run macro economic equilibrium at E_3.

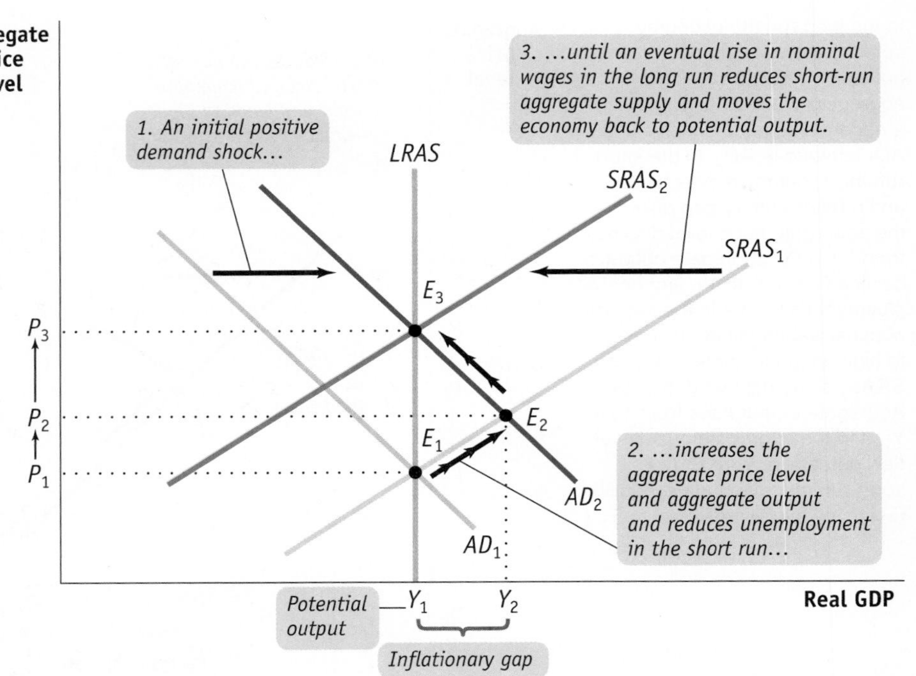

There is an **inflationary gap** when aggregate output is above potential output.

The **output gap** is the percentage difference between actual aggregate output and potential output.

The economy is **self-correcting** when shocks to aggregate demand affect aggregate output in the short run, but not in the long run.

short-run equilibrium is above potential output, and unemployment is low in order to produce this higher level of aggregate output. When this happens, the economy experiences an **inflationary gap.** As in the case of a recessionary gap, this isn't the end of the story.

In the face of low unemployment, nominal wages will rise, as will other sticky prices. An inflationary gap causes the short-run aggregate supply curve to shift gradually to the left as producers reduce output in the face of rising nominal wages. This process continues until $SRAS_1$ reaches its new position at $SRAS_2$, bringing the economy into equilibrium at E_3, where AD_2, $SRAS_2$, and *LRAS* all intersect. At E_3, the economy is back in long-run macroeconomic equilibrium. It is back at potential output, but at a higher price level, P_3, reflecting a long-run rise in the aggregate price level. Again, the economy is self-correcting in the long run.

To summarize the analysis of how the economy responds to recessionary and inflationary gaps, we can focus on the **output gap,** the percentage difference between actual aggregate output and potential output. The output gap is calculated as follows:

$$\textbf{(65-1)}\ \text{Output gap} = \frac{\text{Actual aggregate output} - \text{Potential output}}{\text{Potential output}} \times 100$$

Our analysis says that the output gap always tends toward zero.

If there is a recessionary gap, so that the output gap is negative, nominal wages eventually fall, moving the economy back to potential output and bringing the output gap back to zero. If there is an inflationary gap, so that the output gap is positive, nominal wages eventually rise, also moving the economy back to potential output and again bringing the output gap back to zero. So in the long run the economy is **self-correcting:** shocks to aggregate demand affect aggregate output in the short run but not in the long run.

ECONOMICS ▶ IN ACTION

SUPPLY SHOCKS VERSUS DEMAND SHOCKS IN PRACTICE

How often do supply shocks and demand shocks, respectively, cause recessions? The verdict of most, though not all, macroeconomists is that recessions are mainly caused by demand shocks. But when a negative supply shock does happen, the resulting recession tends to be particularly severe.

Let's get specific. Officially there have been twelve recessions in the United States since World War II. However, two of these, in 1979–1980 and 1981–1982, are often treated as a single "double-dip" recession, bringing the total number down to eleven. Of these eleven recessions, only two—the recession of 1973–1975 and the double-dip recession of 1979–1982—showed the distinctive combination of falling aggregate output and a surge in the price level that we call stagflation.

In each case, the cause of the supply shock was political turmoil in the Middle East—the Arab–Israeli war of 1973 and the Iranian revolution of 1979—that disrupted world oil supplies and sent oil prices skyrocketing. In fact, economists sometimes refer to the two slumps as "OPEC I" and "OPEC II," after the Organization of Petroleum Exporting Countries, the world oil cartel. A third recession that began in 2007 and lasted until 2009 was at least partially exacerbated, if not at least partially caused, by a spike in oil prices.

FIGURE 65-7 Negative Supply Shocks Are Relatively Rare but Nasty

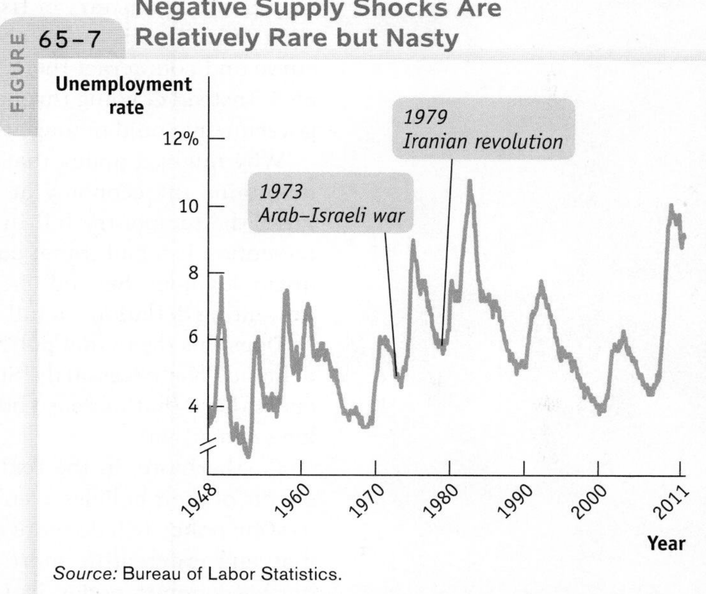

Source: Bureau of Labor Statistics.

So eight of eleven postwar recessions were purely the result of demand shocks, not supply shocks. The few supply-shock recessions, however, were the worst as measured by the unemployment rate. Figure 65-7 shows the U.S. unemployment rate from 1948 through 2011, with the dates of the 1973 Arab–Israeli war and the 1979 Iranian revolution highlighted. Some of the highest unemployment rates since World War II came after these big negative supply shocks.

There's a reason the aftermath of a supply shock tends to be particularly severe for the economy: macroeconomic policy has a much harder time dealing with supply shocks than with demand shocks. Indeed, the reason the Federal Reserve was having a hard time in 2008, as described in the section-opening story, was the fact that in early 2008 the U.S. economy was in a recession partially caused by a supply shock (although it was also facing a demand shock). We'll see in a moment why supply shocks present such a problem.

Macroeconomic Policy

We've just seen that the economy is self-correcting in the long run: it will eventually trend back to potential output.

Most macroeconomists believe, however, that the process of self-correction typically takes a decade or more. In particular, if aggregate output is below potential output, the economy can suffer an extended period of depressed aggregate output and high unemployment before it returns to normal.

This belief is the background to one of the most famous quotations in economics: John Maynard Keynes's declaration, "In the long run we are all dead." Economists usually interpret Keynes as having recommended that governments not wait for the

Stabilization policy is the use of government policy to reduce the severity of recessions and rein in excessively strong expansions.

economy to correct itself. Instead, it is argued by many economists, but not all, that the government should use fiscal policy to get the economy back to potential output in the aftermath of a shift of the aggregate demand curve.

This is the rationale for active **stabilization policy,** which is the use of government policy to reduce the severity of recessions and rein in excessively strong expansions.

Can stabilization policy improve the economy's performance? As we saw in Figure 64-4, the answer certainly appears to be yes. Under active stabilization policy, the U.S. economy returned to potential output in 1996 after an approximately five-year recessionary gap. Likewise, in 2001, it also returned to potential output after an approximately four-year inflationary gap. These periods are much shorter than the decade or more that economists believe it would take for the economy to self-correct in the absence of active stabilization policy. However, the ability to improve the economy's performance is not always guaranteed. It depends on the kinds of shocks the economy faces.

Policy in the Face of Demand Shocks

Imagine that the economy experiences a negative demand shock, like the one shown by the shift from AD_1 to AD_2 in Figure 65-5. As we know, fiscal policy shifts the aggregate demand curve. If policy makers react quickly to the fall in aggregate demand, they can use monetary or fiscal policy to shift the aggregate demand curve back to the right. And if policy were able to perfectly anticipate shifts of the aggregate demand curve and counteract them, it could short-circuit the whole process shown in Figure 65-5. Instead of going through a period of low aggregate output and falling prices, the government could manage the economy so that it would stay at E_1.

Why might a policy that short-circuits the adjustment shown in Figure 65-5 and maintains the economy at its original equilibrium be desirable? For two reasons: First, the temporary fall in aggregate output that would happen without policy intervention is a bad thing, particularly because such a decline is associated with high unemployment. Second, *price stability* is generally regarded as a desirable goal. So preventing deflation—a fall in the aggregate price level—is a good thing.

Does this mean that policy makers should always act to offset declines in aggregate demand? Not necessarily. Some policy measures to increase aggregate demand, especially those that increase budget deficits, may have long-term costs in terms of lower long-run growth.

Furthermore, in the real world policy makers aren't perfectly informed, and the effects of their policies aren't perfectly predictable. This creates the danger that stabilization policy will do more harm than good; that is, attempts to stabilize the economy may end up creating more instability. We'll describe the long-running debate over macroeconomic policy in later modules. Despite these qualifications, most economists believe that a good case can be made for using macroeconomic policy to offset major negative shocks to the *AD* curve.

Should policy makers also try to offset positive shocks to aggregate demand? It may not seem obvious that they should. After all, even though inflation may be a bad thing, isn't more output and lower unemployment a good thing? Again, not necessarily. Most economists now believe that any short-run gains from an inflationary gap must be paid back later. So policy makers today usually try to offset positive as well as negative demand shocks. For reasons we'll explain later, attempts to eliminate recessionary gaps and inflationary gaps usually rely on monetary rather than fiscal policy. But how should macroeconomic policy respond to supply shocks?

Responding to Supply Shocks

In panel (a) of Figure 65-3 we showed the effects of a negative supply shock: in the short run such a shock leads to lower aggregate output but a higher aggregate price level. As we've noted, policy makers can respond to a negative *demand* shock by using monetary and fiscal policy to return aggregate demand to its original level. But what can or should they do about a negative *supply* shock?

In contrast to the case of a demand shock, there are no easy remedies for a supply shock. That is, there are no government policies that can easily counteract the changes in production costs that shift the short-run aggregate supply curve. So the policy response to a negative supply shock cannot aim to simply push the curve that shifted back to its original position.

And if you consider using monetary or fiscal policy to shift the aggregate demand curve in response to a supply shock, the right response isn't obvious. Two bad things are happening simultaneously: a fall in aggregate output, leading to a rise in unemployment, *and* a rise in the aggregate price level. Any policy that shifts the aggregate demand curve helps one problem only by making the other worse. If the government acts to increase aggregate demand and limit the rise in unemployment, it reduces the decline in output but causes even more inflation. If it acts to reduce aggregate demand, it curbs inflation but causes a further rise in unemployment.

It's a trade-off with no good answer. In the end, the United States and other economically advanced nations suffering from the supply shocks of the 1970s eventually chose to stabilize prices even at the cost of higher unemployment. But being an economic policy maker in the 1970s, or in early 2008, meant facing even harder choices than usual.

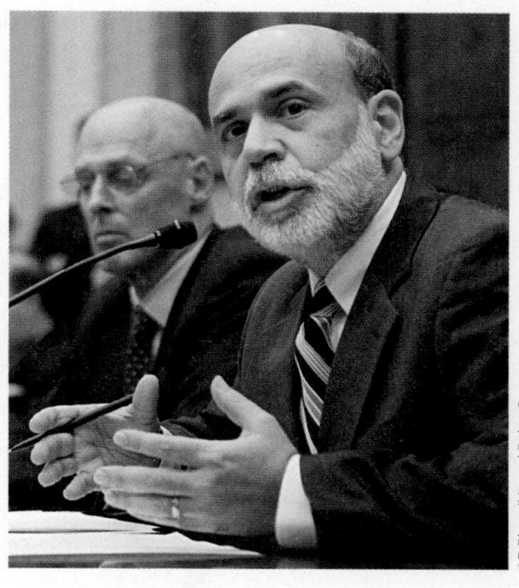

AP Photo/Manuel Balce Ceneta

In 2008, stagflation made for difficult policy choices for the Federal Reserve chairman at the time, Ben Bernanke.

MODULE 65 Review

Solutions appear at the back of the book.

Check Your Understanding

1. Describe the short-run effects of each of the following shocks on the aggregate price level and on aggregate output.
   - a. The government sharply increases the minimum wage, raising the wages of many workers.
   - b. Solar energy firms launch a major program of investment spending.
   - c. Congress raises taxes and cuts spending.
   - d. Severe weather destroys crops around the world.
2. A rise in productivity increases potential output, but some worry that demand for the additional output will be insufficient even in the long run. How would you respond?
3. Suppose someone says, "Using monetary or fiscal policy to pump up the economy is counterproductive—you get a brief high, but then you have the pain of inflation."
   - a. Explain what this means in terms of the *AD–AS* model.
   - b. Is this a valid argument against stabilization policy? Why or why not?
4. In 2008, in the aftermath of the collapse of the housing bubble and a sharp rise in the price of commodities, particularly oil, there was much internal disagreement within the Fed about how to respond, with some advocating lowering interest rates and others contending that this would set off a rise in inflation. Explain the reasoning behind each of these views in terms of the *AD–AS* model.

Multiple-Choice Questions

1. Which of the following causes a negative supply shock?
   - I. a technological advance
   - II. increasing productivity
   - III. an increase in oil prices

   - a. I only
   - b. II only
   - c. III only
   - d. I and III only
   - e. I, II, and III
2. Which of the following causes a positive demand shock?
   - a. an increase in wealth
   - b. pessimistic consumer expectations
   - c. a decrease in government spending
   - d. an increase in taxes
   - e. an increase in the existing stock of capital

3. During stagflation, what happens to the aggregate price level and real GDP?

	Aggregate price level	*Real GDP*
a.	decreases	increases
b.	decreases	decreases
c.	increases	increases
d.	increases	decreases
e.	stays the same	stays the same

Refer to the graph for questions 4 and 5.

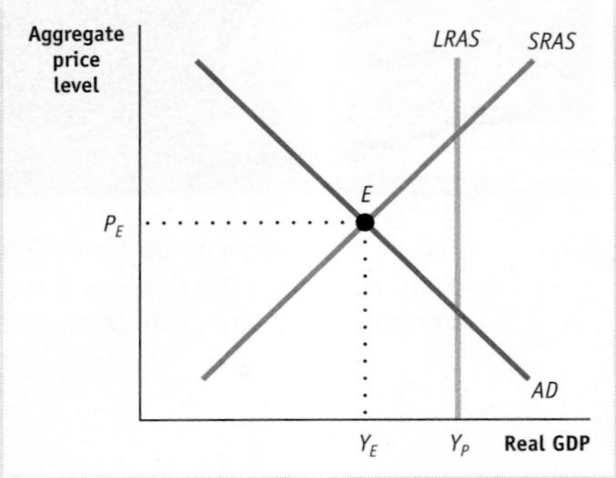

4. Which of the following statements is true if this economy is operating at P_E and Y_E?
   I. The level of aggregate output equals potential output.
   II. It is in short-run macroeconomic equilibrium.
   III. It is in long-run macroeconomic equilibrium.
   a. I only
   b. II only
   c. III only
   d. II and III
   e. I and III

5. The economy depicted in the graph is experiencing a(n)
   a. contractionary gap.
   b. recessionary gap.
   c. inflationary gap.
   d. demand gap.
   e. supply gap.

Critical-Thinking Question

Draw a graph to illustrate an economy in the midst of an inflationary gap. Explain and illustrate why the economy will eventually return to long-run equilibrium.

PITFALLS

WHERE'S THE DEFLATION?

? The *AD–AS* model tells us that either a negative demand shock or a positive supply shock should lead to a fall in the aggregate price level—that is, it should lead to deflation. But, how often does deflation actually occur?

> RARELY. SINCE 1949, AN ACTUAL FALL IN THE AGGREGATE PRICE LEVEL HAS BEEN A RARE OCCURRENCE IN THE UNITED STATES. SIMILARLY, MOST OTHER COUNTRIES HAVE HAD LITTLE OR NO EXPERIENCE WITH DEFLATION. Japan, which experienced sustained mild deflation in the late 1990s and the early part of the next decade, is the big (and much discussed) exception. What happened to deflation?

The basic answer is that since World War II economic fluctuations have largely taken place around a long-run inflationary trend. Before the war, it was common for prices to fall during recessions, but since then negative demand shocks have largely been reflected in a decline in the rate of inflation rather than an actual fall in prices. For example, the rate of consumer price inflation fell from more than 3% at the beginning of the 2001 recession to 1.1% a year later, but it never went below zero. All of this changed during the recession of 2007–2009. The negative demand shock that followed the 2008 financial crisis was so severe that, for most of 2009, consumer prices in the United States indeed fell. But the deflationary period didn't last long: beginning in 2010, prices again rose, at a rate of between 1% and 4% per year.

To learn more, see pages 669–673, especially Figure 65-5.

BUSINESS CASE • United in Pain

BSTAR IMAGES/Alamy

The airline industry is notoriously "cyclical." That is, instead of making profits all through the business cycle, it tends to plunge into losses during recessions, only regaining profitability sometime after recovery begins. Mainly this is because airlines have large fixed costs that remain high even if ticket sales slump. The cost of operating a flight from one city to another is pretty much the same whether the flight is fully booked or two-thirds empty, so when business slumps for whatever reason, even highly profitable routes quickly become money-losers.

It's true that airlines can to some extent adapt to a decline in business by switching to smaller planes, consolidating flights, and so on, but this process takes time and still tends to leave costs per passenger higher than before.

But some recessions are worse for airlines than for other businesses, because operating costs rise even as demand falls. This was very much the case in early 2008. In the spring of that year, the Great Recession of 2007–2009 was still in its early stages, with unemployment just starting to rise. Yet airlines were already, as an article in the *Los Angeles Times* put it, in a "sea of red ink." The article highlighted the case of United Airlines, which had suddenly plunged into large losses and was planning large layoffs.

Why was United in so much trouble? Business travel had started to slacken, but at that point leisure travel, such as flights to Disney World, was still holding up. What was hurting United and its sister airlines was the cost of fuel, which soared in late 2007 and early 2008.

Fuel prices fell back down in late 2008. But by that time United was suffering from a sharp drop in ticket sales. The airline finally returned to profitability in 2010, which was also the year it agreed to merge with Continental. But in early 2011 fuel prices rose again, putting airlines once more in a difficult position.

Questions for Thought

1. How did United's problems in early 2008 relate to our analysis of the causes of recessions?
2. The chairman of the Fed at the time, Ben Bernanke, had to make a choice between fighting two evils in early 2008. How would that choice affect United compared with, say, a company producing a service without expensive raw-material inputs, like health care?
3. In early 2008, business travel was beginning to slacken, but leisure travel was still holding up. Given the situation the overall economy was in, what would you expect to happen to leisure travel as the economy moved further into recession?

SECTION 20 REVIEW

Summary

Aggregate Demand

1. The **aggregate demand curve** shows the relationship between the aggregate price level and the quantity of aggregate output demanded.
2. The aggregate demand curve is downward sloping for two reasons. The first is the **wealth effect of a change in the aggregate price level**—a higher aggregate price level reduces the purchasing power of households' wealth and reduces consumer spending. The second is the **interest rate effect of a change in the aggregate price level**—a higher aggregate price level reduces the purchasing power of households' and firms' money holdings, leading to a rise in interest rates and a fall in investment spending and consumer spending.
3. The aggregate demand curve shifts because of changes in expectations, changes in wealth not due to changes in the aggregate price level, and the effect of the size of the existing stock of physical capital. Policy makers can use *fiscal policy* and *monetary policy* to shift the aggregate demand curve.

Aggregate Supply

4. The **aggregate supply curve** shows the relationship between the aggregate price level and the quantity of aggregate output supplied.
5. The **short-run aggregate supply curve** is upward sloping because **nominal wages** are **sticky** in the short run: a higher aggregate price level leads to higher profit per unit of output and increased aggregate output in the short run.
6. Changes in commodity prices, nominal wages, and productivity lead to changes in producers' profits and shift the short-run aggregate supply curve.
7. In the long run, all prices, including nominal wages, are flexible and the economy produces at its **potential output.** If actual aggregate output exceeds potential output, nominal wages will eventually rise in response to low unemployment and aggregate output will fall. If potential output exceeds actual aggregate output, nominal wages will eventually fall in response to high unemployment and aggregate output will rise. So the **long-run aggregate supply curve** is vertical at potential output.

The *AD–AS* Model

8. In the ***AD–AS* model,** the intersection of the short-run aggregate supply curve and the aggregate demand curve is the point of **short-run macroeconomic equilibrium.** It determines the **short-run equilibrium aggregate price level** and the level of **short-run equilibrium aggregate output.**
9. Economic fluctuations occur because of a shift of the aggregate demand curve (a *demand shock*) or the short-run aggregate supply curve (a *supply shock*). A **demand shock** causes the aggregate price level and aggregate output to move in the same direction as the economy moves along the short-run aggregate supply curve. A **supply shock** causes them to move in opposite directions as the economy moves along the aggregate demand curve. A particularly nasty occurrence is **stagflation**—inflation and falling aggregate output—which is caused by a negative supply shock.
10. Demand shocks have only short-run effects on aggregate output because the economy is **self-correcting** in the long run. In a **recessionary gap,** an eventual fall in nominal wages moves the economy to **long-run macroeconomic equilibrium,** in which aggregate output is equal to potential output. In an **inflationary gap,** an eventual rise in nominal wages moves the economy to long-run macroeconomic equilibrium. We can use the **output gap,** the percentage difference between actual aggregate output and potential output, to summarize how the economy responds to recessionary and inflationary gaps. Because the economy tends to be self-correcting in the long run, the output gap always tends toward zero.
11. The high cost—in terms of unemployment—of a recessionary gap and the future adverse consequences of an inflationary gap lead many economists to advocate active **stabilization policy:** using fiscal or monetary policy to offset demand shocks. There can be drawbacks, however, because such policies may contribute to a long-term rise in the budget deficit, leading to lower long-run growth. Also, poorly timed policies can increase economic instability.
12. Negative supply shocks pose a policy dilemma: a policy that counteracts the fall in aggregate output by increasing aggregate demand will lead to higher inflation, but a policy that counteracts inflation by reducing aggregate demand will deepen the output slump.

Key Terms

Aggregate demand curve, p. 646
Wealth effect of a change in the aggregate price level, p. 648
Interest rate effect of a change in the aggregate price level, p. 648
Aggregate supply curve, p. 656
Nominal wage, p. 657
Sticky wages, p. 657
Short-run aggregate supply curve, p. 658
Long-run aggregate supply curve, p. 662
Potential output, p. 663
AD–AS model, p. 668
Short-run macroeconomic equilibrium, p. 668
Short-run equilibrium aggregate price level, p. 668
Short-run equilibrium aggregate output, p. 668
Demand shock, p. 669
Supply shock, p. 670
Stagflation, p. 671
Long-run macroeconomic equilibrium, p. 672
Recessionary gap, p. 673
Inflationary gap, p. 674
Output gap, p. 674
Self-correcting, p. 674
Stabilization policy, p. 676

Problems

1. A fall in the value of the dollar against other currencies makes U.S. final goods and services cheaper to foreigners even though the U.S. aggregate price level stays the same. As a result, foreigners demand more American aggregate output. Your study partner says that this represents a movement down the aggregate demand curve because foreigners are demanding more in response to a lower price. You, however, insist that this represents a rightward shift of the aggregate demand curve. Who is right? Explain.

2. Your study partner is confused by the upward-sloping short-run aggregate supply curve and the vertical long-run aggregate supply curve. How would you explain this?

3. Suppose that in Wageland all workers sign annual wage contracts each year on January 1. No matter what happens to prices of final goods and services during the year, all workers earn the wage specified in their annual contract. This year, prices of final goods and services fall unexpectedly after the contracts are signed. Answer the following questions using a diagram and assume that the economy starts at potential output.

a. In the short run, how will the quantity of aggregate output supplied respond to the fall in prices?

b. What will happen when firms and workers renegotiate their wages?

4. In each of the following cases, in the short run, determine whether the events cause a shift of a curve or a movement along a curve. Determine which curve is involved and the direction of the change.

a. As a result of an increase in the value of the dollar in relation to other currencies, American producers now pay less in dollar terms for foreign steel, a major commodity used in production.

b. An increase in the quantity of money by the Federal Reserve increases the quantity of money that people wish to lend, lowering interest rates.

c. Greater union activity leads to higher nominal wages.

d. A fall in the aggregate price level increases the purchasing power of households' and firms' money holdings. As a result, they borrow less and lend more.

5. The economy is at point *A* in the accompanying diagram. Suppose that the aggregate price level rises from P_1 to P_2. How will aggregate supply adjust in the short run and in the long run to the increase in the aggregate price level? Illustrate with a diagram.

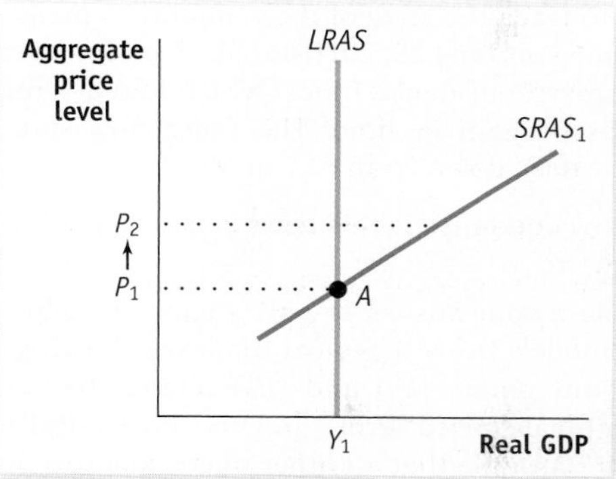

6. Suppose that all households hold all their wealth in assets that automatically rise in value when the aggregate price level rises (an example of this is what is called an "inflation-indexed bond"—a bond whose interest rate, among other things, changes one-for-one with the inflation rate). What happens to the wealth effect of a change in the aggregate price level as a result of this allocation of assets? What happens to the slope of the aggregate demand curve? Will it still slope downward? Explain.

7. Suppose that the economy is currently at potential output. Also suppose that you are an economic policy maker and that a college economics student asks you to rank, if possible, your most preferred to least preferred type of shock: positive demand shock, negative demand shock, positive supply shock, negative supply shock. How would you rank them and why?

8. Explain whether the following government policies affect the aggregate demand curve or the short-run aggregate supply curve and how.

a. The government reduces the minimum nominal wage.

b. The government increases Temporary Assistance to Needy Families (TANF) payments, which are government transfers to families with dependent children.

c. To reduce the budget deficit, the government announces that households will pay much higher taxes beginning next year.

d. The government reduces military spending.

9. In Wageland, all workers sign an annual wage contract each year on January 1. In late January, a new computer operating system is introduced that increases labor productivity dramatically. Explain how Wageland will move from one short-run macroeconomic equilibrium to another. Illustrate with a diagram.

10. The Conference Board publishes the Consumer Confidence Index (CCI) every month based on a survey of 5,000 representative U.S. households. It is used by many economists to track the state of the economy. A press release by the Board on June 28, 2011 stated: "The Conference Board Consumer Confidence Index, which had declined in May, decreased again in June. The Index now stands at 58.5 (1985 = 100), down from 61.7 in May."

a. To an economist, is this news encouraging for economic growth?

b. Explain your answer to part a with the help of the *AD–AS* model. Draw a typical diagram showing two equilibrium points (E_1) and (E_2). Label the vertical axis "Aggregate price level" and the horizontal axis "Real GDP." Assume that all other major macroeconomic factors remain unchanged.

c. How should the government respond to this news? What are some policy measures that could be used to help neutralize the effect of falling consumer confidence?

11. There were two major shocks to the U.S. economy in 2007, leading to the severe recession of 2007–2009. One shock was related to oil prices; the other was the slump in the housing market. This question analyzes the effect of these two shocks on GDP using the *AD–AS* framework.

a. Draw typical aggregate demand and short-run aggregate supply curves. Label the horizontal axis "Real GDP" and the vertical axis "Aggregate price level." Label the equilibrium point E_1, the equilibrium quantity Y_1, and equilibrium price P_1.

b. Data taken from the Department of Energy indicate that the average price of crude oil in the world increased from $54.63 per barrel on January 5, 2007, to $92.93 on December 28, 2007. Would an increase in oil prices cause a demand shock or a supply shock? Redraw the diagram from part a to illustrate the effect of this shock by shifting the appropriate curve.

c. The Housing Price Index, published by the Office of Federal Housing Enterprise Oversight, calculates that U.S. home prices fell by an average of 3.0% in the 12 months between January 2007 and January 2008. Would the fall in home prices cause a supply shock or demand shock? Redraw the diagram from part b to illustrate the effect of this shock by shifting the appropriate curve. Label the new equilibrium point E_3, the equilibrium quantity Y_3, and equilibrium price P_3.

d. Compare the equilibrium points E_1 and E_3 in your diagram for part c. What was the effect of the two shocks on real GDP and the aggregate price level (increase, decrease, or indeterminate)?

12. Using aggregate demand, short-run aggregate supply, and long-run aggregate supply curves, explain the process by which each of the following economic events will move the economy from one long-run macroeconomic equilibrium to another. Illustrate with diagrams. In each case, what are the short-run and long-run effects on the aggregate price level and aggregate output?

a. There is a decrease in households' wealth due to a decline in the stock market.

b. The government lowers taxes, leaving households with more disposable income, with no corresponding reduction in government purchases.

13. Using aggregate demand, short-run aggregate supply, and long-run aggregate supply curves, explain the process by which each of the following government policies will move the economy from one long-run macroeconomic equilibrium to another. Illustrate with diagrams. In each case, what are the short-run and long-run effects on the aggregate price level and aggregate output?

a. There is an increase in taxes on households.

b. There is an increase in the quantity of money.

c. There is an increase in government spending.

14. The economy is in short-run macroeconomic equilibrium at point E_1 in the accompanying diagram. Based on the diagram, answer the following questions.

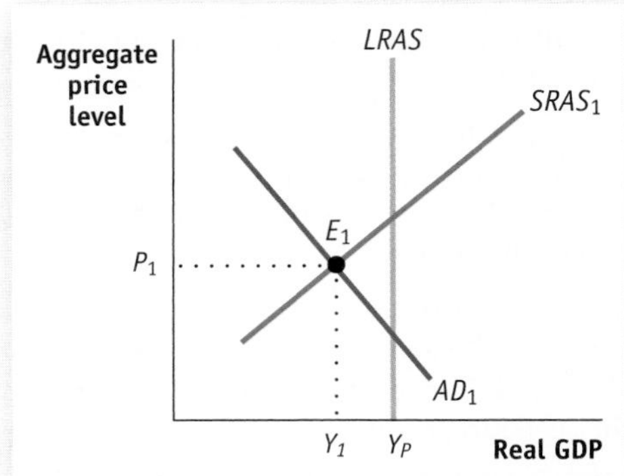

a. Is the economy facing an inflationary or a recessionary gap?

b. What policies can the government implement that might bring the economy back to long-run macroeconomic equilibrium? Illustrate with a diagram.

c. If the government did not intervene to close this gap, would the economy return to long-run macroeconomic equilibrium? Explain and illustrate with a diagram.

d. What are the advantages and disadvantages of the government implementing policies to close the gap?

15. In the accompanying diagram, the economy is in long-run macroeconomic equilibrium at point E_1 when an oil shock shifts the short-run aggregate supply curve to $SRAS_2$. Based on the diagram, answer the following questions.

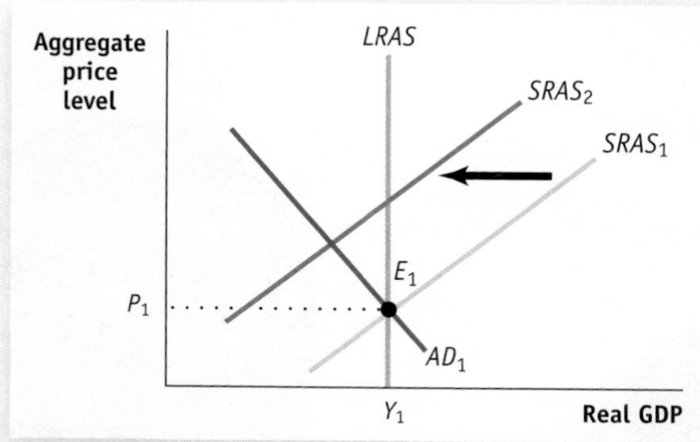

a. How do the aggregate price level and aggregate output change in the short run as a result of the oil shock? What is this phenomenon known as?

b. What fiscal or monetary policies can the government use to address the effects of the supply shock? Use a diagram that shows the effect of policies chosen to address the change in real GDP. Use another diagram to show the effect of policies chosen to address the change in the aggregate price level.

c. Why do supply shocks present a dilemma for government policy makers?

16. The late 1990s in the United States was characterized by substantial economic growth with low inflation; that is, real GDP increased with little, if any, increase in the aggregate price level. Explain this experience using aggregate demand and aggregate supply curves. Illustrate with a diagram.

United States
Pay to
the order of
FIFTY
TEN
NATIONAL DEBT:
Family share

Module 66: Fiscal Policy Basics
Module 67: Fiscal Policy and the Multiplier
Module 68: Budget Deficits and Public Debt

SECTION 21

Fiscal Policy

TO STIMULATE OR NOT TO STIMULATE?

On February 17, 2009, President Obama signed the American Recovery and Reinvestment Act, a $787 billion package of spending, aid, and tax cuts intended to help the struggling U.S. economy reverse a severe recession that began in December 2007. A week earlier, as the bill neared final passage in Congress, Obama hailed the measure: "It is the right size; it is the right scope. Broadly speaking it has the right priorities to create jobs that will jumpstart our economy and transform it for the twenty-first century."

Others weren't so sure. Some argued that the government should be cutting spending, not increasing it, at a time when American families were suffering. "It's time for government to tighten their belts and show the American people that we 'get' it," said John Boehner, the leader of Republicans in the House of Representatives. Some economic analysts warned that the stimulus bill, as the Recovery Act was commonly called, would drive up interest rates and increase the burden of national debt.

Others had the opposite complaint—that the stimulus was too small given the economy's troubles. For example, Joseph Stiglitz, the 2001 recipient of the Nobel Prize in economics, stated about the stimulus, "First of all that it was not enough should be pretty apparent from what I just said: It is trying to offset the deficiency in aggregate demand and it is just too small."

Nor did the passage of time resolve these disputes. True, some predictions were proved false. On one side, Obama's hope that the bill would "jumpstart" the economy fell short: although the recession officially ended in June 2009, unemployment remained high through 2011 and into 2012, by which time the stimulus had largely run its course. On the other side, the soaring interest rates predicted by stimulus opponents failed to materialize, as U.S. borrowing costs remained low by historical standards. But the net effect of the stimulus remained controversial, with opponents arguing that it had failed to help the economy and defenders arguing that things would have been much worse without the bill.

Whatever the verdict—and this is one of those issues that economists and historians will probably be arguing about for decades to come—the Recovery Act of 2009 was a classic example of *fiscal policy,* the use of government spending and taxes to manage aggregate demand. In this section we'll see how fiscal policy fits into the models of economic fluctuations we studied in the last section. We'll also see why budget deficits and government debt can be a problem and how short-run and long-run concerns can pull fiscal policy in different directions.

MODULE 66 Fiscal Policy Basics

Shutterstock

Andrew Zarivny/Shutterstock

WHAT YOU WILL LEARN

1. What fiscal policy is
2. Why fiscal policy is an important tool for managing economic fluctuations
3. Which policies constitute expansionary fiscal policy and which constitute contractionary fiscal policy

What Is Fiscal Policy?

Let's begin with the obvious: modern governments in economically advanced countries spend a great deal of money and collect a lot in taxes. Figure 66-1 shows government spending and tax revenue as percentages of GDP for a selection of high-income countries in 2007. We focus on 2007, rather than a more recent year, because it was a largely "normal" year. The numbers for later years were very much affected by the financial crisis of 2008 and its aftermath.

FIGURE 66-1 Government Spending and Tax Revenue for Some High-Income Countries in 2007

We focus on 2007 because it was a "normal" year, not a year of deep economic slump. Government spending and tax revenue are represented as a percentage of GDP. Sweden has a particularly large government sector, representing more than half of its GDP. The U.S. government sector, although sizable, is smaller than those of Canada and most European countries as a percentage of GDP.
Source: OECD.

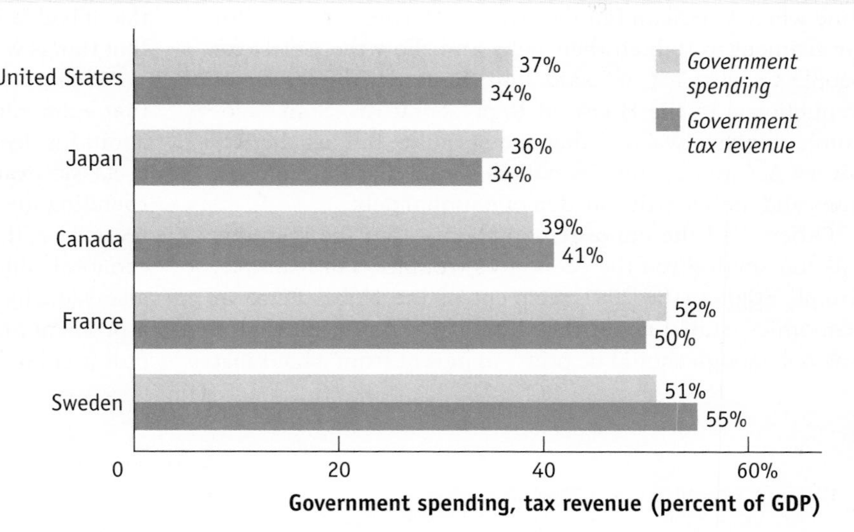

As you can see, the Swedish government sector is relatively large, accounting for more than half of the Swedish economy. The government of the United States plays a smaller role in the economy than those of Canada or most European countries. But that role is still sizable, with the government playing a major role in the U.S. economy. As a result, changes in the federal budget—changes in government spending or in taxation—can have large effects on the American economy.

To analyze these effects, we begin by showing how taxes and government spending affect the economy's flow of income. Then we can see how changes in spending and tax policy affect aggregate demand.

Taxes, Purchases of Goods and Services, Government Transfers, and Borrowing

In Figure 46-2 on page 479 we showed the circular flow of income and spending in the economy as a whole. One of the sectors represented in that figure was the government. Funds flow *into* the government in the form of taxes and government borrowing; funds flow *out* in the form of government purchases of goods and services and government transfers to households.

What kinds of taxes do Americans pay, and where does the money go? Figure 66-2 shows the composition of U.S. tax revenue in 2007. Taxes, of course, are required payments to the government. In the United States, taxes are collected at the national level by the federal government; at the state level by each state government; and at local levels by counties, cities, and towns. At the federal level, the taxes that generate the greatest revenue are income taxes on both personal income and corporate profits as well as *social insurance* taxes, which we'll explain shortly. At the state and local levels, the picture is more complex: these governments rely on a mix of sales taxes, property taxes, income taxes, and fees of various kinds.

Overall, taxes on personal income and corporate profits accounted for 48% of total government revenue in 2007; social insurance taxes accounted for 25%; and a variety of other taxes, collected mainly at the state and local levels, accounted for the rest.

FIGURE 66-2

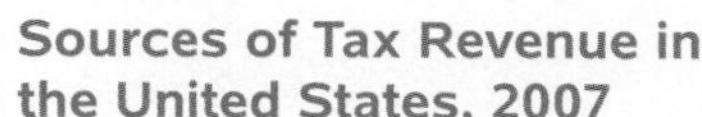

Sources of Tax Revenue in the United States, 2007

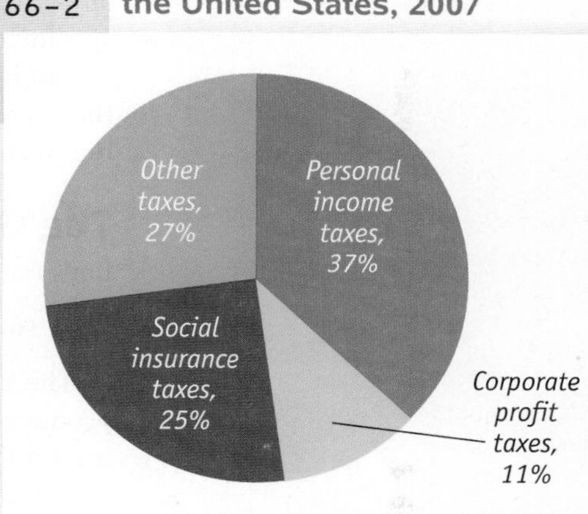

Personal income taxes, taxes on corporate profits, and social insurance taxes account for most government tax revenue. The rest is a mix of property taxes, sales taxes, and other sources of revenue.

Source: Bureau of Economic Analysis.

Figure 66-3 shows the composition of total U.S. government spending in 2007, which takes two broad forms. One form is purchases of goods and services. This includes everything from ammunition for the military to the salaries of public school teachers (who are treated in the national accounts as providers of a service—education). The big items here are national defense and education. The large category labeled "Other goods and services" consists mainly of state and local spending

FIGURE 66-3 **Government Spending in the United States, 2007**

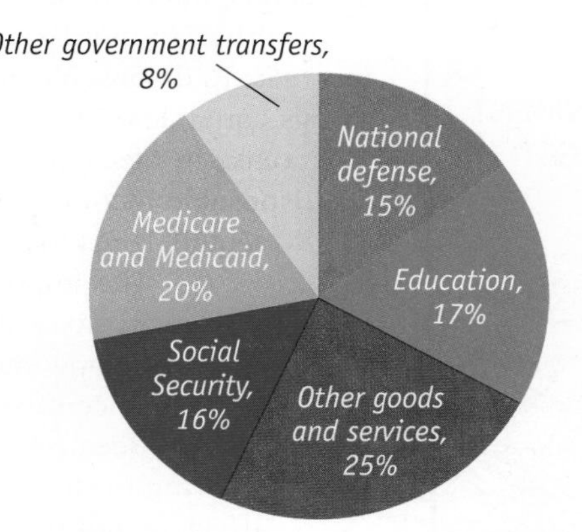

The two types of government spending are purchases of goods and services and government transfers. The big items in government purchases are national defense and education. The big items in government transfers are Social Security and the Medicare and Medicaid health care programs. (Numbers do not add to 100% due to rounding.)

Source: Bureau of Economic Analysis.

Social insurance programs are government programs intended to protect families against economic hardship.

on a variety of services, from police and firefighters, to highway construction and maintenance, to building and operating dams.

The other form of government spending is government transfers, which are payments by the government to households for which no good or service is provided in return. In the modern United States, as well as in Canada and Europe, government transfers represent a very large proportion of the budget. Most U.S. government spending on transfer payments is accounted for by three big programs:

1. **Social Security,** which provides guaranteed income to older Americans, disabled Americans, and the surviving spouses and dependent children of deceased or retired beneficiaries
2. **Medicare,** which covers much of the cost of health care for Americans over age 65
3. **Medicaid,** which covers much of the cost of health care for Americans with low incomes

The term **social insurance** is used to describe government programs that are intended to protect families against economic hardship. These include Social Security, Medicare, and Medicaid, as well as smaller programs such as unemployment insurance and food stamps (also known as the Supplemental Nutrition Assistance Program, or SNAP). In the United States, social insurance programs are largely paid for with special, dedicated taxes on wages—the social insurance taxes we mentioned earlier.

But how do tax policy and government spending affect the economy? The answer is that taxation and government spending have a strong effect on total aggregate spending in the economy.

The Government Budget and Total Spending

Let's recall the basic equation of national income accounting:

(66-1) $\text{GDP} = C + I + G + X - IM$

The left-hand side of this equation is GDP, the value of all final goods and services produced in the economy. The right-hand side is aggregate spending, total spending on final goods and services produced in the economy. It is the sum of consumer spending (C), investment spending (I), government purchases of goods and services (G), and the value of exports (X) minus the value of imports (IM). It includes all the sources of aggregate demand.

The government directly controls one of the variables on the right-hand side of Equation 66-1: government purchases of goods and services (G). But that's not the only effect fiscal policy has on aggregate spending in the economy. Through changes in taxes and transfers, it also influences consumer spending (C) and, in some cases, investment spending (I).

To see why the budget affects consumer spending, recall that *disposable income,* the total income households have available to spend, is equal to the total income they receive from wages, dividends, interest, and rent, *minus* taxes, *plus* government transfers. So either an increase in taxes or a reduction in government transfers *reduces* disposable income. And a fall in disposable income, other things equal, leads to a fall in consumer spending. Conversely, either a decrease in taxes or an increase in government transfers *increases* disposable income. And a rise in disposable income, other things equal, leads to a rise in consumer spending.

The important point to remember is that the government taxes profits, and changes in the rules that determine how much a business owes can increase or reduce the incentive to spend on investment goods.

Because the government itself is one source of spending in the economy, and because taxes and transfers can affect spending by consumers and firms, the government can

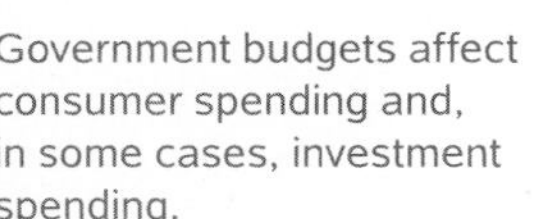
Government budgets affect consumer spending and, in some cases, investment spending.

GOVERNMENT BUDGET

Shutterstock

use changes in taxes or government spending to *shift the aggregate demand curve.* And as we saw in the previous module, there are sometimes good reasons to shift the aggregate demand curve. As this section-opening story explained, in 2009, the Obama administration believed it was crucial that the U.S. government act to increase aggregate demand—that is, to move the aggregate demand curve to the right of where it would otherwise be. The 2009 stimulus package was a classic example of *fiscal policy:* the use of taxes, government transfers, or government purchases of goods and services to stabilize the economy by shifting the aggregate demand curve.

Expansionary fiscal policy is fiscal policy that increases aggregate demand.

Expansionary and Contractionary Fiscal Policy

Why would the government want to shift the aggregate demand curve? Because it wants to close either a recessionary gap, created when aggregate output falls below potential output, or an inflationary gap, created when aggregate output exceeds potential output.

Figure 66-4 shows the case of an economy facing a recessionary gap. *SRAS* is the short-run aggregate supply curve, *LRAS* is the long-run aggregate supply curve, and AD_1 is the initial aggregate demand curve. At the initial short-run macroeconomic equilibrium, E_1, aggregate output is Y_1, below potential output, Y_P. What the government would like to do is increase aggregate demand, shifting the aggregate demand curve rightward to AD_2. This would increase aggregate output, making it equal to potential output. Fiscal policy that increases aggregate demand, called **expansionary fiscal policy,** normally takes one of three forms:

1. An increase in government purchases of goods and services
2. A cut in taxes
3. An increase in government transfers

The 2009 American Recovery and Reinvestment Act, or simply, the Recovery Act, was a combination of all three: a direct increase in federal spending and aid to state governments to help them maintain spending, tax cuts for most families, and increased aid to the unemployed.

FIGURE 66-4 **Expansionary Fiscal Policy Can Close a Recessionary Gap**

The economy is in short-run macroeconomic equilibrium at E_1, where the aggregate demand curve, AD_1, intersects the *SRAS* curve. However, it is not in long-run macroeconomic equilibrium. At E_1, there is a recessionary gap of $Y_P - Y_1$. An expansionary fiscal policy—an increase in government purchases of goods and services, a reduction in taxes, or an increase in government transfers—shifts the aggregate demand curve rightward. It can close the recessionary gap by shifting AD_1 to AD_2, moving the economy to a new short-run macroeconomic equilibrium, E_2, which is also a long-run macroeconomic equilibrium.

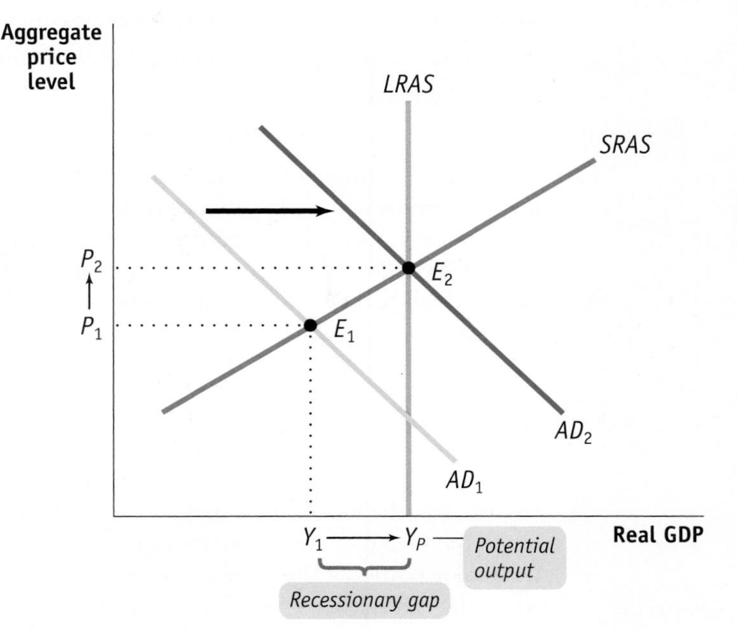

FIGURE 66-5 Contractionary Fiscal Policy Can Close an Inflationary Gap

The economy is in short-run macroeconomic equilibrium at E_1, where the aggregate demand curve, AD_1, intersects the $SRAS$ curve. But it is not in long-run macroeconomic equilibrium. At E_1, there is an inflationary gap of $Y_1 - Y_P$. A contractionary fiscal policy—such as reduced government purchases of goods and services, an increase in taxes, or a reduction in government transfers—shifts the aggregate demand curve leftward. It closes the inflationary gap by shifting AD_1 to AD_2, moving the economy to a new short-run macroeconomic equilibrium, E_2, which is also a long-run macroeconomic equilibrium.

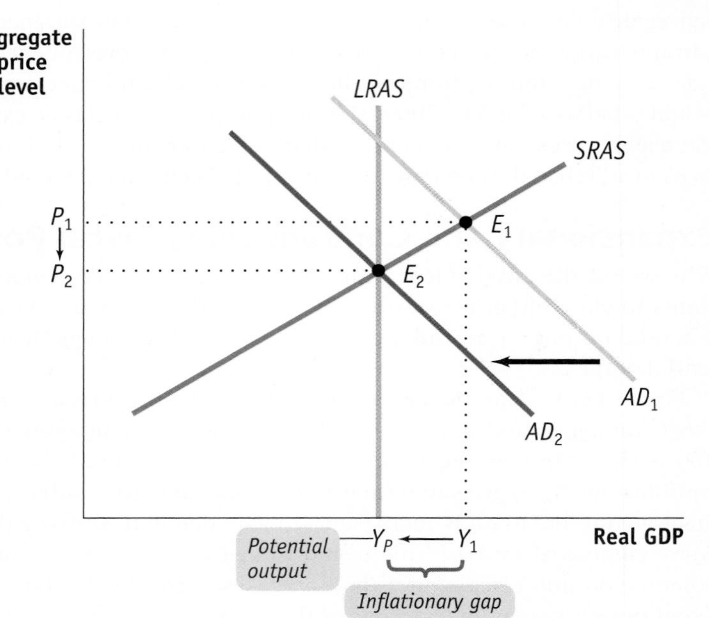

Figure 66-5 shows the opposite case—an economy facing an inflationary gap. Again, *SRAS* is the short-run aggregate supply curve, *LRAS* is the long-run aggregate supply curve, and AD_1 is the initial aggregate demand curve. At the initial equilibrium, E_1, aggregate output is Y_1, above potential output, Y_P.

Policy makers often try to head off inflation by eliminating inflationary gaps. To eliminate the inflationary gap shown in Figure 66-5, fiscal policy must reduce aggregate demand and shift the aggregate demand curve leftward to AD_2. This reduces aggregate output and makes it equal to potential output. Fiscal policy that reduces aggregate demand, called **contractionary fiscal policy,** is the opposite of expansionary fiscal policy. It is implemented in three possible ways:

1. A reduction in government purchases of goods and services
2. An increase in taxes
3. A reduction in government transfers

A classic example of contractionary fiscal policy occurred in 1968, when U.S. policy makers grew worried about rising inflation. President Lyndon Johnson imposed a temporary 10% surcharge on taxable income—everyone's income taxes were increased by 10%. He also tried to scale back government purchases of goods and services, which had risen dramatically because of the cost of the Vietnam War.

Can Expansionary Fiscal Policy Actually Work?

In practice, the use of fiscal policy—in particular, the use of expansionary fiscal policy in the face of a recessionary gap—is often controversial. Let's quickly summarize the major points of the debate over expansionary fiscal policy, so we can understand when the critiques are justified and when they are not.

Broadly speaking, there are three arguments against the use of expansionary fiscal policy. We'll examine each in turn.

Contractionary fiscal policy is fiscal policy that reduces aggregate demand.

1. Government spending always crowds out private spending (this claim, although wrong in principle, has played a prominent role in public debates)
2. Government borrowing always crowds out private investment spending (this claim is valid under some, but not all, circumstances)
3. Government budget deficits lead to reduced private spending (although this claim raises some important issues, it isn't a good reason to believe that expansionary fiscal policy doesn't work).

Shutterstock

CLAIM 1: GOVERNMENT SPENDING ALWAYS CROWDS OUT PRIVATE SPENDING Some claim that expansionary fiscal policy can never raise aggregate spending and therefore can never raise aggregate income, with reasons that go something like this: "Every dollar that the government spends is a dollar taken away from the private sector. So any rise in government spending must be offset by an equal fall in private spending." In other words, every dollar spent by the government *crowds out,* or displaces, a dollar of private spending. So what's wrong with this view?

The answer is that the statement is wrong because it assumes that resources in the economy are always fully employed and, as a result, the aggregate income earned in the economy is always a fixed sum—which isn't true. In particular, when the economy is suffering from a recessionary gap, there are unemployed resources in the economy and output, and therefore income, is below its potential level. Expansionary fiscal policy during these periods puts unemployed resources to work and generates higher spending and higher income. So the argument that expansionary fiscal policy always crowds out private spending is wrong in principle.

CLAIM 2: GOVERNMENT BORROWING ALWAYS CROWDS OUT PRIVATE INVESTMENT SPENDING We've discussed the possibility that government borrowing uses funds that would have otherwise been used for private investment spending—that is, it crowds out private investment spending. How valid is that argument?

The answer is it depends on whether the economy is depressed or not. If the economy is not depressed, then increased government borrowing, by increasing the demand for loanable funds, can raise interest rates and crowd out private investment spending. However, if the economy *is* depressed, crowding out is much less likely.

When the economy is at far less than full employment, a fiscal expansion will lead to higher incomes, which in turn lead to increased savings at any given interest rate. This larger pool of savings allows the government to borrow without driving up interest rates. The Recovery Act of 2009 was a case in point: despite high levels of government borrowing, U.S. interest rates stayed near historic lows.

CLAIM 3: GOVERNMENT BUDGET DEFICITS LEAD TO REDUCED PRIVATE SPENDING Other things equal, expansionary fiscal policy leads to a larger budget deficit and greater government debt. And higher debt will eventually require the government to raise taxes to pay it off. So, according to this argument against expansionary fiscal policy, consumers, anticipating that they must pay higher taxes in the future to pay off today's government debt, will cut their spending today in order to save money.

This argument, known as *Ricardian equivalence,* is often taken to imply that expansionary fiscal policy will have no effect on the economy because far-sighted consumers will undo any attempts at expansion by the government. (And will also undo any contractionary fiscal policy.)

In reality, however, it's doubtful that consumers behave with such foresight and budgeting discipline. Most people, when provided with extra cash (generated by the fiscal expansion), will spend at least some of it. So even fiscal policy that takes the form of temporary tax cuts or transfers of cash to consumers probably does have an expansionary effect.

Moreover, it's possible to show that a temporary rise in government spending that involves direct purchases of goods and services—such as a program of road construction—would still lead to a boost in total spending in the near term. That's because even if consumers cut back their current spending in anticipation of higher future taxes, their reduced spending will take place over an extended period as consumers save over time to pay the future tax bill. Meanwhile, the additional government spending will be concentrated in the near future, when the economy needs it.

So although the effects emphasized by Ricardian equivalence may reduce the impact of fiscal expansion, the claim that it makes fiscal expansion completely ineffective is neither consistent with how consumers actually behave nor a reason to believe that increases in government spending have no effect. So, in the end, it's not a valid argument against expansionary fiscal policy.

In sum, then, the extent to which we should expect expansionary fiscal policy to work depends upon the circumstances. When the economy has a recessionary gap—as it did when the 2009 Recovery Act was passed—economics tells us that this is just the kind of situation in which expansionary fiscal policy helps the economy. However, when the economy is already at full employment, expansionary fiscal policy is the wrong policy and will lead to crowding out, an overheated economy, and higher inflation.

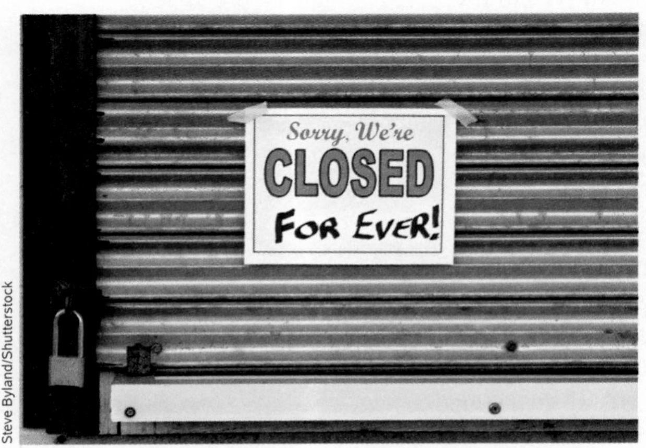

Steve Byland/Shutterstock

Time lags create real challenges for policy makers who are considering the use of expansionary fiscal policy to fight a recessionary gap.

A Cautionary Note: Lags in Fiscal Policy

Looking back at Figures 66-4 and 66-5, it may seem obvious that the government should actively use fiscal policy—always adopting an expansionary fiscal policy when the economy faces a recessionary gap and always adopting a contractionary fiscal policy when the economy faces an inflationary gap. But many economists caution against an extremely active stabilization policy, arguing that a government that tries too hard to stabilize the economy—through either fiscal policy or monetary policy—can end up making the economy less stable.

One key reason for caution is that there are important *time lags* between when the policy is decided upon and when it is implemented. To understand the nature of these lags, think about what has to happen before the government increases spending to fight a recessionary gap.

- First, the government has to realize that the recessionary gap exists: economic data take time to collect and analyze, and recessions are often recognized only months after they have begun.
- Second, the government has to develop a spending plan, which can itself take months, particularly if politicians take time debating how the money should be spent and passing legislation.
- Finally, it takes time to spend money. For example, a road construction project begins with activities such as surveying that don't involve spending large sums. It may be quite some time before the big spending begins.

Because of these lags, an attempt to increase spending to fight a recessionary gap may take so long to get going that the economy has already recovered on its own. In fact, the recessionary gap may have turned into an inflationary gap by the time the fiscal policy takes effect. In that case, the fiscal policy will make things worse instead of better.

This doesn't mean that fiscal policy should never be actively used. In early 2009 there was good reason to believe that the slump facing the U.S. economy would be both deep and long and that a fiscal stimulus designed to arrive over the next year or two would almost surely push aggregate demand in the right direction. In fact, the 2009 stimulus arguably faded out too soon, leaving the economy still deeply depressed. But the problem of lags makes the use of both fiscal and monetary policy harder than you might think from a simple analysis like the one we have just given.

ECONOMICS IN ACTION

WHAT WAS IN THE RECOVERY ACT?

As we've just learned, fiscal stimulus can take three forms: increased government purchases of goods and services, increased transfer payments, and tax cuts. So what form did the Recovery Act of 2009 take? The answer is that it's a bit complicated.

Figure 66-6 shows the composition of the budget impact of the Recovery Act, a measure that adds up the dollar value of tax cuts, transfer payments, and government spending. Here, the numbers are broken down into *four* categories, not three.

FIGURE 66-6 The American Recovery and Reinvestment Act of 2009 (Billions of Dollars)

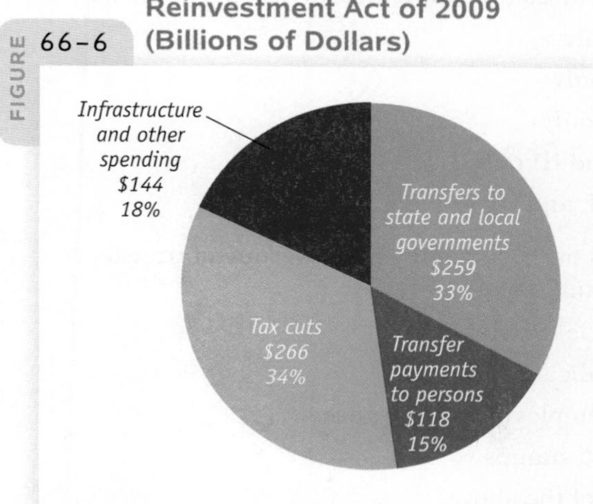

"Infrastructure and other spending" means spending on roads, bridges, and schools as well as "nontraditional" infrastructure like research and development, all of which fall under government purchases of goods and services. "Tax cuts" are self-explanatory. "Transfer payments to persons" mostly took the form of expanded benefits for the unemployed. But a fourth category, "transfers to state and local governments," accounted for roughly a third of the funds. Why this fourth category?

Because America has multiple levels of government. The authors live in Princeton Township, which has its own budget, which is part of Mercer County, which has its own budget, which is part of the state of New Jersey, which has its own budget, which is part of the United States. One effect of the recession was a sharp drop in revenues at the state and local levels, which in turn forced these lower levels of government to cut spending. Federal aid—those transfers to state and local governments—was intended to mitigate these spending cuts.

Perhaps the most surprising aspect of the Recovery Act was how little direct federal spending on goods and services was involved. The great bulk of the program involved giving money to other people, one way or another, in the hope that they would spend it.

MODULE 66 Review

Solutions appear at the back of the book.

Check Your Understanding

1. In each of the following cases, determine whether the policy is an expansionary or contractionary fiscal policy.
   a. Several military bases around the country, which together employ tens of thousands of people, are closed.
   b. The number of weeks an unemployed person is eligible for unemployment benefits is increased.
   c. The federal tax on gasoline is increased.
2. Explain why federal disaster relief, which quickly disburses funds to victims of natural disasters such as hurricanes, floods, and large-scale crop failures, will stabilize the economy more effectively after a disaster than relief that must be legislated.
3. Suppose someone says, "Using fiscal policy to pump up the economy is counterproductive—you get a brief high, but then you have the pain of inflation."
   a. Explain what this means in terms of the *AD–AS* model.
   b. Is this a valid argument against stabilization policy? Why or why not?

Multiple-Choice Questions

1. Which of the following contributes to the lag in implementing fiscal policy?
   - I. It takes time for Congress and the president to pass spending and tax changes.
   - II. Current economic data take time to collect and analyze.
   - III. It takes time to realize an output gap exists.

   a. I only
   b. II only
   c. III only
   d. I and III only
   e. I, II, and III

2. Which of the following is a government transfer program?

   a. Social Security
   b. Medicare/Medicaid
   c. unemployment insurance
   d. food stamps
   e. all of the above

3. Which of the following is an example of expansionary fiscal policy?

   a. increasing taxes
   b. increasing government spending
   c. decreasing government transfers
   d. decreasing interest rates
   e. increasing the money supply

4. Which of the following is a fiscal policy that is appropriate to combat inflation?

   a. decreasing taxes
   b. decreasing government spending
   c. increasing government transfers
   d. increasing interest rates
   e. expansionary fiscal policy

5. An income tax rebate is an example of

   a. an expansionary fiscal policy.
   b. a contractionary fiscal policy.
   c. an expansionary monetary policy.
   d. a contractionary monetary policy.
   e. none of the above.

Critical-Thinking Questions

Draw a graph showing an economy experiencing a recessionary gap, then answer the following questions.

1. What type of fiscal policy is appropriate in this situation?
2. Give an example of what the government could do to implement the type of policy you listed in question 1.

Fiscal Policy and the Multiplier

Shutterstock

Dmitriy Shironosov/Alamy

WHAT YOU WILL LEARN

1. Why fiscal policy has a multiplier effect
2. How the multiplier effect is influenced by automatic stabilizers

Multiplier Effects of Fiscal Policy

An expansionary fiscal policy, like the 2009 U.S. stimulus, pushes the aggregate demand curve to the right. A contractionary fiscal policy, like Lyndon Johnson's tax surcharge, pushes the aggregate demand curve to the left. For policy makers, however, knowing the direction of the shift isn't enough: they need estimates of *how much* a given policy will shift the aggregate demand curve. To get these estimates, they use the concept of the *multiplier,* which we learned about in Module 60.

Multiplier Effects of an Increase in Government Purchases of Goods and Services

Suppose that a government decides to spend $50 billion building bridges and roads. The government's purchases of goods and services will directly increase total spending on final goods and services by $50 billion.

But as we learned, there will also be an indirect effect: the government's purchases will start a chain reaction throughout the economy. The firms that produce the goods and services purchased by the government earn revenues that flow to households in the form of wages, profits, interest, and rent. This increase in disposable income leads to a rise in consumer spending. The rise in consumer spending, in turn, induces firms to increase output, leading to a further rise in disposable income, which leads to another round of consumer spending increases, and so on.

As we know, the *multiplier* is the ratio of the change in real GDP caused by an autonomous change in aggregate spending to the size of that autonomous change. An increase in government purchases of goods and services is a prime example of such an autonomous increase in aggregate spending.

In Module 60 we considered a simple case in which there are no taxes or international trade, so that any change in GDP accrues entirely to households. We also assumed that the aggregate price level is fixed, so that any increase in nominal GDP is also a rise in real GDP, and that the interest rate is fixed. In that case the multiplier is $1/(1 - MPC)$. Recall that *MPC* is the *marginal propensity to consume,* the fraction of an additional dollar in disposable income that is spent.

For example, if the marginal propensity to consume is 0.5, the multiplier is $1/(1 - 0.5) = 1/0.5 = 2$. Given a multiplier of 2, a $50 billion increase in government

Expansionary or contractionary fiscal policy will start a chain reaction throughout the economy.

Ralf Hettler/Getty Images

purchases of goods and services would increase real GDP by $100 billion. Of that $100 billion, $50 billion is the initial effect from the increase in *G*, and the remaining $50 billion is the subsequent effect arising from the increase in consumer spending.

What happens if government purchases of goods and services are reduced instead? The math is exactly the same, except that there's a minus sign in front: if government purchases of goods and services fall by $50 billion and the marginal propensity to consume is 0.5, real GDP falls by $100 billion.

Multiplier Effects of Changes in Government Transfers and Taxes

Expansionary or contractionary fiscal policy need not take the form of changes in government purchases of goods and services. Governments can also change transfer payments or taxes. In general, however, a change in government transfers or taxes shifts the aggregate demand curve by *less* than an equal-sized change in government purchases, resulting in a smaller effect on real GDP.

To see why, imagine that instead of spending $50 billion on building bridges, the government simply hands out $50 billion in the form of government transfers. In this case, there is no direct effect on aggregate demand, as there was with government purchases of goods and services. Real GDP goes up only because households spend some of that $50 billion—and they probably won't spend it all.

Table 67-1 shows a hypothetical comparison of two expansionary fiscal policies assuming an *MPC* equal to 0.5 and a multiplier equal to 2: one in which the government directly purchases $50 billion in goods and services and one in which the government makes transfer payments instead, sending out $50 billion in checks to consumers. In each case there is a first-round effect on real GDP, either from purchases by the government or from purchases by the consumers who received the checks, followed by a series of additional rounds as rising real GDP raises disposable income.

TABLE 67-1

Hypothetical Effects of a Fiscal Policy with Multiplier of 2

Effect on real GDP	$50 billion rise in government purchases of goods and services	$50 billion rise in government transfer payments
First round	$50 billion	$25 billion
Second round	$25 billion	$12.5 billion
Third round	$12.5 billion	$6.25 billion
• • •	• • •	• • •
Eventual effect	$100 billion	$50 billion

However, the first-round effect of the transfer program is smaller; because we have assumed that the *MPC* is 0.5, only $25 billion of the $50 billion is spent, with the other $25 billion saved. And as a result, all the further rounds are smaller, too. In the end, the transfer payment increases real GDP by only $50 billion. In comparison, a $50 billion increase in government purchases produces a $100 billion increase in real GDP.

Overall, when expansionary fiscal policy takes the form of a rise in transfer payments, real GDP may rise by either more or less than the initial government outlay—that is, the multiplier may be either more or less than 1 depending upon the size of the *MPC*. In Table 67-1, with an *MPC* equal to 0.5, the multiplier is exactly 1: a $50 billion rise in transfer payments increases real GDP by $50 billion. If the *MPC* is less than 0.5, so that a smaller share of the initial transfer is spent, the multiplier on that transfer is *less* than 1. If a larger share of the initial transfer is spent, the multiplier is *more* than 1.

A tax cut has an effect similar to the effect of a transfer. It increases disposable income, leading to a series of increases in consumer spending. But the overall effect is smaller than that of an equal-sized increase in government purchases of goods and services: the autonomous increase in aggregate spending is smaller because households save part of the amount of the tax cut.

In practice, economists often argue that the size of the multiplier determines *who* among the population should get tax cuts or increases in government transfers. For example, compare the effects of an increase in unemployment benefits with a cut in taxes on profits distributed to shareholders as dividends.

Consumer surveys suggest that the average unemployed worker will spend a higher share of any increase in his or her disposable income than would the average recipient of dividend income. That is, people who are unemployed tend to have a higher *MPC* than people who own a lot of stocks because the latter tend to be wealthier and tend to save more of any increase in disposable income. If that's true, a dollar spent on unemployment benefits increases aggregate demand more than a dollar's worth of dividend tax cuts.

How Taxes Affect the Multiplier

When we introduced the analysis of the multiplier, we simplified matters by assuming that a $1 increase in real GDP raises disposable income by $1. In fact, however, government taxes capture some part of the increase in real GDP that occurs in each round of the multiplier process, since most government taxes depend positively on real GDP. As a result, disposable income increases by considerably less than $1 once we include taxes in the model.

The increase in government tax revenue when real GDP rises isn't the result of a deliberate decision or action by the government. It's a consequence of the way the tax laws are written, which causes most sources of government revenue to increase *automatically* when real GDP goes up.

The income taxes individuals pay to the government are a percentage of their income. Therefore, when real GDP rises, this increase in aggregate income leads to an increase in government tax revenue. In the real world, governments rarely impose **lump-sum taxes,** in which the amount of tax an individual owes is independent of his or her income.

In addition, sales tax receipts increase when real GDP rises because people with more income spend more on goods and services. And corporate profit tax receipts increase when real GDP rises because profits increase when the economy expands.

The effect of these automatic increases in tax revenue is to reduce the size of the multiplier. Remember, the multiplier is the result of a chain reaction in which higher real GDP leads to higher disposable income, which leads to higher consumer spending, which leads to further increases in real GDP. The fact that the government siphons off some of any increase in real GDP means that at each stage of this process, the increase in consumer spending is smaller than it would be if taxes weren't part of the picture. The result is to reduce the multiplier.

Many macroeconomists believe it's a good thing that in real life taxes reduce the multiplier. Earlier we argued that most, though not all, recessions are the result of negative demand shocks. The same mechanism that causes tax revenue to increase when the economy expands causes it to decrease when the economy contracts. Since tax receipts decrease when real GDP falls, the effects of these negative demand shocks are smaller than they would be if there were no taxes. The decrease in tax revenue reduces the adverse effect of the initial fall in aggregate demand.

The automatic decrease in government tax revenue generated by a fall in real GDP—caused by a decrease in the amount of taxes households pay—acts like an automatic expansionary fiscal policy implemented in the face of a recession.

Similarly, when the economy expands, the government finds itself automatically pursuing a contractionary fiscal policy—a tax increase. Government spending and taxation rules that cause fiscal policy to be automatically expansionary when the economy contracts and automatically contractionary when the economy expands, without requiring any deliberate action by policy makers, are called **automatic stabilizers.**

The rules that govern tax collection aren't the only automatic stabilizers, although they are the most important ones. Some types of government transfers also play a stabilizing role. For example, more people receive unemployment insurance when the economy is depressed than when it is booming. The same is true of Medicaid and food stamps, or SNAP.

So transfer payments tend to rise when the economy is contracting and fall when the economy is expanding. Like changes in tax revenue, these automatic changes in

Lump-sum taxes are taxes that don't depend on the taxpayer's income.

Automatic stabilizers are government spending and taxation rules that cause fiscal policy to be automatically expansionary when the economy contracts and automatically contractionary when the economy expands.

AP Photo

The Works Progress Administration (WPA), a Depression-era relief measure that put millions of unemployed Americans to work building bridges, roads, and parks, is an example of discretionary fiscal policy.

transfers tend to reduce the size of the multiplier because the total change in disposable income that results from a given rise or fall in real GDP is smaller.

As in the case of government tax revenue, many macroeconomists believe that it's a good thing that government transfers reduce the multiplier. Expansionary and contractionary fiscal policies that are the result of automatic stabilizers are widely considered helpful to macroeconomic stabilization because they blunt the extremes of the business cycle.

But what about fiscal policy that *isn't* the result of automatic stabilizers? **Discretionary fiscal policy** is fiscal policy that is the direct result of deliberate actions by policy makers rather than automatic adjustment. For example, during a recession, the government may pass legislation that cuts taxes and increases government spending in order to stimulate the economy. In general, economists tend to support the use of discretionary fiscal policy only in special circumstances, such as an especially severe recession.

ECONOMICS IN ACTION

MULTIPLIERS AND THE OBAMA STIMULUS

The American Recovery and Reinvestment Act, also known as the Obama stimulus, was the largest example of discretionary fiscal expansion in U.S. history. The total stimulus was $787 billion, although not all of that was spent at once: only about half, or roughly $400 billion, of the stimulus arrived in 2010, the year of peak impact. Still, even that was a lot—roughly 2.7% of GDP. But was that enough? From the beginning, there were doubts.

Used with the permission of Karl Wimer and the Cartoonist Group. All rights reserved.

The first description of the planned stimulus and its expected effects came in early January 2009, from two of the incoming administration's top economists. They were explicit about the assumed multipliers: based on models developed at the Federal Reserve and elsewhere, they assumed that government spending would have a multiplier of 1.57 and that tax cuts would have a multiplier of 0.99.

These assumptions yielded an overall multiplier for the stimulus of almost 1.4, implying that the stimulus would, at its peak in 2010, add about 3.7% to real GDP. It would also, they estimated, reduce unemployment by about 1.8 percentage points relative to what it would otherwise have been.

But here's the problem: the slump the Obama stimulus was intended to fight was brought on by a major financial crisis—and such crises tend to produce very deep, prolonged slumps. Around this time, two Harvard economists, Carmen Reinhart and Kenneth Rogoff, circulated a paper with their findings that major crises are followed, on average, by a 7-percentage-point rise in the unemployment rate and that it takes years before unemployment falls to anything like normal levels (based on an analysis of historical episodes).

Compared with the economy's problems, then, the Obama stimulus was actually small: it cut only 1.8 points off the unemployment rate in 2010 and faded out rapidly thereafter. And given its small size relative to the problem, the failure of the stimulus to avert persistently high unemployment should not have come as a surprise.

Discretionary fiscal policy is fiscal policy that is the result of deliberate actions by policy makers rather than automatic adjustments.

MODULE 67 Review

Solutions appear at the back of the book.

Check Your Understanding

1. Explain why a $500 million increase in government purchases of goods and services will generate a larger rise in real GDP than a $500 million increase in government transfers.

2. Explain why a $500 million reduction in government purchases of goods and services will generate a larger fall in real GDP than a $500 million reduction in government transfers.

3. The country of Boldovia has no unemployment insurance benefits and a tax system using only lump-sum taxes. The neighboring country of Moldovia has generous unemployment benefits and a tax system in which residents must pay a percentage of their income. Which country will experience greater variation in real GDP in response to demand shocks, positive and negative? Explain.

Multiple-Choice Questions

1. The marginal propensity to consume
   - I. is inversely related to the multiplier.
   - II. is equal to 1.
   - III. represents the proportion of consumers' disposable income that is spent.

   a. I only
   b. II only
   c. III only
   d. I and III only
   e. I, II, and III

2. Assume that taxes and interest rates remain unchanged when government spending increases, and that both savings and consumer spending increase when income increases. The ultimate effect on real GDP of a $100 million increase in government purchases of goods and services will be
   a. an increase of $100 million.
   b. an increase of more than $100 million.
   c. an increase of less than $100 million.
   d. an increase of either more than or less than $100 million, depending on the *MPC*.
   e. a decrease of $100 million.

3. Taxes have what effect on the multiplier? They
   a. increase it.
   b. decrease it.
   c. destabilize it.
   d. negate it.
   e. have no effect on it.

4. A lump-sum tax is
   a. higher as income increases.
   b. lower as income increases.
   c. independent of income.
   d. the most common form of tax.
   e. a type of business tax.

5. Which of the following is NOT an automatic stabilizer?
   a. income taxes
   b. unemployment insurance
   c. Medicaid
   d. food stamps
   e. monetary policy

Critical-Thinking Questions

A change in government purchases of goods and services results in a change in real GDP equal to $200 million. Assuming the absence of taxes, international trade, and changes in the aggregate price level, answer the following.

1. Suppose that the *MPC* is equal to 0.75. What was the size of the change in government purchases of goods and services that resulted in the increase in real GDP of $200 million?

2. Now suppose that the change in government purchases of goods and services was $20 million. What value of the multiplier would result in an increase in real GDP of $200 million?

3. Given the value of the multiplier you calculated in the preceding question, what marginal propensity to save would have led to that value of the multiplier?

68 Budget Deficits and Public Debt

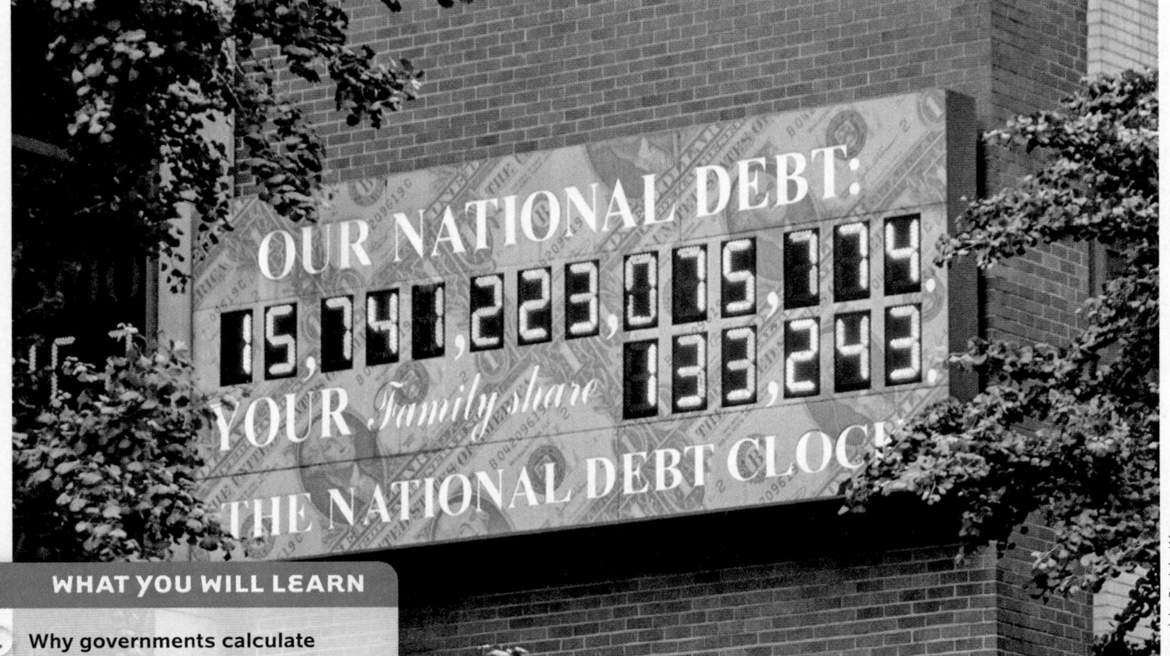

Marmaduke St. John/Alamy

WHAT YOU WILL LEARN

1. Why governments calculate the cyclically adjusted budget balance
2. Why a large public debt may be a cause for concern
3. Why implicit liabilities of the government can also be a cause for concern

Headlines about the government's budget tend to focus on just one point: whether the government is running a surplus or a deficit and, in either case, how big. People usually think of surpluses as good: when the federal government ran a record surplus in 2000, many people regarded it as a cause for celebration. Conversely, people usually think of deficits as bad: the record deficits run by the U.S. federal government from 2009–2012 were a cause of concern for many people.

The Budget Balance

How do surpluses and deficits fit into the analysis of fiscal policy? Are deficits ever a good thing and surpluses a bad thing? To answer those questions, let's look at the causes and consequences of surpluses and deficits.

The Budget Balance as a Measure of Fiscal Policy

What do we mean by surpluses and deficits? The budget balance, which we defined earlier, is the difference between the government's revenue, in the form of tax revenue, and its spending, both on goods and services and on government transfers, in a given year. That is, the budget balance—savings by government—is defined by Equation 68-1 (which is the same as Equation 56-7):

$$\textbf{(68-1)} \quad S_{Government} = T - G - TR$$

where T is the value of tax revenues, G is government purchases of goods and services, and TR is the value of government transfers. A budget surplus is a positive budget balance and a budget deficit is a negative budget balance.

Other things equal, expansionary fiscal policies—increased government purchases of goods and services, higher government transfers, or lower taxes—reduce the budget balance for that year. That is, expansionary fiscal policies make a budget surplus smaller or a budget deficit bigger. Conversely, contractionary fiscal policies—reduced government purchases of goods and services, lower government transfers, or higher taxes—increase the budget balance for that year, making a budget surplus bigger or a budget deficit smaller.

You might think this means that changes in the budget balance can be used to measure fiscal policy. In fact, economists often do just that: they use changes in the budget balance as a "quick-and-dirty" way to assess whether current fiscal policy is expansionary or contractionary. But they always keep in mind two reasons this quick-and-dirty approach is sometimes misleading:

1. Two different changes in fiscal policy that have equal-sized effects on the budget balance may have quite unequal effects on the economy. As we have already seen, changes in government purchases of goods and services have a larger effect on real GDP than equal-sized changes in taxes and government transfers.
2. Often, changes in the budget balance are themselves the result, not the cause, of fluctuations in the economy.

To understand the second point, we need to examine the effects of the business cycle on the budget.

The Business Cycle and the Cyclically Adjusted Budget Balance

Historically there has been a strong relationship between the federal government's budget balance and the business cycle. The budget tends to move into deficit when the economy experiences a recession, but deficits tend to get smaller or even turn into surpluses when the economy is expanding. Figure 68-1 shows the federal budget deficit as a percentage of GDP from 1970 to 2013. Shaded areas indicate recessions; unshaded areas indicate expansions. As you can see, the federal budget deficit increased around the time of each recession and usually declined during expansions. In fact, in the late stages of the long expansion from 1991 to 2000, the deficit actually became negative—the budget deficit became a budget surplus.

FIGURE 68-1 **The U.S. Federal Budget Deficit and the Business Cycle, 1970–2013**

The budget deficit as a percentage of GDP tends to rise during recessions (indicated by shaded areas) and fall during expansions.

Sources: Bureau of Economic Analysis; National Bureau of Economic Research.

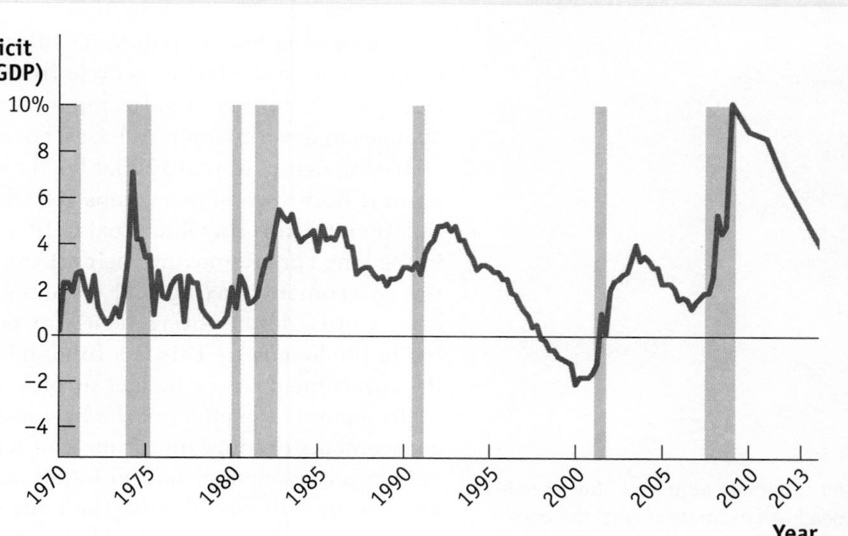

The relationship between the business cycle and the budget balance is even clearer if we compare the budget deficit as a percentage of GDP with the unemployment rate, as we do in Figure 68-2. The budget deficit almost always rises when the unemployment rate rises and falls when the unemployment rate falls.

Is this relationship between the business cycle and the budget balance evidence that policy makers engage in discretionary fiscal policy, using expansionary fiscal policy during recessions and contractionary fiscal policy during expansions? Not necessarily. To a large extent the relationship in Figure 68-2 reflects automatic stabilizers at work. As we learned in the discussion of automatic stabilizers, government tax revenue tends to rise and some government transfers, like unemployment benefit payments, tend to fall when the economy expands. Conversely, government tax revenue tends to fall and some government transfers tend to rise when the economy contracts. So the budget balance tends to move toward surplus during expansions and toward deficit during recessions even without any deliberate action on the part of policy makers.

FIGURE 68-2 The U.S. Federal Budget Deficit and the Unemployment Rate

There is a close relationship between the budget balance and the business cycle: a recession moves the budget balance toward deficit, but an expansion moves it toward surplus. Here, the unemployment rate serves as an indicator of the business cycle, and we should expect to see a higher unemployment rate associated with a higher budget deficit. This is confirmed by the figure: the budget deficit as a percentage of GDP moves closely in tandem with the unemployment rate.

Source: Federal Reserve Bank of St. Louis.

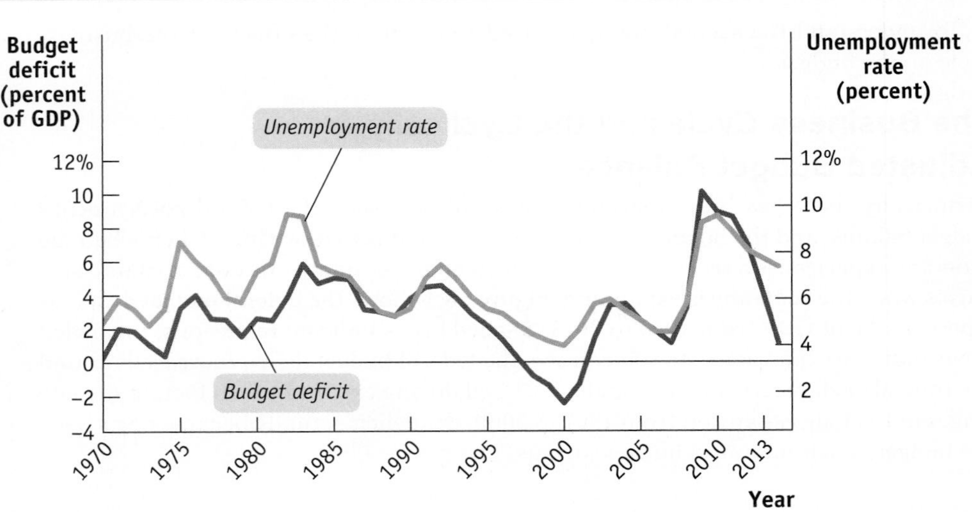

In assessing budget policy, it's often useful to separate movements in the budget balance due to the business cycle from movements due to discretionary fiscal policy changes. The former are affected by automatic stabilizers and the latter by deliberate changes in government purchases, government transfers, or taxes.

It's important to realize that business-cycle effects on the budget balance are temporary: both recessionary gaps (in which real GDP is below potential output) and inflationary gaps (in which real GDP is above potential output) tend to be eliminated in the long run. Removing their effects on the budget balance sheds light on whether the government's taxing and spending policies are sustainable in the long run. In other words, do the government's tax policies yield enough revenue to fund its spending in the long run? This is a fundamentally more important question than whether the government runs a budget surplus or deficit in the current year.

To separate the effect of the business cycle from the effects of other factors, many governments produce an estimate of what the budget balance would be if there were neither a recessionary nor an inflationary gap. The **cyclically adjusted budget balance** is an estimate of what the budget balance would be if real GDP were exactly equal to potential output. It takes into account the extra tax revenue the government would collect and the transfers it would save if a recessionary gap were eliminated—

The **cyclically adjusted budget balance** is an estimate of what the budget balance would be if real GDP were exactly equal to potential output.

or the revenue the government would lose and the extra transfers it would make if an inflationary gap were eliminated.

Figure 68-3 shows the actual budget deficit and the Congressional Budget Office estimate of the cyclically adjusted budget deficit, both as a percentage of GDP, from 1970 to 2013. As you can see, the cyclically adjusted budget deficit doesn't fluctuate as much as the actual budget deficit. In particular, large actual deficits, such as those of 1975, 1983, and 2009, are usually caused in part by a depressed economy.

FIGURE 68-3 The Actual Budget Deficit versus the Cyclically Adjusted Budget Deficit

The cyclically adjusted budget deficit is an estimate of what the budget deficit would be if the economy was at potential output. It fluctuates less than the actual budget deficit because years of large budget deficits also tend to be years when the economy has a large recessionary gap.

Sources: Congressional Budget Office; Bureau of Economic Analysis.

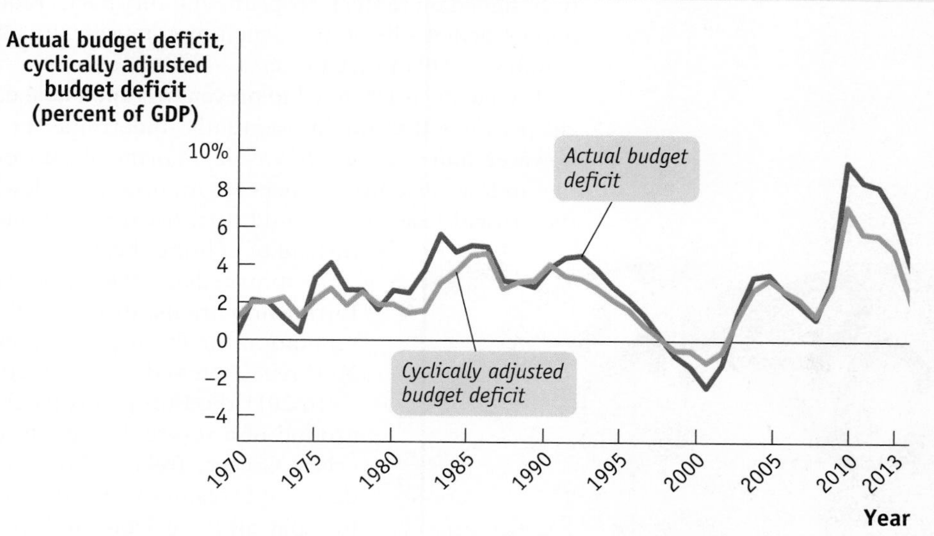

Should the Budget Be Balanced?

Persistent budget deficits can cause problems for both the government and the economy. Yet politicians are always tempted to run deficits because this allows them to cater to voters by cutting taxes without cutting spending or by increasing spending without increasing taxes. As a result, there are occasional attempts by policy makers to force fiscal discipline by introducing legislation—even a constitutional amendment—forbidding the government from running budget deficits. This is usually stated as a requirement that the budget be "balanced"—that revenues at least equal spending each fiscal year. Would it be a good idea to require a balanced budget annually?

Most economists don't think so. They believe that the government should only balance its budget on average—that it should be allowed to run deficits in bad years, offset by surpluses in good years. They don't believe the government should be forced to run a balanced budget *every year* because this would undermine the role of taxes and transfers as automatic stabilizers.

As we've learned, the tendency of tax revenue to fall and transfers to rise when the economy contracts helps to limit the size of recessions. But falling tax revenue and rising transfer payments generated by a downturn in the economy push the budget toward deficit. If constrained by a balanced-budget rule, the government would have to respond to this deficit with contractionary fiscal policies that would tend to deepen a recession.

Yet policy makers concerned about excessive deficits sometimes feel that rigid rules prohibiting—or at least setting an upper limit on—deficits are necessary. As the following Economics in Action explains, Europe has had a lot of trouble reconciling rules to enforce fiscal responsibility with the challenges of short-run fiscal policy.

ECONOMICS ▶ IN ACTION

EUROPE'S SEARCH FOR A FISCAL RULE

In 1999 a group of European nations took a momentous step when they adopted a common currency, the euro, to replace their various national currencies, such as the French franc, the German mark, and the Italian lira. Along with the introduction of the euro came the creation of the European Central Bank, which sets monetary policy for the whole region.

As part of the agreement creating the new currency, governments of member countries signed on to the European "stability pact," requiring each government to keep its budget deficit—its actual deficit, not a cyclically adjusted number—below 3% of the country's GDP or face fines.

The pact was intended to prevent irresponsible deficit spending arising from political pressure that might eventually undermine the new currency. The stability pact, however, had a serious downside: in principle, it would force countries to slash spending and/or raise taxes whenever an economic downturn pushed their deficits above the critical level. This would turn fiscal policy into a force that worsens recessions instead of fighting them.

Image source photography/Veer

Although several European nations have adopted a common currency—the euro—many of them have struggled to establish effective fiscal policy.

As it turned out, the stability pact proved impossible to enforce: European nations, including France and even Germany, with its reputation for fiscal probity, simply ignored the rule during the 2001 recession and its aftermath.

In 2011 the Europeans tried again, this time against the background of a severe debt crisis. In the wake of the 2008 financial crisis, Greece, Ireland, Portugal, Spain, and Italy lost the confidence of investors worried about their ability and/or willingness to repay all their debt—and the efforts of these nations to reduce their deficits seemed likely to push Europe back into recession.

Yet a return to the old stability pact didn't seem to make sense. Among other things, the stability pact's rule on the size of budget deficits would not have done much to prevent the crisis—in 2007 all of the problem debtors except Greece were running deficits under 3% of GDP. Ireland and Spain were actually running surpluses.

So the agreement reached in December 2011 was framed in terms of the "structural" budget balance, more or less corresponding to the cyclically adjusted budget balance as we defined it in the text. According to the new rule, the structural budget balance of each country should be very nearly zero, with deficits not to exceed 0.5% of GDP. This seemed like a much better rule than the old stability pact.

Yet big problems remained. One was a question about the reliability of the estimates of the structural budget balances. Also, the new rule seemed to ban the use of discretionary fiscal policy, under any circumstances. Was this wise?

Before patting themselves on the back over the superiority of their own fiscal rules, Americans should note that the United States has its own version of the original, flawed European stability pact. The federal government's budget acts as an automatic stabilizer, but 49 of the 50 states are required by their state constitutions to balance their budgets every year. When recession struck in 2008, most states were forced to—guess what?—slash spending and raise taxes, exactly the wrong thing from a macroeconomic point of view.

Long-Run Implications of Fiscal Policy

In 2009 the government of Greece ran into a financial wall. Like most other governments in Europe (and the U.S. government, too), the Greek government was running a large budget deficit, which meant that it needed to keep borrowing more funds, both to cover its expenses and to pay off existing loans as they came due. But governments, like companies or individuals, can only borrow if lenders believe there's a good chance they are willing or able to repay their debts. By 2009 most investors, having lost confidence in Greece's financial future, were no longer willing to lend to the Greek government. Those few who were willing to lend demanded very high interest rates to compensate them for the risk of loss.

Figure 68-4 compares interest rates on 10-year bonds issued by the governments of Greece and Germany. At the beginning of 2007, Greece could borrow at almost the same rate as Germany, widely considered a very safe borrower. By the end of 2013, however, Greece had to pay an interest rate around 10 times the rate Germany paid.

Slavoljub Pantelic/Shutterstock

The severe economic downturn that followed Greece's debt crisis continued into 2014.

Why was Greece having these problems? Largely because investors had become deeply worried about the level of its debt (in part because it became clear that the Greek government had been using creative accounting to hide just how much debt it had already taken on). Government debt is, after all, a promise to make future payments to lenders. By 2009 it seemed likely that the Greek government had already promised more than it could possibly deliver.

FIGURE 68-4 **Greek and German Long-Term Interest Rates**

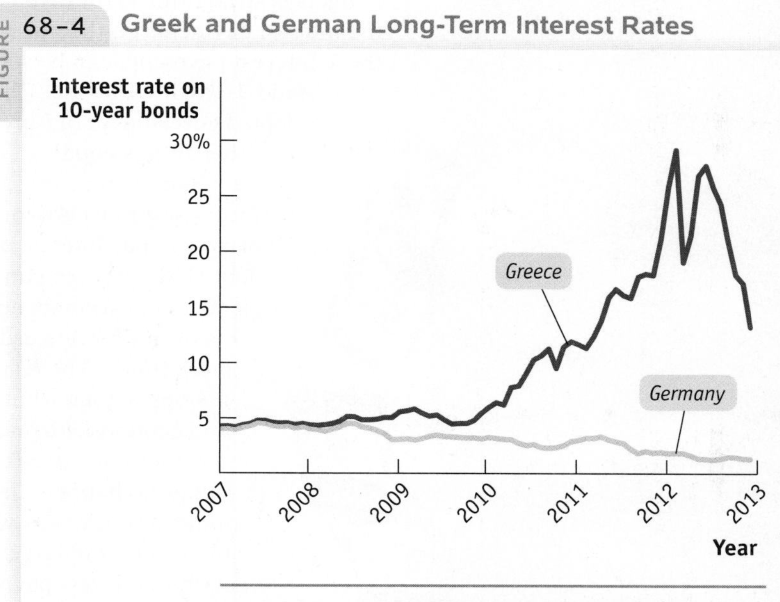

As late as 2008, the government of Greece could borrow at interest rates only slightly higher than those facing Germany, widely considered a very safe borrower. But in early 2009, as it became clear that both Greek debt and Greek deficits were larger than previously reported, investors lost confidence, sending Greek borrowing costs sky-high.
Source: European Central Bank.

The result was that Greece found itself unable to borrow more from private lenders; it received emergency loans from other European nations and the International Monetary Fund, but these loans came with the requirement that the Greek government make severe spending cuts, which wreaked havoc with its economy, imposed severe economic hardship on Greeks, and led to massive social unrest.

No discussion of fiscal policy is complete if it doesn't take into account the long-run implications of government budget surpluses and deficits, especially for government debt. We now turn to those long-run implications.

Deficits, Surpluses, and Debt

When a family spends more than it earns over the course of a year, it has to raise the extra funds either by selling assets or by borrowing. And if a family borrows year after year, it will eventually end up with a lot of debt.

The same is true for governments. With a few exceptions, governments don't raise large sums by selling assets such as national parkland. Instead, when a government spends more than the tax revenue it receives—when it runs a budget deficit—it almost always borrows the extra funds. And governments that run persistent budget deficits end up with substantial debts.

To interpret the numbers that follow, you need to know a slightly peculiar feature of federal government accounting. For historical reasons, the U.S. government does not keep books by calendar years. Instead, budget totals are kept by **fiscal years,** which run from October 1 to September 30 and are labeled by the calendar year in which they end. For example, fiscal 2010 began on October 1, 2009, and ended on September 30, 2010.

At the end of fiscal 2013, the U.S. federal government had total debt equal to $16.7 trillion. However, part of that debt represented special accounting rules specifying that the federal government as a whole owes funds to certain government programs, especially Social Security. We'll explain those rules shortly. For now, however, let's

A **fiscal year** runs from October 1 to September 30 and is labeled according to the calendar year in which it ends.

Public debt is government debt held by individuals and institutions outside the government.

focus on **public debt:** government debt held by individuals and institutions outside the government. At the end of fiscal 2013, the federal government's public debt was "only" $12.0 trillion, or 71% of GDP. If we include the debts of state and local governments, total public debt at the end of fiscal 2013 was larger than it was at the end of fiscal 2012 because the federal government ran a budget deficit during fiscal 2013. A government that runs persistent budget deficits will experience a rising level of public debt. Why is this a problem?

Problems Posed by Rising Government Debt

There are two reasons to be concerned when a government runs persistent budget deficits. We described the first reason in an earlier module: when the economy is at full employment and the government borrows funds in the financial markets, it is competing with firms that plan to borrow funds for investment spending. As a result, the government's borrowing may crowd out private investment spending, increasing interest rates and reducing the economy's long-run rate of growth.

But there's a second reason: today's deficits, by increasing the government's debt, place financial pressure on future budgets. The impact of current deficits on future budgets is straightforward. Like individuals, governments must pay their bills, including interest payments on their accumulated debt. When a government is deeply in debt, those interest payments can be substantial. In fiscal 2013, the U.S. federal government paid 1.3% of GDP—$221 billion—in interest on its debt. The more heavily indebted government of Italy paid interest of 5.3% of its GDP in 2013.

Colin Anderson/Brand X Pictures/Getty Images

Other things equal, a government paying large sums in interest must raise more revenue from taxes or spend less than it would otherwise be able to afford—or it must borrow even more to cover the gap. And a government that borrows to pay interest on its outstanding debt pushes itself even deeper into debt. This process can eventually push a government to the point where lenders question its ability to repay. Like a consumer who has maxed out his or her credit cards, it will find that lenders are unwilling to lend any more funds. The result can be that the government defaults on its debt—it stops paying what it owes. Default is often followed by deep financial and economic turmoil.

Americans aren't used to the idea of government default, but such things do happen. In the 1990s Argentina, a relatively high-income developing country, was widely praised for its economic policies—and it was able to borrow large sums from foreign lenders. By 2001, however, Argentina's interest payments were spiraling out of control, and the country stopped paying the sums that were due. In the end, it reached a settlement with most of its lenders under which it paid less than a third of the amount originally due. By late 2011 investors were placing a fairly high probability on an Argentine-type default by Greece, Ireland, and Portugal—and were seriously worried about Italy and Spain. Each one was forced to pay high interest rates on its debt by nervous lenders, raising the risk of default.

Default creates havoc in a country's financial markets and badly shakes public confidence in the government and the economy. Argentina's debt default was accompanied by a crisis in the country's banking system and a very severe recession.

And even if a highly indebted government avoids default, a heavy debt burden typically forces it to slash spending or raise taxes, politically unpopular measures that can also damage the economy. In some cases, "austerity" measures intended to reassure lenders that the government can indeed pay end up depressing the economy so much that lender confidence continues to fall, a situation faced to varying degrees by Greece, Ireland, Portugal, Spain, and Italy at the end of 2013.

Some may ask, why can't a government that has trouble borrowing just print money to pay its bills? Yes, it can if it has its own currency (which the troubled European nations don't). But printing money to pay the government's bills can lead to another problem: inflation. Governments do not want to find themselves in a position where the choice is between defaulting on their debts and inflating those debts away by printing money.

The **debt–GDP ratio** is the government's debt as a percentage of GDP.

Concerns about the long-run effects of deficits need not rule out the use of expansionary fiscal policy to stimulate the economy when it is depressed. However, these concerns do mean that governments should try to offset budget deficits in bad years with budget surpluses in good years. In other words, governments should run a budget that is approximately balanced over time. Have they actually done so?

Deficits and Debt in Practice

Figure 68-5 shows how the U.S. federal government's budget deficit and its debt evolved from 1940 to 2013. Panel (a) shows the federal deficit as a percentage of GDP. As you can see, the federal government ran huge deficits during World War II. It briefly ran surpluses after the war, but it has normally run deficits ever since, especially after 1980. This seems inconsistent with the advice that governments should offset deficits in bad times with surpluses in good times.

However, panel (b) of Figure 68-5 shows that for most of the period these persistent deficits didn't lead to runaway debt. To assess the ability of governments to pay their debt, we use the **debt–GDP ratio,** the government's debt as a percentage of GDP. We use this measure, rather than simply looking at the size of the debt, because GDP, which measures the size of the economy as a whole, is a good indicator of the potential taxes the government can collect. If the government's debt grows more slowly than GDP, the burden of paying that debt is actually falling compared with the government's potential tax revenue.

What we see from panel (b) is that although the federal debt grew in almost every year, the debt–GDP ratio fell for 30 years after the end of World War II. This shows that the debt–GDP ratio can fall, even when debt is rising, as long as GDP grows faster than debt.

FIGURE 68-5 U.S. Federal Deficits and Debt

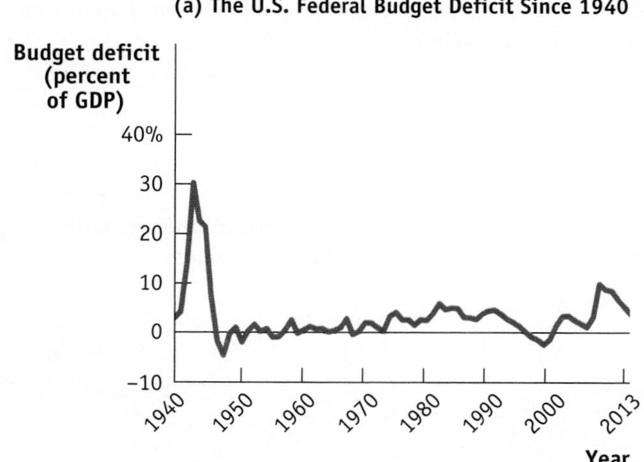

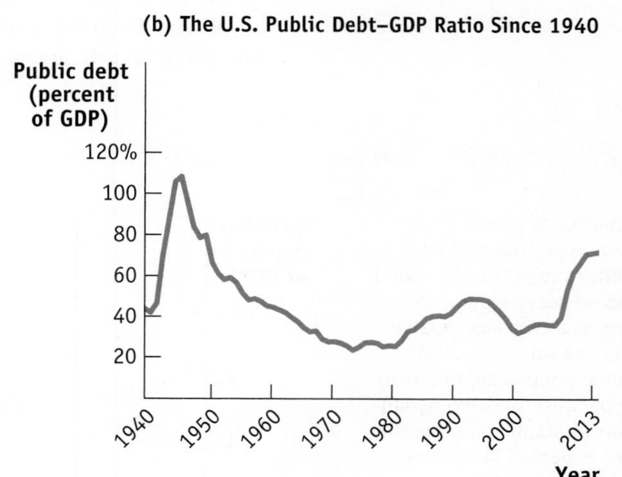

Panel (a) shows the U.S. federal budget deficit as a percentage of GDP from 1940 to 2013. The U.S. government ran huge deficits during World War II and has run smaller deficits, or a surplus, ever since. Panel (b) shows the U.S. debt–GDP ratio. Comparing panels (a) and (b), you can see that in many years the debt–GDP ratio has declined in spite of government deficits. This seeming paradox reflects the fact that the debt–GDP ratio can fall, even when debt is rising, as long as GDP grows faster than debt. The rising debt–GDP ratio in recent years can be attributed to the aftermath of the 2008 financial crisis when deficits were much larger than average and growth in GDP was well below average.

Source: Office of Management and Budget.

Implicit liabilities are spending promises made by governments that are effectively a debt despite the fact that they are not included in the usual debt statistics.

Still, a government that runs persistent *large* deficits will have a rising debt–GDP ratio when debt grows faster than GDP. In the aftermath of the financial crisis of 2008, the U.S. government began running deficits much larger than anything seen since World War II, and the debt–GDP ratio began rising sharply. Similar surges in the debt–GDP ratio could be seen in a number of other countries in 2008.

Economists and policy makers agreed that this was not a sustainable trend, that governments would need to get their spending and revenues back in line. But *when* to bring spending in line with revenue was a source of great disagreement. Some argued for fiscal tightening right away; others argued that this tightening should be postponed until the major economies had recovered from their slump.

Implicit Liabilities

Looking at Figure 68-5, you might be tempted to conclude that until the 2008 crisis struck, the U.S. federal budget was in fairly decent shape: the return to budget deficits after 2001 caused the debt–GDP ratio to rise a bit, but that ratio was still low compared with both historical experience and some other wealthy countries. In fact, however, experts on long-run budget issues view the situation of the United States (and other countries such as Japan and Italy) with alarm. The reason is the problem of *implicit liabilities*. **Implicit liabilities** are spending promises made by governments that are effectively a debt despite the fact that they are not included in the usual debt statistics.

The largest implicit liabilities of the U.S. government arise from two transfer programs that principally benefit older Americans: Social Security and Medicare. The third-largest implicit liability, Medicaid, benefits low-income families. In each of these cases, the government has promised to provide transfer payments to future as well as current beneficiaries. So these programs represent a future debt that must be honored, even though the debt does not currently show up in the usual statistics. Together, these three programs currently account for almost 40% of federal spending.

The implicit liabilities created by these transfer programs worry fiscal experts. Figure 68-6 shows why. It shows actual spending on Social Security and on Medicare, Medicaid, and CHIP (a program that provides health care coverage to uninsured children) as percentages of GDP from 2000 to 2013, together with Congressional Budget Office projections of spending through 2085. According to these projections, spending on Social Security will rise substantially over the next few decades and spending on the three health care programs will soar. Why?

FIGURE 68-6 **Future Demands on the Federal Budget**

This figure shows Congressional Budget Office projections of spending on social insurance programs as a share of GDP. Partly as a result of an aging population, but mainly because of rising health care costs, these programs are expected to become much more expensive over time, posing problems for the federal budget.

Source: Congressional Budget Office.

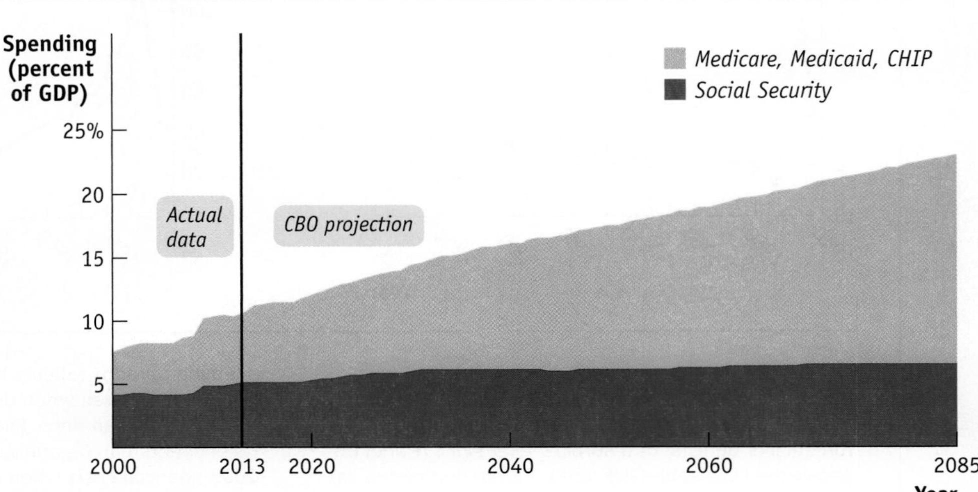

In the case of Social Security, the answer is demography. Social Security is a "pay-as-you-go" system: current workers pay payroll taxes that fund the benefits of current retirees. So the ratio of the number of retirees drawing benefits to the number of workers paying into Social Security has a major impact on the system's finances.

There was a huge surge in the U.S. birth rate between 1946 and 1964, commonly called the "baby boom." Most baby boomers are currently of working age—which means they are paying taxes, not collecting benefits. But some are starting to retire, and as more of them do so, they will stop earning taxable income and start collecting benefits. As a result, the ratio of retirees receiving benefits to workers paying into the Social Security system will rise.

In 2013 there were 35 retirees receiving benefits for every 100 workers paying into the system. By 2030, according to the Social Security Administration, that number will rise to 46; by 2050, it will rise to 48; and by 2080, that number will be 51. So as baby boomers move into retirement, benefit payments will continue to rise relative to the size of the economy.

The aging of the baby boomers, by itself, poses only a moderately sized long-run fiscal problem. The projected rise in Medicare and Medicaid spending is a much more serious concern. The main story behind projections of higher Medicare and Medicaid spending is the long-run tendency of health care spending to rise faster than overall spending, both for government-funded and for privately funded health care.

To some extent, the implicit liabilities of the U.S. government are already reflected in debt statistics. We mentioned earlier that the government had a total debt of $16.7 trillion at the end of fiscal 2013 but that only $12.0 trillion of that total was owed to the public. The main explanation for that discrepancy is that both Social Security and part of Medicare (the hospital insurance program) are supported by *dedicated taxes:* their expenses are paid out of special taxes on wages. At times, these dedicated taxes yield more revenue than is needed to pay current benefits.

In particular, since the mid-1980s the Social Security system has been taking in more revenue than it currently needs in order to prepare for the retirement of the baby boomers. This surplus in the Social Security system has been used to accumulate a *Social Security trust fund,* which was $2.7 trillion at the end of fiscal 2013.

The money in the trust fund is held in the form of U.S. government bonds, which are included in the $16.7 trillion in total debt. You could say that there's something funny about counting bonds in the Social Security trust fund as part of government debt. After all, these bonds are owed by one part of the government (the government outside the Social Security system) to another part of the government (the Social Security system itself). But the debt corresponds to a real, if implicit, liability: promises by the government to pay future retirement benefits.

So many economists argue that the gross debt of $16.7 trillion, the sum of public debt and government debt held by Social Security and other trust funds, is a more accurate indication of the government's fiscal health than the smaller amount owed to the public alone.

MODULE 68 Review

Solutions appear at the back of the book.

Check Your Understanding

1. Why is the cyclically adjusted budget balance a better measure of whether government policies are sustainable in the long run than the actual budget balance?

2. Explain why states required by their constitutions to balance their budgets are likely to experience more severe economic fluctuations than states not held to that requirement.

3. Explain how each of the following events would affect the public debt or implicit liabilities of the U.S. government, other things equal. Would the public debt or implicit liabilities be greater or smaller?
   a. A higher growth rate of real GDP
   b. Retirees live longer
   c. A decrease in tax revenue
   d. Government borrowing to pay interest on its current public debt

Multiple-Choice Questions

1. Over the course of the business cycle
   a. the budget deficit tends to increase during expansions.
   b. the budget deficit tends to decrease during expansions.
   c. Congress will take steps to ensure the budget balance does not change.
   d. the budget balance does not change due to automatic stabilizers.
   e. the level of government debt tends to decline.
2. The total debt of the U.S. federal government
   a. is the same as the public debt.
   b. is measured by the difference between the government's revenue and spending for a particular year.
   c. increases when the government runs a budget deficit.
   d. decreases when the government runs a budget deficit.
   e. is measured by the size of its implicit liabilities.
3. The budget balance tends to decline during a recession because
   a. tax revenue automatically declines.
   b. transfer payments automatically decline.
   c. government spending automatically declines.
   d. the government must cut spending as tax revenue automatically declines.
   e. the government is likely to pursue contractionary fiscal policy.
4. During a recession the budget balance tends to __________ because of __________
   a. increase : discretionary fiscal policy
   b. decrease : discretionary fiscal policy
   c. increase : automatic stabilizers
   d. decrease : automatic stabilizers
   e. remain unchanged : discretionary fiscal policy
5. The cyclically adjusted budget balance estimates
   a. the budget balance during a recession.
   b. the budget balance during an expansion.
   c. the change in the budget balance during the business cycle.
   d. the budget balance if real GDP was equal to potential output.
   e. how much tax revenues should change to balance the budget.

Critical-Thinking Question

Suppose the economy is in a slump and the current public debt is quite large. Explain the trade-off of short-run versus long-run objectives that policy makers face when deciding whether or not to engage in fiscal policy.

PITFALLS

DEFICITS AND DEBT DO DIFFER

? What Is the difference between deficit and debt? Confusing deficit and debt is a common mistake—it happens all the time in news reports, for example.

\> A *DEFICIT* IS THE DIFFERENCE BETWEEN THE AMOUNT OF MONEY A GOVERNMENT SPENDS AND THE AMOUNT IT RECEIVES IN TAXES OVER A GIVEN PERIOD—USUALLY, THOUGH NOT ALWAYS, A YEAR. A *DEBT* IS THE SUM OF MONEY A GOVERNMENT OWES AT A PARTICULAR POINT IN TIME. Deficit numbers always come with a statement about the time period to which they apply, as in "the U.S. budget deficit *in fiscal 2013* was $683 billion." Debt numbers usually come with a specific date, as in "U.S. public debt *at the end of fiscal 2013* was $17 trillion."

Although deficits and debt are linked, because government debt grows when governments run deficits, they aren't the same thing, and they can even tell different stories. For example, Italy, which found itself in debt trouble in 2011, had a fairly small deficit by historical standards, but it had very high debt, a legacy of past policies.

To learn more, see pages 705–706.

BUSINESS CASE • Priming the Pumps

Courtesy Garney Companies, Inc.

In the old days, when fewer Americans had cars but many more people lived in rural areas and drew their water from wells, advocates of fiscal expansion used different metaphors. Instead of talking, as President Obama did, about giving the economy a "jump start," they'd talk about "priming the pump." You see, it was often necessary to add water to old-fashioned hand pumps before they would work; similarly, people would argue, you need to add funds to the economy before it will get back to producing jobs and income.

In the case of the Obama stimulus, priming the pump was more than a metaphor: some of the most obvious beneficiaries were companies that made . . . pumps. The Recovery Act allocated $7 billion for drinking-water and wastewater projects, creating a number of new opportunities for companies in the business of moving water around.

A case in point was Garney Construction, a Kansas-City-based company specializing in water and sewage projects whose slogan is "Advancing Water." By the summer of 2009, Garney had won contracts to work on nine water- and sewer-related projects that were being financed in whole or in part by the Recovery Act.

None of these infrastructure projects were dreamed up as ways to spend more money; they were all things that state or local governments had been planning to do eventually. "I think most of these projects were sitting on a shelf, waiting for funding," Garney's president told a local business journal.

Although the stimulus was good for Garney, it was not exactly a financial gusher. In 2007, the United States spent about $100 billion on water-supply and wastewater infrastructure; the extra $7 billion coming from the stimulus, not all of it coming in one year, was basically a, well, drop in the bucket by comparison. Indeed, Garney said that only about 10% of its business was coming from stimulus money. And despite the stimulus, the company had less business than it had two years earlier.

Still, Garney and other companies in the water-infrastructure business were clearly getting some benefit from the Recovery Act.

Questions for Thought

1. Some opponents of fiscal expansion have accused it of consisting of make-work projects of little social value. What does the Garney story say about this view?
2. Based on this case, would you say that government spending was competing with the private sector for scarce resources?
3. If a water or sewer project is something we want to do eventually, is the depth of a recession a good or a bad time to undertake that project? Why?

SECTION 21 REVIEW

Summary

Fiscal Policy Basics

1. The government plays a significant role in the economy by collecting a large share of GDP in taxes and spending a large share both to purchase goods and services and to make transfer payments, mainly for **social insurance.**
2. Fiscal policy is the use of taxes, government transfers, or government purchases of goods and services to shift the aggregate demand curve.
3. Government purchases of goods and services directly affect aggregate demand, and changes in taxes and government transfers affect aggregate demand indirectly by changing households' disposable income.
4. **Expansionary fiscal policy** shifts the aggregate demand curve rightward, and leads to an increase in real GDP. **Contractionary fiscal policy** shifts the aggregate demand curve leftward, and leads to a reduction in real GDP.
5. Only when the economy is at full employment is there potential for crowding out of private spending and private investment spending by expansionary fiscal policy.
6. The argument that expansionary fiscal policy won't work because of Ricardian equivalence—that consumers will cut back spending today to offset expected future tax increases—appears to be untrue in practice.
7. Very active fiscal policy may make the economy less stable due to time lags in policy formulation and implementation.

Fiscal Policy and the Multiplier

8. Expansionary and contractionary fiscal policies have a multiplier effect on the economy, the size of which depends on the fiscal policy. Except in the case of **lump-sum taxes,** an increase in taxes will reduce the size of the multiplier.
9. Since part of any change in taxes or transfers is absorbed by savings in the first round of spending, changes in government purchases of goods and services have a more powerful effect on the economy than equal-sized changes in taxes or transfers.
10. Some taxes and transfers act as **automatic stabilizers,** reducing the size of the multiplier and automatically reducing the size of fluctuations in the business cycle. Lump-sum taxes do not change as real GDP changes, and therefore do not act as automatic stabilizers.
11. **Discretionary fiscal policy** arises from deliberate actions by policy makers rather than automatic adjustment caused by the business cycle.

Budget Deficits and Public Debt

12. Some of the fluctuations in the budget balance are due to the effects of the business cycle. In order to separate the effects of the business cycle from the effects of discretionary fiscal policy, governments estimate the **cyclically adjusted budget balance,** an estimate of the budget balance if the economy were at potential output.
13. U.S. government budget accounting is calculated on the basis of **fiscal years.**
14. Persistent budget deficits have long-run consequences because they lead to an increase in **public debt.** This can be a problem for two reasons. Public debt may crowd out investment spending, which reduces long-run economic growth. In extreme cases, rising debt may lead to government default, resulting in economic and financial turmoil.
15. A widely used measure of fiscal health is the **debt–GDP ratio.** This number can remain stable or fall even in the face of moderate budget deficits if GDP rises over time.
16. A stable debt–GDP ratio may give a misleading impression that all is well because modern governments often have large **implicit liabilities.** The largest implicit liabilities of the U.S. government come from Social Security, Medicare, and Medicaid, the costs of which are increasing due to the aging of the population and rising medical costs.

Key Terms

Problems

1. The accompanying diagram shows the current macroeconomic situation for the economy of Albernia. You have been hired as an economic consultant to help the economy move to potential output, Y_P.

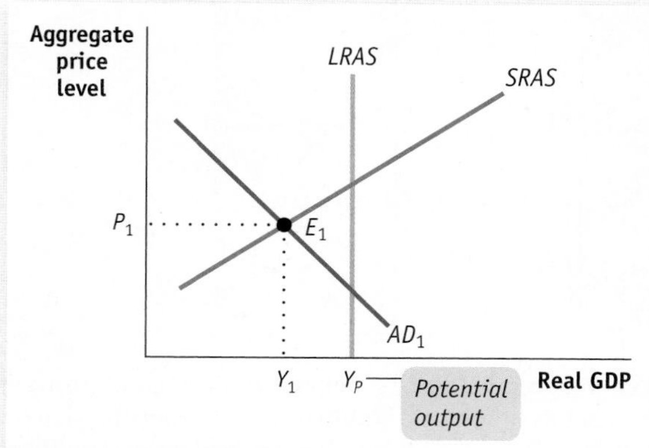

a. Is Albernia facing a recessionary or inflationary gap?

b. Which type of fiscal policy—expansionary or contractionary—would move the economy of Albernia to potential output, Y_P? What are some examples of such policies?

c. Draw a diagram illustrating the macroeconomic situation in Albernia after the successful fiscal policy has been implemented.

2. The accompanying diagram shows the current macroeconomic situation for the economy of Brittania; real GDP is Y_1, and the aggregate price level is P_1. You have been hired as an economic consultant to help the economy move to potential output, Y_P.

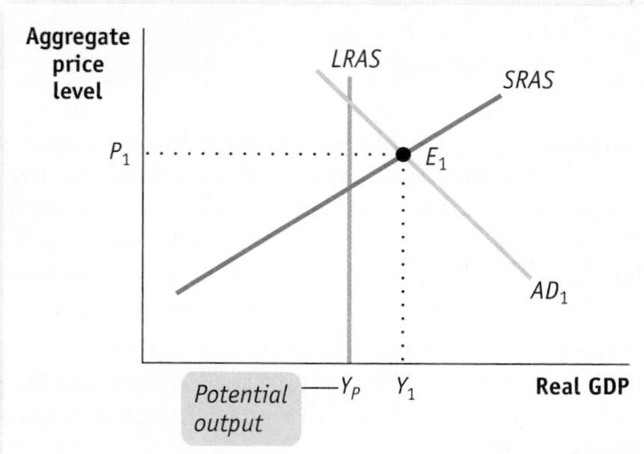

a. Is Brittania facing a recessionary or inflationary gap?

b. Which type of fiscal policy—expansionary or contractionary—would move the economy of Brittania to potential output, Y_P? What are some examples of such policies?

c. Draw a diagram illustrating the macroeconomic situation in Brittania after the successful fiscal policy has been implemented.

3. An economy is in long-run macroeconomic equilibrium when each of the following aggregate demand shocks occurs. What kind of gap—inflationary or recessionary—will the economy face after the shock, and what type of fiscal policies would help move the economy back to potential output? How would your recommended fiscal policy shift the aggregate demand curve?

a. A stock market boom increases the value of stocks held by households.

b. Firms come to believe that a recession in the near future is likely.

c. Anticipating the possibility of war, the government increases its purchases of military equipment.

d. The quantity of money in the economy declines and interest rates increase.

4. During a recent interview, the German finance minister said, "We have to watch out that in Europe and beyond, nothing like a combination of downward economic [growth] and high inflation rates emerges—something that experts call stagflation." Such a situation can be depicted by the movement of the short-run aggregate supply curve from its original position, $SRAS_1$, to its new position, $SRAS_2$, with the new equilibrium point E_2 in the accompanying figure. In this question, we try to understand why stagflation is particularly hard to fix using fiscal policy.

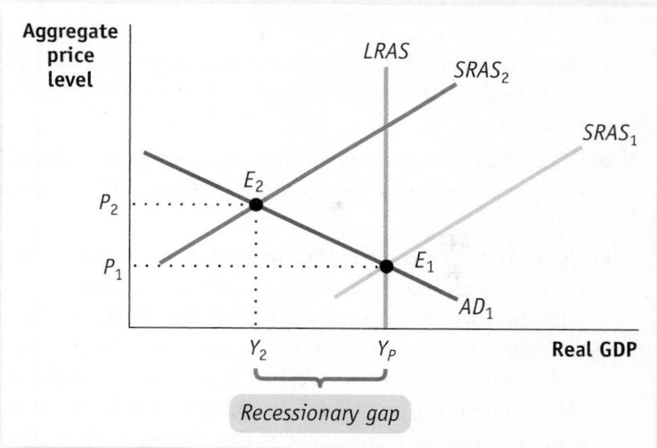

a. What would be the appropriate fiscal policy response to this situation if the primary concern of the government was to maintain economic growth? Illustrate the effect of the policy on the equilibrium point and the aggregate price level using the diagram.

b. What would be the appropriate fiscal policy response to this situation if the primary concern of the government was to maintain price stability? Illustrate the effect of the policy on the equilibrium point and the aggregate price level using the diagram.

c. Discuss the effectiveness of the policies in parts a and b in fighting stagflation.

5. Show why a \$10 billion reduction in government purchases of goods and services will have a larger effect on real GDP than a \$10 billion reduction in government transfers by completing the following table for an economy with a marginal propensity to consume (MPC) of 0.6.

Rounds	Decrease in G = −$10 billion (Billions of dollars)			Decrease in TR = −$10 billion (Billions of dollars)		
	Change in G or C	Change in real GDP	Change in YD	Change in TR or C	Change in real GDP	Change in YD
1	ΔG = −$10.00	−$10.00	−$10.00	ΔTR = −$10.00	$0.00	−$10.00
2	ΔC = −6.00	−6.00	−6.00	ΔC = −6.00	−6.00	−6.00
3	ΔC = ?	?	?	ΔC = ?	?	?
4	ΔC = ?	?	?	ΔC = ?	?	?
5	ΔC = ?	?	?	ΔC = ?	?	?
6	ΔC = ?	?	?	ΔC = ?	?	?
7	ΔC = ?	?	?	ΔC = ?	?	?
8	ΔC = ?	?	?	ΔC = ?	?	?
9	ΔC = ?	?	?	ΔC = ?	?	?
10	ΔC = ?	?	?	ΔC = ?	?	?

The first and second rows of the table are filled in for you: on the left side of the table, in the first row, the $10 billion reduction in government purchases decreases real GDP and disposable income, *YD*, by $10 billion, leading to a reduction in consumer spending of $6 billion (*MPC* × change in disposable income) in row 2. However, on the right side of the table, the $10 billion reduction in transfers has no effect on real GDP in round 1 but does lower *YD* by $10 billion, resulting in a decrease in consumer spending of $6 billion in round 2.

a. When government purchases decrease by $10 billion, what is the sum of the changes in real GDP after the 10 rounds?

b. When the government reduces transfers by $10 billion, what is the sum of the changes in real GDP after the 10 rounds?

c. Using the formula for the multiplier for changes in government purchases and for changes in transfers, calculate the total change in real GDP due to the $10 billion decrease in government purchases and the $10 billion reduction in transfers. What explains the difference? (*Hint:* The multiplier for government purchases of goods and services is 1/(1 − *MPC*). But since each $1 change in government transfers only leads to an initial change in real GDP of *MPC* × $1, the multiplier for government transfers is *MPC*/(1 − *MPC*).)

6. In each of the following cases, either a recessionary or inflationary gap exists. Assume that the aggregate supply curve is horizontal, so that the change in real GDP arising from a shift of the aggregate demand curve equals the size of the shift of the curve. Calculate both the change in government purchases of goods and services and the change in government transfers necessary to close the gap.

a. Real GDP equals $100 billion, potential output equals $160 billion, and the marginal propensity to consume is 0.75.

b. Real GDP equals $250 billion, potential output equals $200 billion, and the marginal propensity to consume is 0.5.

c. Real GDP equals $180 billion, potential output equals $100 billion, and the marginal propensity to consume is 0.8.

7. Most macroeconomists believe it is a good thing that taxes act as automatic stabilizers and lower the size of the multiplier. However, a smaller multiplier means that the change in government purchases of goods and services, government transfers, or taxes needed to close an inflationary or recessionary gap is larger. How can you explain this apparent inconsistency?

8. The accompanying table shows how consumers' marginal propensities to consume in a particular economy are related to their level of income.

Income range	Marginal propensity to consume
$0–$20,000	0.9
$20,001–$40,000	0.8
$40,001–$60,000	0.7
$60,001–$80,000	0.6
Above $80,000	0.5

a. Suppose the government engages in increased purchases of goods and services. For each of the income groups in the table, what is the value of the multiplier—that is, what is the "bang for the buck" from each dollar the government spends on government purchases of goods and services in each income group?

b. If the government needed to close a recessionary or inflationary gap, at which group should it primarily aim its fiscal policy of changes in government purchases of goods and services?

9. The government's budget surplus in Macroland has risen consistently over the past five years. Two government policy makers disagree as to why this has happened. One argues that a rising budget surplus indicates a growing economy; the other argues that it shows that the government is using contractionary fiscal policy. Can you determine which policy maker is correct? If not, why not?

10. Figure 68-3 shows the actual budget deficit and the cyclically adjusted budget deficit as a percentage of GDP in the United States from 1970 to 2013. Assuming that potential output was unchanged, use this figure to determine which of the years from 1990 to 2011 the government used expansionary fiscal policy and in which years it used contractionary fiscal policy.

11. You are an economic adviser to a candidate for national office. She asks you for a summary of the economic consequences of a balanced-budget rule for the federal government and for your recommendation on whether she should support such a rule. How do you respond?

12. In 2012, the policy makers of the economy of Eastlandia projected the debt–GDP ratio and the ratio of the budget deficit to GDP for the economy for the next 10 years under different scenarios for growth in the government's deficit. Real GDP is currently \$1,000 billion per year and is expected to grow by 3% per year, the public debt is \$300 billion at the beginning of the year, and the deficit is \$30 billion in 2012.

Year	Real GDP (billions of dollars)	Debt (billions) of dollars)	Budget deficit (billions of dollars)	Debt (percent of real GDP)	Budget deficit (percent of real GDP)
2012	\$1,000	\$300	\$30	?	?
2013	1,030	?	?	?	?
2014	1,061	?	?	?	?
2015	1,093	?	?	?	?
2016	1,126	?	?	?	?
2017	1,159	?	?	?	?
2018	1,194	?	?	?	?
2019	1,230	?	?	?	?
2020	1,267	?	?	?	?
2021	1,305	?	?	?	?
2022	1,344	?	?	?	?

a. Complete the accompanying table to show the debt–GDP ratio and the ratio of the budget deficit to GDP for the economy if the government's budget deficit remains constant at \$30 billion over the next 10 years. (Remember that the government's debt will grow by the previous year's deficit.)

b. Redo the table to show the debt–GDP ratio and the ratio of the budget deficit to GDP for the economy if the government's budget deficit grows by 3% per year over the next 10 years.

c. Redo the table again to show the debt–GDP ratio and the ratio of the budget deficit to GDP for the economy if the government's budget deficit grows by 20% per year over the next 10 years.

d. What happens to the debt–GDP ratio and the ratio of the budget deficit to GDP for the economy over time under the three different scenarios?

13. Your study partner argues that the distinction between the government's budget deficit and debt is similar to the distinction between consumer savings and wealth. He also argues that if you have large budget deficits, you must have a large debt. In what ways is your study partner correct and in what ways is he incorrect?

14. In which of the following cases does the size of the government's debt and the size of the budget deficit indicate potential problems for the economy?

a. The government's debt is relatively low, but the government is running a large budget deficit as it builds a high-speed rail system to connect the major cities of the nation.

b. The government's debt is relatively high due to a recently ended deficit-financed war, but the government is now running only a small budget deficit.

c. The government's debt is relatively low, but the government is running a budget deficit to finance the interest payments on the debt.

15. How did or would the following affect the current public debt and implicit liabilities of the U.S. government?

a. In 2003, Congress passed and President Bush signed the Medicare Modernization Act, which provides seniors and individuals with disabilities with a prescription drug benefit. Some of the benefits under this law took effect immediately, but others will not begin until sometime in the future.

b. The age at which retired persons can receive full Social Security benefits is raised to age 70 for future retirees.

c. Social Security benefits for future retirees are limited to those with low incomes.

d. Because the cost of health care is increasing faster than the overall inflation rate, annual increases in Social Security benefits are increased by the annual increase in health care costs rather than the overall inflation rate.

16. Unlike households, governments are often able to sustain large debts. For example, in 2011, the U.S. government's total debt reached \$14.8 trillion, approximately equal to 102.7% of GDP. At the time, according to the U.S. Treasury, the average interest rate paid by the government on its debt was 2.2%. However, running budget deficits becomes hard when very large debts are outstanding.

a. Calculate the dollar cost of the annual interest on the government's total debt assuming the interest rate and debt figures cited above.

b. If the government operates on a balanced budget before interest payments are taken into account, at what rate must GDP grow in order for the debt–GDP ratio to remain unchanged?

c. Calculate the total increase in national debt if the government incurs a deficit of \$600 billion in 2012.

d. At what rate would GDP have to grow in order for the debt–GDP ratio to remain unchanged when the deficit in 2012 is \$600 billion?

e. Why is the debt–GDP ratio the preferred measure of a country's debt rather than the dollar value of the debt? Why is it important for a government to keep this number under control?

SECTION 22

Money, Banking, and the Federal Reserve System

FUNNY MONEY

In 2013, police in Lima, Peru, were stunned when they arrested a 13-year-old boy carrying a sack filled with $700,000 in counterfeit U.S. dollars. The boy, along with other children, worked for one of the many highly successful counterfeiting rings in Peru.

In recent years, Peru has become a major source for the production of counterfeit U.S. currency. Workers in these rings meticulously add decorative details to printed bills by hand, creating high-quality fakes that are very hard to detect.

The funny thing is that elaborately decorated pieces of paper have little or no intrinsic value. Indeed, a $100 bill printed with blue or orange ink wouldn't be worth the paper it was printed on.

But if the ink on that piece of paper is just the right shade of green, people will think that it's *money* and will accept it as payment for very real goods and services. Why? Because they believe, correctly, that they can do the same thing: exchange that piece of green paper for real goods and services.

In fact, here's a riddle: If a fake $100 bill from Peru enters the United States and is successfully exchanged for a good or service with nobody ever realizing it's fake, who gets hurt? Accepting a fake $100 bill isn't like buying a car that turns out to be a lemon or a meal that turns out to be inedible; as long as the bill's counterfeit nature remains undiscovered, it will pass from hand to hand just like a real $100 bill.

The answer to the riddle is that the actual victims of the counterfeiting are U.S. taxpayers because counterfeit dollars reduce the revenues available to pay for the operations of the U.S. government. Accordingly, the Secret Service diligently monitors the integrity of U.S. currency, promptly investigating any reports of counterfeit dollars.

The efforts of the Secret Service attest to the fact that money isn't like ordinary goods and services. In this section we'll look at the role money plays, the workings of a modern monetary system, and the institutions that sustain and regulate it, including the *Federal Reserve*.

Module 69 Defining and Measuring Money

Shutterstock

WHAT YOU WILL LEARN

1. The definition and functions of money
2. The various roles money plays and the many forms it takes in the economy
3. How the amount of money in the economy is measured

The Meaning of Money

People often use the word *money* to mean "wealth." If you ask, "How much money does Bill Gates have?" the answer will be something like, "Oh, $50 billion or so, but who's counting?" That is, the number will include the value of the stocks, bonds, real estate, and other assets he owns.

But the economist's definition of money doesn't include all forms of wealth. The dollar bills in your wallet are money; other forms of wealth—such as cars, houses, and stock certificates—aren't money. What, according to economists, distinguishes money from other forms of wealth?

What Is Money?

Money is defined in terms of what it does: **money** is any asset that can easily be used to purchase goods and services. Earlier, we defined an asset as *liquid* if it can easily be converted into cash. Money consists of cash itself, which is liquid by definition, as well as other assets that are highly liquid.

You can see the distinction between money and other assets by asking yourself how you pay for groceries. The person at the cash register will accept dollar bills in return for milk and frozen pizza—but he or she won't accept stock certificates or a collection of vintage baseball cards. If you want to convert stock certificates or vintage baseball cards into groceries, you have to sell them—trade them for money—and then use the money to buy groceries.

Money is any asset that can easily be used to purchase goods and services.

Of course, many stores allow you to write a check on your bank account in payment for goods (or to pay with a debit card that is linked to your bank account).

Does that make your bank account money, even if you haven't converted it into cash? Yes. **Currency in circulation**—actual cash in the hands of the public—is considered money. So are **checkable bank deposits**—bank accounts on which people can write checks.

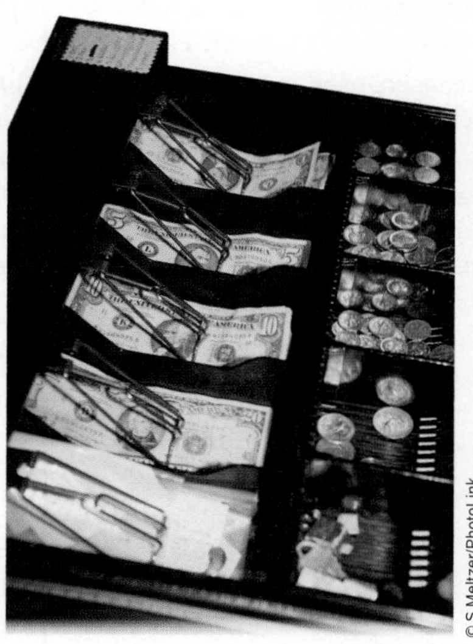

© S Meltzer/PhotoLink

Money is the essential channel that links the various parts of the modern economy.

Are currency and checkable bank deposits the only assets that are considered money? It depends. As we'll see later, there are two widely used definitions of the **money supply,** the total value of financial assets in the economy that are considered money. The narrower definition considers only the most liquid assets to be money: currency in circulation, traveler's checks, and checkable bank deposits. The broader definition includes these three categories plus other assets that are "almost" checkable, such as savings account deposits that can be transferred into a checking account online with a few mouse clicks. Both definitions of the money supply, however, make a distinction between those assets that can easily be used to purchase goods and services, and those that can't.

Money plays a crucial role in generating *gains from trade* because it makes indirect exchange possible. Think of what happens when a cardiac surgeon buys a new refrigerator. The surgeon has valuable services to offer—namely, performing heart operations. The owner of the store has valuable goods to offer: refrigerators and other appliances. It would be extremely difficult for both parties if, instead of using money, they had to directly barter the goods and services they sell. In a barter system, a cardiac surgeon and an appliance store owner could trade only if the store owner happened to want a heart operation *and* the surgeon happened to want a new refrigerator.

This is known as the problem of finding a "double coincidence of wants": in a barter system, two parties can trade only when each wants what the other has to offer. Money solves this problem: individuals can trade what they have to offer for money and trade money for what they want.

Because the ability to make transactions with money rather than relying on bartering makes it easier to achieve gains from trade, the existence of money increases welfare, even though money does not directly produce anything.

Let's take a closer look at the roles money plays in the economy.

Roles of Money

Money plays three main roles in any modern economy: it is a *medium of exchange,* a *store of value,* and a *unit of account.*

1. MEDIUM OF EXCHANGE Our cardiac surgeon/refrigerator store owner example illustrates the role of money as a **medium of exchange**—an asset that individuals use to trade for goods and services rather than for consumption. People can't eat dollar bills; rather, they use dollar bills to trade for edible goods and their accompanying services.

In normal times, the official money of a given country—the dollar in the United States, the peso in Mexico, and so on—is also the medium of exchange in virtually all transactions in that country. During troubled economic times, however, other goods or assets often play that role instead. For example, people often turn to other countries' moneys as the medium of exchange in times of economic turmoil: U.S. dollars have played this role in troubled Latin American countries, as have euros in troubled Eastern European countries.

In a famous example, cigarettes functioned as the medium of exchange in World War II prisoner-of-war camps. Even nonsmokers traded goods and services for cigarettes because the cigarettes could in turn be easily traded for other items. During the extreme German inflation of 1923, goods such as eggs and lumps of coal became, briefly, mediums of exchange.

Currency in circulation is cash held by the public.

Checkable bank deposits are bank accounts on which people can write checks.

The **money supply** is the total value of financial assets in the economy that are considered money.

A **medium of exchange** is an asset that individuals acquire for the purpose of trading goods and services rather than for their own consumption.

A **store of value** is a means of holding purchasing power over time.

A **unit of account** is a measure used to set prices and make economic calculations.

Commodity money is a good used as a medium of exchange that has intrinsic value in other uses.

Commodity-backed money is a medium of exchange with no intrinsic value whose ultimate value is guaranteed by a promise that it can be converted into valuable goods.

2. STORE OF VALUE In order to act as a medium of exchange, money must also be a **store of value**—a means of holding purchasing power over time. To see why this is necessary, imagine trying to operate an economy in which ice-cream cones were the medium of exchange. Such an economy would quickly suffer from, well, monetary meltdown: your medium of exchange would often turn into a sticky puddle before you could use it to buy something else.

Of course, money is by no means the only store of value. Any asset that holds its purchasing power over time is a store of value. So the store-of-value role is a necessary but not distinctive feature of money.

3. UNIT OF ACCOUNT Finally, money normally serves as the **unit of account**—the commonly accepted measure individuals use to set prices and make economic calculations. To understand the importance of this role, consider a historical fact: during the Middle Ages, peasants typically were required to provide landowners with goods and labor rather than money. A peasant might, for example, be required to work on the landowner's land one day a week and hand over one-fifth of his harvest.

Today, rents, like other prices, are almost always specified in money terms. That makes things much clearer: imagine how hard it would be to decide which apartment to rent if modern landowners followed medieval practice. Suppose, for example, that Mr. Smith says he'll let you have a place if you clean his house twice a week and bring him a pound of steak every day, whereas Ms. Jones wants you to clean her house just once a week but wants four pounds of chicken every day. Who's offering the better deal? It's hard to say. If, on the other hand, Smith wants $600 a month and Jones wants $700, the comparison is easy. In other words, without a commonly accepted measure, the terms of a transaction are harder to determine, making it more difficult to make transactions and achieve gains from trade.

Thinkstock

For centuries, people used goods with value, like gold and silver, as a medium of exchange.

Types of Money

In some form or another, money has been in use for thousands of years. For most of that period, people used **commodity money:** the medium of exchange was a good, normally gold or silver, that had intrinsic value in other uses. These alternative uses gave commodity money value independent of its role as a medium of exchange. For example, the cigarettes that served as money in World War II prisoner-of-war camps were valuable because many prisoners smoked. Gold was valuable because it was used for jewelry and ornamentation, aside from the fact that it was minted into coins.

By 1776, the year in which the United States declared its independence and Adam Smith published *The Wealth of Nations,* there was widespread use of paper money in addition to gold or silver coins. Unlike modern dollar bills, however, this paper money consisted of notes issued by private banks, which promised to exchange their notes for gold or silver coins on demand. So the paper currency that initially replaced commodity money was **commodity-backed money,** a medium of exchange with no intrinsic value whose ultimate value was guaranteed by a promise that it could always be converted into valuable goods on demand.

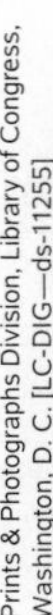

Prints & Photographs Division, Library of Congress, Washington, D. C. [LC-DIG—ds-11255]

Early paper money consisted of bank-issued promissory notes that functioned in a different way than cash does today.

The big advantage of commodity-backed money over simple commodity money, like gold and silver coins, was that it tied up fewer valuable resources. Although a note-issuing bank still had to keep some gold and silver on hand, it had to keep only enough to satisfy demands for redemption of its notes. And it could rely on the fact that on a normal day only a fraction of its paper notes would be redeemed. So the bank needed to keep only a portion of the total value of its notes in circulation in the form of gold and silver in its vaults. It could lend out the remaining gold and silver to those who wished to use it. This allowed society to use the remaining gold and silver for other purposes, all with no loss in the ability to achieve gains from trade.

Fiat money is a medium of exchange whose value derives entirely from its official status as a means of payment.

At this point you may ask, why make any use at all of gold and silver in the monetary system, even to back paper money? In fact, today's monetary system has eliminated any role for gold and silver. A U.S. dollar bill isn't commodity money, and it isn't even commodity-backed. Rather, its value arises entirely from the fact that it is generally accepted as a means of payment, a role that is ultimately decreed by the U.S. government. Money whose value derives entirely from its official status as a means of exchange is known as **fiat money** because it exists by government *fiat,* a historical term for a policy declared by a ruler.

Fiat money has two major advantages over commodity-backed money. First, creating it doesn't use up any real resources, except for the paper it's printed on. Second, the money supply can be adjusted based on the needs of the economy, instead of being determined by the amount of gold and silver prospectors happen to discover.

Fiat money, though, poses some risks. One such risk is counterfeiting, as we saw in the section-opening story. Counterfeiters usurp a privilege of the U.S. government, which has the sole legal right to print dollar bills. And the benefit that counterfeiters get by exchanging fake bills for real goods and services comes at the expense of the U.S. federal government, which covers a small but nontrivial part of its own expenses by issuing new currency to meet growing demand for money.

The larger risk is that governments that can create money whenever they feel like it will be tempted to abuse the privilege by printing so much money that they create inflation.

ECONOMICS ▶ *IN ACTION*

THE HISTORY OF THE DOLLAR

U.S. dollar bills are pure fiat money: they have no intrinsic value, and they are not backed by anything that does. But American money wasn't always like that.

In the early days of European settlement, the colonies that would become the United States used commodity money, partly consisting of gold and silver coins minted in Europe. But such coins were scarce on this side of the Atlantic, so the colonists relied on a variety of other forms of commodity money. For example, settlers in Virginia used tobacco as money and settlers in the Northeast used "wampum," a type of clamshell.

Later in American history, commodity-backed paper money came into widespread use. But this wasn't paper money as we now know it, issued by the U.S. government and bearing the signature of the Secretary of the Treasury. Before the Civil War, the U.S. government didn't issue any paper money. Instead, dollar bills were issued by private banks, which promised that their bills could be redeemed for silver coins on demand.

These promises weren't always credible because banks sometimes failed, leaving holders of their bills with worthless pieces of paper. Understandably, people were reluctant to accept currency from any bank rumored to be in financial trouble. In other words, in this private money system, some dollars were less valuable than others.

A curious legacy of that time was notes issued by the Citizens' Bank of Louisiana, based in New Orleans. They became among the most widely used bank notes in the southern states. These notes were printed in English on one side and French on the other. (At the time, many people in New Orleans, originally a colony of France, spoke French.) Thus, the $10 bill read *Ten* on one side and *Dix,* the French word for "ten," on the other. These $10 bills became known as "dixies," probably the source of the nickname of the U.S. South.

SB Photography/Alamy

Not until the Civil War did the U.S. government issue official paper money.

During the Civil War, the U.S. government began issuing official paper money, called "greenbacks," as a way to help pay for the war. At first greenbacks had no fixed value in terms of commodities. After 1873, the U.S. government guaranteed the value of a dollar in terms of gold, effectively turning dollars into commodity-backed money.

In 1933, when President Franklin D. Roosevelt broke the link between dollars and gold, his own federal budget director—who feared that the public would lose confidence in the dollar if it wasn't ultimately backed by gold—declared ominously, "This will be the end of Western civilization." It wasn't. The link between the dollar and gold was restored a few years later, and then dropped again—seemingly for good—in August 1971. Despite the warnings of doom, the U.S. dollar is still the world's most widely used currency.

Measuring the Money Supply

The Federal Reserve (an institution we'll talk about shortly) calculates the size of two **monetary aggregates,** overall measures of the money supply, which differ in how strictly money is defined. The two aggregates are known, rather cryptically, as M1 and M2. (There used to be a third aggregate named—you guessed it—M3, but in 2006 the Federal Reserve concluded that measuring it was no longer useful.)

M1, the narrowest definition, contains only currency in circulation (also known as cash), traveler's checks, and checkable bank deposits. M2 starts with M1 and adds several other kinds of assets, often referred to as **near-moneys**—financial assets that aren't directly usable as a medium of exchange but can be readily converted into cash or checkable bank deposits, such as savings accounts. Examples are time deposits such as small denomination CDs, which aren't checkable but can be withdrawn at any time before their maturity date by paying a penalty. Because currency and checkable deposits are directly usable as a medium of exchange, M1 is the most liquid measure of money.

A **monetary aggregate** is an overall measure of the money supply.

Near-moneys are financial assets that can't be directly used as a medium of exchange but can be readily converted into cash or checkable bank deposits.

Figure 69-1 shows the actual composition of M1 and M2 in April 2013, in billions of dollars. As you can see, M1 was valued at $2,514.1 billion, with approximately 44%

FIGURE 69-1 Monetary Aggregates, April 2013

The Federal Reserve uses two definitions of the money supply, M1 and M2. As panel (a) shows, more than half of M1 consists of checkable bank deposits with currency in circulation making up virtually all of the rest. M2, as panel (b) shows, has a much broader definition: it includes M1 plus a range of other deposits and deposit-like assets, making it over four times as large.

Source: Federal Reserve Bank of St. Louis.

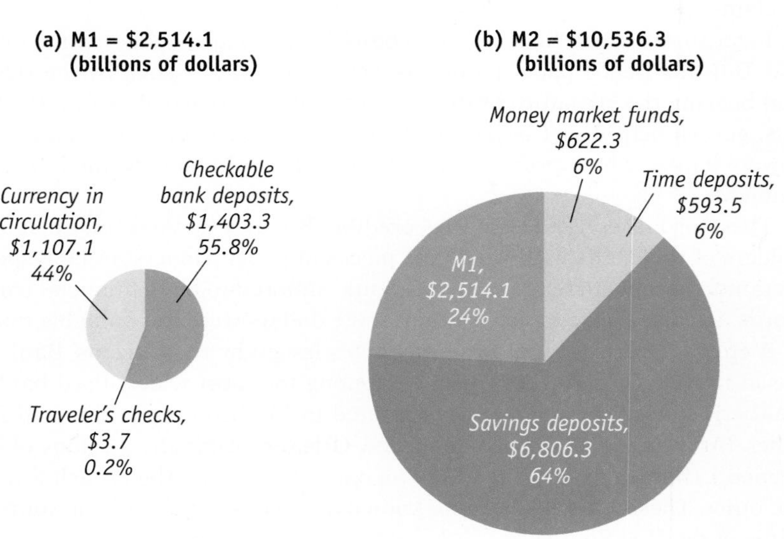

accounted for by currency in circulation, approximately 56% accounted for by checkable bank deposits, and a tiny slice accounted for by traveler's checks. In turn, M1 made up 24% of M2, valued at $10,536.3 billion. M2 consists of M1 plus other types of assets: two types of bank deposits, known as savings deposits and time deposits, both of which are considered noncheckable, plus money market funds, which are mutual funds that invest only in liquid assets and bear a close resemblance to bank deposits. These near-moneys pay interest while cash (currency in circulation) does not, and they typically pay higher interest rates than any offered on checkable bank deposits.

MODULE 69 Review

Solutions appear at the back of the book.

Check Your Understanding

1. Suppose you hold a gift certificate, good for certain products at participating stores. Is this gift certificate money? Why or why not?
2. Although most bank accounts pay some interest, depositors can get a higher interest rate by buying a certificate of deposit, or CD. The difference between a CD and a checking account is that the depositor pays a penalty for withdrawing the money before the CD comes due—a period of months or even years. Small CDs are counted in M2, but not in M1. Explain why they are not part of M1.
3. Explain why a system of commodity-backed money uses resources more efficiently than a system of commodity money.

Multiple-Choice Questions

1. When you use money to purchase your lunch, money is serving which role(s)?
   - I. medium of exchange
   - II. store of value
   - III. unit of account
   - a. I only
   - b. II only
   - c. III only
   - d. I and III only
   - e. I, II, and III
2. When you decide you want "$10 worth" of a product, money is serving which role(s)?
   - I. medium of exchange
   - II. store of value
   - III. unit of account
   - a. I only
   - b. II only
   - c. III only
   - d. I and II only
   - e. I, II, and III
3. In the United States, the dollar is
   - a. backed by silver.
   - b. backed by gold and silver.
   - c. commodity-backed money.
   - d. commodity money.
   - e. fiat money.
4. Which of the following is the most liquid monetary aggregate?
   - a. M1
   - b. M2
   - c. M3
   - d. near-moneys
   - e. dollar bills
5. Which of the following is the best example of using money as a store of value?
   - a. A customer pays in advance for $10 worth of gasoline at a gas station.
   - b. A babysitter puts her earnings in a dresser drawer while she saves to buy a bicycle.
   - c. Travelers buy meals on board an airline flight.
   - d. Foreign visitors to the United States convert their currency to dollars at the airport.
   - e. You use $1 bills to purchase soda from a vending machine.

Critical-Thinking Questions

1. The U.S. dollar derives its value from what? That is, what "backs" U.S. currency?
2. What is the term used to describe the type of money used in the United States today?
3. What other two types of money have been used throughout history? Define each.

PITFALLS

TO BE IN THE MONEY SUPPLY, OR NOT TO BE?

? Are financial assets such as stocks and bonds part of the money supply?

> NO, STOCKS AND BONDS ARE NOT IN THE MONEY SUPPLY, UNDER ANY DEFINITION, BECAUSE THEY'RE NOT LIQUID ENOUGH. Think of M1 as including assets you can use to buy groceries: currency, traveler's checks, and checkable deposits. M2 is broader, because it includes things like savings accounts that can easily and quickly be converted into M1. You can, for example, switch funds between your savings and checking accounts electronically. By contrast, converting a stock or a bond into cash requires selling the stock or bond—something that usually takes some time and also involves paying a broker's fee. That makes these assets much less liquid than bank deposits. So, unlike bank deposits, stocks and bonds aren't considered money.

To learn more, see pages 722–723.

Banking and Money Creation

Jund Lund/Getty Images

WHAT YOU WILL LEARN

1. The role of banks in the economy
2. The reasons for and types of banking regulation
3. How banks create money

The Monetary Role of Banks

A little less than half of M1, the narrowest definition of the money supply, consists of currency in circulation—$1 bills, $5 bills, and so on. It's obvious where currency comes from: it's printed by the U.S. Treasury. But the rest of M1 consists of bank deposits, and deposits account for the great bulk of M2, the broader definition of the money supply. By either measure, then, bank deposits are a major component of the money supply. And this fact brings us to our next topic: the monetary role of banks.

What Banks Do

A bank is a *financial intermediary* that uses liquid assets in the form of bank deposits to finance the illiquid investments of borrowers. Banks can create liquidity because it isn't necessary for a bank to keep all of the funds deposited with it in the form of highly liquid assets. Except in the case of a *bank run*—which we'll get to shortly—all of a bank's depositors won't want to withdraw their funds at the same time. So a bank can provide its depositors with liquid assets yet still invest much of the depositors' funds in illiquid assets, such as mortgages and business loans.

Banks can't, however, lend out all the funds placed in their hands by depositors because they have to satisfy any depositor who wants to withdraw his or her funds. In order to meet these demands, a bank must keep substantial quantities of liquid assets on hand. In the modern U.S. banking system, these assets take the form either of currency in the bank's vault or deposits held in the bank's own account at the Federal Reserve. The latter can be converted into currency more or less instantly. Currency in bank vaults and bank deposits held at the Federal Reserve are called **bank reserves.** Because bank reserves are in bank vaults and at the Federal Reserve, not held by the public, they are not part of currency in circulation.

Bank reserves are the currency banks hold in their vaults plus their deposits at the Federal Reserve.

To understand the role of banks in determining the money supply, we start by introducing a simple tool for analyzing a bank's financial position: a **T-account.** A business's T-account summarizes its financial position by showing, in a single table, the business's assets and liabilities, with assets on the left and liabilities on the right.

Figure 70-1 shows the T-account for a hypothetical business that *isn't* a bank—Samantha's Smoothies. According to Figure 70-1, Samantha's Smoothies owns a building worth $30,000 and has $15,000 worth of smoothie-making equipment. These are assets, so they're on the left side of the table. To finance its opening, the business borrowed $20,000 from a local bank. That's a liability, so the loan is on the right side of the table. By looking at the T-account, you can immediately see what Samantha's Smoothies owns and what it owes. Oh, and it's called a T-account because the lines in the table make a T-shape.

FIGURE 70-1 A T-Account for Samantha's Smoothies

Assets		Liabilities	
Building	$30,000	Loan from bank	$20,000
Smoothie-making machines	$15,000		

A T-account summarizes a business's financial position. Its assets, in this case consisting of a building and some smoothie-making machinery, are on the left side. Its liabilities, consisting of the money it owes to a local bank, are on the right side.

Samantha's Smoothies is an ordinary, nonbank business. Now let's look at the T-account for a hypothetical bank, First Street Bank, which is the repository of $1 million in bank deposits.

Figure 70-2 shows First Street Bank's financial position. The loans First Street Bank has made are on the left side because they're assets: they represent funds that those who have borrowed from the bank are expected to repay. The bank's only other assets, in this simplified example, are its reserves, which, as we've learned, can take the form either of cash in the bank's vault or deposits at the Federal Reserve. On the right side we show the bank's liabilities, which in this example consist entirely of deposits made by customers at First Street Bank. These are liabilities because they represent funds that must ultimately be repaid to depositors.

FIGURE 70-2 Assets and Liabilities of First Street Bank

Assets		Liabilities	
Loans	$1,000,000	Deposits	$1,000,000
Reserves	$100,000		

First Street Bank's assets consist of $1,000,000 in loans and $100,000 in reserves. Its liabilities consist of $1,000,000 in deposits—money owed to people who have placed funds in First Street's hands.

Notice, by the way, that in this example First Street Bank's assets are larger than its liabilities. That's the way it's supposed to be! In fact, as we'll see shortly, banks are required by law to maintain assets larger by a specific percentage than their liabilities.

In this example, First Street Bank holds reserves equal to 10% of its customers' bank deposits. The fraction of bank deposits that a bank holds as reserves is its **reserve ratio.**

In the modern American system, the Federal Reserve—which, among other things, regulates banks operating in the United States—sets a **required reserve ratio,** which is the smallest fraction of bank deposits that a bank must hold. To understand why banks are regulated, let's consider a problem banks can face: *bank runs.*

The Problem of Bank Runs

A bank can lend out most of the funds deposited in its care because in normal times only a small fraction of its depositors want to withdraw their funds on any given day. But what would happen if, for some reason, all or at least a large fraction of its depositors *did* try to withdraw their funds during a short period of time, such as a couple of days?

If a significant share of its depositors demanded their money back at the same time, the bank wouldn't be able to raise enough cash to meet those demands. The reason is that banks convert most of their depositors' funds into loans made to borrowers; that's how banks earn revenue—by charging interest on loans.

Bank loans, however, are illiquid: they can't easily be converted into cash on short notice. To see why, imagine that First Street Bank has lent $100,000 to Drive-a-Peach Used Cars, a local dealership. To raise cash to meet demands for withdrawals, First Street Bank can sell its loan to Drive-a-Peach to someone else—another bank or an

A **T-account** is a tool for analyzing a business's financial position by showing, in a single table, the business's assets (on the left) and liabilities (on the right).

The **reserve ratio** is the fraction of bank deposits that a bank holds as reserves.

The **required reserve ratio** is the smallest fraction of deposits that the Federal Reserve allows banks to hold.

individual investor. But if First Street Bank tries to sell the loan quickly, potential buyers will be wary: they will suspect that First Street Bank wants to sell the loan because there is something wrong and the loan might not be repaid. As a result, First Street Bank can sell the loan quickly only by offering it for sale at a deep discount—say, a discount of 50%, or $50,000.

A **bank run** is a phenomenon in which many of a bank's depositors try to withdraw their funds due to fears of a bank failure.

The upshot is that if a significant number of First Street Bank's depositors suddenly decided to withdraw their funds, the bank's efforts to raise the necessary cash quickly would force it to sell off its assets very cheaply. Inevitably, this leads to a *bank failure*: the bank would be unable to pay off its depositors in full.

What might start this whole process? That is, what might lead First Street Bank's depositors to rush to pull their money out? A plausible answer is a spreading rumor that the bank is in financial trouble. Even if depositors aren't sure the rumor is true, they are likely to play it safe and get their money out while they still can. And it gets worse: a depositor who simply thinks that *other* depositors are going to panic and try to get their money out will realize that this could "break the bank." So he or she joins the rush. In other words, fear about a bank's financial condition can be a self-fulfilling prophecy: depositors who believe that other depositors will rush to the exit will rush to the exit themselves.

A **bank run** is a phenomenon in which many of a bank's depositors try to withdraw their funds due to fears of a bank failure. Bank runs aren't bad only for the bank in question and its depositors. Historically, they have often proved contagious, with a run on one bank leading to a loss of faith in other banks, causing additional bank runs. The upcoming Economics in Action describes an actual case of just such a contagion, the wave of bank runs that swept across the United States in the early 1930s. In response to that experience and similar experiences in other countries, most modern governments established a system of bank regulations, which we'll look at next.

ECONOMICS IN ACTION

WORLD VIEW

IT'S A WONDERFUL BANKING SYSTEM

Next Christmastime, it's a sure thing that at least one TV channel will show the 1946 film *It's a Wonderful Life,* featuring Jimmy Stewart as George Bailey. The movie's climactic scene is a run on Bailey's bank, as fearful depositors rush to take their funds out.

When the movie was made, such scenes were still fresh in Americans' memories. There was a wave of bank runs in late 1930, a second wave in the spring of 1931, and a third wave in early 1933. By the end, more than a third of the nation's banks had failed. To bring the panic to an end, in 1933, the newly inaugurated president, Franklin Delano Roosevelt, closed all banks for a week to give bank regulators time to shut down unhealthy banks and certify healthy ones.

Gabriel Bouys/AFP/Getty Images

Panicky IndyMac depositors lined up to pull their money out of the troubled California bank in 2008.

Since then, regulation has protected the United States and other wealthy countries against most bank runs. In fact, the scene in *It's a Wonderful Life* was already out of date when the movie was made. But the last 15 years have seen several waves of bank runs in developing countries. For example, bank runs played a role in an economic crisis that swept Southeast Asia in 1997–1998 and in the severe economic crisis in Argentina, which began in late 2001.

Notice that we said "most bank runs." There are some limits on deposit insurance. As a result, there can still be a rush to pull money out of a bank perceived as troubled. In fact, that's exactly what happened to IndyMac, a California-based lender that had made a large number of questionable home loans. In 2008, as questions about IndyMac's financial soundness were raised, depositors began pulling out funds, forcing federal regulators to step in and close the bank. Unlike in the bank runs of the 1930s, however, most depositors got all their funds back—and the panic at IndyMac did not spread to other institutions.

Bank Regulation

Should you worry about losing money in the United States due to a bank run? No. After the banking crises of the 1930s, the United States and most other countries put into place a system designed to protect depositors and the economy as a whole against bank runs. This system has three main features: *deposit insurance, capital requirements,* and *reserve requirements.* In addition, banks have access to the *discount window,* a source of cash when it's needed.

Ted Foxx/Alamy

The FDIC guarantees that bank deposits up to a certain amount will be paid even if a bank runs short or fails.

1. DEPOSIT INSURANCE Almost all banks in the United States advertise themselves as a "member of the FDIC"—the Federal Deposit Insurance Corporation. The FDIC provides **deposit insurance,** a guarantee that depositors will be paid even if the bank can't come up with the funds, up to a maximum amount per account. Currently, the FDIC guarantees the first $250,000 per depositer, per insured bank.

Deposit insurance doesn't just protect depositors if a bank actually fails. The insurance also eliminates the main reason for bank runs: since depositors know their funds are safe even if a bank fails, they have no incentive to rush to pull them out because of a rumor that the bank is in trouble.

2. CAPITAL REQUIREMENTS Deposit insurance, although it protects the banking system against bank runs, creates a well-known incentive problem. Because depositors are protected from loss, they have no incentive to monitor their bank's financial health, allowing risky behavior by the bank to go undetected. At the same time, the owners of banks have an incentive to engage in overly risky investment behavior, such as making questionable loans at high interest rates. That's because if all goes well, the owners profit; and if things go badly, the government covers the losses through federal deposit insurance.

To reduce the incentive for excessive risk-taking, regulators require that the owners of banks hold substantially more assets than the value of bank deposits. That way, the bank will still have assets larger than its deposits even if some of its loans go bad, and losses will accrue against the bank owners' assets, not the government. The excess of a bank's assets over its bank deposits and other liabilities is called the *bank's capital.* For example, First Street Bank has capital of $100,000, equal to 9% of the total value of its assets. In practice, banks' capital is required to equal at least 7% of the value of their assets.

3. RESERVE REQUIREMENTS Another regulation used to reduce the risk of bank runs is **reserve requirements,** rules set by the Federal Reserve that specify the minimum reserve ratio for banks. For example, in the United States, the required reserve ratio for checkable bank deposits is 10%.

4. THE DISCOUNT WINDOW One final protection against bank runs is the fact that the Federal Reserve, which we'll discuss more thoroughly later, stands ready to lend money to banks in trouble, an arrangement known as the **discount window.** The ability to borrow money means a bank can avoid being forced to sell its assets at fire-sale prices in order to satisfy the demands of a sudden rush of depositors demanding cash. Instead, it can turn to the Federal Reserve and borrow the funds it needs to pay off depositors.

Deposit insurance guarantees that a bank's depositors will be paid even if the bank can't come up with the funds, up to a maximum amount per account.

Reserve requirements are rules set by the Federal Reserve that determine the required reserve ratio for banks.

The **discount window** is an arrangement in which the Federal Reserve stands ready to lend money to banks.

Determining the Money Supply

Without banks, there would be no checkable deposits, and so the quantity of currency in circulation would equal the money supply. In that case, the money supply would be determined solely by whoever controls government minting and printing presses.

But banks do exist, and through their creation of checkable bank deposits, they affect the money supply in two ways.

1. Banks remove some currency from circulation: dollar bills that are sitting in bank vaults, as opposed to sitting in people's wallets, aren't part of the money supply.
2. Much more importantly, banks create money by accepting deposits and making loans—that is, they make the money supply larger than just the value of currency in circulation.

Next we cover how banks create money and what determines the amount of money they create.

How Banks Create Money

To see how banks create money, let's examine what happens when someone decides to deposit currency in a bank. Consider the example of Silas, a miser, who keeps a shoebox full of cash under his bed. Suppose Silas realizes that it would be safer, as well as more convenient, to deposit that cash in the bank and to use his debit card when shopping. Assume that he deposits $1,000 into a checkable account at First Street Bank. What effect will Silas's actions have on the money supply?

Alina Vincent Photography, LLC/Getty Images

Money creation begins when cash is deposited into a checkable bank account.

Panel (a) of Figure 70-3 shows the initial effect of his deposit. First Street Bank credits Silas with $1,000 in his account, so the economy's checkable bank deposits rise by $1,000. Meanwhile, Silas's cash goes into the vault, raising First Street Bank's reserves by $1,000 as well.

This initial transaction has no effect on the money supply. Currency in circulation, part of the money supply, falls by $1,000; checkable bank deposits, also part of the money supply, rise by the same amount.

But this is not the end of the story because First Street Bank can now lend out part of Silas's deposit. Assume that it holds 10% of Silas's deposit—$100—in reserves and lends the rest out in cash to Silas's neighbor, Mary. The effect of this second stage is shown in panel (b). First Street Bank's deposits remain unchanged, and so does the value of its assets. But the composition of its assets changes: by making the loan, it reduces its reserves by $900, so that they are only $100 larger than they were before Silas made his deposit. In the place of the $900 reduction in reserves, the bank has acquired an IOU, its $900 cash loan to Mary.

FIGURE 70-3 **Effect on the Money Supply of Turning Cash into a Checkable Deposit at First Street Bank**

(a) Initial Effect Before Bank Makes a New Loan

Assets		Liabilities	
Loans	No change	Checkable deposits	+$1,000
Reserves	+$1,000		

(b) Effect When Bank Makes a New Loan

Assets		Liabilities
Loans	+$900	No change
Reserves	−$900	

When Silas deposits $1,000 (which had been stashed under his bed) into a checkable bank account, there is initially no effect on the money supply: currency in circulation falls by $1,000, but checkable bank deposits rise by $1,000. The corresponding entries on the bank's T-account, depicted in panel (a), show deposits initially rising by $1,000 and the bank's reserves initially rising by $1,000. In the second stage, depicted in panel (b), the bank holds 10% of Silas's deposit ($100) as reserves and lends out the rest ($900) to Mary. As a result, its reserves fall by $900 and its loans increase by $900. Its liabilities, including Silas's $1,000 deposit, are unchanged. The money supply, the sum of checkable bank deposits and currency in circulation, has now increased by $900—the $900 now held by Mary.

Turhan/Shutterstock

The money supply increases when banks lend out a portion of their cash deposits.

So by putting $900 of Silas's cash back into circulation by lending it to Mary, First Street Bank has, in fact, increased the money supply. That is, the sum of currency in circulation and checkable bank deposits has risen by $900 compared to what it had been when Silas's cash was still under his bed. Although Silas is still the owner of $1,000, now in the form of a checkable deposit, Mary has the use of $900 in cash from her borrowings.

And this may not be the end of the story. Suppose that Mary uses her cash to buy a television and a tablet from Acme Electronics. What does Anne Acme, the store's owner, do with the cash? If she holds on to it, the money supply doesn't increase any further. But suppose she deposits the $900 into a checkable bank deposit—say, at Second Street Bank. Second Street Bank, in turn, will keep only part of that deposit in reserves, lending out the rest, creating still more money.

Assume that Second Street Bank, like First Street Bank, keeps 10% of any bank deposit in reserves and lends out the rest. Then it will keep $90 in reserves and lend out $810 of Anne's deposit to another borrower, further increasing the money supply.

Table 70-1 shows the process of money creation we have described so far. At first the money supply consists only of Silas's $1,000. After he deposits the cash into a checkable bank deposit and the bank makes a loan, the money supply rises to $1,900. After the second deposit and the second loan, the money supply rises to $2,710. And the process will, of course, continue from there. (Although we have considered the case in which Silas places his cash in a checkable bank deposit, the results would be the same if he put it into any type of near-money.)

TABLE 70-1

How Banks Create Money

	Currency in circulation	Checkable bank deposits	Money supply
First stage Silas keeps his cash under his bed.	$1,000	$0	$1,000
Second stage Silas deposits cash in First Street Bank, which lends out $900 to Mary, who then pays it to Anne Acme.	900	1,000	1,900
Third stage Anne Acme deposits $900 in Second Street Bank, which lends out $810 to another borrower.	810	1,900	2,710

This process of money creation may sound familiar. Recall the *multiplier process* that we described earlier: an initial increase in real GDP leads to a rise in consumer spending, which leads to a further rise in real GDP, which leads to a further rise in consumer spending, and so on. What we have here is another kind of multiplier—the *money multiplier.* Next, we'll learn what determines the size of this multiplier.

Reserves, Bank Deposits, and the Money Multiplier

In tracing out the effect of Silas's deposit in Table 70-1, we assumed that the funds a bank lends out always end up being deposited either in the same bank or in another bank—so funds disbursed as loans come back to the banking system, even if not to the lending bank itself.

In reality, some of these loaned funds may be held by borrowers in their wallets and not deposited in a bank, meaning that some of the loaned amount "leaks" out of the banking system. Such leaks reduce the size of the money multiplier, just as leaks of real income into savings reduce the size of the real GDP multiplier. (Bear in mind, however, that the "leak" here comes from the fact that borrowers keep some of their funds in currency, rather than the fact that consumers save some of their income.)

But let's set that complication aside for a moment and consider how the money supply is determined in a "checkable-deposits-only" monetary system, where funds are always deposited in bank accounts and none are held in wallets as currency. That is, in our checkable-deposits-only monetary system, any and all funds borrowed from a bank are immediately deposited into a checkable bank account. We'll assume that banks are required to satisfy a minimum reserve ratio of 10% and that every bank lends out all of its **excess reserves,** reserves over and above the amount needed to satisfy the minimum reserve ratio.

Excess reserves are a bank's reserves over and above its required reserves.

The **monetary base** is the sum of currency in circulation and bank reserves.

Now suppose that for some reason a bank suddenly finds itself with \$1,000 in excess reserves. What happens? The answer is that the bank will lend out that \$1,000, which will end up as a checkable bank deposit somewhere in the banking system, launching a money multiplier process very similar to the process shown in Table 70-1.

In the first stage, the bank lends out its excess reserves of \$1,000, which becomes a checkable bank deposit somewhere. The bank that receives the \$1,000 deposit keeps 10%, or \$100, as reserves and lends out the remaining 90%, or \$900, which again becomes a checkable bank deposit somewhere. The bank receiving this \$900 deposit again keeps 10%, which is \$90, as reserves and lends out the remaining \$810. The bank receiving this \$810 keeps \$81 in reserves and lends out the remaining \$729, and so on.

As a result of this process, the total increase in checkable bank deposits is equal to a sum that looks like:

$$\$1{,}000 + \$900 + \$810 + \$729 + \ldots$$

We'll use the symbol rr for the reserve ratio. More generally, the total increase in checkable bank deposits that is generated when a bank lends out \$1,000 in excess reserves is the:

(70-1) Increase in checkable bank deposits from \$1,000 in excess reserves =
$\$1{,}000 + (\$1{,}000 \times (1 - rr)) + (\$1{,}000 \times (1 - rr)^2) + (\$1{,}000 \times (1 - rr)^3) + \ldots$

As we have seen, an infinite series of this form can be simplified to:

(70-2) Increase in checkable bank deposits from \$1,000 in excess reserves =
$\$1{,}000/rr$

Given a reserve ratio of 10%, or 0.1, a \$1,000 increase in excess reserves will increase the total value of checkable bank deposits by \$1,000/0.1 = \$10,000. In fact, in a checkable-deposits-only monetary system, the total value of checkable bank deposits will be equal to the value of bank reserves divided by the reserve ratio. Or to put it a different way, if the reserve ratio is 10%, each \$1 of reserves held by a bank supports $\$1/rr = \$1/0.1 = \$10$ of checkable bank deposits.

The Money Multiplier in Reality

In reality, the determination of the money supply is more complicated than our simple model suggests because it depends not only on the ratio of reserves to bank deposits but also on the fraction of the money supply that individuals choose to hold in the form of currency. In fact, we already saw this in our example of Silas depositing the cash under his bed: when he chose to hold a checkable bank deposit instead of currency, he set in motion an increase in the money supply.

To define the money multiplier in practice, it's important to recognize that the Federal Reserve controls the *sum* of bank reserves and currency in circulation, called the *monetary base,* but it does not control the allocation of that sum between bank reserves and currency in circulation. Consider Silas and his deposit one more time: by taking the cash from under his bed and depositing it in a bank, he reduces the quantity of currency in circulation but increases bank reserves by an equal amount—leaving the monetary base, on net, unchanged. The **monetary base,** which is the quantity the monetary authorities control, is the sum of currency in circulation and reserves held by banks.

The monetary base is different from the money supply in two ways.

1. Bank reserves, which are part of the monetary base, aren't considered part of the money supply. A $1 bill in someone's wallet is considered money because it's available for an individual to spend, but a $1 bill held as bank reserves in a bank vault or deposited at the Federal Reserve isn't considered part of the money supply because it's not available for spending.
2. Checkable bank deposits, which are part of the money supply because they are available for spending, aren't part of the monetary base.

Figure 70-4 shows the two concepts schematically. The circle on the left represents the monetary base, consisting of bank reserves plus currency in circulation. The circle on the right represents the money supply, consisting mainly of currency in circulation plus checkable or near-checkable bank deposits. As the figure indicates, currency in circulation is part of both the monetary base and the money supply. But bank reserves aren't part of the money supply, and checkable or near-checkable bank deposits aren't part of the monetary base. In normal times, most of the monetary base actually consists of currency in circulation, which also makes up about half of the money supply.

FIGURE 70-4 **The Monetary Base and the Money Supply**

The monetary base is equal to bank reserves plus currency in circulation. It is different from the money supply, consisting mainly of checkable or near-checkable bank deposits plus currency in circulation. Each dollar of bank reserves backs several dollars of bank deposits, making the money supply larger than the monetary base.

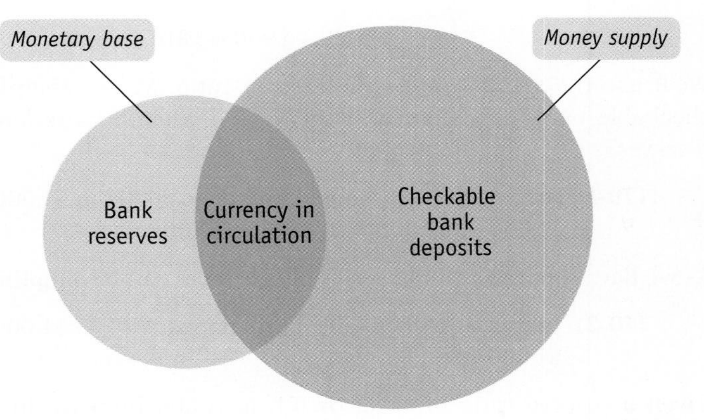

Now we can formally define the **money multiplier:** it's the ratio of the money supply to the monetary base. In normal times the money multiplier in the United States, using M1 as our measure of money, has fluctuated between 3.0 and 1.5. During the recession of 2007–2009, it fell to about 0.7. Even in normal times, that's a lot smaller than 1/0.1 = 10, the money multiplier in a checkable-deposits-only system with a reserve ratio of 10% (the minimum required ratio for most checkable deposits in the United States).

The reason the actual money multiplier is so small arises from the fact that people hold significant amounts of cash, and a dollar of currency in circulation, unlike a dollar in reserves, doesn't support multiple dollars of the money supply. In fact, currency in circulation normally accounts for more than 90% of the monetary base. However, in April 2013, currency in circulation was $1,107 billion, compared with a monetary base of $3,061 billion—just about 36%. What had happened?

Notice that earlier we said "in normal times." As we'll see in upcoming modules, a very abnormal situation developed after Lehman Brothers, a key financial institution, failed in September 2008. Banks, seeing few opportunities for safe, profitable lending, began parking large sums at the Federal Reserve in the form of deposits—deposits that counted as part of the monetary base. As a result, currency in circulation in April 2013 made up only 36% of the monetary base, and the monetary base was actually larger than M1, with the money multiplier therefore less than 1.

The **money multiplier** is the ratio of the money supply to the monetary base.

MODULE 70 Review

Solutions appear at the back of the book.

Check Your Understanding

1. Suppose you are a depositor at First Street Bank. You hear a rumor that the bank has suffered serious losses on its loans. Every depositor knows that the rumor isn't true, but each thinks that most other depositors believe the rumor. Why, in the absence of deposit insurance, could this lead to a bank run? How does deposit insurance change the situation?

2. A con artist has a great idea: he'll open a bank without investing any capital and lend all the deposits at high interest rates to real estate developers. If the real estate market booms, the loans will be repaid and he'll make high profits. If the real estate market goes bust, the loans won't be repaid and the bank will fail—but he will not lose any of his own wealth. How would modern bank regulation frustrate his scheme?

3. Assume that total reserves are equal to $200 and total checkable bank deposits are equal to $1,000. Also assume that the public does not hold any currency and banks hold no excess reserves. Now suppose that the required reserve ratio falls from 20% to 10%. Trace out how this leads to an expansion in bank deposits.

4. Take the example of Silas depositing his $1,000 in cash into First Street Bank and assume that the required reserve ratio is 10%. But now assume that each recipient of a bank loan keeps half the loan in cash and deposits the rest. Trace out the resulting expansion in the money supply through at least three rounds of deposits.

Multiple-Choice Questions

1. Bank reserves include which of the following?
   - I. currency in bank vaults
   - II. bank deposits held in accounts at the Federal Reserve
   - III. customer deposits in bank checking accounts

   a. I only
   b. II only
   c. III only
   d. I and II only
   e. I, II, and III

2. The fraction of bank deposits actually held as reserves is the
   a. reserve ratio.
   b. required reserve ratio.
   c. excess reserve ratio.
   d. reserve requirement.
   e. monetary base.

3. Bank regulation includes which of the following?
   - I. deposit insurance
   - II. capital requirements
   - III. reserve requirements

   a. I only
   b. II only
   c. III only
   d. I and II
   e. I, II, and III

4. Which of the following changes would be the most likely to reduce the size of the money multiplier?
   a. a decrease in the required reserve ratio
   b. a decrease in excess reserves
   c. an increase in cash holding by consumers
   d. a decrease in bank runs
   e. an increase in deposit insurance

5. The monetary base equals
   a. currency in circulation.
   b. reserves held by banks.
   c. currency in circulation – reserves held by banks.
   d. currency in circulation + reserves held by banks.
   e. currency in circulation/reserves held by banks.

Critical-Thinking Questions

Assume that the required reserve ratio is 5% to answer the following.

1. If a bank has deposits of $100,000 and holds $10,000 as reserves, how much are its excess reserves? Explain.

2. If a bank holds no excess reserves and it receives a new deposit of $1,000, how much of that $1,000 can the bank lend out and how much is the bank required to add to its reserves? Explain.

3. By how much can an increase in excess reserves of $2,000 change the money supply in a checkable-deposits-only system? Explain.

MODULE 71 The Federal Reserve System

WHAT YOU WILL LEARN

1. The structure of the Federal Reserve System
2. The history of the Federal Reserve System
3. How the Federal Reserve has responded to major financial crises

Who's in charge of ensuring that banks maintain enough reserves? Who decides how large the monetary base will be? The answer, in the United States, is an institution known as the Federal Reserve (or, informally, as "the Fed"). The Federal Reserve is a **central bank**—an institution that oversees and regulates the banking system and controls the monetary base. Other central banks include the Bank of England, the Bank of Japan, and the European Central Bank, or ECB. The ECB acts as a common central bank for 18 European countries.

The Structure of the Fed

The legal status of the Fed, which was created in 1913, is unusual: it is not exactly part of the U.S. government, but it is not really a private institution either. Strictly speaking, the Federal Reserve System consists of two parts: the Board of Governors and the 12 regional Federal Reserve Banks.

The Board of Governors, which oversees the entire system from its offices in Washington, D.C., is constituted like a government agency: its seven members are appointed by the president and must be approved by the Senate. However, they are appointed for 14-year terms.

Although the chair is appointed more frequently—every four years—it is traditional for the chair to be reappointed and serve much longer terms. For example, William McChesney Martin was chair of the Fed from 1951 until 1970. Alan Greenspan, appointed in 1987, served as the Fed's chair until 2006. By comparison, Ben Bernanke's tenure as chair, from 2006 to early 2014, was on the brief side.

The 12 Federal Reserve Banks each serve a region of the country, providing various banking and supervisory services. One of their jobs, for example, is to audit the books of private-sector banks to ensure their financial health. Each regional bank is run by a board of directors chosen from the local banking and business community. The

A **central bank** is an institution that oversees and regulates the banking system and controls the monetary base.

FIGURE 71-1 The Federal Reserve System

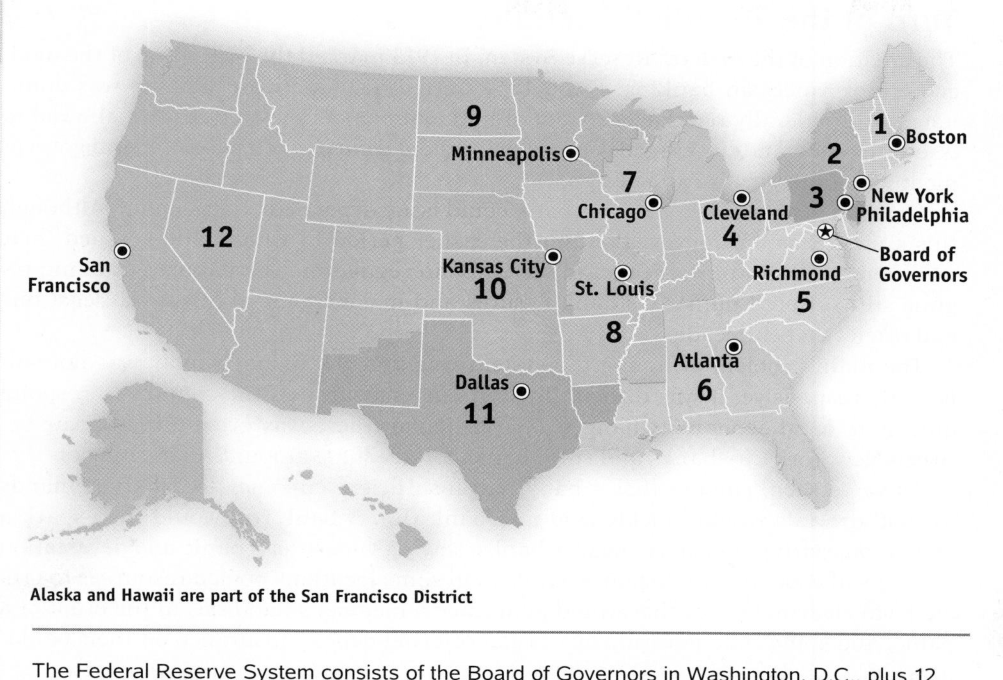

The Federal Reserve System consists of the Board of Governors in Washington, D.C., plus 12 regional Federal Reserve Banks. This map shows each of the 12 Federal Reserve districts.
Source: Board of Governors of the Federal Reserve System.

Federal Reserve Bank of New York plays a special role: it carries out *open-market operations,* usually the main tool of monetary policy. Figure 71-1 shows the 12 Federal Reserve districts and the city in which each regional Federal Reserve Bank is located.

John Keith/Shutterstock

Decisions about monetary policy are made by the Federal Open Market Committee, which consists of the Board of Governors plus five of the regional bank presidents. The president of the Federal Reserve Bank of New York is always on the committee, and the other four seats rotate among the 11 other regional bank presidents. The chair of the Board of Governors normally also serves as the chair of the Federal Open Market Committee.

The effect of this complex structure is to create an institution that is ultimately accountable to the voting public because the Board of Governors is chosen by elected officials. But the long terms served by board members, as well as the indirectness of their appointment process, largely insulate them from short-term political pressures.

The Evolution of the American Banking System

Up to this point in the section, we have been describing the U.S. banking system and how it works. To fully understand that system, however, it is helpful to understand how and why it was created—a story that is closely intertwined with the story of how and when things went wrong. For the key elements of twenty-first-century U.S. banking weren't created out of thin air: efforts to change both the regulations that govern banking and the Federal Reserve System that began in 2008 have propelled financial reform to the forefront. This reform promises to continue reshaping the financial system well into future years.

The Crisis in American Banking at the Turn of the Twentieth Century

The creation of the Federal Reserve System in 1913 marked the beginning of the modern era of American banking. From 1864 until 1913, American banking was dominated by a federally regulated system of national banks. They alone were allowed to issue currency, and the currency notes they issued were printed by the federal government with uniform size and design.

How much currency a national bank could issue depended on its capital. Although this system was an improvement on the earlier period in which banks issued their own notes with no uniformity and virtually no regulation, the national banking regime still suffered numerous bank failures and major financial crises—at least one and often two per decade.

The main problem afflicting the system was that the money supply was not sufficiently responsive: it was difficult to shift currency around the country to respond quickly to local economic changes. (In particular, there was often a tug-of-war between New York City banks and rural banks for adequate amounts of currency.)

As we've seen, rumors that a bank had insufficient currency to satisfy demands for withdrawals would quickly lead to a bank run. A bank run would then spark a contagion, setting off runs at nearby banks, sowing widespread panic and devastation in the local economy. In response, bankers in some locations pooled resources to create local clearinghouses that would guarantee a member's liabilities in the event of a panic, and some state governments began offering deposit insurance on their banks' deposits.

However, the cause of the Panic of 1907 was different from those of previous crises; in fact, its cause was eerily similar to the roots of the 2008 crisis. Ground zero of the 1907 panic was New York City, but the consequences devastated the entire country, leading to a deep four-year recession.

The crisis originated in institutions in New York known as *trusts,* bank-like institutions that accepted deposits but that were originally intended to manage only inheritances and estates for wealthy clients. Because these trusts were supposed to engage only in low-risk activities, they were less regulated, had lower reserve requirements, and had lower cash reserves than national banks.

In both the Panic of 1907 and the financial crisis of 2008, large losses from risky speculation destabilized the banking system.

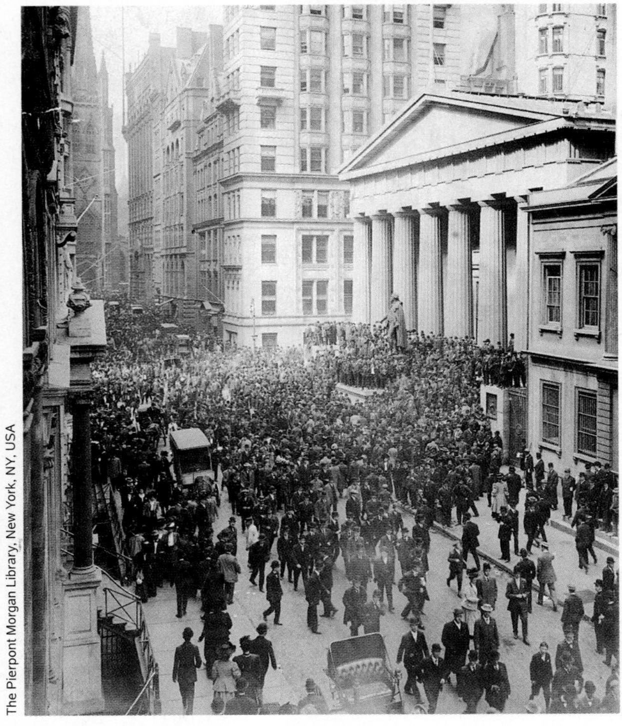

The Pierpont Morgan Library, New York, NY, USA

However, as the American economy boomed during the first decade of the twentieth century, trusts began speculating in real estate and the stock market, areas forbidden to national banks. Less regulated than national banks, trusts were able to pay their depositors higher returns. Yet trusts took a free ride on national banks' reputation for soundness, with depositors considering them equally safe.

As a result, trusts grew rapidly: by 1907, the total assets of trusts in New York City were as large as those of national banks. Meanwhile, the trusts declined to join the New York Clearinghouse, a consortium of New York City national banks that guaranteed one another's soundness; that would have required the trusts to hold higher cash reserves, reducing their profits.

The Panic of 1907 began with the failure of the Knickerbocker Trust, a large New York City trust that failed when it suffered massive losses in unsuccessful stock market speculation. Quickly, other New York trusts came under pressure, and frightened depositors began queuing in long lines to withdraw their funds. The New York Clearinghouse declined to step in and lend to the trusts, and even healthy trusts came under serious assault.

Within two days, a dozen major trusts had gone under. Credit markets froze, the stock market fell dramatically as stock traders were unable to get credit to finance their trades, and business confidence evaporated.

Fortunately, one of New York City's wealthiest men, the banker J. P. Morgan, quickly stepped in to stop the panic. Understanding that the crisis would spread and soon engulf healthy institutions, trusts and banks alike, he worked with other bankers, wealthy men such as John D. Rockefeller, and the U.S. Secretary of the Treasury to shore up the reserves of banks and trusts to withstand the onslaught of withdrawals. Once people were assured that they could withdraw their money, the panic ceased.

Although the panic itself lasted little more than a week, it and the stock market collapse decimated the economy. A four-year recession ensued, with production falling 11% and unemployment rising from 3% to 8%.

Responding to Banking Crises: The Creation of the Federal Reserve

Concerns over frequent banking crises and the unprecedented role of J. P. Morgan in saving the financial system prompted the federal government to initiate banking reform. In 1913 the national banking system was eliminated and the Federal Reserve System was created as a way to compel all deposit-taking institutions to hold adequate reserves and open their accounts to inspection by regulators.

The Panic of 1907 convinced many that the time for centralized control of bank reserves had come. In addition, the Federal Reserve was given the sole right to issue currency in order to make the money supply sufficiently responsive to satisfy economic conditions around the country.

THE EFFECTIVENESS OF THE FEDERAL RESERVE SYSTEM Although the Federal Reserve System standardized and centralized the holding of bank reserves, it did not eliminate the potential for bank runs because banks' reserves were still less than the total value of their deposits. The potential for more bank runs became a reality during the Great Depression. Plunging commodity prices hit American farmers particularly hard, precipitating a series of bank runs in 1930, 1931, and 1933, each of which started at midwestern banks and then spread throughout the country.

After the failure of a particularly large bank in 1930, federal officials realized that the economy-wide effects compelled them to take a less hands-off approach and to intervene more vigorously. In 1932, the Reconstruction Finance Corporation (RFC) was established and given the authority to make loans to banks in order to stabilize the banking sector.

Also, the Glass-Steagall Act of 1933, which increased the ability of banks to borrow from the Federal Reserve System, was passed. A loan to a leading Chicago bank from the Federal Reserve appears to have stopped a major banking crisis in 1932. However, the beast had not yet been tamed. Banks became fearful of borrowing from the RFC because doing so signaled weakness to the public.

During the midst of the catastrophic bank run of 1933, the new U.S. president, Franklin Delano Roosevelt, was inaugurated. He immediately declared a "bank holiday," closing all banks until regulators could get a handle on the problem.

In March 1933, emergency measures were adopted that gave the RFC extraordinary powers to stabilize and restructure the banking industry by providing capital to banks either by loans or by outright purchases of bank shares. With the new regulations, regulators closed nonviable banks and recapitalized viable ones by allowing the RFC to buy preferred shares in banks (shares that gave the U.S. government more rights than regular shareholders) and by greatly expanding banks' ability to borrow from the Federal Reserve.

By 1933, the RFC had invested over $17 billion (2013 dollars) in bank capital—one-third of the total capital of all banks in the United States at that time—and purchased shares in almost one-half of all banks. The RFC loaned more than $34 billion (2013 dollars) to banks during this period.

Economic historians uniformly agree that the banking crises of the early 1930s greatly exacerbated the severity of the Great Depression, rendering monetary policy ineffective as the banking sector broke down and currency, withdrawn from banks and stashed under beds, reduced the money supply.

A **commercial bank** accepts deposits and is covered by deposit insurance.

An **investment bank** trades in financial assets and is not covered by deposit insurance.

A **savings and loan (thrift)** is another type of deposit-taking bank, usually specialized in issuing home loans.

THE GLASS-STEAGALL ACT Although the powerful actions of the RFC stabilized the banking industry, new legislation was needed to prevent future banking crises. The Glass-Steagall Act separated banks into two categories: **commercial banks,** depository banks that accepted deposits and were covered by deposit insurance, and **investment banks,** which engaged in creating and trading financial assets such as stocks and corporate bonds but were not covered by deposit insurance because their activities were considered more risky.

Regulation Q prevented commercial banks from paying interest on checking accounts, in the belief that this would promote unhealthy competition between banks. In addition, investment banks were much more lightly regulated than commercial banks. The most important measure for the prevention of bank runs, however, was the adoption of federal deposit insurance (with an original limit of $2,500 per deposit).

These measures were clearly successful, and the United States enjoyed a long period of financial and banking stability. As memories of the bad old days dimmed, Depression-era bank regulations were lifted. In 1980 Regulation Q was eliminated, and by 1999, the Glass-Steagall Act had been so weakened that offering services like trading financial assets were no longer off-limits to commercial banks.

The Savings and Loan Crisis of the 1980s

Along with banks, the banking industry also included **savings and loans** (also called S&Ls or **thrifts**), institutions designed to accept savings and turn them into long-term mortgages for home-buyers. S&Ls were covered by federal deposit insurance and were tightly regulated for safety. However, trouble hit in the 1970s, as high inflation led savers to withdraw their funds from low-interest-paying S&L accounts and put them into higher-interest-paying money market accounts. In addition, the high inflation rate severely eroded the value of the S&Ls' assets, the long-term mortgages they held on their books.

In order to improve S&Ls' competitive position vis-à-vis banks, Congress eased regulations to allow S&Ls to undertake riskier investments in addition to long-term home mortgages. However, the new freedom did not bring with it increased oversight, leaving S&Ls with less oversight than banks. Unsurprisingly, during the real estate boom of the 1970s and 1980s, S&Ls engaged in overly risky real estate lending. There was also corruption as some S&L executives used their institutions as private piggy banks.

Unfortunately, during the late 1970s and early 1980s, political interference from Congress kept insolvent S&Ls open when a bank in a comparable situation would have been quickly shut down by regulators. By the early 1980s, many S&Ls had failed. Because accounts were covered by federal deposit insurance, the liabilities of a failed S&L became liabilities of the federal government, and depositors had to be paid from taxpayer funds. From 1986 through 1995, the government closed over 1,000 failed S&Ls, costing U.S. taxpayers over $124 billion dollars.

In a classic case of shutting the barn door after the horse has escaped, in 1989 Congress put in place comprehensive oversight of S&L activities. It also empowered Fannie Mae and Freddie Mac to take over much of the home mortgage lending previously done by S&Ls. Fannie Mae and Freddie Mac are quasi-governmental agencies created during the Great Depression to make homeownership more affordable for low- and moderate-income households. It has been calculated that the S&L crisis helped cause a steep slowdown in the finance and real estate industries, leading to the recession of the early 1990s.

Back to the Future: The Financial Crisis of 2008

The financial crisis of 2008 shared features of previous crises. Like the Panic of 1907 and the S&L crisis, it involved institutions that were not as strictly regulated as deposit-taking banks, as well as excessive speculation. Like the crises of the early 1930s, it involved a U.S. government that was reluctant to take aggressive action until the scale of the devastation became clear. In addition, by the late 1990s, advances in technology and financial innovation had created yet another systemic weakness that played a central role in 2008. The story of Long-Term Capital Management, or LTCM, highlights these problems.

A financial institution engages in **leverage** when it finances its investments with borrowed funds.

The **balance sheet effect** is the reduction in a firm's net worth from falling asset prices.

A **vicious cycle of deleveraging** takes place when asset sales to cover losses produce negative balance sheet effects on other firms and force creditors to call in their loans, forcing sales of more assets and causing further declines in asset prices.

LONG-TERM CAPITAL (MIS)MANAGEMENT Created in 1994, LTCM was a *hedge fund*, a private investment partnership open only to wealthy individuals and institutions. Hedge funds are virtually unregulated, allowing them to make much riskier investments than mutual funds, which are open to the average investor. Using vast amounts of **leverage**—that is, borrowed money—in order to increase its returns, LTCM used sophisticated computer models to make money by taking advantage of small differences in asset prices in global financial markets to buy at a lower price and sell at a higher price. In one year, LTCM made a return as high as 40%.

LTCM was also heavily involved in *derivatives,* complex financial instruments that are constructed—derived—from the obligations of more basic financial assets. Derivatives are popular investment tools because they are cheaper to trade than basic financial assets and can be constructed to suit a buyer's or seller's particular needs. Yet their complexity can make it extremely hard to measure their value. LTCM believed that its computer models allowed it to accurately gauge the risk in the huge bets that it was undertaking in derivatives using borrowed money.

However, LTCM's computer models hadn't factored in a series of financial crises in Asia and in Russia during 1997 and 1998. Through its large borrowing, LTCM had become such a big player in global financial markets that attempts to sell its assets depressed the prices of what it was trying to sell. As the markets fell around the world and LTCM's panic-stricken investors demanded the return of their funds, LTCM's losses mounted as it tried to sell assets to satisfy those demands. Quickly, its operations collapsed because it could no longer borrow money and other parties refused to trade with it. Financial markets around the world froze in panic.

The Federal Reserve realized that allowing LTCM's remaining assets to be sold at panic-stricken prices presented a grave risk to the entire financial system through the **balance sheet effect:** as sales of assets by LTCM depressed asset prices all over the world, other firms would see the value of their balance sheets fall as assets held on these balance sheets declined in value.

Moreover, falling asset prices meant the value of assets held by borrowers on their balance sheet would fall below a critical threshold, leading to a default on the terms of their credit contracts and forcing creditors to call in their loans. This in turn would lead to more sales of assets as borrowers tried to raise cash to repay their loans, more credit defaults, and more loans called in, creating a **vicious cycle of deleveraging.**

The Federal Reserve Bank of New York arranged a $3.625 billion bailout of LTCM in 1998, in which other private institutions took on shares of LTCM's assets and obligations, liquidated them in an orderly manner, and eventually turned a small profit. Quick action by the Federal Reserve Bank of New York prevented LTCM from sparking a contagion, yet virtually all of LTCM's investors were wiped out.

SUBPRIME LENDING AND THE HOUSING BUBBLE After the LTCM crisis, U.S. financial markets stabilized. They remained more or less stable even as stock prices fell sharply from 2000 to 2002 and the U.S. economy went into recession. During the recovery from the 2001 recession, however, the seeds for another financial crisis were planted.

The story begins with low interest rates: by 2003, U.S. interest rates were at historically low levels, partly because of Federal Reserve policy and partly because of large inflows of capital from other countries, especially China. These low interest rates helped cause a boom in housing, which in turn led the U.S. economy out of recession. As housing boomed,

The New Yorker Collection 2008 Leo Cullum from cartoonbank.com. All Rights Reserved.

"Honey, we're homeless."

Subprime lending is lending to home buyers who don't meet the usual criteria for being able to afford their payments.

In **securitization** a pool of loans is assembled and shares of that pool are sold to investors.

however, financial institutions began taking on growing risks—risks that were not well understood.

Traditionally, people were able to borrow money to buy homes only if they had sufficient income to meet the mortgage payments. Making home loans to people who didn't meet the usual criteria for borrowing, called **subprime lending,** was only a minor part of overall lending. But in the booming housing market of 2003–2006, subprime lending started to seem like a safe bet. Since housing prices kept rising, borrowers who couldn't make their mortgage payments could always pay off their mortgages, if necessary, by selling their homes. As a result, subprime lending exploded.

Who was making these subprime loans? For the most part, it wasn't traditional banks lending out depositors' money. Instead, most of the loans were made by "loan originators," who quickly sold mortgages to other investors. These sales were made possible by a process known as **securitization:** financial institutions assembled pools of loans and sold shares in the income from these pools. These shares were considered relatively safe investments since it was considered unlikely that large numbers of home-buyers would default on their payments at the same time.

But that's exactly what happened. The housing boom turned out to be a bubble, and when home prices started falling in late 2006, many subprime borrowers were unable either to meet their mortgage payments or sell their houses for enough to pay off their mortgages. As a result, investors in securities backed by subprime mortgages started taking heavy losses. Many of the mortgage-backed assets were held by financial institutions, including banks and other institutions playing bank-like roles. Like the trusts that played a key role in the Panic of 1907, these "nonbank banks" were less regulated than commercial banks, which allowed them to offer higher returns to investors but left them extremely vulnerable in a crisis. Mortgage-related losses, in turn, led to a collapse of trust in the financial system.

Figure 71-2 shows one measure of this loss of trust: the TED spread, which is the difference between the interest rate on three-month loans that banks make to each other and the interest rate the federal government pays on three-month bonds. Since government bonds are considered extremely safe, the TED spread shows how much risk banks think they're taking on when lending to each other. Normally, the spread is around a quarter of a percentage point, but it shot up in August 2007 and surged to an unprecedented 4.58 percentage points in October 2008 before returning to more normal levels in mid-2009.

FIGURE 71-2 The TED Spread

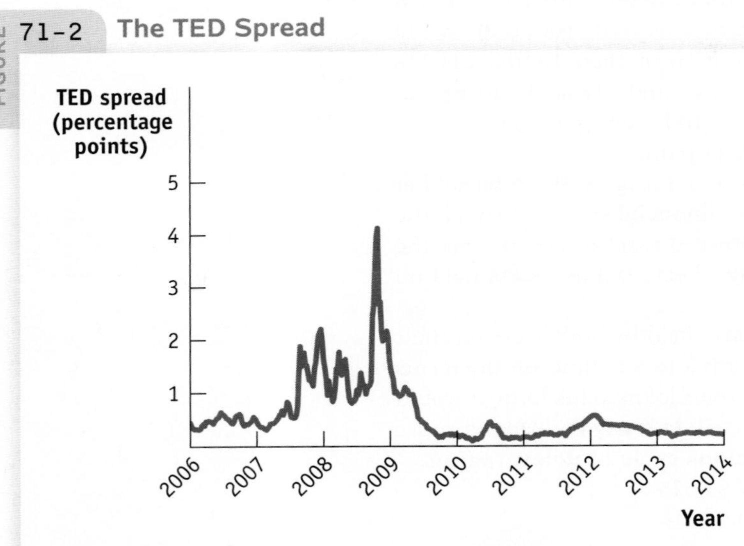

The TED spread is the difference between the interest rate at which banks lend to each other and the interest rate on U.S. government debt. It's widely used as a measure of financial stress. The TED spread soared as a result of the financial crisis of 2007–2008.
Source: Federal Reserve Bank of St. Louis.

CRISIS AND RESPONSE The collapse of trust in the financial system, combined with the large losses suffered by financial firms, led to a severe cycle of deleveraging and a credit crunch for the economy as a whole. Firms found it difficult to borrow, even for short-term operations; individuals found home loans unavailable and credit card limits reduced.

Overall, the negative economic effect of the financial crisis bore a distinct and troubling resemblance to the effects of the banking crisis of the early 1930s, which helped cause the Great Depression. Policy makers noticed the resemblance and tried to prevent a repeat performance. Beginning in August 2007, the Federal Reserve engaged in a series of efforts to provide cash to the financial system, lending funds to a widening range of institutions and buying private-sector debt. The Fed and the

Treasury Department also stepped in to rescue individual firms that were deemed too crucial to be allowed to fail, such as the investment bank Bear Stearns and the insurance company AIG.

In September 2008, however, policy makers decided that one major investment bank, Lehman Brothers, could be allowed to fail. They quickly regretted the decision. Within days of Lehman's failure, widespread panic gripped the financial markets, as illustrated by the late surge in the TED spread shown in Figure 71-2. In response to the intensified crisis, the U.S. government intervened further to support the financial system, as the U.S. Treasury began "injecting" capital into banks. Injecting capital, in practice, meant that the U.S. government would supply cash to banks in return for shares—in effect, partially nationalizing the financial system.

The crisis of 2008 led to major changes in the financial system, the largest changes since the 1930s. The crisis raised new questions about the appropriate scope of safety nets and regulations and, like the crises preceding it, exerted a powerful negative effect on the rest of the economy. There is a detailed discussion of the crisis and its impact in Module 78.

Official White House Photo by Pete Souza

Like FDR, President Obama was faced with a major financial crisis upon taking office.

ECONOMICS IN ACTION

REGULATION AFTER THE 2008 CRISIS

In 2010, President Obama signed the Wall Street Reform and Consumer Protection Act—generally known as Dodd-Frank, after its sponsors in the Senate and House, respectively—into law. It was the biggest financial reform enacted since the 1930s—not surprising given that the nation had just gone through the worst financial crisis since the 1930s. How did Dodd-Frank change regulation?

For the most part, it left regulation of traditional deposit-taking banks more or less as it was. The main change facing these banks was the creation of a new agency, the Bureau of Consumer Financial Protection, whose mission was to protect borrowers from being exploited through seemingly attractive financial deals they didn't understand.

The major changes came in the regulation of financial institutions other than banks—institutions that, as the fall of Lehman Brothers showed, could trigger banking crises.

The new law gave a special government committee, the Financial Stability Oversight Council, the right to designate certain institutions as "systemically important" even if they weren't ordinary deposit-taking banks. These systemically important institutions would be subjected to bank-style regulation, including relatively high capital requirements and limits on the kinds of risks they could take. In addition, the federal government would acquire "resolution authority," meaning the right to seize troubled financial institutions in much the same way that it routinely takes over troubled banks.

Thinkstock

Dodd-Frank was an attempt to extend the spirit of old-fashioned bank regulation to today's more complex financial system.

Beyond this, the law established new rules on the trading of derivatives: most derivatives would have to be bought and sold on exchanges, where everyone could observe their prices and the volume of transactions. The idea was to make the risks taken by financial institutions more transparent. Will Dodd-Frank succeed in heading off future banking crises? Stay tuned.

MODULE 71 Review

Solutions appear at the back of the book.

Check Your Understanding

1. What are the similarities between the Panic of 1907, the S&L crisis, and the crisis of 2008?
2. Why did the creation of the Federal Reserve fail to prevent the bank runs of the Great Depression? What measures did stop the bank runs?
3. Describe the balance sheet effect. Describe the vicious cycle of deleveraging. Why is it necessary for the government to step in to halt a vicious cycle of deleveraging?

Multiple-Choice Questions

1. Which of the following contributed to the creation of the Federal Reserve System?
   - I. the bank panic of 1907
   - II. the Great Depression
   - III. the savings and loan crisis of the 1980s

   a. I only
   b. II only
   c. III only
   d. I and II only
   e. I, II, and III
2. Which of the following is a part of both the Federal Reserve System and the federal government?
   a. the Federal Reserve Board of Governors
   b. the 12 regional Federal Reserve Banks
   c. the Reconstruction Finance Corporation
   d. commercial banks
   e. the Treasury Department
3. Which of the following is NOT a role of the Federal Reserve System?
   a. controlling bank reserves
   b. printing currency (Federal Reserve notes)
   c. carrying out monetary policy
   d. supervising and regulating banks
   e. holding reserves for commercial banks
4. Who oversees the Federal Reserve System?
   a. the presidents of the Regional Federal Reserve Banks
   b. the president of the United States
   c. the Federal Open Market Committee
   d. the Board of Governors of the Federal Reserve System
   e. the Reconstruction Finance Corporation
5. Which of the following contributed to the financial crisis of 2008?
   a. subprime lending
   b. securitization
   c. deleveraging
   d. low interest rates leading to a housing boom
   e. all of the above

Critical-Thinking Questions

Answer the following questions about the Board of Governors of the Federal Reserve System.

1. What does the Board of Governors of the Federal Reserve System do?
2. How many members serve on the group?
3. Who appoints members?
4. How long do members serve?
5. Why do they serve a term of this length?
6. How long does the chair serve?

BUSINESS CASE: The Perfect Gift: Cash or a Gift Card?

Jeff Greenberg/Alamy

Over the past few years, more and more people have been buying gift cards, prepaid plastic cards issued by a retailer that can be redeemed for merchandise.

Several websites are now making a profit from the fact that gift card recipients are often willing to sell their cards at a discount—sometimes at a fairly sizable discount. Cashcard.com is one such site. At the time of writing, it offers to pay cash to a seller of a Whole Foods gift card equivalent to 90% of the card's face value (for example, the seller of a card with a value of $100 would receive $90 in cash). But it offers cash equal to only 70% of a Gap card's face value.

Cashcard.com profits by reselling the card for more than what it paid; for example, it buys a Gap card for 70% of its face value and then resells it for 88% of its face value.

Many consumers may be willing to sell at a sizable discount to turn their gift cards into cash, but retailers are eager to promote the use of gift cards over cash. According to GiftCardUSA.com, 5% to 15% of gift cards are never redeemed. Those unredeemed dollars accrue to the retailer, making gift cards a highly profitable line of business. The Tower Group, a financial consulting firm, has estimated that the value of "breakage," the amount of a gift card that accrues to the retailer rather than to the card holder, amounts to billions of dollars annually.

How does breakage occur? People lose cards. Or they spend only $47 of a $50 gift card, figuring it's not worth the effort to return to the store to spend that last $3. Also, retailers impose fees on the use of the card or make cards subject to expiration dates, which customers forget about. And if a retailer goes out of business, the value of any outstanding gift cards disappears with it.

In addition to breakage, retailers benefit when customers intent on using up the value of their gift card find that it is too difficult to spend exactly the amount of the card; instead, they spend more than the card's face value, sometimes even spending more than they would have in the absence of the gift card.

Gift cards are so beneficial to retailers that those which used to reward customer loyalty with rebate checks have largely switched to dispensing gift cards. As one commentator noted in explaining why retailers prefer gift cards to rebate checks, "Nobody neglects to spend cash."

Questions for Thought

1. Why are gift card owners willing to sell their cards for a cash amount less than their face value?
2. Why do gift cards for retailers like Walmart, Home Depot, and Whole Foods sell for a smaller discount than those for retailers like the Gap and Aeropostale?
3. Use your answer from Question 2 to explain why cash never "sells" at a discount.
4. Explain why retailers prefer to reward loyal customers with gift cards instead of rebate checks.
5. Congress has enacted legislation restricting the ability of retailers to impose fees and expiration dates on their gift cards and mandating greater disclosure of their terms. Why do you think Congress did this?

SECTION 22 REVIEW

Summary

Defining and Measuring Money

1. **Money** is any asset that can easily be used to purchase goods and services. **Currency in circulation** and **checkable bank deposits** are both considered part of the **money supply.** Money plays three roles: it is a **medium of exchange** used for transactions, a **store of value** that holds purchasing power over time, and a **unit of account** in which prices are stated.
2. Over time, **commodity money,** which consists of goods possessing value aside from their role as money, such as gold and silver coins, was replaced by **commodity-backed money,** such as paper currency backed by gold. Today the dollar is pure **fiat money,** whose value derives solely from its official role.
3. The Federal Reserve calculates two measures of the money supply. M1 is the narrowest **monetary aggregate;** it contains only currency in circulation, traveler's checks, and checkable bank deposits. M2 includes a wider range of assets called **near-moneys,** mainly other forms of bank deposits, that can easily be converted into checkable bank deposits.

Banking and Money Creation

4. Banks allow depositors immediate access to their funds, but they also lend out most of the funds deposited in their care. To meet demands for cash, they maintain **bank reserves** composed of both currency held in vaults and deposits at the Federal Reserve. The **reserve ratio** is the ratio of bank reserves to bank deposits. A **T-account** summarizes a bank's financial position, with loans and reserves counted as assets, and deposits counted as liabilities.
5. Banks have sometimes been subject to **bank runs,** most notably in the early 1930s. To avert this danger, depositors are now protected by **deposit insurance,** bank owners face capital requirements that reduce the incentive to make overly risky loans with depositors' funds, and banks must satisfy **reserve requirements,** a legally mandated **required reserve ratio.**
6. When currency is deposited in a bank, it starts a multiplier process in which banks lend out **excess reserves,** leading to an increase in the money supply—so banks create money. If the entire money supply consisted of checkable bank deposits, the money supply would be equal to the value of reserves divided by the reserve ratio. In reality, much of the **monetary base** consists of currency in circulation, and the **money multiplier** is the ratio of the money supply to the monetary base.

The Federal Reserve System

7. In response to the Panic of 1907, the Fed was created to centralize holding of reserves, inspect banks' books, and make the money supply sufficiently responsive to varying economic conditions.
8. The Great Depression sparked widespread bank runs in the early 1930s, which greatly worsened and lengthened the depth of the Depression. Federal deposit insurance was created, and the government recapitalized banks by lending to them and by buying shares of banks. By 1933, banks had been separated into two categories: **commercial** (covered by deposit insurance) and **investment** (not covered). Public acceptance of deposit insurance finally stopped the bank runs of the Great Depression.
9. The **savings and loan (thrift)** crisis of the 1980s arose because insufficiently regulated S&Ls engaged in overly risky speculation and incurred huge losses. Depositors in failed S&Ls were compensated with taxpayer funds because they were covered by deposit insurance. However, the crisis caused steep losses in the financial and real estate sectors, resulting in a recession in the early 1990s.
10. During the mid-1990s, the hedge fund LTCM used huge amounts of **leverage** to speculate in global financial markets, incurred massive losses, and collapsed. LTCM was so large that, in selling assets to cover its losses, it caused **balance sheet effects** for firms around the world, leading to the prospect of a **vicious cycle of deleveraging.** As a result, credit markets around the world froze. The New York Fed coordinated a private bailout of LTCM and revived world credit markets.
11. **Subprime lending** during the U.S. housing bubble of the mid-2000s spread through the financial system via **securitization.** When the bubble burst, massive losses by banks and nonbank financial institutions led to widespread collapse in the financial system. To prevent another Great Depression, the Fed and the U.S. Treasury expanded lending to bank and nonbank institutions, provided capital through the purchase of bank shares, and purchased private debt. Because much of the crisis originated in nontraditional bank institutions, the crisis of 2008 raised the question of whether a wider safety net and broader regulation were needed in the financial sector.

Key Terms

Money, p. 718
Currency in circulation, p. 719
Checkable bank deposits, p. 719
Money supply, p. 719
Medium of exchange, p. 719
Store of value, p. 720
Unit of account, p. 720
Commodity money, p. 720
Commodity-backed money, p. 720
Fiat money, p. 721
Monetary aggregate, p. 722
Near-moneys, p. 722
Bank reserves, p. 725
T-account, p. 726
Reserve ratio, p. 726
Required reserve ratio, p. 726
Bank run, p. 727
Deposit insurance, p. 728
Reserve requirements, p. 728
Discount window, p. 728
Excess reserves, p. 731
Monetary base, p. 731
Money multiplier, p. 732
Central bank, p. 734
Commercial bank, p. 738
Investment bank, p. 738
Savings and loan (thrift), p. 738
Leverage, p. 739
Balance sheet effect, p. 739
Vicious cycle of deleveraging, p. 739
Subprime lending, p. 740
Securitization, p. 740

Problems

1. For each of the following transactions, what is the initial effect (increase or decrease) on M1? On M2?
   a. You sell a few shares of stock and put the proceeds into your savings account.
   b. You sell a few shares of stock and put the proceeds into your checking account.
   c. You transfer money from your savings account to your checking account.
   d. You discover $0.25 under the floor mat in your car and deposit it in your checking account.
   e. You discover $0.25 under the floor mat in your car and deposit it in your savings account.

2. There are three types of money: commodity money, commodity-backed money, and fiat money. Which type of money is used in each of the following situations?
   a. Bottles of rum were used to pay for goods in colonial Australia.
   b. Salt was used in many European countries as a medium of exchange.
   c. For a brief time, Germany used paper money (the "Rye Mark") that could be redeemed for a certain amount of rye, a type of grain.
   d. The town of Ithaca, New York, prints its own currency, the Ithaca HOURS, which can be used to purchase local goods and services.

3. The following table shows the components of M1 and M2 in billions of dollars for the month of December in the years 2001 to 2011 as published in the 2012 Economic Report of the President. Complete the table by calculating M1, M2, currency in circulation as a percentage of M1, and currency in circulation as a percentage of M2. What trends or patterns about M1, M2, currency in circulation as a percentage of M1, and currency in circulation as a percentage of M2 do you see? What might account for these trends?

Year	Currency in circulation	Traveler's checks	Checkable deposits	Savings deposits	Time deposits	Money market funds	M1	M2	Currency in circulation as a percentage of M1	Currency in circulation as a percentage of M2
2001	$581.1	$8.0	$592.9	$2,309.5	$974.5	$962.5	?	?	?	?
2002	626.2	7.8	585.7	2,773.4	894.5	887.5	?	?	?	?
2003	662.5	7.7	636.2	3,162.8	817.8	777.0	?	?	?	?
2004	697.7	7.6	671.1	3,508.8	827.9	694.7	?	?	?	?
2005	724.1	7.2	643.5	3,606.0	993.1	699.4	?	?	?	?
2006	749.6	6.7	610.0	3,694.6	1,205.3	799.0	?	?	?	?
2007	759.7	6.3	607.6	3,872.6	1,275.0	972.7	?	?	?	?
2008	815.0	5.5	782.1	4,106.1	1,455.7	1,080.5	?	?	?	?
2009	861.5	5.1	827.0	4,836.9	1,177.4	820.8	?	?	?	?
2010	915.7	4.7	911.7	5,357.6	926.6	700.0	?	?	?	?
2011	$1,000.0	4.3	1,169.7	6,023.2	759.7	683.3	?	?	?	?

Source: 2012 Economic Report of the President.

4. Indicate whether each of the following is part of M1, M2, or neither:

   a. $95 on your campus meal card
   b. $0.55 in the change cup of your car
   c. $1,663 in your savings account
   d. $459 in your checking account
   e. 100 shares of stock worth $4,000
   f. A $1,000 line of credit on your Sears credit card

5. Tracy Williams deposits $500 that was in her sock drawer into a checking account at the local bank.

   a. How does the deposit initially change the T-account of the local bank? How does it change the money supply?
   b. If the bank maintains a reserve ratio of 10%, how will it respond to the new deposit?
   c. If every time the bank makes a loan, the loan results in a new checkable bank deposit in a different bank equal to the amount of the loan, by how much could the total money supply in the economy expand in response to Tracy's initial cash deposit of $500?
   d. If every time the bank makes a loan, the loan results in a new checkable bank deposit in a different bank equal to the amount of the loan and the bank maintains a reserve ratio of 5%, by how much could the money supply expand in response to Tracy's initial cash deposit of $500?

6. Ryan Cozzens withdraws $400 from his checking account at the local bank and keeps it in his wallet.

   a. How will the withdrawal change the T-account of the local bank and the money supply?
   b. If the bank maintains a reserve ratio of 10%, how will it respond to the withdrawal? Assume that the bank responds to insufficient reserves by reducing the amount of deposits it holds until its level of reserves satisfies its required reserve ratio. The bank reduces its deposits by calling in some of its loans, forcing borrowers to pay back these loans by taking cash from their checking deposits (at the same bank) to make repayment.
   c. If every time the bank decreases its loans, checkable bank deposits fall by the amount of the loan, by how much will the money supply in the economy contract in response to Ryan's withdrawal of $400?
   d. If every time the bank decreases its loans, checkable bank deposits fall by the amount of the loan and the bank maintains a reserve ratio of 20%, by how much will the money supply contract in response to a withdrawal of $400?

7. The government of Eastlandia uses measures of monetary aggregates similar to those used by the United States, and the central bank of Eastlandia imposes a required reserve ratio of 10%. Given the following information, answer the questions below.

   Bank deposits at the central bank = $200 million
   Currency held by public = $150 million
   Currency in bank vaults = $100 million
   Checkable bank deposits = $500 million
   Traveler's checks = $10 million

   a. What is M1?
   b. What is the monetary base?
   c. Are the commercial banks holding excess reserves?
   d. Can the commercial banks increase checkable bank deposits? If yes, by how much can checkable bank deposits increase?

8. In Westlandia, the public holds 50% of M1 in the form of currency, and the required reserve ratio is 20%. Estimate how much the money supply will increase in response to a new cash deposit of $500 by completing the accompanying table. (*Hint:* The first row shows that the bank must hold $100 in minimum reserves—20% of the $500 deposit—against this deposit, leaving $400 in excess reserves that can be loaned out. However, since the public wants to hold 50% of the loan in currency, only $400 × 0.5 = $200 of the loan will be deposited in round 2 from the loan granted in round 1.) How does your answer compare to an economy in which the total amount of the loan is deposited in the banking system and the public doesn't hold any of the loan in currency? What does this imply about the relationship between the public's desire for holding currency and the money multiplier?

Round	Deposits	Required reserves	Excess reserves	Loans	Held as currency
1	$500.00	$100.00	$400.00	$400.00	$200.00
2	200.00	?	?	?	?
3	?	?	?	?	?
4	?	?	?	?	?
5	?	?	?	?	?
6	?	?	?	?	?
7	?	?	?	?	?
8	?	?	?	?	?
9	?	?	?	?	?
Total after 10 rounds	?	?	?	?	?

9. What will happen to the money supply under the following circumstances in a checkable-deposits-only system?

   a. The required reserve ratio is 25%, and a depositor withdraws $700 from his checkable bank deposit.
   b. The required reserve ratio is 5%, and a depositor withdraws $700 from his checkable bank deposit.
   c. The required reserve ratio is 20%, and a customer deposits $750 to her checkable bank deposit.
   d. The required reserve ratio is 10%, and a customer deposits $600 to her checkable bank deposit.

10. Although the U.S. Federal Reserve doesn't use changes in reserve requirements to manage the money supply, the central bank of Albernia does. The commercial banks of Albernia have $100 million in reserves and $1,000 million in checkable deposits; the initial required reserve ratio is 10%. The commercial banks follow a policy of holding no excess reserves. The public holds no currency, only checkable deposits in the banking system.

a. How will the money supply change if the required reserve ratio falls to 5%?

b. How will the money supply change if the required reserve ratio rises to 25%?

11. Using Figure 71-1, find the Federal Reserve district in which you live. Go to http://www.federalreserve.gov/bios/pres.htm and click on your district to identify the president of the Federal Reserve Bank in your district. Go to http://www.federalreserve.gov/fomc/ and determine if the president of the regional Federal Reserve bank in your district is currently a voting member of the Federal Open Market Committee (FOMC).

12. The Congressional Research Service estimates that at least $45 million of counterfeit U.S. $100 notes produced by the North Korean government are in circulation.

a. Why do U.S. taxpayers lose because of North Korea's counterfeiting?

b. As of March 2013, the interest rate earned on one-year U.S. Treasury bills was 0.14%. At a 0.14% rate of interest, what is the amount of money U.S. taxpayers are losing per year because of these $45 million in counterfeit notes?

13. The accompanying figure shows new U.S. housing starts, in thousands of units per month, between January 1980 and August 2011. The graph shows a large drop in new housing starts in 1984–1991 and 2006–2009. New housing starts are related to the availability of mortgages.

a. What caused the drop in new housing starts in 1984–1991?

b. What caused the drop in new housing starts in 2006–2009?

c. How could better regulation of financial institutions have prevented these two instances?

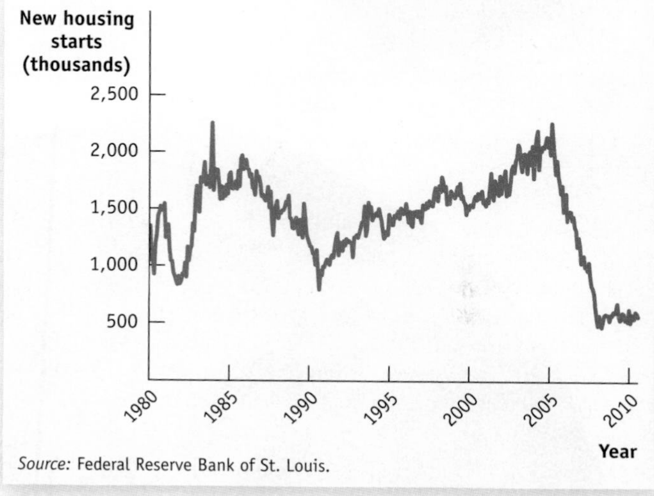

Source: Federal Reserve Bank of St. Louis.

SECTION 23

Monetary Policy

PERSON OF THE YEAR

"A bald man with a gray beard and tired eyes is sitting in his oversize Washington office, talking about the economy. He doesn't have a commanding presence. He isn't a mesmerizing speaker. He has none of the look-at-me swagger or listen-to-me charisma so common among men with oversize Washington offices. His arguments aren't partisan or ideological; they're methodical, grounded in data and the latest academic literature. When he doesn't know something, he doesn't bluster or bluff. He's professorial, which makes sense, because he spent most of his career as a professor."

So began *Time* magazine's profile of Ben Bernanke, whom the magazine named Person of the Year for 2009. Who is this mild-mannered man, and why did he matter so much? The answer is that Bernanke was chairman of the Board of Governors of the Federal Reserve System—the body that controls *monetary policy*. In 2014, Bernanke was succeeded in the post by Janet Yellen.

People sometimes say that the Fed chair decides how much money to print. That's not quite true: for one thing, the Fed doesn't literally print money, and beyond that, monetary decisions are actually made by a committee rather than by one person. But, as we will see, the Federal Reserve can use open-market operations and other actions, such as changes in reserve requirements, to alter the money supply—and, like others who held the job of Fed chair, Ben Bernanke had more influence over these actions than anyone else in America.

And these actions matter a lot. Roughly half of the recessions the United States has experienced since World War II can be attributed, at least in part, to the decisions of the Federal Reserve to tighten policy to fight inflation.

In a number of other cases, the Fed has played a key role in fighting slumps and promoting recovery. The financial crisis of 2008 put the Fed at center stage. Bernanke's aggressive response to the crisis included a tripling of the monetary base, inspiring both praise (including his designation as Person of the Year) and condemnation.

In this section we'll learn how monetary policy works—how the Fed's actions can have a powerful effect on the economy. We'll start by looking at what the Federal Reserve does and the tools it uses. We'll proceed to consider the demand for money from households and firms. And then we'll see how the Fed's ability to change the *supply of money* allows it to move interest rates in the short run and thereby affect real GDP. We conclude by examining U.S. monetary policy and its long-run effects.

72 The Federal Reserve and Monetary Policy

Drew Angerer/Bloomberg via Getty Images

WHAT YOU WILL LEARN

1. The functions of the Federal Reserve System
2. The major tools the Federal Reserve uses to serve its functions

In the previous section, we learned that the Federal Reserve System serves as the central bank of the United States. It has two parts: the Board of Governors, which is part of the U.S. government, and the 12 regional Federal Reserve Banks, which are privately owned.

Functions of the Federal Reserve System

The Federal Reserve's functions fall into four categories. We touched on these functions of the Federal Reserve in the previous section. We examine them again here, but then turn our full attention to the fourth function, conducting monetary policy.

1. PROVIDE FINANCIAL SERVICES The 12 regional Federal Reserve Banks provide financial services to depository institutions such as banks and other large institutions, including the U.S. government. The Federal Reserve is sometimes referred to as the "banker's bank" because it holds reserves, clears checks, provides cash, and transfers funds for commercial banks—all services that banks provide for their customers. The Federal Reserve also acts as the banker and fiscal agent for the federal government. The U.S. Treasury has its checking account with the Federal Reserve, so when the federal government writes a check, it is written on an account at the Fed.

2. SUPERVISE AND REGULATE BANKING INSTITUTIONS The Federal Reserve is responsible for ensuring the safety and soundness of the nation's banking and financial system. The regional Federal Reserve Banks examine and regulate commercial banks in their district. The Board of Governors also engages in regulation and supervision of financial institutions.

3. MAINTAIN THE STABILITY OF THE FINANCIAL SYSTEM One of the major reasons the Federal Reserve System was created was to provide the nation with a safe and stable monetary and financial system. As part of this function, Federal Reserve banks provide liquidity to financial institutions to ensure their safety and soundness.

4. CONDUCT MONETARY POLICY One of the Federal Reserve's most important functions is the conduct of *monetary policy*, which involves the Fed using changes in the quantity of money to alter interest rates, which in turn affect the level of overall spending. The goal of monetary policy is to prevent or address extreme macroeconomic fluctuations in the U.S. economy.

AP Photo/Britt K. Leckman, Federal Reserve

The Federal Reserve Board of Governors, the main governing body of the Federal Reserve System, oversees Federal Reserve Banks and helps to implement monetary policy.

How the Fed Conducts Policy

The Federal Reserve has three main policy tools at its disposal: reserve requirements, the discount rate, and, most importantly for the conduct of monetary policy, *open-market operations*. These tools give the Fed the ability to adjust the money supply to achieve its policy goals.

The Reserve Requirement

In our discussion of bank runs, we noted that the Fed sets a minimum required reserve ratio, currently equal to 10% for checkable bank deposits. Banks that fail to maintain at least the required reserve ratio on average over a two-week period face penalties.

What does a bank do if it looks as if it has insufficient reserves to meet the Fed's reserve requirement? Normally, it borrows additional reserves from other banks via the **federal funds market,** a financial market that allows banks that fall short of the reserve requirement to borrow reserves (usually just overnight) from banks that are holding excess reserves. The interest rate in this market is determined by supply and demand but the supply and demand for bank reserves are both strongly affected by Federal Reserve actions. The **federal funds rate,** the interest rate at which funds are borrowed and lent in the federal funds market, plays a key role in modern monetary policy.

In order to alter the money supply, the Fed can change reserve requirements. If the Fed reduces the required reserve ratio, banks will lend a larger percentage of their deposits, leading to more loans and an increase in the money supply via the money multiplier. Alternatively, if the Fed increases the required reserve ratio, banks are forced to reduce their lending, leading to a fall in the money supply via the money multiplier.

Under current practice, however, the Fed doesn't use changes in reserve requirements to actively manage the money supply. The last significant change in reserve requirements was in 1992.

The Discount Rate

Banks in need of reserves can also borrow from the Fed itself via the discount window. The **discount rate** is the interest rate the Fed charges on those loans. Normally, the discount rate is set 1 percentage point above the federal funds rate in order to discourage banks from turning to the Fed when they are in need of reserves.

In order to alter the money supply, the Fed can change the discount rate. Beginning in the fall of 2007, the Fed reduced the spread between the federal funds rate and the discount rate as part of its response to an ongoing financial crisis. As a result, by the spring of 2008 the discount rate was only 0.25 percentage points above the federal funds rate. And by January 2014 the discount rate was still only 0.68 percentage points above the federal funds rate.

If the Fed reduces the spread between the discount rate and the federal funds rate, the cost to banks of being short of reserves falls; banks respond by increasing their lending, and the money supply increases via the money multiplier. If the Fed increases the spread between the discount rate and the federal funds rate, bank lending falls—and so will the money supply via the money multiplier.

The Fed normally doesn't use the discount rate to actively manage the money supply. Although, as we mentioned earlier, there was a temporary surge in lending through the discount window from the middle of 2007 through 2008 in response to a financial crisis.

The **federal funds market** allows banks that fall short of the reserve requirement to borrow funds from banks with excess reserves.

The **federal funds rate** is the interest rate determined in the federal funds market.

The **discount rate** is the interest rate the Fed charges on loans to banks.

An **open-market operation** is a purchase or sale of government debt by the Fed.

Today, normal monetary policy is conducted almost exclusively using the Fed's third policy tool: open-market operations.

Open-Market Operations

Like the banks it oversees, the Federal Reserve has assets and liabilities. The Fed's assets consist of its holdings of debt issued by the U.S. government, mainly short-term U.S. government bonds with a maturity of less than one year, known as U.S. Treasury bills. Remember, the Fed isn't exactly part of the U.S. government, so U.S. Treasury bills held by the Fed are a liability of the government but an asset of the Fed. The Fed's liabilities consist of currency in circulation and bank reserves. Figure 72-1 summarizes the normal assets and liabilities of the Fed in the form of a T-account.

FIGURE 72-1 The Federal Reserve's Assets and Liabilities

Assets	Liabilities
Government debt (Treasury bills)	Monetary base (Currency in circulation + bank reserves)

The Federal Reserve holds its assets mostly in short-term government bonds called U.S. Treasury bills. Its liabilities are the monetary base—currency in circulation plus bank reserves.

In an **open-market operation** the Federal Reserve buys or sells U.S. Treasury bills, normally through a transaction with *commercial banks*—banks that mainly make business loans, as opposed to home loans. The Fed never buys U.S. Treasury bills directly from the federal government. There's a good reason for this: when a central bank buys government debt directly from the government, it is lending directly to the government—in effect, the central bank is "printing money" to finance the government's budget deficit. This has historically been a formula for disastrous levels of inflation.

The two panels of Figure 72-2 show the changes in the financial position of both the Fed and commercial banks that result from open-market operations. When the Fed buys U.S. Treasury bills from a commercial bank, it pays by crediting the bank's reserve account by an amount equal to the value of the Treasury bills. This is shown in panel (a): the Fed buys $100 million of U.S. Treasury bills from commercial banks, increasing the monetary base by $100 million because it increases bank reserves by $100 million.

FIGURE 72-2 Open-Market Operations by the Federal Reserve

(a) An Open-Market Purchase of $100 Million

	Assets		Liabilities	
Federal Reserve	Treasury bills	+$100 million	Monetary base	+$100 million

	Assets		Liabilities
Commercial banks	Treasury bills	−$100 million	No change
	Reserves	+$100 million	

(b) An Open-Market Sale of $100 Million

	Assets		Liabilities	
Federal Reserve	Treasury bills	−$100 million	Monetary base	−$100 million

	Assets		Liabilities
Commercial banks	Treasury bills	+$100 million	No change
	Reserves	−$100 million	

In panel (a), the Federal Reserve increases the monetary base by purchasing U.S. Treasury bills from private commercial banks in an open-market operation. Here, a $100 million purchase of U.S. Treasury bills by the Federal Reserve is paid for by a $100 million increase in the monetary base. This will ultimately lead to an increase in the money supply via the money multiplier as banks lend out some of these new reserves. In panel (b), the Federal Reserve reduces the monetary base by selling U.S. Treasury bills to private commercial banks in an open-market operation. Here, a $100 million sale of U.S. Treasury bills leads to a $100 million reduction in commercial bank reserves, resulting in a $100 million decrease in the monetary base. This will ultimately lead to a fall in the money supply via the money multiplier as banks reduce their loans in response to a fall in their reserves.

When the Fed sells U.S. Treasury bills to commercial banks, it debits the banks' accounts, reducing their reserves. This is shown in panel (b), where the Fed sells $100 million of U.S. Treasury bills. Here, bank reserves and the monetary base decrease.

You might wonder where the Fed gets the funds to purchase U.S. Treasury bills from banks. The answer is that it simply creates them with a stroke of the pen or a click of the mouse, crediting the banks' accounts with extra reserves. (The Fed issues currency to pay for Treasury bills only when banks want the additional reserves in the form of currency.) Remember, the modern dollar is fiat money, which isn't backed by anything. So the Fed can increase the monetary base at its own discretion.

The change in bank reserves caused by an open-market operation doesn't directly affect the money supply. Instead, it sets the money multiplier in motion. After the $100 million increase in reserves shown in panel (a), commercial banks would lend out their additional reserves, immediately increasing the money supply by $100 million. Some of those loans would be deposited back into the banking system, increasing reserves again and permitting a further round of loans, and so on, leading to a rise in the money supply. An open-market sale has the reverse effect: bank reserves fall, requiring banks to reduce their loans, leading to a fall in the money supply.

Shutterstock

The Fed buys or sells U.S. Treasury bills in transactions with commercial banks in an effort to influence the money supply and interest rates.

Economists often say, loosely, that the Fed controls the money supply—checkable deposits plus currency in circulation. In fact, it controls only the monetary base—bank reserves plus currency in circulation. But by increasing or reducing the monetary base, the Fed can exert a powerful influence on both the money supply and interest rates, which is the basis of monetary policy.

ECONOMICS IN ACTION

WHO GETS THE INTEREST ON THE FED'S ASSETS?

As we've just learned, the Fed owns a lot of assets—Treasury bills—which it bought from commercial banks in exchange for the monetary base in the form of credits to banks' reserve accounts. These assets pay interest. Yet the Fed's liabilities consist mainly of the monetary base, liabilities on which the Fed *doesn't* pay interest. So the Fed is, in effect, an institution that has the privilege of borrowing funds at a zero interest rate and lending them out at a positive interest rate. That sounds like a pretty profitable business. Who gets the profits?

You do—or rather, U.S. taxpayers do. The Fed keeps some of the interest it receives to finance its operations but turns most of it over to the U.S. Treasury. For example, in 2012 the Federal Reserve System earned net income of $91.0 billion—largely in interest on its holdings of Treasury bills, of which $88.9 billion was returned to the Treasury.

Taxpayers profit from interest earned on Fed assets and pay when counterfeit bills enter the money supply, reducing those interest payments.

Consider what happens when a fake $100 bill enters circulation. It has the same economic effect as a real $100 bill printed by the U.S. government. That is, as long as the forgery isn't caught, the fake bill is, for all practical purposes, part of the monetary base.

Meanwhile, the Fed decides on the size of the monetary base based on economic considerations—in particular, the Fed doesn't let the monetary base get too large because that can cause inflation. So every fake $100 bill that enters circulation basically means that the Fed prints one less real $100 bill. When the Fed prints a $100 bill legally, however, it gets Treasury bills in return—and the interest on those bills helps pay for the U.S. government's expenses.

So a counterfeit $100 bill reduces the amount of Treasury bills the Fed can acquire and thereby reduces the interest payments going to the Fed and the U.S. Treasury. In the end, taxpayers bear the real cost of counterfeiting.

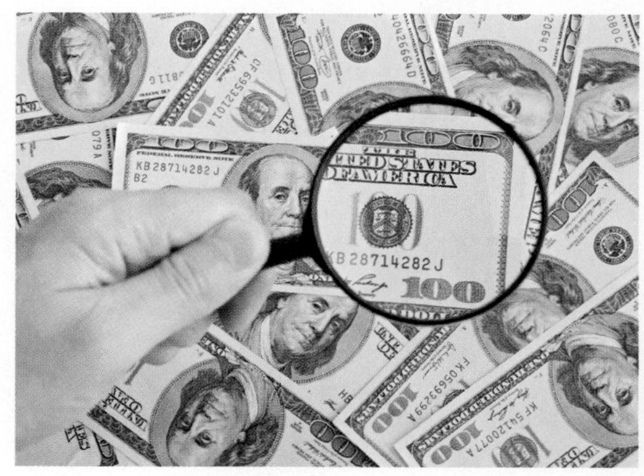
Shutterstock

MODULE 72 Review

Solutions appear at the back of the book.

Check Your Understanding

1. Assume that any money lent by a bank is deposited back in the banking system as a checkable deposit and that the reserve ratio is 10%. Trace out the effects of a $100 million open-market purchase of U.S. Treasury bills by the Fed on the value of checkable bank deposits. What is the size of the money multiplier?

Multiple-Choice Questions

1. Which of the following is a function of the Federal Reserve System?
   - I. examine commercial banks
   - II. print Federal Reserve notes
   - III. conduct monetary policy
   - a. I only
   - b. II only
   - c. III only
   - d. I and III only
   - e. I, II, and III

2. Which of the following financial services does the Federal Reserve provide for commercial banks?
   - I. clearing checks
   - II. holding reserves
   - III. making loans
   - a. I only
   - b. II only
   - c. III only
   - d. I and II
   - e. I, II, and III

3. When the Fed makes a loan to a commercial bank, it charges
   - a. no interest.
   - b. the prime rate.
   - c. the federal funds rate.
   - d. the discount rate.
   - e. the market interest rate.

4. If the Fed purchases U.S. Treasury bills from a commercial bank, what happens to bank reserves and the money supply?

	Bank reserves	*Money supply*
a.	increase	decrease
b.	increase	increase
c.	decrease	decrease
d.	decrease	increase
e.	increase	no change

5. When banks make loans to each other, they charge the
   - a. prime rate.
   - b. discount rate.
   - c. federal funds rate.
   - d. CD rate.
   - e. mortgage rate.

Critical-Thinking Question

What are the four basic functions of the Federal Reserve System?

The Money Market

Shutterstock

WHAT YOU WILL LEARN

1. What the money demand curve is
2. Why the liquidity preference model determines the interest rate in the short run

The Demand for Money

In Module 69 we learned about the various types of monetary aggregates: M1, the most commonly used definition of the money supply, consists of currency in circulation (cash), plus checkable bank deposits, plus traveler's checks; and M2, a broader definition of the money supply, consists of M1 plus deposits that can easily be transferred into checkable deposits. We also learned why people hold money—to make it easier to purchase goods and services. Now we'll go deeper, examining what determines how much money individuals and firms want to hold at any given time.

The Opportunity Cost of Holding Money

Most economic decisions involve trade-offs at the margin. That is, individuals decide how much of a good to consume by determining whether the benefit they'd gain from consuming a bit more of any given good is worth the cost. The same decision process is used when deciding how much money to hold.

Individuals and firms find it useful to hold some of their assets in the form of money because of the convenience money provides: money can be used to make purchases directly, but other assets can't. But there is a price to be paid for that convenience: money normally yields a lower rate of return than nonmonetary assets.

As an example of how convenience makes it worth incurring some opportunity costs, consider the fact that even today—with the prevalence of credit cards, debit cards, and ATMs—people continue to keep cash in their wallets rather than leave the funds in an interest-bearing account. They do this because they don't want to have to go to an ATM to withdraw money every time they want to buy lunch from a place that doesn't accept credit cards or won't accept them for small amounts because of the processing fee. In other words, the convenience of keeping some cash in your wallet is more valuable than the interest you would earn by keeping that money in the bank.

Derek E. Rothchild/Media Bakery

There is a price to be paid for the convenience of holding money.

Even holding money in a checking account involves a trade-off between convenience and earning interest. That's because you can earn a higher interest rate by putting your money in assets other than a checking account. For example, many banks offer certificates of deposit, or CDs, which pay a higher interest rate than ordinary bank accounts. But CDs also carry a penalty if you withdraw the funds before a certain amount of time—say, six months—has elapsed. An individual who keeps funds in a checking account is forgoing the higher interest rate those funds might earn if placed in a CD in return for the convenience of having cash readily available when needed.

So making sense of the demand for money is about understanding how individuals and firms trade off the benefit of holding cash—that provides convenience but no interest—versus the benefit of holding interest-bearing nonmonetary assets—that provide interest but not convenience. And that trade-off is affected by the interest rate. (As before, when we say *the interest rate* it is with the understanding that we mean a nominal interest rate—that is, it's unadjusted for inflation.) Next, we'll examine how that trade-off changed dramatically from June 2007 to June 2008, when there was a big fall in interest rates.

Table 73-1 illustrates the opportunity cost of holding money in a specific month, June 2007. The first row shows the interest rate on one-month certificates of deposit—that is, the interest rate individuals could get if they were willing to tie their funds up for one month. In June 2007, one-month CDs yielded 5.30%. The second row shows the interest rate on interest-bearing demand deposits (specifically, those included in M2, minus small time deposits). Funds in these accounts were more accessible than those in CDs, but the price of that convenience was a much lower interest rate, only 2.30%. Finally, the last row shows the interest rate on currency—cash in your wallet—which was, of course, zero.

TABLE 73-1

Selected Interest Rates, June 2007

One-month certificates of deposit (CDs)	5.30%
Interest-bearing demand deposits	2.30%
Currency	0

Source: Federal Reserve Bank of St. Louis.

Table 73-1 shows the opportunity cost of holding money at one point in time, but the opportunity cost of holding money changes when the overall level of interest rates changes. Specifically, when the overall level of interest rates falls, the opportunity cost of holding money falls, too.

Table 73-2 illustrates this point by showing how selected interest rates changed between June 2007 and June 2008, a period when the Federal Reserve was slashing rates in an (unsuccessful) effort to fight off a rapidly worsening recession.

A comparison between interest rates in June 2007 and June 2008 illustrates what happens when the opportunity cost of holding money falls sharply. Between June 2007 and June 2008, the federal funds rate, which is the rate the Fed controls most directly, fell by 3.25 percentage points. The interest rate on one-month CDs fell almost as much, 2.8 percentage points. These interest rates are **short-term interest rates**—rates on financial assets that come due, or mature, within less than a year.

TABLE 73-2

Interest Rates and the Opportunity Cost of Holding Money

	June 2007	June 2008
Federal funds rate	5.25%	2.00%
One-month certificates of deposit (CDs)	5.30%	2.50%
Interest-bearing demand deposits	2.30%	1.24%
Currency	0	0
CDs minus interest-bearing demand deposits (percentage points)	**3.00**	**1.26**
CDs minus currency (percentage points)	**5.30**	**2.50**

Source: Federal Reserve Bank of St. Louis.

As short-term interest rates fell between June 2007 and June 2008, the interest rates on money didn't fall by the same amount. The interest rate on currency, of course, remained at zero. The interest rate paid on demand deposits did fall, but by much less than short-term interest rates.

As a comparison of the two columns of Table 73-2 shows, the opportunity cost of holding money fell. The last two rows of Table 73-2 summarize this comparison: they give the differences between the interest rates on demand deposits and on currency and the interest rate on CDs. These differences—the opportunity cost of holding money rather than interest-bearing assets—declined sharply between June 2007 and June 2008. This reflects a general result: *The higher the short-term interest rate, the higher the opportunity cost of holding money; the lower the short-term interest rate, the lower the opportunity cost of holding money.*

Short-term interest rates are the interest rates on financial assets that mature within less than a year.

The fact that the federal funds rate in Table 73-2 and the interest rate on one-month CDs fell by almost the same percentage is not an accident: all short-term interest rates tend to move together, with rare exceptions. The reason short-term interest rates tend to move together is that CDs and other short-term assets (like one-month and three-month U.S. Treasury bills) are in effect competing for the same business. Any short-term asset that offers a lower-than-average interest rate will be sold by investors, who will move their wealth into a higher-yielding short-term asset. The selling of the asset, in turn, forces its interest rate up, because investors must be rewarded with a higher rate in order to induce them to buy it.

Conversely, investors will move their wealth into any short-term financial asset that offers an above-average interest rate. The purchase of the asset drives its interest rate down when sellers find they can lower the rate of return on the asset and still find willing buyers. So interest rates on short-term financial assets tend to be roughly the same because no asset will consistently offer a higher-than-average or a lower-than-average interest rate.

Table 73-2 contains only short-term interest rates. At any given moment, **long-term interest rates**—rates of interest on financial assets that mature, or come due, a number of years into the future—may be different from short-term interest rates. The difference between short-term and long-term interest rates is sometimes important as a practical matter.

Long-term interest rates are interest rates on financial assets that mature a number of years in the future.

Moreover, it's short-term rates rather than long-term rates that affect money demand, because the decision to hold money involves trading off the convenience of holding cash versus the payoff from holding assets that mature in the short term—a year or less.

For the moment, however, let's ignore the distinction between short-term and long-term rates and assume that there is only one interest rate.

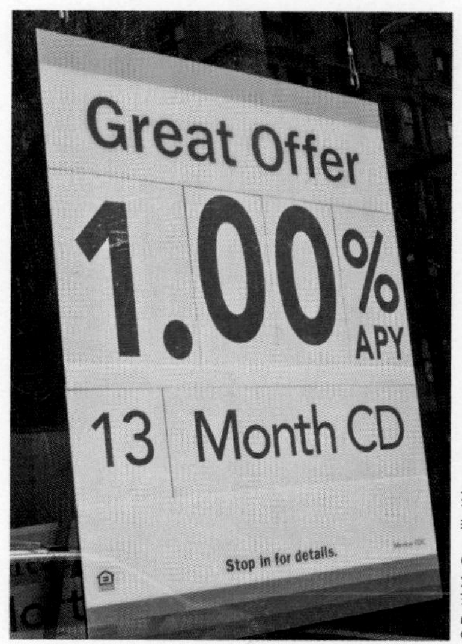

© Patti McConville/Alamy

Short-term interest rates tend to move together.

The Money Demand Curve

Because the overall level of interest rates affects the opportunity cost of holding money, the quantity of money individuals and firms want to hold is, other things equal, negatively related to the interest rate.

In Figure 73-1, the horizontal axis shows the quantity of money demanded and the vertical axis shows the interest rate, r, which you can think of as a representative short-term interest rate such as the rate on one-month CDs. (Recall that it is the

FIGURE 73-1 The Money Demand Curve

The money demand curve illustrates the relationship between the interest rate and the quantity of money demanded. It slopes downward: a higher interest rate leads to a higher opportunity cost of holding money and reduces the quantity of money demanded. Correspondingly, a lower interest rate reduces the opportunity cost of holding money and increases the quantity of money demanded.

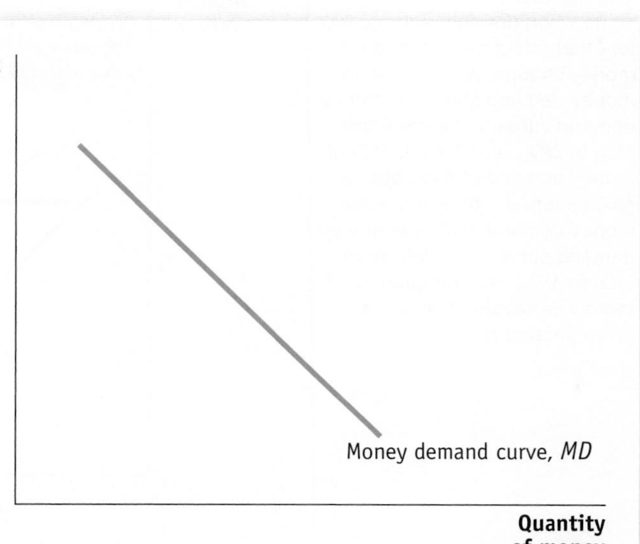

The **money demand curve** shows the relationship between the interest rate and the quantity of money demanded.

nominal interest rate, not the real interest rate, that influences people's money allocation decisions. Hence, *r* in Figure 73-1 and all subsequent figures is the nominal interest rate.)

The relationship between the interest rate and the quantity of money demanded by the public is illustrated by the **money demand curve,** *MD,* in Figure 73-1. The money demand curve slopes downward because, other things equal, a higher interest rate increases the opportunity cost of holding money, leading the public to reduce the quantity of money it demands. For example, if the interest rate is very low—say, 1%—the interest forgone by holding money is relatively small. As a result, individuals and firms will tend to hold relatively large amounts of money to avoid the cost and nuisance of converting other assets into money when making purchases.

By contrast, if the interest rate is relatively high—say, 15%, a level it reached in the United States in the early 1980s—the opportunity cost of holding money is high. People will respond by keeping only small amounts in cash and deposits, converting assets into money only when needed.

You might ask why we draw the money demand curve with the interest rate—as opposed to rates of return on other assets, such as stocks or real estate—on the vertical axis. The answer is that for most people the relevant question in deciding how much money to hold is whether to put the funds in the form of other assets that can be turned fairly quickly and easily into money.

Stocks don't fit that definition because there are significant transaction fees when you sell stock (which is why stock market investors are advised not to buy and sell too often). Real estate doesn't fit the definition either because selling real estate involves even larger fees and can take a long time as well. So the relevant comparison is with assets that are "close to" money—fairly liquid assets like CDs. And as we've already seen, the interest rates on all these assets normally move closely together.

Shifts of the Money Demand Curve

A number of factors other than the interest rate affect the demand for money. When one of these factors changes, the money demand curve shifts. Figure 73-2 shows shifts of the money demand curve: an increase in the demand for money corresponds

FIGURE 73-2 Increases and Decreases in the Demand for Money

The demand curve for money shifts when non-interest rate factors that affect the demand for money change. An increase in money demand shifts the money demand curve to the right, from MD_1 to MD_2, and the quantity of money demanded rises at any given interest rate. A decrease in money demand shifts the money demand curve to the left, from MD_1 to MD_3, and the quantity of money demanded falls at any given interest rate.

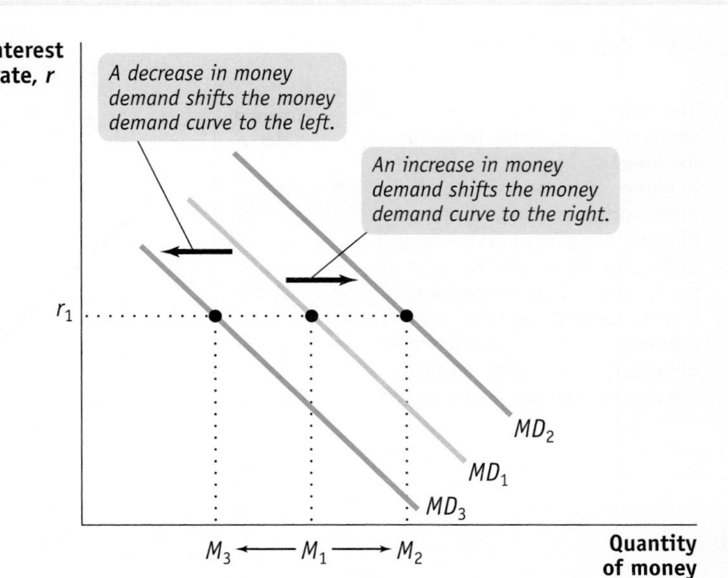

to a rightward shift of the *MD* curve, raising the quantity of money demanded at any given interest rate; a decrease in the demand for money corresponds to a leftward shift of the *MD* curve, reducing the quantity of money demanded at any given interest rate.

The most important factors causing the money demand curve to shift are changes in the aggregate price level, changes in real GDP, changes in credit markets and banking technology, and changes in institutions.

CHANGES IN THE AGGREGATE PRICE LEVEL Americans keep a lot more cash in their wallets and funds in their checking accounts today than they did in the 1950s. One reason is that they have to if they want to be able to buy anything: almost everything costs more now than it did when you could get a burger, fries, and a drink at McDonald's for 45 cents and a gallon of gasoline for 29 cents.

So, other things equal, higher prices increase the demand for money (a rightward shift of the *MD* curve), and lower prices decrease the demand for money (a leftward shift of the *MD* curve).

We can actually be more specific than this: other things equal, the demand for money is *proportional* to the price level. That is, if the aggregate price level rises by 20%, the quantity of money demanded at any given interest rate, such as r_1 in Figure 73-2, also rises by 20%—the movement from M_1 to M_2. Why? Because if the price of everything rises by 20%, it takes 20% more money to buy the same basket of goods and services.

And if the aggregate price level falls by 20%, at any given interest rate the quantity of money demanded falls by 20%—shown by the movement from M_1 to M_3 at the interest rate r_1. As we'll see later, the fact that money demand is proportional to the price level has important implications for the long-run effects of monetary policy.

CHANGES IN REAL GDP Households and firms hold money as a way to facilitate purchases of goods and services. The larger the quantity of goods and services they buy, the larger the quantity of money they will want to hold at any given interest rate. So an increase in real GDP—the total quantity of goods and services produced and sold in the economy—shifts the money demand curve rightward. A fall in real GDP shifts the money demand curve leftward.

CHANGES IN CREDIT MARKETS AND BANKING TECHNOLOGY Credit cards are everywhere in American life today, but it wasn't always so. The first credit card that allowed customers to carry a balance from month to month (called a "revolving balance") was issued in 1959. Before then, people had to either pay for purchases in cash or pay off their balance every month.

The invention of revolving-balance credit cards allowed people to hold less money in order to fund their purchases and decreased the demand for money. In addition, changes in banking technology that made credit cards widely available and widely accepted magnified the effect, making it easier for people to make purchases without having to convert funds from their interest-bearing assets, further reducing the demand for money.

Shutterstock

Credit cards allow people to hold less money to fund their purchases, decreasing the demand for money.

CHANGES IN INSTITUTIONS Changes in institutions can increase or decrease the demand for money. For example, until Regulation Q was eliminated in 1980, U.S. banks weren't allowed to offer interest on checking accounts. So the interest you would forgo by holding funds in a checking account instead of an interest-bearing asset made the opportunity cost of holding funds in checking accounts very high. When banking regulations changed, allowing banks to pay interest on checking account funds, the demand for money rose and shifted the money demand curve to the right.

ECONOMICS ▶ IN ACTION

Sakarin Sawasdinaka/Shutterstock

No matter what they are shopping for, Japanese consumers tend to pay with cash rather than plastic.

A YEN FOR CASH

Japan, say financial experts, is still a "cash society." Visitors from the United States or Europe are surprised at how little use the Japanese make of credit cards and how much cash they carry around in their wallets. Yet Japan is an economically and technologically advanced country and, according to some measures, ahead of the United States in the use of telecommunications and information technology.

So why do the citizens of this economic powerhouse still do business the way Americans and Europeans did a generation ago? The answer highlights the factors affecting the demand for money.

One reason the Japanese use cash so much is that their institutions never made the switch to heavy reliance on plastic. For complex reasons, Japan's retail sector is still dominated by small mom-and-pop stores, which are reluctant to invest in credit card technology. Japan's banks have also been slow about pushing transaction technology; visitors are often surprised to find that ATMs close early in the evening rather than staying open all night.

But there's another reason the Japanese hold so much cash: there's little opportunity cost to doing so. Short-term interest rates in Japan have been below 1% since the mid-1990s. It also helps that the Japanese crime rate is quite low, so you are unlikely to have your wallet full of cash stolen. So why not hold cash?

Money and Interest Rates

The Federal Open Market Committee decided today to lower its target for the federal funds rate 75 basis points to 2¼ percent.

Recent information indicates that the outlook for economic activity has weakened further. Growth in consumer spending has slowed and labor markets have softened. Financial markets remain under considerable stress, and the tightening of credit conditions and the deepening of the housing contraction are likely to weigh on economic growth over the next few quarters.

So read the beginning of a press release from the Federal Reserve issued on March 18, 2008. (A basis point is equal to 0.01 percentage point. So the statement implies that the Fed lowered the target from 3% to 2.25%.) Recall that the federal funds rate is the rate at which banks lend reserves to each other to meet the required reserve ratio.

As the statement implies, at each of its eight-times-a-year meetings, a group called the Federal Open Market Committee sets a target value for the federal funds rate. It's then up to Fed officials to achieve that target. This is done by the Open Market Desk at the Federal Reserve Bank of New York, which buys and sells short-term U.S. government debt, known as Treasury bills, to achieve that target.

As we've already seen, other short-term interest rates, such as the rates on CDs, move with the federal funds rate. So when the Fed reduced its target for the federal funds rate from 3% to 2.25% in March 2008, many other short-term interest rates also fell by about three-quarters of a percentage point.

How does the Fed go about achieving a *target federal funds rate*? And more to the point, how is the Fed able to affect interest rates at all?

The Equilibrium Interest Rate

According to the **liquidity preference model of the interest rate,** the interest rate is determined by the supply and demand for money.

Remember that, for simplicity, we're assuming there is only one interest rate paid on nonmonetary financial assets, both in the short run and in the long run. To understand how the interest rate is determined, consider Figure 73-3, which illustrates the **liquidity preference model of the interest rate;** this model says that the interest rate is determined by the supply and demand for money in the market for money.

Figure 73-3 combines the money demand curve, *MD*, with the **money supply curve,** *MS*, which shows how the quantity of money supplied by the Federal Reserve varies with the interest rate.

The **money supply curve** shows how the quantity of money supplied varies with the interest rate.

In the previous module we learned how the Federal Reserve can increase or decrease the money supply: it usually does this through open-market operations, buying or selling Treasury bills, but it can also lend via the discount window or change reserve requirements.

Let's assume for simplicity that the Fed, using one or more of these methods, simply chooses the level of the money supply that it believes will achieve its interest rate target. Then the money supply curve is a vertical line, *MS* in Figure 73-3, with a horizontal intercept corresponding to the money supply chosen by the Fed, $\overline{M}$. The money market equilibrium is at *E*, where *MS* and *MD* cross. At this point the quantity of money demanded equals the money supply, $\overline{M}$, leading to an equilibrium interest rate of r_E.

To understand why r_E is the equilibrium interest rate, consider what happens if the money market is at a point like *L*, where the interest rate, r_L, is below r_E. At r_L the public wants to hold the quantity of money M_L, an amount larger than the actual money supply, $\overline{M}$. This means that at point *L*, the public wants to shift some of its wealth out of interest-bearing assets such as CDs into money.

This has two implications. One is that the quantity of money demanded is *more* than the quantity of money supplied. The other is that the quantity of interest-bearing money assets demanded is less than the quantity supplied. So those trying to sell nonmoney assets will find that they have to offer a higher interest rate to attract buyers. As a result, the interest rate will be driven up from r_L until the public wants to hold the quantity of money that is actually available, $\overline{M}$. That is, the interest rate will rise until it is equal to r_E.

Now consider what happens if the money market is at a point such as *H* in Figure 73-3, where the interest rate r_H is above r_E. In that case the quantity of money demanded, M_H, is less than the quantity of money supplied, $\overline{M}$. Correspondingly, the quantity of interest-bearing nonmoney assets demanded is greater than the quantity supplied. Those trying to sell interest-bearing nonmoney assets will find that they can

FIGURE 73-3 **Equilibrium in the Money Market**

The money supply curve, *MS*, is vertical at the money supply chosen by the Federal Reserve, $\overline{M}$. The money market is in equilibrium at the interest rate r_E: *the quantity of money demanded by the public is equal to* $\overline{M}$, the quantity of money supplied.

At a point such as *L*, the interest rate, r_L, is below r_E and the corresponding quantity of money demanded, M_L, exceeds the money supply, $\overline{M}$. In an attempt to shift their wealth out of nonmoney interest-bearing financial assets and raise their money holdings, investors drive the interest rate up to r_E. At a point such as *H*, the interest rate r_H exceeds r_E and the corresponding quantity of money demanded, M_H, is less than the money supply, $\overline{M}$. In an attempt to shift out of money holdings into nonmoney interest-bearing financial assets, investors drive the interest rate down to r_E.

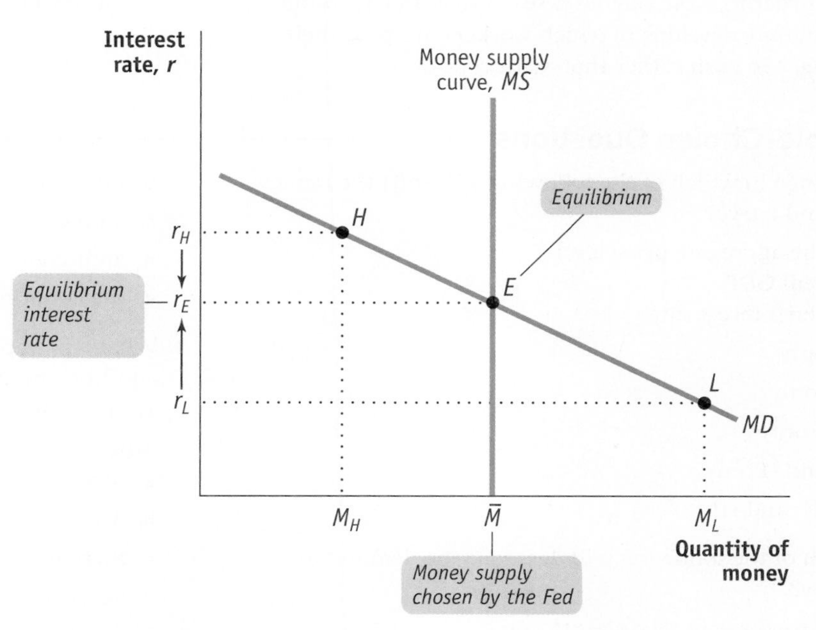

offer a lower interest rate and still find willing buyers. This leads to a fall in the interest rate from r_H. It falls until the public wants to hold the quantity of money that is actually available, $\overline{M}$. Again, the interest rate will end up at r_E.

Two Models of Interest Rates?

You might have noticed that this is the second time we have discussed the determination of the interest rate. In an earlier module, we studied the *loanable funds model* of the interest rate; according to that model, the interest rate is determined by the equalization of the supply of funds from lenders and the demand for funds by borrowers in the market for loanable funds. But here we have described a seemingly different model in which the interest rate is determined by the equalization of the supply and demand for money in the money market.

Which of these models is correct? The answer is both, depending on context. The loanable funds model is focused on the interest rate in the long run. The money market model, however, focuses on the interest rate in the short run.

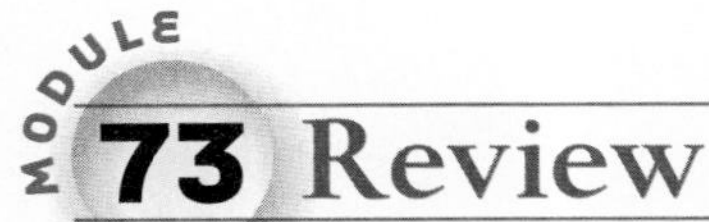

MODULE 73 Review

Solutions appear at the back of the book.

Check Your Understanding

1. Explain how each of the following would affect the quantity of money demanded, and indicate whether each change would cause a movement along the money demand curve or a shift of the money demand curve.
   a. Short-term interest rates rise from 5% to 30%.
   b. All prices fall by 10%.
   c. New wireless technology automatically charges supermarket purchases to credit cards, eliminating the need to stop at the cash register.
   d. In order to avoid paying taxes, a vast underground economy develops in which workers are paid their wages in cash rather than with checks.

2. Will each of the following increase the opportunity cost of holding cash, reduce it, or have no effect on it? Explain your answers.
   a. Merchants charge a 1% processing fee on debit/credit card transactions for purchases of less than $50.
   b. To attract more deposits, banks raise the interest paid on six-month CDs.
   c. Real estate prices fall significantly.
   d. The cost of food rises significantly.

Multiple-Choice Questions

1. A change in which of the following will shift the money demand curve?
   I. the aggregate price level
   II. real GDP
   III. the interest rate
   a. I only
   b. II only
   c. III only
   d. I and II only
   e. I, II, and III

2. Which of the following will decrease the demand for money?
   a. an increase in the interest rate
   b. inflation
   c. an increase in real GDP
   d. an increase in the availability of ATMs
   e. the adoption of Regulation Q

3. What will happen to the money supply and the equilibrium interest rate if the Federal Reserve sells Treasury securities?

	Money supply	*Equilibrium interest rate*
a.	increase	increase
b.	decrease	increase
c.	increase	decrease
d.	decrease	decrease
e.	decrease	no change

4. Which of the following is true regarding short-term and long-term interest rates?
   a. Short-term interest rates are always above long-term interest rates.
   b. Short-term interest rates are always below long-term interest rates.
   c. Short-term interest rates are always equal to long-term interest rates.
   d. Short-term interest rates are more important for determining the demand for money.
   e. Long-term interest rates are more important for determining the demand for money.

5. The quantity of money demanded rises (that is, there is a movement along the money demand curve) when
   a. the aggregate price level increases.
   b. the aggregate price level falls.
   c. real GDP increases.
   d. new technology makes banking easier.
   e. short-term interest rates fall.

Critical-Thinking Question

Draw a graph showing equilibrium in the money market. Select an interest rate below the equilibrium interest rate and explain what occurs in the market at that interest rate and how the market will eventually return to equilibrium.

74 Monetary Policy and the Interest Rate

Harrer/Bloomberg via Getty Images

WHAT YOU WILL LEARN

1. How the Federal Reserve implements monetary policy, moving the interest rate to affect aggregate output
2. Why monetary policy is the main tool for stabilizing the economy

In the previous module we developed a model of the money market to show how the interest rate is determined in the short run. Now we are ready to use this model to explain how the Federal Reserve can use monetary policy to stabilize the economy in the short run.

The Fed, the Money Supply, and the Interest Rate

Let's examine how the Federal Reserve can use changes in the money supply to change the interest rate. Figure 74-1 shows what happens when the Fed increases the money supply from $\overline{M}_1$ to $\overline{M}_2$.

The economy is originally in equilibrium at E_1, with the equilibrium interest rate r_1 and the money supply $\overline{M}_1$. An increase in the money supply by the Fed to $\overline{M}_2$ shifts the money supply curve to the right, from MS_1 to MS_2, and leads to a fall in the equilibrium interest rate to r_2. Why? Because r_2 is the only interest rate at which the public is willing to hold the quantity of money actually supplied, $\overline{M}_2$.

So an increase in the money supply drives the interest rate down. Similarly, a reduction in the money supply drives the interest rate up. By adjusting the money supply up or down, the Fed can set the interest rate.

In practice, at each meeting the Federal Open Market Committee decides on the interest rate to prevail for the next six weeks, until its next meeting. The Fed sets a **target federal funds rate,** a desired level for the federal funds rate. This target is then enforced by the Open Market Desk of the Federal Reserve Bank of New York, which adjusts the money supply through *open-market operations*—the purchase or sale of Treasury bills—until the actual federal funds rate equals the target rate.

The **target federal funds rate** is the Federal Reserve's desired federal funds rate.

FIGURE 74-1 **The Effect of an Increase in the Money Supply on the Interest Rate**

The Federal Reserve can lower the interest rate by increasing the money supply. Here, the equilibrium interest rate falls from r_1 to r_2 in response to an increase in the money supply from $\overline{M}_1$ to $\overline{M}_2$. In order to induce people to hold the larger quantity of money, the interest rate must fall from r_1 to r_2.

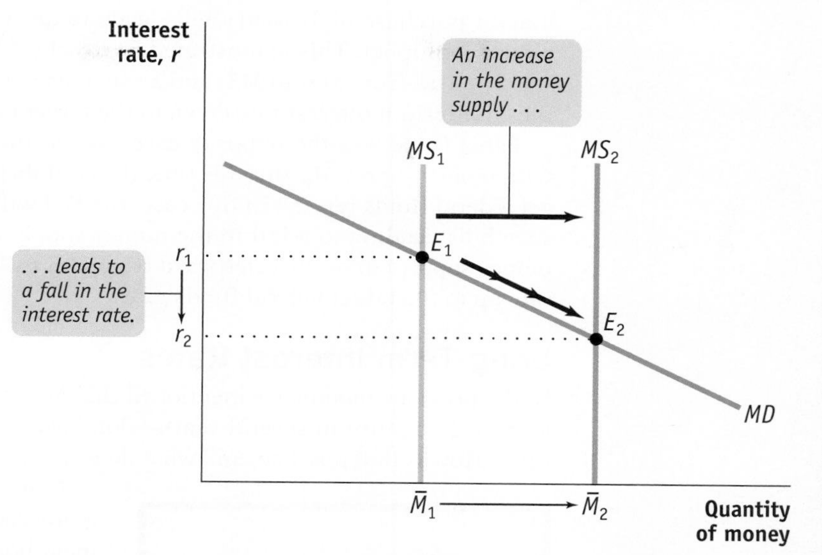

The other tools of monetary policy, lending through the discount window and changes in reserve requirements, aren't used on a regular basis, although the Fed used discount window lending in its efforts to address the 2008 financial crisis.

Figure 74-2 shows how the Fed adjusts the money supply in order to change the interest rate and achieve its target federal funds rate. In both panels, r_T is the target federal funds rate. In panel (a), the initial money supply curve is MS_1 with money

FIGURE 74-2 **Setting the Federal Funds Rate**

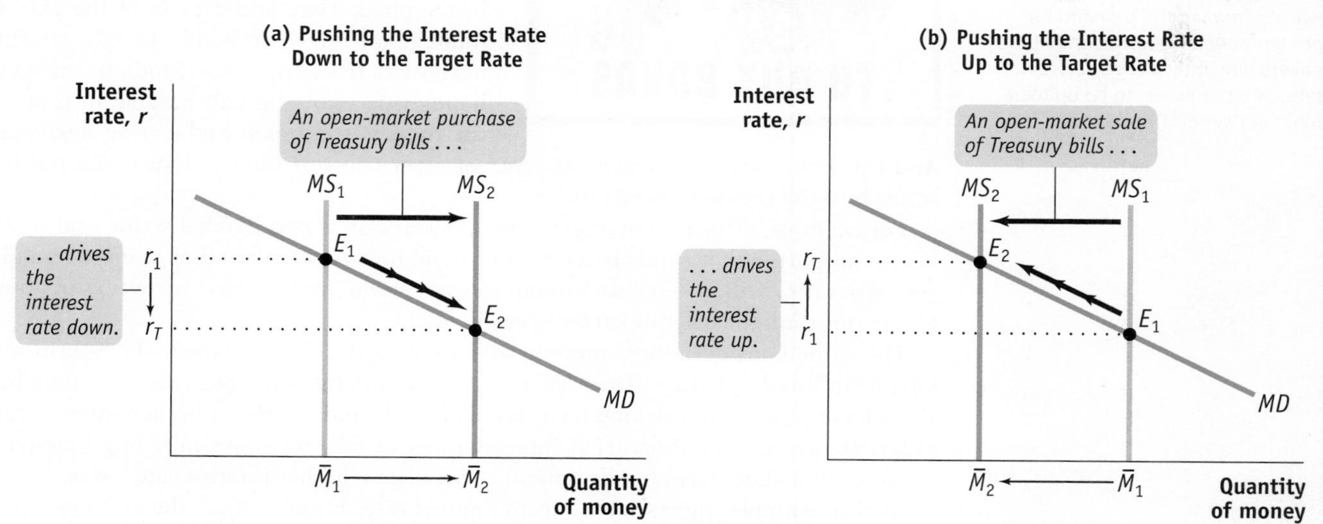

The Federal Reserve sets a target for the federal funds rate and uses open-market operations to achieve that target. In both panels the target rate is r_T. In panel (a) the initial equilibrium interest rate, r_1, is above the target rate. The Fed increases the money supply by making an open-market purchase of Treasury bills, pushing the money supply curve rightward, from MS_1 to MS_2, and driving the interest rate down to r_T. In panel (b) the initial equilibrium interest rate, r_1, is below the target rate. The Fed reduces the money supply by making an open-market sale of Treasury bills, pushing the money supply curve leftward, from MS_1 to MS_2, and driving the interest rate up to r_T.

supply $\overline{M}_1$, and the equilibrium interest rate, r_1, is above the target rate. To lower the interest rate to r_T, the Fed makes an open-market purchase of Treasury bills. An open-market purchase of Treasury bills leads to an increase in the money supply via the money multiplier. This is illustrated in panel (a) by the rightward shift of the money supply curve from MS_1 to MS_2 and an increase in the money supply to $\overline{M}_2$. This drives the equilibrium interest rate down to the target rate, r_T.

Panel (b) shows the opposite case. Again, the initial money supply curve is MS_1 with money supply $\overline{M}_1$. But this time the equilibrium interest rate, r_1, is below the target federal funds rate, r_T. In this case, the Fed will make an open-market sale of Treasury bills, leading to a fall in the money supply to $\overline{M}_2$ via the money multiplier. The money supply curve shifts leftward from MS_1 to MS_2, driving the equilibrium interest rate up to the target federal funds rate, r_T.

Long-Term Interest Rates

In the previous module we mentioned that *long-term interest rates*—rates on bonds or loans that mature in several years—don't necessarily move with short-term interest rates. How is that possible, and what does it say about monetary policy?

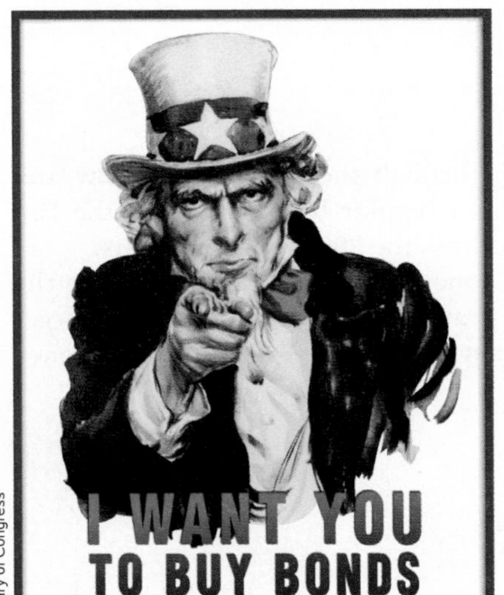

Library of Congress

Advertising during the two world wars increased the demand for government long-term bonds from savers who may have been reluctant, at other times, to tie up their funds for several years.

Consider the case of Millie, who has already decided to place $10,000 in U.S. government bonds for the next two years. However, she hasn't decided whether to put the money in one-year bonds, at a 4% rate of interest, or two-year bonds, at a 5% rate of interest. If she buys the one-year bond, then in one year, Millie will receive the $10,000 she paid for the bond (the *principal*) plus interest earned. If instead she buys the two-year bond, Millie will have to wait until the end of the second year to receive her principal and her interest.

You might think that the two-year bonds are a clearly better deal—but they may not be. Suppose that Millie expects the rate of interest on one-year bonds to rise sharply next year. If she puts her funds in one-year bonds this year, she will be able to reinvest the money at a much higher rate next year. And this could give her a two-year rate of return that is higher than if she put her funds into the two-year bonds today.

For example, if the rate of interest on one-year bonds rises from 4% this year to 8% next year, putting her funds in a one-year bond today and in another one-year bond a year from now will give her an annual rate of return over the next two years of about 6%, better than the 5% rate on two-year bonds.

The same considerations apply to all investors deciding between short-term and long-term bonds. If they expect short-term interest rates to rise, investors may buy short-term bonds even if long-term bonds bought today offer a higher interest rate today. If they expect short-term interest rates to fall, investors may buy long-term bonds even if short-term bonds bought today offer a higher interest rate today.

As this example suggests, long-term interest rates largely reflect the average expectation in the market about what's going to happen to short-term rates in the future. When long-term rates are higher than short-term rates, the market is signaling that it expects short-term rates to rise in the future.

This is not, however, the whole story: risk is also a factor. Return to the example of Millie, deciding whether to buy one-year or two-year bonds. Suppose that there is some chance she will need to cash in her investment after just one year—say, to meet an emergency medical bill. If she buys two-year bonds, she would have to sell those bonds to meet the unexpected expense. But what price will she get for those bonds? It depends on what has happened to interest rates in the rest of the economy. Recall that bond prices and interest rates move in opposite directions: if interest rates rise, bond prices fall, and vice versa.

This means that Millie will face extra risk if she buys two-year rather than one-year bonds, because if a year from now bond prices fall and she must sell her bonds in order to raise cash, she will lose money on the bonds.

Owing to this risk factor, long-term interest rates are, on average, higher than short-term rates in order to compensate long-term bond purchasers for the higher risk they face (although this relationship is reversed when short-term rates are unusually high).

The fact that long-term rates don't necessarily move with short-term rates is sometimes an important consideration for monetary policy.

ECONOMICS IN ACTION

FED REVERSES COURSE

The Fed's decision in March 2008 to cut its target interest rate represented a dramatic reversal of Fed policy that began in September 2007.

Figure 74-3 shows two interest rates from the beginning of 2004 through 2013: the target federal funds rate, decided by the Federal Open Market Committee, and the effective, or actual, rate in the market.

As you can see, the Fed raised its target rate in a series of steps from late 2004 until the middle of 2006; it did this to head off the possibility of an overheating economy and rising inflation.

But the Fed dramatically reversed course beginning in September 2007, as falling housing prices triggered a growing financial crisis and ultimately a severe recession. And in December 2008, the Fed decided to allow the federal funds rate to move inside a target band between 0% and 0.25%. From 2009 through 2013, the Fed funds rate was kept close to zero in response to a very weak economy and high unemployment.

Figure 74-3 also shows that the Fed doesn't always hit its target. There were a number of days, especially in 2008, when the effective federal funds rate was significantly above or below the target rate. But these episodes didn't last long, and overall the Fed got what it wanted, at least as far as short-term interest rates were concerned.

FIGURE 74-3 The Fed Reverses Course

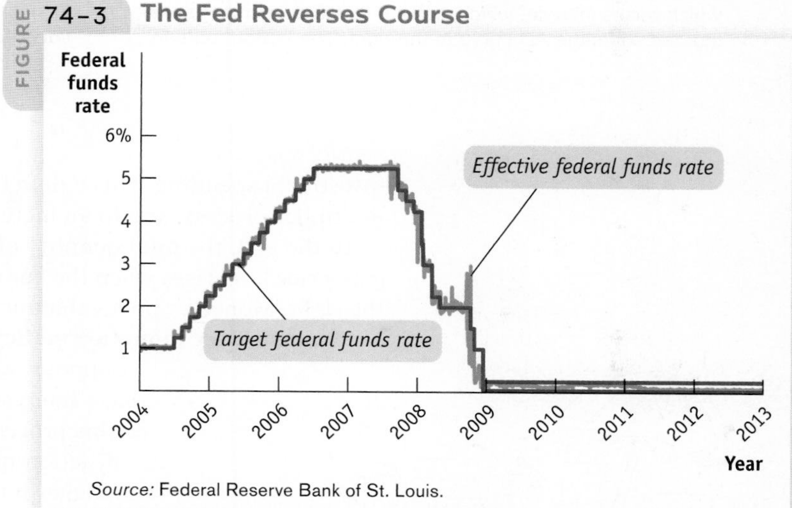

Source: Federal Reserve Bank of St. Louis.

Monetary Policy and Aggregate Demand

In an earlier section we saw how fiscal policy can be used to stabilize the economy. Now we will see how monetary policy—changes in the money supply and the interest rate—can play the same role.

Expansionary and Contractionary Monetary Policy

In Module 63 we learned that monetary policy shifts the aggregate demand curve. We can now explain how that works: through the effect of monetary policy on the interest rate.

Figure 74-4 illustrates the process. Suppose, first, that the Federal Reserve wants to reduce interest rates, so it expands the money supply. As you can see in the top portion of the figure, a lower interest rate, in turn, will lead, other things equal, to more

FIGURE 74-4 Expansionary and Contractionary Monetary Policy

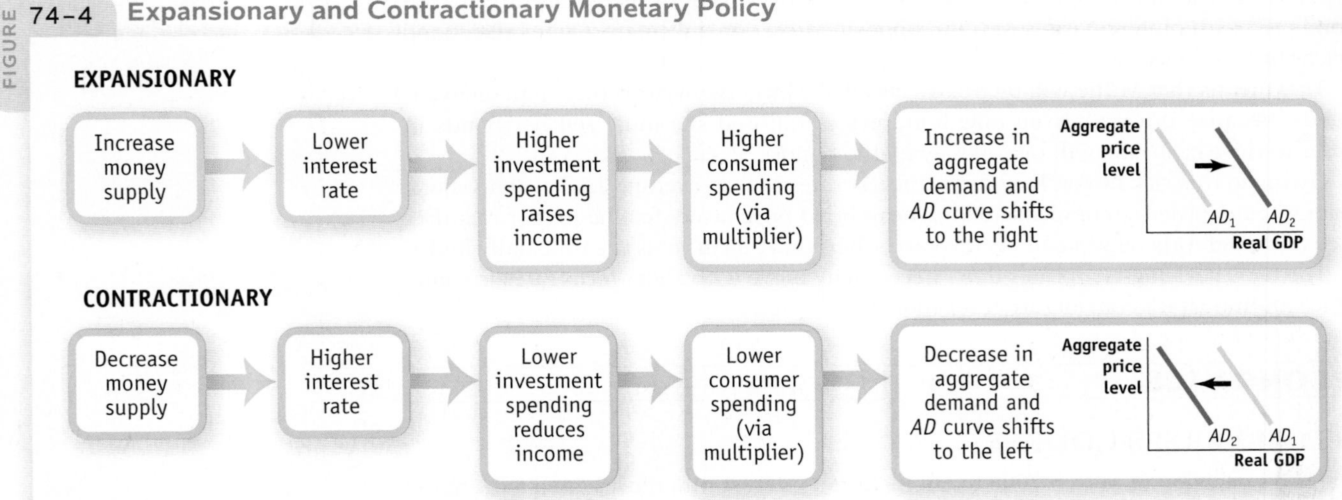

The top portion shows what happens when the Fed adopts an expansionary monetary policy and increases the money supply. Interest rates fall, leading to higher investment spending, which raises income, which, in turn, raises consumer spending and shifts the *AD* curve to the right. The bottom portion shows what happens when the Fed adopts a contractionary monetary policy and reduces the money supply. Interest rates rise, leading to lower investment spending and a reduction in income. This lowers consumer spending and shifts the *AD* curve to the left.

investment spending. This will in turn lead to higher consumer spending, through the multiplier process, and to an increase in aggregate output demanded.

In the end, the total quantity of goods and services demanded at any given aggregate price level rises when the quantity of money increases, and the *AD* curve shifts to the right. Monetary policy that increases the demand for goods and services is known as **expansionary monetary policy.**

Suppose, alternatively, that the Federal Reserve wants to increase interest rates, so it contracts the money supply. You can see this process illustrated in the bottom portion of the diagram. Contraction of the money supply leads to a higher interest rate. The higher interest rate leads to lower investment spending, then to lower consumer spending, and then to a decrease in aggregate output demanded.

So the total quantity of goods and services demanded falls when the money supply is reduced, and the *AD* curve shifts to the left. Monetary policy that decreases the demand for goods and services is called **contractionary monetary policy.**

"I told you the Fed should have tightened."

© The New Yorker Collection 1997 Robert Mankoff from cartoonbank.com. All Rights Reserved.

Monetary Policy in Practice

How does the Fed decide whether to use expansionary or contractionary monetary policy? And how does it decide how much is enough? As we know, policy makers try to fight recessions, as well as try to ensure *price stability*: low (though usually not zero) inflation. Actual monetary policy reflects a combination of these goals.

In general, the Federal Reserve and other central banks tend to engage in expansionary monetary policy when actual real GDP is below potential output. Panel (a) of Figure 74-5 shows the U.S. output gap, which we've previously defined as the percentage difference between actual real GDP and potential output, versus the federal funds rate since 1985. (Recall that the output gap is positive when actual real GDP exceeds potential output.) As you can see, the Fed has tended to raise interest rates when the

Expansionary monetary policy is monetary policy that increases aggregate demand.

Contractionary monetary policy is monetary policy that decreases aggregate demand.

FIGURE 74-5 Tracking Monetary Policy Using the Output Gap and Inflation

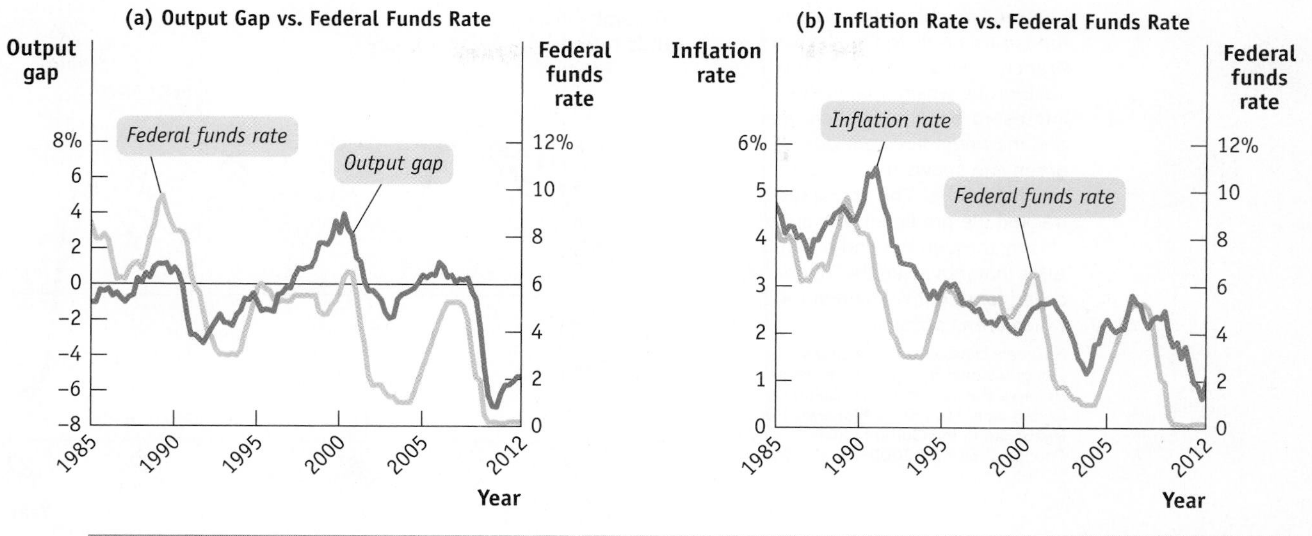

Panel (a) shows that the federal funds rate usually rises when the output gap is positive—that is, when actual real GDP is above potential output—and falls when the output gap is negative. Panel (b) illustrates that the federal funds rate tends to be high when inflation is high and low when inflation is low.

Sources: Bureau of Labor Statistics; Congressional Budget Office; Federal Reserve Bank of St. Louis.

output gap is rising—that is, when the economy is developing an inflationary gap—and cut rates when the output gap is falling.

The big exception was the late 1990s, when the Fed left rates steady for several years even as the economy developed a positive output gap (which went along with a low unemployment rate). One reason the Fed was willing to keep interest rates low in the late 1990s was that inflation was low.

Panel (b) of Figure 74-5 compares the inflation rate, measured as the rate of change in consumer prices excluding food and energy, with the federal funds rate. You can see how low inflation during the mid-1990s, the early 2000s, and the late 2000s helped encourage loose monetary policy in the late 1990s, in 2002–2003, and again beginning in 2008.

The Taylor Rule Method of Setting Monetary Policy

In 1993 Stanford economist John Taylor suggested that monetary policy should follow a simple rule that takes into account concerns about both the business cycle and inflation. He also suggested that actual monetary policy often looks as if the Federal Reserve was, in fact, more or less following the proposed rule. A **Taylor rule for monetary policy** is a rule for setting interest rates that takes into account the inflation rate and the output gap or, in some cases, the unemployment rate.

A widely cited example of a Taylor rule is a relationship among Fed policy, inflation, and unemployment estimated by economists at the Federal Reserve Bank of San Francisco. These economists found that between 1988 and 2008 the Fed's behavior was well summarized by the following Taylor rule:

$$\text{Federal funds rate} = 2.07 + 1.28 \times \text{inflation rate} - 1.95 \times \text{unemployment gap}$$

where the inflation rate was measured by the change over the previous year in consumer prices excluding food and energy, and the unemployment gap was the difference between the actual unemployment rate and Congressional Budget Office estimates of the natural rate of unemployment.

A **Taylor rule for monetary policy** is a rule that sets the federal funds rate according to the level of the inflation rate and either the output gap or the unemployment rate.

FIGURE 74-6 **The Taylor Rule and the Federal Funds Rate**

The red line shows the federal funds rate predicted by the San Francisco Fed's version of the Taylor rule, which relates the interest rate to the inflation rate and the unemployment rate. The green line shows the actual federal funds rate. The actual rate tracked the predicted rate quite closely through the end of 2008. After that, however, the Taylor rule called for negative interest rates, which aren't possible.

Sources: Bureau of Labor Statistics; Congressional Budget Office; Federal Reserve Bank of St. Louis; Glenn D. Rudebusch, "The Fed's Monetary Policy Response to the Current Crisis," *FRBSF Economic Letter* #2009-17 (May 22, 2009).

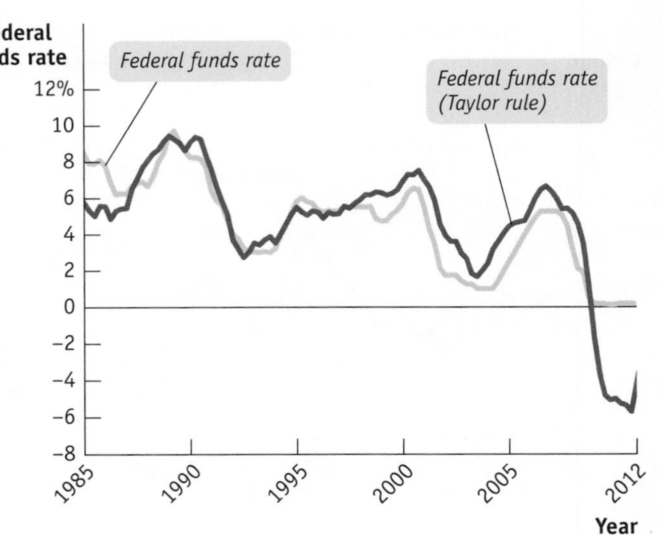

Figure 74-6 compares the federal funds rate predicted by this rule with the actual federal funds rate from 1985 to 2012. As you can see, the Fed's decisions were quite close to those predicted by this particular Taylor rule from 1988 through the end of 2008. We'll talk about what happened after 2008 shortly.

Inflation Targeting

Until January 2012, the Fed did not explicitly commit itself to achieving a particular inflation rate. However, in January 2012, the Fed chairman at the time, Ben Bernanke, announced that the Fed would set its policy to maintain an approximately 2% inflation rate per year. With that statement, the Fed joined a number of other central banks that have explicit inflation targets.

So rather than using a Taylor rule to set monetary policy, they instead announced the inflation rate that they want to achieve—the *inflation target*—and set policy in an attempt to hit that target. This method of setting monetary policy, called **inflation targeting,** involves having the central bank announce the inflation rate it is trying to achieve and set policy in an attempt to hit that target. The central bank of New Zealand, which was the first country to adopt inflation targeting, specified a range for that target of 1% to 3%.

Other central banks commit themselves to achieving a specific number. For example, the Bank of England has committed to keeping inflation at 2%. In practice, there doesn't seem to be much difference between these versions: central banks with a target range for inflation seem to aim for the middle of that range, and central banks with a fixed target tend to give themselves considerable wiggle room.

One major difference between inflation targeting and the Taylor rule method is that inflation targeting is forward-looking rather than backward-looking. That is, the Taylor rule method adjusts monetary policy in response to *past* inflation, but inflation targeting is based on a forecast of future inflation.

Advocates of inflation targeting argue that it has two key advantages over a Taylor rule: *transparency* and *accountability*. First, economic uncertainty is reduced because the central bank's plan is transparent: the public knows the objective of an inflation-targeting central bank. Second, the central bank's success can be judged by seeing how closely actual inflation rates have matched the inflation target, making central bankers accountable.

Inflation targeting occurs when the central bank sets an explicit target for the inflation rate and sets monetary policy in order to hit that target.

Critics of inflation targeting argue that it's too restrictive because there are times when other concerns—like the stability of the financial system—should take priority over achieving any particular inflation rate. Indeed, in late 2007 and early 2008 the Fed cut interest rates much more than either a Taylor rule or inflation targeting would have dictated because it feared that turmoil in the financial markets would lead to a major recession. (In fact, it did.)

Many American macroeconomists have had positive things to say about inflation targeting—including Bernanke. And in January 2012 the Fed declared that what it means by the "price stability" it seeks is 2 percent inflation, although there was no explicit commitment about when this inflation rate would be achieved.

The Zero Lower Bound Problem

As Figure 74-6 shows, a Taylor rule based on inflation and the unemployment rate does a good job of predicting Federal Reserve policy from 1988 through 2008. After that, however, things go awry, and for a simple reason: with very high unemployment and low inflation, the same Taylor rule called for an interest rate less than zero, which isn't possible.

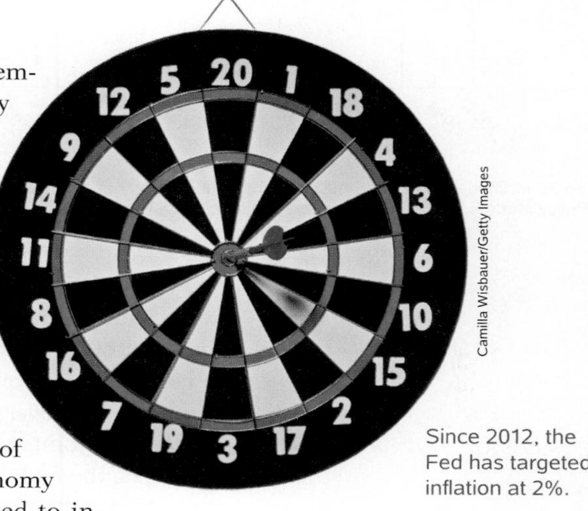

Camilla Wisbauer/Getty Images

Since 2012, the Fed has targeted inflation at 2%.

Why aren't negative interest rates possible? Because people always have the alternative of holding cash, which offers a zero interest rate. Nobody would ever buy a bond yielding an interest rate less than zero because holding cash would be a better alternative.

The fact that interest rates can't go below zero—called the **zero lower bound for interest rates**—sets limits to the power of monetary policy. In 2009 and 2010, inflation was low and the economy was operating far below potential, so the Federal Reserve wanted to increase aggregate demand. Yet the normal way it does this—open-market purchases of short-term government debt to expand the money supply—had run out of room to operate because short-term interest rates were already at or near zero.

In November 2010 the Fed began an attempt to circumvent this problem, which went by the somewhat obscure name *quantitative easing.* Instead of purchasing only short-term government debt, it began buying longer-term government debt—five-year or six-year bonds, rather than three-month Treasury bills.

As we have already pointed out, long-term interest rates don't exactly follow short-term rates. At the time the Fed began this program, short-term rates were near zero, but rates on longer-term bonds were between 2% and 3%. The Fed hoped that direct purchases of these longer-term bonds would drive down interest rates on long-term debt, exerting an expansionary effect on the economy.

Long-term interest rates did decline to about 1% in 2010, then rose back up to 2% in 2011, before once again returning to 1% where they stayed until mid-2013. Although the Fed's policy may have boosted spending from 2010 to 2013, recovery remained slow.

ECONOMICS IN ACTION

WHAT THE FED WANTS, THE FED GETS

What's the evidence that the Fed can actually cause an economic contraction or expansion? You might think that finding such evidence is just a matter of looking at what happens to the economy when interest rates go up or down. But it turns out that there's a big problem with that approach: the Fed usually changes interest rates in an attempt to tame the business cycle, raising rates if the economy is expanding and reducing rates if the economy is slumping. So in the actual data, it often looks as if low interest rates go along with a weak economy and high rates go along with a strong economy.

The **zero lower bound for interest rates** means that interest rates cannot fall below zero.

FIGURE 74-7 When the Fed Wants a Recession

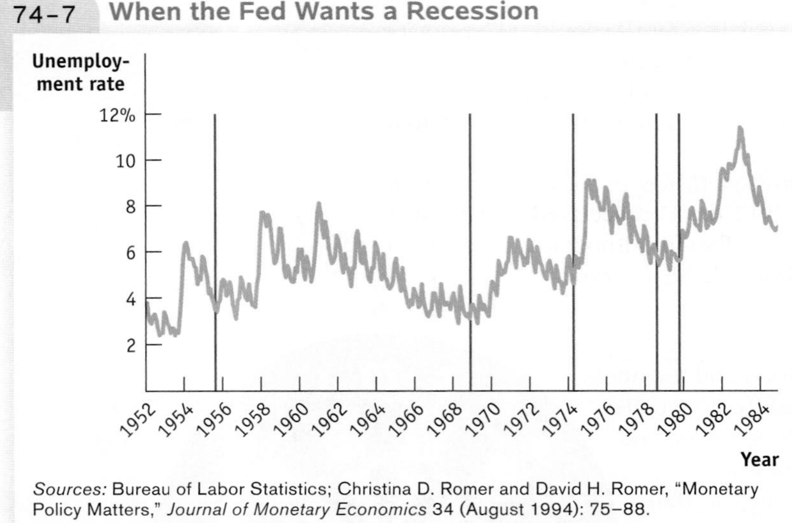

Sources: Bureau of Labor Statistics; Christina D. Romer and David H. Romer, "Monetary Policy Matters," *Journal of Monetary Economics* 34 (August 1994): 75–88.

In a famous paper titled "Monetary Policy Matters," the macroeconomists Christina Romer and David Romer solved this problem by focusing on episodes in which monetary policy wasn't a reaction to the business cycle. Specifically, they used minutes from the Federal Open Market Committee and other sources to identify episodes "in which the Federal Reserve in effect decided to attempt to create a recession to reduce inflation."

Rather than just using monetary policy as a tool of macroeconomic stabilization, sometimes it is used to eliminate *embedded* inflation—inflation that people believe will persist into the future. In such a case, the Fed needs to create a recessionary gap—not just eliminate an inflationary gap—to wring embedded inflation out of the economy.

Figure 74-7 shows the unemployment rate between 1952 and 1984 (orange) and also identifies five dates on which, according to Romer and Romer, the Fed decided that it wanted a recession (vertical red lines). In four out of the five cases, the decision to contract the economy was followed, after a modest lag, by a rise in the unemployment rate. On average, Romer and Romer found, the unemployment rate rises by 2 percentage points after the Fed decides that unemployment needs to go up.

So yes, the Fed gets what it wants.

MODULE 74 Review

Solutions appear at the back of the book.

Check Your Understanding

1. Assume that there is an increase in the demand for money at every interest rate. Draw a diagram that shows what effect this will have on the equilibrium interest rate for a given money supply.

2. Now assume that the Fed is following a policy of targeting the federal funds rate. What will the Fed do in the situation described in Problem 1 to keep the federal funds rate unchanged? Illustrate with a diagram.

3. Suppose the economy is currently suffering from a recessionary gap and the Federal Reserve uses an expansionary monetary policy to close that gap. Describe the short-run effect of this policy on the following.
   - **a.** the money supply curve
   - **b.** the equilibrium interest rate
   - **c.** investment spending
   - **d.** consumer spending
   - **e.** aggregate output

Multiple-Choice Questions

1. At each meeting of the Federal Open Market Committee, the Federal Reserve sets a target for which of the following?
   - I. the federal funds rate
   - II. the prime interest rate
   - III. the market interest rate

   - **a.** I only
   - **b.** II only
   - **c.** III only
   - **d.** I and III only
   - **e.** I, II, and III

2. Which of the following actions can the Fed take to decrease the equilibrium interest rate?
   a. increase the money supply
   b. increase money demand
   c. decrease the money supply
   d. decrease money demand
   e. both (a) and (d)

3. Contractionary monetary policy attempts to __________ aggregate demand by __________ interest rates.
   a. decrease; increasing
   b. increase; decreasing
   c. decrease; decreasing
   d. increase; increasing
   e. increase; maintaining

4. Which of the following is a goal of monetary policy?
   a. zero inflation
   b. deflation
   c. price stability
   d. increased potential output
   e. decreased actual real GDP

5. When implementing monetary policy, the Federal Reserve attempts to achieve
   a. an explicit target inflation rate.
   b. zero inflation.
   c. a low rate of deflation.
   d. a low but positive inflation rate.
   e. between 4% and 5% inflation.

Critical-Thinking Questions

1. What can the Fed do with each of its tools to implement expansionary monetary policy during a recession?
2. Use a graph of the money market to explain how the Fed's use of expansionary monetary policy affects interest rates in the short run.
3. Explain how the interest rate changes you graphed in Problem 2 affect aggregate supply and demand in the short run.
4. Use an aggregate demand and supply graph to illustrate how expansionary monetary policy affects aggregate output in the short run.

PITFALLS

THE TARGET VERSUS THE MARKET

? Over the years, the Federal Reserve has changed the way in which monetary policy is implemented. In the late 1970s and early 1980s, it set a target level for the money supply and altered the monetary base to achieve that target. Under this way of operating, the federal funds rate fluctuated freely. Today the Fed uses the reverse procedure, setting a target for the federal funds rate and allowing the money supply to fluctuate as it pursues that target. Do these changes in the way the Fed operates alter the way the money market works?

> NOT AT ALL. THE MONEY MARKET WORKS THE SAME WAY AS ALWAYS: THE INTEREST RATE IS DETERMINED BY THE SUPPLY AND DEMAND FOR MONEY. THE ONLY DIFFERENCE IS THAT NOW THE FED ADJUSTS THE SUPPLY OF MONEY TO ACHIEVE ITS TARGET INTEREST RATE Although you may hear people say that the interest rate no longer reflects the supply and demand for money because the Fed sets the interest rate, this is a common misconception. It's important not to confuse a change in the Fed's operating procedure with a change in the way the economy works.

To learn more, see pages 764–766.

MODULE 75 Money, Output, and Prices in the Long Run

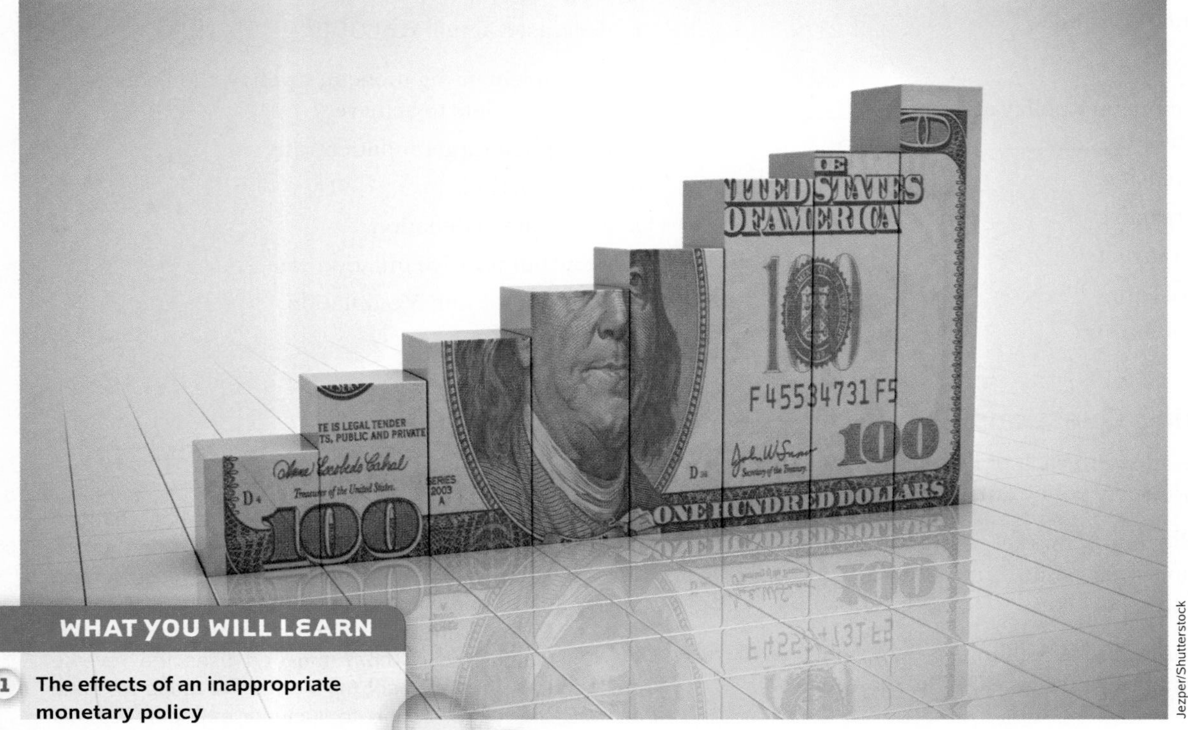
Jezper/Shutterstock

WHAT YOU WILL LEARN

1. **The effects of an inappropriate monetary policy**
2. **The concept of monetary neutrality and its relationship to the long-run economic effects of monetary policy**

In the previous module we discussed how expansionary and contractionary monetary policy can be used to stabilize the economy. The Federal Reserve can use its monetary policy tools to change the money supply and cause the equilibrium interest rate in the money market to increase or decrease.

But what if a central bank pursues a monetary policy that is not appropriate? That is, what if a central bank pursues expansionary policy during an expansion or contractionary policy during a recession? In this module we consider how a counterproductive action by a central bank can actually destabilize the economy in the short run.

We also introduce the long-run effects of monetary policy. As we've seen, the money market (where monetary policy has its effect on the money supply) determines the interest rate only in the short run. In the long run, the interest rate is determined in the market for loanable funds. Now we turn to long-run adjustments and consider the long-run effects of monetary policy.

Money, Output, and Prices

Because of its expansionary and contractionary effects, monetary policy is generally the policy tool of choice to help stabilize the economy. However, not all actions by central banks are productive. Central banks sometimes print money not to fight a recessionary gap but to help the government pay its bills, an action that typically destabilizes the economy.

What happens when a change in the money supply pushes the economy away from, rather than toward, long-run equilibrium? The economy is self-correcting in the long run: a demand shock has only a temporary effect on aggregate output. If the demand shock is the result of a change in the money supply, we can make a stronger statement: in the long run, changes in the quantity of money affect the aggregate price level, but they do not change real aggregate output or the interest rate.

To see why, let's look at what happens if the central bank permanently increases the money supply.

Short-Run and Long-Run Effects of an Increase in the Money Supply

To analyze the long-run effects of monetary policy, it's helpful to think of the central bank as choosing a target for the money supply rather than for the interest rate. In assessing the effects of an increase in the money supply, we return to the analysis of the long-run effects of an increase in aggregate demand.

Figure 75-1 shows the short-run and long-run effects of an increase in the money supply when the economy begins at potential output, Y_1. The initial short-run aggregate supply curve is $SRAS_1$, the long-run aggregate supply curve is *LRAS*, and the initial aggregate demand curve is AD_1. The economy's initial equilibrium is at E_1, a point of both short-run and long-run macroeconomic equilibrium because it is on both the short-run and the long-run aggregate supply curves. Real GDP is at potential output, Y_1.

Now suppose there is an increase in the money supply. Other things equal, an increase in the money supply reduces the interest rate, which increases investment spending, which leads to a further rise in consumer spending, and so on. So an increase in

FIGURE 75-1 The Short-Run and Long-Run Effects of an Increase in the Money Supply

An increase in the money supply generates a positive short-run effect, but no long-run effect, on real GDP. Here, the economy begins at E_1, a point of short-run and long-run macroeconomic equilibrium. An increase in the money supply shifts the *AD* curve rightward, and the economy moves to a new short-run equilibrium at E_2 and a new real GDP of Y_2. But E_2 is not a long-run equilibrium: Y_2 exceeds potential output, Y_1, leading over time to an increase in nominal wages. In the long run, the increase in nominal wages shifts the short-run aggregate supply curve leftward, to a new position at $SRAS_2$. The economy reaches a new short-run and long-run macroeconomic equilibrium at E_3 on the *LRAS* curve, and output falls back to potential output, Y_1. The only long-run effect of an increase in the money supply is an increase in the aggregate price level from P_1 to P_3.

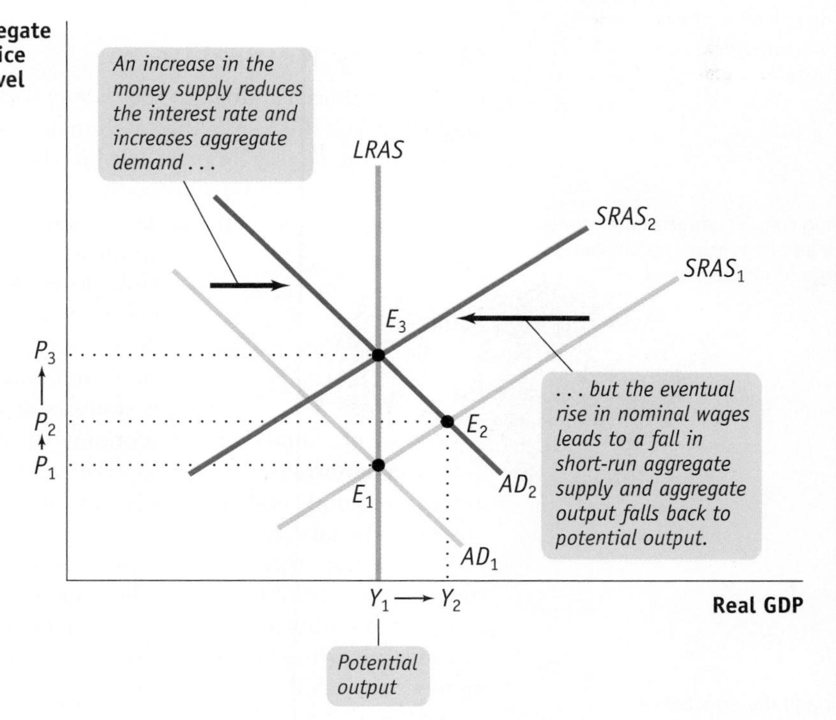
Aggregate price level
An increase in the money supply reduces the interest rate and increases aggregate demand . . .
LRAS
SRAS2
SRAS1
E3
P3
P2
P1
E2
E1
AD2
AD1
. . . but the eventual rise in nominal wages leads to a fall in short-run aggregate supply and aggregate output falls back to potential output.
Y1 → Y2
Real GDP
Potential output

the money supply increases the quantity of goods and services demanded, shifting the *AD* curve rightward to AD_2.

In the short run, the economy moves to a new short-run macroeconomic equilibrium at E_2. The price level rises from P_1 to P_2, and real GDP rises from Y_1 to Y_2. That is, both the aggregate price level and aggregate output increase in the short run.

But the aggregate output level Y_2 is above potential output. As a result, nominal wages will rise over time, causing the short-run aggregate supply curve to shift leftward. This process stops only when the *SRAS* curve ends up at $SRAS_2$ and the economy ends up at point E_3, a point of both short-run and long-run macroeconomic equilibrium.

The long-run effect of an increase in the money supply, then, is that the aggregate price level has increased from P_1 to P_3, but aggregate output is back at potential output, Y_1. In the long run, a monetary expansion raises the aggregate price level but has no effect on real GDP.

If the money supply decreases, the story we have just told plays out in reverse. Other things equal, a decrease in the money supply raises the interest rate, which decreases investment spending, which leads to a further decrease in consumer spending, and so on. So a decrease in the money supply decreases the quantity of goods and services demanded at any given aggregate price level, shifting the aggregate demand curve to the left.

In the short run, the economy moves to a new short-run macroeconomic equilibrium at a level of real GDP below potential output and a lower aggregate price level. That is, both the aggregate price level and aggregate output decrease in the short run.

But what happens over time? When the aggregate output level is below potential output, nominal wages fall. When this happens, the short-run aggregate supply curve shifts rightward. This process stops only when the *SRAS* curve ends up at a point of both short-run and long-run macroeconomic equilibrium.

The long-run effect of a decrease in the money supply, then, is that the aggregate price level decreases, but aggregate output is back at potential output. In the long run, a monetary contraction decreases the aggregate price level but has no effect on real GDP.

Monetary Neutrality

How much does a change in the money supply change the aggregate price level in the long run? The answer is that a change in the money supply leads to a proportional change in the aggregate price level in the long run. For example, if the money supply falls 25%, the aggregate price level falls 25% in the long run; if the money supply rises 50%, the aggregate price level rises 50% in the long run.

In the long run, a change in the money supply leads to a proportional change in the aggregate price level.

FeaturePics

How do we know this? Consider the following thought experiment: suppose all prices in the economy—prices of final goods and services and also factor prices, such as nominal wage rates—double. And suppose the money supply doubles at the same time. What difference does this make to the economy in real terms? None. All real variables in the economy—such as real GDP and the real value of the money supply (the amount of goods and services it can buy)—are unchanged. So there is no reason for anyone to behave any differently.

We can state this argument in reverse: if the economy starts out in long-run macroeconomic equilibrium and the money supply changes, restoring long-run macroeconomic equilibrium requires restoring all real values to their original values. This includes restoring the real value of the money supply to its original level. So if the money supply falls 25%, the aggregate price level must fall 25%; if the money supply rises 50%, the price level must rise 50%; and so on.

According to the concept of **monetary neutrality**, changes in the money supply have no real effects on the economy in the long run.

This analysis demonstrates the concept known as **monetary neutrality,** in which changes in the money supply have no real effects on the economy. In the long run, the only effect of an increase in the money supply is to raise the aggregate price level by an equal percentage. Economists argue that *money is neutral in the long run.*

This is, however, a good time to recall the dictum of John Maynard Keynes: "In the long run we are all dead." In the long run, changes in the money supply don't have any effect on real GDP, interest rates, or anything else except the price level.

But it would be foolish to conclude from this that the Fed is irrelevant. Monetary policy does have powerful real effects on the economy in the short run, often making the difference between recession and expansion. And that matters a lot for society's welfare.

Changes in the Money Supply and the Interest Rate in the Long Run

In the short run, an increase in the money supply leads to a fall in the interest rate, and a decrease in the money supply leads to a rise in the interest rate. We have explained that in the long run it's a different story: changes in the money supply don't affect the interest rate at all. Let's look at why.

Figure 75-2 shows why. It shows the money supply curve and the money demand curve before and after the Fed increases the money supply. We assume that the economy is initially at E_1, in long-run macroeconomic equilibrium at potential output, and with money supply $\overline{M}_1$. The initial equilibrium interest rate, determined by the intersection of the money demand curve MD_1 and the money supply curve MS_1, is r_1.

FIGURE 75-2 **The Long-Run Determination of the Interest Rate**

In the short run, an increase in the money supply from $\overline{M}_1$ to $\overline{M}_2$ pushes the interest rate down from r_1 to r_2 and the economy moves to E_2, a short-run equilibrium. In the long run, however, the aggregate price level rises in proportion to the increase in the money supply, leading to an increase in money demand at any given interest rate in proportion to the increase in the aggregate price level, as shown by the shift from MD_1 to MD_2. The result is that the quantity of money demanded at any given interest rate rises by the same amount as the quantity of money supplied. The economy moves to long-run equilibrium at E_3 and the interest rate returns to r_1.

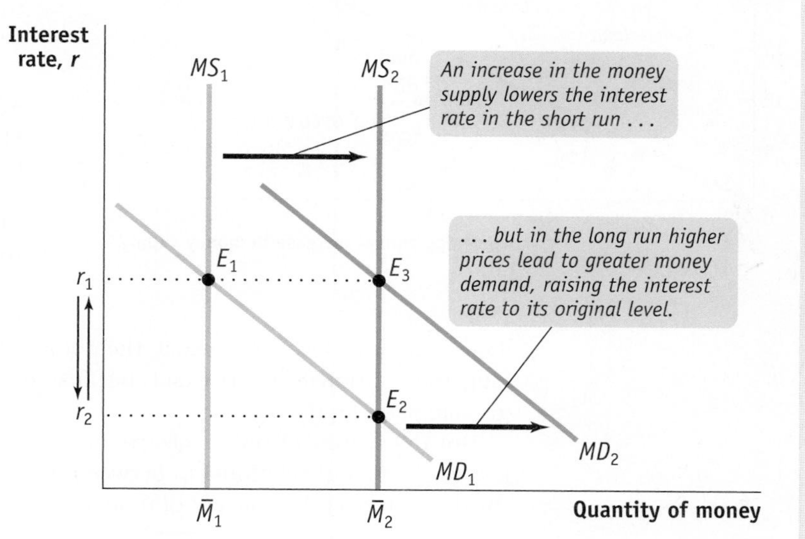
Interest rate, r
MS1
MS2
An increase in the money supply lowers the interest rate in the short run . . .
. . . but in the long run higher prices lead to greater money demand, raising the interest rate to its original level.
r1
E1
E3
E2
r2
MD1
MD2
M̄1
M̄2
Quantity of money

Now suppose the money supply increases from $\overline{M}_1$ to $\overline{M}_2$. In the short run, the economy moves from E_1 to E_2 and the interest rate falls from r_1 to r_2. Over time, however, the aggregate price level rises, and this raises money demand, shifting the money demand curve rightward from MD_1 to MD_2. The economy moves to a new long-run equilibrium at E_3, and the interest rate rises to its original level at r_1.

And it turns out that the long-run equilibrium interest rate is the original interest rate, r_1. We know this for two reasons.

1. Because of monetary neutrality, in the long run the aggregate price level rises by the same proportion as the money supply; so if the money supply rises by, say, 50%, the price level will also rise by 50%.

2. The demand for money is, other things equal, proportional to the aggregate price level. So a 50% increase in the money supply raises the aggregate price level by 50%, which increases the quantity of money demanded at any given interest rate by 50%. As a result, the quantity of money demanded at the initial interest rate, r_1, rises exactly as much as the money supply—so that r_1 is still the equilibrium interest rate.

In the long run, then, changes in the money supply do not affect the interest rate.

ECONOMICS ▶ IN ACTION

INTERNATIONAL EVIDENCE OF MONETARY NEUTRALITY

These days monetary policy is quite similar among wealthy countries. Each major nation (or, in the case of the euro, the euro area) has a central bank that is insulated from political pressure. All of these central banks try to keep the aggregate price level roughly stable, which usually means inflation of, at most, 2% to 3% per year.

But if we look at a longer period and a wider group of countries, we see large differences in the growth of the money supply. Between 1970 and the present, the money supply rose only a few percent per year in some countries, such as Switzerland and the United States, but rose much more rapidly in some poorer countries, such as South Africa.

These differences allow us to see whether increases in the money supply in the long run really do lead to equal percent rises in the aggregate price level.

Figure 75-3 shows the annual percentage increases in the money supply and average annual increases in the aggregate price level—that is, the average rate of inflation—for a sample of countries during the period 1970–2010, with each point representing a country.

If the relationship between increases in the money supply and changes in the aggregate price level were exact, the points would lie precisely on a 45-degree line. In fact, the relationship isn't exact, because other factors besides money affect the aggregate price level.

But the scatter of points clearly lies close to a 45-degree line, showing a more or less proportional relationship between money and the aggregate price level. That is, the data support the concept of monetary neutrality in the long run.

FIGURE 75-3 The Long-Run Relationship Between Money and Inflation

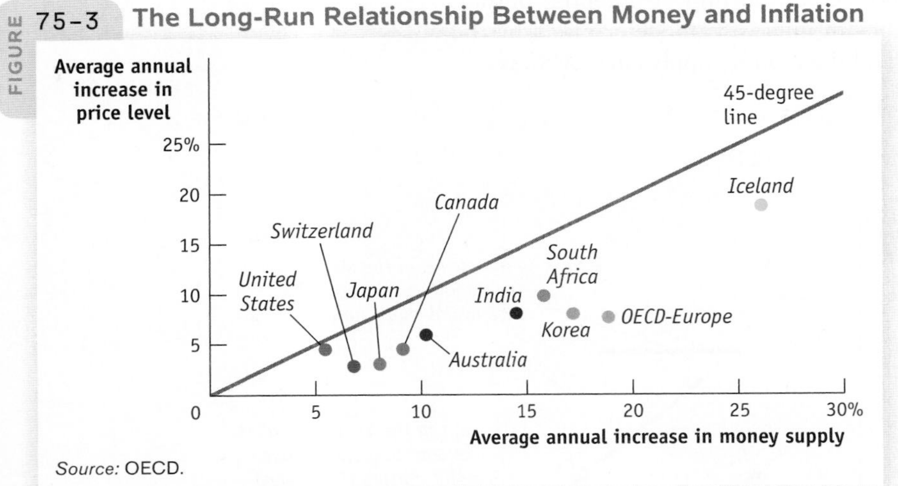

Source: OECD.

MODULE 75 Review

Solutions appear at the back of the book.

Check Your Understanding

1. Suppose the economy begins in long-run macroeconomic equilibrium. What is the long-run effect on the aggregate price level of a 5% increase in the money supply? Explain.

2. Again supposing the economy begins in long-run macroeconomic equilibrium, what is the long-run effect on the interest rate of a 5% increase in the money supply? Explain.

Multiple-Choice Questions

1. In the long run, changes in the quantity of money affect which of the following?
   I. real aggregate output
   II. interest rates
   III. the aggregate price level
   a. I only
   b. II only
   c. III only
   d. I and II only
   e. I, II, and III

2. An increase in the money supply will lead to which of the following in the short run?
   a. higher interest rates
   b. decreased investment spending
   c. decreased consumer spending
   d. increased aggregate demand
   e. lower real GDP

3. A 10% decrease in the money supply will change the aggregate price level in the long run by
   a. zero.
   b. less than 10%.
   c. 10%.
   d. 20%.
   e. more than 20%.

4. Monetary neutrality means that, in the long run, changes in the money supply
   a. cannot happen.
   b. have no effect on the economy.
   c. have no real effect on the economy.
   d. increase real GDP.
   e. change real interest rates.

5. A graph of percentage increases in the money supply and average annual increases in the price level for various countries provides evidence that
   a. changes in the two variables are exactly equal.
   b. the money supply and aggregate price level are unrelated.
   c. money neutrality holds only in wealthy countries.
   d. monetary policy is ineffective.
   e. money is neutral in the long run.

Critical-Thinking Questions

1. Draw a graph of aggregate demand and supply showing an economy in long-run macroeconomic equilibrium.
2. On your graph, show what happens in the short run if the central bank increases the money supply to pay off a government deficit. Explain.
3. On your graph, show what will happen in the long run. Explain.

BUSINESS CASE: PIMCO Bets on Cheap Money

Stephen VanHorn/Shutterstock

Pacific Investment Management Company, generally known as PIMCO, is one of the world's largest investment companies. Among other things, it runs PIMCO Total Return, the world's second-largest mutual fund. The head of PIMCO, Bill Gross, is legendary for his ability to predict trends in financial markets, especially bond markets, where PIMCO does much of its investing.

In the fall of 2009, Gross decided to put more of PIMCO's assets into long-term U.S. government bonds. This amounted to a bet that long-term interest rates would fall. This bet was especially interesting because it was the opposite of the bet many other investors were making. For example, in November 2009 the investment bank Morgan Stanley told its clients to expect a sharp rise in long-term interest rates.

What lay behind PIMCO's bet? Gross explained the firm's thinking in his September 2009 commentary. He suggested that unemployment was likely to stay high and inflation low. "Global policy rates," he asserted—meaning the federal funds rate and its equivalents in Europe and elsewhere—"will remain low for extended periods of time."

The Federal Funds Rate and Long-Term Interest Rates, 2009–2011

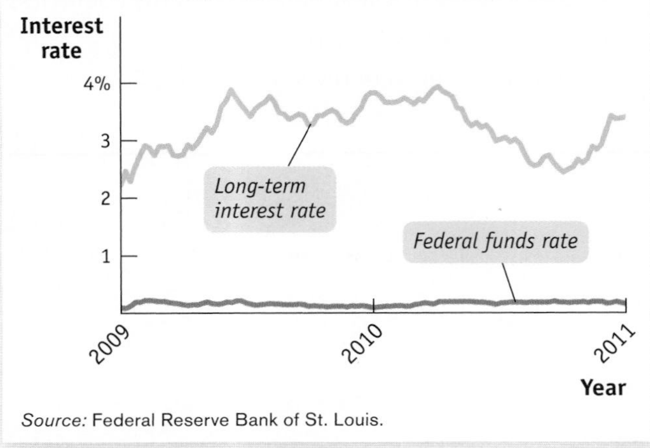

Source: Federal Reserve Bank of St. Louis.

PIMCO's view was in sharp contrast to those of other investors: Morgan Stanley expected long-term rates to rise in part because it expected the Fed to raise the federal funds rate in 2010.

Who was right? PIMCO, mostly. As the accompanying figure shows, the federal funds rate stayed near zero, and long-term interest rates fell through much of 2010, although they rose somewhat very late in the year as investors became somewhat more optimistic about economic recovery.

Morgan Stanley, which had bet on rising rates, actually apologized to investors for getting it so wrong.

Bill Gross's foresight, however, was a lot less accurate in 2011. Anticipating a significantly stronger U.S. economy by mid-2011 that would result in inflation, Gross bet heavily against U.S. government bonds early that year. But this time he was wrong, as weak growth continued. By late summer 2011, Gross realized his mistake as U.S. bonds rose in value and the value of his funds sank. He admitted to the *Wall Street Journal* that he had "lost sleep" over his bet, and called it a "mistake."

Questions for Thought

1. Why did PIMCO's view that unemployment would stay high and inflation low lead to a forecast that policy interest rates would remain low for an extended period?
2. Why would low policy rates suggest low long-term interest rates?
3. What might have caused long-term interest rates to rise in late 2010, even though the federal funds rate was still zero?

SECTION 23 REVIEW

Summary

The Federal Reserve and Monetary Policy

1. The monetary base is controlled by the Federal Reserve, the central bank of the United States. The Fed regulates banks and sets reserve requirements. To meet those requirements, banks borrow and lend reserves in the **federal funds market** at the **federal funds rate.** Through the discount window facility, banks can borrow from the Fed at the **discount rate.**
2. **Open-market operations** by the Fed are the principal tool of monetary policy: the Fed can increase or reduce the monetary base by buying U.S. Treasury bills from banks or selling U.S. Treasury bills to banks.

The Money Market

3. The **money demand curve** arises from a trade-off between the opportunity cost of holding money and the liquidity that money provides. The opportunity cost of holding money depends on **short-term interest rates,** not **long-term interest rates.** Changes in the aggregate price level, real GDP, technology, and institutions shift the money demand curve.
4. According to the **liquidity preference model of the interest rate,** the interest rate is determined in the money market by the money demand curve and the **money supply curve.** The Federal Reserve can change the interest rate in the short run by shifting the money supply curve.

Monetary Policy and the Interest Rate

5. In practice, the Fed uses open-market operations to achieve a **target federal funds rate,** which other short-term interest rates generally track. Although long-term interest rates don't necessarily move with short-term interest rates, they reflect expectations about what's going to happen to short-term rates in the future.
6. **Expansionary monetary policy** reduces the interest rate by increasing the money supply. This increases investment spending and consumer spending, which in turn increases aggregate demand and real GDP in the short run. **Contractionary monetary policy** raises the interest rate by reducing the money supply. This reduces investment spending and consumer spending, which in turn reduces aggregate demand and real GDP in the short run.
7. The Federal Reserve and other central banks try to stabilize the economy, limiting fluctuations of actual output around potential output, while also keeping inflation low but positive. Under a **Taylor rule for monetary policy,** the target federal funds rate rises when there is high inflation and either a positive output gap or very low unemployment; it falls when there is low or negative inflation and either a negative output gap or high unemployment. Some central banks (including the Fed as of January 2012) engage in **inflation targeting,** which is a forward-looking policy rule, whereas the Taylor rule method is a backward-looking policy rule.
8. Because monetary policy is subject to fewer implementation lags than fiscal policy, it is the preferred policy tool for stabilizing the economy. Because interest rates cannot fall below zero—the **zero lower bound for interest rates**—the power of monetary policy is limited.

Money, Output, and Prices in the Long Run

9. In the long run, changes in the money supply affect the aggregate price level but not real GDP or the interest rate. Data show that the concept of **monetary neutrality** holds: changes in the money supply have no real effect on the economy in the long run.

Key Terms

Problems

1. Show the changes to the T-accounts for the Federal Reserve and for commercial banks when the Federal Reserve buys \$50 million in U.S. Treasury bills. If the public holds a fixed amount of currency (so that all loans create an equal amount of deposits in the banking system), the minimum reserve ratio is 10%, and banks hold no excess reserves, by how much will deposits in the commercial banks change? By how much will the money supply change? Show the final changes to the T-account for commercial banks when the money supply changes by this amount.

2. Show the changes to the T-accounts for the Federal Reserve and for commercial banks when the Federal Reserve sells \$30 million in U.S. Treasury bills. If the public holds a fixed amount of currency (so that all new loans create an equal amount of checkable bank deposits in the banking system) and the minimum reserve ratio is 5%, by how much will checkable bank deposits in the commercial banks change? By how much will the money supply change? Show the final changes to the T-account for the commercial banks when the money supply changes by this amount.

3. Go to the FOMC page of the Federal Reserve Board's website (http://www.federalreserve.gov/FOMC/) to find the statement issued after the most recent FOMC meeting. (Click on "Meeting calendars and information" and then click on the most recent statement listed in the calendar.)

   a. What is the target federal funds rate?

   b. Is the target federal funds rate different from the target federal funds rate in the previous FOMC statement? If yes, by how much does it differ?

   c. Does the statement comment on current macroeconomic conditions in the United States? How does it describe the U.S. economy?

4. How will the following events affect the demand for money? In each case, specify whether there is a shift of the demand curve or a movement along the demand curve and its direction.

   a. There is a fall in the interest rate from 12% to 10%.

   b. Thanksgiving arrives and, with it, the beginning of the holiday shopping season.

   c. McDonald's and other fast-food restaurants begin to accept credit cards.

   d. The Fed engages in an open-market purchase of U.S. Treasury bills.

5. a. Go to www.treasurydirect.gov. Under "Individuals," go to "Treasury Bills, Notes, Bonds, TIPS, and FRNs." Click on "Treasury Bills." Under "at a glance," click on "rates in recent auctions." What is the investment rate for the most recently issued 26-week T-bills?

   b. Go to the website of your favorite bank. What is the interest rate for six-month CDs?

   c. Why are the rates for six-month CDs higher than for 26-week Treasury bills?

6. Go to www.treasurydirect.gov. Under "Individuals," go to "Treasury Bills, Notes, Bonds, TIPS, and FRNs." Click on "Treasury Notes." Under "at a glance," click on "rates in recent auctions." Use the list of Recent Note, Bond, and TIPS Auction Results to answer the following questions.

   a. What are the interest rates on 2-year and 10-year notes?

   b. How do the interest rates on the 2-year and 10-year notes relate to each other? Why is the interest rate on the 10-year note higher (or lower) than the interest rate on the 2-year note?

7. An economy is facing the recessionary gap shown in the accompanying diagram. To eliminate the gap, should the central bank use expansionary or contractionary monetary policy? How will the interest rate, investment spending, consumer spending, real GDP, and the aggregate price level change as monetary policy closes the recessionary gap?

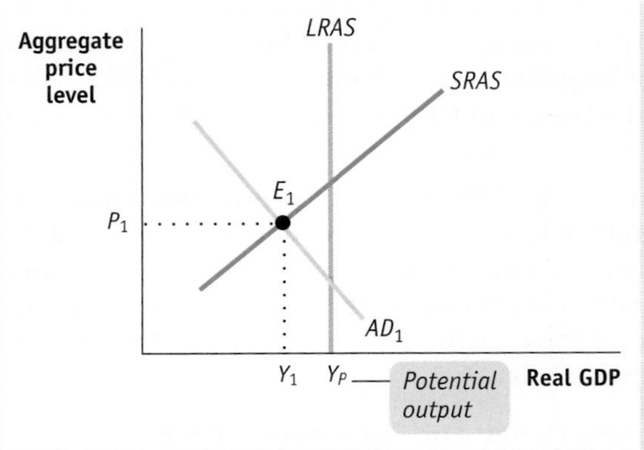

8. An economy is facing the inflationary gap shown in the accompanying diagram. To eliminate the gap, should the central bank use expansionary or contractionary monetary policy? How will the interest rate, investment spending, consumer spending, real GDP, and the aggregate price level change as monetary policy closes the inflationary gap?

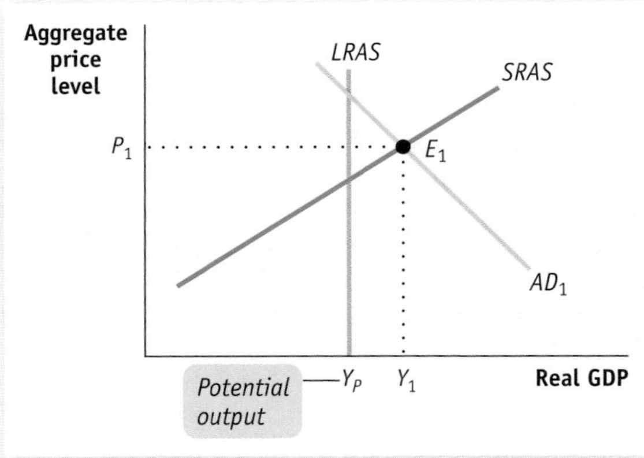

9. In the economy of Eastlandia, the money market is initially in equilibrium when the economy begins to slide into a recession.

a. Using the accompanying diagram, explain what will happen to the interest rate if the central bank of Eastlandia keeps the money supply constant at $\overline{M}_1$.

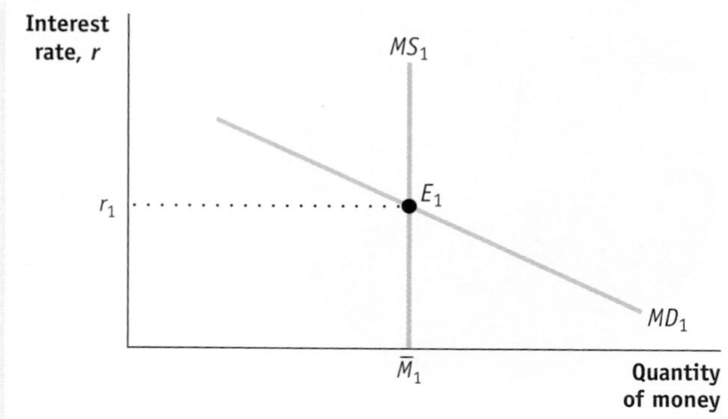

b. If the central bank is instead committed to maintaining an interest rate target of r_1, then as the economy slides into recession, how should the central bank react? Using your diagram from part a, demonstrate the central bank's reaction.

10. Suppose that the money market in Westlandia is initially in equilibrium and the central bank decides to decrease the money supply.

a. Using a diagram like the one in Problem 9, explain what will happen to the interest rate in the short run.

b. What will happen to the interest rate in the long run?

11. An economy is in long-run macroeconomic equilibrium with an unemployment rate of 5% when the government passes a law requiring the central bank to use monetary policy to lower the unemployment rate to 3% and keep it there. How could the central bank achieve this goal in the short run? What would happen in the long run? Illustrate with a diagram.

12. According to the European Central Bank website, the treaty establishing the European Community "makes clear that ensuring price stability is the most important contribution that monetary policy can make to achieve a favourable economic environment and a high level of employment." If price stability is the only goal of monetary policy, explain how monetary policy would be conducted during recessions. Analyze both the case of a recession that is the result of a demand shock and the case of a recession that is the result of a supply shock.

13. The effectiveness of monetary policy depends on how easy it is for changes in the money supply to change interest rates. By changing interest rates, monetary policy affects investment spending and the aggregate demand curve. The economies of Albernia and Brittania have very different money demand curves, as shown in the accompanying diagram. In which economy will changes in the money supply be a more effective policy tool? Why?

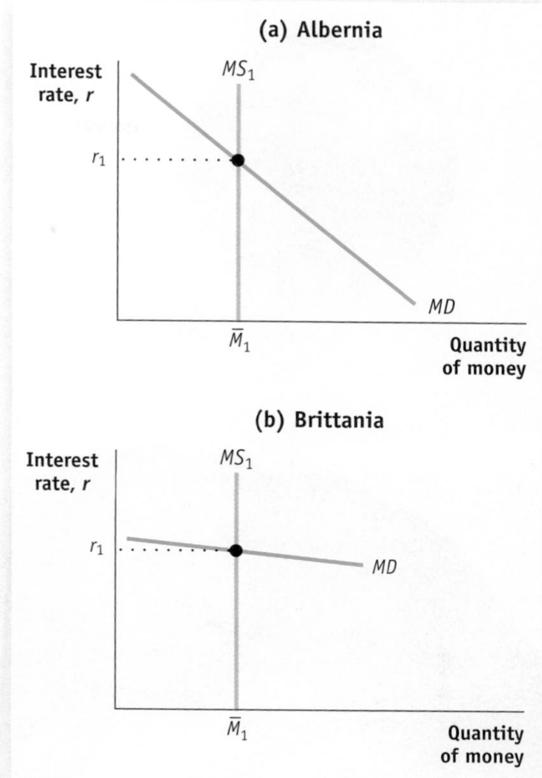

14. During the Great Depression, businesspeople in the United States were very pessimistic about the future of economic growth and reluctant to increase investment spending even when interest rates fell. How did this limit the potential for monetary policy to help alleviate the Depression?

15. Because of the economic slowdown associated with the 2007–2009 recession, the Federal Open Market Committee of the Federal Reserve, between September 18, 2007 and December 16, 2008, lowered the federal funds rate in a series of steps from a high of 5.25% to a rate between zero and 0.25%. The idea was to provide a boost to the economy by increasing aggregate demand.

a. Use the liquidity preference model to explain how the Federal Open Market Committee lowers the interest rate in the short run. Draw a typical graph that illustrates the mechanism. Label the vertical axis "Interest rate" and the horizontal axis "Quantity of money." Your graph should show two interest rates, r_1 and r_2.

b. Explain why the reduction in the interest rate causes aggregate demand to increase in the short run.

c. Suppose that in 2016 the economy is at potential output but that this is somehow overlooked by the Fed, which continues its monetary expansion. Demonstrate the effect of the policy measure on the *AD* curve. Use the *LRAS* curve to show that the effect of this policy measure on the *AD* curve, other things equal, causes the aggregate price level to rise in the long run. Label the vertical axis "Aggregate price level" and the horizontal axis "Real GDP."

TRUNK

Module 76: Inflation, Disinflation, and Deflation
Module 77: The Phillips Curve
Module 78: Crises and Consequences

SECTION 24

Policy Responses to Unemployment and Inflation

BRINGING A SUITCASE TO THE BANK

The African nation of Zimbabwe achieved a dubious distinction in 2008: it exhibited one of the highest inflation rates ever recorded, peaking at around 500 billion percent.

Although the government kept introducing ever-larger denominations of the Zimbabwe dollar—for example, in May 2008 it introduced a half-billion-dollar bill—it still took a lot of currency to pay for the necessities of life: a stack of the cash worth $100 U.S. dollars weighed about 40 pounds. The currency was worth so little that some people making bank withdrawals brought suitcases along in order to be able to walk away with enough cash to pay for basic living expenses. In the end, the Zimbabwe dollar lost all value—literally. By October 2008, the currency more or less vanished from circulation, replaced by U.S. dollars and South African rands.

Zimbabwe's experience was shocking, but not unprecedented. In 1994 the inflation rate in Armenia hit 27,000%. In 1991 Nicaraguan inflation exceeded 60,000%. And Zimbabwe's experience was more or less matched by history's most famous example of extreme inflation, which took place in Germany in 1922–1923. Toward the end of the German hyperinflation, prices were rising 16% a *day*, which—through compounding—meant an increase of approximately 500 billion percent over the course of five months. People were so reluctant to hold paper money, which lost value by the hour, that eggs and lumps of coal began to circulate as currency.

German firms would pay their workers several times a day so that they could spend their earnings before they lost value (lending new meaning to the term *hourly wage*). Legend has it that men sitting down at a bar would order two beers at a time, out of fear that the price of a beer would rise before they could order a second round!

The United States has never experienced that kind of inflation. The worst U.S. inflation in modern times took place at the end of the 1970s, when consumer prices were rising at an annual rate of 13%. Yet inflation at even that rate was profoundly troubling to the American public, and the policies the Federal Reserve pursued in order to get U.S. inflation back down to an acceptable rate led to a very deep recession.

In this section we look at the reasons inflation rises and falls. We'll see that the causes of very high inflation, the type of inflation suffered by Zimbabwe, are quite different from the causes of more moderate inflation. We'll also learn about *disinflation,* a reduction in the inflation rate, and the special problems associated with a falling price level, or *deflation*. Finally we'll look at the causes and consequences of banking crises and discuss policy options for helping an economy recover from them.

MODULE 76

Inflation, Disinflation, and Deflation

Thinkstock

WHAT YOU WILL LEARN

1. The classical model of the price level
2. Why efforts to collect an inflation tax by printing money can lead to high rates of inflation and even hyperinflation

Money and Inflation

To understand what causes inflation, we need to revisit the effect of changes in the money supply on the overall price level. Then we'll turn to the reasons why governments sometimes increase the money supply very rapidly.

The Classical Model of Money and Prices

We learned that in the short run an increase in the money supply increases real GDP by lowering the interest rate and stimulating investment spending and consumer spending. However, in the long run, as nominal wages and other sticky prices rise, real GDP falls back to its original level. So in the long run, an increase in the money supply does not change real GDP. Instead, other things equal, it leads to an equal percentage rise in the overall price level; that is, the prices of all goods and services in the economy, including nominal wages and the prices of intermediate goods, rise by the same percentage as the money supply. And when the overall price level rises, the aggregate price level—the prices of all final goods and services—rises as well.

As a result, a change in the *nominal* money supply, M, leads in the long run to a change in the aggregate price level, P, that leaves the *real* quantity of money, M/P, at its original level. There is also no long-run effect on aggregate demand or real GDP. For example, when Turkey dropped six zeros from its currency, the Turkish lira, in 2005, the country's real GDP did not change. The only thing that changed was the number of zeros in prices: instead of something costing 2,000,000 lira, it cost 2 lira.

This is, to repeat, what happens in the long run. When analyzing large changes in the aggregate price level, however, macroeconomists often find it useful to ignore the distinction between the short run and the long run. Instead, they work with a simplified model in which the effect of a change in the money supply on the aggregate price level takes place instantaneously rather than over a long period of time. You might be concerned about this assumption given the emphasis we've placed on the difference between the short run and the long run. However, for reasons we'll explain shortly, this is a reasonable assumption to make in the case of high inflation.

According to the **classical model of the price level,** the real quantity of money is always at its long-run equilibrium level.

The simplified model in which the real quantity of money, *M/P,* is always at its long-run equilibrium level is known as the **classical model of the price level** because it was commonly used by "classical" economists prior to the influence of John Maynard Keynes. To understand the classical model and why it is useful in the context of high inflation, let's revisit the *AD–AS* model and what it says about the effects of an increase in the money supply. (Unless otherwise noted, we will always be referring to changes in the *nominal* supply of money.)

Figure 76-1 reviews the effects of an increase in the money supply according to the *AD–AS* model. The economy starts at E_1, a point of short-run and long-run macroeconomic equilibrium. It lies at the intersection of the aggregate demand curve, AD_1, and the short-run aggregate supply curve, $SRAS_1$. It also lies on the long-run aggregate supply curve, *LRAS*. At E_1, the equilibrium aggregate price level is P_1.

Now suppose there is an increase in the money supply. This is an expansionary monetary policy, which shifts the aggregate demand curve to the right, to AD_2, and moves the economy to a new short-run macroeconomic equilibrium at E_2. Over time, however, nominal wages adjust upward in response to the rise in the aggregate price level, and the *SRAS* curve shifts to the left, to $SRAS_2$. The new long-run macroeconomic equilibrium is at E_3, and real GDP returns to its initial level. The long-run increase in the aggregate price level from P_1 to P_3 is proportional to the increase in the money supply. As a result, in the long run changes in the money supply have no effect on the real quantity of money, *M/P,* or on real GDP. In the long run, money—as we learned—is *neutral.*

The classical model of the price level ignores the short-run movement from E_1 to E_2, assuming that the economy moves directly from one long-run equilibrium to another long-run equilibrium. In other words, it assumes that the economy moves directly from E_1 to E_3 and that real GDP never changes in response to a change in the money supply. In effect, in the classical model the effects of money supply changes are analyzed as if the short-run as well as the long-run aggregate supply curves were vertical.

FIGURE 76-1 **The Classical Model of the Price Level**

Starting at E_1, an increase in the money supply shifts the aggregate demand curve rightward, as shown by the movement from AD_1 to AD_2. There is a new short-run macroeconomic equilibrium at E_2 and a higher price level at P_2. In the long run, nominal wages adjust upward and push the *SRAS* curve leftward to $SRAS_2$. The total percent increase in the price level from P_1 to P_3 is equal to the percent increase in the money supply. In the *classical model of the price level,* we ignore the transition period and think of the price level as rising to P_3 immediately. This is a good approximation under conditions of high inflation.

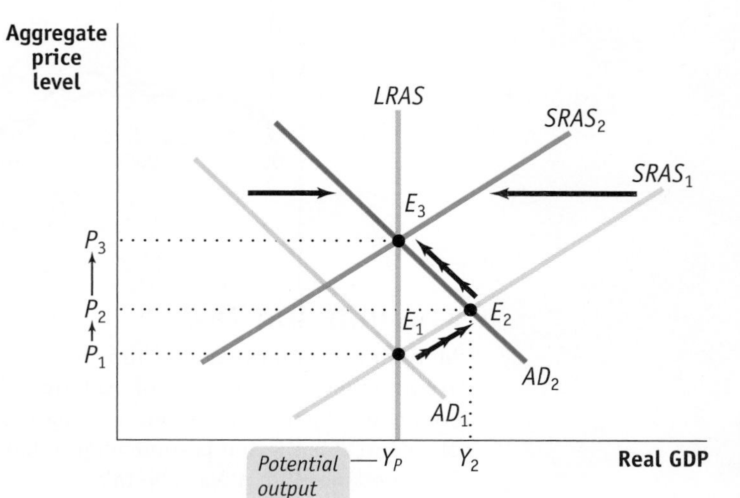

In reality, this is a poor assumption during periods of low inflation. With a low inflation rate, it may take a while for workers and firms to react to a monetary expansion by raising wages and prices. In this scenario, some nominal wages and the prices of some goods are sticky in the short run. As a result, under low inflation there is an upward-sloping *SRAS* curve, and changes in the money supply can indeed change real GDP in the short run.

But what about periods of high inflation? In the face of high inflation, economists have observed that the short-run stickiness of nominal wages and prices tends to vanish. Workers and businesses, sensitized to inflation, are quick to raise their wages and prices in response to changes in the money supply. This implies that under high inflation there is a quicker adjustment of wages and prices of intermediate goods than occurs in the case of low inflation. So the short-run aggregate supply curve shifts leftward more quickly and there is a more rapid return to long-run equilibrium under high inflation. As a result, the classical model of the price level is much more likely to be a good approximation of reality for economies experiencing persistently high inflation.

The consequence of this rapid adjustment of all prices in the economy is that in countries with persistently high inflation, changes in the money supply are quickly translated into changes in the inflation rate. Let's look at Zimbabwe, which we read about in the story at the start of the section. Figure 76-2 shows the annual rate of growth in the money supply and the annual rate of change of consumer prices from 2003 through April 2008. As you can see, the surge in the growth rate of the money supply coincided closely with a roughly equal surge in the inflation rate. Note that to fit these very large percentage increases—exceeding 100,000 percent—onto the figure, we have drawn the vertical axis using a logarithmic scale that allows us to draw equal sized percent changes as the same size.

What leads a country to increase its money supply so much that the result is an inflation rate in the millions, or even billions, of percent?

FIGURE 76-2 **Money Supply Growth and Inflation in Zimbabwe**

This figure, drawn on a logarithmic scale, shows the annual rates of change of the money supply and the price level in Zimbabwe from 2003 through April 2008. The surges in the money supply were quickly reflected in a roughly equal surge in the price level.
Source: International Monetary Fund.

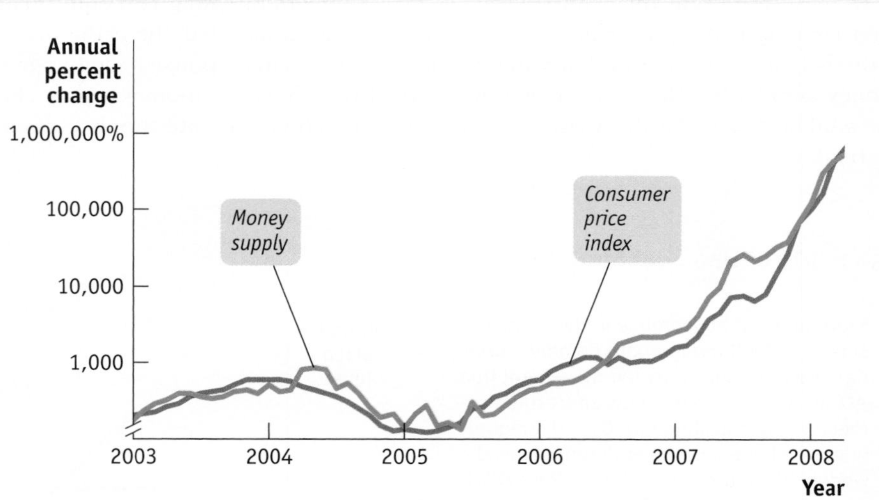

The Inflation Tax

Modern economies use fiat money—pieces of paper that have no intrinsic value but are accepted as a medium of exchange. In the United States and most other wealthy countries, the decision about how many pieces of paper to issue is placed in the hands of a central bank that is somewhat independent of the political process. However, this independence can always be taken away if politicians decide to seize control of monetary policy.

So what is to prevent a government from paying for some of its expenses not by raising taxes or borrowing but simply by printing money? Nothing. In fact, governments, including the U.S. government, do it all the time. How can the U.S. government do this, given that the Federal Reserve, not the U.S. Treasury, issues money? The answer is that the Treasury and the Federal Reserve work in concert. The Treasury issues debt to finance the government's purchases of goods and services, and the Fed *monetizes* the debt by creating money and buying the debt back from the public through open-market purchases of Treasury bills. In effect, the U.S. government can and does raise revenue by printing money.

Nate Beeler © Cagel Cartoons

For example, in May 2013, the U.S. monetary base—bank reserves plus currency in circulation—was $388 billion larger than it had been a year earlier. This occurred because, over the course of that year, the Federal Reserve had issued $388 billion in money or its electronic equivalent and put it into circulation mainly through open-market operations. To put it another way, the Fed created money out of thin air and used it to buy valuable government securities from the private sector.

It's true that the U.S. government pays interest on debt owned by the Federal Reserve—but the Fed, by law, hands the interest payments it receives on government debt back to the Treasury, keeping only enough to fund its own operations. In effect, then, the Federal Reserve's actions enabled the government to pay off $388 billion in outstanding government debt by printing money.

An alternative way to look at this is to say that the right to print money is itself a source of revenue. Economists refer to the revenue generated by the government's right to print money as *seignorage,* an archaic term that goes back to the Middle Ages. It refers to the right to stamp gold and silver into coins, and charge a fee for doing so, that medieval lords—seigneurs, in France—reserved for themselves.

Seignorage accounts for only a tiny fraction (less than 1%) of the U.S. government's budget. Furthermore, concerns about seignorage don't have any influence on the Federal Reserve's decisions about how much money to print; the Fed is worried about inflation and unemployment, not revenue. But this hasn't always been true, even in the United States: both sides relied on seignorage to help cover budget deficits during the Civil War.

In fact, there have been many occasions in history when governments turned to their printing presses as a crucial source of revenue. According to the usual scenario, a government finds itself running a large budget deficit—and lacks either the competence or the political will to eliminate this deficit by raising taxes or cutting spending. Furthermore, the government can't borrow to cover the gap because potential lenders won't extend loans, given the fear that the government's weakness will continue and leave it unable to repay its debts.

In such a situation, governments end up printing money to cover the budget deficit. But by printing money to pay its bills, a government increases the quantity of money in circulation. And as we've just seen, increases in the money supply translate into equally large increases in the aggregate price level. So printing money to cover a budget deficit leads to inflation.

Who ends up paying for the goods and services the government purchases with newly printed money? The people who currently hold money pay. They pay because inflation erodes the purchasing power of their money holdings. In other words, a government imposes an **inflation tax,** a reduction in the value of the money held by the public, by printing money to cover its budget deficit and creating inflation.

An **inflation tax** is a reduction in the value of money held by the public caused by inflation.

It's helpful to think about what this tax represents. If the inflation rate is 5%, then a year from now $1 will buy goods and services worth only about $0.95 today. So a 5% inflation rate in effect imposes a tax rate of 5% on the value of all money held by the public.

But why would any government push the inflation tax to rates of hundreds or thousands of percent? We turn next to the process by which high inflation turns into explosive hyperinflation.

Keystone/Getty Images

In the 1920s, hyperinflation made German currency worth so little that children made kites from banknotes.

The Logic of Hyperinflation

Inflation imposes a tax on individuals who hold money. And, like most taxes, it will lead people to change their behavior. In particular, when inflation is high, people will try to avoid holding money and will instead substitute real goods as well as interest-bearing assets for money. During the German hyperinflation, people began using eggs or lumps of coal as a medium of exchange. They did this because lumps of coal maintained their real value over time but money didn't.

Indeed, during the peak of German hyperinflation, people often burned paper money, which was less valuable than wood. Moreover, people don't just reduce their nominal money holdings—they reduce their *real* money holdings, cutting the amount of money they hold so much that it actually has less purchasing power than the amount of money they would hold if inflation were low. Why? Because the more real money holdings they have, the greater the real amount of resources the government captures from them through the inflation tax.

We are now prepared to understand how countries can get themselves into situations of extreme inflation. High inflation arises when the government must print a large quantity of money, imposing a large inflation tax, to cover a large budget deficit.

Now, the seignorage collected by the government over a short period—say, one month—is equal to the change in the money supply over that period. Let's use M to represent the money supply and the symbol Δ to mean "monthly change in." Then:

(76-1) $\text{Seignorage} = \Delta M$

The money value of seignorage, however, isn't very informative by itself. After all, the whole point of inflation is that a given amount of money buys less and less over time. So it's more useful to look at *real* seignorage, the revenue created by printing money divided by the price level, P:

(76-2) $\text{Real seignorage} = \Delta M/P$

Equation 76-2 can be rewritten by dividing and multiplying by the current level of the money supply, M, giving us:

(76-3) $\text{Real seignorage} = (\Delta M/M) \times (M/P)$

or

Real seignorage = Rate of growth of the money supply × Real money supply

But as we've just explained, in the face of high inflation the public reduces the real amount of money it holds, so that the far right-hand term in Equation 76-3, M/P, gets smaller. Suppose that the government needs to print enough money to pay for a given quantity of goods and services—that is, it needs to collect a given *real* amount of seignorage. Then, as people hold smaller amounts of real money due to a high rate of inflation, the government has to respond by accelerating the rate of growth of the money supply, $\Delta M/M$. This will lead to an even higher rate of inflation. And people will respond to this new higher rate of inflation by reducing their real money holdings, M/P, yet again.

As the process becomes self-reinforcing, it can easily spiral out of control. Although the amount of real seignorage that the government must ultimately collect to pay off its deficit does not change, the inflation rate the government needs to impose to collect that amount rises. So the government is forced to increase the money supply more rapidly, leading to an even higher rate of inflation, and so on.

Here's an analogy: imagine a city government that tries to raise a lot of money with a special fee on taxi rides. The fee will raise the cost of taxi rides, and this will cause people to turn to substitutes, such as walking or taking the bus. As taxi use declines, the government finds that its tax revenue declines and it must impose a higher fee to raise the same amount of revenue as before. You can imagine the ensuing vicious circle: the government imposes fees on taxi rides, which leads to less taxi use, which causes the government to raise the fee on taxi rides, which leads to even less taxi use, and so on.

Substitute the real money supply for taxi rides and the inflation rate for the increase in the fee on taxi rides, and you have the story of hyperinflation. A race develops between the government printing presses and the public: the presses churn out money at a faster and faster rate to try to compensate for the fact that the public is reducing its real money holdings. At some point the inflation rate explodes into hyperinflation, and people are unwilling to hold any money at all (and resort to trading in eggs and lumps of coal). The government is then forced to abandon its use of the inflation tax and shut down the printing presses.

ECONOMICS IN ACTION WORLD VIEW

WHAT CAUSED ZIMBABWE'S INFLATION?

As noted in this section's opening story, Zimbabwe offers a recent example of a country experiencing very high inflation. Figure 76-2 showed that surges in Zimbabwe's money supply growth were matched by almost simultaneous surges in its inflation rate. But looking at rates of change doesn't give a true feel for just how much prices went up.

Figure 76-3 shows Zimbabwe's consumer price index from January 2000 to July 2008, with the January 2000 level set equal to 100. As in Figure 76-2, we also use a logarithmic scale. Over the course of just over eight years, consumer prices rose by approximately 80 trillion percent.

Why did Zimbabwe's government pursue policies that led to runaway inflation? The reason boils down to political instability, which in turn had its roots in Zimbabwe's history.

Until the 1970s, Zimbabwe had been ruled by its small white minority; even after the shift to majority rule, many of the country's farms remained in the hands of whites. Eventually Robert Mugabe, Zimbabwe's president, tried to solidify his position by seizing these farms and turning them over to his political supporters. But because this seizure disrupted production, the result was to undermine the country's economy and its tax base. It became impossible for the country's government to balance its budget either by raising taxes or by cutting spending. At the same time, the regime's instability left Zimbabwe unable to borrow money in world markets. Like many others before it, Zimbabwe's government turned to the printing press to cover the gap—leading to massive inflation.

FIGURE 76-3 Consumer Prices in Zimbabwe, 2000–2008

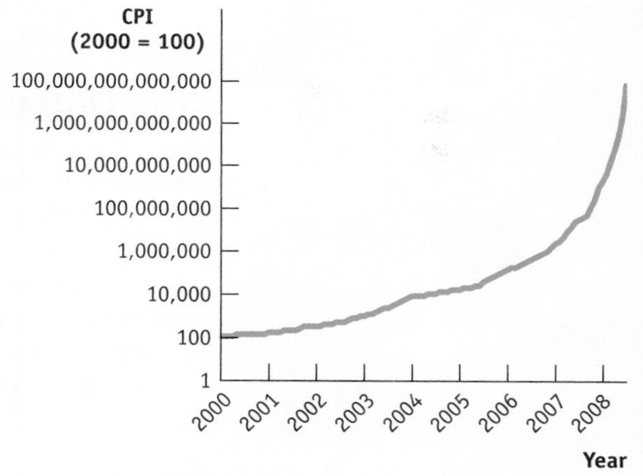

Source: International Monetary Fund.

Moderate Inflation and Disinflation

The governments of wealthy, politically stable countries like the United States and Britain don't find themselves forced to print money to pay their bills. Yet over the past 40 years both countries, along with a number of other nations, have experienced uncomfortable episodes of inflation. In the United States, the inflation rate peaked at

13% in 1980. In Britain, the inflation rate reached 26% in 1975. Why did policy makers allow this to happen?

The answer, in brief, is that in the short run, policies that produce a booming economy also tend to lead to higher inflation, and policies that reduce inflation tend to depress the economy. This creates both temptations and dilemmas for governments.

Imagine yourself as a politician facing an election in a year, and suppose that inflation is fairly low at the moment. You might well be tempted to pursue expansionary policies that will push the unemployment rate down, as a way to please voters, even if your economic advisers warn that this will eventually lead to higher inflation. You might also be tempted to find different economic advisers, who will tell you not to worry: in politics, as in ordinary life, wishful thinking often prevails over realistic analysis.

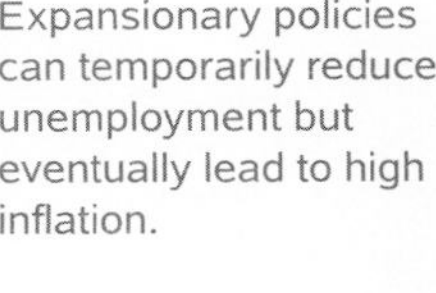
Expansionary policies can temporarily reduce unemployment but eventually lead to high inflation.

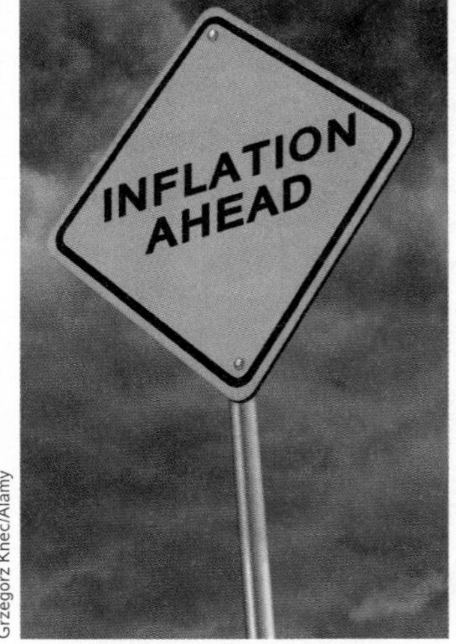

Grzegorz Knec/Alamy

Conversely, imagine yourself as a politician in an economy suffering from inflation. Your economic advisers will probably tell you that the only way to bring inflation down is to push the economy into a recession, which will lead to temporarily higher unemployment. Are you willing to pay that price? Maybe not.

This political asymmetry—inflationary policies often produce short-term political gains, but policies to bring inflation down carry short-term political costs—explains how countries with no need to impose an inflation tax sometimes end up with serious inflation problems. For example, that 26% rate of inflation in Britain was largely the result of the British government's decision in 1971 to pursue highly expansionary monetary and fiscal policies. Politicians disregarded warnings that these policies would be inflationary and were extremely reluctant to reverse course even when it became clear that the warnings had been correct.

But why do expansionary policies lead to inflation? To answer that question, we need to look first at the relationship between output and unemployment.

The Output Gap and the Unemployment Rate

Earlier we introduced the concept of *potential output,* the level of real GDP that the economy would produce once all prices had fully adjusted. Potential output typically grows steadily over time, reflecting long-run growth. However, as we learned from the aggregate demand–aggregate supply model, actual aggregate output fluctuates around potential output in the short run: a recessionary gap arises when actual aggregate output falls short of potential output; an inflationary gap arises when actual aggregate output exceeds potential output.

Recall that the percentage difference between the actual level of real GDP and potential output is called the *output gap.* A positive or negative output gap occurs when an economy is producing more than or less than what would be "expected" because all prices have not yet adjusted. And wages, as we've learned, are the prices in the labor market.

Meanwhile, we learned that the unemployment rate is composed of cyclical unemployment and natural unemployment, the portion of the unemployment rate unaffected by the business cycle. So there is a relationship between the unemployment rate and the output gap. This relationship is defined by two rules:

1. When actual aggregate output is equal to potential output, the actual unemployment rate is equal to the natural rate of unemployment.
2. When the output gap is positive (an inflationary gap), the unemployment rate is *below* the natural rate. When the output gap is negative (a recessionary gap), the unemployment rate is *above* the natural rate.

In other words, fluctuations of aggregate output around the long-run trend of potential output correspond to fluctuations of the unemployment rate around the natural rate.

This makes sense. When the economy is producing less than potential output—when the output gap is negative—it is not making full use of its productive resources. Among the resources that are not fully used is labor, the economy's most important resource. So we would expect a negative output gap to be associated with unusually high unemployment. Conversely, when the economy is producing more than potential output, it is temporarily using resources at higher-than-normal rates. With this positive output gap, we would expect to see lower-than-normal unemployment.

Figure 76-4 confirms this rule. Panel (a) shows the actual and natural rates of unemployment, as estimated by the Congressional Budget Office (CBO). Panel (b) shows two series. One is cyclical unemployment: the difference between the actual unemployment rate and the CBO estimate of the natural rate of unemployment, measured on the left. The other is the CBO estimate of the output gap, measured on the right. To make the relationship clearer, the output gap series is inverted—shown upside down—so that the line goes down if actual output rises above potential output and up if actual output falls below potential output.

As you can see, the two series move together quite closely, showing the strong relationship between the output gap and cyclical unemployment. Years of high cyclical unemployment, like 1982, 1992, or 2009, were also years of a strongly negative output gap. Years of low cyclical unemployment, like the late 1960s or 2000, were also years of a strongly positive output gap.

FIGURE 76-4 Cyclical Unemployment and the Output Gap

Panel (a) shows the actual U.S. unemployment rate from 1950 to early 2013, together with the Congressional Budget Office estimate of the natural rate of unemployment. The actual rate fluctuates around the natural rate, often for extended periods. Panel (b) shows cyclical unemployment—the difference between the actual unemployment rate and the natural rate of unemployment—and the output gap, also estimated by the CBO. The unemployment rate is measured on the left vertical axis, and the output gap is measured with an inverted scale on the right vertical axis. With an inverted scale, it moves in the same direction as the unemployment rate: when the output gap is positive, the actual unemployment rate is below its natural rate; when the output gap is negative, the actual unemployment rate is above its natural rate. The two series track one another closely, showing the strong relationship between the output gap and cyclical unemployment.

Sources: Congressional Budget Office; Bureau of Labor Statistics; Bureau of Economic Analysis.

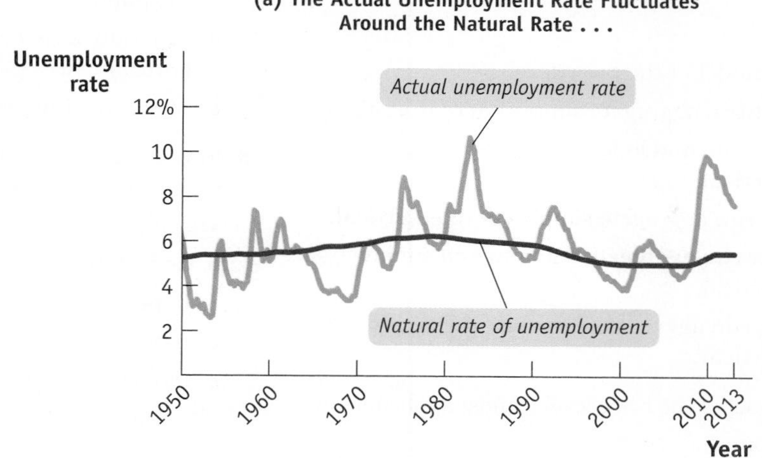

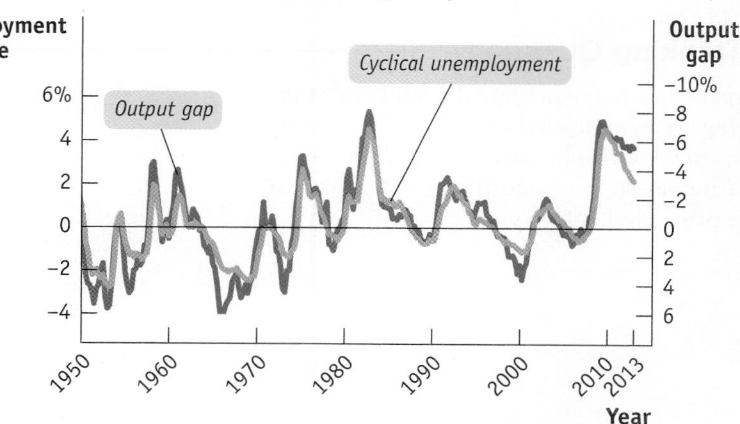

MODULE 76 Review

Solutions appear at the back of the book.

Check Your Understanding

1. Suppose there is a large increase in the money supply in an economy that previously had low inflation. As a consequence, aggregate output expands in the short run. What does this say about situations in which the classical model of the price level applies?

2. Suppose that all wages and prices in an economy are indexed to inflation. Can there still be an inflation tax?

Multiple-Choice Questions

1. The real quantity of money is
   - I. equal to M/P.
   - II. the money supply adjusted for inflation.
   - III. higher in the long run when the Fed buys government securities.

   a. I only
   b. II only
   c. III only
   d. I and II only
   e. I, II, and III

2. In the classical model of the price level
   a. only the short-run aggregate supply curve is vertical.
   b. both the short-run and long-run aggregate supply curves are vertical.
   c. only the long-run aggregate supply curve is vertical.
   d. both the short-run aggregate demand and supply curves are vertical.
   e. both the long-run aggregate demand and supply curves are vertical.

3. The classical model of the price level is most applicable in
   a. the United States.
   b. periods of high inflation.
   c. periods of low inflation.
   d. recessions.
   e. depressions.

4. An inflation tax is
   a. imposed by governments to offset price increases.
   b. paid directly as a percentage of the sale price on purchases.
   c. the result of a decrease in the value of money held by the public.
   d. generally levied by states rather than the federal government.
   e. higher during periods of low inflation.

5. Revenue generated by the government's right to print money is known as
   a. seignorage.
   b. an inflation tax.
   c. hyperinflation.
   d. fiat money.
   e. monetary funds.

Critical-Thinking Question

Draw a correctly labeled aggregate demand and supply graph showing an economy in long-run macroeconomic equilibrium. On your graph, show the effect of an increase in the money supply, according to the classical model of the price level.

The Phillips Curve

Tom Bonaventure/Photographer's Choice RF/Getty Images

WHAT YOU WILL LEARN

1. What the Phillips curve is and the nature of the short-run trade-off between inflation and unemployment
2. Why there is no long-run trade-off between inflation and unemployment
3. Why expansionary policies are limited due to the effects of expected inflation
4. Why deflation is a problem for economic policy

Inflation and Unemployment in the Short Run

We've just seen that expansionary policies lead to a lower unemployment rate. Our next step in understanding the temptations and dilemmas facing governments is to show that there is a short-run trade-off between unemployment and inflation—lower unemployment tends to lead to higher inflation, and vice versa. The key concept is that of the *Phillips curve*.

The Short-Run Phillips Curve

The origins of this concept lie in a famous 1958 paper by the New Zealand–born economist A. W. H. Phillips. Looking at historical data for Britain, he found that when the unemployment rate was high, the wage rate tended to fall, and when the unemployment rate was low, the wage rate tended to rise. Using data from Britain, the United States, and elsewhere, other economists soon found a similar apparent relationship between the unemployment rate and the rate of inflation—that is, the rate of change in the aggregate price level. For example, Figure 77-1 shows the U.S. unemployment rate and the rate of consumer price inflation over each subsequent year from 1955 to 1968, with each dot representing one year's data.

Looking at evidence like Figure 77-1, many economists concluded that there is a negative short-run relationship between the unemployment rate and the inflation rate, represented by the **short-run Phillips curve,** or *SRPC.* (We'll explain the difference between the short-run and the long-run Phillips curve soon.) Figure 77-2 shows a hypothetical short-run Phillips curve.

Early estimates of the short-run Phillips curve for the United States were very simple: they showed a negative relationship between the unemployment rate and the inflation rate, without taking account of any other variables. During the 1950s and 1960s

The **short-run Phillips curve** is the negative short-run relationship between the unemployment rate and the inflation rate.

FIGURE 77-1 Unemployment and Inflation, 1955–1968

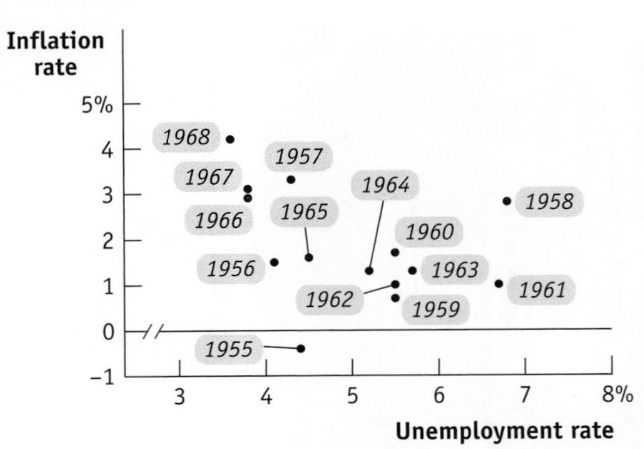

Each dot shows the average U.S. unemployment rate for one year and the percentage increase in the consumer price index over the subsequent year. Data like this lay behind the initial concept of the Phillips curve.

Source: Bureau of Labor Statistics.

this simple approach seemed, for a while, to be adequate. And this simple relationship is clear in the data in Figure 77-1.

Even at the time, however, some economists argued that a more accurate short-run Phillips curve would include other factors. Previously, we discussed the effect of *supply shocks,* such as sudden changes in the price of oil, that shift the short-run aggregate supply curve. Such shocks also shift the short-run Phillips curve: surging oil prices were an important factor in the inflation of the 1970s and also played an important role in the acceleration of inflation in 2007–2008.

In general, a negative supply shock shifts *SRPC* up, as the inflation rate increases for every level of the unemployment rate, and a positive supply shock shifts it down as the inflation rate falls for every level of the unemployment rate. Both outcomes are shown in Figure 77-3.

But supply shocks are not the only factors that can change the inflation rate. In the early 1960s, Americans had little experience with inflation as inflation rates had been low for decades. But by the late 1960s, after inflation had been steadily increasing for a number of years, Americans had come to expect future inflation. In 1968 two economists—Milton Friedman of the University of Chicago and Edmund Phelps of Columbia University—independently set forth a crucial hypothesis: that expectations about future inflation directly affect the present inflation rate. Today most economists accept that the *expected inflation rate*—the rate of inflation that employers and workers expect in the near future—is the most important factor, other than the unemployment rate, affecting inflation.

FIGURE 77-2 The Short-Run Phillips Curve

The short-run Phillips curve, *SRPC,* slopes downward because the relationship between the unemployment rate and the inflation rate is negative.

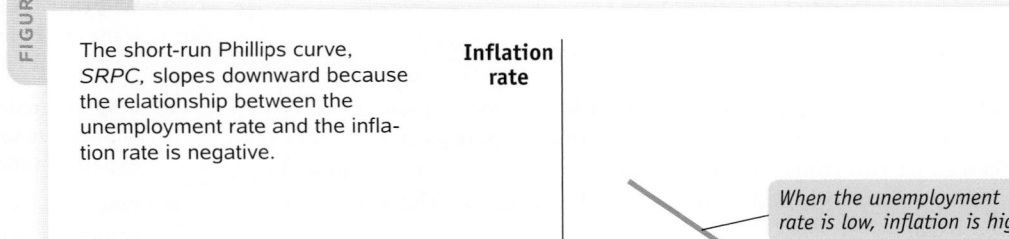

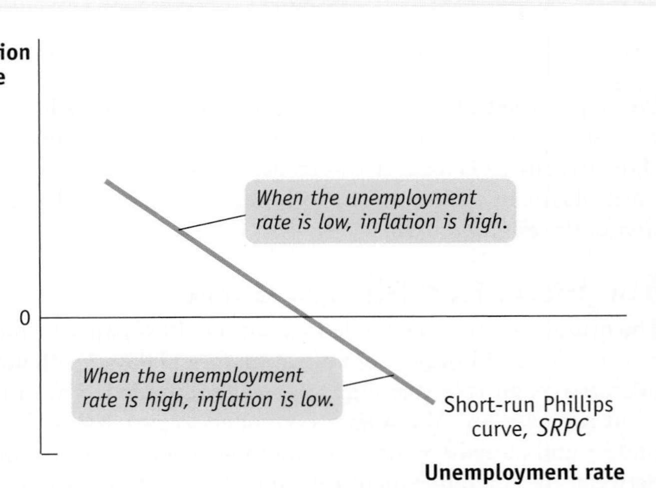

Inflation Expectations and the Short-Run Phillips Curve

The expected rate of inflation is the rate that employers and workers expect in the near future. One of the crucial discoveries of modern macroeconomics is that changes in the expected rate of inflation affect the short-run trade-off between unemployment and inflation and shift the short-run Phillips curve.

Why do changes in expected inflation affect the short-run Phillips curve? Put yourself in the position of a worker or employer about to sign a contract setting the worker's wages over the next year. For a number of reasons, the wage rate they agree

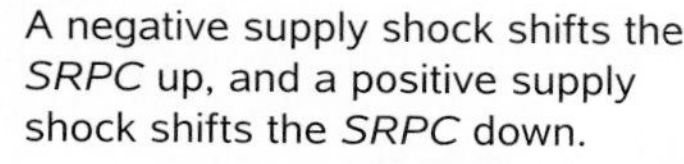

77-3 The Short-Run Phillips Curve and Supply Shocks

A negative supply shock shifts the *SRPC* up, and a positive supply shock shifts the *SRPC* down.

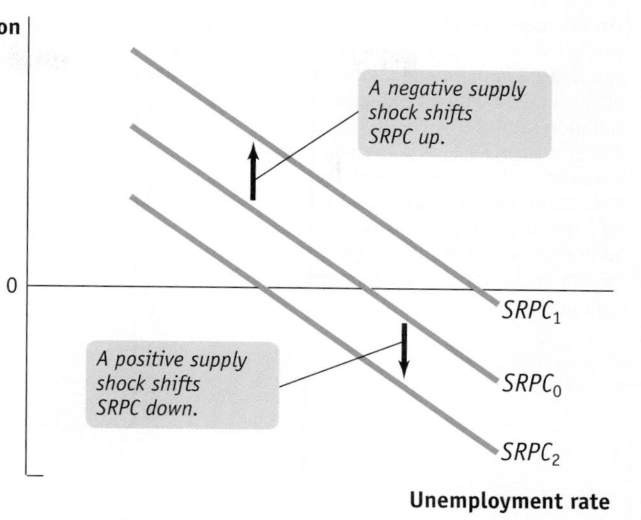

to will be higher if everyone expects high inflation (including rising wages) than if everyone expects prices to be stable. The worker will want a wage rate that takes into account future declines in the purchasing power of earnings. He or she will also want a wage rate that won't fall behind the wages of other workers. And the employer will be more willing to agree to a wage increase now if hiring workers later will be even more expensive. Also, rising prices will make paying a higher wage rate more affordable for the employer because the employer's output will sell for more.

For these reasons, an increase in expected inflation shifts the short-run Phillips curve upward: the actual rate of inflation at any given unemployment rate is higher when the expected inflation rate is higher. In fact, macroeconomists believe that the relationship between changes in expected inflation and changes in actual inflation is one-to-one. That is, when the expected inflation rate increases, the actual inflation rate at any given unemployment rate will increase by the same amount. When the expected inflation rate falls, the actual inflation rate at any given level of unemployment will fall by the same amount.

Figure 77-4 shows how the expected rate of inflation affects the short-run Phillips curve. First, suppose that the expected rate of inflation is 0%. $SRPC_0$ is the short-run Phillips curve when the public expects 0% inflation. According to $SRPC_0$, the actual inflation rate will be 0% if the unemployment rate is 6%; it will be 2% if the unemployment rate is 4%.

Alternatively, suppose the expected rate of inflation is 2%. In that case, employers and workers will build this expectation into wages and prices: at any given unemployment rate, the actual inflation rate will be 2 percentage points higher than it would be if people expected 0% inflation. $SRPC_2$, which shows the Phillips curve when the expected inflation rate is 2%, is $SRPC_0$ shifted upward by 2 percentage points at every level of unemployment. According to $SRPC_2$, the actual inflation rate will be 2% if the unemployment rate is 6%; it will be 4% if the unemployment rate is 4%.

What determines the expected rate of inflation? In general, people base their expectations about inflation on experience. If the inflation rate has hovered around 0% in the last few years, people will expect it to be around 0% in the near future. But if the inflation rate has averaged around 5% lately, people will expect inflation to be around 5% in the near future.

Since expected inflation is an important part of the modern discussion about the short-run Phillips curve, you might wonder why it was not in the original formulation

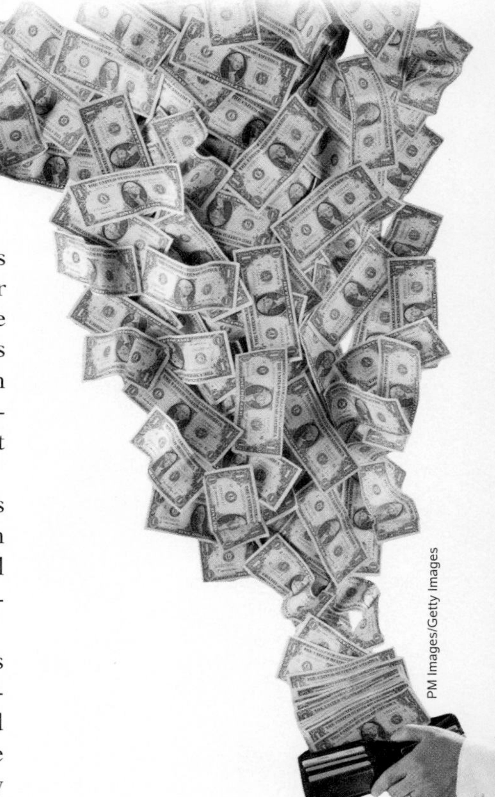
PM Images/Getty Images

The expected inflation rate is the most important factor, other than unemployment, that affects inflation.

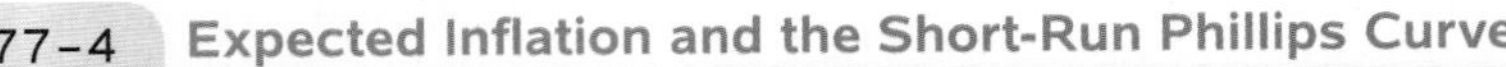

FIGURE 77-4 Expected Inflation and the Short-Run Phillips Curve

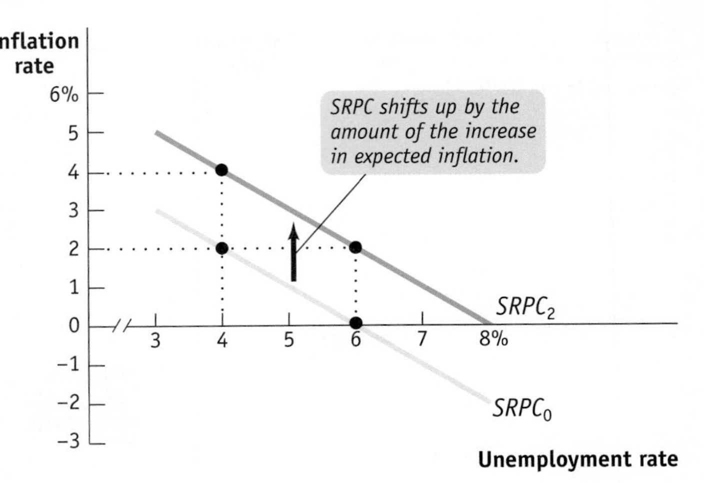

An increase in expected inflation shifts the short-run Phillips curve up. $SRPC_0$ is the initial short-run Phillips curve with an expected inflation rate of 0%; $SRPC_2$ is the short-run Phillips curve with an expected inflation rate of 2%. Each additional percentage point of expected inflation raises the actual inflation rate at any given unemployment rate by 1 percentage point.

of the Phillips curve. The answer lies in history. Think back to what we said about the early 1960s: at that time, people were accustomed to low inflation rates and reasonably expected that future inflation rates would also be low. It was only after 1965 that persistent inflation became a fact of life. So only then did it become clear that expected inflation would play an important role in price-setting.

Inflation and Unemployment in the Long Run

The short-run Phillips curve says that at any given point in time there is a trade-off between unemployment and inflation. According to this view, policy makers have a choice: they can choose to accept the price of high inflation in order to achieve low unemployment, or they can reject high inflation and pay the price of high unemployment. In fact, during the 1960s many economists believed that this trade-off represented a real choice.

However, this view was greatly altered by the later recognition that expected inflation affects the short-run Phillips curve. In the short run, expectations often diverge from reality. In the long run, however, any consistent rate of inflation will be reflected in expectations. If inflation is consistently high, as it was in the 1970s, people will come to expect more of the same; if inflation is consistently low, as it has been in recent years, that, too, will become part of expectations.

So what does the trade-off between inflation and unemployment look like in the long run, when actual inflation is incorporated into expectations? Most macroeconomists believe that there is, in fact, no long-run trade-off. That is, it is not possible to achieve lower unemployment in the long run by accepting higher inflation. To see why, we need to introduce another concept: the *long-run Phillips curve*.

The Long-Run Phillips Curve

Figure 77-5 reproduces the two short-run Phillips curves from Figure 77-4, $SRPC_0$ and $SRPC_2$. It also includes an additional short-run Phillips curve, $SRPC_4$, representing a 4% expected rate of inflation. In a moment, we'll explain the significance of the vertical long-run Phillips curve, *LRPC*.

Suppose that the economy has, in the past, had a 0% inflation rate. In that case, the current short-run Phillips curve will be $SRPC_0$, reflecting a 0% expected inflation rate. If the unemployment rate is 6%, the actual inflation rate will be 0%.

Also suppose that policy makers decide to trade off lower unemployment for a higher rate of inflation. They use monetary policy, fiscal policy, or both to drive the unemployment rate down to 4%. This puts the economy at point *A* on $SRPC_0$, leading to an actual inflation rate of 2%.

Over time, the public will come to expect a 2% inflation rate. *This increase in inflationary expectations will shift the short-run Phillips curve upward* to $SRPC_2$. Now, when the unemployment rate is 6%, the actual inflation rate will be 2%. Given this new short-run Phillips curve, policies adopted to keep the unemployment rate at 4% will lead to a 4% actual inflation rate—point *B* on $SRPC_2$—rather than point *A* with a 2% actual inflation rate.

Eventually, the 4% actual inflation rate gets built into expectations about the future inflation rate, and the short-run Phillips curve shifts upward yet again to $SRPC_4$. To keep the unemployment rate at 4% would now require accepting a 6% actual inflation rate, point *C* on $SRPC_4$, and so on. In short, a persistent attempt to trade off lower unemployment for higher inflation leads to *accelerating* inflation over time.

To avoid accelerating inflation over time, the unemployment rate must be high enough that the actual rate of inflation matches the expected rate of inflation. This is the situation at E_0 on $SRPC_0$: when the expected inflation rate is 0% and the unemployment rate is 6%, the actual inflation rate is 0%. It is also the situation at E_2 on $SRPC_2$: when the expected inflation rate is 2% and the unemployment rate is 6%, the actual inflation rate is 2%. And it is the situation at E_4 on $SRPC_4$: when the expected inflation rate is 4% and the unemployment rate is 6%, the actual inflation rate is 4%. As we'll learn shortly, this relationship between accelerating inflation and the unemployment rate is known as the *natural rate hypothesis.*

The unemployment rate at which inflation does not change over time—6% in Figure 77-5—is known as the **nonaccelerating inflation rate of unemployment,** or **NAIRU** for short. Keeping the unemployment rate below the NAIRU leads to ever-accelerating inflation and cannot be maintained. Most macroeconomists believe that there is a NAIRU and that there is no long-run trade-off between unemployment and inflation.

We can now explain the significance of the vertical line *LRPC.* It is the **long-run Phillips curve,** the relationship between unemployment and inflation in the long run, after expectations of inflation have had time to adjust to experience. It is vertical because any unemployment rate below the NAIRU leads to ever-accelerating

The **nonaccelerating inflation rate of unemployment,** or **NAIRU,** is the unemployment rate at which inflation does not change over time.

The **long-run Phillips curve** shows the relationship between unemployment and inflation after expectations of inflation have had time to adjust to experience.

NAIRU is the unemployment rate at which inflation does not change over time.

Everett Collection/Shutterstock

FIGURE 77-5 The NAIRU and the Long-Run Phillips Curve

$SRPC_0$ is the short-run Phillips curve when the expected inflation rate is 0%. At a 4% unemployment rate, the economy is at point *A* with an actual inflation rate of 2%. The higher inflation rate will be incorporated into expectations, and the *SRPC* will shift upward to $SRPC_2$. If policy makers act to keep the unemployment rate at 4%, the economy will be at *B* and the actual inflation rate will rise to 4%. Inflationary expectations will be revised upward again, and *SRPC* will shift to $SRPC_4$. At a 4% unemployment rate, the economy will be at *C* and the actual inflation rate will rise to 6%. Here, an unemployment rate of 6% is the NAIRU, or nonaccelerating inflation rate of unemployment. As long as unemployment is at the NAIRU, the actual inflation rate will match expectations and remain constant. An unemployment rate below 6% requires ever-accelerating inflation. The long-run Phillips curve, *LRPC*, which passes through E_0, E_2, and E_4, is vertical: no long-run trade-off between unemployment and inflation exists.

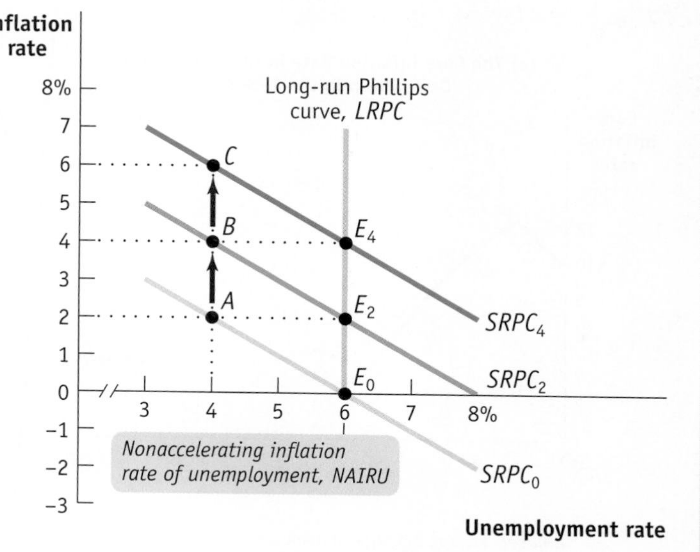

inflation. In other words, the long-run Phillips curve shows that there are limits to expansionary policies because an unemployment rate below the NAIRU cannot be maintained in the long run. Moreover there is a corresponding point we have not yet emphasized: any unemployment rate above the NAIRU leads to decelerating inflation.

The Natural Rate of Unemployment, Revisited

Recall the concept of the natural rate of unemployment, the portion of the unemployment rate unaffected by the swings of the business cycle. Now we have introduced the concept of the NAIRU. How do these two concepts relate to each other?

The answer is that the NAIRU is another name for the natural rate. The level of unemployment the economy "needs" in order to avoid accelerating inflation is equal to the natural rate of unemployment.

In fact, economists estimate the natural rate of unemployment by looking for evidence about the NAIRU from the behavior of the inflation rate and the unemployment rate over the course of the business cycle. For example, the way major European countries learned, to their dismay, that their natural rates of unemployment were 9% or more was through unpleasant experience. In the late 1980s, and again in the late 1990s, European inflation began to accelerate as European unemployment rates, which had been above 9%, began to fall, approaching 8%.

ECONOMICS IN ACTION

THE GREAT DISINFLATION OF THE 1980s

As we've mentioned several times, the United States ended the 1970s with a high rate of inflation, at least by its own peacetime historical standards—13% in 1980. Part of this inflation was the result of one-time events, especially a world oil crisis. But expectations of future inflation at 10% or more per year appeared to be firmly embedded in the economy.

By the mid-1980s, however, inflation was running at about 4% per year. Panel (a) of Figure 77-6 shows the annual rate of change in the "core" consumer price index (CPI)—also called the *core inflation rate*. This index, which excludes volatile energy and food prices, is widely regarded as a better indicator of underlying inflation trends than the overall CPI. By this measure, inflation fell from about 12% at the end of the 1970s to about 4% by the mid-1980s.

How was this disinflation achieved? At great cost. Beginning in late 1979, the Federal Reserve imposed strongly contractionary monetary policies, which pushed the

FIGURE 77-6 The Great Disinflation

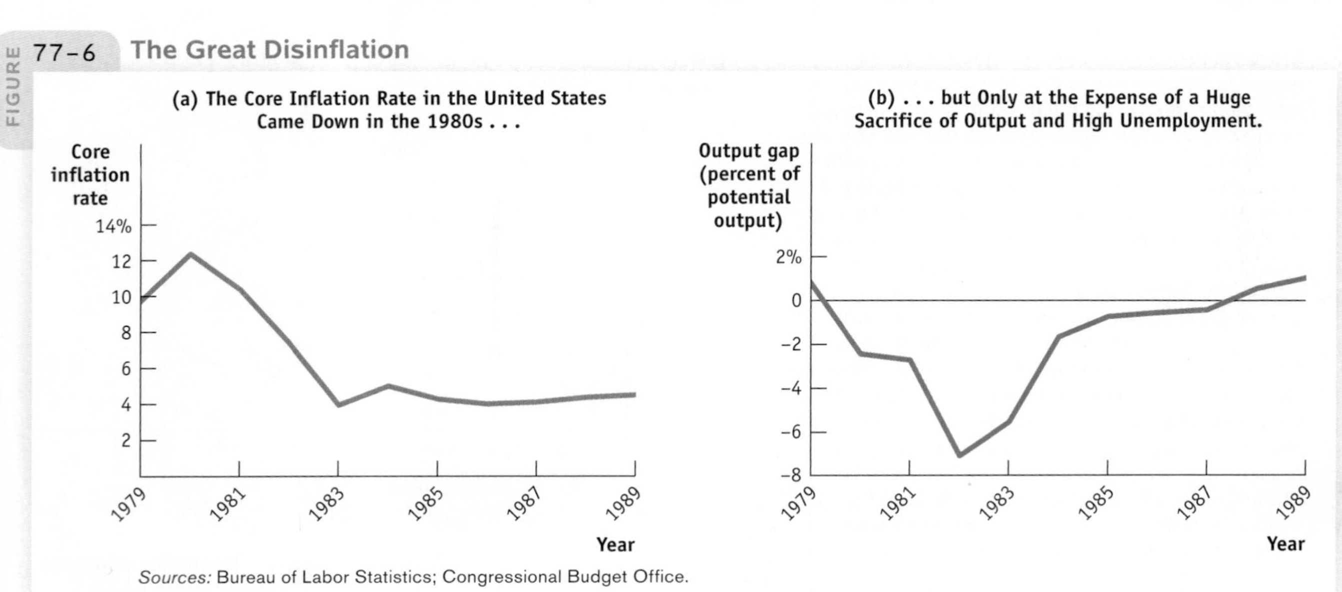

Sources: Bureau of Labor Statistics; Congressional Budget Office.

economy into its worst recession since the Great Depression. Panel (b) shows the Congressional Budget Office estimate of the U.S. output gap from 1979 to 1989: by 1982, actual output was 7% below potential output, corresponding to an unemployment rate of more than 9%. Aggregate output didn't get back to potential output until 1987.

Our analysis of the Phillips curve tells us that a temporary rise in unemployment, like that of the 1980s, is needed to break the cycle of inflationary expectations. Once expectations of inflation are reduced, the economy can return to the natural rate of unemployment at a lower inflation rate. And that's just what happened.

But the cost was huge. If you add up the output gaps over 1980–1987, you find that the economy sacrificed approximately 18% of an average year's output over the period. If we had to do the same thing today, that would mean giving up roughly $2.6 trillion worth of goods and services.

In Figure 77-3 we cited Congressional Budget Office estimates of the U.S. natural rate of unemployment. The CBO has a model that predicts changes in the inflation rate based on the deviation of the actual unemployment rate from the natural rate. Given data on actual unemployment and inflation, this model can be used to deduce estimates of the natural rate—and that's where the CBO numbers come from.

The Costs of Disinflation

Through experience, policy makers have found that bringing inflation down is a much harder task than increasing it. The reason is that once the public has come to expect continuing inflation, bringing inflation down is painful.

A persistent attempt to keep unemployment below the natural rate leads to accelerating inflation that becomes incorporated into expectations. To reduce inflationary expectations, policy makers need to run the process in reverse, adopting contractionary policies that keep the unemployment rate above the natural rate for an extended period of time. The process of bringing down inflation that has become embedded in expectations is known as *disinflation.*

Disinflation can be very expensive. The U.S. retreat from high inflation at the beginning of the 1980s appears to have cost the equivalent of about 18% of a year's real GDP, the equivalent of roughly $2.6 trillion today. The justification for paying these costs is that they lead to a permanent gain. Although the economy does not recover the short-term production losses caused by disinflation, it no longer suffers from the costs associated with persistently high inflation. In fact, the United States, Britain, and other wealthy countries that experienced inflation in the 1970s eventually decided that the benefit of bringing inflation down was worth the required suffering—the large reduction in real GDP in the short term.

Some economists argue that the costs of disinflation can be reduced if policy makers explicitly state their determination to reduce inflation. A clearly announced, credible policy of disinflation, they contend, can reduce expectations of future inflation and so shift the short-run Phillips curve downward. Some economists believe that the clear determination of the Federal Reserve to combat the inflation of the 1970s was credible enough that the costs of disinflation, huge though they were, were lower than they might otherwise have been.

Deflation

Before World War II, *deflation*—a falling aggregate price level—was almost as common as inflation. In fact, the U.S. consumer price index on the eve of World War II was 30% lower than it had been in 1920. After World War II, inflation became the norm in all countries. But in the 1990s, deflation reappeared in Japan and proved difficult to reverse. Concerns about potential deflation played a crucial role in U.S. monetary policy in the early 2000s and again in late 2008. In fact, in late 2008, the U.S. experienced a brief period of deflation.

Why is deflation a problem? And why is it hard to end?

Debt Deflation

Deflation, like inflation, produces both winners and losers—but in the opposite direction. Due to the falling price level, a dollar in the future has a higher real value than a dollar today. So lenders, who are owed money, gain under deflation because the real value of borrowers' payments increases. Borrowers lose because the real burden of their debt rises.

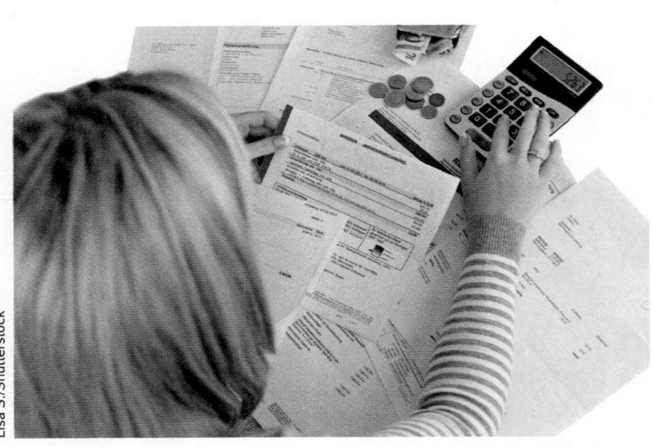

Lisa S./Shutterstock

The effects of deflation on borrowers and lenders can worsen an economic slump.

In a famous analysis at the beginning of the Great Depression, economist Irving Fisher claimed that the effects of deflation on borrowers and lenders can worsen an economic slump. Deflation, in effect, takes real resources away from borrowers and redistributes them to lenders. Fisher argued that borrowers, who lose from deflation, are typically short of cash and will be forced to cut their spending sharply when their debt burden rises. Lenders, however, are less likely to increase spending sharply when the values of the loans they own rise. The overall effect, said Fisher, is that deflation reduces aggregate demand, deepening an economic slump, which, in a vicious circle, may lead to further deflation. The effect of deflation in reducing aggregate demand, known as **debt deflation,** probably played a significant role in the Great Depression.

Effects of Expected Deflation

Like expected inflation, expected deflation affects the nominal interest rate. Consider Figure 77-7 (which you may recall seeing in an earlier section). It demonstrates how expected inflation affects the equilibrium interest rate. As shown, the equilibrium nominal interest rate is 4% if the expected inflation rate is 0%. Clearly, if the expected inflation rate is −3%—if the public expects deflation at 3% per year—the equilibrium nominal interest rate will be 1%.

But what would happen if the expected rate of inflation were −5%? Would the nominal interest rate fall to −1%, meaning that lenders are paying borrowers 1% on their debt? No. Nobody would lend money at a negative nominal rate of interest because they could do better by simply holding cash. This illustrates what economists call the **zero bound** on the nominal interest rate: it cannot go below zero.

Debt deflation is the reduction in aggregate demand arising from the increase in the real burden of outstanding debt caused by deflation.

There is a **zero bound** on the nominal interest rate: it cannot go below zero.

This zero bound can limit the effectiveness of monetary policy. Suppose the economy is depressed, with output below potential output and the unemployment rate above the natural rate. Normally, the central bank can respond by cutting interest rates so as to increase aggregate demand. If the nominal interest rate is already zero, however, the central bank cannot push it down any further. Banks refuse to lend and consumers and firms refuse to spend because, with a negative inflation rate and a 0%

FIGURE 77-7 The Fisher Effect

D_0 and S_0 are the demand and supply curves for loanable funds when the expected future inflation rate is 0%. At an expected inflation rate of 0%, the equilibrium nominal interest rate is 4%. An increase in expected future inflation pushes both the demand and supply curves upward by 1 percentage point for every percentage point increase in expected future inflation. D_{10} and S_{10} are the demand and supply curves for loanable funds when the expected future inflation rate is 10%. The 10 percentage point increase in expected future inflation raises the equilibrium nominal interest rate to 14%. The expected real interest rate remains at 4%, and the equilibrium quantity of loanable funds also remains unchanged.

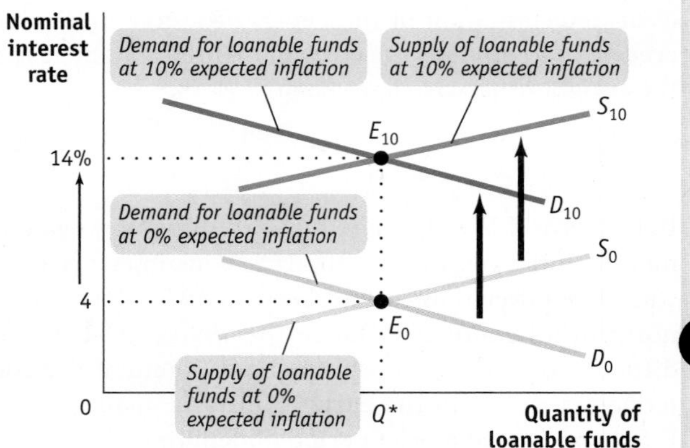

FIGURE 77-8 The Zero Bound in U.S. History

This figure shows U.S. short-term interest rates, specifically the interest rate on three-month Treasury bills, from 1920 to 2013. As shown by the shaded area at left, for much of the 1930s, interest rates were very close to zero, leaving little room for expansionary monetary policy. After World War II, persistent inflation generally kept interest rates well above zero. However, in late 2008, in the wake of the housing bubble bursting and the financial crisis, the interest rate on three-month Treasury bills was again virtually zero.

Source: Federal Reserve Bank of St. Louis.

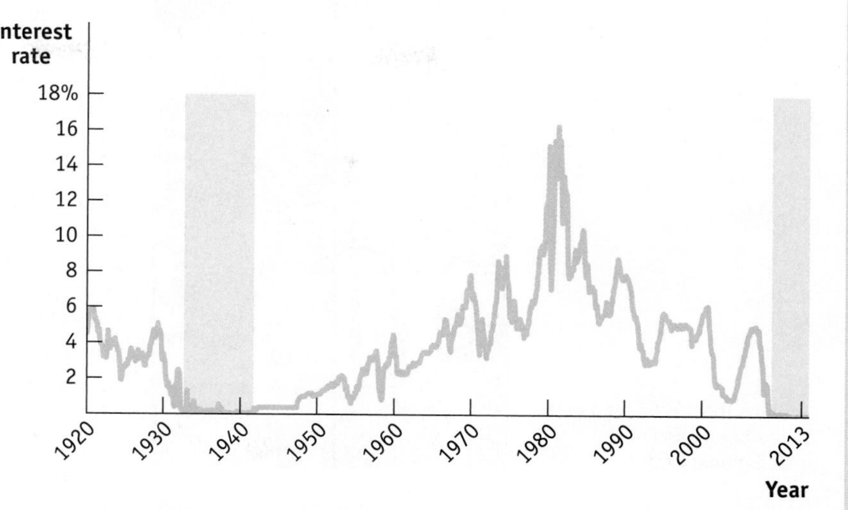

nominal interest rate, holding cash yields a positive real rate of return. Any further increases in the monetary base will either be held in bank vaults or held as cash by individuals and firms, without being spent.

A situation in which conventional monetary policy to fight a slump—cutting interest rates—can't be used because nominal interest rates are up against the zero bound is known as a **liquidity trap.** A liquidity trap can occur whenever there is a sharp reduction in demand for loanable funds—which is exactly what happened during the Great Depression. Figure 77-8 shows the interest rate on short-term U.S. government debt from 1920 to 2013. As you can see, starting in 1933 and ending when World War II brought a full economic recovery, the U.S. economy was either close to or up against the zero bound. After World War II, when inflation became the norm around the world, the zero bound problem largely vanished as the public came to expect inflation rather than deflation.

However, the recent history of the Japanese economy, shown in Figure 77-9, provides a modern illustration of the problem of deflation and the liquidity trap.

A **liquidity trap** is a situation in which conventional monetary policy is ineffective because nominal interest rates are up against the zero bound.

FIGURE 77-9 Japan's Lost Decade

A prolonged economic slump in Japan led to deflation from the late 1990s on. The Bank of Japan responded by cutting interest rates—but eventually ran up against the zero bound.

Source: OECD; Bank of Japan.

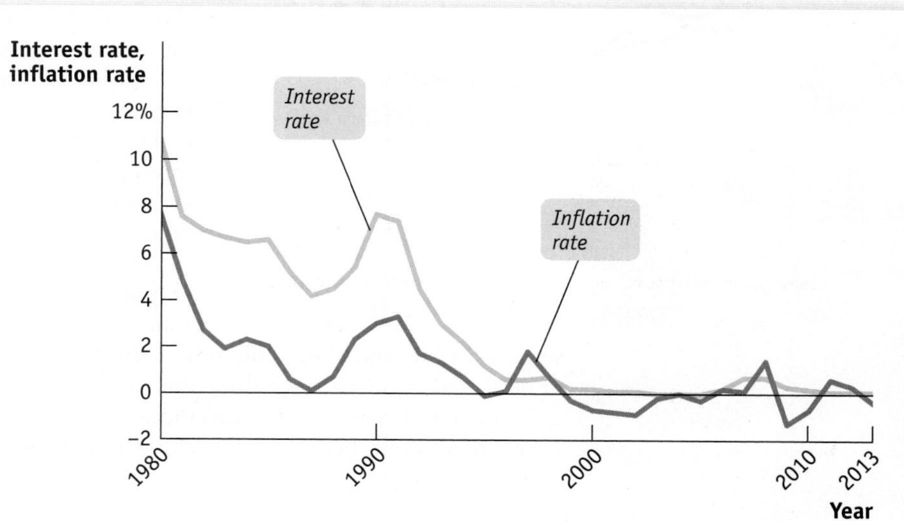

Tom Bonaventure/Getty Images

Since the 1990s, Japan has been stuck in a deflationary trap.

Japan experienced a huge boom in the prices of both stocks and real estate in the late 1980s, and then saw both bubbles burst. The result was a prolonged period of economic stagnation, the so-called Lost Decade, which gradually reduced the inflation rate and eventually led to persistent deflation.

In an effort to fight the weakness of the economy, the Bank of Japan—the equivalent of the Federal Reserve—repeatedly cut interest rates. Eventually, it arrived at the ZIRP: the zero interest rate policy. The call money rate, the equivalent of the U.S. federal funds rate, was literally set equal to zero. Because the economy was still depressed, it would have been desirable to cut interest rates even further. But that wasn't possible: Japan was up against the zero bound.

In the aftermath of the 2008 financial crisis, the Federal Reserve also found itself up against the zero bound with the interest on short-term U.S. government debt virtually at zero. As the following Economics in Action explains, this led to fears of a Japan-type trap and spurred the Fed to take some unconventional action.

ECONOMICS IN ACTION WORLD VIEW

THE DEFLATION SCARE OF 2010

Ever since the financial crisis of 2008, U.S. policy makers have been worried about the possibility of "Japanification"—that is, they have worried that, like Japan since the 1990s, the United States might find itself stuck in a deflationary trap. Indeed, Ben Bernanke, chairman of the Federal Reserve during the crisis, studied Japan intensively before he went to the Fed and sought to do better than his Japanese counterparts.

FIGURE 77-10 Expected vs. Actual Inflation, 2010

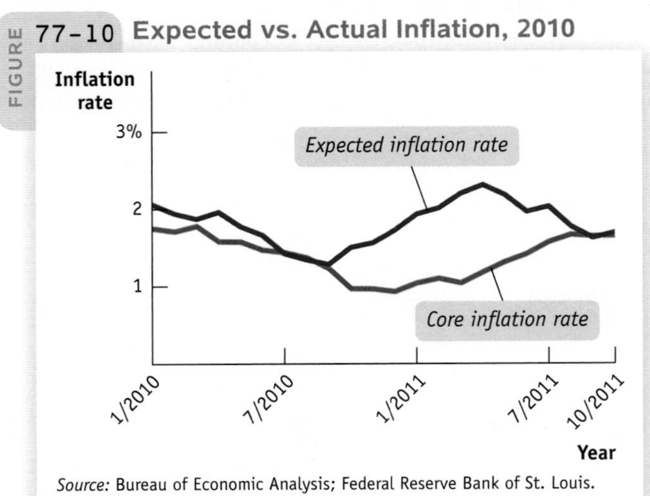

Source: Bureau of Economic Analysis; Federal Reserve Bank of St. Louis.

Fears of deflation were particularly intense in the summer and early fall of 2010. Figure 77-10 shows why, by tracking two numbers the Fed watches carefully when making policy. One of these numbers is the "core" inflation rate over the past year—the percentage rise in a measure of consumer prices (the personal consumption expenditure deflator) that excludes volatile food and energy prices. The Fed normally regards this core inflation rate as its best guide to underlying inflation and tries to keep it at around 2%. The other number is a measure of expected inflation derived by calculating the difference between the interest rate on ordinary government bonds and the rate on government bonds whose yield is protected against inflation.

As you can see, by the late summer of 2010 both actual inflation and expected inflation were sliding to levels well below the Fed's 2% target. Fed officials were worried, and they took action. In August 2010 Bernanke gave a speech at the annual Fed meeting, signaling that he would take special actions to head off the deflationary threat. And in November the Fed, which normally buys only short-term government debt, began a program of long-term bond purchases, hoping to give the economy a boost.

The figure shows that Bernanke's speech and the Fed's action led to a major change in expectations, as investors' fears of deflation ebbed. Actual inflation also picked up significantly.

What was far from clear, however, was whether the Fed had achieved more than a temporary reprieve. A year after Bernanke's big speech, expected inflation was sagging again, and deflation fears were on the rise. And those fears linger, given that core inflation averaged only 1.8% in 2013.

MODULE 77 Review

Solutions appear at the back of the book.

Check Your Understanding

1. Explain how the short-run Phillips curve illustrates the negative relationship between cyclical unemployment and the actual inflation rate for a given level of the expected inflation rate.
2. Why is there no long-run trade-off between unemployment and inflation?
3. Why is disinflation so costly for an economy? Are there ways to reduce these costs?
4. Why won't anyone lend money at a negative nominal rate of interest? How can this pose problems for monetary policy?

Multiple-Choice Questions

1. The long-run Phillips curve is
   - I. the same as the short-run Phillips curve.
   - II. vertical.
   - III. the short-run Phillips curve plus expected inflation.
   - a. I only
   - b. II only
   - c. III only
   - d. I and II only
   - e. I, II, and III
2. The short-run Phillips curve shows a ___________ relationship between ___________.
   - a. negative; the aggregate price level and aggregate output
   - b. positive; the aggregate price level and aggregate output
   - c. negative; unemployment and inflation
   - d. positive; unemployment and aggregate output
   - e. positive; unemployment and the aggregate price level
3. An increase in expected inflation will shift
   - a. the short-run Phillips curve downward.
   - b. the short-run Phillips curve upward.
   - c. the long-run Phillips curve upward.
   - d. the long-run Phillips curve downward.
   - e. neither the short-run nor the long-run Phillips curve.
4. Bringing down inflation that has become embedded in expectations is called
   - a. deflation.
   - b. negative inflation.
   - c. anti-inflation.
   - d. unexpected inflation.
   - e. disinflation.
5. Debt deflation is
   - a. the effect of deflation in decreasing aggregate demand.
   - b. an idea proposed by Irving Fisher.
   - c. a contributing factor in causing the Great Depression.
   - d. due to differences in how borrowers/lenders respond to inflation losses/gains.
   - e. all of the above.

Critical-Thinking Questions

Use the accompanying diagram to answer the questions that follow.

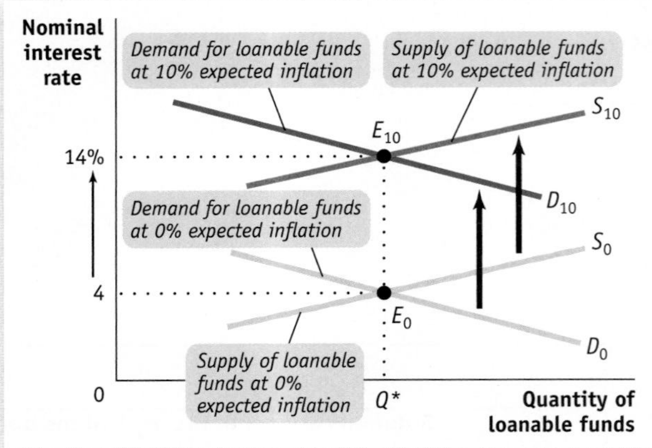

1. What is the nominal interest rate if expected inflation is 0%?
2. What would the nominal interest rate be if the expected inflation rate were –2%? Explain.
3. What would the nominal interest rate be if the expected inflation rate were –6%? Explain.
4. What would a negative nominal interest rate mean for lenders? How much lending would take place at a negative nominal interest rate? Explain.
5. What effect does a nominal interest rate of zero have on monetary policy? What is this situation called?

Crises and Consequences

Igor Stevanovic/Shutterstock

WHAT YOU WILL LEARN

1. **How depository banks and shadow banks differ and why both are subject to bank runs**
2. **What happens during financial panics and banking crises and why their effects are so severe and long-lasting**
3. **The causes of the 2008 financial crisis**
4. **How new regulation seeks to avoid another crisis**

Banking: Benefits and Dangers

As we learned earlier, banks perform an essential role in any modern economy. In this module we examine what makes banking vulnerable to a crisis—even to full-blown financial panic. We'll explore the history of such crises, how destructive they are to the economy, and how governments respond to the risks of financial crises.

The Purpose of Banking

We defined commercial banks and savings and loans as financial intermediaries that provide liquid financial assets in the form of deposits to savers and use their funds to finance the illiquid investment spending needs of borrowers. Deposit-taking banks perform the important functions of providing liquidity to savers and directly influencing the level of the money supply.

Banks will accept the savings of individuals, promising to return them on demand, but put most of those funds to work by taking advantage of the fact that not everyone wants access to those funds at the same time. A typical bank account lets you withdraw as much of your funds as you want, anytime you want—but the bank doesn't actually keep everyone's cash in its safe or even in a form that can be turned quickly into cash. Instead, the bank lends out most of the funds, keeping limited reserves to meet day-to-day withdrawals. And because deposits can be put to use, banks don't charge you (or charge very little) for the privilege of keeping your savings safe. Depending on the type of account, they might even pay interest on your deposits.

In contrast, investment banks, hedge funds, and money market funds do not take deposits from consumers. These institutions are sometimes referred to as *shadow banks*. "Shadow" refers to the fact that before the 2008 crisis these financial institutions were neither closely watched nor effectively regulated. Like deposit-taking

Maturity transformation is the conversion of short-term liabilities into long-term assets.

A **shadow bank** is a nondepository financial institution that engages in maturity transformation.

A **banking crisis** occurs when a large part of the depository banking sector or the shadow banking sector fails or threatens to fail.

banks, shadow banks are vulnerable to bank runs. From now on, we will use the term *depository banks* for banks that accept deposits (commercial banks and savings and loans) to better distinguish them from shadow banks (investment banks, hedge funds, and money market funds), which do not.

More generally, depository banks borrow on a short-term basis from depositors (who can demand to be repaid at any time) and lend on a long-term basis to others (who cannot be forced to repay until the end date of their loan). This is what economists call **maturity transformation:** converting short-term liabilities (deposits in this case) into long-term assets (bank loans that earn interest).

A **shadow bank** is any financial institution that does not accept deposits but does engage in maturity transformation—borrowing over the short term and lending or investing over the longer term. And just as bank depositors benefit from the liquidity and higher return that banking provides compared to sitting on their money, lenders to shadow banks benefit from liquidity (their loans must be repaid quickly, often overnight) and higher return compared to other ways of investing their funds.

A generation ago, depository banks accounted for most banking. After about 1980, however, there was a steady rise in shadow banking. Shadow banking has grown so popular because it has not been subject to the regulations, such as capital requirements and reserve requirements, that are imposed on depository banking. So, like the unregulated trusts that set off the Panic of 1907, shadow banks can offer their customers a higher rate of return on their funds.

Shadow Banks and the Re-emergence of Bank Runs

Because a depository bank keeps on hand just a small fraction of its depositors' funds, a bank run typically results in a bank failure: the bank is unable to meet depositors' demands for their money and closes its doors. Ominously, bank runs can be self-fulfilling prophecies: although a bank may be in fine financial shape, if enough depositors believe it is in trouble and try to withdraw their money, their beliefs end up dooming the bank.

To prevent such occurrences, after the 1930s the United States (and most countries) adopted wide-ranging banking regulation in the form of regular audits by the Federal Reserve, deposit insurance, capital requirements and reserve requirements, and provisions allowing troubled banks to borrow from the Fed's discount window.

Shadow banks, though, don't take deposits. So how can they be vulnerable to a bank run? The reason is that a shadow bank, like a depository bank, engages in maturity transformation: it borrows short term and lends or invests longer term. If a shadow bank's lenders suddenly decide one day that it's no longer safe to lend it money, the shadow bank can no longer fund its operations. Unless it can sell its assets immediately to raise cash, it will quickly fail. This is exactly what happened in 2008 to the once venerable investment bank Lehman Brothers, which is the topic of the upcoming Economics in Action.

A typical scene outside a bank during the banking crisis of the Great Depression.

FPG/Hulton Archive/Getty Images.

Banking Crises and Financial Panics

Bank failures are common: even in a good year, several U.S. banks typically go under for one reason or another. And shadow banks sometimes fail, too. **Banking crises**—episodes in which a large part of the depository banking sector or the shadow banking sector fails or threatens to fail—are relatively rare by comparison. Yet they do happen, often with severe negative effects on the broader economy. What would cause so many of these institutions to get into trouble at the same time? Let's take a look at the two reasons why many banks—either depository banks or shadow banks—get into trouble. First, many of them could have made similar mistakes, often due to an *asset bubble*. Second, there may be *financial contagion*, in which one institution's problems spread and create trouble for others.

In an **asset bubble**, the price of an asset is pushed to an unreasonably high level due to expectations of further price gains.

A **financial contagion** is a vicious downward spiral among depository banks or shadow banks: each bank's failure worsens fears and increases the likelihood that another bank will fail.

A **financial panic** is a sudden and widespread disruption of the financial markets that occurs when people suddenly lose faith in the liquidity of financial institutions and markets.

SHARED MISTAKES Banking crises usually owe their origins to many banks making the same mistake of investing in an *asset bubble*. In an **asset bubble,** the price of some kind of asset, such as housing, is pushed to an unreasonably high level by investors' expectations of further price gains. For a while, such bubbles feed on themselves.

A good example of such a bubble is the savings and loan crisis of the 1980s, when there was a huge boom in the construction of commercial real estate, especially office buildings. Many banks extended large loans to real estate developers, believing that the boom would continue indefinitely. By the late 1980s, it became clear that developers had gotten carried away, building far more office space than the country needed. Unable to rent out their space or forced to slash rents, a number of developers defaulted on their loans—and the result was a wave of bank failures.

A similar phenomenon occurred between 2002 and 2006, when rapidly rising housing prices led many people to borrow heavily to buy a house in the belief that prices would keep rising. This process accelerated as more buyers rushed into the market and pushed housing prices up even faster.

Eventually the market runs out of new buyers and the bubble bursts. At this point asset prices fall. This, in turn, undermines confidence in financial institutions that are exposed to losses due to falling asset prices. This loss of confidence, if it's sufficiently severe, can set in motion a financial contagion.

FINANCIAL CONTAGION In especially severe banking crises, an economy-wide vicious downward spiral that occurs among depository banks or shadow banks is known as a **financial contagion.** Each institution's failure worsens depositors' or lenders' fears and increases the odds that another bank will fail. The shadow banking sector, because it is largely unregulated, is especially prone to fear- and rumor-driven contagion.

When a financial institution is under pressure to reduce debt and raise cash, it tries to sell assets. To sell assets quickly, though, it often has to sell them at a deep discount. The contagion comes from the fact that other financial institutions own similar assets, whose prices decline as a result of the "fire sale." This decline in asset prices hurts the other financial institutions' financial positions, too, leading their creditors to stop lending to them. This knock-on effect forces more financial institutions to sell assets, reinforcing the downward spiral of asset prices.

Combine an asset bubble with a huge, unregulated shadow banking system and a vicious cycle of deleveraging and it is easy to see, as the U.S. economy did in 2008, how a full-blown **financial panic**—a sudden and widespread disruption of financial markets that happens when people suddenly lose faith in the liquidity of financial institutions and markets—can arise. A financial panic almost always involves a banking crisis, either in the depository banking sector, or the shadow banking sector, or both.

Because banking provides much of the liquidity needed for trading financial assets like stocks and bonds, severe banking crises almost always lead to disruptions of the stock and bond markets. Disruptions of these markets, along with a headlong rush to sell assets and raise cash, lead to a vicious circle of deleveraging. As the panic unfolds, savers and investors come to believe that the safest place for their money is under their bed, and their hoarding of cash further deepens the distress.

ECONOMICS IN ACTION

LIGHTS OUT AT LEHMAN

Press Association via AP Images

The collapse of Lehman Brothers, the once-venerable investment bank, set off a chain of events that led to a worldwide financial panic.

By 1850, Lehman Brothers had established itself on Wall Street; by 2008, thanks to its skill at trading financial assets, Lehman Brothers was one of the nation's top investment banks. But in September of that year, Lehman's luck ran out.

The firm had invested heavily in subprime mortgages—loans to home-buyers with too little income or too few assets to qualify for standard (also called "prime") mortgages. In the summer and fall of 2008, as the U.S. housing market plunge intensified and investments related to subprime mortgages lost much of their value, Lehman was hit hard.

Lehman had been borrowing heavily in the short-term credit market (also known as the *repo market*)—often using overnight loans that must be repaid the next business day—to finance its ongoing operations and trading. As rumors began to spread about how heavily Lehman was exposed to the tanking housing market, its sources of credit dried up. On September 15, 2008, after being denied a government bailout, the firm declared the largest bankruptcy in history. What happened would shock the world.

When Lehman fell, it set off a chain of events that came close to taking down the entire world financial system. Through securitization (a concept we defined in Module 71) financial institutions throughout the world were exposed to real estate loans that were quickly deteriorating in value as default rates on those loans rose. Credit markets froze because those with funds to lend decided it was better to sit on the funds rather than lend them out and risk losing them to a borrower who might go under like Lehman had.

Around the world, borrowers either lost their access to credit or found themselves forced to pay drastically higher interest rates. Stocks plunged, and within weeks the Dow had fallen almost 3,000 points.

Nor were the consequences limited to financial markets. The U.S. economy was already in recession when Lehman fell, but the pace of the downturn accelerated drastically in the months that followed. By the time U.S. employment bottomed out in early 2010, more than 8 million jobs had been lost. Europe and Japan were also suffering their worst recessions since the 1930s, and world trade plunged even faster than it had in the first year of the Great Depression.

Economists who knew their history quickly recognized what they were seeing: it was a modern version of a financial panic, a sudden and widespread disruption of financial markets.

Financial panics were a regular feature of the U.S. financial system before World War II. The financial panic that hit the United States in 2008 shared many features with the Panic of 1907, whose devastation prompted the creation of the Federal Reserve system. Financial panics almost always include a banking crisis, in which a significant portion of the banking sector ceases to function.

Financial panics and banking crises have happened fairly often, sometimes with disastrous effects on output and employment. Chile's 1981 banking crisis was followed by a 19% decline in real GDP per capita and a slump that lasted through most of the following decade. Finland's 1990 banking crisis was followed by a surge in the unemployment rate from 3.2% to 16.3%. Japan's banking crisis of the early 1990s led to more than a decade of economic stagnation.

The Consequences of Banking Crises

If banking crises affected only banks, they wouldn't be as serious a concern. In fact, however, banking crises are almost always associated with recessions, and severe banking crises are associated with the worst economic slumps. Furthermore, history shows that recessions caused in part by banking crises inflict sustained economic damage, with economies taking years to recover.

Banking Crises, Recessions, and Recovery

A severe banking crisis is one in which a large fraction of the banking system either fails outright (that is, goes bankrupt) or suffers a major loss of confidence and must be bailed out by the government. Such crises almost invariably lead to deep recessions, which are usually followed by slow recoveries.

Figure 78-1 illustrates this phenomenon by tracking unemployment in the aftermath of two banking crises widely separated in space and time: the Panic of 1893 in the United States and the Swedish banking crisis of 1991. In the figure, t represents the year of the crisis: 1893 for the United States, 1991 for Sweden. As the figure shows, these crises on different continents, almost a century apart, produced similarly devastating results: unemployment shot up and came down only slowly and erratically so that, even five years after the crisis, the number of jobless remained high by pre-crisis standards.

FIGURE 78-1 **Unemployment Rates, Before and After a Banking Crisis**

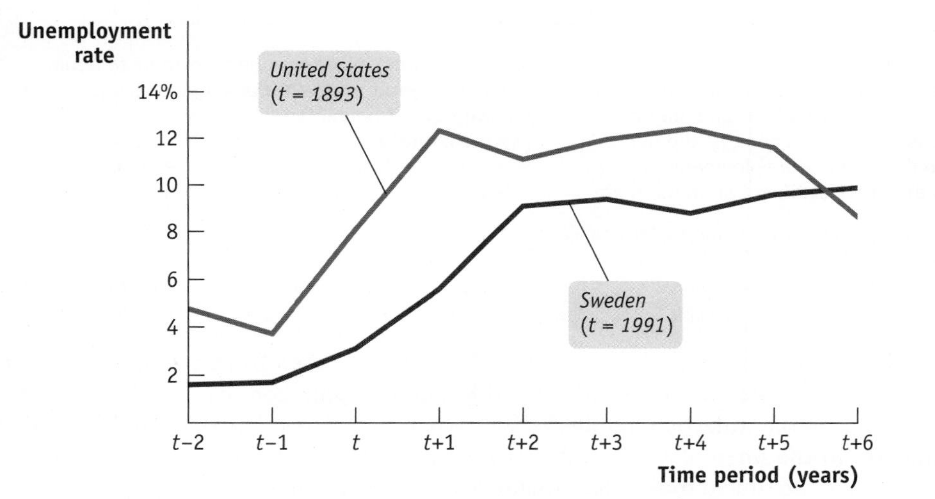

This figure tracks unemployment in the wake of two banking crises: the Panic of 1893 in the United States and the Swedish banking crisis of 1991. t represents the year of the crisis—1893 for the United States, 1991 for Sweden. $t - 2$ is the date two years before the crisis hit; $t + 5$ is the date five years after. In both cases, the economy suffered severe damage from the banking crisis: unemployment shot up and came down only slowly and erratically. In both cases, five years after the crisis the unemployment rate remained high compared to pre-crisis levels.

Sources: Christina D. Romer, "Spurious Volatility in Historical Unemployment Data," *Journal of Political Economy* 94, no. 1 (1986): 1–37; Eurostat.

FIGURE 78-2 Episodes of Banking Crises and Unemployment

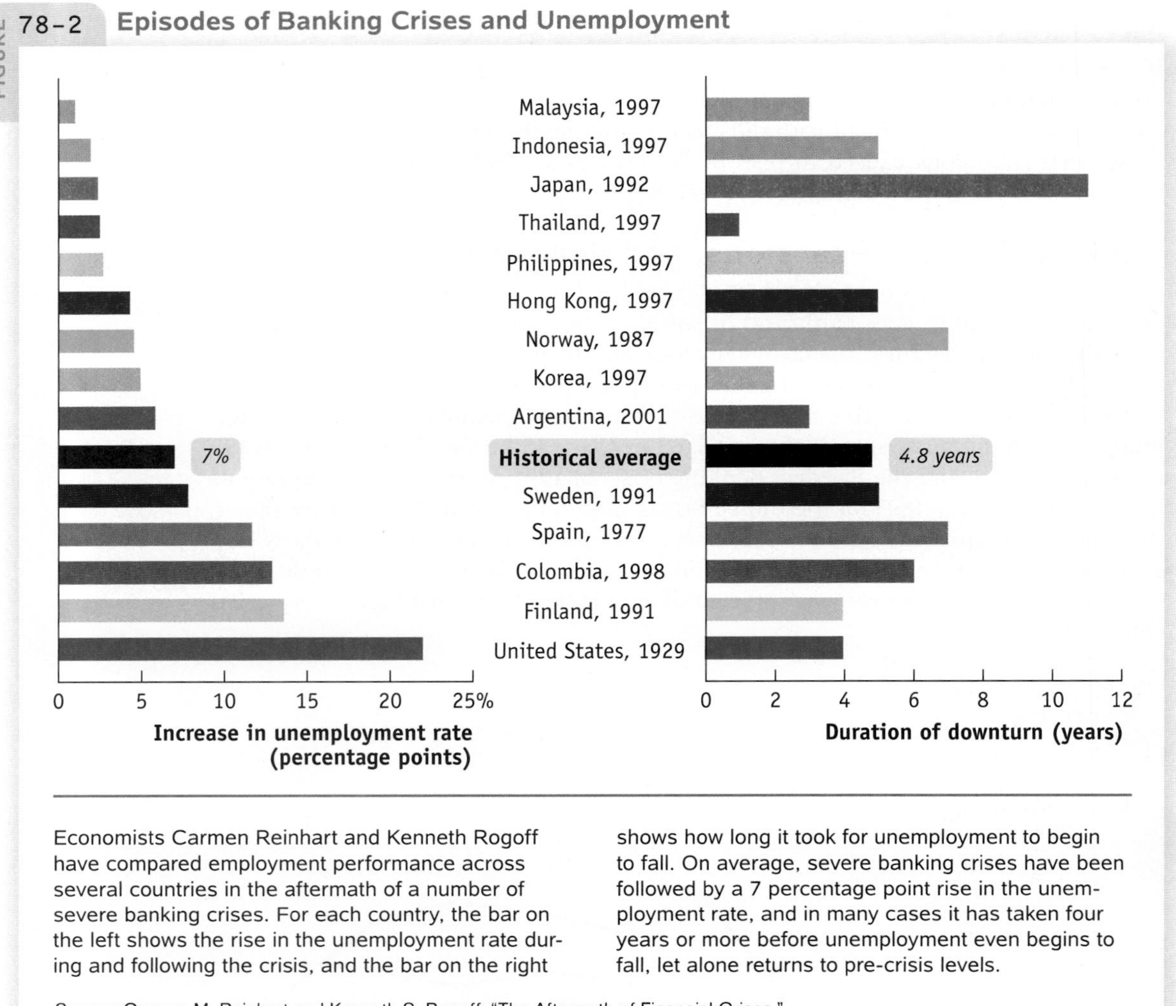

Economists Carmen Reinhart and Kenneth Rogoff have compared employment performance across several countries in the aftermath of a number of severe banking crises. For each country, the bar on the left shows the rise in the unemployment rate during and following the crisis, and the bar on the right shows how long it took for unemployment to begin to fall. On average, severe banking crises have been followed by a 7 percentage point rise in the unemployment rate, and in many cases it has taken four years or more before unemployment even begins to fall, let alone returns to pre-crisis levels.

Source: Carmen M. Reinhart and Kenneth S. Rogoff, "The Aftermath of Financial Crises," *American Economic Review* 99, no. 2 (2009): 466–472.

These historical examples are typical. Figure 78-2, taken from a widely cited study by the economists Carmen Reinhart and Kenneth Rogoff, compares employment performance in the wake of a number of severe banking crises. The bars on the left show the rise in the unemployment rate during and following the crisis; the bars on the right show the time it took before unemployment began to fall.

The numbers in the figure are shocking: on average, severe banking crises have been followed by a 7 percentage point rise in the unemployment rate, and in many cases it has taken four years or more before the unemployment rate even begins to fall, let alone returns to pre-crisis levels.

Why Are Banking-Crisis Recessions So Bad?

It's not difficult to see why banking crises normally lead to recessions. There are three main reasons: a *credit crunch* arising from reduced availability of credit, financial distress caused by a *debt overhang,* and the loss of monetary policy effectiveness.

In a **credit crunch,** potential borrowers either can't get credit at all or must pay very high interest rates.

1. *Credit crunch.* The disruption of the banking system typically leads to a reduction in the availability of credit called a **credit crunch,** in which potential borrowers either can't get credit at all or must pay very high interest rates. Unable to borrow or unwilling to pay higher interest rates, businesses and consumers cut back on spending, pushing the economy into a recession.

2. *Debt overhang.* A banking crisis typically pushes down the prices of many assets through a vicious cycle of deleveraging, as distressed borrowers try to sell assets to raise cash, pushing down asset prices and causing further financial distress. As we have already seen, deleveraging is a factor in the spread of the crisis, lowering the value of the assets banks hold on their balance sheets and so undermining their solvency. It also creates problems for other players in the economy.

   To take an example all too familiar from recent events, falling housing prices can leave consumers substantially poorer, especially because they are still stuck with the debt they incurred to buy their homes. A banking crisis, then, tends to leave consumers and businesses with a **debt overhang:** high debt but diminished assets. Like a credit crunch, this also leads to a fall in spending and a recession as consumers and businesses cut back in order to reduce their debt and rebuild their assets.
3. *Loss of monetary policy effectiveness.* A key feature of banking-crisis recessions is that when they occur, monetary policy—the main tool of policy makers for fighting negative demand shocks caused by a fall in consumer and investment spending—loses much of its effectiveness. The ineffectiveness of monetary policy makes banking-crisis recessions especially severe and long-lasting.

A **debt overhang** occurs when a vicious cycle of deleveraging leaves a borrower with high debt but diminished assets.

A **lender of last resort** is an institution, usually a country's central bank, that provides funds to financial institutions when they are unable to borrow from the private credit markets.

Recall how the Fed normally responds to a recession: it engages in open-market operations, purchasing short-term government debt from banks. This leaves banks with excess reserves, which they lend out, leading to a fall in interest rates and causing an economic expansion through increased consumer and investment spending.

Under normal conditions, this policy response is highly effective. In the aftermath of a banking crisis, though, the whole process tends to break down. Banks, fearing runs by depositors or a loss of confidence by their creditors, tend to hold on to excess reserves rather than lend them out. Meanwhile, businesses and consumers, finding themselves in financial difficulty due to the plunge in asset prices, may be unwilling to borrow even if interest rates fall. As a result, even very low interest rates may not be enough to push the economy back to full employment.

In the previous module we described the problem of the economy's falling into a liquidity trap, when even pushing short-term interest rates to zero isn't enough. In fact, all the historical episodes in which the zero bound on interest rates became an important constraint on policy—the 1930s, Japan in the 1990s, and a number of countries after 2008—have occurred after a major banking crisis.

The inability of the usual tools of monetary policy to offset the macroeconomic devastation caused by banking crises is the major reason such crises produce deep, prolonged slumps. The obvious solution is to look for other policy tools. In fact, governments do typically take a variety of special steps when banks are in crisis.

Governments Step In

Before the Great Depression, policy makers often allowed banks to fail in the belief that market forces should be allowed to work. Since the catastrophe of the 1930s, though, almost all policy makers have believed that it's necessary to take steps to contain the damage from bank failures. In general, central banks and governments take three main kinds of action in an effort to limit the fallout from banking crises:

1. They act as the *lender of last resort.*
2. They offer guarantees to depositors and others with claims on banks.
3. In an extreme crisis, a central bank will step in and provide financing to private credit markets.

1. LENDER OF LAST RESORT An institution, usually a country's central bank, that provides funds to financial institutions when they are unable to borrow from the private credit markets is known as a **lender of last resort.** In particular, the central bank can provide cash to a bank that is facing a run by depositors but is fundamentally solvent, making it unnecessary for the bank to engage in fire sales of its assets to raise cash.

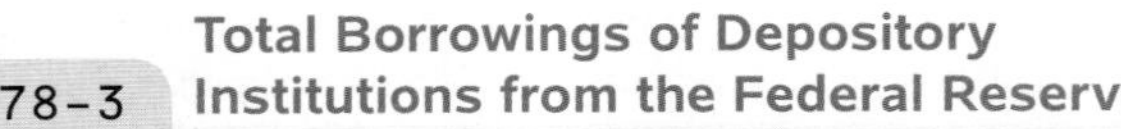

FIGURE 78-3 Total Borrowings of Depository Institutions from the Federal Reserve

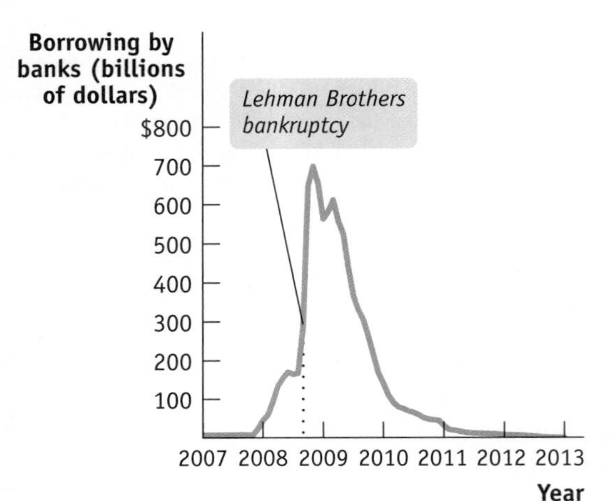

Although commercial banks borrowed negligible amounts from the Fed before the crisis hit in 2008, in the months after Lehman's collapse their borrowing surged to $700 billion—an amount 14 times total bank reserves before the crisis.

Source: Federal Reserve Bank of St. Louis.

This acts as a lifeline, working to prevent a loss of confidence in the bank's solvency from turning into a self-fulfilling prophecy.

Did the Federal Reserve act as a lender of last resort in the 2008 financial crisis? Very much so. Figure 78-3 shows borrowing by banks from the Fed: commercial banks borrowed negligible amounts from the central bank before the crisis, but their borrowing rose to $700 billion in the months following Lehman's failure. To get a sense of how large this borrowing was, note that total bank reserves before the crisis were less than $50 billion—so these loans were 14 times the banks' initial reserves.

2. GOVERNMENT GUARANTEES There are limits, though, to how much a lender of last resort can accomplish: it can't restore confidence in a bank if there is good reason to believe the bank is fundamentally insolvent. If the public believes that the bank's assets aren't worth enough to cover its debts even if it doesn't have to sell these assets on short notice, a lender of last resort isn't going to help much. And in major banking crises there are often good reasons to believe that many banks are truly bankrupt.

In such cases, governments often step in to guarantee banks' liabilities. In 2007, a bank run hit the British bank Northern Rock, ceasing only when the British government stepped in and guaranteed all deposits at the bank, regardless of size. Ireland's government eventually stepped in to guarantee repayment of not just deposits at all of the nation's banks, but all bank debts. Sweden did the same thing after its 1991 banking crisis.

When governments take on banks' risk, they often take ownership of the banks they are rescuing. Northern Rock was nationalized in 2008. Sweden nationalized a significant part of its banking system in 1992. In the United States, the Federal Deposit Insurance Corporation routinely seizes banks that are no longer solvent; it seized 140 banks in 2009. Ireland, however, chose not to seize any of the banks whose debts were guaranteed by taxpayers.

These government takeovers are almost always temporary. In general, modern governments want to save banks, not run them. So they "reprivatize" nationalized banks, selling them to private buyers, as soon as they believe they can.

3. PROVIDER OF DIRECT FINANCING During the depths of the 2008 financial crisis the Federal Reserve expanded its operations beyond the usual measures of open-market operations and lending to depository banks. It also began lending to shadow banks and buying commercial paper—short-term bonds issued by private companies—as well as buying the debt of Fannie Mae and Freddie Mac, the government-sponsored home mortgage agencies. In this way, the Fed provided credit to keep the economy afloat when private credit markets had dried up.

The 2008 Crisis and Its Aftermath

As we've just seen, banking crises have typically been followed by major economic problems. How did the aftermath of the financial crisis of 2008 compare with this historical experience? The answer, unfortunately, is that history has proved a very good guide: once again, the economic damage from the financial crisis was both large and prolonged.

Severe Crisis, Slow Recovery

Figure 78-4 shows real GDP in the United States and the European Union, the world's two largest economies, during the crisis and aftermath, with the peak pre-crisis quarter—the last quarter of 2007 for the United States, the first quarter of 2008 for the European Union—set equal to 100. What you can see is that both economies suf-

FIGURE 78-4 Crisis and Recovery in the United States and the European Union

In the aftermath of the 2008 financial crisis, aggregate output in the European Union and in the United States fell dramatically. Real GDP, shown here as an index with each economy's peak pre-crisis quarter set to 100, declined by more than 5%. As you can see, by 2013, real GDP in the United States had recovered beyond pre-crisis levels, and aggregate output in the European Union had still not reached its pre-crisis peak.

Sources: Bureau of Economic Analysis; Eurostat.

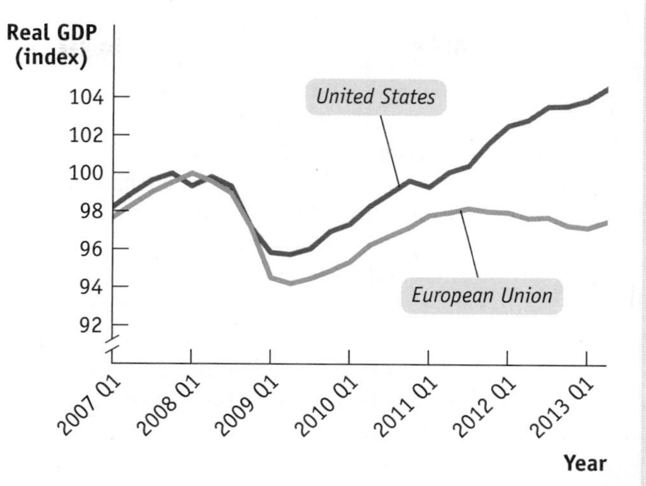

fered severe downturns, shrinking more than 5%, followed by relatively slow recoveries. The United States returned to its pre-crisis level of real GDP in the second quarter of 2011, and managed to exceed it in 2013. While as of late 2013, the European Union had yet to regain its pre-crisis level of output.

The severe slump and the slow recovery were very bad news for workers, since a healthy job market depends on an economy growing fast enough to accommodate both a growing workforce and rising productivity. Figure 78-5 shows two indicators of unemployment in the United States—the overall unemployment rate and the percentage of the unemployed who had been out of work 27 weeks or more. Both measures shot up during the crisis and remained very high through 2012, when the unemployment rate dropped below 8% for the first time in over three years. Nonetheless, it remained well above the pre-crisis level, indicating a labor market in which it was hard to find a job.

This outcome was, sad to say, about what one should have expected given the severity of the initial financial shock and the historical experience with such shocks.

FIGURE 78-5 Unemployment in the Aftermath of the 2008 Crisis

After 2008, the unemployment rate increased dramatically. Long-term unemployment, measured by the percentage of the unemployed who were out of work for 27 weeks or longer, increased at the same time. By 2011, almost half of all unemployed workers were long-term unemployed. Although the unemployment rate dips slightly starting in late 2012, throughout 2013, both unemployment rates remained above their pre-crisis levels.

Source: Bureau of Labor Statistics.

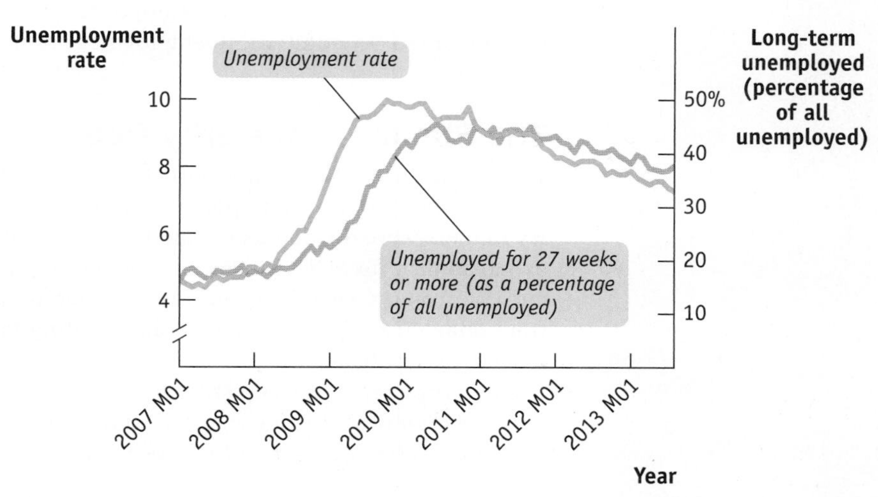

Aftershocks in Europe

One important factor bedeviling hopes for recovery was the emergence of special difficulties in several European nations.

The 2008 crisis was caused by problems with private debt, mainly home loans, which then triggered a crisis of confidence in banks. In 2011 and 2012, fears of a second crisis were focused on public debt, specifically the public debts of Southern European countries plus Ireland.

Europe's troubles first surfaced in Greece, a country with a long history of fiscal irresponsibility. In late 2009, it was revealed that a previous Greek government had understated the size of the budget deficits and the amount of government debt, prompting lenders to refuse further loans to Greece. Other European countries provided emergency loans to the Greek government in return for harsh budget cuts. But these budget cuts depressed the Greek economy, and by late 2011 there was general agreement that Greece could not pay back its debts in full.

By itself, this was probably a manageable shock for the European economy since Greece accounts for less than 3% of European GDP. Unfortunately, foot-dragging by European officials in confronting Greece's problems and the effects of the harsh budget cuts on the Greek economy spooked investors. By the fall of 2011, the crisis had spread beyond the Greek borders, hitting two major European economies: Spain and Italy.

Spain also ran into trouble, the result of fallout from the 2008 crisis. It suffered a housing bubble between 2000 and 2007 that eventually burst, leading to a deep economic slump that depressed tax receipts and caused large budget deficits. There were worries that the Spanish government might have to spend large amounts bailing out banks. As a result, investors began to worry about the solvency of the government and a possible default, driving up interest rates.

The youth unemployment rate in Spain, shockingly high at almost 58% in late 2013, is one example of the difficulties Europeans face in the aftermath of the 2008 crisis.

Giorgio Fochesato/Getty Images

Italy's government also faced insolvency fears in 2010 because in the aftermath of the 2008 crisis, investors feared that the Italian economy was growing too slowly to generate enough tax revenue to repay its public debt. These doubts drove up interest rates on Italian public debt, in turn creating a vicious circle: higher interest payments, caused by fears about Italian government solvency, worsened Italy's fiscal position even further and pushed it closer to the edge.

Heading into 2014, the growth rate of real GDP in Greece, Spain, and Italy is forecast to be slightly positive for the first time since the crisis began. However, the level of real GDP in these countries remains well below pre-crisis levels, partly due to the spending cuts and tax increases imposed as a condition of their bailout by the European Union. In addition, unemployment remains high, indicating that recovery is ongoing.

The Stimulus–Austerity Debate

The persistence of economic difficulties after the 2008 financial crisis led to fierce debates about appropriate policy responses. Broadly speaking, economists and policy makers were divided as to whether the situation called for more fiscal stimulus—expansionary fiscal measures such as more government spending and possibly tax cuts to promote spending and reduce unemployment—or for fiscal "austerity," contractionary fiscal measures such as spending cuts and possibly tax increases to reduce budget deficits.

The proponents of more stimulus pointed to the continuing poor performance of major economies, arguing that the combination of high unemployment and relatively low inflation clearly pointed to the need for expansionary policies. And since monetary policy was limited by the zero bound on interest rates, stimulus proponents advocated expansionary fiscal policy to fill the gap.

The austerity camp took a very different view. Strongly influenced by the solvency troubles of Greece, Ireland, Spain, and Italy, they argued that the common source of all the problems were high levels of government deficits and debts. In their view, countries like the United States that continued to run large government deficits several years after the 2008 crisis were at risk of suffering a similar loss of investor confidence in their ability to repay their debts. Moreover, austerity advocates claimed that cuts in government spending would not actually be contractionary because they would improve investor confidence and keep interest rates on government debt low.

Each side of the debate argued that recent experience refuted the other side's claims. Austerity proponents argued that the persistence of high unemployment despite the fiscal stimulus programs adopted by the United States and other major economies in 2009 showed that stimulus doesn't work. Stimulus advocates argued that these programs were simply inadequate in size, pointing out that many economists had warned of their inadequacy from the start.

Stimulus advocates further argued that warnings about the dangers of deficits were overblown, that far from rising, borrowing costs for Japan, the United States, and Britain—nations that, unlike the troubled European debtors, still had their own currencies with all the flexibility that implies—had fallen to record lows. And they dismissed claims that spending cuts would raise confidence as mainly fantasy.

At the time of writing, neither side was giving much ground. Clearly, any resolution of the debate would hinge on future economic developments and how they were interpreted.

The Lesson of the Post-Crisis Slump

Almost all major economies had great difficulty dealing with the aftermath of the 2008 financial crisis—high unemployment, low growth and, for some, solvency concerns, and high interest rates on public debt.

Clearly, then, the best way to avoid the terrible problems that arise after a financial crisis is not to have a crisis in the first place. How can you do that? In part, one might hope, through better regulation of financial institutions.

Regulation in the Wake of the Crisis

By late 2009, interventions by governments and central banks around the world had restored calm to financial markets. However, huge damage had been done to the global economy.

The banking crisis of 2008 demonstrated, all too clearly, that financial regulation is a continuing process—that regulations will and should change over time to keep up with a changing world. The dependence on very short-term loans (called repo), the lack of regulation, and being outside the lender-of-last-resort system made the shadow-banking sector vulnerable to crises and panics.

So what changes will the most recent crisis bring? One thing that became all too clear in the 2008 crisis was that the traditional scope of banking regulation was too narrow. Regulating only depository institutions was clearly inadequate in a world in which a large part of banking, properly understood, is undertaken by the shadow banking sector.

In the aftermath of the crisis, then, an overhaul of financial regulation was clearly needed. And in 2010 the U.S. Congress

Signed into law in 2010, Dodd-Frank is seen by many on Wall Street as too much regulation, while others wonder if it is enough.

AP Photo/Charles Dharapak, File

passed the Wall Street Reform and Consumer Protection Act—often referred to as the Dodd-Frank Act (named for the two legislators who introduced the bill to Congress). President Obama signed Dodd-Frank into law that same year. It represented an effort to respond to the events of the preceding years. These are its four main elements:

1. Consumer protection
2. Derivatives regulation
3. Regulation of shadow banks
4. Resolution authority over nonbank financial institutions that face bankruptcy

1. CONSUMER PROTECTION One factor in the financial crisis was the fact that many borrowers accepted offers they didn't understand, such as mortgages that were easy to pay in the first two years but required sharply higher payments later on. In an effort to limit future abuses, the new law creates a special office, the Consumer Financial Protection Bureau, dedicated to policing financial industry practices and protecting borrowers.

2. DERIVATIVES REGULATION Another factor in the crisis was the proliferation of derivatives, complex financial instruments that were supposed to help spread risk but arguably simply concealed it. Under the new law, most derivatives have to be bought and sold in open, transparent markets, hopefully limiting the extent to which financial players can take on invisible risk.

3. REGULATION OF SHADOW BANKS A key element in the financial crisis, as we've seen, was the rise of institutions that didn't fit the conventional definition of a bank but played the role of banks and created the risk of a banking crisis. How can regulation be extended to such institutions?

Dodd-Frank does not offer an explicit new definition of what it means to be a bank. Instead, it offers a sort of financial version of "you know it when you see it." Specifically, it gives a special panel the ability to designate financial institutions as "systemically important," meaning that their activities have the potential to create a banking crisis. Such institutions will be subject to bank-like regulation of their capital, their investments, and so on.

4. RESOLUTION AUTHORITY The events of 2008 made it clear that governments would often feel the need to guarantee a wide range of financial institution debts in a crisis, not just deposits. Yet how can this be done without creating huge incentive problems, motivating financial institutions to undertake overly risky behavior in the knowledge that they will be bailed out by the government if they get into trouble?

Part of the answer is to empower the government to seize control of financial institutions that require a bailout, the way it already does with failing commercial banks and thrifts. This new power, known as *resolution authority,* should be viewed as solving a problem that seemed acute in early 2009, when several major financial institutions were teetering on the brink. Yet it wasn't clear whether Washington had the legal authority to orchestrate a rescue that was fair to taxpayers.

It has been several years since the crisis ended and Dodd-Frank took effect. But, two questions about the law remain:

1. How will these regulations be worked into the international financial system? Will other nations adopt similar policies? If they do, how will conflicts among different national policies be resolved?
2. Will these regulations do the trick? Post-1930s bank regulation produced decades of stability, but will that happen again? Or will the new system fail in the face of a serious test?

Nobody knows the answers to these questions. We'll just have to continue to wait and see.

MODULE 78 Review

Solutions appear at the back of the book.

Check Your Understanding

1. Which of the following are examples of maturity transformations? Which are subject to a bank-run-like phenomenon in which fear of a failure becomes a self-fulfilling prophecy? Explain.
   a. You sell tickets to a lottery in which each ticket holder has a chance of winning a $10,000 jackpot.
   b. Dana borrows on her credit card to pay her living expenses while she takes a year-long course to upgrade her job skills. Without a better-paying job, she will not be able to pay her accumulated credit card balance.
   c. An investment partnership invests in office buildings. Partners invest their own funds and can redeem them only by selling their partnership share to someone else.
   d. The local student union savings bank offers checking accounts to students and invests those funds in student loans.
2. In November 2011, the government of France announced that it was reducing its forecast for economic growth in 2012. It was also reducing its estimates of tax revenue for 2012, since a weaker economy would mean smaller tax receipts. To offset the effect of lower revenue on the budget deficit, the government also announced a new package of tax increases and spending cuts. Which side of the stimulus–austerity debate was France taking?
3. Why does the use of short-term borrowing and being outside of the lender-of-last-resort system make shadow banks vulnerable to events similar to bank runs?
4. How do you think the crisis of 2008 would have been mitigated if there had been no shadow banking sector but only the formal depository banking sector?
5. Describe the incentive problem facing the U.S. government in responding to the 2007–2009 crisis with respect to the shadow banking sector. How did the Dodd-Frank Act attempt to address those incentive problems?

Multiple-Choice Questions

1. What makes a shadow bank different from a depository bank?
   a. Shadow banks do not engage in maturity transformation.
   b. Shadow banks do not make loans.
   c. Shadow banks do not accept deposits.
   d. Shadow banks are not vulnerable to bank runs.
   e. Shadow banks are government institutions.
2. The conversion of short-term liabilities into long-term assets is called
   a. an asset bubble.
   b. a shadow bank.
   c. maturity transformation.
   d. financial contagion.
   e. financial panic.
3. People in a coastal community believe housing prices in their area have been pushed to unreasonably high levels due to expectations of rising demand for housing by retiring baby boomers. This situation is termed
   a. an asset bubble.
   b. a shadow bubble.
   c. financial panic.
   d. maturity transformation.
   e. financial contagion.
4. A severe banking crisis typically leads to
   a. a deep recession followed by a quick recovery.
   b. a deep recession followed by a slow recovery.
   c. a shallow recession followed by a quick recovery.
   d. an asset bubble.
   e. an increase in shadow banking.
5. When a borrower is left with high debt but diminished assets this situation is called
   a. an asset bubble.
   b. a credit crunch.
   c. financial contagion.
   d. financial panic.
   e. debt overhang.

Critical-Thinking Question

Why does a banking crisis normally lead to a deep recession?

BUSINESS CASE: Licenses to Print Money

Thinkstock

People sometimes talk about profitable companies as having a "license to print money." Well, the British firm De La Rue actually does. In 1930, De La Rue, printer of items such as postage stamps, expanded into the money-printing business, producing banknotes for the then-government of China. Today it produces the currencies of about 150 countries.

De La Rue's business received some unexpected attention in 2011 when Muammar Gaddafi, who, at the time, was the dictator who had ruled Libya since 1969, was fighting to suppress a fierce popular uprising. To finance his efforts, he turned to seignorage, ordering around $1.5 billion worth of Libyan dinars printed.

But Libyan banknotes weren't printed in Libya; they were printed in Britain at one of De La Rue's facilities. The British Government, an enemy of the Gaddafi regime, seized the new banknotes before they could be flown to Libya, refusing to release them until Gaddafi was overthrown, which happened later that year.

Why do so many countries turn to private companies like De La Rue and its main rival, the German firm Giesecke and Devrient, to print their currencies? The short answer is that printing money isn't as easy as it sounds: producing high-quality banknotes that are hard to counterfeit requires highly specialized equipment and expertise.

Large, wealthy nations like the United States can easily afford to do this for themselves: U.S. currency is printed by the Bureau of Engraving and Printing, a division of the Treasury Department. But smaller, poorer countries do better by turning to experts like De La Rue, which can include high-tech features like security threads and holography to fight counterfeiters.

Actually, De La Rue has had its own problems with quality control: a scandal erupted in 2010, when it emerged that one of its plants had been producing defective security paper and that employees had covered up the problems. Nonetheless, many countries will surely continue relying on expert private firms to produce their currency.

Questions for Thought

1. How can a government obtain revenue by printing money when someone else actually prints the money?
2. Why, exactly, would Gaddafi have resorted to the printing press in early 2011?
3. Were there risks to the Libyan economy in releasing those dinars to its new government?

SECTION 24 REVIEW

Summary

Inflation, Disinflation, Deflation

1. In analyzing high inflation, economists use the **classical model of the price level,** which says that changes in the money supply lead to proportional changes in the aggregate price level even in the short run.
2. Governments sometimes print money in order to finance budget deficits. When they do, they impose an **inflation tax,** generating tax revenue equal to the inflation rate times the money supply, on those who hold money. Revenue from the real inflation tax, the inflation rate times the real money supply, is the real value of resources captured by the government. In order to avoid paying the inflation tax, people reduce their real money holdings and force the government to increase inflation to capture the same amount of real inflation tax revenue. In some cases, this leads to a vicious circle of a shrinking real money supply and a rising rate of inflation, leading to hyperinflation and a fiscal crisis.
3. Countries that don't need to print money to cover government deficits can still stumble into moderate inflation, either because of political opportunism or because of wishful thinking.

The Phillips Curve

4. At a given point in time, there is a downward-sloping relationship between unemployment and inflation known as the **short-run Phillips curve.** This curve is shifted by changes in the expected rate of inflation. The **long-run Phillips curve,** which shows the relationship between unemployment and inflation once expectations have had time to adjust, is vertical. It defines the **nonaccelerating inflation rate of unemployment,** or **NAIRU,** which is equal to the natural rate of unemployment.
5. Once inflation has become embedded in expectations, getting inflation back down can be difficult because *disinflation* can be very costly, requiring the sacrifice of large amounts of aggregate output and imposing high levels of unemployment. However, policy makers in the United States and other wealthy countries were willing to pay that price of bringing down the high inflation of the 1970s.
6. Deflation poses several problems. It can lead to **debt deflation,** in which a rising real burden of outstanding debt intensifies an economic downturn. Also, interest rates are more likely to run up against the **zero bound** in an economy experiencing deflation. When this happens, the economy enters a **liquidity trap,** rendering conventional monetary policy ineffective.

Crises and Consequences

7. Banks engage in **maturity transformation,** transforming short-term liabilities into long-term assets. **Shadow banks** have grown greatly since 1980. Largely unregulated, they can pay savers a higher rate of return than depository banks. Like depository banks, shadow banks engage in maturity transformation, depending on short-term borrowing to operate and investing in long-term assets. Therefore, shadow banks can also be subject to bank runs.
8. Although **banking crises** are rare, they typically inflict severe damage on the economy. They have two main sources: shared mistakes, such as investing in an **asset bubble,** and **financial contagion.** Contagion is spread through bank runs or via a vicious cycle of deleveraging. When unregulated, shadow banking is particularly vulnerable to contagion. In 2008, a **financial panic** hit the United States, arising from the combination of an asset bubble, a huge shadow banking sector, and a vicious cycle of deleveraging.
9. Severe banking crises almost invariably lead to deep and long recessions, with unemployment remaining high for several years after the crisis began. There are three main reasons why banking crises are so damaging to the economy: they result in a **credit crunch,** the vicious cycle of deleveraging leads to a **debt overhang,** and monetary policy is rendered ineffective as the economy falls into a liquidity trap. As a result, households and businesses are either unable or unwilling to spend, deepening the downturn.
10. Unlike during the Great Depression, governments now step in to try to limit the damage from a banking crisis by acting as the **lender of last resort** and by guaranteeing the banks' liabilities. Sometimes, but not always, governments nationalize the banks and then later reprivatize them. In an extreme crisis, the central bank may directly finance commercial transactions.
11. Economic damage from the financial crisis of 2008 was large and prolonged. The world's two largest economies, the United States and the European Union, suffered severe downturns. The persistence of economic difficulties after 2008 led to fierce debates about appropriate policy responses between economists and policy makers calling for more fiscal stimulus—more government spending and possibly tax cuts to promote spending and reduce unemployment—and those favoring fiscal austerity—spending cuts and possibly tax increases to reduce budget deficits.

12. The banking regulatory system put in place during the 1930s has eroded due to the rise of shadow banking. In the aftermath of the crisis, the U.S. Congress enacted the Dodd-Frank Act in the hope of preventing a replay of the crisis. The main elements of the law are stronger consumer protection, greater regulation of derivatives, regulation of shadow banking, and resolution authority for a variety of financial institutions. We have yet to see whether these changes will be adequate or whether they will be adopted by other countries.

Key Terms

Classical model of the price level, p. 787
Inflation tax, p. 789
Short-run Phillips curve, p. 795
Nonaccelerating inflation rate of unemployment (NAIRU), p. 799
Long-run Phillips curve, p. 799
Debt deflation, p. 802
Zero bound, p. 802
Liquidity trap, p. 803
Maturity transformation, p. 808
Shadow bank, p. 808
Banking crisis, p. 808
Asset bubble, p. 809
Financial contagion, p. 809
Financial panic, p. 809
Credit crunch, p. 812
Debt overhang, p. 813
Lender of last resort, p. 813

Problems

1. In the economy of Scottopia, policy makers want to lower the unemployment rate and raise real GDP by using monetary policy. Using the accompanying diagram, show why this policy will ultimately result in a higher aggregate price level but no change in real GDP.

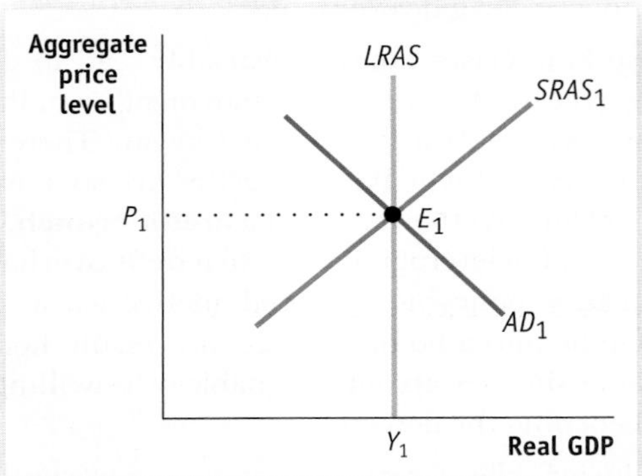

2. In the following examples, would the classical model of the price level be relevant?

   a. There is a great deal of unemployment in the economy and no history of inflation.

   b. The economy has just experienced five years of hyperinflation.

   c. Although the economy experienced inflation in the 10% to 20% range three years ago, prices have recently been stable and the unemployment rate has approximated the natural rate of unemployment.

3. Answer the following questions about the (real) inflation tax, assuming that the price level starts at 1.

   a. Maria Moneybags keeps $1,000 in her sock drawer for a year. Over the year, the inflation rate is 10%. What is the real inflation tax paid by Maria for this year?

   b. Maria continues to keep the $1,000 in her drawer for a second year. What is the real value of this $1,000 at the beginning of the second year? Over the year, the inflation rate is again 10%. What is the real inflation tax paid by Maria for the second year?

   c. For a third year, Maria keeps the $1,000 in the drawer. What is the real value of this $1,000 at the beginning of the third year? Over the year, the inflation rate is again 10%. What is the real inflation tax paid by Maria for the third year?

   d. After three years, what is the cumulative real inflation tax paid?

   e. Redo parts a through d with an inflation rate of 25%. Why is hyperinflation such a problem?

4. Concerned about the crowding-out effects of government borrowing on private investment spending, a candidate for president argues that the United States should just print money to cover the government's budget deficit. What are the advantages and disadvantages of such a plan?

5. After experiencing a recession for the past two years, the residents of Albernia were looking forward to a decrease in the unemployment rate. Yet after six months of strong positive economic growth, the unemployment rate has fallen only slightly below what it was at the end of the recession. How can you explain why the unemployment rate did not fall as much although the economy was experiencing strong economic growth?

6. Due to historical differences, countries often differ in how quickly a change in actual inflation is incorporated into a change in expected inflation. In a country such as Japan, which has had very little inflation in recent memory, it will take longer for a change in the actual inflation rate to be reflected in a corresponding change in the expected inflation rate. In contrast, in a country such as Zimbabwe, which has recently had very high inflation, a change in the actual inflation rate will immediately be reflected in a corresponding change in the expected inflation rate. What does this imply about the short-run and long-run Phillips curves in these two types of countries? What does this imply about the effectiveness of monetary and fiscal policy to reduce the unemployment rate?

7. a. Go to www.bls.gov. Click on "Subject Areas"; on the left, under "Inflation & Prices," click on the link "Consumer Price Index." Scroll down to the section "CPI Tables," and find the link under the head that reads "Table Containing History of CPI-U U.S." and click on it. What is the value of the percent change in the CPI from 2008 to 2009?

   b. Now go to www.treasury.gov and click on "Resource Center." From there, click on "Data and Charts Center." Then click on "Interest Rate Statistics." In the scroll-down windows, select "Daily Treasury Bill Rates" and "2009." Examine the data in "4 Weeks Bank Discount." What is the maximum? The minimum? Then do the same for 2007. How do the data for 2009 and 2007 compare? How would you relate this to your answer in part (a)? From the data on Treasury bill interest rates, what would you infer about the level of the inflation rate in 2007 compared to 2009? (You can check your answer by going back to the www.bls.gov website to find the percent change in the CPI from 2006 to 2007.)

   c. How would you characterize the change in the U.S. economy from 2007 to 2009?

8. The economy of Brittania has been suffering from high inflation with an unemployment rate equal to its natural rate. Policy makers would like to disinflate the economy with the lowest economic cost possible. Assume that the state of the economy is not the result of a negative supply shock. How can they try to minimize the unemployment cost of disinflation? Is it possible for there to be no cost of disinflation?

9. Who are the winners and losers when a mortgage company lends $100,000 to the Miller family to buy a house worth $105,000 and during the first year prices unexpectedly fall by 10%? What would you expect to happen if the deflation continued over the next few years? How would continuing deflation affect borrowers and lenders throughout the economy as a whole?

10. Which of the following are examples of debt overhang? Which examples are likely to lead to a cutback in spending? Explain.

   a. Your uncle starts a restaurant, borrowing to fund his investment. The restaurant fails, and your uncle must shut down but still must pay his debt.

   b. Your parents take out a loan to buy a house. Your father is transferred to a new city, and now your parents must sell the house. The value of the house has gone up during the time your family has lived there.

   c. Your friend's parents take out a loan to buy her a condo to live in while she is at college. Meanwhile, the housing market plummets. By the time your friend leaves college, the condo is worth significantly less than the value of the loan.

   d. You finish college with an honors degree in a field with many good job prospects and with $25,000 in student loans that you must repay.

11. Which of the following are *not* examples of a vicious cycle of deleveraging? Explain.

   a. Your university decides to sell several commercial buildings in the middle of town in order to upgrade buildings on campus.

   b. A company decides to sell its large and valuable art collection because other asset prices on its balance sheet have fallen below a critical level, forcing creditors to call in their loans to the company because of provisions written into the original loan contract.

   c. A company decides to issue more stock in order to voluntarily pay off some of its debt.

   d. A shadow bank must sell its holdings of corporate bonds because falling asset prices have led to a default on the terms of its loans with some creditors.

12. Figure 78-1 tracks the unemployment rate in the years before and after the Panic of 1893 in the United States and the banking crisis of 1991 in Sweden.

   a. In Figure 78-1, how many years after the Panic of 1893 did unemployment peak in the United States?

   b. In Figure 78-1, how many years after the banking crisis of 1991 did unemployment peak in Sweden?

13. In 2007–2009, the Federal Reserve, acting as a lender of last resort, stepped in to provide funds when private markets were unable to do so. The Fed also took over many banks. In 2007, it seized 3 banks; in 2008, it seized 25 banks; and in 2009, it seized 140 banks. Go to www.fdic.gov; under "Bank Closing Information," click on "Complete Failed Bank List." Then count the number of banks that the Federal Reserve has seized so far this year. Have bank failures decreased since the crisis in 2008?

Schweiz
Currency Exchange

SECTION 25

Open-Economy Macroeconomics

SWITZERLAND DOESN'T WANT YOUR MONEY

Parking your money in a Swiss bank is no way to get rich, given the low interest rates Swiss bankers offer. In fact, Swiss banks have even paid negative interest on deposits, charging customers for the service of keeping their funds.

But for generations, Swiss bank accounts have been seen as a way to *stay* rich, a safe place to store your wealth. In the troubled years that followed the 2008 financial crisis, the Swiss reputation for safety became especially important. European investors, in particular, poured money into Switzerland.

And the Swiss hated it—the result of the inflow of foreign funds was a surge in the value of the Swiss franc that wreaked havoc with Swiss exports.

At the beginning of 2008, one Swiss franc traded for about 0.6 euro. By mid-2011, the franc was trading for around 0.9 euro. That meant that Swiss exports, other things equal, had seen a 50% rise in their labor costs relative to competitors elsewhere in Europe.

Thanks to its reputation for quality, Switzerland has been remarkably successful over the years at selling goods to the world market, despite high labor costs. Nobody expects to get a bargain on Swiss watches or Swiss chocolate. But this was pushing matters to the breaking point.

So what was to be done? Starting in early 2009, the Swiss National Bank, Switzerland's equivalent of the Federal Reserve, began selling francs on the foreign exchange market in an attempt to hold down the franc's value. In return for these francs, it received other currencies, mainly dollars and euros, which it added to its reserves.

We're talking about a *lot* of sales: over a period of 2½ years, the bank added $180 billion to its foreign exchange reserves, which was about a third of Switzerland's GDP—the equivalent for the United States of selling $5 trillion dollars.

Yet even that wasn't enough to stop the franc's rise. In September 2011, as the franc seemed headed for a value of 1 euro or more, the Swiss National Bank announced that it would do whatever it took—sell an unlimited amount of francs—to keep the franc below a maximum of 0.833 euro per franc (that is, 1.2 francs per euro, which was the way the target was stated). That announcement finally seemed to stop the franc's rise, at least at first.

What the extraordinary efforts of the Swiss National Bank illustrated was the importance of a dimension of macroeconomics that we haven't emphasized so far—the fact that modern national economies are *open economies* that trade goods, services, and assets with the rest of the world. *Open-economy macroeconomics* is a branch of macroeconomics that deals with the relationships between national economies.

In this section we'll learn about some of the key issues in open-economy macroeconomics: the determinants of a country's *balance of payments,* the factors affecting *exchange rates,* the different forms of *exchange rate policy* adopted by various countries, and the relationship between exchange rates and macroeconomic policy.

MODULE 79

Capital Flows and the Balance of Payments

© Sadik Demiroz/Thinkstock

WHAT YOU WILL LEARN

1. The meaning of the balance of payments accounts
2. The determinants of international capital flows

The Balance of Payments Accounts

In 2012, people living in the United States sold about $3.5 trillion worth of stuff to people living in other countries and bought about $3.5 trillion worth of stuff in return. What kind of stuff? All kinds. Residents of the United States (including employees of firms operating in the United States) sold airplanes, bonds, wheat, and many other items to residents of other countries. Residents of the United States bought cars, stocks, oil, and many other items from residents of other countries.

How can we keep track of these transactions? Earlier we learned that economists keep track of the domestic economy using the national income and product accounts. Economists keep track of international transactions using a different but related set of numbers, the *balance of payments accounts.*

Understanding the Balance of Payments

A country's **balance of payments accounts** are a summary of the country's transactions with other countries.

To understand the basic idea behind the balance of payments accounts, let's consider a small-scale example: not a country, but a family farm. Let's say that we know the following about how last year went financially for the Costas, who own a small artichoke farm in California:

- They made $100,000 by selling artichokes.
- They spent $70,000 on running the farm, including purchases of new farm machinery, and another $40,000 buying food, paying utility bills for their home, replacing their worn-out car, and so on.
- They received $500 in interest on their bank account but paid $10,000 in interest on their mortgage.
- They took out a new $25,000 loan to help pay for farm improvements but didn't use all the money immediately. So they put the extra in the bank.

A country's **balance of payments accounts** are a summary of the country's transactions with other countries.

How could we summarize the Costas' year? One way would be with a table like Table 79-1, which shows sources of cash coming in and money going out, characterized under a few broad headings.

The first row of Table 79-1 shows sales and purchases of goods and services: sales of artichokes; purchases of groceries, heating oil, that new car, and so on. The second row shows interest payments: the interest the Costas received from their bank account and the interest they paid on their mortgage. The third row shows cash coming in from new borrowing versus money deposited in the bank.

In each row we show the net inflow of cash from that type of transaction. So the net in the first row is −$10,000 because the Costas spent $10,000 more than they earned. The net in the second row is −$9,500, the difference between the interest the Costas received on their bank account and the interest they paid on the mortgage. The net in the third row is $19,500: the Costas brought in $25,000 with their new loan but put only $5,500 of that sum in the bank.

Rob MacDougall/Getty Images

The last row shows the sum of cash coming in from all sources and the sum of all cash used. These sums are equal, by definition: every dollar has a source, and every dollar received gets used somewhere. (What if the Costas hid money under the mattress? Then that would be counted as another "use" of cash.)

A country's balance of payments accounts summarize its transactions with the world using a table similar to the one we just used to summarize the Costas' financial year.

TABLE 79-1

The Costas' Financial Year

	Sources of cash	Uses of cash	Net
Purchases or sales of goods and services	Artichoke sales: $100,000	Farm operation and living expenses: $110,000	−$10,000
Interest payments	Interest received on bank account: $500	Interest paid on mortgage: $10,000	−$9,500
Loans and deposits	Funds received from new loan: $25,000	Funds deposited in bank: $5,500	+$19,500
Total	**$125,500**	**$125,500**	**$0**

Table 79-2 on the next page shows a simplified version of the U.S. balance of payments accounts for 2012. Where the Costa family's accounts show sources and uses of cash, the U.S. balance of payments accounts show payments from foreigners—in effect, sources of cash for the United States as a whole—and payments to foreigners.

Row 1 of Table 79-2 shows payments that arise from sales and purchases of goods and services. For example, the value of U.S. wheat exports and the fees foreigners pay to U.S. consulting companies appear in the second column; the value of U.S. oil imports and the fees American companies pay to Indian call centers—the people who often answer your 1-800 calls—appear in the third column.

Row 2 shows *factor income*—payments for the use of factors of production owned by residents of other countries. Mostly this means investment income: interest paid on loans from overseas, the profits of foreign-owned corporations, and so on. For example, the profits earned by Disneyland Paris, which is owned by the U.S.-based Walt Disney Company, appear in the second column; the profits earned by the U.S. operations of Japanese auto companies appear in the third column. Factor income also includes labor income. For example, the wages of an American engineer who works temporarily on a construction site in Dubai are counted in the second column.

Row 3 shows *international transfers*—funds sent by residents of one country to residents of another. The main element here is the remittances that immigrants, such as the millions of Mexican-born workers employed in the United States, send to their families in their country of origin. Notice that Table 79-2 shows only the net value of transfers. That's because the U.S. government provides only an estimate of the net, not a breakdown between payments to foreigners and payments from foreigners.

The next two rows of Table 79-2 show payments resulting from sales and purchases of assets, broken down by who is doing the buying and selling. Row 4 shows transactions that involve governments or government agencies, mainly central banks. As we'll learn later, in 2012 most of the U.S. sales in this category involved the accumulation of *foreign exchange reserves* by the central banks of China and oil-exporting countries. Row 5 shows private sales and purchases of assets. For example, the 2012 purchase

TABLE 79-2

The U.S. Balance of Payments in 2012 (billions of dollars)

		Payments from foreigners	Payments to foreigners	Net
1	Sales and purchases of goods and services	2,211	2,745	–534
2	Factor income	776	552	224
3	Transfers	—	—	–130
	Current account (1 + 2 + 3)			–440
4	Official asset sales and purchases	394	–81	475
5	Private sales and purchases of assets	150	178	–28
	Financial account (4 + 5)			447
	Total	—	—	7

Source: Bureau of Economic Analysis.

of the American-owned AMC Cinema chain, by the Chinese company Dalian Wanda, showed up in the "Payments from foreigners" column of row 5; purchases of European stocks by U.S. investors show up as positive values in the "Payments to foreigners" column.

In laying out Table 79-2, we have separated rows 1, 2, and 3 into one group and rows 4 and 5 into another. This reflects a fundamental difference in how these two groups of transactions affect the future.

When a U.S. resident sells a good, such as wheat, to a foreigner, that's the end of the transaction. But a financial asset, such as a bond, is different. Remember, a bond is a promise to pay interest and principal in the future. So when a U.S. resident sells a bond to a foreigner, that sale creates a liability: the U.S. resident will have to pay interest and repay principal in the future. The balance of payments accounts distinguish between transactions that don't create liabilities and those that do.

Transactions that don't create liabilities are considered part of the **balance of payments on the current account,** often referred to simply as the **current account:** the balance of payments on goods and services plus factor income and net international transfer payments. The balance of row 1 of Table 79-2, −$534 billion, corresponds to the most important part of the current account: **the balance of payments on goods and services,** the difference between the value of exports and the value of imports during a given period.

A country's **balance of payments on the current account,** or the **current account,** is its balance of payments on goods and services plus net international transfer payments and factor income.

A country's **balance of payments on goods and services** is the difference between its exports and its imports of both goods and services during a given period.

The **merchandise trade balance,** or **trade balance,** is the difference between a country's exports and imports of goods.

A country's **balance of payments on the financial account,** or simply the **financial account,** is the difference between its sales of assets to foreigners and its purchases of assets from foreigners during a given period.

If you read news reports on the economy, you may well see references to another measure, the **merchandise trade balance,** sometimes referred to as the **trade balance** for short. This is the difference between a country's exports and imports of goods alone—not including services. Economists sometimes focus on the merchandise trade balance, even though it's an incomplete measure, because data on international trade in services aren't as accurate as data on trade in physical goods, and they are also slower to arrive.

The current account, as we've just learned, consists of international transactions that don't create liabilities. Transactions that involve the sale or purchase of assets, and therefore do create future liabilities, are considered part of the **balance of payments on the financial account,** or the **financial account** for short. (Until a few years ago, economists often referred to the financial account as the *capital account.* We'll use the modern term, but you may run across the older term.)

So how does it all add up? The first two unnumbered rows of Table 79-2 show the bottom lines: the overall U.S. current account and financial account for 2012. As you can see, in 2012, the United States ran a current account deficit: the amount it paid to foreigners for goods, services, factors, and transfers was greater than the amount it received. Simultaneously, it ran a financial account surplus: the value of the assets it sold to foreigners was greater than the value of the assets it bought from foreigners.

In the official data, the U.S. current account deficit and financial account surplus almost, but not quite, offset each other: the financial account surplus was $7 billion larger than the current account deficit. But that's just a statistical error, reflecting the imperfection of official data. (And a $7 billion error when you're measuring inflows and outflows of $3.5 trillion isn't bad!) In fact, it's a basic rule of balance of payments accounting that the current account and the financial account must sum to zero:

(79-1) Current account (CA) + Financial account (FA) = 0

or

$$CA = -FA$$

Why must Equation 79-1 be true? We already saw the fundamental explanation in Table 79-1, which showed the accounts of the Costa family: in total, the sources of cash must equal the uses of cash. The same applies to balance of payments accounts. Figure 79-1, a variant on the circular-flow diagram we have found useful in discussing domestic macroeconomics, may help you visualize how this adding up works. Instead of showing the flow of money *within* a national economy, Figure 79-1 shows the flow of money *between* national economies.

Money flows into the United States from the rest of the world as payment for U.S. exports of goods and services, as payment for the use of U.S.-owned factors of production, and as transfer payments. These flows (indicated by the lower yellow arrow) are the positive components of the U.S. current account. Money also flows into the United States from foreigners who purchase U.S. assets (as shown by the lower green arrow)—the positive component of the U.S. financial account.

At the same time, money flows from the United States to the rest of the world as payment for U.S. imports of goods and services, as payment for the use of foreign-owned factors of production, and as transfer payments. These flows, indicated by the upper yellow arrow, are the negative components of the U.S. current account. Money also flows from the United States to purchase foreign assets, as shown by the upper green arrow—the negative component of the U.S. financial account. As in all circular-flow diagrams, the flow into a box and the flow out of a box are equal. This means that the

FIGURE 79-1 **The Balance of Payments**

The yellow arrows represent payments that are counted in the current account. The green arrows represent payments that are counted in the financial account. Because the total flow into the United States must equal the total flow out of the United States, the sum of the current account plus the financial account is zero.

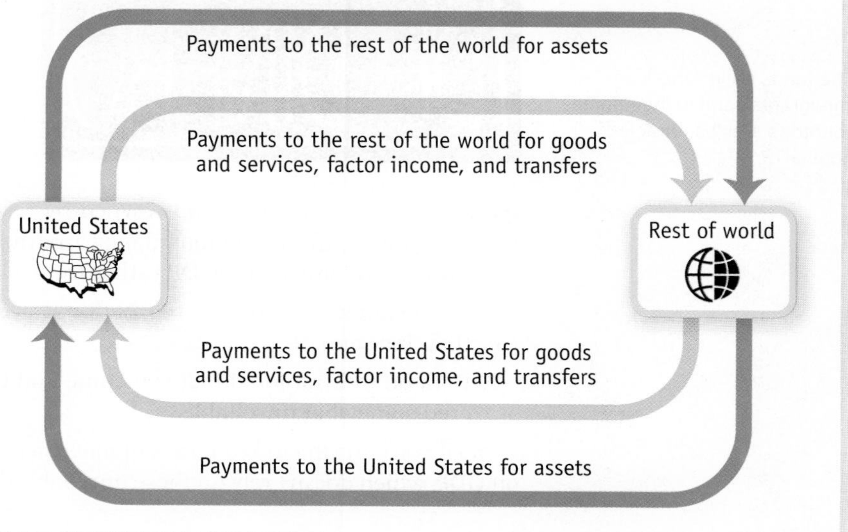

sum of the yellow and green arrows going into the United States is equal to the sum of the yellow and green arrows going out of the United States. That is,

(79-2) Positive entries on the current account (lower yellow arrow) + Positive entries on the financial account (lower green arrow) = Negative entries on the current account (upper yellow arrow) + Negative entries on the financial account (upper green arrow)

Equation 79-2 can be rearranged as follows:

(79-3) Positive entries on the current account − Negative entries on the current account + Positive entries on the financial account − Negative entries on the financial account = 0

Equation 79-3 is equivalent to Equation 79-1: the current account plus the financial account—both equal to positive entries minus negative entries—is equal to zero.

But what determines the current account and the financial account?

ECONOMICS IN ACTION WORLD VIEW

GDP, GNP, AND THE CURRENT ACCOUNT

When we discussed national income accounting, we derived the basic equation relating GDP to the components of spending:

$$Y = C + I + G + X - IM$$

where X and IM are exports and imports, respectively, of goods and services. But as we've learned, the balance of payments on goods and services is only one component of the current account balance. Why doesn't the national income equation use the current account as a whole?

The answer is that gross domestic product, GDP, is the value of goods and services produced domestically. So it doesn't include international factor income and international transfers, two sources of income that are included in the calculation of the current account balance. The profits of Ford Motors U.K. aren't included in America's GDP, and the funds Latin American immigrants send home to their families aren't subtracted from GDP.

Mikeledray/Shutterstock

The funds Latin American immigrants send to their home countries aren't subtracted from GDP.

Shouldn't we have a broader measure that does include these sources of income? Actually, gross national product—GNP—does include international factor income. Estimates of U.S. GNP differ slightly from estimates of GDP because GNP adds in items such as the earnings of U.S. companies abroad and subtracts items such as the interest payments on bonds owned by residents of China and Japan. There isn't, however, any regularly calculated measure that includes transfer payments.

Why do economists use GDP rather than a broader measure? Two reasons:

1. The original purpose of the national accounts was to track production rather than income.
2. Data on international factor income and transfer payments are generally considered somewhat unreliable.

So if you're trying to keep track of movements in the economy, it makes sense to focus on GDP, which doesn't rely on these unreliable data.

Modeling the Financial Account

A country's financial account measures its net sales of assets, such as currencies, securities, and factories, to foreigners. Those assets are exchanged for a type of capital called *financial capital,* which is funds from savings that are available for investment spending. We can thus think of the financial account as a measure of *capital inflows* in the form of foreign savings that become available to finance domestic investment spending.

What determines these capital inflows?

Part of our explanation will have to wait for a little while because some international capital flows are created by governments and central banks, which sometimes act very differently from private investors. But we can gain insight into the motivations for capital flows that are the result of private decisions by using the *loanable funds model* we developed previously. In using this model, we make two important simplifications:

1. We simplify the reality of international capital flows by assuming that all flows are in the form of loans. In reality, capital flows take many forms, including purchases of shares of stock in foreign companies and foreign real estate as well as *foreign direct investment,* in which companies build factories or acquire other productive assets abroad.
2. We also ignore the effects of expected changes in *exchange rates,* the relative values of different national currencies. We'll analyze the determination of exchange rates later.

Figure 79-2 recaps the loanable funds model for a closed economy. Equilibrium corresponds to point *E,* at an interest rate of 4%, at which the supply of loanable funds, *S,* intersects the demand for loanable funds curve, *D.* But if international capital flows are possible, this diagram changes and *E* may no longer be the equilibrium. We can analyze the causes and effects of international capital flows using Figure 79-3, which places the loanable funds market diagrams for two countries side by side.

Figure 79-3 illustrates a world consisting of only two countries, the United States and Britain. Panel (a) shows the loanable funds market in the United States, where

FIGURE 79-2 **The Loanable Funds Model Revisited**

According to the loanable funds model of the interest rate, the equilibrium interest rate is determined by the intersection of the supply of loanable funds curve, *S,* and the demand for loanable funds curve, *D.* At point *E,* the equilibrium interest rate is 4%.

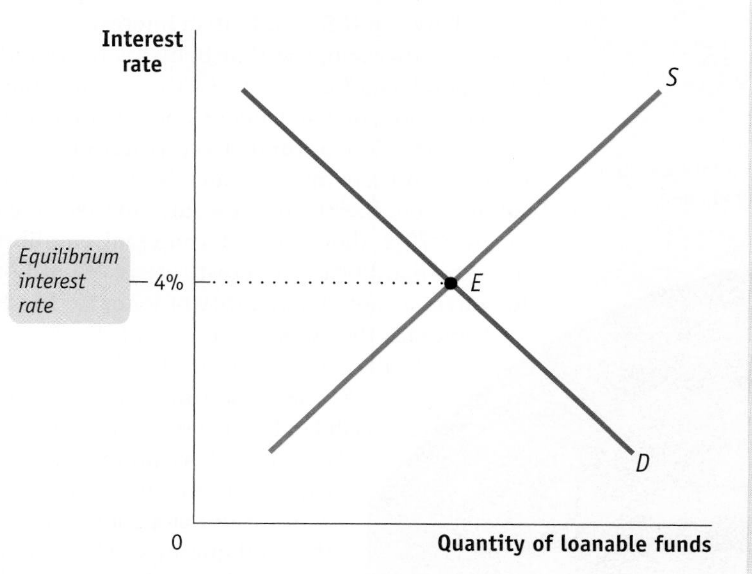

FIGURE 79-3 Loanable Funds Markets in Two Countries

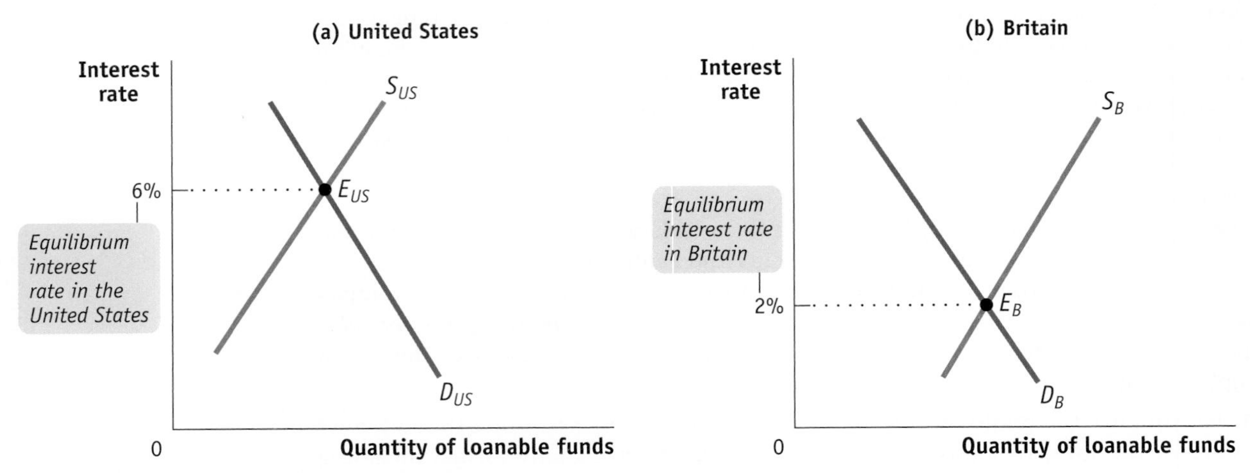

Here we show two countries, the United States and Britain, each with its own loanable funds market. The equilibrium interest rate is 6% in the U.S. market but only 2% in the British market. This creates an incentive for capital to flow from Britain to the United States.

the equilibrium in the absence of international capital flows is at point E_{US} with an interest rate of 6%. Panel (b) shows the loanable funds market in Britain, where the equilibrium in the absence of international capital flows is at point E_B with an interest rate of 2%.

Will the actual interest rate in the United States remain at 6% and that in Britain at 2%? Not if it is easy for British residents to make loans to Americans. In that case, British lenders, attracted by high American interest rates, will send some of their loanable funds to the United States. This capital inflow will increase the quantity of loanable funds supplied to American borrowers, pushing the U.S. interest rate down. At the same time, it will reduce the quantity of loanable funds supplied to British borrowers, pushing the British interest rate up. So international capital flows will narrow the gap between U.S. and British interest rates.

Let's further suppose that British lenders regard a loan to an American as being just as good as a loan to one of their own compatriots, and American borrowers regard a debt to a British lender as no more costly than a debt to an American lender. In that case, the flow of funds from Britain to the United States will continue until the gap between their interest rates is eliminated. In other words, international capital flows will equalize the interest rates in the two countries.

International flows of capital resemble international flows of goods and services.

BLOOMimage/Getty Images

Figure 79-4 shows an international equilibrium in the loanable funds markets where the equilibrium interest rate is 4% in both the United States and Britain. At this interest rate, the quantity of loanable funds demanded by American borrowers exceeds the quantity of loanable funds supplied by American lenders. This gap is filled by "imported" funds—a capital inflow from Britain.

At the same time, the quantity of loanable funds supplied by British lenders is greater than the quantity of loanable funds demanded by British borrowers. This excess is "exported" in the form of a capital outflow to the United States. And the two markets are in equilibrium at a common interest rate of 4%. At that interest rate, the total quantity of loans demanded by borrowers across the two markets is equal to the total quantity of loans supplied by lenders across the two markets.

FIGURE 79-4 International Capital Flows

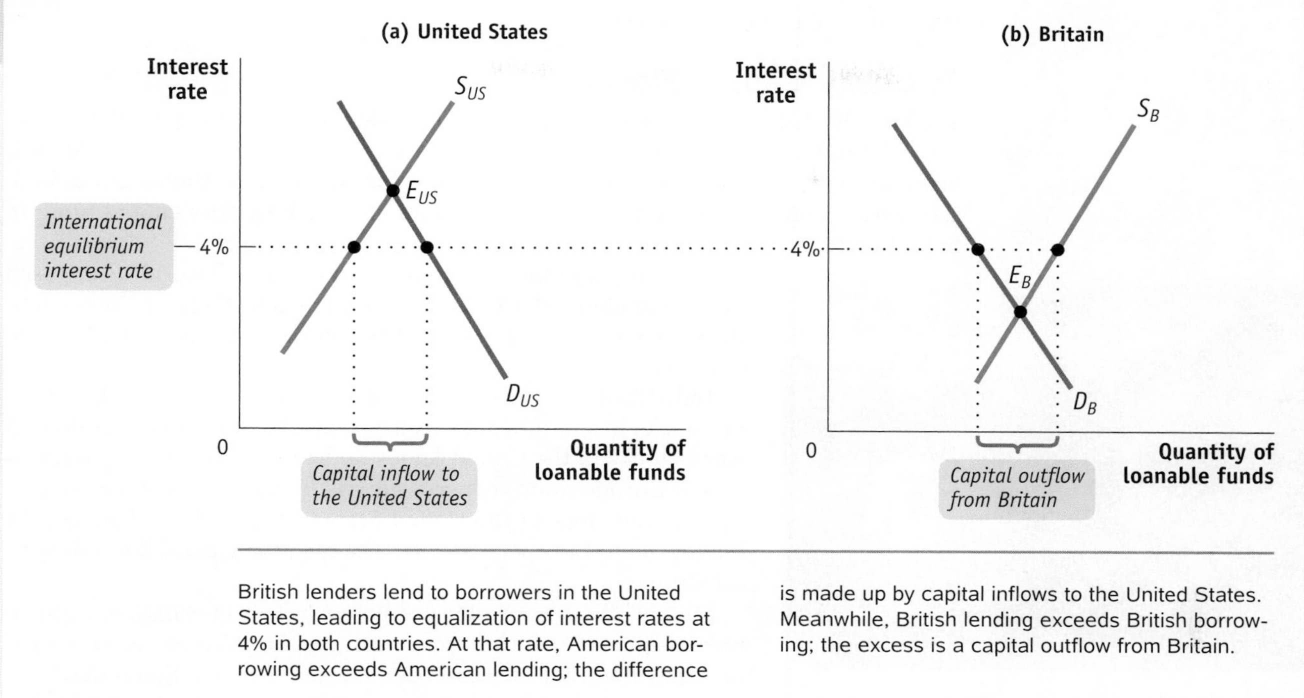

British lenders lend to borrowers in the United States, leading to equalization of interest rates at 4% in both countries. At that rate, American borrowing exceeds American lending; the difference is made up by capital inflows to the United States. Meanwhile, British lending exceeds British borrowing; the excess is a capital outflow from Britain.

In short, international flows of capital are like international flows of goods and services. Capital moves from places where it would be cheap in the absence of international capital flows to places where it would be expensive in the absence of such flows.

Underlying Determinants of International Capital Flows

The open-economy version of the loanable funds model helps us understand international capital flows in terms of the supply and demand for funds. But what underlies differences across countries in the supply and demand for funds? Why, in the absence of international capital flows, would interest rates differ internationally, creating an incentive for international capital flows?

International differences in the demand for funds reflect underlying differences in investment opportunities. In particular, a country with a rapidly growing economy, other things equal, tends to offer more investment opportunities than a country with a slowly growing economy. So a rapidly growing economy typically—though not always—has a higher demand for capital and offers higher returns to investors than a slowly growing economy in the absence of capital flows. As a result, capital tends to flow from slowly growing to rapidly growing economies.

The classic example is the flow of capital from Britain to the United States, among other countries, between 1870 and 1914. During that era, the U.S. economy was growing rapidly as the population increased and spread westward and as the nation industrialized. This created a demand for investment spending on railroads, factories, and so on. Meanwhile, Britain had a much more slowly growing population, was already industrialized, and already had a railroad network covering the country. This left Britain with savings to spare, much of which were lent to the United States and other New World economies.

International differences in the supply of funds reflect differences in savings across countries. These may be the result of differences in private savings rates, which vary widely among countries. For example, in 2012, private savings were 22% of Japan's

GDP but only 17% of U.S. GDP. They may also reflect differences in savings by governments. In particular, government budget deficits, which reduce overall national savings, can lead to capital inflows.

Two-way Capital Flows

The loanable funds model helps us understand the direction of *net* capital flows—the excess of inflows into a country over outflows, or vice versa. As we saw in Table 79-2, however, *gross* flows take place in both directions: for example, the United States both sells assets to foreigners and buys assets from foreigners. Why does capital move in both directions?

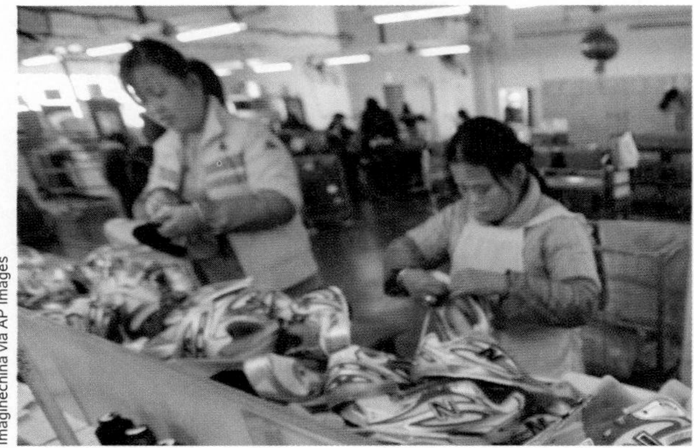

Imaginechina via AP Images

Many American companies have opened plants in China for easier access to the growing Chinese market and to take advantage of low labor costs.

The answer to this question is that in the real world, as opposed to the simple model we've just constructed, there are other motives for international capital flows besides seeking a higher rate of interest.

Individual investors often seek to diversify against risk by buying stocks in a number of countries. Stocks in Europe may do well when stocks in the United States do badly, or vice versa, so investors in Europe try to reduce their risk by buying some U.S. stocks, even as investors in the United States try to reduce their risk by buying some European stocks. The result is capital flows in both directions.

Meanwhile, corporations often engage in international investment as part of their business strategy—for example, auto companies may find that they can compete better in a national market if they assemble some of their cars locally. Such business investments can also lead to two-way capital flows, as, say, European carmakers build plants in the United States even as U.S. computer companies open facilities in Europe.

Finally, some countries, including the United States, are international banking centers: people from all over the world put money in U.S. financial institutions, which then invest many of those funds overseas.

The result of these two-way flows is that modern economies are typically both debtors (countries that owe money to the rest of the world) and creditors (countries to which the rest of the world owes money). Due to years of both capital inflows and outflows, at the end of 2012, the United States had accumulated foreign assets worth $20.8 trillion and foreigners had accumulated assets in the United States worth $25.2 trillion.

MODULE 79 Review

Solutions appear at the back of the book.

Check Your Understanding

1. Which of the balance of payments accounts do the following events affect?
   a. Boeing, a U.S.-based company, sells a newly built airplane to China.
   b. Chinese investors buy stock in Boeing from Americans.
   c. A Chinese company buys a used airplane from American Airlines and ships it to China.
   d. A Chinese investor who owns property in the United States buys a corporate jet, which he will keep in the United States so he can travel around America.
2. What effect do you think the collapse of the U.S. housing bubble and the ensuing recession had on international capital flows into the United States?

Multiple-Choice Questions

1. The current account includes which of the following?
   I. payments for goods and services
   II. transfer payments
   III. factor income
   a. I only
   b. II only
   c. III only
   d. I and II only
   e. I, II, and III

2. The balance of payments on the current account plus the balance of payments on the financial account is equal to
   a. zero.
   b. one.
   c. the trade balance.
   d. net capital flows.
   e. the size of the trade deficit.

3. The financial account was previously known as the
   a. gross national product.
   b. capital account.
   c. trade deficit.
   d. investment account.
   e. trade balance.

4. The trade balance includes which of the following?
   I. imports and exports of goods
   II. imports and exports of services
   III. net capital flows
   a. I only
   b. II only
   c. III only
   d. I and II only
   e. I, II, and III

5. Which of the following will increase the demand for loanable funds in a country?
   a. economic growth
   b. decreased investment opportunities
   c. a recession
   d. decreased private savings rates
   e. government budget surpluses

Critical-Thinking Question

Draw two side-by-side graphs of the loanable funds market in the United States and in China to show how a higher interest rate in the United States will lead to capital flows between the two countries. On your graphs, label the starting and ending interest rates and the size of the capital inflows and outflows.

MODULE 80 The Foreign Exchange Market

© Image Source Plus/Alamy

WHAT YOU WILL LEARN

1. The role of the foreign exchange market and the exchange rate
2. The importance of real exchange rates and their role in the current account

The Role of the Exchange Rate

We've just seen how differences in the supply of loanable funds from savings and the demand for loanable funds for investment spending lead to international capital flows. We've also learned that a country's balance of payments on the current account plus its balance of payments on the financial account add up to zero: a country that receives net capital inflows must run a matching current account deficit, and a country that generates net capital outflows must run a matching current account surplus.

The behavior of the financial account—reflecting inflows or outflows of capital—is best described as equilibrium in the international loanable funds market. At the same time, the balance of payments on goods and services, the main component of the current account, is determined by decisions in the international markets for goods and services.

So given that the financial account reflects the movement of capital and the current account reflects the movement of goods and services, what ensures that the balance of payments really does balance? That is, what ensures that the two accounts actually offset each other?

The answer lies in the role of the *exchange rate,* which is determined in the *foreign exchange market.*

Understanding Exchange Rates

In general, goods, services, and assets produced in a country must be paid for in that country's currency. American products must be paid for in dollars; European products must be paid for in euros; Japanese products must be paid for in yen. Occasionally, sellers will accept payment in foreign currency, but they will then exchange that currency for domestic money.

International transactions, then, require a market—the **foreign exchange market**—in which currencies can be exchanged for each other. This market determines **exchange rates,** the prices at which currencies trade. You will not find the foreign exchange market located in any one geographic spot. Rather, it is a global electronic market that traders around the world use to buy and sell currencies.

TABLE 80-1

Exchange Rates, May 13, 2013 7:50 A.M.

	U.S. dollars	Yen	Euros
One U.S. dollar exchanged for	1	101.6500	0.7701
One yen exchanged for	0.0098	1	0.0076
One euro exchanged for	1.2985	132.0300	1

Table 80-1 shows exchange rates among the world's three most important currencies as of 7:50 A.M., EST, on May 13, 2013. Each entry shows the price of the "row" currency in terms of the "column" currency. For example, at that time US$1 exchanged for €0.7701, so it took €0.7701 to buy US$1. Similarly, it took US$1.2985 to buy €1. These two numbers reflect the same rate of exchange between the euro and the U.S. dollar: 1/1.2985 = €0.7701.

There are two ways to write any given exchange rate. In this case, there were €0.7701 to US$1 and US$1.2985 to €1. Which is the correct way to write it? The answer is that there is no fixed rule. In most countries, people tend to express the exchange rate as the price of a dollar in domestic currency. However, this rule isn't universal, and the U.S. dollar–euro rate is commonly quoted both ways. The important thing is to be sure you know which one you are using!

When discussing movements in exchange rates, economists use specialized terms to avoid confusion. When a currency becomes more valuable in terms of other currencies, economists say that the currency **appreciates.** When a currency becomes less valuable in terms of other currencies, it **depreciates.** Suppose, for example, that the value of €1 went from $1 to $1.25, which means that the value of US$1 went from €1 to €0.80 (because 1/1.25 = 0.80). In this case, we would say that the euro appreciated and the U.S. dollar depreciated.

Movements in exchange rates, other things equal, affect the relative prices of goods, services, and assets in different countries. Suppose, for example, that the price of an American hotel room is US$100 and the price of a French hotel room is €100. If the exchange rate is €1 = US$1, these hotel rooms have the same price. If the exchange rate is €1.25 = US$1, the French hotel room is 20% cheaper than the American hotel room. If the exchange rate is €0.80 = US$1, the French hotel room is 25% more expensive than the American hotel room.

But what determines exchange rates? Supply and demand in the foreign exchange market.

Bruce Laurance/Getty Images

When the dollar appreciates, an American vacation becomes more expensive for European tourists.

The Equilibrium Exchange Rate

Imagine, for the sake of simplicity, that there are only two currencies in the world: U.S. dollars and euros. Europeans wanting to purchase American goods, services, and assets come to the foreign exchange market to exchange euros for U.S. dollars. That is, Europeans demand U.S. dollars from the foreign exchange market and, correspondingly, supply euros to that market.

Americans wanting to buy European goods, services, and assets come to the foreign exchange market to exchange U.S. dollars for euros. That is, Americans supply U.S. dollars to the foreign exchange market and, correspondingly, demand euros from that market. (International transfers and payments of factor income also enter into the foreign exchange market, but to make things simple, we'll ignore these.)

Figure 80-1 shows how the foreign exchange market works. The quantity of dollars demanded and supplied at any given euro–U.S. dollar exchange rate is shown on the horizontal axis, and the euro–U.S. dollar exchange rate is shown on the vertical axis. The exchange rate plays the same role as the price of a good or service in an ordinary supply and demand diagram.

The figure shows two curves, the demand curve for U.S. dollars and the supply curve for U.S. dollars. The key to understanding the slopes of these curves is that the level of the exchange rate affects exports and imports. When a country's currency

Currencies are traded in the **foreign exchange market.**

The prices at which currencies trade are known as **exchange rates.**

When a currency becomes more valuable in terms of other currencies, it **appreciates.**

When a currency becomes less valuable in terms of other currencies, it **depreciates.**

FIGURE 80-1 The Foreign Exchange Market

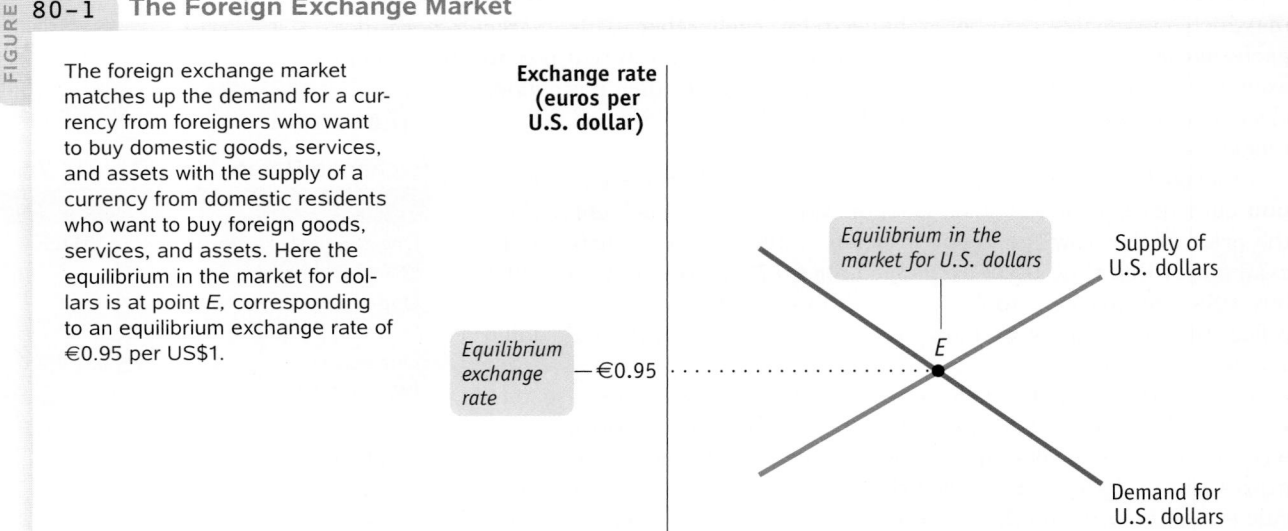

The foreign exchange market matches up the demand for a currency from foreigners who want to buy domestic goods, services, and assets with the supply of a currency from domestic residents who want to buy foreign goods, services, and assets. Here the equilibrium in the market for dollars is at point *E*, corresponding to an equilibrium exchange rate of €0.95 per US$1.

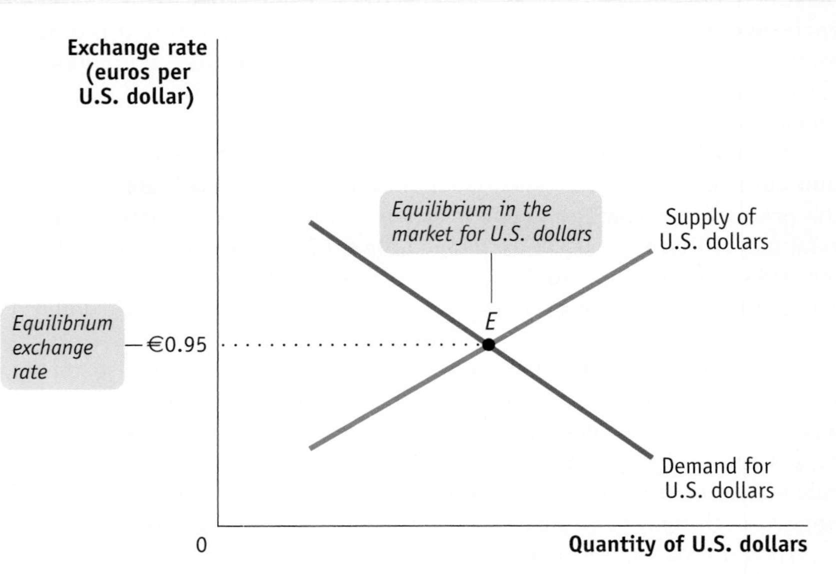

The **equilibrium exchange rate** is the exchange rate at which the quantity of a currency demanded in the foreign exchange market is equal to the quantity supplied.

appreciates (becomes more valuable), exports fall and imports rise. When a country's currency depreciates (becomes less valuable), exports rise and imports fall.

To understand why the demand curve for U.S. dollars slopes downward, recall that the exchange rate, other things equal, determines the prices of American goods, services, and assets relative to those of European goods, services, and assets. If the U.S. dollar rises against the euro (the dollar appreciates), American products will become more expensive to Europeans relative to European products. So Europeans will buy less from the United States and will acquire fewer dollars in the foreign exchange market: the quantity of U.S. dollars demanded falls as the number of euros needed to buy a U.S. dollar rises.

If the U.S. dollar falls against the euro (the dollar depreciates), American products will become relatively cheaper for Europeans. Europeans will respond by buying more from the United States and acquiring more dollars in the foreign exchange market: the quantity of U.S. dollars demanded rises as the number of euros needed to buy a U.S. dollar falls.

A similar argument explains why the supply curve of U.S. dollars in Figure 80-1 slopes upward: the more euros required to buy a U.S. dollar, the more dollars Americans will supply. Again, the reason is the effect of the exchange rate on relative prices. If the U.S. dollar rises against the euro, European products look cheaper to Americans—who will demand more of them. This will require Americans to convert more dollars into euros.

The **equilibrium exchange rate** is the exchange rate at which the quantity of U.S. dollars demanded in the foreign exchange market is equal to the quantity of U.S. dollars supplied. In Figure 80-1, the equilibrium is at point *E*, and the equilibrium exchange rate is 0.95. That is, at an exchange rate of €0.95 per US$1, the quantity of U.S. dollars supplied to the foreign exchange market is equal to the quantity of U.S. dollars demanded.

To understand the significance of the equilibrium exchange rate, it's helpful to consider a numerical example of what equilibrium in the foreign exchange market looks like. A hypothetical example

TABLE 80-2

A Hypothetical Example of Equilibrium in the Foreign Exchange Market

European purchases of U.S. dollars (trillions of U.S. dollars)	To buy U.S. goods and services: 1.0	**To buy U.S. assets: 1.0**	**Total purchases of U.S. dollars: 2.0**
U.S. sales of U.S. dollars (trillions of U.S. dollars)	To buy European goods and services: 1.5	**To buy European assets: 0.5**	**Total sales of U.S. dollars: 2.0**
	U.S. balance of payments on the current account: −0.5	**U.S. balance of payments on the financial account: +0.5**	

is shown in Table 80-2. The first row shows European purchases of U.S. dollars, either to buy U.S. goods and services or to buy U.S. assets. The second row shows U.S. sales of U.S. dollars, either to buy European goods and services or to buy European assets. At the equilibrium exchange rate, the total quantity of U.S. dollars Europeans want to buy is equal to the total quantity of U.S. dollars Americans want to sell.

Remember that the balance of payments accounts divide international transactions into two types. Purchases and sales of goods and services are counted in the current account. (Again, we're leaving out transfers and factor income to keep things simple.) Purchases and sales of assets are counted in the financial account. At the equilibrium exchange rate, then, we have the situation shown in Table 80-2: the sum of the balance of payments on the current account plus the balance of payments on the financial account is zero.

Now let's briefly consider how a shift in the demand for U.S. dollars affects equilibrium in the foreign exchange market. Suppose that for some reason capital flows from Europe to the United States increase—say, due to a change in the preferences of European investors. The effects are shown in Figure 80-2. The demand for U.S. dollars in the foreign exchange market increases as European investors convert euros into dollars to fund their new investments in the United States. This is shown by the shift of the demand curve from D_1 to D_2. As a result, the U.S. dollar appreciates: the number of euros per U.S. dollar at the equilibrium exchange rate rises from XR_1 to XR_2.

FIGURE 80-2 An Increase in the Demand for U.S. Dollars

An increase in the demand for U.S. dollars might result from a change in the preferences of European investors. The demand curve for U.S. dollars shifts from D_1 to D_2. So the equilibrium number of euros per U.S. dollar rises—the dollar *appreciates*. As a result, the balance of payments on the current account falls as the balance of payments on the financial account rises.

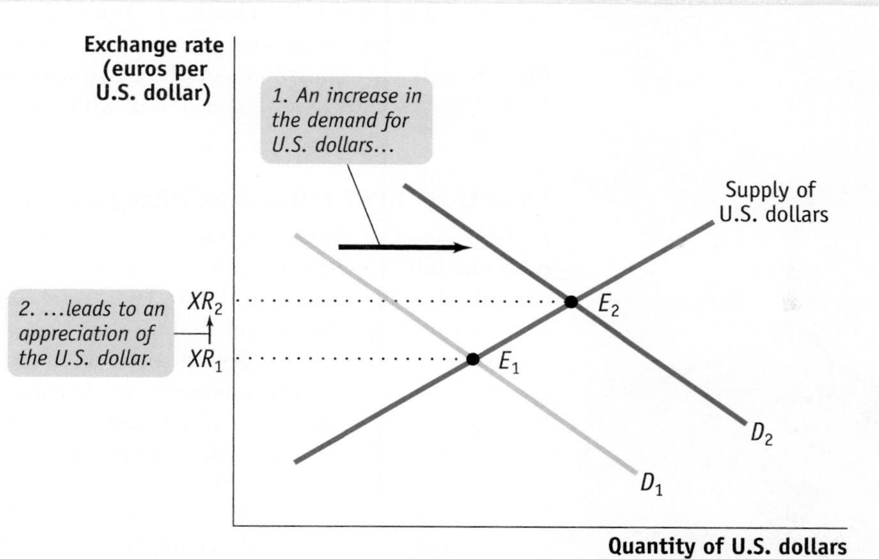

What are the consequences of this increased capital inflow for the balance of payments? The total quantity of U.S. dollars supplied to the foreign exchange market still must equal the total quantity of U.S. dollars demanded. So the increased capital inflow to the United States—an increase in the balance of payments on the financial account—must be matched by a decline in the balance of payments on the current account. What causes the balance of payments on the current account to decline? The appreciation of the U.S. dollar. A rise in the number of euros per U.S. dollar leads Americans to buy more European goods and services and Europeans to buy fewer American goods and services.

Table 80-3 shows a hypothetical example of how this might work. Europeans are buying more U.S. assets, increasing the balance of payments on the financial account from 0.5 to 1.0 trillion dollars. This is offset by a reduction in European purchases

TABLE 80-3

A Hypothetical Example of Effects of Increased Capital Inflows

European purchases of U.S. dollars (trillions of U.S. dollars)	To buy U.S. goods and services: 0.75 (down 0.25)	To buy U.S. assets: 1.5 (up 0.5)	**Total purchases of U.S. dollars: 2.25**
U.S. sales of U.S. dollars (trillions of U.S. dollars)	To buy European goods and services: 1.75 (up 0.25)	To buy European assets: 0.5 (no change)	**Total sales of U.S. dollars: 2.25**
	U.S. balance of payments on the current account: –1.0 (down 0.5)	**U.S. balance of payments on the financial account: +1.0 (up 0.5)**	

of U.S. goods and services and a rise in U.S. purchases of European goods and services, both the result of the dollar's appreciation. *So any change in the U.S. balance of payments on the financial account generates an equal and opposite reaction in the balance of payments on the current account.* Movements in the exchange rate ensure that changes in the financial account and in the current account offset each other.

Let's briefly run this process in reverse. Suppose there is a reduction in capital flows from Europe to the United States—again due to a change in the preferences of European investors. The demand for U.S. dollars in the foreign exchange market falls, and the dollar depreciates: the number of euros per U.S. dollar at the equilibrium exchange rate falls. This leads Americans to buy fewer European products and Europeans to buy more American products. Ultimately, this generates an increase in the U.S. balance of payments on the current account. So a fall in capital flows into the United States leads to a weaker dollar, which in turn generates an increase in U.S. net exports.

Inflation and Real Exchange Rates

In 1993, one U.S. dollar exchanged, on average, for 3.1 Mexican pesos. By 2013, the peso had fallen against the dollar by more than 75%, with an average exchange rate in early 2013 of 12.1 pesos per dollar. Did Mexican products also become much cheaper relative to U.S. products over that 20-year period? Did the price of Mexican products expressed in terms of U.S. dollars also fall by more than 75%?

Javier Correa/Alamy

The answer is no because Mexico had much higher inflation than the United States over that period. In fact, the relative price of U.S. and Mexican products changed little between 1993 and 2013, although the exchange rate changed a lot.

To take account of the effects of differences in inflation rates, economists calculate **real exchange rates,** exchange rates adjusted for international differences in aggregate price levels. Suppose that the exchange rate we are looking at is the number of Mexican pesos per U.S. dollar. Let P_{US} and P_{Mex} be indexes of the aggregate price levels in the United States and Mexico, respectively. Then the real exchange rate between the Mexican peso and the U.S. dollar is defined as:

$$\textbf{(80-1)}\quad \text{Real exchange rate} = \text{Mexican pesos per U.S. dollar} \times \frac{P_{US}}{P_{Mex}}$$

To distinguish it from the real exchange rate, the exchange rate unadjusted for aggregate price levels is sometimes called the *nominal* exchange rate.

Real exchange rates are exchange rates adjusted for international differences in aggregate price levels.

To understand the significance of the difference between the real and nominal exchange rates, let's consider the following example. Suppose that the Mexican peso depreciates against the U.S. dollar, with the exchange rate going from 10 pesos per U.S. dollar to 15 pesos per U.S. dollar, a 50% change. But suppose that at the same time the price of everything in Mexico, measured in pesos, increases by 50%, so that the

Mexican price index rises from 100 to 150. We'll assume that there is no change in U.S. prices, so that the U.S. price index remains at 100. Then the initial real exchange rate is:

$$\text{Pesos per dollar} \times \frac{P_{US}}{P_{Mex}} = 10 \times \frac{100}{100} = 10$$

After the peso depreciates and the Mexican price level increases, the real exchange rate is:

$$\text{Pesos per dollar} \times \frac{P_{US}}{P_{Mex}} = 15 \times \frac{100}{150} = 10$$

In this example, the peso has depreciated substantially in terms of the U.S. dollar, but the *real* exchange rate between the peso and the U.S. dollar hasn't changed at all. And because the real peso–U.S. dollar exchange rate hasn't changed, the nominal depreciation of the peso against the U.S. dollar will have no effect either on the quantity of goods and services exported by Mexico to the United States or on the quantity of goods and services imported by Mexico from the United States.

To see why, consider again the example of a hotel room. Suppose that this room initially costs 1,000 pesos per night, which is $100 at an exchange rate of 10 pesos per dollar. After both Mexican prices and the number of pesos per dollar rise by 50%, the hotel room costs 1,500 pesos per night—but 1,500 pesos divided by 15 pesos per dollar is $100, so the Mexican hotel room still costs $100. As a result, a U.S. tourist considering a trip to Mexico will have no reason to change plans.

The current account responds only to changes in real exchange rates, which have been adjusted for differing levels of inflation.

The same is true for all goods and services that enter into trade: *the current account responds only to changes in the real exchange rate, not the nominal exchange rate.* A country's products become cheaper to foreigners only when that country's currency depreciates in real terms, and those products become more expensive to foreigners only when the currency appreciates in real terms. As a consequence, economists who analyze movements in exports and imports of goods and services focus on the real exchange rate, not the nominal exchange rate.

Figure 80-3 illustrates just how important it can be to distinguish between nominal and real exchange rates. The line labeled "Nominal exchange rate" shows the number of pesos it took to buy a U.S. dollar from November 1993 to December 2011. As you can see, the peso depreciated massively over that period. But the line labeled "Real

FIGURE 80-3 **Real versus Nominal Exchange Rates, 1993–2011**

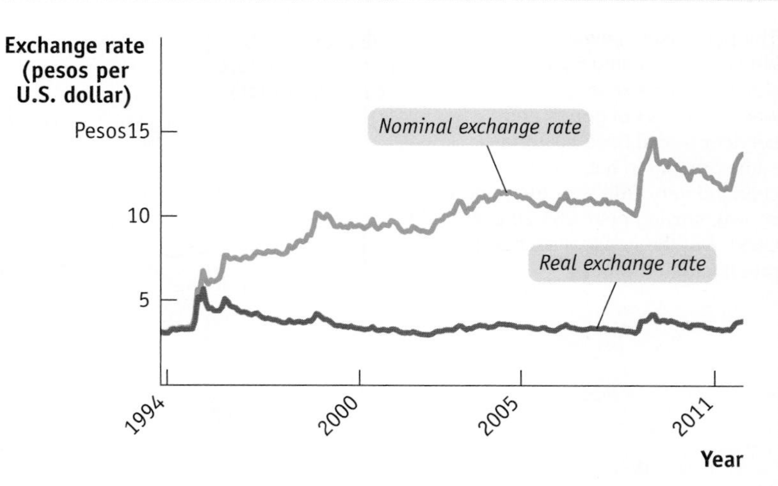

Between November 1993 and December 2011, the price of a dollar in Mexican pesos increased dramatically. But because Mexico had higher inflation than the United States, the real exchange rate, which measures the relative price of Mexican goods and services, ended up roughly where it started.

Source: Federal Reserve Bank of St. Louis.

The **purchasing power parity** between two countries' currencies is the nominal exchange rate at which a given basket of goods and services would cost the same amount in each country.

exchange rate" shows the real exchange rate: it was calculated using Equation 80-1, with price indexes for both Mexico and the United States set so that the value in 1993 was 100. In real terms, the peso depreciated between 1994 and 1995, but not by nearly as much as the nominal depreciation. By the end of 2011, the real peso–U.S. dollar exchange rate was just about back where it started.

Purchasing Power Parity

A useful tool for analyzing exchange rates, closely connected to the concept of the real exchange rate, is known as *purchasing power parity.* The **purchasing power parity** between two countries' currencies is the nominal exchange rate at which a given basket of goods and services would cost the same amount in each country. Suppose, for example, that a basket of goods and services that costs $100 in the United States costs 1,000 pesos in Mexico. Then the purchasing power parity is 10 pesos per U.S. dollar: at that exchange rate, 1,000 pesos = $100, so the market basket costs the same amount in both countries.

Calculations of purchasing power parities are usually made by estimating the cost of buying broad market baskets containing many goods and services—everything from automobiles and groceries to housing and telephone calls. But once a year the magazine *The Economist* publishes a list of purchasing power parities based on the cost of buying a market basket that contains only one item—a McDonald's Big Mac.

Nominal exchange rates almost always differ from purchasing power parities. Some of these differences are systematic: in general, aggregate price levels are lower in poor countries than in rich countries because services tend to be cheaper in poor countries. But even among countries at roughly the same level of economic development, nominal exchange rates vary quite a lot from purchasing power parity.

Figure 80-4 shows the nominal exchange rate between the Canadian dollar and the U.S. dollar, measured as the number of Canadian dollars per U.S. dollar, from 1990 to 2012, together with an estimate of the purchasing power parity exchange rate between the United States and Canada over the same period. The purchasing power parity didn't change much over the whole period because the United States and Canada had about the same rate of inflation.

But at the beginning of the period the nominal exchange rate was below purchasing power parity, so a given market basket was more expensive in Canada than in the United States. By 2002, the nominal exchange rate was far above the purchasing power parity, so a market basket was much cheaper in Canada than in the United States.

Over the long run, however, purchasing power parities are pretty good at predicting actual changes in nominal exchange rates. In particular, nominal exchange rates

FIGURE 80-4 **Purchasing Power Parity versus the Nominal Exchange Rate, 1990–2012**

The purchasing power parity between the United States and Canada—the exchange rate at which a basket of goods and services would have cost the same amount in both countries—changed very little over the period shown, staying near C$1.20 per US$1. But the nominal exchange rate fluctuated widely.

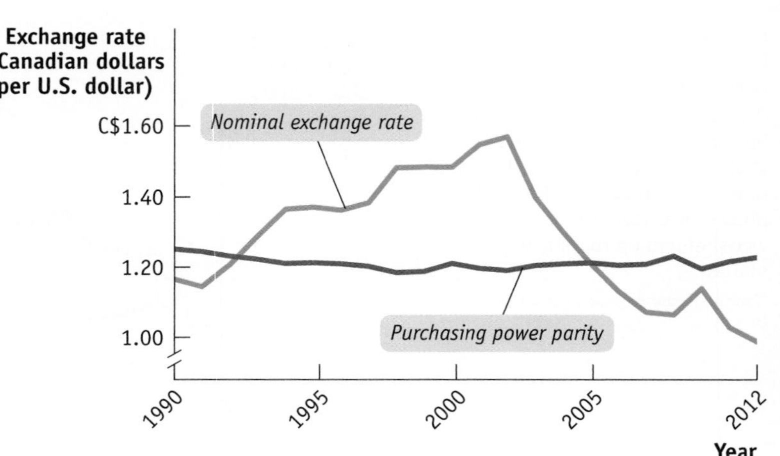

Source: Federal Reserve Bank of St. Louis

between countries at similar levels of economic development tend to fluctuate around levels that lead to similar costs for a given market basket. In fact, by July 2005, the nominal exchange rate between the United States and Canada was C$1.22 per US$1—just about the purchasing power parity. And by 2012, the cost of living was once again higher in Canada than in the United States.

ECONOMICS IN ACTION

BURGERNOMICS

For a number of years the British magazine *The Economist* has produced an annual comparison of the cost in different countries of one particular consumption item that is found around the world—a McDonald's Big Mac.

The magazine finds the price of a Big Mac in local currency, then computes two numbers: the price of a Big Mac in U.S. dollars using the prevailing exchange rate and the exchange rate at which the price of a Big Mac would equal the U.S. price. If purchasing power parity held for Big Macs, the dollar price of a Big Mac would be the same everywhere. If purchasing power parity is a good theory for the long run, the exchange rate at which a Big Mac's price matches the U.S. price should offer some guidance about where the exchange rate will eventually end up.

Table 80-4 shows the *Economist* estimates for selected countries as of July 2013, ranked in increasing order of the dollar price of a Big Mac. The countries with the cheapest Big Macs, and therefore by this measure with the most undervalued currencies, are India and China, both developing countries.

But not all developing countries have low-priced Big Macs: the price of a Big Mac in Brazil, converted into dollars, is considerably higher than in the United States. This reflects a sharp appreciation of the *real*, Brazil's currency, in recent years as the country has become a favorite of international investors. And topping the list, with a Big Mac some 47% more expensive than in the United States, is Switzerland.

TABLE 80-4

Purchasing Power Parity and the Price of a Big Mac

	Big Mac price		Local currency per dollar	
Country	In local currency	In U.S. dollars	Implied PPP	Actual exchange rate
India	Rupee 90	1.50	19.75	59.98
China	Yuan 16	2.61	3.51	6.13
Mexico	Peso 37	2.86	8.12	12.94
Japan	¥ 320	3.20	70.23	100.11
Britain	£ 2.69	4.02	0.59	0.67
United States	$4.56	4.56	1.00	1.00
Euro area	€ 3.62	4.66	0.80	0.78
Brazil	Real 12	5.28	2.63	2.27
Switzerland	SFr 6.5	6.72	1.43	0.97

MODULE 80 Review

Solutions appear at the back of the book.

Check Your Understanding

1. Suppose Mexico discovers huge reserves of oil and starts exporting oil to the United States. Describe how this affects the following:
   a. the nominal peso–U.S. dollar exchange rate
   b. Mexican exports of other goods and services
   c. Mexican imports of goods and services
2. A basket of goods and services that costs $100 in the United States costs 800 pesos in Mexico and the current nominal exchange rate is 10 pesos per U.S. dollar. Over the next five years, the cost of that market basket rises to $120 in the United States and to 1,200 pesos in Mexico, although the nominal exchange rate remains at 10 pesos per U.S. dollar. Calculate the following:
   a. the real exchange rate now and five years from now, if today's price index in both countries is 100
   b. purchasing power parity today and five years from now

Multiple-Choice Questions

1. When the U.S. dollar buys more Japanese yen, the U.S. dollar has
   - I. become more valuable in terms of the yen
   - II. appreciated
   - III. depreciated

   a. I only
   b. II only
   c. III only
   d. I and II only
   e. I and III only

2. The nominal exchange rate at which a given basket of goods and services would cost the same in each country describes
   a. the international consumer price index (ICPI).
   b. appreciation.
   c. depreciation.
   d. purchasing power parity.
   e. the balance of payments on the current account.

3. What happens to the real exchange rate between the euro and the U.S. dollar (expressed as euros per dollar) if the aggregate price levels in Europe and the United States both fall? It
   a. is unaffected.
   b. increases.
   c. decreases.
   d. may increase, decrease, or stay the same.
   e. cannot be calculated.

4. Which of the following would cause the real exchange rate between pesos and U.S. dollars (in terms of pesos per dollar) to decrease?
   a. an increase in net capital flows from Mexico to the United States
   b. an increase in the real interest rate in Mexico relative to the United States
   c. a doubling of prices in both Mexico and the United States
   d. a decrease in oil exports from Mexico to the United States
   e. an increase in the balance of payments on the current account in the United States

5. Which of the following will decrease the supply of U.S. dollars in the foreign exchange market?
   a. U.S. residents increase their travel abroad
   b. U.S. consumers demand fewer imports
   c. Foreigners increase their demand for U.S. goods
   d. Foreigners increase their travel to the United States
   e. Foreign investors see increased investment opportunities in the United States

Critical-Thinking Question

Draw a graph of the foreign exchange market between the United States and Europe. Illustrate what would happen to the value of the U.S. dollar if there were an increase in the U.S. demand for imports from Europe.

PITFALLS

WHICH WAY IS UP?

? You are a tourist in Mexico and need to exchange dollars for pesos. You've heard that the U.S. exchange rate is up, which sounds like good news. But, is it?

\> IT DEPENDS. TO DETERMINE IF THE DOLLAR HAS APPRECIATED OR DEPRECIATED, YOU NEED TO CHECK THE EXCHANGE RATE DATA TO FIND OUT WHICH WAY THE EXCHANGE RATE IS BEING MEASURED. Sometimes the exchange rate is measured as the price of a dollar in terms of foreign currency, sometimes it's measured as the price of foreign currency in terms of dollars. Most countries, other than the United States, report their exchange rates in terms of the price of a dollar in their domestic currency—for example, Mexican officials will say that the exchange rate is 12, meaning 12 pesos per dollar. But Britain, for historical reasons, usually states its exchange rate the other way. For example, On May 13, 2013, US$1 was worth £0.6514, and £1 was worth US$1.5350. More often than not, this number is reported as an exchange rate of 1.5350. In fact, on occasion, even professional economists and consultants embarrass themselves by getting the direction in which the pound is moving wrong! And Americans generally follow other countries' lead: we usually say that the exchange rate against Mexico is 12 pesos per dollar but that the exchange rate against Britain is 1.53 dollars per pound. But this rule isn't reliable; exchange rates against the euro are often stated both ways.

To learn more about exchange rates, see pages 836–837.

Exchange Rate Policy

Greg Balfour Evans/Alamy

WHAT YOU WILL LEARN

1. The difference between fixed exchange rates and floating exchange rates
2. Considerations that lead countries to choose different exchange rate regimes

Exchange Rate Regimes

As we saw in the previous module, the nominal exchange rate, like other prices, is determined by supply and demand. Unlike the price of wheat or oil, however, the exchange rate is the price of a country's money (in terms of another country's money). Money isn't a good or service produced by the private sector; it's an asset whose quantity is determined by government policy. As a result, governments have much more power to influence nominal exchange rates than they have to influence ordinary prices.

The nominal exchange rate is a very important price for many countries: the exchange rate determines the price of imports; it determines the price of exports; in economies where exports and imports are large relative to GDP, movements in the exchange rate can have major effects on aggregate output and the aggregate price level. What do governments do with their power to influence this important price?

The answer is, it depends. At different times and in different places, governments have adopted a variety of **exchange rate regimes.** An *exchange rate regime* is a *rule governing policy toward the exchange rate*. Let's talk about these regimes, how they are enforced, and how governments choose a regime. (From now on, we'll adopt the convention that we mean the nominal exchange rate when we refer to the exchange rate.)

An **exchange rate regime** is a rule governing policy toward the exchange rate.

Fixed and Floating Exchange Rates

There are two main kinds of exchange rate regimes. A country has a **fixed exchange rate** when the government keeps the exchange rate against some other currency at or near a particular target. For example, Hong Kong has an official policy of setting an exchange rate of HK$7.80 per US$1. A country has a **floating exchange rate** when the government lets the exchange rate go wherever the market takes it. This is the policy followed by Britain, Canada, and the United States.

A country has a **fixed exchange rate** when the government keeps the exchange rate against some other currency at or near a particular target.

A country has a **floating exchange rate** when the government lets the exchange rate go wherever the market takes it.

Fixed exchange rates and floating exchange rates aren't the only possibilities. At various times, countries have adopted compromise policies that lie somewhere between fixed and floating exchange rates. These include exchange rates that are fixed at any given time but are adjusted frequently, exchange rates that aren't fixed but are "managed" by the government to avoid wide swings, and exchange rates that float within a "target zone" but are prevented from leaving that zone. In this book, however, we'll focus on the two main exchange rate regimes.

The immediate question about a fixed exchange rate is how it is possible for governments to fix the exchange rate when the exchange rate is determined by supply and demand.

How Can an Exchange Rate Be Held Fixed?

To understand how it is possible for a country to fix its exchange rate, let's consider a hypothetical country, Genovia, which for some reason has decided to fix the value of its currency, the geno, at US$1.50.

The obvious problem is that $1.50 may not be the equilibrium exchange rate in the foreign exchange market: the equilibrium rate may be either higher or lower than the target exchange rate. Figure 81-1 shows the foreign exchange market for genos, with the quantities of genos supplied and demanded on the horizontal axis and the exchange rate of the geno, measured in U.S. dollars per geno, on the vertical axis. Panel (a) shows the case in which the equilibrium value of the geno is *below* the target exchange rate. Panel (b) shows the case in which the equilibrium value of the geno is *above* the target exchange rate.

Consider first the case in which the equilibrium value of the geno is below the target exchange rate. As panel (a) shows, at the target exchange rate there is a surplus of genos in the foreign exchange market, which would normally push the value of the geno down. How can the Genovian government support the value of the geno to keep the rate where it wants? There are three possible ways the Genovian government can support the geno, all of which have been used by governments at some point.

1. It can "soak up" the surplus of genos by buying its own currency in the foreign exchange market. Government purchases or sales of currency in the foreign ex-

FIGURE 81-1 Exchange Market Intervention

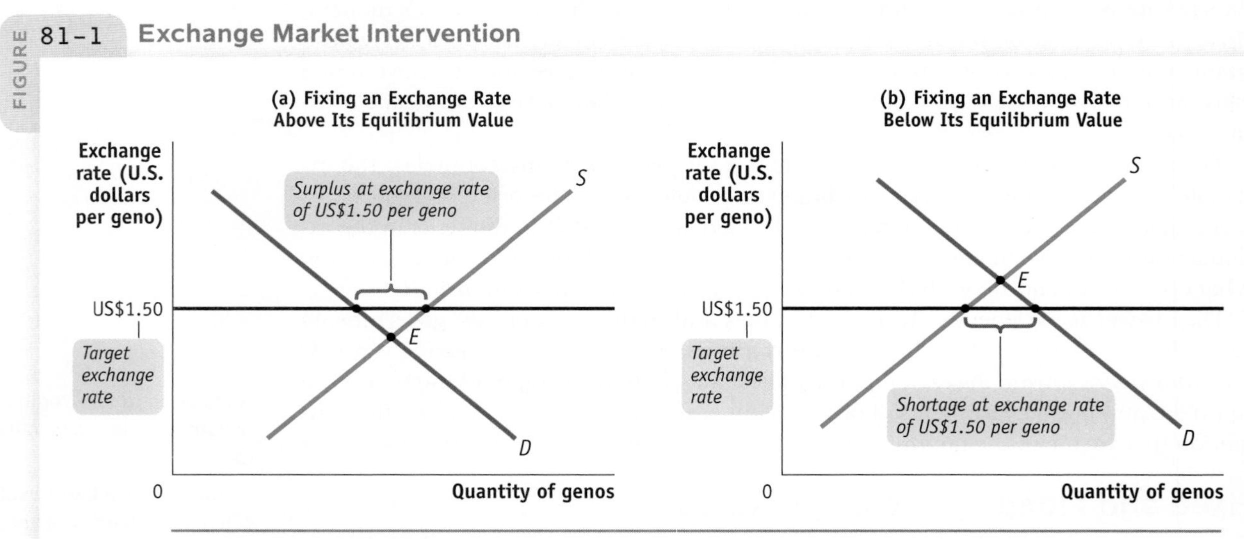

In both panels, the imaginary country of Genovia is trying to keep the value of its currency, the geno, fixed at US$1.50. In panel (a), there is a surplus of genos on the foreign exchange market. To keep the geno from falling, the Genovian government can buy genos and sell U.S. dollars. In panel (b), there is a shortage of genos. To keep the geno from rising, the Genovian government can sell genos and buy U.S. dollars.

change market are called **exchange market intervention.** To buy genos in the foreign exchange market, of course, the Genovian government must have U.S. dollars to exchange for genos. In fact, most countries maintain **foreign exchange reserves,** stocks of foreign currency (usually U.S. dollars or euros) that they can use to buy their own currency to support its price.

We mentioned earlier that an important part of international capital flows is the result of purchases and sales of foreign assets by governments and central banks. Now we can see why governments sell foreign assets: they are supporting their currency through exchange market intervention. As we'll see in a moment, governments that keep the value of their currency *down* through exchange market intervention must *buy* foreign assets. First, however, let's talk about the other ways governments fix exchange rates.

Government purchases or sales of currency in the foreign exchange market constitute **exchange market intervention.**

Foreign exchange reserves are stocks of foreign currency that governments maintain to buy their own currency on the foreign exchange market.

Foreign exchange controls are licensing systems that limit the right of individuals to buy foreign currency.

2. The Genovian government can try to shift the supply and demand curves for the geno in the foreign exchange market. Governments usually do this by changing monetary policy. For example, to support the geno, the Genovian central bank can raise the Genovian interest rate. This will increase capital flows into Genovia, increasing the demand for genos, at the same time that it reduces capital flows out of Genovia, reducing the supply of genos. So, other things equal, an increase in a country's interest rate will increase the value of its currency.
3. It can reduce the supply of genos to the foreign exchange market by requiring domestic residents who want to buy foreign currency to get a license and giving these licenses only to people engaging in approved transactions (such as the purchase of imported goods the Genovian government thinks are essential). Licensing systems that limit the right of individuals to buy foreign currency are called **foreign exchange controls.** Other things equal, foreign exchange controls increase the value of a country's currency.

So far we've been discussing a situation in which the government is trying to prevent a depreciation of the geno. Suppose, instead, that the situation is as shown in panel (b) of Figure 81-1, where the equilibrium value of the geno is *above* the target exchange rate and there is a shortage of genos.

To maintain the target exchange rate, the Genovian government can apply the same three basic options in the reverse direction. It can intervene in the foreign exchange market, in this case *selling* genos and acquiring U.S. dollars, which it can add to its foreign exchange reserves. It can *reduce* interest rates to increase the supply of genos and reduce the demand. Or it can impose foreign exchange controls that limit the ability of foreigners to buy genos. All of these actions, other things equal, will reduce the value of the geno.

As we said, all three techniques have been used to manage fixed exchange rates. But we haven't said whether fixing the exchange rate is a good idea. In fact, the choice of exchange rate regime poses a dilemma for policy makers because fixed and floating exchange rates each have both advantages and disadvantages.

The Exchange Rate Regime Dilemma

Few questions in macroeconomics produce as many arguments as that of whether a country should adopt a fixed or a floating exchange rate. The reason there are so many arguments is that both sides have a case.

To understand the case for a fixed exchange rate, consider for a moment how easy it is to conduct business across state lines in the United States. There are a number of things that make interstate commerce trouble-free, but one of them is the absence of any uncertainty about the value of money: a dollar is a dollar, in both New York City and Los Angeles.

By contrast, a dollar isn't a dollar in transactions between New York City and Toronto. The exchange rate between the Canadian

Once you cross the border into Canada, a dollar is no longer worth a dollar.

Robert Nickelsberg/Getty Images

dollar and the U.S. dollar fluctuates, sometimes widely. If a U.S. firm promises to pay a Canadian firm a given number of U.S. dollars a year from now, the value of that promise in Canadian currency can vary by 10% or more. This uncertainty has the effect of deterring trade between the two countries. So one benefit of a fixed exchange rate is certainty about the future value of a currency.

There is also, in some cases, an additional benefit to adopting a fixed exchange rate: by committing itself to a fixed rate, a country is also committing not to engage in inflationary policies because such policies would destabilize the exchange rate. For example, in 1991, Argentina, which has a long history of irresponsible policies leading to severe inflation, adopted a fixed exchange rate of US$1 per Argentine peso in an attempt to commit itself to non-inflationary policies in the future. (Argentina's fixed exchange rate regime collapsed disastrously in late 2001. But that's another story.)

The point is that there is some economic value in having a stable exchange rate. Indeed, the presumed benefits of stable exchange rates motivated the international system of fixed exchange rates created after World War II. It was also a major reason for the creation of the euro.

However, there are also costs to fixing the exchange rate.

- To stabilize an exchange rate through intervention, a country must keep large quantities of foreign currency on hand, and that currency is usually a low-return investment. Furthermore, even large reserves can be quickly exhausted when there are large capital flows out of a country.
- If a country chooses to stabilize an exchange rate by adjusting monetary policy rather than through intervention, it must divert monetary policy from other goals, notably stabilizing the economy and managing the inflation rate.
- Finally, foreign exchange controls, like import quotas and tariffs, distort incentives for importing and exporting goods and services. They can also create substantial costs in terms of red tape and corruption.

So there's a dilemma. Should a country let its currency float, which leaves monetary policy available for macroeconomic stabilization but creates uncertainty for everyone affected by trade? Or should it fix the exchange rate, which eliminates the uncertainty but means giving up monetary policy, adopting exchange controls, or both?

Different countries reach different conclusions at different times. Most European countries, except for Britain, have long believed that exchange rates among major European economies, which do most of their international trade with each other, should be fixed. But Canada seems happy with a floating exchange rate with the United States, even though the United States accounts for most of Canada's trade.

In the next module we'll consider macroeconomic policy under each type of exchange rate regime.

ECONOMICS IN ACTION

WORLD VIEW

CHINA PEGS THE YUAN

In the early years of the twenty-first century, China provided a striking example of the lengths to which countries sometimes go to maintain a fixed exchange rate. Here's the background: China's spectacular success as an exporter led to a rising surplus on current account. At the same time, non-Chinese private investors became increasingly eager to shift funds into China, to invest in its growing domestic economy. These capital flows were somewhat limited by foreign exchange controls—but kept coming in anyway.

As a result of the current account surplus and private capital inflows, China found itself in the position described by panel (b) of Figure 81-1: at the target exchange rate, the demand for yuan exceeded the supply. Yet the Chinese government was determined to keep the exchange rate fixed at a value below its equilibrium level.

To keep the rate fixed, China had to engage in large-scale exchange market intervention, selling yuan, buying up other countries' currencies (mainly U.S. dollars) on the foreign exchange market, and adding them to its reserves. In 2010, China added $450 billion to its foreign exchange reserves, and by the summer of 2011, those reserves had risen to $3.2 trillion.

To get a sense of how big these totals are, in 2010 China's GDP was approximately $5.9 trillion. This means that in 2010 China bought U.S. dollars and other currencies equal to about 7½% of its GDP, making its accumulated reserves equal to more than half its GDP. That's as if the U.S. government had bought well over $1 trillion worth of yen and euros in a single year, even though it was already sitting on an $8 trillion pile of foreign currencies. Not surprisingly, China's exchange rate policy has led to some friction with its trading partners who feel that it has had the effect of subsidizing Chinese exports.

Since late 2011, China has significantly reduced its intervention in the foreign exchange market. In fact, in 2013, the International Monetary Fund declared the yuan to be only moderately undervalued, a big change from past years.

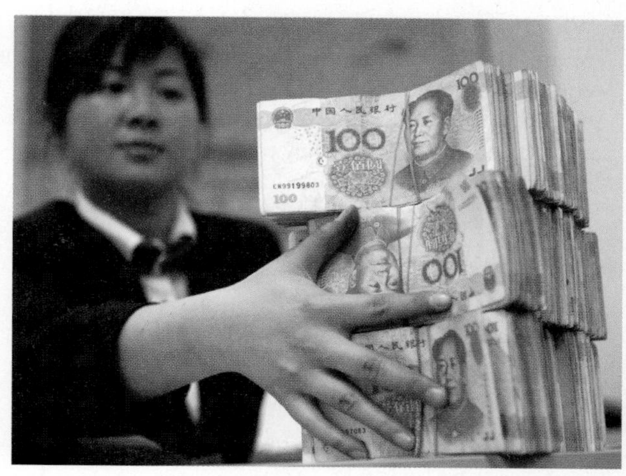

AFP/Getty Images

China provides a striking example of the lengths to which countries sometimes go to maintain a fixed exchange rate.

MODULE 81 Review

Solutions appear at the back of the book.

Check Your Understanding

1. Draw a diagram, similar to Figure 81-1, representing the foreign exchange situation of China when it kept the exchange rate fixed at a target rate of $0.121 per yuan and the market equilibrium rate was higher than the target rate. Then show with a diagram how each of the following policy changes might eliminate the disequilibrium in the market.
   - a. allowing the exchange rate to float more freely
   - b. placing restrictions on foreigners who want to invest in China
   - c. removing restrictions on Chinese who want to invest abroad
   - d. imposing taxes on Chinese exports, such as clothing

Multiple-Choice Questions

1. Which of the following methods can be used to fix a country's exchange rate at a predetermined level?
   - I. using foreign exchange reserves to buy its own currency
   - II. using monetary policy to change interest rates
   - III. implementing foreign exchange controls

   - a. I only
   - b. II only
   - c. III only
   - d. I and II only
   - e. I, II, and III
2. Changes in exchange rates affect which of the following?
   - a. the price of imports
   - b. the price of exports
   - c. aggregate demand
   - d. aggregate output
   - e. all of the above
3. The United States has which of the following exchange rate regimes?
   - a. fixed
   - b. floating
   - c. fixed, but adjusted frequently
   - d. fixed, but managed
   - e. floating within a target zone

4. Which of the following interventions would be required to keep a country's exchange rate fixed if the equilibrium exchange rate in the foreign exchange market were below the fixed exchange rate (measured as units of foreign currency per unit of domestic currency)? The government/central bank
   - a. buys the domestic currency.
   - b. sells the domestic currency.
   - c. buys the foreign currency.
   - d. lowers domestic interest rates.
   - e. removes foreign exchange controls.

5. Which of the following is a benefit of a fixed exchange rate regime?
   - a. certainty about the value of domestic currency
   - b. commitment to inflationary policies
   - c. no need for foreign exchange reserves
   - d. allows unrestricted use of monetary policy
   - e. all of the above

Critical-Thinking Question

List three tools used to fix exchange rates and explain the major costs resulting from their use.

Exchange Rates and Macroeconomic Policy

Millennium Images/SuperStock

WHAT YOU WILL LEARN

1. **The meaning and purpose of devaluation and revaluation of a currency under a fixed exchange rate regime**
2. **Why open-economy considerations affect macroeconomic policy under floating exchange rates**

When the euro was created in 1999, there were celebrations across the nations of Europe—with a few notable exceptions. You see, some countries chose not to adopt the new currency. The most important of these was Britain, but other European countries, such as Switzerland and Sweden, also decided that the euro was not for them.

Why did Britain say no? Part of the answer was national pride: for example, if Britain gave up the pound, it would also have to give up currency that bears the portrait of the queen. But there were also serious economic concerns about giving up the pound in favor of the euro.

British economists who favored adoption of the euro argued that if Britain used the same currency as its neighbors, the country's international trade would expand and its economy would become more productive. But other economists pointed out that adopting the euro would take away Britain's ability to have an independent monetary policy and might lead to macroeconomic problems.

As this discussion suggests, the fact that modern economies are open to international trade and capital flows adds a new level of complication to our analysis of macroeconomic policy. Let's now look at these three policy issues raised by open-economy macroeconomics:

1. Devaluation and revaluation of fixed exchange rates
2. Monetary policy under a floating exchange rate regime
3. International business cycles

Devaluation and Revaluation of Fixed Exchange Rates

Historically, fixed exchange rates haven't been permanent commitments. Sometimes countries with a fixed exchange rate switch to a floating rate. In other cases, they retain a fixed exchange rate but change the target exchange rate. Such adjustments in the target were common during the Bretton Woods era described in the upcoming Economics in Action. For example, in 1967 Britain changed the exchange rate of the pound against the U.S. dollar from US$2.80 per £1 to US$2.40 per £1. Another example is Argentina, which maintained a fixed exchange rate against the dollar from 1991 to 2001, but switched to a floating exchange rate at the end of 2001.

A reduction in the value of a currency that is set under a fixed exchange rate regime is called **devaluation.** As we've already learned, a *depreciation* is a downward move in a currency. A devaluation is a depreciation that is due to a revision in a fixed exchange rate target. An increase in the value of a currency that is set under a fixed exchange rate regime is called a **revaluation.**

A devaluation, like any depreciation, makes domestic goods cheaper in terms of foreign currency, which leads to higher exports. At the same time, it makes foreign goods more expensive in terms of domestic currency, which reduces imports. The effect is to increase the balance of payments on the current account. Similarly, a revaluation makes domestic goods more expensive in terms of foreign currency, which reduces exports, and makes foreign goods cheaper in domestic currency, which increases imports. So a revaluation reduces the balance of payments on the current account.

Devaluations and revaluations serve two purposes under a fixed exchange rate regime. First, they can be used to eliminate shortages or surpluses in the foreign exchange market. For example, in 2010, some economists and politicians were urging China to revalue the yuan because they believed that China's exchange rate policy unfairly aided Chinese exports. China eventually took action at the end of 2011, discontinuing much of their exchange rate intervention and allowing the yuan to gradually appreciate in value.

Second, devaluation and revaluation can be used as tools of macroeconomic policy. A devaluation, by increasing exports and reducing imports, increases aggregate demand. So a devaluation can be used to reduce or eliminate a recessionary gap. A revaluation has the opposite effect, reducing aggregate demand. So a revaluation can be used to reduce or eliminate an inflationary gap.

A **devaluation** is a reduction in the value of a currency that is set under a fixed exchange rate regime.

A **revaluation** is an increase in the value of a currency that is set under a fixed exchange rate regime.

ECONOMICS IN ACTION WORLD VIEW

FROM BRETTON WOODS TO THE EURO

In 1944, while World War II was still raging, representatives of the Allied nations met in Bretton Woods, New Hampshire, to establish a postwar international monetary system of fixed exchange rates among major currencies. The system was highly successful at first, but it broke down in 1971. After a confusing interval during which policy makers tried unsuccessfully to establish a new fixed exchange rate system, by 1973 most economically advanced countries had moved to floating exchange rates.

In Europe, however, many policy makers were unhappy with floating exchange rates, which they believed created too much uncertainty for business. From the late 1970s onward they tried several times to create a system of more or less fixed exchange rates in Europe, culminating in an arrangement known as the Exchange Rate Mechanism. (The Exchange Rate Mechanism was, strictly speaking, a "target zone" system—European exchange rates were free to move within a narrow band, but not outside it.)

And in 1991 they agreed to move to the ultimate in fixed exchange rates: a common European currency, the euro. To the surprise of many analysts, they pulled it off: today most of Europe has abandoned national currencies for the euro.

Figure 82-1 illustrates the history of European exchange rate arrangements. It shows the exchange rate between the French franc and the German mark, measured as francs per mark, from 1971 until their replacement by the euro. The exchange rate fluctuated widely at first. The "plateaus" you can see in the data—eras when the exchange rate fluctuated only modestly—are periods when attempts to restore fixed exchange rates were in process.

The Exchange Rate Mechanism, after a couple of false starts, became effective in 1987, stabilizing the exchange rate at about 3.4 francs per mark. (The wobbles in the early 1990s reflect two currency crises—episodes in which widespread expectations of imminent devaluations led to large but temporary capital flows.)

In 1999 the exchange rate was "locked"—no further fluctuations were allowed as the countries prepared to switch from francs and marks to the euro. At the end of 2001, the franc and the mark ceased to exist.

FIGURE 82-1 The Exchange Rate Between the Franc and the Mark, 1971–2002

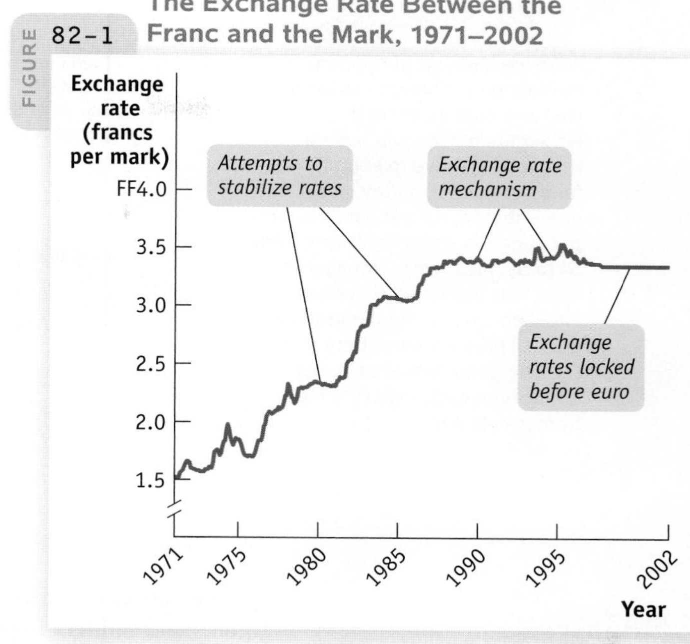

The transition to the euro has not been without costs. Countries that adopted the euro sacrificed some important policy tools: they could no longer tailor monetary policy to their specific economic circumstances or lower their costs relative to other European nations simply by letting their currencies depreciate.

In 2013, the euro area remained under stress as many countries struggled to recover from severe recession following the 2008 financial crisis. Several nations—including Greece, Spain, and Italy, three big economies—were in such serious economic straits that economists and policy makers wondered about their ability to make critically important economic adjustments without defaulting on their debts and abandoning the euro.

Monetary Policy Under a Floating Exchange Rate Regime

Under a floating exchange rate regime, a country's central bank retains its ability to pursue independent monetary policy: it can increase aggregate demand by cutting the interest rate or decrease aggregate demand by raising the interest rate. But the exchange rate adds another dimension to the effects of monetary policy. To see why, let's return to the hypothetical country of Genovia as discussed in the preceding module and ask what happens if the central bank cuts the interest rate.

Just as in a closed economy, a lower interest rate leads to higher investment spending and higher consumer spending. But the decline in the interest rate also affects the foreign exchange market. Foreigners have less incentive to move funds into Genovia because they will receive a lower rate of return on their loans. As a result, they have less need to exchange U.S. dollars for genos, so the demand for genos falls. At the same time, Genovians have *more* incentive to move funds abroad because the rate of return on loans at home has fallen, making investments outside the country more attractive. Thus, they need to exchange more genos for U.S. dollars and the supply of genos rises.

Figure 82-2 shows the effect of an interest rate reduction on the foreign exchange market. The demand curve for genos shifts leftward, from D_1 to D_2, and the supply curve shifts rightward, from S_1 to S_2. The equilibrium exchange rate, as measured in U.S. dollars per geno, falls from XR_1 to XR_2. That is, a reduction in the Genovian interest rate causes the geno to *depreciate*.

The depreciation of the geno, in turn, affects aggregate demand. We've already seen that a devaluation—a depreciation that is the result of a change in a fixed exchange rate—increases exports and reduces imports, thereby increasing aggregate demand.

FIGURE 82-2 **Monetary Policy and the Exchange Rate**

Here we show what happens in the foreign exchange market if Genovia cuts its interest rate. Residents of Genovia have a reduced incentive to keep their funds at home, so they invest more abroad. As a result, the supply of genos shifts rightward, from S_1 to S_2. Meanwhile, foreigners have less incentive to put funds into Genovia, so the demand for genos shifts leftward, from D_1 to D_2. The geno depreciates: the equilibrium exchange rate falls from XR_1 to XR_2.

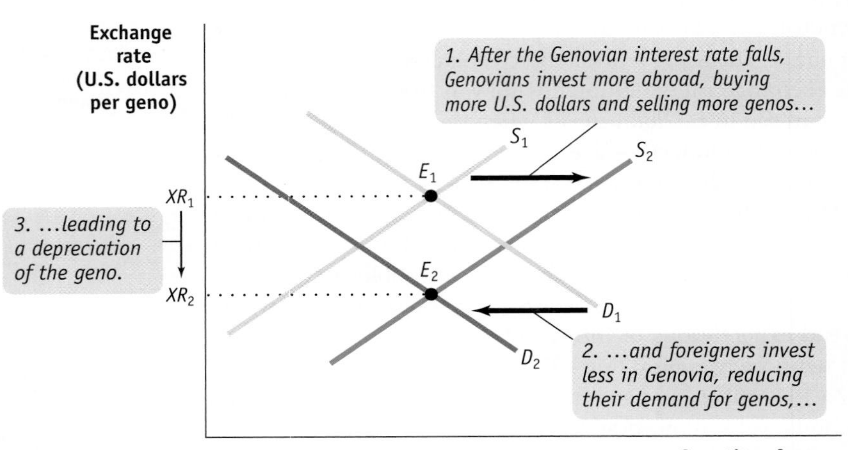

A depreciation that results from an interest rate cut has the same effect: it increases exports and reduces imports, increasing aggregate demand.

In other words, monetary policy under floating rates has effects beyond those we've described in looking at closed economies.

In a closed economy, a reduction in the interest rate leads to a rise in aggregate demand because it leads to more investment spending and consumer spending.

In an open economy with a floating exchange rate, the interest rate reduction leads to increased investment spending and consumer spending, but it also increases aggregate demand in another way: it leads to a currency depreciation, which increases exports and reduces imports, further increasing aggregate demand.

International Business Cycles

Up to this point, we have discussed macroeconomics, even in an open economy, as if all demand changes or *shocks* originated from the domestic economy. In reality, however, economies sometimes face shocks coming from abroad. For example, recessions in the United States have historically led to recessions in Mexico.

The key point is that changes in aggregate demand affect the demand for goods and services produced abroad as well as at home: other things equal, a recession leads to a fall in imports and an expansion leads to a rise in imports. And one country's imports are another country's exports. This link between aggregate demand in different national economies is one reason business cycles in different countries sometimes—but not always—seem to be synchronized. The prime example is the Great Depression, which affected countries around the world.

For better or worse, trading partners tend to import each other's business cycles as well as each other's goods.

John Sturrock/Alamy

The extent of this link depends, however, on the exchange rate regime. To see why, think about what happens if a recession abroad reduces the demand for Genovia's exports. A reduction in foreign demand for Genovian goods and services is also a reduction in demand for genos on the foreign exchange market. If Genovia has a fixed exchange rate, it responds to this decline with exchange market intervention.

But if Genovia has a floating exchange rate, the geno depreciates. Because Genovian goods and services become cheaper to foreigners when the demand for exports falls, the quantity of goods and services exported doesn't fall by as much as it would under a fixed rate. At the same time, the fall in the geno makes imports more expensive to Genovians, leading to a fall in imports. Both effects limit the decline in Genovia's aggregate demand compared to what it would have been under a fixed exchange rate regime.

One of the virtues of floating exchange rates, according to their advocates, is that they help insulate countries from recessions originating abroad. This theory looked pretty good in the early 2000s: Britain, with a floating exchange rate, managed to stay out of a recession that affected the rest of Europe, and Canada, which also has a floating rate, suffered a less severe recession than the United States.

In 2008, however, the financial crisis that began in the United States produced a recession in virtually every country. In this case, it appears that the international linkages between financial markets were much stronger than any insulation from overseas disturbances provided by floating exchange rates.

Module 82 Review

Solutions appear at the back of the book.

Check Your Understanding

1. Look at Figure 82-1. Where do you see devaluations and revaluations of the franc against the mark?
2. In the late 1980s, Canadian economists argued that the high interest rate policies of the Bank of Canada weren't just causing high unemployment—they were also making it hard for Canadian manufacturers to compete with U.S. manufacturers. Explain this complaint, using our analysis of how monetary policy works under floating exchange rates.

Multiple-Choice Questions

1. Devaluation of a currency occurs when which of the following happens?
   - I. The supply of a currency with a floating exchange rate increases.
   - II. The demand for a currency with a floating exchange rate decreases.
   - III. The government decreases the fixed exchange rate.
   - a. I only
   - b. II only
   - c. III only
   - d. I and II only
   - e. I, II, and III
2. Devaluation of a currency will lead to which of the following?
   - a. appreciation of the currency
   - b. an increase in exports
   - c. an increase in imports
   - d. a decrease in exports
   - e. floating exchange rates
3. Devaluation of a currency is used to achieve which of the following?
   - a. an elimination of a surplus in the foreign exchange market
   - b. an elimination of a shortage in the foreign exchange market
   - c. a reduction in aggregate demand
   - d. a lower inflation rate
   - e. a floating exchange rate
4. Monetary policy that reduces the interest rate will do which of the following?
   - a. appreciate the domestic currency
   - b. decrease exports
   - c. increase imports
   - d. depreciate the domestic currency
   - e. prevent inflation
5. Which of the following will happen in a country if a trading partner's economy experiences a recession?
   - a. It will experience an expansion.
   - b. Exports will decrease.
   - c. The demand for the country's currency will increase.
   - d. The country's currency will appreciate.
   - e. All of the above will occur.

Critical-Thinking Question

Explain how a floating exchange rate system can help insulate a country from recessions abroad.

BUSINESS CASE: War of the Earthmovers

Philip Lewis/Alamy

Visit a construction site almost anywhere in the world, and odds are that the earthmoving equipment you see—the tractors, dump trucks, excavators, graders, scrapers, and so on—is made by one of two companies, America's Caterpillar or Japan's Komatsu.

Caterpillar and Komatsu both rely heavily on exports, rather than selling only to their domestic markets, and have been fierce competitors for three decades, with first one company, then the other, seemingly on the ropes.

Ask the companies' leaders to explain the course of this see-sawing competitive struggle, and they will tell a tale of corporate cultures and management decisions. Caterpillar, the story goes, entered the 1980s filled with complacency thanks to its longtime dominance of the earthmoving industry, only to face a shock from Komatsu that almost drove it to the brink. Then Caterpillar reformed its management practices, regaining the upper hand in the 1990s, and Komatsu found itself in danger of failing, until reinvigorated management stabilized the company again.

Comparing Real Exchange Rates, 1980–2011

Source: Federal Reserve Bank of St. Louis.

But is this the whole story? Not exactly. Management decisions were no doubt crucial to both firms, but so were movements in the exchange rate. The accompanying figure shows the real exchange rate between the United States and Japan, using consumer prices, from 1980 to 2011.

The figure immediately suggests one reason Caterpillar was able to recover from the shock of competition in the 1980s: a sharp appreciation of the Japanese yen beginning in 1985. And Komatsu's ability to survive Caterpillar's resurgence was surely helped by the slide in the yen after 1995, and especially after 2000.

Recently, the two companies seem to have settled into relatively stable positions, with Caterpillar the bigger firm but Komatsu also doing well thanks in part to rapid growth in demand from China. But Japanese executives at Komatsu (and other firms) are always on the alert for signs that the yen is once again on the rise.

Questions for Thought

1. Why does the yen–dollar exchange rate matter so much for the fortunes of Caterpillar and Komatsu?
2. Why does the figure present the real rather than the nominal exchange rate? Do you think this makes an important difference to the story?
3. In 2011, Japanese policy makers were discussing possible sales of yen on the foreign exchange market. How would this affect the Caterpillar/Komatsu rivalry?

SECTION 25 REVIEW

Summary

Capital Flows and the Balance of Payments

1. A country's **balance of payments accounts** summarize its transactions with the rest of the world. The **balance of payments on the current account,** or the **current account,** includes the **balance of payments on goods and services** together with balances on factor income and transfers. The **merchandise trade balance,** or **trade balance,** is a frequently cited component of the balance of payments on goods and services. The **balance of payments on the financial account,** or **the financial account,** measures capital flows. By definition, the balance of payments on the current account plus the balance of payments on the financial account is zero.
2. Capital flows respond to international differences in interest rates and other rates of return; they can be usefully analyzed using an international version of the loanable funds model, which shows how a country where the interest rate would be low in the absence of capital flows sends funds to a country where the interest rate would be high in the absence of capital flows. The underlying determinants of capital flows are international differences in savings and opportunities for investment spending.

The Foreign Exchange Market

3. Currencies are traded in the **foreign exchange market;** the prices at which they are traded are **exchange rates.** When a currency rises against another currency, it **appreciates;** when it falls, it **depreciates.** The **equilibrium exchange rate** matches the quantity of that currency supplied to the foreign exchange market to the quantity demanded.
4. To correct for international differences in inflation rates, economists calculate **real exchange rates,** which multiply the exchange rate between two countries' respective currencies by the ratio of the countries' price levels. The current account responds only to changes in the real exchange rate, not the nominal exchange rate. **Purchasing power parity** is the exchange rate that makes the cost of a basket of goods and services equal in two countries. While purchasing power parity and the nominal exchange rate almost always differ, purchasing power parity is a good predictor of actual changes in the nominal exchange rate.

Exchange Rate Policy

5. Countries adopt different **exchange rate regimes,** rules governing exchange rate policy. The main types are **fixed exchange rates,** where the government takes action to keep the exchange rate at a target level, and **floating exchange rates,** where the exchange rate is free to fluctuate. Countries can fix exchange rates using **exchange market intervention,** which requires them to hold **foreign exchange reserves** that they use to buy any surplus of their currency. Alternatively, they can change domestic policies, especially monetary policy, to shift the demand and supply curves in the foreign exchange market. Finally, they can use **foreign exchange controls.**
6. Exchange rate policy poses a dilemma: there are economic payoffs to stable exchange rates, but the policies used to fix the exchange rate have costs. Exchange market intervention requires large reserves, and exchange controls distort incentives. If monetary policy is used to help fix the exchange rate, it isn't available to use for domestic policy.

Exchange Rates and Macroeconomic Policy

7. Fixed exchange rates aren't always permanent commitments: countries with a fixed exchange rate sometimes engage in **devaluations** or **revaluations.** In addition to helping eliminate a surplus of domestic currency on the foreign exchange market, a devaluation increases aggregate demand. Similarly, a revaluation reduces shortages of domestic currency and reduces aggregate demand.
8. The fact that one country's imports are another country's exports creates a link between the business cycles in different countries. Floating exchange rates, however, may reduce the strength of that link.

Key Terms

Balance of payments accounts, p. 826
Balance of payments on the current account (the current account), p. 828
Balance of payments on goods and services, p. 828
Merchandise trade balance (trade balance), p. 828
Balance of payments on the financial account (the financial account), p. 828
Foreign exchange market, p. 837
Exchange rates, p. 837
Appreciates, p. 837
Depreciates, p. 837
Equilibrium exchange rate, p. 838
Real exchange rate, p. 840
Purchasing power parity, p. 842
Exchange rate regime, p. 845
Fixed exchange rate, p. 845
Floating exchange rate, p. 845
Exchange market intervention, p. 847
Foreign exchange reserves, p. 847
Foreign exchange controls, p. 847
Devaluation, p. 852
Revaluation, p. 852

Problems

1. How would the following transactions be categorized in the U.S. balance of payments accounts? Would they be entered in the current account (as a payment to or from a foreigner) or the financial account (as a sale of assets to or purchase of assets from a foreigner)? How will the balance of payments on the current and financial accounts change?

   a. A French importer buys a case of California wine for $500.

   b. An American who works for a French company deposits her paycheck, drawn on a Paris bank, into her San Francisco bank.

   c. An American buys a bond from a Japanese company for $10,000.

   d. An American charity sends $100,000 to Africa to help local residents buy food after a harvest shortfall.

2. The accompanying diagram shows foreign-owned assets in the United States and U.S.-owned assets abroad, both as a percentage of foreign GDP. As you can see from the diagram, both increased around fivefold from 1980 to 2010.

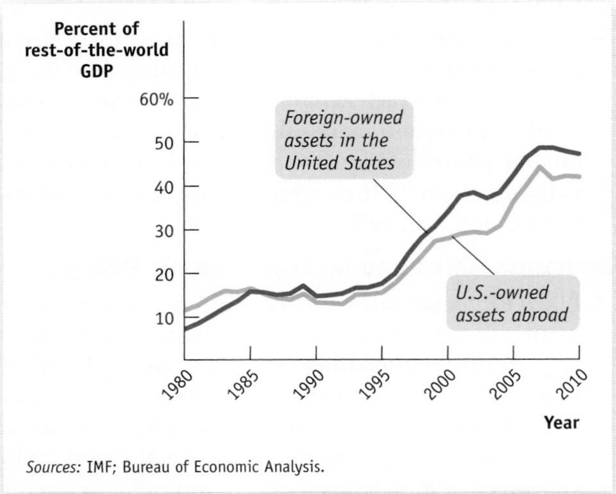

Sources: IMF; Bureau of Economic Analysis.

   a. As U.S.-owned assets abroad increased as a percentage of foreign GDP, does this mean that the United States, over the period, experienced net capital outflows?

   b. Does this diagram indicate that world economies were more tightly linked in 2010 than they were in 1980?

3. In the economy of Scottopia in 2013, exports equaled $400 billion of goods and $300 billion of services, imports equaled $500 billion of goods and $350 billion of services, and the rest of the world purchased $250 billion of Scottopia's assets. What was the merchandise trade balance for Scottopia? What was the balance of payments on current account in Scottopia? What was the balance of payments on financial account? What was the value of Scottopia's purchases of assets from the rest of the world?

4. In the economy of Popania in 2013, total Popanian purchases of assets in the rest of the world equaled $300 billion, purchases of Popanian assets by the rest of the world equaled $400 billion, and Popania exported goods and services equal to $350 billion. What was Popania's balance of payments on financial account in 2013? What was its balance of payments on current account? What was the value of its imports?

5. Suppose that Northlandia and Southlandia are the only two trading countries in the world, that each nation runs a balance of payments on both current and financial accounts equal to zero, and that each nation sees the other's assets as identical to its own. Using the accompanying diagrams, explain how the demand and supply of loanable funds, the interest rate, and the balance of payments on current and financial accounts will change in each country if international capital flows are possible.

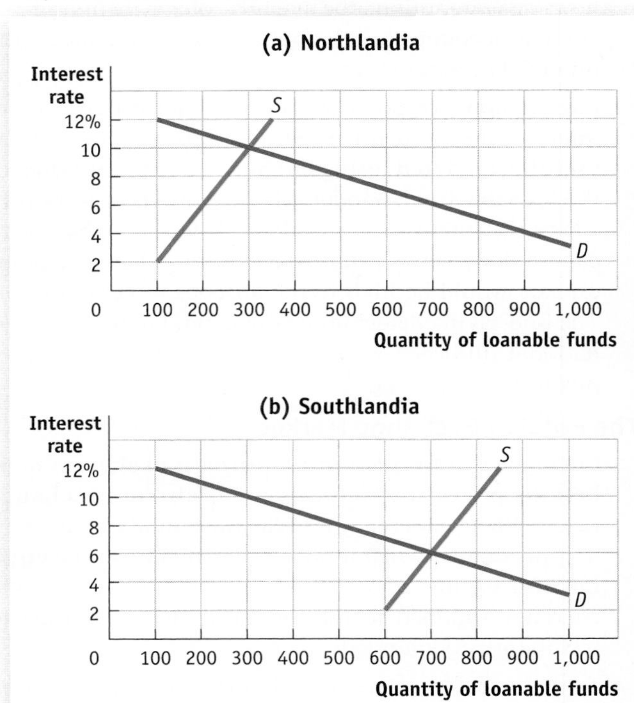

6. Based on the exchange rates for the first trading days of 2011 and 2012 shown in the accompanying table, did the U.S. dollar appreciate or depreciate during 2011? Did the movement in the value of the U.S. dollar make American goods and services more or less attractive to foreigners?

January 3, 2011	January 3, 2012
US$1.55 to buy 1 British pound sterling	US$1.57 to buy 1 British pound sterling
29.08 Taiwan dollars to buy US$1	30.28 Taiwan dollars to buy US$1
US$0.99 to buy 1 Canadian dollar	US$1.01 to buy 1 Canadian dollar
81.56 Japanese yen to buy US$1	76.67 Japanese yen to buy US$1
US$1.34 to buy 1 euro	US$1.31 to buy 1 euro
0.93 Swiss franc to buy US$1	0.93 Swiss franc to buy US$1

7. Go to http://fx.sauder.ubc.ca. Using the table labeled "The Most Recent Cross-Rates of Major Currencies," determine whether the British pound (GBP), the Canadian dollar (CAD), the Japanese yen (JPY), the euro (EUR), and the Swiss franc (CHF) have appreciated or depreciated against the U.S. dollar (USD) since January 3, 2012. The exchange rates on January 3, 2012, are listed in the table in Problem 6.

8. Suppose the United States and Japan are the only two trading countries in the world. What will happen to the value of the U.S. dollar if the following occur, other things equal?

  a. Japan relaxes some of its import restrictions.
  b. The United States imposes some import tariffs on Japanese goods.
  c. Interest rates in the United States rise dramatically.
  d. A report indicates that Japanese cars last much longer than previously thought, especially compared with American cars.

9. From January 1, 2001, to June 2003, the U.S. federal funds rate decreased from 6.5% to 1%. During the same period, the marginal lending facility rate at the European Central Bank decreased from 5.75% to 3%.

  a. Considering the change in interest rates over the period and using the loanable funds model, would you have expected funds to flow from the United States to Europe or from Europe to the United States over this period?
  b. The accompanying diagram shows the exchange rate between the euro and the U.S. dollar from January 1, 2001, through September 2008. Is the movement of the exchange rate over the period January 2001 to June 2003 consistent with the movement in funds predicted in part a?

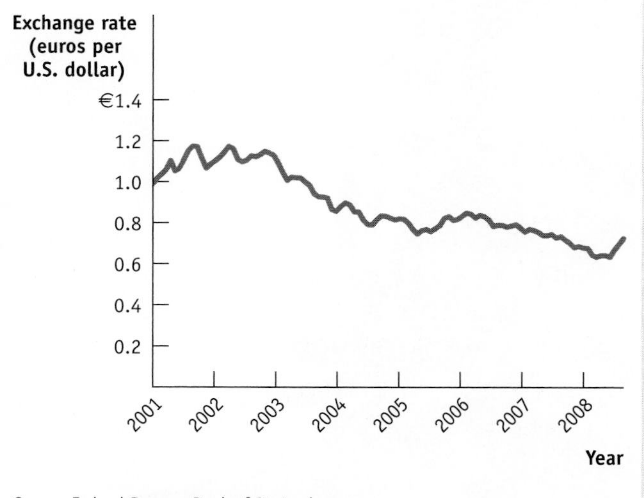

Source: Federal Reserve Bank of St. Louis.

10. In each of the following scenarios, suppose that the two nations are the only trading nations in the world. Given inflation and the change in the nominal exchange rate, which nation's goods become more attractive?

  a. Inflation is 10% in the United States and 5% in Japan; the U.S. dollar–Japanese yen exchange rate remains the same.
  b. Inflation is 3% in the United States and 8% in Mexico; the price of the U.S. dollar falls from 12.50 to 10.25 Mexican pesos.
  c. Inflation is 5% in the United States and 3% in the euro area; the price of the euro falls from \$1.30 to \$1.20.
  d. Inflation is 8% in the United States and 4% in Canada; the price of the Canadian dollar rises from US\$0.60 to US\$0.75.

11. Starting from a position of equilibrium in the foreign exchange market under a fixed exchange rate regime, how must a government react to an increase in the demand for the nation's goods and services by the rest of the world to keep the exchange rate at its fixed value?

12. Suppose that Albernia's central bank has fixed the value of its currency, the bern, to the U.S. dollar (at a rate of US\$1.50 to 1 bern) and is committed to that exchange rate. Initially, the foreign exchange market for the bern is also in equilibrium, as shown in the accompanying diagram. However, both Albernians and Americans begin to believe that there are big risks in holding Albernian assets; as a result, they become unwilling to hold Albernian assets unless they receive a higher rate of return on them than they do on U.S. assets. How would this affect the diagram? If the Albernian central bank tries to keep the exchange rate fixed using monetary policy, how will this affect the Albernian economy?

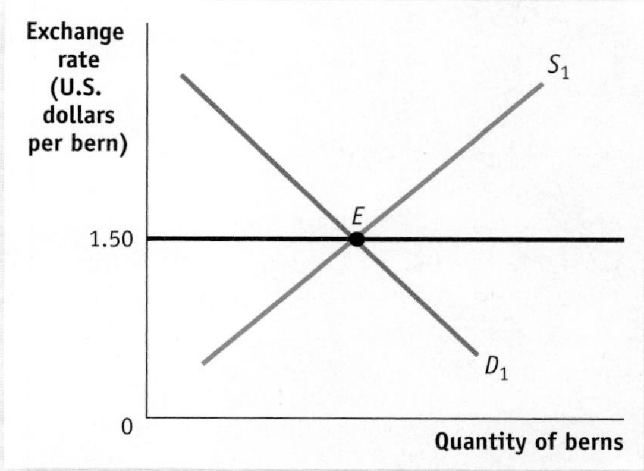

13. Your study partner asks you, "If central banks lose the ability to use discretionary monetary policy under fixed exchange rates, why would nations agree to a fixed exchange rate system?" How do you respond?

WHY CAN'T
GIVE MY DAD
A JOB?
Need $
4 FOOD
DIAPERS
HELPS

Module 83: History and Alternative Views of Macroeconomics

Module 84: The Modern Macroeconomic Consensus

SECTION 26

Macroeconomics: Events and Ideas

A TALE OF TWO SLUMPS

In November 2002, the Federal Reserve held a special conference to honor Milton Friedman on the occasion of his 90th birthday. Among those delivering tributes was Ben Bernanke, then a member of the Board of Governors, who later served as Fed Chairman. In his tribute, Bernanke surveyed Friedman's intellectual contributions, with particular focus on the argument made by Friedman and his collaborator Anna Schwartz that the Great Depression of the 1930s could have been avoided if only the Fed had done its job properly.

At the close of his talk, Bernanke directly addressed Friedman and Schwartz, who were sitting in the audience: "Let me end my talk by abusing slightly my status as an official representative of the Federal Reserve. I would like to say to Milton and Anna: Regarding the Great Depression. You're right, we did it. We're very sorry. But thanks to you, we won't do it again."

Today, in the aftermath of a devastating financial crisis that continues to inflict high unemployment, those words ring somewhat hollow. Avoiding severe economic downturns, it turned out, wasn't as easy as Friedman, Schwartz, and Bernanke had believed. Yet, as bad as they were, the crisis of 2008 and its aftermath were less devastating than the Great Depression.

It can be reasonably argued that part of the reason was that macroeconomics had evolved in the 78 years from 1930 to 2008. As a result, policy makers knew more about the causes of depressions and how to fight them than they did during the Great Depression.

In this section we'll trace the development of macroeconomic ideas over the past 80 years. As we'll see, this development has been strongly influenced by economic events, from the Great Depression of the 1930s, to the stagflation of the 1970s, to the surprising period of economic stability achieved between 1985 and 2007. And as we'll also see, the process continues, as the economic difficulties since 2008 have spurred many macroeconomists to rethink what they thought they knew.

83 History and Alternative Views of Macroeconomics

© Minnesota HistoricalSociety/CORBIS

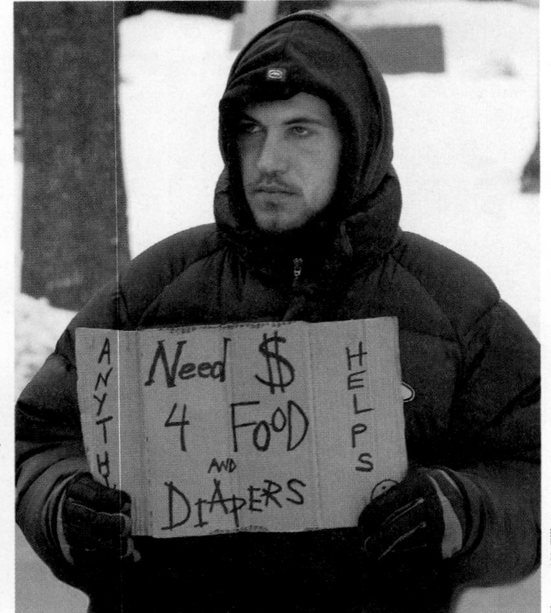

Thomas W. Elliott

WHAT YOU WILL LEARN

1. Why classical macroeconomics wasn't adequate for the problems posed by the Great Depression
2. How Keynes and the experience of the Great Depression legitimized macroeconomic policy activism
3. What monetarism is and its views about the limits of discretionary monetary policy
4. How challenges led to a revision of Keynesian ideas and the emergence of the new classical macroeconomics

Classical Macroeconomics

The term *macroeconomics* appears to have been coined in 1933 by the Norwegian economist Ragnar Frisch. The timing, during the worst year of the Great Depression, was no accident. Still, there were economists analyzing what we now consider macroeconomic issues—the behavior of the aggregate price level and aggregate output—before then.

Money and the Price Level

Previously, we described the *classical model of the price level.* According to the classical model, prices are flexible, making the aggregate supply curve vertical even in the short run. In this model, an increase in the money supply leads, other things equal, to a proportional rise in the aggregate price level, with no effect on aggregate output. As a result, increases in the money supply lead to inflation, and that's all. Before the 1930s, the classical model of the price level dominated economic thinking about the effects of monetary policy.

Did classical economists really believe that changes in the money supply affected only aggregate prices, without any effect on aggregate output? Probably not. Historians of economic thought argue that before 1930 most economists were aware that changes in the money supply affected aggregate output as well as aggregate prices in the short run—or, to use modern terms, they were aware that the short-run aggregate supply curve sloped upward. But they regarded such short-run effects as unimportant, stressing the long run instead. It was this attitude that led John Maynard Keynes to scoff at the focus on the long run, in which, as he said, "we are all dead."

The Business Cycle

Classical economists were, of course, also aware that the economy did not grow smoothly. The American economist Wesley Mitchell pioneered the quantitative study of business cycles. In 1920, he founded the National Bureau of Economic Research, an independent, nonprofit organization that to this day has the official role of declaring the beginnings of recessions and expansions. Thanks to Mitchell's work, the *measurement* of business cycles was well advanced by 1930. But there was no widely accepted *theory* of business cycles.

In the absence of any clear theory, views about how policy makers should respond to a recession were conflicting. Some economists favored expansionary monetary and fiscal policies to fight a recession. Others believed that such policies would worsen the slump or merely postpone the inevitable. When the Great Depression hit, the policy making process was paralyzed by this lack of consensus. In many cases, economists now believe, policy makers took steps in the wrong direction.

Necessity was, however, the mother of invention. As we'll explain next, the Great Depression provided a strong incentive for economists to develop theories that could serve as a guide to policy—and economists responded.

The Great Depression and the Keynesian Revolution

The Great Depression demonstrated, once and for all, that economists cannot safely ignore the short run. Not only was the economic pain severe, it threatened to destabilize societies and political systems.

The whole world wanted to know how this economic disaster could be happening and what should be done about it. But because there was no widely accepted theory of the business cycle, economists gave conflicting and, we now believe, often harmful advice. Some believed that only a huge change in the economic system—such as having the government take over much of private industry and replace markets with a command economy—could end the slump. Others argued that slumps were natural—even beneficial—and that nothing should be done.

Some economists, however, argued that the slump both could have and should have been cured—without giving up on the basic idea of a market economy. In 1930, the British economist John Maynard Keynes compared the problems of the U.S. and British economies to those of a car with a defective alternator. Getting the economy running, he argued, would require only a modest repair, not a complete overhaul.

Nice metaphor. But what was the nature of the trouble?

Tim Gidal/Picture Post/Getty Images

Some people use *Keynesian economics* as a synonym for *left-wing economics*—but, in truth, Keynes's ideas have been accepted across a broad part of the political spectrum.

Keynes's Theory

In 1936, Keynes presented his analysis of the Great Depression—his explanation of what was wrong with the economy's alternator—in a book titled *The General Theory of Employment, Interest, and Money*. *The General Theory* stands with Adam Smith's *The Wealth of Nations* as one of the most influential books on economics ever written.

Keynes's book is a vast stew of ideas. And Keynesian economics mainly reflected two innovations. First, Keynes emphasized the short-run effects of shifts in aggregate demand on aggregate output, rather than the long-run determination of the aggregate price level. As Keynes's famous remark about being dead in the long run suggests, until his book appeared most economists had treated short-run macroeconomics as a minor issue. Keynes focused the attention of economists on situations in which the short-run aggregate supply curve slopes upward and shifts in the aggregate demand curve affect aggregate output and employment as well as aggregate prices.

FIGURE 83-1 Classical Versus Keynesian Macroeconomics

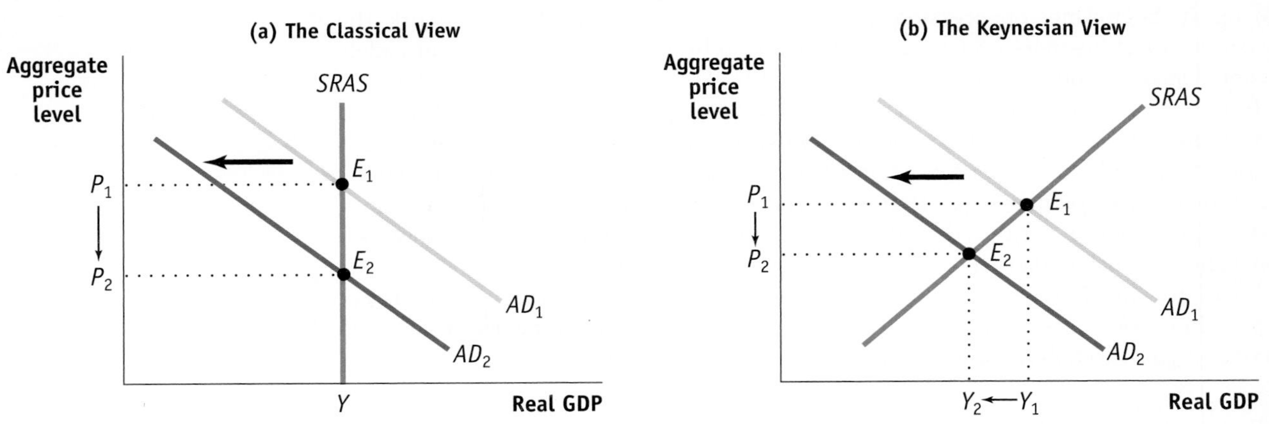

One important difference between classical and Keynesian economics involves the short-run aggregate supply curve. Panel (a) shows the classical view: the *SRAS* curve is vertical, so shifts in aggregate demand affect the aggregate price level but not aggregate output. Panel (b) shows the Keynesian view: in the short run the *SRAS* curve slopes upward, so shifts in aggregate demand affect aggregate output as well as aggregate prices.

Figure 83-1 illustrates the difference between Keynesian and classical macroeconomics. Both panels of the figure show the short-run aggregate supply curve, *SRAS;* in both it is assumed that for some reason the aggregate demand curve shifts leftward from AD_1 to AD_2—let's say in response to a fall in stock market prices that leads households to reduce consumer spending.

Panel (a) shows the classical view: the short-run aggregate supply curve is vertical. The decline in aggregate demand leads to a fall in the aggregate price level, from P_1 to P_2, but no change in aggregate output. Panel (b) shows the Keynesian view: the short-run aggregate supply curve slopes upward, so the decline in aggregate demand leads to both a fall in the aggregate price level, from P_1 to P_2, and a fall in aggregate output, from Y_1 to Y_2.

As we've already explained, many classical macroeconomists would have agreed that panel (b) was an accurate story in the short run—but they regarded the short run as unimportant. Keynes disagreed. (Just to be clear, there isn't any diagram that looks like panel (b) of Figure 83-1 in Keynes's *General Theory*. But Keynes's discussion of aggregate supply, translated into modern terminology, clearly implies an upward-sloping *SRAS* curve.)

Second, classical economists emphasized the role of changes in the money supply in shifting the aggregate demand curve, paying little attention to other factors. Keynes, however, argued that other factors, especially changes in "animal spirits"—these days usually referred to with the bland term *business confidence*—are mainly responsible for business cycles. Before Keynes, economists often argued that a decline in business confidence would have no effect on either the aggregate price level or aggregate output, as long as the money supply stayed constant. Keynes offered a very different picture.

Keynes's ideas have penetrated deeply into the public consciousness, to the extent that many people who have never heard of Keynes, or have heard of him but think they disagree with his theory, use Keynesian ideas all the time. For example, suppose that a business commentator says something like this: "Because of a decline in business confidence, investment spending slumped, causing a recession." Whether the commentator knows it or not, that statement is pure Keynesian economics.

Policy to Fight Recessions

The main practical consequence of Keynes's work was that it legitimized **macroeconomic policy activism**—the use of monetary and fiscal policy to smooth out the business cycle.

Macroeconomic policy activism is the use of monetary and fiscal policy to smooth out the business cycle.

Macroeconomic policy activism wasn't something completely new. Before Keynes, many economists had argued for using monetary expansion to fight economic downturns—though others were fiercely opposed. In fact, many governments followed policies that we would now call Keynesian. In the United States, the administration of Franklin Roosevelt engaged in modest deficit spending in an effort to create jobs. But these efforts were half-hearted. Roosevelt's advisers were deeply divided over the appropriate policies to adopt, and in 1937 Roosevelt gave in to advice from non-Keynesian economists who urged him to balance the budget and raise interest rates, even though the economy was still depressed. The result was a renewed slump.

After World War II, Keynesian ideas were broadly accepted by U.S. economists. There were, however, a series of challenges to those ideas, which led to a considerable shift in views even among economists who continued to believe that Keynes was broadly right about the causes of recessions. In the upcoming section, we'll learn about those challenges and the schools, *new classical economics* and *new Keynesian economics*, that emerged.

ECONOMICS IN ACTION

THE END OF THE GREAT DEPRESSION

It would make a good story if Keynes's ideas had led to a change in economic policy that brought the Great Depression to an end. Unfortunately, that's not what happened. Still, the way the Depression ended did a lot to convince economists that Keynes was right.

The basic message many of the young economists who adopted Keynes's ideas in the 1930s took from his work was that economic recovery requires aggressive fiscal expansion—deficit spending on a large scale to create jobs. And that is what they eventually got, but it wasn't because politicians were persuaded. Instead, what happened was a very large and expensive war, World War II.

FIGURE 83-2 The Unemployment Rate and Federal Budget Deficit as a Share of GDP, 1930–1947

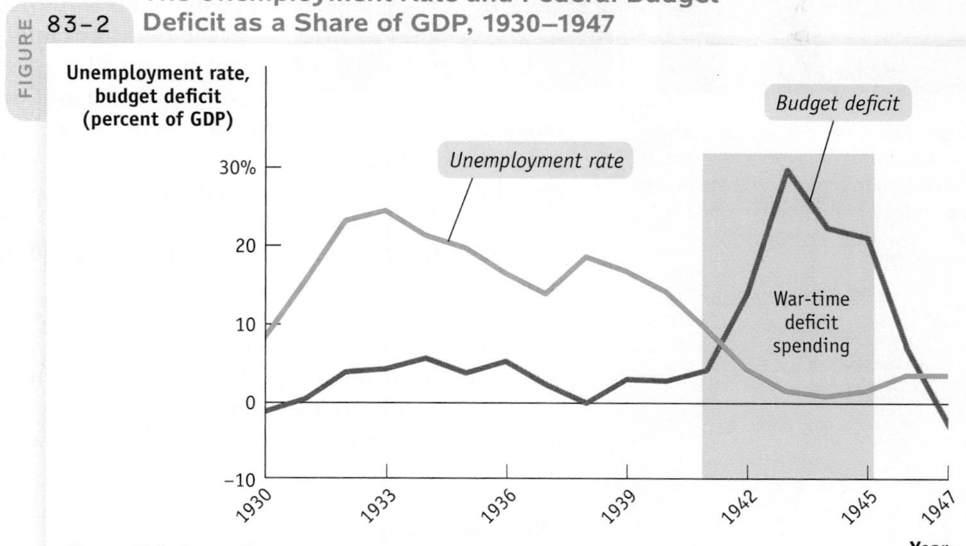

Source: U.S. Census Bureau.

Figure 83-2 shows the U.S. unemployment rate and the federal budget deficit as a share of GDP from 1930 to 1947. As you can see, deficit spending during the 1930s was on a modest scale. In 1940, as the risk of war grew larger, the United States began a large military buildup, and the budget moved deep into deficit. After the attack on Pearl Harbor on December 7, 1941, the country began deficit spending on an enormous scale: in fiscal 1943, which began in July 1942, the deficit was 30% of GDP. Today that would be a deficit of $5.0 trillion.

And the economy recovered. World War II wasn't intended as a Keynesian fiscal policy, but it demonstrated that expansionary fiscal policy can, in fact, create jobs in the short run.

Challenges to Keynesian Economics

Keynes's ideas fundamentally changed the way economists think about business cycles. They did not, however, go unquestioned. In the decades that followed the publication of *The General Theory,* Keynesian economics faced a series of challenges. As a result, the consensus of macroeconomists retreated somewhat from the strong version of Keynesianism that prevailed in the 1950s. In particular, economists became much more aware of the limits to macroeconomic policy activism.

The Revival of Monetary Policy

Keynes's *General Theory* suggested that monetary policy wouldn't be very effective in depression conditions. Many modern macroeconomists agree: earlier we introduced the concept of a *liquidity trap,* a situation in which monetary policy is ineffective because the interest rate is down against the zero bound. In the 1930s, when Keynes wrote, interest rates were, in fact, very close to 0%.

But even when the era of near-0% interest rates came to an end after World War II, many economists continued to emphasize fiscal policy and downplay the usefulness of monetary policy. Eventually, however, macroeconomists reassessed the importance of monetary policy. A key milestone in this reassessment was the 1963 publication of *A Monetary History of the United States, 1867–1960* by Milton Friedman, of the University of Chicago, and Anna Schwartz, of the National Bureau of Economic Research.

Roger Ressmeyer/Corbis

Teresa Zabala/The New York Times/Redux

Milton Friedman and his co-author Anna Schwartz played a key role in convincing macroeconomists of the importance of monetary policy.

Friedman and Schwartz showed that business cycles had historically been associated with fluctuations in the money supply. In particular, the money supply fell sharply during the onset of the Great Depression. Friedman and Schwartz persuaded many, though not all, economists that the Great Depression could have been avoided if the Federal Reserve had acted to prevent that monetary contraction and that monetary policy should play a key role in economic management.

The revival of interest in monetary policy was significant because it suggested that the burden of managing the economy could be shifted away from fiscal policy—meaning that economic management could largely be taken out of the hands of politicians. Fiscal policy, which must involve changing tax rates or government spending, necessarily involves political choices. If the government tries to stimulate the economy by cutting taxes, it must decide whose taxes will be cut. If it tries to stimulate the economy with government spending, it must decide what to spend the money on.

Monetary policy, in contrast, does not involve such choices: when the central bank cuts interest rates to fight a recession, it cuts everyone's interest rate at the same time. So a shift from relying on fiscal policy to relying on monetary policy makes macroeconomics a more technical, less political issue. In fact, monetary policy in most major economies is set by an independent central bank that is insulated from the political process.

Monetarism

After the publication of *A Monetary History,* Milton Friedman led a movement, called *monetarism,* that sought to eliminate macroeconomic policy activism while maintaining the importance of monetary policy. **Monetarism** asserted that GDP will grow steadily if the money supply grows steadily. The monetarist policy prescription was to have the central bank target a constant rate of growth of the money supply, such as 3% per year, and maintain that target regardless of any fluctuations in the economy.

Monetarism asserts that GDP will grow steadily if the money supply grows steadily.

It's important to realize that monetarism retained many Keynesian ideas. Like Keynes, Friedman asserted that the short run is important and that short-run changes in aggregate demand affect aggregate output as well as aggregate prices. Like Keynes, he argued that policy should have been much more expansionary during the Great Depression.

Monetarists argued, however, that most of the efforts of policy makers to smooth out the business cycle actually make things worse. We have already discussed concerns over the usefulness of *discretionary fiscal policy*—changes in taxes or government spending, or both—in response to the state of the economy. As we explained, government perceptions about the economy often lag behind reality, and there are further lags in changing fiscal policy and in its effects on the economy. As a result, discretionary fiscal policies intended to fight a recession often end up feeding a boom, and vice versa. According to monetarists, **discretionary monetary policy,** changes in the interest rate or the money supply by the central bank in order to stabilize the economy, faces the same problem of lags as fiscal policy, but to a lesser extent.

Discretionary monetary policy is the use of changes in the interest rate or the money supply to stabilize the economy.

Friedman also argued that if the central bank followed his advice and refused to change the money supply in response to fluctuations in the economy, fiscal policy would be much less effective than Keynesians believed. Earlier we analyzed the phenomenon of *crowding out,* in which government deficits drive up interest rates and lead to reduced investment spending. Friedman and others pointed out that if the money supply is held fixed while the government pursues an expansionary fiscal policy, crowding out will limit the effect of the fiscal expansion on aggregate demand.

Figure 83-3 illustrates this argument. Panel (a) shows aggregate output and the aggregate price level. AD_1 is the initial aggregate demand curve and $SRAS$ is the short-run aggregate supply curve. At the initial equilibrium, E_1, the level of aggregate output is Y_1 and the aggregate price level is P_1. Panel (b) shows the money market. MS is the money supply curve and MD_1 is the initial money demand curve, so the initial interest rate is r_1.

FIGURE 83-3 **Fiscal Policy with a Fixed Money Supply**

(a) The increase in aggregate demand from an expansionary fiscal policy is limited when the money supply is fixed...

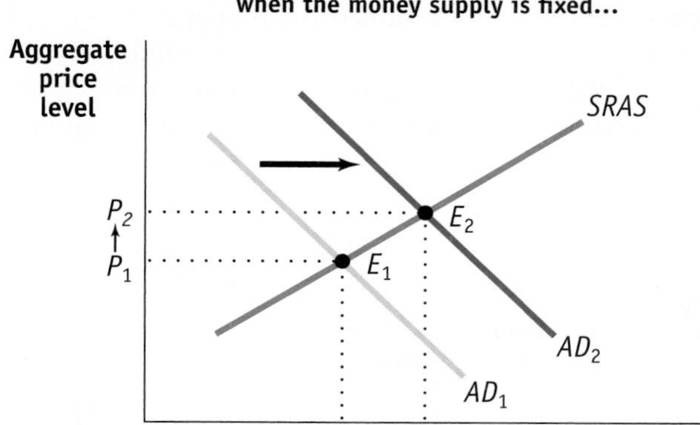

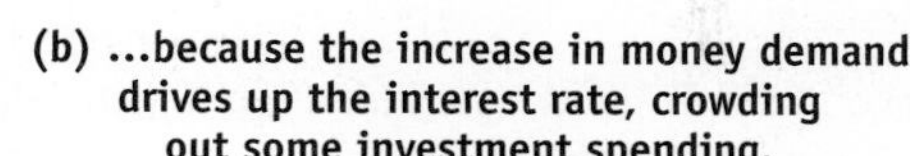

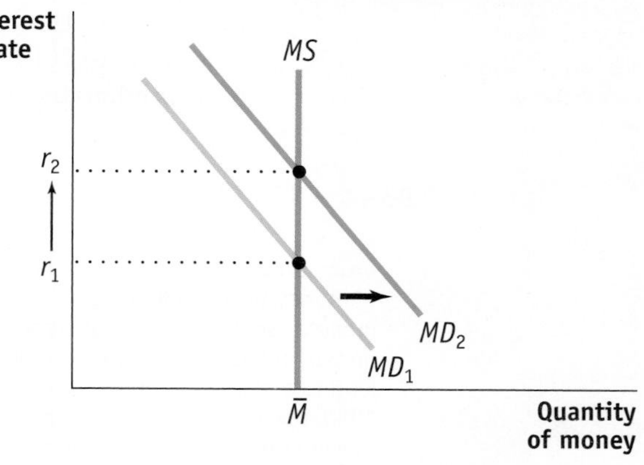

In panel (a) an expansionary fiscal policy shifts the *AD* curve rightward, driving up both the aggregate price level and aggregate output. However, this leads to an increase in the demand for money. If the money supply is held fixed, as in panel (b), the increase in money demand drives up the interest rate, reducing investment spending and offsetting part of the fiscal expansion. So the shift of the *AD* curve is less than it would otherwise be: fiscal policy becomes less effective when the money supply is held fixed.

A **monetary policy rule** is a formula that determines the central bank's actions.

The **Quantity Theory of Money** emphasizes the positive relationship between the price level and the money supply. It relies on the velocity equation ($M \times V = P \times Y$).

The **velocity of money** is the ratio of nominal GDP to the money supply. It is a measure of the number of times the average dollar bill is spent per year.

Now suppose the government increases purchases of goods and services. We know that this will shift the *AD* curve rightward, as illustrated by the shift from AD_1 to AD_2; that aggregate output will rise, from Y_1 to Y_2; and that the aggregate price level will rise, from P_1 to P_2. Both the rise in aggregate output and the rise in the aggregate price level will, however, increase the demand for money, shifting the money demand curve rightward from MD_1 to MD_2. This drives up the equilibrium interest rate to r_2. Friedman's point was that this rise in the interest rate reduces investment spending, partially offsetting the initial rise in government spending. As a result, the rightward shift of the *AD* curve is smaller than multiplier analysis indicates. And Friedman argued that with a constant money supply, the multiplier is so small that there's not much point in using fiscal policy, even in a depressed economy.

But Friedman didn't favor activist monetary policy either. He argued that the problem of time lags that limit the ability of discretionary fiscal policy to stabilize the economy also apply to discretionary monetary policy. Friedman's solution was to put monetary policy on "autopilot." The central bank, he argued, should follow a **monetary policy rule,** a formula that determines its actions and leaves it relatively little discretion. During the 1960s and 1970s, most monetarists favored a monetary policy rule of slow, steady growth in the money supply.

Underlying this view was the **Quantity Theory of Money,** which relies on the concept of the **velocity of money,** the ratio of nominal GDP to the money supply. Velocity is a measure of the number of times the average dollar bill in the economy turns over per year between buyers and sellers (e.g., I tip the Starbucks barista a dollar, she uses it to buy lunch, and so on). This concept gives rise to the *velocity equation:*

(83-1) $M \times V = P \times Y$

Where M is the money supply, V is velocity, P is the aggregate price level, and Y is real GDP.

Monetarists believed, with considerable historical justification, that the velocity of money was stable in the short run and changed only slowly in the long run. As a result, they claimed, steady growth in the money supply by the central bank would ensure steady growth in spending, and therefore in GDP.

Monetarism strongly influenced actual monetary policy in the late 1970s and early 1980s. It quickly became clear, however, that steady growth in the money supply didn't ensure steady growth in the economy: the velocity of money wasn't stable enough for such a simple policy rule to work.

Figure 83-4 shows how events eventually undermined the monetarists' view. The figure shows the velocity of money, as measured by the ratio of nominal GDP to M1, from 1960 to 2013. As you can see, until 1980, velocity followed a fairly smooth, seemingly predictable trend. After the Fed began to adopt monetarist ideas in the late 1970s

FIGURE 83-4 **The Velocity of Money**

From 1960 to 1980, the velocity of money was stable, leading monetarists to believe that steady growth in the money supply would lead to a stable economy. After 1980, however, velocity began moving erratically, undermining the case for traditional monetarism. As a result, traditional monetarism fell out of favor.

Source: Bureau of Economic Analysis; Federal Reserve Bank of St. Louis.

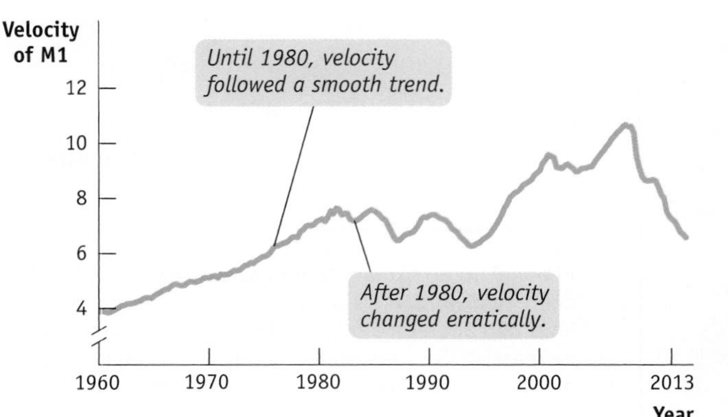

and early 1980s, however, the velocity of money began moving erratically—probably due to financial market innovations.

Traditional monetarists are hard to find among today's macroeconomists. As we'll see later, however, the concern that originally motivated the monetarists—that too much discretionary monetary policy can actually destabilize the economy—has become widely accepted.

According to the **natural rate hypothesis,** to avoid accelerating inflation over time, the unemployment rate must be high enough that the actual inflation rate equals the expected inflation rate.

Inflation and the Natural Rate of Unemployment

At the same time that monetarists were challenging Keynesian views about how macroeconomic policy should be conducted, other economists—some, but not all, monetarists—were emphasizing the limits to what activist macroeconomic policy could achieve.

In the 1940s and 1950s, many Keynesian economists believed that expansionary fiscal policy could be used to achieve full employment on a permanent basis. In the 1960s, however, many economists realized that expansionary policies could cause problems with inflation, but they still believed policy makers could choose to trade off low unemployment for higher inflation even in the long run.

In 1968, however, Edmund Phelps of Columbia University and Milton Friedman, working independently, proposed the concept of the *natural rate of unemployment.* Earlier you learned that the natural rate of unemployment is also the nonaccelerating inflation rate of unemployment, or NAIRU. According to the **natural rate hypothesis,** because inflation is eventually embedded in expectations, to avoid accelerating inflation over time, the unemployment rate must be high enough that the actual inflation rate equals the expected rate of inflation. Attempts to keep the unemployment rate below the natural rate will lead to an ever-rising inflation rate.

The natural rate hypothesis limits the role of activist macroeconomic policy compared to earlier theories. Because the government can't keep unemployment below the natural rate, its task is not to keep unemployment low but to keep it *stable*—to prevent large fluctuations in unemployment in either direction.

The Friedman–Phelps hypothesis made a strong prediction: that the apparent trade-off between unemployment and inflation would not survive an extended period of rising prices. Once inflation was embedded in the public's expectations, inflation would continue even in the face of high unemployment. Sure enough, that's exactly what happened in the 1970s. This accurate prediction was one of the triumphs of macroeconomic analysis, and it convinced the great majority of economists that the natural rate hypothesis was correct. In contrast to traditional monetarism, which declined in influence as more evidence accumulated, the natural rate hypothesis has become almost universally accepted among macroeconomists, with a few qualifications. But some macroeconomists believe that at very low or negative rates of inflation the hypothesis doesn't work.

The Political Business Cycle

One final challenge to Keynesian economics focused not on the validity of the economic analysis but on its political consequences. A number of economists and political scientists pointed out that activist macroeconomic policy lends itself to political manipulation.

Statistical evidence suggests that election results tend to be determined by the state of the economy in the months just before the election. In the United States, if the economy is growing rapidly and the unemployment rate is falling in the six months or so before Election Day, the incumbent party tends to be re-elected even if the economy performed poorly in the preceding three years.

Shutterstock

This creates an obvious temptation to abuse activist macroeconomic policy: pump up the economy in an election year, and pay the price in higher inflation and/or

AWesleyFloyd/Shutterstock

higher unemployment later. The result can be unnecessary instability in the economy, a **political business cycle** caused by the use of macroeconomic policy to serve political ends.

An often-cited example is the combination of expansionary fiscal and monetary policy that led to rapid growth in the U.S. economy just before the 1972 election and a sharp acceleration in inflation after the election. Kenneth Rogoff, a respected macroeconomist who served as chief economist at the International Monetary Fund, proclaimed Richard Nixon, the president at the time, "the all-time hero of political business cycles."

One way to avoid a political business cycle is to place monetary policy in the hands of an independent central bank, insulated from political pressure. The political business cycle is also a reason to limit the use of discretionary fiscal policy to extreme circumstances.

Rational Expectations, Real Business Cycles, and New Classical Macroeconomics

As we have seen, one key difference between classical economics and Keynesian economics is that classical economists believed that the short-run aggregate supply curve is vertical, but Keynes emphasized the idea that the aggregate supply curve slopes upward in the short run. As a result, Keynes argued that demand shocks—shifts in the aggregate demand curve—can cause fluctuations in aggregate output.

The challenges to Keynesian economics that arose in the 1950s and 1960s—the renewed emphasis on monetary policy and the natural rate hypothesis—didn't question the view that an increase in aggregate demand leads to a rise in aggregate output in the short run nor that a decrease in aggregate demand leads to a fall in aggregate output in the short run.

In the 1970s and 1980s, however, some economists developed an approach to the business cycle known as **new classical macroeconomics,** which returned to the classical view that shifts in the aggregate demand curve affect only the aggregate price level, not aggregate output. The new approach evolved in two steps. First, some economists challenged traditional arguments about the slope of the short-run aggregate supply curve based on the concept of *rational expectations.* Second, some economists suggested that changes in productivity caused economic fluctuations, a view known as *real business cycle theory.*

Rational Expectations

In the 1970s, a concept known as *rational expectations* had a powerful impact on macroeconomics. **Rational expectations,** a theory originally introduced by John Muth in 1961, is the view that individuals and firms make decisions optimally, using all available information.

For example, workers and employers bargaining over long-term wage contracts need to estimate the inflation rate they expect over the life of that contract. Rational expectations says that in making estimates of future inflation, they won't just look at past rates of inflation; they will also take into account available information about monetary and fiscal policy. Suppose that prices didn't rise last year, but that the monetary and fiscal policies announced by policy makers made it clear to economic analysts that there would be substantial inflation over the next few years. According to rational expectations, long-term wage contracts will be adjusted today to reflect this future inflation, even though prices didn't rise in the past.

A **political business cycle** results when politicians use macroeconomic policy to serve political ends.

New classical macroeconomics is an approach to the business cycle that returns to the classical view that shifts in the aggregate demand curve affect only the aggregate price level, not aggregate output.

Rational expectations is the view that individuals and firms make decisions optimally, using all available information.

Rational expectations can significantly alter policy makers' beliefs about the effectiveness of government policy. According to the original version of the natural rate hypothesis, a government attempt to trade off higher inflation for lower unemployment would work in the short run but would eventually fail because higher inflation would get built into expectations.

According to rational expectations, we should remove the word *eventually:* if it's clear that the government intends to trade off higher inflation for lower unemployment, the public will understand this, and expected inflation will immediately rise. So, under rational expectations, government intervention fails in the short run and the long run.

In the 1970s, Robert Lucas of the University of Chicago used this logic to argue that monetary policy can change the level of unemployment only if it comes as a surprise to the public. If his analysis was right, monetary policy isn't useful in stabilizing the economy after all. In 1995 Lucas won the Nobel Prize in economics for this work, which remains widely admired. However, many—perhaps most—macroeconomists, especially those advising policy makers, now believe that his conclusions were overstated.

Why, in the view of many macroeconomists, doesn't the rational expectations hypothesis accurately describe how the economy behaves? **New Keynesian economics,** a set of ideas that became influential in the 1990s, provides an explanation. It argues that market imperfections interact to make many prices in the economy temporarily sticky. For example, one new Keynesian argument points out that monopolists don't have to be too careful about setting prices exactly "right": if they set a price a bit too high, they'll lose some sales but make more profit on each sale; if they set the price too low, they'll reduce the profit per sale but sell more. As a result, even small costs to changing prices can lead to substantial price stickiness and make the economy as a whole behave in a Keynesian fashion.

Over time, new Keynesian ideas combined with actual experience have reduced the practical influence of the rational expectations concept. Nonetheless, the idea of rational expectations served as a useful caution for macroeconomists who had become excessively optimistic about their ability to manage the economy.

According to **new Keynesian economics,** market imperfections can lead to price stickiness for the economy as a whole.

Real business cycle theory claims that fluctuations in the rate of growth of total factor productivity cause the business cycle.

Real Business Cycles

Earlier we introduced the concept of *total factor productivity,* the amount of output that can be generated with a given level of factor inputs. Total factor productivity grows over time, but that growth isn't smooth. In the 1980s, a number of economists argued that slowdowns in productivity growth, which they attributed to pauses in technological progress, are the main cause of recessions. **Real business cycle theory** claims that fluctuations in the rate of growth of total factor productivity cause the business cycle.

Believing that the aggregate supply curve is vertical, real business cycle theorists attribute the source of business cycles to shifts of the aggregate supply curve: a recession occurs when a slowdown in productivity growth shifts the aggregate supply curve leftward, and a recovery occurs when a pickup in productivity growth shifts the aggregate supply curve rightward. In the early days of real business cycle theory, the theory's proponents denied that changes in aggregate demand—and likewise, macroeconomic policy activism—had any effect on aggregate output.

This theory was strongly influential, but the current status of real business cycle theory is somewhat similar to that of rational expectations. The theory is widely recognized as having made valuable contributions to our understanding of the economy, and it serves as a useful caution against too much emphasis on aggregate demand.

But many of the real business cycle theorists themselves now acknowledge that their models need an upward-sloping aggregate supply curve to fit the economic data—and that this gives aggregate demand a potential role in determining aggregate output. And as we have seen, policy makers strongly believe that aggregate demand policy has an important role to play in fighting recessions.

MODULE 83 Review

Solutions appear at the back of the book.

Check Your Understanding

1. When Ben Bernanke, in his tribute to Milton Friedman, said that "Regarding the Great Depression . . . we did it," he was referring to the fact that the Federal Reserve at the time did not pursue expansionary monetary policy. Why would a classical economist have thought that action by the Federal Reserve would not have made a difference in the length or depth of the Great Depression?

2. Consider Figure 83-4.
   a. If the Federal Reserve had pursued a monetarist policy of a constant rate of growth in the money supply, what would have happened to output beginning in 2008 according to the velocity equation?
   b. In fact, the Federal Reserve accelerated the rate of growth in M1 rapidly beginning in 2008, partly in order to counteract a large increase in unemployment. Would a monetarist have agreed with this policy? What limits are there, according to a monetarist point of view, to changing the unemployment rate?

3. What are the limits of macroeconomic policy activism?

4. In late 2008, as it became clear that the United States was experiencing a recession, the Fed reduced its target for the federal funds rate to near zero, as part of a larger aggressively expansionary monetary policy stance (including what the Fed called "quantitative easing"). Most observers agreed that the Fed's aggressive monetary expansion helped reduce the length and severity of the 2007–2009 recession.
   a. What would rational expectations theorists say about this conclusion?
   b. What would real business cycle theorists say?

Multiple-Choice Questions

1. Which of the following was an important point emphasized in Keynes's influential work?
   I. In the short run, shifts in aggregate demand affect aggregate output.
   II. Animal spirits are an important determinant of business cycles.
   III. In the long run we're all dead.
   a. I only
   b. II only
   c. III only
   d. I and II only
   e. I, II, and III

2. Which of the following is a central point of monetarism?
   a. Business cycles are associated with fluctuations in money demand.
   b. Activist monetary policy is the best way to address business cycles.
   c. Discretionary monetary policy is effective while discretionary fiscal policy is not.
   d. The Fed should follow a monetary policy rule.
   e. All of the above.

3. The natural rate hypothesis says that the unemployment rate should be
   a. below the NAIRU.
   b. high enough that the actual rate of inflation equals the expected rate.
   c. as close to zero as possible.
   d. 5%.
   e. left wherever the economy sets it.

4. The main difference between the classical model of the price level and Keynesian economics is that
   a. the classical model assumes a vertical short-run aggregate supply curve.

b. Keynesian economics assumes a vertical short-run aggregate supply curve.
c. the classical model assumes an upward sloping long-run aggregate supply curve.
d. Keynesian economics assumes a vertical long-run aggregate supply curve.
e. the classical model assumes aggregate demand can not change in the long run.

5. That fluctuations in total factor productivity growth cause the business cycle is the main tenet of which theory?
   a. Keynesian
   b. classical
   c. rational expectations
   d. real business cycle
   e. natural rate

Critical-Thinking Question

For each of the following economic theories, identify its fundamental conclusion.

a. the classical model of the price level
b. Keynesian economics
c. monetarism
d. the natural rate hypothesis
e. rational expectations
f. real business cycle theory

MODULE

84 The Modern Macroeconomic Consensus

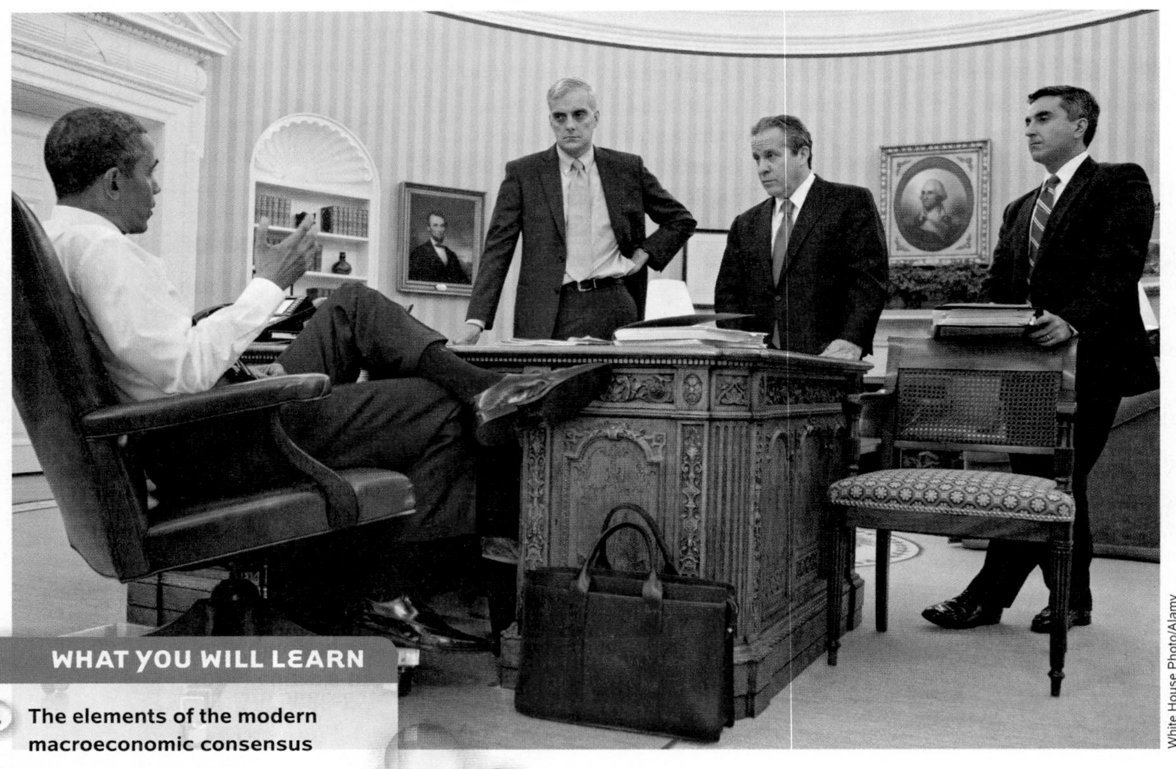
White House Photo/Alamy

WHAT YOU WILL LEARN

1. The elements of the modern macroeconomic consensus
2. The main remaining disputes

Consensus and Conflict in Modern Macroeconomics

The 1970s and the first half of the 1980s were a stormy period for the U.S. economy (and for other major economies, too). There was a severe recession in 1974–1975, then two back-to-back recessions in 1979–1982 that sent the unemployment rate to almost 11%. At the same time, the inflation rate soared into double digits—and then plunged. As we have seen, these events left a strong mark on macroeconomic thought.

After about 1985, however, the economy settled down. The recession of 1990–1991 was much milder than the 1974–1975 recession or the double-dip slump from 1979 to 1982, and the inflation rate generally stayed below 4%. The period of relative calm in the economy from 1985 to 2007 came to be known as the **Great Moderation.** And the calmness of the economy was to a large extent marked by a similar calm in macroeconomic policy discussion. In fact, it seemed that a broad consensus had emerged about several key macroeconomic issues.

The **Great Moderation** is the period from 1985 to 2007 when the U.S. economy experienced relatively small fluctuations and low inflation.

The **Great Moderation consensus** combines a belief in monetary policy as the main tool of stabilization, with skepticism toward the use of fiscal policy, and an acknowledgement of the policy constraints imposed by the natural rate of unemployment and the political business cycle.

The Great Moderation was, unfortunately, followed by the *Great Recession,* the severe and persistent slump that followed the 2008 financial crisis. We'll talk shortly about the policy disputes caused by the Great Recession. First, however, let's examine the apparent consensus that emerged during the Great Moderation, which we call the **Great Moderation consensus.** It combines a belief in monetary policy as the main tool of stabilization, with skepticism toward the use of fiscal policy, and an acknowledgement of the policy constraints imposed by the natural rate of unemployment and the political business cycle.

To understand where the consensus came from and what still remains in dispute, we'll look at how macroeconomists have changed their answers to five key questions about macroeconomic policy. The five questions and the various answers given by schools of macroeconomics over the decades are summarized in Table 84-1. (In the table, new classical economics is subsumed under classical economics, and new Keynesian economics is subsumed under the Great Moderation consensus.) Notice that classical macroeconomics said no to each question; basically, classical macroeconomists didn't think macroeconomic policy could accomplish very much. But let's go through the questions one by one.

TABLE 84-1

Five Key Questions About Macroeconomic Policy

	Classical macroeconomics	Keynesian macroeconomics	Monetarism	Great Moderation consensus
1. Is expansionary monetary policy helpful in fighting recessions?	No	Not very	Yes	Yes, except in special circumstances
2. Is expansionary fiscal policy effective in fighting recessions?	No	Yes	No	Yes
3. Can monetary and/or fiscal policy reduce unemployment in the long run?	No	Yes	No	No
4. Should fiscal policy be used in a discretionary way?	No	Yes	No	No, except possibly in special circumstances
5. Should monetary policy be used in a discretionary way?	No	Yes	No	Still in dispute

QUESTION 1: IS EXPANSIONARY MONETARY POLICY HELPFUL IN FIGHTING RECESSIONS? As we've seen, classical macroeconomists generally believed that expansionary monetary policy was ineffective or even harmful in fighting recessions. In the early years of Keynesian economics, macroeconomists weren't against monetary expansion during recessions, but they tended to believe that it was of doubtful effectiveness. Milton Friedman and his followers convinced economists that monetary policy is effective after all.

Nearly all macroeconomists now agree that monetary policy can be used to shift the aggregate demand curve and to reduce economic instability. The classical view that changes in the money supply affect only aggregate prices, not aggregate output, has few supporters today. The view held by early Keynesian economists—that changes in the money supply have little effect—has equally few supporters. Now it is generally agreed that monetary policy is ineffective only in the case of a liquidity trap.

QUESTION 2: IS EXPANSIONARY FISCAL POLICY EFFECTIVE IN FIGHTING RECESSIONS? Classical macroeconomists were, if anything, even more opposed to fiscal expansion than monetary expansion. Keynesian economists, on the other hand, gave fiscal policy a central role in fighting recessions. Monetarists argued that fiscal policy was ineffective if the money supply was held constant. But that strong view has become relatively rare.

Most macroeconomists now agree that fiscal policy, like monetary policy, can shift the aggregate demand curve. Most macroeconomists also agree that the government should not seek to balance the budget regardless of the state of the economy: they agree that the role of the budget as an automatic stabilizer helps keep the economy on an even keel.

QUESTION 3: CAN MONETARY AND/OR FISCAL POLICY REDUCE UNEMPLOYMENT IN THE LONG RUN? Classical macroeconomists didn't believe the government could do anything about unemployment. Some Keynesian economists moved to the opposite extreme, arguing that expansionary policies could be used to achieve a permanently low unemployment rate, perhaps at the cost of some inflation. Monetarists believed that unemployment could not be kept below the natural rate.

Almost all macroeconomists now accept the natural rate hypothesis. This hypothesis leads them to accept sharp limits to what monetary and fiscal policy can accomplish. Effective monetary and fiscal policy, most macroeconomists believe, can limit the size of fluctuations of the actual unemployment rate around the natural rate, but they can't be used to keep unemployment below the natural rate.

QUESTION 4: SHOULD FISCAL POLICY BE USED IN A DISCRETIONARY WAY? As we've already seen, views about the effectiveness of fiscal policy have gone back and forth, from rejection by classical macroeconomists, to a positive view by Keynesian economists, to a negative view once again by monetarists. Today most macroeconomists believe that tax cuts and spending increases are at least somewhat effective in increasing aggregate demand.

Many, but not all, macroeconomists, however, believe that *discretionary fiscal policy* is usually counterproductive. They believe that the lags in adjusting fiscal policy mean that, all too often, policies intended to fight a slump end up intensifying a boom.

As a result, the macroeconomic consensus gives monetary policy the lead role in economic stabilization. Some, but not all, economists believe that fiscal policy must be brought back into the mix under special circumstances, in particular when interest rates are at or near the zero lower bound and the economy is in a liquidity trap. As we'll see shortly, the proper role of fiscal policy became a huge point of contention after 2008.

QUESTION 5: SHOULD MONETARY POLICY BE USED IN A DISCRETIONARY WAY? Classical macroeconomists didn't think that monetary policy should be used to fight recessions; Keynesian economists didn't oppose discretionary monetary policy, but they were skeptical about its effectiveness. Monetarists argued that discretionary monetary policy was doing more harm than good. Where are we today? This remains an area of dispute. Today, under the Great Moderation consensus, most macreconomists agree on these three points:

- Monetary policy should play the main role in stabilization policy.
- The central bank should be independent, insulated from political pressures, in order to avoid a political business cycle.
- Discretionary fiscal policy should be used sparingly, both because of policy lags and because of the risks of a political business cycle.

However, the Great Moderation was up-ended by events that posed very difficult questions. We'll now examine what happened and why the ongoing debate is so fierce.

Crisis and Aftermath

The Great Recession shattered any sense among macroeconomists that they had entered a permanent era of agreement over key policy questions. Given the nature of the slump, however, this should not have come as a surprise. Why? Because the severity of the slump arguably made the policies that seemed to work during the Great Moderation inadequate.

Under the Great Moderation consensus, there had been broad agreement that the job of stabilizing the economy was best carried out by having the Federal Reserve and its counterparts abroad raise or lower interest rates as the economic situation warranted. But what should be done if the economy is deeply depressed, but the interest rates the Fed normally controls are already close to zero and can go no lower (that is, when the economy is in a liquidity trap)? Some economists called for the aggressive use of discretionary fiscal policy and/or unconventional monetary policies that might achieve results despite the zero lower bound. Others strongly opposed these measures, arguing either that they would be ineffective or that they would produce undesirable side effects.

The Debate over Fiscal Policy

In 2009 a number of governments, including that of the United States, responded with expansionary fiscal policy, or "stimulus," generally taking the form of a mix of temporary spending measures and temporary tax cuts. From the start, however, these efforts were highly controversial.

Supporters of fiscal stimulus offered three main arguments for breaking with the normal presumption against discretionary fiscal policy:

1. They argued that discretionary fiscal expansion was needed because the usual tool for stabilizing the economy, monetary policy, could no longer be used now that interest rates were near zero.
2. They argued that one normal concern about expansionary fiscal policy—that deficit spending would drive up interest rates, crowding out private investment spending—was unlikely to be a problem in a depressed economy. Again, this was because interest rates were close to zero and likely to stay there as long as the economy was depressed.
3. Finally, they argued that another concern about discretionary fiscal policy—that it might take a long time to get going—was less of a concern than usual given the likelihood that the economy would be depressed for an extended period.

These arguments generally won the day in early 2009. However, opponents of fiscal stimulus raised two main objections:

1. They argued that households and firms would see any rise in government spending as a sign that tax burdens were likely to rise in the future, leading to a fall in private spending that would undo any positive effect. (As you will recall, this is the *Ricardian equivalence* argument.)
2. They also warned that spending programs might undermine investors' faith in the government's ability to repay its debts, leading to an increase in long-term interest rates despite loose monetary policy.

In fact, by 2010 a number of economists were arguing that the best way to boost the economy was actually to cut government spending, which they argued would increase private-sector confidence and lead to a rise in output and employment. This notion, often referred to as the doctrine of "expansionary austerity," was especially popular in Europe at the time.

One might have hoped that events would resolve this dispute. But the debate continues to rage today. At the time, critics of fiscal stimulus pointed out that the U.S. stimulus had failed to deliver a convincing fall in unemployment; stimulus advocates, however, had warned from the start that this was likely to happen because the stimulus was too small compared with the depth of the slump. Meanwhile, austerity programs in Britain and elsewhere had also failed to deliver an economic turnaround and, in fact, had seemed to deepen the slump; supporters of these programs, however, argued that they were nonetheless necessary to head off a potential collapse of confidence.

One thing that was clear, however, was that those who had predicted a sharp rise in U.S. interest rates due to budget deficits, leading to conventional crowding out, were wrong: by the fall of 2011, U.S. long-term rates were hitting record lows despite continuing large deficits. Interest rates remained low through 2013, even as the budget deficit declined.

In 2008, the Fed took a series of unconventional monetary policy actions in response to the deepening financial crisis.

AP Photo/Carolyn Kaster

The Debate over Monetary Policy

As we've seen, a central bank that wants to increase aggregate demand normally does this by buying short-term government debt, pushing short-term interest rates down and causing spending to rise. By the fall of 2008, however, this conventional form of monetary policy had already reached its limit because the relevant interest rates were close to zero. The question then became whether there were other things the Federal Reserve and other central banks could do.

In 2008–2009 and again in the fall of 2010, the Fed pursued one such alternative, known as *quantitative easing,* which involved buying assets other than short-term government debt, notably long-term debt whose interest rate was still significantly above zero. For example, in November 2010 the Fed began buying $600 billion worth of longer-term U.S. debt in a program generally referred to as "QE2" (quantitative easing 2). The idea was to drive down longer-term interest rates, which arguably matter more for private spending than short-term rates. In September 2011 the Fed announced another program that involved selling shorter-term assets with interest rates already near zero and buying longer-term assets instead.

The policy of quantitative easing was controversial, facing criticisms both from those who believed the Fed was doing too much and from those who believed it wasn't doing enough. Those who thought the Fed was doing too much were concerned about possible future inflation; they argued that the Fed would find its unconventional measures hard to reverse as the economy recovered and that the end result would be a much too expansionary monetary policy.

© Gahan Wilson The New York Collection www.cartoonbank.com

"I'll pause for a moment so you can let this information sink in."

Critics from the other side argued that the Fed's actions were likely to be ineffective: long-term interest rates, they suggested, mainly reflected expectations about future short-term rates, and even large purchases of long-term bonds by the Fed would have little impact.

Many of those calling for even more active policy advocated an official rise in the Fed's inflation target. Recall the distinction between the nominal interest rate, which is the number normally cited, and the *real* interest rate—the nominal rate minus expected inflation—which is what should matter for investment decisions. Advocates of a higher inflation target argued that by promising to raise prices over, say, the next 10 years by an annual average rate of 3% or 4%, the Fed could push the real interest rate down even though the nominal rate was up against the zero lower bound.

Such proposals, however, led to fierce disputes. Some economists pointed out that the Fed had fought hard to drive inflation expectations down and argued that changing course would undermine hard-won credibility. Others argued that given the enormous economic and human damage being done by high unemployment, it was time for extraordinary measures, and inflation-fighting could no longer be given first priority.

These same debates continue to rage today, and it seems unlikely that a new consensus about macroeconomic policy will emerge any time soon.

ECONOMICS IN ACTION

WORLD VIEW

AN IRISH ROLE MODEL?

Over the course of 2010 and 2011 a fierce debate raged, among both economists and policy makers, about whether countries suffering large budget deficits should move quickly to reduce those deficits if they were also suffering from high unemployment. Many economists argued that spending cuts and/or tax increases should be delayed until economies had recovered. As we explained in the text, however, others argued that fast action on deficits would actually help the economy even in the short run, by improving confidence—a claim that came to be known as *expansionary austerity.*

How could this dispute be settled? Researchers turned their attention to historical episodes, in particular to cases in which nations had managed to combine sharp reductions in budget deficits with strong economic growth. One case in particular became a major intellectual battleground: Ireland in the second half of the 1980s.

Panel (a) of Figure 84-1 shows why Ireland's experience drew attention. It compares Ireland's cyclically adjusted budget deficit as a percentage of GDP with its growth rate. Between 1986 and 1989 Ireland drastically reduced its underlying deficits with a combination of spending cuts and tax hikes, and the Irish economy's growth sharply accelerated. A number of observers suggested that nations facing large deficits in the aftermath of the 2008 financial crisis should seek to emulate that experience.

FIGURE 84-1 **Economic Indicators for Ireland**

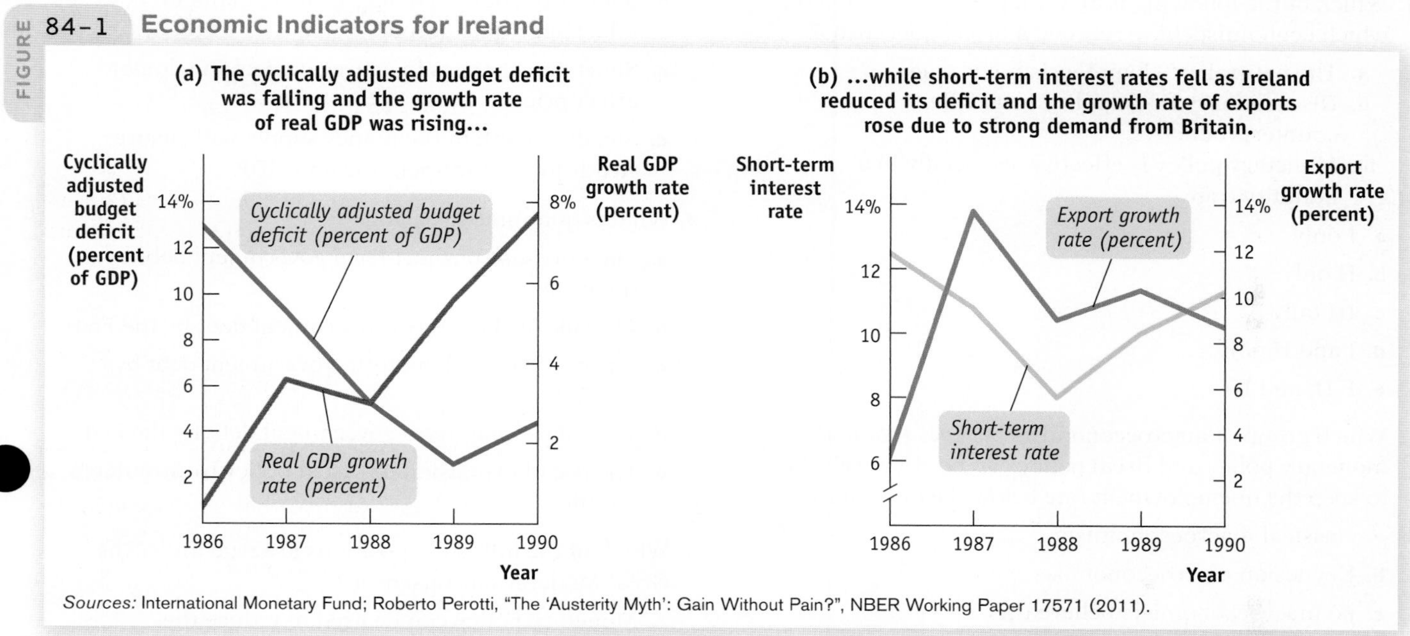

Sources: International Monetary Fund; Roberto Perotti, "The 'Austerity Myth': Gain Without Pain?", NBER Working Paper 17571 (2011).

A closer look, however, suggested that Ireland's situation in the 1980s was very different from that facing Western economies in 2010 and 2011. Panel (b) of Figure 84-1 shows two other economic indicators for Ireland from 1986 to 1990: short-term interest rates and export growth. Ireland entered into fiscal austerity with high interest rates, which fell sharply between 1986 and 1988 as investors gained more confidence in its solvency (although they rose thereafter).

At the same time, Ireland had a major export boom, partly due to rapid economic growth in neighboring Britain. Both factors helped offset any contractionary effects from lower spending and higher taxes.

The point was that these "cushioning" factors would not be available if, say, the United States were to slash spending. Short-term interest rates were already near zero and couldn't fall further, and America had no booming neighbors to export to.

By the end of 2011 careful study of the historical record convinced most, though not all, economists studying the issue that hopes for expansionary austerity were probably misplaced. However, the debate about what the United States and other troubled economies should do raged on.

MODULE 84 Review

Solutions appear at the back of the book.

Check Your Understanding

1. Why did the Great Recession lead to the decline of the Great Moderation consensus? Given events, why is it predictable that a new consensus has not emerged?

Multiple-Choice Questions

1. Which of the following is an example of an opinion on which economists have reached a broad consensus?
   - I. The natural rate hypothesis holds true.
   - II. Discretionary fiscal policy is usually counterproductive.
   - III. Monetary policy is effective, especially in a liquidity trap.

   a. I only
   b. II only
   c. III only
   d. I and II only
   e. I, II, and III

2. Which group of macroeconomists believes that both monetary policy and fiscal policy can be effectively used to keep the unemployment rate below the natural rate?

   a. classical macroeconomists
   b. Keynesian macroeconomists
   c. no macroeconomists believe this
   d. monetarists
   e. Keynesians and monetarists

3. Which of the following policy positions would a monetarist support?

   a. Fiscal policy cannot effectively fight a recession.
   b. Short-run changes in aggregate demand do not affect aggregate output.
   c. Short-run changes in aggregate demand do not affect prices.
   d. Steady growth in the money supply will ensure steady growth in spending and GDP.

4. What is quantitative easing?

   a. The purchase of short-term government debt by the Fed.
   b. The sale of short-term government debt by the Fed.
   c. The purchase of long-term government debt by the Fed.
   d. The sale of long-term government debt by the Fed.
   e. The use of expansionary fiscal policy to stimulate output.

5. Which of the following positions are true under the Great Moderation consensus?

   a. Monetary policy can be used to reduce the unemployment rate in the long run.
   b. Expansionary fiscal policy is not effective in fighting a recession.
   c. Monetary policy is effective in fighting a recession.
   d. Monetary policy and fiscal policy cannot effectively reduce unemployment in the short run.

Critical-Thinking Questions

1. What arguments were made in favor of using expansionary fiscal policy to help the U.S. economy recover from the Great Recession?

2. What arguments were made against the use of fiscal stimulus during the Great Recession?

SECTION 26 REVIEW

Summary

History and Alternative Views of Macroeconomics

1. Classical macroeconomics asserted that monetary policy affected only the aggregate price level, not aggregate output, and that the short run was unimportant. By the 1930s, measurement of business cycles was a well-established subject, but there was no widely accepted theory of business cycles.
2. Keynesian economics attributed the business cycle to shifts of the aggregate demand curve, often the result of changes in business confidence. Keynesian economics also offered a rationale for **macroeconomic policy activism.**
3. In the decades that followed Keynes's work, economists came to agree that monetary policy as well as fiscal policy is effective under certain conditions. **Monetarism,** a doctrine that called for a **monetary policy rule** as opposed to **discretionary monetary policy** and that argued—based on a belief that the **velocity of money** was stable—that GDP would grow steadily if the money supply grew steadily, was influential for a time but was eventually rejected by many macroeconomists.
4. The **natural rate hypothesis** became almost universally accepted, limiting the role of macroeconomic policy to stabilizing the economy rather than seeking a permanently lower unemployment rate. Fears of a **political business cycle** led to a consensus that monetary policy should be insulated from politics.
5. **Rational expectations** claims that individuals and firms make decisions using all available information and only unexpected changes in monetary policy affect aggregate output and employment; expected changes merely alter the price level. **Real business cycle theory** claims that changes in the rate of growth of total factor productivity are the main cause of business cycles. Both of these versions of **new classical macroeconomics** received wide attention and respect, but policy makers and many economists haven't accepted the conclusion that monetary and fiscal policy are ineffective in changing aggregate output.
6. **New Keynesian economics** argues that market imperfections can lead to price stickiness, so that changes in aggregate demand have effects on aggregate output after all.

The Modern Macroeconomic Consensus

7. The **Great Moderation** from 1985 to 2007 generated the **Great Moderation consensus:** belief in monetary policy as the main tool of stabilization; skepticism toward use of fiscal policy, except possibly in exceptional circumstances such as a liquidity trap; and acknowledgement of the policy constraints imposed by the natural rate of unemployment and the political business cycle. But the Great Moderation consensus was challenged by the post-2008 crisis events, as monetary policy lost its effectiveness in the midst of a liquidity trap. As a result, many advocated the use of fiscal policy to address the deep recession.
8. In 2009, a number of governments, including the United States, used fiscal stimulus to support their deeply depressed economies in the face of a liquidity trap. The use of fiscal policy remained highly controversial. In the United States, it failed to significantly reduce unemployment, with critics citing that as proof of its general ineffectiveness, while supporters argued the size of the stimulus was too small. Yet the crowding out predicted by its critics failed to occur.
9. Monetary policy was also hotly debated in the wake of the Great Recession, as the Fed pursued "quantitative easing" and other unconventional monetary policies to address the liquidity trap. Critics claimed the Fed was doing too much and would sacrifice its hard-won credibility as an inflation fighter. Others countered that the Fed was doing too little, yet others claimed the Fed's actions would have little impact. Some proposed the Fed adopt a higher inflation target to push the real interest rate down.

Key Terms

Macroeconomic policy activism, p. 865
Monetarism, p. 866
Discretionary monetary policy, p. 867
Monetary policy rule, p. 868
Quantity Theory of Money, p. 868
Velocity of money, p. 868
Natural rate hypothesis, p. 869
Political business cycle, p. 870
New classical macroeconomics, p. 870
Rational expectations, p. 870
New Keynesian economics, p. 871
Real business cycle theory, p. 871
Great Moderation, p. 874
Great Moderation consensus, p. 874

Problems

1. After the crash of its stock market in 1989, the Japanese economy saw little economic growth and some deflation. The accompanying table from the Organization for Economic Co-operation and Development (OECD) shows some key macroeconomic data for Japan for 1991 (a "normal" year) and 1995–2003.

   a. From the data, determine the type of policies Japan's policy makers undertook at that time to promote growth.

   b. We can safely consider a short-term interest rate that is less than 0.1% to effectively be a 0% interest rate. What is this situation called? What does it imply about the effectiveness of monetary policy? Of fiscal policy?

Year	Real GDP annual growth rate	Short-term interest rate	Government debt (percent of GDP)	Government budget deficit (percent of GDP)
1991	3.4%	7.38%	64.8%	−1.81%
1995	1.9	1.23	87.1	4.71
1996	3.4	0.59	93.9	5.07
1997	1.9	0.60	100.3	3.79
1998	−1.1	0.72	112.2	5.51
1999	0.1	0.25	125.7	7.23
2000	2.8	0.25	134.1	7.48
2001	0.4	0.12	142.3	6.13
2002	−0.3	0.06	149.3	7.88
2003	2.5	0.04	157.5	7.67

2. The National Bureau of Economic Research (NBER) maintains the official chronology of past U.S. business cycles. Go to its website at http://www.nber.org/cycles/cyclesmain.html to answer the following questions.

   a. How many business cycles have occurred since the end of World War II in 1945?

   b. What was the average duration of a business cycle when measured from the end of one expansion (its peak) to the end of the next? That is, what was the average duration of a business cycle in the period from 1945 to 2001?

   c. When was the last announcement by the NBER's Business Cycle Dating Committee, and what was it?

3. The fall of America's military rival, the Soviet Union, in 1989 allowed the United States to significantly reduce its defense spending in subsequent years. Using the data in the following table from the Economic Report of the President, replicate Figure 83-2 for the 1990–2000 period. Given the strong economic growth in the United States during the late 1990s, why would a Keynesian see the reduction in defense spending during the 1990s as a good thing?

Year	Budget deficit (percent of GDP)	Unemployment rate
1990	3.9%	5.6%
1991	4.5	6.8
1992	4.7	7.5
1993	3.9	6.9
1994	2.9	6.1
1995	2.2	5.6
1996	1.4	5.4
1997	0.3	4.9
1998	−0.8	4.5
1999	−1.4	4.2
2000	−2.4	4.0

4. In the modern world, central banks are free to increase or reduce the money supply as they see fit. However, some people harken back to the "good old days" of the gold standard. Under the gold standard, the money supply could expand only when the amount of available gold increased.

   a. Under the gold standard, if the velocity of money were stable when the economy was expanding, what would have had to happen to keep prices stable?

   b. Why would modern macroeconomists consider the gold standard a bad idea?

5. Monetarists believed for a period of time that the velocity of money was stable within a country. However, with financial innovation, the velocity began shifting around erratically after 1980. As would be expected, the velocity of money is different across countries depending upon the sophistication of their financial systems—velocity of money tends to be higher in countries with developed financial systems. The accompanying table provides an example of a single year's money supply and GDP information for six countries.

Country	National currency	M1 (billions in national currency)	Nominal GDP (billions in national currency)
Egypt	Egyptian pounds	101	539
South Korea	Korean won	77,274	806,622
Thailand	Thai baht	863	7,103
United States	U.S. dollars	1,369	12,456
Kenya	Kenyan pounds	231	1,415
India	Indian rupees	7,213	35,314

Source: Datastream.

   a. Calculate the velocity of money for each of the countries. The accompanying table shows an example of a single year's GDP per capita data for each of these countries in U.S. dollars.

Country	Nominal GDP per capita (U.S. dollars)
Egypt	$1,270
South Korea	16,444
Thailand	2,707
United States	41,886
Kenya	572
India	710

Source: IMF.

b. Rank the countries in descending order of per capita income and velocity of money. Do wealthy countries or poor countries tend to "turn over" their money more times per year? Would you expect wealthy countries to have more sophisticated financial systems?

6. Kenneth Rogoff proclaimed Richard Nixon "the all-time hero of political business cycles." Using the following table of data from the Economic Report of the President, explain why Nixon may have earned that title. (*Note:* Nixon entered office in January 1969 and was reelected in November 1972. He resigned in August 1974.)

Year	Government receipts (billions of dollars)	Government spending (billions of dollars)	Government budget balance (billions of dollars)	M1 growth	M2 growth	3-month Treasury bill rate
1969	$186.9	$183.6	$3.2	3.3%	3.7%	6.68%
1970	192.8	195.6	−2.8	5.1	6.6	6.46
1971	187.1	210.2	−23.0	6.5	13.4	4.35
1972	207.3	230.7	−23.4	9.2	13.0	4.07
1973	230.8	245.7	−14.9	5.5	6.6	7.04

7. The economy of Albernia is facing a recessionary gap, and the leader of that nation calls together five of its best economists representing the classical, Keynesian, monetarist, real business cycle, and Great Moderation consensus views of the macroeconomy. Explain what policies each economist would recommend and why.

8. Which of the following policy recommendations are consistent with the classical, Keynesian, monetarist, and/or Great Moderation consensus views of the macroeconomy?

a. Since the long-run growth of GDP is 2%, the money supply should grow at 2%.

b. Decrease government spending in order to decrease inflationary pressure.

c. Increase the money supply in order to alleviate a recessionary gap.

d. Always maintain a balanced budget.

e. Decrease the budget deficit as a percent of GDP when facing a recessionary gap.

9. Using a graph like Figure 83-3, show how a monetarist can argue that a contractionary fiscal policy need not lead to a fall in real GDP given a fixed money supply. Explain.

APPENDIX A Graphs in Economics

Whether you're reading about economics in the news or in your economics textbook, you will see many graphs. Visual presentations can make it easier to understand verbal descriptions, numerical information, or ideas. In economics, graphs are used to facilitate understanding. But to get the full benefit from these visual aids, you need to know how to interpret them. This appendix explains how graphs are constructed, interpreted, and used in economics.

Graphs, Variables, and Economic Models

If you were reading an article about the relationship between educational attainment and income, you would probably see a graph showing the income levels for workers with different levels of education. This graph would depict the idea that, in general, having more education increases a person's income. This graph, like most graphs in economics, would depict the relationship between two economic variables. A **variable** is a quantity that can take on more than one value, such as the number of years of education a person has, the price of a can of soda, or a household's income.

Earlier we discussed how economic analysis relies heavily on *models,* simplified descriptions of real situations. Most economic models describe the relationship between two variables, simplified by holding constant other variables that may affect the relationship. For example, an economic model might describe the relationship between the price of a can of soda and the number of cans of soda that consumers will buy, assuming that everything else that affects consumers' purchases of soda stays constant. This type of model can be described mathematically or verbally, but illustrating the relationship in a graph makes it easier to understand. Next we show how graphs that depict economic models are constructed and interpreted.

How Graphs Work

Most graphs in economics are based on a grid built around two perpendicular lines that show the values of two variables, helping you visualize the relationship between them. So a first step in understanding the use of such graphs is to see how this system works.

Two-Variable Graphs

Figure A-1 shows a typical two-variable graph. It illustrates the data in the accompanying table on outside temperature and the number of sodas a typical vendor can expect to sell at a baseball stadium during one game. The first column shows the values of outside temperature (the first variable) and the second column shows the values of the number of sodas sold (the second variable). Five combinations or pairs of the two variables are shown, denoted by points *A* through *E* in the third column.

Now let's turn to graphing the data in this table. In any two-variable graph, one variable is called the *x*-variable and the other is called the *y*-variable. Here we have made outside temperature the *x*-variable and number of sodas sold the *y*-variable.

The solid horizontal line in the graph is called the **horizontal axis** or ***x*-axis,** and values of the *x*-variable—outside temperature—are measured along it. Similarly, the solid vertical line in the graph is called the **vertical axis** or ***y*-axis,** and values of the *y*-variable—number of sodas sold—are measured along it. At the **origin,** the point where the two axes meet, each variable is equal to zero. As you move rightward from the origin along the *x*-axis, values of the *x*-variable are positive and increasing. As

A quantity that can take on more than one value is called a **variable**.

The line along which values of the x-variable are measured is called the **horizontal axis** or ***x*-axis**. The line along which values of the y-variable are measured is called the **vertical axis** or ***y*-axis**. The point where the axes of a two-variable graph meet is the **origin**.

FIGURE A-1 Plotting Points on a Two-Variable Graph

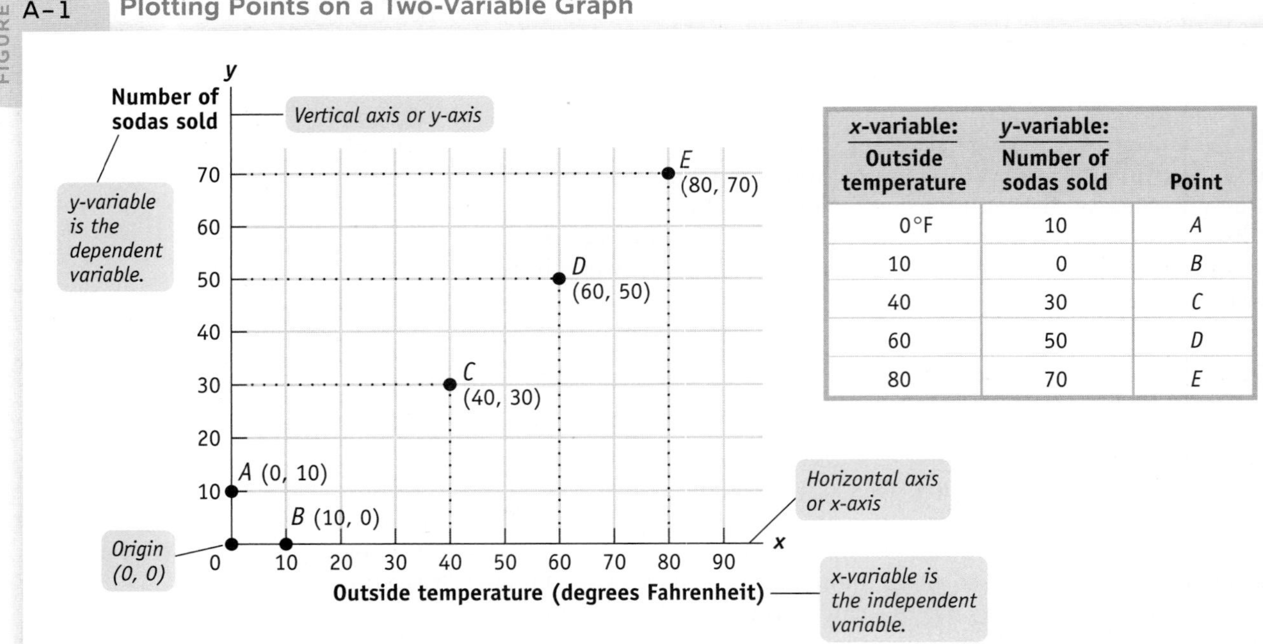

x-variable: Outside temperature	y-variable: Number of sodas sold	Point
0°F	10	*A*
10	0	*B*
40	30	*C*
60	50	*D*
80	70	*E*

The data from the table are plotted where outside temperature (the independent variable) is measured along the horizontal axis and number of sodas sold (the dependent variable) is measured along the vertical axis. Each of the five combinations of temperature and sodas sold is represented by a point: *A*, *B*, *C*, *D*, and *E*. Each point in the graph is identified by a pair of values. For example, point *C* corresponds to the pair (40, 30)—an outside temperature of 40°F (the value of the *x*-variable) and 30 sodas sold (the value of the *y*-variable).

you move up from the origin along the *y*-axis, values of the *y*-variable are positive and increasing.

You can plot each of the five points *A* through *E* on this graph by using a pair of numbers—the values that the *x*-variable and the *y*-variable take on for a given point. In Figure A-1, at point *C*, the *x*-variable takes on the value 40 and the *y*-variable takes on the value 30. You plot point *C* by drawing a line straight up from 40 on the *x*-axis and a horizontal line across from 30 on the *y*-axis. We write point *C* as (40, 30). We write the origin as (0, 0).

Looking at point *A* and point *B* in Figure A-1, you can see that when one of the variables for a point has a value of zero, it will lie on one of the axes. If the value of the *x*-variable is zero, the point will lie on the vertical axis, like point *A*. If the value of the *y*-variable is zero, the point will lie on the horizontal axis, like point *B*.

Most graphs that depict relationships between two economic variables represent a **causal relationship,** a relationship in which the value taken by one variable directly influences or determines the value taken by the other variable. In a causal relationship, the determining variable is called the **independent variable;** the variable it determines is called the **dependent variable.** In our example of soda sales, the outside temperature is the independent variable. It directly influences the number of sodas that are sold, which is the dependent variable in this case.

A **causal relationship** exists between two variables when the value taken by one variable directly influences or determines the value taken by the other variable. In a causal relationship, the determining variable is called the **independent variable;** the variable it determines is called the **dependent variable.**

By convention, we put the independent variable on the horizontal axis and the dependent variable on the vertical axis. Figure A-1 follows this convention: the independent variable (outside temperature) is on the horizontal axis and the dependent variable (number of sodas sold) is on the vertical axis.

An important exception to this convention is in graphs showing the economic relationship between the price of a product and quantity of the product: although price is generally the independent variable that determines quantity, it is always measured on the vertical axis.

Curves on a Graph

Panel (a) of Figure A-2 contains some of the same information as Figure A-1, with a line drawn through the points *B, C, D,* and *E*. Such a line on a graph is called a **curve,** regardless of whether it is a straight line or a curved line. If the curve that shows the relationship between two variables is a straight line, or linear, the variables have a **linear relationship.** When the curve is not a straight line, or nonlinear, the variables have a **nonlinear relationship.**

A **curve** is a line on a graph that depicts a relationship between two variables. It may be either a straight line or a curved line. If the curve is a straight line, the variables have a **linear relationship**. If the curve is not a straight line, the variables have a **nonlinear relationship**.

A point on a curve indicates the value of the *y*-variable for a specific value of the *x*-variable. For example, point *D* indicates that at a temperature of 60°F, a vendor can expect to sell 50 sodas. The shape and orientation of a curve reveal the general nature of the relationship between the two variables. The upward tilt of the curve in panel (a) of Figure A-2 suggests that vendors can expect to sell more sodas at higher outside temperatures.

When variables are related in this way—that is, when an increase in one variable is associated with an increase in the other variable—the variables are said to have a **positive relationship.** It is illustrated by a curve that slopes upward from left to right. Because this curve is also linear, the relationship between outside temperature and number of sodas sold illustrated by the curve in panel (a) of Figure A-2 is a positive linear relationship.

Two variables have a **positive relationship** when an increase in the value of one variable is associated with an increase in the value of the other variable. It is illustrated by a curve that slopes upward from left to right.

When an increase in one variable is associated with a decrease in the other variable, the two variables are said to have a **negative relationship.** It is illustrated by a curve that slopes downward from left to right, like the curve in panel (b) of Figure A-2. Because this curve is also linear, the relationship it depicts is a negative linear relationship. Two variables that might have such a relationship are the outside temperature and the number of hot drinks a vendor can expect to sell at a baseball stadium.

Two variables have a **negative relationship** when an increase in the value of one variable is associated with a decrease in the value of the other variable. It is illustrated by a curve that slopes downward from left to right.

FIGURE A-2 Drawing Curves

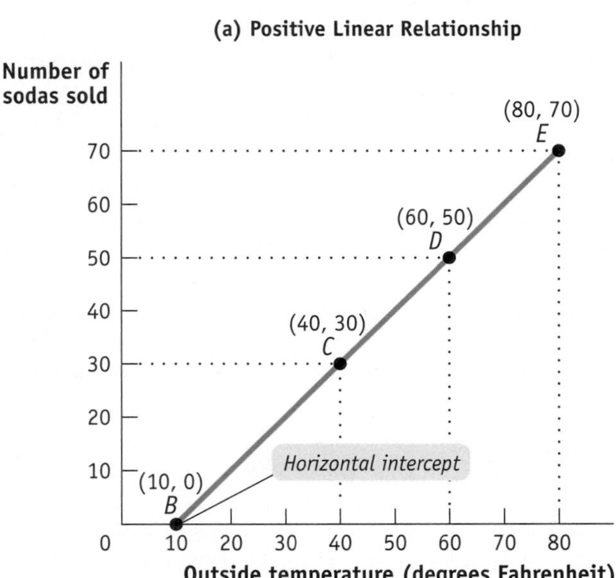

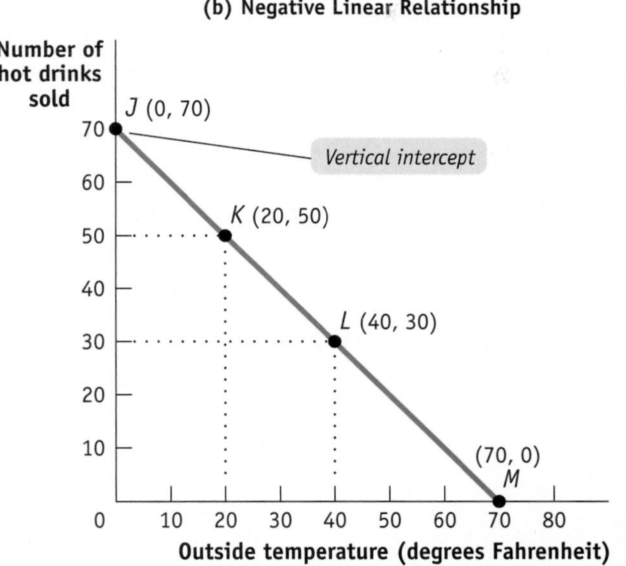

The curve in panel (a) illustrates the relationship between the two variables, outside temperature and number of sodas sold. The two variables have a positive linear relationship: positive because the curve has an upward tilt, and linear because it is a straight line. The curve implies that an increase in the *x*-variable (outside temperature) leads to an increase in the *y*-variable (number of sodas sold). The curve in panel (b) is also a straight line, but it tilts downward. The two variables here, outside temperature and number of hot drinks sold, have a negative linear relationship: an increase in the *x*-variable (outside temperature) leads to a decrease in the *y*-variable (number of hot drinks sold). The curve in panel (a) has a horizontal intercept at point *B*, where it hits the horizontal axis. The curve in panel (b) has a vertical intercept at point *J*, where it hits the vertical axis, and a horizontal intercept at point *M*, where it hits the horizontal axis.

The **horizontal intercept** of a curve is the point at which it hits the horizontal axis; it indicates the value of the x-variable when the value of the y-variable is zero.

The **vertical intercept** of a curve is the point at which it hits the vertical axis; it shows the value of the y-variable when the value of the x-variable is zero. The slope of a line or curve is a measure of how steep it is.

The **slope** of a line is measured by "rise over run"—the change in the y-variable between two points on the line divided by the change in the x-variable between those same two points.

Return for a moment to the curve in panel (a) of Figure A-2, and you can see that it hits the horizontal axis at point B. This point, known as the **horizontal intercept,** shows the value of the x-variable when the value of the y-variable is zero. In panel (b) of Figure A-2, the curve hits the vertical axis at point J. This point, called the **vertical intercept,** indicates the value of the y-variable when the value of the x-variable is zero.

A Key Concept: The Slope of a Curve

The **slope** of a curve is a measure of how steep it is; the slope indicates how sensitive the y-variable is to a change in the x-variable. In our example of outside temperature and the number of cans of soda a vendor can expect to sell, the slope of the curve would indicate how many more cans of soda the vendor could expect to sell with each 1° increase in temperature. Interpreted this way, the slope gives meaningful information.

Even without numbers for x and y, it is possible to arrive at important conclusions about the relationship between the two variables by examining the slope of a curve at various points.

The Slope of a Linear Curve

Along a linear curve the slope, or steepness, is measured by dividing the "rise" between two points on the curve by the "run" between those same two points. The rise is the amount that y changes, and the run is the amount that x changes. Here is the formula:

$$\frac{\text{Change in } y}{\text{Change in } x} = \frac{\Delta y}{\Delta x} = \text{Slope}$$

In the formula, the symbol Δ (the Greek uppercase delta) stands for "change in." When a variable increases, the change in that variable is positive; when a variable decreases, the change in that variable is negative.

The slope of a curve is positive when the rise (the change in the y-variable) has the same sign as the run (the change in the x-variable). That's because when two numbers have the same sign, the ratio of those two numbers is positive.

The curve in panel (a) of Figure A-2 has a positive slope: along the curve, both the y-variable and the x-variable increase. The slope of a curve is negative when the rise and the run have different signs. That's because when two numbers have different signs, the ratio of those two numbers is negative. The curve in panel (b) of Figure A-2 has a negative slope: along the curve, an increase in the x-variable is associated with a decrease in the y-variable.

Figure A-3 illustrates how to calculate the slope of a linear curve. Let's focus first on panel (a). From point A to point B the value of the y-variable changes from 25 to 20 and the value of the x-variable changes from 10 to 20. So the slope of the line between these two points is

$$\frac{\text{Change in } y}{\text{Change in } x} = \frac{\Delta y}{\Delta x} = \frac{-5}{10} = -\frac{1}{2} = -0.5$$

Because a straight line is equally steep at all points, the slope of a straight line is the same at all points. In other words, a straight line has a constant slope. You can check this by calculating the slope of the linear curve between points A and B and between points C and D in panel (b) of Figure A-3.

$$\frac{\Delta y}{\Delta x} = \frac{10}{2} = 5$$

$$\frac{\Delta y}{\Delta x} = \frac{20}{4} = 5$$

FIGURE A-3 Calculating the Slope

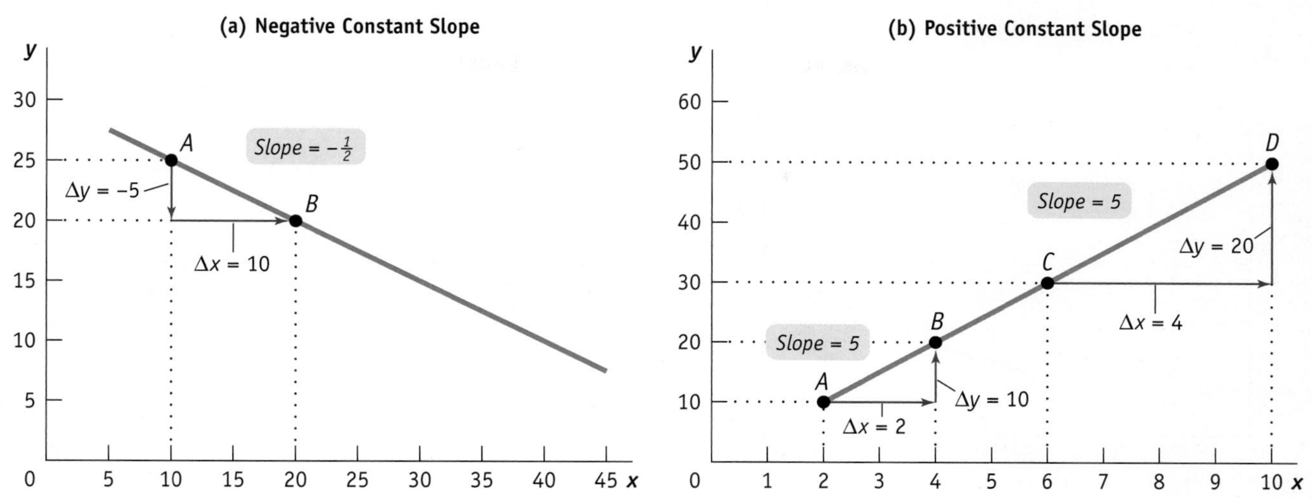

Panels (a) and (b) show two linear curves. Between points *A* and *B* on the curve in panel (a), the change in *y* (the rise) is −5 and the change in *x* (the run) is 10. So the slope from *A* to *B* is $\frac{\Delta y}{\Delta x} = \frac{-5}{10} = -\frac{1}{2} = -0.5$, where the negative sign indicates that the curve is downward sloping. In panel (b), the curve has a slope from *A* to *B* of $\frac{\Delta y}{\Delta x} = \frac{10}{2} = 5$. The slope from *C* to *D* is $\frac{\Delta y}{\Delta x} = \frac{20}{4} = 5$. The slope is positive, indicating that the curve is upward sloping. Furthermore, the slope between *A* and *B* is the same as the slope between *C* and *D*, making this a linear curve. The slope of a linear curve is constant: it is the same regardless of where it is calculated along the curve.

Horizontal and Vertical Curves and Their Slopes

When a curve is horizontal, the value of *y* along that curve never changes—it is constant. Everywhere along the curve, the change in *y* is zero. Now, zero divided by any number is zero. So regardless of the value of the change in *x*, the slope of a horizontal curve is always zero.

If a curve is vertical, the value of *x* along the curve never changes—it is constant. Everywhere along the curve, the change in *x* is zero. This means that the slope of a vertical line is a ratio with zero in the denominator. A ratio with zero in the denominator is equal to infinity—that is, an infinitely large number. So the slope of a vertical line is equal to infinity.

A vertical or a horizontal curve has a special implication: it means that the *x*-variable and the *y*-variable are unrelated. Two variables are unrelated when a change in one variable (the independent variable) has no effect on the other variable (the dependent variable). To put it a slightly different way, two variables are unrelated when the dependent variable is constant regardless of the value of the independent variable. If, as is usual, the *y*-variable is the dependent variable, the curve is horizontal. If the dependent variable is the *x*-variable, the curve is vertical.

The Slope of a Nonlinear Curve

A **nonlinear curve** is one in which the slope changes as you move along it. Panels (a), (b), (c), and (d) of Figure A-4 show various nonlinear curves. Panels (a) and (b) show nonlinear curves whose slopes change as you follow the line's progression, but the slopes always remain positive.

Although both curves tilt upward, the curve in panel (a) gets steeper as the line moves from left to right in contrast to the curve in panel (b), which gets flatter. A

A **nonlinear curve** is one in which the slope is not the same between every pair of points.

FIGURE A-4 Nonlinear Curves

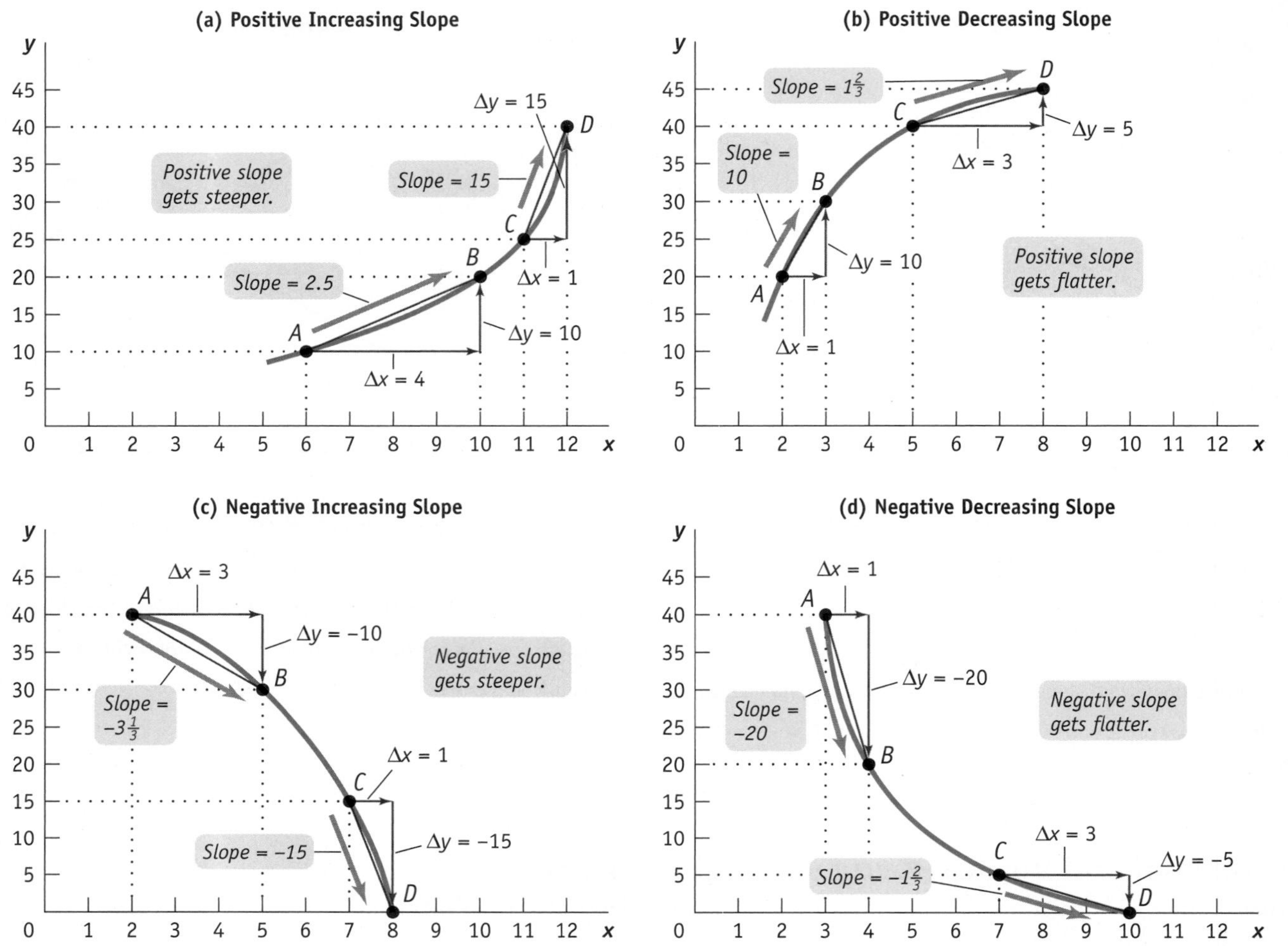

In panel (a) the slope of the curve from *A* to *B* is $\frac{\Delta y}{\Delta x} = \frac{10}{4} = 2.5$, and from *C* to *D* it is $\frac{\Delta y}{\Delta x} = \frac{15}{1} = 15$. The slope is positive and increasing; it gets steeper as it moves to the right. In panel (b) the slope of the curve from *A* to *B* is $\frac{\Delta y}{\Delta x} = \frac{10}{1} = 10$, and from *C* to *D* it is $\frac{\Delta y}{\Delta x} = \frac{5}{3} = 1\frac{2}{3}$. The slope is positive and decreasing; it gets flatter as it moves to the right. In panel (c) the slope from *A* to *B* is $\frac{\Delta y}{\Delta x} = \frac{-10}{3} = -3\frac{1}{3}$, and from *C* to *D* it is $\frac{\Delta y}{\Delta x} = \frac{-15}{1} = -15$. The slope is negative and increasing; it gets steeper as it moves to the right. And in panel (d) the slope from *A* to *B* is $\frac{\Delta y}{\Delta x} = \frac{-20}{1} = -20$, and from *C* to *D* it is $\frac{\Delta y}{\Delta x} = \frac{-5}{3} = -1\frac{2}{3}$. The slope is negative and decreasing; it gets flatter as it moves to the right.

The slope in each case has been calculated by using the *arc method*—that is, by drawing a straight line connecting two points along a curve. The average slope between those two points is equal to the slope of the straight line between those two points.

curve that is upward sloping and gets steeper, as in panel (a), is said to have *positive increasing* slope. A curve that is upward sloping but gets flatter, as in panel (b), is said to have *positive decreasing* slope.

When we calculate the slope along these nonlinear curves, we obtain different values for the slope at different points. How the slope changes along the curve determines the curve's shape. For example, in panel (a) of Figure A-4, the slope of the curve is a positive number that steadily increases as the line moves from left to right, whereas in panel (b), the slope is a positive number that steadily decreases.

ABSOLUTE VALUE The slopes of the curves in panels (c) and (d) are negative numbers. Economists often prefer to express a negative number as its **absolute value,** which is the value of the negative number without the minus sign.

In general, we denote the absolute value of a number by two parallel bars around the number; for example, the absolute value of −4 is written as |−4| = 4. In panel (c), the absolute value of the slope steadily increases as the line moves from left to right. The curve therefore has *negative increasing* slope. And in panel (d), the absolute value of the slope of the curve steadily decreases along the curve. This curve therefore has *negative decreasing* slope.

The **absolute value** of a negative number is the value of the negative number without the minus sign.

A nonlinear curve may have a **maximum** point, the highest point along the curve. At the maximum, the slope of the curve changes from positive to negative.

A nonlinear curve may have a **minimum** point, the lowest point along the curve. At the minimum, the slope of the curve changes from negative to positive.

Maximum and Minimum Points

The slope of a nonlinear curve can change from positive to negative or vice versa. When the slope of a curve changes from positive to negative, it creates what is called a *maximum* point of the curve. When the slope of a curve changes from negative to positive, it creates a *minimum* point.

Panel (a) of Figure A-5 illustrates a curve in which the slope changes from positive to negative as the line moves from left to right. When x is between 0 and 50, the slope of the curve is positive. At x equal to 50, the curve attains its highest point—the largest value of y along the curve. This point is called the **maximum** of the curve. When x exceeds 50, the slope becomes negative as the curve turns downward. Many important curves in economics, such as the curve that represents how the profit of a firm changes as it produces more output, are hill-shaped like this one.

FIGURE A-5 Maximum and Minimum Points

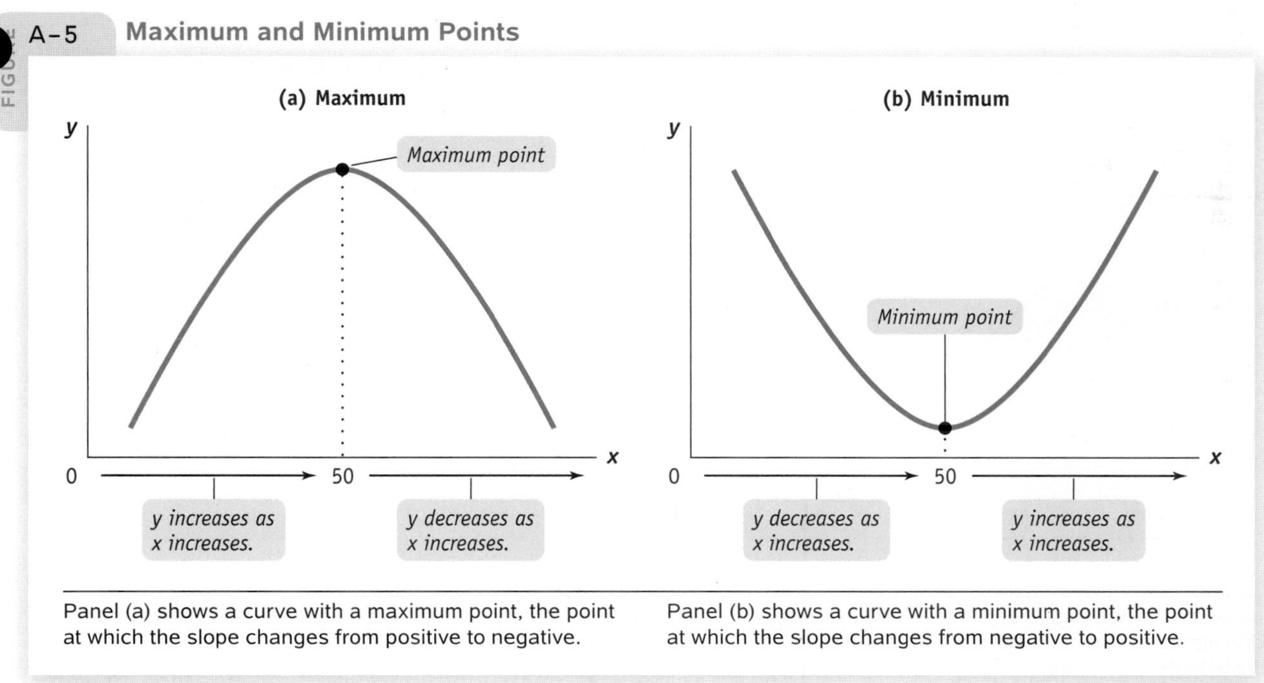

Panel (a) shows a curve with a maximum point, the point at which the slope changes from positive to negative.

Panel (b) shows a curve with a minimum point, the point at which the slope changes from negative to positive.

In contrast, the curve shown in panel (b) of Figure A-5 is U-shaped: it has a slope that changes from negative to positive. At x equal to 50, the curve reaches its lowest point—the smallest value of y along the curve. This point is called the **minimum** of the curve. Various important curves in economics, such as the curve that represents how a firm's cost per unit changes as output increases, are U-shaped like this one.

A **time-series graph** has dates on the horizontal axis and values of a variable that occurred on those dates on the vertical axis.

A **scatter diagram** shows points that correspond to actual observations of the *x*- and *y*-variables. A curve is usually fitted to the scatter of points.

Calculating the Area Below or Above a Curve

Sometimes it is useful to be able to measure the size of the area below or above a curve. To keep things simple, we'll only calculate the area below or above a linear curve.

How large is the shaded area below the linear curve in panel (a) of Figure A-6? First, note that this area has the shape of a right triangle. A *right triangle* is a triangle in which two adjacent sides form a 90° angle. We will refer to one of these sides as the *height* of the triangle and the other side as the *base* of the triangle. For our purposes, it doesn't matter which of these two sides we refer to as the base and which as the height.

Calculating the area of a right triangle is straightforward: multiply the height of the triangle by the base of the triangle, and divide the result by 2. The height of the triangle in panel (a) of Figure A-6 is 10 – 4 = 6. And the base of the triangle is 3 – 0 = 3. So the area of that triangle is

$$\frac{6 \times 3}{2} = 9$$

How about the shaded area above the linear curve in panel (b) of Figure A-6? We can use the same formula to calculate the area of this right triangle. The height of the triangle is 8 – 2 = 6. And the base of the triangle is 4 – 0 = 4. So the area of that triangle is

$$\frac{6 \times 4}{2} = 12$$

FIGURE A-6 Calculating the Area Below and Above a Linear Curve

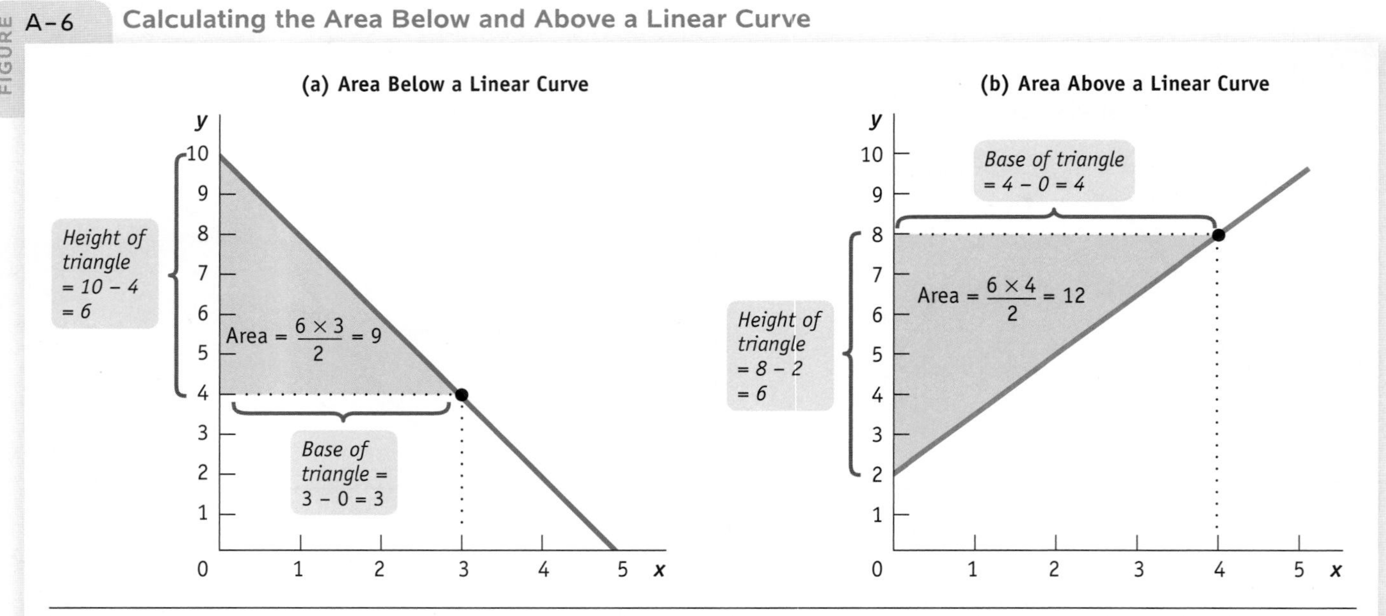

The area below or above a linear curve forms a right triangle. The area of a right triangle is calculated by multiplying the height of the triangle by the base of the triangle, and dividing the result by 2. In panel (a) the area of the shaded triangle is 9. In panel (b) the area of the shaded triangle is 12.

Graphs That Depict Numerical Information

Graphs are also used as a convenient way to summarize and display data without assuming some underlying causal relationship. Graphs that simply display numerical information are called *numerical graphs*.

Here we will consider the four most widely used types of numerical graphs: *time-series graphs, scatter diagrams, pie charts,* and *bar graphs.* These graphs are used to display real, empirical data about different economic variables and help economists and policy makers identify patterns or trends in the economy.

TIME-SERIES GRAPH You have probably seen graphs that show what happens over time to economic variables such as the unemployment rate or stock prices. A **time-series graph** has successive dates on the horizontal axis and the values of a variable that occurred on those dates on the vertical axis. For example, Figure A-7 shows real gross domestic product (GDP) per capita—a rough measure of a country's standard of living—in the United States from 1947 to late 2010. A line connecting the points that correspond to real GDP per capita for each calendar quarter during those years gives a clear idea of the overall trend in the standard of living over these years.

FIGURE A-7 Time-Series Graph

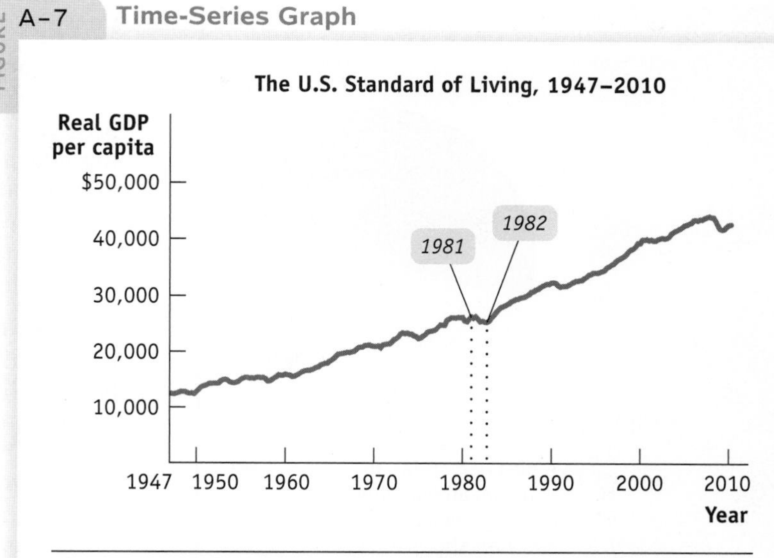

Time-series graphs show successive dates on the *x*-axis and values for a variable on the *y*-axis. This time-series graph shows real gross domestic product per capita, a measure of a country's standard of living, in the United States from 1947 to late 2010.

Source: Bureau of Economic Analysis.

SCATTER DIAGRAM Figure A-8 is an example of a different kind of numerical graph. It represents information from a sample of 184 countries on the standard of living, measured by GDP per capita, and the amount of carbon emissions per capita, a measure of environmental pollution. This type of graph is a **scatter diagram.** In these graphs, each point corresponds to an actual observation of the *x*-variable and the *y*-variable. Typically, a curve is fitted to the scatter of points; that is, a curve is drawn to approximate, as closely as possible, the general relationship between the variables. Each point in Figure A-8 indicates an average resident's standard of living and his or her annual carbon emissions for a given country.

The points lying in the upper right of the graph, which show combinations of a high standard of living and high carbon emissions, represent economically advanced countries such as the United States. (The country with the highest carbon emissions, at the top of the graph, is Qatar.) Points lying in the bottom left of the graph, which show combinations of a low standard of living and low carbon emissions, represent economically less advanced countries such as Afghanistan and Sierra Leone.

The pattern of points indicates that there is a positive relationship between living standard and carbon emissions per capita:

FIGURE A-8 Scatter Diagram

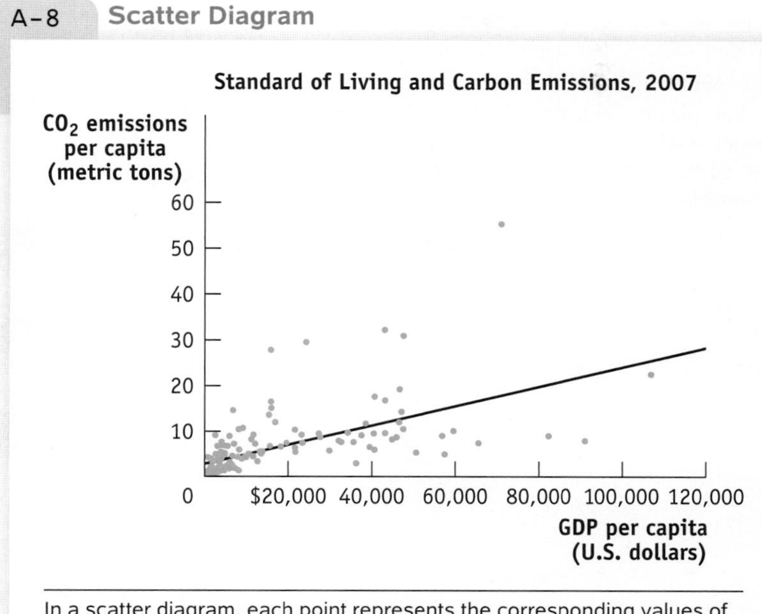

In a scatter diagram, each point represents the corresponding values of the *x*- and *y*-variables for a given observation. Here, each point indicates the GDP per capita and the amount of carbon emissions per capita for a given country for a sample of 184 countries. The upward-sloping fitted line here is the best approximation of the general relationship between the two variables.

Source: World Bank.

FIGURE A-9 Pie Chart

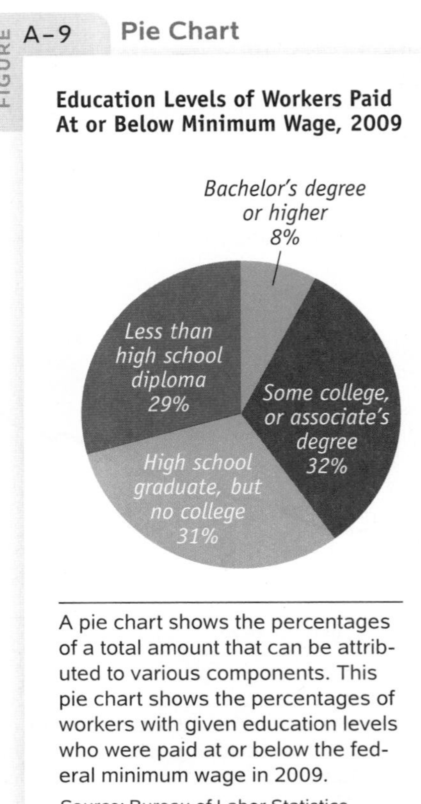

A pie chart shows the percentages of a total amount that can be attributed to various components. This pie chart shows the percentages of workers with given education levels who were paid at or below the federal minimum wage in 2009.

Source: Bureau of Labor Statistics.

on the whole, people create more pollution in countries with a higher standard of living. As you can see, the fitted line in Figure A-8 is upward sloping, indicating the underlying positive relationship between the two variables.

Scatter diagrams are often used to show how a general relationship can be inferred from a set of data.

PIE CHART A **pie chart** shows the share of a total amount that is accounted for by various components, usually expressed in percentages. Figure A-9 is a pie chart that depicts the education levels of workers who in 2009 were paid the federal minimum wage or less. As you can see, the majority of workers paid at or below the minimum wage had no college degree. Only 8% of workers who were paid at or below the minimum wage had a bachelor's degree or higher.

BAR GRAPH A graph that uses bars of various heights or lengths to indicate values of a variable is a **bar graph**. In the bar graph in Figure A-10, the bars show the percent change in the number of unemployed workers in the United States from 2009 to 2010, separately for White, Black or African-American, and Asian workers. Exact values of the variable that is being measured may be written at the end of the bar, as in this figure. For instance, the number of unemployed Black or African-American workers in the United States increased by 9.4% between 2009 and 2010. But even without the precise values, comparing the heights or lengths of the bars can give useful insight into the relative magnitudes of the different values of the variable.

A pie chart shows how some total is divided among its components, usually expressed in percentages.

A bar graph uses bars of varying height or length to show the comparative sizes of different observations of a variable.

FIGURE A-10 Bar Graph

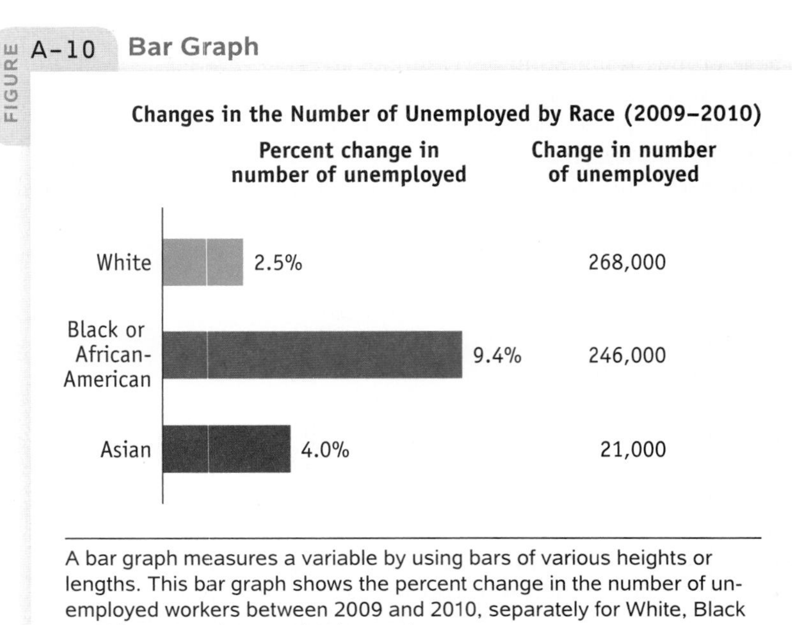

A bar graph measures a variable by using bars of various heights or lengths. This bar graph shows the percent change in the number of unemployed workers between 2009 and 2010, separately for White, Black or African-American, and Asian workers.

Source: Bureau of Labor Statistics.

Appendix B Macroeconomic Data

This appendix includes the following data tables:

Table 1.
MACROECONOMIC DATA FOR THE UNITED STATES 1929–2012[1]

	1929	1933	1939	1945	1950	1955	1960
Nominal GDP and Its Components							
1. + Consumer spending (*C*)	77.4	45.9	67.2	120	192.2	258.7	331.6
2. + Investment spending (*I*)	17.2	2.3	10.2	12.4	56.5	73.8	86.5
3. + Government purchases of goods and services (*G*)	9.6	8.9	15.2	96.6	50.7	93.3	121
4. + Exports (*X*)	5.9	2	4	6.8	12.4	17.7	27
5. – Imports (*IM*)	5.6	1.9	3.1	7.5	11.6	17.2	22.8
6. = Gross domestic product (GDP)	**104.6**	**57.2**	**93.5**	**228.2**	**300.2**	**426.2**	**543.3**
7. + Income from abroad earned by Americans	1.1	0.4	0.7	0.8	2.2	3.5	4.9
8. – Income paid to foreigners	0.4	0.1	0.3	0.5	0.7	1.1	1.8
9. = Gross national product	**105.3**	**57.5**	**93.9**	**228.5**	**301.7**	**428.6**	**546.4**
10. National income	94.2	49	82.5	201.4	267	377.6	479.9
11. Government transfers	1.2	1.7	2.5	5.6	14	15.7	25.7
12. Taxes	1.7	0.8	1.5	19.4	18.9	32.9	46.1
13. Disposable income	83.5	46.4	72.1	156.3	215	291.7	376.5
14. Private savings	3.9	–0.4	3.9	35.2	20	28.2	37.8
Real GDP and Growth Measures							
15. Real GDP (billions of 2009 dollars)	1055.6	777.6	1162.6	2215.9	2181.9	2736.4	3105.8
16. Real GDP growth (percent change from previous year)	-	–1.3	8	–1	8.7	7.1	2.6
17. Real GDP per capita (2009 dollars)	8661	6187	8873	15836	14384	16557	17182
18. Real GDP per capita growth (percent change from previous year)	-	–1.8	7.1	–2.0	6.9	5.3	0.5
Prices and Inflation							
19. Consumer Price Index (1982 – 1984 = 100)	17.1	13.0	13.9	18.0	24.1	26.8	29.6
20. CPI inflation rate	-	-5.1	–1.4	2.3	1.3	-0.4	1.7
21. Producer Price Index (all commodities, 1982 = 100)	16.4	11.4	13.3	18.2	27.3	29.4	31.7
22. PPI inflation rate (%)		1.8	–2.2	1.7	3.8	0.3	0.0
23. GDP deflator (2009 = 100)	9.9	7.4	8.0	10.3	13.8	15.6	17.5
24. GDP deflator inflation rate (%)		–2.8	–0.9	2.6	1.2	1.7	1.4
Population and Employment							
25. Population (thousands)	121,878	125,690	131,028	139,928	151,684	165,872	180,639
26. Labor force (thousands)[2]	49,180	51,590	55,230	53,860	62,122	64,964	69,659
27. Unemployed (thousands)[2]	1,550	12,830	9,480	1,040	3,230	2,834	3,874
28. Unemployment rate	3.2	24.9	17.2	1.9	5.2	4.4	5.6
Government Finance and Money							
29. Government (federal, state and local) budget balance	2.1	–0.9	–0.8	–31	2.2	1.6	2.8
30. Budget balance (percent of GDP)	2.0	–1.6	–0.9	–13.6	0.7	0.4	0.5
31. M1	-	-	-	-	-	-	140.3
32. M2	-	-	-	-	-	-	304.3
33. Federal funds rate (yearly average)	-	-	-	-	-	1.8	3.2
International Trade							
34. Current account balance	0.8	0.2	1	–1.3	–1.8	0.4	3.2

Sources: Bureau of Economic Analysis, Bureau of Labor Statistics, Federal Reserve Bank of St. Louis.

1. Data in billions of current dollars unless otherwise stated. Only select dates shown for 1929 through 1965; annual data supplied for 1965 through 2012.
2. Until 1947, includes workers 14 years and older; 1948 and after, includes workers 16 years and older.

1965	1966	1967	1968	1969	1970	1971	1972	1973	1974	1975
443.6	480.6	507.4	557.4	604.5	647.7	701	769.4	851.1	932	1032.8
129.6	144.2	142.7	156.9	173.6	170.1	196.8	228.1	266.9	274.5	257.3
164.9	186.4	208.1	226.8	240.4	254.2	269.3	288.2	306.4	343.1	382.9
37.1	40.9	43.5	47.9	51.9	59.7	63	70.8	95.3	126.7	138.7
31.5	37.1	39.9	46.6	50.5	55.8	62.3	74.2	91.2	127.5	122.7
743.7	**815**	**861.7**	**942.5**	**1019.9**	**1075.9**	**1167.8**	**1282.4**	**1428.5**	**1548.8**	**1688.9**
7.9	8.1	8.7	10.1	11.8	12.8	14	16.3	23.5	29.8	28
2.6	3	3.3	4	5.7	6.4	6.4	7.7	10.9	14.3	15
749	**820.1**	**867.1**	**948.6**	**1026**	**1082.3**	**1175.4**	**1291**	**1441.1**	**1564.3**	**1701.9**
660.3	719.7	760.2	832.1	899.5	940.1	1017	1123	1257	1350.8	1451.1
36.2	39.6	48	56.1	62.3	74.7	88.1	97.9	112.6	133.3	170
57.7	66.4	73	87	104.5	103.1	101.7	123.6	132.4	151	147.6
513.2	554.2	592.8	643.8	695.8	761.5	830.4	899.9	1006.1	1098.3	1219.3
58.3	61.4	72.2	72.1	75	96.1	110.1	109.2	131.8	141.7	159
3972.9	4234.9	4351.2	4564.7	4707.9	4717.7	4873	5128.8	5418.2	5390.2	5379.5
6.5	6.6	2.7	4.9	3.1	0.2	3.3	5.2	5.6	–0.5	–0.2
20442	21541	21893	22739	23222	23003	23463	24432	25565	25200	24907
5.2	5.4	1.6	3.9	2.1	–0.9	2.0	4.1	4.6	–1.4	–1.2
31.5	32.4	33.4	34.8	36.7	38.8	40.5	41.8	44.4	49.3	53.8
1.6	2.9	3.1	4.2	5.5	5.7	4.4	3.2	6.2	11.0	9.1
32.3	33.3	33.4	34.2	35.6	36.9	38.1	39.8	45.0	53.5	58.4
2.2	3.1	0.3	2.4	4.1	3.7	3.3	4.5	13.1	18.9	9.2
18.7	19.2	19.8	20.6	21.7	22.8	24.0	25.0	26.4	28.7	31.4
1.8	2.8	2.9	4.3	4.9	5.3	5.1	4.3	5.4	9.0	9.3
194,250	196,508	198,664	200,664	202,649	204,982	207,589	209,838	211,857	213,815	215,891
74,424	75,745	77,348	78,710	80,705	82,796	84,376	87,011	89,411	91,976	93,770
3,354	2,867	2,972	2,797	2,830	4,127	5,022	4,876	4,359	5,173	7,940
4.5	3.8	3.8	3.6	3.5	5.0	6.0	5.6	4.9	5.6	8.5
–1.4	–1.8	–14.8	–9.5	–1	–31.8	–50.2	–40.5	–28	–38.3	–102.5
–0.2	–0.2	–1.7	–1.0	–0.1	–3.0	–4.3	–3.2	–2.0	–2.5	–6.1
163.5	171.0	177.7	190.1	201.4	209.1	223.2	239.0	256.4	269.2	281.4
442.5	471.4	503.6	545.3	578.7	601.4	674.4	758.1	831.8	880.7	963.7
4.1	5.1	4.2	5.7	8.2	7.2	4.7	4.4	8.7	10.5	5.8
6.2	3.8	3.5	1.5	1.6	3.7	0.3	-4	8.9	6	19.8

(continued on next page)

Table 1, continued
MACROECONOMIC DATA FOR THE UNITED STATES 1929–2012[1]

	1976	1977	1978	1979	1980	1981	1982
Nominal GDP and Its Components							
1. + Consumer spending (*C*)	1150.2	1276.7	1426.2	1589.5	1754.6	1937.5	2073.9
2. + Investment spending (*I*)	323.2	396.6	478.4	539.7	530.1	631.2	581
3. + Government purchases of goods and services (*G*)	405.8	435.8	477.4	525.5	590.8	654.7	710
4. + Exports (*X*)	149.5	159.4	186.9	230.1	280.8	305.2	283.2
5. – Imports (*IM*)	151.1	182.4	212.3	252.7	293.8	317.8	303.2
6. = Gross domestic product (GDP)	**1877.6**	**2086**	**2356.6**	**2632.1**	**2862.5**	**3210.9**	**3345**
7. + Income from abroad earned by Americans	32.4	37.2	46.3	68.3	79.1	92	101
8. – Income paid to foreigners	15.5	16.9	24.7	36.4	44.9	59.1	64.5
9. = Gross national product	**1894.5**	**2106.3**	**2378.2**	**2664**	**2896.7**	**3243.8**	**3381.5**
10. National income	1614.8	1798.7	2029.9	2248.2	2426.8	2722.1	2840.4
11. Government transfers	184	194.2	209.6	235.3	279.5	318.4	354.8
12. Taxes	172.3	197.5	229.4	268.7	298.9	345.2	354.1
13. Disposable income	1325.8	1456.7	1630.1	1809.3	2018	2250.7	2424.7
14. Private savings	147.3	148.2	166.6	177.5	213.2	252.5	277.7
Real GDP and Growth Measures							
15. Real GDP (billions of 2009 dollars)	5669.3	5930.6	6260.4	6459.2	6443.4	6610.6	6484.3
16. Real GDP growth (percent change from previous year)	5.4	4.6	5.6	3.2	–0.2	2.6	–1.9
17. Real GDP per capita (2009 dollars)	25996	26922	28120	28694	28295	28741	27923
18. Real GDP per capita growth (percent change from previous year)	4.4	3.6	4.4	2.0	–1.4	1.6	–2.8
Prices and Inflation							
19. Consumer Price Index (1982 – 1984 = 100)	56.9	60.6	65.2	72.6	82.4	90.9	96.5
20. CPI inflation rate	5.8	6.5	7.6	11.3	13.5	10.3	6.2
21. Producer Price Index (all commodities, 1982 = 100)	61.1	64.9	69.9	78.7	89.8	98.0	100.0
22. PPI inflation rate (%)	4.6	6.2	7.7	12.6	14.1	9.1	2.0
23. GDP deflator (2009 = 100) (%)	33.1	35.2	37.6	40.8	44.4	48.6	51.6
24. GDP deflator inflation rate (%)	5.5	6.2	7.0	8.3	9.0	9.3	6.2
Population and Employment							
25. Population (thousands)	217,999	220,193	222,525	225,003	227,622	229,916	232,128
26. Labor force (thousands)[2]	96,151	98,984	102,233	104,961	106,974	108,676	110,244
27. Unemployed (thousands)[2]	7,398	6,967	6,187	6,135	7,671	8,276	10,715
28. Unemployment rate	7.7	7.0	6.1	5.8	7.2	7.6	9.7
Government Finance and Money							
29. Government (federal, state and local) budget balance	–77.1	–63.5	–46.4	–36.3	–80.9	–81.7	–169.7
30. Budget balance (percent of GDP)	–4.1	–3.0	–2.0	–1.4	–2.8	–2.5	–5.1
31. M1	297.2	320.0	346.3	372.7	395.7	424.9	453.0
32. M2	1086.6	1221.4	1322.4	1425.8	1540.4	1679.6	1831.4
33. Federal funds rate (yearly average)	5.1	5.5	7.9	11.2	13.4	16.4	12.3
International Trade							
34. Current account balance	7.1	–10.9	–12.6	–1.2	8.5	3.4	–3.3

Sources: Bureau of Economic Analysis, Bureau of Labor Statistics, Federal Reserve Bank of St. Louis.

1. Data in billions of current dollars unless otherwise stated. Only select dates shown for 1929 through 1965; annual data supplied for 1965 through 2012.
2. Until 1947, includes workers 14 years and older; 1948 and after, includes workers 16 years and older.

1983	1984	1985	1986	1987	1988	1989	1990	1991	1992	1993
2286.5	2498.2	2722.7	2898.4	3092.1	3346.9	3592.8	3825.6	3960.2	4215.7	4471
637.5	820.1	829.6	849.1	892.2	937	999.7	993.5	944.3	1013	1106.8
765.7	825.2	908.4	974.5	1030.8	1078.2	1151.9	1238.4	1298.2	1345.4	1366.1
277	302.4	303.2	321	363.9	444.6	504.3	551.9	594.9	633	654.8
328.6	405.1	417.2	452.9	508.7	554	591	629.7	623.5	667.8	720
3638.1	**4040.7**	**4346.7**	**4590.1**	**4870.2**	**5252.6**	**5657.7**	**5979.6**	**6174**	**6539.3**	**6878.7**
101.9	121.9	112.7	111.3	123.3	152.1	177.7	188.8	168.4	152.1	155.6
64.8	85.6	87.3	94.4	105.8	129.5	152.9	154.2	136.8	121	123.6
3675.2	**4077**	**4372.1**	**4607**	**4887.7**	**5275.2**	**5682.5**	**6014.2**	**6205.6**	**6570.4**	**6910.7**
3060.5	3444	3684.2	3848.2	4119.2	4493.4	4782.2	5036.1	5186.1	5499.7	5754.8
383.7	400.1	424.9	451	467.6	496.5	542.6	594.9	665.9	745.8	790.8
352.3	377.4	417.3	437.2	489.1	504.9	566.1	592.7	586.6	610.5	646.5
2617.4	2903.9	3098.5	3287.9	3466.3	3770.4	4052.1	4311.8	4484.5	4800.3	5000.2
247	312.1	265.1	269.4	252.1	294.7	316.5	335.4	365.9	426	367.6
6784.7	7277.2	7585.7	7852.1	8123.9	8465.4	8777	8945.4	8938.9	9256.7	9510.8
4.6	7.3	4.2	3.5	3.5	4.2	3.7	1.9	–0.1	3.6	2.7
28953	30784	31805	32624	33453	34544	35479	35756	35258	36029	36540
3.7	6.3	3.3	2.6	2.5	3.3	2.7	0.8	–1.4	2.2	1.4
99.6	103.9	107.6	109.6	113.6	118.3	124.0	130.7	136.2	140.3	144.5
3.2	4.3	3.6	1.9	3.6	4.1	4.8	5.4	4.2	3.0	3.0
101.3	103.7	103.2	100.2	102.8	106.9	112.2	116.3	116.5	117.2	118.9
1.3	2.4	–0.5	–2.9	2.6	4.0	5.0	3.7	0.2	0.6	1.5
53.6	55.5	57.3	58.5	59.9	62.0	64.5	66.8	69.1	70.6	72.3
3.9	3.5	3.2	2.0	2.6	3.5	3.9	3.7	3.3	2.3	2.4
234,247	236,307	238,416	240,593	242,751	244,968	247,286	250,047	253,392	256,777	260,146
111,515	113,532	115,467	117,846	119,853	121,671	123,851	125,857	126,352	128,099	129,185
10,694	8,529	8,313	8,245	7,414	6,697	6,524	7,061	8,640	9,611	8,927
9.6	7.5	7.2	7.0	6.2	5.5	5.3	5.6	6.8	7.5	6.9
–203.7	–171.4	–175.4	–192.2	–151.1	–140.4	–149.2	–207.4	–271.3	–370.2	–349
–5.6	–4.2	–4.0	–4.2	–3.1	–2.7	–2.6	–3.5	–4.4	–5.7	–5.1
503.2	538.6	587.0	666.4	743.5	774.8	782.2	810.6	859.0	965.9	1078.5
2054.8	2219.3	2416.7	2613.5	2783.8	2933.4	3056.1	3223.6	3342.2	3403.6	3438.0
9.1	10.2	8.1	6.8	6.7	7.6	9.2	8.1	5.7	3.5	3.0
–35.1	–90.1	–114.3	–142.7	–154.1	–115.7	–92.4	–74.9	7.9	–45.6	–78.6

(continued on next page)

Table 1, continued
MACROECONOMIC DATA FOR THE UNITED STATES 1929–2012[1]

	1994	1995	1996	1997	1998	1999	2000
Nominal GDP and Its Components							
1. + Consumer spending (*C*)	4741	4984.2	5268.1	5560.7	5903	6316.9	6801.6
2. + Investment spending (*I*)	1256.5	1317.5	1432.1	1595.6	1735.3	1884.2	2033.8
3. + Government purchases of goods and services (*G*)	1403.7	1452.2	1496.4	1554.2	1613.5	1726	1834.4
4. + Exports (*X*)	720.9	812.8	867.6	953.8	952.9	989.2	1094.3
5. – Imports (*IM*)	813.4	902.6	964	1055.8	1115.7	1250.6	1474.4
6. = Gross domestic product (GDP)	**7308.7**	**7664**	**8100.2**	**8608.5**	**9089.1**	**9665.7**	**10289.7**
7. + Income from abroad earned by Americans	184.5	229.8	246.4	280.1	286.8	321.4	382.7
8. – Income paid to foreigners	160.7	201.1	214.6	256	268.5	294.3	345.7
9. = Gross national product	**7332.5**	**7692.7**	**8132**	**8632.6**	**9107.4**	**9692.8**	**10326.7**
10. National income	6140.2	6479.5	6899.4	7380.4	7857.3	8324.4	8907
11. Government transfers	826.4	878.9	924.1	949.2	977.9	1021.6	1083
12. Taxes	690.5	743.9	832	926.2	1026.4	1107.5	1232.3
13. Disposable income	5244.2	5532.6	5829.9	6148.9	6561.3	6876.3	7400.5
14. Private savings	331.4	352.9	345.2	352.2	405.3	293	297.9
Real GDP and Growth Measures							
15. Real GDP (billions of 2009 dollars)	9894.7	10163.7	10549.5	11022.9	11513.4	12071.4	12565.2
16. Real GDP growth (percent change from previous year)	4	2.7	3.8	4.5	4.4	4.8	4.1
17. Real GDP per capita (2009 dollars)	37557	38125	39114	40383	41692	43216	44495
18. Real GDP per capita growth (percent change from previous year)	2.8	1.5	2.6	3.2	3.2	3.7	3.0
Prices and Inflation							
19. Consumer Price Index (1982 – 1984 = 100)	148.2	152.4	156.9	160.5	163.0	166.6	172.2
20. CPI inflation rate (%)	2.6	2.8	3.0	2.3	1.6	2.2	3.4
21. Producer Price Index (all commodities, 1982 = 100)	120.5	124.8	127.7	127.6	124.4	125.5	132.7
22. PPI inflation rate (%)	1.3	3.6	2.3	–0.1	–2.5	0.9	5.7
23. GDP deflator (2009 = 100)	73.9	75.4	76.8	78.1	78.9	80.1	81.9
24. GDP deflator inflation rate	2.1	2.1	1.8	1.7	1.1	1.4	2.3
Population and Employment							
25. Population (thousands)	263,325	266,458	269,581	272,822	276,022	279,195	282,296
26. Labor force (thousands)[2]	131,047	132,315	133,951	136,301	137,680	139,380	142,586
27. Unemployed (thousands)[2]	7,976	7,407	7,231	6,729	6,204	5,879	5,685
28. Unemployment rate	6.1	5.6	5.4	4.9	4.5	4.2	4.0
Government Finance and Money							
29. Government (federal, state and local) budget balance	–280.7	–272.4	–191	–89.5	18.1	75.8	165.8
30. Budget balance (percent of GDP)	–3.8	–3.6	–2.4	–1.0	0.2	0.8	1.6
31. M1	1145.2	1143.1	1106.5	1070.1	1080.6	1102.3	1103.6
32. M2	3482.1	3552.7	3722.8	3909.8	4188.9	4496.9	4769.3
33. Federal funds rate (yearly average)	4.2	5.8	5.3	5.5	5.4	5.0	6.2
International Trade							
34. Current account balance	–114.7	–105.1	–114.1	–129.3	–204.5	–291.9	–409.1

Sources: Bureau of Economic Analysis, Bureau of Labor Statistics, Federal Reserve Bank of St. Louis.

1. Data in billions of current dollars unless otherwise stated. Only select dates shown for 1929 through 1965; annual data supplied for 1965 through 2012.
2. Until 1947, includes workers 14 years and older; 1948 and after, includes workers 16 years and older.

2001	2002	2003	2004	2005	2006	2007	2008	2009	2010	2011	2012
7106.9	7385.3	7764.4	8257.8	8790.3	9297.5	9744.4	10005.5	9842.9	10201.9	10711.8	11149.6
1928.6	1925	2027.9	2276.7	2527.1	2680.6	2643.7	2424.8	1878.1	2100.8	2232.1	2475.2
1958.8	2094.9	2220.8	2357.4	2493.7	2642.2	2801.9	3003.2	3089.1	3174	3158.7	3167
1028.8	1004.7	1043.4	1183.1	1310.4	1478.5	1665.7	1843.1	1583.8	1843.5	2101.2	2195.9
1397.8	1429.7	1544.3	1797.9	2026.1	2240.9	2375.5	2556.4	1976	2362	2669.9	2743.1
10625.3	**10980.2**	**11512.2**	**12277**	**13095.4**	**13857.9**	**14480.3**	**14720.3**	**14417.9**	**14958.3**	**15533.8**	**16244.6**
325.3	315.8	356.1	451.4	575.8	724.2	875.5	856.8	643.7	720	802.8	818.6
273.5	267.2	288.1	361.4	482.3	655.7	749.1	683.8	496.5	514.1	542.1	565.7
10677.1	**11028.8**	**11580.2**	**12367**	**13188.9**	**13926.4**	**14606.7**	**14893.3**	**14565.1**	**15164.2**	**15794.5**	**16497.5**
9184.6	9436.8	9865.1	10541.9	11240.8	12005.6	12322.3	12430.8	12124.5	12739.5	13395.7	13971.6
1188.1	1280.3	1342.9	1416.7	1512	1609.6	1722.8	1884	2140.2	2276.9	2306.9	2358.3
1234.8	1050.3	1000.9	1046	1208.5	1352.1	1487.9	1435.2	1144.9	1191.5	1404	1498
7752.3	8099.2	8486.7	9003.2	9401.8	10037.7	10507.9	10995.4	10937.2	11243.7	11787.4	12245.8
331.2	403.9	410.8	413.2	242.7	336.9	317.2	551.3	670.7	634.2	668.2	687.4
12684.4	12909.7	13270	13774	14235.6	14615.2	14876.8	14833.6	14417.9	14779.4	15052.4	15470.7
1	1.8	2.8	3.8	3.4	2.7	1.8	–0.3	–2.8	2.5	1.8	2.8
44472	44832	45660	46968	48094	48910	49311	48708	46927	47710	48239	49226
–0.1	0.8	1.8	2.9	2.4	1.7	0.8	–1.2	–3.7	1.7	1.1	2.0
177.1	179.9	184.0	188.9	195.3	201.6	207.342	215.303	214.537	218.056	224.939	229.594
2.8	1.6	2.3	2.7	3.4	3.2	2.8	3.8	–0.4	1.6	3.2	2.1
134.2	131.1	138.1	146.7	157.4	164.8	172.7	189.6	172.9	184.7	201.1	202.2
1.1	–2.3	5.3	6.2	7.3	4.7	4.8	9.8	–8.8	6.8	8.9	0.5
83.8	85.1	86.8	89.1	92.0	94.8	97.3	99.2	100.0	101.2	103.2	105.0
2.3	1.5	2.0	2.7	3.2	3.1	2.7	2.0	0.8	1.2	2.0	1.7
285,216	288,019	290,733	293,389	296,115	298,930	301,903	304,718	307,374	309,733	311,943	314,184
143,769	144,856	146,500	147,380	149,289	151,409	153,123	154,322	154,189	153,888	153,619	154,966
6,830	8,375	8,770	8,140	7,579	6,991	7,073	8,948	14,295	14,810	13,737	12,497
4.8	5.8	6.0	5.5	5.1	4.6	4.6	5.8	9.3	9.6	8.9	8.1
–51.3	–391.9	–524.9	–508.1	–372	–267.5	–339.4	–800.2	–1521.7	–1566.8	–1461.3	–1362.3
–0.5	–3.6	–4.6	–4.1	–2.8	–1.9	–2.3	–5.4	–10.6	–10.5	–9.4	–8.4
1140.3	1196.7	1273.8	1344.3	1371.6	1374.7	1372.6	1434.9	1637.7	1742.3	2010.0	2310.9
5179.4	5562.4	5950.1	6236.0	6504.3	6845.3	7267.1	7763.7	8385.3	8593.4	9221.3	10006.9
3.9	1.7	1.1	1.4	3.2	5.0	5.0	1.9	0.2	0.2	0.1	0.1
–389.8	–449.9	–513.5	–621.7	–737.1	–795.7	–709.1	–678.5	–381.2	–454.5	–457	–439

Table 2.
MACROECONOMIC DATA FOR SELECT COUNTRIES
GDP (Billions of U.S. Dollars)

Country	1985	1986	1987	1988	1989	1990	1991	1992	1993
Argentina	88.18	106.04	108.72	127.34	81.70	141.33	189.58	228.76	236.49
Australia	176.88	183.57	216.18	274.38	310.98	328.20	328.79	321.64	312.89
Austria	68.03	96.53	120.71	132.41	132.06	165.26	172.78	193.52	188.39
Bangladesh	21.34	22.37	24.68	26.64	29.34	30.50	31.43	31.44	32.95
Belgium	85.76	118.88	147.79	160.47	162.45	203.31	208.53	231.79	222.26
Brazil	253.08	293.58	319.55	356.98	490.05	507.78	445.24	426.52	478.62
Bulgaria	27.39	24.24	28.10	45.92	46.77	20.62	2.02	8.20	4.45
Canada	355.71	368.87	421.53	498.16	555.52	582.74	598.20	579.52	563.68
Chile	16.49	17.72	20.90	24.64	28.39	31.56	36.43	44.47	47.69
China	307.02	297.59	323.97	404.15	451.31	390.28	409.17	488.22	613.22
Colombia	48.68	48.75	50.75	54.71	55.17	56.19	57.54	68.75	77.85
Cyprus	2.43	3.09	3.71	4.27	4.56	5.59	5.77	6.91	6.61
Czech Republic	n/a	n/a	n/a	n/a	n/a	n/a	n/a	n/a	n/a
Denmark	61.20	86.37	107.37	113.23	110.06	135.84	136.70	150.20	140.63
Dominican Republic	6.49	7.88	8.30	7.60	8.58	7.99	9.79	11.49	12.95
Ecuador	16.18	11.87	11.10	10.55	10.36	10.52	11.80	12.90	15.07
Egypt	46.45	51.43	73.57	88.00	109.71	91.38	46.06	42.01	47.10
Estonia	n/a	n/a	n/a	n/a	n/a	n/a	n/a	n/a	1.73
Finland	55.25	72.33	90.12	107.26	116.73	139.12	125.66	110.72	87.39
France	547.90	761.35	923.68	1,004.44	1,009.84	1,248.56	1,249.22	1,374.07	1,292.12
Germany	639.70	913.64	1,136.93	1,225.73	1,216.80	1,547.03	1,815.06	2,066.73	2,005.56
Ghana	5.33	6.03	4.76	5.15	5.94	6.53	6.85	6.66	5.97
Greece	45.13	53.10	61.78	71.95	74.56	92.20	99.42	109.56	102.61
Guatemala	10.39	5.62	6.50	7.04	8.12	7.07	8.70	9.60	10.46
Hungary	21.14	24.35	26.77	29.29	29.90	33.89	34.27	38.19	39.57
Iceland	2.94	3.93	5.44	6.02	5.59	6.36	6.80	6.97	6.12
India	229.56	252.45	278.20	304.46	302.14	325.93	289.36	291.86	285.33
Ireland	20.99	28.14	33.36	36.55	37.70	47.77	48.42	54.44	50.44
Israel	25.32	31.17	37.23	46.06	46.81	55.09	62.10	69.03	69.19
Italy	437.10	619.08	777.01	860.86	895.34	1,135.54	1,198.99	1,271.91	1,022.66
Jamaica	2.16	2.57	2.90	3.46	4.01	5.06	4.75	4.25	5.92
Japan	1,352.06	2,003.32	2,429.60	2,950.00	2,951.77	3,030.05	3,464.93	3,781.78	4,340.89
Kenya	8.75	10.39	11.39	11.81	11.71	12.18	11.50	11.33	7.87
Korea	98.50	113.74	143.38	192.11	236.23	270.41	315.58	338.17	372.21
Latvia	n/a	n/a	n/a	n/a	n/a	n/a	n/a	1.55	2.47
Lithuania	n/a	n/a	n/a	n/a	n/a	n/a	n/a	1.99	2.81
Luxembourg	4.57	6.65	8.26	9.36	9.96	12.71	13.77	15.42	15.81
Malaysia	31.77	28.24	32.18	35.27	38.85	44.03	49.88	60.05	67.90
Mexico	211.52	146.45	160.60	196.48	239.44	282.56	338.74	392.84	436.13
Netherlands	133.17	185.60	226.44	241.38	238.18	295.46	303.46	334.65	324.39
New Zealand	22.38	27.23	36.29	44.67	43.07	44.68	42.79	40.62	43.94
Nigeria	25.97	20.56	21.91	24.31	23.49	31.48	28.34	25.52	15.79
Norway	64.26	77.20	92.45	100.06	100.77	117.62	119.67	128.32	118.17
Peru	17.21	25.82	42.64	33.73	41.63	28.98	34.55	35.95	34.82
Philippines	30.73	29.87	33.20	37.89	42.65	44.16	45.32	52.98	54.37
Poland	70.78	73.68	63.71	68.61	66.90	62.08	80.45	88.71	90.37
Portugal	26.78	37.25	46.61	54.52	58.82	78.13	88.43	106.34	93.57
Romania	47.80	51.77	57.89	59.93	53.69	38.24	28.85	19.58	26.36
Russia	n/a	n/a	n/a	n/a	n/a	n/a	n/a	85.59	183.82
Saudi Arabia	103.89	86.95	85.70	88.26	95.34	116.78	131.34	136.30	132.15
Singapore	18.46	18.73	21.55	26.48	31.41	38.84	45.19	52.01	60.47
South Africa	57.27	65.42	85.79	92.24	95.98	112.00	120.24	130.53	130.45
Spain	176.69	244.48	309.75	363.91	401.39	520.71	560.80	613.02	514.95
Sweden	106.38	140.79	171.61	193.88	204.45	244.55	257.90	267.17	202.04
Switzerland	99.47	142.60	178.58	193.20	186.53	238.22	241.00	250.98	244.09
Thailand	38.90	43.10	50.54	61.67	72.25	85.64	96.19	109.43	121.80
Turkey	90.38	101.80	117.18	122.13	144.03	202.38	202.72	213.58	242.14
Ukraine	n/a	n/a	n/a	n/a	n/a	n/a	n/a	20.78	32.71
United Arab Emirates	27.35	21.67	23.80	24.19	27.92	35.99	33.19	33.49	36.72
United Kingdom	468.96	570.88	702.54	852.40	861.29	1,017.79	1,059.26	1,098.30	982.62
United States	4,217.48	4,460.05	4,736.35	5,100.43	5,482.13	5,800.53	5,992.10	6,342.30	6,667.33
Vietnam	15.00	33.87	42.05	23.23	6.29	6.47	7.64	9.87	13.18

Sources: International Monetary Fund, World Economic Outlook Database, April 2013.

1994	1995	1996	1997	1998	1999	2000	2001	2002	2003	2004
257.43	258.02	272.22	292.99	299.08	283.76	284.41	268.96	97.40	127.55	151.82
356.64	382.25	428.03	428.44	382.28	413.57	399.60	376.65	423.69	539.17	654.98
201.64	238.55	234.23	207.13	212.44	211.21	192.63	191.84	208.27	254.43	291.81
35.80	39.58	41.52	43.39	44.76	46.53	47.05	47.19	49.56	54.48	59.12
242.62	284.79	275.17	249.76	255.57	254.38	233.35	232.69	253.69	312.29	362.16
596.76	769.74	840.05	871.52	841.30	573.12	644.28	554.41	505.71	552.24	663.55
7.82	13.11	9.90	10.37	12.85	12.98	12.94	13.88	16.03	20.71	25.32
564.48	590.50	613.78	637.53	616.78	661.25	739.66	732.90	752.63	887.81	1018.12
55.16	71.35	75.77	82.81	79.37	72.99	78.00	71.29	70.11	76.10	99.29
559.22	727.95	856.08	952.65	1,019.48	1,083.28	1198.48	1324.81	1453.83	1640.96	1931.65
97.87	110.81	120.00	112.70	109.12	96.89	99.90	98.21	97.82	94.70	118.80
7.45	9.25	9.35	8.9	9.56	9.78	9.20	9.61	10.48	13.18	15.66
n/a	55.26	62.01	57.14	61.85	60.19	58.80	64.38	78.43	95.29	113.98
153.59	181.99	184.44	170.44	173.65	173.94	160.08	160.48	173.88	212.62	244.73
13.99	15.52	17.07	19.19	20.08	21.48	23.66	24.51	24.91	20.21	21.56
18.59	20.22	21.29	23.66	23.28	16.69	18.69	24.79	28.77	32.39	37.21
51.88	60.16	67.63	75.87	84.82	89.94	99.16	95.40	87.51	81.38	78.80
2.42	3.78	4.73	5.05	5.59	5.71	5.70	6.25	7.35	9.86	12.04
100.99	130.85	128.28	123.07	129.84	130.39	122.15	124.75	135.66	164.57	189.31
1,366.16	1,572.38	1,574.32	1,425.80	1,474.24	1,458.37	1330.22	1339.49	1457.14	1795.64	2058.41
2,151.03	2,524.95	2,439.35	2,163.23	2,187.48	2,146.43	1891.93	1882.51	2013.69	2428.45	2729.92
5.45	6.46	6.93	6.89	7.48	7.72	7.36	7.44	9.48	11.19	14.56
109.82	128.90	136.27	133.13	133.87	137.83	127.60	131.14	147.91	194.99	230.34
11.84	13.32	14.20	16.09	17.31	16.49	17.19	18.70	20.78	21.92	23.97
42.55	45.79	46.59	47.18	48.75	49.13	46.39	52.72	66.39	83.54	101.93
6.29	7.01	7.31	7.42	8.27	8.73	8.68	7.90	8.91	10.97	13.25
323.94	367.73	378.99	424.14	427.55	456.52	476.35	487.80	510.29	590.97	689.03
55.35	67.13	74.09	81.29	88.12	96.42	97.74	105.36	123.60	159.25	186.74
78.37	96.06	105.37	108.39	109.89	110.79	124.89	122.94	112.97	118.67	126.57
1,054.90	1,126.63	1,259.95	1,193.62	1,218.67	1,202.40	1107.25	1124.67	1229.52	1517.40	1737.80
7.66	5.81	7.84	8.20	8.62	8.76	9.07	9.20	9.72	9.43	10.17
4,778.99	5,264.38	4,642.55	4,261.84	3,857.03	4,368.73	4731.20	4159.86	3980.82	4302.94	4655.82
9.42	11.94	12.05	13.28	13.77	12.88	12.32	13.06	13.19	15.04	16.09
435.59	531.14	573	532.24	357.51	461.81	533.39	504.58	575.93	643.76	721.98
4.15	4.96	5.68	6.25	6.73	7.29	7.78	8.22	9.23	11.15	13.74
4.40	6.47	8.17	9.96	11.23	10.97	11.50	12.22	14.24	18.70	22.66
17.59	20.70	20.59	18.54	19.38	21.22	20.33	20.22	22.65	29.20	34.12
75.61	90.17	102.38	101.68	73.27	80.34	93.79	92.78	100.85	110.20	124.75
456.12	310.10	360.06	434.23	455.59	520.45	671.87	709.98	721.79	700.32	759.56
348.91	419.35	418.11	387.01	403.20	412.00	386.20	401.00	439.36	539.34	610.69
51.77	61.06	67.80	67.69	55.60	57.61	53.44	52.55	61.40	81.64	100.68
18.09	36.95	46.02	35.39	32.75	35.94	46.39	44.14	59.12	67.66	87.85
124.48	148.92	160.00	158.23	151.14	159.05	168.29	170.92	191.93	224.88	260.03
44.92	53.66	55.85	59.14	56.76	51.53	53.36	53.96	56.78	61.36	69.70
64.08	75.53	84.37	83.74	66.60	76.16	81.02	76.26	81.36	83.91	91.37
103.68	139.10	156.66	157.08	172.00	167.79	171.26	190.42	198.21	216.81	253.02
98.05	116.24	121.01	115.67	122.73	126.28	117.64	120.44	132.75	162.24	185.64
30.07	35.48	35.32	35.29	42.12	35.59	37.33	40.59	45.99	59.47	75.80
276.90	313.45	391.78	404.95	271.04	195.91	259.72	306.62	345.13	430.35	590.94
134.33	142.46	157.74	164.99	145.97	161.17	194.81	189.36	194.88	221.47	258.74
73.24	87.06	95.18	99.30	85.01	84.88	94.31	87.70	90.64	95.96	112.70
135.82	151.12	143.83	148.84	134.22	133.11	132.97	118.56	111.36	168.22	219.42
516.72	597.28	622.65	573.38	601.63	618.69	582.05	609.38	688.73	885.53	1045.98
217.55	253.68	276.46	253.18	254.72	258.81	247.53	227.89	251.61	315.98	361.78
270.22	315.95	304.75	264.58	272.63	268.22	256.04	262.65	286.66	334.59	374.23
144.31	168.02	181.95	150.89	111.86	122.63	122.73	115.54	126.88	142.64	161.34
174.45	227.51	243.90	255.07	269.13	249.82	266.44	195.55	232.28	303.26	392.21
36.76	37.01	44.56	50.15	41.88	31.58	31.26	38.01	42.39	50.13	64.88
37.44	40.73	48.01	51.22	48.51	55.18	103.89	103.31	109.82	124.35	147.82
1,061.38	1,157.44	1,220.85	1,359.44	1,456.16	1,502.89	1478.65	1468.53	1604.24	1857.62	2197.94
7,085.15	7,414.63	7,838.48	8,332.35	8,793.48	9,353.50	9951.48	10286.18	10642.30	11142.23	11853.25
16.28	20.80	24.69	26.89	27.23	28.70	31.18	32.52	35.10	39.56	45.45

(continued on next page)

Table 2, continued
MACROECONOMIC DATA FOR SELECT COUNTRIES
GDP (Billions of U.S. Dollars)

Country	2005	2006	2007	2008	2009	2010	2011	2012
Argentina	181.36	212.51	260.07	324.41	305.76	367.57	444.61	474.95
Australia	730.75	777.94	945.38	1051.26	993.24	1247.11	1490.52	1541.80
Austria	305.51	325.26	375.58	416.12	384.62	380.02	418.41	398.59
Bangladesh	61.13	65.28	73.99	84.47	94.87	106.23	113.89	122.72
Belgium	378.01	400.34	460.28	509.77	474.63	472.54	514.60	484.69
Brazil	881.75	1089.16	1366.22	1650.39	1622.31	2142.93	2492.91	2395.97
Bulgaria	28.97	33.25	42.18	52.14	48.65	47.84	53.58	51.02
Canada	1164.21	1309.92	1457.98	1542.47	1368.90	1616.02	1781.08	1819.08
Chile	123.07	154.71	173.06	179.52	172.11	217.31	250.99	268.18
China	2256.92	2712.92	3494.24	4519.95	4990.53	5930.39	7321.99	8227.04
Colombia	146.59	160.69	210.57	235.26	231.60	284.88	327.63	366.02
Cyprus	16.92	18.42	21.77	25.25	23.47	23.10	25.02	23.01
Czech Republic	130.07	148.37	180.48	225.43	197.19	198.95	217.08	196.07
Denmark	257.68	274.38	311.42	343.88	310.55	313.14	333.70	313.64
Dominican Republic	33.53	35.67	40.99	45.52	46.71	51.67	55.64	59.00
Ecuador	41.77	46.80	51.01	60.75	57.86	63.75	73.04	80.93
Egypt	89.79	107.38	130.35	162.44	188.61	218.46	235.58	256.73
Estonia	13.93	16.82	22.02	23.87	19.18	19.02	22.20	21.86
Finland	196.12	208.14	246.48	273.25	240.00	237.24	263.66	250.13
France	2140.21	2257.78	2586.12	2845.12	2626.54	2570.59	2778.09	2608.70
Germany	2771.06	2905.45	3328.59	3640.73	3307.20	3312.19	3607.36	3400.58
Ghana	17.41	20.41	24.76	28.53	25.80	32.19	38.39	38.94
Greece	240.49	261.96	305.87	343.20	321.85	294.77	290.15	249.20
Guatemala	27.21	30.23	34.11	39.14	37.73	41.34	46.98	49.88
Hungary	110.32	112.53	136.09	154.22	126.65	127.96	138.97	126.87
Iceland	16.32	16.73	20.43	16.83	12.12	12.56	14.06	13.65
India	806.78	909.47	1160.15	1275.73	1259.07	1614.83	1838.17	1824.83
Ireland	203.10	223.17	258.68	263.26	224.62	207.64	221.22	210.42
Israel	133.70	145.14	166.34	201.51	194.79	217.69	243.65	240.89
Italy	1789.38	1874.72	2130.24	2318.16	2116.63	2059.19	2196.33	2014.08
Jamaica	11.23	11.94	12.88	13.85	12.28	13.49	14.78	15.25
Japan	4571.87	4356.75	4356.35	4849.19	5035.14	5495.39	5897.02	5963.97
Kenya	18.74	22.50	27.24	30.47	30.60	32.18	34.06	41.12
Korea	844.87	951.77	1049.24	931.41	834.06	1014.89	1116.25	1155.87
Latvia	15.94	19.85	28.65	33.45	25.85	24.10	28.48	28.38
Lithuania	26.10	30.24	39.32	47.48	37.12	36.63	42.87	42.16
Luxembourg	37.71	42.58	51.39	55.00	50.19	52.95	59.31	56.74
Malaysia	143.54	162.75	193.61	231.07	202.28	246.83	287.94	303.53
Mexico	848.57	951.68	1035.03	1093.74	882.83	1034.15	1158.30	1177.12
Netherlands	639.58	678.32	783.69	874.91	798.40	781.20	837.59	773.12
New Zealand	112.32	108.66	132.70	133.06	118.80	142.02	161.84	169.68
Nigeria	112.25	145.43	165.92	207.12	168.59	228.64	243.99	268.71
Norway	304.06	340.04	393.48	453.89	378.85	420.95	490.66	501.10
Peru	79.39	92.32	107.25	126.87	126.95	153.88	178.49	199.00
Philippines	103.07	122.21	149.36	173.60	168.49	199.59	224.77	250.44
Poland	303.98	341.67	425.32	529.43	430.89	469.80	514.02	487.67
Portugal	192.18	201.98	232.08	253.11	234.69	229.33	237.99	212.72
Romania	99.17	122.70	170.62	204.34	164.34	164.79	182.61	169.38
Russia	764.02	989.93	1299.70	1660.85	1222.65	1525.35	1899.06	2021.96
Saudi Arabia	328.46	376.90	415.97	519.80	429.10	526.81	669.51	727.31
Singapore	125.43	145.64	177.87	190.59	188.83	231.70	265.62	276.52
South Africa	246.95	261.18	285.81	273.45	285.22	363.20	402.25	384.32
Spain	1132.76	1237.50	1443.50	1600.91	1459.74	1391.76	1479.56	1352.06
Sweden	370.17	399.62	463.63	486.61	406.41	462.46	538.62	526.19
Switzerland	384.76	405.18	450.53	524.29	509.47	550.69	660.76	632.40
Thailand	176.35	207.09	246.98	272.58	263.71	318.91	345.67	365.56
Turkey	482.69	529.19	649.13	730.32	614.42	731.29	774.34	794.47
Ukraine	86.18	107.75	142.72	180.12	117.23	136.42	163.42	176.24
United Arab Emirates	180.62	221.97	257.92	314.45	259.73	283.92	341.96	358.94
United Kingdom	2298.64	2456.52	2826.61	2670.40	2193.18	2267.48	2431.53	2440.51
United States	12622.95	13377.20	14028.68	14291.55	13973.65	14498.93	15075.68	15684.75
Vietnam	52.93	60.93	71.11	90.30	93.17	103.58	122.72	138.07

Sources: International Monetary Fund, World Economic Outlook Database, April 2013.

Table 3.
MACROECONOMIC DATA FOR SELECT COUNTRIES GDP PER PERSON (1985–2012)

Country	1985	1986	1987	1988	1989	1990	1991	1992	1993
Argentina	2,928.87	3,477.26	3,525.01	4,079.01	2,584.99	4,379.50	5,796.41	6,900.12	7,028.62
Australia	10,964.10	11,241.64	12,994.53	16,241.83	18,157.93	18,858.22	18,668.05	18,089.07	17,429.52
Austria	8,988.26	12,740.75	15,911.50	17,431.46	17,309.05	21,511.83	22,259.58	24,678.01	23,847.20
Bangladesh	226.296	230.972	248.09	260.802	280.059	283.992	285.918	279.626	286.814
Belgium	8,464.36	11,729.28	14,561.04	15,813.79	15,902.22	19,875.05	20,313.44	22,545.24	21,459.22
Brazil	1,710.10	1,942.66	2,072.19	2,270.25	3,058.46	3,113.03	2,683.78	2,529.35	2,793.36
Bulgaria	3,130.67	2,777.17	3,232.54	5,313.24	5,449.81	2,422.35	239.505	981.877	538.524
Canada	14,060.69	14,438.27	16,291.17	19,001.44	20,828.27	21,518.68	21,809.72	20,877.26	20,074.52
Chile	1,448.02	1,529.42	1,772.85	2,054.62	2,327.48	2,545.46	2,876.74	3,442.28	3,618.89
China	290.046	276.81	296.408	364.013	400.439	341.353	353.268	416.675	517.414
Colombia	1,573.62	1,543.74	1,573.96	1,662.06	1,641.85	1,638.97	1,644.09	1,926.10	2,140.21
Cyprus	4,390.66	5,512.95	6,541.58	7,466.26	7,858.91	9,428.03	9,476.93	11,064.83	10,322.07
Czech Republic	n/a	n/a	n/a	n/a	n/a	n/a	n/a	n/a	n/a
Denmark	11,974.67	16,880.56	20,950.32	22,075.41	21,454.88	26,451.46	26,560.90	29,095.51	27,144.62
Dominican Republic	1,061.73	1,258.73	1,292.91	1,156.44	1,277.82	1,166.21	1,404.34	1,611.67	1,768.14
Ecuador	2,109.31	1,508.40	1,374.50	1,273.93	1,220.13	1,210.42	1,327.52	1,419.45	1,622.85
Egypt	997.959	1,077.02	1,507.61	1,767.07	2,155.49	1,779.26	878.615	785.038	862.411
Estonia	n/a	n/a	n/a	n/a	n/a	n/a	n/a	n/a	1,145.29
Finland	11,259.11	14,696.74	18,262.52	21,666.93	23,486.11	27,854.86	25,006.32	21,920.30	17,223.04
France	9,932.14	13,713.16	16,501.33	17,924.31	17,912.96	22,046.99	21,984.99	24,090.71	22,632.31
Germany	8,397.49	11,985.43	14,911.90	15,979.26	15,705.89	19,592.68	22,692.73	25,671.42	24,742.34
Ghana	638.019	521.185	506.054	531.591	531.463	617.604	757.762	748.149	575.869
Greece	4,543.24	5,325.20	6,174.13	7,163.58	7,387.05	9,073.88	9,702.81	10,585.18	9,807.41
Guatemala	1,431.50	754.669	852.191	900.109	1,012.37	860.29	1,034.15	1,112.25	1,181.10
Hungary	1,985.30	2,295.26	2,534.76	2,785.72	2,855.53	3,250.63	3,287.86	3,663.94	3,799.05
Iceland	12,211.18	16,228.24	22,274.72	24,289.84	22,154.55	25,077.03	26,568.62	26,825.10	23,336.04
India	312.036	324.955	357.042	369.101	362.165	386.193	318.628	333.21	315.951
Ireland	5,863.83	7,861.61	9,304.87	10,239.26	10,624.69	13,478.01	13,583.60	15,147.74	13,959.02
Israel	6,529.38	7,910.34	9,297.91	11,316.35	11,271.15	12,957.64	14,247.65	15,373.02	14,897.07
Italy	7,882.06	11,161.62	14,009.86	15,517.72	16,127.82	20,111.95	21,226.03	22,512.31	18,087.21
Jamaica	879.434	1,036.04	1,160.02	1,374.42	1,590.50	1,974.11	1,800.91	1,803.94	2,279.03
Japan	11,464.24	16,890.81	20,367.18	24,604.40	24,522.43	25,139.58	28,541.69	30,972.98	35,376.66
Kenya	444.559	509.703	539.628	540.668	518.42	522.332	478.464	457.953	309.76
Korea	2,413.94	2,759.70	3,444.79	4,570.73	5,565.10	6,307.66	7,288.84	7,729.98	8,422.05
Latvia	n/a	n/a	n/a	n/a	n/a	n/a	n/a	582.078	928.28
Lithuania	n/a	n/a	n/a	n/a	n/a	n/a	n/a	n/a	n/a
Luxembourg	12,442.97	18,021.25	22,237.43	24,974.22	26,331.00	33,198.13	35,486.78	39,216.06	39,639.77
Malaysia	1,978.11	1,711.46	1,900.58	2,032.66	2,185.66	2,374.17	2,649.14	3,102.25	3,412.71
Mexico	2,960.57	2,008.52	2,159.17	2,590.36	3,096.75	3,586.12	4,219.65	4,804.19	5,801.94
Netherlands	9,189.30	12,736.41	15,501.24	16,471.39	16,132.50	19,767.94	20,201.82	22,191.00	21,430.99
New Zealand	6,891.89	8,310.97	11,093.14	13,532.61	12,943.73	13,278.32	12,331.48	11,635.06	12,389.85
Nigeria	331.052	254.845	263.86	284.384	266.904	347.625	304.172	266.615	160.529
Norway	15,449.40	18,495.98	22,020.51	23,706.38	23,805.28	27,677.12	27,996.21	29,842.34	27,323.22
Peru	881.63	1,293.11	2,088.09	1,616.27	1,952.82	1,331.72	1,557.49	1,599.87	1,542.74
Philippines	620.246	590.895	640.726	715.079	784.881	796.274	797.084	911.418	914.073
Poland	1,896.08	1,961.68	1,687.80	1,815.82	1,768.61	1,625.84	2,101.35	2,311.09	2,347.12
Portugal	2,673.63	3,713.00	4,644.16	5,438.16	5,873.52	7,815.76	8,868.07	10,670.24	9,380.55
Romania	2,083.00	2,243.90	2,495.19	2,569.62	2,293.82	1,631.94	1,233.00	839.917	1,137.13
Russia	n/a	n/a	n/a	n/a	n/a	n/a	n/a	575.99	1,238.65
Saudi Arabia	8,714.81	6,940.77	6,510.77	6,385.68	6,569.77	7,683.59	8,267.14	8,063.88	7,953.12
Singapore	6,748.29	6,853.03	7,767.00	9,303.40	10,715.16	12,745.06	14,412.55	16,099.09	18,250.52
South Africa	1,735.62	1,937.54	2,485.04	2,614.36	2,662.24	3,039.44	3,192.05	3,389.85	3,315.64
Spain	4,597.63	6,343.30	8,017.91	9,400.09	10,347.54	13,400.01	14,393.43	15,681.87	13,132.27
Sweden	12,643.39	16,689.33	20,253.00	22,761.72	23,805.06	28,273.05	29,645.84	30,523.05	23,102.87
Switzerland	15,783.83	22,524.91	28,045.15	30,136.76	28,863.83	36,564.25	36,540.67	37,559.36	36,184.71
Thailand	750.973	813.604	938.093	1,122.03	1,306.77	1,521.05	1,688.66	1,893.55	2,087.83
Turkey	1,837.97	2,024.85	2,281.01	2,416.97	2,810.15	3,862.75	3,795.75	3,920.70	4,373.52
Ukraine	n/a	n/a	n/a	n/a	n/a	n/a	n/a	415.009	652.902
United Arab Emirates	27,036.00	20,533.02	21,644.07	18,435.20	20,478.53	26,621.51	25,847.41	25,960.97	25,654.37
United Kingdom	8,292.23	10,071.38	12,395.15	15,035.66	15,171.88	17,900.11	18,626.91	19,325.67	17,298.24
United States	18,231.83	19,078.41	20,062.55	21,442.13	22,878.98	23,913.66	24,365.53	25,466.73	26,441.65
Vietnam	251.202	556.019	674.88	365.892	97.158	98.032	113.654	144.149	189.261

Sources: International Monetary Fund, World Economic Outlook Database, 2013.

1994	1995	1996	1997	1998	1999	2000	2001	2001	2003	2004
7,576.83	7,531.45	7,862.15	8,381.06	8,478.20	7,970.20	7,917.15	7,417.62	2,656.23	3,439.37	4,048.33
19,725.52	20,929.85	23,201.57	23,017.57	20,340.85	21,778.63	20,876.31	19,457.24	21,610.11	27,193.09	32,673.23
25,439.40	30,043.89	29,497.01	26,113.72	26,780.11	26,598.11	24,044.50	23,854.31	25,769.47	31,340.72	35,720.10
305.035	330.191	339.18	347.256	351.097	358.01	355.392	350.287	361.732	391.388	418.594
23,336.92	28,111.96	27,199.40	24,589.22	25,111.41	24,950.44	22,790.54	22,671.37	24,606.76	30,155.42	34,835.03
3,428.43	4,755.95	5,111.60	5,222.80	4,982.75	3,413.60	3,696.33	3,133.16	2,822.49	3,041.20	3,609.73
956.589	1,617.78	1,232.72	1,300.59	1,622.99	1,647.47	1,588.37	1,758.27	2,042.61	2,654.15	3,261.87
19,888.86	20,572.16	21,202.83	21,795.99	20,961.72	22,205.35	24,127.69	23,658.81	24,037.51	28,094.78	31,923.94
4,103.67	5,199.27	5,322.60	5,734.23	5,437.33	4,951.66	5,065.26	4,578.24	4,452.59	4,780.29	6,169.16
466.603	601.008	699.478	770.59	817.147	861.212	945.597	1,038.04	1,131.80	1,269.83	1,486.02
2,642.68	2,942.08	3,134.98	2,906.21	2,770.85	2,429.31	2,479.97	2,406.64	2,366.90	2,262.95	2,803.95
11,398.57	14,011.84	13,922.15	13,056.25	13,829.80	13,996.55	13,185.64	13,615.20	14,676.35	18,226.81	21,360.22
n/a	5,592.28	6,287.48	5,768.12	6,200.85	6,041.60	5,721.18	6,270.45	7,683.91	9,339.41	11,161.65
29,556.47	34,891.59	35,123.93	32,309.50	32,796.45	32,735.71	30,033.99	29,999.90	32,389.91	39,495.21	45,339.84
1,898.15	2,052.67	2,210.62	2,455.39	2,564.03	2,641.34	2,862.80	2,914.30	2,909.36	2,318.37	2,430.18
1,917.41	2,043.34	2,101.90	2,324.87	2,329.65	1,649.60	1,508.31	1,971.96	2,254.87	2,525.33	2,808.91
930.632	1,057.35	1,162.07	1,277.18	1,397.39	1,450.67	1,566.42	1,474.48	1,301.79	1,210.20	1,148.71
1,641.19	2,609.58	3,317.06	3,596.63	4,021.33	4,147.08	4,151.15	4,568.35	5,397.58	7,273.07	8,914.16
19,822.50	25,592.36	25,013.86	23,928.37	25,184.63	25,234.25	23,576.21	24,013.85	26,057.31	31,528.53	36,151.81
23,810.08	27,238.24	27,152.86	24,487.66	25,230.31	24,930.36	22,600.49	22,600.48	24,413.99	29,876.70	34,019.75
26,439.46	30,920.73	29,767.35	26,323.24	26,589.97	25,994.91	23,019.52	22,862.72	24,413.62	29,428.65	33,089.57
496.58	517.757	551.547	621.73	680.683	705.42	399.838	393.731	489.639	563.211	714.67
10,387.83	12,352.02	12,949.18	12,664.05	12,654.18	12,966.90	11,702.85	11,997.21	13,484.68	17,716.15	20,863.05
1,301.69	1,425.39	1,480.48	1,633.57	1,711.32	1,588.07	1,530.34	1,625.48	1,761.78	1,812.72	1,933.15
4,091.42	4,408.84	4,450.22	4,517.35	4,664.55	4,706.43	4,537.82	5,168.72	6,524.77	8,236.87	10,074.70
23,729.08	26,255.31	27,280.43	27,479.36	30,355.48	31,678.60	31,094.08	27,879.06	31,106.72	38,026.10	45,602.99
363.025	391.987	419.31	435.418	432.829	459.82	461.111	470.168	491.244	572.129	657.521
15,266.86	18,860.13	20,516.34	22,209.16	23,841.08	25,847.66	25,759.86	27,359.37	31,515.30	39,959.31	46,110.44
16,418.21	18,890.55	20,120.06	20,186.90	19,911.59	19,576.84	21,514.03	20,761.78	18,806.43	19,413.38	20,302.71
18,648.74	19,919.85	22,282.90	21,096.53	21,547.92	21,257.87	19,451.50	19,744.64	21,572.80	26,471.98	30,019.91
2,262.90	2,655.30	2,975.14	3,347.37	3,467.54	3,473.44	3,510.58	3,529.72	3,700.06	3,562.46	3,816.38
38,758.66	42,516.46	37,424.79	34,307.37	30,981.06	35,014.33	37,303.81	32,711.10	31,241.17	33,717.88	36,444.19
361.756	448.134	441.811	476.342	483.632	442.43	426.344	426.351	419.139	461.269	483.442
9,757.50	11,778.76	12,586.61	11,582.11	7,723.84	9,906.50	11,346.66	10,654.82	12,093.73	13,451.10	15,028.82
1,584.66	1,988.82	2,293.81	2,568.52	2,858.36	3,056.42	3,264.81	3,493.18	3,974.67	4,847.76	6,033.31
n/a	n/a	n/a	n/a	n/a	3,113.15	3,286.36	3,510.15	4,104.12	5,413.15	6,594.32
43,478.77	50,532.67	49,664.00	44,157.70	45,572.68	49,184.07	46,513.81	45,745.09	50,712.10	64,559.68	74,420.64
3,697.94	4,295.15	4,752.05	4,601.40	3,231.71	3,454.84	3,991.91	3,846.24	4,078.35	4,352.36	4,815.65
5,964.93	3,810.38	4,339.67	5,175.12	5,332.32	6,072.74	7,063.98	7,354.31	7,436.01	7,079.74	7,519.94
22,881.25	27,126.46	26,922.47	24,791.02	25,670.20	26,055.94	24,249.91	24,990.55	27,206.45	33,241.45	37,507.13
14,415.37	16,737.11	18,285.63	18,012.92	14,702.99	15,175.99	13,832.93	13,501.87	15,503.65	20,224.41	24,584.17
178.953	355.757	431.264	322.73	290.675	309.855	389.951	361.112	470.703	524.261	662.472
28,635.64	34,078.34	36,459.94	35,851.38	34,036.02	35,554.23	37,390.55	37,819.98	42,206.93	49,176.47	56,537.85
1,956.72	2,302.93	2,361.12	2,459.80	2,324.91	2,078.00	2,116.95	2,107.94	2,184.22	2,324.51	2,600.53
1,051.68	1,200.43	1,311.13	1,273.33	960.71	1,080.95	1,055.12	970.377	1,014.94	1,024.77	1,093.48
2,687.41	3,605.31	4,057.58	4,065.33	4,448.94	4,339.24	4,475.91	4,977.81	5,182.89	5,672.93	6,625.21
9,813.67	11,602.51	12,048.14	11,480.82	12,146.45	12,445.05	11,504.58	11,700.72	12,803.71	15,538.76	17,676.71
1,305.21	1,548.97	1,550.50	1,557.48	1,868.29	1,586.44	1,671.53	1,817.91	2,061.24	2,742.19	3,502.87
1,864.66	2,113.63	2,641.77	2,739.83	1,837.54	1,333.61	1,775.13	2,095.58	2,376.90	2,967.51	4,096.86
7,889.53	8,157.46	8,795.62	8,976.16	7,790.87	8,359.73	9,515.06	9,027.49	9,067.84	10,057.69	11,469.08
21,419.97	24,702.00	25,929.64	26,158.10	21,647.26	21,441.38	23,413.77	21,194.09	21,705.06	23,319.87	27,047.14
3,382.24	3,684.84	3,439.25	3,495.07	3,100.05	3,029.06	2,986.51	2,632.86	2,445.22	3,656.12	4,722.68
13,141.99	15,155.44	15,762.76	14,477.11	15,137.33	15,486.74	14,455.74	14,964.58	16,670.51	21,081.77	24,500.85
24,675.35	28,705.08	31,257.62	28,615.37	28,768.35	29,206.66	27,835.73	25,519.75	28,069.13	35,062.93	40,181.34
39,707.59	46,157.58	44,184.22	38,450.50	39,304.06	38,399.27	35,739.31	36,488.59	39,506.20	45,746.13	50,818.24
2,441.95	2,825.72	3,026.60	2,481.11	1,819.86	1,988.75	1,983.32	1,835.78	1,999.30	2,228.26	2,479.03
3,115.00	3,961.64	4,167.43	4,281.13	4,310.68	3,941.70	4,148.66	3,009.34	3,522.76	4,531.10	5,790.59
710.711	721.409	875.865	995.07	838.095	637.416	636.497	781.055	878.771	1,048.30	1,367.74
25,762.53	26,394.42	29,058.86	29,535.55	25,897.65	27,321.04	34,688.98	32,621.29	32,790.71	35,017.31	39,304.51
18,679.57	20,353.52	21,373.35	23,742.74	25,275.24	25,875.93	25,415.29	25,132.28	27,370.06	31,520.54	37,129.76
27,755.48	28,762.68	30,047.22	31,553.44	32,928.95	34,619.90	36,450.14	37,253.44	38,123.18	39,597.37	41,845.61
229.847	288.874	337.524	361.908	360.925	374.722	401.567	413.342	440.209	489.034	603.668

(continued on next page)

Table 3, continued
MACROECONOMIC DATA FOR SELECT COUNTRIES GDP PER PERSON (1985–2012)

Country	2005	2006	2007	2008	2009	2010	2011	2012
Argentina	4,781.86	5,540.64	6,705.04	8,270.21	7,707.99	9,162.21	10,958.90	11,582.48
Australia	35,976.04	37,713.29	44,982.82	48,951.34	45,429.71	56,250.57	66,201.52	67,304.47
Austria	37,143.21	39,339.41	45,245.56	49,915.00	46,003.57	45,111.55	49,444.29	46,642.88
Bangladesh	427.061	450.089	505.053	570.804	634.593	702.83	747.12	797.159
Belgium	36,187.16	38,086.06	43,486.09	47,789.59	44,134.37	43,585.79	46,796.78	43,615.17
Brazil	4,742.50	5,795.20	7,201.62	8,632.72	8,395.03	10,992.27	12,583.64	11,358.54
Bulgaria	3,753.28	4,329.16	5,520.39	6,854.99	6,432.50	6,374.12	7,311.80	7,006.25
Canada	36,149.39	40,290.98	44,336.26	46,372.50	40,709.04	47,367.38	51,645.22	52,299.76
Chile	7,565.31	9,414.66	10,426.27	10,709.21	10,166.62	12,712.54	14,551.69	15,410.12
China	1,726.05	2,063.87	2,644.56	3,403.53	3,739.62	4,422.66	5,434.36	6,071.47
Colombia	3,417.82	3,702.09	4,793.63	5,292.55	5,149.15	6,273.01	7,182.36	7,919.17
Cyprus	22,742.03	24,305.65	28,039.01	31,685.54	28,657.35	27,501.53	29,021.34	26,388.99
Czech Republic	12,725.94	14,474.00	17,544.02	21,715.05	18,837.96	18,891.89	20,603.29	18,624.30
Denmark	47,617.12	50,553.49	57,171.43	62,800.30	56,345.41	56,576.98	60,010.50	56,426.45
Dominican Republic	3,712.24	3,879.11	4,378.36	4,776.56	4,815.83	5,233.14	5,535.34	5,766.16
Ecuador	3,140.91	3,490.61	3,749.19	4,473.93	4,464.10	4,752.81	5,324.55	5,742.65
Egypt	1,282.77	1,505.96	1,771.00	2,160.04	2,452.63	2,775.85	2,930.12	3,111.87
Estonia	10,333.63	12,510.63	16,404.50	17,800.95	14,522.92	14,237.81	16,836.13	16,720.16
Finland	37,316.14	39,443.69	46,501.68	51,302.50	44,848.61	44,118.26	48,605.15	45,634.93
France	35,107.47	36,772.17	41,849.57	45,789.29	42,046.84	40,943.40	44,140.20	41,223.31
Germany	33,603.03	35,274.92	40,463.14	44,334.37	40,388.15	40,493.05	44,405.33	41,865.52
Ghana	833.397	952.739	1,126.86	1,266.11	1,116.45	1,358.16	1,594.43	1,622.24
Greece	21,699.72	23,546.25	27,379.01	30,605.23	28,582.40	26,074.16	25,654.78	22,072.45
Guatemala	2,140.94	2,320.30	2,554.52	2,859.65	2,690.09	2,875.31	3,236.13	3,325.68
Hungary	10,925.11	11,166.95	13,519.92	15,352.90	12,625.81	12,777.74	13,916.32	12,652.04
Iceland	55,590.44	55,786.89	66,390.20	53,354.20	37,933.65	39,556.32	44,163.99	42,725.04
India	748.85	839.927	1,080.70	1,052.67	1,158.91	1,432.25	1,546.55	1,500.76
Ireland	49,090.31	52,675.44	59,405.71	59,146.02	49,858.39	46,056.37	49,452.99	45,984.37
Israel	20,984.22	22,339.21	25,330.42	30,190.17	28,523.42	31,420.31	34,264.73	33,432.68
Italy	30,607.34	31,909.23	36,025.61	38,882.76	35,250.64	34,126.26	36,227.33	33,115.01
Jamaica	4,186.20	4,429.58	4,754.77	5,053.91	4,436.94	4,838.49	5,251.25	5,358.30
Japan	35,780.57	34,076.75	34,038.35	37,865.07	39,321.22	42,916.74	46,101.82	46,706.72
Kenya	546.57	637.226	748.701	813.052	792.75	810.995	839.158	966.587
Korea	17,550.88	19,676.11	21,590.17	19,028.07	16,958.65	20,540.18	22,388.40	22,588.92
Latvia	7,084.34	8,911.82	12,971.07	15,262.65	11,953.72	11,364.95	13,728.02	13,899.89
Lithuania	7,644.31	8,909.56	11,647.88	14,139.73	11,094.68	11,127.45	14,148.40	14,009.01
Luxembourg	80,971.13	90,049.03	106,915.85	112,428.82	100,741.58	104,335.44	114,186.25	106,406.42
Malaysia	5,421.34	6,065.61	7,121.82	8,390.27	7,203.34	8,658.67	9,979.39	10,344.87
Mexico	8,366.99	9,166.16	9,736.17	10,111.47	8,085.20	9,158.24	10,033.52	10,058.50
Netherlands	39,189.91	41,497.70	47,838.63	53,198.73	48,300.07	46,861.68	49,932.22	46,010.95
New Zealand	27,118.27	25,918.65	31,329.09	31,119.79	27,470.50	32,459.07	36,687.08	38,254.62
Nigeria	823.824	1,038.76	1,153.40	1,401.24	1,110.04	1,465.15	1,521.66	1,640.11
Norway	65,646.21	72,784.95	83,335.71	94,815.85	78,231.37	85,764.72	98,664.44	99,170.20
Peru	2,916.68	3,340.24	3,800.44	4,427.11	4,362.46	5,204.83	5,943.85	6,525.36
Philippines	1,208.93	1,405.21	1,683.69	1,918.26	1,851.48	2,155.41	2,378.93	2,611.50
Poland	7,962.95	8,954.31	11,155.83	13,890.16	11,313.67	12,308.93	13,383.56	12,709.27
Portugal	18,217.25	19,082.78	21,876.73	23,827.95	22,076.37	21,562.45	22,334.04	20,037.74
Romania	4,589.37	5,686.89	7,916.74	9,496.90	7,649.49	7,683.84	8,539.55	7,939.30
Russia	5,310.88	6,912.93	9,101.56	11,630.58	8,567.94	10,671.21	13,335.23	14,302.09
Saudi Arabia	14,078.90	15,624.75	16,677.92	20,157.30	16,095.19	19,413.05	23,599.11	24,523.92
Singapore	29,403.39	33,088.75	38,762.59	39,382.95	37,859.79	45,639.35	51,241.74	52,051.81
South Africa	5,266.81	5,511.09	5,851.56	5,544.53	5,732.84	7,244.72	7,971.62	7,525.39
Spain	26,101.60	28,081.47	32,168.13	35,112.83	31,746.74	30,113.76	31,563.40	28,670.09
Sweden	40,958.21	43,790.68	50,366.61	52,521.66	43,442.55	49,180.46	56,523.12	54,814.80
Switzerland	51,888.75	54,321.34	59,998.62	69,049.02	65,442.05	69,771.89	82,834.72	78,880.93
Thailand	2,707.51	3,172.30	3,756.87	4,110.00	3,943.07	4,740.33	5,114.73	5,390.41
Turkey	7,044.10	7,650.66	9,216.55	10,272.53	8,529.77	10,015.27	10,477.01	10,526.80
Ukraine	1,829.76	2,304.92	3,071.49	3,899.27	2,550.45	2,979.67	3,583.97	3,877.28
United Arab Emirates	43,988.56	44,283.30	41,472.29	39,074.84	31,073.63	34,778.05	40,951.45	43,773.84
United Kingdom	38,584.96	41,043.58	46,866.34	44,131.12	35,885.37	36,891.37	39,286.35	39,160.58
United States	44,224.13	46,358.36	47,963.56	48,307.78	46,906.90	48,294.19	49,796.95	51,703.95
Vietnam	699.682	796.928	920.463	1,154.49	1,181.51	1,297.85	1,532.06	1,752.62

Sources: International Monetary Fund, World Economic Outlook Database, 2013.

GLOSSARY

absolute advantage the advantage conferred by the ability to produce more of a good or service with a given amount of time and resources; not the same thing as comparative advantage.

accelerator principle the proposition that a higher rate of growth in real GDP results in a higher level of planned investment spending, and a lower growth rate in real GDP leads to lower planned investment spending.

accounting profit a business's revenue minus the explicit cost and depreciation.

actual investment spending the sum of planned investment spending and unplanned inventory investment.

***AD–AS* model** the basic model used to understand fluctuations in aggregate output and the aggregate price level. It uses the aggregate demand curve and the aggregate supply curve together to analyze the behavior of the economy in response to shocks or government policy.

administrative costs (of a tax) the resources used (which is a cost) by government to collect the tax, and by taxpayers to pay it, over and above the amount of the tax, as well as to evade it.

adverse selection occurs when an individual knows more about the way things are than other people do. Adverse selection problems can lead to market problems: private information leads buyers to expect hidden problems in items offered for sale, leading to low prices and the best items being kept off the market.

aggregate consumption function the relationship for the economy as a whole between aggregate current disposable income and aggregate consumer spending.

aggregate demand curve a graphical representation of the relationship between the aggregate price level and the quantity of aggregate output demanded by households, businesses, the government, and the rest of the world.

aggregate output the economy's total production of final goods and services for a given time period, usually a year. Real GDP is the numerical measure of aggregate output typically used by economists.

aggregate price level a measure of the overall level of prices in the economy.

aggregate production function a hypothetical function that shows how productivity (real GDP per worker) depends on the quantities of physical capital per worker and human capital per worker as well as the state of technology.

aggregate spending the total spending on domestically produced final goods and services; the sum of consumer spending (C), investment spending (I), government purchases of goods and services (G), and exports minus imports ($X - IM$).

aggregate supply curve a graphical representation of the relationship between the aggregate price level and the total quantity of aggregate output supplied.

antitrust policy legislative and regulatory efforts undertaken by the government to prevent oligopolistic industries from becoming or behaving like monopolies.

appreciation (of currency) a rise in the value of one currency in terms of other currencies.

artificially scarce good a good that is excludable but nonrival in consumption.

asset bubble a phenomenon in which the price of a particular good or service is pushed to an unreasonably high level due to expectations of further price gains.

autarky a situation in which a country does not trade with other countries.

automatic stabilizers government spending and taxation rules that cause fiscal policy to be automatically expansionary when the economy contracts and automatically contractionary when the economy expands. Taxes that depend on disposable income are the most important example of automatic stabilizers.

autonomous consumer spending the amount of money a household would spend if it had no disposable income.

average cost total cost divided by quantity of output produced. Also referred to as average total cost.

average fixed cost the fixed cost per unit of output.

average total cost total cost divided by quantity of output produced. Also referred to as average cost.

average variable cost the variable cost per unit of output.

balance of payments accounts a summary of a country's transactions with other countries, including two main elements: the balance of payments on the current account and the balance of payments on the financial account.

balance of payments on the current account (current account) a country's balance of payments on goods and services plus net international transfer payments and factor income.

balance of payments on the financial account (financial account) the difference between a country's sales of assets to foreigners and its purchases of assets from foreigners during a given period.

balance of payments on goods and services the difference between the value of exports and the value of imports during a given period.

balance sheet effect the reduction in a firm's net worth from falling asset prices.

bank a financial intermediary that provides liquid assets in the form of bank deposits to lenders and uses those funds to finance the illiquid investments or investment spending needs of borrowers.

bank deposit a claim on a bank that obliges the bank to give the depositor his or her cash when demanded.

bank reserves currency held by banks in their vaults plus their deposits at the Federal Reserve.

bank run a phenomenon in which many of a bank's depositors try to withdraw their funds due to fears of a bank failure.

banking crisis an episode in which a large part of the depository banking sector or the shadow banking sector fails or threatens to fail.

barrier to entry something that prevents other firms from entering an industry. Crucial in protecting the profits of a monopolist. There are four types of barriers to entry: control over scarce resources or inputs, increasing returns to scale, technological superiority, and government-created barriers such as licenses.

black market a market in which goods or services are bought and sold illegally, either because it is illegal to sell them at all or because the prices charged are legally prohibited by a price ceiling.

bond a loan in the form of an IOU that pays interest.

bounded rationality a basis for decision making that leads to a choice that is close to but not exactly the one that leads to the best possible economic outcome; the "good enough" method of decision making.

brand name a name owned by a particular firm that distinguishes its products from those of other firms.

break-even price the market price at which a firm earns zero profits.

budget balance the difference between tax revenue and government spending. A positive budget balance is referred to as a budget surplus; a negative budget balance is referred to as a budget deficit.

budget constraint the cost of a consumer's consumption bundle cannot exceed the consumer's income.

budget deficit the difference between tax revenue and government spending when government spending exceeds tax revenue.

budget line all the consumption bundles available to a consumer who spends all of his or her income.

budget surplus the difference between tax revenue and government spending when tax revenue exceeds government spending.

business cycle the short-run alternation between economic downturns, known as recessions, and economic upturns, known as expansions.

business-cycle peak the point in time at which the economy shifts from expansion to recession.

business-cycle trough the point in time at which the economy shifts from recession to expansion.

capital the total value of assets owned by an individual or firm—physical assets plus financial assets.

cartel an agreement among several producers to obey output restrictions in order to increase their joint profits.

central bank an institution that oversees and regulates the banking system and controls the monetary base.

chained dollars describes a method of calculating real GDP that splits the difference between growth rates calculated using early base years and the growth rates calculated using late base years.

change in demand a shift of the demand curve, which changes the quantity demanded at any given price.

change in supply a shift of the supply curve, which changes the quantity supplied at any given price.

checkable bank deposits bank accounts on which people can write checks.

circular-flow diagram a diagram that represents the transactions in an economy by two kinds of flows around a circle: flows of physical things such as goods or labor in one direction and flows of money to pay for these physical things in the opposite direction.

classical model of the price level a model of the price level in which the real quantity of money is always at its long-run equilibrium level. This model ignores the distinction between the short run and the long run but is useful for analyzing the case of high inflation.

Coase theorem the proposition that even in the presence of externalities an economy can always reach an efficient solution as long as transaction costs are sufficiently low.

collusion cooperation among producers to limit production and raise prices so as to raise one another's profits.

commercial bank a bank that accepts deposits and is covered by deposit insurance.

commodity output of different producers regarded by consumers as the same good; also referred to as a standardized product.

commodity money a medium of exchange that is a good, normally gold or silver, that has intrinsic value in other uses.

commodity-backed money a medium of exchange that has no intrinsic value whose ultimate value is guaranteed by a promise that it can be converted into valuable goods on demand.

common resource a resource that is nonexcludable and rival in consumption.

comparative advantage the advantage conferred if the opportunity cost of producing the good or service is lower for another producer.

compensating differentials wage differences across jobs that reflect the fact that some jobs are less pleasant or more dangerous than others.

competitive market a market in which there are many buyers and sellers of the same good or service, none of whom can influence the price at which the good or service is sold.

complements pairs of goods for which a rise in the price of one good leads to a decrease in the demand for the other good.

constant marginal cost each additional unit costs the same to produce as the previous one.

constant returns to scale long-run average total cost is constant as output increases.

consumer price index (CPI) a measure of the cost of a market basket intended to represent the consumption of a typical urban American family of four. It is the most commonly used measure of prices in the United States.

consumer spending household spending on goods and services from domestic and foreign firms.

consumer surplus a term often used to refer both to individual consumer surplus and to total consumer surplus.

consumption function an equation showing how an individual household's consumer spending varies with the household's current disposable income.

consumption possibilities the set of all consumption bundles that are affordable, given a consumer's income and prevailing prices.

contractionary fiscal policy fiscal policy that reduces aggregate demand by decreasing government purchases, increasing taxes, or decreasing transfers.

contractionary monetary policy monetary policy that, through the raising of the interest rate, reduces aggregate demand and therefore output.

convergence hypothesis a theory of economic growth that holds that international differences in real GDP per capita tend to narrow over time because countries with low GDP per capita generally have higher growth rates.

copyright the exclusive legal right of the creator of a literary or artistic work to profit from that work; like a patent, it is a temporary monopoly.

cost (of seller) the lowest price at which a seller is willing to sell a good.

cost-minimization rule hire factors so that the marginal product per dollar spent on each factor is the same; a firm uses this rule to determine the cost-minimizing combination of inputs.

credit crunch a time during which potential borrowers either can't get credit at all or must pay very high interest rates.

cross-price elasticity of demand a measure of the effect of the change in the price of one good on the quantity demanded of the other; it is equal to the percent change in the quantity demanded of one good divided by the percent change in the price of another good.

crowding out the negative effect of budget deficits on private investment, which occurs because government borrowing drives up interest rates.

currency in circulation actual cash held by the public.

cyclical unemployment unemployment resulting from the business cycle; equivalently, the difference between the actual rate of unemployment and the natural rate of unemployment.

cyclically adjusted budget balance an estimate of what the budget balance would be if real GDP were exactly equal to potential output.

deadweight loss losses associated with quantities of output that are greater than or less than the efficient level, as can result from market intervention such as taxes, or from externalities such as pollution.

debt deflation the reduction in aggregate demand arising from the increase in the real burden of outstanding debt caused by deflation; occurs because borrowers, whose real debt rises as a result of deflation, are likely to cut spending sharply, and lenders, whose real assets are now more valuable, are less likely to increase spending.

debt–GDP ratio government debt as a percentage of GDP, frequently used as a measure of a government's ability to pay its debts.

debt overhang high debt but diminished assets, resulting from a vicious cycle of deleveraging.

decreasing marginal benefit each additional unit of an activity yields less benefit than the previous unit.

decreasing marginal cost each additional unit costs less to produce than the previous one.

decreasing returns to scale long-run average total cost increases as output increases (also known as diseconomies of scale).

deductible a sum specified in an insurance policy that the insured individuals must pay before being compensated for a claim; deductibles reduce moral hazard.

default the failure of a borrower to make payments as specified by the bond contract.

deflation a fall in the overall level of prices.

demand curve a graphical representation of the demand schedule, showing the relationship between quantity demanded and price.

demand price the price of a given quantity at which consumers will demand that quantity.

demand schedule a list or table showing how much of a good or service consumers will want to buy at different prices.

demand shock any event that shifts the aggregate demand curve. A positive demand shock is associated with higher demand for aggregate output at any price level and shifts the curve to the right. A negative demand shock is associated with lower demand for aggregate output at any price level and shifts the curve to the left.

deposit insurance a guarantee that a bank's depositors will be paid even if the bank can't come up with the funds, up to a maximum amount per account.

depreciation (of currency) a fall in the value of one currency in terms of other currencies.

derived demand demand for a factor that results from (or is derived from) the demand for the output being produced.

devaluation a reduction in the value of a currency that is set under a fixed exchange rate regime.

diminishing returns to an input the effect observed when an increase in the quantity of an input, while holding the levels of all other inputs fixed, leads to a decline in the marginal product of that input.

diminishing returns to physical capital describes the effect on an aggregate production function when the amount of human capital per worker and the state of technology are held fixed: each successive increase in the amount of physical capital per worker leads to a smaller increase in productivity.

discount rate the interest rate the Fed charges on loans to banks in trouble.

discount window an arrangement in which the Federal Reserve stands ready to lend money to banks in trouble.

discouraged workers nonworking people who are capable of working but have given up looking for a job due to the state of the job market.

discretionary fiscal policy fiscal policy that is the direct result of deliberate actions by policy makers rather than rules.

discretionary monetary policy the use of changes in the interest rate or the money supply to stabilize the economy.

disinflation the process of bringing down inflation that has become embedded in expectations.

disposable income income plus government transfers minus taxes; the total amount of household income available to spend on consumption and saving.

diversification investment in several different assets with unrelated, or independent, risks, so that the possible losses are independent events.

domestic demand curve a demand curve that shows how the quantity of a good demanded by domestic consumers depends on the price of that good.

domestic supply curve a supply curve that shows how the quantity of a good supplied by domestic producers depends on the price of that good.

dominant strategy in game theory, an action that is a player's best action regardless of the action taken by the other player.

duopolist one of the two firms in a duopoly.

duopoly an oligopoly consisting of only two firms.

economic aggregates economic measures that summarize data across different markets for goods, services, workers, and assets.

economic profit a business's revenue minus the opportunity cost of resources; usually less than the accounting profit.

economic signal any piece of information that helps people make better economic decisions.

economics the study of scarcity and choice.

economy a system for coordinating a society's productive and consumptive activities.

efficiency wages wages that employers set above the equilibrium wage rate as an incentive for workers to deliver better performance.

efficiency-wage model a model in which some employers pay an above-equilibrium wage as an incentive for better performance.

efficient describes a market or economy that takes all opportunities to make some people better off without making other people worse off.

elastic demand the case in which the price elasticity of demand is greater than 1.

emissions tax a tax that depends on the amount of pollution a firm produces.

employed refers to people currently holding a job in the economy, either full time or part time.

environmental standards rules established by a government to protect the environment by specifying actions by producers and consumers.

equilibrium an economic situation in which no individual would be better off doing something different.

equilibrium exchange rate the exchange rate at which the quantity of a currency demanded in the foreign exchange market is equal to the quantity supplied.

equilibrium price the price at which the market is in equilibrium, that is, the quantity of a good or service demanded equals the quantity of that good or service supplied; also referred to as the market-clearing price.

equilibrium quantity the quantity of a good or service bought and sold at the equilibrium (or market-clearing) price.

equilibrium value of the marginal product the additional value produced by the last unit of a factor employed in the factor market as a whole.

excess capacity when firms produce less than the output at which average total cost is minimized; characteristic of monopolistically competitive firms.

excess reserves a bank's reserves over and above the reserves required by law or regulation.

exchange market intervention government purchases or sales of currency in the foreign exchange market.

exchange rate the price at which currencies trade, determined by the foreign exchange market.

exchange rate regime a rule governing policy toward the exchange rate.

excise tax a tax on sales of a particular good or service.

excludable referring to a good, describes the case in which the supplier can prevent those who do not pay from consuming the good.

expansion a period of economic upturn in which output and employment are rising; most economic numbers are following their normal upward trend; also referred to as a recovery.

expansionary fiscal policy fiscal policy that increases aggregate demand by increasing government purchases, decreasing taxes, or increasing transfers.

expansionary monetary policy monetary policy that, through the lowering of the interest rate, increases aggregate demand and therefore output.

explicit cost a cost that involves actually laying out money.

exporting industries industries that produce goods or services that are sold abroad.

exports goods and services sold to other countries.

external benefit an uncompensated benefit that an individual or firm confers on others; also known as positive externalities.

external cost an uncompensated cost that an individual or firm imposes on others; also known as negative externalities.

externalities external costs and external benefits.

factor distribution of income the division of total income among land, labor, physical capital, and human capital.

factor intensity the difference in the ratio of factors used to produce a good in various industries. For example, oil refining is capital-intensive compared to clothing manufacture because oil refiners use a higher ratio of capital to labor than do clothing producers.

factor markets markets in which resources, especially capital and labor, are bought and sold.

factors of production the resources used to produce goods and services. The main factors of production are land, labor, physical capital, and human capital.

federal funds market the financial market that allows banks that fall short of reserve requirements to borrow funds from banks with excess reserves.

federal funds rate the interest rate at which funds are borrowed and lent in the federal funds market.

fiat money a medium of exchange whose value derives entirely from its official status as a means of payment.

final goods and services goods and services sold to the final, or end, user.

financial asset a paper claim that entitles the buyer to future income from the seller. Loans, stocks, bonds, and bank deposits are types of financial assets.

financial contagion a vicious downward spiral among depository banks as well as shadow banks: each institution's failure increases the likelihood that another will fail.

financial intermediary an institution, such as a mutual fund, pension fund, life insurance company, or bank, that transforms the funds it gathers from many individuals into financial assets.

financial markets the banking, stock, and bond markets, which channel private savings and foreign lending into investment spending, government borrowing, and foreign borrowing.

financial panic a sudden and widespread disruption of the financial markets that occurs when peope lose faith in the liquidity of financial institutions and markets.

financial risk uncertainty about future outcomes that involve financial losses and gains.

firm an organization that produces goods and services for sale.

fiscal year the time period used for much of government accounting; the U.S. fiscal year runs from October 1 to September 30. Fiscal years are labeled by the calendar year in which they end.

Fisher effect the principle by which an increase in expected future inflation drives up the nominal interest rate, leaving the expected real interest rate unchanged.

fixed cost cost that does not depend on the quantity of output produced. It is the cost of the fixed input.

fixed exchange rate an exchange rate regime in which the government keeps the exchange rate against some other currency at or near a particular target.

fixed input an input whose quantity is fixed for a period of time and cannot be varied (for example, land).

floating exchange rate an exchange rate regime in which the government lets the exchange rate go wherever the market takes it.

foreign exchange controls licensing systems that limit the right of individuals to buy foreign currency.

foreign exchange market the market in which currencies are traded.

foreign exchange reserves stocks of foreign currency that governments can use to buy their own currency on the foreign exchange market.

free entry and exit describes an industry that potential producers can easily enter or current producers can leave.

free trade trade that is unregulated by government tariffs or other artificial barriers; the levels of exports and imports occur naturally, as a result of supply and demand.

free-rider problem the problem that results when individuals who have no incentive to pay for their own consumption of a good take a "free ride" on anyone who does pay; a problem with goods that are nonexcludable.

frictional unemployment unemployment due to time workers spend in job search.

gains from trade an economic principle that states that by dividing tasks and trading, people can get more of what they want through trade than they could if they tried to be self-sufficient.

game theory the study of behavior in situations of interdependence. Used to explain the behavior of an oligopoly.

GDP deflator a price measure for a given year that is equal to 100 times the ratio of nominal GDP to real GDP in that year.

GDP per capita GDP divided by the size of the population; equivalent to the average GDP per person.

Gini coefficient a number that summarizes a country's level of income inequality based on how unequally income is distributed across the quintiles.

globalization the phenomenon of growing economic linkages among countries.

government borrowing the amount of funds borrowed by the government in financial markets to buy goods and services.

government purchases of goods and services total purchases by federal, state, and local governments on goods and services.

government transfer a government payment to an individual or a family.

Great Moderation the period from 1985 to 2007 when the U.S. economy experienced small fluctuations and low inflation.

Great Moderation consensus a belief in monetary policy as the main tool of stabilization combined with skepticism toward the use of fiscal policy and an acknowledgment of the policy constraints imposed by the natural rate of unemployment and the political business cycle.

gross domestic product (GDP) the total value of all final goods and services produced in the economy during a given period, usually a year.

growth accounting estimation of the contribution of each of the major factors (physical and human capital, labor, and technology) in the aggregate production function.

Heckscher–Ohlin model a model of international trade in which a country has a comparative advantage in a good whose production is intensive in the factors that are abundantly available in that country.

Herfindahl–Hirschman Index the square of each firm's share of market sales summed over the industry. It gives a picture of the industry market structure.

household a person or a group of people who share income.

human capital the improvement in labor created by the education and knowledge embodied in the workforce.

illiquid describes an asset that cannot be quickly converted into cash without much loss of value.

imperfect competition a market structure in which no firm is a monopolist, but producers nonetheless have market power they can use to affect market prices.

implicit cost a cost that does not require the outlay of money; it is measured by the value, in dollar terms, of forgone benefits.

implicit cost of capital the opportunity cost of the capital used by a business; that is, the income that could have been realized had the capital been used in the next best alternative way.

implicit liabilities spending promises made by governments that are effectively a debt despite the fact that they are not included in the usual debt statistics. In the United States, the largest implicit liabilities arise from Social Security and Medicare, which promise transfer payments to current and future retirees (Social Security) and to the elderly (Medicare).

import quota a legal limit on the quantity of a good that can be imported.

import-competing industries industries that produce goods or services that are also imported.

imports goods and services purchased from other countries.

income effect the change in the quantity of a good consumed that results from the change in a consumer's purchasing power due to the change in the price of the good.

income elasticity of demand the percent change in the quantity of a good demanded when a consumer's income changes divided by the percent change in the consumer's income.

income–expenditure equilibrium a situation in which aggregate output, measured by real GDP, is equal to planned aggregate spending and firms have no incentive to change output.

income–expenditure equilibrium GDP the level of real GDP at which real GDP equals planned aggregate spending.

income-elastic demand the case in which the income elasticity of demand for a good is greater than 1.

income-inelastic demand the case in which the income elasticity of demand for a good is positive but less than 1.

increasing marginal cost each additional unit costs more to produce than the previous one.

increasing returns to scale long-run average total cost declines as output increases (also referred to as economies of scale).

individual choice the decision by an individual of what to do, which necessarily involves a decision of what not to do.

individual consumer surplus the net gain to an individual buyer from the purchase of a good; equal to the difference between the buyer's willingness to pay and the price paid.

individual demand curve a graphical representation of the relationship between quantity demanded and price for an individual consumer.

individual labor supply curve a graphical representation showing how the quantity of labor supplied by an individual depends on that individual's wage rate.

individual producer surplus the net gain to an individual seller from selling a good; equal to the difference between the price received and the seller's cost.

individual supply curve a graphical representation of the relationship between quantity supplied and price for an individual producer.

industry supply curve a graphical representation that shows the relationship between the price of a good and the total output of the industry for that good.

inefficient describes a market or economy in which there are missed opportunities: some people could be made better off without making other people worse off.

inefficient allocation of sales among sellers a form of inefficiency in which sellers who would be willing to sell a good at the lowest price are not always those who actually manage to sell it; often the result of a price floor.

inefficient allocation to consumers a form of inefficiency in which people who want a good badly and are willing to pay a high price don't get it, and those who care relatively little about the good and are only willing to pay a low price do get it; often a result of a price ceiling.

inefficiently high quality a form of inefficiency in which sellers offer high-quality goods at a high price even though buyers would prefer a lower quality at a lower price; often the result of a price floor.

inefficiently low quality a form of inefficiency in which sellers offer low-quality goods at a low price even though buyers would prefer a higher quality at a higher price; often a result of a price ceiling.

inelastic demand the case in which the price elasticity of demand is less than 1.

inferior good a good for which a rise in income decreases the demand for the good.

inflation a rise in the overall level of prices.

inflation rate the annual percent change in a price index—typically the consumer price index. The inflation rate is positive when the aggregate price level is rising (inflation) and negative when the aggregate price level is falling (deflation).

inflation targeting an approach to monetary policy that requires that the central bank try to keep the inflation rate near a predetermined target rate.

inflation tax the reduction in the value of money held by the public caused by inflation.

inflationary gap the gap that exists when aggregate output is above potential output.

infrastructure physical capital, such as roads, power lines, ports, information networks, and other parts of an economy, that provides the underpinnings, or foundation, for economic activity.

in-kind benefit a benefit given in the form of goods or services.

input a good or service used to produce another good or service.

interdependent the relationship among firms in which the outcome (profit) of each firm depends on the actions of the other firms in the market.

interest rate effect of a change in the aggregate price level the effect on consumer spending and investment spending caused by a change in the purchasing power of consumers' money holdings when the aggregate price level changes. A rise (fall) in the aggregate price level decreases (increases) the purchasing power of consumers' money holdings. In response, consumers try to increase (decrease) their money holdings, which drives up (down) interest rates, thereby decreasing (increasing) consumption and investment.

intermediate goods and services goods and services, bought from one firm by another firm, that are inputs for production of final goods and services.

internalize the externalities take into account external costs and external benefits.

inventories stocks of goods and raw materials held to satisfy future sales.

inventory investment the value of the change in total inventories held in the economy during a given period. Unlike other types of investment spending, inventory investment can be negative, if inventories fall.

investment bank a bank that creates and trades in financial assets and is not covered by deposit insurance.

investment spending spending on productive physical capital, such as machinery and construction of structures, and on changes to inventories.

invisible hand a phrase used by Adam Smith to refer to the way in which an individual's pursuit of self-interest can lead, without the individual's intending it, to good results for society as a whole.

irrational describes a decision maker who chooses an option that leaves him or her worse off than choosing another available option.

job search the period in which workers spend time looking for employment.

jobless recovery a period in which GDP growth rate is positive but the unemployment rate is still rising.

Keynesian cross a diagram that identifies income–expenditure equilibrium as the point where the planned aggregate spending line crosses the 45-degree line.

Keynesian economics a school of thought emerging out of the works of John Maynard Keynes; according to Keynesian economics, a depressed economy is the result of inadequate spending and government intervention can help a depressed economy through monetary policy and fiscal policy.

labor the effort of workers.

labor force the number of people who are either actively employed for pay or unemployed and actively looking for work; the sum of employment and unemployment.

labor force participation rate the percentage of the population age 16 or older that is in the labor force.

labor productivity output per worker; also known simply as productivity.

land all resources that come from nature, such as minerals, timber, and petroleum.

law of demand the principle that a higher price for a good or service, other things equal, leads people to demand a smaller quantity of that good or service.

law of supply the general proposition that, other things equal, the price and quantity supplied of a good are positively related.

leisure the time available for purposes other than earning money to buy marketed goods.

lender of last resort an institution, usually a country's central bank, that provides funds to financial institutions when they are unable to borrow from the private credit markets.

leverage the degree to which a financial institution is financing its investments with borrowed funds.

liability a requirement to pay income in the future.

license the right, conferred by the government or an owner, to supply a good or service.

life insurance company a financial intermediary that sells policies guaranteeing a payment to a policyholder's beneficiaries when the policyholder dies.

liquid describes an asset that can be quickly converted into cash without much loss of value.

liquidity preference model of the interest rate a model of the market for money in which the interest rate is determined by the supply and demand for money.

liquidity trap a situation in which monetary policy is ineffective because nominal interest rates are up against the zero bound.

loan a lending agreement between an individual lender and an individual borrower. Loans are usually tailored to the individual borrower's needs and ability to pay but carry relatively high transaction costs.

loanable funds market a hypothetical market in which the demand for funds is generated by borrowers and the supply of funds is provided by lenders. The market equilibrium determines the quantity and price, or interest rate, of loanable funds.

loan-backed securities assets created by pooling individual loans and selling shares in that pool.

long run the time period in which all inputs can be varied.

long-run aggregate supply curve a graphical representation of the relationship between the aggregate price level and the quantity of aggregate output supplied if all prices, including nominal wages, were fully flexible. The long-run aggregate supply curve is vertical because the aggregate price level has no effect on aggregate output in the long run; in the long run, aggregate output is determined by the economy's potential output.

long-run average total cost curve a graphical representation showing the relationship between output and average total cost when fixed cost has been chosen to minimize average total cost for each level of output.

long-run economic growth the sustained rise in the quantity of goods and services the economy produces.

long-run industry supply curve a graphical representation that shows how quantity supplied responds to price once producers have had time to enter or exit the industry.

long-run macroeconomic equilibrium a situation in which the short-run macroeconomic equilibrium is also on the long-run aggregate supply curve; so short-run equilibrium aggregate output is equal to potential output.

long-run market equilibrium an economic balance in which, given sufficient time for producers to enter or exit an industry, the quantity supplied equals the quantity demanded.

long-run Phillips curve a graphical representation of the relationship between unemployment and inflation in the long run after expectations of inflation have had time to adjust to experience.

long-term interest rate the interest rate on financial assets that mature a number of years into the future.

loss aversion oversensitivity to loss, leading to unwillingness to recognize a loss and move on.

lump-sum taxes taxes that don't depend on the taxpayer's income.

macroeconomic policy activism the use of monetary policy and fiscal policy to smooth out the business cycle.

macroeconomics the branch of economics that is concerned with the overall ups and downs in the economy.

marginal analysis comparison of the benefit of doing a little bit more of some activity with the cost of doing a little bit more of that activity.

marginal benefit the additional benefit derived from producing one more unit of a good or service.

marginal benefit curve a graphical representation showing how the benefit from producing one more unit depends on the quantity that has already been produced.

marginal cost the additional cost incurred by producing one more unit of a good or service.

marginal cost curve a graphical representation showing how the cost of producing one more unit depends on the quantity that has already been produced.

marginal product the additional quantity of output produced by using one more unit of that input.

marginal productivity theory of income distribution every factor of production is paid its equilibrium value of the marginal product.

marginal propensity to consume (*MPC*) the increase in consumer spending when income rises by $1. Because consumers normally spend part but not all of an additional dollar of disposable income, *MPC* is between 0 and 1.

marginal propensity to save (*MPS*) the increase in household savings when disposable income rises by $1.

marginal revenue the change in total revenue generated by an additional unit of output.

marginal revenue curve a graphical representation showing how marginal revenue varies as output varies.

marginal revenue product of labor (*MRPL*) equals the marginal product of labor times the marginal revenue received from selling the additional output. The marginal revenue product of land and the marginal revenue product of capital are equivalent concepts.

marginal social benefit of pollution the additional gain to society as a whole from an additional unit of pollution.

marginal social cost of pollution the additional cost imposed on society as a whole by an additional unit of pollution.

marginal utility the change in total utility generated by consuming one additional unit of a good or service.

marginal utility curve a graphical representation showing how marginal utility depends on the quantity of a good or service consumed.

marginal utility per dollar the= additional utility from spending one more dollar on a good or service.

marginally attached workers nonworking individuals who say they would like a job and have looked for work in the recent past but are not currently looking for work.

market basket a hypothetical consumption bundle of consumer purchases of goods and services, used to measure changes in overall price level.

market economy an economy in which decisions of individual producers and consumers largely determine what, how, and for whom to produce, with little government involvement in the decisions.

market failure the failure of a market to be efficient.

market share the fraction of the total industry output accounted for by a firm's output.

market-clearing price the price at which the market is in equilibrium; that is, the quantity of a good or service demanded equals the quantity of that good or service supplied. Also referred to as the equilibrium price.

maturity transformation the conversion of short-term liabilities into long-term assets.

mean household income the average income across all households.

means-tested program a program in which benefits are available only to individuals or families whose incomes fall below a certain level.

median household income the income of the household lying in the middle of the income distribution.

medium of exchange an asset that individuals acquire for the purpose of trading for goods and services rather than for their own consumption.

mental accounting the habit of mentally assigning dollars to different accounts so that some dollars are worth more than others.

menu cost the real cost of changing a listed price.

merchandise trade balance (trade balance) the difference between a country's exports and imports of goods alone—not including services.

microeconomics the branch of economics that studies how people make decisions and how those decisions interact.

midpoint method a technique for calculating the percent change in which changes in a variable are compared with the average, or midpoint, of the starting and final values.

minimum wage a legal floor on the wage rate. The wage rate is the market price of labor.

minimum-cost output the quantity of output at which average total cost is lowest—the bottom of the U-shaped average total cost curve.

model a simplified representation of a real situation that is used to better understand real-life situations.

monetarism a theory of business cycles, associated primarily with Milton Friedman, that asserts that GDP will grow steadily if the money supply grows steadily.

monetary aggregate an overall measure of the money supply. The most common monetary aggregates in the United States are M1, which includes currency in circulation, traveler's checks, and checkable bank deposits, and M2, which includes M1 as well as near-moneys.

monetary base the sum of currency in circulation and bank reserves.

monetary neutrality the concept that changes in the money supply have no real effects on the economy in the long run and only result in a proportional change in the price level.

monetary policy rule a formula that determines the central bank's actions.

money any asset that can easily be used to purchase goods and services.

money demand curve a graphical representation of the negative relationship between the quantity of money demanded and the interest rate. The money demand curve slopes downward because, other things equal, a higher interest rate increases the opportunity cost of holding money.

money multiplier the ratio of the money supply to the monetary base; indicates the total number of dollars created in the banking system by each $1 addition to the monetary base.

money supply the total value of financial assets in the economy that are considered money.

money supply curve a graphical representation of the relationship between the quantity of money supplied by the Federal Reserve and the interest rate.

monopolist a firm that is the only producer of a good that has no close substitutes.

monopolistic competition a market structure in which there are many competing firms in an industry, each firm sells a differentiated product, and there is free entry into and exit from the industry in the long run.

monopoly an industry controlled by a monopolist.

monopsonist a single buyer in a market.

monopsony a market in which there is only one buyer.

moral hazard the situation that can exist when an individual knows more about his or her own actions than other people do. This leads to a distortion of incentives to take care or to exert effort when someone else bears the costs of the lack of care or effort.

movement along the demand curve a change in the quantity demanded of a good that results from a change in the price of that good.

movement along the supply curve a change in the quantity supplied of a good that results from a change in the price of that good.

multiplier the ratio of total change in real GDP caused by an autonomous change in aggregate spending to the size of that autonomous change.

mutual fund a financial intermediary that creates a stock portfolio by buying and holding shares in companies and then selling shares of this portfolio to individual investors.

Nash equilibrium in game theory, the equilibrium that results when all players choose the action that maximizes their payoffs given the actions of other players, ignoring the effect of that action on the payoffs of other players; also known as noncooperative equilibrium.

national income and product accounts (national accounts) an accounting of consumer spending, sales of producers, business investment spending, and other flows of money between different sectors of the economy. Calculated by the Bureau of Economic Analysis.

national savings the sum of private savings and the government's budget balance; the total amount of savings generated within the economy.

natural monopoly a monopoly that exists when increasing returns to scale provide a large cost advantage to having all output produced by a single firm.

natural rate hypothesis the hypothesis that the unemployment rate is stable in the long run at a particular natural rate. According to this hypothesis, attempts to lower the unemployment rate below the natural rate of unemployment will cause an ever-rising inflation rate.

natural rate of unemployment the unemployment rate that arises from the effects of frictional plus structural unemployment.

near-money a financial asset that can't be directly used as a medium of exchange but can be readily converted into cash or checkable bank deposits.

negative externalities external costs.

negative income tax a government program that supplements the income of low-income working families.

net exports the difference between the value of exports and the value of imports. A positive value for net exports indicates that a country is a net exporter of goods and services; a negative value indicates that a country is a net importer of goods and services.

net present value the present value of current and future benefits minus the present value of current and future costs.

network externality the case in which the value of a good to an individual is greater when more people also use the good.

new classical macroeconomics an approach to the business cycle that returns to the classical view that shifts in the aggregate demand curve affect only the aggregate price level, not aggregate output.

new Keynesian economics a theory that argues that market imperfections can lead to price stickiness for the economy as a whole.

nominal GDP the value of all final goods and services produced in the economy during a given year, calculated using the prices current in the year in which the output is produced.

nominal interest rate the interest rate actually paid for a loan, not adjusted for inflation.

nominal wage the dollar amount of any given wage paid.

nonaccelerating inflation rate of unemployment (NAIRU) the unemployment rate at which, other things equal, inflation does not change over time.

noncooperative behavior actions by firms that ignore the effects of those actions on the profits of other firms.

noncooperative equilibrium in game theory, the equilibrium that results when all players choose the action that maximizes their payoffs given the actions of other players, ignoring the effect of that action on the payoffs of other players; also known as Nash equilibrium.

nonexcludable referring to a good, describes the case in which the supplier cannot prevent those who do not pay from consuming the good.

nonprice competition competition in areas other than price to increase sales, such as new product features and advertising; especially engaged in by firms that have a tacit understanding not to compete on price.

nonrival in consumption referring to a good, describes the case in which the same unit can be consumed by more than one person at the same time.

normal good a good for which a rise in income increases the demand for that good—the "normal" case.

normative economics the branch of economic analysis that makes prescriptions about the way the economy should work.

offshore outsourcing the practice in which businesses hire people in another country to perform various tasks.

oligopolist a firm in an industry with only a small number of producers.

oligopoly an industry with only a small number of producers.

open economy an economy that trades goods and services with other countries.

open-market operation a purchase or sale of U.S. Treasury bills by the Federal Reserve, undertaken to change the monetary base, which in turn changes the money supply.

opportunity cost the real cost of an item: what you must give up in order to get it.

optimal consumption bundle the consumption bundle that maximizes the consumer's total utility given his or her budget constraint.

optimal consumption rule when a consumer maximizes utility, the marginal utility per dollar spent must be the same for all goods and services in the consumption bundle.

optimal output rule profit is maximized by producing the quantity of output at which the marginal revenue of the last unit produced is equal to its marginal cost.

optimal quantity the quantity that generates the highest possible total net gain.

other things equal assumption in the development of a model, the assumption that all relevant factors except the one under study remain unchanged.

output gap the percentage difference between actual aggregate output and potential output.

overuse the depletion of a common resource that occurs when individuals ignore the fact that their use depletes the amount of the resource remaining for others.

patent a temporary monopoly given by the government to an inventor for the use or sale of an invention.

payoff in game theory, the reward received by a player in a game (for example, the profit earned by an oligopolist).

payoff matrix in game theory, a diagram that shows how the payoffs to each of the participants in a two-player game depend on the actions of both; a tool in analyzing interdependence.

pension fund a type of mutual fund that holds assets in order to provide retirement income to its members.

perfect price discrimination a situation in which a monopolist charges each consumer his or her willingness to pay—the maximum that the consumer is willing to pay.

perfectly competitive industry an industry in which all producers are price-takers.

perfectly competitive market a market in which all market participants are price-takers.

perfectly elastic demand the case in which any price increase will cause the quantity demanded to drop to zero; the demand curve is a horizontal line.

perfectly elastic supply the case in which even a tiny increase or reduction in the price will lead to very large changes in the quantity supplied, so that the price elasticity of supply is infinite; the perfectly elastic supply curve is a horizontal line.

perfectly inelastic demand the case in which the quantity demanded does not respond at all to changes in the price; the demand curve is a vertical line.

perfectly inelastic supply the case in which the price elasticity of supply is zero, so that changes in the price of the good have no effect on the quantity supplied; the perfectly inelastic supply curve is a vertical line.

physical asset a claim on a tangible object that gives the owner the right to dispose of the object as he or she wishes.

physical capital human-made goods such as buildings and machines used to produce other goods and services.

Pigouvian subsidy a payment designed to encourage activities that yield external benefits.

Pigouvian taxes taxes designed to reduce external costs.

planned aggregate spending the total amount of planned spending in the economy; includes consumer spending and planned investment spending.

planned investment spending the investment spending that firms intend to undertake during a given period. Planned investment spending may differ from actual investment spending due to unplanned inventory investment.

political business cycle a business cycle that results from the use of macroeconomic policy to serve political ends.

positive economics the branch of economic analysis that describes the way the economy actually works.

positive externalities external benefits.

positive feedback put simply, success breeds success, failure breeds failure; the effect is seen with goods that are subject to network externalities.

potential output the level of real GDP the economy would produce if all prices, including nominal wages, were fully flexible.

poverty program a government program designed to aid the poor.

poverty rate the percentage of the population with incomes below the poverty threshold.

poverty threshold the annual income below which a family is officially considered poor.

present value (of *X*) the amount of money needed today in order to receive *X* at a future date given the interest rate.

price ceiling the maximum price sellers are allowed to charge for a good or service; a form of price control.

price controls legal restrictions on how high or low a market price may go.

price discrimination charging different prices to different consumers for the same good.

price elasticity of demand the ratio of the percent change in the quantity demanded to the percent change in the price as we move along the demand curve (dropping the minus sign).

price elasticity of supply a measure of the responsiveness of the quantity of a good supplied to the price of that good; the ratio of the percent change in the quantity supplied to the percent change in the price as we move along the supply curve.

price floor the minimum price buyers are required to pay for a good or service; a form of price control.

price index a measure of the cost of purchasing a given market basket in a given year, where that cost is normalized so that it is equal to 100 in the selected base year; a measure of overall price level.

price leadership a pattern of behavior in which one firm sets its price and other firms in the industry follow.

price regulation a limitation on the price that a monopolist is allowed to charge.

price stability a period in which the aggregate price level is changing only slowly.

price war a collapse of prices when tacit collusion breaks down.

price-taking consumer a consumer whose actions have no effect on the market price of the good or service he or she buys.

price-taking firm a firm whose actions have no effect on the market price of the good or service it sells.

price-taking firm's optimal output rule the profit of a price-taking firm is maximized by producing the quantity of output at which the market price is equal to the marginal cost of the last unit produced.

principle of diminishing marginal utility the proposition that each successive unit of a good or service consumed adds less to total utility than does the previous unit.

principle of "either–or" decision making the principle that, in a decision between two activities, the one with the positive economic profit should be chosen.

prisoners' dilemma a game based on two premises: (1) Each player has an incentive to choose an action that benefits itself at the other player's expense; and (2) When both players act in this way, both are worse off than if they had acted cooperatively.

private good a good that is both excludable and rival in consumption.

private information information that some people have that others do not.

private savings disposable income minus consumer spending; disposable income that is not spent on consumption but rather goes into financial markets.

producer price index (PPI) a measure of the cost of a typical basket of goods and services purchased by producers. Because these commodity prices respond quickly to changes in demand, the PPI is often regarded as a leading indicator of changes in the inflation rate.

producer surplus a term often used to refer to either individual producer surplus or to total producer surplus.

product differentiation the attempt by firms to convince buyers that their products are different from those of other firms in the industry. If firms can so convince buyers, they can charge a higher price.

product markets markets where goods and services are bought and sold.

production function the relationship between the quantity of inputs a firm uses and the quantity of output it produces.

production possibility frontier (PPF) a model that illustrates the trade-offs facing an economy that produces only two goods; shows the maximum quantity of one good that can be produced for each possible quantity of the other good produced.

productivity output per worker; an alternative term for labor productivity.

profit-maximizing principle of marginal analysis the proposition that in a profit-maximizing "how much" decision the optimal quantity is the largest quantity at which marginal benefit is greater than or equal to marginal cost.

progressive tax a tax that takes a larger share of the income of high-income taxpayers than of low-income taxpayers.

property rights the rights of owners of valuable items, whether resources or goods, to dispose of those items as they choose.

proportional tax a tax that is the same percentage of the tax base regardless of the taxpayer's income or wealth.

protection policies that limit imports; an alternative term for trade protection.

public debt government debt held by individuals and institutions outside the government.

public good a good that is both nonexcludable and nonrival in consumption.

public ownership the case in which goods are supplied by the government or by a firm owned by the government to protect the interests of the consumer in response to natural monopoly.

purchasing power parity (between two countries' currencies) the nominal exchange rate at which a given basket of goods and services would cost the same amount in each country.

quantity control an upper limit, set by the government, on the quantity of some good that can be bought or sold; also referred to as a quota.

quantity demanded the actual amount of a good or service consumers are willing to buy at some specific price.

quantity supplied the actual amount of a good or service producers are willing to sell at some specific price.

Quantity Theory of Money a theory that emphasizes the positive relationship between the price level and the money supply. It relies on the equation ($M \times V = P \times Y$).

quota an upper limit, set by the government, on the quantity of some good that can be bought or sold; also referred to as a quantity control.

quota rent the earnings that accrue to the license-holder from ownership of the right to sell the good.

rational describes a decision maker who chooses the available option that leads to the outcome he or she most prefers.

rational expectations a theory of expectation formation that holds that individuals and firms make decisions optimally, using all available information.

real business cycle theory a theory of business cycles that asserts that fluctuations in the growth rate of total factor productivity cause the business cycle.

real exchange rate the exchange rate adjusted for international differences in aggregate price levels.

real GDP the total value of all final goods and services produced in the economy during a given year, calculated using the prices of a selected base year.

real GDP per capita the average GDP per person.

real income income divided by the price level.

real interest rate the nominal interest rate minus the inflation rate.

real wage the wage rate divided by the price level.

recession a period of economic downturn when output and unemployment are falling; also referred to as a contraction.

recessionary gap exists when aggregate output is below potential output.

regressive tax a tax that takes a smaller share of the income of high-income taxpayers than of low-income taxpayers.

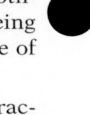

reputation a long-term standing in the public regard that serves to reassure others that private information is not being concealed; a valuable asset in the face of adverse selection.

required reserve ratio the smallest fraction of deposits that the Federal Reserve allows banks to hold.

research and development (R&D) spending to create and implement new technologies.

reserve ratio the fraction of bank deposits that a bank holds as reserves. In the United States, the minimum required reserve ratio is set by the Federal Reserve.

reserve requirements rules set by the Federal Reserve that set the minimum reserve ratio for banks. For checkable bank deposits in the United States, the minimum reserve ratio is set at 10%.

resource anything, such as land, labor, human capital, and physical capital, that can be used to produce something else; includes natural resources (from the physical environment) and human resources (labor, skill, intelligence).

revaluation an increase in the value of a currency that is set under a fixed exchange rate regime.

risk aversion the willingness to sacrifice some economic payoff in order to avoid a potential loss.

rival in consumption referring to a good, describes the case in which one unit cannot be consumed by more than one person at the same time.

Rule of 70 a mathematical formula that states that the time it takes real GDP per capita, or any other variable that grows gradually over time, to double is approximately 70 divided by that variable's annual growth rate.

savings and loans (thrifts) deposit-taking banks, usually specialized in issuing home loans.

savings–investment spending identity an accounting fact that states that savings and investment spending are always equal for the economy as a whole.

scarce in short supply; a resource is scarce when there is not enough of the resource available to satisfy all the various ways a society wants to use it.

screening using observable information about people to make inferences about their private information; a way to reduce adverse selection.

securitization the pooling of loans and mortgages made by a financial institution and the sale of shares in such a pool to other investors.

self-correcting describes the economy, referring to the fact that in the long run, shocks to aggregate demand affect aggregate output in the short run, but not in the long run.

self-regulating describes an economy in which problems such as unemployment are resolved without government intervention, through the working of the invisible hand, and in which government attempts to improve the economy's performance would be ineffective at best, and would probably make things worse.

shadow bank a nondepository financial institution that engages in maturity transformation.

shoe-leather costs (of inflation) the increased costs of transactions caused by inflation.

short run the time period in which at least one input is fixed.

shortage the insufficiency of a good or service that occurs when the quantity demanded exceeds the quantity supplied; shortages occur when the price is below the equilibrium price.

short-run aggregate supply curve a graphical representation of the relationship between the aggregate price level and the quantity of aggregate output supplied that exists in the short run, the time period when many production costs can be taken as fixed. The short-run aggregate supply curve has a positive slope because a rise in the aggregate price level leads to a rise in profits, and therefore output, when production costs are fixed.

short-run equilibrium aggregate output the quantity of aggregate output produced in short-run macroeconomic equilibrium.

short-run equilibrium aggregate price level the aggregate price level in short-run macroeconomic equilibrium.

short-run industry supply curve a graphical representation that shows how the quantity supplied by an industry depends on the market price, given a fixed number of producers.

short-run macroeconomic equilibrium the point at which the quantity of aggregate output supplied is equal to the quantity demanded.

short-run market equilibrium an economic balance that results when the quantity supplied equals the quantity demanded, taking the number of producers as given.

short-run Phillips curve a graphical representation of the negative short-run relationship between the unemployment rate and the inflation rate.

short-term interest rate the interest rate on financial assets that mature within less than a year.

shut-down price the price at which a firm ceases production in the short run because the price has fallen below the minimum average variable cost.

signaling taking some action to establish credibility despite possessing private information; a way to reduce adverse selection.

single-price monopolist a monopolist that offers its product to all consumers at the same price.

social insurance government programs—like Social Security, Medicare, unemployment insurance, and food stamps—intended to protect families against economic hardship.

social insurance program a government program designed to provide protection against unpredictable financial distress.

socially optimal quantity of pollution the quantity of pollution that society would choose if all the costs and benefits of pollution were fully accounted for.

specialization a situation in which each person engages in the task that he or she is good at performing.

stabilization policy the use of government policy to reduce the severity of recessions and to rein in excessively strong expansions. There are two main tools of stabilization policy: monetary policy and fiscal policy.

stagflation the combination of inflation and falling aggregate output.

standardized product output of different producers regarded by consumers as the same good; also referred to as a commodity.

status quo bias the tendency to avoid making a decision.

sticky wages nominal wages that are slow to fall even in the face of high unemployment and slow to rise even in the face of labor shortages.

stock a share in the ownership of a company held by a shareholder.

store of value an asset that is a means of holding purchasing power over time.

strategic behavior actions taken by a firm that attempt to influence the future behavior of other firms.

structural unemployment unemployment that results when there are more people seeking jobs in a labor market than there are jobs available at the current wage rate.

subprime lending lending to home buyers who don't meet the usual criteria for borrowing.

substitutes pairs of goods for which a rise in the price of one of the goods leads to an increase in the demand for the other good.

substitution effect the change in the quantity of a good demanded as the consumer substitutes the good that has become relatively cheaper for the good that has become relatively more expensive.

sunk cost a cost that has already been incurred and is nonrecoverable.

supply and demand model a model of how a competitive market works.

supply curve a graphical representation of the supply schedule, showing the relationship between quantity supplied and price.

supply price the price of a given quantity at which producers will supply that quantity.

supply schedule a list or table showing how much of a good or service producers will supply at different prices.

supply shock an event that shifts the short-run aggregate supply curve. A negative supply shock raises production costs and reduces the quantity supplied at any aggregate price level, shifting the curve leftward. A positive supply shock decreases production costs and increases the quantity supplied at any aggregate price level, shifting the curve rightward.

surplus the excess of a good or service that occurs when the quantity supplied exceeds the quantity demanded; surpluses occur when the price is above the equilibrium price.

sustainable long-run economic growth long-run growth that can continue in the face of the limited supply of natural resources and the impact of growth on the environment.

T-account a simple tool that summarizes a business's financial position by showing, in a single table, the business's assets and liabilities, with assets on the left and liabilities on the right.

tacit collusion cooperation among producers, without a formal agreement, to limit production and raise prices so as to raise one anothers' profits.

target federal funds rate the Federal Reserve's desired level for the federal funds rate. The Federal Reserve adjusts the money supply through the purchase and sale of Treasury bills until the actual rate equals the desired rate.

tariff a tax levied on imports.

tax incidence the distribution of the tax burden.

Taylor rule for monetary policy a rule for setting the federal funds rate that takes into account both the inflation rate and the output gap.

technological progress an advance in the technical means of the production of goods and services.

technology the technical means for the production of goods and services.

technology spillover an external benefit that results when knowledge spreads among individuals and firms.

time allocation the decision about how many hours to spend on different activities, which leads to a decision about how much labor to supply.

tit for tat in game theory, a strategy that involves playing cooperatively at first, then doing whatever the other player did in the previous period.

total consumer surplus the sum of the individual consumer surpluses of all the buyers of a good in a market.

total cost the sum of the fixed cost and the variable cost of producing a quantity of output.

total cost curve a graphical representation of the total cost, showing how total cost depends on the quantity of output.

total factor productivity the amount of output that can be produced with a given amount of factor inputs.

total producer surplus the sum of the individual producer surpluses of all the sellers of a good in a market.

total product curve a graphical representation of the production function, showing how the quantity of output depends on the quantity of the variable input for a given quantity of the fixed input.

total revenue the total value of sales of a good or service (the price of the good or service multiplied by the quantity sold).

total surplus the total net gain to consumers and producers from trading in a market; the sum of the consumer surplus and the producer surplus.

tradable emissions permits licenses to emit limited quantities of pollutants that can be bought and sold by polluters.

trade the practice, in a market economy, in which individuals provide goods and services to others and receive goods and services in return.

trade deficit describes the situation in which the value of the goods and services bought from foreigners is more than the value of the goods and services sold to consumers abroad.

trade protection policies that limit imports; also known simply as protection.

trade surplus describes the situation in which the value of goods and services bought from foreigners is less than the value of the goods and services sold to them.

trade-off the giving up of something in order to have something else.

transaction costs the costs to individuals of making a deal.

underemployed refers to people who work part time because they cannot find full-time jobs.

unemployed refers to people who are actively looking for work but are not currently employed.

unemployment rate the percentage of the total number of people in the labor force who are unemployed, calculated as unemployment/(unemployment + employment).

unions organizations of workers that try to raise wages and improve working conditions for their members by bargaining collectively.

unit of account a measure used to set prices and make economic calculations.

unit-elastic demand the case in which the price elasticity of demand is exactly 1.

unit-of-account costs (of inflation) costs arising from the way inflation makes money a less reliable unit of measurement.

unplanned inventory investment unplanned changes in inventories, which occur when actual sales are more or less than businesses expected; sales in excess of expectations result in negative unplanned inventory investment.

U-shaped average total cost curve a distinctive graphical representation of the relationship between output and average total cost; the average total cost curve at first falls when output is low and then rises as output increases.

util a unit of utility.

utility (of a consumer) a measure of the satisfaction derived from consumption of goods and services.

value added (of a producer) the value of a producer's sales minus the value of input purchases.

value of the marginal product the value of the additional output generated by employing one more unit of a given factor, such as labor.

value of the marginal product curve a graphical representation showing how the value of the marginal product of a factor depends on the quantity of the factor employed.

variable cost a cost that depends on the quantity of output produced; the cost of the variable input.

variable input an input whose quantity the firm can vary at any time (for example, labor).

velocity of money the ratio of nominal GDP to the money supply.

vicious cycle of deleveraging describes the sequence of events that takes place when a firm's asset sales to cover losses produce negative balance sheet effects on other firms and force creditors to call in their loans, forcing sales of more assets and causing further declines in asset prices.

wasted resources a form of inefficiency in which people expend money, effort, and time to cope with the shortages caused by a price ceiling.

wealth (of a household) the value of accumulated savings.

wealth effect of a change in the aggregate price level the effect on consumer spending caused by the change in the purchasing power of consumers' assets when the aggregate price level changes. A rise in the aggregate price level decreases the purchasing power of consumers' assets, so they decrease their consumption; a fall in the aggregate price level increases the purchasing power of consumers' assets, so they increase their consumption.

wedge the difference between the demand price of the quantity transacted and the supply price of the quantity transacted for a good when the supply of the good is legally restricted. Often created by a quota or a tax.

welfare state the collection of government programs designed to alleviate economic hardship.

willingness to pay the maximum price a consumer is prepared to pay for a good.

world price the price at which a good can be bought or sold abroad.

zero bound the lower bound of zero on the nominal interest rate.

zero lower bound for interest rates statement of the fact that interest rates cannot fall below zero.

zero-profit equilibrium an economic balance in which each firm makes zero profit at its profit-maximizing quantity.

SOLUTIONS TO MODULE REVIEW QUESTIONS

This section offers suggested answers to the Review Questions that appear at the end of each module.

MODULE 1

Check Your Understanding

1. Land, labor, physical capital, and human capital are the four categories of resources. Possible examples include fisheries (land), time spent working on a fishing boat (labor), fishing nets (physical capital), and experienced fishermen and fish farmers (human capital).

2. a. time spent flipping burgers at a restaurant: labor
   b. a bulldozer: capital
   c. a river: land

3. a. Yes. The increased time spent commuting is a cost you will incur if you accept the new job. That additional time spent commuting—or equivalently, the benefit you would get from spending that time doing something else—is an opportunity cost of the new job.
   b. Yes. One of the benefits of the new job is that you will be making $50,000. But if you take the new job, you will have to give up your current job; that is, you have to give up your current salary of $45,000, so $45,000 is one of the opportunity costs of taking the new job.
   c. No. A more spacious office is an additional benefit of your new job and does not involve forgoing something else, so it is not an opportunity cost.

4. a. This is a normative statement because it stipulates what should be done. In addition, it may have no "right" answer. That is, should people be prevented from all dangerous personal behavior if they enjoy that behavior—like skydiving? Your answer will depend on your point of view.
   b. This is a positive statement because it is a description of fact.

Multiple-Choice Questions

1. d
2. d
3. b (The opportunity cost needs to take into account only the next-best alternative, which in this case is watching TV. The opportunity cost of watching TV, in turn, is its next best alternative: listening to music.)
4. b
5. a

Critical-Thinking Question

In positive economics there is a "right" or "wrong" answer. In normative economics there is not necessarily a "right" or "wrong" answer. There is more disagreement in normative economics because there is no "right" or "wrong" answer. Economists disagree because of (1) differences in values and (2) disagreements about models and about which simplifications are appropriate.

MODULE 2

Check Your Understanding

1. As households spend more on goods and services, firms increase their production of goods and services. As firms increase production, additional workers are hired and other workers can receive additional income for their labor. The result is an increase in the number of jobs in the economy. In addition, with more income, workers consume more goods and services and then the cycle begins again.

2. This illustrates the principle that one person's spending is another person's income. As oil companies increase their spending on labor by hiring more workers, or pay existing workers higher wages, those workers' incomes rise. In turn, these workers increase their consumer spending, which becomes income to restaurants and other consumer businesses.

Multiple-Choice Questions

1. b
2. c
3. c
4. d
5. e

Critical-Thinking Questions

The accompanying diagram illustrates the circular flow for Atlantis.

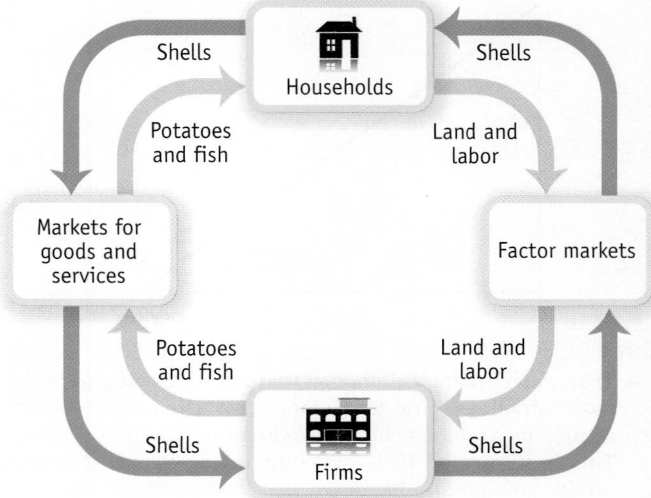

1. The flooding of the fields will destroy the potato crop. Destruction of the potato crop reduces the flow of goods

from firms to households: fewer potatoes produced by firms now are sold to households. An implication, of course, is that fewer cowry shells flow from households to firms as payment for the potatoes in the market for goods and services. Since firms now earn fewer shells, they have fewer shells to pay to households in the factor markets. As a result, the number of factors flowing from households to firms is also reduced.

2. The productive fishing season leads to greater quantity of fish produced by firms to flow to households. An implication is that more money flows from households to firms through the markets for goods and services. As a result, firms will want to buy more factors from households (the flow of shells from firms to households increases) and, in return, the flow of factors from households to firms increases.

3. Time spent at dancing festivals reduces the flow of labor from households to firms and therefore reduces the number of shells flowing from firms to households through the factor markets. In return, households now have fewer shells to buy goods with (the flow of shells from households to firms in the markets for goods and services is reduced), implying that fewer goods flow from firms to households.

MODULE 3

Check Your Understanding

1. a. False. An increase in the resources available to Boeing for use in producing Dreamliners and small jets changes the production possibility curve by shifting it outward. This is because Boeing can now produce more small jets and Dreamliners than before. In the accompanying figure, the line labeled "Boeing's original *PPF*" represents Boeing's original production possibility curve, and the line labeled "Boeing's new *PPF*" represents the new production possibility curve that results from an increase in resources available to Boeing.

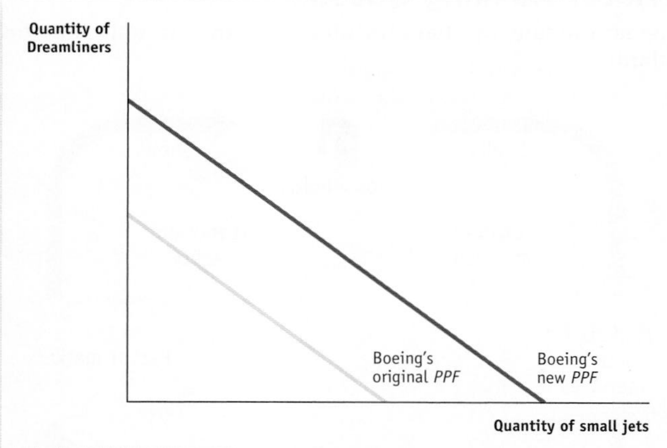

b. True. A technological change that allows Boeing to build more small jets for any amount of Dreamliners built results in a change in its production possibility curve. This is illustrated in the accompanying figure: the new production possibility curve is represented by the line labeled "Boeing's new *PPF*," and the original production curve is represented by the line labeled "Boeing's original *PPF*." Since the maximum quantity of Dreamliners that Boeing can build is the same as before, the new production possibility curve intersects the vertical axis at the same point as the original curve. But since the maximum possible quantity of small jets is now greater than before, the new curve intersects the horizontal axis to the right of the original curve.

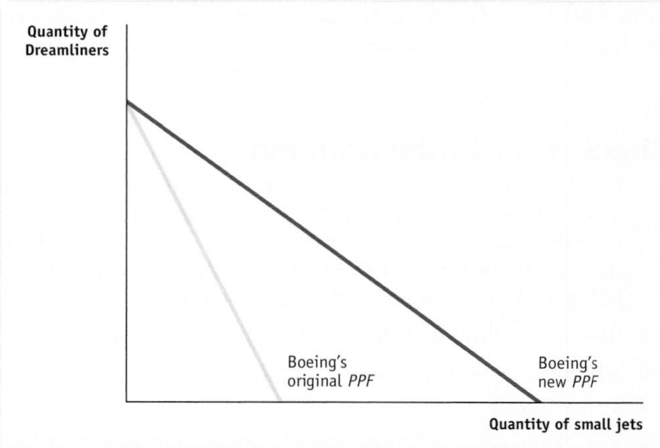

c. False. The production possibility frontier illustrates how much of one good an economy must give up to get more of another good only when resources are used efficiently in production. If an economy is producing inefficiently—that is, inside the frontier—then it does not have to give up a unit of one good in order to get another unit of the other good. Instead, by becoming more efficient in production, this economy can have more of both goods.

Multiple-Choice Questions

1. c
2. d
3. d
4. e
5. a

Critical-Thinking Question

Your graph should look like this.

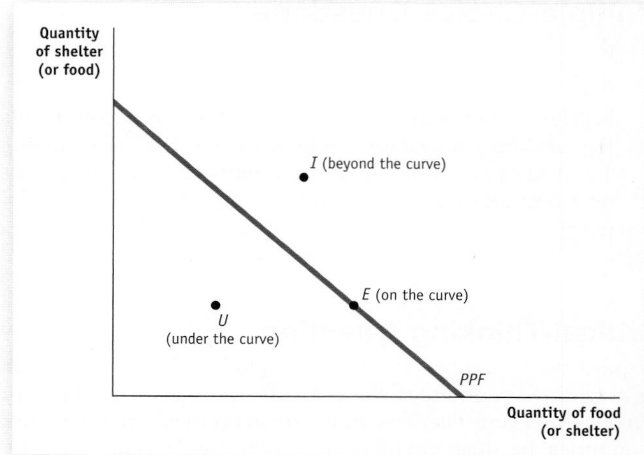

MODULE 4

Check Your Understanding

1. **a.** The United States has an absolute advantage in automobile production because it takes fewer Americans (6) to produce a car in one day than it takes Italians (8). The United States also has an absolute advantage in washing machine production because it takes fewer Americans (2) to produce a washing machine in one day than it takes Italians (3).

   b. In Italy the opportunity cost of a washing machine in terms of an automobile is $3/8$. In other words, $3/8$ of a car can be produced with the same number of workers and in the same time it takes to produce 1 washing machine. In the United States the opportunity cost of a washing machine in terms of an automobile is $2/6 = 1/3$. In other words, $1/3$ of a car can be produced with the same number of workers and in the same time it takes to produce 1 washing machine. Since $1/3 < 3/8$, the United States has a comparative advantage in the production of washing machines: to produce a washing machine, only $1/3$ of a car must be given up in the United States but $3/8$ of a car must be given up in Italy. This means that Italy has a comparative advantage in automobiles. This can be checked as follows. The opportunity cost of an automobile in terms of a washing machine in Italy is $8/3$, equal to $2\frac{2}{3}$. In other words, $2\frac{2}{3}$ washing machines can be produced with the same number of workers and in the time it takes to produce 1 car in Italy. And the opportunity cost of an automobile in terms of a washing machine in the United States is $6/2$, equal to 3. In other words, 3 washing machines can be produced with the same number of workers and in the time it takes to produce 1 car in the United States.

   c. The greatest gains are realized when each country specializes in producing the good for which it has a comparative advantage. Therefore, based on this example, the United States should specialize in washing machines and Italy should specialize in automobiles.

2. At a trade of 10 U.S. large jets for 15 Brazilian small jets, Brazil gives up less for a large jet than it would if it were building large jets itself. Without trade, Brazil gives up 3 small jets for each large jet it produces. With trade, Brazil gives up only 1.5 small jets for each large jet from the United States. Likewise, the United States gives up less for a small jet than it would if it were producing small jets itself. Without trade, the United States gives up $3/4$ of a large jet for each small jet. With trade, the United States gives up only $2/3$ of a large jet for each small jet from Brazil.

Multiple-Choice Questions

1. a
2. a
3. a
4. d
5. d

Critical-Thinking Questions

1. Country A: opportunity cost of 1 bushel of wheat = 4 units of textiles

   Country B: opportunity cost of 1 bushel of wheat = 6 units of textiles

2. Country A has an absolute advantage in the production of wheat (15 versus 10)

3. Country A: opportunity cost of 1 unit of textiles = $1/4$ bushel of wheat

   Country B: opportunity cost of 1 unit of textiles = $1/6$ bushel of wheat

   Country B has the comparative advantage in textile production because it has a lower opportunity cost of producing textiles. (Alternate answer: Country B has the comparative advantage in the production of textiles because Country A has a comparative advantage in the production of wheat based on opportunity costs shown in part a.)

MODULE 5

Check Your Understanding

1. **a.** The quantity of umbrellas demanded is higher at any given price on a rainy day than on a dry day. This is a rightward *shift* of the demand curve, since at any given price the quantity demanded rises. This implies that any specific quantity can now be sold at a higher price.

   b. The quantity of weekend calls demanded rises in response to a price reduction. This is a *movement along* the demand curve for weekend calls.

   c. The demand for roses increases the week of Valentine's Day. This is a rightward *shift* of the demand curve.

   d. The quantity of gasoline demanded falls in response to a rise in price. This is a *movement along* the demand curve.

Multiple-Choice Questions

1. e
2. a
3. c
4. d
5. a

Critical-Thinking Question

Your graph would look like this.

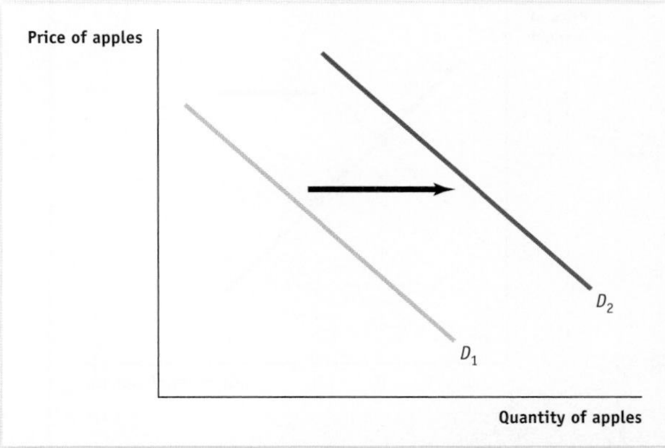

MODULE 6

Check Your Understanding

1. **a.** The quantity of houses supplied rises as a result of an increase in prices. This is a *movement along* the supply curve.

b. The quantity of strawberries supplied is higher at any given price. This is an *increase* in supply, which shifts the supply curve to the right.

c. The quantity of labor supplied is lower at any given wage. This is a *decrease* in supply, which shifts the supply curve leftward compared to the supply curve during school vacation. So, in order to attract workers, fast-food chains have to offer higher wages.

d. The quantity of labor supplied rises in response to a rise in wages. This is a *movement along* the supply curve.

e. The quantity of cabins supplied is higher at any given price. This is an *increase* in supply, which shifts the supply curve to the right.

2. a. This is an increase in supply, so the supply curve shifts rightward. At the original equilibrium price of the year before, the quantity of grapes supplied exceeds the quantity demanded, and the result is a surplus. The price of grapes will fall.

b. This is a decrease in demand, so the demand curve shifts leftward. At the original equilibrium price, the quantity of hotel rooms supplied exceeds the quantity demanded. The result is a surplus. The rates for hotel rooms will fall.

c. Demand increases, so the demand curve for second-hand snowblowers shifts rightward. At the original equilibrium price, the quantity of second-hand snowblowers demanded exceeds the quantity supplied. This is a case of shortage. The equilibrium price of second-hand snowblowers will rise.

Multiple-Choice Questions

1. d
2. d
3. c
4. b
5. d

Critical-Thinking Question

Your graph would look like this.

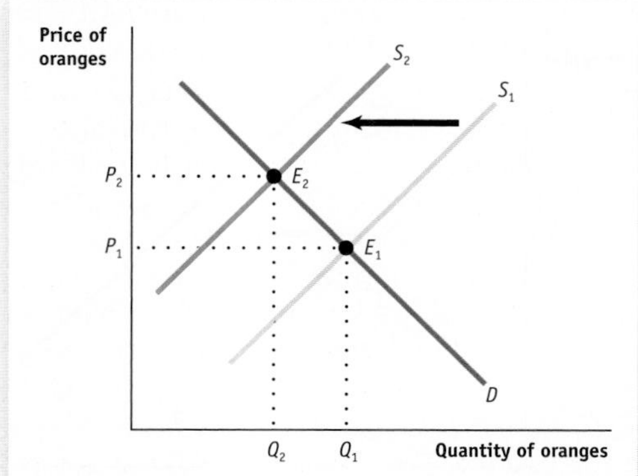

MODULE 7

Check Your Understanding

1. a. The decrease in the price of gasoline caused a rightward shift in the demand for large cars. As a result of the shift, the equilibrium price of large cars rose and the equilibrium quantity of large cars bought and sold also rose.

b. The technological innovation has caused a rightward shift in the supply of fresh paper made from recycled stock. As a result of this shift, the equilibrium price of fresh paper made from recycled stock has fallen and the equilibrium quantity bought and sold has risen.

c. The fall in the price of pay-per-view movies causes a leftward shift in the demand for movies at local movie theaters. As a result of this shift, the equilibrium price of movie tickets falls and the equilibrium number of people who go to the movies also falls.

2. Upon the announcement of the new chip, the demand curve for computers using the earlier chip shifts leftward (demand decreases), and the supply curve for these computers shifts rightward (supply increases).

a. If demand decreases relatively more than supply increases, then the equilibrium quantity falls, as shown here:

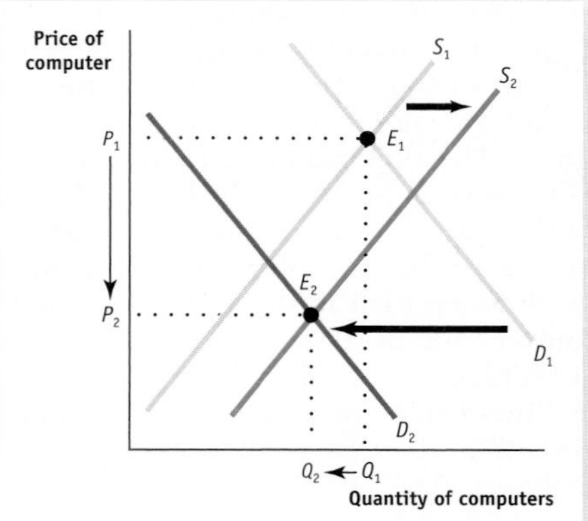

b. If supply increases relatively more than demand decreases, then the equilibrium quantity rises, as shown here:

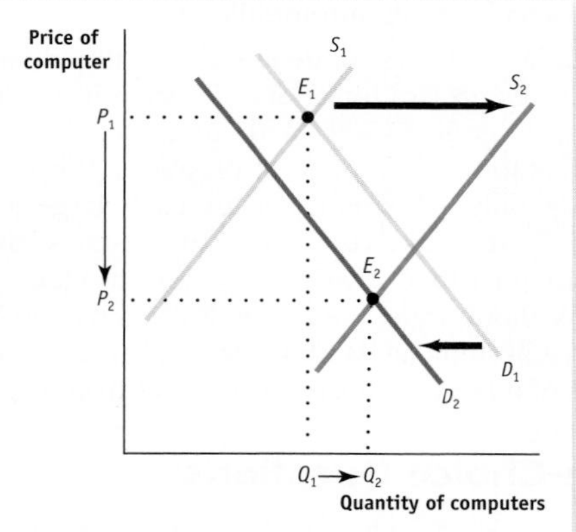

In both cases, the equilibrium price falls.

Multiple-Choice Questions

1. d
2. b
3. a
4. a
5. c

Critical-Thinking Question

Your graph would look like this.

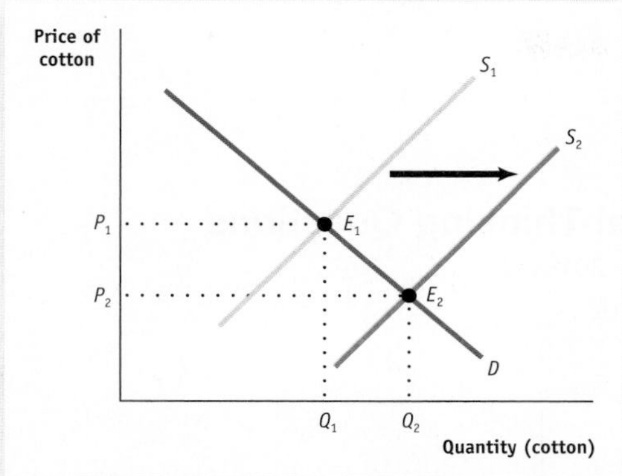

MODULE 8

Check Your Understanding

1. a. Since spending on orange juice is a small share of Clare's spending, the income effect from a rise in the price of orange juice is insignificant. Only the substitution effect, represented by the substitution of lemonade for orange juice, is significant.

   b. Since rent is a large share of Delia's expenditures, the increase in rent generates an income effect, making Delia feel poorer. Since housing is a normal good for Delia, the income and substitution effects move in the same direction, leading her to reduce her consumption of housing by moving to a smaller apartment.

   c. Since a meal ticket is a significant share of the students' living costs, an increase in its price will generate an income effect. Students respond to the price increase by eating more often in the cafeteria. So the substitution effect (which would induce them to eat in the cafeteria less often as they substitute restaurant meals in place of meals at the cafeteria) and the income effect (which would induce them to eat in the cafeteria more often because they are poorer) move in opposite directions. This happens because cafeteria meals are an inferior good. In fact, since the income effect outweighs the substitution effect (students eat in the cafeteria more as the price of meal tickets increases), cafeteria meals are a Giffen good.

2. By the midpoint method, the percent change in the quantity of strawberries demanded is

$$\frac{200{,}000 - 100{,}000}{(100{,}000 + 200{,}000)/2} \times 100 = \frac{100{,}000}{150{,}000} \times 100 = 67\%$$

Similarly, the percent change in the price of strawberries is

$$\frac{\$1.00 - \$1.50}{(\$1.50 + \$1.00)/2} \times 100 = \frac{-\$0.50}{\$1.25} \times 100 = -40\%$$

Dropping the minus sign, the price elasticity of demand using the midpoint method is 67%/40% = 1.7.

3. By the midpoint method, the percent change in the quantity of movie tickets demanded in going from 4,000 tickets to 5,000 tickets is

$$\frac{5{,}000 - 4{,}000}{(4{,}000 + 5{,}000)/2} \times 100 = \frac{1{,}000}{4{,}500} \times 100 = 22\%$$

Since the price elasticity of demand is 1 at the current consumption level, it will take a 22% reduction in the price of movie tickets to generate a 22% increase in quantity demanded.

4. Since price rises, we know that quantity demanded must fall. Given the current price of $0.50, a $0.05 increase in price represents a 10% change, using the method in Equation 8-2. So the price elasticity of demand is

$$\frac{\text{\% change in quantity demanded}}{10\%} = 1.2$$

so that the percent change in quantity demanded is 12%. A 12% decrease in quantity demanded represents 100,000 × 0.12, or 12,000 sandwiches.

Multiple-Choice Questions

1. d
2. c
3. b
4. e
5. c

Critical-Thinking Questions

a. The substitution effect will decrease the quantity demanded. As price increases, consumers will buy other goods instead.

b. The income effect will increase the quantity demanded. As price increases, real income decreases, so consumers will purchase more of the inferior good.

c. The substitution effect is larger than the income effect. If the income effect were larger than the substitution effect, more of the good would be purchased as the price increased, and the demand curve would be upward sloping.

MODULE 9

Check Your Understanding

1. a. Elastic demand. Consumers are highly responsive to changes in price. For a rise in price, the quantity effect (which tends to reduce total revenue) outweighs the price effect (which tends to increase total revenue). Overall, this leads to a fall in total revenue.

   b. Unit-elastic demand. Here the revenue lost to the fall in price is exactly equal to the revenue gained from higher sales. The quantity effect exactly offsets the price effect.

   c. Inelastic demand. Consumers are relatively unresponsive to changes in price. For consumers to purchase a given percent more, the price must fall by an even greater percent. The price effect of a fall in price (which tends to reduce total revenue) outweighs the quantity effect (which tends to increase total revenue). As a result, total revenue decreases.

   d. Inelastic demand. Consumers are not very responsive to changes in price. For a rise in price, the quantity effect (which tends to reduce total revenue) is outweighed by the price effect (which tends to increase total revenue). Overall, this leads to an increase in total revenue.

2. a. Once bitten by a venomous snake, the victim's demand for an antidote is very likely to be perfectly inelastic because there is no substitute and it is necessary for survival. The demand curve will be vertical at a quantity equal to the needed dose.

b. Students' demand for blue pencils is likely to be perfectly elastic because there are readily available substitutes, such as yellow pencils. The demand curve will be horizontal at a price equal to that of non-blue pencils.

Multiple-Choice Questions

1. d
2. d
3. c
4. b
5. c

Critical-Thinking Question

a.

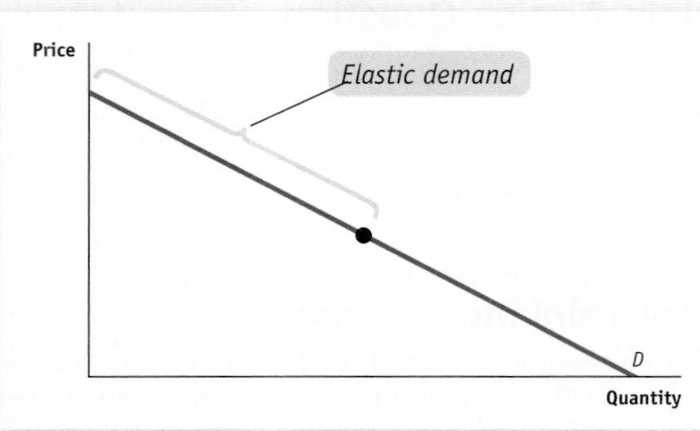

b. An increase in price will decrease total revenue because the negative quantity effect of the price increase is greater than the positive price effect of the price increase.

MODULE 10

Check Your Understanding

1. By the midpoint method, the percent increase in Chelsea's consumption of DVDs is

$$\frac{40 - 10}{(10 + 40)/2} \times 100 = \frac{30}{25} \times 100 = 120\%$$

Similarly, the percent increase in her income is

$$\frac{\$18{,}000 - \$12{,}000}{(\$12{,}000 + \$18{,}000)/2} \times 100 = \frac{\$6{,}000}{\$15{,}000} \times 100 = 40\%$$

Chelsea's income elasticity of demand for DVDs is therefore 120%/40% = 3.

2. The cross-price elasticity of demand is 5%/20% = 0.25. Since the cross-price elasticity of demand is positive, the two goods are substitutes.

3. By the midpoint method, the percent change in the number of hours of web-design services contracted is

$$\frac{500{,}000 - 300{,}000}{(300{,}000 + 500{,}000)/2} \times 100 = \frac{200{,}000}{400{,}000} \times 100 = 50\%$$

Similarly, the percent change in the price of web-design services is:

$$\frac{\$150 - \$100}{(\$100 + \$150)/2} \times 100 = \frac{\$50}{\$125} \times 100 = 40\%$$

The price elasticity of supply is 50%/40% = 1.25. Hence supply is elastic.

Multiple-Choice Questions

1. b
2. d
3. d
4. d
5. c

Critical-Thinking Questions

a. 40%/20% = 2

b. elastic

c.

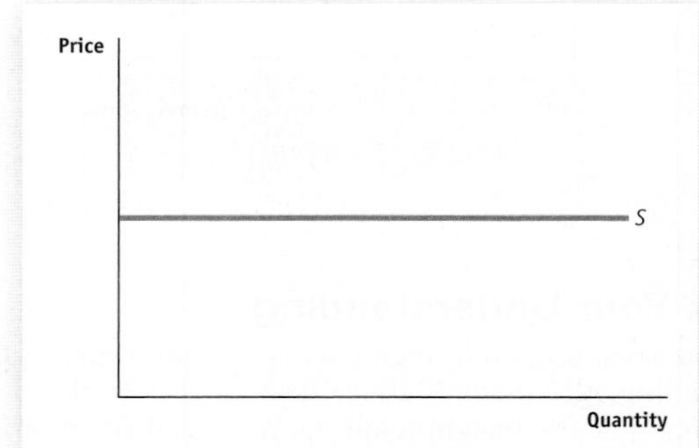

d. Inputs are readily available and can be shifted into/out of production at low cost.

MODULE 11

Check Your Understanding

1. A consumer buys each pepper if the price is less than (or just equal to) the consumer's willingness to pay for that pepper. The demand schedule is constructed by asking how many peppers will be demanded at any given price. The accompanying table illustrates the demand schedule.

Price of pepper	Quantity of peppers demanded	Quantity of peppers demanded by Casey	Quantity of peppers demanded by Josey
$0.90	1	1	0
0.80	2	1	1
0.70	3	2	1
0.60	4	2	2
0.50	5	3	2
0.40	6	3	3
0.30	8	4	4
0.20	8	4	4
0.10	8	4	4
0.00	8	4	4

When the price is $0.40, Casey's consumer surplus from the first pepper is $0.50, from his second pepper $0.30, from his third pepper $0.10, and he does not buy any more peppers. Casey's individual consumer surplus is therefore $0.90. Josey's consumer surplus from her first pepper is $0.40, from her second pepper $0.20, from her third pepper $0.00 (since the price is exactly equal to her willingness to pay, she buys the third pepper but receives no consumer surplus from it), and she does not buy any more peppers. Josey's individual consumer surplus is therefore $0.60. Total consumer surplus at a price of $0.40 is therefore $0.90 + $0.60 = $1.50.

2. A producer supplies each pepper if the price is greater than (or just equal to) the producer's cost of producing that pepper. The supply schedule is constructed by asking how many peppers will be supplied at any price. The accompanying table illustrates the supply schedule.

Price of pepper	Quantity of peppers supplied	Quantity of peppers supplied by Cara	Quantity of peppers supplied by Jamie
$0.90	8	4	4
0.80	7	4	3
0.70	7	4	3
0.60	6	4	2
0.50	5	3	2
0.40	4	3	1
0.30	3	2	1
0.20	2	2	0
0.10	2	2	0
0.00	0	0	0

When the price is $0.70, Cara's producer surplus from the first pepper is $0.60, from her second pepper $0.60, from her third pepper $0.30, from her fourth pepper $0.10, and she does not supply any more peppers. Cara's individual producer surplus is therefore $1.60. Jamie's producer surplus from his first pepper is $0.40, from his second pepper $0.20, from his third pepper $0.00 (since the price is exactly equal to his cost, he sells the third pepper but receives no producer surplus from it), and he does not supply any more peppers. Jamie's individual producer surplus is therefore $0.60. Total producer surplus at a price of $0.70 is therefore $1.60 + $0.60 = $2.20.

Multiple-Choice Questions

1. c
2. c
3. c
4. b
5. a

Critical-Thinking Question

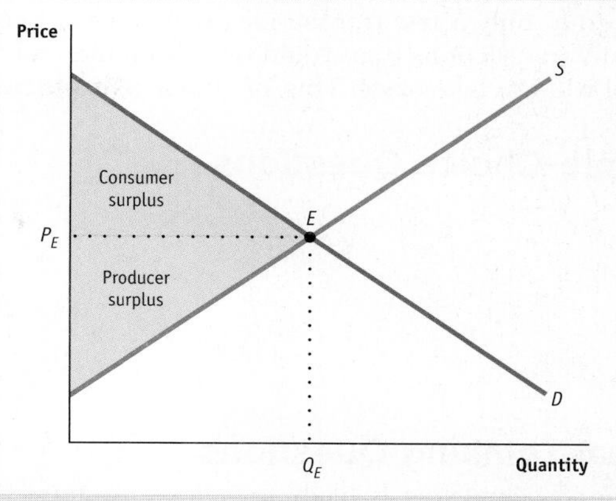

MODULE 12

Check Your Understanding

1. The quantity demanded equals the quantity supplied at a price of $0.50, the equilibrium price. At that price, a total quantity of five peppers will be bought and sold. Casey will buy three peppers and receive consumer surplus of $0.40 on his first, $0.20 on his second, and $0.00 on his third pepper. Josey will buy two peppers and receive consumer surplus of $0.30 on her first and $0.10 on her second pepper. Total consumer surplus is therefore $1.00. Cara will supply three peppers and receive producer surplus of $0.40 on her first, $0.40 on her second, and $0.10 on her third pepper. Jamie will supply two peppers and receive producer surplus of $0.20 on his first and $0.00 on his second pepper. Total producer surplus is therefore $1.10. Total surplus in this market is therefore $1.00 + $1.10 = $2.10.

2. **a.** If Josey consumes one fewer pepper, she loses $0.10 (her consumer surplus on the second pepper when market price is $0.50); if Casey consumes one more pepper, he loses $0.20 (his willingness to pay for his fourth pepper is only $0.30 but the market price is $0.50). This results in an overall loss of consumer surplus of $0.10 + $0.20 = $0.30.

   b. Cara's producer surplus on the last pepper she supplied (the third pepper) at a market price of $0.50 is $0.10, and Jamie's loss in terms of producer surplus of producing one more (his third pepper, which costs $0.70 to produce) is $0.20 at a market price of $0.50. Total producer surplus therefore falls by $0.10 + $0.20 = $0.30.

   c. Josey's consumer surplus from her second pepper is $0.10; this is what she would lose if she were to consume one fewer pepper. Cara's producer surplus from producing her third pepper is $0.10; this is what she would forego if she were to produce one fewer pepper. Therefore, if we reduced quantity by one pepper, we would lose $0.10 + $0.10 = $0.20 of total surplus.

3. There will be many sellers willing to sell their books but only a few buyers who want to buy books at that price. As a result, only a few transactions will actually occur, and many transactions that would have been mutually beneficial will not take place. This, of course, is inefficient.

Multiple-Choice Questions

1. c
2. e
3. b
4. d
5. d

Critical-Thinking Questions

1. The new guideline is likely to reduce the total life span of kidney recipients because older recipients (those with small children) are more likely to get a kidney compared to the original guideline. As a result, total surplus is likely to fall. However, this new policy can be justified as an acceptable sacrifice of efficiency for fairness, because society is likely to agree that it is a desirable goal to reduce the chance of a small child losing a parent.
2. Markets, alas, do not always lead to efficiency. When there is market failure, the market outcome may be inefficient. This can occur for three main reasons. Markets can fail when, in an attempt to capture more surplus, one party—a monopolist, for instance—prevents mutually beneficial trades from occurring. Markets can also fail when one individual's actions have side effects—externalities—on the welfare of others. Finally, markets can fail when the goods themselves—such as goods about which some relevant information is private—are unsuited for efficient management by markets.

MODULE 13

Check Your Understanding

1.

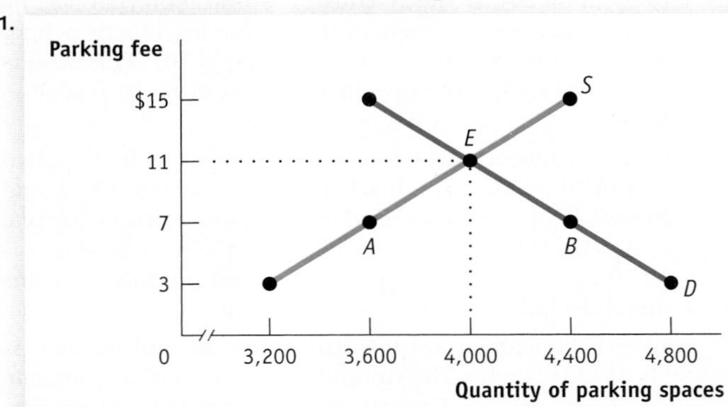

a. Fewer homeowners are willing to rent out their driveways because the price ceiling has reduced the payment they receive. This is an example of a fall in price leading to a fall in the quantity supplied. This is shown in the accompanying diagram by the movement from point E to point A along the supply curve, a reduction in quantity of 400 parking spaces.

b. The quantity demanded increases by 400 spaces as the price decreases. At a lower price, more fans are willing to drive and rent a parking space. It is shown in the diagram by the movement from point E to point B along the demand curve.

c. Under a price ceiling, the quantity demanded exceeds the quantity supplied; as a result, shortages arise. In this case, there will be a shortage of 800 parking spaces. It is shown by the horizontal distance between points A and B.

d. Price ceilings result in wasted resources. The additional time fans spend to secure a parking space is wasted time.

e. Price ceilings lead to the inefficient allocation of goods—here, the parking spaces—to consumers. If less serious fans with connections end up with the parking spaces, diehard fans have no place to park.

f. Price ceilings lead to black markets.

2. a. False. By lowering the price that producers receive, a price ceiling leads to a decrease in the quantity supplied.

b. True. A price ceiling leads to a lower quantity supplied than in an efficient, unregulated market. As a result, some people who would have been willing to pay the market price, and so would have gotten the good in an unregulated market, are unable to obtain it when a price ceiling is imposed.

c. True. Those producers who still sell the product now receive less for it and are therefore worse off. Other producers will no longer find it worthwhile to sell the product at all and so will also be made worse off.

3.

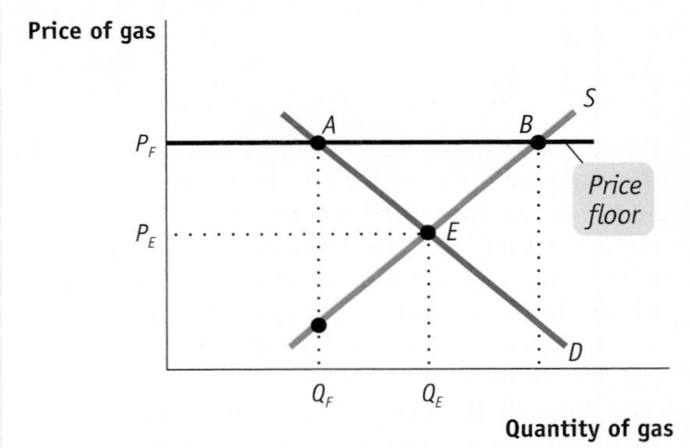

a. Some gas station owners will benefit from getting a higher price. Q_F indicates the sales made by these owners. But some will lose; there are those who make sales at the market equilibrium price of P_E but do not make sales at the regulated price of P_F. These missed sales are indicated on the graph by the fall in the quantity demanded along the demand curve, from point E to point A.

b. Those who buy gas at the higher price of P_F will probably receive better service; this is an example of *inefficiently high quality* caused by a price floor as gas station owners compete on quality rather than price. But opponents are correct to claim that consumers are generally worse off—those who buy at P_F would have been happy to buy at P_E, and many who were willing to buy at a price between P_E and P_F are now unwilling to buy. This is indicated on the graph by the fall in the quantity demanded along the demand curve, from point E to point A.

c. Proponents are wrong because consumers and some gas station owners are hurt by the price floor, which creates "missed opportunities"—desirable transactions between consumers and station owners that never take place. Moreover, the inefficiency of wasted resources arises as consumers spend time and money driving to other states. The price floor also tempts people to engage in black market activity. With the price floor, only Q_F units are sold. But at prices between P_E and P_F, there are drivers who together want to buy more than Q_F and owners who are willing to sell to them, a situation likely to lead to illegal activity.

Multiple-Choice Questions

1. e
2. b
3. e
4. b
5. c

Critical-Thinking Question

Your graph should look like this.

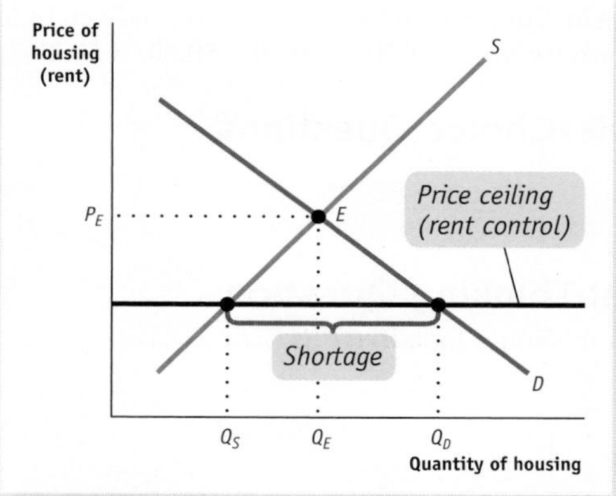

MODULE 14

Check Your Understanding

1. a. The price of a ride is $7 since the quantity demanded at this price is 6 million: $7 is the *demand price* of 6 million rides. This is represented by point *A* in the accompanying figure.

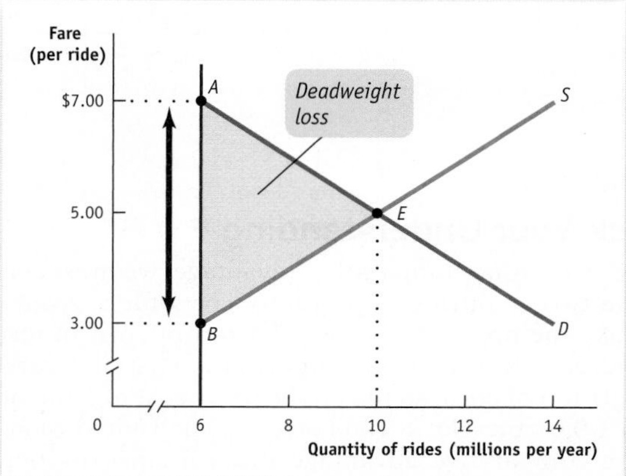

b. At 6 million rides, the supply price is $3 per ride, represented by point *B* in the figure. The wedge between the demand price of $7 per ride and the supply price of $3 per ride is the quota rent per ride, $4. This is represented in the figure above by the vertical distance between points *A* and *B*.

c. The quota discourages 4 million mutually beneficial transactions. The shaded triangle in the figure represents the deadweight loss.

d. At 9 million rides, the demand price is $5.50 per ride, indicated by point *C* in the accompanying figure, and the supply price is $4.50 per ride, indicated by point *D*. The quota rent is the difference between the demand price and the supply price: $1. The deadweight loss is represented by the shaded triangle in the figure. Compare that area to the figure above, and you can see that the deadweight loss is smaller when the quota is set at 9 million rides than when it is set at 6 million rides (illustrated above).

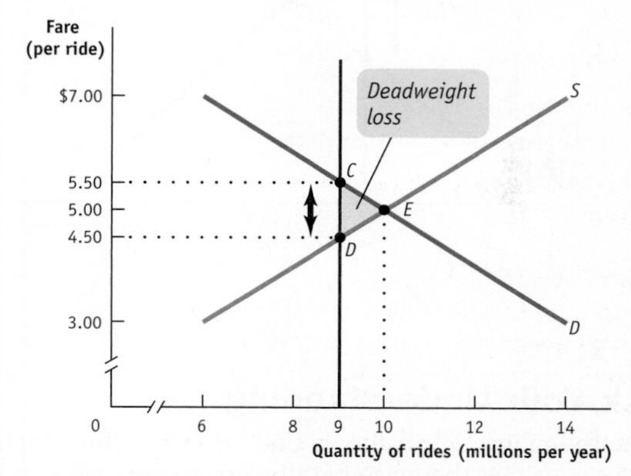

2. The accompanying figure shows a decrease in demand by 4 million rides, represented by a leftward shift of the demand curve from D_1 to D_2: at any given price, the quantity demanded falls by 4 million rides. (For example, at a price of $5, the quantity demanded falls from 10 million to 6 million rides per year.) This eliminates the effect of a quota limit of 8 million rides. At point E_2, the new market equilibrium, the equilibrium quantity is equal to the quota limit; as a result, the quota has no effect on the market.

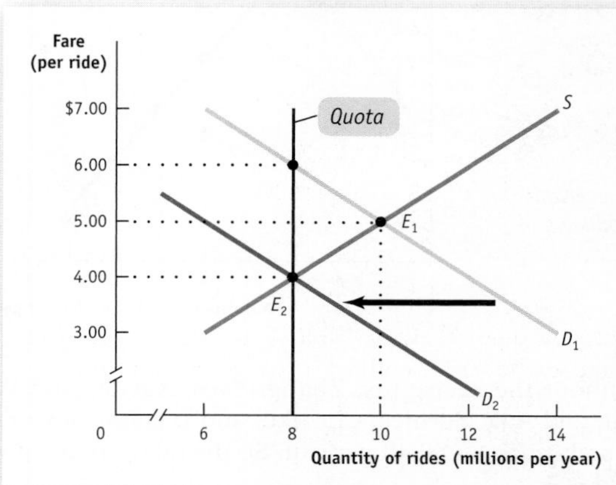

Multiple-Choice Questions

1. d
2. b
3. b
4. d
5. a

Critical-Thinking Question

Your graph should look like this.

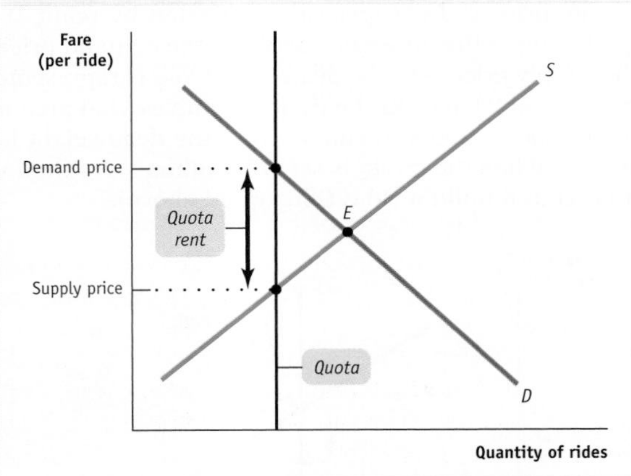

MODULE 15

Check Your Understanding

1. The following figure shows that, after the introduction of the excise tax, the price paid by consumers rises to $1.20; the price received by producers falls to $0.90. Consumers bear $0.20 of the $0.30 tax per pound of butter; producers bear $0.10 of the tax. The tax drives a wedge of $0.30 between the price paid by consumers and the price received by producers. As a result, the quantity of butter sold is now 9 million pounds.

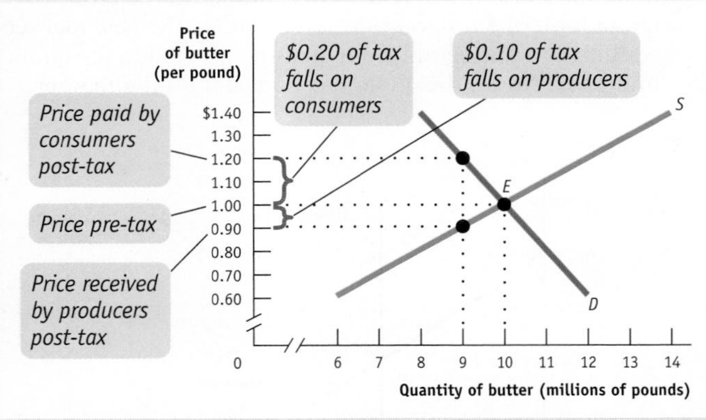

2. a. Without the excise tax, Zhang, Yves, Xavier, and Walter sell, and Ana, Bernice, Chizuko, and Dagmar buy one can of soda each, at $0.40 per can. So the quantity bought and sold is 4.

b. With the excise tax, Zhang and Yves sell, and Ana and Bernice buy one can of soda each. So the quantity sold is 2.

c. Without the excise tax, Ana's individual consumer surplus is $0.70 – $0.40 = $0.30, Bernice's is $0.60 – $0.40 = $0.20, Chizuko's is $0.50 – $0.40 = $0.10, and Dagmar's is $0.40 – $0.40 = $0.00. Total consumer surplus is $0.30 + $0.20 + $0.10 + $0.00 = $0.60. With the tax, Ana's individual consumer surplus is $0.70 – $0.60 = $0.10 and Bernice's is $0.60 – $0.60 = $0.00. Total consumer surplus post-tax is $0.10 + $0.00 = $0.10. So the total consumer surplus lost because of the tax is $0.60 – $0.10 = $0.50.

d. Without the excise tax, Zhang's individual producer surplus is $0.40 – $0.10 = $0.30, Yves's is $0.40 – $0.20 = $0.20, Xavier's is $0.40 – $0.30 = $0.10, and Walter's is $0.40 – $0.40 = $0.00. Total producer surplus is $0.30 + $0.20 + $0.10 + $0.00 = $0.60. With the tax, Zhang's individual producer surplus is $0.20 – $0.10 = $0.10 and Yves's is $0.20 – $0.20 = $0.00. Total producer surplus post-tax is $0.10 + $0.00 = $0.10. So the total producer surplus lost because of the tax is $0.60 – $0.10 = $0.50.

e. With the tax, two cans of soda are sold, so the government tax revenue from this excise tax is 2 × $0.40 = $0.80.

f. Total surplus without the tax is $0.60 + $0.60 = $1.20. With the tax, total surplus is $0.10 + $0.10 = $0.20, and government tax revenue is $0.80. So deadweight loss from this excise tax is $1.20 – ($0.20 + $0.80) = $0.20.

Multiple-Choice Questions

1. d
2. c

Critical-Thinking Question

Your graph should look like this.

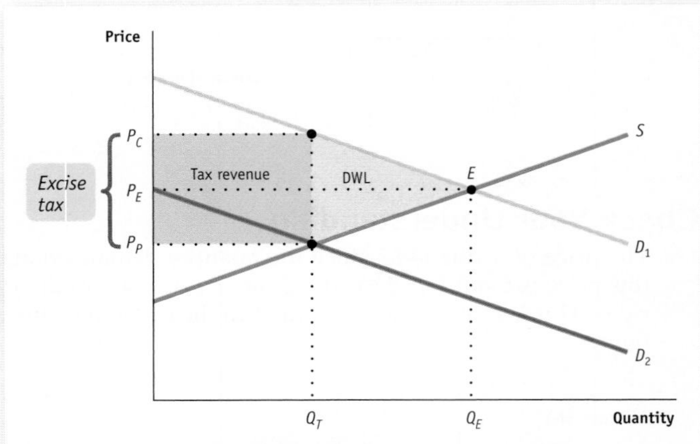

MODULE 16

Check Your Understanding

1. a. To determine comparative advantage, we must compare the two countries' opportunity costs for a given good. Take the opportunity cost of 1 ton of corn in terms of bicycles. In China, the opportunity cost of 1 bicycle is 0.01 ton of corn; so the opportunity cost of 1 ton of corn is 1/0.01 bicycles = 100 bicycles. The United States has the comparative advantage in corn since its opportunity cost in terms of bicycles is 50, a smaller number.

Similarly, the opportunity cost in the United States of 1 bicycle in terms of corn is 1/50 ton of corn = 0.02 ton of corn. This is greater than 0.01, the Chinese opportunity cost of 1 bicycle in terms of corn, implying that China has a comparative advantage in bicycles.

b. Given that the United States can produce 200,000 bicycles if no corn is produced, it can produce 200,000 bicycles × 0.02 ton of corn/bicycle = 4,000 tons of corn when no bicycles are produced. Likewise, if China can produce 3,000 tons of corn if no bicycles are produced, it can produce 3,000 tons of corn × 100 bicycles/ton of corn = 300,000 bicycles if no corn is produced. These points determine the vertical and horizontal intercepts of the U.S. and Chinese production possibilities, as shown in the accompanying diagram.

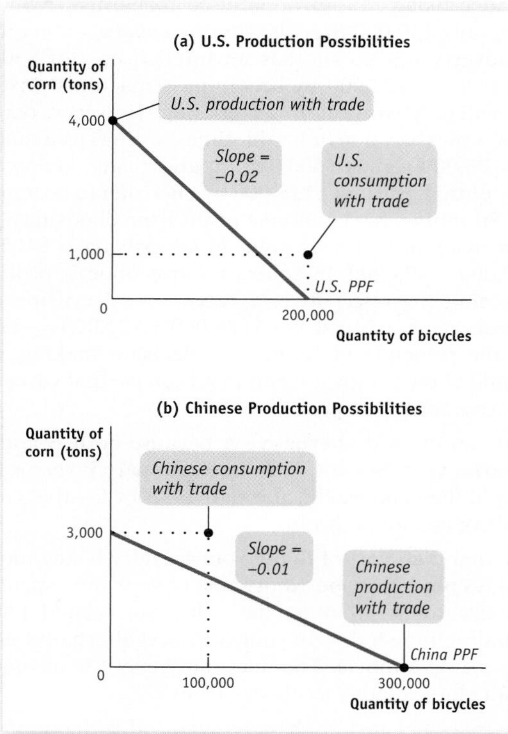

c. The diagram shows the production and consumption points of the two countries. Each country is clearly better off with international trade because each now consumes a bundle of the two goods that lies outside its own production possibility curve, indicating that these bundles were unattainable in autarky.

2. a. The resources required to produce wine are more abundant in France, while the resources required to produce movies are abundant in the U.S. As a result, France exports wine to the United States, and the United States exports movies to France.

b. The resources required to produce shoes, such as labor, are more abundant in Brazil, while the U.S. has the resources to produce shoe-making machinery. As a result, Brazil exports shoes to the United States, and the United States exports shoe-making machinery to Brazil.

Multiple-Choice Questions

1. b
2. c
3. a
4. b
5. c

Critical-Thinking Question

The country will become an importer of the good because it can buy the good for a lower price from another country. This will cause the domestic price of the good to fall to the world price of $8. As a result, quantity demanded will increase and domestic quantity produced will decrease.

MODULE 17

Check Your Understanding

1. a. If the tariff is $0.50, the price paid by domestic consumers for a pound of imported butter is $0.50 + $0.50 = $1.00, the same price as a pound of domestic butter. Imported butter will no longer have a price advantage over domestic butter, imports will cease, and domestic producers will capture all the feasible sales to domestic consumers, selling amount Q_A in the accompanying figure. But if the tariff is less than $0.50—say, only $0.25—the price paid by domestic consumers for a pound of imported butter is $0.50 + $0.25 = $0.75, $0.25 cheaper than a pound of domestic butter. American butter producers will gain sales in the amount of $Q_2 - Q_1$ as a result of the $0.25 tariff. But this is smaller than the amount they would have gained under the $0.50 tariff, the amount $Q_A - Q_1$.

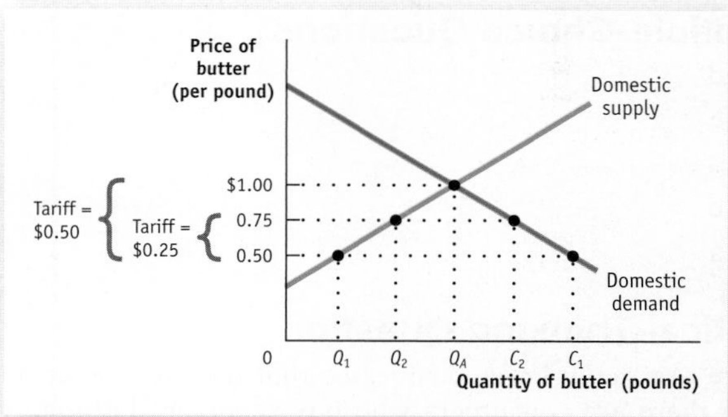

b. As long as the tariff is at least $0.50, increasing it more has no effect. At a tariff of $0.50, all imports are effectively blocked.

2. Because a tariff of $0.50 reduces imports to zero, the only quota that would provide the same results would be a total halt to all imports of butter.

3. In the accompanying diagram, P_A is the U.S. price of grapes in autarky and P_W is the world price of grapes under international trade. With trade, U.S. consumers pay a price of P_W for grapes and consume quantity Q_D, U.S. grape producers produce quantity Q_S, and the difference, $Q_D - Q_S$, represents imports of Mexican grapes. As a consequence of the strike by truckers, imports are halted,

the price paid by American consumers rises to the autarky price, P_A, and U.S. consumption falls to the autarky quantity Q_A.

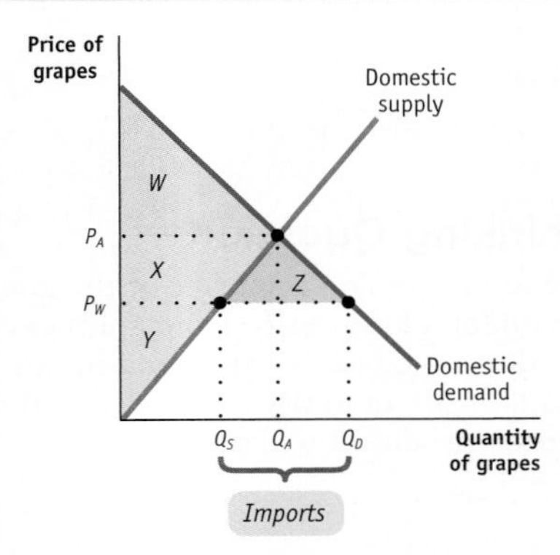

The strike also had these effects:

a. U.S. grape consumers' surplus is decreased by the areas X and Z.

b. U.S. grape producers' surplus is increased by area X.

c. U.S. total surplus is decreased by area Z.

4. Mexican grape producers will not be able to export grapes to the United States, which will raise the supply of grapes in Mexico. This will reduce the Mexican price of grapes, harming Mexican grape producers. Mexican grape pickers will likely see their wages reduced because of the reduction in price of grapes. Mexican grape consumers will be better off because there will be greater supply on the Mexican market, reducing price. U.S. grape pickers will be better off because demand for their services will rise.

Multiple-Choice Questions

1. d
2. e
3. a
4. d
5. a

Critical-Thinking Question

There are many fewer businesses that use steel as an input than there are consumers who buy sugar or clothing. So it will be easier for such businesses to communicate and coordinate among themselves to lobby against tariffs than it will be for consumers. In addition, each business will perceive that the cost of a steel tariff is quite costly to its profits, but an individual consumer is either unaware of or perceives little loss from tariffs on sugar or clothing. The tariffs were indeed lifted a year after they were imposed.

MODULE 18

Check Your Understanding

1. a. Supplies are an explicit cost because they require an outlay of money.

b. If the basement could be used in some other way that generates money, such as renting it to a student, then the implicit cost is that money forgone. Otherwise, the implicit cost is zero.

c. Wages are an explicit cost.

d. By using the van for their business, Karma and Don forgo the money they could have gained by selling it. So use of the van is an implicit cost.

e. Karma's forgone wages from her job are an implicit cost.

2. We need only compare the choice of becoming a machinist to the choice of taking a job in advertising in order to make the right choice. We can discard the choice of acquiring a teaching degree because we already know that taking a job in advertising is always superior to it. Now let's compare the remaining two alternatives: becoming a skilled machinist versus immediately taking a job in advertising. As an apprentice machinist, Ashley will earn only \$30,000 over the first two years, versus \$57,000 in advertising. So she has an implicit cost of \$30,000 – \$57,000 = – \$27,000 by becoming a machinist instead of immediately working in advertising. However, two years from now the value of her lifetime earnings as a machinist is \$725,000 versus \$600,000 in advertising, giving her an accounting profit of \$125,000 by choosing to be a machinist. Summing, her economic profit from choosing a career as a machinist over a career in advertising is \$125,000 – \$27,000 = \$98,000. In contrast, her economic profit from choosing the alternative, a career in advertising over a career as a machinist, is –\$125,000 + \$27,000 = –\$98,000. By the principle of "either–or" decision making, Ashley should choose to be a machinist because that career has a positive economic profit.

3. You can discard alternative A because both B and C are superior to it. But you must now compare B versus C. You should then choose the alternative—B or C—that carries a positive economic profit.

4. a. The marginal cost of doing your laundry is any monetary outlays plus the opportunity cost of your time spent doing laundry today—that is, the value you would place on spending time today on your next best alternative activity, like seeing a movie. The marginal benefit is having more clean clothes today to choose from.

b. The marginal cost of changing your oil is the opportunity cost of time spent changing your oil now as well as the explicit cost of the oil change. The marginal benefit is the improvement in your car's performance.

c. The marginal cost is the unpleasant feeling of a burning mouth that you receive from it plus any explicit cost of the jalapeno. The marginal benefit of another jalapeno on your nachos is the pleasant taste that you receive from it.

d. The marginal benefit of hiring another worker in your company is the value of the output that worker produces. The marginal cost is the wage you must pay that worker.

e. The marginal cost is the value lost due to the increased side effects from this additional dose. The marginal benefit of another dose of the drug is the value of the reduction in the patient's disease.

f. The marginal cost is the opportunity cost of your time—what you would have gotten from the next best use of your time. The marginal benefit is the probable increase in your grade.

5. The accompanying table shows Alex's new marginal cost and his new profit. It also reproduces Alex's marginal benefit from Table 18-5.

Years of schooling	Total cost	Marginal cost	Marginal benefit	Profit
0	$0			
		$90,000	$300,000	$210,000
1	90,000			
		30,000	150,000	120,000
2	120,000			
		50,000	90,000	40,000
3	170,000			
		80,000	60,000	−20,000
4	250,000			
		120,000	50,000	−80,000
5	370,000			

Alex's marginal cost is decreasing until he has completed two years of schooling, after which marginal cost increases because of the value of his forgone income. The optimal amount of schooling is still three years. For less than three years of schooling, marginal benefit exceeds marginal cost; for more than three years, marginal cost exceeds marginal benefit.

6. a. Your sunk cost is $8,000 because none of the $8,000 spent on the truck is recoverable.

b. Your sunk cost is $4,000 because 50% of the $8,000 spent on the truck is recoverable.

7. a. This is an invalid argument because the time and money already spent are a sunk cost at this point.

b. This is also an invalid argument because what you should have done two years ago is irrelevant to what you should do now.

c. This is a valid argument because it recognizes that sunk costs are irrelevant to what you should do now.

d. This is a valid argument given that you are concerned about disappointing your parents. But your parents' views are irrational because they do not recognize that the time already spent is a sunk cost.

Multiple-Choice Questions

1. d
2. b
3. c
4. d
5. c

Critical-Thinking Question

The cost of the ticket is a sunk cost and cannot be recovered. The decision to remain at the game should be based on the marginal benefits of continued attendance, and the marginal cost of continuing to watch your favorite team lose.

MODULE 19

Check Your Understanding

1. a. Jenny is exhibiting loss aversion. She has an oversensitivity to loss, leading to an unwillingness to recognize a loss and move on.

b. Dan is doing mental accounting. Dollars from his unexpected overtime earnings are worth less—spent on a weekend getaway—than the dollars earned from his regular hours that he uses to pay down his student loan.

c. Carol may have unrealistic expectations of future behavior. Even if she does not want to participate in the plan now, she should find a way to commit to participating at a later date.

d. Jeremy is showing signs of status quo bias. He is avoiding making a decision altogether; in other words, he is sticking with the status quo.

Multiple-Choice Questions

1. c
2. d
3. c
4. c
5. a

Critical-Thinking Question

You would determine whether a decision was rational or irrational by first accurately accounting for all the costs and benefits of the decision. In particular, you must accurately measure all opportunity costs. Then calculate the economic payoff of the decision relative to the next best alternative. If you would still make the same choice after this comparison, then you have made a rational choice. If not, then the choice was irrational.

MODULE 20

Check Your Understanding

1. Consuming a unit that generates negative marginal utility leaves the consumer with lower total utility than not consuming that unit at all. A rational consumer, a consumer who maximizes utility, would not do that. For example, Figure 20-3 shows that Cassie receives 64 utils if she consumes 8 clams, but if she consumes a 9th clam, she loses a util, decreasing her total utility to only 63 utils. Whenever consuming a unit generates negative marginal utility, the consumer is made better off by not consuming that unit, even when that unit is free.

2. a. The accompanying table shows the consumer's consumption possibilities, bundles *A* through *C*. These consumption possibilities are plotted in the accompanying diagram, along with the consumer's budget line.

Consumption Bundle	Quantity of popcorn (buckets)	Quantity of movie tickets
A	0	2
B	2	1
C	4	0

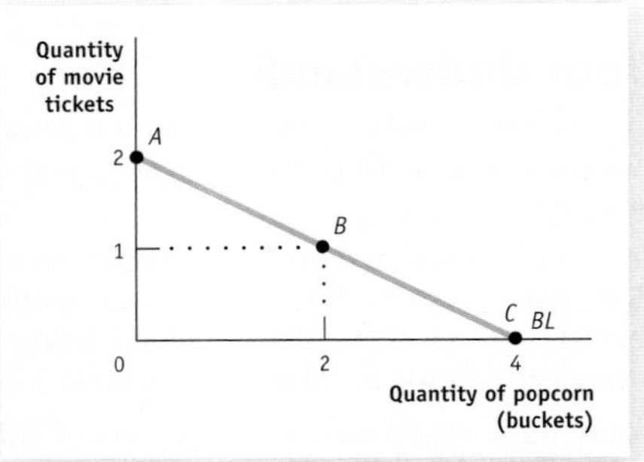

b. The accompanying table shows the consumer's consumption possibilities, *A* through *D*. These consumption possibilities are plotted in the accompanying diagram, along with the consumer's budget line.

Consumption Bundle	Quantity of underwear (pairs)	Quantity of socks (pairs)
A	0	6
B	1	4
C	2	2
D	3	0

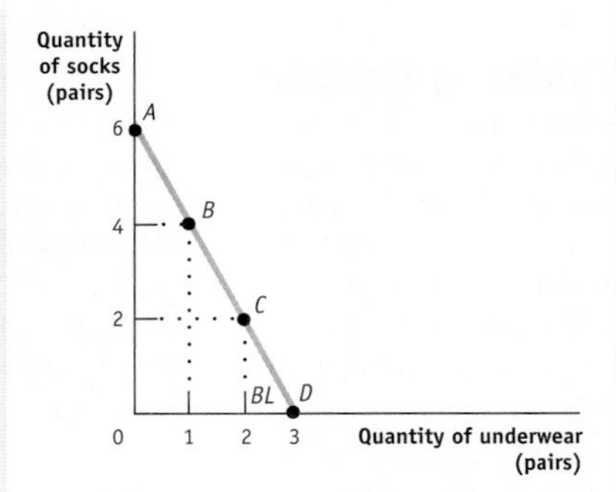

3. From Table 20-3 you can see that Sammy's marginal utility per dollar from increasing his consumption of clams from 3 to 4 pounds and his marginal utility per dollar from increasing his consumption of potatoes from 9 to 10 pounds are the same, 0.75 utils. But a consumption bundle consisting of 4 pounds of clams and 10 pounds of potatoes is not Sammy's optimal consumption bundle because it is not affordable given his income of $20; a bundle of 4 pounds of clams and 10 pounds of potatoes costs $4 × 4 + $2 × 10 = $36, $16 more than Sammy's income. This can be illustrated with Sammy's budget line from Figure 20-3: a bundle of 4 pounds of clams and 10 pounds of potatoes is represented by point *X* in the accompanying diagram, a point that lies outside Sammy's budget line. If you look at the horizontal axis of Figure 20-4, it is quite clear that there is no such thing in Sammy's consumption possibilities as a bundle consisting of 4 pounds of clams and 10 pounds of potatoes.

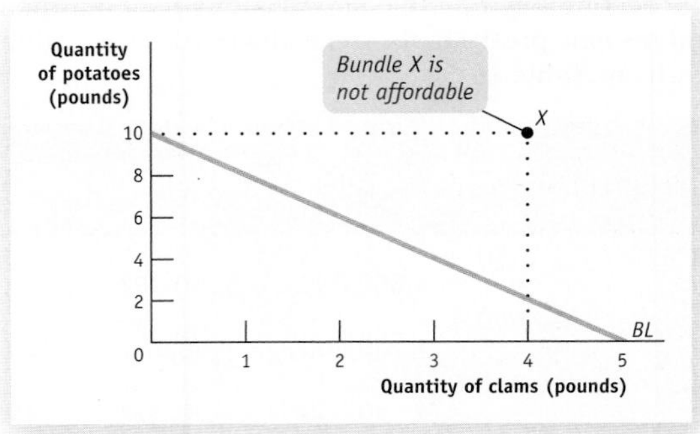

Multiple-Choice Questions

1. d
2. b
3. a
4. b
5. d

Critical-Thinking Questions

a.

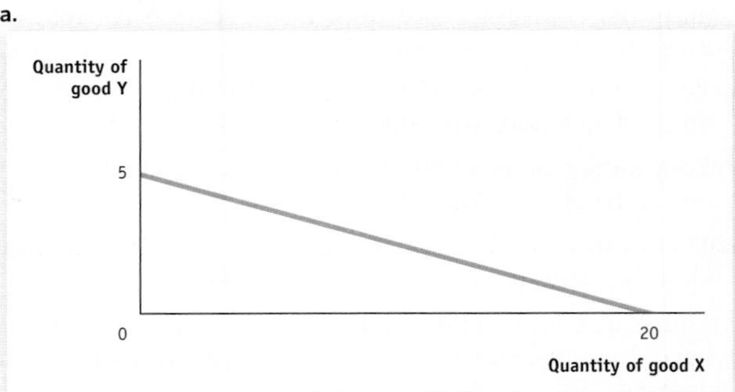

b. Yes, 100/$5 = 400/$20

c. Total utility will increase because marginal utility is positive, while marginal utility will decrease due to the principle of diminishing marginal utility.

MODULE 21

Check Your Understanding

1. a. The fixed input is the 10-ton machine and the variable input is electricity.

   b. As you can see from the declining numbers in the third column of the accompanying table, electricity does indeed exhibit diminishing returns: the marginal product of each additional kilowatt of electricity is less than that of the previous kilowatt.

Quantity of electricity (kilowatts)	Quantity of ice (pounds)	Marginal product of electricity (pounds per kilowatt)
0	0	
		1,000
1	1,000	
		800
2	1,800	
		600
3	2,400	
		400
4	2,800	

c. A 50% increase in the size of the fixed input means that Bernie now has a 15-ton machine, so the fixed input is now the 15-ton machine. Since it generates a 100% increase in output for any given amount of electricity, the quantity of output and the marginal product are now as shown in the accompanying table.

Quantity of electricity (kilowatts)	Quantity of ice (pounds)	Marginal product of electricity (pounds per kilowatt)
0	0	
		2,000
1	2,000	
		1,600
2	3,600	
		1,200
3	4,800	
		800
4	5,600	

Multiple-Choice Questions

1. d
2. e
3. a
4. b
5. a

Critical-Thinking Question

As you can see from the graph, the data exhibit diminishing returns to labor because the *MPL* curve is downward sloping.

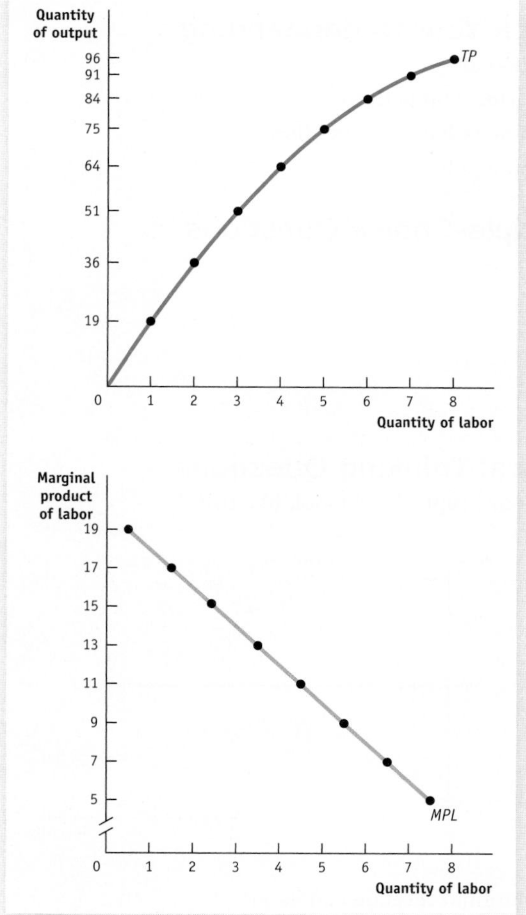

MODULE 22

Check Your Understanding

1. a. As shown in the accompanying table, the marginal cost for each pie is found by multiplying the marginal cost of the previous pie by 1.5. The variable cost for each output level is found by summing the marginal cost for all the pies produced to reach that output level. So, for example, the variable cost of three pies is $1.00 + $1.50 + $2.25 = $4.75. Average fixed cost for *Q* pies is calculated as $9.00/*Q* since fixed cost is $9.00. Average variable cost for *Q* pies is equal to the variable cost for the *Q* pies divided by *Q*; for example, the average variable cost of five pies is $13.19/5, or approximately $2.64. Finally, average total cost can be calculated in two equivalent ways: as *TC*/*Q* or as *AVC* + *AFC*.

Quantity of pies	Marginal cost of pie	Variable cost	Average fixed cost of pie	Average variable cost of pie	Average total cost of pie
0		$0.00	—	—	—
	$1.00				
1		1.00	$9.00	$1.00	$10.00
	1.50				
2		2.50	4.50	1.25	5.75
	2.25				
3		4.75	3.00	1.58	4.58
	3.38				
4		8.13	2.25	2.03	4.28
	5.06				
5		13.19	1.80	2.64	4.44
	7.59				
6		20.78	1.50	3.46	4.96

b. The spreading effect dominates the diminishing returns effect when average total cost is falling: the fall in *AFC* dominates the rise in *AVC* for pies 1 to 4. The diminishing returns effect dominates when average total cost is rising: the rise in *AVC* dominates the fall in *AFC* for pies 5 and 6.

c. Alicia's minimum-cost output is 4 pies; this generates the lowest average total cost, $4.28. When output is less than 4, the marginal cost of a pie is less than the average total cost of the pies already produced. So making an additional pie lowers average total cost. For example, the marginal cost of pie 3 is $2.25, whereas the average total cost of pies 1 and 2 is $5.75. So making pie 3 lowers average total cost to $4.58, equal to (2 × $5.75 + $2.25)/3. When output is more than 4, the marginal cost of a pie is greater than the average total cost of the pies already produced. Consequently, making an additional pie raises average total cost. So, although the marginal cost of pie 6 is $7.59, the average total cost of pies 1 through 5 is $4.44. Making pie 6 raises average total cost to $4.96, equal to (5 × $4.44 + $7.59)/6.

Multiple-Choice Questions

1. c
2. e
3. e
4. e
5. a

Critical-Thinking Question

Your graph should look like this.

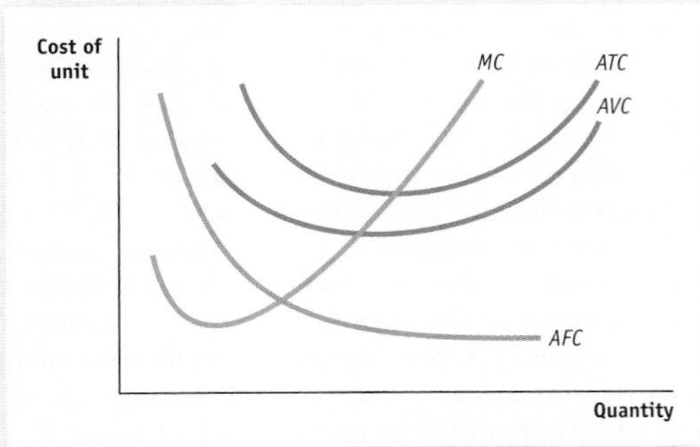

MODULE 23

Check Your Understanding

1. a. The accompanying table shows the average total cost of producing 12,000, 22,000, and 30,000 units for each of the three choices of fixed cost. For example, if the firm makes choice 1, the total cost of producing 12,000 units of output is $8,000 + 12,000 × $1.00 = $20,000. The average total cost of producing 12,000 units of output is therefore $20,000/12,000 = $1.67. The other average total costs are calculated similarly.

	12,000 units	22,000 units	30,000 units
Average total cost from choice 1	$1.67	$1.36	$1.27
Average total cost from choice 2	1.75	1.30	1.15
Average total cost from choice 3	2.25	1.34	1.05

So if the firm wanted to produce 12,000 units, it would make choice 1 because this gives it the lowest average total cost. If it wanted to produce 22,000 units, it would make choice 2. If it wanted to produce 30,000 units, it would make choice 3.

b. Having historically produced 12,000 units, the firm would have adopted choice 1. When producing 12,000 units, the firm would have had an average total cost of $1.67. When output jumps to 22,000 units, the firm cannot alter its choice of fixed cost in the short run, so its average total cost in the short run will be $1.36. In the long run, however, it will adopt choice 2, making its average total cost fall to $1.30.

c. If the firm believes that the increase in demand is temporary, it should not alter its fixed cost from choice 1 because choice 2 generates higher average total cost as soon as output falls back to its original quantity of 12,000 units: $1.75 versus $1.67.

2. a. This firm is likely to experience diseconomies of scale. As the firm takes on more projects, the costs of communication and coordination required to implement the expertise of the firm's owner are likely to increase.

b. This firm is likely to experience economies of scale. Because diamond mining requires a large initial setup cost for excavation equipment, long-run average total cost will fall as output increases.

Multiple-Choice Questions

1. a
2. e
3. e
4. d
5. e

Critical-Thinking Question

Your graph should look like this.

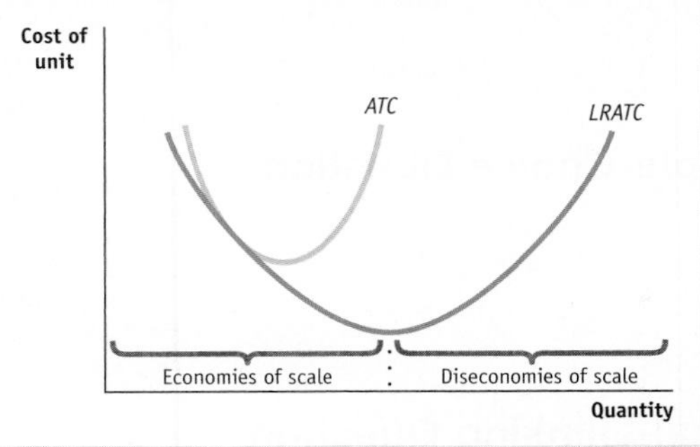

MODULE 24

Check Your Understanding

1. a. oligopoly
   b. perfect competition
   c. monopolistic competition
   d. monopoly

Multiple-Choice Questions

1. b
2. a
3. d
4. a
5. a

Critical-Thinking Questions

1. Your graph should look like this.

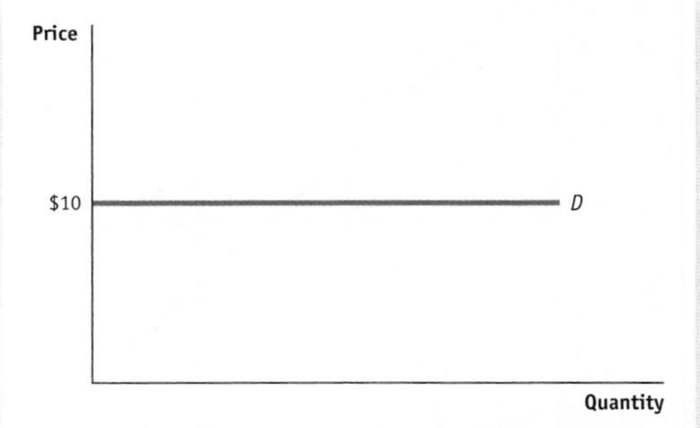

2. Marginal revenue equals $10.

MODULE 25

Check Your Understanding

1. a. The firm maximizes profit at a quantity of 4, because it is at that quantity that $MC = MR$.

   b. At a quantity of 4 the firm just breaks even. This is because at a quantity of 4, $P = ATC$, so the amount the firm takes in for each unit—the price—exactly equals the average total cost per unit.

2. The lowest price that would allow the firm to break even is \$10, because the minimum average total cost is \$500/50 = \$10, and price must at least equal minimum average total cost for the firm to break even.

Multiple-Choice Questions

1. d
2. e
3. d
4. c
5. c

Critical-Thinking Questions

1. This is how the firm's marginal cost at each quantity is calculated.

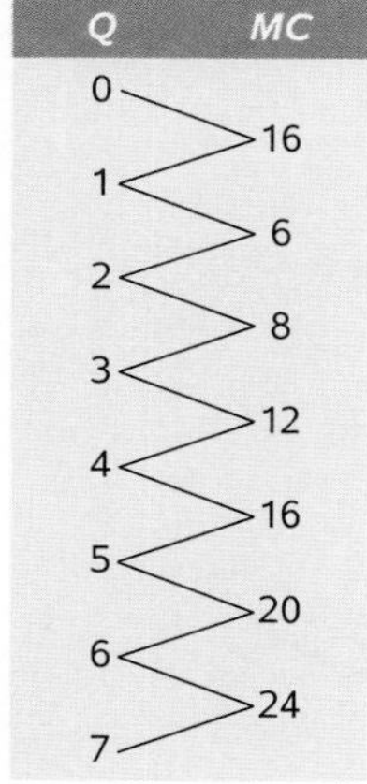

Q	MC
0	
	16
1	
	6
2	
	8
3	
	12
4	
	16
5	
	20
6	
	24
7	

2. The profit-maximizing quantity is 4.
3. The firm's maximum profit is $TR - TC = (4 \times \$14) - \$56 = \$56 - \$56 = \$0$.

MODULE 26

Check Your Understanding

1. a. The firm should shut down immediately when price is less than minimum average variable cost, the shut-down price. In the accompanying diagram, this is optimal for prices in the range from 0 to P_1.

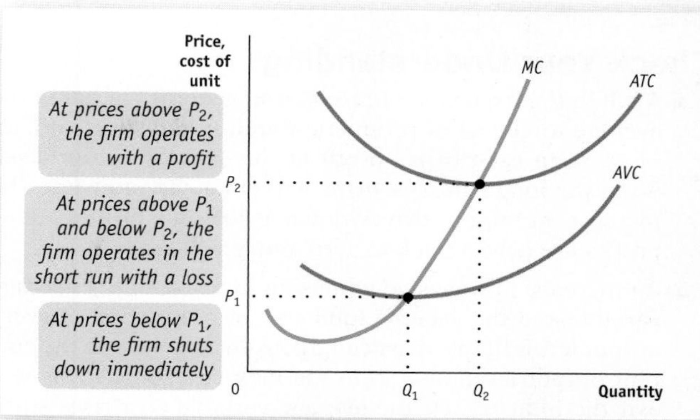

   b. When the price is greater than the minimum average variable cost (the shut-down price) but less than the minimum average total cost (the break-even price), the firm should continue to operate in the short run even though it is incurring a loss. This is optimal for prices in the range from P_1 to P_2.

   c. When the price exceeds the minimum average total cost (the break-even price), the firm makes a profit. This happens for prices in excess of P_2.

2. This is an example of a temporary shut-down by a firm when the market price lies below the shut-down price, the minimum average variable cost. The market price is the price of a lobster meal and the variable cost is the cost of the lobster, employee wages, and other expenses that increase as more meals are served. In this example, however, it is the average variable cost curve rather than the market price that shifts over time, due to seasonal changes in the cost of lobsters. Maine lobster shacks have relatively low average variable cost during the summer, when cheap Maine lobsters are available; during the rest of the year, their average variable cost is relatively high due to the high cost of imported lobsters. So the lobster shacks are open for business during the summer, when their minimum average variable cost lies below price; but they close during the rest of the year, when the price lies below their minimum average variable cost.

Multiple-Choice Questions

1. e
2. d
3. b
4. d
5. c

Critical-Thinking Questions

1. 6
2. $\$20 \times 6 = \$120$
3. $\$29.50 \times 6 = \$177$
4. $\$120 - \$177 = -\$57$ (or a loss of \$57)
5. No, because $P < AVC$

MODULE 27

Check Your Understanding

1. a. A fall in the fixed cost of production generates a fall in the average total cost of production and, in the short run, an increase in each firm's profit at the current output level. So in the long run new firms will enter the industry. The increase in supply drives down price and profits. Once profits are driven back to zero, entry will cease.

   b. An increase in wages generates an increase in the average variable and the average total cost of production at every output level. In the short run, firms incur losses at the current output level, and so in the long run some firms will exit the industry. (If the average variable cost rises sufficiently, some firms may even shut down in the short run.) As firms exit, supply decreases, price rises, and losses are reduced. Exit will cease once losses return to zero.

   c. Price will rise as a result of the increased demand, leading to a short-run increase in profits at the current output level. In the long run, firms will enter the industry, generating an increase in supply, a fall in price, and a fall in profits. Once profits are driven back to zero, entry will cease.

   d. The shortage of a key input causes that input's price to increase, resulting in an increase in average variable and average total cost for producers. Firms incur losses in the short run, and some firms will exit the industry in the long run. The fall in supply generates an increase in price and decreased losses. Exit will cease when the losses for remaining firms have returned to zero.

2. In the accompanying diagram, point X_{MKT} in panel (b), the intersection of S_1 and D_1, represents the long-run industry equilibrium before the change in consumer tastes. When tastes change, demand falls and the industry moves in the short run to point Y_{MKT} in panel (b), at the intersection of the new demand curve D_2 and S_1, the short-run supply curve representing the same number of egg producers as in the original equilibrium at point X_{MKT}. As the market price falls, each individual firm reacts by producing less—as shown in panel (a)—as long as the market price remains above the minimum average variable cost. If market price falls below minimum average variable cost, the firm would shut down immediately. At point Y_{MKT} the price of eggs is below minimum average total cost, creating losses for producers. This leads some firms to exit, which shifts the short-run industry supply curve leftward to S_2. A new long-run equilibrium is established at point Z_{MKT}. As this occurs, the market price rises again, and, as shown in panel (c), each remaining producer reacts by increasing output (here, from point *Y* to point *Z*). All remaining producers again make zero profits. The decrease in the quantity of eggs supplied in the industry comes entirely from the exit of some producers from the industry. The long-run industry supply curve is the curve labeled *LRS* in panel (b).

Multiple-Choice Questions

1. d
2. b
3. a
4. e
5. b

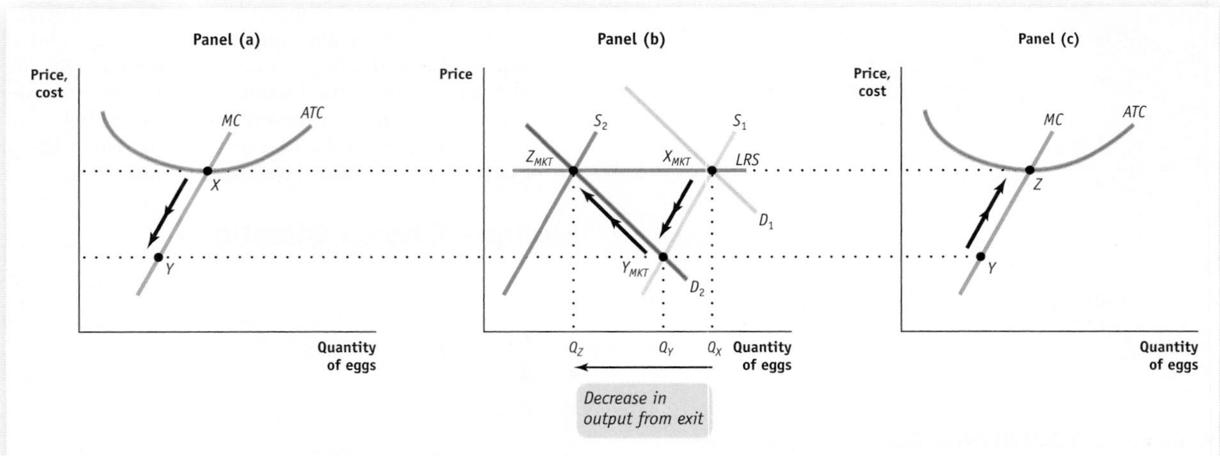

Critical-Thinking Question

Your graphs should look like this.

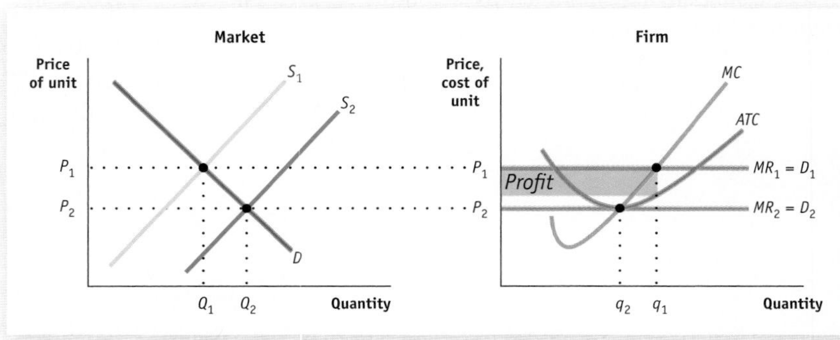

MODULE 28

Check Your Understanding

1. a. The demand schedule is found by determining the price at which each quantity would be demanded. This price is the average revenue, found at each output level by dividing the total revenue by the number of emeralds produced. For example, the price when 3 emeralds are produced is $252/3 = $84. The price at the various output levels is then used to construct the demand schedule in the accompanying table.

   b. The marginal revenue schedule is found by calculating the change in total revenue as output increases by one unit. For example, the marginal revenue generated by increasing output from 2 to 3 emeralds is ($252 – $186) = $66.

   c. The quantity effect component of marginal revenue is the additional revenue generated by selling one more unit of the good at the market price. For example, as shown in the accompanying table, at 3 emeralds, the market price is $84; so, when going from 2 to 3 emeralds the quantity effect is equal to $84.

   d. The price effect component of marginal revenue is the decline in total revenue caused by the fall in price when one more unit is sold. For example, as shown in the table, when only 2 emeralds are sold, each emerald sells at a price of $93. However, when Emerald, Inc. sells an additional emerald, the price must fall by $9 to $84. So the price effect component in going from 2 to 3 emeralds is (–$9) × 2 = –$18. That's because when just 2 emeralds are sold, each is sold at a price of $93. But when 3 emeralds are sold, those same 2 diamonds are sold for only $84 each, a $9 loss per diamond.

Quantity of emeralds demanded	Price of emerald	Total revenue	Marginal revenue	Quantity effect component	Price effect component
1	$100	$100			
			$86	$93	–$7
2	93	186			
			66	84	–18
3	84	252			
			28	70	–42
4	70	280			
			–30	50	–80
5	50	250			

   e. In order to determine Emerald, Inc.'s profit-maximizing output level, you must know its marginal cost at each output level. Its profit-maximizing output level is the one at which marginal revenue is equal to marginal cost.

2. As the accompanying diagram shows, the marginal cost curve shifts upward to $400. The profit-maximizing price rises to $700 and quantity falls to 6. Profit falls from $3,200 to $300 × 6 = $1,800. The quantity a perfectly competitive industry would produce decreases to 12, but profits remain unchanged at zero.

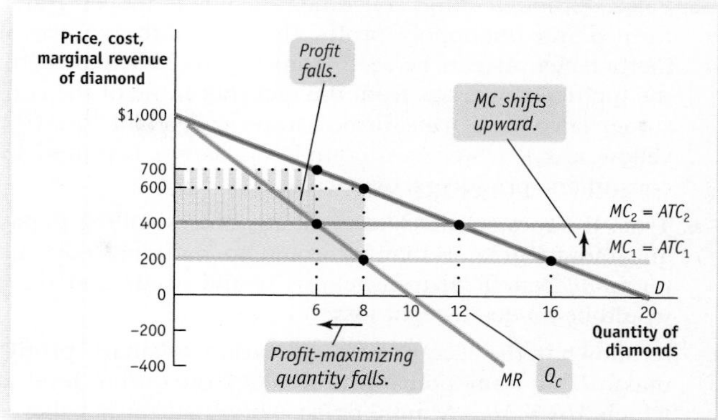

Multiple-Choice Questions

1. b
2. c
3. b
4. d
5. d

Critical-Thinking Questions

1. Your graph should look like this.

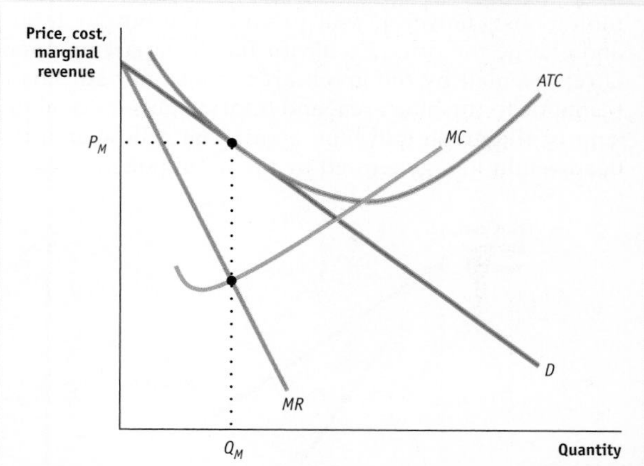

2. Yes, with the help of barriers to entry that keep competitors out.

MODULE 29

Check Your Understanding

1. a. Cable Internet service is a natural monopoly. So the government should intervene if it believes that the current price exceeds average total cost, which includes the cost of laying the cable. In this case it should impose a price ceiling equal to average total cost. If the price does not exceed average total cost, the government should do nothing.

   b. The government should approve the merger only if it fosters competition by transferring some of the company's landing slots to another, competing airline.

2. a. False. Although some consumer surplus is indeed transformed into monopoly profit, this is not the source of inefficiency. As can be seen from Figure 29-1, panel (b), the inefficiency arises from the fact that some of the consumer surplus is transformed into deadweight loss (the yellow area), which is a complete loss not captured by consumers, producers, or anyone else.

   b. True. If a monopolist sold to all customers willing to pay an amount greater than or equal to marginal cost, all mutually beneficial transactions would occur and there would be no deadweight loss.

3. As shown in the accompanying diagram, a "smart" profit–maximizing monopolist produces Q_M, the output level at which $MR = MC$. A monopolist who mistakenly believes that $P = MR$ produces the output level at which $P = MC$ (when, in fact, $P > MR$, and at the true profit-maximizing level of output, $P > MR = MC$). This misguided monopolist will produce the output level Q_C, where the demand curve crosses the marginal cost curve—the same output level that would be produced if the industry were perfectly competitive. It will charge the price P_C, which is equal to marginal cost, and make zero profit. The entire shaded area is equal to the consumer surplus, which is also equal to total surplus in this case (since the monopolist receives zero producer surplus). There is no deadweight loss because every consumer who is willing to pay as much as or more than marginal cost gets the good. A smart monopolist, however, will produce the output level Q_M and charge the price P_M. Profit for the smart monopolist is represented by the green area, consumer surplus corresponds to the blue area, and total surplus is equal to the sum of the green and blue areas. The yellow area is the deadweight loss generated by the monopolist.

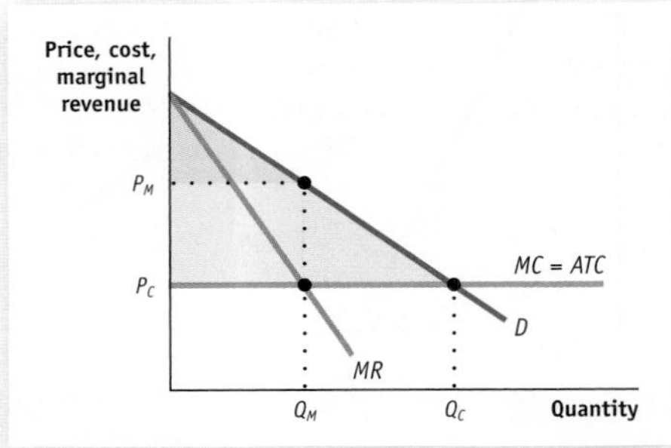

Multiple-Choice Questions

1. a
2. b
3. c
4. a
5. b

Critical-Thinking Question

This graph illustrates a natural monopoly.

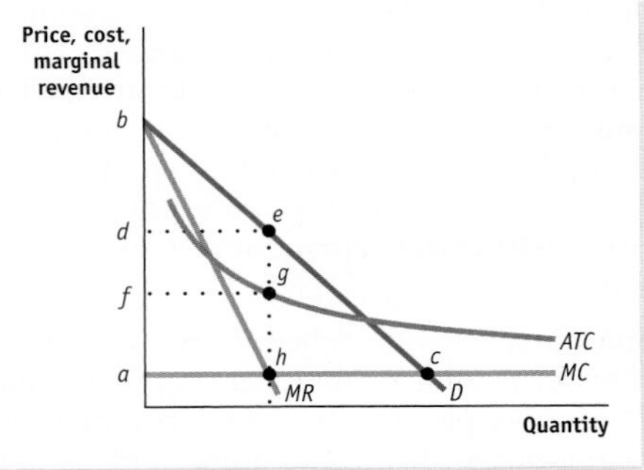

a. triangle *bca*

b. triangle *bed*

c. rectangle *degf*

d. triangle *ech*

MODULE 30

Check Your Understanding

1. a. False. The opposite is true. A price-discriminating monopolist will sell to some customers that would not find the product affordable if purchasing from a single-price monopolist—namely, customers with a high price elasticity of demand who are willing to pay only a relatively low price for the good.

   b. False. Although a price-discriminating monopolist does indeed capture more of the consumer surplus, less inefficiency is created: more mutually beneficial transactions occur because the monopolist makes more sales to customers with a low willingness to pay for the good.

   c. True. Under price discrimination consumers are charged prices that depend on their price elasticity of demand. A consumer with highly elastic demand will pay a lower price than a consumer with inelastic demand.

2. a. This is not a case of price discrimination because the product itself is different and all consumers, regardless of their price elasticities of demand, value the damaged merchandise less than undamaged merchandise. So the price must be lowered to sell the merchandise.

   b. This is a case of price discrimination. Senior citizens have a higher price elasticity of demand for restaurant meals (their demand for restaurant meals is more responsive to price changes) than other patrons. Restaurants lower the price to high-elasticity consumers (senior citizens). Consumers with low price elasticity of demand will pay the full price.

   c. This is a case of price discrimination. Consumers with a high price elasticity of demand will pay a lower price by collecting and using discount coupons. Consumers with a low price elasticity of demand will not collect or use coupons.

   d. This is not a case of price discrimination; it is simply a case of supply and demand.

Multiple-Choice Questions

1. d
2. c
3. b
4. e
5. a

Critical-Thinking Question

This graph shows a monopoly practicing perfect price discrimination. In this case, consumer surplus is zero because each consumer is charged the maximum he or she is willing to pay.

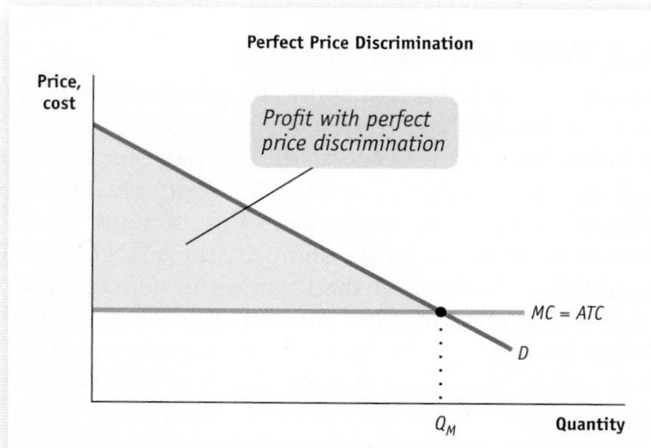

MODULE 31

Check Your Understanding

1. a. This will decrease the likelihood that the firm will collude to restrict output. By increasing output, the firm will generate a negative price effect. But because the firm's current market share is small, the price effect will fall mostly on its rivals' revenues rather than on its own. At the same time, the firm will benefit from a positive quantity effect.

   b. This will decrease the likelihood that the firm will collude to restrict output. By acting noncooperatively and raising output, the firm will cause the price to fall. Because its rivals have higher costs, they will lose money at the lower price while the firm continues to make profits. So the firm may be able to drive its rivals out of business by increasing its output.

   c. This will increase the likelihood that the firm will collude. Because it is costly for consumers to switch products, the firm would have to lower its price substantially (with a commensurate increase in quantity) to induce consumers to switch to its product. So increasing output is likely to be unprofitable, given the large negative price effect.

   d. This will increase the likelihood that the firm will collude. It cannot increase sales because it is currently at maximum production capacity, making attempts to undercut rivals' prices fruitless due to the inability to produce the output needed to steal the rivals' customers. This makes the option to cooperate in restricting output relatively attractive.

Multiple-Choice Questions

1. a
2. c
3. d
4. e
5. b

Critical-Thinking Question

The first major reason is that cartels are illegal in the United States. The second major reason is that cartels set prices above marginal cost, which creates an incentive for each firm to cheat on the cartel agreement in order to make more profit. This incentive to cheat tends to cause cartels to fall apart.

MODULE 32

Check Your Understanding

1. a. A Nash equilibrium is a set of actions from which neither side wants to deviate (change actions), given what the other is doing. Both sides building a missile is a Nash equilibrium because neither player wants to deviate from the decision to build a missile. To switch from building to not building a missile, given that the other player is building a missile, would result in a change from −10 to −20 utils. There is no other Nash equilibrium in this game because for any other set of actions, at least one side is not building a missile, and would be better off switching to building a missile.

   b. Their total payoff is greatest when neither side builds a missile, in which case their total payoff is $0 + 0 = 0$.

   c. This outcome would require cooperation because each side sees itself as better off by building a missile. If Margaret builds a missile but Nikita does not, Margaret gets a payoff of +8, rather than the 0 she gets if she doesn't build a missile. Similarly, Nikita is better off if he builds a missile but Margaret doesn't: he gets a payoff of +8, rather than the 0 he gets if he doesn't build a missile. Indeed, both players have an incentive to build a missile regardless of what the other side does. So unless Nikita and Margaret are able to communicate in some way to enforce cooperation, they will act in their own individual interests and each will pursue its dominant strategy of building a missile.

2. a. Future entry by several new firms will increase competition and drive down industry profits. As a result, there is less future profit to protect by behaving cooperatively today. This makes each oligopolist more likely to behave noncooperatively today.

   b. When it is very difficult for a firm to detect if another firm has raised output, it is very difficult to enforce cooperation by playing tit for tat. So it is more likely that a firm will behave noncooperatively.

   c. When firms have coexisted while maintaining high prices for a long time, each expects cooperation to continue. So the value of behaving cooperatively today is high, and it is likely that firms will engage in tacit collusion.

Multiple-Choice Questions

1. b
2. b
3. c
4. a
5. c

Critical-Thinking Question

Your payoff matrix should look like this.

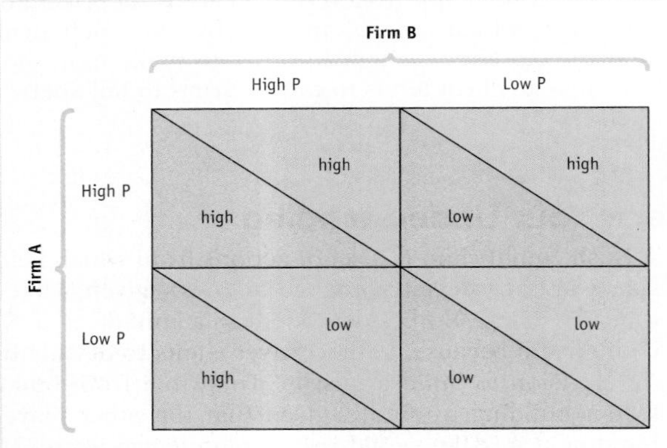

MODULE 33

Check Your Understanding

1. a. This is evidence of tacit collusion. Firms in the industry are able to tacitly collude by setting their prices according to the published "suggested" price of the largest firm in the industry. This is a form of price leadership.

   b. This is not evidence of tacit collusion. Considerable variation in market shares indicates that firms have been competing to capture each other's business.

   c. This is not evidence of tacit collusion. These features make it less likely that consumers will switch products in response to lower prices. So this is a way for firms to avoid any temptation to gain market share by lowering price. This is a form of product differentiation used to avoid direct competition.

   d. This is evidence of tacit collusion. In the guise of discussing sales targets, firms can create a cartel by designating quantities to be produced by each firm.

   e. This is evidence of tacit collusion. By raising prices together, each firm in the industry is refusing to undercut its rivals by leaving its price unchanged or lowering it. Because it could gain market share by doing so, refusing to do so supports the conclusion that there is tacit collusion.

Multiple-Choice Questions

1. d
2. d
3. c
4. e
5. a

Critical-Thinking Question

a. A large number of firms: having more firms means there is less incentive for any firm to behave cooperatively.

b. Complex products/pricing schemes: keeping track of adherence to an agreement is more difficult.

c. Differences in interests: firms often have different views of their own interests and of what a fair agreement would entail.

d. Bargaining power of buyers: firms are less able to raise prices for buyers with significant bargaining power, which can result from size or access to many options.

MODULE 34

Check Your Understanding

1. a. An increase in fixed cost shifts the average total cost curve upward. In the short run, firms incur losses because price is below average total cost. In the long run, some firms will exit the industry, resulting in a rightward shift of the demand curves for those firms that remain, since each firm now serves a larger share of the market. Long-run equilibrium is reestablished when the demand curve for each remaining firm has shifted rightward to the point where it is tangent to the firm's new, higher average total cost curve. At this point each firm's price just equals its average total cost, and each firm makes zero profit.

   b. A decrease in marginal cost shifts the average total cost curve and the marginal cost curve downward. In the short run, firms earn positive economic profit. In the long run new entrants are attracted into the industry by the profit. This results in a leftward shift of each existing firm's demand curve because each firm now has a smaller share of the market. Long-run equilibrium is reestablished when each firm's demand curve has shifted leftward to the point where it is tangent to the new, lower average total cost curve. At this point each firm's price just equals average total cost, and each firm makes zero profit.

2. If all the existing firms in the industry joined together to create a monopoly, they could achieve positive economic profit in the short run. But this would induce new firms to create new, differentiated products and then enter the industry and capture some of the profit. So, in the long run, thanks to the lack of barriers to entry, it would be impossible to maintain such a monopoly.

3. a. False. As illustrated in panel (b) of Figure 34.4, a monopolistically competitive firm sells its output at a price that exceeds marginal cost—unlike a perfectly competitive firm, which sells at a price equal to marginal cost.

   b. True. Firms in a monopolistically competitive industry could achieve higher profit (*monopoly profit*) if they all joined together as a single firm with a single product. Because each of the smaller firms possesses excess capacity, a single firm producing a larger quantity would have a lower average total cost. The effect on consumers, however, is ambiguous. They would experience less choice. But if consolidation substantially reduced industry-wide average total cost and increases industry-wide output, consumers could experience lower prices with the monopoly.

   c. True. Fads and fashions are promulgated by advertising and a desire for product differentiation, which are common in oligopolies and monopolistically competitive industries, but not in monopolies or perfectly competitive industries.

Multiple-Choice Questions

1. b
2. e
3. b
4. b
5. e

Critical-Thinking Question

Your graph should look like this.

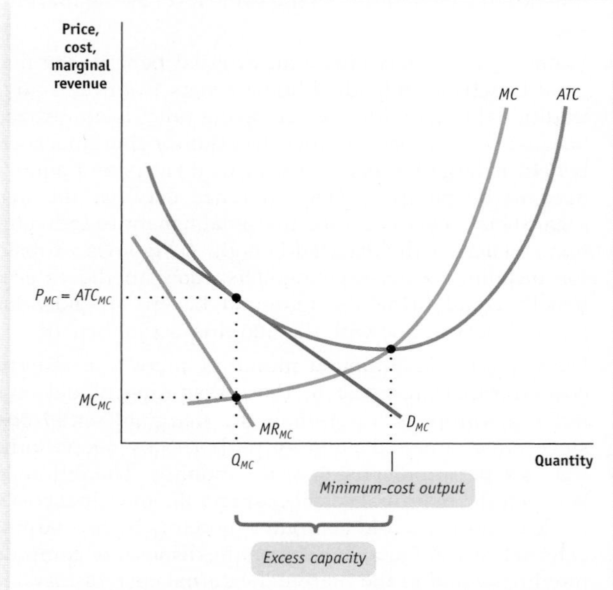

MODULE 35

Check Your Understanding

1. a. Ladders are not differentiated as a result of monopolistic competition. A ladder producer makes different ladders (tall ladders versus short ladders) to satisfy different consumer needs, not to avoid competition with rivals. So two tall ladders made by two different producers will be indistinguishable by consumers.

   b. Soft drinks are an example of product differentiation as a result of monopolistic competition. For example, several producers make colas; each is differentiated in terms of taste, which fast-food chains sell it, and so on.

   c. Department stores are an example of product differentiation as a result of monopolistic competition. They serve different clientele that have different price sensitivities and different tastes. They also offer different levels of customer service and are situated in different locations.

   d. Steel is not differentiated as a result of monopolistic competition. Different types of steel (beams versus sheets) are made for different purposes, not to distinguish one steel manufacturer's products from another's.

2. a. Perfectly competitive industries and monopolistically competitive industries both have many sellers. So it may be hard to distinguish between them solely in terms of number of firms. And in both market structures, there is free entry into and exit from the industry in the long run. But in a perfectly competitive industry, one standardized product is sold; in a monopolistically competitive industry, products are differentiated. So you should ask whether products are differentiated in the industry.

   b. In a monopoly there is only one firm, but a monopolistically competitive industry contains many firms. So you should ask whether or not there is a single firm in the industry.

3. a. This type of advertising is likely to be useful because it provides new information on an important product.

   b. This type of advertising is likely to be wasteful because it is focused on promoting Bayer aspirin over a rival's aspirin despite the two products being medically indistinguishable.

   c. This is useful because the longevity of a business gives a potential customer information about its quality.

4. A successful brand name indicates a desirable attribute, such as quality, to a potential buyer. So, other things equal—such as price—a firm with a successful brand name will achieve higher sales than a rival with a comparable product but without a successful brand name. This is likely to deter new firms from entering an industry in which an existing firm has a successful brand name.

Multiple-Choice Questions

1. e
2. d
3. a
4. e
5. d

Critical-Thinking Question

Product differentiation is efficient when it conveys useful information to consumers and the marginal benefit of the product differentiation exceeds the marginal cost. It is not efficient from a societal standpoint if it does not convey useful information or other benefits worth more than the resources devoted to it. This is likely to be the case, for example, if it misleads consumers or creates undesirable market power.

MODULE 36

Check Your Understanding

1. a. This is an externality problem because the cost of wastewater runoff is imposed on the farms' neighbors with no compensation and no other way for the farms to internalize the cost.

   b. Since the large poultry farmers do not take the external cost of their actions into account when making decisions about how much wastewater to generate, they will create more runoff than is socially optimal. They will produce runoff up to the point at which the marginal social benefit of an additional unit of runoff is zero; however, their neighbors experience a high, positive level of marginal social cost of runoff from this output level. So the quantity of wastewater runoff is inefficient: reducing runoff by one unit would reduce total social benefit by less than it would reduce total social cost.

c. At the socially optimal quantity of wastewater runoff, the marginal social benefit is equal to the marginal social cost. This quantity is lower than the quantity of wastewater runoff that would be created in the absence of government intervention or a private deal.

2. Yasmin's reasoning is not correct: allowing some late returns of books is likely to be socially optimal. Although you impose a marginal social cost on others every day that you are late in returning a book, there is some positive marginal social benefit to you of returning a book late—you get a longer period during which to use it for education and pleasure. If you need it for a book report, the additional benefit from another day might be large indeed.

The socially optimal number of days that a book is returned late is the number at which the marginal social benefit equals the marginal social cost. A fine so stiff that it prevents any late returns is likely to result in a situation in which people return books although the marginal social benefit of keeping them another day is greater than the marginal social cost—an inefficient outcome. In that case, allowing an overdue patron another day would increase total social benefit more than it would increase total social cost. So charging a moderate fine that reduces the number of days that books are returned late to the socially optimal number of days is appropriate.

Multiple-Choice Questions

1. a

2. a

3. d

4. b

5. d

Critical-Thinking Questions

1. The marginal social cost of pollution is the additional cost imposed on society by an additional unit of pollution.

2. The marginal social benefit of pollution is the additional benefit to society from an additional unit of pollution. Even when a firm could provide the same quantity of output without polluting as much, there is a benefit from polluting more because the firm can devote less money and resources to pollution avoidance.

3. The socially optimal level of pollution is that level at which the marginal social benefit of pollution equals the marginal social cost.

MODULE 37

Check Your Understanding

1. This is a misguided argument. Allowing polluters to sell emissions permits makes polluters face a cost of polluting: the opportunity cost of not being able to sell the permits that cover that pollution. If a polluter chooses not to reduce its emissions, it cannot sell its emissions permits. As a result, it forgoes the opportunity of making money from the sale of the permits. So, despite the fact that the polluter receives a monetary benefit from selling the permits, the scheme has the desired effect: to make polluters internalize the externality of their actions and reduce the total amount of pollution.

2. College education provides external benefits through the creation of knowledge. And student aid acts like a Pigouvian subsidy on higher education. If the marginal social benefit of higher education is indeed $35 billion, then student aid is an optimal policy.

3. a. Planting trees imposes an external benefit: the marginal social benefit of planting trees is higher than the marginal benefit to individual tree planters because many people (not just those who plant the trees) can enjoy the improved air quality and lower summer temperatures. The difference between the marginal social benefit and the marginal benefit to individual tree planters is the external benefit. A Pigouvian subsidy equal to the external benefit could be placed on each tree planted in urban areas in order to increase the marginal private benefit to individual tree planters to the same level as the marginal social benefit.

b. Water-saving toilets create an external benefit: the marginal benefit to individual homeowners from replacing a traditional toilet with a water-saving toilet is almost zero because water is very inexpensive. But the marginal social benefit is large because fewer critical rivers and aquifers need to be pumped. The difference between the marginal social benefit and the marginal benefit to individual homeowners is the external benefit. A Pigouvian subsidy for installing water-saving toilets equal to the external benefit could bring the marginal benefit to individual homeowners in line with the marginal social benefit.

c. Disposing of old computer monitors imposes an external cost: the marginal cost to those disposing of old computer monitors is lower than the marginal social cost, since environmental pollution is borne by people other than the person disposing of the monitor. The difference between the marginal social cost and the marginal cost to those disposing of old computer monitors is the marginal external cost. A Pigouvian tax on the disposal of computer monitors equal to the marginal external cost, or a system of tradable permits for their disposal, could raise the marginal cost to those disposing of old computer monitors up to the level of the marginal social cost.

Multiple-Choice Questions

1. a

2. d

3. b

4. a

5. e

Critical-Thinking Question

It depends. The Pigouvian tax should be set at the price where the marginal social benefits of the pollution caused by water bottle usage is equal to the marginal social costs of such usage. If this is equal to $0.50 per bottle, then it is optimal. If it is either greater or less than $0.50, it is an inefficient tax.

MODULE 38

Check Your Understanding

1. a. A public space is generally nonexcludable, but it may or may not be rival in consumption, depending on the level of congestion. For example, if you and I are the only users of a jogging path in the public park, then your use will not prevent my use—the path is nonrival in consumption. In this case the public space is a public good. But the space is rival in consumption if there are many people trying to use the jogging path at the same time or if my use of the public tennis court prevents your use of the same court. In this case the public space becomes a common resource.

b. A cheese burrito is both excludable and rival in consumption. Hence it is a private good.

c. Information from a password-protected website is excludable but nonrival in consumption. So it is an artificially scarce good.

d. Publicly announced information about the path of an incoming hurricane is nonexcludable and nonrival in consumption, so it is a public good.

2. A private producer will supply only a good that is excludable; otherwise, the producer won't be able to charge a price for it that covers the cost of production. So a private producer would be willing to supply a cheese burrito and information from a password-protected website but unwilling to supply a public park or publicly announced information about an incoming hurricane.

3. a. With 10 Homebodies and 6 Revelers, the marginal social benefit schedule of money spent on the party is as shown in the accompanying table.

Money spent on party	Marginal social benefit
$0	
	(10 × $0.05) + (6 × $0.13) = $1.28
1	
	(10 × $0.04) + (6 × $0.11) = $1.06
2	
	(10 × $0.03) + (6 × $0.09) = $0.84
3	
	(10 × $0.02) + (6 × $0.07) = $0.62
4	

The efficient spending level is $2, the highest level for which the marginal social benefit is greater than the marginal cost ($1).

b. With 6 Homebodies and 10 Revelers, the marginal social benefit schedule of money spent on the party is as shown in the accompanying table.

Money spent on party	Marginal social benefit
$0	
	(6 × $0.05) + (10 × $0.13) = $1.60
1	
	(6 × $0.04) + (10 × $0.11) = $1.34
2	
	(6 × $0.03) + (10 × $0.09) = $1.08
3	
	(6 × $0.02) + (10 × $0.07) = $0.82
4	

The efficient spending level is now $3, the highest level for which the marginal social benefit is greater than the marginal cost ($1). The efficient level of spending has increased from that in part a because with relatively more Revelers than Homebodies, an additional dollar spent on the party generates a higher level of social benefit compared to when there are relatively more Homebodies than Revelers.

c. When the numbers of Homebodies and Revelers are unknown but residents are asked their preferences, Homebodies will pretend to be Revelers to induce a higher level of spending on the public party. That's because a Homebody still receives a positive individual marginal benefit from an additional $1 spent, despite the fact that his or her individual marginal benefit is lower than that of a Reveler for every additional $1. In this case the "reported" marginal social benefit schedule of money spent on the party will be as shown in the accompanying table.

Money spent on party	Marginal social benefit
$0	
	16 × $0.13 = $2.08
1	
	16 × $0.11 = $1.76
2	
	16 × $0.09 = $1.44
3	
	16 × $0.07 = $1.12
4	

As a result, $4 will be spent on the party, the highest level for which the "reported" marginal social benefit is greater than the marginal cost ($1). Regardless of whether there are 10 Homebodies and 6 Revelers (part a) or 6 Homebodies and 10 Revelers (part b), spending $4 in total on the party is clearly inefficient because marginal cost exceeds marginal social benefit at this spending level.

4. When individuals are allowed to harvest freely, the government-owned forest becomes a common resource, and individuals will overuse it—they will harvest more trees than is efficient. In economic terms, the marginal social cost of harvesting a tree is greater than a private logger's individual marginal cost.

5. The three methods consistent with economic theory are (i) Pigouvian taxes, (ii) a system of tradable licenses, and (iii) allocation of property rights.

i. *Pigouvian taxes.* You would enforce a tax on loggers that equals the difference between the marginal social cost and the individual marginal cost of logging a tree at the socially efficient harvest amount. In order to do this, you must know the marginal social cost schedule and the individual marginal cost schedule.

ii. *System of tradable licenses.* You would issue tradable licenses, setting the total number of trees harvested equal to the socially efficient harvest number. The market that arises in these licenses will allocate the right to log efficiently when loggers differ in their costs of logging: licenses will be purchased by those who have a relatively lower cost of logging. The market price of a license will be equal to the difference between the marginal social cost and the individual marginal cost of logging a tree at the socially efficient harvest amount. In order to implement this level, you need to know the socially efficient harvest amount.

iii. *Allocation of property rights.* Here you would sell or give the forest to a private party. This party will have the right to exclude others from harvesting trees. Harvesting is now a private good—it is excludable and rival in consumption. As a result, there is no longer any divergence between social and private costs, and the private party will harvest the efficient level of trees. You need no additional information to use this method.

Multiple-Choice Questions

1. a
2. b
3. e
4. d
5. e

Critical-Thinking Questions

1. Nonrival in consumption: the same unit of the good can be consumed by more than one person at the same time. Nonexcludable: suppliers of the good can't prevent people who don't pay from consuming the good.
2. The additional cost is zero. Public goods are nonrival, so the same unit can be provided to additional community members at no added cost.

MODULE 39

Check Your Understanding

1. a. A pension guarantee program is a social insurance program. The possibility of an employer declaring bankruptcy and defaulting on its obligation to pay employee pensions creates insecurity. By providing pension income to those employees, such a program alleviates this source of economic insecurity.
   b. The SCHIP program is a poverty program. By providing health care to children in low-income households, it targets its spending specifically to the poor.
   c. The Section 8 housing program is a poverty program. By targeting its support to low-income households, it specifically helps the poor.
   d. The federal flood program is a social insurance program. For many people, the majority of their wealth is tied up in the home they own. The potential for a loss of that wealth creates economic insecurity. By providing assistance to those hit by a major flood, the program alleviates this source of insecurity.
2. The poverty threshold is an absolute measure of poverty. It defines individuals as poor if their incomes fall below a level that is considered adequate to purchase the necessities of life, irrespective of how well other people are doing. And that measure is fixed: in 2010, for instance, it took $11,139 for an individual living alone to purchase the necessities of life, regardless of how well-off other Americans were. In particular, the poverty threshold is not adjusted for an increase in living standards: even if other Americans are becoming increasingly well-off over time, in real terms (that is, how many goods an individual at the poverty threshold can buy) the poverty threshold remains the same.
3. a. To determine mean (or average) income, we take the total income of all individuals in this economy and divide it by the number of individuals. Mean income is ($39,000 + $17,500 + $900,000 + $15,000 + $28,000)/5 = $999,500/5 = $199,900. To determine median income, look at the accompanying table, which lines up the five individuals in order of their income.

	Income
Vijay	$15,000
Kelly	17,500
Oskar	28,000
Sephora	39,000
Raul	900,000

   The median income is the income of the individual in the exact middle of the income distribution: Oskar, with an income of $28,000. So the median income is $28,000.

   Median income is more representative of the income of individuals in this economy: almost everyone earns income between $15,000 and $39,000, close to the median income of $28,000. Only Raul is the exception: it is his income that raises the mean income to $199,900, which is not representative of most incomes in this economy.

   b. The first quintile is made up of the 20% (or one-fifth) of individuals with the lowest incomes in the economy. Vijay makes up the 20% of individuals with the lowest incomes. His income is $15,000, so that is the average income of the first quintile. Oskar makes up the 20% of individuals with the third-lowest incomes. His income is $28,000, so that is the average income of the third quintile.
4. As the Economics in Action pointed out, much of the rise in inequality reflects growing differences among highly educated workers. That is, workers with similar levels of education earn very dissimilar incomes. As a result, the principal source of rising inequality in the United States today is reflected by statement b: the rise in the bank CEO's salary relative to that of the branch manager.
5. The Earned Income Tax Credit (EITC), a negative income tax, applies only to those workers who earn income; over a certain range of incomes, the more a worker earns, the higher the amount of EITC received. A person who earns no income receives no income tax credit. By contrast, poverty programs that pay individuals based solely on low income still make those payments even if the individual does not work at all; once the individual earns a certain amount of income, these programs discontinue payments. As a result, such programs contain an incentive not to work and earn income, since earning more than a certain amount makes individuals ineligible for their benefits. The negative income tax, however, provides an incentive to work and earn income because its payments increase the more an individual works.
6. According to the data in Table 39-4, the U.S. welfare state reduces the poverty rate for every age group. It does so particularly dramatically for those aged 65 and over, where it cuts the poverty rate by 80%.
7. Over the past 40 years, polarization in Congress has increased. Forty years ago, some Republicans were to the left of some Democrats. Today, the rightmost Democrats appear to be to the left of the leftmost Republicans.

Multiple-Choice Questions

1. a
2. b
3. e
4. c
5. a

Critical-Thinking Question

(Answers to the first part of the question will differ.) Economics can add to our knowledge of the facts regarding trade-offs involved in implementing government programs to redistribute income. However, economics can't resolve differences in values and philosophies.

MODULE 40

Check Your Understanding

1. Many college professors will depart for other lines of work if the government imposes a wage that is lower than the market wage. Fewer professors will result in fewer courses taught and therefore fewer college degrees produced. It will adversely affect sectors of the economy that depend directly on colleges, such as the local shopkeepers who sell goods and services to students and faculty, college textbook publishers, and so on. It will also adversely affect firms that use the "output" produced by colleges: new college graduates. Firms that need to hire new employees with college degrees will be hurt as a smaller supply results in a higher market wage for college graduates. Ultimately, the reduced supply of college-educated workers will result in a lower level of human capital in the entire economy relative to what it would have been without the policy. And this will hurt all sectors of the economy that depend on human capital. The sectors of the economy that might benefit are firms that compete with colleges in the hiring of would-be college professors. For example, accounting firms will find it easier to hire people who would otherwise have been professors of accounting, and publishers will find it easier to hire people who would otherwise have been professors of English (easier in the sense that the firms can recruit would-be professors with a lower wage than before). In addition, workers who already have college degrees will benefit; they will command higher wages as the supply of college-educated workers falls.

2. a. The demand curve for labor shifts to the right.
   b. The demand curve for labor shifts to the left.

Multiple-Choice Questions

1. b
2. e
3. d
4. b
5. a

Critical-Thinking Question

The three graphs should appear as shown here.

1.

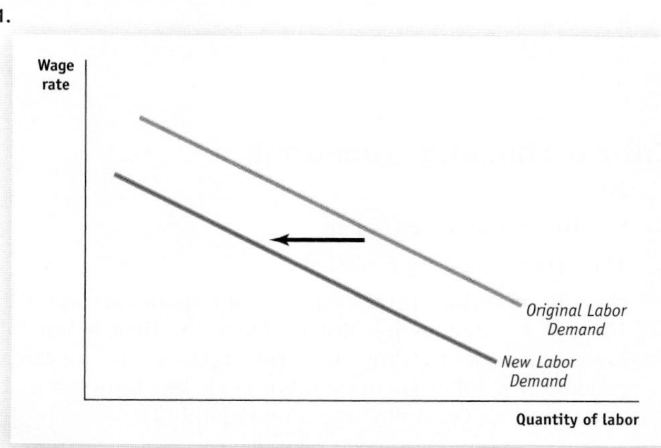

2.

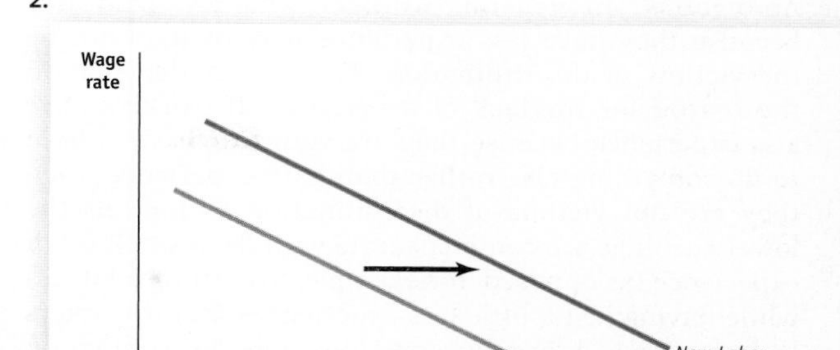

3.

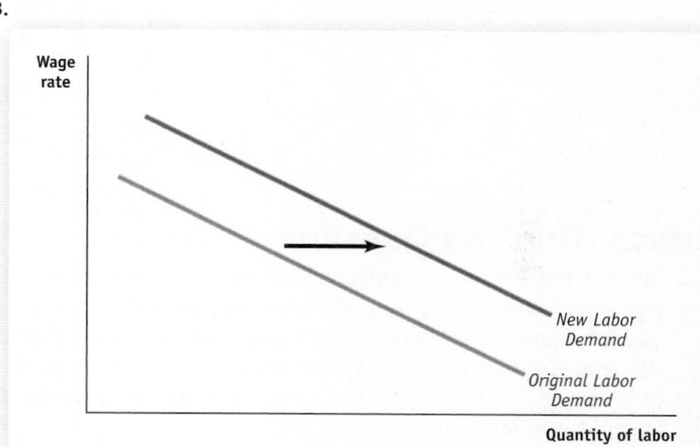

MODULE 41

Check Your Understanding

1. a. False. Income disparities associated with gender, race, and ethnicity can be explained by the marginal productivity theory of income distribution, provided that differences in marginal productivity across people are correlated with gender, race, or ethnicity. One possible source for such correlation is past discrimination. Such discrimination can lower individuals' marginal productivity by, for example, preventing them from acquiring the human capital that would raise their productivity. Another possible source of the correlation is differences in work experience that are associated with gender, race, or ethnicity. For example, in jobs for which work experience or length of tenure is important, women may earn lower wages because on average more women than men take child-care-related absences from work.

   b. True. Companies that discriminate when their competitors do not are likely to hire less able workers because they discriminate against more able workers who are considered to be of the wrong gender, race, ethnicity, or other characteristic. And with less able workers, such companies are likely to earn less profit than their competitors who don't discriminate.

c. Ambiguous. In general, workers who are paid less because they have less experience may or may not be the victims of discrimination. The answer depends on the reason for the lack of experience. If workers have less experience because they are young or have chosen to do something else rather than gain experience, then they are not victims of discrimination as long as the lower earnings are commensurate with the lower level of experience (as opposed, for example, to earning a lot less while having just a little less experience). But if workers lack experience because previous job discrimination prevented them from gaining experience, then they are indeed victims of discrimination when they are paid less.

Multiple-Choice Questions

1. a
2. a
3. a
4. b
5. e

Critical-Thinking Question

1. Market power—firms with market power can organize to pay lower wages than would result in a perfectly competitive labor market. Monopsonies pay less than the value of the marginal product of labor. And unions can organize to demand higher wages than would result in a perfectly competitive labor market.
2. Efficiency wages—some firms pay high wages to boost worker performance and encourage loyalty.
3. Discrimination—some firms pay workers differently solely on the basis of worker characteristics that do not affect marginal productivity.

MODULE 42

Check Your Understanding

1. **a.** Clive is made worse off if, before the new law, he had preferred to work more than 35 hours per week. As a result of the law, he can no longer choose his preferred time allocation; he now consumes fewer goods and more leisure than he would like.

   b. Clive's utility is unaffected by the law if, before the law, he had preferred to work 35 or fewer hours per week. The law has not changed his preferred time allocation.

   c. Clive can never be made better off by a law that restricts the number of hours he can work. He can only be made worse off (case a) or equally as well off (case b).
2. The substitution effect would induce Clive to work fewer hours and consume more leisure after his wage rate falls—the fall in the wage rate means the price of an hour of leisure falls, leading Clive to consume more leisure. But a fall in his wage rate also generates a fall in Clive's income. The income effect of this is to induce Clive to consume less leisure and therefore work more hours, since he is now poorer and leisure is a normal good. If the income effect dominates the substitution effect, Clive will in the end work more hours than before.

Multiple-Choice Questions

1. d
2. a
3. e
4. c
5. d

Critical-Thinking Questions

1 and 2. Your graph should look like this.

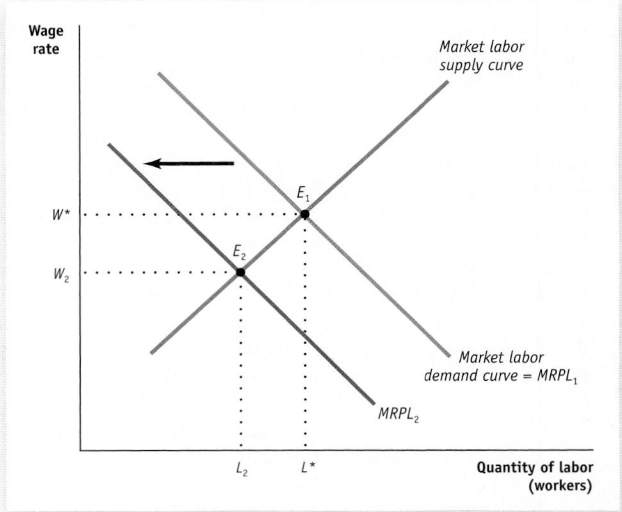

MODULE 43

Check Your Understanding

1. Yes, the firm is employing the cost-minimizing combination of inputs because the marginal product per dollar is equal for capital and labor: 500/$100 = 1,000/$200 = 5 units of output per dollar.

Multiple-Choice Questions

1. c
2. b
3. c
4. a
5. d

Critical-Thinking Questions

1. 20
2. 10/$10 = 1 pencil per dollar
3. The firm would hire 6 workers.
4. No. The marginal product per dollar spent on capital is 100/$50 = 2 pencils per dollar. Thus, the firm is not following the cost-minimization rule because the marginal product per dollar spent on labor (1) is less than the marginal product per dollar spent on capital (2).

MODULE 44

Check Your Understanding

1. The inefficiency caused by adverse selection is that an insurance policy with a premium based on the average risk of all drivers will attract only an adverse selection of bad drivers. Good (that is, safe) drivers will find this insurance premium too expensive and so will remain uninsured. This is inefficient. However, safe drivers are also those drivers who have had fewer moving violations for several years. Lowering premiums for only those drivers allows the insurance company to screen its customers and sell insurance to safe drivers, too. This means that at least some of the good drivers now are also insured, which decreases the inefficiency that arises from adverse selection. In a way, having no moving violations for several years is a way of building a reputation as a safe driver.
2. The moral hazard problem in home construction arises from private information about what the contractor does: whether she takes care to reduce the cost of construction or allows costs to increase. The homeowner cannot, or can only imperfectly, observe the cost-reduction efforts of the contractor. If the contractor were fully reimbursed for all costs incurred during construction, she would have no incentive to reduce costs. Making the contractor responsible for any additional costs above the original estimate means that she now has an incentive to keep costs low. However, this imposes risk on the contractor. For instance, if the weather is bad, home construction will take longer, and will be more costly, than if the weather had been good. Since the contractor pays for any additional costs (such as weather-induced delays) above the original estimate, she now faces risk that she cannot control.
3. **a.** True. Drivers with higher deductibles have more incentive to take care in their driving in order to avoid paying the deductible. This is a moral hazard phenomenon.

   b. True. Suppose you know that you are a safe driver. You have a choice of a policy with a high premium but a low deductible or one with a lower premium but a higher deductible. In this case, you would be more inclined to choose the cheap policy with the high deductible because you know that you will be unlikely to have to pay the deductible. When there is adverse selection, insurance companies use screening devices such as this to infer private information about how careful people are as drivers.

Multiple-Choice Questions

1. d
2. a
3. b
4. a
5. b

Critical-Thinking Questions

1. This is an example of moral hazard. The government bears the cost of any lack of care in the individual/corporate decisions.
2. Distorted incentives lead the individual/corporation to make riskier decisions because, if a decision is bad, the cost falls on others.
3. The individuals/corporations must be given a personal stake in the result of their decisions. This could be achieved by making the individuals/corporations repay at least some portion of the bailout cost.

MODULE 45

Check Your Understanding

1. We talk about business cycles for the economy as a whole because recessions and expansions are not confined to a few industries—they reflect downturns and upturns for the economy as a whole. In downturns, almost every sector of the economy reduces output and the number of people employed. Moreover, business cycles are an international phenomenon, sometimes moving in rough synchrony across countries.
2. Countries with high rates of population growth will have to maintain higher growth rates of overall output than countries with low rates of population growth in order to achieve an increased standard of living per person because aggregate output will have to be divided among a larger number of people.
3. **a.** As some prices have risen but other prices have fallen, there may be overall inflation or deflation. The answer is ambiguous.

   b. As all prices have risen significantly, this sounds like inflation.

   c. As most prices have fallen and others have not changed, this sounds like deflation.

Multiple-Choice Questions

1. a
2. c
3. e
4. c
5. a

Critical-Thinking Question

No, Argentina is not poorer than it was in the past. Both Argentina and Canada have experienced long-run growth. However, after World War II, Argentina did not make as much progress as Canada, perhaps because of political instability and bad macroeconomic policies. Canada's economy grew much faster than Argentina's. Although Canada is now about three times as rich as Argentina, Argentina still had long-run growth of its economy.

MODULE 46

Check Your Understanding

1. **a.** Households are linked to firms through the sale of factors of production to firms, through purchases from firms of final goods and services, and through lending funds to firms in the financial markets.

   b. Households are linked to the government through their payment of taxes, their receipt of transfers, and their lending of funds to the government to finance government borrowing via the financial markets.

c. Finally, households are linked to the rest of the world through their purchases of imports and transactions with foreigners in financial markets.

2. The four types of income received by households are wages, profit, interest, and rent. Wage income is received as payment for selling labor hours to firms. Some of the profit earned by firms is distributed to households who own stock in a company. Interest income is paid to households who hold bonds. In the case of bonds, some households have elected to lend money to firms in return for interest income. Finally, households receive rental income from firms when they rent land or physical structures they own to a firm. Households use their income to pay for consumption spending, taxes, and private savings.

Multiple-Choice Questions

1. a
2. b
3. e
4. c
5. d

Critical-Thinking Question

In the market for goods and services, firms sell the goods and services they produce to households. Firms buy the resources they need to produce the goods and services in factor markets. The banking, stock, and bond markets are collectively known as the financial market. The financial market links lenders (those with savings) and borrowers (such as firms that require funds to pay for investment spending).

MODULE 47

Check Your Understanding

1. Let's start by considering the relationship between the total value added of all domestically produced final goods and services, and aggregate spending on domestically produced final goods and services. These two quantities are equal because every final good and service produced in the economy is either purchased by someone or added to inventories, and additions to inventories are counted as spending by firms. Next, consider the relationship between aggregate spending on domestically produced final goods and services and total factor income. These two quantities are equal because all spending that is channeled to firms to pay for purchases of domestically produced final goods and services is revenue for firms. Those revenues must be paid out by firms to their factors of production in the form of wages, profit, interest, and rent. Taken together, this means that all three methods of calculating GDP are equivalent.

2. The investment spending category of GDP measures purchases of new capital by firms, changes to the stock of firm's inventories, and residential investment (the value of new houses constructed during the given time period).

3. You would be counting the value of the steel twice—once as it was sold by American Steel to American Motors and once as part of the car sold by American Motors.

Multiple-Choice Questions

1. e
2. a
3. c
4. b
5. a

Critical-Thinking Questions

1. Some of the new goods and services produced are intermediate goods. We do not want to count intermediate goods separately because they are part of the value of the final goods.

2. The concept of value added allows the government to measure GDP by counting only the value added by each firm as opposed to the total value of the firm's output. Value added by definition is the value of the firm's output minus the value of any purchased intermediate goods used in production.

MODULE 48

Check Your Understanding

1. a. In 2012 nominal GDP was (1,000,000 × \$0.40) + (800,000 × \$0.60) = \$400,000 + \$480,000 = \$880,000. The total value of sales of french fries in 2013 was 900,000 × \$0.50 = \$450,000. The total value of sales of onion rings in 2013 was 840,000 × \$0.51 = \$428,400. Nominal GDP in 2013 was \$450,000 + \$428,400 = \$878,400. To find real GDP in 2013, we must calculate the value of sales in 2013 using 2012 prices: (900,000 × \$0.40) + (840,000 × \$0.60) = \$360,000 + \$504,000 = \$864,000.

b. A comparison of nominal GDP in 2012 to nominal GDP in 2013 shows a decline of ((\$880,000 – \$878,400) / \$880,000) × 100 = 0.18%. But a comparison using real GDP shows a decline of ((\$880,000 – \$864,000) / \$880,000) × 100 = 1.8%. That is, a calculation based on real GDP shows a drop 10 times larger (1.8%) than a calculation based on nominal GDP (0.18%): in this case, the calculation based on nominal GDP underestimates the true magnitude of the change because it incorporates both quantity changes and price changes.

2. A price index based on 1990 prices will contain a relatively low price of housing compared to a price index based on 2000 prices. This means that a 2000 price index used to calculate real GDP in 2010 will magnify the value of housing production in the economy and increase the relative size of the housing sector as a component of real GDP.

Multiple-Choice Questions

1. d
2. b
3. c
4. c
5. c

Critical-Thinking Questions

1. Country A: (4,000–2,000/2,000) × 100 = 100%
Country B: (6,000–2,000/2,000) × 100 = 200%

2. Country A: It stayed the same.
Country B: It doubled.

3. Country A: $4,000 (There was no price increase so it is the same.)
Country B: $6,000/2 = $3,000 (Prices doubled.)

4. Country A: (4,000–2,000/2,000) × 100 = 100%
Country B: (3,000–2,000/2,000) × 100 = 50%

5. Country A: 4,000/20 = $200 versus
Country B: 3,000/15 = $200. It is the same.

MODULE 49

Check Your Understanding

1. The advent of websites that enable job-seekers to find jobs more quickly will reduce the unemployment rate over time. However, websites that induce discouraged workers to begin actively looking for work again will lead to an increase in the unemployment rate over time.

2. a. Not counted as unemployed because not actively looking for work, but counted in broader measures of labor underutilization as a discouraged worker.
   b. Not counted as unemployed—considered employed because the teacher has a job.
   c. Unemployed: not working, actively looking for work.
   d. Not unemployed, but underemployed: working part-time for economic reasons. Counted in broader measures of labor underutilization.
   e. Not unemployed, but considered "marginally attached." Counted in broader measures of labor underutilization.

3. Items (a) and (b) are consistent with the observed relationship between growth in GDP and changes in the unemployment rate. Item (c) is not.

Multiple-Choice Questions

1. e
2. b
3. a
4. d
5. b

Critical-Thinking Questions

1. Employed (underemployed); she is not working up to her full potential.
2. Not in the labor force (discouraged). Once a worker stops actively seeking work, he or she falls out of the labor force.
3. Employed (part-time); individuals are classified as employed if they work full or part time.
4. Not in the labor force; he is not actively seeking employment.

MODULE 50

Check Your Understanding

1. a. Frictional unemployment is unemployment due to the time workers spend searching for jobs. It is inevitable because workers may leave one job in search of another for a variety of reasons. Furthermore, there will always be new entrants into the labor force who are seeking a first job. During the search process, these individuals will be counted as part of the frictionally unemployed.
   b. When the unemployment rate is low, frictional unemployment will account for a larger share of total unemployment because other sources of unemployment will be diminished. So the share of total unemployment composed of the frictionally unemployed will rise.

2. A binding minimum wage represents a price floor below which wages cannot fall. As a result, actual wages cannot move toward equilibrium. So a minimum wage causes the quantity of labor supplied to exceed the quantity of labor demanded. Because this surplus of labor reflects unemployed workers, it affects the unemployment rate. Collective bargaining has a similar effect—unions are able to raise the wage above the equilibrium level. This will act like a minimum wage by causing the number of job seekers to be larger than the number of workers firms are willing to hire. Collective bargaining causes the unemployment rate to be higher than it otherwise would be, as shown in the accompanying figure.

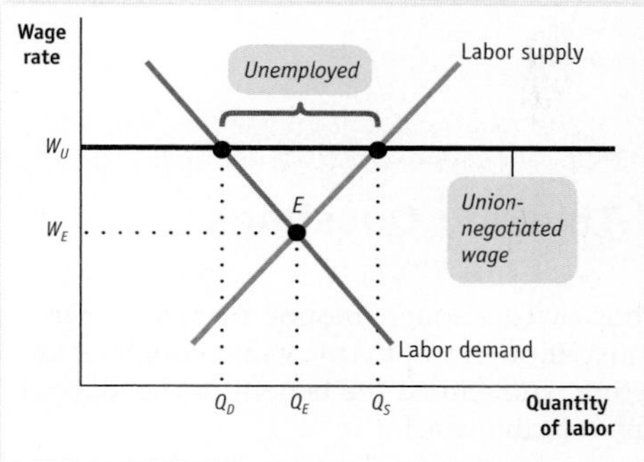

3. An increase in unemployment benefits reduces the cost to individuals of being unemployed, causing them to spend more time searching for a new job. So the natural rate of unemployment would increase.

Multiple-Choice Questions

1. a
2. c
3. b
4. d
5. e

Critical-Thinking Question

This statement is true only if there is no change in the size of the labor force. The size of the labor force will decrease if some employed people quit their jobs and leave the labor force. An example would be people who decide to retire. The size of the labor force will increase if some people who are currently not in the labor force decide to enter the labor force and either become employed or unemployed. An example would be full-time students who graduate and enter the labor force. The size of the labor force will decrease if some unemployed people give up looking for work and exit the labor force.

MODULE 51

Check Your Understanding

1. Shoe-leather costs as a result of inflation will be lower because it is now less costly for individuals to manage their assets in order to economize on their money holdings. ATM machines, for example, give customers 24-hour access to cash in thousands of locations. This reduction in the cost of obtaining money translates into lower shoe-leather costs.
2. If inflation came to a complete stop for several years, the inflation rate of zero would be less than the expected inflation rate of 2–3%. Because the real interest rate is the nominal interest rate minus the inflation rate, the real interest rates on loans would be higher than expected, and lenders would gain at the expense of borrowers. Borrowers would have to repay their loans with funds that had a higher real value than had been expected.

Multiple-Choice Questions

1. e
2. c
3. b
4. d
5. c

Critical-Thinking Questions

1. 0%
2. You borrowed enough money to buy a couch and paid back just enough to buy the same couch (after inflation). Therefore, you gained the benefit of the loan without paying any real interest for it.
3. Whoever gave you the loan lost. The loan was paid back after prices unexpectedly increased, so the lender received a real interest rate of 0% for letting you use the money for a year.

MODULE 52

Check Your Understanding

1. Pre–frost, this market basket costs (100 × $0.20) + (50 × $0.60) + (200 × $0.25) = $20 + $30 + $50 = $100. The same market basket, post-frost, costs (100 × $0.40) + (50 × $1.00) + (200 × $0.45) = $40 + $50 + $90 = $180. So the price index is ($100/$100) × 100 = 100 before the frost and ($180/$100) × 100 = 180 after the frost, implying a rise in the price index of 80%. This increase in the price index is less than the 84.2% increase calculated in the text. The reason for this difference is that the new market basket of 100 oranges, 50 grapefruit, and 200 lemons contains proportionately more of an item that has experienced a relatively small price increase (the lemons, the price of which has increased by 80%) and proportionately fewer of an item that has experienced a relatively large price increase (the oranges, the price of which has increased by 100%). This shows that the price index can be very sensitive to the composition of the market basket. If the market basket contains a large proportion of goods whose prices have risen faster than the prices of other goods, it will lead to a higher estimate of the increase in the price level. If it contains a large proportion of goods whose prices have risen more slowly than the prices of other goods, it will lead to a lower estimate of the increase in the price level.
2. a. A market basket determined 10 years ago will contain fewer cars than at present. Given that the average price of a car has grown faster than the average prices of other goods, this basket will underestimate the true increase in the price level because it contains relatively too few cars.
   b. A market basket determined 10 years ago will not contain Internet access, so it cannot track the fall in prices of Internet access over the past few years. As a result, it will overestimate the true increase in the price level.
3. Using Equation 52-2, the inflation rate from 2011 to 2012 is (229.6 – 224.9)/224.9 × 100 = 2.1%.

Multiple-Choice Questions

1. d
2. c
3. e
4. b
5. b

Critical-Thinking Question

To calculate the inflation rate from 2010 to 2011 using either the GDP deflator or the CPI, start with the 2011 price index value and subtract the 2010 price index value to find the change in the price index. Divide this change in the price index by the 2011 value and then multiply by 100. Do the same to calculate the inflation rate from 2011 to 2012. The results are shown in the following table.

Year	GDP Deflator	CPI
2010–2011	(2.4/111.0) × 100 = 2.2%	(6.8/218.1) × 100 = 3.1%
2011–2012	(2.0/113.4) × 100 = 1.8%	(4.7/224.9) × 100 = 2.1%

MODULE 53

Check Your Understanding

1. Economists want a measure of economic progress that rises with increases in the living standard of the average resident of a country. An increase in overall real GDP does not accurately reflect an increase in an average resident's living standard because it does not account for growth in the number of residents. If, for example, real GDP rises by 10% but population grows by 20%, the living standard of the average resident falls: after the change, the average resident has only (110/120) × 100 = 91.6% as much real income as before the change. Similarly, an increase in nominal GDP per capita does not accurately reflect an increase in living standards because it does not account for any change in prices. For example, a 5% increase in nominal GDP per capita generated by a 5% increase in prices results in no change in living standards. Real GDP per capita is the only measure that accounts for both changes in the population and changes in prices.
2. Using the Rule of 70, the amount of time it will take China to double its real GDP per capita is (70/8.9) = 7.9 years; India, (70/4.2) = 16.7 years; Ireland, (70/3.1) = 22.6 years; the United States, (70/1.7) = 41.2 years; France,

(70/1.3) = 53.8 years; and Argentina (70/1.2) = 58.3 years. Since the Rule of 70 can be applied to only a positive growth rate, we cannot apply it to the case of Zimbabwe, which experienced negative growth. If India continues to have a higher growth rate of real GDP per capita than the United States, then India's real GDP per capita will eventually surpass that of the United States.

3. The United States began growing rapidly over a century ago, but China and India have begun growing rapidly only recently. As a result, the living standard of the typical Chinese or Indian household has not yet caught up with that of the typical American household.

Multiple-Choice Questions

1. d
2. c
3. c
4. b
5. b

Critical-Thinking Question

Increases in real GDP per capita result mostly from changes in productivity (or labor productivity). Productivity is defined as output per worker or output per hour. Increased labor force participation could also lead to higher real GDP per capita, but the rate of employment growth is rarely very different from the rate of population growth, meaning that the corresponding increase in output does not lead to an increase in output per capita.

MODULE 54

Check Your Understanding

1. a. Significant technological progress will result in a positive growth rate of productivity even though physical capital per worker and human capital per worker are unchanged.
   b. Productivity will grow, but due to diminishing marginal returns, each successive increase in physical capital per worker results in a smaller increase in productivity than the one before it.
2. a. If the economy has grown 3% per year and the labor force has grown 1% per year, then productivity—output per worker—has grown at approximately 3% − 1% = 2% per year.
   b. If physical capital has grown 4% per year and the labor force has grown 1% per year, then physical capital per worker has grown at approximately 4% − 1% = 3% per year.
   c. According to estimates, each 1% rise in physical capital, other things equal, increases productivity by 0.3%. So, as physical capital per worker has increased by 3%, productivity growth that can be attributed to an increase in physical capital per worker is 0.3 × 3% = 0.9%. As a percentage of total productivity growth, this is 0.9%/2% × 100% = 45%.
   d. If the rest of productivity growth is due to technological progress, then technological progress has contributed 2% − 0.9% = 1.1% to productivity growth. As a percentage of total productivity growth, this is 1.1%/2% × 100% = 55%.
3. It will take time for workers to learn how to use the new computer system and to adjust their routines. And because there are often setbacks in learning a new system, such as accidentally erasing your computer files, productivity at Multinomics may decrease for a period of time.
4. Growth increases a country's greenhouse gas emissions. The current best estimates are that a large reduction in emissions will result in only a modest reduction in growth. The international burden sharing of greenhouse gas emissions reduction is contentious because rich countries are reluctant to pay the costs of reducing their emissions only to see newly emerging countries like China rapidly increase their emissions. Yet most of the current accumulation of gases is due to the past actions of rich countries. Poorer countries like China are equally reluctant to sacrifice their growth to pay for the past actions of rich countries.

Multiple-Choice Questions

1. e
2. a
3. a
4. c
5. b

Critical-Thinking Questions

1. Growing physical capital per worker is responsible for 1% productivity growth per year. 2% × 0.5 = 1%
2. There was no growth in total factor productivity because there was no technological progress. According to the Rule of 70, over 70 years (from 1942 to 2012), a 1% growth rate would cause output to double. Real GDP per capita in this case doubled, as would be expected from a 1% productivity growth rate alone; therefore, there was no change in technological progress.

MODULE 55

Check Your Understanding

1. A country that has high domestic savings is able to achieve a high rate of investment spending as a percentage of GDP. This, in turn, allows the country to achieve a high growth rate.
2. Although it is important in determining the growth rate for some countries (such as those of Western Europe), the initial level of GDP per capita isn't the only factor. High rates of saving and investment appear to be better predictors of future growth than today's standard of living.
3. The evidence suggests that both sets of factors matter: better infrastructure is important for growth, but so is political and financial stability. Policies should try to address both areas.

Multiple-Choice Questions

1. e
2. e
3. d
4. e
5. b

Critical-Thinking Question

The convergence hypothesis says a country grows more slowly, other things equal, when its real GDP per capita is relatively higher. This points to lower future growth for East Asian countries. However, other things might not be equal: if Asian economies continue investing in human capital, if savings rates continue to be high, if governments invest in infrastructure, and so on, growth might continue to accelerate.

MODULE 56

Check Your Understanding

1. **a.** False. In an open economy, investment spending is equal to national savings plus net capital inflow. If the budget balance is zero, then government savings is zero and national savings is equal to private savings. In this case, investment is equal to private savings plus net capital inflow. Investment spending is being financed by private savings and from funds flowing into the country from abroad.

   b. True. In an open economy, investment spending is equal to national savings plus net capital inflow, so investment spending minus national savings equals net capital inflow. If national savings is less than investment spending then investment spending minus national savings is positive, and therefore so is net capital inflow. Investment spending is being financed by national savings and from funds flowing into the country from abroad.

2. $I = GDP - C - G - X + M = \$2{,}081$

   $S_{National} = GDP - C - G = \$1{,}548$

   $T = S_{Government} + G = \$1{,}822$

   $NCI = IM - X = \$533$

   $S_{Private} = I - S_{Government} - NCI = \$2{,}775$

   Note that the budget balance is the same as government saving.

Multiple-Choice Questions

1. a
2. a
3. e
4. a
5. a

Critical-Thinking Question

Investment spending is equal to national savings plus net capital inflow. This means investment spending can be financed with funds saved by national residents of the country, or by funds that flow into the country from abroad.

MODULE 57

Check Your Understanding

1. **a.** As capital flows into the economy, the supply of loanable funds increases. This is illustrated by the shift of the supply curve from S_1 to S_2 in the accompanying diagram. As the equilibrium moves from E_1 to E_2, the equilibrium interest rate falls from r_1 to r_2, and the equilibrium quantity of loanable funds increases from Q_1 to Q_2.

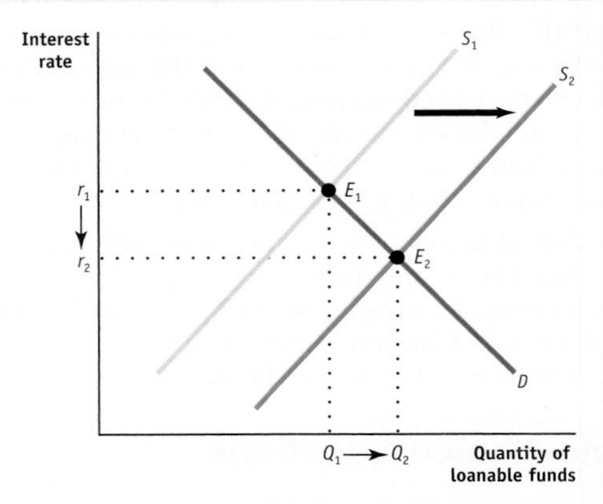

   b. Savings fall due to the higher proportion of retired people, and the supply of loanable funds decreases. This is illustrated by the leftward shift of the supply curve from S_1 to S_2 in the accompanying diagram. The equilibrium moves from E_1 to E_2, the equilibrium interest rate rises from r_1 to r_2, and the equilibrium quantity of loanable funds falls from Q_1 to Q_2.

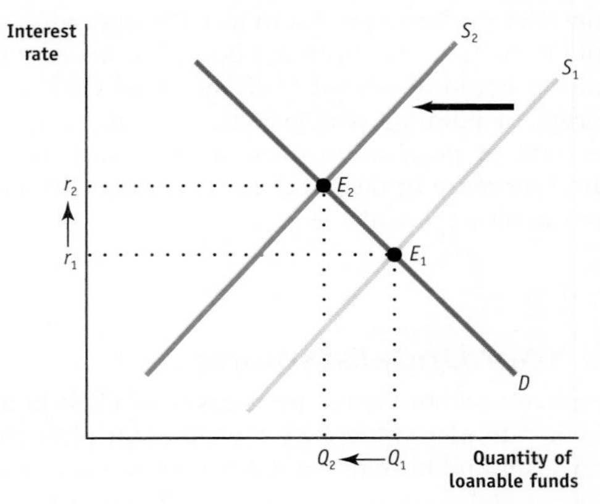

2. We know from the loanable funds market that as the interest rate rises, households want to save more and consume less. But at the same time, an increase in the interest rate lowers the number of investment spending projects with returns at least as high as the interest rate. The statement "households will want to save more money than businesses will want to invest" cannot represent an equilibrium in the loanable funds market because it says that the quantity of loanable funds offered exceeds the quantity of loanable funds demanded. If that were to occur, the interest rate would fall to make the quantity of loanable funds offered equal to the quantity of loanable funds demanded.

3. **a.** The real interest rate will not change. According to the Fisher effect, an increase in expected inflation drives up the nominal interest rate, leaving the real interest rate unchanged.

   b. The nominal interest rate will rise by 3%. Each additional percentage point of expected inflation drives up the nominal interest rate by 1 percentage point.

   c. As long as inflation is expected, it does not affect the equilibrium quantity of loanable funds. Both the supply and demand curves for loanable funds are pushed upward, leaving the equilibrium quantity of loanable funds unchanged.

Multiple-Choice Questions

1. e
2. b
3. b
4. c
5. a

Critical-Thinking Questions

1. This causes an increase (rightward shift) in the supply of loanable funds.
2. This causes a decrease (leftward shift) in the demand for loanable funds.
3. This causes an increase (rightward shift) in the demand for loanable funds.
4. This causes a decrease (leftward shift) in the supply of loanable funds.

MODULE 58

Check Your Understanding

1. a. The net present value of project A is unaffected by the interest rate since it is money received today; its present value is still \$100. The net present value of project B is now −\$10 + \$115/1.02 = \$102.75. The net present value of project C is now \$119 – \$20/1.02 = \$99.39. Project B is now preferred.

   b. When the interest rate is lower, the cost of waiting for money that arrives in the future is lower. For example, at a 10% interest rate, \$1 arriving one year from today is worth only \$1/1.10 = \$0.91. But when the interest rate is 2%, \$1 arriving one year from today is worth \$1/1.02 = \$0.98, a sizable increase. As a result, project B, which has a benefit one year from today, becomes more attractive. And project C, which has a cost one year from today, becomes less attractive.

Multiple-Choice Questions

1. e
2. b
3. c
4. d
5. b

Critical-Thinking Questions

1. $\$1{,}000 \times (1.05)^3 = \$1{,}000 \times 1.16 = \$1{,}157.63$
2. $\$1{,}000/(1.05)^3 = \$863.84$

MODULE 59

Check Your Understanding

1. The transaction costs for (a) a bank deposit and (b) a share of a mutual fund are approximately equivalent because each can typically be accomplished by making a phone call, going online, or visiting a branch office. Transaction costs are highest for (c) a share of a family business since finding a buyer for the share consumes time and resources. The level of risk is lowest for (a) a bank deposit, since these deposits are insured by the Federal Deposit Insurance Corporation (FDIC) up to \$250,000; somewhat higher for (b) a share of a mutual fund since despite diversification, there is still risk associated with holding stocks; and highest for (c) a share of a family business since this investment is not diversified. The level of liquidity is the lowest for (c) a share of a family business, since it can be sold only with the unanimous agreement of other members and it will take some time to find a buyer; higher for (b) a share of a mutual fund, since it will take only a few days between selling your shares and the payment being processed; and highest for (a) a bank deposit, since withdrawals can usually be made immediately.
2. Economic development and growth are the result of, among other factors, investment spending on physical capital. Since investment spending is equal to savings, the greater the amount saved, the higher investment spending will be, and so the higher growth and economic development will be. So the existence of institutions that facilitate savings will help a country's growth and economic development. As a result, a country with a financial system that provides low transaction costs, opportunities for diversification of risk, and high liquidity to its savers will experience faster growth and economic development than a country that doesn't.

Multiple-Choice Questions

1. d
2. a
3. c
4. d
5. b

Critical-Thinking Question

1) **Mutual fund**—a financial intermediary that creates a stock portfolio by buying and holding shares in companies and then selling shares of the stock portfolio to individual investors.
2) **Life insurance company**—a firm that guarantees a payment to the policyholder's beneficiaries (typically, the family) when the policyholder dies.
3) **Bank**—an institution that helps resolve the conflict between lenders' needs for liquidity and the illiquid financing needs of borrowers who don't want to use the stock or bond markets.
4) **Pension fund**—a nonprofit institution that collects the savings of its members and invests those funds in a variety of assets, providing its members with income when they retire.

MODULE 60

Check Your Understanding

1. A decline in investment spending, like a rise in investment spending, has a multiplier effect on real GDP—the only difference in this case is that real GDP falls instead of

rises. The fall in I leads to an initial fall in real GDP, which leads to a fall in disposable income, which leads to lower consumer spending, which leads to another fall in real GDP, and so on. So consumer spending falls as an indirect result of the fall in investment spending.

2. When the *MPC* is 0.5, the multiplier is equal to 1/(1 – 0.5) = 1/0.5 = 2. When the *MPC* is 0.8, the multiplier is equal to 1/(1 – 0.8) = 1/0.2 = 5.

3. The greater the share of GDP that is saved rather than spent, the lower the *MPC*. Disposable income that goes to savings is like a "leak" in the system, reducing the amount of spending that fuels a further expansion. So it is likely that Amerigo will have the larger multiplier.

Multiple-Choice Questions

1. e
2. a
3. b
4. b
5. c

Critical-Thinking Question

An autonomous change in aggregate spending, such as a $100 million increase in investment spending, has a multiple effect on real GDP. In other words, real GDP will in this example increase by more than $100 million. The initial $100 million increase in investment spending leads to an increase in real GDP, which leads to an increase in disposable income and more consumption spending. This increase in consumption spending is what causes real GDP to increase by an amount larger than the initial increase in autonomous aggregate spending.

MODULE 61

Check Your Understanding

1. a. Angelina's autonomous consumer spending is $8,000. When her current disposable income rises by $10,000, her consumer spending rises by $12,000 – $8,000 = $4,000. So her *MPC* is $4,000/$10,000 = 0.4 and her consumption function is c = $8,000 + 0.4 × yd. Felicia's autonomous consumer spending is $6,500. When her current disposable income rises by $10,000, her consumer spending rises by $14,500 – $6,500 = $8,000. So her *MPC* is $8,000/$10,000 = 0.8 and her consumption function is c = $6,500 + 0.8 × yd. Marina's autonomous consumer spending is $7,250. When her current disposable income rises by $10,000, her consumer spending rises by $14,250 – $7,250 = $7,000. So her *MPC* is $7,000/$10,000 = 0.7 and her consumption function is c = $7,250 + 0.7 × yd.

   b. The aggregate autonomous consumer spending in this economy is $8,000 + $6,500 + $7,250 = $21,750. A $30,000 increase in disposable income (3 × $10,000) leads to a $4,000 + $8,000 + $7,000 = $19,000 increase in consumer spending. So the economy-wide *MPC* is $19,000/$30,000 = 0.63 and the aggregate consumption function is C = $21,750 + 0.63 × YD.

2. If you expect your future disposable income to fall, you would like to save some of today's disposable income to tide you over in the future. But you cannot do this if you cannot save. If you expect your future disposable income to rise, you would like to spend some of tomorrow's higher income today. But you cannot do this if you cannot borrow. If you cannot save or borrow, your expected future disposable income will have no effect on your consumer spending today. In fact, your *MPC* must always equal 1: you must consume all your current disposable income today, and you will be unable to smooth your consumption over time.

3. a. An unexpected increase in consumer spending will result in a reduction in inventories as producers sell items from their inventories to satisfy this short-term increase in demand. This is negative unplanned inventory investment: it reduces the value of producers' inventories.

   b. A rise in the cost of borrowing is equivalent to a rise in the interest rate: fewer investment spending projects are now profitable to producers, whether they are financed through borrowing or retained earnings. As a result, producers will reduce the amount of planned investment spending.

   c. A sharp increase in the rate of real GDP growth leads to a higher level of planned investment spending by producers, according to the accelerator principle, as they increase production capacity to meet higher demand.

   d. As sales fall, producers sell less, and their inventories grow. This leads to positive unplanned inventory investment.

4. When consumer spending is sluggish, firms with excess production capacity will cut back on planned investment spending because they think their existing capacities are sufficient for expected future sales. Similarly, when consumer spending is sluggish and firms have a large amount of unplanned inventory investment, they are likely to cut back their production of output because they think their existing inventories are sufficient for expected future sales. So an inventory overhang is likely to depress current economic activity as firms cut back on their planned investment spending and on their output.

Multiple-Choice Questions

1. d
2. c
3. b
4. d
5. a

Critical-Thinking Question

The three most important factors are these:

1. The interest rate is the price (or opportunity cost) of investing, thus they are negatively related.
2. Expected future real GDP—if a firm expects its sales to grow rapidly in the future, it will invest in expanded production capacity.
3. Production capacity—if a firm finds its existing production capacity insufficient for its future production needs, it will undertake investment spending to meet those needs.

MODULE 62

Check Your Understanding

1. A slump in planned investment spending will lead to a fall in real GDP in response to an unanticipated increase in inventories. The fall in real GDP will translate into a fall in households' disposable income, and households will respond by reducing consumer spending. The decrease in consumer spending leads producers to further decrease output, further lowering disposable income and leading to further reductions in consumer spending. So although the slump originated in investment spending, it will cause a reduction in consumer spending.

2. a. After an autonomous fall in planned aggregate spending, the economy is no longer in equilibrium: real GDP is greater than planned aggregate spending. The accompanying figure shows this autonomous fall in planned aggregate spending by the shift of the aggregate spending curve from AE_1 to AE_2. The difference between the two results in positive unplanned inventory investment: there is an unanticipated increase in inventories. Firms will respond by reducing production. This will eventually move the economy to a new equilibrium. In the accompanying figure, this is illustrated by the movement from the initial income–expenditure equilibrium at E_1 to the new income–expenditure equilibrium at E_2. As the economy moves to its new equilibrium, real GDP falls from its initial income–expenditure equilibrium level at Y_1^* to its new lower level, Y_2^*.

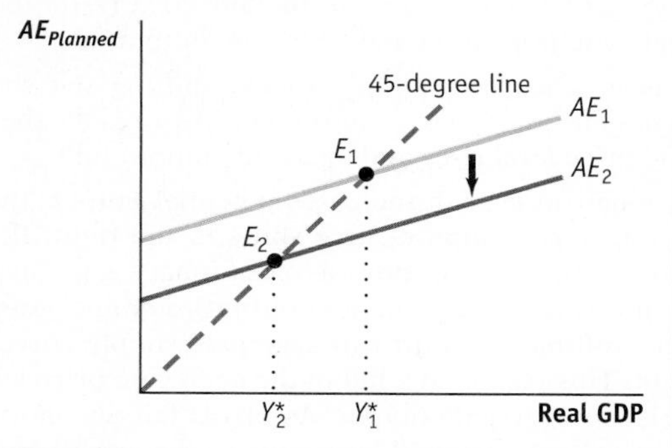

b. We know that the change in income–expenditure equilibrium GDP is given by Equation 62-7: $\Delta Y^* =$ Multiplier $\times$ $\Delta AAE_{Planned}$. Here, the multiplier $= 1/(1 - 0.5) = 1/0.5 = 2$. So a \$300 million autonomous reduction in planned aggregate spending will lead to a $2 \times$ \$300 million = \$600 million (\$0.6 billion) fall in income–expenditure equilibrium GDP. The new Y^* will be \$500 billion – \$0.6 billion = \$499.4 billion.

Multiple-Choice Questions

1. c
2. b
3. c
4. b
5. c

Critical-Thinking Question

In income–expenditure equilibrium, unplanned inventory investment is equal to zero. Firms have produced enough output to match expected sales, and to adjust inventories to their desired level. When sales are above or below expected levels, then there will be unplanned inventory changes and the economy will not be in income–expenditure equilibrium.

MODULE 63

Check Your Understanding

1. a This is a shift of the aggregate demand curve. A decrease in the quantity of money raises the interest rate, since people now want to borrow more and lend less. A higher interest rate reduces investment and consumer spending at any given aggregate price level, so the aggregate demand curve shifts to the left.

b. This is a movement up along the aggregate demand curve. As the aggregate price level rises, the real value of money holdings falls. This is the interest rate effect of a change in the aggregate price level: as the value of money falls, people want to hold more money. They do so by borrowing more and lending less. This leads to a rise in the interest rate and a reduction in consumer and investment spending. So it is a movement along the aggregate demand curve.

c. This is a shift of the aggregate demand curve. Expectations of a poor job market, and so lower average disposable incomes, will reduce people's consumer spending today at any given aggregate price level. So the aggregate demand curve shifts to the left.

d. This is a shift of the aggregate demand curve. A fall in tax rates raises people's disposable income. At any given aggregate price level, consumer spending is now higher. So the aggregate demand curve shifts to the right.

e. This is a movement down along the aggregate demand curve. As the aggregate price level falls, the real value of assets rises. This is the wealth effect of a change in the aggregate price level: as the value of assets rises, people will increase their consumption plans. This leads to higher consumer spending. So it is a movement along the aggregate demand curve.

f. This is a shift of the aggregate demand curve. A rise in the real value of assets in the economy due to a surge in real estate values raises consumer spending at any given aggregate price level. So the aggregate demand curve shifts to the right.

Multiple-Choice Questions

1. d
2. c
3. c
4. a
5. a

Critical-Thinking Question

The two effects that cause the aggregate demand curve to have a downward slope are the wealth effect and the interest rate effect of a change in the aggregate price level.

The wealth effect: When the price level increases, the purchasing power of money decreases, causing consumers to scale back on spending. Because consumer spending is a component of aggregate demand, increases in the aggregate price level lead to decreases in the quantity of aggregate output demanded. The opposite is true for decreases in the price level. This negative relationship between the price level and the quantity of aggregate output demanded results in a downward-sloping aggregate demand curve.

The interest rate effect: Increases in the aggregate price level cause people to want to hold more money, which increases the demand for money and drives interest rates up. Higher interest rates reduce investment spending because it costs more to borrow money. Thus, a rise in the price level leads to less investment spending, which is a component of aggregate demand, and causes the quantity of aggregate output demanded to decrease (and vice versa). The result is a downward-sloping aggregate demand curve.

MODULE 64

Check Your Understanding

1. a. This represents a movement along the *SRAS* curve because the CPI—like the GDP deflator—is a measure of the aggregate price level, the overall price level of final goods and services in the economy.

   b. This represents a shift of the *SRAS* curve because oil is a commodity. The *SRAS* curve will shift to the right because production costs are now lower, leading to a higher quantity of aggregate output supplied at any given aggregate price level.

   c. This represents a shift of the *SRAS* curve because it involves a change in nominal wages. An increase in legally mandated benefits to workers is equivalent to an increase in nominal wages. As a result, the *SRAS* curve will shift leftward because production costs are now higher, leading to a lower quantity of aggregate output supplied at any given aggregate price level.

2. You would need to know what happened to the aggregate price level. If the increase in the quantity of aggregate output supplied was due to a movement along the *SRAS* curve, the aggregate price level would have increased at the same time as the quantity of aggregate output supplied increased. If the increase in the quantity of aggregate output supplied was due to a rightward shift of the *LRAS* curve, the aggregate price level might not rise. Alternatively, you could make the determination by observing what happened to aggregate output in the long run. If it fell back to its initial level in the long run, then the temporary increase in aggregate output was due to a movement along the *SRAS* curve. If it stayed at the higher level in the long run, the increase in aggregate output was due to a rightward shift of the *LRAS* curve.

Multiple-Choice Questions

1. e
2. a
3. c
4. d
5. e

Critical-Thinking Questions

1. If there is a fall in the aggregate price level, then the price received by the perfectly competitive firm for its output will also fall. Since many production costs are fixed in the short run, the price will fall by more than production costs will fall. This will reduce profit per unit and, therefore, the perfectly competitive firm will reduce output.

2. An imperfectly competitive firm is not a price taker and can change price in response to changes in demand. If there is an increase in demand, then the firm can sell more output. The imperfectly competitive firm is likely to increase the price it charges in order to increase profit per unit.

MODULE 65

Check Your Understanding

1. a. An increase in the minimum wage raises the nominal wage and, as a result, shifts the short-run aggregate supply curve to the left. As a result of this negative supply shock, the aggregate price level rises and aggregate output falls.

   b. Increased investment spending shifts the aggregate demand curve to the right. As a result of this positive demand shock, both the aggregate price level and aggregate output rise.

   c. An increase in taxes and a reduction in government spending both result in negative demand shocks, shifting the aggregate demand curve to the left. As a result, both the aggregate price level and aggregate output fall.

   d. This is a negative supply shock, shifting the short-run aggregate supply curve to the left. As a result, the aggregate price level rises and aggregate output falls.

2. As long-run growth increases potential output, the long-run aggregate supply curve shifts to the right. If, in the short run, there is now a recessionary gap (aggregate output is less than potential output), nominal wages will fall, shifting the short-run aggregate supply curve to the right. This results in a fall in the aggregate price level and a rise in aggregate output. As prices fall, we move along the aggregate demand curve due to the wealth and interest rate effects of a change in the aggregate price level. Eventually, as long-run macroeconomic equilibrium is reestablished, aggregate output will rise to be equal to potential output, and the aggregate price level will fall to the level that equates the quantity of aggregate output demanded with potential output.

3. a. An economy is overstimulated when an inflationary gap is present. This will arise if an expansionary monetary or fiscal policy is implemented when the economy is currently in long-run macroeconomic equilibrium. This shifts the aggregate demand curve to the right, in the short run raising the aggregate price level and aggregate output and creating an inflationary gap. Eventually nominal wages will rise and shift the short-run aggregate supply curve to the left, and aggregate output will fall back to potential output. This is the scenario envisaged by the speaker.

   b. No, this is not a valid argument. When the economy is not currently in long-run macroeconomic equilibrium, an expansionary monetary or fiscal policy does not lead to the outcome described. Suppose a negative demand shock has shifted the aggregate demand curve to the left, resulting in a recessionary gap. An expansionary monetary or fiscal policy can shift the aggregate demand curve back to its original position in long-run macroeconomic equilibrium. In this way, the short-run fall in aggregate output and deflation caused by the original negative demand shock can be avoided. So, if used in response to demand shocks, fiscal or monetary policy is an effective policy tool.

4. Those within the Fed who advocated lowering interest rates were focused on boosting aggregate demand in order to counteract the negative demand shock caused by the collapse of the housing bubble. Lowering interest rates will result in a rightward shift of the aggregate demand curve, increasing aggregate output but raising the aggregate price level. Those within the Fed who advocated holding interest rates steady were focused on the fact that fighting the slump in aggregate demand in the face of a negative supply shock could result in a rise in inflation. Holding interest rates steady relies on the ability of the economy to self-correct in the long run, with the aggregate price level and aggregate output only gradually returning to their levels before the negative supply shock.

Multiple-Choice Questions

1. c
2. a
3. d
4. b
5. b

Critical-Thinking Question

Since output Y_1 is above potential output, there is an inflationary gap. The low level of unemployment will cause nominal wages to rise, causing production cost to rise. This will shift the *SRAS* curve up and to the left. As the price level rises, there is a movement along the *AD* curve and output returns to its potential level.

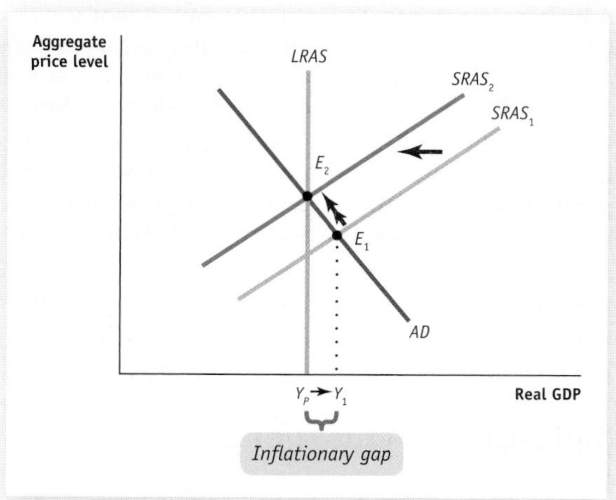

MODULE 66

Check Your Understanding

1. a. This is a contractionary fiscal policy because it is a reduction in government purchases of goods and services.

   b. This is an expansionary fiscal policy because it is an increase in government transfers that will increase disposable income.

   c. This is a contractionary fiscal policy because it is an increase in taxes, which will reduce disposable income.

2. Federal disaster relief that is quickly disbursed is more effective at stabilizing the economy than legislated aid because there is very little time lag between the time of the disaster and the time when relief is received by victims. In contrast, the process of creating new legislation is relatively slow, so legislated aid is likely to entail a time lag in its disbursement, potentially destabilizing the economy.

3. a. An economy is overstimulated when an inflationary gap is present. This will arise if expansionary fiscal policy is implemented when the economy is currently in long-run macroeconomic equilibrium. This shifts the aggregate demand curve to the right, in the short run raising the aggregate price level and aggregate output and creating an inflationary gap. Eventually, nominal wages will rise and shift the short-run aggregate supply curve to the left, and aggregate output will fall back to potential output. This is the scenario envisaged by the speaker.

   b. No, this is not a valid argument. When the economy is not currently in long-run macroeconomic equilibrium, expansionary fiscal policy does not lead to the outcome just described. Suppose a negative demand shock has shifted the aggregate demand curve to the left, resulting in a recessionary gap. Expansionary fiscal policy can shift the aggregate demand curve back to its original position in long-run macroeconomic equilibrium. In this way, the short-run fall in aggregate output and deflation caused by the original negative demand shock can be avoided. So, if used in response to demand shocks, fiscal policy is an effective policy tool.

Multiple-Choice Questions

1. e
2. e
3. b
4. b
5. a

Critical-Thinking Questions

Your graph should look like this.

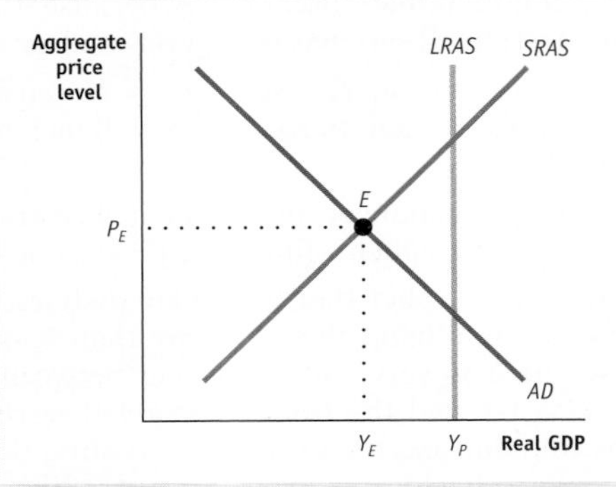

1. Expansionary
2. Decrease taxes, increase government purchases of goods and services, or increase government transfers

MODULE 67

Check Your Understanding

1. A \$500 million increase in government purchases of goods and services directly increases aggregate spending by \$500 million, which then starts the multiplier in motion. It will increase real GDP by \$500 million × $1/(1 - MPC)$. A \$500 million increase in government transfers increases aggregate spending only to the extent that it leads to an increase in consumer spending. Consumer spending rises by MPC × \$1 for every \$1 increase in disposable income, where MPC is less than 1. So a \$500 million increase in government transfers will cause a rise in real GDP only MPC times as much as a \$500 million increase in government purchases of goods and services. It will increase real GDP by \$500 million × $MPC/(1 - MPC)$.
2. If government purchases of goods and services fall by \$500 million, the initial fall in aggregate spending is \$500 million. If there is a \$500 million tax increase, the initial fall in aggregate spending is MPC × \$500 million, which is less than \$500 million because some of the tax payments are made with money that would otherwise have been saved rather than spent.
3. Boldovia will experience greater variation in its real GDP than Moldovia because Moldovia has automatic stabilizers while Boldovia does not. In Moldovia the effects of slumps will be lessened by unemployment insurance benefits, which will support residents' incomes, while the effects of booms will be diminished because tax revenues will go up. In contrast, incomes will not be supported in Boldovia during slumps because there is no unemployment insurance. In addition, because Boldovia has lump-sum taxes, its booms will not be diminished by increases in tax revenue.

Multiple-Choice Questions

1. c
2. b
3. b
4. c
5. e

Critical-Thinking Questions

1. \$50 million
   multiplier = $1/(1 - MPC) = 1/(1 - 0.75) = 1/0.25 = 4$
   change in $G \times 4$ = \$200 million
   change in G = \$50 million
2. 10
   \$20 million × multiplier = \$200 million
   multiplier = 200/20 = 10
3. 0.1
   $1/(1 - \text{MPC}) = 1/\text{MPS} = 10$
   MPS = 0.1

MODULE 68

1. The actual budget balance takes into account the effects of the business cycle on the budget deficit. During recessionary gaps, it incorporates the effect of lower tax revenues and higher transfers on the budget balance; during inflationary gaps, it incorporates the effect of higher tax revenues and reduced transfers. In contrast, the cyclically adjusted budget balance factors out the effects of the business cycle and assumes that real GDP is at potential output. Since, in the long run, real GDP tends to potential output, the cyclically adjusted budget balance is a better measure of the long-run sustainability of government policies.
2. In recessions, real GDP falls. This implies that consumers' incomes, consumer spending, and producers' profits also fall. So in recessions, states' tax revenue (which depends in large part on consumers' incomes, consumer spending, and producers' profits) falls. In order to balance the state budget, states have to cut spending or raise taxes. But that deepens the recession. Without a balanced-budget requirement, states could use expansionary fiscal policy during a recession to lessen the fall in real GDP.
3. a. A higher growth rate of real GDP implies that tax revenue will increase. If government spending remains constant and the government runs a budget surplus, the size of the public debt will be less than it would otherwise have been.
   b. If retirees live longer, the average age of the population increases. As a result, the implicit liabilities of the government increase because spending on programs for older Americans, such as Social Security and Medicare, will rise.
   c. A decrease in tax revenue without offsetting reductions in government spending will cause the public debt to increase.
   d. Public debt will increase as a result of government borrowing to pay interest on its current public debt.

Multiple-Choice Questions

1. b
2. c
3. a
4. c
5. d

Critical-Thinking Question

To stimulate the economy in the short run, the government can use fiscal policy to increase real GDP. This entails borrowing, which runs the risk of increasing the debt even more and, in extreme cases, of forcing the government to default on its debts. Even in less extreme cases, a large public debt is undesirable because government borrowing crowds out borrowing for private investment spending. The result is a decrease in investment spending and reduced long-run growth of the economy.

MODULE 69

Check Your Understanding

1. The defining characteristic of money is its liquidity: how easily it can be used to purchase goods and services. Although a gift certificate can easily be used to purchase a very defined set of goods or services (the goods or services available at the store issuing the gift certificate), it cannot be used to purchase any other goods or services. A gift certificate is therefore not money since it cannot easily be used to purchase all goods or services.
2. Again, the important characteristic of money is its liquidity: how easily it can be used to purchase goods and services. M1, the narrowest definition of the money supply, consists only of currency in circulation, traveler's checks, and checkable bank deposits. CDs aren't checkable—and they can't be made checkable without incurring a cost because there's a penalty for early withdrawal. This makes them less liquid than the assets counted in M1.
3. Commodity-backed money uses resources more efficiently than simple commodity money, like gold and silver coins, because commodity-backed money ties up fewer valuable resources. Although a bank must keep some of the commodity—generally gold and silver—on hand, it has to keep only enough to satisfy demand for redemptions. It can then lend out the remaining gold and silver, which allows society to use these resources for other purposes, with no loss in the ability to achieve gains from trade.

Multiple-Choice Questions

1. d
2. c
3. e
4. a
5. b

Critical-Thinking Questions

1. its official status given by the U.S. government
2. fiat money
3. **i.** commodity money—money that has intrinsic value in other uses

   ii. commodity-backed money—money that has no intrinsic value but can be converted into valuable goods on demand

MODULE 70

Check Your Understanding

1. Even though you know that the rumor about the bank is not true, you are concerned about other depositors pulling their money out of the bank. And you know that if enough other depositors pull their money out, the bank will fail. In that case, it is rational for you to pull your money out before the bank fails. All depositors will think like this, so even if they all know that the rumor is false, they may still rationally pull their money out, leading to a bank run. Deposit insurance leads depositors to worry less about the possibility of a bank run. Even if a bank fails, the FDIC will currently pay each depositor up to $250,000 per account. This will make you much less likely to pull your money out in response to a rumor. Since other depositors will think the same, there will be no bank run.
2. The aspects of modern bank regulation that would frustrate this scheme are *capital requirements* and *reserve requirements*. Capital requirements mean that a bank has to have a certain amount of capital—the difference between its assets (loans plus reserves) and its liabilities (deposits). So the con artist could not open a bank without putting any of his own wealth in because his bank would need the required amount of capital—that is, it needs to hold more assets (loans plus reserves) than deposits. So the con artist would be at risk of losing his own wealth if his loans turn out badly.
3. Since they have to hold only $100 in reserves, instead of $200, banks now lend out $100 of their reserves. Whoever borrows the $100 will deposit it in a bank (or spend it, and the recipient will deposit it in a bank), which will lend out $\$100 \times (1 - rr) = \$100 \times 0.9 = \$90$. The borrowed $90 will likewise find its way into a bank, which will lend out $\$90 \times 0.9 = \$81$, and so on. Overall, deposits will increase by $\$100/0.1 = \$1{,}000$.
4. Silas puts $1,000 in the bank, of which the bank lends out $\$1{,}000 \times (1 - rr) = \$1{,}000 \times 0.9 = \$900$. Whoever borrows the $900 will keep $450 in cash and deposit $450 in the bank. The bank will lend out $\$450 \times 0.9 = \$405$. Whoever borrows the $405 will keep $202.50 in cash and deposit $202.50 in the bank. The bank will lend out $\$202.50 \times 0.9 = \$182.25$, and so on. Overall this leads to an increase in deposits of $1,000 + $450 + $202.50 + . . . But it decreases the amount of currency in circulation: the amount of cash is reduced by the $1,000 Silas puts into the bank. This is offset, but not fully, by the amount of cash held by each borrower. The amount of currency in circulation therefore changes by –$1,000 + $450 + $202.50 + . . . The money supply therefore increases by the sum of the increase in deposits and the change in currency in circulation, which is $1,000 – $1,000 + $450 + $450 + $202.50 + $202.50 + . . . and so on.

Multiple-Choice Questions

1. d
2. a
3. e
4. c
5. d

Critical-Thinking Questions

1. The bank must hold $5,000 as required reserves (5% of $100,000). It is holding $10,000, so $5,000 must be excess reserves.
2. The bank must hold an additional $50 as reserves because that is the reserve requirement multiplied by the deposit: 5% of $1,000. The bank can lend out $950.
3. The money multiplier is 1/0.05 = 20. An increase of $2,000 in excess reserves can increase the money supply by $2,000 × 20 = $40,000.

MODULE 71

Check Your Understanding

1. The Panic of 1907, the S&L crisis, and the crisis of 2008 all involved losses by financial institutions that were less regulated than banks. In the crises of 1907 and 2008, there was a widespread loss of confidence in the financial sector and collapse of credit markets. Like the crisis of 1907 and the S&L crisis, the crisis of 2008 exerted a powerful negative effect on the economy.
2. The creation of the Federal Reserve failed to prevent bank runs because it did not eradicate the fears of depositors that a bank collapse would cause them to lose their money. The bank runs eventually stopped after federal deposit insurance was instituted and the public came to understand that their deposits were protected.
3. The balance sheet effect occurs when asset sales cause declines in asset prices, which then reduce the value of other firms' net worth as the value of the assets on their balance sheets declines. In the vicious cycle of deleveraging, the balance sheet effect on firms forces their creditors to call in their loan contracts, forcing the firms to sell assets to pay back their loans, leading to further asset sales and price declines. Because the vicious cycle of deleveraging occurs across different firms and no single firm can stop it, it is necessary for the government to step in to stop it.

Multiple-Choice Questions

1. a
2. a
3. b
4. d
5. e

Critical-Thinking Questions

1. oversee the Federal Reserve System and serve on the Federal Open Market Committee
2. 7
3. the president of the United States
4. 14-year terms
5. to insulate appointees from political pressure
6. 4 years; may be reappointed

MODULE 72

Check Your Understanding

1. An open-market purchase of $100 million by the Fed increases banks' reserves by $100 million as the Fed credits their accounts with additional reserves. In other words, this open-market purchase increases the monetary base (currency in circulation plus bank reserves) by $100 million. Banks lend out the additional $100 million. Whoever borrows the money puts it back into the banking system in the form of deposits. Of these deposits, banks lend out $100 million × (1 − *rr*) = $100 million × 0.9 = $90 million. Whoever borrows the money deposits it back into the banking system. And banks lend out $90 million × 0.9 = $81 million, and so on. As a result, bank deposits increased by $100 million + $90 million + $81 million + . . . = $100 million/*rr* = $100 million/0.1 = $1,000 million = $1 billion. Since in this simplified example all money lent out is deposited back into the banking system, there is no increase of currency in circulation, so the increase in bank deposits is equal to the increase in the money supply. In other words, the money supply increases by $1 billion. This is greater than the increase in the monetary base by a factor of 10: in this simplified model in which deposits are the only component of the money supply and in which banks hold no excess reserves, the money multiplier is 1/*rr* = 10.

Multiple-Choice Questions

1. d
2. e
3. d
4. b
5. c

Critical-Thinking Question

1. provide financial services to depository institutions
2. supervise and regulate banking institutions
3. maintain the stability of the financial system
4. conduct monetary policy

MODULE 73

Check Your Understanding

1. a. By increasing the opportunity cost of holding money, a high interest rate reduces the quantity of money demanded. This is a movement up and to the left along the money demand curve.
   b. A 10% fall in prices reduces the quantity of money demanded at any given interest rate, shifting the money demand curve leftward.
   c. This technological change reduces the quantity of money demanded at any given interest rate, so it shifts the money demand curve leftward.
   d. Payments in cash require employers to hold more money, increasing the quantity of money demanded at any given interest rate. So it shifts the money demand curve rightward.

2. a. A 1% processing fee on debit/credit card transactions for purchases less than $50 reduces the opportunity cost of holding cash because consumers will save money by paying with cash.

   b. An increase in the interest paid on six-month CDs raises the opportunity cost of holding cash because holding cash requires forgoing the higher interest paid.

   c. A fall in real estate prices has no effect on the opportunity cost or benefit of holding cash because real estate is an illiquid asset and therefore isn't relevant in the decision of how much cash to hold. Also, real estate transactions are generally not carried out using cash.

   d. Because many purchases of food are made in cash, a significant increase in the cost of food reduces the opportunity cost of holding cash.

Multiple-Choice Questions

1. d
2. d
3. b
4. d
5. e

Critical-Thinking Question

Your graph should look like the following. At an interest rate below equilibrium, the quantity of money demanded exceeds the quantity of money supplied. People want to shift more of their wealth out of interest-bearing assets such as CDs and hold it as money instead. Because the quantity of interest-bearing nonmoney assets demanded is less than the quantity supplied, those trying to sell these assets will have to offer a higher interest rate to attract buyers. As the interest rate rises, the quantity of money demanded decreases. This process continues until the market returns to equilibrium.

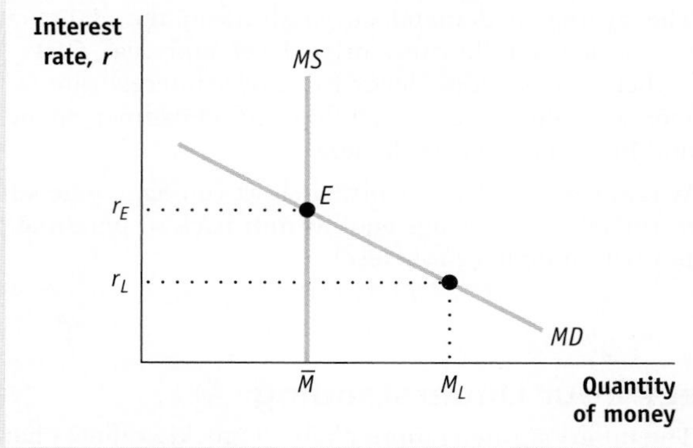

MODULE 74

Check Your Understanding

1. In the accompanying diagram, the increase in the demand for money is shown as a rightward shift of the money demand curve, from MD_1 to MD_2. This raises the equilibrium interest rate from r_1 to r_2.

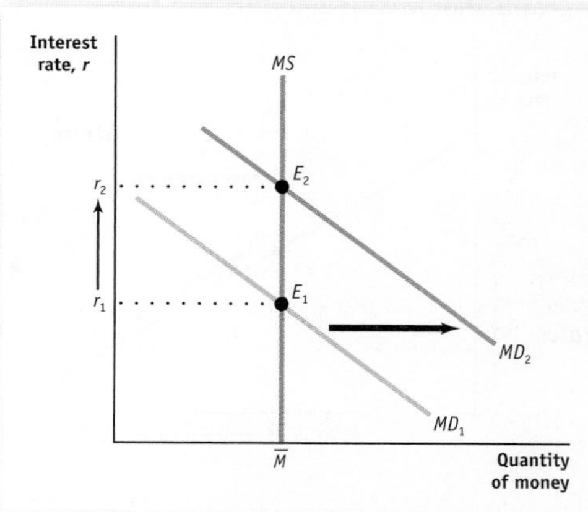

2. In order to prevent the interest rate from rising, the Federal Reserve must make an open-market purchase of Treasury bills, shifting the money supply curve rightward. This is shown in the accompanying diagram as the move from MS_1 to MS_2.

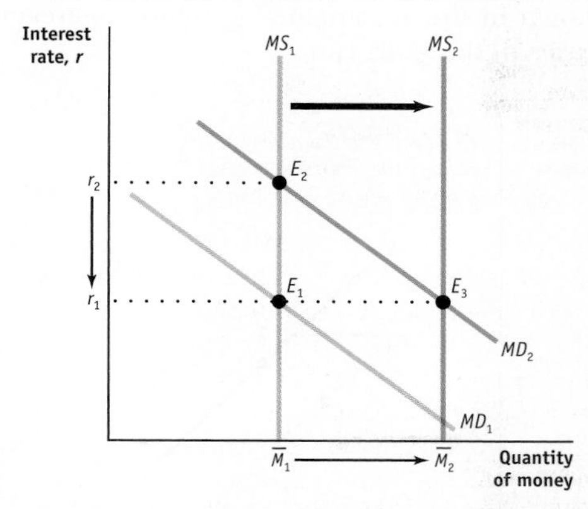

3. a. The money supply curve shifts to the right.

   b. The equilibrium interest rate falls.

   c. Investment spending rises, due to the fall in the interest rate.

   d. Consumer spending rises, due to the multiplier process.

   e. Aggregate output rises because of the rightward shift of the aggregate demand curve.

Multiple-Choice Questions

1. a
2. a
3. a
4. c
5. a

Critical-Thinking Questions

1. decrease the discount rate, decrease the reserve requirement, open-market purchases

2. Your graph should look like this.

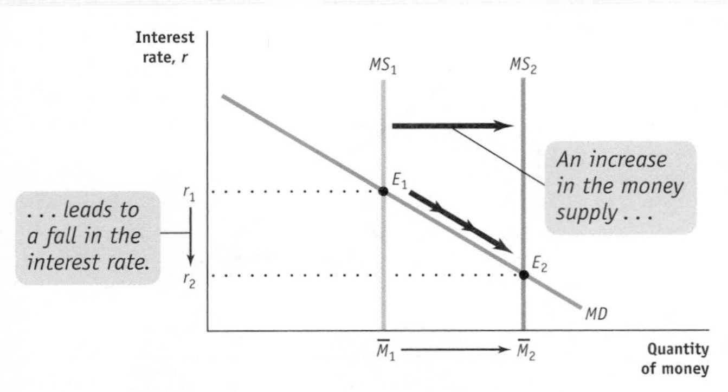

3. There is no change in aggregate supply; aggregate demand increases. Lower interest rates lead to greater investment spending (and more interest-sensitive consumer spending). Aggregate demand is made up of $C + I + G + (X - IM)$, so an increase in I and C increases AD. Interest rate changes don't affect short-run aggregate supply.

4. As shown in the accompanying figure, aggregate output increases in the short run.

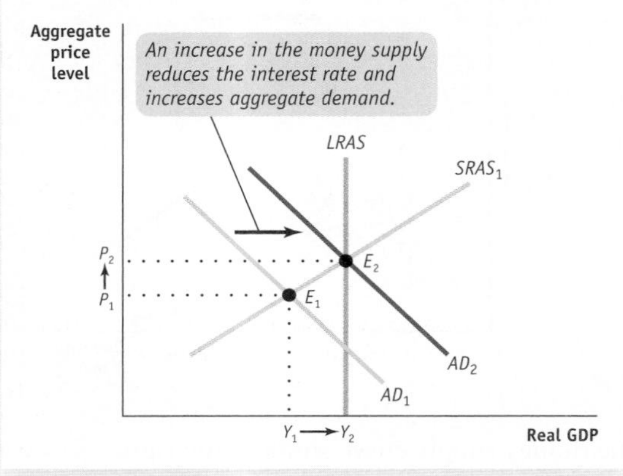

MODULE 75

Check Your Understanding

1. A 5% increase in the money supply will cause a 5% increase in the aggregate price level in the long run. The process begins in the short run, when the larger money supply decreases the interest rate and promotes investment spending. Investment spending is a component of aggregate demand, so the increase in investment spending leads to an increase in aggregate demand, which causes real GDP to increase beyond potential output. The resulting upward pressure on nominal wages and other input prices shifts aggregate supply to the left until a new long-run equilibrium is reached. Although real GDP returns to its original level, both the increase in aggregate demand and the decrease in aggregate supply cause the aggregate price level to increase. The end result is 5% more money being spent on the same quantity of goods and services, which could only mean a 5% increase in the aggregate price level.

2. A 5% increase in the money supply will have no effect on the interest rate in the long run. As explained in the previous answer, a 5% increase in the money supply is matched by a 5% increase in the aggregate price level in the long run. Changes in the aggregate price level, in turn, cause proportional changes in the demand for money. So a 5% increase in the aggregate price level increases the quantity of money demanded at any given interest rate by 5%. This means that at the initial interest rate, the quantity of money demanded rises exactly as much as the money supply, and the new, long-run interest rate is therefore no different from the initial interest rate.

Multiple-Choice Questions

1. c
2. d
3. c
4. c
5. e

Critical-Thinking Questions

1. Your graph should look like this.

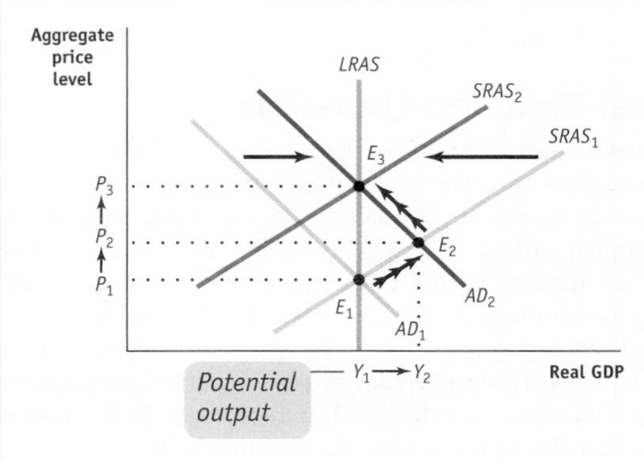

2. The aggregate demand curve shifts to the right, creating a new equilibrium price level and real GDP. The higher money supply leads to a lower interest rate, which increases investment spending and consumer spending, and in turn aggregate demand.

3. Wages rise over time, shifting short-run aggregate supply to the left. This brings equilibrium back to potential output with a higher price level.

MODULE 76

Check Your Understanding

1. The inflation rate is more likely to quickly reflect changes in the money supply when the economy has had an extended period of high inflation. That's because an extended period of high inflation sensitizes workers and firms to raise nominal wages and prices of intermediate goods when the aggregate price level rises. As a result, there will be little or no increase in real output in the short run after an increase in the money supply, and the increase in the money supply will simply be reflected in a proportional increase in prices. In an economy where people are not sensitized to high inflation because of low inflation in the past, an increase in the money supply will

lead to an increase in real output in the short run. This illustrates the fact that the classical model of the price level best applies to economies with *persistently* high inflation, not those with little or no history of high inflation even though they may currently have high inflation.

2. Yes, there can still be an inflation tax because the tax is levied on people who hold money. As long as people hold money, regardless of whether prices are indexed or not, the government is able to use seignorage to capture real resources from the public.

Multiple-Choice Questions

1. d
2. b
3. b
4. c
5. a

Critical-Thinking Question

Your diagram should look like this.

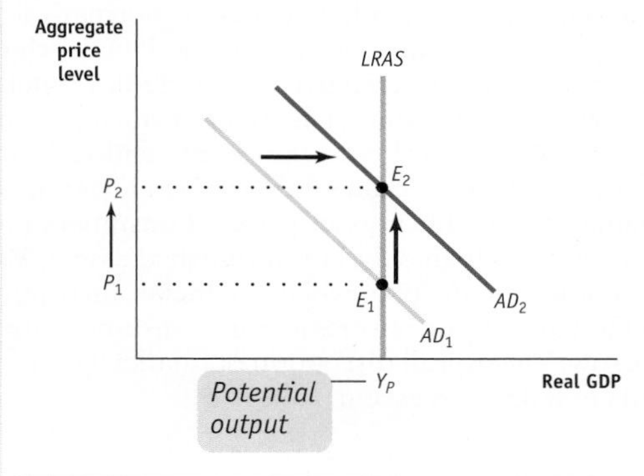

MODULE 77

Check Your Understanding

1. When real GDP equals potential output, cyclical unemployment is zero and the unemployment rate is equal to the natural rate. This is the case at point E_1 in the figure assuming a natural rate of 6%. Any unemployment in excess of this 6% rate represents cyclical unemployment. An increase in aggregate demand leads to a fall in the unemployment rate below the natural rate (negative cyclical unemployment) and an increase in the inflation rate. This is given by the movement from E_1 to E_2 in the figure and traces a movement upward along the short-run Phillips curve. A reduction in aggregate demand leads to a rise in the unemployment rate above the natural rate (positive cyclical unemployment) and a fall in the inflation rate. This would be represented by a movement down along the short-run Phillips curve from point E_1. So for a given expected inflation rate, the short-run Phillips curve illustrates the relationship between cyclical unemployment and the actual inflation rate.

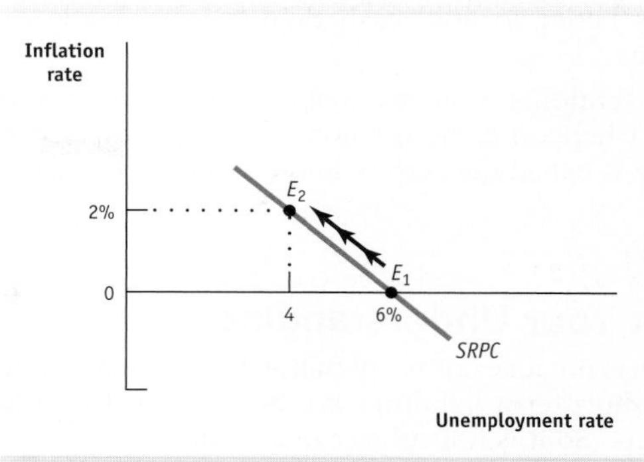

2. There is no long-run trade-off between inflation and unemployment because after expectations of inflation change, wages will adjust to the change, returning employment and the unemployment rate to their equilibrium (natural) levels. This implies that once expectations of inflation fully adjust to any change in actual inflation, the unemployment rate will return to the natural rate of unemployment, or NAIRU. This also implies that the long-run Phillips curve is vertical.

3. Disinflation is costly because to reduce the inflation rate, aggregate output in the short run must typically fall below potential output. This, in turn, results in an increase in the unemployment rate above the natural rate. In general, we would observe a reduction in real GDP. The costs of disinflation can be reduced by not allowing inflation to increase in the first place. The costs of any disinflation will also be lower if the central bank is credible and it announces in advance its policy to reduce inflation. In this situation, the adjustment to the disinflationary policy will be more rapid, resulting in a smaller loss of aggregate output.

4. If the nominal interest rate is negative, an individual is better off simply holding cash, which has a 0% nominal rate of return. If the options facing an individual are to lend and receive a negative nominal interest rate or to hold cash and receive a 0% nominal rate of return, the individual will hold cash. Such a scenario creates the possibility of a liquidity trap, in which monetary policy is ineffective because the nominal interest rate cannot fall below zero. Once the nominal interest rate falls to zero, further increases in the money supply will lead firms and individuals to simply hold the additional cash.

Multiple-Choice Questions

1. b
2. c
3. b
4. e
5. e

Critical-Thinking Questions

1. 4%
2. 2%, because 4% – 2% = 2%
3. 0%, because although 4% – 6% = –2%, nominal interest rates can't go below zero
4. Lenders would effectively have to pay people to borrow money, in that what the lenders received back would be less than what they lent out. No lending would take place.

It is better to hold cash than to pay people to borrow money.

5. Conventional monetary policy (decreasing interest rates) can't happen if the nominal interest rate is already zero. This is called the zero bound or a liquidity trap.

MODULE 78

Check Your Understanding

1. a. This is not an example of maturity transformation because no short-term liabilities are being turned into long-term assets. So it is not subject to a bank run.

   b. This is an example of maturity transformation: Dana incurs a short-term liability, credit card debt, to fund the acquisition of a long-term asset, better job skills. It can result in a bank-run-like phenomenon if her credit card lender becomes fearful of her ability to repay and stops lending to her. If this happens, she will not be able to finish her course and, as a result, will not be able to get the better job that would allow her to pay off her credit card loans.

   c. This is not an example of maturity transformation because there are no short-term liabilities. The partnership itself has no obligation to repay an individual partner's investment and so has no liabilities, short term or long term.

   d. This is an example of maturity transformation: the checking accounts are short-term liabilities of the student union savings bank, and the student loans are long-term assets.

2. According to standard macroeconomics, a government should adopt expansionary policies to increase aggregate demand to address an economic slump. France, however, did just the opposite, responding to a weaker economy with a contractionary fiscal policy that would make the economy even weaker. This shows that the French government had adopted the austerity view, believing that it was more important to try to assure markets of its solvency than to support the economy.

3. Because shadow banks like Lehman relied on short-term borrowing to fund their operations, fears about their soundness could quickly lead lenders to immediately cut off their credit and force them into failure. And without membership in the lender-of-last-resort system, shadow banks like Lehman could not borrow from the Federal Reserve to make up for the short-term loans it had lost.

4. If there had been only a formal depository banking sector, several factors would have mitigated the potential and scope of a banking crisis. First, there would have been no repo financing; the only short-term liabilities would have been customers' deposits, and these would have been largely covered by deposit insurance. Second, capital requirements would have reduced banks' willingness to take on excessive risk, such as holding onto subprime mortgages. Also, direct oversight by the Federal Reserve would have prevented so much concentration of risk within the banking sector. Finally, depository banks are within the lender-of-last-resort system; as a result, depository banks had another layer of protection against the fear of depositors and other creditors that they couldn't meet their obligations. All of these factors would have reduced the potential and scope of a banking crisis.

5. Because the shadow banking sector had become such a critical part of the U.S. economy, the crisis of 2008 made it clear that in the event of another crisis, the government would need to guarantee a wide range of financial institution debts, including those of shadow banks (in addition to those of depository banks). The result was an incentive problem: shadow banks would be able to take more risk, knowing that the government would bail them out in the event of a meltdown. To counteract this, the Dodd-Frank Act gave the government the power to regulate "systemically important" shadow banks (those likely to wreak havoc on the economy should they fail) in order to reduce their risk taking. It also gave the government the power to seize control of failing shadow banks in a way that was fair to taxpayers and and that did not enrich the bankers involved.

Multiple-Choice Questions

1. c
2. c
3. a
4. b
5. e

Critical-Thinking Question

A banking crisis occurs when a large part of the banking sector is in danger of failing. A banking crisis normally leads to a deep recession because of a credit crunch, debt overhang, and a loss of monetary policy effectiveness. A credit crunch occurs when borrowers either cannot get credit or must pay very high interest rates. The reduction in borrowing will reduce spending and output. Debt overhang occurs when a vicious cycle of deleveraging pushes down asset prices. Consumers and businesses are left with high debt but diminished assets. Monetary policy becomes ineffective when financial institutions are unwilling to lend and/or businesses and consumers are unwilling to borrow. The overall disruption of financial markets typically leads to a deep recession.

MODULE 79

Check Your Understanding

1. a. The sale of the new airplane to China represents an export of a good to China and so enters the current account.

   b. The sale of Boeing stock to Chinese investors is a sale of a U.S. asset and so enters the financial account.

   c. Even though the plane already exists, when it is shipped to China it is an export of a good from the United States. So the sale of the plane enters the current account.

   d. Because the plane stays in the United States, the Chinese investor is buying a U.S. asset. So this is identical to the answer in part b: the sale of the jet enters the financial account.

2. The collapse of the U.S. housing bubble and the ensuing recession led to a dramatic fall in interest rates in the United States because of the deeply depressed economy. Consequently, capital inflows into the United States dried up.

Multiple-Choice Questions

1. e
2. a
3. b
4. a
5. a

Critical-Thinking Question

Your graphs should look like the following.

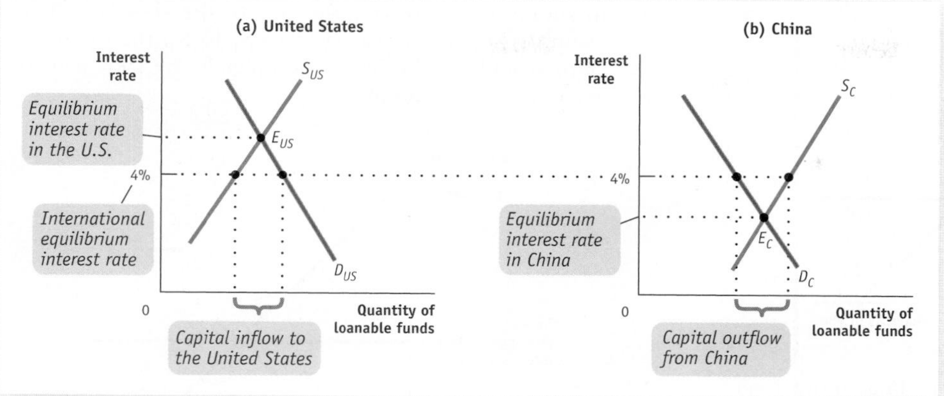

MODULE 80

Check Your Understanding

1. a. The increased purchase of Mexican oil would cause U.S. individuals (and firms) to increase their demand for the peso. To purchase pesos, individuals would increase their supply of U.S. dollars to the foreign exchange market, causing a rightward shift in the supply curve of U.S. dollars. This would cause the peso price of the dollar to fall (the amount of pesos per dollar would fall). The peso would appreciate and the U.S. dollar would depreciate as a result.

   b. With the appreciation of the peso it would take more U.S. dollars to obtain the same quantity of Mexican pesos. If we assume that the price level (measured in Mexican pesos) of other Mexican goods and services would not change, other Mexican goods and services would become more expensive to U.S. households and firms. The dollar cost of other Mexican goods and services would rise as the peso appreciated. So Mexican exports of goods and services other than oil would fall.

   c. U.S. goods and services would become cheaper in terms of pesos, so Mexican imports of goods and services would rise.

2. a. The real exchange rate equals pesos per U.S. dollar × aggregate price level in the U.S./aggregate price level in Mexico. Today, the aggregate price level in both countries is 100. The real exchange rate today is: 10 × (100/100) = 10. The aggregate price level in five years in the U.S. will be 100 × (120/100) = 120, and in Mexico it will be 100 × (1,200/800) = 150. Thus, the real exchange rate in five years, assuming the nominal exchange rate does not change, will be 10 × (120/150) = 8.

   b. Today, a basket of goods and services that costs $100 costs 800 pesos, so the purchasing power parity is 8 pesos per U.S. dollar. In five years, a basket that costs $120 will cost 1,200 pesos, so the purchasing power parity will be 10 pesos per U.S. dollar.

Multiple-Choice Questions

1. d
2. d
3. d
4. b
5. b

Critical-Thinking Question

In order to purchase more imports from Europe, U.S. consumers must supply more dollars in exchange for euros. As shown in the diagram, the increase in the supply of dollars shifts the dollar supply curve to the right and decreases the exchange rate from XR_1 to XR_2.

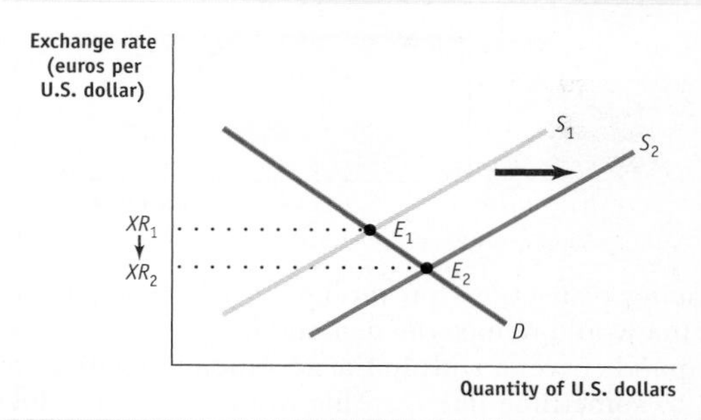

MODULE 81

Check Your Understanding

1. The accompanying diagram shows the supply of and demand for the yuan, with the U.S. dollar price of the yuan on the vertical axis. In 2005, prior to the revaluation, the exchange rate was pegged at 8.28 yuan per U.S. dollar or, equivalently, 0.121 U.S. dollars per yuan ($0.121). At the target exchange rate of $0.121, the quantity of yuan demanded exceeded the quantity of yuan supplied, creating the shortage depicted in the diagram. Without any intervention by the Chinese government, the U.S. dollar price of the yuan would be bid up, causing an appreciation

of the yuan. The Chinese government, however, intervened to prevent this appreciation.

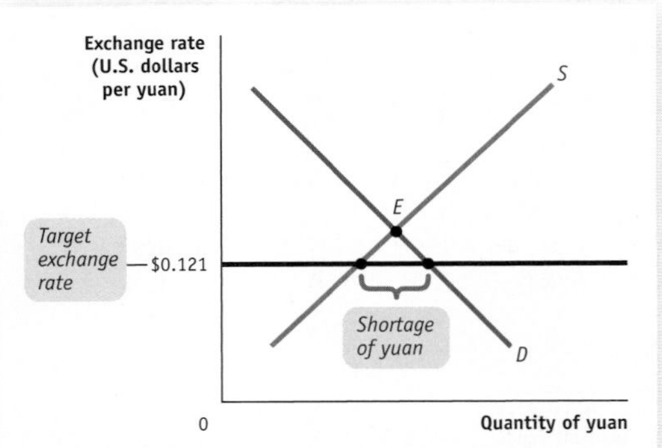

a. If the exchange rate were allowed to float more freely, the U.S. dollar price of the exchange rate would move toward the equilibrium exchange rate (labeled *XR** in the accompanying diagram). This would occur as a result of the shortage, when buyers of the yuan would bid up its U.S. dollar price. As the exchange rate increased, the quantity of yuan demanded would fall and the quantity of yuan supplied would increase. If the exchange rate were allowed to increase to *XR**, the disequilibrium would be entirely eliminated.

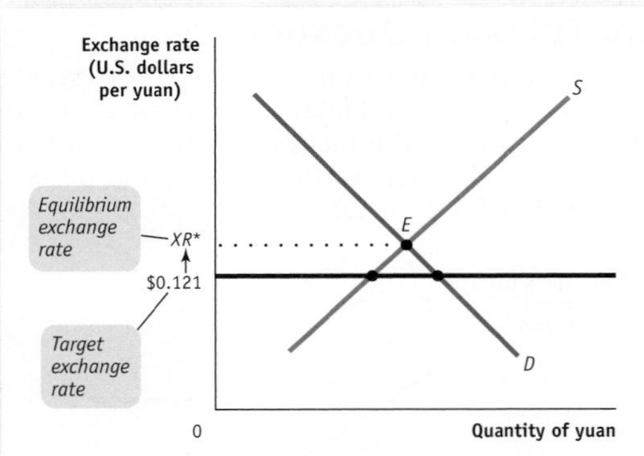

b. Placing restrictions on foreigners who want to invest in China would reduce the demand for the yuan, causing the demand curve to shift in the accompanying diagram from D_1 to something like D_2. This would cause a reduction in the shortage of the yuan. If demand fell to D_3, the disequilibrium would be completely eliminated.

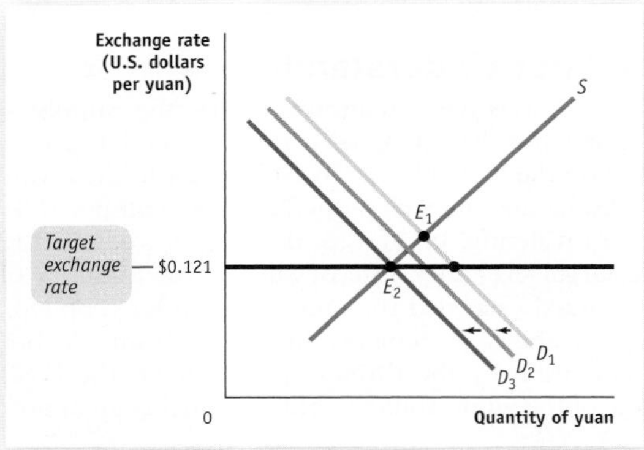

c. Removing restrictions on Chinese who wish to invest abroad would cause an increase in the supply of the yuan and a rightward shift of the supply curve. This increase in supply would reduce the size of the shortage. If, for example, supply increased from S_1 to S_2, the disequilibrium would be eliminated completely, as shown in the accompanying diagram.

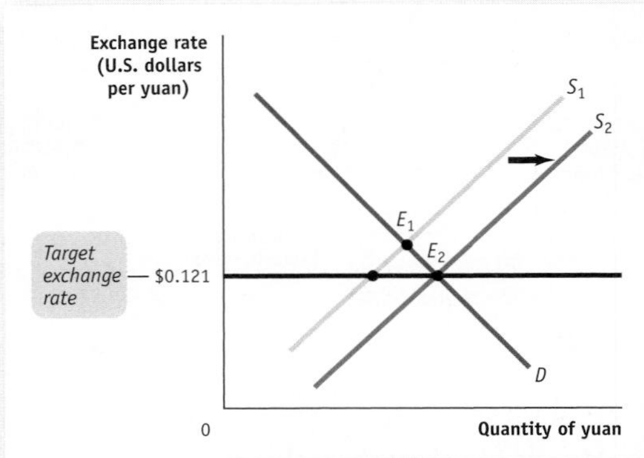

d. Imposing a tax on exports (Chinese goods sold to foreigners) would raise the price of these goods and decrease the amount of Chinese goods purchased. This would also decrease the demand for yuan with which to purchase those goods. The graphical analysis here is virtually identical to that found in the figure accompanying part b.

Multiple-Choice Questions

1. e
2. e
3. b
4. a
5. a

Critical-Thinking Question

1) Use foreign exchange reserves. To stabilize an exchange rate through exchange market intervention (e.g., buying its own currency), a country must keep large quantities of foreign currency on hand, which is usually a low-return investment. And large reserves can be quickly exhausted when there are large capital flows out of a country.

2) Shifting supply and demand curves for currency through monetary policy. If a country chooses to stabilize an exchange rate by adjusting monetary policy rather than through intervention, it must divert monetary policy from other goals, notably stabilizing the economy and managing the inflation rate.

3) Foreign exchange controls. These regulations distort incentives for importing and exporting goods and services. They can also create substantial costs in terms of red tape and corruption.

MODULE 82

Check Your Understanding

1. The devaluations and revaluations most likely occurred in those periods when there was a sudden change in the franc–mark exchange rate: 1974, 1976, the early 1980s, 1986, and 1993–1994.

2. The high Canadian interest rates caused an increase in capital inflows to Canada. To obtain assets that yielded a relatively high interest rate in Canada, investors first had to obtain Canadian dollars. The increase in the demand for the Canadian dollar caused the Canadian dollar to appreciate. This appreciation of the Canadian currency raised the price of Canadian goods to foreigners (measured in terms of the foreign currency). This made it more difficult for Canadian firms to compete in other markets.

Multiple-Choice Questions

1. c
2. b
3. a
4. d
5. b

Critical-Thinking Question

The decrease in aggregate demand that occurs during a recession includes the demand for goods and services produced abroad as well as at home. When a trading partner experiences a recession, it leads to a fall in their imports. The trading partner's imports are the country's exports.

A reduction in foreign demand for the country's domestic goods and services leads to a reduction in demand for the domestic currency. With a floating exchange rate, the currency depreciates. This makes domestic goods and services cheaper, so exports don't fall by as much as they would have, and it makes imports more expensive, leading to a fall in imports. Both effects limit the decline in domestic aggregate demand.

MODULE 83

Check Your Understanding

1. A classical economist would have said that although expansionary monetary policy would probably have some effect in the short run, the short run was unimportant. Instead, a classical economist would have stressed the long run, claiming expansionary monetary policy would result only in an increase in the aggregate price level without affecting aggregate output.

2. a. According to the velocity equation, $M \times V = P \times Y$, where M is the money supply, V the velocity of money, P the aggregate price level, and Y real GDP. If the Federal Reserve had pursued a monetary policy rule of constant money supply growth, the collapse in the velocity of money beginning in 2008 and visible in Figure 83-4 would have resulted in a dramatic decline in aggregate output.

   b. Although monetarists generally believe that monetary policy is not only effective but, in fact, more effective than fiscal policy, they also generally do not favor macroeconomic policy activism. Instead, monetarists generally advocate monetary policy rules, such as a low but constant rate of money supply growth. In addition, the natural rate hypothesis states that although monetary policy may be effective in helping return unemployment to its natural rate, it cannot permanently reduce unemployment below the natural rate.

3. Fiscal policy is limited by time lags in recognizing economic problems, forming a response, passing legislation, and implementing the policies. Monetary policy is also limited by time lags, but these lags are not as severe as those for fiscal policy because the Federal Reserve tends to act more quickly than Congress. Attempts to reduce unemployment below the natural rate via both fiscal and monetary policy are limited by predictions of the natural rate hypothesis: that these attempts will result in accelerating inflation. Also, both fiscal and monetary policy are limited by concerns about the political business cycle: that they will be used to satisfy political ends and will end up destabilizing the economy.

4. a. Rational expectations theorists would argue that only unexpected changes in the money supply would have any short-run effect on economic activity. They would also argue that expected changes in the money supply would affect only the aggregate price level, with no short-run effect on aggregate output. So such theorists would give credit to the Fed for limiting the severity of the 2007–2009 recession only if the Fed's monetary policy had been more aggressive than individuals expected during this period.

   b. Real business cycle theorists would argue that the Fed's policy had no effect on ending the 2007–2009 recession because they believe that fluctuations in aggregate output are caused largely by changes in total factor productivity.

Multiple-Choice Questions

1. e
2. d
3. b
4. a
5. d

Critical-Thinking Question

a. The aggregate supply curve is vertical so changes in the money supply affect only the aggregate price level.

b. Changes in aggregate demand will affect aggregate output because the short-run aggregate supply curve is upward sloping.

c. Business cycles are associated with fluctuations in the money supply.

d. To avoid inflation, the unemployment rate must be set so that actual inflation equals expected inflation.

e. Individuals and firms make optimal decisions using all available information.

f. Fluctuations in total factor productivity growth cause the business cycle by causing the vertical aggregate supply curve to shift.

MODULE 84

Check Your Understanding

The liquidity trap brought on by the Great Recession greatly diminished the Great Moderation consensus because it considered monetary policy to be the main policy tool and monetary policy was now largely ineffective. The continuing disagreements over fiscal policy were now brought to the forefront as fiscal policy was used by policy makers to support their deeply depressed economies. A new consensus is unlikely to emerge anytime soon because results of the various policies have been unclear or disappointing: fiscal stimulus has failed to bring down unemployment substantially (although some say the stimulus was too small); conventional monetary policy does not work; and the Fed's unconventional monetary policy seemed to have relatively little effect.

Multiple-Choice Questions

1. d
2. c
3. d
4. c
5. c

Critical-Thinking Questions

1. Supporters of expansionary fiscal policy, or fiscal stimulus, offered three main arguments:
   - Monetary policy was not effective due to interest rates being near zero.
   - Given the already near zero interest rates, expansionary fiscal policy was unlikely to result in crowding out of investment.
   - Even if fiscal policy took time to implement, the economy was still likely to be in need of stimulus.
2. Opponents of fiscal stimulus offered two main arguments:
   - People would see any increase in government spending as a sign that taxes were sure to rise in the future. This would reduce spending now and negate the effects of the increase in government spending.
   - People might lose faith in the government's ability to repay its debt if the level of debt continued to rise.

INDEX

Key terms and the pages on which they are defined appear in **boldface.**

A

B

F

G

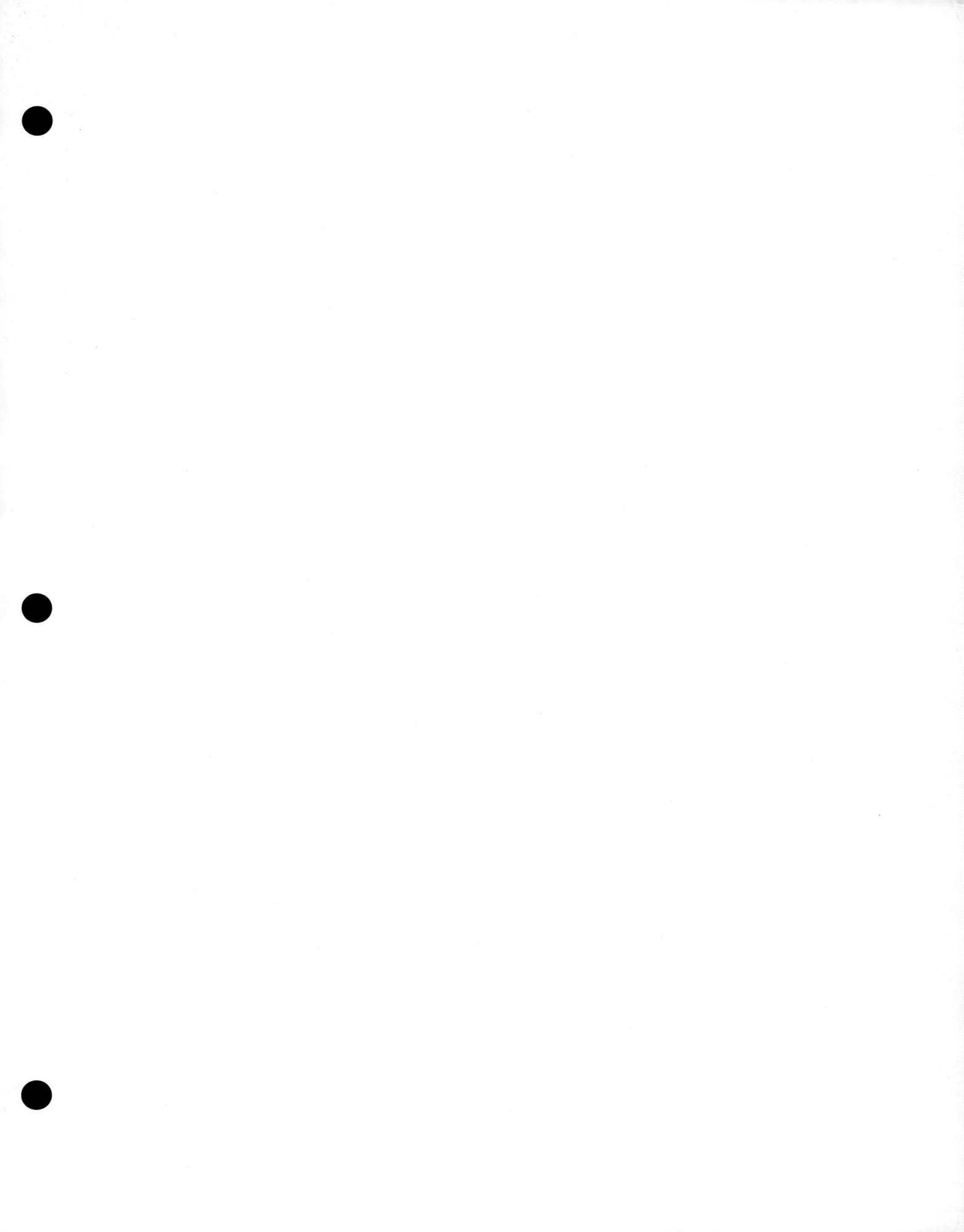

Applications in Economics in Modules

Continued from the inside front cover

SECTION	SECTION-OPENING STORIES
15: Macroeconomic Measurement	15: The New #2
16: Unemployment and Inflation	16: A Very British Dilemma
17: Long-Run Economic Growth	17: Tall Tales
18: Savings, Investment Spending, and the Financial System	18: Funds for Facebook
19: Income and Expenditure	19: From Boom to Bust
20: Aggregate Demand and Aggregate Supply	20: Shocks to the System
21: Fiscal Policy	21: To Stimulate or Not to Stimulate?
22: Money, Banking, and the Federal Reserve System	22: Funny Money
23: Monetary Policy	23: Person of the Year
24: Policy Responses to Unemployment and Inflation	24: Bringing a Suitcase to the Bank
25: Open-Economy Macroeconomics	25: Switzerland Doesn't Want Your Money
26: Macroeconomics: Events and Ideas	26: A Tale of Two Slumps